RUSSIAN COMPANY AND COMMERCIAL LEGISLATION

RUSSIAN
COMPANY AND
COMMERCIAL
LEGISLATION

Compiled and Edited,
with translations from the Russian and an Introduction, by
W. E. BUTLER

OXFORD
UNIVERSITY PRESS

OXFORD
UNIVERSITY PRESS

Great Clarendon Street, Oxford OX2 6DP

Oxford University Press is a department of the University of Oxford.
It furthers the University's objective of excellence in research, scholarship,
and education by publishing worldwide in

Oxford New York

Auckland Bangkok Buenos Aires Cape Town Chennai
Dar es Salaam Delhi Hong Kong Istanbul Karachi Kolkata
Kuala Lumpur Madrid Melbourne Mexico City Mumbai Nairobi
São Paulo Shanghai Taipei Tokyo Toronto

Oxford is a registered trade mark of Oxford University Press
in the UK and in certain other countries

Published in the United States
by Oxford University Press Inc., New York

British Library Cataloguing-in-Publication Data
A catalogue record for this book is available from
The British Library

Library of Congress Cataloging in Publication Data
Data available

ISBN 0–19–926152–0

1 3 5 7 9 10 8 6 4 2

Typeset by Hope Services (Abingdon) Ltd.
Printed in Great Britain
on acid-free paper by
Biddles Ltd., Guildford and King's Lynn

William E. Butler is Professor of Comparative Law in the University of London; Academician of the Russian Academy of Natural Sciences and of the National Academy of Sciences of Ukraine; Director of The Vinogradoff Institute, University College London. He was the founder and Dean (1993–98) of the Faculty of Law, Moscow Higher School of Social and Economic Sciences and continues to teach there as the M. M. Speranskii Professor of International and Comparative Law, and in spring 2002 as professor at the Chair of Civil and Family Law, Moscow State Legal Academy. In 1999 he was elected to the Russian Academy of Legal Sciences. He read law at Harvard University, where he has been Visiting Professor of Law, and holds a Master of Russian Law (LL.M.) from the School of Law, Institute of State and Law, Russian Academy of Sciences, and higher doctorates from The Johns Hopkins University (Ph.D.) and the University of London (LL.D.). He has advised the Governments of the USSR, Belarus, Russian Federation, Republic Azerbaidzhan, Republic Kazakhstan, Kyrgyz Republic, Tadzhikistan, Turkmenistan, Ukraine, Uzbekistan, and Lithuania on aspects of law reform and participated in the drafting of a number of key legislative acts. He served as a member of the EC/IS Joint Task Force on Law Reform in the Independent States and has advised The World Bank, the European Bank of Reconstruction and Development, the European Commission, the United Kingdom Know-How Fund, the Department for International Development (UK), and specialised agencies of the United Nations on law reform in the Independent States. In 1995 he was elected a member of the Russian Court of International Commercial Arbitration, and in 1999 to the Court of Economic Arbitration attached to the Urals Chamber of Trade and Industry (Ekaterinburg). In 2002 he co-founded Phoenix Law Associates, a law firm based in Moscow and specialising in the legal systems of the CIS.

CONTENTS

On the Development of Russian Company and Commercial
Legislation—W. E. Butler   xiii

Abbreviations   xxxvii

GENERAL PROVISIONS

Federal Law on the State Registration of Juridical Persons (8 August 2001)   1

Federal Law on Licensing Individual Types of Activity (8 August
2001, as amended)   16

Federal Law on Competition and the Limitation of Monopolistic
Activity on Goods Markets (22 March 1991, as amended)   31

Law of the Russian Federation on the Organisation of Insurance
Affairs in the Russian Federation (27 November 1992, as amended)   59

Land Code of the Russian Federation (25 October 2001)   72

Federal Law on Introduction into Operation of the Land Code of the
Russian Federation (25 October 2001)   144

Federal Law on the Turnover of Lands of Agricultural Designation
(24 July 2002)   151

ECONOMIC SOCIETIES AND PARTNERSHIPS

Federal Law on Limited Responsibility Societies (8 February 1998, as
amended)   165

Federal Law on Joint-Stock Societies (26 December 1995, as amended)   215

Federal Law on the Peculiarities of the Legal Status of Joint-Stock
Societies of Workers (People's Enterprises) (19 July 1998, as
amended)   300

Federal Law on Financial-Industrial Groups (30 November 1995)   317

Contents

Federal Law on Banks and Banking Activity (2 December 1990, as
amended)   328

Federal Law on Insolvency (or Bankruptcy) (26 October 2002)   366

Federal Law on the Insolvency (or Bankruptcy) of Credit Organisations
(25 February 1999, as amended)   544

STATE AND MUNICIPAL UNITARY ENTERPRISES

Federal Law on State and Municipal Unitary Enterprises
(14 November 2002)   577

NONCOMMERCIAL ORGANISATIONS

Federal Law on Noncommercial Organisations (12 January 1996, as
amended)   601

Federal Law on Philanthropic Activity and Philanthropic
Organisations (11 August 1995, as amended)   621

OBJECTS OF CIVIL RIGHTS

Federal Law on the Securities Market (20 March 1996, as amended)   633

Federal Law on Defence of the Rights and Legal Interests of Investors
on the Securities Market (5 March 1999, as amended)   705

Federal Law on Counteracting the Legalisation (or Laundering) of
Revenues Received by Criminal Means and Financing of Terrorism
(7 August 2001, as amended)   717

Law of the Russian Federation on Pledge (29 May 1992, as affected) 731

Federal Law on Mortgage (or Pledge of Immoveable) (16 July 1998,
as amended)   747

Federal Law on Finance Lease (Finance Leasing) (29 October 1998,
as amended)   794

Contents

FOREIGN INVESTMENT AND INTERNATIONAL ARBITRATION

Federal Law on Foreign Investments in the Russian Federation (9 July 1999, as amended)   811

Federal Law on Investment Activity in the Russian Federation Effectuated in the Form of Capital Investments (25 February 1999, as amended)   825

Law of the Russian Federation on International Commercial Arbitration (7 July 1993)   839
    Annexe 1: Statute on International Commercial Arbitration Court   854
    Annexe 2: Statute on the Maritime Arbitration Commission   855
    Decree on the Introduction into Operation of the Law of the Russian Federation 'On International Commercial Arbitration' (7 July 1993)   857

Federal Law on Arbitration Courts in the Russian Federation (24 July 2002)   859

PREFACE

This volume collects in specially prepared translations the principal enactments of civil legislation which elaborate the Civil Code of the Russian Federation (published separately by Oxford University Press) and are classified by Russian legal doctrine as falling within the general domain of commercial and company law. All translations have been made from the official Russian texts, incorporating all amendments, changes, and additions, including, where applicable, relevant decrees of the Constitutional Court of the Russian Federation.

Although the volume stands independently as a resource on Russian law, it accompanies and complements my treatise on the subject, *Russian Law*, the second edition of which is appearing simultaneously, and my translation of the Civil Code of the Russian Federation, which all of the enactments in this volume elaborate or augment in one way or another.

Status juris: 1 February 2003

W. E. Butler
Bicester, Oxon.

ON THE DEVELOPMENT OF RUSSIAN COMPANY AND COMMERCIAL LEGISLATION

W. E. Butler

The Civil Code of the Russian Federation[1] makes specific mention of most of the laws translated in this volume; that is, those laws mentioned are an integral part of Russian civil legislation, were enacted in pursuance of the Civil Code, and are concerned principally with the commercial and company law aspects of civil law.

The terms 'commercial' [коммерческое] and 'company' are used with some reluctance and diffidence in the title of this volume. Although they are routine in the English language for materials of the nature translated here, in the Russian language they are inapt and controversial, and in the case of 'company', there is no adjectival form.

The controversy surrounding the expression 'commercial' is not without interest to the foreign lawyer. In prerevolutionary Russia many jurists used 'commercial' and 'trade' [торговое] law as synonyms. Shershenevich wrote: 'by commercial (or trade) law is understood the aggregate of norms of private law, general and special, intended to service trade (or commercial) turnover and regulate the mutual relations of professional entrepreneurs (or commercants)'.[2] Modern commercial law in Russia, however, is regarded by its proponents not as a revival or reconstruction of prerevolutionary Russian legal concepts. Rather, it is '. . . a new instructional discipline structured on the principles which take into account the importance of commercial law for resolving strategic tasks of building a civilised market and determining the purposes, means, and methods of activity of organisations, institutions, and trade turnover of the country as a whole'.[3]

Some would go further and characterise commercial law as an autonomous branch of law whose subject is the broad commercial relations that exist in the domain of economic activity. This approach had its supporters prior to 1917,

---

[1] See W. E. Butler (transl.), *The Russian Civil Code* (Oxford University Press, 2002). The Civil Code was enacted in three parts. Part Three entered into force on 1 March 2002.

[2] G. F. Shershenevich, *Учебник торгового права* [Textbook of Trade Law] (1914 ed.; 1994), pp. 13–29.

[3] See M. M. Rassolov (ed.), *Коммерческое право* [Commercial Law] (2001), p. 3.

amongst them P. P. Tsitovich[4] and A. I. Kaminka.[5] In this view, the entrepreneur is the subject of these relations, and the method of legal regulation is the linkage between objects that pursue a single purpose—to derive profit. Proposals have been made to actually produce a Trade (or Commercial) Code separate from the Civil Code.[6]

The relationship between civil and commercial law is understood variously. That they overlap is beyond doubt. Some Russian jurists speak of the 'organic unity', the 'inner community' of civil and commercial law, while observing at the same time that this overlap and shared unity does not preclude singling out commercial law from civil.[7] In the 1920s Soviet jurists referred to the 'trade spirit' (in both the positive and negative senses) which informs 'trade law', which 'penetrates all turnover and part of the respective legislation', and which would be undesirable to extend to civil law as a whole. V. M. Gordon wrote that 'the spirit of trade laws absolutely must be other than the spirit of civil laws'.[8]

The distinction between commerce and trade is merely one aspect of the problem. A similar issue arises when differentiating between 'commerce' and 'entrepreneurship', and between the 'commersant' and the 'entrepreneur' (the term 'trader' often has a negative connotation in Russian and is not widely used in legal writings, at least). In prerevolutionary Russia the entrepreneur and commersant were widely seen as synonymous. After the October 1917 revolution the concept of commercial or trade law was narrowly defined, and in the transition to a market economy a broader definition of entrepreneur has come to be accepted.

The State Educational Standard for Higher Professional Education has distinguished between entrepreneurial and commercial law and established two distinct syllabuses for each. Some Russian faculties of law disagree with the distinction and effectively treat the two terms as synonymous, among them the Chair of Commercial Law at St. Petersburg State University. Their fundamental textbook in its third edition in two volumes, they observe, might just as well have been entitled 'commercial law', 'entrepreneurial law', or 'trade law'. Although they chose the first, they point out that the subject-matter is a 'sub-branch of civil law' which has no distinct section in the Civil Code of the Russian Federation.[9] They define

---

[4] See P. P. Tsitovich, *Очерк основных понятий торгового права* [Essays on Basic Concepts of Trade Law] (1912 ed.; 2001).

[5] See A. I. Kaminka, *Очерки торговово права* [Essays on Trade Law] (1912 ed.; 2002).

[6] See, for example, Iu. K. Tolstoi, 'На путях кодификации гражданского законодательства' [On the Path of Codification of Civil Legislation], *Правоведение*, no. 3 (1994), p. 26.

[7] See, among others, B. I. Puginskii (ed.), *Коммерческое право в России* [Commercial Law in Russia] (1999), pp. 7–8.

[8] V. M. Gordon, *Система советского торгового права* [System of Soviet Trade Law] (Kharkov, 1924), pp. 6–7.

[9] See V. F. Popondopulo and V. F. Iakovleva, in their introduction to *Коммерческое право* [Commercial Law] (2002), I, p. 10. In *Russian Law* (1999; 2nd ed 2002) I have found it convenient to devote separate chapters to civil law and to entrepreneurial law. The fashion for 'commercial law'

commercial law as '. . . the aggregate of general and special norms of civil law regulating property and connected personal nonproperty relations between persons effectuating entrepreneurial activity, or with the participation thereof, based on equality, autonomy, and the property autonomy of the participants thereof'.[10]

The predominant view in Russian legal doctrine today distinguishes entrepreneurial, commercial, and trade law, however they may differ among themselves, from 'economic law' (sometimes translated very misleadingly as 'business' law). Those partial to economic law believe that the concept of economic activity is inextricably linked with economic management: 'Economic activity and the management thereof comprise a unified sphere of socialist economic management which forms a unified branch of legal regulation . . . An enterprise enters into economic legal relations with another enterprise (horizontal relations) which together with vertial relations comprise a unified complex economic legal relation'.[11] This approach combines the public and private law dimensions of commercial, entrepreneurial, trade, or economic relations and operation, hence the reference to 'vertical' relations of administrative subordination and 'horizontal' relations of legal equality. An 'Economic Code', strongly favoured during the Soviet era, continues to be an ideal supported by proponents of economic law in a market-orientated economy, although such a code in a market economy would, of course, be different from the drafts prepared for a planned economy.[12] In Ukraine both economic and civil codes were adopted at third reading on 29 November 2001 by the Supreme Rada, but vetoed by the President of Ukraine.[13]

is reflected to some extent in Western writings, although without the theoretical 'baggage'. An example is H. Oda, *Russian Commercial Law* (2002).

[10] Popondopulo (n 9 above) p. 14. Elsewhere the same author writes that 'Commercial (entrepreneurial) law is private law, comprising (although a special) part of civil law' (p. 37). E. A. Sukhanov defined 'commercial law' as a sub-branch of civil law together with other such sub-branches as the right to a thing, the law of obligations, inheritance law, family law, and private international law. See E. A. Sukhanov, '*Система частного права*' [System of Private Law], *Вестник Московского университета, Серия 11.* Право (1994), no. 4, pp. 30–31.

[11] See V. V. Laptev (ed.), *Теоретические проблемы хозяйственного права* [Theoretical Problems of Economic Law] (1975), p. 13. An early post-Soviet work on economic law is V. S. Martem'ianov, *Хозяйственное право* [Economic Law] (1994) in two volumes. The view that economic and entrepreneurial law are the same or similar is set out in O. M. Oleinik (ed.), *Предпринимательское (хозяйственное) право. Учебник* [Entrepreneurial (Economic) Law. Textbook] (1999), in two volumes. Also see V. V. Laptev, *Предпринимательское право: понятие и субъекты* [Entrepreneurial Law: Concept and Subjects] (1997); I. V. Doinikov, *Предпринимательское право* [Entrepreneurial Law] (1999); I. V. Ershova and T. M. Ivanova, *Предпринимательское право* [Entrepreneurial Law] (2000).

[12] See, among other writings, V. V. Laptev, '*Хозяйственное право—право предпринимательской деятельности*' [Economic Law—Law of Entrepreneurial Activity], *Государство право*, no. 1 (1993), pp. 36–39.

[13] See V. K. Mamutov (ed.), *Хозяйственное право* [Economic Law] (Kiev, 2002). The authors observe: 'The authors of this book proceed from the fact that the branch of law regulating relations with regard to the organisation and effectuation of economic activity do not reduce merely to what is called entrepreneurship or commerce. Entrepreneurship is one of the orientations of economic activity, one of whose features is receiving profit. But, first, tens of thousands of subjects of

Opponents of economic law reject, amongst other things, the mixture or combining of public and private law regulation into an autonomous branch of law.[14]

So much for conceptual definitions. The substantive scope of works on commercial, trade, entrepreneurial, and economic law shares a certain common core, albeit with divergent emphases and formulations. Kruglova concentrates upon the 'field' of commercial activity of an enterprise, the legal mechanism and subjects (economic partnerships and societies) of commercial law, the people's enterprise (which in practice is apparently almost nonexistent), the general provisions on obligations, antimonopoly activity, the legal regulation of purchase-sale and delivery of goods, trade turnover of production assets of an enterprise (immoveables, lease, finance leasing), State regulation of foreign trade activity, including frontier trade and free economic zones, and the legal foundations of the securities market.[15] Rassolov concentrates upon economic societies and partnerships (subjects of commercial activity), the law of ownership, general provisions on obligations and types of commercial contracts in commercial activity, settlements of accounts and provision of credit, insurance, delict, dispute settlement, elements of taxation, and foreign economic activity. Popondopulo and Iakovleva also include intellectual property, privatisation, and legal services for enterprises in their understanding of commercial law.

From this brief conspectus of the principal Russian works on commercial law, it is apparent that the enactments translated in this volume are central to all approaches to the subject. The term 'company law', which does not translate into Russian literally, during the early 1990s was called 'enterprise' law, but as enterprises figured merely in passing in the Civil Code and the early Russian market legislation on enterprises has been repealed, modern parlance prefers to speak of 'organisations' or 'societies'. The term 'enterprise' is reserved principally for the 'unitary enterprise' in State ownership. Moreover, until the introduction into Russian law of 'holding companies', the expression 'company' for most of the twentieth century in Russian legal terminology referred to foreign business entities.[16] The inclination of many Anglo-American sources to refer to Russian 'companies' (as they commonly do with respect to the French *société* or the German *Gesellschaft*) instead of the literal Russian terminology of a 'society' [*общество*] obscures the true legal nature of the Russian 'economic society' and its distinctive conceptual origins in Soviet approaches to the concept of a 'juridical person', fully

economic activity are created and function not to derive profit, but for the purposes of resolving social tasks. Second, industrial, construction, transport, and other enterprises are created and effectuate economic activity not only for the purposes of receiving profit' (p. 3).

[14] The principle of distinguishing between public and private law, they stress, originates in the Digests of Justinian.

[15] See N. Iu. Kruglova, *Коммерческое право* [Commercial Law] (2001).

[16] But not entirely, at least in the prerevolutionary period. See A. I. Kaminka, *Акционерные компании: Юридическое исследование* [Joint-Stock Companies: Legal Study] (1902). Only volume one appeared.

xvi

reflected in the Russian Civil Code.[17] With these qualifications, we use the expression 'company' as a convenient shorthand expression for the principal commercial and noncommercial organisations that may be created under Russian legislation and the laws regulating their formation, licensing, competitive relations, insurance, and land relations.

Many Russian conceptions of commercial law are sufficiently broad to encompass securities regulation, pledge and mortgage, regulation of money laundering, and finance leasing within their purview. However, we transcend Russian conceptions by including foreign investment laws, which seem to fall outside all Russian doctrinal formulations of the subject. I have yet to discover a reasoned argument to explain why they should be overlooked.

Certain background information is given on each enactment below, together with references to, principally, subordinate normative legal acts of relevance in applying or construing them.

GENERAL PROVISIONS

Registration of Juridical Persons

The Federal Law on the State Registration of Juridical Persons was adopted by the State Duma on 13 July 2001, approved by the Soviet of the Federation on 20 July 2001, and signed by the President of the Russian Federation on 8 August 2001. It entered into force on 1 July 2002, except for Article 27(2), which entered into force on the date of official publication, 10 August 2001.

Charges for the registration of juridical persons under the Federal Law are determined by the 1991 Law on State Duty, as amended.

Licensing

The Federal Law on Licensing Individual Types of Activity was adopted by the State Duma on 13 July 2001, approved by the Soviet of the Federation on 20 July 2001, was signed by the President of Russia on 8 August 2001, and entered into force six months after the day of its official publication, in February 2002. It replaced an identically-titled Federal Law of 25 September 1998, as amended.

The List of federal agencies of executive power which effectuate licensing and the List of types of activity to be licensed by agencies of executive power of subjects of the Russian Federation and federal agencies of executive power were

---

[17] The definition of a juridical person in the Russian Civil Code reads as follows: 'A juridical person shall be deemed to be an organisation which has solitary property in ownership, economic jurisdiction, or operative management and is liable for its obligations with such property and may in its own name acquire and effectuate property and personal nonproperty rights, bear duties, and be a plaintiff or defendant in court. Juridical persons must have an autonomous balance sheet or estimate' (Article 48(1), Civil Code of the Russian Federation). See W. E. Butler (transl.), *Civil Code of the Russian Federation* (2001), p. 99.

confirmed by Decree of the Government of the Russian Federation of 11 February 2002, No. 135. The number of individual statutes to be adopted is extensive; those confirmed by the Federal Government are enumerated with sources in an Annexe to the present Introduction below.

Competition and Antimonopoly Legislation

The Law on Competition and Limitation of Monopolistic Activity on the Goods Market was one of the early Russian Federation enactments in the transition to a market economy. Adopted on 22 March 1991, the original version closely followed an analogous enactment adopted by the USSR. The Law is addressed to competition of the 'goods market'. Competition on the securities, banking services, insurance, and other financial services markets is regulated by Federal Law No. 117-ФЗ of 23 June 1999. The procedure for submitting petitions to antimonopoly agencies to obtain authorisations to create, reorganise, or liquidate commercial organisations or associations thereof in compliance with antimonopoly requirements is regulated by an Order of the Ministry of Antimonopoly Policy of the Russian Federation of 13 August 1999, No. 276. The same Order governs the procedure for presenting notifications under Articles 17 and 18 of the Law.

Insurance

The Law on Insurance was adopted on 27 November 1992, No. 4015–1, and amended a number of times before being issued in a new version under a changed title: 'Law on the Organisation of Insurance Affairs in the Russian Federation'. Chapter 2 of the Law on insurance contracts was repealed on 31 December 1997 by reason of the enactment of the Civil Code of the Russian Federation. The provisions of Article 3, paragraph one, concerning prohibitions against certain types of insurance do not extend to societies subsidiary to foreign investors if on the day the Federal Law of 20 November 1999, No. 204-ФЗ, entered into force those societies had licenses to engage in the respective types of insurance. Similarly, the limitations contained in Article 6(4) do not apply to subsidiary societies grandfathered before the Federal Law of 20 November 1999 entered into force.

The calculation of the ratio of charter capital to foreign participation provided for by Article 6(3) of the Law on Insurance as of 1 January 2002 was confirmed by an Order of the Ministry of Finances of the Russian Federation of 6 March 2002, No. 44.

Mutual insurance societies provided for in Article 7 of the Law on Insurance are registered at the Department of Insurance Supervision of the Ministry of Finances of the Russian Federation pursuant to the Letter of the Ministry of Finances of 28 March 2001, No. 24–00/05.

The minimum paid-up capital established by Article 25 of the Law on Insurance does not extend to juridical persons who submitted documents to receive a license for insurance activity prior to the entry into force of Federal Law No. 157-ФЗ, of

31 December 1997. Prudential reserves are regulated in the Letter of the Ministry of Finances of the Russian Federation of 15 April 2002, No. 24–00/КП–51. The solvency of insurers provided for by the guarantees required in Article 27 of the Law on Insurance is secured by normative correlations provided for in the Statute on the Procedure for Calculation by Insurers of the Normative Correlation of Assets and Insurance Obligations Assumed by Them, confirmed by Order of the Ministry of Finances of the Russian Federation of 2 November 2001, No. 90н, which repealed an earlier Instruction of 30 October 1995, No. 02–02/20.

Land Code

The Land Code, which is Federal Law No. 136-ФЗ, was adopted by the State Duma on 28 September 2001, approved by the Soviet of the Federation on 10 October 2001, and signed by the President of the Russian Federation on 25 October 2001. The Land Code entered into force on the day of official publication, 30 October 2001.

The Land Code must be read against Chapter 17 of the Civil Code of the Russian Federation. The procedure for land tenure operations (Article 69, Land Code) is regulated by the Federal Law No. 78-ФЗ, 18 June 2001, 'On Land Tenure'. Juridical persons, with certain exceptions, are required to reformalise the right of permanent or in perpetuity land use or to acquire the land plots they occupy in ownership before 1 January 2004 pursuant to Article 36 of the Land Code. Russian citizens who previously held land by right of permanent or in perpetuity use or inheritable possession for life have the right, without limitation, to acquire their land plots in ownership.

The issue of private land ownership in Russia has turned principally on the question as to whether foreign citizens would be able to acquire agricultural lands in ownership or would be confined to lease arrangements. That question, together with the special regime of agricultural lands, was addressed in the Federal Law on the Turnover of Lands of Agricultural Designation, No. 101-ФЗ, adopted by the State Duma on 26 June 2002, approved by the Soviet of the Federation on 10 July 2002, and signed by the President of the Russian Federation on 24 July 2002. The Law entered into force six months after first official publication, which occurred on 27 July 2002.

ECONOMIC SOCIETIES AND PARTNERSHIPS

Limited Responsibility Societies

The Federal Law on Limited Responsibility Societies of 8 February 1998, No. 14-ФЗ, was adopted by the State Duma on 14 January 1998 and approved by the Soviet of the Federation on 28 January 1998. It has been twice amended. The name of the Law illustrates the dangers in referring loosely to 'limited liability companies' in English, for the Russian legislator has used the general concept of 'limited liability', a feature of all Russian juridical persons, to describe one particular type of economic society. The OOO, as it is known from its Russian acronym, is widely used by Russian entrepreneurs, though more sparingly by foreign investors because of VAT consequences in the event that participatory shares in the OOO are transferred to another person. Foreign investors must read the Law on Limited Responsibility Societies against the 1999 Law on Foreign Investments in the Russian Federation.

Disputes arising out of the conclusion of 'interested' or 'large-scale' transactions by economic societies have been addressed by an Information Letter of the Presidium of the Supreme Arbitrazh Court of the Russian Federation, No. 62, of 13 March 2001.

Joint-Stock Societies

The Law on Joint-Stock Societies was signed by the President of the Russian Federation on 26 December 1995, officially published on 29 December 1995, and entered into force as from 1 January 1996. The Law superseded a subordinate normative act, the Statute on Joint-Stock Societies confirmed by Decree of the RSFSR Council of Ministers, No. 601, on 25 December 1990.[18] All joint-stock societies registered prior to 1 January 1996 were required to bring their constitutive documents in accordance with the 1995 Law not later than 1 July 1997.

The 1990 Statute on Joint-Stock Societies was supplemented directly and indirectly by the Edict of 4 July 1992 on privatisation,[19] which dealt with a number of issues relating to the management of joint-stock societies formed by way of joint-stockisation within the privatisation programme. Many joint-stock charters registered after July 1992 drew upon the model of the Presidential Edict, although they were not obliged to, finding the provisions of Decree 601 somewhat basic.

Certain collateral and subordinate legislation is of relevance when applying the Law on Joint-Stock Societies. On defending the rights of stockholders and the interests of the State in its capacity as owner and stockholder, see the Edict of the President of the Russian Federation of 18 August 1996, No. 1210. The requirements for the charter of an investment fund, in addition to those set out in Article 11 of the Law on Joint-Stock Societies, are augmented by the Federal Law on Investment Funds of 29 November 2001, No. 156-ФЗ. The paying up of stocks, under Article 34 of the Law on Joint-Stock Societies, or participatory shares issued by credit organisations through the use of federal loan bonds having permanent coupon revenues or by using monetary means, is regulated by an Instructive Regulation of the Central Bank of the Russian Federation of 8 June 1999, No.

---

[18] СП РСФСР (1991), no. 6, item 92; transl. in W. E. Butler, *Basic Legal Documents of the Russian Federation* (1992), pp. 209–225; and in W. E. Butler and M. E. Gashi-Butler, *Legal Aspects of Doing Business in Russia* (1993), pp. 67–76.

[19] See W. E. Butler (transl.), *Soviet Business Legislation* (1992).

571-У. The procedure for valuing net assets of a society, in conformity with Article 35(3) of the Law on Joint-Stock Societies, is in the case of credit organisations governed by a joint Order of the Ministry of Finances of the Russian Federation, No. 108, and of the Federal Securities Commission of the Russian Federation, No. 235, of 24 December 1996. Under Article 35(4) of the Law on Joint-Stock Societies, should the yearly audit disclose a shortfall of charter capital in comparison with net assets the procedure for credit organisations to rectify the situation is addressed in an Instructive Regulation of the Central Bank of the Russian Federation, 27 August 2001, No. 1024-У.

Stockholder registers referred to in Article 44 of the Law on Joint-Stock Societies are kept in accordance with the Statute on Keeping the Register of Possessors of Inscribed Securities, confirmed by Decree of the Federal Securities Commission of the Russian Federation of 2 October 1997, No. 27. Stockholder meetings in which a so-called 'golden stock' may be voted are conducted pursuant to the Federal Law of 21 July 1997, No. 123-ФЗ. External voting at a general stockholder meeting is regulated by Decree of the Federal Securities Commission of the Russian Federation, No. 8, of 20 April 1998. The information to be contained in ballots at a general stockholder meeting is stipulated by a Letter of the Federal Securities Commission of the Russian Federation of 16 June 2000, No. ИК–07/2861, and the requirements for keeping ballots cast at such meetings, by the Information Letter of the Federal Securities Commission of 28 November 2000, No. ИК–07/6364.

Whether and how juridical persons participate as members of a council of directors (Article 64, Law on Joint-Stock Societies) is addressed in the Letter of the Federal Securities Commission of the Russian Federation of 31 March 2000, No. ИК–04/1608. Joint-stock investment funds must relegate other issues than those enumerated in Article 65 of the Law on Joint-Stock Societies to the exclusive competence of the council of directors; these are set out in the Federal Law of 29 November 2001, No. 156-ФЗ.

The term of powers of an internal audit commission, an institution unknown in western company practice, is governed by the Letter of the Federal Securities Commission of the Russian Federation of 28 February 2000, No. ИК–07/883.

Article 92(1) of the Law on Joint-Stock Societies concerning information to be provided to stockholders by a society must be read against Article 67(1) of the Civil Code of the Russian Federation. Publication of yearly bookkeeping reports by open joint-stock societies is affected by the Order of the Ministry of Finances of the Russian Federation of 28 November 1996, No. 101. Affiliated societies mentioned in Article 93 of the Law on Joint-Stock Societies are determined to be such in accordance with the Federal Law of 22 March 1991, No. 948–1. Affiliated persons must be recorded and information about them submitted to the Bank of Russia pursuant to a Statute of the Central Bank of the Russian Federation of 19 March 2002, No 184-П.

People's Enterprises

The Federal Law on the Peculiarities of the Legal Status of Joint-Stock Societies of Workers (People's Enterprises) was adopted by the State Duma on 24 June 1998, approved by the Soviet of the Federation on 9 July 1998, and signed by the President of the Russian Federation on 19 July 1998. The Law entered into force on 1 October 1998 and was amended on 21 March 2002.

Financial-Industrial Groups

The Federal Law on Financial-Industrial Groups was adopted by the State Duma on 27 October 1995, approved by the Soviet of the Federation on 15 November 1995, and signed by the President of the Russian Federation on 30 November 1995. The Law entered into force on the day of official publication, 6 December 1995.

On 22 May 1996 the Decree of the Government of the Russian Federation, No. 621, confirmed the Statute on the Procedure for Keeping the State Register of Financial-Industrial Groups of the Russian Federation.

Banks and Banking Activity

The Law on Banks and Banking Activity of 2 December 1990 remains the foundation enactment for all banks in the Russian Federation. On 3 February 1996 it was issued in a revised version, which has been amended with some frequency thereafter and been the subject of constitutional litigation. The key concept is the 'credit organisation', of which a 'bank' is merely one type and to be distinguished from a nonbanking credit organisation.

The procedure for regulating the activities of nonbanking credit organisations, mentioned in Article 1 of the Law on Banks, is regulated by the Statute of the Central Bank of the Russian Federation of 21 September 2001, No. 153-П. The procedure for opening and the activity in Russia of representations of foreign credit organisations (Article 2, Law on Banks) is governed by Order of the Central Bank of the Russian Federation of 7 October 1997, No. 02–437. Transfers of monetary means on behalf of natural persons without opening bank accounts (Article 5(9), Law on Banks) are treated in Letter of the Central Bank of the Russian Federation of 23 November 1998, No. 327-T. Trust management operations by credit organisations are addressed in an Instruction confirmed by Order of the Central Bank of the Russian Federation of 2 July 1997, No. 02–287. A credit organisation which engages in production, trade, or insurance activity, contrary to Article 5 of the Law on Banks, is subject to administrative responsibility under Article 15.26 of the 2001 Code on Administrative Violations.

On the use of special words and word combinations in the names of credit organisations (Article 7, Law on Banks), see the Decree of the Government of the

Russian Federation of 7 December 1996, No. 1463, and the Telegram of the Central Bank of the Russian Federation, 15 March 1996, No. 42–96.

The acquisition by natural persons of participatory shares or stocks in the charter capital of a credit organisation is regulated by the Statute confirmed by the Central Bank of the Russian Federation on 26 March 1999, No. 72-П, and the procedure generally for obtaining prior consent to acquire 20% or more participatory share or stocks in a credit organisation, by the Instruction of the Central Bank of the Russian Federation of 23 July 1998, No. 75-И.

The reference in Article 16 of the Law on Banks to Article 254(2) of the 1971 Code of Laws on Labour of the RSFSR has not yet been amended, but the equivalent is Article 81(7) of the 2001 Labour Code of the Russian Federation.

Revocation of the license of a credit organisation referred to in Article 20 of the Law on Banks may be initiated in accordance with the Directive of the Central Bank of the Russian Federation of 27 August 2001, No. 1025-У.

A number of subordinate acts are directed towards reinforcing the financial reliability of a credit organisation. Important among them are the Statute on the procedure for forming and using the reserve fund of a credit organisation, confirmed by the Central Bank of the Russian Federation on 24 April 2000, No. 112-П; and the Instruction of the Central Bank of the Russian Federation on the procedure for forming and using the reserve for possible loan losses, of 30 June 1997, No. 62a. The Statute on the Organisation of Internal Control in Banks was confirmed by Order of the Central Bank of the Russian Federation on 28 August 1997, No. 02–372.

Article 31, paragraph three, of the Law on Banks should be read as applicable when Article 856 of the Civil Code of the Russian Federation is not applicable, pursuant to the Decree of the Plenum of the Supreme Court of the Russian Federation and Plenum of the Supreme Arbitrazh Court of the Russian Federation of 8 October 1998, No. 13/14.

Bankruptcy and Insolvency

Bankruptcy legislation has been regarded by many observers, including international financial institutions, as the keystone of the transition to a market economy. Without a concept of bankruptcy, State enterprises were at liberty to continue to operate, usually under highly subsidised arrangements, rather than pay the economic price of their inefficiencies. The second Federal Law on Insolvency (or Bankruptcy) was adopted by the State Duma on 10 December 1997 and approved by the Soviet of the Federation on 24 December 1997. It was signed by the President of the Russian Federation on 8 January 1998 as Federal Law No. 6-ФЗ. On three occasions the Constitutional Court of the Russian Federation held individual provisions of the Law to be unconstitutional. It was replaced by the third Federal Law on the subject on 26 October 2002 with effect from 1 January 2003.

What the legislation on bankruptcy designates as the 'State agency for cases concerning bankruptcy and financial recuperation' (Article 25) is the Federal Service of Russia for Financial Recuperation and Bankruptcy, established by Edict of the President of the Russian Federation of 25 May 1999, No. 651, as amended on 29 February 2000. The Statute on the Federal Service was confirmed by Decree of the Government of the Russian Federation of 4 April 2000, No. 301.

The remuneration of arbitrazh managers provided for by Article 22 of the Federal Law is regulated by an Order of the Federal Service of Russia for Financial Recuperation and Bankruptcy of 18 September 2000, No. 301.

Articles 141–143 of the 1998 Law on Bankruptcy made provision for the enactment of a special Federal Law on the Insolvency (or Bankruptcy) of Credit Organisations, duly adopted by the State Duma on 18 September 1998, approved by the Soviet of the Federation on 14 October 1998, and signed by the President not until 25 February 1999, No. 40-ФЗ. Whether the adoption of this Law before the so-called 'August Crisis' of 1998 would have cushioned the impact of that crisis on the hundreds of Russian banks that became insolvent, one can only speculate. The Constitutional Court of the Russian Federation has declared certain provisions of the Federal Law to be unconstitutional.

Instruction of the Central Bank of the Russian Federation of 12 July 1999, No. 84-И, addresses the procedure for taking measures to prevent the insolvency or bankruptcy of credit organisations. The reorganisation of credit organisations by way of merger or accession is addressed in the Statute confirmed by the Central Bank of Russia on 30 December 1997, No. 12-П. The procedure for publishing announcements concerning the liquidation of a credit organisation in the *Вестник Банка России* is laid down in a Directive of the Central Bank of 7 July 1999, No. 602-У. These enactments will be replaced or changed to take account of the 2002 Federal Law.

Unitary Enterprises

Unitary enterprises in State or municipal ownership are regulated by the Civil Code of the Russian Federation to some extent. Being in State ownership, they are governed by the Conception of the Management of State Property and Privatisation in the Russian Federation, approved by Decree of the Government of the Russian Federation, No. 1024, of 9 September 1999.

Pursuant to the Civil Code of the Russian Federation, they are regulated in detail by the Federal Law on State and Municipal Unitary Enterprises, No. 161-ФЗ, of 14 November 2002.

Noncommercial Organisations

Notwithstanding their designation, noncommercial organisations are coming to play a significant part in commercial activity as an 'organisational-legal form' because legislation requires them to be used for certain commercial structures. Examples are to be found in the field of securities legislation and the formation of advocate organisations.

The Federal Law on Noncommercial Organisations, No. 7-ФЗ, was adopted by the State Duma on 8 December 1995 and apparently not considered by the Soviet of the Federation. The President of the Russian Federation signed the Law on 12 January 1996. The Law does not extend to consumer cooperative societies, which are regulated by the Law of 19 June 1992, No. 3085-1, 'On Consumer Cooperative Societies (Consumer Societies and Unions Thereof) in the Russian Federation'. The legal status of social associations, a species of noncommercial organisation, is regulated by the Federal Law on Social Associations.

The Federal Law on Philanthropic Activity and Philanthropic Organisations was adopted by the State Duma on 7 July 1995 and signed by the President of the Russian Federation on 11 August 1995. The Law entered into force on the date of official publication, 17 August 1995, and was amended on 21 March 2002, with effect from 1 July 2002.

OBJECTS OF CIVIL RIGHTS

Securities Regulation

The Federal Law on the Securities Market, No. 39-ФЗ, was adopted by the State Duma on 20 March 1996, approved by the Soviet of the Federation on 11 April 1996, and signed by the President of the Russian Federation on 22 April 1996. Although the 1995 Federal Law on Joint-Stock Societies required that all stocks be inscribed, it should be noted that the Federal Law on Securities permitted bearer stocks to be issued in accordance with normative standards to be established by the Federal Securities Commission of the Russian Federation.

The Rules for the Effectuation of Broker and Dealer Activity on the Securities Market of the Russian Federation were confirmed by Decree of the Federal Securities Commission on 11 October 1999, No. 9. Securities management is affected by the Statute on Trust Management of Securities and Means of Investing in Securities confirmed by Decree of the Federal Securities Commission of 17 October 1997, No. 37. The Statute on Clearing Activity on the Securities Market of the Russian Federation was confirmed by Decree of the Federal Securities Commission on 12 November 1998, No. 51. The Statute on Depositary Activity in the Russian Federation was confirmed by Decree of the Federal Securities Commission of 16 October 1997, No. 36.

Stockholder registers are governed by the Statute on Conducting the Register of Possessors of Inscribed Securities, confirmed by Decree of the Federal Securities Commission on 2 October 1997, No. 27. Nominee holders of securites who fail to provide lists of true holders fall under the Statute on the Procedure for Termination of the Performance of Functions of the Nominee Holder of Securities, confirmed by Decree of the Federal Securities Commission of 10 November 1998, No. 46. So-called market-makers, or what the Federal Law on Securities calls the 'organisers of trade on the securities market' are regulated by the Statute on the System of Control of Organisers of Trade on the Securities Market and Additional Requirements for Participants of Public Sales and Emitents of Securities, confirmed by Decree of the Federal Securities Commission of 26 October 2001, No. 28, and by the Statute on Requirements for Organisers of Trade on the Securities Market, confirmed by the Federal Securities Commission on 4 January 2002, No. 1-пс.

The registration of securities issues is governed by the Statute on Registering Agencies Effectuating the State Registration of Issues of Securities, confirmed by the Federal Securities Commission of 4 March 1997, No. 11. The notifications required in connection with the acquisition of securities by foreigners are addressed in an Information Letter of the Federal Securities Commission of 2 August 2001, No. ИК–04/5159.

The procedure for the publication and entry into force of decrees of the Federal Securities Commission which in the opinion of the Ministry of Justice of the Russian Federation do not require State registration is governed by the Decree of the Federal Securities Commission of 27 December 2000, No. 22.

The procedure for the Federal Securities Commission to issue authorisations permitting emission securities of Russian emitents to circulate outside Russia in the form of securities of foreign emitents issued in accordance with foreign law is addressed by a Statute confirmed by the Federal Securities Commission on 13 March 2001, No. 3.

Certain violations of securities legislation constitute crimes under the Criminal Code of the Russian Federation; see Articles 185 and 185[1]. Administrative responsibility for securities violations is provided for in the 2001 Code on Administrative Violations; see Articles 15.17–15.24.

On 5 March 1999 the President of the Russian Federation signed the Federal Law No. 46-ФЗ, On Defence of the Rights and Legal Interests of Investors on the Securities Market, which had been approved by the State Duma on 12 February 1999 and approved by the Soviet of the Federation on 18 February 1999. The Law entered into force from the day of official publication, 11 March 1999, and has been amended on 27 December 2000 and twice on 30 December 2001.

Article 5(4) of the Federal Law lost force in connection with amendments made on 7 August 2001 to the Law on Joint-Stock Societies and is now repealed.

Article 17 remains in force, but only until changes are made to the Federal Law on the Securities Market (Article 20(4)).

Money Laundering

The Federal Law on Counteracting the Legalisation (or Laundering) of Revenues Received by Criminal Means and Financing of Terrorism, No. 115-ФЗ, was adopted by the State Duma on 13 July 2001, approved by the Soviet of the Federation on 20 July 2001, and signed by the President of the Russian Federation on 7 August 2001. The Law entered into force on 1 February 2002.

The empowered agency under the Law is the Committee of the Russian Federation for Financial Monitoring (KFM RF), created in accordance with Article 8 of the Federal Law by Edict of the President of the Russian Federation, No. 1263, of 1 November 2001. The Statute on the Committee was confirmed by Decree of the Government of the Russian Federation, No. 211, on 2 April 2002. The forms for the submission of information concerning operations subject to obligatory control under Article 7 of the Federal Law were notified by Letter of the Committee for Financial Monitoring, No. 02–1–27/632, of 17 May 2002. Credit organisations submit information to the Committee for Financial Monitoring pursuant to a Statute confirmed by the Central Bank of the Russian Federation, No. 161-П, 28 November 2001. The Central Bank of the Russian Federation effectuates control over compliance by credit organisations with the requirement to submit information under a Statute confirmed by the Central Bank, No. 160-П, of 28 November 2001.

Pursuant to Article 9 of the Law against money laundering, the Statute on the Provision of Information and Documents to the Committee of the Russian Federation for Financial Monitoring by Agencies of State Power of the Russian Federation, Agencies of State Power of Subjects of the Russian Federation, and Agencies of Local Self-Government was confirmed by Decree of the Government of the Russian Federation on 14 June 2002, No. 425.

Pledge and Mortgage

The Law on Pledge was an early foundation-stone in the transition to a market economy in the Russian Federation. It was signed by the President of the Russian Federation on 29 May 1992, No. 2872–1. The Law has never been formally amended; however, the Law on Mortgage (or Pledge of Immoveables) of 29 October 1998 provides that the Law on Pledge continues to operate in so far as not inconsistent with the Law on Mortgage.

The Federal Law on Mortgage (or Pledge of Immoveables), No. 102-ФЗ, was adopted by the State Duma on 24 June 1997, approved by the Soviet of the Federation on 9 July 1998, and signed by the President of the Russian Federation on 16 July 1998. The Law entered into force on the day of official publication, 22 July 1998, and has been amended on 9 November 2001, 11 February 2002, and 24 December 2002.

Valuations required by the Law on Mortgage are made under the Federal Law No. 135-ФЗ 'On Valuation Activity in the Russian Federation' of 29 July 1998. An Instruction on the Procedure for the Registration of the Mortgage of a Dwelling Premise Which Arose by Virtue of a Law or Contract, and also on the Procedure for Changing the Pledgeholder in Connection with the Transfer of Rights of Demand Under Mortgage Credits was confirmed jointly by Order of the Ministry of Justice of the Russian Federation, No. 289, Gosstroi RF, No. 235, and the Federal Securities Commission, No. 290, of 16 October 2000.

Finance Leasing

The Federal Law on Finance Leasing, No. 164-ФЗ, was adopted by the State Duma on 11 September 1998, approved by the Soviet of the Federation on 14 October 1998, and signed by the President of the Russian Federation on 29 October 1998. The Law entered into force from the day of official publication, 5 November 1998, and was amended extensively on 29 January 2002.

Foreign Investments

The Federal Law on Foreign Investments in the Russian Federation, No. 160-ФЗ, was adopted by the State Duma on 25 June 1999, approved by the Soviet of the Federation on 2 July 1999, and signed by the President of the Russian Federation on 9 July 1999. The Law entered into force from the day of official publication, 14 July 1999, and was amended on 21 March 2002 and 25 July 2002. It replaced the 1991 Law on foreign investments.[20]

On goods brought in to Russia as a contribution to charter capital of an enterprise with foreign investments, see the Letter of the State Customs Committee of the Russian Federation, No. 01–15/21733, of 12 August 1999. The State registration of commercial organisations with foreign investments is addressed in a Letter of the Ministry of Justice of the Russian Federation of 26 July 1999, No. 5893-ЭР, and of 24 September 1999, No. 7659-ЭР.

The Federal Law on Investment Activity in the Form of Capital Investments was adopted by the State Duma on 15 July 1998, approved by the Soviet of the Federation on 17 July 1998, and signed by the President of the Russian Federation on 25 February 1999 as Federal Law No. 39-ФЗ. The Law entered into force from the day of official publication, 4 March 1999, and was amended on 2 January 2000. The 1991 Law on Investment Activity in the RSFSR remains in force in so far as not contrary to the provisions of the 1999 Law on Investment Activity.

State guarantees mentioned in Article 11 of the 1999 Federal Law are regulated by the Statute on Granting State Guarantees for Investment Projects of Social and National Economic Significance, confirmed by Decree of the Government of the Russian Federation, No. 1249, of 12 November 1999.

---

[20] See W. E. Butler, *Foreign Investment Law in the Commonwealth of Independent States* (2002), which contains all present and previous CIS foreign investment legislation.

International Arbitration

The Law of the Russian Federation on International Commercial Arbitration, No. 5338–1, was adopted by the Supreme Soviet of the Russian Federation on 7 July 1993. Official publication was in *Ведомости СНД и ВС РФ* (1993), no. 32, item 1240.

Russia has been a progenitor of arbitration as an instrument for the peaceful settlement of disputes since the nineteenth century. Even in the Soviet era, when there was profound suspicion about the possibility of 'neutral' arbitrators, the response was to encourage domestic international arbitral tribunals rather than to abandon arbitration entirely. The present Law marks the full return of Russian arbitration to the international community. Based upon the UNCITRAL Model Law, the law extends to all international commercial arbitration in Russia and not merely arbitrations conducted within the International Court of Commercial Arbitration attached to the Chamber of Commerce and Industry of the Russian Federation. Appended to the Law in the form of Annexes are the Statute on the International Commercial Arbitration Court and the Statute on the Maritime Arbitration Commission, which must be read against the Decree on the introduction of the Law into force.

So-called 'domestic arbitration', long regulated by various enactments profoundly inconsistent with one another, became the subject of a single codification in the form of the Federal Law on Arbitration Courts in the Russian Federation, No. 102-ФЗ, adopted by the State Duma on 21 June 2002, approved by the Soviet of the Federation on 10 July 2002, and signed by the President of the Russian Federation on 24 July 2002, with effect from the first day of official publication, which occurred on 27 July 2002. From that date Annexe 3 of the 1964 Code of Civil Procedure of the Russian Federation lost force, together with other designated relevant enactments.

INDIVIDUAL STATUTES ON LICENSING CERTAIN TYPES OF ACTIVITY

The List below is given in the sequence of types of activity contained in Article 17 of the 2001 Law on the Licensing of Individual Types of Activity. Each Statute has been confirmed by a Decree of the Government of the Russian Federation on the date designated; sources of official publication are given where available.

Statute on Licensing the Working Out of Aviation Technology, Including Aviation Technology of Dual Designation, confirmed by Decree of 27 May 2002, No. 346. СЗ РФ (2002), no. 23, item 2159

Statute on Licensing of Production of Aviation Technology, Including Aviation Technology of Dual Designation, confirmed by Decree of 27 May 2002, No. 346. СЗ РФ (2002), no. 23, item 2159

Statute on Licensing of Repair of Aviation Technology, Including Aviation Technology of Dual Designation, confirmed by Decree of 27 May 2002, No. 346. СЗ РФ (2002), no. 23, item 2159

Statute on Licensing the Testing of Aviation Technology, Including Aviation Technology of Dual Designation, confirmed by Degree of 27 May 2002, No. 346. СЗ РФ (2002), no. 23, item 2159

Statute on Licensing Activity With Regard to Working Out and/or Production of Means of Defence of Confidential Information, confirmed by Decree of 27 May 2002, No. 348. СЗ РФ (2002), no. 23, item 2161; РГ, 22 June 2002, p. 12

Statute on Licensing Activity With Regard to Technical Defence of Confidential Information, confirmed by Decree of 30 April 2002, No. 290. СЗ РФ(2002), no. 18, item 1775

Statute on Licensing Activity With Regard to the Working Out, Production, Realisation, and Acquisition for the Purposes of Sale of Special Technical Means Intended for Nontransparent Receipt of Information by Individual Entrepreneurs and Juridical Persons Effectuating Entrepreneurial Activity, confirmed by Decree of 15 July 2002, No. 526. СЗ РФ (2002), no. 29, item 2965; РГ, 9 August 2002, p. 30

Statute on Licensing of Activity in Armaments and Military Technology, confirmed by Decree No. 456, 21 June 2002 СЗ РФ (2002), no 26, item 2599; РГ, 10 July 2002, p. 14

Statute on Licensing of Production of Weapon and Basic Parts of FIrearm, confirmed by Decree No. 455, 21 June 2002. СЗ РФ (2002), no. 26, item 2598; РГ, 10 July 2002, p. 11

Statute on Licensing of Production of Cartridges for Weapon and Component Parts of Cartridges, confirmed by Decree No. 457, 21 June 2002. СЗ РФ (2002), no. 26, item 2600; РГ, 10 July 2002, p. 11

Statute on Licensing of Working Out and Production of Ammunition, confirmed by Decree No. 467, 26 June 2002. СЗ РФ (2002), no. 26, item 2607

Statute on Licensing Utilisation of Ammunition, confirmed by Decree No. 467, 26 June 2002. СЗ РФ (2002), no. 26, item 2607

Statute on Licensing Activity With Regard to Fulfilment of Work and Rendering of Services With Regard to Keeping, Carriages, and Destruction of Chemical Weapons, confirmed by Decree of 27 May 2002, No. 347. СЗ РФ (2002), no. 23, item 2160

Statute on Licensing Activity With Regard to the Operation of Explosive Production Objects, confirmed by Decree of 4 June 2002, No. 382. СЗ РФ (2002), no. 23, item 2182; РГ, 26 June 2002, p. 11

Statute on Licensing Activity With Regard to the Operation of Chemically-Dangerous Production Objects, confirmed by Decree of 4 June 2002, No. 382. СЗ РФ (2002), no. 23, item 2182; РГ, 26 June 2002, pp. 11–12

Statute on Licensing Activity With Regard to the Operation of Main Pipeline Transport, confirmed by Decree of 4 June 2002, No. 382. СЗ РФ (2002), no. 23, item 2182; РГ, 26 June 2002, p. 12

Statute on Licensing Activity With Regard to the Operation of Oil and Gas Extractive Production Entities, confirmed by Decree of 4 June 2002, No. 382. СЗ РФ (2002), no. 23, item 2182; РГ, 26 June 2002, p. 12

Statute on Licensing Activity With Regard to the Prevention and Extinguishing of Fires, confirmed by Decree of 31 May 2002, No. 373. СЗ РФ (2002), no. 23, item 2175

Statute on Licensing Production of Work With Regard to Assembly, Repair, and Servicing of Means of Ensuring Fire Safety of Buildings and Installations, confirmed by Decree of 31 May 2002, No. 373. СЗ РФ (2002), no. 23, item 2175

Statute on Licensing Activity With Regard to Operation of Gas Networks, confirmed by Decree of 4 June 2002, No. 382. СЗ РФ (2002), no. 23, item 2182

Statute on Licensing Activity With Regard to Operation of Oil and Gas Extractive Production Entities, confirmed by Decree of 4 June 2002, No. 382. СЗ РФ (2002), no. 23, item 2182; РГ, 26 June 2002, p. 12

Statute on Licensing Activity With Regard to Conducting Expert Examination of Industrial Safety, confirmed by Decree of 4 June 2002, No. 382. СЗ РФ (2002), no. 23, item 2182; РГ, 26 June 2002, p. 12

Statute on Licensing Production of Explosive Materials of Industrial Designation, confirmed by Decree of 26 June 2002, No. 468. СЗ РФ (2002), no. 26, item 2608

Statute on Licensing Keeping of Explosive Materials of Industrial Designation, confirmed by Decree of 26 June 2002, No. 468. СЗ РФ (2002), no. 26, item 2608

Statute on Licensing Use of Explosive Materials of Industrial Designation, confirmed by Decree of 26 June 2002, No. 468. СЗ РФ (2002), no. 26, item 2608

Statute on Licensing Activity With Regard to Dissemination of Explosive Materials of Industrial Designation, confirmed by Decree of 26 June 2002, No. 468. СЗ РФ (2002), no. 26, item 2608

Statute on Licensing Production of Pyrotechnical Articles, confirmed by Decree of 26 June 2002, No. 467. СЗ РФ (2002), no. 26, item 2607

Statute on Licensing Production of Pyrotechnical Articles, confirmed by Degree of 26 June 2002, No. 467. СЗ РФ (2002), no. 26, item 2607

Statute on Licensing Activity With Regard to Dissemination of Pyrotechnical Articles of IV and V Classes in Accordance with State Standard, confirmed by Decree of 26 June 2002, No. 467. СЗ РФ (2002), no. 26, item 2607

Statute on Licensing Activity in Domain of Fire Safety, confirmed by Decree of 31 May 2002, No. 373. СЗ РФ (2002), no. 23, item 2175; РГ, 22 June 2002, p. 12

Statute on Licensing Performance of Work With Regard to Assembly, Repair, and Servicing of Means of Ensuring Fire Safety of Buildings and Installations, confirmed by Decree of 31 May 2002, No. 373. СЗ РФ (2002), no. 23, item 2175; РГ, 22 June 2002, p. 12

Statute on Licensing Activity With Regard to Operation of Gas Networks, confirmed by Decree of 4 June 2002, No.382. СЗ РФ (2002), no. 23, item 2182; РГ, 26 June 2002, p. 12

Statute on Licensing Activity With Regard to Designing Buildings and Installations of I and II Levels of Responsibility in Accordance with State Standard, confirmed by Decree of 21 March 2002, No. 174. СЗ РФ (2002), no. 12, item 1149

Statute on Licensing Activity With Regard to Construction of Buildings and Installations of I and II Levels of Responsibility in Accordance with State Standard, confirmed by Decree of 21 March 2002, No. 174. СЗ РФ (2002), no. 12, item 1149

Statute on Licensing Activity With Regard to Engineering Surveys for Construction of Buildings and Installations of I and II Levels of Responsibility in Accordance with State Standard, confirmed by Decree of 21 March 2002, No. 174. СЗ РФ (2002), no. 12, item 1149

Statute on Licensing Activity With Regard to Performance of Land Survey Work, confirmed by Decree of 4 June 2002, No. 382. СЗ РФ (2002), no. 23, item 2182; РГ, 26 June 2002, p. 12

Statute on Licensing of Geodesic Activity, confirmed by Decree of 28 May 2002, No. 360. СЗ РФ (2002), no. 23, item 2168; РГ, 22 June 2002, p. 10

Statute on Licensing of Cartographic Activity, confirmed by Decree of 28 May 2002, No. 360. СЗ РФ (2002), no. 23, itcm 2168; РГ, 22 June 2002, p. 10

Statute on Licensing Work With Regard to Active Impact on Hydro-meteorological Processes and Phenomena, confirmed by Decree of 20 May 2002, No. 324. СЗ РФ (2002), no. 21, item 1997

Statute on Licensing Work With Regard to Active Impact on Geophysical Processes and Phenomena, confirmed by Decree of 20 May 2002, No. 324. СЗ РФ (2002), no. 21, item 1997

Statute on Licensing Activity in Domain of Hydrometeorology and Neighbouring Domains, confirmed by Decree of 20 May 2002, No. 324. СЗ РФ (2002), no. 21, item 1997

Statute on Licensing of Pharmaceutical Activity, confirmed by Decree of 1 July 2002, No. 489. СЗ РФ (2002), no. 27, item 2700; РГ, 11 July 2002, p. 11

Statute on Licensing Production of Medicinal Means, confirmed by Decree of 4 July 2002, No. 500. СЗ РФ (2002), no. 27, item 2711; РГ, 11 July 2002, p. 11

Statute on Licensing Medical Activity, confirmed by Decree of 4 July 2002, No. 499. СЗ РФ (2002), no. 27, item 2710; РГ, 11 July 2002, p. 11

Statute on Licensing Activity With Regard to Rendering Prosthetic and

Orthopedic Assistance, confirmed by Decree of 13 May 2002, No. 309. СЗ РФ (2002), no. 20, item 1864

Statute on Licensing Activity With Regard to Cultivating Flora to be Used for Production of Narcotic Means and Psychotropic Substances, confirmed by Decree of 14 June 2002, No. 423. СЗ РФ (2002), no. 25, item 2455; РГ, 22 June 2002, p. 10

Statute on Licensing Activity Connected with Turnover of Narcotic Means and Psychotropic Substances included in List II in accordance with the Federal Law 'On Narcotic Means and Psychotropic Substances', confirmed by Decree of 21 June 2002, No. 454. СЗ РФ (2002), no. 26, item 2597; РГ, 3 July 2002, p. 10

Statute on Licensing Activity Connected with Turnover of Narcotic Means and Psychotropic Substances included in List III in accordance with the Federal Law 'On Narcotic Means and Psychotropic Substances', confirmed by Decree of 21 June 2002, No. 454. СЗ РФ (2002), no. 26, item 2597; РГ, 3 July 2002, p. 10

Statute on Licensing Activity Connected with the Use of Pathogens of Contagious Diseases, confirmed by Decree of 4 July 2002, No. 501. СЗ РФ (2002, no. 27, item 2712

Statute on Licensing Activity Connected with Production of Disinfection, Fumigation, and Rodent Control Means, confirmed by Decree of 4 July 2002, No. 501. СЗ РФ (2002), no. 27, item 2712

Statute on Licensing Carriages of Maritime Transport of Passengers, confirmed by Decree of 19 June 2002, No. 447. СЗ РФ (2002), no. 26, item 2590

Statute on Licensing Carriages of Maritime Transport of Cargo, confirmed by Decree of 19 June 2002, No. 447. СЗ РФ (2002), no. 26, item 2590

Statute on Licensing Carriages of Cargo by Internal Water Transport, confirmed by Decree of 27 May 2002, No. 345. СЗ РФ (2002), no. 23, item 2158

Statute on Licensing Carriages of Passengers by Internal Water Transport, confirmed by Decree of 27 May 2002, No. 345. СЗ РФ (2002), no. 23, item 2158

Statute on Licensing of Loading and Unloading Activity on Internal Water Transport, confirmed by Decree of 27 May 2002, No. 345. СЗ РФ (2002), no. 23, item 2158

Statute on Licensing Carriages of Passengers and Freight by Motor Vehicle Transport, confirmed by Decree of 10 June 2002, No. 402. СЗ РФ (2002), no. 24, item 2306; РГ, 19 June 2002, p. 11

Statute on Licensing Carriages of Passengers by Railway Transport, confirmed by Decree of 5 June 2002, No. 383. СЗ РФ (2002), no. 23, item 2183; РГ, 18 June 2002, p. 13

Statute on Licensing Carriages of Goods by Railway Transport, confirmed by Decree of 5 June 2002, No. 383. СЗ РФ (2002), no. 23, item 2183; РГ, 18 June 2002, p. 14

Statute on Licensing Surveyor Servicing of Sea-Going Vessels in Sea Ports, confirmed by Decree of 19 June 2002, No. 447. СЗ РФ (2002), no. 26, item 2590

Statute on Licensing Loading and Unloading Activity in Sea Ports, confirmed by Decree of 19 June 2002, No. 447. СЗ РФ (2002), no. 26, item 2590

Statute on Licensing Loading and Unloading Activity on Railway Transport, confirmed by Decree of 5 June 2002, No. 383. СЗ РФ (2002), no. 23, item 2183; РГ, 18 June 2002, p. 14

Statute on Licensing Activity With Regard to Effectuation of Towages of Maritime Transport, confirmed by Decree of 19 June 2002, No. 447. СЗ РФ (2002), no. 26, item 2590

Statute on Licensing Activity With Regard to Technical Servicing and Repair of Rolling Stock on Railway Transport, confirmed by Decree of 5 June 2002, No. 383. СЗ РФ (2002), no. 23, item 2183; РГ, 18 June 2002, p. 13

Statute on Licensing Activity With Regard to Technical Servicing and Repair of Technical Means Used on Railway Transport, confirmed by Decree of 5 June 2002, No. 383. СЗ РФ (2002), no. 23, item 2183

Statute on Licensing Activity With Regard to Treatment of Dangerous Wastes, confirmed by Decree of 23 May 2002, No. 340. СЗ РФ (2002), no. 23, item 2157

Statute on Licensing Activity With Regard to the Organisation and Maintenance of Totalisers and Gambling Institutions, confirmed by Decree of 15 July 2002, No. 525. СЗ РФ (2002), no. 29, item 2964; РГ, 1 August 2002, p. 4

Statute on Licensing Valuation Activity, confirmed by Decree of 7 June 2002, No. 395. СЗ РФ (2002), no. 23, item 2192; РГ, 18 June 2002, p. 14

Statute on Licensing Tour Operator Activity, confirmed by Decree of 11 February 2002, No. 95. СЗ РФ (2002), no. 7, item 695

Statute on Licensing Tourist Agency Activity, confirmed by Decree of 11 February 2002, No. 95. СЗ РФ (2002), no. 7, item 695

Statute on Licensing the Procurement, Processing, and Realisation of Scrap of Nonferrous Metals, confirmed by Decree of 23 July 2002, No. 552. СЗ РФ (2002), no. 30, item 000; РГ, 1 August 2002, p. 4

Statute on Licensing the Procurement, Processing, and Realisation of Scrap of Ferrous Metals, confirmed by Decree of 23 July 2002, No. 553. СЗ РФ (2002), no. 30, item 000; РГ, 1 August 2002, p. 4

Statute on Licensing Activity Connected with Arrangement of Employment of Citizens of Russian Federation Beyond Limits of Russian Federation, confirmed by Decree of 14 June 2002, No. 424. СЗ РФ (2002), no. 25, item 2456; РГ, 21 June 2002, p. 29

Statute on Licensing Activity With Regard to Public Showing of Audiovisual Works if the Said Activity is Effectuated in Cinema Hall, confirmed by Decree of 13 May 2002, No. 308. СЗ РФ (2002), no. 20, item 1863

Statute on Licensing Activity With Regard to Reproduction (or Manufacture of Examples) of Audiovisual Works and Phonograms on Any Types of Carriers, confirmed by Decree of 4 June 2002, No. 381. СЗ РФ (2002), no. 23, item 2181; РГ, 19 June 2002, p. 12

Statute on Licensing Auditor Activity, confirmed by Decree of 29 March 2002, No. 190. СЗ РФ (2002), no. 14, item 1298

Statute on Licensing Activity with Regard to Raising Pedigree Livestock (except for Instance when said activity is effectuated to ensure own needs of juridical person or individual entrepreneur), confirmed by Decree of 4 July 2002, No. 497. СЗ РФ (2002), no. 27, item 2708

Statute on Licensing Activity with Regard to Production and Use of Pedigree Livestock (or Material), except for instance when said activity is effectuated to ensure own needs of juridical person or individual entrepreneur, confirmed by Decree of 4 July 2002, No. 497. СЗ РФ (2002), no. 27, item 2708

Statute on Licensing Activity of Investment Funds, confirmed by Decree of 7 June 2002, No. 394. СЗ РФ (2002), no. 23, item 2191; РГ, 19 June 2002, p. 12

Statute on Licensing Activity with regard to Management of Investment Funds, Share Investment Funds, and Non-State Investment Funds, confirmed by Decree of 4 July 2002, No. 495. СЗ РФ (2002), no. 27, item 2707

Statute on Licensing Activity of Specialised Depositaries of Investment Funds, Share Investment Funds, and Non-State Investment Funds, confirmed by Decree of 5 June 2002, No. 384. СЗ РФ (2002), no. 23, item 2184; РГ, 18 June 2002, p. 5

Statute on Licensing of Non-State Pension FUnds, confirmed by Decree of 22 July 2002, No. 546. СЗ РФ (2002), no. 30, item 000; РГ, 1 August 2002, p. 4

Statute on Licensing Activity With Regard to Production of Elite Seeds (or Seeds of Best Specimens), confirmed by Decree of 13 June 2002, No. 415. СЗ РФ(2002), no. 25, item 2450; РГ, 22 June 2002, p. 9

Statute on Licensing Activity With Regard to the Production of Tobacco Manufactures, confirmed by Decree of 22 July 2002, No. 548. СЗ РФ (2002), no. 30, item 000; РГ, 1 August 2002, p. 4

Statute on Licensing Activity With Regard to Manufacture and Repair of Means of Measurement, confirmed by Decree of 27 May 2002, No. 352. СЗ РФ (2002), no. 23, item 2162

Statute on Licensing Activity Effectuated at Sea with Regard to the Acceptance and Transporting of Catches of Aquatic Biological Resources, Including Fish, and also Other Aquatic Fauna and Flora, confirmed by Decree of 4 July 2002, No. 496. СЗ РФ (2002), no. 30, item 2860; РГ, 17 July 2002, p. 12

Statute on Licensing Activity With Regard to Keeping Grain and Products of Processing Thereof, confirmed by Decree of 13 June 2002, No. 414. СЗ РФ (2002), no. 25, item 2449; РГ, 22 June 2002, p. 9

Statute on Licensing of Outer Space Activity, confirmed by Decree of 14 June 2002, No. 422. СЗ РФ (2002), no. 25, item 2454; РГ, 22 June 2002, p. 10

Statute on Licensing of Veterinary Activity, confirmed by Decree of 5 July 2002, No. 504. СЗ РФ (2002), no. 28, item 2862; РГ, 18 July 2002, p. 6

ABBREVIATIONS

Ведомости СНД и ВС РФ	*Ведомости Съезда народных депутатов и Верховного Совета Российской Федерадии* [Vedomosti of the Congress of People's Deputies and Supreme Soviet of the Russian Federation]
KFM RF	Committee of the Russian Federation for Financial Monitoring
РГ	*Российская газета* [Russian Newspaper]
СЗ РФ	*Собрание законодательства Российской Федерадии* [Collection of Legislation of the Russian Federation]

FEDERAL LAW ON THE STATE REGISTRATION OF JURIDICAL PERSONS

[Federal Law No. 129-ФЗ. 8 August 2001.
СЗ РФ (2001), no. 33(I), item 3431]

Chapter I	General Provisions	1
Chapter II	State Register	2
Chapter III	Procedure of State Registration	5
Chapter IV	State Registration of Juridical Persons in Event of Creation Thereof	7
Chapter V	State of Juridicial Persons Created by Means of Reorganisation	8
Chapter VI	State Registration of Changes Made in Constitutive Documents of Juridical Person and Making Changes in Information Concerning Juridical Person Contained in State Register	10
Chapter VII	State Registration of Juridical Person in Connection with Liquidation Thereof	12
Chapter VIII	Refusal of State Registration, Responsibility for Violation of the Procedure of State Registration	13
Chapter IX	Transitional and Concluding Provisions	14

Chapter I. General Provisions

Article 1. Relations Regulated by Present Federal Law

The present Federal Law regulates relations arising in connection with the State registration of juridical persons, in the event of their creation, reorganisation, and liquidation, when making changes in their constitutive documents, and when keeping the unified State register of juridical persons (hereinafter—State register).

State registration of juridical persons (hereinafter—State registration) is an act of an empowered federal agency of executive power effectuated by means of inserting information in the State register concerning the creation, reorganisation, and liquidation of juridical persons, and also other information concerning juridical persons in accordance with the present Federal Law.

Legislation of the Russian Federation on State registration shall consist of the Civil Code of the Russian Federation, the present Federal Law, and other normative legal acts of the Russian Federation issued in accordance therewith.

Article 2. Agency Effectuating State Registration of Juridical Persons

State registration shall be effectuated by the federal agency of executive power (hereinafter—registering agency) empowered in the procedure established by the Constitution of the Russian Federation and Federal Constitutional Law 'On the Government of the Russian Federation'.

Article 3. State Duty for State Registration

State duty shall be paid for State registration in accordance with legislation on taxes and charges.

Chapter II. State Register

Article 4. Principles of Keeping State Register

1. A State register shall be kept in the Russian Federation containing information concerning the creation, reorganisation, and liquidation of juridical persons and respective documents.

The uniformity and comparability of the said information shall be ensured at the expense of complying with the unity of principles, methods, and forms of keeping the State register.

The State register shall be a federal information resource.

The State register shall be kept on paper and electronic carriers. In the event of a nonconformity between entries on paper carriers and electronic carriers the entries on paper carriers shall have priority unless another procedure for keeping the State register has been established.

The keeping of the State register on electronic carriers shall be effectuated in accordance with uniform organisational, methodological, and programme-technical principles ensuring the compatibility and interaction of the State register with other federal information systems and networks.

2. The keeping of the State register shall be effectuated by the registering agency in the procedure established by the Government of the Russian Federation.

Article 5. Content of State Register

1. The following information and documents on a juridical person shall be contained in the State register:

(a) full and (if there is such) abbreviated name, including firm name, for commercial organisations in the Russian language. If in the constitutive documents of a juridical person the name thereof has been indicated in one of the languages of the peoples of the Russian Federation and/or in a foreign language, the name of the juridical person in these languages also shall be indicated in the State register;

(b) the organisational-legal form;

(c) the address (or location) of the permanently operating executive organ of the juridical person (in the absence of a permanently operating executive organ of the juridical person—another organ or person having the right to operate in the name of the juridical person without a power of attorney) with regard to which the link with the juridical person is effectuated;

(d) the means of formation of the juridical person (creation or reorganisation);

(e) information concerning the founders of the juridical person;

(f) copies of the constitutive documents of the juridical person;

(g) information concerning legal succession—for juridical person created as a result of the reorganisation of other juridical persons, for juridical persons in whose constitutive documents are entered changes in connection with reorganisation, and also for juridical persons who have terminated their activity as a result of reorganisation;

(h) the date of registration of changes entered in the constitutive documents of a juridical person, or in instances established by a law, the date of receipt by the registering agency of information concerning changes entered in constitutive documents;

(i) the means of termination of the activity of the juridical person (by means of reorganisation or by means of liquidation);

(j) the amount of charter capital (or contributed capital, charter fund, share contributions, or other) specified in the constitutive documents of a commercial organisation;

(k) the surname, forename, patronymic, and post of the person having the right without a power of attorney to act in the name of the juridical person, and also the passport data of this person or data of other documents certifying identity in accordance with legislation of the Russian Federation, and the taxpayer identification number if there is such;

(l) information concerning licenses received by the juridical person.

2. In the event of a change in the State register information previously inserted shall be preserved. The procedure and periods for exclusion from the State register of obsolete information and the destruction of obsolete documents shall be determined by the Government of the Russian Federation.

3. Entries shall be inserted in the State register on the basis of documents submitted by applicant in the event of State registration of juridical persons and making of entries in the State register. Each entry shall be conferred with a State registration number and for each entry the date shall be indicated of the inserting thereof in the register. In the event of the failure of the information of the State register specified in point 1 of the present Article to conform to information contained in documents submitted during the State registration, the information specified in point 1 of the present Article shall be considered to be reliable until the inserting of respective corrections therein.

The information specified in point 1(l) of the present Article shall be submitted by licensing agencies not later than five work days from the moment of the adoption of the respective decision.

4. A juridical person shall be obliged within three days from the moment of changing the information specified in point 1 of the present Article, except for information specified in subpoint (l), to inform the registering agency thereof at the place of its location. If a change of the said information has occurred in connection with the inserting of changes in the constitutive documents, the making of changes in the State register shall be effectuated in the procedure provided for by Chapter VI of the present Federal Law.

5. All documents submitted to the registering agency in accordance with the present Federal Law must be contained in the registration file of the juridical person, information concerning the State registration of which has been inserted in the State register.

Registration files of juridical persons shall be part of the State register.

Article 6. Provision of Information Contained in State Register

1. Information contained in the State register shall be open and generally accessible, except for the passport data of natural persons and their taxpayer identification numbers.

Passport data of natural persons and their taxpayer identification numbers may be provided exclusively with regard to inquiries of agencies of State power in accordance with their competence.

2. Information contained in the State register concerning a specific juridical person shall be provided in the form of:

extracts from the State register;

copies of a document(s) contained in the registration file;

reference concerning the absence of the information requested.

The form and procedure for the provision of information contained in the State register shall be established by the Government of the Russian Federation.

3. The period for the provision of information contained in the State register shall be established by the Government of the Russian Federation and may not comprise more than five days from the day of receipt by the registering agency of the respective inquiry.

4. A refusal to provide information contained in the State register shall not be permitted.

Article 7. Conditions for Receipt of Information Contained in State Register

1. The provision of information contained in the State register shall be effectuated for payment, unless established otherwise by federal laws.

The amount of payment for the provision of information contained in the State register shall be established by the Government of the Russian Federation.

2. In the instances and in the procedure which have been established by federal laws and normative legal acts of the Government of the Russian Federation the registering agency shall provide free of charge information contained in the State register with regard to inquiries of agencies of State power, including law enforcement agencies and courts with regard to cases under proceedings, agencies of local self-government, and also other persons determined by federal laws.

3. The means received in the form of payment for the provision of information contained in the State register shall be used exclusively for the purposes of the creation, maintenance, and development of the system of State registration, including for the purposes of keeping the State register.

Chapter III. Procedure of State Registration

Article 8. Periods and Place of State Registration

1. State registration shall be effectuated within a period of not more than five work days from the day of submission of documents to the registering agency.

2. State registration of a juridical person shall be effectuated at the location of the permanently operating executive organ specified by the founders in the application concerning State registration, and in the absence of such executive organ— at the location of another organ or person having the right to act in the name of the juridical person without a power of attorney.

Article 9. Procedure for Submission of Documents During State Registration

1. Documents shall be submitted to the registering agency by the empowered person directly or shall be sent by post with a declared value on the parcel and a list of the enclosures. Other means of submitting documents to the registering agency may be determined by the Government of the Russian Federation.

The requirements for the formalisation of documents submitted to the registering agency established by the Government of the Russian Federation.

The following natural persons may be empowered persons (hereinafter— applicant):

executive of the permanently operating executive organ of the juridical person being registered or other person having the right without a power of attorney to act in the name of his juridical person;

founder(s) of the juridical person during the creation thereof;

executive of the juridical person acting as the founder of the juridical person being registered;

bankruptcy manager or head of the liquidation commission (or liquidator) in the event of liquidation of the juridical person;

other person acting on the basis of a power of attorney or other power provided for by a federal law, or act of specially empowered State agency, or act of agency of local self-government.

The applicant shall certify the application by his signature submitted to the registering agency and shall indicate his passport date or data of another document certifying identity in accordance with legislation of the Russian Federation and taxpayer identification number (if there is such).

The signature of the applicant on the said application must be notarially certified.

2. The day of receipt thereof by the registering agency shall be the date of submission of the documents when effectuating State registration.

3. To the applicant shall be issued a receipt of receipt of the documents, specifying the enumeration and date thereof by the registering agency. The receipt must be issued on the day of receipt of the documents by the registering agency.

When documents are received by the registering agency sent by post, the receipt shall be sent within the work day following the day of receipt of the documents by the registering agency to the postal address specified by the application with notice concerning receipt thereof.

The registering agency shall ensure the recording and keeping of all documents submitted during State registration.

4. The registering agency shall not have the right to demand the submission of other documents except the documents established by the present Federal Law.

5. Notarial certification of documents submitted during State registration shall be necessary only in the instances provided for by federal laws.

Article 10. Peculiarities of Registration of Individual Types of Juridical Persons

A special procedure for the registration of individual types of juridical persons may be established by federal laws.

Article 11. Decision Concerning State Registration

1. The decision concerning State registration adopted by the registering agency shall be grounds for making a respective entry in the State register.

2. The making of the respective entry in the State register by the registering agency shall be deemed to be the moment of State registration.

3. The registering agency shall not later than one work day from the moment of State registration issue (or send) to the applicant a document confirming the

fact of the making of the entry in the State register. The form and content of the document shall be established by the Government of the Russian Federation.

4. The registering agency within a period of not more than five work days from the moment of State registration submit information concerning the registration to the State agencies determined by the Government of the Russian Federation. The composition of the information to be sent to the said State agency, and also the procedure and periods for the provision to the respective juridical person of information concerning its record data, shall be established by the Government of the Russian Federation.

Chapter IV. State Registration of Juridical Persons in Event of Creation Thereof

Article 12. Documents to be Submitted During State Registration for Juridical Person Being Created

There shall be submitted to the registering agency during State registration of a juridical person being created:

(a) an application signed by the applicant concerning State registration according to the form confirmed by the Government of the Russian Federation. It shall be confirmed in the application that the constitutive documents confirmed correspond to the requirements established by legislation of the Russian Federation for constitutive documents of a juridical person of the said organisational-legal form that the information contained in these constitutive documents, other documents submitted for State registration and application concerning State registration, are reliable, that when creating the juridical person the procedure for the founding thereof has complied with established for juridical persons of the particular organisational-legal form, including paying up of the charter capital (or charter fund, contributed capital, share contributions) at the moment of State registration, and in the instances established by a law the questions of the creation of the juridical person have been agreed with the respective State agency(ies) and/or agencies of local self-government;

(b) the decision concerning the creation of a juridical person in the form of a protocol, contract, or other document in accordance with legislation of the Russian Federation;

(c) the constitutive documents of the juridical person (originals or notarially certified copies);

(d) extract from the register of foreign juridical persons of the respective country of origin or other evidence equal in legal force of the legal status of the foreign juridical person-founder;

(e) document concerning the payment of State duty.

Article 13. Procedure for State Registration of Juridical Persons in Event of Creation Thereof

1. State registration of juridical persons in the event of the creation thereof shall be effectuated by registering agencies at the location of the permanently operating executive organ, and in the absence of the permanently operating executive organ—at the location of another organ or person having the right to act in the name of the juridical person without a power of attorney.

2. The submission of documents during State registration shall be effectuated in the procedure provided for by Article 9 of the present Federal Law.

3. State registration shall be effectuated within the periods provided for by Article 8 of the present Federal Law.

Chapter V. State of Juridical Persons Created by Means of Reorganisation

Article 14. Documents to be Submitted When Registering Juridical Person Created by Means of Reorganisation

1. The following documents shall be submitted in the event of the State registration of a juridical person created by way of reorganisation (transformation, merger, division, separation):

(a) the application signed by the applicant concerning the State registration of each newly arising juridical person created by means of reorganisation according to the form confirmed by the Government of the Russian Federation. It shall be confirmed in the application that the constitutive documents of the juridical persons created by way of reorganisation correspond to the requirements established by legislation of the Russian Federation to the constitutive documents of a juridical person of the particular organisational-legal form, that the information contained in these constitutive documents and application concerning State registration is reliable, that the act of transfer or separation balance sheet contains provisions concerning legal succession with regard to all obligations of the newly arising juridical person with respect to all of its creditors, and that all creditors of the person being reorganised have been notified in written form about the reorganisation and in the instances established by a law the questions concerning the reorganisation of the juridical person have been agreed with the respective State agencies and/or agencies of local self-government;

(b) the constitutive documents of each newly arising juridical person created by means of reorganisation (originals or notarially certified copies);

(c) the decision concerning the reorganisation of the juridical person;

(d) the contract concerning merger or accession in the instances provided for by federal laws;

(e) the act of transfer or separation balance sheet;

(f) the document concerning payment of State duty.

2. If changes are made in the constitutive documents of a juridical person created by means of reorganisation, the State registration of such changes shall be effectuated in accordance with the rules established by Chapter VI of the present Federal Law.

Article 15. Procedure of State Registration of Juridical Person Created by Way of Reorganisation

1. State registration of juridical persons created by way of reorganisation shall be effectuated by registering agencies at the location of the juridical persons being reorganised.

If the location of juridical persons to be created by means of reorganisation is different from the location of the juridical person being reorganised, the procedure for interaction of the registering agencies shall be determined by the Government of the Russian Federation.

2. If the reorganisation entails termination of the activity of one or several juridical persons, the registering agency shall make an entry in the State register concerning the termination of the activity of such juridical persons upon receipt of information from the respective registering agency concerning the State registration of the newly arisen juridical persons, except for instances specified in Article 16(5) of the present Federal Law.

3. The submission of documents of juridical persons created by way of reorganisation shall be effectuated in the procedure provided for by Article 9 of the present Federal Law.

4. State registration of juridical persons created by way of reorganisation shall be effectuated within the periods provided for by Article 8 of the present Federal Law.

Article 16. Completion of State Registration of Juridical Person to be Created by Way of Reorganisation

1. The reorganisation of a juridical person in the form of transformation shall be considered to be completed from the moment of State registration of the juridical person newly arisen, and the transformed juridical person—to have terminated its activity.

2. The reorganisation of juridical persons in the form of merger shall be considered to be completed from the moment of State registration of the juridical person which newly arose, and juridical persons reorganised in the form of merger shall be considered to have terminated their activity.

3. The reorganisation of a juridical in the form of division shall be considered to be completed from the moment of State registration of the last from the juridical persons which newly arose, and the juridical person reorganised in the form of separation shall be considered to have terminated its activity.

4. The reorganisation of a juridical person in the form of separation shall be considered to be completed from the moment of State registration of the last of the juridical persons which newly arose.

5. The reorganisation of a juridical person in the form of accession shall be considered to be completed from the moment of the making of an entry in the State register concerning termination of the activity of the last of the acceding juridical persons.

Chapter VI. State Registration of Changes Made in Constitutive Documents of Juridical Person and Making Changes in Information Concerning Juridical Person Contained in State Register

Article 17. Documents to be Submitted for State Registration of Changes Made in Constitutive Documents of Juridical Person and Making Changes in Information Concerning Juridical Person Contained in State Register

1. For the State registration of changes made in constitutive documents of a juridical person there shall be submitted to the registering agency:

(a) the application signed by the applicant concerning State registration according to the form confirmed by the Government of the Russian Federation. It shall be confirmed in the application that the changes made in the constitutive documents of a juridical person correspond to the requirements established by legislation of the Russian Federation, that the information contained in these documents and in the application is reliable, and that the procedure for adoption of the decision concerning the making of changes in the constitutive documents of the juridical person established by a federal law has been complied with;

(b) the decision concerning the making of changes in the constitutive documents of the juridical person;

(c) the changes made in the constitutive documents of the juridical person;

(d) the document concerning the payment of State duty.

2. In order to make changes in the State register affecting information concerning a juridical person but not connected with the making of changes in the constitutive documents of the juridical person, an application signed by the applicant shall be submitted to the registering agency concerning the making of changes in the State register according to the form confirmed by the Government of the Russian Federation. It shall be confirmed in the application that the changes made correspond to the requirements established by legislation of the Russian Federation and the information contained in the application is reliable.

Article 18. Procedure of State Registration of Changes Made in Constitutive Documents of Juridical Person and Making Changes in Information Concerning Juridical Person Contained in State Register

1. State registration of changes made in the constitutive documents of a juridical person and/or the making of changes in the State register affecting information concerning the juridical person but not connected with the making of changes in the constitutive documents of a juridical person shall be effectuated by the registering agency at the location of the juridical person.

2. The submission of documents for registration of changes made in constitutive documents of a juridical person and/or the making of changes in the State register affecting information concerning the juridical person but not connected with changes of the constitutive documents of the juridical person shall be effectuated in the procedure provided for by Article 9 of the present Federal Law.

3. State registration of changes made in the constitutive documents of a juridical person, and/or the making of changes in the State register affecting information concerning the juridical person but not connected with the changes made in the constitutive documents of the juridical person shall be effectuated within the periods provided for by Article 8 of the present Federal Law.

4. In the event of making changes in information concerning a juridical person in connection with a change of location of the juridical person, the registering agency shall make a respective entry in the State register and send the registration file to the registering agency at the new location of the juridical person.

5. In the event of the State registration of constitutive documents in a new version and/or making of changes in the State register affecting information concerning the juridical person but not connected with changes made in the constitutive documents of a juridical person, a respective entry shall be made in the State register.

Article 19. Notification Concerning Making of Changes in Constitutive Documents of Juridical Person

1. In instances established by federal law, a juridical person shall submit to the registering agency at its location a notification signed by the applicant concerning the making of changes in constitutive documents, the decision concerning the making of changes in the constitutive documents, and the change.

2. When making changes in the constitutive documents of a juridical person the registering agency within a period of not more than five days from the moment of receipt of the said notification shall make a respective entry in the State register, of which the juridical shall be notified in written form.

3. In the instances provided for by federal law, the changes made in constitutive documents shall acquire force for third persons from the moment of notification of the registering agency about such changes.

Chapter VII. State Registration of Juridical Person in Connection with Liquidation Thereof

Article 20. Notification Concerning Liquidation of Juridical Person

1. The founders (or participants) of a juridical person or organ which adopted the decision concerning liquidation of a juridical person shall be obliged within a three-day period in written form to notify the registering agency thereof at the location of the juridical person being liquidated, appending the decision concerning liquidation of the juridical person.

2. The registering agency shall make an entry in the State register that the juridical person is in the process of liquidation. From that moment the State registration of changes made in the constitutive documents of the juridical person being liquidated, and also the State registration of juridical persons, a founder of which the said juridical person acts or the State registration of juridical persons which arise as a result of the reorganisation thereof, shall not be permitted.

3. The founders (or participants) of a juridical person or organ which adopted the decision concerning the liquidation of the juridical person shall notify the registering agency about the formation of the liquidation commission or about the appointment of a liquidator, and also about the drawing up of the interim liquidation balance sheet.

Article 21. Documents to be Submitted for State Registration in Event of Liquidation of Juridical Person

1. The following documents shall be submitted for State registration in connection with the liquidation of a juridical person to the registering agency:
(a) application signed by the applicant concerning State registration according to the form confirmed by the Government of the Russian Federation. It shall be confirmed in the application that the procedure for liquidation of the juridical person established by a federal law has been complied with, settlements of accounts with creditors have been completed, and questions of the liquidation of a juridical person have been agreed with the respective State agencies and/or municipal agencies in the instances established by a federal law;
(b) liquidation balance sheet;
(c) document concerning the payment of State duty.

2. When liquidating a juridical person in the event of the application of bankruptcy procedures, there shall be submitted to the registering agency:

(a) the ruling of the arbitrazh court concerning the completion of the bankruptcy proceedings;

(b) document concerning the payment of State duty.

Article 22. Procedure of State Registration in Event of Liquidation of Juridical Person

1. State registration in the event of the liquidation of a juridical person shall be effectuated by the registering agency at the location of the juridical person being liquidated.

2. A liquidation commission (or liquidator) shall notify the registering agency about the completion of the process of liquidation of the juridical person not earlier than two months from the moment of placement by the liquidation commission (or liquidator) in press organs of the publication concerning liquidation of the juridical person.

3. The documents provided for by Article 21 of the present Federal Law shall be submitted to the registering agency after completion of the process of liquidation of the juridical person.

4. The submission of documents for State registration in connection with the liquidation of a juridical person shall be effectuated in the procedure provided for by Article 9 of the present Federal Law.

5. State registration in the event of liquidation of a juridical person shall be effectuated within the periods provided for by Article 8 of the present Federal Law.

6. The liquidation of a juridical person shall be considered to be completed, and the juridical person—to have terminated its existence, after the making of the entry thereof in the State register. The registering agency shall publish information concerning the liquidation of the juridical person.

Chapter VIII. Refusal of State Registration, Responsibility for Violation of the Procedure of State Registration

Article 23. Refusal of State Registration

1. A refusal of State registration shall be permitted in the event of:

(a) the failure to submit necessary documents for State registration determined by the present Federal Law;

(b) the submission of documents to the improper registering agency.

2. A decision concerning refusal of State registration must contain the grounds for the refusal with an obligatory reference to the violation provided for by point 1 of the present Article.

3. A decision concerning a refusal of State registration must be adopted not later than the period established by Article 8 of the present Federal Law for State registration.

4. A decision concerning refusal of State registration shall be sent to the person specified in the application concerning State registration, with notification concerning the handing over of such decision.

5. A decision concerning refusal of State registration may be appealed in a judicial proceeding.

Article 24. Responsibility of Registering Agency for Violation of Procedure of State Registration

1. For an unsubstantiated, that is, failure to correspond to the grounds specified in Article 23 of the present Federal Law, refusal of State registration, failure to effectuate State registration within the established periods, or other violation of the procedure of State registration established by the present Federal Law, and also for a refusal to provide or the untimely provision of information contained in the State register, officials of registering agencies shall bear the responsibility established by legislation of the Russian Federation.

2. A registering agency shall compensate damage caused by a refusal of State registration, evasion of State registration, or violation of the procedure of State registration permitted through its fault.

Article 25. Responsibility of Applicant and/or Juridical Person for Unlawful Actions

1. For the failure to submit, or the untimely submission, or submission of unreliable information necessary for inclusion in the State register, the applicants and/or juridical persons shall bear the responsibility established by legislation of the Russian Federation.

2. The registering agency shall have the right to apply to a court with a demand concerning liquidation of the juridical person in the event flagrant violations of a law or other legal acts are permitted when creating such juridical person, if these violations are ineradicable, and also in the event of repeated or flagrant violations o laws or other normative legal acts concerning the State registration of juridical persons.

Chapter IX. Transitional and Concluding Provisions

Article 26. Transitional Provisions

1. Registration files concerning juridical persons previously registered kept in agencies effectuating State registration of juridical persons before the introduction of the present Federal Law into operation shall be part of the federal information centre.

2. The procedure and periods for the transfer of the said registration files to the registering agency shall be established by the Government of the Russian Federation.

3. An empowered person of a juridical person registered before the entry of the present Federal Law into force shall be obliged within six months from the day of entry of the present Federal Law into force to submit to the registering agency information provided for by Article 5(1)(a)-(e) and (k) of the present Federal Law.

The failure to fulfil the said requirement shall be grounds for the adoption by a court of a decision concerning the liquidation of such juridical person on the basis of the application of the registering agency.

Article 27. Introduction of Present Federal Law into Operation

1. The present Federal Law shall be introduced into operation from 1 July 2002, except for point 2 of the present Article, which shall be introduced into operation from the day of official publication of the present Federal Law.

2. Normative legal acts provided for by the present Federal Law shall be adopted by the Government of the Russian Federation from the day of official publication of the present Federal Law and before the introduction thereof into operation.

3. The President of the Russian Federation and the Government of the Russian Federation shall bring their normative legal acts into conformity with the present Federal Law.

FEDERAL LAW ON LICENSING INDIVIDUAL TYPES OF ACTIVITY

[Signed 8 August 2001, No. 128-ФЗ,
as amended 13 March 2002, No. 28-ФЗ, 21 March 2002,
No. 31-ФЗ, 9 December 2002, No. 164-ФЗ, and
10 January 2003, No. 17-ФЗ
СЗ РФ (2001), no. 33(I), item 3430; (2002), no. 11,
item 1020; no. 12, item 1093; no. 50, item 4925; (2003), no. 2]

Article 1. Sphere of Application of Present Federal Law

1. The present Federal Law shall regulate relations arising between federal agencies of executive power, agencies of executive power of subjects of the Russian Federation, juridical persons, and individual entrepreneurs in connection with the effectuation of the licensing of individual types of activity in accordance with a List provided for by Article 17(1) of the present Federal Law.

2. The operation of the present Federal Law shall not extend to the following types of activity:
    activity of credit organisations;
    activity connected with the defence of State secrecy;
    activity in the domain of the production and turnover of ethyl spirit, alcoholic and spirit-containing products;
    activity in the domain of communications;
    stock exchange activity;
    activity in the domain of customs;
    notarial activity;
    insurance activity;
    activity of professional participants of the securities market;
    effectuation of foreign economic operations;
    effectuation of international motor vehicle carriages of goods and passengers;
    acquisition of weapons and cartridges for them;
    use of results of intellectual activity;
    use of orbital-frequency resources and radio frequencies for the effectuation of television broadcasting and radiobroadcasting (including broadcasting of additional information);

use of natural resources, including the subsoil, forest fund, and objects of flora and fauna;

activity, work, and services in the domain of the use of atomic energy;

educational activity.

Article 2. Basic Concepts

For the purposes of the present Federal Law the following basic concepts shall be applied:

license: a special authorisation for the effectuation of a specific type of activity with obligatory compliance with the license requirements and conditions issued by a licensing agency to a juridical person or individual entrepreneur;

licensed type of activity: type of activity for the effectuation of which on the territory of the Russian Federation the receipt of a license is required in accordance with the present Federal Law;

licensing: measures connected with the granting of licenses, reformalisation of documents confirming the existence of licenses, suspension and renewal of the operation of licenses, annulment of licenses, and control of licensing agencies over compliance by the licensee when effectuating licensed types of activity with the respective license requirements and conditions;

license requirements and conditions: the aggregate of requirements and conditions established by statutes on the licensing of individual types of activity, the fulfilment of which by the licensee is obligatory when effectuating the licensed type of activity;

licensing agencies: federal agencies of executive power and agencies of executive power of subjects of the Russian Federation effectuating licensing in accordance with the present Federal Law;

licensee: juridical person or individual entrepreneur having a license for the effectuation of a specific type of activity;

aspirant licensee: juridical person or individual entrepreneur who has applied to a licensing agency concerning the granting of a license for the effectuation of a specific type of activity;

register of licenses: aggregate data concerning the granting of licenses, reformalisation of documents confirming the existence of licenses, and the suspension and renewal of the operation of licenses and the annulment of licenses.

Article 3. Basic Principles for Effectuation of Licensing

The basic principles for the effectuation of licensing shall be:

ensuring the unity of economic space on the territory of the Russian Federation;

establishment of the unified List of licensed types of activity;

establishment of the unified procedure of licensing on the territory of the Russian Federation;

establishment of the licensing requirements and conditions by statutes on the licensing of specific types of activity;

glasnost and openness of licensing;

compliance with legality when effectuating licensing.

Article 4. Criteria for Determining Licensed Types of Activity

There shall be relegated to licensed types of activity the types of activity whose effectuation may entail the causing of harm to the rights, legal interests, and health of citizens, defence and security of the State, the cultural heritage of the peoples of the Russian Federation, and the regulation of which may not be effectuated by other methods than by licensing.

Article 5. Determination of Powers of Russian Federation When Effectuating Licensing

For the purposes of ensuring the unity of economic space on the territory of the Russian Federation, the Government of the Russian Federation in accordance with the basic orientations of internal policy of the State determined by the President of the Russian Federation shall:

confirm statutes on licensing specific types of activity;

determine the federal agencies of executive power effectuating the licensing of specific types of activity;

establish the types of activity whose licensing is effectuated by agencies of executive power of subjects of the Russian Federation.

Article 6. Powers of Licensing Agencies

1. Licensing agencies shall effectuate the following powers:

granting of licenses;

reformalisation of documents confirming the existence of licenses;

suspension of the operation of licenses;

renewal of the operation of licenses;

annulment of licenses (in the event provided for by Article 13(3) of the present Federal Law);

keeping the register of licenses;

control over compliance by licensees when effectuating licensed types of activity of the respective license requirements and conditions.

The procedure for the effectuation of powers of licensing agencies shall be established by statutes concerning the licensing of specific types of activity.

2. Federal agencies of executive power may by agreement with agencies of executive power of subjects of the Russian Federation transfer to them the effectuation of their powers provided for by point 1 of the present Article.

Article 7. Operation of License

1. A license shall be granted for each type of activity specified in Article 17(1) of the present Federal Law.

The type of activity for the effectuation of which a license has been granted may be fulfilled only by the juridical person or individual entrepreneur who has received the license.

2. Activity for the effectuation of which a license is granted by a federal agency of executive power or agency of executive power of a subject of the Russian Federation may be effectuated throughout the entire territory of the Russian Federation. Activity for the effectuation of which a license is granted by a licensing agency of a subject of the Russian Federation may be effectuated on the territory of other subjects of the Russian Federation on condition of notification by the licensee of the licensing agencies of the respective subjects of the Russian Federation in the procedure established by the Government of the Russian Federation.

Article 8. Period of Operation of License

The period of operation of a license may not be less than five years. The operation of a license may upon the completion thereof be extended upon the application of the licensee.

Extension of the period of operation of a license shall be effectuated by way of reformalisation of a document confirming the existence of a license.

The operation of a license in perpetuity may be provided for by statutes on the licensing of specific types of activity.

Article 9. Adoption of Decision Concerning Issuance of License

1. In order to receive a license the aspirant for the license shall submit to the respective licensing agency the following documents:

an application concerning the granting of a license, specifying the name and organisational-legal form of the juridical person, and location—for a juridical person; surname, forename, and patronymic, place of residence and data of the document certifying the identity of a citizen—for an individual entrepreneur; licensed type of activity which the juridical person or individual entrepreneur intends to effectuate;

copies of the constitutive documents and copy of the document concerning State registration of the aspirant for the license as a juridical person (with the presentation of originals if copies have not been attested by a notary)—for a juridical person [as amended by Federal Law of 21 March 2002, No. 31-ФЗ];

a copy of the certificate concerning the State registration of a citizen as an individual entrepreneur (with the presentation of the original if the copy has not been attested by a notary)—for an individual entrepreneur;

a copy of the certificate concerning registration of the aspirant for the license in a tax agency (with the presentation of the original if the copy is not attested by a notary);

document confirming payment of the license charge for consideration by the licensing agency of the application concerning the granting of the license;

information concerning the skills of workers of the aspirant for the license.

It shall not be permitted to require from the aspirant for the license the presentation of documents not provided for by the present Federal Law and other federal laws.

All documents submitted to the respective licensing agency for the granting of a license shall be accepted according to an inventory, a copy of which shall be sent (or handed over) to the aspirant for the license with a notation concerning the date of acceptance of the documents by the said agency.

The aspirant for a license shall bear responsibility in accordance with legislation of the Russian Federation for the provision of unreliable or distorted information.

2. The licensing agency shall adopt a decision concerning the granting or a refusal to grant the license within a period not exceeding sixty days from the day of receipt of the application concerning the granting of a license with all necessary documents. The respective decision shall be formalised by an order of the licensing agency.

Briefer periods for adoption of the decision concerning the granting or refusal to grant the license may be established by the statutes on licensing specific types of activity.

The licensing agency shall be obliged to inform the aspirant for the license within the said period about the adoption of the decision concerning the granting or the refusal to grant the license.

Notification concerning the granting of the license shall be sent (or handed over) to the aspirant for the license in written form specifying the requisites of the bank account and the period for payment of the license charge for granting the license.

Notification concerning the refusal to grant a license shall be sent (or handed over) to the aspirant for the license in written form specifying the reasons for the refusal.

The licensing agency shall issue a document confirming the existence of a license to the licensee free of charge within three days after the submission by the aspirant for the license of the document confirming payment of the license charge for granting the license.

The licensee shall have the right to receive duplicates of the said document. Duplicates of the said document shall be granted to the licensee for payment equal to the payment established for providing the information contained in the register of licenses.

3. The grounds for a refusal to grant a license shall be:

the existence in the documents submitted by the aspirant for the license of unreliable or distorted information;

the failure of the aspirant for the license or of objects belonging to or used by it to conform to the license requirements and conditions.

A refusal to issue a license on the grounds of the amount of volume of products (or work, services) to be produced or planned for production by the aspirant for the license shall not be permitted.

4. An aspirant for a license shall have the right to appeal in the procedure established by legislation of the Russian Federation a refusal of the licensing agency to provide a license or the failure of the licensing agency to act.

Article 10. Content of Document Confirming Existence of License and Decision on Granting of License

There shall be specified in the decision concerning the granting of a license and in the document confirming the existence of a license:

the name of the licensing agency;

the name and organisational-legal form of the juridical person and location—for a juridical person;

the surname, forename, patronymic, place of residence, and data of the document certifying identity—for an individual entrepreneur;

licensed type of activity;

period of operation of the license;

taxpayer identification number;

number of the license;

date of adoption of the decision concerning the granting of a license.

Article 11. Reformalisation of Document Confirming Existence of License

1. In the event of the transformation of a juridical person or the change of its name or location, or the change of name or place of residence of an individual entrepreneur, or loss of the document confirming the existence of a license, the licensee—juridical person (or its legal successor) or individual entrepreneur—shall be obliged within not later than fifteen days to file an application concerning the reformalisation of the document confirming the existence of the license, appending the documents confirming the said changes or loss of document confirming the existence of a license.

2. In the event of the reformalisation of the document confirming the existence of a license the licensing agency shall make respective changes in the register of licenses. Reformalisation of the document confirming the existence of the license shall be effectuated within ten days from the day of receipt by the licensing agency of the respective application.

21

3. For reformalisation of the document confirming the existence of a license payment shall be recovered in the amount of 100 rubles, which shall be credited to the respective budget.

Article 12. Effectuation of Control

1. Control over compliance by the licensee with the license requirements and conditions determined by the statute on licensing of a specific type of activity shall be effectuated by licensing agencies within the limits of their competence.

2. Licensing agencies shall have the right to:
conduct verifications of the activity of the licensee on the subject of the conformity thereof to the license requirements and conditions;
request from the licensee necessary explanations and documents when conducting the verifications;
draw up on the basis of the results of verifications acts (or protocols) specifying specific violations;
render decisions obliging the licensee to eliminate elicited violations and establish the periods for the elimination of such violations;
render a warning to the licensee.

Article 13. Suspension of Operation of License and Annulment of License

1. Licensing agencies shall have the right to suspend the operation of a license in the event of the eliciting by licensing agencies of repeated violations or a flagrant violation by the licensee of license requirements and conditions.

A licensing agency shall be obliged to establish the period for the elimination of violations by the licensee which entailed suspension of the operation of a license. The said period may not exceed six months. If within the established period the licensee has not eliminated the said violations, the licensing agency shall be obliged to apply to a court concerning annulment of the license.

The licensee shall be obliged to inform the licensing agency in written form about the elimination by it of violations which entailed suspension of operation of the license. The licensing agency which suspended the operation of the license shall adopt a decision concerning renewal of the operation thereof and notify the licensee in written form within three days after receipt of the respective notification and verification of the elimination by the licensee of the violations which entailed suspension of operation of the license.

Payment shall not be recovered for renewal of the operation of a license. The period of operation of a license shall not be extended for the time of suspension of the operation thereof.

2. A license shall lose legal force in the event of the liquidation of the juridical person or termination of its activity as a result of a reorganisation, except for the

transformation thereof or the termination of the operation of the certificate concerning the State registration of a citizen as an individual entrepreneur.

3. Licensing agencies may annul a license without recourse to a court in the event of the licensee's failure to pay the license charge within three months for the granting of the license.

4. A license may be annulled by decision of a court on the basis of an application of a licensing agency if a violation by the licensee of license requirements and conditions entailed the infliction of damage to the rights, legal interests, health of citizens, defence and security of the State, cultural heritae of peoples of the Russian Federation, and/or in the event provided for by point 1, paragraph two, of the present Article. Simultaneously with the filing of an application in court the licensing agency shall have the right to suspend the operation of the said license for the period up to entry of the decision of the court into force.

5. The decision concerning suspension of the operation of a license, annulment of a license, or sending to a court of an application concerning the annulment of a license shall be communicated by the licensing agency to the licensee in written form with a reasoned substantiation of such decision not later than three days after the adoption thereof.

6. The decision concerning suspension of the operation of the license and annulment of the license may be appealed in the procedure established by legislation of the Russian Federation.

7. A licensing agency shall not have the right to conduct verifications with regard to a subject of jurisdiction of other agencies of State power and agencies of local self-government.

Article 14. Conducting of Registers of Licenses

1. Licensing agencies shall conduct the registers of licenses for types of activity, the licensing of which they effectuate.

There must be specified in the registers of licenses, besides the information specified in Article 10 of the present Federal Law:

information concerning the registration of licenses in the register of a license;

grounds and dates of the suspension and renewal of the operation of licenses;

grounds and date of the annulment of a license;

other information determined by the statutes on licensing of specific types of activity.

2. The information contained in the register of licenses shall be open for familiarisation by natural and juridical persons.

Information contained in the register of licenses shall be provided in the form of extracts concerning specific licensees to natural and juridical persons for payment. The amount of payment for the provision of the said information shall be 10 rubles.

Payment for the provision of information contained in the register of licenses shall be credited to the respective budget.

Information from the register of licenses shall be provided free of charge to agencies of State power and agencies of local self-government.

The period for provision of the information from a register of licenses may not exceed three days from the day of receipt of the respective application.

Article 15. License Charges

A license charge in the amount of 300 rubles shall be recovered for the consideration by a licensing agency of an application concerning the granting of a license.

A license charge in the amount of 1000 rubles shall be recovered for the granting of a license.

The amounts of license charges specified in the present Article shall be credited to the respective budgets.

Article 16. Financing of Licensing

The financing of licensing shall be effectuated within the limits of the means allotted for the maintenance of licensing agencies from the respective budgets.

Article 17. List of Types of Activity for Effectuation of Which Licenses Are Required

In accordance with the present Federal Law the following types of activity shall be subject to licensing:

development of aviation technology, including aviation technology of dual designation;

production of aviation technology, including aviation technology of dual designation;

repair of aviation technology, including aviation technology of dual designation;

testing of aviation technology, including aviation technology of dual designation;

activity with regard to dissemination of encoding (or cryptographic) means;

activity with regard to technical servicing of encoding (or cryptographic) means;

provision of services in domain of the encoding of information;

development and production of encoded (or cryptographic) means defended with use of encoded (or cryptographic) means of information systems and telecommunications systems;

activity with regard to issuance of certificates of keys for electronic encoded signatures, registration of possessors of electronic encoded signatures, rendering of services connected with use of electronic encoded signatures, and confirmation of genuineness of electronic encoded signatures;

activity with regard to eliciting electronic devices intended for nontransparent receipt of information in premises and technical means (except if the said activity is effectuated to ensure own needs of juridical person or individual entrepreneur);

activity with regard to the development and/or production of means of defence of confidential information;

activity with regard to technical defence of confidential information;

activity with regard to the development, production, realisation, and acquisition for the purposes of sale of special technical means intended for nontransparent receipt of information by individual entrepreneurs and juridical persons effectuating entrepreneurial activity;

activity with regard to manufacture of polygraphic product defended against counterfeits, including forms for securities, and also trade in the said product;

development of armament and military technology;

production of armament and military technology;

repair of armament and military technology;

utilisation of armament and military technology;

trade in armaments and military technology;

production of weapon and basic parts of firearm;

production of cartridges for weapon and components of cartridges;

trade in weapon and basic parts of firearm;

trade in cartridges for weapon;

exhibiting of weapon, basic parts of firearm, cartridges for weapon;

collecting of weapons, basic parts of firearm, cartridges for weapon;

development and production of ammunition;

utilisation of ammunition;

fulfillment of work and rendering of services with regard to keeping, carriage, and destruction of chemical weapon;

operation of explosively-dangerous production objects;

operation of flammable production objects;

operation of chemically-dangerous production objects;

operation of main pipeline transport;

operation of oil and gas extractive production entities;

processing of oil, gas, and products of processing thereof;

transporting on main pipelines of oil, as, and products of processing thereof;

keeping of oil, gas, and products of processing thereof;

[repealed by Federal Law of 9 December 2002, No. 164-ФЗ].

activity with regard to conducting expert examination of industrial safety;

production of explosive materials of industrial designation;

keeping of explosive materials of industrial designation;

use of explosive materials of industrial designation;

activity with regard to dissemination of explosive materials of industrial designation;

production of pyrotechnic manufactures;

activity with regard to dissemination of pyrotechnic manufactures of IV and V class in accordance with a State standard;

activity with regard to prevention and extinguishing of fires;

performance of work with regard to assembly, repair, and servicing of means for ensuring fire safety of buildings and installations;

activity with regard to operation of electricity networks (except if the said activity is effectuated to ensure own needs of juridical person or individual entrepreneur);

activity with regard to operation of gas networks;

activity with regard to operation of thermal networks (except if the said activity is effectuated to ensure own needs of juridical person or individual entrepreneur);

designing of buildings and installations of I and II levels of responsibility in accordance with State standard;

construction of buildings and installations of I and II levels of responsibility in accordance with State standard;

engineering surveys for construction of building and installations of I and II levels of responsibility in accordance with State standard;

performance of land-survey work;

activity with regard to restoration of objects of cultural heritage (monuments of history and culture);

geodesic activity;

cartographic activity;

fulfillment of work with regard to active impact on hydrometeorological processes and phenomena;

fulfillment of work with regard to active impact on geophysical processes and phenomena;

activity in domain of hydrometeorological and neighbouring domains;

pharmaceutical activity;

production of medicinal means;

production of medical technology;

activity with regard to dissemination of medicinal means and manufactures of medical designation;

technical servicing of medical technology (except if the said activity is effectuated to ensure own needs of juridical person or individual entrepreneur);

activity with regard to rendering prosthetic-orthopedic assistance;

cultivating of flora used for production of narcotic means and psychotropic substances;

activity connected with turnover of narcotic means and psychotropic substances (development, production, manufacture, processing, keeping, carriages, release, realisation, distribution, acquisition, use, destruction) in List II in accordance with the Federal Law 'On Narcotic Means and Psychotropic Substances';

activity connected with turnover of psychotropic substances (development, production, manufacture, processing, keeping, carriages, release, realisation, distribution, acquisition, use, destruction) in List III in accordance with the Federal Law 'On Narcotic Means and Psychotropic Substances';

activity connected with use of pathogens of contagious diseases;

production of disinfection, fumigation, and rodent control means;

carriages of passengers by maritime transport;

carriages of cargo by maritime transport;

carriages of passengers by internal water transport;

carriages of cargo by internal water transport;

carriages of passengers by air transport;

carriages of freight by air transport;

carriages of passengers by motor vehicle transport equipped for carriages of more than 8 persons (except if the said activity is effectuated to ensure own needs of juridical person or individual entrepreneur);

carriages of passengers on a commercial basis by light motor vehicle transport;

carriages by motor vehicle transport of freight exceeding 3.5 tons (except if the said activity is effectuated to ensure own needs of a juridical person or individual entrepreneur);

[paragraph repealed by Federal Law of 10 January 2003, No. 17-ФЗ].

[paragraph repealed by Federal Law of 10 January 2003, No. 17-ФЗ].

surveyor servicing of sea-going vessels in sea ports;

loading and unloading activity on internal water transport;

loading and unloading activity in sea ports;

loading and unloading activity on railway transport;

activity with regard to effectuation of towage of maritime transport (except if the said activity is effectuated to ensure own needs of juridical person or individual entrepreneur);

activity with regard to technical servicing of air traffic;

activity with regard to technical servicing of aircraft;

activity with regard to repair of aircraft;

activity with regard to use of aviation in branches of the economy;

activity with regard to technical servicing and repair of rolling stock on railway transport;

activity with regard to technical servicing and repair of technical means used for railway transport;

activity with regard to circulation of dangerous wastes;

organisation and maintenance of totalisors and gambling institutions;

valuation activity;

tourist operator activity;

tourist agency activity;

activity with regard to sale of rights for club leisure;

non-State (private) protection activity;

non-State (private) detective activity;

procurement, processing, and realisation of scrap nonferrous metals;

procurement, processing, and realisation of scrap ferrous metals;

activity connected with arrangment of employment of citizens of Russian Federation beyond the limits of the Russian Federation;

activity with regard to raising pedigree livestock (except if the said activity is effectuated to ensure own needs of a juridical person or individual entrepreneur);

activity with regard to the production and use of pedigree products (or material) (except if the said activity is effectuated to ensure own needs of a juridical person or individual entrepreneur);

public showing of audiovisual works if the said activity is effectuated in a cinema hall;

reproduction (or manufacture of examples) of audiovisual works and phonograms on any types of carrier;

auditor activity;

activity of investment funds;

activity with regard to management of investment funds, share investment funds, and non-State pension funds;

activity of specialised depositaries of investment funds, share investment funds, and non-State pension funds;

activity of non-State pension funds;

activity with regard to production of elite seeds (seeds of best specimens);

production of tobacco manufactures;

activity with regard to manufacture and repair of means of measurement;

effectuation at sea of activity with regard to acceptance and transporting of catches of aquatic biological resources, including fish, and also other aquatic fauna and flora;

activity with regard to keeping of grain and products of processing thereof;

outer space activity;

veterinary activity;

medical activity;

[added and repealed by Federal Law of 13 March 2002, No. 28-ФЗ].

carriage of passengers and baggage by railway transport [paragraph added by Federal Law of 10 January 2003, No. 17-ФЗ];

carriage of freight and baggage by railway transport [paragraph added by Federal Law of 10 January 2003, No. 17-ФЗ];

carriage of freight-baggage by railway transport [paragraph added by Federal Law of 10 January 2003, No. 17-ФЗ].

activity with regard to provision of infrastructure of railway transport of general use for the effectuation of carriages [paragraph added by Federal Law of 10 January 2003, No. 17-ФЗ].

transporting of freight (or movement of freight without the conclusion of a contract of carriage) along railway tracks of general use, except for clearing up freight which has arrived from railway removal rails and return thereof to railway removal rails [paragraph added by Federal Law of 10 January 2003, No. 17-ФЗ].

2. A List of work and services with regard to outer space activity, veterinary activity, and medical activity shall be established by statutes on licensing the said types of activity.

3. The introduction of licensing of other types of activity shall be possible only by means of making additions to the list of types of activity for whose effectuation a license is required provided for by the present Federal Law.

Article 18. Transitional Provisions

1. Federal laws and other normative legal acts regulating the procedure for licensing of individual types of activity, except for types of activity provided for by Article 1(2) of the present Federal Law, shall operate in the part which is not contrary to the present Federal Law and shall be subject to being brought into conformity with the present Federal Law.

2. The licensing of types of activity not specified in Article 17(1) of the present Federal Law shall terminate from the day of entry into force of the present Federal Law.

3. Federal aviation rules for licensing activity in the domain of civil aviation shall operate until the moment of entry into force of a federal law on making respective changed in the Air Code of the Russian Federation.

4. Licensing the activity of arbitrazh managers shall terminate from 1 July 2002 [added by Federal Law of 13 March 2002, No. 28-ФЗ].

Article 19. Deeming to Have Lost Force Certain Legislative Acts in Connection with Adoption of Present Federal Law

From the day of entry into force of the present Federal Law there shall be deemed to have lost force:

Federal Law of 25 September 1998, No. 158-ФЗ 'On Licensing Individual Types of Activity' (СЗ РФ (1998), no. 39, item 4857);

Federal Law of 26 November 1998, No. 178-ФЗ 'On Making Additions to the Federal Law "On Licensing Individual Types of Activity" ' (СЗ РФ (1998), no. 48, item 5853);

Federal Law of 22 December 1999, No. 215-ФЗ 'On Making Additions to Article 17 of the Federal Law "On Licensing Individual Types of Activity" ' (СЗ РФ (1999), no. 52, item 6365);

Federal Law of 22 December 1999, No. 216-ФЗ 'On Making Additions to Article 17 of the Federal Law "On Licensing Individual Types of Activity" ' (СЗ РФ (1999), no. 52, item 6366);

Federal Law of 12 May 2000, No. 69-ФЗ 'On Making Changes in Article 17 of the Federal Law "On Licensing Individual Types of Activity" ' (СЗ РФ (2000), no. 20, item 2104);

Article 2 of the Federal Law of 29 December 2000, No. 169-ФЗ 'On Making Changes in and Additions to Federal Law 'On Production and Consumption Wastes' and Federal Law "On Licensing Individual Types of Activity" ' (СЗ РФ (2001), no. 1, item 21).

Article 20. Entry into Force of Present Federal Law

The present Federal Law shall enter into force upon the expiry of six months from the day of its official publication.

The President of the Russian Federation and Government of the Russian Federation shall bring their normative legal acts into conformity with the present Federal Law.

FEDERAL LAW ON COMPETITION AND THE LIMITATION OF MONOPOLISTIC ACTIVITY ON GOODS MARKETS

[Law of 22 March 1991, as amended by Laws of the
Russian Federation No. 3119-1, 24 June 1991 and
No. 3310-1, 15 July 1992, and by Federal Law
No. 83-ФЗ, 25 May 1995, Federal Law No. 70-ФЗ,
6 May 1998, Federal Law No. 3-ФЗ, 2 January 2000,
Federal Law No. 196-ФЗ, 30 December 2001,
Federal Law No. 31-ФЗ, 21 March 2002, and Federal Law No.
122-ФЗ, 9 October 2002.
Ведомости СНД и ВС РСФСР (1991), no. 16, item 499;
Ведомости СНД и ВС РФ (1992), no. 34, item 1966; no. 32,
item 1882; СЗ РФ (1995), no. 22, item 1977; (1998),
no. 19, item 2066; (2000), no. 2, item 124;
(2002), no. 1(I), item 2; no. 12, item 1093; no. 41, item 3969]

Section I	General Provisions	31
Section II	Monopolistic Activity	37
Section II[1]	Acts, Actions, Agreements or Agreed Actions Limiting Competition of Federal Agencies of Executive Power, Agencies of State Power of Subjects of Russian Federation, Agencies of Local Self-Government, and Other Agencies or Organisations Endowed With Functions or Rights of Said Agencies of Power	40
Section III	Unfair Competition	43
Section IV	Antimonopoly Agency	44
Section V	Individual Types of State Antimonopoly Control	48
Section VI	Responsibility for Violation of Antimonopoly Legislation	55
Section VII	Procedure for Adoption of Decisions and Issuance of Prescriptions by Federal Antimonopoly Agency and Appeal Thereof	57

Section I. General Provisions

Article 1. Purposes of Present Law [as amended by Federal Law No. 122-ФЗ, 9 October 2002]

1. The present Law shall determine the organisational and legal foundations for the prevention and suppression of:

monopolistic activity and unfair competition on the goods market in the Russian Federation;

limitation of competition by federal agencies of executive power, agencies of State power of subjects of the Russian Federation, agencies of local self-government, and by other agencies or organisations endowed with functions or rights of the said agencies of power.

2. The present Law is directed towards ensuring the unity of economic space, free movement of goods, support for competition, and freedom of economic activity on the territory of the Russian Federation and the creation of conditions for the effective functioning of goods markets [Article 1 as amended by Federal Law No. 122-ФЗ, 9 October 2002].

Article 1¹. Antimonopoly Legislation and Other Normative Legal Acts on Competition and Limitation of Monopolistic Activity on Goods Markets [as amended by Federal Law No. 122-ФЗ, 9 October 2002]

1. Antimonopoly legislation of the Russian Federation shall be based on the Constitution of the Russian Federation and consist of the present Law and federal laws regulating relations provided for by Article 2 of the present Law.

2. Relations provided for by Article 2 of the present Law may also be regulated by edicts of the President of the Russian Federation, which must not be contrary to the present Law and federal laws.

3. On the basis of and in execution of the present Law, federal laws, and edicts of the President of the Russian Federation the Government of the Russian Federation shall have the right to adopt decrees regulating the relations provided for by Article 2 of the present Law.

4. In the event an edict of the President of the Russian Federation or decree of the Government of the Russian Federation is contrary to the present Law or a federal law, the present Law or respective federal law shall apply [Article added by Federal Law No. 83-ФЗ, 25 May 1995, as amended by Federal Law No. 122-ФЗ, 9 October 2002]

Article 2. Sphere of Application of Present Law [as amended by Federal Law No. 122-ФЗ, 9 October 2002]

1. The present Law shall operate throughout the territory of the Russian Federation.

The present Law shall extend to relations influencing competition on goods markets in the Russian Federation in which Russian and foreign juridical persons participate, federal agencies of executive power, agencies of State power of subjects of the Russian Federation, agencies of local self-government, and other agencies or organisations endowed with functions or rights of the said agencies of power, and also natural persons, including individual entrepreneurs. The present Law also shall apply in those instances when the actions and agreements respectively performed or concluded by the said persons beyond the limits of the territory of the Russian Federation lead or may lead to a limitation of competition or entail other negative consequences on markets in the Russian Federation [as amended by Federal Law No. 83-ФЗ, 25 May 1995, and by Federal Law No. 122-ФЗ, 9 October 2002].

2. The present Law shall not extend to relations connected with objects of exclusive rights, except for instances when agreements connected with their use have been directed towards the limitation of competition or the acquisition, use and violation of exclusive rights to objects of intellectual property may lead to unfair competition [as amended by Federal Law No. 83-ФЗ, 25 May 1995, and by Federal Law No. 122-ФЗ, 9 October 2002].

3. Relations connected with monopolistic activity and unfair competition on the financial services market, except for instances when relations forming on those markets exert an influence on competition on the goods markets, shall be regulated by federal laws [as amended by Federal Law No. 83-ФЗ, 25 May 1995, and by Federal Law No. 122-ФЗ, 9 October 2002].

4. [point 4 repealed by Federal Law No. 122-ФЗ, 9 October 2002]

Article 3. Antimonopoly Agencies [repealed by Federal Law No. 122-ФЗ, 9 October 2002]

Article 4. Definition of Basic Concepts

The following concepts shall be used in the present Law:

good—product of activity (including work, services) intended for sale, exchange, or other introduction into turnover [as amended by Federal Law No. 122-ФЗ, 9 October 2002];

mutually replaceable goods—group of goods which may be comparable with regard to their functional designation, application, qualitative and technical characteristics, price, and other parameters so that the purchaser actually replaces or is prepared to replace them with one another in the process of consumption (including production);

goods market—sphere of circulation of goods not having replacements, or mutually-replaceable goods on the territory of the Russian Federation or part thereof determined by proceeding from the economic possibility of the acquirer to acquire a good on the respective territory and absence of this possibility beyond the limits thereof [as amended by Federal Law No. 122-ФЗ, 9 October 2002];

economic subjects—Russian and foreign commercial organisations and non-commercial organisations, except those not engaging in entrepreneurial activity, including agricultural consumer cooperatives, and also individual entrepreneurs [as amended by Federal Law No. 122-ФЗ, 9 October 2002];

competition—contentiousness of economic subjects when their autonomous actions effectively limit the possibilities for each of them to influence unilaterally the general conditions for the circulation of goods on the respective goods market;

unfair competition—any actions of an economic subject directed towards the acquisition of preferences in entrepreneurial activity which are contrary to the provisions of prevailing legislation, customs of business turnover, requirements of good order, reasonableness, and justness and may cause or caused losses to other economic subjects-competitors or cause damage to their business reputation;

dominant position—the exclusive position of an economic subject or several economic subjects in the market of a good not having a replacement, or mutually-replaceable goods (hereinafter—determined good) giving it (or them) the possibility to exert a decisive influence on the general conditions of circulation of a good on the respective goods market or to make difficult the access of other economic subjects to the market. A position of an economic subject shall be deemed to be dominant whose participatory share on the market of a determined good comprises 65% or more, except for those instances when the economic subject proves that, despite exceeding the said amount, its position on the market is not dominant. A position of an economic subject also shall be deemed to be dominant whose participatory share on the market of a determined good comprises less than 65% if this was established by the antimonopoly agency by proceeding from the stability of the participatory share of the economic subject on the market relative to the amount of participatory share on the market belonging to competitors and the possibility of access to this market of new competitors or other criteria characterising the goods market. The position of an economic subject may not be deemed to be dominant whose participatory share on the market of a determined good does not exceed 35%;

monopolistic activity—actions (or failure to act) which is contrary to anti-monopoly legislation of economic subjects directed towards not permitting, limiting, or eliminating competition [as amended by Federal Law No. 122-ФЗ, 9 October 2002];

monopoly-high price—price of a good which is established by an economic subject occupying a dominant position on the goods market and under which the particular economic subject contributorily compensates or may contributorily compensate unsubstantiated expenditures and/or receives or may receive profit materially higher than this may be in comparable conditions or conditions of competition [as amended by Federal Law No. 122-ФЗ, 9 October 2002];

monopoly-low price—price of acquired good established by economic subject occupying a dominant position on the goods market as purchaser for the purposes of receiving additional profit and/or contributory compensation of unsubstantiated expenditures at the expense of the seller, or price of a good consciously established by an economic subject occupying a dominant position on the goods market as seller at a level bringing losses from the sale of this good, as a result of establishing which there is or may be limitation of competition by means of squeezing competitors from the market;

antimonopoly agency—federal antimonopoly agency and territorial agencies thereof [added by Federal Law No. 122-ФЗ, 9 October 2002];

acquisition of stocks (or participatory shares) in charter capital of economic subjects—purchase, and also receipt of another possibility of effectuating autonomously or through representatives of the rights of vote embodies in these stocks (or participatory shares) on the basis of contracts of trust management, joint activity, commission, other transactions, or on other grounds [as amended by Federal Law No. 122-ФЗ, 9 October 2002];

group of persons—group of juridical and/or natural persons with regard to which one or several of the following conditions is fulfilled [as amended by Federal Law No. 70-ФЗ, 6 May 1998]:

a person or several persons jointly as a result of agreement (or agreed actions) has the right directly or indirectly to dispose (including on the basis of contracts of purchase-sale, trust management, joint activity, commission, other transactions, or on other grounds) of more than 50% of the total number of votes for voting stocks or contributions or participatory share of one juridical person comprising charter (or contributed) capital. In so doing the possibility of the actual disposition thereof through third persons with respect to whom the first person possesses the aforementioned right or power shall be understood as the indirect disposition of votes of a juridical person [as amended by Federal Law No. 122-ФЗ, 9 October 2002];

a person or several persons have received the possibility on the basis of a contract or otherwise to determine decisions adopted by another person or persons, including to determine conditions for the other person or persons to conduct entrepreneurial activity, or to effectuate powers of the executive organ of other persons or person on the basis of a contract [as amended by Federal Law No. 70-ФЗ, 6 May 1998];

a person has the right to appoint the one-man executive organ and/or more than 50% of the composition of a collegial executive organ of a juridical person and/or upon the proposal of the person more than 50% of the composition of the council of directors (or supervisory council) or other collegial management organ of a juridical person is elected [as amended by Federal Law No. 70-ФЗ, 6 May 1998];

a natural person effectuates the powers of a one-man executive organ of a juridical person [as amended by Federal Law No. 70-ФЗ, 6 May 1998];

one and the same natural persons, spouse thereof, parents, children, brothers, sisters, and/or persons proposed by one and the same juridical person comprise more than 50% of the composition of a collegial executive organ and/or council of directors (or supervisory council) or other collegial management organ of two or more juridical persons or upon the proposal of one and the same juridical persons more than 50% of the composition of the council of directors (or supervisory council) or other collegial management organ of two or more juridical persons is elected [added by Federal Law No. 70-ФЗ, 6 May 1998];

a natural person performing labour duties in a juridical person or within one group of persons of juridical persons simultaneously being a one-man executive organ of another juridical person or natural persons performing labour duties in a juridical person or within one group of persons of juridical persons, shall comprise more than 50% of the composition of a collegial executive organ and/or council of directors (or supervisory council) or other collegial management organ of another juridical person [added by Federal Law No. 122-ФЗ, 9 October 2002];

one and the same natural persons, spouse thereof, parents, children, brothers, sisters, and/or juridical persons have the right autonomously or through representatives (or attornies) to dispose of more than 50% of voting stocks or contributions and participatory shares of the particular juridical person comprising the charter or contributed capital [added by Federal Law No. 70-ФЗ, 6 May 1998, as amended by Federal Law No. 122-ФЗ, 9 October 2002];

natural persons and/or juridical persons have the right autonomously or through representatives (or attornies) to dispose in total or more than 50% of the votes of voting stocks or comprising the charter or contributed capital of contributions or participatory share of the particular juridical person and simultaneously the said natural persons, spouse, parents, children, brothers, sisters, and/or persons proposed by one and the same juridical person comprise more than 50% of the composition of a collegial executive organ and/or council of directors (or supervisory council) or other collegial management organ of another juridical person [added by Federal Law No. 70-ФЗ, 6 May 1998, as amended by Federal Law No. 122-ФЗ, 9 October 2002];

juridical persons are participants of a single financial-industrial group [added by Federal Law No. 70-ФЗ, 6 May 1998];

natural persons are spouses, parents and children, brothers, and/or sisters [added by Federal Law No. 70-ФЗ, 6 May 1998];

provisions relating to a group of persons shall extend to each person within the said group [added by Federal Law No. 122-ФЗ, 9 October 2002];

affiliated persons—natural and juridical persons capable of exerting influence on the activity of juridical and/or natural persons effectuating entrepreneurial activity [added by Federal Law No. 70-ФЗ, 6 May 1998];

affiliated persons of juridical person shall be [added by Federal Law No. 70-ФЗ, 6 May 1998]:

a member of its council of directors (or supervisory council) or other collegial management organ, member of the collegial executive organ thereof, and also person effectuating powers of its one-man executive organ [added by Federal Law No. 70-ФЗ, 6 May 1998];

a person belonging to the group of persons to which the said juridical person belongs [added by Federal Law No. 70-ФЗ, 6 May 1998];

persons who have the right to dispose of more than 20% of the total number of votes of stocks for voting stocks or contributions and participatory shares of the particular juridical person comprising the charter or contributed capital [added by Federal Law No. 70-ФЗ, 6 May 1998, as amended by Federal Law No. 122-ФЗ, 9 October 2002];

a juridical person in which the particular juridical person has the right to dispose of more than 20% of the total number of votes of voting stocks or contributions or participatory shares of the particular juridical person comprising the charter or contributed capital [added by Federal Law No. 70-ФЗ, 6 May 1998, as amended by Federal Law No. 122-ФЗ, 9 October 2002];

if a juridical person is a participant of a financial-industrial group, to the affiliated persons thereof also shall be relegated members of the councils of directors (or supervisory councils) or other collegial management organs, collegial executive organs of participants of the financial-industrial group, and also persons effectuating the powers of one-man executive organs of participants of the financial-industrial group [added by Federal Law No. 70-ФЗ, 6 May 1998];

affiliated persons of a natural person effectuating entrepreneurial activity shall be [added by Federal Law No. 70-ФЗ, 6 May 1998]:

persons belonging to the same group of persons to which the said natural person belongs [added by Federal Law No. 70-ФЗ, 6 May 1998];

a juridical person in which the particular natural person has the right to dispose of more than 20% of the total number of votes of voting stocks or contributions and participatory shares of the particular juridical person comprising the charter or contributed capital [added by Federal Law No. 70-ФЗ, 6 May 1998, as amended by Federal Law No. 122-ФЗ, 9 October 2002].

The provisions of the present Law relating to economic subjects shall extend to a group of persons.

Section II. Monopolistic Activity

Article 5. Abuse by Economic Subject of Dominant Position in Market

1. There shall be prohibited the actions (or failure to act) of an economic subject (or group of persons) occupying a dominant position which has or may have

as its result the nonadmission, limitation, and elimination of competition and/or impinging of the interests of other economic subjects, including such actions (or failure to act) as [as amended by Federal Law No. 83-ФЗ, 25 May 1995, and by Federal Law No. 122-ФЗ, 9 October 2002]:

the withdrawal of goods from circulation for the purpose or as a result of which there is the creation or maintenance of a deficit in the market or an increase of prices [as amended by Federal Law No. 83-ФЗ, 25 May 1995];

tying up a contracting party through the conditions of a contract which are not advantageous to him or do not relate to the subject of the contract (unsubstantiated demand to transfer financial means, other property, property rights, work force of the contracting party, consent to conclude a contract merely on condition of inserting therein provisions concerning goods in which the contracting party is not interested, and others) [as amended by Federal Law No. 83-ФЗ, 25 May 1995, and by Federal Law No. 122-ФЗ, 9 October 2002];

creation of conditions of access to the goods market, exchange, consumption, acquisition, production, and realisation of a good which places one or several economic subjects in an unequal position in comparison with another or other economic subjects (discriminatory conditions) [as amended by Federal Law No. 122-ФЗ, 9 October 2002];

[paragraph five repealed by Federal Law No. 122-ФЗ, 9 October 2002]

creation of obstacles to access to the market (or withdrawal from the market) by other economic subjects;

violation of the procedure for price-formation established by normative acts;

establishment and maintenance of monopoly-high (or low) prices [added by Federal Law No. 83-ФЗ, 25 May 1995, as amended by Federal Law No. 122-ФЗ, 9 October 2002];

reduction or termination of production of goods for which there is demand or orders of consumers when there exists a non-lossmaking possibility for the production thereof [added by Federal Law No. 83-ФЗ, 25 May 1995];

unsubstantiated refusal to conclude contract with individual purchasers (or customers) when there exists the possibility for production or delivery of the respective good [added by Federal Law No. 83-ФЗ, 25 May 1995].

2. In exceptional instances the actions (or failure to act) of an economic subject specified in point 1 of the present Article may be deemed to be lawful if the economic subject proves that the positive effect of its actions, including in the socio-economic sphere, exceeds the negative consequences for the goods market being considered [added by Federal Law No. 83-ФЗ, 25 May 1995, as amended by Federal Law No. 122-ФЗ, 9 October 2002].

Article 6. Agreements (or Agreed Actions) of Economic Subjects Limiting Competition

1. There shall be prohibited the conclusion of a contract, other transaction, and agreement (hereinafter—agreement) or the effectuation of agreed actions by economic subjects operating on the market of one good (or mutually replaceable goods) which leads or might lead to: [as amended by Federal Law No. 83-ФЗ, 25 May 1995, and by Federal Law No. 122-ФЗ, 9 October 2002]:

the establishment (or maintenance) of prices (or tariffs), discounts, increments (or surcharges), or increases;

the increase, reduction, or maintenance of prices at auctions and public sales;

the division of the market according to a territorial principle, by volume of sales or purchases, by assortment of goods being realised, or by group of sellers or purchasers (or customers);

the limitation of access to the market or elimination therefrom of other economic subjects as the sellers of specified goods or the purchasers (or customers) thereof;

the refusal to conclude contracts with determined sellers or purchasers (or customers) [grammatical changes as introduced by Federal Law No. 122-ФЗ, 9 October 2002].

2. The conclusion by economic subjects operating on the market of one good (or mutually replaceable goods) of other agreements or the effectuation of agreed actions, as a result of which there are or could occur the nonadmission, limitation, and elimination of competition and impingement on the interests of other economic subjects also shall be prohibited [added by Federal Law No. 122-ФЗ, 9 October 2002].

3. The conclusion of an agreement or effectuation of agreed actions by economic subjects not competing between themselves on a respective goods market who are receiving (potential acquirers) and providing (potential sellers) a good (or mutually replaceable goods) shall be prohibited if as a result of such agreements or agreed actions there are or may occur the nonadmission, limitation, or elimination of competition.

The provisions of the present point shall not apply to economic subjects whose aggregate participatory share on the market of a determined good does not exceed 35% [as amended by Federal Law No. 83-ФЗ, 25 May 1995, as renumbered and amended by Federal Law No. 122-ФЗ, 9 October 2002].

4. In exceptional instances agreements or agreed actions of economic subjects specified in points 2 and 3 of the present Article may be deemed to be lawful by the antimonopoly agency in the procedure provided for by Article 19[1] of the present Law if the economic subjects prove that the positive effect of their actions, including in the socio-economic sphere, exceeds the unfavourable consequences for the goods market being considered, or if the possibility to conclude such an

agreement or effectuate agreed actions by economic subjects has been provided for by federal laws [as amended by Federal Law No. 83-ФЗ, 25 May 1995, as renumbered and amended by Federal Law No. 122-ФЗ, 9 October 2002].

5. The coordination of entrepreneurial activity which has or could have as its result the limitation of competition shall be prohibited.

A violation of the said requirements shall be grounds for liquidation in a judicial procedure of the organisations effectuating the coordination of entrepreneurial activity upon the suit of the antimonopoly agency [point 4 added by Federal Law No. 83-ФЗ, 25 May 1995, as renumbered and amended by Federal Law No. 122-ФЗ, 9 October 2002].

Section II[1]. Acts, Actions, Agreements or
Agreed Actions Limiting Competition of Federal Agencies of
Executive Power, Agencies of State Power of Subjects
of Russian Federation, Agencies of Local Self-
Government, and Other Agencies or Organisations Endowed
With Functions or Rights of Said Agencies of Power
[added by Federal Law No. 122-ФЗ, 9 October 2002]

Article 7. Acts and Actions of Federal Agencies of Executive Power, Agencies of State Power of Subjects of Russian Federation, Agencies of Local Self-Government, and Other Agencies or Organisations Endowed with Functions or Rights of Said Agencies of Power [as amended by Federal Law No. 83-ФЗ, 25 May 1995, and by Federal Law No. 122-ФЗ, 9 October 2002]

1. Federal agencies of executive power, agencies of State power of subjects of Russian Federation, agencies of local self-government, and other agencies or organisations endowed with functions and rights of the said agencies of power shall be prohibited from adopting acts and/or performing actions which limit the autonomy of economic subjects, create discriminatory conditions for the activity of individual economic subjects, if such acts or actions have as their result the non-admission, limitation, and elimination of competition and impinging upon the interests of economic subjects, including it shall be prohibited [as amended by Federal Law No. 83-ФЗ, 25 May 1995]:

to introduce limitations on the creation of new economic subjects in any sphere of activity, and also to establish prohibitions on the effectuation of individual types of activity or production of determined types of goods, except for instances established by legislation of the Russian Federation [as amended by Federal Law No. 83-ФЗ, 25 May 1995];

to obstruct without grounds the effectuation of activity of economic subjects in any sphere whatsoever;

to establish prohibitions against the sale (or purchase, exchange, or acquisition) of goods from one region of the Russian Federation (or republic, territory, region, district, city, or district in city) to another or otherwise limit the rights of economic subjects in the sale (or acquisition, purchase, or exchange) of goods;

to give economic subjects instructions concerning the priority delivery of goods (or fulfilment of work, rendering of services) to a specified group of purchasers (or customers) or concerning the priority of concluding contracts without taking into account the priorities established by legislative or other normative acts of the Russian Federation;

to obstruct unfoundedly the creation of new economic subjects in any sphere of activity whatsoever;

to grant unfoundedly to an individual economic subject or several economic subjects tax or other privileges which place them in a preferential position with regard to other economic subjects working in the market of the same good [as amended by Federal Law No. 83-ФЗ, 25 May 1995].

2. Draft decisions of federal agencies of executive power, agencies of executive power of subjects of the Russian Federation, agencies of local self-government, and other agencies or organisations endowed with functions or rights of the said agencies of power, with regard to questions of the granting of privileges and preferences to an individual economic subject or several economic subjects, shall be subject to agreement with the antimonopoly agency [added by Federal Law No. 83-ФЗ, 25 May 1995, as amended by Federal Law No. 122-ФЗ, 9 October 2002].

3. The endowing of federal agencies of executive power, agencies of State power of subjects of the Russian Federation, agencies of local self-government, and other agencies or organisations endowed with functions or rights of the said agencies of power with powers whose effectuation has or may have as its result the limitation of competition shall be prohibited [as amended by Federal Law No. 83-ФЗ, 25 May 1995, and renumbered and amended by Federal Law No. 122-ФЗ, 9 October 2002].

The combining of functions of federal agencies of executive power, agencies of executive power of subjects of the Russian Federation, agencies of local self-government, and other agencies or organisations endowed with functions or rights of the said agencies of power with the functions of economic subjects, and also endowing economic subjects with the functions and rights of the said agencies, including functions and rights of agencies of State supervision, except for instances provided for by legislative acts of the Russian Federation, shall be prohibited [added by Federal Law No. 83-ФЗ, 25 May 1995, as amended by Federal Law No. 122-ФЗ, 9 October 2002].

Article 8. Agreements (or Agreed Actions) of Federal Agencies of Executive Power, Agencies of State Power of Subjects of Russian Federation, Agencies of Local Self-Government, and Other Agencies or Organisations Endowed with Functions or Rights of Said Agencies of Power [as amended by Federal Law No. 83-ФЗ, 25 May 1995, and by Federal Law No. 122-ФЗ, 9 October 2002]

There shall be prohibited the conclusion in any form of agreements or the effectuation of agreed actions of federal agencies of executive power, agencies of State power of subjects of the Russian Federation, agencies of local self-government, and other agencies or organisation endowed with functions or rights of the said agencies of power between themselves or between them and an economic subject, as a result of which there is or may occur the nonadmission, limitation, or elimination of competition and impingement of interests of economic subjects, including agreements or agreed actions which lead or may lead to [as amended by Federal Law No. 83-ФЗ, 25 May 1995, and by Federal Law No. 122-ФЗ, 9 October 2002]:

the increase, reduction, or maintenance of prices (or tariffs), except for instances when the conclusion of such agreements is permitted by federal laws or normative legal acts of the President of the Russian Federation or Government of the Russian Federation [as amended by Federal Law No. 122-ФЗ, 9 October 2002];

the division of the market according to the territorial principle, by volume of sales or purchases, by assortment of goods being realised, or by group of sellers or purchasers (or customers);

the limitation of access to the market or elimination of economic subjects therefrom [paragraphs three and four amended to reflect grammatical changes by Federal Law No. 122-ФЗ, 9 October 2002].

Article 9. Antimonopoly Requirements for Conducting Competition for Placement of Orders for Delivery of Goods, Fulfilment of Work, and Rendering of Services for State Needs and Needs of Local Self-Government [as amended by Federal Law No. 122-ФЗ, 9 October 2002]

1. When conducting a competition there shall not be permitted:

the creation of preferential conditions of participation in a competition, including access to confidential information, reduction of payment of participation in the competition for individual participants of the competition;

the participation in the competition of the organisers of the competition, personnel thereof, and affiliated persons;

the effectuation by the organiser of the competition of the coordination of activity of participants thereof, as a result of which there is or may occur a limitation of competition between participants of the competition or impingement of the interests of participants thereof;

unsubstantiated limitation of access to participation in the competition.

2. A violation of the rules established by the present Article shall be grounds for the deeming by a court of the competition to be invalid [Article 9 as amended by Federal Law No. 122-Ф3, 9 October 2002].

Section III. Unfair Competition

Article 10. Forms of Unfair Competition

1. Unfair competition shall not be permitted, including [numbering introduced by Federal Law No. 122-Ф3, 9 October 2002]:

the dissemination of false, inaccurate, or distorted information capable of causing losses to another economic subject or causing damage to its business reputation;

the misleading of consumers as to the character, means, and place of manufacture, consumer properties, and quality and quantity of a good or the manufacture thereof [as amended by Federal Law No. 122-Ф3, 9 October 2002];

the incorrect comparison by an economic subject of the goods it produces or realises with the goods of other economic subjects [as amended by Federal Law No. 83-Ф3, 25 May 1995];

the sale, exchange, or other introduction into turnover of a good with the illegal use of the results of intellectual activity and means of individualisation of a juridical person equated thereto, individualisation of a product, and fulfilment of work or services [as amended by Federal Law No. 83-Ф3, 25 May 1995, and by Federal Law No. 122-Ф3, 9 October 2002];

the receipt, use, or divulgence of information comprising a commercial or employment secret and secret protected by a law [as amended by Federal Law No. 122-Ф3, 9 October 2002].

2. Unfair competition connected with the acquisition and use of exclusive rights to means of individualisation of a juridical person, individualisation of a product, work fulfilled, or services rendered shall not be permitted [point 2 added by Federal Law No. 122-Ф3, 9 October 2002].

3. A decision of an antimonopoly agency concerning a violation of the provisions of point 2 of the present Article with respect to the individualisation of a product, work fulfilled, or services rendered shall be sent to the federal agency of executive power in the domain of patents and trademarks to decide the question concerning the termination before time of the registration of the object of exclusive rights or deeming of the registration of that object to be invalid in the procedure established by legislation on trademarks, service marks, and names of places of origin of goods [point 3 added by Federal Law No. 122-Ф3, 9 October 2002].

Section IV. Antimonopoly Agency
[as amended by Federal Law No. 83-ФЗ, 25 May 1995,
and by Federal Law No. 122-ФЗ, 9 October 2002]

Article 11. Antimonopoly Agency [as amended by Federal Law No. 83-ФЗ, 25 May 1995, and by Federal Law No. 122-ФЗ, 9 October 2002]

1. The conducting of State policy with regard to promoting the development of trade markets and competition, effectuation of State control over compliance with antimonopoly legislation, and also prevention and suppression of monopolistic activity, unfair competition, and other actions limiting competition shall be effectuated by the antimonopoly agency [as amended by Federal Law No. 122-ФЗ, 9 October 2002]

2. The powers of the federal antimonopoly agency shall be determined by the present Law and other normative legal acts of the Russian Federation [as amended by Federal Law No. 83-ФЗ, 25 May 1995, and by Federal Law No. 122-ФЗ, 9 October 2002].

3. The federal antimonopoly agency shall in order to effectuate its powers have the right to create territorial agencies and to appoint the respective officials [as amended by Federal Law No. 83-ФЗ, 25 May 1995, and by Federal Law No. 122-ФЗ, 9 October 2002].

4. [repealed by Federal Law No. 83-ФЗ, 25 May 1995].

4. Territorial agencies shall be within the jurisdiction of the federal antimonopoly agency and shall effectuate their activity in accordance with legislation of the Russian Federation on the basis of a Statute confirmed by the federal antimonopoly agency.
The federal antimonopoly agency shall endow territorial agencies with powers within the limits of its competence [point 4 added by Federal Law No. 122-ФЗ, 9 October 2002].

Article 12. Powers of Antimonopoly Agency [as amended by Federal Law No. 83-ФЗ, 25 May 1995, and by Federal Law No. 122-ФЗ, 9 October 2002]

In accordance with the present Law the antimonopoly agency shall have the right to [as amended by Federal Law No. 83-ФЗ, 25 May 1995, and by Federal Law No. 122-ФЗ, 9 October 2002]:
(1) when there are the indicia of a violation of antimonopoly legislation, initiate a case, with regard to the results of the consideration of which adopt a decision or issue a prescription;
(2) issue to economic subjects prescriptions binding for execution on:
the non-permitting of actions creating the threat of a violation of antimonopoly legislation;

the elimination of the consequences of a violation of antimonopoly legislation;

the restoration of the position which existed before the violation of anti-monopoly legislation;

on the compulsory division of a commercial organisation or noncommercial organisation or separation from the composition thereof of one or several organisations;

on the change of the conditions or dissolution of contracts and other transactions;

on the conclusion of contracts with economic subjects;

on the transfer to the federal budget of revenue received as a result of a violation of antimonopoly legislation;

on the change or limitation of the use of a firm name;

on the fulfilment of economic, technical, informational, and other requirements directed towards prevention of the creation of discriminatory conditions;

on the performance of actions directed towards ensuring competition [as amended by Federal Law No. 83-Ф3, 25 May 1995, and by Federal Law No. 122-Ф3, 9 October 2002];

(3) issue to federal agencies of executive power, agencies of executive power of subjects of the Russian Federation, agencies of local self-government, and other agencies or organisations endowed with functions or rights of the said agencies of power, as well as officials thereof, prescriptions binding for execution on:

the repeal or change of acts adopted by them which are contrary to anti-monopoly legislation;

the termination of violations of antimonopoly legislation;

the dissolution or change of agreements concluded by them and contrary to antimonopoly legislation;

the performance of actions directed towards ensuring competition [as amended by Federal Law No. 83-Ф3, 25 May 1995, and by Federal Law No. 122-Ф3, 9 October 2002].

(4) bring commercial organisations and noncommercial organisations, executives thereof, natural persons, including individual entrepreneurs, and also officials of federal agencies of executive power, agencies of executive power of subjects of the Russian Federation, agencies of local self-government, and other agencies and organisations endowed with functions or rights of the said agencies of power to administrative responsibility for a violation of antimonopoly legislation in the instances and in the procedure which have been established by legislation concerning administrative violations;

(5) conduct a verification of compliance with antimonopoly legislation by economic subjects, federal agencies of executive power, agencies of executive power of subjects of the Russian Federation, agencies of local self-government, and other agencies and organisations endowed with functions or rights of the said agencies of power, and receive from them necessary documents and information and explanations in written and oral forms;

(6) apply to a court or arbitrazh court with applications concerning a violation of antimonopoly legislation, including:

the deeming invalid wholly or in part:

acts and agreements of federal agencies of executive power, agencies of State power of subjects of the Russian Federation, agencies of local self-government, and other agencies and organisations endowed with functions or rights of the said agencies of power which are contrary to antimonopoly legislation;

contracts and other transactions which do not correspond to antimonopoly legislation;

the obligatory conclusion of a contract with an economic subject;

the liquidation of commercial organisations and noncommercial organisations;

(7) participate in the consideration by a court or arbitrazh court of cases connected with the application or violation of antimonopoly legislation;

(8) establish the existence of a dominant position of an economic subject;

(9) give explanations with regard to questions of the application of antimonopoly legislation;

(10) form and conduct the register of economic subjects having a participatory share in the market of a determined good in an amount of more than 35%;

(11) give opinions in the established form concerning the existence or absence of a limitation of competition on the goods market when introducing, changing, and terminating the operation of customs tariffs and introducing nontariff measures;

(12) effectuate cooperation with international organisations and State agencies of foreign States, take part in the working out and realisation of international treaties of the Russian Federation, work of intergovernmental and interdepartmental commissions which coordinate international cooperation of the Russian Federation, effectuate international programmes and drafts with regard to questions of the competence of the antimonopoly agency;

(13) effectuate the exchange of information with federal agencies of executive power, agencies of executive power of subjects of the Russian Federation, agencies of local self-government, international organisations, and State agencies of foreign States within the limits of their competence;

(14) send recommendations concerning the development of competition to respective federal agencies of executive power, agencies of executive power of subjects of the Russian Federation, agencies of local self-government, and other agencies and organisations endowed with functions or rights of the said agencies of power;

(15) conduct an analysis of the state of the goods markets;

(16) effectuate other powers provided for by the present Law [Article 12 as amended by Federal Law No. 83-ФЗ, 25 May 1995, and by Federal Law No. 122-ФЗ, 9 October 2002].

Article 13. Right of Access to Information

Personnel of the antimonopoly agency duly empowered shall, for the purposes of fulfilling functions placed on them and upon the presentation by them of employment cards and the decision of the executive (or deputy thereof) of the antimonopoly agency concerning the conducting of a verification, have the right of unobstructed access to federal agencies of executive power, agencies of executive power of subjects of the Russian Federation, and agencies of local self-government, and other agencies and organisations endowed with functions or rights of the said agencies of power, and also economic subjects, in order to receive in the established procedure documents and information necessary for the antimonopoly agency in order to fulfill the functions placed on it [as amended by Federal Law No. 83-ФЗ, 25 May 1995, and by Federal Law No. 122-ФЗ, 9 October 2002].

Internal affairs agencies shall be obliged within the limits of their powers to render assistance to personnel of the antimonopoly agency for the fulfillment by them of employment duties [added by Federal Law No. 83-ФЗ, 25 May 1995, and by Federal Law No. 122-ФЗ, 9 October 2002].

Article 14. Duty With Regard to Submission of Information to Antimonopoly Agency [as amended by Federal Law No. 83-ФЗ, 25 May 1995, and by Federal Law No. 122-ФЗ, 9 October 2002]

Commercial and noncommercial organisations (or executives thereof), federal agencies of executive power, agencies of executive power of subjects of the Russian Federation, agencies of local self-government, and other agencies and organisations endowed with functions or rights of the said agencies of power (or officials thereof), and natural persons, including individual entrepreneurs, shall be obliged upon the demand of the antimonopoly agency to submit reliable documents, written and oral explanations, and other information necessary for the effectuation by the antimonopoly agency of its legal activity [as amended by Federal Law No. 83-ФЗ, 25 May 1995, and by Federal Law No. 122-ФЗ, 9 October 2002].

Article 15. Duties of Antimonopoly Agency Regarding Compliance with Commercial and Employment Secrecy and Secrecy Protected by Law [as amended by Federal Law No. 83-ФЗ, 25 May 1995, and by Federal Law No. 122-ФЗ, 9 October 2002]

Information constituting a commercial or employment secret or secret protected by a law which has been received by an antimonopoly agency when effectuating its powers shall not be subject to divulgence, except for instances established by a federal law [as amended by Federal Law No. 83-ФЗ, 25 May 1995, and by Federal Law No. 122-ФЗ, 9 October 2002].

In the event of the divulgence by personnel of the antimonopoly agency of information constituting a commercial and employment secret, the losses caused shall be subject to compensation in accordance with civil legislation [as amended by Federal Law No. 83-ФЗ, 25 May 1995, and by Federal Law No. 122-ФЗ, 9 October 2002].

Article 16. Promoting Development of Goods Markets, Competition, and Support of Entrepreneurship [repealed by Federal Law No. 122-ФЗ, 9 October 2002]

Section V. Individual Types of State Antimonopoly Control
[as amended by Federal Law No. 83-ФЗ, 25 May 1995,
and by Federal Law No. 122-ФЗ, 9 October 2002]

Article 17. State Control Over Creation, Reorganisation, and Liquidation of Commercial and Noncommercial Organisations [as amended by Federal Law No. 83-ФЗ, 25 May 1995, and by Federal Law No. 122-ФЗ, 9 October 2002]

1. The merger and accession of commercial organisations whose total balance sheet value according to the last balance sheet exceeds 200,000 times the minimum amounts of payment for labour established by a federal law shall be effectuated with the prior consent of the antimonopoly agency [point 1 as amended by Federal Law No. 83-ФЗ, 25 May 1995, and by Federal Law No. 122-ФЗ, 9 October 2002].

2. Persons or agencies adopting a decision concerning the merger or accession of commercial organisations shall submit to the antimonopoly agency, besides the documents submitted to the registering agency in accordance with legislation of the Russian Federation, a petition concerning the giving of consent to the merger or accession of commercial organisations, information concerning the basic types of activity and volumes of products (or work, services) produced and realised on the respective goods markets and other information, including on a magnetic carrier, provided by a List confirmed by the federal antimonopoly agency [as amended by Federal Law No. 122-ФЗ, 9 October 2002].

[paragraph two repealed by Federal Law No. 122-ФЗ, 9 October 2002].

The antimonopoly agency shall not later than 30 days from the day of receipt of the necessary documents inform the applicant in written form about the decision adopted [as amended by Federal Law No. 122-ФЗ, 9 October 2002].

In the event the necessity arises, the said period may be increased by the antimonopoly agency, but not by more than 20 days [point 2 as amended by Federal Law No. 83-ФЗ, 25 May 1995, and by Federal Law No. 122-ФЗ, 9 October 2002].

3. The antimonopoly agency shall reject a petition if when considering the documents submitted it is discovered that the information contained therein having significance for adoption of the decision is unreliable, and likewise if satisfaction of the petition may lead to a limitation of competition on the goods market, including as a result of the arising or intensification of the dominant position of the economic subject(s) [as amended by Federal Law No. 122-ФЗ, 9 October 2002].

[paragraph two repealed by Federal Law No. 122-ФЗ, 9 October 2002].

4. The antimonopoly agency shall have the right to satisfy the petition even if the ensuing of the unfavourable consequences is possible specified in point 3 of the present Article in the event of:

the persons or agencies adopting the decision concerning merger or accession of commercial organisations prove that the positive effect of their actions, including in the socio-economic sphere, exceeds the unfavourable consequences for the goods market being considered;

the issuance of a prescription concerning the commission by persons or agencies adopting a decision concerning merger or accession of commercial organisations of actions directed towards ensuring competition [added by Federal Law No. 122-ФЗ, 9 October 2002].

5. The federal antimonopoly agency must be informed by the founders (or participants) (or one of the founders or participants) within 45 days from the day of State registration (or from the day of making of changes in and additions to the Unified State Register of Juridical Persons) about:

the creation, merger, and accession of noncommercial organisations (or associations, unions, noncommercial partnerships) if not less than two commercial organisations are within the composition of participants (or members) of these organisations;

the change of the composition of participants (or members) of noncommercial organisations (or associations, unions, noncommercial partnerships) if not less than two commercial organisations are within the composition of participants (or members) of these organisations;

the creation of commercial organisations if the total value of assets of the founders (or participants) with regard to the last balance sheet exceeds 200,000 minimum amounts of payment of labour established by a federal law, and also the merger of and accession of commercial organisations if the total of their assets according to the last balance sheet exceeds 100,000 minimim amounts of payment for labour established by a federal law.

When informing the antimonopoly agency, the applicant shall submit the information provided for by point 2 of the present Article.

The requirements of the present point shall extend to noncommercial organisations effectuating or having the intention to effectuate the coordination of entrepreneurial activity of its participants (or members) [point 4 as amended by Federal Law No. 83-ФЗ, 25 May 1995, and as renumbered and amended by Federal Law No. 122-ФЗ, 9 October 2002].

5. [point 5 repealed by Federal Law No. 122-ФЗ, 9 October 2002].

6. If the actions provided for by point 5 of the present Article may lead or led to the limitation of competition, the antimonopoly agency shall issue to the founders (or participants) of a commercial or noncommercial organisation, persons, or agencies which adopted the respective decision a prescription on the

commission of the actions directed towards ensuring competition [point 6 as amended by Federal Law No. 83-ФЗ, 25 May 1995, and by Federal Law No. 122-ФЗ, 9 October 2002].

7. In the instances provided for by point 5 of the present Article the persons or organs adopting the decision concerning the creation, merger, or accession shall have the right before adopting such decisions to request the consent of the anti-monopoly agency, which shall be obliged to consider the respective petitions in the procedure established by point 2 of the present Article [point 7 as amended by Federal Law No. 83-ФЗ, 25 May 1995, and by Federal Law No. 122-ФЗ, 9 October 2002].

8. The State registration of commercial organisations, and also the making of entries concerning exclusion from the unified State register of juridical persons of commercial organisations, shall be effectuated by the registering agency when there is the prior consent of the antimonopoly agency [point 8 added by Federal Law No. 83-ФЗ, 25 May 1995, as amended by Federal Law No. 122-ФЗ, 9 October 2002].

[paragraph repealed by Federal Law No. 31-ФЗ, 21 March 2002].

9. The creation, merger, and accession of commercial and noncommercial organisations and a change of the composition of participants of noncommercial organisations in violation of the procedure established by points 1 and 5 of the present Article which led to a limitation of competition, including as a result of the arising or intensifying of dominance, and likewise the failure to perform a pre-scription of an antimonopoly agency which was issued in accordance with points 4 and 6 of the present Article, shall be grounds for the liquidation thereof in a judicial procedure upon the suit of the antimonopoly agency [point 9 added by Federal Law No. 83-ФЗ, 25 May 1995, as amended by Federal Law No. 31-ФЗ, 21 March 2002, and by Federal Law No. 122-ФЗ, 9 October 2002].

Article 18. State Control Over Compliance with Antimonopoly Legislation When Acquiring Stocks (or Participatory Shares) in Charter Capital of Commercial Organisations and Other Instances [as amended by Federal Law No. 83-ФЗ, 25 May 1995]

1. With the prior consent of the antimonopoly agency there shall be effectuated on the basis of a petition of a juridical or natural person [as amended by Federal Law No. 122-ФЗ, 9 October 2002]:

the acquisition by a person (or group of persons) the stocks (or participatory shares) with the right of vote in the charter capital of an economic society, such person (or group of persons) receiving the right to dispose of more than 20% of the said stocks (or participatory shares). This requirement shall not extend to the founders of the economic society when it is formed;

the receiving in ownership, use, or possession by one economic subject (or group of persons) the basic production means or nonmaterial assets of another economic subject if the balance sheet value of the property comprising the subject of the transaction (or mutually connected transactions) exceeds 10% of the balance sheet value of the basic production means and nonmaterial assets of the economic subject alienating or transferring the property;

the acquisition by a person (or group of persons) of rights enabling to determine the conditions for the conducting by the economic subject of its entrepreneurial activity or to effectuate functions of the executive organ thereof [point 1 as amended by Federal Law No. 83-ФЗ, 25 May 1995].

2. The prior consent to the effectuation of transactions specified in point 1 of the present Article shall be required if the total value of assets with regard to the last balance sheet of the persons specified in point 1 of the present Article exceeds 200,000 minimum amounts of payment of labour established by a federal law or one of them is an economic subject entered in the Register of economic subjects having a participatory share in the market of a determined good of less than 35%, or the acquirer is a group of persons controlling the activity of the said economic subject [as amended by Federal Law No. 122-ФЗ, 9 October 2002].

The procedure for forming the Register of economic subjects having a participatory share in the market of a determined good is more than 35% (hereinafter— Register) shall be determined by the Government of the Russian Federation [point 2 as amended by Federal Law No. 83-ФЗ, 25 May 1995].

3. In order to conclude the transactions specified in point 1 of the present Article, the persons shall be obliged to submit to the antimonopoly agency a petition concerning the giving of consent to the conclusion thereof and communicate the information necessary for adopting a decision provided for by Article 17(2) of the present Law.

State control over the conclusion of transactions provided for by the present Article shall be effectuated by the antimonopoly agency in the procedure provided for by Article 17(2) of the present Law [point 3 as amended by Federal Law No. 83-ФЗ, 25 May 1995, and by Federal Law No. 122-ФЗ, 9 October 2002].

4. The antimonopoly agency shall reject the petition if when considering the documents submitted it is discovered that the information contained therein having significance for adoption of the decision is unreliable or information has not been submitted by participants of transactions upon the demand of the antimonopoly agency within the period established by it in accordance with point 3 of the present Article, and also information concerning the sources, conditions of receiving, and amounts of monetary means and other property necessary for the conclusion of the transactions specified in point 1 of the present Article, and likewise if satisfaction of the petition may lead to limitation of competition on the goods market, including as a result of the arising or intensification of a dominant position of the economic subject(s) [point 4 as amended by Federal Law No.

83-ФЗ, 25 May 1995, and by Federal Law No. 3-ФЗ, 2 January 2000, and by Federal Law No. 122-ФЗ, 9 October 2002].

[paragraph two repealed by Federal Law No. 122-ФЗ, 9 October 2002].

[paragraph three repealed by Federal Law No. 122-ФЗ, 9 October 2002].

[paragraph four repealed by Federal Law No. 122-ФЗ, 9 October 2002].

5. The antimonopoly agency shall have the right to satisfy a petition even when the ensuing of unfavourable consequences specified in point 4 of the present Article is possible if:

participants of transactions prove that the positive effect from their actions, including in the socio-economic sphere, exceeds the unfavourable consequences for the goods market being considered;

a prescription concerning the commission of actions directed towards ensuring competition is issued.

A decision of the antimonopoly agency concerning consent to the conclusion of transactions specified in point 1 of the present Article shall terminate its operation if such transactions are not concluded within a year from the day of adoption of the said decision [point 5 as amended by Federal Law No. 122-ФЗ, 9 October 2002].

6. The antimonopoly agency shall be subject to being informed upon the application of a juridical or natural person within 45 days from the moment of the conclusion of the transaction specified in point 1 of the present Article if the total value of assets with regard to the last balance sheet of the persons specified in point 1 of the present Article exceeds 100,000 minimum amounts of payment of labour established by a federal law.

The economic subjects whose total value of assets with regard to the last balance sheet exceeds 100,000 minimum amounts of payment of labour established by a federal law, or economic subjects entered in the register of economic subjects having a participatory share in the market of a determined good of more than 35%, shall be obliged to inform the antimonopoly agency about the election of natural persons to executive organs and councils of directors (or supervisory councils) within 45 days from the moment of election. When informing the antimonopoly agency, the applicant shall provide it together with the application the information provided for by point 3 of the present Article [point 6 as amended by Federal Law No. 83-ФЗ, 25 May 1995, and by Federal Law No. 122-ФЗ, 9 October 2002].

7. If in the instances provided for by point 6 of the present Article the actions have led or may lead to the limitation of competition, including as a result of the arising or intensification of the dominant position of an economic subject(s), the persons effectuating the said actions shall be obliged upon the prescription of the antimonopoly agency to perform the actions directed towards ensuring competition [point 7 as amended by Federal Law No. 83-ФЗ, 25 May 1995, and by Federal Law No. 122-ФЗ, 9 October 2002].

8. In the instances provided for by point 6, paragraph one, of the present Article, the persons shall have the right to preliminarily request consent for performance of the said actions from the antimonopoly agency, which shall be obliged to consider the respective applications in the established procedure [point 8 as amended by Federal Law No. 83-ФЗ, 25 May 1995, and by Federal Law No. 122-ФЗ, 9 October 2002].

9. Transactions concluded in violation of the procedure established by the present Article leading to the limitation of competition, including as a result of the arising or intensification of domination, may be deemed invalid in a judicial procedure upon the suit of the antimonopoly agency.

The failure to perform decisions and prescriptions of the antimonopoly agency rendered in accordance with points 5 and 7 of the present Article shall be grounds for deeming the respective transaction invalid upon the suit of the antimonopoly agency.

[paragraph three repealed by Federal Law No. 122-ФЗ, 9 October 2002].

[point 9 as amended by Federal Law No. 83-ФЗ, 25 May 1995, and by Federal Law No. 122-ФЗ, 9 October 2002].

Article 19. Compulsory Division (or Separation) of Commercial Organisations and Noncommercial Organisations Effectuating Entrepreneurial Activity [as amended by Federal Law No. 83-ФЗ, 25 May 1995, and by Federal Law No. 122-ФЗ, 9 October 2002]

1. The antimonopoly agency shall have the right to issue a prescription concerning the compulsory division of a commercial organisation or noncommercial organisation effectuating entrepreneurial activity occupying a dominant position, or the separation thereof from the composition or one or several organisations in the event of the systematic effectuation by them of monopolistic activity [point 1 as amended by Federal Law No. 83-ФЗ, 25 May 1995, and by Federal Law No. 122-ФЗ, 9 October 2002].

By systematic effectuation of monopolistic activity is understood the commission within three years more than two facts of monopolistic activity elicited in the established procedure [added by Federal Law No. 122-ФЗ, 9 October 2002].

2. A prescription concerning compulsory division (or separation) of a commercial organisation shall be adopted when the following conditions are present [as amended by Federal Law No. 122-ФЗ, 9 October 2002]:

if this leads to the development of competition [added by Federal Law No. 122-ФЗ, 9 October 2002];

the possibility of an organisational and territorial solitariness of the structural subdivisions thereof;

the absence between the structural subdivisions thereof of a close technological interlinkage (in particular, if the volume of products (or work, services) of a structural subdivision thereof consumed by a juridical person does not exceed 30% of the total volume of products (or work, services) produced by this structural subdivision;

the possibilities of juridical persons as a result of a reorganisation autonomously to work on the market of a determined good [point 2 as amended by Federal Law No. 83-ФЗ, 25 May 1995].

3. The prescription of the antimonopoly agency concerning compulsory division (or separation) of commercial organisations or noncommercial organisations effectuating entrepreneurial activity shall be subject to performance by the owner or organ empowered by it, taking into account the requirements provided for in the said prescription and within the period determined by it, which may not be less than six months [point 3 as amended by Federal Law No. 83-ФЗ, 25 May 1995, and by Federal Law No. 122-ФЗ, 9 October 2002].

Article 19¹. State Control Over Agreements of Agreed Actions of Economic Subjects Limiting Competition [added by Federal Law No. 122-ФЗ, 9 October 2002]

1. In accordance with Article 6(4) of the present Law economic subjects having the intention to conclude an agreement or effectuate agreed actions shall have the right to apply to the antimonopoly agency with an application concerning the verification of the conformity of the agreement or effectuation of agreed actions to the requirements of antimonopoly legislation.

2. In the event of the submission of an application by economic subjects having the intention to conclude an agreement or to effectuate agreed actions, or by an empowered from among them, also shall submit to the antimonopoly agency information in accordance with the list of information confirmed by the federal antimonopoly agency.

3. The antimonopoly agency shall within 30 days from the day of receipt of all information necessary for consideration of the application adopt a decision concerning the conformity or nonconformity of the agreement or agreed actions to the requirements of antimonopoly legislation.

The grounds for refusal to adopt a decision concerning the conformity of the agreement or agreed actions to the requirements of antimonopoly legislation shall be:

the conditions provided for by Article 6(1), (2), and (3) of the present Law;

the unreliability of information submitted by economic subjects having significance for adoption of the decision.

The failure to submit information provided for by point 2 of the present Article shall be grounds for a refusal to adopt the decision with regard to the application.

When necessary, the period for consideration of an application may be extended by the antimonopoly agency, but not more than 20 days. The anti-monopoly agency shall communicate to the applicant in written form about the extension of the period for consideration of the application, specifying the reasons for the extension.

4. The decision of an antimonopoly agency concerning the conformity of the agreement or agreed actions to the requirements of antimonopoly legislation shall terminate its operation if such agreement was not reached nor agreed actions effectuated within two years from the day of adoption of the said decision.

5. The antimonopoly agency shall, together with the decision concerning the conformity of the agreement or agreed actions to the requirements of anti-monopoly legislation, have the right to issue to participants of the agreement or agreed actions a prescription directed towards ensuring competition.

6. The antimonopoly agency shall have the right to repeal a decision concern-ing the conformity of an agreement or agreed actions to the requirements of anti-monopoly legislation if:

after the adoption of the decision it was established than when considering the application unreliable information was submitted by the parties having significance for the adoption of the decision;

the prescription of the antimonopoly agencies provided for by point 5 of the present Article was not fulfilled by the participants of the agreement or agreed actions.

Article 20. Appeal Against Decisions of Federal Antimonopoly Agency (or Territorial Agency) Adopted on Basis of Articles 17, 18, and 19 of Present Law [repealed by Federal Law No. 122-ФЗ, 9 October 2002]

Article 21. Recording of Affiliated Persons [repealed by Federal Law No. 122-ФЗ, 9 October 2002]

Section VI. Responsibility for Violation of
Antimonopoly Legislation
[as amended by Federal Law No. 83-ФЗ, 25 May 1995]

Article 22. Obligatoriness of Performance of Decisions and Prescriptions of Antimonopoly Agency [as amended by Federal Law No. 83-ФЗ, 25 May 1995, and by Federal Law No. 122-ФЗ, 9 October 2002]

Commercial and noncommercial organisations (or their executives), federal agencies of executive power, agencies of executive power of subjects of the Russian Federation, agencies of local self-government, other agencies or organisations endowed with functions or rights of the said agencies of power (or their officials), and natural persons, including individual entrepreneurs, shall be obliged to fulfill actions provided for by the decision or prescription of the antimonopoly agency within the period established by it [as amended by Federal Law No. 83-ФЗ, 25 May 1995, and by Federal Law No. 122-ФЗ, 9 October 2002],

[paragraph repealed by Federal Law No. 122-ФЗ, 9 October 2002].

[pararaph repealed by Federal Law No. 83-ФЗ, 25 May 1995];

[pararaph repealed by Federal Law No. 83-ФЗ, 25 May 1995].

2. [repealed by Federal Law No. 122-ФЗ, 9 October 2002].

3. [repealed by Federal Law No. 83-ФЗ, 25 May 1995].

Article 22¹. Types of Responsibility for Violation of Antimonopoly Legislation

1. For a violation of antimonopoly legislation the officials of federal agencies of executive power, agencies of executive power of subjects of the Russian Federation, agencies of local self-government and other agencies or organisations endowed with functions or rights of the said agencies of power, commercial and noncommercial organisations, and the executives thereof, and also natural persons, including individual entrepreneurs, shall bear civil-law, administrative, or criminal responsibility [added by Federal Law No. 83-ФЗ, 25 May 1995, as amended by Federal Law No. 122-ФЗ, 9 October 2002].

2. The bringing to responsibility of persons specified in point 1 of the present Article shall not relieve them from the duty to perform the decision or prescription of the antimonopoly agency, submit a petition (or notification) for consideration, or perform actions provided for by antimonopoly legislation [added by Federal Law No. 122-ФЗ, 9 October 2002].

Article 23. Grounds for Imposition of Fines on Economic Subjects
[repealed by Federal Law No. 196-ФЗ, 30 December 2001]

Article 23¹. Recovery of Revenue Received as Result of Monopolistic Activity and Unfair Competition [added by Federal Law No. 122-ФЗ, 9 October 2002]

Revenue received as a result of a violation of antimonopoly legislation by an economic subject whose actions were deemed in the established procedure to be monopolistic activity or unfair competition shall in the event of the failure to perform the respective prescription be subject to recovery to the federal budget in a judicial procedure upon the suit of the antimonopoly agency.

Article 24. Responsibility of Officials of Agencies of Administration and Economic Subjects for Violation of Present Law [repealed by Federal Law No. 196-ФЗ, 30 December 2001]

Article 25. Responsibility of Officials of Antimonopoly Committee of RSFSR for Violation of Present Law [repealed by Federal Law No. 196-ФЗ, 30 December 2001]

Article 26. Compensation of Losses Caused to Economic Subjects [as amended by Federal Law No. 83-ФЗ, 25 May 1995, and by Federal Law No. 122-ФЗ, 9 October 2002]

Losses caused to a natural or juridical person as a result of illegal actions (or failure to act) of a federal agency of executive power, agency of State power of a subject of the Russian Federation, agency of local self-government, or other agencies or organisations endowed with functions or rights of the said agencies of power, including losses caused as a result of the issuance by them of legal acts in violation of antimonopoly legislation or the failure to perform or improper performance by the said agencies of their duties, shall be subject to compensation by the Russian Federation, respective subject of the Russian Federation, or municipal formation [as amended by Federal Law No. 83-ФЗ, 25 May 1995, and by Federal Law No. 122-ФЗ, 9 October 2002].

[paragraph two repealed by Federal Law No. 122-ФЗ, 9 October 2002]

Section VII. Procedure for Adoption of Decisions and Issuance of Prescriptions by Federal Antimonopoly Agency and Appeal Thereof
[as amended by Federal Law No. 83-ФЗ, 25 May 1995, and by Federal Law No. 122-ФЗ, 9 October 2002]

Article 27. Adoption of Decisions and Issuance of Prescriptions by Federal Antimonopoly Agency [as amended by Federal Law No. 83-ФЗ, 25 May 1995, and by Federal Law No. 122-ФЗ, 9 October 2002]

1. The antimonopoly agency shall adopt decisions and issue prescriptions provided for by the present Law within the limits of its competence.

2. The grounds for the initiation and consideration of cases, the adoption of decisions, and issuance of prescriptions by an antimonopoly agency shall be the representations of agencies, applications of organisations and natural persons, and also the initiative of the antimonopoly agency [as amended by Federal Law No. 122-ФЗ, 9 October 2002].

3. Decisions and prescriptions directed against prevention of the creation of discriminatory conditions must, if possible, be orientated towards competition principles and may contain requirements concerning ensuring the access of interested persons to information enabling them to ensure comparison of conditions of the circulation of goods and/or access to the market, and/or publication of the said information in the mass media, and also economic, technical, and other requirements.

Requirements shall be established by federal laws and other normative legal acts of the Russian Federation directed towards prevention of the creation of discriminatory conditions and not contrary to the provisions of the present Law.

4. Consideration by the antimonopoly agency of representations of agencies and applications of organisations and natural persons, the adoption of decisions and issuance of prescriptions provided for by the present Law, and also control over compliance with antimonopoly legislation, shall be effectuated in the procedure established by the federal antimonopoly agency [Article 27 as amended by Federal Law No. 83-ФЗ, 25 May 1995, and by Federal Law No. 122-ФЗ, 9 October 2002].

Article 28. Procedure for Appeal of Decisions and Prescriptions of Antimonopoly Agency [as amended by Federal Law No. 83-ФЗ, 25 May 1995, and by Federal Law No. 122-ФЗ, 9 October 2002]

1. Federal agencies of executive power, agencies of executive power of subjects of the Russian Federation, agencies of local self-government, other agencies or organisations endowed with functions or rights of the said agencies of power (or officials thereof), commercial and noncommercial organisations (or executives thereof), and natural persons, including individual entrepreneurs, shall have the right to apply to a court or arbitrazh court with an application concerning the deeming of decisions and prescriptions of the antimonopoly agency to be invalid fully or partly [as amended by Federal Law No. 196-ФЗ, 30 December 2001, and by Federal Law No. 122-ФЗ, 9 October 2002].

2. The filing of an application shall suspend the execution of the decision and prescription of the antimonopoly agency concerning the crediting to the federal budget of revenue received as a result of a violation of antimonopoly legislation, the compulsory separation of a commercial or noncommercial organisation, or separation from the composition thereof of one or several organisations, a change of conditions or dissolution of contracts and other transactions, and the conclusion of contracts with economic subjects for the time of consideration thereof in court or arbitrazh court until the entry of the decision of the court or arbitrazh court into legal force [as amended by Federal Law No. 83-ФЗ, 25 May 1995, and by Federal Law No. 122-ФЗ, 9 October 2002].

In other instances provided for by Article 12(2) of the present Law, the filing of an application shall not suspend performance of the decision and prescription of the antimonopoly agency [added by Federal Law No. 122-ФЗ, 9 October 2002].

The decision or prescription of the antimonopoly agency may be appealed within three months from the day of adoption or issuance of the decision or prescription [as amended by Federal Law No. 122-ФЗ, 9 October 2002].

Article 29. Procedure for Execution of Prescriptions and Other Decisions of Federal Antimonopoly Agency (or Territorial Agency) [repealed by Federal Law No. 122-ФЗ, 9 October 2002]

LAW OF THE RUSSIAN FEDERATION ON THE ORGANISATION OF INSURANCE AFFAIRS IN THE RUSSIAN FEDERATION

[Adopted 27 November 1992, Law No. 4015–1, as amended
31 December 1997, No. 157-ФЗ, 20 November 1999,
No. 204-ФЗ, 21 March 2002, No. 31-ФЗ,
and 25 April 2002, No. 41-ФЗ.
Ведомости Съезда народных депутатов Российской Федерации
(1993), no. 2, item 56; СЗ РФ (1998), no. 1, item 4;
(1999), no. 29, item 3703; (2002), no. 12, item 1093;
no. 18, item 1721]

Chapter I   General Provisions   59
Chapter II   Contract of Insurance   65
Chapter III Ensuring Financial Stability of Insurers   66
Chapter IV   State Supervision Over Insurance Activity   68
Chapter V   Concluding Provisions   71

Chapter I. General Provisions

Article 1. Relations Regulated by Present Law

1. The present Law regulates relations in the domain of insurance between insurance organisations and citizens, enterprises, institutions, and organisations, relations of insurance organisations between themselves, and also establishes the basic principles of State regulation of insurance activity.

2. Relations in the domain of insurance shall be regulated also by other acts of legislation of the Russian Federation adopted on the basis of the present Law.

3. The operation of the present Law shall not extend to State social insurance.

Article 2. Concept of Insurance

Insurance shall be relations relating to the protection of property interests of natural and juridical persons when specified events (insured events) ensue at the expense of monetary funds formed from insurance contributions (insurance premiums) paid by them.

Article 3. Forms of Insurance

1. Insurance may be effectuated in voluntary and obligatory forms.

2. Voluntary insurance shall be effectuated on the basis of a contract between the insurant and the insurer. The rules of voluntary insurance determining the general conditions and procedure for carrying it out shall be established by the insurer autonomously in accordance with the provisions of the present Law. The specific conditions of insurance shall be determined when the insurance contract is concluded.

3. Insurance effectuated by virtue of law shall be obligatory. The types, conditions, and procedure for carrying out obligatory insurance shall be determined by the respective laws of the Russian Federation.

Article 4. Objects of Insurance

Property interests which are not contrary to legislation of the Russian Federation may be the objects of insurance:

connected with the life, health, capacity to labour, and pension security of the insurant or insured person (personal insurance);

connected with the possession, use, and disposition of property (property insurance);

connected with compensating the insurant for harm of the person caused to him or to the property of a natural person, and also harm caused to a juridical person (insurance of responsibility).

Insurance of property interests of juridical persons situated on the territory of the Russian Federation (except for reinsurance and mutual insurance) and of property interests of natural persons-residents of the Russian Federation may be effectuated only by juridical persons having a license for the effectuation of insurance activity on the territory of the Russian Federation [added by Federal Law of 17 December 1997].

Article 5. Insurants

1. Juridical persons and natural persons who have dispositive legal capacity and have concluded insurance contracts with insurers or who are insurants by virtue of law shall be deemed to be insurants.

2. Insurants shall have the right to conclude contracts with insurers concerning insurance of third persons to the benefit of the latter (insured persons).

3. Insurants shall have the right when concluding insurance contracts to designate natural or juridical persons (beneficiaries) in order to receive insurance payments under the insurance contracts, and also to replace them at their discretion until the insured event ensues.

Article 6. Insurers

1. Juridical persons of any organisational-legal form provided for by legislation of the Russian Federation created in order to effectuate insurance activity (insurance organisations and mutual insurance societies) and which have received in the procedure established by the present Law a license to effectuate insurance activity on the territory of the Russian Federation shall be deemed to be insurers. Limitations may be established by legislative acts of the Russian Federation when insurance organisations are created by foreign juridical persons and foreign citizens on the territory of the Russian Federation.

Production, intermediary trading, and banking activity may not be the subject of direct activity by insurers

2. Juridical persons which do not meet the requirements provided for by point 1 of the present Article shall not have the right to engage in insurance activity.

3. Insurance organisations which are subsidiary societies with respect to foreign investors (or principal organisations) or have a participatory share of foreign investors in their charter capital of more than 49% may not effectuate in the Russian Federation the insurance of life, obligatory insurance, obligatory State insurance, property insurance connected with the effectuation of deliveries or fulfilment of independent-contract work for State needs, and also the insurance of property interests of State and municipal organdistions.

If the amount (or quota) of participation of foreign capital in the charter capital of insurance organisations exceeds 15%, the federal agency of executive power for supervision over insurance activity shall terminate the issuance of licenses for the effectuation of insurance activity to insurance organisations which are subsidiary societies with respect to foreign investors (or principal organisations) or have a participatory share of foreign investors in their charter capital of more than 49%.

The aforesaid amount (or aforesaid quota) shall be calculated as the relation of the total capital belonging to foreign investors and their subsidiary societies in the charter capital of insurance organisations to the aggregate charter capital of the insurance organisations.

An insurance organisation shall be obliged to receive the prior authoristion of the federal agency of executive power for supervision over insurance activity for an increase of the amount of its charter capital at the expense of means of foreign investors and/or their subsidiary societies, for the alienation to the benefit of a foreign investor (including for sale to foreign investors) of their stocks (or participatory shares in charter capital), and Russian stockholders (or participants), for alienation of stocks belonging to them (or participatory shares in charter capital) of an insurance organisation to the benefit of foreign investors and/or their subsidiary societies. The said prior authorisation shall be refused to insurance organisations which are subsidiary societies with respect to foreign investors (or principal organisations), or have a participatory share of foreign investors in their charter capital of more than 49%, or become such as a result of the said transactions, if the amount (or quota) established by the present point is exhausted or will be exceeded when concluding them.

The paying up by foreign investors of stocks of insurance organisations belonging to them (or participatory shares in charter capital) shall be made exclusively in monetary form in the currency of the Russian Federation.

Persons effectuating the functions of a one-man executive organ and chief bookkeeper of an insurance organisation with foreign investments must have citizenship of the Russian Federation [point 3 added by Federal Law of 20 November 1999].

4. An insurance organisation which is a subsidiary society with respect to a foreign investor (or principal organisation) shall have the right to effectuate insurance activity in the Russian Federation if the foreign investor (or principal organisation) for not less than 15 years is an insurance organisation effectuating its activity in accordance with legislation of the respective State and not less than two years participates in the activity of insurance organisations created on the territory of the Russian Federation.

Insurance organisations which are subsidiary societies with respect to foreign investors (or principal organisations) or have a participatory share of foreign investors in its charter capital or more than 49% may open their branches on the territory of the Russian Federation, participate in subsidiary insurance organisations after receiving the prior autorisation therefor of the federal agency of executive power for supervision for insurance activity. The said prior authorisations shall be refused if the amount (or quota) of participation of foreign capital in insurance organisations of the Russian Federation specified in point 3 of the present Article is exceeded [point 4 added by Federal Law of 20 November 1999].

Article 7. Mutual Insurance Societies

Juridical and natural persons may, for the insurance protection of their property interests, create mutual insurance societies in the procedure and on the conditions determined by the Statute on the Mutual Insurance Society, confirmed by the Supreme Soviet of the Russian Federation.

Article 8. Insurance Agents and Insurance Brokers

1. Insurers may effectuate insurance activity through insurance agents and insurance brokers.

2. Insurance agents shall be natural or juridical persons operating in the name of the insurer and on his behalf in accordance with the powers granted.

3. Insurance brokers shall be juridical or natural persons registered in the established procedure as entrepreneurs effectuating intermediary activity relating

to insurance in their own name on the basis of commissions of the insurant or insurer.

Insurance brokers shall be obliged to send to the federal agency of executive power for supervision over insurance activity a notice concerning the intention to effectuate intermediary activity relating to insurance 10 days before commencement of this activity. To the notice must be appended a copy of the document concerning State registration of the broker as a juridical person or entrepreneur [as amended by Federal Laws of 17 December 1997 and 21 March 2002].

4. Intermediary activity relating to insurance connected with the concluding of insurance contracts in the name of foreign insurance organisations, except for contracts of insurance of civil responsibility of possessors of motor vehicle means of transport travelling beyond the limits of the Russian Federation, on the territory of the Russian Federation shall not be permitted unless inter-State agreements with the participation of the Russian Federation have provided otherwise [as amended by Federal Law of 17 December 1997].

Intermediary activity connected with the conclusion on the territory of the Russian Federation in the name of foreign insurers of contracts of insurance of civil responsibility of possessors of motor vehicles means of transport travelling beyond the limits of the Russian Federation shall be authorised from the commencement of insurance activity of the insurance organisation effectuating the said intermediary activity [added by Federal Law of 17 December 1997].

Article 9. Insured Risk, Insured Event, Insurance Payment

1. An insured risk shall be the presupposed event, in the event of the ensuing of which the insurance is carried out.

An event considered as an insured risk must possess the indicia of the probability and fortuitousness of its ensuing.

2. An insured event shall be an event which has occurred, provided for by the insurance contract or law, with the ensuing of which the duty of the insurer arises to make an insurance payment to the insurant, insured person, beneficiary, or other third persons.

3. In the case of an insured event with property, the insurance payment shall be made in the form of insurance compensation, and in the case of an insured event with the person of the insurant or a third person, in the form of insurance security.

Article 10. Insurance Sum, Insurance Compensation, Insurance Security

1. An insurance sum shall be the monetary sum specified by the insurance contract or established by law, proceeding from which the amounts of insurance contribution and insurance payment shall be established, unless provided otherwise by the contract or by legislative acts of the Russian Federation.

2. In the event of property insurance, the insurance sum may not exceed its real value at the moment of concluding the contract (insurance value). The parties may not dispute the insurance value of property specified in an insurance contract except for instances when the insurer proves that he was intentionally deceived by the insurant.

If the insurance sum specified by the contract of insurance exceeds insurance value of the property, it shall be void by virtue of law in that portion of the insurance sum which exceeds the real value of the property at the moment of conclusion of the contract.

3. Insurance compensation may not exceed the amount of direct damage to the insured property of the insurant or third person under the insured event unless the payment of insurance compensation has been provided by the insurance contract in a specified amount.

When the insurance sum is lower than the insurance value of property, the amount of insurance compensation shall be reduced proportionately by the relation of the insurance sum of the property to the insurance value of the property, unless provided otherwise by the conditions of the insurance contract.

When the insurant has concluded a property insurance contract with several insurers for a sum exceeding the total aggregate insurance value of the property (double insurance), the insurance compensation received by him from all the insurers with respect to the insurance of this property may not exceed its insurance value. In so doing each of the insurers shall pay insurance compensation in the amount proportionally of the relation of the insurance sum regarding the contract concluded by it to the total amount with regard to all insurance contracts for the said property concluded by this insurer.

The conditions of an insurance contract may provide for the substitution of insurance payment by compensation for damage in kind within the limits of the amount of insurance compensation.

4. In a contract of personal insurance the insurance sum shall be established by the insurant by agreement with the insurer.

Insurance security shall be paid to the insurant or to a third person irrespective of the amounts due to them under other insurance contracts, and also under social insurance, social security, and by way of compensation of harm. In so doing the insurance security with regard to personal insurance due to a beneficiary in the event of the insurant's death shall not be part of the inheritance property.

Article 11. Insurance Contribution and Insurance Tariff

1. An insurance contribution shall be payment for insurance which the insurant is obliged to make to the insurer in accordance with the insurance contract or law.

2. The insurance tariff shall represent the rate of insurance contribution per unity of insurance sum or object of insurance.

Insurance tariffs relating to obligatory types of insurance shall be established or regulated in accordance with laws on obligatory insurance [as amended by Federal Law of 25 April 2002].

Insurance tariffs relating to voluntary types of personal insurance, property insurance, and insurance of responsibility may be calculated by the insurers autonomously. The specific amount of insurance tariff shall be specified in the insurance contract by agreement of the parties.

Article 12. Co-Insurance

An object of insurance may be insured under one contract jointly by several insurers (co-insurance). In so doing the conditions specifying the rights and duties of each insurer must be contained in the contract.

Article 13. Reinsurance

1. Reinsurance shall be the insurance by one insurer (or reinsurer) on conditions specified by the contract of the risk of performance of all or part of their obligations to the insurant by another insurer (or reinsurer).

2. An insurer who has concluded with a reinsurer a contract concerning reinsurance shall remain responsible to the insurant in full in accordance with the contract of insurance.

Article 14. Associations of Insurers

1. Insurers may form unions, groups, and other associations in order to coordinate their activity, protect the interests of their members, and effectuation of joint programmes, if the creation thereof is not contrary to the requirements of legislation of the Russian Federation. These associations shall not have the right to directly engage in insurance activity.

2. Associations of insurers shall operate on the basis of charters and shall acquire the rights of juridical persons after State registration in accordance with the Federal Law 'On the State Registration of Juridical Persons' [as amended by Federal Laws of 17 December 1997 and 21 March 2002].

Chapter II. Contract of Insurance

Article 15. Concept of Insurance Contract [repealed by Federal Law of 17 December 1997].

Article 16. Conclusion of Insurance Contract [repealed by Federal Law of 17 December 1997].

Article 17. Duties of Insurer [repealed by Federal Law of 17 December 1997].

Article 18. Duties of Insurant [repealed by Federal Law of 17 December 1997].

Article 19. Replacement of Insurant in Contract of Insurance [repealed by Federal Law of 17 December 1997].

Article 20. Procedure and Conditions for Effectuation of Insurance Payment [repealed by Federal Law of 17 December 1997].

Article 21. Refusal of Insurance Payment [repealed by Federal Law of 17 December 1997].

Article 22. Transfer to Insurer of Rights of Insurant Relating to Insurance of Property With Respect to Person Responsible for Causing Damage [repealed by Federal Law of 17 December 1997].

Article 23. Termination of Contract of Insurance [repealed by Federal Law of 17 December 1997].

Article 24. Invalidity of Contract of Insurance [repealed by Federal Law of 17 December 1997].

Chapter III. Ensuring Financial Stability of Insurers

Article 25. Conditions of Ensuring Financial Stability of Insurers

The existence of paid up charter capital and insurance reserves, as well as a system of reinsurance, shall be the basis of the financial stability of insurers.

The minimum amount of paid-up charter capital formed from monetary means on the day of issuance by a juridical person of documents to receive a license for the effectuation of insurance activity must be not less than 25,000 minimum amounts of payment for labour when conducting types of insurance other than the insurance of life, not less than 35,000 minimum amounts of payment for labour when conducting insurance of life and other types of insurance, and not less than 50,000 minimum amounts of payment for labour when conducting reinsurance exclusively [added by Federal Law of 17 December 1997].

The minimum amount of paid-up charter capital formed at the expense of monetary means on the day of filing documents to receive a license for the effectuation of insurance activity by an insurance organisation which is a subsidiary society with respect to a foreign investor (or principal organisation) or has a participatory share of foreign investors in its charter capital of more than 49% must comprise not less than 250,000 minimum amounts of payment for labour, and when conducting exclusively reinsurance—not less than 300,000 minimum amounts of payment for labour [paragraph three added by Federal Law of 20 November 1999].

Article 26. Insurance Reserves and Funds of Insurers

1. In order to ensure the fulfilment of insurance obligations accepted, insurers shall, in the procedure and on the conditions established by legislation of the

Russian Federation, form from the insurance contributions received by them insurance reserves for future insurance payments with regard to personal insurance, property insurance, and responsibility insurance.

In an analogous procedure the insurers shall have the right to create reserves in order to finance measures relating to the prevention of accidents and the loss or damaging of insured property.

Insurance reserves formed by insurers shall not be subject to withdrawal to the federal and other budgets.

2. From the revenues remaining after the payment of taxes and at the disposition of the insurers, they may form funds necessary in order to ensure their activity.

3. Insurers shall have the right to invest or otherwise place insurance reserves and other assets, and also to make loans to insurants who have concluded contracts of personal insurance, within the limits of the insurance amounts under these contracts.

4. Additional requirements may be established by the federal agency of executive power for supervision over insurance activity for the procedure and conditions of forming and placing insurance reserves by insurance organisations with foreign investments [point 4 added by Federal Law of 20 November 1999].

Article 27. Guarantees of Solvency of Insurers

1. In order to ensure their solvency, insurers shall be obliged to comply with normative correlations between assets and insurance obligations accepted by them. The method for calculating these correlations and the normative amounts thereof shall be established by the federal agency of executive power for supervision over insurance activity [as amended by Federal Law of 17 December 1997].

Additional requirements may be established by the federal agency of executive power for supervision over insurance activity for normative correlations between assets and insurance obligations accepted by insurance organisations with foreign investments [paragraph added by Federal Law of 20 November 1999].

2. Insurers who have accepted obligations in volumes exceeding the possibility of performing them at the expense of own assets and insurance reserves shall be obliged to insure the risk of performing the respective obligations with reinsurers.

3. The placement of insurance reserves must be effectuated by insurers on conditions of diversification, repayability, profitableness, and liquidity.

Article 28. Records and Reports of Insurers

1. The plan of accounts and bookkeeping rules, indicators and forms of records of insurance operations, and reports of insurers shall be established by the federal agency of executive power for supervision over insurance activity by

agreement with the Ministry of Finances of the Russian Federation and the State Committee of the Russian Federation for Statistics [as amended by Federal Law of 17 December 1997].

2. Operations with regard to personal insurance shall be taken into account by insurers separately from operations relating to property insurance and to responsibility insurance.

Article 29. Publication of Annual Balance Sheets by Insurers

Insurers shall publish annual balance sheets and profit and loss accounts within the periods established by the federal agency of executive power for supervision over insurance activity after audit confirmation of the reliability of the information contained therein [as amended by Federal Law of 17 December 1997].

Chapter IV. State Supervision Over Insurance Activity

Article 30. State Supervision Over Insurance Activity in Russian Federation

1. State supervision over insurance activity shall be effectuated for the purposes of complying with the requirements of legislation of the Russian Federation concerning insurance, the effective development of insurance services, protection of the rights and interests of insurants, insurers, other interested persons, and the State.

2. State supervision over insurance activity on the territory of the Russian Federation shall be effectuated by the federal agency of executive power for supervision over insurance activity, operating on the basis of a Statute confirmed by the Government of the Russian Federation [as amended by Federal Law of 17 December 1997].

3. The principal functions of the federal agency of executive power for supervision over insurance activity shall be [as amended by Federal Law of 17 December 1997]:
    (a) the issuance to insurers of licenses for the effectuation of insurance activity;
    (b) keeping a unified State register of insurers and associations of insurers, and also a register of insurance brokers;
    (c) control over the well-foundedness of insurance tariffs and ensuring the solvency of insurers;
    (d) establishment of rules for the formation and placing of insurance reserves, indicators, and forms for records of insurance operations and reports on insurance activity;
    (e) issuance in the instances provided for by the present Law of authorisations for increasing amounts of charter capital of insurance organisations at the expense of means of foreign investors for the conclusion of transactions with the partici-

pation of foreign investors with regard to the alienation of stocks (or participatory shares in charter capital) of insurance organisations, and also the opening of branches by insurance organisations with foreign investments [added by Federal Law of 20 November 1999];

(f) working out of normative and methods documents relating to questions of insurance activity relegated by the present Law to the competence of the federal agency of executive power for supervision over insurance activity [as amended by Federal Laws of 31 December 1997 and 20 November 1999];

(g) summarising of the practice of insurance activity, the working out and submission in the established procedure of proposals for the development and improvement of legislation of the Russian Federation on insurance [as amended by Federal Law of 20 November 1999].

4. The federal agency of executive power for supervision over insurance activity shall have the right to [as amended 17 December 1997]:

(a) receive from insurers the established report on insurance activity, information concerning their financial position, receive information needed to fulfil the functions entrusted to it from enterprises, institutions, and organisations, including banks, and also from citizens;

(b) conduct verifications of compliance by insurers with legislation of the Russian Federation on insurance and the reliability of reports submitted by them;

(c) in the event violations by insurers are elicited of the requirements of the present Law, give them instructions regarding the elimination thereof, and in the event of the failure to fulfil the instructions, suspend or limit the operation of licenses of these insurers until the elimination of the elicited violations or adopt decisions to revoke the licenses;

(d) apply to an arbitrazh court with a suit concerning the liquidation of the insurer in the event of a repeated violation by the latter of legislation of the Russian Federation, and also the liquidation of enterprises and organisations effectuating insurance without licenses.

Article 31. Suppression of Monopolistic Activity and Unfair Competition in Insurance Market

The prevention, limitation, and suppression of monopolistic activity and unfair competition on the insurance market shall be ensured by the State Committee of the Russian Federation for Anti-Monopoly Policy and Support of New Economic Structures, in accordance with anti-monopoly legislation of the Russian Federation.

Article 32. Licensing of Insurance Activity

1. Licenses for the effectuation of insurance activity shall be issued by the federal agency of executive power for supervision over insurance activity [as amended by Federal Law of 17 December 1997]:

(a) to insurers on the basis of their application with the following appended:

constitutive documents;

document concerning State registration [as amended by Federal Law of 21 March 2002];

information concerning the amount of paid up charter capital;

economic substantiation of insurance activity;

rules regarding the types of insurance;

calculations of insurance tariffs;

information concerning the directors and their deputies;

(b) to insurers, the subject of whose activity is exclusively reinsurance, on the basis of their applications with the following appended:

constitutive documents;

document concerning State registration [as amended by Federal Law of 21 March 2002];

information concerning the amount of paid up charter capital;

information concerning the directors and their deputies.

2. Licenses shall be issued for the effectuation of voluntary and obligatory personal insurance, property insurance, and responsibility insurance, and also reinsurance, if the subject of activity of the insurer is exclusively reinsurance. In the licenses shall be specified the specific types of insurance which the insurer has the right to effectuate.

3. The federal agency of executive power for supervision over insurance activity shall consider the applications of juridical persons concerning the issuance of licenses to them within a period not exceeding 60 days from the moment of receipt of documents provided for by point 1 of the present Article [as amended by Federal Law of 17 December 1997].

4. The failure of the documents appended to the application to conform to the requirements of legislation of the Russian Federation shall serve as the grounds for a refusal to issue a license to a juridical person for the effectuation of insurance activity.

The federal service of executive power for supervision over insurance activity shall communicate to a juridical person in written form the refusal to issue a license, indicating the reasons for the refusal [as amended by Federal Law of 17 December 1997].

5. An insurer shall be obliged to communicate to the federal agency of executive power for supervision over insurance activity all changes made in constitutive documents within a month of the registration of these changes in the established procedure [as amended by Federal Law of 17 December 1997].

Article 33. Compliance with Commercial Secrecy of Insurer by Officials of Federal Agency of Executive Power for Supervision Over Insurance Activity [as amended by Federal Law of 17 December 1997]

Officials of the federal agency of executive power for supervision over insurance activity shall not have the right to use for mercenary purposes and to divulge in any form whatever information constituting a commercial secret of the insurer [as amended by Federal Law of 17 December 1997].

Chapter V. Concluding Provisions

Article 34. Insurance of Foreign Citizens, Stateless Persons, and Foreign Juridical Persons on Territory of Russian Federation

Foreign citizens, stateless persons, and foreign juridical persons on the territory of the Russian Federation shall enjoy the right to insurance protection equally with citizens and juridical persons of the Russian Federation.

Article 35. Consideration of Disputes

Disputes connected with insurance shall be settled by a court or an arbitrazh or arbitration courts in accordance with their competence.

Article 36. International Treaties

If other rules have been established by international treaties of the Russian Federation or former USSR than those which are contained in legislation of the Russian Federation on insurance, the rules of the international treaty shall apply.

LAND CODE OF THE RUSSIAN FEDERATION

[Federal Law No. 136-ФЗ, 25 October 2001.
СЗ РФ (2001), no. 44, item 4147]

Chapter I	General Provisions	73
Chapter II	Protection of Lands	79
Chapter III	Ownership in Land	81
Chapter IV	Permanent (or In Perpetuity) Use, Inheritable Possession for Life of Land Plots, Limited Use by Others of Land Plots (Servitude), Lease of Land Plots, Uncompensated Fixed Term Use of Land Plots	83
Chapter V	Arising of Rights in Land	88
Chapter VI	Rights and Duties of Owners of Land Plots, Landusers, Land Possessors, and Lessees of Land Plots When Using Land Plots	103
Chapter VII	Termination and Limitation of Rights to Land	104
Chapter VIII	Compensation of Losses and Loss of Agricultural Production and Forestry in Event of Seizure of Land Plots for State and Municipal Needs	112
Chapter IX	Defence of Rights to Land and Consideration of Land Disputes	114
Chapter X	Payment for Land and Valuation of Land	116
Chapter XI	Monitoring of Lands, Land Tenure, and State Land Cadastre	117
Chapter XII	Control Over Compliance with Land Legislation and Protection and Use of Lands (Land Control)	119
Chapter XIII	Responsibility for Violation in Domain of Protection and Use of Lands	120
Chapter XIV	Lands of Agricultural Designation	121
Chapter XV	Lands of Settlements	124
Chapter XVI	Lands of Industry, Electric Power, Transport, Communications, Radiobroadcasting, Television, Information, Lands for Ensuring Outer Space Activity, Lands of Defence and Security, and Lands of Other Special Designation	128
Chapter XVII	Lands of Specially-Protected Territories and Objects	136
Chapter XVIII	Forestry Fund Lands, Water Fund Lands, and Reserve Lands	141

Chapter I. General Provisions

Article 1. Basic Principles of Land Legislation

1. The present Code and other acts of land legislation issued in accordance therewith shall be based on the following principles:

(1) recording the significance of land as the basis of the life and activity of man, according to which the regulation of relations with regard to the use and protection of land is effecutated by proceeding from concepts of land as a natural object to be protected as a major constituent part of nature, a natural resource to be used as a means of production in agriculture and forestry and the foundations for the effectuation of economic and other activity on the territory of the Russian Federation, and simultaneously as immoveable property and an object of the right of ownership and other rights to land;

(2) priority of the protection of land as a major component of the environment and means of production in agriculture and forestry over the use of land as immoveable property, according to which the possession, use, and disposition of land are effectuated by the owners of land plots freely if such does not damage the environment;

(3) priority of the protection of human life and health, according to which when effectuating activity with regard to the use and protection of land such decisions should be taken and such types of activity effectuated which would enable the preservation of human life to be ensured or negative (or harmful) influence on human health to be averted, even if this requires great expenditures;

(4) participation of citizens and social organisations (or associations) in deciding questions affecting their rights to land, according to which citizens of the Russian Federation and social organisations (or associations) shall have the right to take part in the preparation of decisoins whose realisation may exert influence on the state of lands in the event of their use and protection, and agencies of State power, agencies of local self-government, subjects of economic and other activity shall be obliged to ensure the possibility of such activity in the procedure and forms which have been established by legislation;

(5) unity of the fate of land plots and objects durably connected therewith, according to which all objects durably connected with land plots follow the fate of the land plots, except for instances established by federal laws;

(6) priority of the preservation of especially valuable lands and land of specially protected territories, according to which the seizure of valuable lands of agricultural designation, lands of the forestry fund occupied by first-group forests, lands of specially-protected nature territories and objects, lands occupied by objects of cultural heritage, and other especially valuable lands and lands of specially-protected territories for other purposes shall be limited or prohibited in the procedure established by federal laws. The establishment of this principle should not

be construed as a denial or diminution of the significance of lands of other categories;

(7) payment for the use of land, according to which any use of land shall be effectuated for payment, except for instances established by federal laws and by laws of subjects of the Russian Federation;

(8) division of lands by special-purpose designation into categories, according to which the legal regime of lands is determined by proceeding from their affiliation to a particular category and authorised use in accordance with zoning of territories and the requirements of legislation;

(9) delimitation of State ownership in land into the ownership of the Russian Federation, ownership of subjects of the Russian Federation, and ownership of municipal formations, according to which the legal foundations and procedure for such delimitation is established by federal laws;

(10) differentiated approach to the establishment of the legal regime of lands, in accordance with which when determining their legal regime the nature, social, economic, and other factors must be taken into account;

(11) combining of the interests of society and the legal interests of citizens, according to which the regulation of the use and protection of lands is effectuated in the interests of all of society, ensuring the guarantees of each citizen to free possession, use, and disposition of the land plot belonging to him.

When regulating land relations, the principle of delimitation of the operation of norms of civil legislation and norms of land legislation with regard to regulation of relations relating to the use of lands, and also the principle of State regulation of the privatisation of land, shall be applied.

2. Other principles of land legislation which are not contrary to the principles established by point 1 of the present Article also may be established by federal laws.

Article 2. Land Legislation

1. Land legislation in accordance with the Constitution of the Russian Federation is within the joint jurisdiction of the Russian Federation and subjects of the Russian Federation. Land legislation shall consist of the present Code, federal laws, and laws of subjects of the Russian Federation adopted in accordance therewith.

Norms of land law contained in other federal laws and laws of subjects of the Russian Federation must correspond to the present Code.

Land relations also may be regulated by edicts of the President of the Russian Federation, which must not be contrary to the present Code and federal laws.

2. The Government of the Russian Federation shall adopt decisions regulating land relations within the limits of the powers determined by the present Code, federal laws, and also by edicts of the President of the Russian Federation regulating land relations.

3. On the basis of and in execution of the present Code, federal laws, other normative legal acts of the Russian Federation, and laws of subjects of the Russian Federation, agencies of executive power of subjects of the Russian Federation may within the limits of their powers issue acts containing norms of land law.

4. On the basis of and in execution of the present Code, federal laws, other normative legal acts of the Russian Federation, laws, and other normative legal acts of subjects of the Russian Federation, agencies of local self-government may within the limits of their powers issue acts containing norms of land law.

Article 3. Relations to be Regulated by Land Legislation

1. Land legislation shall regulate relations with regard to the use and protection of land in the Russian Federation as the foundation of life and activity of peoples residing on the respective territory (land relations).

2. To relations with regard to the use and protection of the subsoil, waters, forests, fauna, and other natural resources, protection of the natural environment, protection of specially protected nature territories and objects, protection of the atmosphere, and protection of objects of cultural heritage of the peoples of the Russian Federation shall apply respectively legislation on the subsoil, forestry and water legislation, legislation of fauna, on the protection and use of other natural resources, on the protection of the natural environment, on the protection of the atmosphere, on specially protected nature territories and objects, on the protection of objects of cultural heritage of peoples of the Russian Federation, and special federal laws.

Norms of the said branches of legislation shall apply to land relations unless these relations have been regulated by land legislation.

3. Property relations with regard to the possession, use, and disposition of land plots, and also the conclusion of transactions therewith, shall be regulated by civil legislation unless provided otherwise by land, forestry, and water legislation, legislation on the subsoil and protection of the natural environment, and special federal laws.

Article 4. Application of International Treaties of Russian Federation

If other rules have been established by an international treaty of the Russian Federation ratified in the established procedure than those which have been provided for by the present Code, the rules of the international treaty shall apply.

Article 5. Participants of Land Relations

1. Citizens, juridical persons, the Russian Federation, subjects of the Russian Federation, and municipal formations shall be participants of land relations.

2. The rights of foreign citizens, stateless persons, and foreign juridical persons to the acquisition of land plots in ownership shall be determined in accordance with the present Code by federal laws.

3. For the purposes of the present Code the following concepts and definitions shall be used:

owners of land plots—persons who are the owners of land plots;

landusers—persons possessing and using land plots by right of permanent (in perpetuity) use or by right of uncompensated fixed-term use;

land possessors—persons possessing and using land plots by right of inheritable possession for life;

lessees of land plots—persons possessing and using land plots under a contract of lease or contract of sublease;

possessors of servitude—persons having the right of limited use of another's land plots (servitude).

Article 6. Objects of Land Relations

1. There shall be objects of land relations:
(1) land as a natural object or natural resource;
(2) land plots;
(3) parts of land plots.

2. A land plot as an object of land relations is part of the surface of the land (including the soil stratum), the boundaries of which have been described and certified in the established procedure.

A land plot may be divisible and indivisible. A land plot which may be divided into parts, each of which after the division forms an autonomous land plot, the authorised use of which may be effectuated without transfer thereof to lands of another category, shall be divisible, except for instances established by federal laws.

Article 7. Composition of Lands in Russian Federation

1. Lands in the Russian Federation with regard to special-purpose designation shall be subdivided into the following categories:
(1) lands of agricultural designation;
(2) lands of settlements;
(3) lands of industry, electric power, transport, communications, radio broadcasting, television, and information, and lands for ensuring outer space activity, lands of defence and security, and lands of other special designation;
(4) lands of specially protected territories and objects;
(5) forestry fund lands;
(6) water fund lands;
(7) reserve lands.

2. The lands specified in point 1 of the present Article shall be used in accordance with the special-purpose designation established for them. The legal regime of lands shall be determined by proceeding from their affiliation to a particular

category and authorised use in accordance with zoning of territories, the general principles and procedure for conducting of which shall be established by federal laws and by the requirements of special federal laws.

Any type of authorised use from the types provided for by the zoning of territories shall be selected autonomously, without additional authorisations and procedures of agreement.

3. In places of traditional inhabitation and economic activity of native small peoples of the Russian Federation and ethnic communities a special legal regime for the use of lands of the said categories may be established in instances provided for by federal laws, laws and other normative legal acts of subjects of the Russian Federation, and normative legal acts of agencies of local self-government.

Article 8. Relegating of Lands to Categories, Transfer Thereof from One Category to Another

1. The relegating of lands to categories and transfer thereof from one category to another shall be effectuated with respect to:

(1) lands in federal ownership,—by the Government of the Russian Federation;

(2) lands in the ownership of subjects of the Russian Federation and lands of agricultural designation in municipal ownership,—by agencies of executive power of subjects of the Russian Federation;

(3) lands in municipal ownership, except for lands of agricultural designation,—by agencies of local self-government;

(4) lands in private ownership:

lands of agricultural designation—by agencies of executive power of subjects of the Russian Federation;

lands of other special-purpose designation—by agencies of local self-government.

The procedure for the transfer of lands from one category to another shall be established by federal laws.

2. The category of lands shall be specified in:

(1) acts of federal agencies of executive power, acts of agencies of executive power of subjects of the Russian Federation, and acts of local self-government concerning the granting of land plots;

(2) contracts, the subject of which is land plots;

(3) documents of the State land cadastre;

(4) documents concerning State registration of rights to immoveable property and transactions therewith;

(5) other documents in the instances established by federal laws and by laws of subjects of the Russian Federation.

3. A violation of the procedure established by the present Code and federal laws for the transfer of lands from one category to another shall be grounds for deeming invalid acts concerning the relegating of lands to categories and concerning the transfer thereof from one category to another.

Article 9. Powers of Russian Federation in Domain of Land Relations

1. To the powers of the Russian Federation in the domain of land relations shall be relegated:

(1) establishment of the fundamental principles of federal policy in the domain of the regulation of land relations;

(2) establishment of limitations of the rights of owners of land plots, landusers, land possessors, and lessees of land plots, and also limitations on the circulability of land plots;

(3) State administration in the domain of the effectuation of monitoring of lands, State land control, land tenure, and keeping of the State land cadastre;

(4) establishment of the procedure for seizing land plots, including by means of purchase and for State and municipal needs;

(5) seizure for needs of the Russian Federation of land plots, including by means of purchase;

(6) working out and realisation of federal programmes for the use and protection of lands;

(7) other powers relegated to powers of the Russian Federation by the Constitution of the Russian Federation, the present Code, and federal laws.

2. The Russian Federation shall effectuate administration and disposition of land plots in the ownership of the Russian Federation (federal ownership).

Article 10. Powers of Subjects of Russian Federation in Domain of Land Relations

1. To powers of subjects of the Russian Federation shall be relegated the seizure, including by means of purchase, of lands for needs of subjects of the Russian Federation; working out and realisation of regional programmes for the use and protection of lands within the boundaries of subjects of the Russian Federation; other powers not relegated to powers of the Russian Federation or to powers of agencies of local self-government.

2. Subjects of the Russian Federation shall effectuate the administration and disposition of land plots in the ownership of subjects of the Russian Federation.

Article 11. Powers of Agencies of Local Self-Government in Domain of Land Relations

1. To powers of agencies of local self-government in the domain of land relations shall be relegated the seizure, including by means of purchase, of land plots

for municipal needs, establishment by taking into account the requirements of legislation of the Russian Federation of rules for land use and building on territories of city and rural settlements and the territories of other municipal formations, working out and realisation of local programmes for the use and protection of lands, and also other powers to decide questions of local significance in the domain of the use and protection of lands.

2. The administration and disposition of land plots in municipal ownership shall be effectuated by agencies of local self-government.

Chapter II. Protection of Lands

Article 12. Purposes of Protection of Lands

1. Land in the Russian Federation shall be protected as the foundation of the life and activity of peoples inhabiting on the respective territory.

The use of lands must be effectuated by means ensuring the preservation of ecological systems, the capacity of land to be a means of production in agriculture, and the basis of effectuating economic and other types of activity.

2. The purposes of the protection of lands shall be:

(1) prevention of the degradation, pollution, littering, and disturbance of lands and other negative (or harmful) effects of economic activity;

(2) ensuring the improvement and restoration of lands subjected to degradation, pollution, littering, disturbance, and other negative (or harmful) effects of economic activity.

Article 13. Content of Protection of Lands

1. For the purposes of the protection of lands, the owners of land plots, landusers, land possessors, and lessees of land plots shall be obliged to conduct measures with regard to:

(1) preservation of the soils and fertility thereof;

(2) defence of lands against water and wind erosion, settlement, warming, becoming a swamp, secondary salination, drying up, compression, pollution with radioactive and chemical substances, littering with wastes of production and consumption, pollution, including biogenic pollution, and other negative (or harmful) effects, as a result of which degradation of the lands occurs;

(3) defence of agricultural tracts and other lands against infection with bacterial-parasitic and quarantine pests and sicknesses of flora, overgrowing with weeds, bushes, and young forest, and other types of worsening of the state of lands;

(4) liquidation of the consequences of pollution, including biogenic pollution, and littering of lands;

(5) preservation of the achieved level of soil conservation;

(6) recultivation of disturbed lands, restoration of soil fertility, and timely involvement of lands in turnover;

(7) preservation of soil fertility and use thereof when conducting work connected with the disturbance of lands.

2. For the purposes of the protection of lands, federal, regional, and local programmes shall be worked out for the protection of lands, including a List of obligatory measures with regard to the protection of lands, taking into account the peculiarities of economic activity and natural and other conditions.

An assessment of the state of lands and effectiveness of measures provided for with regard to the protection of lands shall be conducted by taking into account ecological expert examination and sanitary-hygienic and other norms and requirements established by legislation.

3. The introduction of new technologies, effectuation of programmes for soil conservation of lands, and increase of soil fertility shall be prohibited in the event of their failure to conform to the ecological, sanitary-hygienic, and other requirements provided for by legislation.

4. When conducting construction work and work with regard to the extraction of minerals connected with a disturbance of the soil stratum, the fertile soil stratum shall be removed and shall be used to improve low-productive lands.

5. In order to assess the state of soil for the purpose of protection of human health and the environment, normative standards of maximally permissible concentrations of harmful substances, harmful micro-organisms, and other biological substances polluting the soil shall be established by the Government of the Russian Federation.

In order to conduct a verification of the conformity of the soil to ecological normative standards, soil, geobotanical, agrochemical, and other investigations shall be conducted.

6. For the purpose of prevention of the degradation of lands, restoration of soil fertility, and polluted territories, the closing down of lands shall be permitted, with the removal thereof from turnover in the procedure established by the Government of the Russian Federation.

7. The protection of lands occupied by reindeer pastures in areas of the Far North, pasturing and seasonal pastures shall be effectuated in accordance with federal laws and other normative legal acts of the Russian Federation and by laws and other normative legal acts of subjects of the Russian Federation.

8. For the purpose of increasing the interest of owners of land plots, landusers, land possessors, and lessees of land plots to preserve and restore soil fertility and defend lands against negative (or harmful) effects of economic activity economic incentives may be effectuated for the protection and use of lands in the procedure established by budget legislation and legislation on taxes and charges.

Article 14. Use of Lands Subject to Radioactive and Chemical Pollution

1. Lands which have been subjected to radioactive and chemical pollution and on which the production of products is not ensured that correspond to the requirements established by legislation shall be subject to limitation in use, exclusion thereof from the categories of lands of agricultural designation, and may be transferred to reserve lands for the closing down thereof. The production and realisation of agricultural products on such lands shall be prohibited.

2. The procedure for the use of lands subject to radioactive and chemical pollution, establishment of protected zones, preservation on these lands of dwelling houses, objects of production designation, objects of social and cultural-domestic servicing of the population, and conducting on these lands of soil conservation and crop engineering work shall be determined by the Government of the Russian Federation, taking into account the normative standards for the maximally admissible levels of radiation and chemical effects.

3. Persons as a result of whose activity radioactive and chemical pollution of lands has occurred which entailed the impossibility of use thereof for the special-purpose designation or worsening of the quality thereof shall compensate losses and reductions of agricultural and forestry production in accordance with the provisions of Articles 57 and 58 of the present Code, and also contributorily compensate expenditures for the deactivation of lands subjected to radioactive and chemical pollution, expenditures for bringing them into a state suitable for use for special-purpose designation, or compensate owners of land plots within the limits of such lands for the value thereof in the event of their transfer to reserve lands for closing down.

Chapter III. Ownership in Land

Article 15. Ownership in Land of Citizens and Juridical Persons

1. Land plots acquired by citizens and juridical persons on the grounds provided for by legislation of the Russian Federation shall be the ownership of citizens and juridical persons (private ownership).

2. Citizens and juridical persons shall have the right of equal access to the acquisition of land plots in ownership. Land plots in State or municipal ownership may be granted to the ownership of citizens and juridical persons, except for land plots which in accordance with the present Code and federal laws may not be in private ownership.

3. Foreign citizens, stateless persons, and foreign juridical persons may not possess by right of ownership in land plots on frontier territories, a List of which shall be established by the President of the Russian Federation in accordance with federal legislation of the State boundary of the Russian Federation and to other

specially established territories of the Russian Federation in accordance with federal laws.

Article 16. State Ownership in Land

1. Lands not in the ownership of citizens, juridical persons, or municipal formations shall be State ownership.

2. Delimitation of State ownership in land into ownership of the Russian Federation (federal ownership), ownership of subjects of the Russian Federation and ownership of municipal formations (municipal ownership) shall be effectuated in accordance with the Federal Law 'On the Delimitation of State Ownership in Land'.

Article 17. Ownership of Russian Federation (Federal Ownership) in Land

1. Land plots shall be in federal ownership:
which have been deemed to be such by federal laws;
the right of ownership of the Russian Federation to which arose when delimiting State ownership in land;
which have been acquired by the Russian Federation on the grounds provided for by civil legislation.

2. Land plots not granted in private ownership on the grounds provided for by the Federal Law 'On the Delimitation of State Ownership in Land' may be in federal ownership.

Article 18. Ownership in Land of Subjects of Russian Federation

1. Land plots shall be in the ownership of subjects of the Russian Federation:
which have been deemed to be such by federal laws;
the right of ownership of subjects of the Russian Federation to which arose when delimiting State ownership in land;
which have been acquired by subjects of the Russian Federation on the grounds provided for by civil legislation.

2. Land plots not granted in private ownership may be in the ownership of subjects of the Russian Federation:
occupied by immoveable property in the ownership of subjects of the Russian Federation;
granted to agencies of State power of subjects of the Russian Federation, State unitary enterprises, and State institutions created by agencies of State power of subjects of the Russian Federation;
relegated to lands of specially-protected territories of regional significance and forestry fund lands in the ownership of subjects of the Russian Federation in accordance with federal laws, water fund lands occupied by water objects in the ownership of subjects of the Russian Federation, and lands of the fund for redistribution of lands;

occupied by privatised property which before privatisation were in the ownership of subjects of the Russian Federation.

Article 19. Municipal Ownership in Land

1. Land plots shall be in municipal ownership:
which have been deemed to be such by federal laws and laws of subjects of the
Russian Federation adopted in accordance therewith;
the right of municipal ownership to which arose when delimiting State ownership in land;
which were acquired on the grounds established by civil legislation.

2. Land plots not granted in private ownership on the grounds provided for by
the Federal Law 'On the Delimitation of State Ownership in Land' may be in
municipal ownership.

3. Lands in State ownership, including beyond the limits of the boundaries of
municipal formations, may be transferred without compensation to the ownership of municipal formations in order to ensure the development thereof.

4. In subjects of the Russian Federation which are cities of federal significance,
Moscow and St. Petersburg, land plots shall not be transferred to municipal ownership when delimiting State ownership in land.
The right of municipal ownership in land plots in these subjects of the Russian
Federation shall arise in the event of the transfer of land plots from ownership of
the cities of Moscow and St. Petersburg to municipal ownership in accordance
with laws of these subjects of the Russian Federation.

**Chapter IV. Permanent (or in Perpetuity) Use, Inheritable Possession
for Life of Land Plots, Limited Use by Others of Land Plots (Servitude),
Lease of Land Plots, Uncompensated Fixed Term Use of
Land Plots**

Article 20. Permanent (or in Perpetuity) Use of Land Plots

1. Land plots shall be granted in permanent (or in perpetuity) to State and
municipal institutions, federal treasury enterprises, and also agencies of State
power and agencies of local self-government.

2. Land plots shall not be granted to citizens in permanent (or in perpetuity)
use.

3. The right of permanent (or in perpetuity) use of land plots in State or
municipal ownership which arose in citizens or juridical persons before the introduction of the present Code into operation shall be preserved.

4. Citizens or juridical persons possessing land plots by right of permanent (or
in perpetuity) use shall not have the right to dispose of these land plots.

5. Citizens possessing land plots by right of permanent (or in perpetuity) use shall have the right to acquire them in ownership. Each citizen shall have the right one time free of charge to acquire in ownership a land plot in his permanent (or in perpetuity) use, in so doing the recovery of additional monetary amounts besides charges established by federal laws shall not be permitted.

Article 21. Inheritable Possession for Life of Land Plots

1. The right of inheritable possession for life of a land plot in State or municipal ownership acquired by a citizen before the introduction of the present Code into operation shall be preserved. The granting of land plots to citizens by right of inheritable possession for life after the introduction of the present Code into operation shall not be permitted.

2. The disposition of a land plot in inheritable possession for life shall not be permitted, except for the transfer of rights to a land plot by inheritance. State registration of the transfer of the right of inheritable possession for life to a land plot by inheritance shall be conducted on the basis of a certificate concerning the right to inheritance.

3. Citizens having land plots by inheritable possession for life shall have the right to acquire them in ownership. Each citizen shall have the right one time free of charge to acquire in ownership a land plot in his inheritable possession for life, in so doing the recovery of additional monetary amounts besides charges established by federal laws shall not be permitted.

Article 22. Lease of Land Plots

1. Foreign citizens and stateless persons may have land plots located within the limits of the territory of the Russian Federation by right of lease, except for instances provided for by the present Code.

2. Land plots, except for those specified in Article 27(4) of the present Code, may be granted by the owners thereof on lease in accordance with civil legislation and the present Code.

3. Upon the expiry of the period of the contract of lease of a land plot, the lessee thereof shall have a preferential right to conclude a new contract of lease of the land plot, except for instances provided for by Article 35(3), Article 36(1), and Article 46 of the present Code.

4. The amount of lease payment shall be determined by the contract of lease. The general principles for determining the lease payment when leasing land plots in State or municipal ownership may be established by the Government of the Russian Federation.

5. The lessee of a land plot shall have the right to transfer his rights and duties under a contract of lease of a land plot to a third person, including to pledge the

lease rights of the land plot and to contribute them as a contribution to the charter capital of an economic partnership or society or a share contribution to a production cooperative within the limits of the period of the contract of lease of the land plot without the consent of the owner of the land plot, on condition of notification thereof unless provided otherwise by the contract of lease of the land plot. In the said instances the new lessee of the land plot shall become responsible under the contract of lease of the land plot to the lessor, except for the transfer of lease rights on pledge. In so doing the conclusin of a new contract of lease of the land plot shall not be required.

6. The lessee of a land plot shall have the right to transfer the leased land plot on sublease within the limits of the period of the contract of lease of the land plot without the consent of the owner of the land plot, on condition of notification thereof unless provided otherwise by the contract of lease of the land plot. All rights of the lessees of land plots provided for by the present Code shall extend to the sublessees.

7. A land plot may be transferred on lease for State or municipal needs or in order to conduct prospecting work for a term of not more than one year. In so doing the lessee of the land plot within the limits of the period of the contract of lease of the land plot shall be obliged at the request of the lessor to bring the land plot into a state fit for the use thereof in accordance with the authorised use; to compensate losses caused when conducting the work; to fulfil necessary work with regard to recultivation of the land plot, and also to perform other duties established by a law and/or the contract of lease of the land plot.

8. In the event of the sale of a land plot in State or municipal ownership, the lessee of the said land plot shall have a preferential right of purchase thereof in the procedure established by civil legislation for instances of the sale of a participatory share in the right of common ownership to an outside person, except for instances provided for by Article 36(1) of the present Code.

9. In the event of the lease of a land plot in State or municipal ownership for a period of more than five years, the lessee of the land plot shall have the right within the limits of the period of the contract of lease of the land plot to transfer his rights and duties under this contract to a third person, including the rights and duties specified in points 4 and 5 of the present Article without the consent of the owner of the land plot, on condition of notification thereof. A change of the conditions of the contract of lease of a land plot without the consent of the lessee and limitation of the rights of the lessee thereof established by the contract of lease of the land plot shall not be permitted. The dissolution before time of a contract of lease of a land plot concluded for a period of more than five years shall be possible at the request of the lessor only on the grounds of a decision of a court in the event of a material violation of the contract of lease of the land plot by the lessee thereof.

10. In the event of inheritance of land plots by persons who have not reached majority, their legal representatives may transfer these land plots on lease for a period up to the attainment of majority by the heirs.

11. Land plots excluded from turnover may not be transferred on lease, except for instances established by federal laws.

Article 23. Right of Limited Use of Another's Land Plot (Servitude)

1. A private servitude shall be established in accordance with civil legislation.

2. A public servitude shall be established by a law or other normative legal act of the Russian Federation, normative legal acts of a subject of the Russian Federation, or normative legal act of an agencies of local self-government in instances if this is necessary in order to ensure the interests of the State, local self-government, or local population without seizure of the land plots. The establishment of a public servitude shall be effectuated by taking into account the results of public hearings.

3. Public servitudes may be established for:
(1) passage or travel across the land plot;
(2) use of the land plot for the purposes of repair of municipal, engineering, electric power, and other lines and networks, and also objects of the transport infrastructure;
(3) siting on the land plot of survey and geodesic marks and accesses to them;
(4) conducting of drainage work on the land plot;
(5) fencing of water and watering-places;
(6) cattle-track of livestock across a land plot;
(7) haying or pasturage of livestock on land plots for periods whose duration corresponds to local conditions and customs, except for those land plots within the limits of forestry fund lands;
(8) use of a land plot for the purposes of hunting, catching of fish in a closed reservoir located on the land plot, collecting of wild fauna within the established periods and in the established procedure;
(9) temporary use of a land plot for the purposes of conducting prospecting, research, and other work;
(10) free access to a coastal belt.

4. A servitude may be fixed-term or permanent.

5. The effectuation of a sevitude must be the least burdensome for the land plot with respect to which it was established.

6. The owner of a land plot encumbered by a private servitude shall have the right to demand commensurate payment from the persons in whose interests the servitude was established unless provided otherwise by federal laws.

7. In instances when the establishment of a public servitude leads to the impossibility of using the land plot, the owner of the land plot, landuser, and land possessor shall have the right to demand the seizure, including by means of purchase, of the land plot with compensation by the agency of State power or agency of local self-government which established the public servitude of losses or the granting of a land plot of equal value with compensation of losses.

In instances when the establishment of a public servitude leads to material difficulties in the use of the land plot, the owner thereof shall have the right to demand commensurate payment from the agency of State power or agency of local self-government which established the public servitude.

8. Persons whose rights and legal interests are affected by the establishment of a public servitude may effectuate the defence of their rights in a judicial proceeding.

9. Servitudes shall be subject to State registration in accordance with the Federal Law 'On State Registration of Immoveable Property and Transactions Therewith'.

Article 24. Uncompensated Fixed-Term Use of Land Plots

1. Land plots may be granted for uncompensated fixed-term use:
(1) from lands in State or municipal ownership by executive agencies of State powr or agencies of local self-government provided for by Article 29 of the present Code, to the juridical persons specified in Article 20(1) of the present Code, for a period of not more than one year;
(2) from lands in the ownership of citizens or juridical persons, to other citizens and juridical persons on the basis of a contract;
(3) from lands of the organisations specified in point 2 of the present Article, to citizens in the form of an employment allotment.

2. Employment allotments shall be granted for uncompensated, fixed-term use to workers of organisations of individual branches of the economy, including transport, forestry, forest industry, hunting, State nature preserve, and national park organisations.

The categories of workers of organisations of those branches having the right to receive employment allotments and the conditions of granting them shall be established by legislation of the Russian Federation and by legislation of subjects of the Russian Federation.

Employment allotments shall be granted to workers of such organisations for the period of establishment of labour relations on the basis of applications of workers by decision of the respective organisations from among the land plots belonging to them.

The rights and duties of persons using employment allotments shall be determined in accordance with the rules of Article 41(1) and Article 42, paragraphs two to four, and paragraphs seven to nine, of the present Code.

Chapter V. Arising of Rights in Land

Article 25. Grounds for Arising of Rights in Land

1. The rights in land plots provided for by Chapters III and IV of the present Code shall arise on the grounds established by civil legislation and federal laws and shall be subject to State registration in accordance with the Federal Law 'On State Registration of Rights to Immoveable Property and Transactions Therewith'.

2. State registration of translations with land plots shall be obligatory in the instances specified in federal laws.

3. Land plots shall not be subject to return, and the value of land plots shall not be subject to compensation or contributory compensation which were nationalised before 1 January 1991 in accordance with legislation which prevailed at the moment of the nationalisation of the land plots.

Article 26. Documents Concerning Rights in Land Plots

1. The rights in land plots provided for by Chapters III and IV of the present Code shall be certified by documents in accordance with the Federal Law 'On State Registration of Rights to Immoveable Property and Transactions Therewith'.

2. Contracts of lease of a land plot, sublease of a land plot, and uncompensated, fixed-term use of a land plot concluded for a period of less than one year shall not be subject to State registration, except for instances established by federal laws.

Article 27. Limitation of Circulability of Land Plots

1. Turnover of land plots shall be effectuated in accordance with civil legislation and the present Code.

2. Land plots relegated to lands removed from turnover may not be granted in private ownership, nor be the objects of transactions provided for by civil legislation.

Land plots relegated to lands limited in turnover shall not be granted in private ownership, except for instances established by federal laws.

3. The content of limitations of turnover of land plots shall be established by the present Code by federal laws.

4. Land plots occupied by the following objects in federal ownership have been removed from turnover:

(1) State nature preserves and national parks (except for instances provided for by Article 95 of the present Code);

(2) buildings, structures, and installations in which the Armed Forces of the

Russian Federation, forces of the Border Service of the Russian Federation, other forces, military formations, and agencies have been placed for permanent activity;

(3) buildings, structures, and installations in which military courts have been placed;

(4) objects of federal security service organisations;

(5) objects of federal State protection agency organisations;

(6) objects for the use of atomic energy, centres for keeping nuclear materials and radioactive substances;

(7) objects in accordance with the types of activity of which closed adminis-trative-territorial formations have been created;

(8) correctional-labour institutions and treatment-labour prophylactic insti-tutions respectively of the Ministry of Justice of the Russian Federation and Ministry of Internal Affairs of the Russian Federation;

(9) military and civilian burials;

(10) engineering-technical installations, lines of communication and com-munications erected in the interests of the defence and protection of the State boundary of the Russian Federation.

5. The following land plots in State or municipal ownership shall be limited in turnover:

(1) within the limits of specially-protected nature territories not specified in point 4 of the present Article;

(2) within the limits of the forestry fund, except for instances established by federal laws;

(3) occupied by water objects within the water fund which are in State or municipal ownership;

(4) occupied by especially valuable objects of cultural heritage of peoples of the Russian Federation, objects included in the List of World Heritage, historical-cul-tural preserves, and objects of archaeological heritage;

(5) granted to ensure defence and security, the defence industry, customs needs, and not specified in point 4 of the present Article;

(6) not specified in point 4 of the present Article within the boundaries of closed administrative-territorial formations;

(7) granted for needs of organisations of transport, including sea and river ports, train stations, aerodromes and airports, installations of navigation provi-sion for air traffice and navigation, terminals and terminal complexes in zones for the formation of international transport corridors;

(8) granted for needs of communications;

(9) occupied by objects of outer space infrastructure;

(10) located beneath objects of hydro-engineering installations;

(11) granted for the production of poisonous substances and narcotic means;

(12) polluted by dangerous wastes, radioactive substances, subjected to bio-genic pollution, and other lands subjected to degradation.

6. Turnover of lands of agricultural designation shall be regulated by the federal law on turnover of lands of agricultural designation.

7. Point 6 of the present Article shall not extend to land plots granted from lands of agricultural designation to citizens for individual housing and garage construction, conducting personal subsidiary and dacha husbandry, gardening, livestock raising, and vegetable gardening, nor to land plots occupied by buildings, structures, and installations.

Article 28. Acquisition of Rights in Land Plots in State or Municipal Ownership

1. Land plots from lands in State or municipal ownership shall be granted to citizens and juridical persons in ownership or on lease, and also shall be granted to juridical persons in permanent (or in perpetuity) use in the instances provided for by Article 20(1) of the present Code, and to citizens and juridical persons in uncompensated fixed-term use in the instances provided for by Article 24(1) of the present Code.

2. The granting of land plots in State or municipal ownership to citizens and juridical persons in ownership shall be effectuated for payment. The granting of land plots to the ownership of citizens and juridical persons may be effectuated free of charge in the instances provided for by the present Code, federal laws, and laws of subjects of the Russian Federation.

3. In the instances provided for by Article 20(5) and by Article 21(3) of the present Code, the procedure for granting land plots established by Articles 30–34 of the present Code shall not apply. A decision concerning the granting of a land plot in ownership must be adopted within a two-week period from the day of filing of the application in written form at the executive agency of State power or agency of local self-government provided for by Article 29 of the present Code.

4. A refusal to grant land plots to the ownership of citizens and juridical persons for construction which are in State or municipal ownership shall not be permitted, except for instances of:
removal of land plots from turnover;
prohibition established by a federal law against the privatisation of land plots;
reserving of land plots for State or municipal needs.
A refusal to grant land plots to the ownership of citizens and juridical persons which are limited in turnover and in State or municipal ownership, if it has been authorised by a federal law to grant them to the ownership of citizens and juridical persons, shall not be permitted.

5. Land plots shall be granted in ownership to foreign citizens, stateless persons, and foreign juridical persons in accordance with the present Article only for payment, the amount of which shall be established by the present Code.

Article 29. Executive Agencies of State Power and Agencies of Local Self-Government Effectuating the Granting of Land Plots

The granting to citizens and juridical persons of land plots from lands in State or municipal ownership shall be effectuated on the basis of a decision of executive agencies of State power or agencies of local self-government possessing the right of granting respective land plots within the limits of their competence in accordance with Articles 9, 10, and 11 of the present Code.

Article 30. Procedure for Granting Land Plots for Construction from Lands in State or Municipal Ownership

1. The granting of land plots for construction from lands in State or municipal ownership shall be effectuated with the conducting of work with regard to the formation of:
   (1) without prior agreement of the sites for placing objects;
   (2) with prior agreement of the sites for placing objects.

2. The granting of land plots for construction in ownership without prior agreement of the sites for placing objects shall be effectuated exclusively at public sales (or competitions, auctions) in accordance with Article 38 of the present Code.

3. The granting of land plots for construction with prior agreement of sites for placing objects shall be effectuated on lease, and to the persons specified in Article 20(1) of the present Code, for permanent (or in perpetuity) use.

4. The granting of a land plot for construction without prior agreement of the site of placing an object shall be effectuated in the following procedure:
   (1) conducting of work with regard to formation of the land plot:
   preparation of the draft boundaries of the land plot and established of the boundaries thereof on location;
   determination of the authorised use of the land plot;
   determination of the technical conditions for connecting objects to networks of engineering-technical provision;
   adoption of decision concerning the conducting of public sales (or competitions, auctions) or granting of land plots without conducting public sales (or competitions, auctions);
   publication of a notice concerning the conducting of public sales (or competitions, auctions) or granting of land plots without conducting public sales (or competitions, auctions);
   (2) State cadastre recording of the land plot in accordance with the rules provided for by Article 70 of the present Code;

(3) conducting of public sales (or competitions, auctions) for the sale of a land plot or saleof the right to conclude a contract of lease of a land plot or granting of the pland plot on lease without conducting public sales (or competitions, auctions) on the basis of an application or a citizen or juridical person interested in the granting of a land plot. The transfer of land plots on lease without conducting public sales (or competitions, auctions) shall be permitted on condition of the prior and timely publication of a notice concering the existence of land plots propsed for such transfer if there is only one application;

(4) signature of a protocol concerning the results of public sales (or competitions, auctions) or signature of a contract of lease of a land plot as a result of the granting of a land plot without conducting public sales (or competitions, auctions).

5. The granting of a land plot for construction with prior agreement of the site of placing an object shall be effectuated in the following procedure:

(1) selection of the land plot and adoption in the procedure established by Article 31 of the present Code of a decision concerning prior agreement of the site of placing the object;

(2) conducting of work with regard to formation of the land plot;

(3) State cadastre recording of the land plot in accordance with the rules provided by Article 70 of the present Code;

(4) adoption of a decision concerning the granting of the land plot for construction in accordance with the rules established by Article 32 of the present Code.

6. If a land plot has been formed but has not been consolidated to a citizen or juridical person, the granting thereof for construction shall be effectuated in accordance with point 4, subpoints (3) and (4), of the present Article.

7. The decision of an executive agency of State power or agency of local self-government provided for by Article 29 of the present Code concerning the granting of a land plot for construction or protocol concerning the results of public sales (or competitions, auctions) shall be grounds for:

(1) State registration of the right of permanent (or in perpetuity) use when the land plot is granted in permanent (or in perpetuity) use;

(2) conclusion of a contract of purchase-sale and State registration of the right of ownership of the purchaser to a land plot when the land plot is granted in ownership;

(3) conclusion of a contract of lease of the land plot and State registration of that contract when the land plot is transferred on lease.

8. The decision or extract therefrom concerning the granting of a land plot for construction or refusal to grant it shall be issued to the applicant within a seven-day period from the day of adoption thereof.

9. A decision concerning a refusal to grant a land plot for construction may be appealed by the applicant to a court.

10. In the event of the deeming of the refusal to grant a land plot for construction to be invalid by a court, the court shall in its decision oblige the executive agency of State power or agency of local self-government provided for by Article 29 of the present Code to grant the land plot, specifying the period and conditions for the granting thereof.

11. The prior agreement of the site of placing an object shall not be conducting when placing the object in a city or rural settlement in accordance with urban construction documentation concerning building and rules for land use and building (or zoning of the territories), and also in the event of granting a land plot for needs of agricultural production or forestry or to a citizen for individual housing construction and conducting of personal subsidiary husbandry.

12. Land plots for construction may be granted to foreign citizens, stateless persons, and foreign juridical persons in the procedure established by the present Article in accordance with Article 5(2), Article 15(3), Article 22(1), and Article 28(4) and (5) of the present Code.

Article 31. Selection of Land Plots for Construction

1. A citizen or juridical person interested in the granting of a land plot for construction shall apply to the executive agency of State power or agency of local self-government provided for by Article 29 of the present Code concerning the selection of a land plot and prior agreement of the site of placing the object. In the application should be specified the designation of the object, the proposed site of placement thereof, a substantiated of the approximate dimensions of the land plot, and the requested right to the land plot. To the application may be appended a feasibility study of the design for construction and necessary calculations.

2. The agency of local self-government upon the application of a citizen or juridical person or upon the appeal of an executive agency of State power provided for by Article 29 of the present Code shall ensure the selection of the land plot on the basis of documents of the State land cadastre and land tenure documents, taking into account the ecological, urban construction, and other conditions of use of the respective territory and subsoil within its boundaries by means of determing the variants of placement of the object and conducting the procedures for agreement in the instances provided for by federal laws with the respective State agencies, agencies of local self-government, and municipal organisations.

The necessary information concerning authorised use of the land plots and provision of these land plots with objects of engineering, transport, and social infrastructures, technical conditions for linking the objects to networks of engineering-technical provision, and also duty cadastre maps (or plans) containing information concerning the site of land plots, shall be granted free of charge by respective State agencies, agencies of local self-government, and municipal organisations within a two-week period from the day of receipt of the inquiry from the agency of local self-government.

3. Agencies of local self-government of city or rural settlements shall inform the population about the possible or forthcoming granting of land plots for construction.

Citizens, social organisations (or associations), and agencies of territorial social self-government shall have the right to participate in deciding questions affecting the interests of the population and connected with the withdrawal, including by means of purchase, of land plots for State and municipal needs and granting of these land plots for construction.

In the event of granting land plots in places of traditional inhabitation and economic activity of native small peoples of the Russian Federation and ethnic communities for purposes not connected with their traditional economic activity and traditional trades, assemblies, and referendums of citizens may be conducted with regard to questions of the removal, including by means of purchase, of land plots for State or municipal needs and granting of land plots for construction of objects, the siting of which affects the legal interests of the said peoples and communities. The executive agencies of State power or agencies of local self-government provided for by Article 29 of the present Code shall adopt decisions concerning the prior agreement of the sites of placing objects, taking into account the results of such assemblies or referendums.

4. An agency of local self-government shall inform landusers, land possessors, and lessees of land plots in State or municipal ownership whose legal interests may be affected as a result of the possible removal for State and municipal needs of land plots respectively in their use and possession in connection with the granting of these land plots for construction. If for the purposes of placing objects it is necessary to purchase land plots for State or municipal needs from lands in the ownership of citizens or juridical persons, the agency of local self-government shall inform the owners of these land plots about the possible purchase thereof. The procedure and conditions for granting such information may be established by federal laws and by laws of subjects of the Russian Federation.

5. The results of the selection of a land plot shall be formalised by an act concerning the selection of a land plot for construction, and in necessary instances also to establish the protection or sanitary-defensive zone thereof. To the said act shall be appended the draft boundaries confirmed by the agency of local self-government for each lan dplot in accoreance with the possible variants of selection thereof.

In the event of a proposed removal, including by means of purchase, of a land plot for State or municipal needs, to the act concerning the selection of the land plot shall also be appended calculations of the losses of owners of the land plots, landusers, land possessors, and lessees of land plots, loss of agricultural production or loss of forestry.

6. The executive agency of State power or agency of local self-government shall adopt the decision provided for by Article 29 of the present Code concerning prior agreement of the site of placing the object confirming the act concerning the selection of the land plot in accordance with one of the variants of selection of the land plot, or concerning a refusal to place the object.

7. A copy of the decision concerning prior agreement of the site of placing the object with the draft boundaries of the land plot appended or concerning a refusal to place the object, shall be issued to the applicant within a seven-day period from the day of confirmation thereof.

8. The decision concerning prior agreement of the site of placing the object shall be grounds for the subsequent adoption of a decision concerning the granting of a land plot for construction and operate for three years.

In the event of the effectuation by the owner of the land plot, landuser, land possessor, and lessee of the land plot of construction on the land plot or other improvement thereof after being informed about the possible removal, including by means of purchase, of the land plot for State or municipal needs, the owner of the land plot, landuser, land possessor, and lessee of the land plot shall bear the risk of relegation to them of expenditures and losses connected with construction on the land plot or other improvements thereof.

If upon the expiry of the period of operation of a decision concerning prior agreement of the site of placing an object the decision concerning the granting of the land plot was not adopted, the persons whose rights were limited shall have the right to demand compensation from the executive agency of State power or agency of local self-government provided for by Article 29 of the present Code and adopted such decision for losses incurred irrespective of extension of the period of operation of the decision concerning prior agreement of the site of placing an object.

9. The decision concerning prior agreement of the site of placing an object or refusal to place an object may be appealed by the interested persons to a court. In the event of the decision being deemed invalid in a judicial proceeding concerning prior agreement of the site of placing an object, the executive agency of State power or agency of local self-government provided for by Article 29 of the present Code and which adopted such decision shall compensate a citizen or juridical person for expenses incurred by them in connection with the preparation of documents necessary in order to adopt the decision concerning prior agreement of the site of placing the object.

10. In subjects of the Russian Federation which are cities of federal signifiance, Moscow and St. Petersburg, the selection of land plots for construction shall be

effectuated by the agency of executive power of the respective subject of the Russian Federation unless provided otherwise by laws of these subjects of the Russian Federation.

Article 32. Adoption of Decision on Granting Land Plot for Construction

1. The decision concerning prior agreement of the site of placing an object and draft boundaries of the land plot shall be grounds for establishing in accordance with applications of citizens or juridical persons interested in the granting of a land plot for construction and at their expense the boundaries of such land plot on site and the State cadastre recording thereof in the procedure established by federal laws.

2. The executive agency of State power or agency of local self-government provided for by Article 29 of the present Code shall, on the basis of an application of a citizen or juridical person interested in the granting of a land plot for construction and the cadastre map (or plan) of the land plot appended thereto, within a two-week period adopt a decision concerning the granting of a land plot for construction.

3. In the event the requested land plot is granted as a result of its seizure, including by purchase, for State or municipal needs, simultaneously with the decision concerning the granting of a land plot shall be adopted a decision concerning the respective form of seizure of such land plot.

4. The conditions for granting land plots for State or municipal needs must provide for compensation of all losses connected with the seizure of these land plots from the landusers and land possessors, dissolution or termination of contracts of lease thereof, and also compensation in accordance with the rules provided for by Article 58 of the present Code, loss of agricultural production or loss of forestry economy. The conditions also may provide for the rights of other persons encumbering the land plots granted or limitations of the use of the land plots provided for by Article 56 of the present Code.

Article 33. Norms for Granting Land Plots

1. The maximum (maximal and minimum) dimensions of land plots to be granted to citizens in ownership from lands in State or municipal ownership for conducting peasant (or farmer) economy, gardening, vegetable-gardening, livestock farming, and dacha construction shall be established by laws of subjects of the Russian Federation, and for conducting personal subsidiary husbandry and individual housing construction—by normative legal acts of agencies of local self-government.

2. The maximal dimensions of land plots to be granted to citizens in ownership free of charge for purposes provided for by the rules of point 1 of the present Article shall be established by:

96

federal laws—from lands in federal ownership;

laws of subjects of the Russian Federation—from lands in the ownership of subjects of the Russian Federation;

normative legal acts of agencies of local self-government—from lands in the ownership of municipal formations.

3. For purposes not specified in point 1 of the present Article the maximum dimensions of land plots shall be established in accordance with norms for the allotment of land for specific types of activity or in accordance with rules for landuse and building, land tenure, urban construction, and design documentation.

Article 34. Procedure for Granting Land Plots to Citizens in State or Municipal Ownership for Purposes Not Connected with Construction

1. Agencies of State power and agencies of local self-government shall be obliged to ensure the administration and disposition of land plots which are in their ownership and/or jurisdiction on the principles of effectiveness, justness, publicness, openness, and transparency of the procedure for granting such land plots. To do so the said agencies shall be obliged to:

adopt the act establishing the procedures and criteria for granting such land plots, including the procedure for consideratio of applications and adoption of decisions. All applications which have arrived before the period determined by the said procedures shall be subject to consideration. The establishment of priorities and special conditions for individual categories of citizens shall not be permitted unless established by a law;

empower a special agency for the administration and disposition of land plots and other immoveables;

ensure the preparation of information concerning land plots which are granted to citizens and juridical persons on a determined right and provided conditions (for payment or free of charge) and timely publication of such information.

2. Citizens interested in the granting or transfer of land plots in ownership or on lease from lands in State or municipal ownership for purposes not connected with construction shall file applications at the executive agency of State power or agency of local self-government provided for by Article 29 of the present Code.

3. In the application specified in point 2 of the present Article must be determined the purpose of use of the land plot, its proposed dimensions and location, and the right to land requested.

4. The agency of local self-government or on its behalf respective land tenure organisation shall on the basis of the application specified in point 2 of the present Article or recourse of the executive agency of State powe provided for by Article 29 of the present Code, taking into account the zoning of territories, within a

month's period ensure the manufacture of the draft boundaries of the land plot and confirm it.

5. The executive agency of State power or agency of local self-government provided for by Article 29 of the present Code shall within a two-week period adopt a decision concerning the granting of the requested land plot in ownership for payment or free of charge or concerning the transfer of the land plot on lease, with the draft boundaries thereof appended.

6. The contract of purchase-sale or lease of the land plot shall be concluded within a week's period after the submission by the applicant of the cadastre map (or plan) of the land plot to the executive agency of State power or agency of local self-government provided for by Article 29 of the present Code.

Article 35. Transfer of Right to Land Plot in Event of Transfer of Right of Ownership to Building, Structure, and Installation

1. In the event of the transfer of the right of ownership to a building, structure, and installation on another's land plot to another person, he shall acquire the right to use of the respective part of the land plot occupied by the building, structure, and installation and necessary for the use thereof on the same conditions and in the same amount as the previous owner thereof.

In the event of the transfer of the right of ownership to a building, structure, and installation to several owners, the procedure for the use of the land plot shall be determined by taking into account the particpatory shares in the right of ownership to the building, structure, and installation or procedure for the use of the land plot which has formed.

2. The space of part of the land plot occupied by the building, structure, and installation and necessary for the use thereof shall be determined in accordance with Article 33(3) of the present Code.

3. The owner of the building, structure, and installation situated on another's land plot shall have preferential right of purchase or lease of the land plot, which shall be effectuated in the procedure established by civil legislation for instances of the sale of a participatory share in a right of common ownership to an outside person. If the land lot is in State or municipal ownership, the rules established by Article 36(1) of the present Code shall apply.

4. The alienation of a building, structure, and installation situated on a land plot and belonging to one person shall be conducted together with the land plot, except for the following instances:

(1) alienation of part of a building, structure, or installation which cannot be apportioned out in kind together with part of the land plot;

(2) alienation of a building, structure, or installation situated on a land plot removed from turnover in accordance with Article 27 of the present Code.

Alienation of a building, structure, or installation situated on a land plot limited in turnover and belonging to one person shall be conducted toether with the land plot if a federal law has authorised such land plot be granted to the ownership of citizens and juridical persons.

The alienation of a land plot without the building, structure, and installation situated on it shall not be permitted if they belong to one person.

The alienation of a participatory share in the right of ownerhsip to a building, structure, and installation situated on a land plot belonging by right of ownership to several persons shall entail alienation of the participatory share in the right of ownership to the land plot, the amount of which is proportional to the participatory share in the right of ownership in the building, structure, and installation.

5. Foreign citizens, stateless persons, and foreign juridical persons who are owners of buildings, structures, and installations situated on another's land plot shall have a preferential right of purchase or lease of the land plot in the procedure established by the present Article and in accordance with Article 5(2), Article 15(3), Article 22(1), and Article 28(4) and (5) of the present Code. The President of the Russian Federation may establish a List of types of buildings, structures, and installations to which this rule shall not extend.

Article 36. Acquisition of Rights to Land Plots Which Are in State or Municipal Ownership and on Which Buildings, Structures, and Installations are Located

1. Citizens and juridical persons having in ownership, economic jurisdiction, or operative management buildings, structures, and installations located on land plots in State or municipal ownership shall acquire the rights to these land plots in accordance with the present Code.

Citizens and juridical persons which are owners of buldings, structures, and installations shall have the exclusive right to privatisation of land plots or acquisition of the right of lease of land plots in the procedure and on the conditions which have been established by the present Code and federal laws.

2. In existing building land plots on which installations are situated that are within the composition of a condominium, dwelling buildings, and other structure shall be granted as common property in common participatory share ownership of the house possessors in the procedure and on the conditions which have been established by the Federal Law 'On Partnerships of Owners of Housing'.

3. If a building (or premise therein) situated on an indivisible land plot belongs to several persons by right of ownership, these persons shall have the right to acquisition of the particular land plot in common participatory share ownership or on lease with the multiplicity of persons on the side of the lessee, unless otherwise provided for by the present Code and federal laws.

If a premise in a building situated on an indivisible land plot belongs to some persons by right of ownership and to other persons by right of economic jurisdiction or to all persons by right of economic jurisdiction, these persons shall have the right to acquisition of the said land plot on lease with the multiplicity of persons on the side of the lessee unless provided otherwise by the present Code and federal laws. In so doing the contract of least of the land plot shall be concluded with a condition of the consent of the parties to enter into this contract of the other right-possessors of the premises in this building.

Federal treasury enterprises and State or municipal institutions which are rights-possessors of premises in this building shall possess the right of limited use of the land plot in order to effectuate their rights to the premise belonging to them.

4. If premises in a building located on an indivisible land plot have been consolidated for several federal treasury enterprises and State or municipal institutions, the said land plot shall be granted to one of those persons on the basis of the decision of the owner of the land plot in permanet (in perpetuity) use, and the others of these persons shall possess the right of limited use of the land plot in order to effectuate their rights to the premises consolidated to them.

5. In order to acquire rights to a land plot citizens or juridical persons specified in the present Article shall jointly apply to the executive agency of State power or agency of local self-government provided for by Article 29 of the present Code concerning the acquisition of the right to the land plot, appending the cadastre map (or plan) thereof.

6. The executive agency of State power or agency of local self-government provided for by Article 29 of the present Code shall within a two-week period from the day of receipt of the application specified in point 5 of the present Article adopt a decision concerning the granting of the land plot in ownership free of charge in accordance with Article 28(2) of the present Code, and in the instances specified in Article 20(1) of the present Code, the right of permanent (in perpetuity) use or prepare a draft contract of purchase-sale or lease of the land plot and send it to the applicant with a proposal concerning the conclusion of the respective contract.

7. In the absence of the cadastre map (or plan) of the land plot, the agency of local self-government on the basis of the application of a citizen or juridical person or upon the recourse of the executive agency of State power provided for by Article 29 of the present Code on the basis of the duty cadastre map (or plan) containing information concerning the location of the land plot and urban construction documentation within a month's period from the day of receipt of the said application or recourse shall ensure the manufacture of the cadastre map (or plan) of the land plot and confirm the draft boundaries thereof.

The boundaries and dimensions of the land plot shall be determined by taking into account the space of the land plot actually used in accordance with the requirements of land and urban construction legislation. The boundaries of the land plot shall be established by taking into account the red lines, boundaries of neighbouring land plots (when they exist), and the natural boundaries of the land plot.

8. The executive agency of State power or agency of local self-government provided for by Article 29 of the present Code shall within a two-week period from the day of submission of the draft boundaries of the land plot adopt a decision concerning the granting of this land plot to persons specified in point 5 of the present Article and send them a copy of the decision with the draft boundaries of the land plot appended.

On the basis of the draft boundaries of the land plot, the boundaries of the land plot on site shall be established and the manufacture of the cadastre map (or plan) of the land plot shall be ensured at the expense of the said persons.

9. Foreign citizens, stateless persons, and foreign juridical persons who are owners of buildings, structures, and installations shall have the right to acquire land plots in ownership in the procedure established by the present Article and in accordance with Article 5(2), Article 15(3), and Article 28(4) and (5) of the present Code.

Article 37. Peculiarities of Purchase-Sale of Land Plots

1. Only land plots which have undergone State cadastre recording may be the object of purchase-sale. The seller when concluding a contract of purchase-sale shall be obliged to provide to the purchaser information which he has concerning encumberments of the land plot and limitations of the use thereof.

2. The following conditions of a contract of purchase-sale of a land plot shall be invalid:

establishing the right of the seller to purchase the land plot back at his own wish;

limiting further disposition of the land plot, including limiting mortgage, transfer of the land plot on lease, and conclusion of other transactions with land;

limiting the responsibility of the seller in the event of the presentation of rights to land plots by third persons.

The said requirements shall also apply to a contract of barter.

3. The purchaser in the event of the provision to him by the seller of information about encumberments of the land plot known to be false and limitations of the use thereof in accordance with authorised use; concerning an authorisation to build on the particular land plot; concerning the use of neighbouring land plots exerting material effects on the use and value of the land plot being sold;

concerning the qualitative properties of lands which may influence the used planned by the purchaser and value of the land plot being sold; other information which may influence the decision of the purchaser concerning purchase of the particular land plot and requirements concerning the provision of which have been established by federal laws shall have the right to demand a reduction of the purchase price or dissolution of the contract of purchase-sale of the land plot and compensation of losses caused to him.

4. The requirements established by point 3 of the present Article shall also apply in instances of the exchange of a land plot and transfer thereof on lease.

Article 38. Acquisition of Land Plot from Lands in State or Municipal Ownership or Rights to Conclude Contract of Lease of Such Land Plot at Public Sales (or Competitions, Auctions)

1. A land plot with established boundaries or the right to conclude a contract of lease of such land plot formalised in accordance with Article 30(4)(1) of the present Code may be the subject of public sales (or competitions, auctions).

2. The executive agency of State powr or agency of local self-government provided for by Article 29 of the present Code shall act as the seller of the land plot or right to conclude a contract of lease of such land plot.
The owner or specialised organisation acting on the basis of a contract with it shall act as the organiser of the public sale (or competition, auction).

3. The owner of a land plot shall determine the form of conducting the public sale (or competition, auction), the starting price of the object of public sale (or competition, auction), and the amount of the deposit.

4. The procedure for the organisation and conducting of a public sale (or competition, auction) with regard to the sale of land plots or rights to conclude contradcts of lease of such land plots shall be determined by the Government of the Russian Federation in accordance with the Civil Code of the Russian Federation and the present Code.

Article 39. Preservation of Right to Land Plot of Persons Who Are Not Owners of Land Plot in Event of Desruction of Building, Structure, and Installation

1. In the event of the destruction of a building, structure, and installation from fire, natural disasters, and dilapidation the rights to the land plot granted for the servicing thereof shall be preserved by the persons possessing the land plot by right of permanent (in perpetuity) use or inheritable possession for life on condition of the commencement of restoration in the established procedure of the building, structure, and installation within three years. The executive agency of State power

or agency of local self-government provided for by Article 29 of the present Code shall have the right to prolong this period.

2. The conditions for the preservation of rights specified in point 1 of the present Article for a lessee and sublessee shall be determined by the contract of lease (or sublease) of the land plot.

Chapter VI. Rights and Duties of Owners of Land Plots, Landusers, Land Possessors, and Lessees of Land Plots When Using Land Plots

Article 40. Rights of Owners of Land Plots to Use of Land Plots

1. The owner of a land plot shall have the right to:

(1) use in the established procedure for own needs generally-disseminated minerals, fresh underground waters, and also closed reservoirs in accordance with legislation of the Russian Federation available on the land plot;

(2) erect dwelling, production, cultural-domestic, and other buildings, structures, and installations in accordance with the special-purpose designation of the land plot and its authorised use, in compliance with the requirements of urban construction reglaments, construction, ecological, sanitary-hygienic, fire prevention, and other rules and normative standards;

(3) conduct in accordance with authorised use irrigation, drainage, crop-engineering, and other soil conservation work, construct ponds and other closed reservoirs in accordance with ecological, construction, sanitary-hygienic, and other special requirements established by legislation;

(4) effectuate other rights to use of the land plot provided for by legislation.

2. An owner of a land plot shall have the right of ownership to:

(1) crops and plantings of agricultural crops, received agricultural products, and revenues from the realisation thereof, except for instances when he transfers the land plot on lease, permanent (in perpetuity) use, or inheritable possession for life, or uncompensated fixed-term use;

(2) perennial plantings located on the land plot, except for instances established by the Forest Code of the Russian Federation.

Article 41. Rights to Use of Land Plots by Landusers, Land Possessors, and Lessees of Land Plots

1. Persons who are not owners of land plots, except for possessors of servitudes, shall effectuate the rights of owners of land plots established by Article 40 of the present Code, except for rights established by point 2(2) of the said Article.

2. In accordance with Article 23(1) of the present Code, the rights of persons using a land plot on the basis of a private servitude shall be determined by a contract, and the rights of persons using the land plot on the basis of a public

servitude shall be determined by a law or other normative legal act by which the public servitude was established.

Article 42. Duties of Owners of Land Plots and Persons Who Are Not Owners of Land Plots With Regard to Use of Land Plots

The owners of land plots and persons who are not owners of land plots shall be obliged to:

use land plots in accordance with their special-purpose designation and affiliation to a particular category of lands and authorised use by means which must not inflict harm on the environment, including land as a nature object;

preserve survey, geodesic, and other special marks established on land plots in accordance with legislation;

effectuate measures with regard to protection of the lands, comply with the procedure for the use of forests, water, and other nature objects;

embark upon the use in a timely way of land plots in instances when periods for exploitation of land plots have been provided for by contracts;

make payments for land in a timely way;

comply when using land plots with requirements of urban construction reglaments, construction, ecological, sanitary-hygienic, fire prevention, and other rules and normative standards;

not permit pollution, littering, degradation, and worsening of fertility of the soil on lands of respective categories;

fulfil other requirements provided for by the present Code and federal laws.

Article 43. Effectuation of Rights to Land Plot

1. Citizens and juridical persons shall effectuate rights to a land plot belonging to them at their discretion, unless established otherwise by the present Code and federal laws.

2. The refusal of citizens and juridical persons to effectuate rights to a land plot belonging to them shall not entail termination of their duties established by Article 42 of the present Code.

Chapter VII. Termination and Limitation of Rights to Land

Article 44. Grounds for Termination of Right of Ownership to Land Plot

The right of ownership to a land plot shall terminate in the event of alienation by the owner of his land plot to other persons, renunciation by the owner of the right of ownership to the land plot, by virtue of compulsory seizure of the land plot from the owner in the procedure established by civil legislation.

Article 45. Grounds for Termination of Right of Permanent (or in Perpetuity) Use of Land Plot and Rights of Inheritable Possession for Life of Land Plot

1. The right of permanent (in perpetuity) use of a land plot and right of inheritable possession for life of a land plot shall terminate in the event of the renunciation by the landuser or land possessor of the rights to the land plot belonging to him on the conditions and in the procedure which have been provided for by Article 53 of the present Code.

2. The right of permanent (or in perpetuity) use of a land plot and the right of inheritable possession for life of a land plot shall terminate compulsorily in the event of:

(1) use of the land plot not in accordance with its special-purpose designation and affiliation to a particular category of lands established by Articles 7 and 8 of the present Code;

(2) use of the land plot by means which lead to a matrial reduction of the fertility of agricultural lands or significant worsening of the ecological situation;

(3) failure to eliminate the following land violations intentionally committed:

poisoning, pollution, spoilage, or destruction of the fertile stratum of soil as a consequence of a violation of rules for treating with fertilisers, flora growth stimulants, chemical pest-killers, and other dangerous chemical or biological substances in the event of their keeping, use, and transport which entailed the causing of harm to human health or the environment;

violation of the regime for the use of lands established by respective norms of Articles 95–100 of the present Code of specially-protected nature territories, lands of nature protection and recreational designation, lands of historico-cultural designation, especially valuable lands, and other lands with special conditions of use, and also lands subjected to radioactive pollution;

systematic failure to fulfil obligatory measures with regard to the improvement of lands, protection of the soil against wind and water erosion, and prevention of other processes worsening the state of the soil;

systematic failure to pay the land tax;

(4) failure to use a land plot in the instances provided for by civil legislation intended for agricultural production or housing or other construction for the said purposes within three years unless a longer period has been established by a federal law, excluding the time during which the land plot could not be used for designation because of natural disasters or in view of other circumstances excluding such use;

(5) seizure of the land plot for State or municipal needs in accordance with the rules provided for by Article 55 of the present Code;

(6) requisition of the land plot in accordance with the rules provided for by Article 51 of the present Code.

3. A decision concerning termination of the rights to land plots in the instances provided for by point 2 of the present Article shall be adopted by a court in accordance with Article 54 of the present Code.

Article 46. Grounds for Termination of Lease of Land Plot

1. The lease of a land plot shall terminate on the grounds and in the procedure which have been provided for by civil legislation.

2. In addition to the instances specified in point 1 of the present Article, the lease of a land plot may be terminated at the initiative of the lessor in the event of:

(1) use of the land plot not in accordance with its special-purpose designation and affiliation to a particular category of lands provided for by Article 8 of the present Code;

(2) use of the land plot which leads to a material reduction of the fertility of agricultural lands or significant worsening of the ecological situation;

(3) failure to eliminate a land violation intentionally committed expressed in poisoning, pollution, spoilage or destruction of fertility of the stratum of soil as a consequence of a violation of rules for treatment with fertilisers, flora growth stimulants, chemical pest-killers, and other dangerous chemical or biological substances in the event of their keeping, use, and transport which entailed the causing of harm to human health or the environment;

(4) failure to use the land plot intended for agricultural production or housing or other construction for the said purposes within three years unless a longer period has been established by a federal law or contract of lease of a landplot except for the time necessary to exploit the land plot, and also the time during which the land plot could not be used for designation because of natural disasters or in view of other circumstances excluding such use;

(5) seizure of the land plot for State or municipal needs in accordance with the rules established by Article 51 of the present Code;

(6) requisition of the land plot in accordance with the rules established by Article 51 of the present Code.

3. Termination of the lease of the land plot on the grounds specified in point 2(2) of the present Article shall not be permitted:

(1) during the period of field agricultural work;

(2) in other instances established by federal laws.

Article 47. Grounds for Termination of Right of Uncompensated Fixed-Term Use of Land Plot

1. The right of uncompensated fixed-term use of a land plot shall terminated by decision of the person who granted the land plot or by agreement of the parties:

(1) upon expiry of the period for which the land plot was granted;

(2) on the grounds specified in Article 45(1) and (2) of the present Code.

2. The right to an employment allotment shall terminate by virtue of termination by a worker of labour relations in connection with which the employment allotment was granted, except for instances specified in points 3 and 4 of the present Article.

3. The right to an employment allotment shall be preserved for a worker who has terminated labour relations in the event of his transfer on old-age pension or disability pension.

4. The right to an employment allotment shall be preserved for one of the members of the family of:

(1) a worker called-up to active fixed-term military service or alternative service for the entire period of undergoing service;

(2) a worker who has commenced studies for the entire period of study in an educational institution;

(3) a worker who has perished in connection with the performance of employment duties.

The right to an employment allotment for a spouse who does not have labour capacity or aged parents of the worker for life, and children of workers until their majority.

5. Termination of the right to an employment allotment shall be formalised by decision of the organisation which granted such employment allotment for use.

6. A worker who has terminated labour relations with the organisation which granted an employment allotment for use shall have the right to use this employment allotment after the termination of labour relations during the period necessary to complete agricultural work.

Article 48. Grounds for Termination of Servitude

1. A private servitude may be terminated on the grounds provided for by civil legislation.

2. A public servitude may be terminated in the absence of social needs for which it was established by means of adoption of an act concerning abolition of the servitude.

Article 49. Seizure, Including by Purchase, of Land Plots for State or Municipal Needs

1. Seizure, including by purchase, of land plots for State or municipal needs shall be effectuated in exceptional instances connected with:

(1) the fulfilment of international obligations of the Russian Federation;

(2) the siting of objects of State or municipal significance in the absence of other variants for possible siting of these objects;

(3) other circumstances in instances established by federal laws, and with regard to seizure, including by purchase, of land plots from lands in the ownership of subjects of the Russian Federation or municipal ownership in the instances established by laws of subjects of the Russian Federation.

2. Limitations of seizure, including by purchase, of land plots for State or municipal needs form lands of individual categories shall be established by Articles 79, 83, 94, and 101 of the present Code.

3. The conditions and procedure for seizure, including by means of purchase, for State or municipal needs shall be established by Article 55 of the present Code.

Article 50. Confiscation of Land Plot

A land plot may be seized without compensation form its owner by decision of a court in the form of a sanction for the commission of a crime (confiscation).

Article 51. Requisition of Land Plot

1. In the event of natural disasters, wrecks, epidemics, epizootics, and under other circumstances of an extraordinary character, a land plot may be temporarily seized from its owner by empowered executive agencies of State power for the purposes of defence of vitally important interests of citizens, society, and the State against threats arising in connection with these extraordinary circumstances with compensation to the owner of the land plot of losses caused (requisition) and issuance to him of a document concerning requisition.

2. The seizure of land plots effectuated by way of seizure, including by purchase, for State or municipal needs on the conditions and in the procedure which have been established by Article 55 of the present Code shall not be requisition.

3. If it is impossible to return a requisitioned land plot, the market value of this land plot shall be compensated to the owner thereof established in accordance with Article 6 of the present Code, or at his wish, a land plot of equal value shall be granted.

4. The owner of a land plot from whom the land plot has been requisitioned shall have the right in the event of the termination of the operation of the circumstances in connection with which requisition is effectuated to demand the return to him of the requisitioned land plot in a judicial proceeding.

5. In the event the circumstances specified in point 1 of the present Article ensue, in the absence of the need for requisition of the land plot it may be temporarily, for the period of operation of these circumstances, occupied for use for the purposes specified in point 1 of the present Article, with compensation to the owner of the land plot for losses caused in connection with the temporary limitation of his rights.

6. The valuation in accordance with which the owner of a land plot shall be contributorily compensated the value of the requisitioned land plot and the losses caused in connection with the requisition thereof or temporary limitation of his rights may be contested by the owner of the land plot in a judicial proceeding.

Article 52. Conditions and Procedure for Alienation of Land Plot

The alienation of a land plot by the owner thereof to other persons shall be effectuated in the procedure established by civil legislation, taking into account the limitations of circulability of land plots provided for by Article 27 of the present Code.

Article 53. Conditions and Procedure for Renunciation by Person of Right to Land Plot

1. The renunciation by a person of the effectuation of the rights to a land plot belonging to him (or filing of application concerning renunciation) shall not entail termination of the respective right.

2. In the event of the renunciation of the right of ownership to a land plot, this land plot shall acquire the legal regime of a masterless immoveable thing, the procedure for the termination of the rights to which shall be established by civil legislation.

3. In the event of the renunciation by a person of the right to inheritable possession for life of a land plot or the right of permanent (in perpetuity) use of a land plot, disposition of the said land plot shall be effectuated by the executive agency of State power or agency of local self-government provided for by Article 29 of the present Code.

Article 54. Conditions and Procedure for Compulsory Termination of Rights to Land Plot of Persons Who Are Not Owners Thereof in View of Improper Use of Land Plot

1. Compulsory termination of the right of inheritable possession for life, right of permanent (in perpetuity) use of the land plot, right of uncompensated fixed-term use of a land plot shall be effectuated in the event of the improper use thereof on the grounds provided for by Article 45(2) of the present Code.

2. Compulsory termination of the right of inheritable possession for life of a land plot, right of permanent (in perpetuity) use of a land plot, right of uncompensated, fixed-term use of the land plot shall be effectuated on condition of the failure to eliminate facts of improper use of the land plot after the imposition of an administrative sanction in the form of a fine.

3. Simultaneously with the imposition of an administrative sanction by an empowered executive agency of State power with regard to the effectuation of

State land control on a person guilty of a violation of land legislation a warning shall be rendered concerning the land violations permitted with consequent notification of the agency provided for by Article 29 of the present Code and which granted the land plot.

The said warning must contain:

(1) an indication of the land violation permitted;

(2) the period during which the land violation must be eliminated;

(3) an indication concerning possible compulsory termination of the right to the land plot in the event of the failure to eliminate the land violation;

(4) an explanation of the rights of the person guilty of a violation of land legislation in the event of the initiation of the procedure for compulsory termination of the rights to the land plot;

(5) other necessary conditions.

The form of warning shall be established by the Government of the Russian Federation.

4. In the event of the failure to eliminate the land violations specified in the warning within the established period, the executive agency of State power which rendered the warning shall send the materials concerning the termination of the right to the land plot in view of the improper use thereof to the executive agency of State power or agency of local self-government provided for by Article 29 of the present Code.

5. The agency of State power or agency of local self-government provided for by Article 29 of the present Code shall send to a court an application concerning termination of the right to a land plot. Upon the expiry of a ten-day period from the moment of adoption of the decision of the court concerning termination of the right to a land plot, the executive agency of State power or agency of local self-government provided for by Article 29 of the present Code shall send the application concerning State registration of termination of the right to a land plot, appending the act, to the agency of State registration of rights to immoveable property and transactions therewith.

6. Termination of the right to a land plot shall not relieve persons guilty of a violation of land legislation from compensation of harm caused provided for by Article 76 of the present Code.

7. A decision concerning seizure of a land plot in view of the improper use of theland plot may be appealed in a judicial proceeding.

Article 55. Conditions and Procedure for Seizure of Land Plots for State or Municipal Needs

1. Seizure, including by purchase, of land plots for State or municipal needs shall be effectuated on the grounds established by Article 49 of the present Code.

2. Compulsory alienation of a land plot for State or municipal needs may be conducted only on condition of prior and equivalent compensation of the value of the land plot on the basis of the decision of a court.

3. The procedure for the purchase of a land plot for State or municipal needs from the owner thereof; procedure for determining the purchase price of the land plot to be purchased for State or municipal needs; the procedure for termination of the rights of possession and use of a land plot in the event of the seizure thereof for State or municipal needs, the rights of the owner of the land plot subject to purchase for State or municipal needs shall be established by civil legislation.

Article 56. Limitation of Rights to Land

1. The rights to land may be limited on the grounds established by the present Code and by federal laws.

2. The following limitation of rights to land may be established:
(1) special conditions for the use of land plots and regime of economic activity in protection and sanitary-defensive zones;
(2) special conditions for the protection of the environment, including fauna and flora, monuments of nature, history, and culture, archaeological objects, preservation of the fertile stratum of the soil, natural feeding environment, and migration routes of wild fauna;
(3) conditions for the commencement and completion of building or exploitation of a land plot within established periods according to a design agreed in the established procedure, construction, repair, or maintenance of a motor vehicle road (or sector of a motor vehicle road) when rights to a land plot are granted which is in State or municipal ownership;
(4) other limitations of use of land plots in instances established by the present Code and federal laws.

3. Limitation of rights to land shall be established by acts of executive agencies of State power, acts of agencies of local self-government, or decision of a court.

4. Limitations of rights to land shall be established in perpetuity or for a determined period.

5. Limitations of rights to land shall be preserved in the event of the transfer of the right of ownership in a land plot to another person.

6. Limitation of rights to land shall be subject to State registration in the procedure established by the Federal Law 'On State Registration of Rights to Immoveable Property and Transactions Therewith'.

7. Limitation of rights to land may be appealed in a judicial proceeding by the person whose rights have been limited.

Chapter VIII. Compensation of Losses and Loss of Agricultural Production and Forestry in Event of Seizure of Land Plots for State and Municipal Needs

Article 57. Compensation of Losses in Event of Seizure of Land Plots for State or Municipal Needs, Worsening of Quality of Lands, Temporary Occupation of Land Plots, Limitation of Rights of Owners of Land Plots, Landusers, Land Possessors, and Lessees of Land Plots

1. Losses shall be subject to compensation in full, including lost advantage, which are caused by:

(1) seizure of land plots for State or municipal needs;

(2) worsening of the quality of lands as a result of the activity of other persons;

(3) temporary occupation of land plots;

(4) limitation of the rights of owners of land plots, landusers, land possessors, and lessees of land plots.

2. Losses shall be compensated to:

(1) landusers, land possessors, and lessees of land plots in the instances provided for by point 1 of the present Article;

(2) owners of land plots in the instances provided for by subpoints (2), (3), and (4) of point 1 of the present Article.

3. Compensation of losses shall be effectuated at the expense of respective budgets or by the persons to whose benefit the land plots are seized or rights to them are limited, and also by persons whose activity gave rise to the need for the establishment of protection and sanitary-defensive zones and entails the limitation of the rights of owners of land plots, landusers, land possessors, and lessees of land plots or worsening of the quality of lands.

4. When calculating the amounts of compensation, the losses of owners of land plots, landusers, land possessors, and lessees of land plots shall be determined by taking into account the value of their property on the day preceding the adoption of the decision concerning seizure of land plots, temporary occupation of land plots, or limitation of the rights of owners of land plots, landusers, land possessors, and lessees of land plots.

5. The procedure for compensation of losses to owners of land plots, landusers, land possessors, and lessees of land plots caused by the seizure or temporary occupation of land plots, limitation of rights of owners of land plots, landusers, land possessors, and lessees of land plots, or worsening of the quality of lands as a result of the activity of other persons shall be established by the Government of the Russian Federation.

Article 58. Compensation for Loss of Agricultural Production and Loss of Forest Economy

1. Losses of agricultural production shall be subject to compensation within a three-month period after the adoption of a decision concerning:

(1) seizure of agricultural tracts and reindeer pastures in State or municipal ownership for the use thereof for purposes not connected with conducting agriculture;

(2) change of the special-purpose designation of agricultural tracts and reindeer pastures in the ownership of citizens or juridical persons.

2. Losses of agricultural production shall be compensated by:

(1) persons to whom lands of agricultural designation and reindeer pastures have been granted for use thereof for purposes not connected with conducting agriculture;

(2) persons for whom protection and sanitary-defensive zones have been established.

3. Losses of agricultural production shall be compensated in the instances when land plots are granted for permanent (in perpetuity) use or are transferred in ownership free of charge. In instances of the sale of land plots or transfer thereof on lease losses of agricultural production shall be included in the value of land plots or taken into account when establishing the lease payment.

4. When calculating the loss of agricultural production normative standards shall be used for the value of exploiting new lands in place of the agricultural tracts seized, and also depending upon the quality of agricultural tracts, other methods established by the Government of the Russian Federation.

5. Means received by way of compensation of loss of agricultural production shall be credited to the respective local budget and may be sent to finance measures for the protection of lands, including measures with regard to raising soil fertility, and when there is a positive opinion of State ecological expert examination on the project for mastering new lands, for their exploitation in accordance with budgetary legislation.

6. In the event of the transfer of forest lands to non-forest lands for the use thereof for purposes not connected with conducting forestry, use of the forest fund, and/or seizure of lands of the forest funds, loss of forestry shall be compensated.

Losses of forestry shall be compensated by persons to whom lands of the forest fund are granted for use thereof for purposes not connected with conducting forestry, use of the forest fund, and/or seizure of forest fund lands from them.

The procedure for compensation of losses of forestry shall be confirmed by the Government of the Russian Federation.

Chapter IX. Defence of Rights to Land and Consideration of Land Disputes

Article 59. Recognition of Right to Land Plot

1. Recognition of a right to a land plot shall be effectuated in a judicial proceeding.

2. A judicial decision which has established a right to land shall be legal groups in the presence of which agencies of State registration of rights to immoveable property and transactions therewith shall be obliged to effectuate State registration of the right to land or transaction with land in the procedure established by the Federal Law 'On State Registration of Rights to Immoveable Property and Transactions Therewith'.

Article 60. Restoration of Position Which Existed Before Violation of Right to Land Plot and Suppression of Actions Violating Right to Land Plot or Creating Threat of Violation Thereof

1. A violated right to a land plot shall be subject to restoration in instances of:
(1) deeming of an act of an executive agency of State power or act of an agency of local self-government which entailed a violation of a right to a land plot to be invalid by a court;
(2) arbitrary occupation of land plot;
(3) other instances provided for by federal law.

2. Actions violating rights to land of citizens and juridical persons or creating a threat of the violation thereof may be suppressed by means of:
(1) deeming invalid in a judicial proceeding in accordance with Article 61 of the present Code acts of executive agencies of State power or acts of agencies of local self-government which do not correspond to legislation;
(2) suspension of performance of acts of executive agencies of State power or acts of agencies of local self-government which do not correspond to legislation;
(3) suspension of industrial, civilian housing and other construction, working of deposits of minerals and peat, operation of objects, conducting of agrochemical, forest soil conservation, geological-prospecting, survey, geodesic, and other work in the procedure established by the Government of the Russian Federation;
(4) restoration of the position which existed before violation of a right and suppression of actions violating the right or creating a threat of the violation thereof.

Article 61. Deeming Invalid Act of Executive Agency of State Power or Act of Agencies of Local Self-Government

1. A non-normative act of an executive agency of State power or a non-normative act of an agency of local self-government, and in instances provided for by

a law, also a normative act, which does not correspond to a law or other normative legal act and violates the rights and interests of a citizen or juridical person protected by a law in the domain of the use and protection of lands, may be deemed invalid by a court.

2. Losses caused to a citizen or juridical person as a result of the issuance of an act of an executive agency of State power which does not correspond to a law and violations rights to land and interests of a citizen or juridical person protected by a law shall be subject to compensation by the executive agency of State power which issued such act.

Article 62. Compensation of Losses

1. Losses caused by a violation of the rights of owners of land plots, landusers, land possessors, and lessees of land plots shall be subject to compensation in full, including lost advantage, in the procedure provided for by civil legislation.

2. On the basis of the decision of a court, the person guilty of violating the rights of owners of land plots, landusers, land possessors, and lessees of land plots may be compelled to perform duties in kind (restoration of fertility of soil, restoration of land plots to previous boundaries, erection of demolished buildings, structures, and installations, or demolition of illegally erected buildings, structures, and installations, restoration of survey and information marks, elimination of other land violations, and performance of obligations which arose).

Article 63. Guarantees of Rights to Land in Event of Seizure of Land Plots for State or Social Needs

1. The seizure of a land plot, including by purchase, for State or municipal needs shall be effectuated after:
(1) granting at the wish of the persons from whom seizure of land plots is being made, including by purchase, land plots of equal value;
(2) compensation of the value of dwelling, production, and other buildings, structures, and installations situated on the land plots being seized;
(3) compensation in accordance with Article 62 of the present Code of losses in full, including lost advantage.

2. Owners of land plots, landusers, land possessors, and lessees of land plots must not later than one year before the forthcoming seizure, including by purchase, of land plots, be notified thereof by the executive agency of State power or agency of local self-government which adopted the decision concerning seizure, including by purchase, of land plots.

Seizure, including by purchase, of land plots before the expiry of a year from the day of receipt of the notice shall be permitted only with the consent of the owners of the land plots, landusers, land possessors, and lessees of land plots.

3. Expenses incurred by owners of land plots, landusers, land possessors, and lessees of land plots for the effectuation of building on land plots of buildings of the capital type and conducting of other measures materially increasing the value of the land shall not be subject to compensation after notice concerning the forthcoming seizure, including by purchase, of land plots.

4. The market value of a land plot, unless a land plot of equal value was granted to him free of charge in ownership, must be compensated to the owner of a land plot in the event of seizure thereof for State or municipal needs together with the guarantees provided for by points 1 and 2 of the present Article.

Article 64. Settlement of Land Disputes

1. Land disputes shall be considered in a judicial proceeding.

2. Before acceptance of a case for proceeding by a court a land dispute may be transferred by the parties for consideration in an arbitration court.

Chapter X. Payment for Land and Valuation of Land

Article 65. Payability of Use of Land

1. The use of land in the Russian Federation shall be for payment. The forms of payment for the use of land shall be the land tax (until the introduction into operation of a tax on immoveables) and lease payment.

2. The procedure for calculating and payment of land tax shall be established by legislation of the Russian Federation on taxes and charges.

3. Lease payment shall be recovered for lands transferred on lease.
The procedure for determining the amount of lease payment, the procedure, conditions, and periods for making lease payment for land in the ownership of the Russian Federation and subjects of the Russian Federation, or municipal ownership shall be established respectively by the Government of the Russian Federation, agencies of State power of subjects of the Russian Federation, and agencies of local self-government.
The amount of lease payment shall be a material condition of the contract of lease of a land plot.

4. The procedure, conditions, and periods for making lease payment for land-plots in private ownership shall be established by contracts of lease of land plots.

5. For the purposes of taxation and in other instances provided for by the present Code and federal laws the cadastre value of a land plot shall be established.

Article 66. Valuation of Land

1. The market value of a land plot shall be established in accordance with the Federal Law on Valuation Activity.

2. In order to establish the cadastre value of land plots, the State cadastre valuation of lands shall be conducted, except for instances determined by point 3 of the present Article. The procedure for conducting the State cadastre valuation of lands shall be established by the Government of the Russian Federation.

3. In instances of determining the market value of a land plot, the cadastre value of the land plot shall be established in percentages of its market value.

Chapter XI. Monitoring of Lands, Land Tenure, and State Land Cadastre

Article 67. State Monitoring of Lands

1. State monitoring of lands shall be the system of observations over the state of lands. All lands in the Russian Federation shall be objects of State monitoring of lands.

2. The tasks of State monitoring of lands shall be:
(1) the timely eliciting of changes of the state of lands, valuation of these changes, forecasting and working out of recommendations concerning the prevention and concerning the elimination of the consequences of negative processes;
(2) the information provision of keeping the State land cadastre, State land control over the use and protection of lands, and other functions of State and municipal administration of land resources, and also land tenure;
(3) provision of citizens with information concerning the state of the environment with regard to the state of lands.

3. Depending upon the purposes of observation and the territory being observed, State monitoring of lands may be federal, regional, and local. State monitoring of lands shall be effectuated in accordance with federal, regional, and local programmes.

4. The procedure of effectuating State monitoring of lands shall be established by the Government of the Russian Federation.

Article 68. Land Tenure

1. Land tenure includes measures with regard to study of the state of lands, planning and organisation of rational use of lands and the protection thereof, formation of new and putting in order of existing objects of land tenure and establishment of the boundaries thereof on site (territorial land tenure), organisation of the rational use by citizens and juridical persons of land plots for the effectuation of agricultural production, and also with regard to organisation of the territories being used by communities of native small peoples of the North, Siberia, and Far East of the Russian Federation.

2. Documents prepared as a result of conducting land tenure shall be use when keeping the State land cadastre and monitoring of lands.

Article 69. Organisation and Procedure for Conducting Land Tenure

1. Land tenure shall be conducted at the initiative of empowered executive agencies of State power, agencies of local self-government, owners of land plots, landusers, land possessors, or by decision of a court.

2. Land tenure shall be conducted in an obligatory procedure in instances provided for by the present Code and federal laws.

3. Information concerning land tenure shall bear an open character, except for information constituting a State secret and information relating to the personality of owners, land plots, landusers, land possessors, or lessees of land plots.

4. When conducting land tenure taking into account the legal interests of persons whose rights may be affected when conducting it shall be ensured by means of notifying them in written form by land tenure personnel not later than seven calendar days before the commencement of work. The absence when conducting land tenure work of duly notified persons shall not be an obstacle to conducting land tenure. Interested persons shall have the right to appeal the actions impinging upon their rights and legal interests in the established procedure.

5. In the event of the seizure, including by means of purchase, of land plots for State or municipal needs, the owners of land plots, landusers, land possessors, and lessees of land plots shall be obliged to ensure access to the land plots in order to conduct land tenure.

6. Juridical persons or individual entrepreneurs may conduct any types of work with regard to land tenure without special authorisations, unless provided otherwise by federal laws.

7. The procedure for conducting land tenure shall be established by federal laws and by laws and other normative legal acts of subjects of the Russian Federation.

Article 70. State Land Cadastre

1. The State land cadastre is the systematised digest of documented information concerning objects of State cadastre recording, the legal regime of lands in the Russian Federation, cadastre value, location and dimensions of land plots and objects of immoveable property stably connected therewith. Information concerning the subjects of rights to land plots shall be included in the State land cadastre.

2. The State land cadastre shall be kept according to a system uniform for the Russian Federation. Land plots and objects of immoveable property stably connected therewith shall be the objects of State cadastre recording.

118

3. The procedure for keeping the State land cadastre shall be established by the Federal Law on the State Land Cadastre.

Chapter XII. Control Over Compliance with Land Legislation and Protection and Use of Lands (Land Control)

Article 71. State Land Control

1. State land control over compliance with land legislation and requirements for the protection and use of lands by organisations, irrespective of their organisational-legal forms and forms of ownership, executives thereof, officials, and also citizens, shall be effectuated by specially empowered State agencies.

2. State land control shall be effectuated in accordance with legislation of the Russian Federation in the procedure established by the Government of the Russian Federation.

Article 72. Municipal and Social Land Control

1. Municipal land control over the use of lands on the territory of a municipal formation shall be effectuated by agencies of local self-government or agencies empowered by them.

2. Municipal land control over the use of lands on the territory of a municipal formation shall be effectuated in accordance with legislation of the Russian Federation and in the procedure established by normative legal acts of agencies of local self-government.

3. Social land control shall be effectuated by agencies of territorial social self-government, other social organisations (or associations), and citizens over compliance with the established procedure for the preparation and adoption by executive agencies of State power and agencies of local self-government provided for by Article 29 of the present Code of decisions affecting the rights and legal interests of citizens and juridical persons provided for by the present Code, and also over compliance with the requirements for the use and protection of lands.

Article 73. Derivative Land Control

1. Derivative land control shall be effectuated by the owner of a land plot, landuser, land possessor, and lessee of a land plot in the course of the effectuation of economic activity on the land plot.

2. A person using a land plot shall be obliged to provide information concerning the organisation of derivative land control to a specially-empowered agency of State land control in the procedure established by the Government of the Russian Federation.

Chapter XIII. Responsibility for Violation in Domain of Protection and Use of Lands

Article 74. Administrative and Criminal Responsibility for Land Violations

1. Persons guilty of the commission of land violations shall bear administrative or criminal responsibility in the procedure established by legislation.

2. The bringing of a person guilty of the commission of land violations to criminal or administrative responsibility shall not relieve him of the duty to eliminate the land violations permitted and to compensate the harm caused by them.

Article 75. Disciplinary Responsibility for Land Violations

1. Officials and workers of organisations guilty of the commission of land violations shall bear disciplinary responsibility in instances when as a result of the improper fulfilment by them of their official or labour duties the organisation incurred administrative responsibility for designing, siting, and introducing into operation objects exerting a negative (or harmful) influence on the state of lands, the pollution thereof by chemical and radioactive substances, production wastes, and sewage waters.

2. The procedure for bringing to disciplinary responsibility shall be determined by labour legislation, legislation on State and municipal service, legislation of disciplinary responsibility of heads of administrations, federal laws, and other normative legal acts of the Russian Federation, and laws and other normative legal acts of subjects of the Russian Federation.

Article 76. Compensation of Harm Caused by Land Violations

1. Juridical persons and citizens shall be obliged to compensate in full harm caused as a result of the commission by them of land violations.

2. Arbitrarily occupied land plots shall be returned to their owners, landusers, land possessors, and lessees of land plots without compensation of expenditures made by the persons guilty of violating land legislation for the time of illegal use of these land plots.

3. Bringing land plots into a state fit for use in the event of the littering thereof, other types of damage, arbitrary occupation, demolition of buildings, structures, and installations during arbitrary occupation of land plots, or arbitrary construction, and also the restoration of destroyed survey marks, shall be effectuated by juridical persons and citizens who are guilty of the said land violations, or at their expense.

Chapter XIV. Lands of Agricultural Designation

Article 77. Concept and Composition of Lands of Agricultural Designation

1. Lands outside the line of settlements granted for needs of agriculture, and also intended for these purposes, shall be deemed to be lands of agricultural designation.

2. Within the composition of lands of agricultural designation shall be singled out agricultural tracts, lands occupied by intra-farm roads, communications, timber and shrubbery flora intended to defend the lands against the influence of negative (or harmful) nature, anthropogenic, and technogenic phenomena, enclosed waters, and also buildings, structures, and installations used for the production, keeping, and primary processing of agricultural products.

Article 78. Use of Lands of Agricultural Designation

Lands of agricultural designation may be used for conducting agricultural production, the creation of defensive plantings, scientific-research, instructional, and other purposes connected with agricultural production by:

citizens, including those conducting peasant (or farmer) economies, personal subsidiary husbandry, gardening, livestock farming, and vegetable-gardening;

economic partnerships and societies, production cooperatives, State and municipal unitary enterprises, and other commercial organisations;

noncommercial organisations, including consumer cooperatives and religious organisations;

Cossack societies;

experimental-production, instructional, instructional-experimental, and instructional-production subdivisions of scientific research organisations, educational institutions of agricultural profile, and institutions of general education;

communities of native small peoples of the North, Siberia, and Far East of the Russian Federation in order to preserve and develop their traditional way of life, economic management, and trades.

Article 79. Peculiarities of Use of Agricultural Tracts

1. Agricultural tracts—ploughed fields, hayfields, pasture, fallow land, lands occupied by perennial plantings (gardens, vineyards, and others),—shall within the composition of lands of agricultural designation have priority in use and shall be subject to special protection.

2. Lands shall be granted for construction of industrial objects and other nonagricultural needs which are unfit for conducting agricultural production, or agricultural tracts from lands of agricultural designation of the worse quality according to cadastre value. For the construction of electric transmission lines,

communications, motor vehicle roads, main pipelines, and other similar installations the granting of agricultural tracts from lands of agricultural designation shall be permitted of a higher quality. The said installations shall be sited principally along motor vehicle roads and boundaries of rotation of crop fields.

3. The seizure, including by means of purchase, for the purposes of granting for nonagricultural use agricultural tracts whose cadastre value exceeds its average-district level shall be permitted only in exceptional instances connected with the fulfilment of international obligations of the Russian Federation, ensuring the defence and security of the State, working of deposits of minerals (except for generally-distributed minerals), maintenance of objects of cultural heritage of the Russian Federation, construction and maintenance of objects of cultural-domestic, social, and educational designation, motor vehicle roads, main pipelines, electric transmission lines, communications, and other similar installations, in the absence of other variants for possible siting of these objects.

4. Especially valuable productive agricultural tracts, including agricultural tracts for experimental-production subdivisions of scientific research organisations and instructional-experimental subdivisions of educational institutions of higher professional education, agricultural tracts whose cadastre value materially exceeds the average-district level, may in accordance with legislation of subjects of the Russian Federation, be included in the List of lands whose use for other purposes is not permitted.

5. The use of land participatory shares which arose as a result of the privatisation of agricultural tracts shall be regulated by the Federal Law on the Turnover of Lands of Agricultural Designation.

Article 80. Fund for Redistribution of Lands

1. For the purposes of redistribution of lands for agricultural production, the creation and expansion of peasant (or farmer) economies, personal subsidiary husbandry, conducting gardening, livestock farming, vegetable-gardening, haying, and pasturage of livestock on lands of agricultural designation, the fund for the redistribution of lands shall be created.

2. The fund for the redistribution of lands shall be formed from the land plots of lands of agricultural designation entering this fund:
(1) in the event of voluntary renunciation of a land plot;
(2) if there are no heirs either by operation of law or by will, or none of the heirs had accepted the inheritance, or all heirs have been deprived by will of the inheritance, of an heir has renounced the inheritance to the benefit of the State, or has renounced the inheritance without an indication of to whose benefit it renounces the inheritance;
(3) in the event of the compulsory seizure of a land plot in the instances provided for by the present Code and federal laws.

3. The use of lands of the fund for redistribution of lands shall be effectuated in accordance with Article 78 of the present Code in the procedure established by laws and other normative legalacts of the Russian Federation.

4. Information concerning the existence of lands in the fund for the redistribution of lands shall be generally-accessible.

Article 81. Granting of Lands of Agricultural Designation to Citizens for Conducting Peasant (or Farmer) Economy and Personal Subsidiary Husbandry and to Citizens and Associations Thereof for Conducting Gardening, Vegetable-Gardening, and Dacha Construction

1. Land plots from lands of agricultural designation shall be granted to citizens who have expressed the wish to conduct peasant (or farmer) economy in accordance with the present Code and the Law on Peasant (or Farmer) Economy.

2. The procedure for granting land plots to citizens and associations thereof in order to conduct gardening, vegetable-gardening, and dacha construction shall be established by the present Code and the Federal Law on Gardening, Vegetable-Gardening, and Dacha Noncommercial Associations of Citizens.

3. Landplots shall be granted to citizens who have expressed the wish to conduct personal subsidiary husbandry in accordance with the present Code and the Federal Law on Personal Subsidiary Husbandry.

4. The conditions for granting land plots to citizens from the lands of agricultural designation for haying and pasturage of livestock shall be established by the present Code, the Federal Law on Turnover of Lands of Agricultural Designation, other federal laws, and laws of subjects of the Russian Federation.

Article 82. Granting of Lands of Agricultural Designation to Economic Societies and Partnerships, Production Cooperatives, State and Municipal Unitary Enterprises, Other Commercial Organisations, Religious Organisations, Cossack Societies, Scientific-Research Organisations, Educational Institutions of Agricultural Profile, Communities of Native Small Peoples of the North, Siberia, and Far East of Russian Federation

The conditions for granting land plots from lands of agricultural designation in ownership to economic partnerships and societies, production cooperatives, State and municipal unitary enterprises, other commercial organisations, religious organisations, Cossack societies, scientific-research organisations, educational institutions of agricultural profile, and communities of native small peoples of the North, Siberia, and Far East of Russian Federation for the effectuation of agricultural production, creation of defensive plantings, scientific-research, instructional, and other purposes connected with agricultural production, and also for the preservation and development of a traditional way of life, economic management, and trades of native small peoples of the North, Siberia, and Far East of the Russian Federation shall be established by a federal law on the turnover of lands of agricultural designation.

Chapter XV. Lands of Settlements

Article 83. Concept of Lands of Settlements

1. Lands used and intended for the building and development of city and rural settlements and separated by the line thereof from the lands of other categories shall be deemed to be the lands of settlements.

2. The procedure for the use of lands of settlements shall be determined in accordance with zoning of the territories thereof. A territory of a settlement within the limits of its administrative boundaries shall be divided into territorial zones. Documents of the zoning of territories shall be confirmed and changed by normative legal acts of local self-government (or rules of landuse and building).

The rules of landuse and building of cities of federal significance, Moscow and St. Petersburg, shall be confirmed and changed by the laws of these subjects of the Russian Federation.

3. Land plots in city and rural settlements may be seized, including by purchase, for State or municipal needs, for the purpose of building in accordance with general plans of city and rural settlements and rules for landuse and building.

Article 84. Line of City and Rural Settlements and Procedure for Establishment Thereof

1. The line of city and rural settlements shall represent the external boundaries of the lands of city and rural settlements, separating those lands from the lands of other categories.

2. The establishment of the line of settlements shall be conducted on the basis of confirmed urban construction and land-tenure documentation. The draft line of a settlement shall be relegated to urban construction documentation.

The line of settlements must be established along the boundaries of land plots granted to citizens and juridical persons.

3. Confirmation and change of a line of city and rural settlements shall be effectuated by agencies of State power of subjects of the Russian Federation, except for instances provided for by points 4 and 5 of the present Article.

4. The line of cities of federal significance, Moscow and St. Petersburg, shall be confirmed and changes by a federal law upon the agreed submission of legislative (or representative) agencies of the City of Moscow and legislative (or representative) agencies of Moscow Region, legislative (or representative) agencies of the

City of St. Petersburg and legislative (or representative) agencies of Leningrad Region.

5. Confirmation and change of a fine of city settlements within the composition of closed administrative-territorial formations shall be effectuated by the Government of the Russian Federation.

6. Inclusion of land plots within the line of settlements shall not entail termination of the rights of owners of the land plots, landusers, land possessors, and lessees of land plots.

Article 85. Composition of Lands of Settlements and Zoning of Territories

1. Within the composition of lands of settlements may be land plots relegated in accordance with urban construction reglaments to the following territorial zones:
   (1) dwelling;
   (2) social-business;
   (3) production;
   (4) engineering and transport infrastructures;
   (5) recreational;
   (6) agricultural use;
   (7) special designation;
   (8) military objects;
   (9) other territorial zones.

2. The boundaries of territorial zones must meet the requirements of affiliation of each land plot only to one zone.

The urban construction reglament shall be established by the rules of land use and building for each territorial zone individually, taking into account the peculiarities of location thereof and development, and also the possibility of a territorial combination of various types of use of land plots (dwelling, social-business, production, recreational, and other types of use of land plots).

A unified urban construction reglament shall be established for land plots located within the boundaries of one territorial zone. The urban construction reglament of a territorial zone shall determine the foundation of the legal regime of land plots, and likewise of everything that is found above and below the surface of the land plots and shall be used in the process of building and subsequent operation of buildings, structures, and installations.

3. Urban construction reglaments shall be binding upon all owners of land plots, landusers, land possessors, and lessees of land plots irrespective of the forms of ownership and other rights to land plots.

The said persons may use land plots in accordance with any type of authorised use provided for by an urban construction reglament for each territorial zone.

4. A land plot and objects of immoveable stably connected therewith shall not correspond to the established urban construction reglament of territorial zones if:

the types of their use are not within the List of types of authorised use;

the dimensions thereof do not correspond to the maximum values established by the urban construction reglament.

The said land plots and objects of immoveable stably connected therewith may be used without the establishment of a period for bringing them into conformity with the urban construction reglament, except for instances of their use being dangerous to human life and health, the environment, and monuments of history and culture.

A prohibition against the use of a land plot and objects of immoveable stably connected therewith until the bringing thereof into conformity with the urban construction reglament or period for bringing the types of use of the land plot and objects of immoveable stably connected therewith in accordance with the urban construction reglament shall be established by the agency of local self-government.

The reconstruction and expansion of existing objects of immoveable, and also construction of new objects of immoveable stably connected with the said land plots, may be effectuated only in accordance with the established urban construction reglaments.

5. Land plots within the composition of dwelling zones shall be intended for the building of dwelling buildings, and also objects of cultural-domestic and other designation. Dwelling zones may be intended for individual dwelling building, mixed dwelling building of a few floors, average-floor mixed dwelling building, and multi-floor dwelling building, and also other types of building, according to urban construction reglaments.

6. Land plots within the composition of social-business zones shall be intended for the building of administrative buildings, objects of educational, cultural-domestic, and social designation and other objects intended for social use according to urban construction reglaments.

7. Land plots within the composition of production zones shall be intended for building industrial, municipal-warehouse, and other production objects intended for these purposes according to urban construction reglaments.

8. Land plots within the composition of zones of engineering and transport infrastructure shall be intended for building objects of railway, motor vehicle, river, sea, air, and pipeline transport, communications, engineering infrastructure, and also objects of other designation according to urban construction reglaments.

9. Land plots within the composition of recreational zones, including land plots occupied by city forests, squares, parks, city gardens, ponds, lakes, and water reservoirs shall be used for the leisure of citizens and tourism.

10. Within the limits of the line of city and rural settlements may be singled out zones of specially-protected territories in which land plots are included having special nature-protection, scientific, historico-cultural, aesthetic, recreational, health, and other specially valuable significance.

Land plots included within the composition of zones of specially-protected territories shall be used in accordance with the requirements established by Articles 94–100 of the present Code.

Land plots on which objects are situated which are not monuments of history and culture, but located within the boundaries of zones for the protection of monuments of history and culture, shall be used in accordance with urban construction reglaments established by taking into account the requirements of protection of monuments of history and culture.

11. Land plots within the composition of zones of agricultural use in settlements—landplots occupied by pastures, perennial plantings, and also buildings, structures, and installations of agricultural designation—shall be used for the purposes of conducting agricultural production up to the moment of a change of type of use thereof in accordance with the general plans of settlements and rules for land use and building.

12. Land plots of common use occupying squares, streets, passages, motor vehicle roads, shore, squares, boulevards, closed reservoirs, beaches, and other objects may be included within the composition of various territorial zones and shall not be subject to privatisation.

Article 86. Suburban Zones

1. Lands situated beyond the line of city settlements comprising with the city a unified social, natural, and economic territory and not within the composition of lands of other settlements may be included within the composition of suburban zones.

2. Territories of agricultural production, zones of leisure for the population, reserve lands for the development of the city shall be separated out in suburban zones.

3. The boundaries and legal regime of suburban zones, except for suburban zones of cities of federal significance, Moscow and St. Petersburg, shall be confirmed and changes by laws of subjects of the Russian Federation.

4. The boundaries and legal regime of suburban zones of cities of federal significance, Moscow and St. Petersburg, shall be confirmed and changed by federal laws.

5. Green zones, which shall fulfil sanitary, sanitary-hygienic, and recreational functions and within whose boundaries economic and other activity is prohibited

which exerts a negative (or harmful) effect on the environment may be singled out within the composition of suburban zones.

6. The transfer of lands within the boundaries of suburban and green zones occupied by first-group forests to the lands of other categories shall be permitted on the basis of a decision of the Government of the Russian Federation.

Chapter XVI. Lands of Industry, Electric Power, Transport, Communications, Radiobroadcasting, Television, Information, Lands for Ensuring Outer Space Activity, Lands of Defence and Security, and Lands of Other Special Designation

Article 87. Composition of Lands of Industry, Electric Power, Transport, Communications, Radiobroadcasting, Television, Information, Lands for Ensuring Outer Space Activity, Lands of Defence and Security, and Lands of Other Special Designation

1. Lands which are located beyond the line of settlements and are used or intended for ensuring activity of organisations and/or operation of objects of industry, electric power, transport, communications, radiobroadcasting, television, information, objects for ensuring outer space activity, objects of defence and security, effectuation of other special tasks and the rights to which arose with participants of land relations on the grounds provided for by the present Code, federal laws, and laws of subjects of the Russian Federation (hereinafter: lands of industry and other special designation), shall be deemed to be lands of industry, electric power, transport, communications, radiobroadcasting, information, lands for ensuring outer space activity, lands of defence and security, and lands of other special designation.

Lands of industry and other special designation shall in accordance with Article 7 of the present Code comprise an autonomous category of lands of the Russian Federation.

2. Lands of industry and other special designation, depending upon the character of special tasks, in order to resolve which they are used or intended, shall be subdivided into:

(1) industry lands;

(2) electric power lands;

(3) transport lands;

(4) lands of communication, radiobroadcasting, television, and information;

(5) lands for ensuring outer space activity;

(6) lands of defence and security;

(7) lands of other special designation.

The peculiarities of the legal regime of these lands shall be established by Articles 88–93 of the present Code and shall be taken into account when conducting the zoning of territories.

3. Protection, sanitary-defensive, and other zones with special conditions for the use of lands may be included in the composition of lands of industry and other special designation for the purposes of ensuring the security of the population and creation of necessary conditions for the operation of objects of industry and electric power, centres for keeping nuclear materials and radioactive substances, transport, and other objects.

Land plots which have been included in the composition of such zones shall not be seized from the owners of land plots, landusers, land possessors, and lessees of land plots, but within the boundaries thereof a special regime for their use may be introduced which limits or prohibits those types of activity that are incompatible with the purposes of the establishment of the zones.

4. Lands of industry and other special designation occupied by federal electric power systems, objects of the use of atomic energy, federal transport, railways, objects of federal information and communication, objects ensuring outer space activity, objects of defence and security, objects of defence production, objects ensuring the status and defence of the State boundary of the Russian Federation, and other objects relegated to the jurisdiction of the Russian Federation in accordance with Article 71 of the Constitution of the Russian Federation shall be federal ownership.

5. The procedure for the use of individual types of lands of industry and other special designation, and also the establishment of zones with special conditions for the use of lands of a particular category, shall be determined by:

(1) the Government of the Russian Federation with respect to the said lands in federal ownership;

(2) agencies of executive power of subjects of the Russian Federation with respect to the said lands in the ownership of subjects of the Russian Federation;

(3) agencies of local self-government with respect to the said lands in municipal ownership.

6. The lands of industry and other special designation may in accordance with Article 24 of the present Code be granted for uncompensated fixed-term use for agricultural production and other use.

Article 88. Industry Lands

1. Lands which are used or intended in order to ensure the activity of organisations and/or operation of objects of industry and rights to which arose with the participants of land relations on the grounds provided for by the present Code, federal laws, and laws of subjects of the Russian Federation shall be deemed to be industry lands.

2. For the purposes of ensuring the activity of organisations and/or operation of objects of industry, land plots may be granted in order to site production and

administrative buildings, structures, installations, and objects servicing them, and also to establish sanitary-defensive and other zones with special conditions of use of lands specified in point 1 of the present Article.

3. The dimensions of land plots granted for the purposes specified in point 2 of the present Article shall be determined in accordance with the norms or design-technical documentation confirmed in the established procedure.

4. Land plots for working minerals shall be granted to organisations of the mining-extractive and oil and gas industries after the formalisation of a mining allotment, confirmation of the design for recultivation of lands, and restoration of previously worked lands. Especially valuable productive agricultural lands shall be granted in accordance with Article 79 of the present Code after working other agricultural lands located within the boundaries of the mining allotment.

Article 89. Electric Power Lands

1. Lands which are used or intended for ensuring the activity of organisations and/or operation of electric power objects and the rights to which arose with participants of land relations on the grounds provided for by the present Code, federal laws, and laws of subjects of the Russian Federation shall be deemed to be electric power lands.

2. For the purposes of ensuring the activity of organisations and electric power objects land plots may be granted for:
(1) the siting of hydro-electric stations, atomic stations, nuclear devices, points for keeping nuclear materials and radioactive substances, heating stations, and other electric power stations servicing the installations and objects thereof;
(2) the siting of air lines of electric transmission, earth installations of cable electric transmission lines, substations, distribution points, and other electric power installations and objects.
In order to ensure the activity of organisations and operation of electric power objects, protection zones for the electric power network may be established.

3. The rules for determining the dimensions of land plots for siting air lines of electric power transmission and support for lines of communications servicing the electric power network shall be established by the Government of the Russian Federation.

Article 90. Transport Lands

1. Lands which are used or intended to ensure the activity of organisations and/or operation of objects of motor vehicle, sea, internal water, railway, air and other types of transport and the rights to which arose with the participants of land relations on grounds provided for by the present Code, federal laws, and laws of subjects of the Russian Federation shall be deemed to be transport lands.

2. For the purposes of ensuring the activity of organisations and operation of objects of railway transport, land plots may be granted for:

(1) the siting of railway tracks;

(2) the siting, operation, expansion, and reconstruction of structures, buildings, installations, including railway terminals, railway stations, and also devices and other objects necessary for the operation, maintenance, construction, reconstruction, repair, and development of earth and underground buildings, structures, installations, devices, and other objects of railway transport;

(3) the establishment of designated belts for protection zones of railways.

Free land plots on designated belts of railways within railway transport lands may be transferred on lease to citizens and juridical persons for agricultural use, rendering services to passengers, warehousing of cargoes, arrangement of loading-unloading spaces, installation of railway warehouses (except for warehouses of inflammable oil materials and petrol stations of any types, and also warehouses intended for the keeping of dangerous substances and materials) and other purposes, on condition of compliance with the requirements for traffic safety established by federal laws.

The procedure for the establishment and use of designated belts and protection zones of railways shall be determined by the Government of the Russian Federation.

3. For the purposes of ensuring the activity of organisations and operation of objects of motor vehicle transport and highway objects land plots may be granted for:

(1) the siting of motor vehicle roads, constructive elements thereof, and road installations;

(2) the siting of motor vehicle terminals and auto stations and other objects of motor vehicle transport and highway objects necessary for the operation, maintenance, construction, reconstruction, repair, and development of earth and underground buildings, installations, and devices;

(3) establishment of designated belts for highways.

Land plots on designated belts of highways within the limits of motor vehicle transport lands may be transferred in the procedure established by the present Code on lease to citizens and juridical persons in order to site objects of road service and outdoor advertising.

On designated belts of highways, except for instances provided for by legislation, there shall be prohibited:

the construction of dwelling and social buildings, and warehouses;

the conducting of construction, geological prospecting, topographic, mining, and prospecting work, and also the installation of earth installations;

the ploughing of land plots, cutting of grass, felling and damaging of perennial plantings, removal of turf and taking of soil;

the installation of outdoor advertisements, information boards and indicators not relating to the safety of road traffic.

In order to create normal conditions for the operation of federal highways and the preservation thereof, ensuring safety requirements of road traffic, and requirements for safety of the population, highway belts shall be created in the form of land plots of designated belts adjacent to both sides of federal highways, with the establishment of a special regime for the use thereof, including the construction of buildings, structures, and installations, limitation of economic activity within the limits of the road belts, installation of advertising boards and posters not relating to traffic safety.

The owners of land plots, landusers, land possessors, and lessees of land plots within the limits of such road belts must be informed by the respective agencies of executive power of subjects of the Russian Federation about the special regime for the use of these land plots.

The procedure for the establishment and use of such road belts and designated belts of federal highways shall be determined by the Government of the Russian Federation.

4. For the purposes of ensuring the activity of organisations and operation of objects of sea and internal water transport, land plots may be granted for:
   (1) the siting of artificially created internal water routes;
   (2) the siting of sea and river ports, piers, jetties, hydro-engineering installations, and other objects necessary for the operation, maintenance, construction, reconstruction, repair, and development of earth and underground buildings, structures, installations, devices, and other objects of sea and internal water transport;
   (3) allotment of coastal belt.

A coastal belt of internal water routes shall be allotted for work connected with navigation and timber floating along internal water routes outside the territories of settlements. The procedure for allocating a coastal belt and the use thereof shall be determined by the Code of Internal Water Transport of the Russian Federation.

5. For the purposes of ensuring the activity of organisations and operation of objects of air transport, land plots may be granted for the siting of airports, aerodromes, air terminals, takeoff and landing belts, and other earth objects necessary for the operation, maintenance, construction, reconstruction, repair, and development of earth and underground buildings, structures, installations, devices, and other objects of air transport.

6. For the purposes of ensuring the activity of organisations and operation of objects of pipeline transport, land plots may be granted for:
   (1) the siting of oil pipelines, gas pipelines, and other pipelines;

(2) the siting of objects necessary for the operation, maintenance, construction, reconstruction, repair, and development of earth and underground buildings, structures, installations, devices, and other objects of pipeline transport;

(3) the establishment of protection zones with special conditions for the use of land plots.

The boundaries of protection zones in which objects of the gas supply system have been sited shall be determined on the basis of construction norms and rules, rules for the protection of main pipelines, and other normative documents confirmed in the established procedure. The construction of any buildings whatsoever, structures, and installations within the limits of established minimum distances up to the objects of the gas supply system shall not be permitted on the said land plots in the event of their economic use. It shall not be authorised to obstruct the owner-organisation of the gas supply system or organisation empowered by it in the fulfilment by it of work with regard to servicing and repair of objects of the gas supply system, liquidation of the consequences of wrecks or catastrophes which have arisen on them.

7. For the purposes of creating conditions for the construction and reconstruction of objects of motor vehicle, water, railway, air, and other types of transport, the reserving of lands shall be effectuated. The procedure for reserving lands for the said purposes shall be established by federal laws.

Article 91. Lands of Communications, Radiobroadcasting, Television, and Information

1. Lands which are used or intended to ensure the activity of organisations and/or objects of communications, radiobroadcasting, television, and information, and the rights to which arose with the participants of land relations on the grounds provided for by the present Code, federal laws, and laws of subjects of the Russian Federation shall be deemed to be land of communications, radiobroadcasting, television, and information.

2. For the purposes of ensuring comunications (except outer space communications), radiobroadcasting, television, and information land plots may be granted in order to site objects of the respective infrastructures, including:

(1) operational enterprises of communications on whose balance sheet there are radio-relay, air, and cable lines of communications and respective belts of alienation;

(2) cable, radio-relay, and air lines of communications and radioification lines on cable lanes and air lines of communications and radiofication, and respective protection zones for lines of communication;

(3) underground cable and air lines of communications and radiofication and respective protection zones for lines of communication;

(4) earth and underground nonservicing reinforcement points for cable lines of communications and respective protection zones;

(5) earth installations and infrastructure of satellite communications.

Article 92. Lands for Ensuring Outer Space Activity

1. Lands which are used or intended for ensuring the activity or organisations and/or objects of outer space activity and the rights to which arose with the participants of land relations on the grounds provided for by the present Code, federal laws, and laws of subjects of the Russian Federation shall be deemed to be lands for ensuring outer space activity.

2. For the purposes of ensuring outer space activity, land plots may be granted to site earth objects of outer space infrastructure, including cosmodromes, launch complexes, and launch devices, command-measuring complexes, centres and points for managing flights of outer space objects, points for the reception, keeping, and processing of information, bases for keeping outer space technology, areas for separating parts of missiles to fall, polygons for the landing of outer space objects and launch-landing belts, objects of an experimental base for working through outer space technology, centres and equipment for the training of cosmonauts, other earth installations and technology to be used when effectuating outer space activity.

3. Land plots to be used in areas for separating parts of missiles episodically fall shall not be seized from the owners of the land plots, landusers, land possessors, and lessees of land plots.

The procedure for compensation of damage to these persons shall be determined by the Government of the Russian Federation.

Article 93. Defence and Security Lands

1. Defence and security lands shall be deemed to be lands which are used or are intended to ensure activity of the Armed Forces of the Russian Federation, forces of the Border Service of the Russian Federation, other forces, military formations, and agencies, organisations, enterprises, and institutions effectuating functions with regard to the armed defence of the integrity and inviolability of the territory of the Russian Federation, defence and protection of the State boundary of the Russian Federation, information security, and other types of security in closed administrative-territorial formations, and rights to which arose with participants of land relations on the grounds provided for by the present Code and federal laws.

2. For the purposes of ensuring defence land plots may be granted for:

(1) construction, training, and maintainin in necessary readiness Armed Forces of the Russian Federation, other forces, military formations, and agencies (siting military organisations, institutions, and other objects, stationing of forces and naval forces, conducting exercises and other measures);

(2) working out, production, and repair of armaments, military, special, and outer space technology and ammunition (experimental testing grounds, sites for the destruction of weapons, and burial of wastes);

(3) creation of stocks of material valuables in State and mobilisation reserves (storehouses, warehouses, and others).

When temporary use of lands (or territories) is necessary in order to conduct exercises and other measures connected with the needs of defence, land plots shall not be seized from the owners of land plots, landusers, land possessors, and lessees of land plots.

The use of these lands shall be effectuated according to the procedure established for conducting prospecting work, and also for zones with special conditions of use.

3. For the purpose of ensuring the defence and protection of the State boundary of the Russian Federation in the procedure established by legislation of the Russian Federation, the use of land belts or plots for arrangement and maintenance of engineering-technical installations and barriers, frontier marks, frontier cuttings, communications, and points for admission across the State boundary of the Russian Federation, and other objects shall be allotted for permanent (in perpetuity) use.

Norms for the allotment of land plots, the dimensions of land plots necessary in order to ensure the defence and protection of the State boundary of the Russian Federation, the procedure for the use thereof, including the peculiarities of economic, trade, and other activity, shall be determined by legislation of the Russian Federation.

4. In order to site objects for the working out, manufacture, keeping, and utilisation of weapons of mass destruction, process radioactive and other materials, military, and other objects inclosed administrative-territorial formations land plots shall be granted in permanent (in perpetuity) use or on lease.

A special regime for the use of lands shall be established in a closed administrative-territorial formation by decision of the Government of the Russian Federation.

Executive agencies of State power and agencies of local self-government provided for by Article 29 of the present Code must take necessary measures with regard to granting land plots in order to satisfy the requirements of the population for the development of gardening, vegetable-gardening, agricultural production, housing and dacha construction beyond the limits of the closed administrative-territorial formation.

5. Executive agencies of State power provided for by Article 29 of the present Code may in the procedure established by the Government of the Russian Federation transfer individual land plots from lands granted for the needs of

defence and security on lease or uncompensated fixed-term use to juridical persons and citizens for agricultural, forestry, and other use.

6. Under conditions of an extraordinary or military situation the use of land plots for the needs of defence and security may be effectuated in the procedure established by Article 51 of the present Code.

7. For the purposes of ensuring the safety of the keeping of armaments and military technology and other military property, defence of the population and objects of production, socio-domestic, and other designation, and also protection of the environment when extraordinary situations arise of a technogenic and natural character on land plots adjacent to arsenals, bases, and warehouses of the Armed Forces of the Russian Federation, forces of the Border Service of the Russian Federation, other forces, military formations, and agencies, prohibited zones may be established.

Chapter XVII. Lands of Specially-Protected Territories and Objects

Article 94. Concept and Composition of Lands of Specially-Protected Territories

1. To lands of specially-protected territories shall be relegated lands which have special nature-protection, scientific, historico-cultural, aesthetic, recreational, health, and other valuable significance that have been removed in accordance with decrees of federal agencies of State power, agencies of State power of subjects of the Russian Federation, or decisions of agencies of local self-government wholly or partly from economic use and turnover and for which a special legal regime has been established.

2. To lands of specially-protected territories shall be relegated lands of:
(1) specially-protected nature territories, including treatment-health localities and resorts;
(2) nature-protection designation;
(3) recreational designation;
(4) historico-cultural designation;
(5) other specially valuable lands in accordance with the present Code and federal laws.

3. The procedure for relegating lands to lands of specially-protected territories of federal significance and the procedure for the use and protection of lands of specially-protected territories of federal significance shall be established by the Government of the Russian Federation on the basis of federal laws.

4. The procedure for relegating lands to lands of specially-protected territories of regional and local significance and the procedure for the use and protection of lands of specially-protected territories of regional and local significance shall be

established by agencies of State power of subjects of the Russian Federation and agencies of local self-government in accordance with federal laws, laws of subjects of the Russian Federation, and normative legal acts of agencies of local self-government.

5. The Government of the Russian Federation and respective agencies of executive power of subjects of the Russian Federation and agencies of local self-government may establish other types of lands of specially-protected territories (lands on which suburban green zones, city forests, city parks, protected coastlines, protected nature landscapes, biological stations, micro-preserves, and others) are situated.

6. Lands of specially-protected nature territories and lands occupied by objects of cultural heritage of the Russian Federation shall be used for the respective purposes. The use of these lands for other purposes shall be limited or prohibited, in instances established by the present Code, by federal laws.

Article 95. Lands of Specially-Protected Nature Territories

1. To lands of specially-protected nature territories shall be relegated lands of State nature preserves, including biospheric, State nature reserves, monuments of nature, national parks, nature parks, dendrological parks, botanical gardens, territories of traditional nature use of native small peoples of the North, Siberia, and Far East of the Russian Federation, and also lands of treatment-health localities and resorts.

2. Lands of specially-protected nature territories shall be relegated to objects of all-national weal and may be in federal ownership, ownership of subjects of the Russian Federation, and municipal ownership. In instances provided for by federal laws the inclusion in lands of specially-protected nature territories of land plots which belong to citizens and juridical citizens by right of ownership shall be permitted.

3. On lands of State nature preserves, including biospheric, national parks, nature parks, State nature reserves, monuments of nature, dendrological parks, and botanical gardens incorporating especially valuable ecological systems and objects, thanks to the preservation of which a specially-protected nature territory has been created, activity shall be prohibited which is not connected with the preservation and study of nature complexes and objects and is not provided for by federal laws and laws of subjects of the Russian Federation. Within the limits of lands of specially-protected nature territories the seizure of land plots or other termination of rights to land for needs which are contrary their special-purpose designation, shall not be permitted.

4. For the purposes of the defence of lands of specially-protected nature territories against unfavourable anthropogenic influences, on land plots adjacent

thereto protection zones or areas with a regulated regime of economic activity may be created. Within the boundaries of those zones activity shall be prohibited which renders a negative (or harmful) influence on the nature complexes of specially-protected nature territories. The boundaries of protected zones should be designated by special informational marks. Land plots within the boundaries of protection zones shall not be seized from owners of the land plots, land users, land possessors, and lessees of the land plots and shall be used by them in compliance with the special legal regime established for these land plots.

5. For the purposes of creating new and expanding existing lands of specially-protected nature territories, agencies of State power of subjects of the Russian Federation shall have the right to adopt decisions concerning the reserving of lands which it is proposed to declare to be lands of specially-protected nature territories, with subsequent seizure of such lands, including by means of purchase, and concerning the limitation of economic activity on them.

6. Lands of State reserves and of national parks in federal ownership also shall be granted to them by right of permanent (in perpetuity) use. Land plots within the boundaries of State reserves and national parks shall not be subject to privatisation. In individual instances the existence within the boundaries of national parks of land plots of other users, and also of owners whose activity does not exert a negative (or harmful) influence on the lands of national parks and does not disturb the regime of use of the lands of State preserves and national parks, shall be permitted. National parks shall have the exclusive right to acquire the said lands.

7. On lands of specially-protected nature territories of federal significance shall be prohibited:
    (1) the granting of garden and dacha plots;
    (2) the construction of federal automobile roads, pipelines, electrical transmission lines and other communications, and also construction and operation of industrial, economic, and dwelling objects not connected with the functioning of specially-protected nature territories;
    (3) the movement and stopping of mechanical means of transport which are not connected with the functioning of specially-protected nature territories, and cattle tracks outside of automobile roads;
    (4) other types of activity prohibited by federal laws.

8. The territories of nature parks shall be located on lands granted to them for permanent (in perpetuity) use; the siting of nature parks on lands of other users, and also of owners, shall be permitted.

9. The declaration of lands to be State nature reserves shall be permitted either with or without seizure, including by means of purchase, of land plots from their owners, landusers, or land possessors.

10. Land plots occupied by nature complexes and objects which are declared in the established procedure to be monuments of nature may be removed from the owners of these plots, landusers, and land possessors.

Article 96. Lands of Treatment-Health Localities and Resorts

1. Lands of treatment-health localities and resorts shall be relegated to specially protected nature territories and intended for treatment and leisure of citizens. Within the composition of these lands shall be included lands possessing nature treatment resources (deposits of mineral waters, treatment muds, brine of estuaries and lakes), favourable climate, and other nature factors and conditions which are used or might be used for the prevention and treatment of human illnesses.

2. For the purposes of preservation of favourable sanitary and ecological conditions in order to organise prevention and treatment of human illnesses on lands of territories of treatment-health localities and resorts a sanitary protection (or mining-sanitary) district shall be established in accordance with legislation. The boundaries and regime of sanitary (or mining-sanitary) protection areas of resorts having federal significance shall be established by the Government of the Russian Federation.

3. Land plots within the boundaries of sanitary zones shall not be seized or purchased from owners of land plots, landusers, land possessors, and lessees of land plots, except for instances when in accordance with the established sanitary regime the complete removal of these land plots from turnover (first zone of sanitary (mining-sanitary) protection of treatment-health localities and resorts) is provided for. Land plots in private ownership shall be subject to purchase from their owners in accordance with Article 55 of the present Code. The use of land plots within the boundaries of second and third zones of sanitary (sanitary-mining) protection shall be limited in accordance with legislation concerning specially-protected nature territories.

Article 97. Lands of Nature-Protection Designation

1. To lands of nature protection designation shall be relegated lands of:
(1) water protection zones of rivers and reservoirs;
(2) prohibited and spawning protection belts;
(3) forests fulfilling defensive functions;
(4) anti-erosion, pasture-defensive, and field-defensive plantings;
(5) other lands fulfilling nature-protection functions.

2. Limited economic activity shall be permitted on lands of nature-protection designation in compliance with the established regime for the protection of these lands in accordance with federal laws, laws of subjects of the Russian Federation, and normative legal acts of agencies of local self-government.

3. Juridical persons in whose interests land plots are allocated with special conditions of use shall be obliged to designate the boundaries thereof with special information marks.

4. Within the limits of lands of nature protection designation shall be introduced a special legal regime of use for lands limiting or prohibiting types of activity which are incompatible with the principal designation of these lands. Land plots within the limits of these lands shall not be seized nor purchased from owners of land plots, landusers, land possessors, and lessees of land plots.

5. In instances provided for by federal laws on native small peoples territories may be formed for traditional nature-use of native small peoples at sites of traditional habitation and economic activity of native small peoples of the Russian Federation and ethnic communities. The procedure for nature use on the said territories shall be established by federal laws, and the boundaries thereof shall be determined by the Government of the Russian Federation.

Article 98. Lands of Recreational Designation

1. To lands of recreational designation shall be relegated lands intended and used for the organisation of leisure, tourism, physical culture-health and sport activity of citizens.

2. Within the composition of lands of recreational designation shall be land plots on which houses of leisure, boarding houses, camping, objects of physical culture and sport, tourist bases, permanent and tent tourist-health camps, houses for fishermen and hunters, children's tourist stations, tourist parks, forest parks, instructional-tourist paths and lanes, children's and sport camps, and other analogous objects are situated.

3. The use of instructional-tourist paths and lanes established by agreement with the owners of land plots, landusers, land possessors, and lessees of land plots may be effectuated on the basis of servitudes, the said land plots not being removed from use.

4. To lands of recreational designation also shall be relegated lands of suburban green zones.

5. Activity shall be prohibited on lands of recreational designation which does not correspond to the special-purpose designation thereof.

Article 99. Lands of Historico-Cultural Designation

1. To lands of historico-cultural designation shall be relegated lands of:
(1) objects of cultural heritage of peoples of the Russian Federation (of monuments of history and culture), including objects of archaeological heritage;
(2) remarkable sites, including sites of historical trades, production sites, and crafts;

(3) military and civil burials.

2. Lands of historico-cultural designation shall be used strictly in accordance with their special-purpose designation.

The seizure of lands of historico-cultural designation and activity not corresponding to the special-purpose designation thereof shall not be permitted.

3. Land plots relegated to lands of historico-cultural designation shall not be seized from the owners of land plots, landusers, land possessors, and lessees of land plots, except for instances established by legislation.

Any economic activity may be prohibited on individual lands of historico-cultural designation, including lands of objects of historico-cultural heritage subject to research and closing down.

4. For the purposes of preservation of the historical, landscape, and urban construction milieu in accordance with federal laws and laws of subjects of the Russian Federation zones for the protection of objects of cultural heritage shall be established. Within the limits of lands of historico-cultural designation beyond the limits of lands of the last a special legal regime shall be introduced for the use of lands prohibiting activity incompatible with the principal designation of these lands. The use of land plots not relegated to lands of historico-cultural designation and located within the said protection zones shall be determined by rules of land use and building in accordance with the requirements for protection of monuments of history and culture.

Article 100. Especially Valuable Lands

1. To especially valuable lands shall be relegated lands within whose limits there are nature objects and objects of cultural heritage representing special scientific, historico-cultural value (typical or rare landscapes, cultural landscapes, communities of flora and fauna organisms, rare geological formations, land plots intended for the effectuation of the activity of scientific research organisations).

2. On the owners of such land plots, landusers, land possessors, and lessees of such land plots shall be placed duties with regard to their preservation. Information concerning especially valuable lands must be specified in documents of the State land cadastre, documents of State registration of the rights to immoveable property and transactions therewith,and other documents certifying rights to land.

Chapter XVIII. Forestry Fund Lands, Water Fund Lands, and Reserve Lands

Article 101. Forestry Fund Lands

1. To forestry fund lands shall be relegated forest lands (or lands covered by forest growth and no covered by it but intended for the restoration thereof—

fellings, ashes, clearings, glades, and others) and non-forest lands intended for the conducting of forestry (cuttings, roads, swamps, and others).

2. The boundaries of forestry fund lands shall be determined by means of demarcating the forestry fund lands from lands of other categories in accordance with the materials of forest tenure. Data concerning the boundaries of forestry fund lands shall be entered in the State land cadastre.

3. The withdrawal of lands occupied by first-group forests for State or municipal needs shall be permitted only in exceptional instances provided for by Article 49(1) and (2) of the present Code.

4. The transfer of forest fund lands to lands of other categories shall be effectuated in accordance with Article 8(1)(1) of the present Code, taking into account the requirements of protection of the environment established by federal laws.

5. Nonforest lands of the forest fund temporarily not used for conducting forestry may on the basis of a decision of the executive agency of State power provided for by Article 29 of the present Code be transferred on lease for a period of up to five years in order to effectuate agricultural production. The conditions of use of such lands and limitations on the use thereof shall be established by contracts of lease of land plots.

6. The procedure for the use and protection of forestry fund lands shall be regulated by the present Code and forestry legislation.

Article 102. Water Fund Lands

1. To water fund lands shall be relegated lands occupied by water objects, lands of water protection zones of water objects, and also lands allocated for the establishment of land strips and protection zones for water barriers, hydro-engineering installations, and other water conservancy installations and objects.

2. Water fund lands may be used for the construction and operation of installations ensuring the satisfaction of requirements of the population for potable water, domestic, recreational, and other requirements of the population, and also for water conservancy, agricultural, nature protection, industrial, fishery, electric power, transport, and other State or municipal needs in compliance with established requirements.

3. Protection zones shall be established in order to protect sources of potable and economic-domestic water supply, within the limits of which a special legal regime shall be introduced for the use of lands.

4. The procedure for the use and protection of water fund lands shall be determined by the present Code and by water legislation.

Article 103. Reserve Lands

1. Lands in State or municipal ownership and not granted to citizens or juridical persons, except for lands of the fund for the redistribution of lands formed in accordance with Article 80 of the present Code, shall be relegated to reserve lands.

2. The use of reserve lands shall be permitted after the transfer thereof to another category.

FEDERAL LAW ON INTRODUCTION INTO OPERATION OF THE LAND CODE OF THE RUSSIAN FEDERATION

[Federal Law No. 137-ФЗ, 25 October 2001.
СЗ РФ (2001), no. 44, item 4148]

Article 1. The Land Code of the Russian Federation shall be introduced into operation from the day of official publication thereof.

Article 2.

1. In the event of the sale in accordance with the rules established by Article 36 of the Land Code of the Russian Federation of land plots in State or municipal ownership to the owners of buildings, structures, and installations located thereon, the value of such land plots shall be determined in the procedure established by points 2 and 3 of the present Article.

2. The price of land shall be established by a subject of the Russian Federation in settlements with a population:

exceeding 3 million persons in an amount from five up to thirty times the rate of land tax per unit of land plot space;

from 500,000 up to 3 million persons in an amount of from five up to seventeen times the rate of land tax per unit of land plot space;

up to 500,000 persons, and also beyond the limits of the boundaries of settlements, in an amount of from three up to ten times the rate of land tax per unit of land plot space (at the beginning of the current calendar year).

The respective minimum rate of land tax shall be applied until the establishment of the price of land by the subject of the Russian Federation.

3. In the event of the sale of a land plot to the value thereof shall be applied a corrective coefficient taking into account the basic type of use of the buildings, structures, and installations located on the land plot. The corrective coefficients taking into account the basic types of use shall be confirmed by the Government of the Russian Federation in an amount of from 0.7 up to 1.3.

Article 3.

1. Rights to land not provided for by Articles 15, 20–24 of the Land Code of the Russian Federation shall be subject to reformalisation from the day of introduction of the Land Code of the Russian Federation into operation.

2. Juridical persons, except for juridical persons specified in Article 20(1) of the Land Code of the Russian Federation, shall be obliged to reformalise the right of permanent (or in perpetuity) use of land plots for the right of lease of land plots or to acquire the land plots in ownership at their wish before 1 January 2004 in accordance with the rules of Article 36 of the Land Code of the Russian Federation. The lease payment for the use of the said land plots shall be established in accordance with a decision of the Government of the Russian Federation.

In so doing the amount of least payment for use of land plots in State or municipal ownership and occupied by transport systems of natural monopolies may not be higher than the amounts of land tax rates established for lands of industry, electric power, transport, communications, radiobroadcasting, television, information, and lands for ensuring outer space activity, lands of defence and security, and lands of other special designation.

In the event of the sale of buildings, structures, and installations located in land plots granted to juridical persons (except for juridical persons specified in Article 20(1) of the Land Code of the Russian Federation) by right of permanent (or in perpetuity) use, the right of permanent (or in perpetuity) use of the land plots shall be subject to reformalisation into the right of lease of land plots or the land plots must be acquired in ownership in accordance with the provisions of the Land Code of the Russian Federation, at the choice of the purchaser of the buildings, structures, and installations.

3. The granting in ownership to citizens of land plots previously granted to them in permanent (or in perpetuity) use or inheritable possession for life shall not be limited by a period in the instances established by land legislation.

4. Citizens of the Russian Federation having in actual use land plots with dwelling houses situated on them which were acquired by them as a result of transactions which were concluded before the entry into force of the Law of the USSR of 6 March 1990, No. 1305-I 'On Ownership in the USSR', but which were not duly formalised and registered shall have the right to register the right of ownership to the said land plots in accordance with the rules established by Article 20 of the Land Code of the Russian Federation.

5. Until the established of the List of frontier territories by the President of the Russian Federation specified in Article 15(3) of the Land Code of the Russian Federation, the granting of land plots located on the said territories to the

ownership of foreign citizens, stateless persons, and foreign juridical persons shall not be permitted.

6. The contribution of the right of permanent (or in perpetuity) use of land plots to the charter (or contributed) capital of commercial organisations shall not be permitted. Commercial and noncommercial organisations may reformalise their right of permanent (or in perpetuity) use of land plots into another right, including the right of lease of land plots, in the procedure established by federal laws.

7. From the day of introduction into operation of the Land Code of the Russian Federation the privatisation of buildings, structures, and installations, including buildings, structures, and installations of industrial designation, without simultaneous privatisation of land plots on which they are located, shall not be permitted except for instances when such land plots have been removed from turnover or limited in turnover.

8. From the day of introduction into operation of the Land Code of the Russian Federation the land plots in State or municipal ownership and in permanent (or in perpetuity) use shall be granted only in the instances established by Article 20(1) of the Land Code of the Russian Federation.

9. State acts, certificates, and other documents certifying the rights to land and issued to citizens or juridical persons before the introduction into operation of the Federal Law 'On State Registration of Rights to Immoveable Property and Transactions Therewith' shall have equal legal force with entries in the Unified State Register of Rights to Immoveable Property and Transactions Therewith.

Certificates concerning the right of ownership to land according to the form confirmed by Edict of the President of the Russian Federation of 27 October 1993, No. 1767, 'On the Regulation of Land Relations and Development of Agrarian Reform in Russia' shall be deemed to be valid and shall have equal legal force with entries in the Unified State Register of Rights to Immoveable Property and Transactions Therewith issued after the introduction into operation of the Federal Law of 21 July 1997, No. 122-ФЗ 'On State Registration of Rights to Immoveable Property and Transactions Therewith' until the commencement of the issue of certificates on State registration of rights according to the form confirmed by Decree of the Government of the Russian Federation of 18 February 1998, No. 219 'On Confirmation of the Rules for Keeping the Unified State Register of Rights to Immoveable Property and Transactions Therewith', and also State acts concerning the right to inheritable possession of land plots for life and the right of permanent (or in perpetuity) use of land plots, according to the forms confirmed by Decree of the Council of Ministers of the RSFSR of 17 September 1991, No. 493 'On Confirmation of the Forms of State Act for the Right of Ownership in Land, Inheritable Possession for Life, and in Perpetuity (or

Permanent) Use of Land', and certificates concerning the right of ownership to land according to the form confirmed by Decree of the Government of the Russian Federation of 19 March 1992, No. 177 'On Confirmation of the Forms of Certificate Concerning the Right of Ownership in Land, Contract of Lease of Lands of Agricultural Designation, and Contract of Temporary Use of Lands of Agricultural Designation'.

10. Until the demarcation of State ownership to land, State registration of the right of State ownership to land in order to effectuate the disposition of lands in State ownership shall not be required.

The disposition of the said lands before the demarcation of State ownership to land shall be effectuated by agencies of local self-government within the limits of their powers unless provided otherwise by legislation.

The procedure for the disposition of the said lands before demarcation of State ownership to land may be determined by the Government of the Russian Federation.

11. From the day of introduction into operation of the Land Code of the Russian Federation all lands situated on the day of introduction into operation of the Land Code of the Russian Federation in funds for the redistribution of lands formed in accordance with the Edict of the President of the Russian Federation of 27 December 1991, No. 323 'On Urgent Measures With Regard to Effectuation of Land Reform in the RSFSR' shall be included in the fund for the redistribution of lands.

12. The right of permanent (or in perpetuity) use of land plots granted to landusers before the introduction into operation of the Land Code of the Russian Federation shall correspond to the permanent (or in perpetuity) use of land plots provided for by the Land Code of the Russian Federation.

13. In instances when the cadastre value of land has not been determined for the purposes specified in Article 65 of the Land Code of the Russian Federation the normative price of theland shall apply.

Note. For the purposes of the present Article the reformalisation of the right to a land plot shall include:

filing an application by a juridical person concerning the granting of a land plot to it for the respective right when reformalising this right in accordance with the present Article or filing an application by a juridical person concerning the granting of a land plot to it for the right provided for by Articles 15 or 22 of the Land Code of the Russian Federation when reformalising this right in accordance with points 2 and 5 of the present Article;

adoption of a decision by the executive agency of State power or agency of local self-government provided for by Article 29 of the Land Code of the Russian Federation concerning the granting of the land plot for the respective right;

147

State registration of the right in accordance with the Federal Law 'On State Registration of Rights to Immoveable Property and Transactions Therewith'.

Article 4.

1. There shall be deemed to have lost force:

Land Code of the RSFSR (Ведомости Съезда народных депутатов РСФСР и Верховного Совета РСФСР (1991), no. 22, item 768);

Decree of the Supreme Soviet of the RSFSR, 25 April 1991, No. 1103/1-I 'On the Introduction of the Land Code of the RSFSR into Operation' (Ведомости Съезда народных депутатов РСФСР и Верховного Совета РСФСР (1991), no. 22, item 769);

Law of the RSFSR of 23 November 1990, No. 374-I 'On Land Reform' (Ведомости Съезда народных депутатов РСФСР и Верховного Совета РСФСР (1990), no. 26, item 327);

Decree of the Supreme Soviet of the RSFSR of 23 November 1990, No. 375-I 'On the Introduction into Operation of the Law of the RSFSR "On Land Reform"' (Ведомости Съезда народных депутатов РСФСР и Верховного Совета РСФСР (1990), no. 26, item 328);

Law of the RSFSR of 27 December 1990, No. 460-I 'On Changes of the Law of the RSFSR "On Land Reform" in Connection with the Adoption of the Decree of the Congress of People's Deputies of the RSFSR "On the Programme for the Renaissance of the Russian Village and Development of the Agro-Industrial Complex" and the Law of the RSFSR "On Changes in and Additions to the Constitution (Basic Law) of the RSFSR" (Ведомости Съезда народных депутатов РСФСР и Верховного Совета РСФСР (1991), no. 1, item 4);

Article 8 of the Law of the Russian Federation of 24 June 1992, No. 3119-I 'On Making Changes in and Additions to the Civil Code of the RSFSR, Code of Civil Procedure of the RSFSR, Reglament of the Supreme Soviet of the RSFSR, Laws of the RSFSR "On the Jewish Autonomous Region", "On Elections of People's Deputies of the RSFSR", "On Additional Powers of Local Soviets of People's Deputies in Conditions of Transition to Market Relations", "On Peasant (or Farmer) Economy", "On Land Reform", "On Banks and Banking Activity in the RSFSR", "On the Central Bank of the RSFSR (Bank of Russia)", "On Ownership in the RSFSR", "On Enterprises and Entrepreneurial Activity", "On the State Tax Service of the RSFSR", "On Competition and Limitation of Monopolist Activity on the Goods Markets"; "On Priority Provision of the Agro-Industrial Complex with Material-Technical Resources", "On Local Self-Government in the RSFSR", "On Privatisation of State and Municipal Enterprises in the RSFSR", "On the Foundations of the Budget Structure and Budgetary Process in the RSFSR", "On State Duty", laws of the Russian Federation "On the Territory and Regional Soviet of People's Deputies and Territory and Regional Administration", "On Goods Exchanges and Exchange Trade"' (Ведомости Съезда народных депутатов РСФСР и Верховного Совета РСФСР (1992), no. 34, item 1966);

Law of the Russian Federation of 20 November 1992, No. 3936-I 'On Making Changes in Article 7 of the Law of the RSFSR "On Land Reform" ' (Ведомости Съезда народных депутатов Российской Федерации и Верховного Совета Российской Федерации (1992), no. 50, item 2962);

Law of the Russian Federation of 23 December 1992, No. 4196-I 'On the Right of Citizens of the Russian Federation to Receive in Private Ownership and to Sell Land Plots for Conducting Personal Subsidiary Husbandry and Dacha Economy, Gardening, and Individual Housing Construction' (Ведомости Съезда народных депутатов Российской Федерации и Верховного Совета Российской Федерации (1993), no. 1, item 26);

Decree of the Supreme Soviet of the Russian Federation of 23 December 1992, No. 4197-I 'On the Procedure for the Introduction into Operation of the Law of the Russian Federation "On the Right of Citizens of the Russian Federation to Receive in Private Ownership and to Sell Land Plots for Conducting Personal Subsidiary Husbandry and Dacha Economy, Gardening, and Individual Housing Construction" ' (Ведомости Съезда народных депутатов Российской Федерации и Верховного Совета Российской Федерации (1993), no. 1, item 27);

Articles 3 and 5 of the Law of the Russian Federation of 28 April 1993, No. 4888-I 'On Making Changes in and Additions to Certain Legislative Acts in Connection with the Adoption of the Law of the RSFSR "On Payment for Land" and Tax Legislation of Russia' (Ведомости Съезда народных депутатов Российской Федерации и Верховного Совета Российской Федерации (1993), no. 21, item 748).

2. The President of the Russian Federation and Government of the Russian Federation shall within a three-month period bring their normative legal acts and treaties concluded with subjects of the Russian Federation into conformity with the Land Code of the Russian Federation.

Article 5. From the day of introduction of the Land Code of the Russian Federation into operation, legislative acts of the USSR containing norms of land law and operating on the territory of the Russian Federation shall not be applied.

Article 6. Normative legal acts of the President of the Russian Federation and normative legal acts of the Government of the Russian Federation issued before the introduction into operation of the Land Code of the Russian Federation and regulating land relations shall apply in the part not contrary to the Land Code of the Russian Federation.

Article 7. To land relations which arose before the introduction into operation of the Land Code of the Russian Federation the Land Code of the Russian

Federation shall apply with respect to those rights and duties which arise after the introduction thereof into operation, except for instances provided for by the present Federal Law.

Article 8. Until the introduction into operation of the federal law on the turnover of lands of agricultural designation, the turnover of land plots of agricultural designation shall be effectuated in accordance with civil legislation and the Land Code of the Russian Federation, taking into account forestry legislation, legislation on the protection of the environment, special federal laws containing norms of land law concerning the particular category of lands, and also taking into account the following provisions:

in the event of the transfer of the right in a land plot from one owner of the land plot, landuser, land possessor, and lessee of the land plot to another category, and the special-purpose designation of such land plot is not subject to change;

foreign citizens, stateless persons, and foreign juridical persons may possess and use land plots of agricultural designation only by right of the lease thereof;

the privatisation of land plots of agricultural designation in State or municipal ownership shall not be permitted.

Article 9. Until the introduction into operation of the federal law on turnover of lands of agricultural designation, subjects of the Russian Federation, the turnover of lands in which before the introduction into operation of the Land Code of the Russian Federation was regulated by respective laws of the said subjects of the Russian Federation, shall continue to effectuate the turnover of lands of agricultural designation in accordance with laws of the said subjects of the Russian Federation.

FEDERAL LAW ON THE TURNOVER OF LANDS OF AGRICULTURAL DESIGNATION

[Federal Law No. 101-ФЗ, 24 July 2002.
СЗ РФ (2002), no. 30, item 3018]

Chapter I	General Provisions	151
Chapter II	Peculiarities of Turnover of Land Plots from Lands of Agricultural Designation	156
Chapter III	Peculiarities of Turnover of Participatory Shares in Right of Common Ownership to Land Plots from Lands of Agricultural Designation	159
Chapter IV	Transitional and Concluding Provisions	162

Chapter I. General Provisions

Article 1. Sphere of Operation of Present Federal Law

1. The present Federal Law shall regulate relations connected with the possession, use, and disposition of land plots from lands of agricultural designation, establish the rules and limitations applicable to the turnover of land plots and participatory shares in the right of common ownership to land plots from lands of agricultural designation—to transactions, the result of the conclusion of which is the arising or termination of rights to land plots from lands of agricultural designation and participatory shares in the right of common ownership to land plots from lands of agricultural designation, determines the conditions for granting land plots from lands of agricultural designation in State or municipal ownership, and also the seizure thereof to State or municipal ownership.

The operation of the present Federal Law shall not extend to land plots granted from lands of agricultural designation to citizens for individual housing and garage construction, conducting of personal subsidiary and dacha husbandry, gardening, livestock and market-gardening, and also land plots occupied by buildings, structures, and installations. Turnover of the said land plots shall be regulated by the Land Code of the Russian Federation.

2. The legal regulation of relations in the domain of the turnover of land plots and participatory shares in the right of common ownership to land plots from

lands of agricultural designation shall be effectuated by the Constitution of the Russian Federation, Land Code of the Russian Federation, Civil Code of the Russian Federation, the present Federal Law, other federal laws, and also other normative legal acts of the Russian Federation adopted in accordance therewith, and laws of subjects of the Russian Federation.

3. Turnover of lands of agricultural designation shall be based on the following principles:

(1) preservation of the special-purpose use of land plots;

(2) establishment of the dimensions of the total space of land plots of agricultural tracts which are located on the territory of one administrative-territorial formation of a subject of the Russian Federation and may simultaneously be in the ownership of a citizen, close relatives thereof, and also juridical persons in which the said citizen or close relatives thereof have the right to dispose of more than 50% of the total quantity of votes due to the stocks or contributions (or participatory shares) comprising the charter (or contributed) capital of the said juridical persons;

(3) preferential right of a subject of the Russian Federation or, in instances established by a law of a subject of the Russian Federation or agency of local self-government, for the purchase of a land plot from lands of agricultural designation in the event of the sale thereof, except for instances of sale by public sale;

(4) preferential right of a subject of the Russian Federation or, in instances established by a law of a subject of the Russian Federation and agency of local self-government, to purchase a participatory share in the right of common ownership to a land plot from lands of agricultural designation in the event of the compensated alienation of such participatory share by a participant of the participatory share ownership if the other participants of the participatory ownership refuse to purchase such participatory share or do not declare an intention to acquire such participatory share in the right of common ownership to a land plot from lands of agricultural designation;

(5) establishment of the peculiarities of granting land plots from lands of agricultural designation to foreign citizens, foreign juridical persons, stateless persons, and also juridical persons in the charter (or contributed) capital of which the participatory share of foreign citizens, foreign juridical persons, and stateless persons comprises more than 50%;

(6) granting to citizens and juridical persons in ownership land plots from lands of agricultural designation in State or municipal ownership on a compensated or uncompensated basis in the instances established by federal laws.

4. The privatisation of land plots from lands of agricultural designation in State or municipal ownership shall be effectuated in the procedure established by the present Federal Law, Land Code of the Russian Federation, and other federal laws. Privatisation of the said land plots located on the territory of a subject of the

Russian Federation shall be effectuated from the moment established by a law of the subject of the Russian Federation.

Land plots from lands of agricultural designation occupied by reindeer pastures in areas of the Far North and pasturing pastures in State or municipal ownership shall not be subject to privatisation.

5. The adoption by subjects of the Russian Federation of laws and other normative legal acts containing additional rules and limitations on the turnover of land plots from lands of agricultural designation shall not be permitted.

6. Norms of other federal laws shall apply to relations arising when using land plots from lands of agricultural designation in accordance with their special-purpose designation and requirements for the protection of land in the part not regulated by the present Federal Law.

Article 2. Participants of Relations Regulated by Present Federal Law

1. Citizens, juridical persons, the Russian Federation, subjects of the Russian Federation, and municipal formations shall be participants of relations regulated by the present Federal Law.

2. Rights of foreign citizens, foreign juridical persons, stateless persons, and also juridical persons in the charter (or contributed) capital of which the participatory share of foreign citizens, foreign juridical persons, and stateless persons comprises more than 50% to land plots from lands of agricultural designation shall be determined in accordance with the present Federal Law.

Article 3. Right of Foreign Citizens, Foreign Juridical Persons, Stateless Persons, and also Juridical Persons in the Charter (or Contributed) Capital of Which the Participatory Share of Foreign Citizens, Foreign Juridical Persons, and Stateless Persons Comprises More than 50% to Land Plots from Lands of Agricultural Designation

Foreign citizens, foreign juridical persons, and stateless persons, and also juridical persons in the charter (or contributed) capital of which the participatory share of foreign citizens, foreign juridical persons, and stateless persons comprises more than 50% may possess land plots from lands of agricultural designation only by right of lease.

Article 4. Maximum Dimensions and Requirements for Positioning Land plots from Lands of Agricultural Designation

1. The minimum dimensions of land plots from lands of agricultural designation may be established by laws of subjects of the Russian Federation in accordance with the requirements of legislation of the Russian Federation on land tenure.

The conclusion of transactions for land plots from lands of agricultural designation, if as a result of such transactions new land plots are formed the dimensions and positioning of which do not correspond to the requirements established by the present Article, shall not be permitted.

The apportionment of a land plot at the expense of a participatory share(s) in the right of common ownership to a land plot from the composition of artificially irrigated agricultural fields, if the dimensions of the land plot apportioned in kind (on the spot) are smaller than the maximum minimum dimension of a land plot for soil conservation lands established by subjects of the Russian Federation in accordance with the requirements of legislation of the Russian Federation on land tenure shall not be permitted.

2. The dimensions of total space of land plots of agricultural tracts which are located on the territory of a single administrative-territorial formation of a subject of the Russian Federation also may be simultaneously situated in the ownership of a citizen, close relatives thereof, and also juridical persons to which the said citizen or close relatives thereof have the right to dispose of more than 50% of the total quantity of votes due to stocks (or contributions, participatory shares) comprising the charter (or contributed) capital of the said juridical persons shall be established by a law of a subject of the Russian Federation.

The dimensions of total space of such land plots of agricultural tracts may not be less than 10% of the total space of agricultural tracts within the boundaries of a single administrative-territorial formation.

Article 5. Duty of Person to Alienate Land Plot from Lands of Agricultural Designation or Participatory Share in Right of Common Ownership to Land Plot from Lands of Agricultural Designation Which May Not Belong Thereto by Right of Ownership

1. If a land plot from lands of agricultural designation or a participatory share in the right of common ownership to a land plot from lands of agricultural designation turns out to be in the ownership of a person on grounds permitted by a law and this entails a violation of the requirements of Articles 3 and 4 of the present Federal Law, such land plot or participatory share must be alienated by the owner. The alienation of a land plot or participatory share in the right of common ownership to a land plot from lands of agricultural designation acquired before the entry of the present Federal Law into force must be effectuated within a year from the day of entry into force of the present Federal Law. Land plots or participatory shares in the right of common ownership to a land plot from lands of agricultural designation acquired after the entry into force of the present Federal Law shall be subject to alienation within a year from the day the right of ownership arises in these land plots or participatory share in the right of common ownership to the land plot or within a year from the day when the owner knew or was obliged to know about the circumstances which entailed a violation of the requirements of Article 3 of the present Federal Law.

If in the event of a violation of the requirements of Article 4 of the present Federal Law the owner does not within the period established by the present point alienate the land plot or participatory share in the right of common ownership to the land plot from lands of agricultural designation, a justice institution effectuating the State registration of rights to immoveable property and transactions therewith shall be obliged in written form to notify the agency of State power of the subject of the Russian Federation thereof.

2. The agency of State power of a subject of the Russian Federation within a month from the day when the violation of the requirements of Articles 3 and 4 of the present Federal Law become known to it shall be obliged to apply to a court concerning the compelling of such owner to sell the land plot or participatory share in common ownership of a land plot from lands of agricultural designation at a public sale (or competition, auction).

3. In the absence of a person who has expressed a wish to acquire the land plot or participatory share in the right of common ownership to a land plot from lands of agricultural designation, this land plot or participatory share must be acquired by the subject of the Russian Federation or in the instances established by a law of the subject of the Russian Federation, agency of local self-government, at the starting price of the subject of public sale.

Article 6. Compulsory Seizure and Termination of Rights to Land Plots from Lands of Agricultural Designation

1. Owners of land plots, land users, land possessors, and lessees of land plots from lands of agricultural designation shall be obliged to use the said land plots in accordance with the special-purpose designation of the particular category of lands and authorised use by means which must not cause harm to the land as a nature object, including lead to the degradation, pollution, and littering of land, poisoning, spoilage, and destruction of the fertile stratum of the soil, and other negative (or harmful) impacts of economic activity.

Determination of the extent of harm caused to the environment, including land as a nature object, shall be effectuated on the basis of normative standards in the domain of environmental protection in accordance with the Federal Law of 10 January 2002, No. 7-ФЗ, 'On Protection of the Environment'.

2. The right of permanent (or in perpetuity) use, right of inheritable possession for life, and right of uncompensated fixed-term use of a land plot from lands of agricultural designation may be terminated compulsorily on the grounds and in the procedure which have been established by the Land Code of the Russian Federation. The lease of a land plot from lands of agricultural designation may be compulsorily terminated in accordance with the requirements of the Land Code of the Russian Federation and Civil Code of the Russian Federation.

3. A land plot from lands of agricultural designation may be seized compulsorily from its owners in a judicial proceeding in the event of improper use. Instances of improper use of the land plot from lands of agricultural designation shall be determined in accordance with the Land Code of the Russian Federation.

An application to a court concerning compulsory seizure from the owner of a land plot from lands of agricultural designation shall be sent by the agency of State power of the subject of the Russian Federation or in instances established by a law of the subject of the Russian Federation or agency of local self-government in the event of the improper use thereof which entailed the causing of harm to the environment, including land as a nature object. The application to the court shall be sent according to the rules established by the Land Code of the Russian Federation for compulsory termination of rights to a land plot of a person who is not the owner thereof in view of the improper use of the land plot.

Article 7. Pledge of Land Plots from Lands of Agricultural Designation

The pledge of land plots from lands of agricultural designation shall be effectuated in accordance with the Federal Law of 16 July 1998, No. 102-ФЗ 'On the Mortgage (or Pledge) of an Immoveable'.

Chapter II. Peculiarities of Turnover of Land Plots from Lands of Agricultural Designation

Article 8. Purchase-Sale of Land Plot from Lands of Agricultural Designation

1. In the event of the sale of a land plot from lands of agricultural designation a subject of the Russian Federation, or in instances established by a law of the subject of the Russian Federation, agency of local self-government, shall have the preferential right to purchase such land plot at the price for which it is sold, except for sale at a public sale.

2. The seller of a land plot from lands of agricultural designation shall be obliged to notify in written form the highest executive agency of State power of the subject of the Russian Federation or in instances established by law of the subject of the Russian Federation, agency of local self-government, about the intention to sell the land plot, specifying the price and other material conditions of the contract.

The notice shall be handed over under receipt or sent by registered letter with notification of handing over.

3. If a subject of the Russian Federation or in instances established by a law of a subject of the Russian Federation, an agency of local self-government, refuses to purchase or does not inform the seller of an intention to acquire a land plot being sold within a month from the day of receipt of the notice, the seller shall have the

right within a year to sell the land plot to a third person at a price not lower than the price specified in the notice. The running of the said period shall commence from the day of receipt of the notice at the highest executive agency of State power of the subject of the Russian Federation or, in instances established by a law of a subject of the Russian Federation, agency of local self-government.

In the event of the sale of a land plot at a price not lower than the price previously declared or with a change of other material conditions of the contract, the seller shall be obliged to send a new notice according to the rules established by the present Article.

4. In the event of the sale of a land plot with a violation of the preferential right of purchase, the subject of the Russian Federation or, in instances established by a law of the subject of the Russian Federation, agency of local self-government, shall have the right within a year from the moment of State registration of the transfer of right of ownership to demand the transfer to it in a judicial proceeding of the rights and duties of the purchaser.

Article 9. Lease of Land Plots from Lands of Agricultural Designation

1. Land plots from lands of agricultural designation which have undergone State cadastre recording, including land plots in participatory ownership, may be transferred on lease.

2. In the event of the transfer on lease of a land plot from lands of agricultural designation in participatory share ownership, the contract of lease of the land plot shall be concluded either with the participants of participatory share ownership or with one of them acting on the basis of a power of attorney issued to him by the other participants of participatory share ownership.

3. The contract of lease of a land plot from lands of agricultural designation may be concluded for a period not exceeding forty-nine years.

A contract of lease concluded for a period exceeding the maximum period established by the present Federal Law shall be considered to be concluded for the period equal to the maximum period.

4. It may be provided in a contract of lease of a land plot from lands of agricultural designation that the leased land plot shall be transferred to the ownership of the lessee upon the expiry of the period of lease or before the expiry thereof on condition of the lessee paying the entire purchase price stipulated by the contract, taking into account the peculiarities established by Articles 8 and 10 of the present Federal Law.

5. Unless provided otherwise by a law or by the contract of lease, the lessee who has duly performed his duties shall upon the expiry of the period of the contract of lease have all conditions being equal a preferential right to conclude a contract of lease for a new period.

6. The space of land plots from lands of agricultural designation which may be on lease to one lessee simultaneously shall not be limited.

7. Economic incentive for a person using land plots from lands of agricultural designation on the basis of a contract of lease concluded for a period of not less than ten years shall be effectuated in the procedure established by budget legislation and legislation on taxes and charges.

Article 10. Granting in Ownership or on Lease to Citizens and Juridical Persons Land Plots from Lands of Agricultural Designation in State or Municipal Ownership

1. Land plots from lands of agricultural designation in State or municipal ownership shall be granted to citizens and juridical persons in ownership at public sales (or competitions, auctions).

The rule of the present point shall not extend to instances provided for by point 4 of the present Article.

2. The transfer on lease of land plots from lands of agricultural designation in State or municipal ownership shall be effectuated in the procedure established by Article 34 of the Land Code of the Russian Federation if there is only one application concerning the transfer on land plots from lands of agricultural designation on lease on condition of the prior publication in good time of a communication concerning the existence of land plots proposed for such transfer in the mass media determined by the subject of the Russian Federation. In so doing the adoption of the decision concerning the transfer of land plots on lease shall be permitted on condition that within a month from the moment of publication of the notification another application has not been received. The provisions of the present point shall not extend to instances provided for by point 5 of the present Article.

If two or more applications were filed concerning the transfer of land plots from lands of agricultural designation on lease, such land plots shall be granted on lease at a public sale (or competition, auction).

3. The organisation and conducting of a public sale (or competition, auction) for the sale of land plots from lands of agricultural designation, and also the right to conclude contracts of lease of such land plots, shall be effectuated in accordance with Article 38 of the Land Code of the Russian Federation.

4. A land plot transferred on lease to a citizen or juridical person may be acquired in ownership by the lessee at the market value thereof upon the expiry of three years from the moment of conclusion of the contract of lease on condition of proper use of such land plot.

The decision concerning the granting of a land plot in ownership must be adopted within a two-week period from the day of filing the application in written form at the executive agency of State owner or agency of local self-government possessing the right to grant the respective land plots within the limits of their competence.

5. Land plots from lands of agricultural designation in State or municipal ownership may be transferred to religious organisations (or associations), cossack societies, scientific-research organisations of an agricultural profile, communities of native small peoples of the North, Siberia, and the Far East of the Russian Federation, and citizens for haying and pasturing of livestock on lease in the procedure established by Article 34 of the Land Code of the Russian Federation.

In so doing the purchase of the leased land plot in ownership shall not be permitted.

6. Land plots from lands of agricultural designation occupied by reindeer pastures in areas of the Far North and pasturing pastures, and in State or municipal ownership, may be transferred to citizens and juridical persons only by right of lease.

Article 11. Inheriting of Land Plots from Lands of Agricultural Designation

If the acceptance of an inheritance has led to a violation of the requirements established by Articles 3 and 4 of the present Federal Law, the requirements established by Article 5 of the present Federal Law shall apply to the heirs.

Chapter III. Peculiarities of Turnover of Participatory Shares in Right of Common Ownership to Land Plots from Lands of Agricultural Designation

Article 12. Peculiarities of Conclusion of Transactions with Participatory Shares in Right of Common Ownership to Land Plots from Lands of Agricultural Designation

1. The rules of the Civil Code of the Russian Federation shall apply to transactions with participatory shares in the right of common ownership to land plots from lands of agricultural designation.

A participant of participatory share ownership shall have the right at his discretion to sell, give, exchange, bequeath, pledge, and contribute to the charter (or contributed) capital of a juridical person his participatory share or to dispose of it otherwise in compliance with the rules for compensated alienation thereof provided for by Article 250 of the Civil Code of the Russian Federation. A participant of participatory share ownership shall have the right to transfer the participatory share in the right of common ownership to a land plot from lands of agricultural designation on trust management.

If the participants of common ownership are more than five, the rules of the Civil Code of the Russian Federation shall be applied by taking into account the peculiarities established by the present Article, and also by Articles 13 and 14 of the present Federal Law.

2. A participant of participatory share ownership shall be obliged to notify in written form the other participants of participatory share ownership or to publish a communication in the mass media determined by the subject of the Russian Federation concerning the intention to sell the participatory share in the right of common ownership to a land plot from lands of agricultural designation to a third person.

If the other participants of participatory share ownership within a month from the moment of receipt of the notice in written form or publication of the said communication refuse to purchase the participatory share in the right of common ownership to the land plot from lands of agricultural designation or do not state an intention to acquire it, the seller shall be obliged to notify in written form the highest executive agency of State power of the subject of the Russian Federation or, in instances established by a law of the subject of the Russian Federation, the agency of local self-government, about the intention to sell the participatory share to the right of common ownership in land plots from lands of agricultural designation, specifying the price and other material conditions of the contract according to the rules established by Article 8 of the present Federal Law, irrespective of the quantity of participants of participatory share ownership.

If a subject of the Russian Federation or in instances established by a law of the subject of the Russian Federation, an agency of local self-government, refuses to purchase a participatory share in the right of common ownership to land plots from lands of agricultural designation or does not inform the seller about the intention to acquire it within a month from the moment of receipt of the notice in written form, the seller shall have the right within a year to sell the participatory share in the right of common ownership to a land plot from lands of agricultural designation to a third person at a price not lower than the price specified in the notice.

In order to sell a participatory share in the right of common ownership to a land plot from lands of agricultural designation at a price lower than the price previously declared or with a change of other material conditions of the contract, the seller shall be obliged to send a new notice in written form according to the rules established by Article 8 of the present Federal Law.

Article 13. Apportionment of Land Plots at Expense of Participatory Shares in Right of Common Ownership in Land Plots from Lands of Agricultural Designation

1. A participant of participatory share ownership shall have the right to demand the apportionment of a land plot at the expense of the participatory share in the right of common ownership to the land plot from lands of agricultural des-

ignation. In order to apportion the land plot at the expense of the participatory share in the right of common ownership in a land plot from lands of agricultural designation the participants of participatory share ownership shall be obliged to notify the intention to apportion the land plot at the expense of the participatory share in the right of common ownership to the land plot from lands of agricultural designation in written form the other participants of participatory share ownership or to publish a communication in the mass media determined by the subject of the Russian Federation, specifying the proposed positioning of the partitioned land plot and the amount of contributory compensation to the other participants of participatory share ownership in the instances established by the present Article.

The positioning of the apportioned land plot must correspond to the requirements established by Article 4(1) of the present Federal Law.

If the market value of the apportioned land plot calculated per unit of space thereof exceeds the market value of the others after the apportionment of the land plot calculated per unit of space thereof, the participant of participatory share ownership effectuating the right of apportionment of the land plot shall be obliged to pay contributory compensation to the other participants of participatory share ownership after the apportionment of the land plot.

The amount of contributory compensation shall be determined as the product of the space of the apportioned land plot and the difference in market value of the apportioned land plot and that of the land plot remaining after the apportionment calculated per unit of space thereof.

2. If within a month from the day of proper notification of participants of participatory share ownership or publication of the communication specified in point 1 of the present Article objections do not ensue from the participants of participatory share ownership, the proposal concerning the positioning of the land plot and amount of contributory compensation in the instances established by the present Article shall be considered to be agreed.

Disputes concerning the positioning of an apportioned land plot and the amount of contributory compensation shall be settled by the participants of participatory share ownership with the use of conciliatory procedures, the procedure for conducting which shall be established by the Government of the Russian Federation.

In the event of the failure to reach an agreed decision, disputes concerning the positioning of the apportioned land plot and the amount of contributory compensation shall be considered in a court.

3. The part of a land plot from lands of agricultural designation unused for two years and in participatory share ownership may be apportioned into an autonomous land plot by the subject of the Russian Federation or in the instances established by a law of the subject of the Russian Federation, agency of local self-government, according to the rules established by the present Article.

The subject of the Russian Federation or in the instances established by a law of the subject of the Russian Federation, agency of local self-government, shall have the right to send an application to a court concerning the recognition of the right of ownership of the subject of the Russian Federation or municipal formation to the said land plot if the participant(s) of participatory share ownership are unknown, or if the participant(s) of participatory share ownership are known, concerning termination of the right of ownership of the participant(s) of participatory share ownership to the participatory share in the right of common ownership to a land plot from lands of agricultural designation and recognition of the right of ownership of the subject of the Russian Federation or municipal formation to the said land plot.

Article 14. Peculiarities of Determination of Procedure of Possession and Use of Land Plot in Participatory Share Ownership

The decision concerning the procedure for the possession and use of a land plot in participatory share ownership shall be adopted by the general meeting of participants of participatory share ownership. Notification of the participants of participatory share ownership about a forthcoming meeting shall be conducted not less than a month in advance of the date of the conducting thereof in written form under receipt and/or by means of publication of a communication in the mass media determined by the subject of the Russian Federation. On condition of proper notification the general meeting of participants of participatory share ownership shall be considered to be empowered if not less than 20% of the participants of participatory share ownership are present at it. The decision shall be adopted by a majority of not less than two-thirds of the votes of the number of participants of participatory share ownership present at the meeting and shall be formalised by a protocol. The protocol shall be signed by all the participants of participatory share ownership present.

Chapter IV. Transitional and Concluding Provisions

Article 15. Concept of Land Participatory Share

A land participatory share received during privatisation of agricultural tracts before the entry into force of the present Federal Law shall be a participatory share in the right of common ownership to land plots from lands of agricultural designation.

Article 16. Regulation of Relations Connected with Contracts of Lease of Land Participatory Shares Concluded Before Entry into Force of Present Federal Law

1. Contracts of lease of land participatory shares concluded before the entry into force of the present Federal Law must be brought into conformity with the rules of the Civil Code of the Russian Federation and Article 9(2) of the present

Federal Law within two years from the day of entry into force of the present Federal Law.

2. If the contract of lease of land participatory shares specified in point 1 of the present Article within two years from the day of entry into force of the present Federal Law have not been brought into conformity with the Civil Code of the Russian Federation and Article 9(2) of the present Federal Law, the rules of contracts of trust management of property shall apply to such contracts. The registration of such contracts shall not be required.

Article 17. Determination on the Spot of Boundaries of Land Plots from Lands of Agricultural Designation in Common Ownership

The participants of participatory share ownership received in ownership in the event of privatisation of agricultural tracts shall be obliged to ensure the determination of the spot land plots in common ownership from lands of agricultural designation in accordance with the requirements of land tenure.

Article 18. Documents Certifying Right to Land Participatory Share

Certificates concerning the right to land participatory shares issued before the entry into force of the Federal Law of 21 July 1997, No. 122-ФЗ 'On State Registration of Rights to Immoveable Property and Transactions Therewith', and in the absence thereof, extracts from decisions of agencies of local self-government adopted before the entry into force of the said Federal Law concerning privatisation of agricultural tracts certifying the rights to a land participatory share, shall have equal legal force with entries in the Unified State Register of Rights to Immoveable Property and Transactions Therewith.

Article 19. Entry into Force of Present Federal Law

The present Federal Law shall enter into force six months after the official publication thereof.

Article 20. Bringing Normative Legal Acts into Conformity with Present Federal Law

1. The President of the Russian Federation and the Government of the Russian Federation shall bring their normative legal acts into conformity with the present Federal Law.

2. The Government of the Russian Federation shall within six months adopt normative legal acts ensuring the realisation of the present Federal Law.

ECONOMIC SOCIETIES AND PARTNERSHIPS

FEDERAL LAW ON LIMITED RESPONSIBILITY SOCIETIES

[Federal Law No. 14-ФЗ,
8 February 1998, as amended by Federal Law No. 96-ФЗ,
11 July 1998; Federal Law No. 193-ФЗ, 31 December 1998;
Federal Law No. 31-ФЗ, 21 March 2002.
СЗ РФ (1998), no. 7, item 785; no. 28, item 3261;
(1999), no. 1, item 2; (2002), no. 12, item 1093]

Chapter I   General Provisions   165
Chapter II   Founding of Society   171
Chapter III   Charter Capital of Society. Property of Society   174
Chapter IV   Management in Society   191
Chapter V   Reorganisation and Liquidation of Society   207
Chapter VI   Concluding Provisions   212

Chapter I. General Provisions

Article 1. Relations Regulated by Present Federal Law

1. The present Federal Law determines in accordance with the Civil Code of the Russian Federation the legal status of the limited responsibility society, the rights and duties of its participants, and the procedure for the creation, reorganisation, and liquidation of the society.

2. The peculiarities of the legal status, and the procedure for the creation, reorganisation, and liquidation of limited responsibility societies in the spheres of banking, insurance, and investment activity, and also in the domain of agricultural production, shall be determined by Federal laws.

Article 2. Basic Provisions on Limited Responsibility Societies

1. A limited responsibility society (hereinafter: 'society') shall be deemed to be an economic society founded by one or several persons whose charter capital is divided into participatory shares in the amounts determined by the constitutive

documents; the participants of the society shall not be liable for its obligations and shall bear the risk of losses connected with the activity of the society within the limits of the value of the contributions made by them.

The participants of a society who have made contributions to the capital of the society not in full shall jointly and severally bear subsidiary responsibility for its obligations within the limits of the value of the unpaid part of the contribution of each of the participants of the society.

2. A society shall have in ownership solitary property taken into account on its autonomous balance sheet, may in its own name acquire and effectuate property and personal nonproperty rights, bear duties, and be a plaintiff and defendant in a court.

A society may have civil rights and bear civil duties necessary for the effectuation of any types of activity not prohibited by Federal laws if this is not contrary to the subject and purposes of activity specifically limited by the charter of the society.

A society may engage in individual types of activity, a list of which is determined by a Federal law, only on the basis of a special authorisation (or license). If the requirement of effectuating such activity as exclusive has been provided for by the conditions of granting the special authorisation (or license) to effectuate the determined type of activity, the society during the period of operation of the special authorisation (or license) shall have the right to effectuate only the types of activity provided for by the special authorisation (or license) and concomitant types of activity.

3. A society shall be considered to be created as a juridical person from the moment of its State registration in the procedure established by the Federal law on State registration of juridical persons.

The society shall be created without limitation of period unless established otherwise by its charter.

4. A society shall have the right in the established procedure to open bank accounts on the territory of the Russian Federation and beyond its limits.

5. A society must have a circular seal containing its full firm name in the Russian language and specifying the location of the society. The seal of the society also may contain the firm name of the society in any language of the peoples of the Russian Federation and/or foreign language.

A society shall have the right to have stamps and letterheads with its own firm name, own emblem, and also trademark and other means of visual individualisation registered in the established procedure.

Article 3. Responsibility of Society

1. A society shall bear responsibility for its obligations with all of the property belonging to it.

2. A society shall not be liable for the obligations of its participants.

3. In the event of the insolvency (or bankruptcy) of a society through the fault of its participants or through the fault of other persons who have the right to give instructions binding upon the society or otherwise have the possibility to determine its actions, subsidiary responsibility for its obligations may be placed on the said participants or other persons in the event the property of the society is insufficient.

4. The Russian Federation, subjects of the Russian Federation, and municipal formations shall not bear responsibility for the obligations of the society, and likewise the society shall not bear responsibility for the obligations of the Russian Federation, subjects of the Russian Federation, and municipal formations.

Article 4. Firm Name of Society and Its Location

1. A society must have a full and shall have the right to have an abbreviated firm name in the Russian language. The society also shall have the right to have a full and/or abbreviated firm name in the languages of the peoples of the Russian Federation and/or in foreign languages.

The full firm name of the society in the Russian language must contain the full name of the society and the words 'limited responsibility'. The abbreviated firm name of the society in the Russian language must contain the full or abbreviated name of the society and the words 'limited responsibility' or the abbreviation 'OOO'.

The firm name of the society in the Russian language may not contain other terms and abbreviations, including borrowed from foreign languages, reflecting its organisational-legal form unless provided otherwise by Federal laws and other legal acts of the Russian Federation.

2. The location of the society shall be determined by the place of its State registration [as amended by Federal Law No. 31-ФЗ, 21 March 2002]

3. [repealed by Federal Law No. 31-ФЗ, 21 March 2002].

Article 5. Branches and Representations of Society

1. A society may create branches and open representations by decision of the general meeting of participants of the society adopted by a majority of not less than two-thirds of the votes of the total number of votes of the participants of the society unless the necessity for a larger number of votes to adopt such a decision has been provided for by the charter of the society.

The creation by a society of branches and the opening of representations on the territory of the Russian Federation shall be effectuated in compliance with the requirements of the present Federal Law and other Federal laws, and beyond the limits of the territory of the Russian Federation also in accordance with the legislation of the foreign State on whose territory branches are created or representations are opened unless provided otherwise by international treaties of the Russian Federation.

2. The branch of a society shall be a solitary subdivision thereof located outside the location of the society, representing the interests of the society, and effectuating all of its functions or part thereof, including the function of representation.

3. The representation of a society shall be a solitary subdivision thereof located outside the location of the society, representing the interests of the society, and effectuating the defence thereof.

4. A branch and a representation of a society shall not be juridical persons and shall operate on the basis of Statutes confirmed by the society. A branch and a representation shall be endowed with property by the society which created them.

The directors of branches and representations of a society shall be appointed by the society and shall operate on the basis of the power of attorney thereof.

Branches and representations of a society shall effectuate their activity in the name of the society which created them. Responsibility for the activity of the branch and representation shall be borne by the society which created them.

5. The charter of a society must contain information concerning its branches and representations. Communications of information concerning changes in the charter of the society about its branches and representations shall be submitted to the agency effectuating the State registration of juridical persons. The said changes in the charter of a society shall enter into force for third persons from the moment of informing the agency effectuating the State registration of juridical persons about such changes.

Article 6. Subsidiary and Dependent Societies

1. A society may have subsidiary and dependent economic societies with the rights of a juridical person created on the territory of the Russian Federation in accordance with the present Federal Law and other federal laws, and beyond the limits of the territory of the Russian Federation, in accordance with the legislation of the foreign State on whose territory the subsidiary or dependent economic society is created, unless provided otherwise by international treaties of the Russian Federation.

2. A society shall be deemed to be subsidiary if another (principal) economic society or partnership by virtue of predominant participation in its charter capital or in accordance with a contract concluded between them, or otherwise has the possibility to determine decisions to be adopted by such society.

3. A subsidiary society shall not be liable for the debts of the principal economic society (or partnership).

The principal economic society (or partnership) which has the right to give to the subsidiary society instructions binding upon it shall be liable jointly and severally with the subsidiary society with regard to transactions concluded by the last in execution of such instructions.

In the event of the insolvency (or bankruptcy) of a subsidiary society through the fault of the principal economic society (or partnership) the last shall bear subsidiary responsibility in the event of the insufficiency of the property of the subsidiary society for its debts.

The participants of a subsidiary society shall have the right to demand compensation by the principal society (or partnership) for losses caused through its fault to the subsidiary society.

4. A society shall be deemed to be dependent if another (predominant, participating) economic society has more than 20% of the charter capital of the first society.

A society which acquired more than 20% of the voting stocks of a joint-stock society or more than 20% of the charter capital of another limited responsibility society shall be obliged immediately to publish information concerning this in the press organ in which data concerning State registration of juridical persons are published.

Article 7. Participants of Society

1. Citizens and juridical persons may be participants of a society.

The participation of individual categories of citizens in societies may be prohibited or limited by a federal law.

2. State agencies and agencies of local self-government shall not have the right to act as participants of societies unless established otherwise by a Federal Law.

A society may be founded by one person, who becomes its sole participant. A society may subsequently become a society with one participant.

A society may not have as a sole participant another economic society consisting of one person.

The provisions of the present Federal Law shall extend to societies with one participant insofar as not provided otherwise by the present Federal Law and this is not contrary to the essence of the respective relations.

3. The number of participants of a society must not be more than fifty.

If the number of participants of a society exceeds the limit established by the present point, the society must within a year be transformed into an open joint-stock society or into a production cooperative. If within the said period a society is not transformed and the number of participants of the society is not reduced to the limit established by the present point, it shall be subject to liquidation in a judicial proceeding at the demand of the agency effectuating the State registration

169

of juridical persons or other State agencies or agencies of local self-government to which the right to present such demand has been granted by a Federal law.

Article 8. Rights of Participants of Society

1. The participants of a society shall have the right to:

participate in the management of the affairs of the society in the procedure established by the present Federal Law and constitutive documents of the society;

receive information concerning the activity of the society and familiarise themselves with its bookkeeping books and other documentation in the procedure established by its constitutive documents;

take part in the distribution of profit;

sell or otherwise assign its participatory share in the charter capital of the society or part thereof to one or several participants of the particular society in the procedure provided for by the present Federal Law and the charter of the society;

at any time withdraw from the society irrespective of the consent of the other participants;

receive in the event of the liquidation of the society the part of the property remaining after the settlement of accounts with creditors or the value thereof.

The participants of a society also shall have other rights provided for by the present Federal Law.

2. Besides the rights provided for by the present Federal Law, the charter of the society may provide for other rights (additional rights) of the participant(s) of the society. The said rights may be provided for by the charter of the society when it is founded or granted to the participant(s) of the society by decision of the general meeting of participants of the society adopted by all participants of the society unanimously.

Additional rights granted to a determined participant of the society in the event of the alienation of its participatory share (or part of the participatory share) shall not pass to the acquirer of the participatory share (or part of the participatory share).

The termination or limitation of additional rights granted to all participants of the society shall be effectuated by decision of the general meeting of participants of the society adopted by all participants of the society unanimously. The termination or limitation of additional rights granted to a determined participant of the society shall be effectuated by decision of the general meeting of participants of the society adopted by a majority of not less than two-thirds of the votes of the total number of votes of participants of the society on condition that the participant to whom such additional rights belong voted for the adoption of such decision or gave written consent.

The participant of the society which was granted additional rights may renounce the effectuation of the additional rights belonging to it, having sent the written notification thereof to the society. From the moment of receipt by the society of the said notification the additional rights of the participant of the society shall terminate.

Article 9. Duties of Participants of Society

1. The participants of a society shall be obliged to:
make contributions in the procedure, in the amounts, in the composition, and within the periods which have been provided for by the present Federal Law and constitutive documents of the society;
not divulge confidential information about the activity of the society.
The participants of the society shall also bear other duties provided for by the present Federal Law.

2. Besides the duties provided for by the present Federal Law, the charter of the society may provide for other duties (additional duties) of a participant(s) of the society. The said duties may be provided for by the charter of the society when it is founded or placed on all participants of the society by decision of the general meeting of participants of the society adopted unanimously by all participants of the society. The placing of additional duties on a determined participant shall be effectuated by decision of the general meeting of participants of the society adopted by a majority of not less than two-thirds of the votes of the total number of votes of participants of the society on condition that the participant on whom such additional duties are placed voted for the adoption of this decision or gave written consent.
Additional duties placed on a determined participant of the society in the event of the alienation of its participatory share (or part of participatory share) shall not pass to the acquirer of the participatory share (or part of participatory share).
Additional duties may be terminated by decision of the general meeting of participants of the society adopted by all participants of the society unanimously.

Article 10. Expulsion of Participant of Society from Society

The participants of a society whose participatory shares in aggregate constitute not less than 10% of the charter capital of the society shall have the right to demand in a judicial proceeding the expulsion from the society of a participant which flagrantly violates its duties or by its actions (or failure to act) makes the activity of the society impossible or materially makes it difficult.

Chapter II. Founding of Society

Article 11. Procedure for Founding of Society

1. The founders of a society shall conclude a constitutive contract and confirm the charter of the society. The constitutive contract and the charter of the society shall be the constitutive documents of the society.

If the society is founded by one person, the constitutive document of the society shall be the charter confirmed by this person. In the event of the increase of the number of participants up to two or more a constitutive contract must be concluded between them.

The founders of the society shall elect (or appoint) the executive organs of the society, and also in the event of making nonmonetary contributions to the charter capital of the society, shall confirm their monetary valuation.

The decision concerning confirmation of the charter of the society, and also the decision concerning confirmation of the monetary valuation of the contributions made by the founders of the society, shall be adopted by the founders unanimously. Other decisions shall be adopted by the founders of the society in the procedure provided for by the present Federal Law and by the constitutive documents of the society.

2. The founders of a society shall bear joint and several responsibility for obligations connected with the founding of the society and which arose before the State registration thereof. The society shall bear responsibility for obligations of the founders of the society connected with its founding only in the event of the subsequent approval of their actions by the general meeting of participants of the society.

3. The peculiarities of founding a society with the participation of foreign investors shall be determined by a Federal law.

Article 12. Constitutive Documents of Society

1. In the constitutive contract the founders of the society shall be obliged to create the society and determine the procedure for the joint activity with regard to its creation. The composition of the founders (or participants) of the society, the amount of charter capital of the society, and the amount of the participatory shares of each of the founders (or participants) of the society, the amount and composition of the contributions and the procedure and periods for them to the charter capital of the society when founding it, the responsibility of the founders (or participants) for a violation of the duty with regard to making contributions, the conditions and the procedure for the distribution among the founders (or participants) of the society of the profit, the composition of the organs of the society, and the procedure for the withdrawal of the participants of the society from the society also shall be determined by the constitutive contract.

2. The charter of the society must contain:
the full and abbreviated firm name of the society;
information concerning the location of the society;
information concerning the composition and competence of the organs of the society, including on questions comprising the exclusive competence of the

general meeting of participants of the society, the procedure for the adoption of decisions by organs of the society, including on questions, the decisions regarding which shall be adopted unanimously or by a qualified majority of votes;

information concerning the amount of charter capital of the society;

information concerning the amount and par value of the participatory share of each participant;

the rights and duties of participants of the society;

information concerning the procedure and consequences of withdrawal of a participant of the society from the society;

information concerning the procedure for the transfer of the participatory share (or part of the participatory share) in the charter capital of the society to another person;

information concerning the procedure for keeping the documents of the society and the procedure for the granting of information by the society to participants of the society and to other persons;

other information provided for by the present Federal Law.

The charter of the society may also contain other provisions which are not contrary to the present Federal Law and to other Federal laws.

3. At the demand of the participant of a society, the auditor or any interested person, the society shall be obliged within reasonable periods to grant them the possibility to familiarise themselves with the constitutive documents of the society, including with changes. The society shall be obliged at the demand of a participant of the society to grant to it copies of the prevailing constitutive contract and charter of the society. Payment recovered by the society for granting copies may not exceed the expenditures for the manufacture thereof.

4. Changes in the constitutive documents of a society shall be made by decision of the general meeting of participants of the society.

Changes made in the constitutive documents of the society shall be subject to State registration in the procedure provided for by Article 13 of the present Federal Law for the registration of the society.

Changes made in the constitutive documents of the society shall acquire force for third persons from the moment of their State registration, and in instances established by the present Federal Law, from the moment of notification of the agency effectuating State registration.

5. In the event of the failure of the provisions of the constitutive contract and the provisions of the charter of the society to conform, the provisions of the charter of the society shall have preferential force for third persons and the participants of the society.

Article 13. State Registration of Society

A society shall be subject to State registration in the agency effectuating the State registration of juridical persons in the procedure provided for by the Federal law on State registration of juridical persons.

Chapter III. Charter Capital of Society. Property of Society

Article 14. Charter Capital of Society. Participatory Shares in Charter Capital of Society

1. The charter capital of a society shall consist of the par value of the participatory shares of its participants.

The amount of charter capital of the society must be not less than one hundred times the minimum amount of payment for labour established by a Federal law on the date of submission of the documents for State registration of the society.

The amount of charter capital of a society and the par value of the participatory shares of participants shall be determined in rubles.

The charter capital of the society shall determine the minimum amount of its property guaranteeing the interests of creditors.

2. The amount of the participatory share of a participant of the society in the charter capital of the society shall be determined in percentages or in the form of fractions. The amount of the participatory share of a participant of the society must correspond to the correlation of the par value of his participatory share and the charter capital of the society.

The actual value of the participatory share shall correspond to the portion of the value of net assets of the society proportional to the amount of the participatory share.

3. The maximum amount of the participatory share of a participant of a society may be limited by the charter of the society. The possibility of changing the correlation of participatory shares of participants of the society may be limited by the charter of the society. Such limitations may not be established with respect to individual participants of the society. The said provisions may be provided for by the charter of the society when it is founded, and also inserted in the charter of the society, changed, or excluded from the charter of the society by decision of the general meeting of participants of the society adopted unanimously by all participants of the society.

Article 15. Contributions to Charter Capital

1. Money, securities, other things or property rights or other rights having monetary value may be a contribution to the charter capital of a society.

2. The monetary value of nonmonetary contributions to the charter capital of a society contributed by participants of the society and by third persons accepted

in the society shall be confirmed by decision of the general meeting of participants of the society adopted by all participants of the society unanimously.

If the par value (or increase of par value) of the participatory share of a participant of the society in the charter capital of the society paid up by a nonmonetary contribution constitutes more than two hundred minimum amounts of payment for labour established by a Federal law on the date of submission of the documents for State registration of the society or respective changes in the charter of the society, such contribution must be valued by an independent valuer. The par value (or increase of par value) of the participatory share of a participant of the society paid up by such nonmonetary contribution may not exceed the amount of valuation of the said contribution determined by the independent valuer.

In the event of making nonmonetary contributions to the charter capital of a society the participants of the society and the independent valuer shall within three years from the moment of State registration of the society or corresponding changes in the charter of the society jointly and severally bear subsidiary responsibility for its obligations, in the event of the insufficiency of the property of the society, in the amount exceeding the value of the nonmonetary contributions.

The types of property which may not be a contribution to the charter capital of the society may be established by the charter of the society.

3. In the event of the termination of the society's right of use of property before the expiry of the period for which such property was transferred for use to the society as a contribution to the charter capital, the participant of the society who transferred the property shall be obliged to grant to the society at its demand monetary contributory compensation equal to the payment for the use of such property under similar conditions during the remaining period. Monetary contributory compensation must be granted in a lump sum within a reasonable period from the moment of presentation by the society of the demand concerning the granting thereof unless another procedure for granting contributory compensation has been established by decision of the general meeting of participants of the society. Such decision shall be adopted by the general meeting of participants of the society without taking into account the votes of the participant of the society which transferred the right of use of the property which was terminated before time to the society for use by it as a contribution to the charter capital.

Other means and the procedure for the granting by a participant of the society of contributory compensation for the termination before time of the right to use property transferred by it to the use of the society as a contribution to the charter capital may be provided for by the constitutive contract.

4. The property transferred by a participant who has been expelled or who has withdrawn from the society to the use of the society as a contribution to the charter capital shall remain in the use of the society during the period for which it was transferred unless provided otherwise by the constitutive contract.

Article 16. Procedure for Making Contributions to Charter Capital of Society When Founding It

1. Each founder of the society must make its contribution in full to the charter capital of the society within the period which has been determined by the constitutive contract and which may not exceed one year from the moment of State registration of the society. In so doing the value of the contribution of each founder of the society must be not less than the par value of its participatory share.

Relieving a founder of the society from the duty to make the contribution to the charter capital of the society shall not be permitted, including by means of set-off of its demands against the society.

2. At the moment of State registration of a society its charter capital must be paid up by the founders by not less than half.

Article 17. Increase of Charter Capital of Society

1. An increase of the charter capital of a society shall be permitted only after it is fully paid up.

2. An increase of the charter capital of a society may be effectuated at the expense of property of the society and/or additional contributions of participants of the society, and/or, if this is not prohibited by the charter of the society, at the expense of contributions of third persons accepted in the society.

Article 18. Increase of Charter Capital of Society at Expense of its Property

1. An increase of charter capital of a society at the expense of its property shall be effectuated by decision of the general meeting of participants of the society adopted by a majority of not less than two-thirds of the votes of the total number of votes of participants of the society unless the necessity for a larger number of votes has been provided for by the charter of the society for the adoption of such a decision.

The decision concerning an increase of the charter capital of the society at the expense of property of the society may be adopted only on the basis of data of the bookkeeping reports of the society for the year preceding the year during which such decision is adopted.

2. The amount by which the charter capital of a society is increased at the expense of property of the society must not exceed the difference between the value of net assets of the society and the amount of charter capital and reserve fund of the society.

3. When increasing the charter capital of a society in accordance with the present Article the par value of the participatory shares of all participants of the society shall be increased proportionally without changing the amounts of their participatory shares.

Article 19. Increase of Charter Capital of Society at Expense of Additional Contributions of Participants Thereof and Contributions of Third Persons Accepted in Society

1. The general meeting of participants of a society may by a majority of not less than two-thirds of the votes of the total number of participants of the society, unless the necessity of a larger number of votes in order to adopt such decision is provided for by the charter of the society, adopt a decision concerning the increase of the charter capital of the society at the expense of making additional contributions by participants of the society. The total value of additional contributions must be determined by such decision, and also a correlation established uniform for all participants of the society between the value of the additional contribution of the participant of the society and the amount by which the par value of its participatory share is increased. The said correlation shall be established by proceeding from the fact that the par value of the participatory share of the participant of the society may be increased by an amount equal to or less than the value of its additional contribution.

Each participant of the society shall have the right to make an additional contribution not exceeding the portion of the total value of the additional contributions proportional to the amount of the participatory share of this participant in the charter capital of the society. The additional contributions may be made by participants of the society within two months from the day of the adoption by the general meeting of participants of the society of the decision specified in paragraph one of the present point unless a different period has been established by the charter of the society or the decision of the general meeting of participants of the society.

Not later than a month from the day of the end of the period for making the additional contributions the general meeting of participants of the society must adopt a decision concerning confirmation of the results of making the additional contributions by the participants of the society and on making changes in the constitutive documents of the society connected with the increase of the amount of the charter capital of the society and the increase of the par value of the participatory shares of the participants of the society which made additional contributions, and, when necessary, also changes connected with the change of the amounts of the participatory shares of the participants of the society. In so doing the par value of the participatory share of each participant of the society which has made an additional contribution shall be increased in accordance with the correlation specified in paragraph one of the present point.

The documents for State registration of the changes provided for by the present point in the constitutive documents of the society, and also the documents confirming the making of the additional contributions by the participants of the society, must be submitted to the agency effectuating the State registration of juridical persons within a month from the date of the adoption of the decision concerning the confirmation of the results of making additional contributions by participants of the society and on making the respective changes in the constitutive documents of the society. The said changes in the constitutive documents of the society shall acquire force for the participants of the society and third persons from the date of their State registration by the agency effectuating the State registration of juridical persons.

In the event of the failure to comply with the periods provided for by paragraphs three and four of the present point, the increase of the charter capital of the society shall be deemed to be unconstituted.

2. The general meeting of participants of the society may adopt a decision concerning an increase of its charter capital on the basis of an application of a participant of the society (or applications of participants of the society) on making an additional contribution and/or, unless this is prohibited by the charter of the society, the application of a third person (or applications of third persons) on the acceptance thereof in the society and the making of a contribution. Such decision shall be adopted by all participants of the society unanimously.

In the application of the participant of the society and the application of a third person there must be specified the amount and composition of the contribution, the procedure and period for making it, and also the amount of the participatory share which the participant of the society or third person wishes to have in the charter capital of the society. Other conditions for making contributions and joining the society also may be specified in the application.

Simultaneously with the decision concerning the increase of the charter capital of the society on the basis of the application of a participant of the society (or application of participants of the society) on the making of an additional contribution by it a decision must be adopted concerning the making of changes in the constitutive documents of the society connected with the increase of the amount of the charter capital of the society and increase of the par value of the participatory share of the participant of the society (or participants of the society) which made the application on making the additional contribution, and, when necessary, also changes connected with a change of the amounts of the participatory shares of participants of the society. In so doing the par value of the participatory share of each participant of the society which made an application to make an additional contribution shall be increased by the amount equal to or less than the value of its additional contribution.

Simultaneously with the decision concerning the increase of the charter capital of the society on the basis of the application of a third person (or applications of third persons) on accepting it (or them) in the society and making a contribution, a decision must be adopted concerning the making of changes in the constitutive documents of the society connected with the acceptance of the third person(s) in the society, the determination of the par value, and the amount of its participatory share (or their participatory shares), increase of the amount of charter capital of the society, and change of the amounts of the participatory shares of the participants of the society. The par value of the participatory share acquired by each third person accepted in the society must be equal to or less than the value of its contribution.

The documents for State registration of the changes provided for by the present point in the constitutive documents of the society, and also the documents confirming the making of the additional contributions by participants of the society and contributions by third persons in the full amount must be submitted to the agency effectuating the State registration of juridical persons within a month from the date of making in full amount the additional contributions by all the participants of the society and contributions of third persons who filed an application but not later than six months from the date of adoption of the decisions of the general meeting of participants of the society provided for by the present point. The said changes in the constitutive documents shall acquire force for the participants of the society and for third persons from the date of their State registration by the agency effectuating the State registration of juridical persons.

In the event of failure to comply with the periods provided for by paragraph five of the present point the increase of the charter capital of the society shall be deemed to be unconstituted.

3. If the increase of the charter capital of the society was unconstituted, the society shall be obliged within a reasonable period to return their contributions to the participants of the society and to third persons which made contribution in money, and in the event of the failure to return the contribution within the said period also to pay interest in the procedure and within the periods provided for by Article 395 of the Civil Code of the Russian Federation.

The society shall be obliged within a reasonable period to return their contributions to the participants of the society and third persons which made nonmonetary contributions, and in the event of the failure to return the contributions within the specified period also to compensate the lost advantage conditioned by the impossibility to use the property contributed.

Article 20. Reduction of Charter Capital of Society

1. A society shall have the right, and in the instances provided for by the present Federal Law, shall be obliged to reduce its charter capital.

A reduction of the charter capital of a society may be effectuated by means of a reduction of the par value of the participatory shares of all participants of the society in the charter capital of the society and/or repayment of the participatory shares belonging to the society.

A society shall not have the right to reduce its charter capital if as a result of such reduction the amount thereof becomes less than the minimum amount of charter capital determined in accordance with the present Federal Law on the date of the submission of documents for State registration of the respective changes in the charter of the society, and in instances when in accordance with the present Federal Law the society is obliged to reduce its charter capital, on the date of State registration of the society.

The reduction of charter capital of a society by means of reducing the par value of the participatory shares of all participants of the society must be effectuated while retaining the amounts of participatory shares of all participants of the society.

2. In the event the charter capital of a society is not paid up in full within a year from the moment of its State registration the society must either declare a reduction of its charter capital to the actual amount thereof paid up and register the reduction thereof in the established procedure or adopt a decision concerning the liquidation of the society.

3. If at the end of the second and each subsequent financial year the value of the net assets of the society prove to be less than its charter capital, the society shall be obliged to declare a reduction of its charter capital to an amount not exceeding the value of its net assets and register such reduction in the established procedure.

If at the end of the second and each subsequent financial year the value of the net assets of the society proves to be less than the minimum amount of charter capital established by the present Federal Law on the date of State registration of the society, the society shall be subject to liquidation.

The value of net assets of a society shall be determined in the procedure established by a Federal law and the normative acts issued in accordance with it.

4. Within thirty days from the date of adoption of the decision to reduce its charter capital the society shall be obliged to inform in writing all creditors of the society known to it about the reduction of the charter capital and the new amount thereof, and also publish in the press organ in which data concerning the State registration of juridical persons is published a notice about the decision adopted. In so doing the creditors of the society shall have the right within thirty days from the date of sending them notification or within thirty days from the date of publication of the notice concerning the decision adopted to demand in writing the termination or performance before time of respective obligations of the society and compensation of losses to them.

The State registration of the reduction of charter capital of the society shall be effectuated only in the event of the submission of evidence of the notification of creditors in the procedure established by the present point.

5. If in the instances provided for by the present Article the society within a reasonable period does not take a decision concerning reduction of its charter capital or concerning its liquidation, the creditors shall have the right to demand

from the society the termination or performance before time of the obligations of the society and compensation of losses to them. The agency effectuating the State registration of juridical persons or other State agencies or agencies of local self-government to which the right to present such a demand has been granted by a Federal law in these instances shall have the right to present a demand in court concerning liquidation of the society.

Article 21. Transfer of Participatory Share (or Part of Participatory Share) of Participant of Society in Charter Capital of Society to Other Participants of Society and Third Persons

1. A participant of a society shall have the right to sell or otherwise assign its participatory share in the charter capital of the society or part thereof to one or several participants of the particular society. The consent of the society or the other participants of the society to the conclusion of such a transaction shall not be required unless provided otherwise by the charter of the society.

2. The sale or assignment otherwise by a participant of the society by its participatory share (or part of the participatory share) to third persons shall be permitted unless this is prohibited by the charter of the society.

3. The participatory share of a participant of the society may be alienated before the full payment thereof only in that part in which it already has been paid up.

4. The participants of a society shall enjoy a preferential right of purchase of the participatory share (or part of the participatory share) at the price of the offer to a third person in proportion to the amounts of their participatory shares unless another procedure for effectuating the particular right has been provided for by the charter of the society or an agreement of the participants of the society. The preferential right of the society to acquire the participatory share (or part of the participatory share) being sold by its participant may be provided for by the charter of the society if the other participants of the society have not taken advantage of their preferential right to purchase the participatory share (or part of the participatory share).

The participant of a society intending to sell its participatory share (or part of the participatory share) to a third person shall be obliged to inform in writing the remaining participants of the society thereof and the society itself, indicating the price and other conditions of the sale thereof. It may be provided by the charter of the society that the notifications to the participants of the society shall be sent through the society. If the participants of the society and/or the society do not take advantage of the preferential right to purchase the entire participatory share (or part of the participatory share) being offered for sale within a month from the date of such notification, unless another period has been provided for by the charter of the society or agreement of the participants of the society, the participatory share (or part of the participatory share) may be sold to a third person at the price and on the conditions communicated to the society and its participants.

The provisions establishing the procedure for effectuating the preferential right of purchase of the participatory share (or part of the participatory share) disproportionate to the amounts of the participatory shares of the participants of the society may be provided for by the charter of the society when founding it, or introduced, changed, or excluded from the charter of the society by decision of the general meeting of participants of the society adopted by all participants of the society unanimously.

In the event of the sale of the participatory share (or part of the participatory share) in violation of the preferential right of purchase any participant of the society shall, if the preferential right of the society to acquire the participatory share (or part of the participatory share) has been provided for by the charter of the society, have the right within three months from the moment when the participant of the society or the society knew or should have known about such violation to demand in a judicial proceeding the transfer to them of the rights and duties of the purchaser.

Assignment of the said preferential right shall not be permitted.

5. The necessity to receive the consent of the society or of the remaining participants of the society to the assignment of the participatory share (or part of the participatory share) of the participant of the society to third persons other than by sale may be provided for by the charter of the society.

6. The assignment of a participatory share (or part of a participatory share) in the charter capital of a society must be concluded in simple written form unless the requirement of concluding it in notarial form has been provided for by the charter of the society. The failure to comply with the form of the transaction with regard to assignment of the participatory share (or part of the participatory share) in the charter capital of the society established by the present point or by the charter of the society shall entail its invalidity.

The society must be informed in writing about the assignment of the participatory share (or part of the participatory share) which has occurred in the charter capital of the society with the submission of evidence of such assignment. The acquirer of the participatory share (or part of the participatory share) in the charter capital of the society shall effectuate the rights and bear the duties of the participant of the society from the moment of informing the society about the said assignment.

To the acquirer of the participatory share (or part of the participatory share) in the charter capital of a society shall pass all rights and duties of the participant of the society which arose before the assignment of the said participatory share (or part of the participatory share), except for the rights and duties provided for respectively by Article 8(2), paragraph two, and Article 9(2), paragraph two, of the present Federal Law. The participant of the society who has assigned its participatory share (or part of the participatory share) in the charter capital of the society shall bear the duty to the society with regard to making the contribution in the property which arose before the assignment of the said participatory share (or part of the participatory share) jointly and severally with the acquirer thereof.

7. The participatory shares in the charter capital of the society shall pass to the heirs of citizens and to the legal successors of juridical persons which are participants of the society.

In the event of the liquidation of a juridical person-participant of the society the participatory share belonging to it remaining after the completion of the settlement of accounts with its creditors shall be distributed among the participants of the juridical person being liquidated unless provided otherwise by a Federal Law, other legal acts, or the constitutive documents of the juridical person being liquidated.

It may be provided by the charter of the society that the transfer and distribution of the participatory share established by paragraphs one and two of the present point shall be permitted only with the consent of the remaining participants of the society.

Until the acceptance by the heir of the deceased participant of a society of the inheritance, the rights of the deceased participant of the society shall be effectuated, and his duties shall be performed, by the person specified in the will, and in the absence of such person, by an administrator appointed by the notary.

8. If the necessity to receive the consent of the participants of the society to the assignment of the participatory share (or part of the participatory share) in the charter capital of the society to participants of the society or to third persons has been provided for by the charter of the society, to the transfer thereof to heirs or to legal successors, or to the distribution of the participatory share among participants of a juridical person being liquidated, such consent shall be considered to be received if within thirty days from the moment of recourse to the participants of the society or within another period determined by the charter of the society, the written consent of all participants of the society has been received or a written refusal of consent has not been received from any of the participants of the society.

If the necessity to receive the consent of the society to the assignment of the participatory share (or part of the participatory share) in the charter capital of the society to the participants of the society or to third persons has been provided for by the charter of the society, such consent shall be considered to be received if within thirty days from the moment of recourse to the society or within another period determined by the charter of the society the written consent of the society has been received or a written refusal to consent from the society has not been received.

9. In the event of the sale of the participatory share (or part of the participatory share) in the charter capital of the society at a public sale in the instances provided for by the present Federal Law or other Federal laws, the acquirer of the said participatory share (or part of the participatory share) shall become a participant of the society irrespective of the consent of the society or its participants.

Article 22. Pledge of Participatory Shares in Charter Capital of Society

The participant of a society shall have the right to pledge the participatory share (or part of the participatory share) belonging to him to another participant of the society or, unless this is prohibited by the charter of the society, to a third person with the consent of the society by decision of the general meeting of participants of the society adopted by a majority of votes of all participants of the society unless the necessity of a larger number of votes for the adoption of such decision has been provided for by the charter of the society. The votes of the participant who intends to pledge the participatory share (or part of the participatory share) shall not be taken into account when determining the results of the voting.

Article 23. Acquisition by Society of Participatory Share (or Part of Participatory Share) in Charter Capital of Society

1. A society shall not have the right to acquire the participatory share (or part of the participatory share) in its charter capital except for the instances provided for by the present Federal Law.

2. If the assignment of the participatory share (or part of the participatory share) of the participant of the society to third persons is prohibited by the charter of the society and other participants of the society refuse to acquire it, and also in the event of the refusal to consent to the assignment of the participatory share (or part of the participatory share) to a participant of the society or to a third person if the necessity to receive such consent has been provided for by the charter of the society, the society shall be obliged to acquire at the demand of a participant of the society the participatory share (or part of the participatory share) belonging to it. In so doing the society shall be obliged to pay to the participant of the society the actual value of this participatory share (or part of the participatory share), which shall be determined on the basis of data of the bookkeeping reports of the society for the last reporting period preceding the date of the recourse of the participant of the society with such demand, or with the consent of the participant of the society to issue it property in kind of the same value.

3. The participatory share of a participant of the society which when founding the society did not make its contribution within the period to the charter capital of the society in full, and also the participatory share of a participant of the society which did not grant monetary or other contributory compensation within the period provided for by Article 15(3) of the present Federal Law, shall pass to the

society. In so doing the society shall be obliged to pay the participant of the society for the actual value of the part of its participatory share proportional to the part of the contribution made by it (or period during which the property was in the use of the society), or with the consent of the participant of the society to issue it property in kind of the same value. The actual value of the part of the participatory share shall be determined on the basis of data of bookkeeping reports of the society for the last reporting period preceding the date of the expiry of the period for making the contribution or granting contributory compensation.

It may be provided for by the charter of the society that part of the participatory share shall pass to the society in proportion to the unpaid part of the contribution or amount (or value) of the contributory compensation.

4. The participatory share of the participant of the society excluded from the society shall pass to the society. In so doing the society shall be obliged to pay to the excluded participant of the society the actual value of its participatory share which shall be determined according to data of the bookkeeping reports of the society for the last reporting period preceding the date of the entry into legal force of the decision of a court concerning exclusion, or with the consent of the excluded participant of the society issue to it property in kind of the same value.

5. In the event of the refusal of the participants of the society to consent to the transfer or distribution of the participatory share in the instances provided for by Article 21(7) of the present Federal Law, if such consent is necessary in accordance with the charter of the society, the participatory share shall pass to the society. In so doing the society shall be obliged to pay to the heirs of the deceased participant of the society or to the legal successors of a reorganised juridical person-participant of the society, or to the participants of the liquidated juridical person-participant of the society the true value of the participatory share determined on the basis of data of the bookkeeping reports of the society for the last reporting period preceding the date of death, reorganisation, or liquidation, or with their consent to issue them property in kind of the same value.

6. In the event of payment by the society in accordance with Article 25 of the present Federal Law of the actual value of the participatory share (or part of the participatory share) of the participant of the society at the demand of its creditor, the part of the participatory share whose actual value was not paid by the other participants of the society shall pass to the society, and the remaining part of the participatory share shall be distributed among the participants of the society in proportion to the payment made by them.

7. The participatory share (or part of the participatory share) shall pass to the society from the moment of presentation by the participant of the society of the demand concerning its creation by the society, or the expiry of the period of making the contribution or granting of contributory compensation, or entry into legal

force of the decision of the court concerning the exclusion of the participant from the society, or receipt from any participant of the society of the refusal to consent to the transfer of the participatory share to the heirs of citizens (or to legal successors of juridical persons) who were participants of the society, or to the distribution thereof among the participants of a liquidated juridical person-participant of the society, or payment by the society of the actual value of the participatory share (or part of the participatory share) of the participant of the society at the demand of its creditors.

8. The society shall be obliged to pay the actual value of the participatory share (or part of the participatory share) or issue property in kind of the same value within one year from the moment of transfer to the society of the participatory share (or part of the participatory share) unless a lesser period has been provided for by the charter of the society.

The actual value of the participatory share (or part of the participatory share) shall be paid from the difference between the value of net assets of the society and the amount of its charter capital. If such difference is insufficient, the society shall be obliged to reduce its charter capital by the insufficient amount.

Article 24. Participatory Shares Belonging to Society

Participatory shares belonging to a society shall not be taken into account when determining the results of voting at a general meeting of participants of the society, and also when distributing the profit and property of the society in the event of its liquidation.

A participatory share belonging to a society must within one year from the date of the transfer thereof to the society be distributed by decision of the general meeting of participants of the society among all participants of the society in proportion to their participatory shares in the charter capital of the society or sold to all or to certain participants of the society and/or, unless this is prohibited by the charter of the society, to third persons and full paid up. The undistributed or unsold part of the participatory share must be cancelled with a respective reduction of the charter capital of the society. The sale of a participatory share to participants of the society as a result of which the amounts of participatory shares of its participants are changed, the sale of a participatory share to third persons, and also the making of changes in the constitutive documents of the society connected therewith, shall be effectuated by decision of the general meeting of participants of the society adopted by all participants of the society unanimously.

The documents for State registration of the changes in the constitutive documents of the society provided for by the present Article, and in the event of the sale of a participatory share also the documents confirming payment of the participatory share sold by the society, must be submitted to the agency effectuating the State registration of juridical persons within one month from the date of adoption of the decision confirming the results of the payment for the participatory shares by participants of the society and making respective changes in the constitutive documents of the society. The said changes in the constitutive documents of the society shall acquire force for participants of the society and third persons from the date of their State registration by the agency effectuating the State registration of juridical persons.

Article 25. Levy of Execution Against Participatory Share (or Part of Participatory Share) of Participant of Society in Charter Capital of Society

1. Levy of execution with regard to a demand of creditors against the participatory share (or part of the participatory share) of the participant of the society in the charter capital of the society with regard to debts of the participant of a society shall be permitted only on the basis of the decision of a court when the other property of the participant of the society is insufficient to cover the debts.

2. In the event of the levy of execution against the participatory share (or part of the participatory share) of the participant of a society with regard to debts of the participant of the society the society shall have the right to pay the creditors the actual value of the participatory share (or part of the participatory share) of the participant of the society.

By decision of the general meeting of participants of the society adopted by all participants of the society unanimously, the actual value of the participatory share (or part of the participatory share) of the participant of a society against whose property execution is levied may be paid to the creditors by the other participants of the society in proportion to their participatory shares in the charter capital of the society unless another procedure for determining the amount of payment has been provided for by the charter of the society or by decision of the general meeting of participants of the society.

The actual value of the participatory share (or part of the participatory share) of the participant of the society in the charter capital of the society shall be determined on the basis of the data of bookkeeping reports of the society for the last reporting period preceding the date of the presentation of the demand to the society concerning the levy of execution against the participatory share (or part of the participatory share) of the participant of the society for his debts.

3. If within three months from the moment of presentation of the demand by creditors the society or the participants thereof do not pay the actual value of the entire participatory share (or entire part of the participatory share) of the participant of the society against which execution is levied, the levy of execution against the participatory share (or part of the participatory share) of the participant of the society shall be effectuated by means of the sale thereof at a public sale.

Article 26. Withdrawal of Participant of Society from Society

1. The participant of a society shall have the right at any time to withdraw from the society irrespective of the consent of the other participants thereof or of the society.

2. In the event of the withdrawal of the participant of the society from the society its participatory share shall pass to the society from the moment of filing application concerning withdrawal from the society. In so doing the society shall be obliged to pay the participant of the society which filed the application concerning withdrawal from the society the actual value of its participatory share determined on the basis of the date of the bookkeeping report of the society for the year during which the application was filed concerning withdrawal from the society, or with the consent of the participant of the society to issue property to it in kind of the same value, and in the event of the failure to pay up its contribution to the charter capital of the society, the actual value of the part of its participatory share in proportion to the part of the contribution paid up.

3. A society shall be obliged to pay the participant of the society which filed the application concerning withdrawal from the society the actual value of its participatory share or issue property to it in kind of the same value within six months from the moment of the end of the financial year during which the application was filed concerning withdrawal from the society unless a lesser period has been provided for by the charter of the society.

The actual value of the participatory share of the participant of the society shall be paid from the difference between the value of the net assets of the society and the amount of the charter capital of the society. If such difference is insufficient to pay the participant of the society which filed the application concerning withdrawal from the society the actual value of its participatory share, the society shall be obliged to reduce its charter capital by the insufficient amount.

4. The withdrawal of the participant of the society from the society shall not relieve it from the duty to the society with regard to making a contribution to the property of the society which arose before filing the application concerning withdrawal from the society.

Article 27. Contributions to Property of Society

1. The participants of the society shall be obliged, if this is provided for by the charter of the society, by decision of the general meeting of participants of the society to make contributions to the property of the society. This duty of participants of the society may be provided for by the charter of the society when founding the society or by means of making changes in the charter of the society by decision of the general meeting of participants of the society adopted by all participants of the society unanimously.

The decision of the general meeting of participants of the society concerning the making of contributions to the property of the society may be adopted by the majority of not less than two-thirds of the votes of the total number of votes of participants of the society unless the necessity of a larger number of votes to adopt such a decision is provided for by the charter of the society.

2. Contributions to the property of a society shall be made by all participants of the society in proportion to their participatory shares in the charter capital of the society unless a different procedure for determining the amounts of the contributions to the property of the society has been provided for by the charter of the society.

The maximum value of the contributions to the property of the society by all or determined participants of the society may be provided for by the charter of the society, and other limitations connected with the making of contributions to the property of the society also may be provided for. Limitations connected with the making of contributions to the property of the society established for a determined participant of the society in the event of the alienation of its participatory share (or part of the participatory share) with respect to the acquirer of a participatory share (or part of a participatory share) shall not operate.

The provisions establishing the procedure for determining the amounts of the contributions to the property of the society disproportionate to the amounts of participatory shares of participants of the society, and also the provisions establishing limitations connected with the making of contributions to the property of the society, may be provided for by the charter of the society when founding it or made in the charter of the society by decision of the general meeting of participants of the society adopted by all participants of the society unanimously.

The change and exclusion of provisions of the charter of the society establishing the procedure for determining the amounts of contributions to the property of the society disproportionate to the amounts of the participatory shares of the participants of the society, and also limitations connected with the making of contributions to the property of the society established for all participants of the society shall be effectuated by decision of the general meeting of participants of the society adopted by all participants of the society unanimously. The change and exclusion of the provisions of the charter of the society establishing specified limitations for a determined participant of the society shall be effectuated by decision of the general meeting of participants of the society adopted by a majority of not less than two-thirds vote from the total number of votes of participants of the society on condition the participant of the society for which such limitations have been established voted for the adoption of such decision or gave written consent.

3. Contributions to the property of the society shall be made in money unless provided otherwise by the charter of the society or by decision of the general meeting of participants of the society.

4. Contributions to the property of the society shall not change the amount and par value of the participatory shares of participants of the society in the charter capital of the society.

Article 28. Distribution of Profit of Society Among Participants of Society

1. A society shall have the right quarterly, once every six months, or once a year to adopt a decision concerning the distribution of its net profit among the participants of the society. The decision concerning the determination of the portion of the profit of the society to be distributed among the participants of the society shall be adopted by the general meeting of participants of the society.

2. The portion of the profit of the society earmarked for distribution among its participants shall be distributed in proportion to their participatory shares in the charter capital of the society.

Another procedure for distribution of profit among the participants of the society may be established by the charter of the society when founding it or by means of making changes in the charter of the society by decision of the general meeting of participants of the society adopted by all participants of the society unanimously. The change and exclusion of provisions of the charter of the society establishing such a procedure shall be effectuated by decision of the general meeting of participants of the society adopted by all participants of the society unanimously.

Article 29. Limitations of Distribution of Profit of Society Among Participants of Society. Limitations of Payment of Profit of Society to Participants of Society

1. A society shall not have the right to adopt a decision concerning the distribution of its profit among participants of the society:

until the payment in full of the entire charter capital of the society;

until the payment of the actual value of the participatory share (or part of the participatory share) of a participant of the society in the instances provided for by the present Federal Law;

if at the moment of the adoption of such decision the society meets the indicia of insolvency (or bankruptcy) in accordance with the Federal Law on insolvency (or bankruptcy) or if the said indicia appear in the society as a result of the adoption of such a decision;

if at the moment of the adoption of such decision the value of net assets of the society is less than its charter capital and reserve fund or will become less than the amount thereof as a result of the adoption of such decision;

in other instances provided for by Federal laws.

2. A society shall not have the right to pay profit to participants of the society, the decision concerning the distribution of which between the participants of the society has been adopted:

if at the moment of payment the society meets the indicia of insolvency (or bankruptcy) in accordance with the Federal law on insolvency (or bankruptcy) or if the said indicia appear in the society as a result of the payment;

if at the moment of payment the value of the net assets of the society are less than its charter capital and the reserve fund or become less than the amount thereof as a result of the payment;

in other instances provided for by Federal laws.

Upon the termination of the circumstances specified in the present point the society shall be obliged to pay profit to the participants of the society, the decision concerning the distribution of which between the participants of the society has been adopted.

Article 30. Reserve Fund and Other Funds of Society

A society may create a reserve fund and other funds in the procedure and in the amounts provided for by the charter of the society.

Article 31. Placement of Bonds by Society

1. A society shall have the right to place bonds and other emission securities in the procedure established by legislation on securities.

2. A society shall have the right to place bonds for an amount not exceeding the amount of its charter capital or the amount of security granted to the society for these purposes by third persons after the payment of the charter capital in full.

3. In the absence of security granted to the society by third persons for the purpose of guaranteeing the fulfilment of obligations to the possessors of the bonds, the placement by the society of bonds shall be permitted not earlier than the third year of existence of the society on condition of the proper confirmation by this time of two yearly balance sheets of the society.

Chapter IV. Management in Society

Article 32. Organs of Society

1. The general meeting of participants of a society shall be the highest organ of the society. The general meeting of participants of the society may be regular or extraordinary.

All participants of the society shall have the right to be present at the general meeting of participants of the society, take part in the discussion of questions on the agenda and vote when adopting decisions.

The provisions of the constitutive documents of the society or decisions of organs of the society limiting the said rights of participants of the society shall be null.

Each participant of the society shall have at the general meeting of participants of the society the number of votes proportional to its participatory share in the charter capital of the society, except for instances provided for by the present Federal Law.

Another procedure for determining the number of votes of participants of the society may be established by the charter of the society when founding it or by means of making changes in the charter of the society by decision of the general meeting of participants of the society unanimously. The change and exclusion of provisions of the charter of the society establishing such a procedure shall be effectuated by decision of the general meeting of participants of the society adopted by all participants of the society unanimously.

2. The formation of a council of directors (or supervisory council) of the society may be provided for by the charter of a society.

The competence of the council of directors (or supervisory council) shall be determined by the charter of the society in accordance with the present Federal Law.

It may be provided by the charter of the society that the formation of the executive organs of the society, termination of their powers before time, deciding of questions concerning the conclusion of large-scale transactions in the instances provided for by Article 46 of the present Federal Law, deciding of questions concerning the conclusion of transactions in the conclusion of which there is an interest in the instances provided for by Article 45 of the present Federal Law, the deciding of questions connected with the preparation, convocation, and conducting of the general meeting of participants of the society, and also the deciding of other questions provided for by the present Federal Law be relegated to the competence of the council of directors (or supervisory council) of the society. If the deciding of questions connected with the preparation, convocation, and conducting of the general meeting of participants of the society is relegated by the charter of the society to the competence of the council of directors (or supervisory council) of the society, the executive organ of the society shall acquire the right to demand the conducting of an extraordinary general meeting of participants of the society.

The procedure for the formation and activity of the council of directors (or supervisory council), and also the procedure for termination of the powers of members of the council of directors (or supervisory council) of the society and competence of the chairman of the council of directors (or supervisory council) of the society shall be determined by the charter of the society.

The members of the collegial executive organ of the society may not comprise more than one-quarter of the composition of the council of directors (or supervisory council) of the society. The person effectuating the functions of one-man executive organ of the society may not be simultaneously the chairman of the council of directors (or supervisory council) of the society.

By decision of the general meeting of participants of the society remuneration and/or expenses contributorily compensated which are connected with the performance of the said duties may be paid to members of the council of directors (or supervisory council) of the society within the period of the performance by them of their duties. The amounts of the said remuneration and contributory compensation shall be established by decision of the general meeting of participants of the society.

3. The members of the council of directors (or supervisory council) of the society, the person effectuating the functions of one-man executive organ of the society, and the members of the collegial executive organ of the society who are not participants of the society may participate in the general meeting of participants of the society with the right of a consultative vote.

4. The direction of the current activity of the society shall be effectuated by the one-man executive organ or by the one-man executive organ of the society and the collegial executive organ of the society. The executive organs of the society shall be accountable to the general meeting of participants of the society and to the council of directors (or supervisory council) of the society.

5. The transfer of the right of vote by a member of the council of directors (or supervisory council) of the society or by a member of the collegial executive organ of the society to other persons, including to other members of the council of directors (or supervisory council) of the society or to other members of the collegial executive organ of the society shall not be permitted.

6. The formation of an audit commission (or election of an internal auditor) of the society may be provided for by the charter of a society. In societies having more than fifteen participants the formation of an audit commission (or election of an internal auditor) of the society shall be obligatory. A person who is not a participant of the society also may be a member of the audit commission (or internal auditor).

The functions of the audit commission (or internal auditor) of the society, if this has been provided for by the charter of the society, may be effectuated by an auditor confirmed by the general meeting of participants of the society who is not connected by the property interests with the society, with members of the council of directors (or supervisory council) of the society, with the person effectuating the functions of one-man executive organ of the society, or by members of the collegial executive organ of the society and participants of the society.

Members of the council of directors (or supervisory council) of the society, the person effectuating the functions of one-man executive organ of the society, and members of the collegial executive organ of the society may not be members of the audit commission (or internal auditor) of the society.

Article 33. Competence of General Meeting of Participants of Society

1. The competence of the general meeting of participants of the society shall be determined by the charter of the society in accordance with the present Federal Law.

2. There shall be relegated to the exclusive competence of the general meeting of participants of the society:

(1) determination of the principal orientations of the activity of the society, and also the adoption of the decision concerning participation in associations [*ассоциации*] and other associations of commercial organisations;

(2) change of the charter of the society, including change of the amount of charter capital of the society;

(3) making of changes in the constitutive contract;

(4) formation of the executive organs of the society and termination before time of their powers, and also the adoption of a decision concerning the transfer of powers of the one-man executive organ of the society to a commercial organisation or individual entrepreneur (hereinafter: manager), confirmation of such manager and the conditions of the contract with him;

(5) election and termination before time of the powers of the audit commission (or internal auditor) of the society;

(6) confirmation of the yearly reports and yearly bookkeeping balance sheets;

(7) adoption of a decision concerning the distribution of the net profit of the society between the participants of the society;

(8) confirmation (or adoption) of documents regulating the internal activity of the society (or internal documents of the society);

(9) adoption of the decision concerning the placement by the society of bonds and other emission securities;

(10) designation of auditor verification, confirmation of the auditor, and determination of the amount of payment for his services;

(11) adoption of decision concerning the reorganisation or liquidation of the society;

(12) appointment of the liquidation commission and confirmation of the liquidation balance sheets;

(13) deciding of other questions provided for by the present Federal Law.

Questions relegated to the exclusive competence of the general meeting of participants of the society may not be transferred by it for decision of the council of directors (or supervisory council) of the society, except for instances provided for by the present Federal Law, and also for decision of the executive organs of the society.

Article 34. Regular General Meeting of Participants of Society

The regular general meeting of participants of the society shall be conducted within the periods determined by the charter of the society, but not less than once a year. The regular general meeting of participants of the society shall be convoked by the executive organ of the society.

The period for conducting the regular general meeting of participants of the society at which the yearly results of the activity of the society are confirmed must be determined by the charter of the society. The said general meeting of participants of the society must be conducted not earlier than two months and not later than four months after the end of the financial year.

Article 35. Extraordinary General Meeting of Participants of Society

1. An extraordinary general meeting of participants of a society shall be conducted in the instances determined by the charter of the society, and also in any other instances if the conducting of such general meeting if the interests of the society and its participants so require.

2. An extraordinary general meeting of participants of the society shall be convoked by the executive organ of the society at its initiative, at the demand of the council of directors (or supervisory committee) of the society, audit commission (or internal auditor) of the society, auditor, and also the participants of the society possessing in aggregate not less than one-tenth of the total number of votes of the participants of the society.

The executive organ of the society shall be obliged within five days from the date of receipt of the demand concerning the conducting of an extraordinary general meeting of participants of the society to consider the particular demand and adopt a decision concerning the conducting of the extraordinary general meeting of participants of the society or a refusal to conduct it. The decision concerning the refusal to conduct an extraordinary general meeting of participants of the society may be adopted by the executive organ of the society only if:

the procedure established by the present Federal Law for presenting the demand concerning the conducting of an extraordinary general meeting of participants of the society has not been complied with;

if none of the questions proposed for inclusion on the agenda of the extraordinary general meeting of participants of the society is relegated to its competence or does not correspond to the requirements of Federal laws.

If one or several questions proposed for inclusion on the agenda of the extraordinary general meeting of participants of the society is not relegated to the competence of the general meeting of participants of the society or does not correspond to the requirements of Federal laws, the said questions shall not be included on the agenda.

The executive organ of the society shall not have the right to make changes in the formulation of the questions proposed for inclusion on the agenda of the general meeting of participants of the society, nor also to change the proposed form for conducting the extraordinary general meeting of participants of the society.

Together with the questions proposed for inclusion on the agenda of the extraordinary general meeting of participants of the society the executive organ of the society shall have the right at its own initiative to include additional questions thereon.

3. In the event of the adoption of a decision concerning the conducting of an extraordinary general meeting of participants of the society, the said general meeting must be conducted not later than forty-five days from the date of receipt of the demand concerning the conducting thereof.

4. If within the period established by the present Federal Law a decision is not adopted concerning the conducting of an extraordinary general meeting of participants of the society or a decision is adopted to refuse to conduct it, the extraordinary general meeting of participants may be convoked by the organs or persons demanding the conducting thereof.

In this event the executive organ of the society shall be obliged to grant to the said agencies or persons a list of participants of the society with their addresses.

The expenses for the preparation, convocation, and conducting of such general meeting may be compensated by decision of the general meeting of participants of the society at the expense of the means of the society.

Article 36. Procedure for Convocation of General Meeting of Participants of Society

1. The organ or person convoking the general meeting of participants of the society shall be obliged not later than thirty days before conducting it to inform each participant of the society thereof by registered letter at the address specified in the list of participants of the society or by the other means provided for by the charter of the society.

2. The time and place of conducting the general meeting of participants of the society, and also the proposed agenda, must be specified in the notification.

Any participant of the society shall have the right to make proposals concerning the inclusion on the agenda of the general meeting of participants of the society of additional questions not later than fifteen days before the conducting thereof. The additional questions, except for questions which are not relegated to the competence of the general meeting of participants of the society or do not correspond to the requirements of Federal laws shall be included on the agenda of the general meeting of participants of the society.

The organ or person convoking the general meeting of participants of the society shall not have the right to make changes in the formulation of additional questions proposed for inclusion on the agenda of the general meeting of participants of the society.

If changes are made upon the proposal of participants of the society in the initial agenda of the general meeting of participants, the organ or persons convoking the general meeting of participants of the society shall be obliged not later than ten days before conducting it to inform all participants of the society about the changes made in the agenda by the means specified in point 1 of the present Article.

3. To the information and materials subject to being granted to participants of the society when preparing the general meeting of participants of the society shall be relegated the yearly report of the society, the opinion of the audit commission (or internal auditor) of the society and the auditor with regard to the results of the verification of the yearly reports and yearly bookkeeping balance sheets of the society, information concerning the candidate(s) for the executive organ of the society, the council of directors (or supervisory council) of the society, draft of changes and additions to be made in the constitutive documents of the society, or draft constitutive documents of the society in a new version, draft internal documents of the society, and also other information (or materials) provided for by the charter of the society.

Unless a different procedure for the familiarisation of participants of the society with information and materials has been provided for by the charter of the society, the organ or persons convoking the general meeting of participants of the society shall be obliged to send them the information and materials together with the notification concerning the conducting of the general meeting of participants of the society, and in the event of a change of the agenda, the respective information and materials shall be sent together with the notification concerning such change.

The said information and materials must within thirty days before conducting the general meeting of participants of the society be granted to all participants of the society for familiarisation at the premise of the executive organ of the society. The society shall be obliged upon the demand of a participant of the society to grant to it copies of the said documents. The payment recovered by the society for granting the said copies may not exceed the expenditures for manufacturing them.

4. Shorter periods than specified in the present Article may be provided for by the charter of the society.

5. In the event of a violation of the procedure established by the present Article for the convocation of the general meeting of participants of the society, such general meeting shall be deemed to be empowered if all participants of the society participate therein.

Article 37. Procedure for Conducting General Meeting of Participants of Society

1. The general meeting of participants of the society shall be conducted in the procedure established by the present Federal Law, the charter of the society, and its internal documents. In the part not regulated by the present Federal Law, the charter of the society, and the internal documents of the society, the procedure for conducting the general meeting of participants of the society shall be established by decision of the general meeting of participants of the society.

2. The registration of participants of the society who have arrived shall be conducted before opening the general meeting of participants of the society.

Participants of the society shall have the right to participate in the general meeting personally or through their representatives. The representatives of the participants of the society must present documents confirming their proper powers. The power of attorney issued to the representative of the participant of the society must contain information concerning the person being represented and the representative (name, place of residence or location, passport data), be formalised in accordance with the requirements of Article 185(4) and (5) of the Civil Code of the Russian Federation, or be notarially certified.

An unregistered participant of the society (or representative of a participant of the society) shall not have the right to take part in the voting.

3. The general meeting of participants of the society shall be opened at the time specified in the notification concerning the conducting of the general meeting of participants of the society or, if all participants of the society already have been registered, earlier.

4. The general meeting of participants of the society shall be opened by the person effectuating the functions of one-man executive organ of the society or by the person heading the collegial executive organ of the society. The general meeting of participants of the society created by the council of directors (or supervisory council) of the society, audit commission (or internal auditor), auditor, or participants of the society shall be opened by the chairman of the council of directors (or supervisory council) of the society, chairman of the audit commission (or internal auditor), auditor, or one of the participants of the society which convoked this general meeting.

5. The person opening the general meeting of participants of the society shall conduct the election of the person presiding from among the participants of the society. Unless provided otherwise by the charter, when voting with regard to the question of electing the presiding person each participant of the general meeting of participants of the society shall have one vote, and the decision with regard to the said question shall be adopted by a majority of votes of the total number of votes of participants of the society having the right to vote at this general meeting.

6. The executive organ of the society shall organise the keeping of the protocol of the general meeting of participants of the society.

The protocols of all general meetings of participants of the society shall be sewn into the book of protocols, which must at any time be granted to any participant of the society for familiarisation. Upon the demand of participants of the society extracts from the book of protocols shall be issued to them certified by the executive organ of the society.

7. The general meeting of participants of the society shall have the right to adopt decisions only with regard to questions of the agenda communicated to par-

ticipants of the society in accordance with Article 36(1) and (2) of the present Federal Law, except for instances when all participants of the society participate in this general meeting

8. Decisions with regard to the questions specified in Article 33(2), subpoint (2) of the present Federal Law, and also with regard to other questions determined by the charter of the society, shall be adopted by a majority of not less than two-thirds of the votes of the total number of votes of the participants of the society, unless the necessity of a larger number of votes in order to adopt such decision is provided for by the present Federal Law or by the charter of the society.

Decisions with regard to questions specified in Article 33(2), subpoints (3) and (11) of the present Federal Law shall be adopted by all participants of the society unanimously.

The remaining decisions shall be adopted by a majority of votes of the total number of votes of the participants of the society unless the necessity of a larger number of votes in order to adopt such decisions is provided for by the present Federal Law or by the charter of the society.

9. The conducting of cumulative voting with regard to questions concerning the election of members of the council of directors (or supervisory council) of the society, members of the collegial executive organ of the society, and/or members of the audit commission of the society may be provided for by the charter of the society.

In the event of cumulative voting the number of votes belonging to each participant of the society shall be multiplied by the number of persons which must be elected to the organ of the society, and a participant of the society shall have the right to cast the number of votes thus received entirely for one candidate or to distribute them among two or more candidates. The candidates who received the largest number of votes shall be considered to be elected.

10. Decisions of the general meeting of participants of the society shall be adopted by open voting unless a different procedure for adopting the decisions has been provided for by the charter of the society.

Article 38. Decision of General Meeting of Participants of Society to be Adopted by Conducting External Voting (by Poll)

1. A decision of the general meeting of participants of the society may be adopted without conducting a meeting (or joint presence of participants of the society in order to discuss questions of the agenda and adoption of decisions with regard to questions put to a vote) by means of conducting an external vote (by poll). Such a vote may be conducted by means of the exchange of documents through the postal, telegraph, teletype, telephone, electronic, or other communications ensuring the authenticity of the communications being transferred and received and the documentary confirmation thereof.

The decision of the general meeting of participants of the society with regard to the questions specified in Article 33(2), subpoint 6, of the present Federal Law may not be adopted by conducting an external vote (by poll).

2. When adopting a decision by the general meeting of participants of the society by means of conducting an external vote (by poll), Article 37(2)(3)(4)(5) and (7) of the present Federal Law shall not apply, and also the provisions of Article 36(1)(2) and (3) of the present Federal Law in the part of the period provided for by them.

3. The procedure for conducting an external vote shall be determined by the internal document of the society which must provide for the obligatoriness of communicating to all participants of the society the proposed agenda, the possibility of familiarisation of all participants of the society before the vote commences with all necessary information and materials, the possibility of making proposals concerning the inclusion of additional questions on the agenda, the obligatoriness of communicating to all participants of the society before the vote commences with a changed agenda, and also the period for completion of the procedure of the voting.

Article 39. Adoption of Decisions With Regard to Questions Relegated to Competence of General Meeting of Participants of Society by Sole Participant of Society

In a society consisting of one participant decisions with regard to questions relegated to the competence of the general meeting of participants of the society shall be adopted by the sole participant of the society as one man and shall be formalised in writing. In so doing the provisions of Articles 34, 35, 36, 37, 38 and 43 of the present Federal Law shall not apply, except for provisions affecting the periods for conducting the yearly general meeting of participants of the society.

Article 40. One-Man Executive Organ of Society

1. The one-man executive organ of a society (director general, president, and others) shall be elected by the general meeting of participants of the society for the term determined by the charter of the society. The one-man executive organ of the society may be elected also not from among the participants of the society.

The contract between the society and the person effectuating the functions of the one-man executive organ of the society shall be signed in the name of the society by the person presiding at the general meeting of participants of the society at which the person effectuating the functions of one-man executive organ of the society is elected or by the participant of the society empowered by decision of the general meeting of participants of the society.

2. Only a natural person, except for the instance provided for by Article 42 of the present Federal Law, may act as the one-man executive organ of the society.

3. The one-man executive organ of the society shall:

(1) act without a power of attorney in the name of the society, including represent its interests and conclude transactions;

(2) issue powers of attorney for the right of representation in the name of the society, including powers of attorney with the right of transfer;

(3) issue orders concerning the appointment to office of workers of the society, their transfer and dismissal, and take measures of incentive and impose disciplinary sanctions;

(4) effectuate other powers not relegated by the present Federal Law or charter of the society to the competence of the general meeting of participants of the society, council of directors (or supervisory council) of the society and collegial executive organ of the society.

4. The procedure for activity of the one-man executive organ of the society and the adoption by it of decisions shall be established by the charter of the society, internal documents of the society, and also the contract concluded between the society and the person effectuating the functions of its one-man executive organ.

Article 41. Collegial Executive Organ of Society

1. If the formation, together with a one-man executive organ of the society, of a collegial executive organ (board, directorate, and others) of the society also has been provided for by the charter of the society, such organ shall be elected by the general meeting of participants of the society in the number and for the period which has been determined by the charter of the society.

Only a natural person, who may be not a participant of the society, may be a member of the collegial executive organ of the society.

The collegial executive organ of the society shall effectuate the powers relegated by the charter of the society to its competence.

The functions of chairman of the collegial executive organ of the society shall be fulfilled by the person effectuating the functions of one-man executive organ of the society, except for the instance when the powers of the one-man executive organ of the society shall be transferred to a manager.

2. The procedure for the activity of the collegial executive organ of the society and the adoption by it of decisions shall be established by the charter of the society and the internal documents of the society.

Article 42. Transfer of Powers of One-Man Executive Organ of Society to Manager

A society shall have the right to transfer under a contract the powers of its one-man executive organ to a manager if such possibility has been expressly provided for by the charter of the society.

The contract with the manager shall be signed in the name of the society by the person presiding at the general meeting of participants of the society which confirmed the conditions of the contract with the manager or by a participant of the society empowered by decision of the general meeting of participants of the society.

Article 43. Appeal Against Decisions of Management Organs of Society

1. The decision of the general meeting of participants of the society adopted in violation of the requirements of the present Federal Law, other legal acts of the Russian Federation, charter of the society, and violating the rights and legal interests of the participant of the society may be deemed by a court to be invalid upon the application of the participant of the society which did not take part in the voting or which voted against the decision being contested. Such application may be filed within two months from the date when the participant of the society knew or should have known about the adoption of the decision. If the participant of the society took part in the general meeting of participants of the society which adopted the decision being appealed, the said application may be filed within two months from the date of the adoption of such decision.

2. A court shall have the right, taking into account all the circumstances of the case, to leave in force the decision being appealed if the vote of the participant of the society which filed the application could not influence the results of the voting, the violation permitted was not material, and the decision did not entail the causing of losses to a particular participant of the society.

3. The decision of the council of directors (or supervisory council) of the society, one-man executive organ of the society, collegial executive organ of the society, or manager adopted in violation of the requirements of the present Federal Law, other legal acts of the Russian Federation, the charter of the society, and violating the rights and legal interests of a participant of the society may be deemed by a court to be invalid upon the application of this participant of the society.

Article 44. Responsibility of Members of Council of Directors (or Supervisory Council) of Society, One-Man Executive Organ of Society, Members of Collegial Executive Organ of Society and Manager

1. Members of the council of directors (or supervisory council) of the society, one-man executive organ of the society, members of the collegial executive organ of the society, and likewise the manager when effectuating their rights and performing duties must act in the interests of the society in good faith and reasonably.

2. Members of the council of directors (or supervisory council) of the society, one-man executive organ of the society, members of the collegial executive organ of the society, and likewise the manager shall bear responsibility to the society for losses caused to the society by their guilty actions (or failure to act) unless other

grounds have been established by Federal laws. In so doing members of the council of directors (or supervisory council) of the society and members of the collegial executive organ of the society who voted against the decision which entailed the causing of losses to the society or who did not take part in the voting shall not bear responsibility.

3. When determining the grounds and amount of responsibility of members of the council of directors (or supervisory council) of the society, one-man executive organ of the society, members of the collegial executive organ of the society, and likewise the manager, the ordinary conditions of business turnover and other circumstances having significance for the matter must be taken into account.

4. If in accordance with the provisions of the present Article several persons bear responsibility, their responsibility to the society shall be joint and several.

5. The society or participant thereof shall have the right to apply to a court with a suit concerning compensation of losses caused to the society by a member of the council of directors (or supervisory council) of the society, one-man executive organ of the society, member of the collegial executive organ of the society, or manager.

Article 45. Interest in Conclusion of Transaction by Society

1. Transactions in the conclusion of which there is an interest of a member of the council of directors (or supervisory council) of the society, the person effectuating the functions of one-man executive organ of the society, member of the collective executive organ of the society, or interest of a participant of the society having jointly with its affiliated persons 20% or more of the votes of the total number of votes of participants of the society may not be concluded by the society without the consent of the general meeting of participants of the society.

The said persons shall be deemed to be interested in the conclusion of a transaction by the society in instances when they, their spouses, parents, children, brothers, sisters, and/or their affiliated persons:

are a party to the transaction or act in the interests of third persons in their relations with the society;

possess (each individually or in aggregate) 20% or more of the stocks (or participatory shares, shares) of the juridical person which is a party to the transaction or acts in the interests of third persons in their relations with the society;

holds an office in the management organs of the juridical persons which is a party to the transaction or acts in the interests of third persons in their relations with the society;

in other instances determined by the charter of the society.

2. The persons specified in point 1, paragraph one, of the present Article must bring to the information of the general meeting of participants of the society information concerning:

juridical persons in which they, their spouses, parents, children, brothers, sisters, and/or their affiliated persons possess 20% or more of the stocks (or participatory shares, shares);

juridical persons in which they, their spouses, parents, children, brothers, sisters, and/or their affiliated persons occupy offices in management organs;

transactions known to them to be concluded or proposed, in the conclusion of which they may be deemed to be interested.

3. The decision concerning the conclusion by the society of a transaction in the conclusion of which there is an interest shall be adopted by the general meeting of participants of the society by a majority of votes of the total number of votes of all participants of the society not interested in the conclusion thereof.

4. The conclusion of a transaction in the conclusion of which there is an interest shall not require the decision of the general meeting of participants of the society provided for by point 3 of the present Article if the transaction is concluded in the process of ordinary economic activity between the society and the other party which occurred before the moment from which the person interested in the conclusion of the transaction is deemed to be such in accordance with point 1 of the present Article (or the decision is not required before the date of conducting the next general meeting of participants of the society).

5. A transaction in the conclusion of which there is an interest and which is concluded in violation of the requirements provided for by the present Article may be deemed to be invalid upon the suit of the society or participant thereof.

6. The present Article shall not apply to societies consisting of one participant which simultaneously effectuates the functions of one-man executive organ of the particular society.

7. In the event of the formation in a society of the council of directors (or supervisory council) of the society the adoption of a decision concerning the conclusion of a transaction in the conclusion of which there is an interest may be relegated by the charter of the society to its competence, except for instances when the amount of payment with regard to the transaction or the value of the property which is the subject of the transaction exceeds 2% of the value of the property of the society determined on the basis of data of the bookkeeping reports for the preceding reporting year.

Article 46. Large-Scale Transactions

1. A large-scale transaction shall be a transaction or several interconnected transactions connected with the acquisition, alienation, or possibility of alienation by the society directly or indirectly of property whose value comprises more than 25% of the value of the property of the society determined on the basis of data of bookkeeping reports for the last reporting period preceding the date of the

adoption of the decision concerning the conclusion of such transactions unless a higher amount of a large-scale transaction has been provided for by the charter of the society. Transactions concluded in the process of ordinary economic activity of the society shall not be deemed to be large-scale transactions.

2. For the purposes of the present Article the value of the property being alienated by the society as a result of the large-scale transaction shall be determined on the basis of data of the bookkeeping records thereof, and the value of the property being acquired by the society, on the basis of the price of the offer.

3. The decision concerning the conclusion of the large-scale transaction shall be adopted by the general meeting of participants of the society.

4. In the event of the formation in the society of a council of directors (or supervisory council) of the society the adoption of decisions concerning the conclusion of large-scale transactions connected with the acquisition, alienation, or possible alienation by the society directly or indirectly of property whose value comprises from 25% up to 50% of the value of the property of the society may be relegated by the charter of the society to the competence of the council of directors (or supervisory council) of the society.

5. A large-scale transaction concluded in violation of the requirements provided for by the present Article may be deemed to be invalid upon the suit of the society or participant thereof.

6. It may be provided by the charter of the society that the decision of the general meeting of participants of the society and the council of directors (or supervisory council) of the society is not required in order to conclude large-scale transactions.

Article 47. Audit Commission (or Internal Auditor) of Society

1. The audit commission (or internal auditor) of a society shall be elected by the general meeting of participants of the society for the term determined by the charter of the society.

The number of members of the audit commission of the society shall be determined by the charter of the society.

2. The audit commission (or internal auditor) of the society shall have the right at any time to conduct verifications of the financial-economic activity of the society and have access to all documentation affecting the activity of the society. At the demand of the audit commission (or internal auditor) of the society the members of the council of directors (or supervisory council) of the society, the person effectuating the functions of one-man executive organ of the society, members of the collegial executive organ of the society, and also workers of the society shall be obliged to give necessary explanations in oral or written form.

3. The audit commission (or internal auditor) of the society shall in an oblig-atory procedure conduct the verification of the yearly reports and bookkeeping balance sheets of the society until their confirmation by the general meeting of participants of the society. The general meeting of participants of the society shall not have the right to confirm the yearly reports and bookkeeping balance sheets of the society in the absence of opinions of the audit commission (or internal audi-tor) of the society.

4. The work procedure of the audit commission (or internal auditor) of the society shall be determined by the charter and internal documents of the society.

5. The present Article shall apply in instances when the formation of the audit commission or election of the internal auditor of the society has been provided for by the charter of the society or is obligatory in accordance with the present Federal Law.

Article 48. Audit Verification of Society

In order to verify and confirm the correctness of yearly reports and bookkeep-ing balance sheets of the society, and also in order to verify the state of current affairs of the society, it shall have the right by decision of the general meeting of participants of the society to enlist a professional auditor not connected by prop-erty interests with the society, members of the council of directors (or supervisory council) of the society, the person effectuating the function of one-man executive organ of the society, members of the collegial executive organ of the society, and participants of the society.

At the demand of any participant of the society an auditor verification may be conducted by a professional auditor selected by it who must meet the require-ments established by paragraph one of the present Article. In the event of con-ducting such verification, payment for the services of the auditor shall be effectuated at the expense of the participant of the society upon whose demand it is conducted. The expenses of the participant of the society for payment for the services of the auditor may be compensated to it by decision of the general meet-ing of participants of the society at the expense of means of the society.

Enlistment of an auditor in order to verify and confirm the correctness of the yearly reports and bookkeeping balance sheets of the society shall be obligatory in the instances provided for by Federal laws and by other legal acts of the Russian Federation.

Article 49. Public Reports of Society

1. A society shall not be obliged to publish the reports concerning its activity, except for instances provided for by the present Federal Law and other Federal laws.

2. In the event of the public placement of bonds and other emission securities a society shall be obliged annually to publish yearly reports and bookkeeping bal-

ance sheets, and also to disclose other information concerning its activity provided for by Federal laws and normative acts adopted in accordance with them.

Article 50. Keeping Documents of Society

1. A society shall be obliged to keep the following documents:

constitutive documents of the society, and also changes in and additions made to the constitutive documents of the society and registered in the established procedure;

protocol(s) of the meeting of founders of the society containing the decision concerning the creation of the society and confirmation of the monetary valuation of nonmonetary contributions to the charter fund of the society, and also other decisions connected with the creation of the society;

document confirming the State registration of the society;

documents confirming the rights of the society to property situated on its balance sheet;

internal documents of the society;

statutes on branches and representations of the society;

documents connected with the emission of bonds and other emission securities of the society;

protocols of general meetings of participants of the society, sessions of the council of directors (or supervisory council) of the society, collegial executive organ of the society, and audit commission of the society;

lists of affiliated persons of the society;

opinions of the audit commission (or internal auditor) of the society, auditor, State and municipal financial control agencies;

other documents provided for by Federal laws and other legal acts of the Russian Federation, charter of the society, internal documents of the society, decisions of the general meeting of participants of the society, council of directors (or supervisory council) of the society, and executive organs of the society.

2. The society shall keep the documents provided for by point 1 of the present Article at the location of its one-man executive organ or other place known to and accessible to the participants of the society.

Chapter V. Reorganisation and Liquidation of Society

Article 51. Reorganisation of Society

1. A society may be voluntarily reorganised in the procedure provided for by the present Federal Law.

Other grounds and the procedure for the reorganisation of the society shall be determined by the Civil Code of the Russian Federation and other Federal laws.

2. The reorganisation of a society may be effectuated in the form of merger, accession, separation, division, and transformation.

3. A society shall be considered to be reorganised, except for instances of reorganisation in the form of accession, from the moment of State registration of the juridical persons created as a result of the reorganisation.

In the event of the reorganisation of a society in the form of accession to it of another society, the first of them shall be considered to be reorganised from the moment of making an entry in the unified State register of juridical persons concerning the termination of the activity of the acceding society.

4. The State registration of a society created as a result of reorganisation and the making of entries concerning the termination of activity of the reorganised societies, and also the State registration of changes in the charter, shall be effectuated in the procedure established by Federal laws.

5. Not later than thirty days from the date of adoption of the decision concerning reorganisation of the society, and in the event of the reorganisation of a society in the form of merger or accession, from the date of adoption of the decision concerning this by the last of the societies participating in the merger or accession, the society shall be obliged in writing to inform all the creditors of the society known to it thereof and to publish in the press organ in which data concerning the State registration of juridical persons is published a communication concerning the decision adopted. In so doing the creditors of the society within thirty days from the date of sending notifications to them or within thirty days from the date of publication of the communication concerning the decision adopted shall have the right in writing to demand the termination or performance before time of the respective obligations of the society and compensation of losses to them.

The State registration of the societies created as a result of the reorganisation and the making of entries concerning the termination of the activity of the reorganised societies shall be effectuated only in the event of the submission of evidence of notification of the creditors in the procedure established by the present point.

If the separation balance sheet does not make it possible to determine the legal successor of the reorganised society, the juridical persons created as a result of the reorganisation shall bear joint and several responsibility for the obligations of the reorganised society to its creditors.

Article 52. Merger of Society

1. The merger of societies shall be deemed to be the creation of a new society with the transfer thereto of all rights and duties of two or several societies and the termination of the last.

2. The general meeting of the participants of each society participating in the reorganisation in the form of merger shall adopt a decision concerning such reorganisation, confirmation of the contract on the merger and the charter of the

society being created as a result of the merger, and also confirmation of the act of transfer.

3. The contract on the merger signed by all the participants of the society being created as a result of the merger is, together with its charter, the constitutive document thereof and must correspond to all the requirements presented by the Civil Code of the Russian Federation and the present Federal Law for a constitutive contract.

4. In the event of the adoption by the general meeting of participants of each society participating in the reorganisation in the form of merger of a decision concerning such reorganisation and confirmation of the contract on merger, the charter of the society created as a result of the merger, and the act of transfer, the election of the executive organs of the society created as a result of the merger shall be effectuated at a joint general meeting of the participants of the societies participating in the merger. The periods and procedure for conducting such general meeting shall be determined by the contract on merger.

The one-man executive organ of the society created as a result of the merger shall effectuate the actions connected with the State registration of the particular society.

5. In the event of the merger of a society all the rights and duties of each of them shall pass to the society created as a result of the merger in accordance with the act of transfer.

Article 53. Accession to Society

1. The accession of a society shall be deemed to be the termination of one or several societies with the transfer of all of their rights and duties to another society.

2. The general meeting of participants of each society participating in the reorganisation in the form of accession shall adopt a decision concerning such reorganisation and confirmation of the contract on accession, and the general meeting of participants of the acceding society also shall adopt a decision concerning confirmation of the act of transfer.

3. A joint general meeting of participants of the societies participating in the accession shall make the changes in the constitutive documents of the society to which accession is being effectuated which are connected with the change of the composition of the participants of the society, determination of the amounts of their participatory shares, other changes provided for by the contract on accession, and also, when necessary, decide other questions, including questions concerning the election of the organs of the society to which accession is being effectuated. The periods and procedure for conducting such a general meeting shall be determined by the contract on accession.

4. In the event of the accession of one society to another, to the last shall pass all the rights and duties of the acceding society in accordance with the act of transfer.

Article 54. Division of Society

1. The division of a society shall be deemed to be the termination of the society with the transfer of all of its rights and duties to the newly created societies.

2. The general meeting of participants of the society being reorganised in the form of division shall adopt a decision concerning such reorganisation, on the procedure and conditions for division of the society, the creation of the new societies, and confirmation of the division balance sheet.

3. The participants of each society created as a result of the division shall sign the constitutive document. The general meeting of participants of each society created as a result of the division shall confirm the charter and elect the organs of the society.

4. In the event of the division of a society all of its rights and duties shall pass to the societies created as a result of the division in accordance with the division balance sheet.

Article 55. Separation of Society

1. The separation of a society shall be deemed to be the creation of one or several societies with the transfer to it (or to them) of part of the rights and duties of the society being reorganised without termination of the last.

2. The general meeting of participants of the society being reorganised in the form of separation shall adopt a decision concerning such reorganisation, the procedure and conditions of the separation, the creation of the new society (or societies), and the confirmation of the division balance sheet, make changes in the constitutive documents of the society being reorganised in the form of separation connected with the change of the composition of the participants of the society, determination of their participatory shares, and other changes provided for by the decision concerning separation, and also, when necessary, decide other questions, including questions concerning the election of the organs of the society.

The participants of the separating society shall sign a constitutive contract. The general meeting of participants of the separating society shall confirm its charter and elect the organs of the society.

If the sole participant of the separating society is the reorganised society, the general meeting of the last shall adopt a decision concerning the reorganisation of the society in the form of separation, the procedure and conditions of separation, and also confirm the charter of the separating society and the division balance sheet, and elect the organs of the separating society.

3. In the event of the separation from a society of one or several societies, to each of them shall pass part of the rights and duties of the reorganised society in accordance with the division balance sheet.

Article 56. Transformation of Society

1. A society shall have the right to transform itself into a joint-stock society, additional responsibility society, or production cooperative.

2. The general meeting of participants of the society being reorganised in the form of transformation shall adopt a decision concerning such reorganisation, the procedure and conditions of transformation, the procedure for the exchange of participatory shares of the participants of the society into stocks of the joint-stock society, participatory shares of participants of an additional responsibility society, or shares of members of a production cooperative, confirmation of the charter of the joint-stock society, additional responsibility society, or production cooperative being created as a result of the transformation, and also confirmation of the act of transfer.

3. The participants of a juridical person created as a result of the transformation shall adopt a decision concerning the election of its organs in accordance with the requirements of Federal laws on such juridical persons and shall commission the respective organ to effectuate the actions connected with the State registration of the juridical person created as a result of the transformation.

4. In the event of the transformation of a society, to the juridical person created as a result of the transformation shall pass all the rights and duties of the reorganised society in accordance with the act of transfer.

Article 57. Liquidation of Society

1. A society may be liquidated voluntarily in the procedure established by the Civil Code of the Russian Federation, taking into account the requirements of the present Federal Law and the charter of the society. A society may be liquidated also by decision of a court on the grounds provided for by the Civil Code of the Russian Federation.

The liquidation of a society shall entail its termination without the transfer of rights and duties by way of legal succession to other persons.

2. The decision of the general meeting of participants of a society concerning voluntary liquidation of the society and the appointment of the liquidation commission shall be adopted upon the proposal of the council of directors (or supervisory council) of the society, executive organ, or participant of the society being liquidated.

The general meeting of participants of a society being liquidated voluntarily shall adopt a decision concerning the liquidation of the society and appointment of the liquidation commission [as amended by Federal Law No. 31-ФЗ, 21 March 2002].

3. From the moment of the appointment of the liquidation commission to it shall pass all powers relating to the management of the affairs of the society. The liquidation commission shall act in court in the name of the society being liquidated.

4. If the Russian Federation, subject of the Russian Federation, or municipal formation is a participant of the society being liquidated, the composition of the liquidation commission shall include a representative of the Federal agency for the administration of State property, specialised institution effectuating the sale of Federal property, agency for the administration of State property of the subject of the Russian Federation, seller of State property of the subject of the Russian Federation, or agency of local self-government [as amended by Federal Law No. 31-ФЗ, 21 March 2002].

5. The procedure for liquidation of the society shall be determined by the Civil Code of the Russian Federation and other Federal laws.

Article 58. Distribution of Property of Society Being Liquidated Among its Participants

1. The property of a society being liquidated which remains after the completion of the settlement of accounts with creditors shall be distributed by the liquidation commission among the participants in the following priority:
in first priority shall be effectuated the payment to participants of the society of the portion of profit distributed but not paid;
in second priority shall be effectuated the distribution of property of the society being liquidated among the participants of the society in proportion to their participatory shares in the charter capital of the society.

2. The demands of each priority shall be satisfied after the complete satisfaction of demands of the preceding priority.
If the property of the society available is insufficient to pay the part of the profit which has been distributed but not paid, the property of the society shall be distributed among the participants thereof in proportion to their participatory shares in the charter capital of the society.

Chapter VI. Concluding Provisions

Article 59. Introduction of Present Federal Law into Operation

1. The present Federal Law shall be introduced into operation from 1 March 1998.

2. From the moment of the introduction of the present Federal Law into operation the legal acts operating on the territory of the Russian Federation before

being brought into conformity with the present Federal Law shall apply in the part which is not contrary to the present Federal Law.

The constitutive documents of limited responsibility societies (or limited responsibility partnerships) shall from the moment of the introduction of the present Federal Law into force apply in the part which is not contrary to the present Federal Law.

3. The constitutive documents of limited responsibility societies (or limited responsibility partnerships) created before the introduction of the present Federal Law into operation shall be subject to being brought into conformity with the norms of the present Federal Law not later than 1 July 1999 [as amended 31 December 1998].

Limited responsibility societies (or limited responsibility partnerships), the number of participants of which at the moment of the introduction of the present Federal Law into operation exceeds fifty must be transformed into joint-stock societies or production cooperatives before 1 July 1999, or the number of participants reduced to the limit established by the present Federal Law. When transforming such limited responsibility societies (or limited responsibility partnerships) into joint-stock societies, their transformation into closed joint-stock societies shall be permitted without the limitation of the maximum number of stockholders of the closed joint-stock society established by the Federal Law 'On Joint-Stock Societies'. The provisions of Article 7(3), paragraphs 2 and 3, of the Federal Law 'On Joint-Stock Societies' shall not apply to the said closed joint-stock societies [as amended by Federal Law No. 96-ФЗ, 11 July 1998 and Federal Law No. 193-ФЗ, 31 December 1998].

When transforming limited responsibility societies (or limited responsibility partnerships) into joint-stock societies or production cooperatives in the procedure provided for by the present point, the provisions of Article 51(5) of the present Federal Law also shall not apply [as amended by Federal Law No. 193-ФЗ, 31 December 1998].

The decision of the general meeting of participants of a limited responsibility society (or limited responsibility partnership) concerning the transformation of the limited responsibility society (or limited responsibility partnership), the number of whose participants at the moment of introduction of the present Federal Law into operation exceeds fifty, shall be adopted by a majority of not less than two-thirds of the votes of the total number of votes of participants of the limited responsibility society (or limited responsibility partnership). The participants of the limited responsibility society (or limited responsibility partnership) who have voted against the adoption of the decision concerning its transformation or who have not taken part in the voting shall have the right to withdraw from the limited responsibility society (or limited responsibility partnership) in the procedure established by Article 26 of the present Federal Law [added by Federal Law No. 193-ФЗ, 31 December 1998].

Limited responsibility societies (or limited responsibility partnerships) which have not brought their constitutive documents into conformity with the present Federal Law or have not been transformed into joint-stock societies or production cooperatives, may be liquidated in a judicial proceeding upon the demand of the agency effectuating State registration of juridical persons or other State agencies or agencies of local self-government to which the right to present such demands has been granted by a Federal law.

4. The limited responsibility societies (or limited responsibility partnerships) specified in point 3 of the present Article shall be exempt from the payment of a registration fee when registering changes of their legal status in connection with bringing it into conformity with the present Federal Law.

FEDERAL LAW ON JOINT-STOCK SOCIETIES

[Federal Law No. 208-ФЗ, 26 December 1995,
as changed on 13 June 1996, No. 65-ФЗ; 24 May 1999,
No. 101-ФЗ; 7 August 2001, No. 120-ФЗ;
21 March 2002, No. 31-ФЗ, and 31 October 2002.
СЗ РФ (1996), no. 1, item 1; no. 25, item 2956;
(1999), no. 22, item 2672; (2001), no. 33(I), item 3423;
(2002), no. 12, item 1093; no. 45, item 4436]

Chapter I	General Provisions	215
Chapter II	Founding, Reorganisation, and Liquidation of Society	223
Chapter III	Charter Capital of Society. Stocks, Bonds, and Other Emission Securities of Society. Net Assets of Society	234
Chapter IV	Placement by Society of Stocks and Other Emission Securities	245
Chapter V	Dividends of Society	249
Chapter VI	Register of Stockholders of Society	251
Chapter VII	General Meeting of Stockholders	253
Chapter VIII	Council of Directors (or Supervisory Council) of Society and Executive Organ of Society	271
Chapter IX	Acquisition and Purchase by Society of Placed Stocks	281
Chapter X	Large-Scale Transactions	287
Chapter XI	Interest in Conclusion of Transaction by Society	290
Chapter XII	Control Over Financial-Economic Activity of Society	294
Chapter XIII	Records, Reports, and Documents of Society. Information Concerning the Society	295
Chapter XIV	Concluding Provisions	298

Chapter I. General Provisions

Article 1. Sphere of Application of Present Federal Law

1. In accordance with the Civil Code of the Russian Federation, the present Federal Law determines the procedure for the creation, reorganisation, and liquidation, and the legal status of joint-stock societies, the rights and duties of their stockholders, and also ensures the defence of the rights and interests of stockholders [as amended by Federal Law No. 120-ФЗ, 7 August 2001].

2. The present Federal Law shall extend to all joint-stock societies created or to be created on the territory of the Russian Federation unless established otherwise by the present Federal Law and by other federal laws.

3. The peculiarities of the creation, reorganisation, and liquidation, and legal status of joint-stock societies in the spheres of banking, investment, and insurance activity shall be determined by federal laws [as amended by Federal Law No. 120-ФЗ, 7 August 2001].

4. The peculiarities of the creation, reorganisation, and liquidation, and legal status of joint-stock societies created on the base of collective farms, State farms, and other agricultural enterprises reorganised in accordance with the Edict of the President of the Russian Federation of 27 December 1991, No. 323, 'On Urgent Measures Relating to the Effectuation of Land Reform in the RSFSR', and also peasant (or farmer) economies, servicing and service enterprises for agricultural producers, to wit: enterprises of material-technical supply, repair-technical enterprises, enterprises for agricultural chemistry, forestry farms, construction inter-farm organisations, rural electric power enterprises, seed-growing stations, flax plants, and enterprises for the processing of vegetables shall be determined by federal laws [as amended by Federal Law No. 120-ФЗ, 7 August 2001].

5. The peculiarities for the creation of joint-stock societies during privatisation of State and municipal enterprises shall be determined by a federal law and other legal acts of the Russian Federation on the privatisation of State and municipal enterprises. The peculiarities of the legal status of joint-stock societies created during privatisation of State and municipal enterprises, more than 25% of the stocks of which have been consolidated in State or municipal ownership or with respect to which a special right is used for the participation of the Russian Federation, subjects of the Russian Federation, or municipal formations to manage the said joint-stock societies ('golden stock'), shall be determined by a federal law on the privatisation of State and municipal enterprises [as amended by Federal Law No. 120-ФЗ, 7 August 2001].

The peculiarities of the legal status of joint-stock societies created during the privatisation of State and municipal enterprises shall operate from the moment of the adoption of the decision concerning privatisation until the moment of alienation by the State or municipal formation of 75% of the stocks belonging to them in such joint-stock society, but not later than the end of the period for privatisation determined by the privatisation plan of the said enterprise.

Article 2. Basic Provisions on Joint-Stock Societies [as amended by Federal Law No. 120-ФЗ, 7 August 2001]

1. A commercial organisation whose charter capital is divided into a specified number of stocks certifying the rights of obligation of the participants of the soci-

ety (stockholders) with respect to the society shall be deemed to be a joint-stock society (hereinafter: society).

Stockholders shall not be liable for obligations of the society and shall bear the risk of losses connected with its activity within the limits of the value of the stocks belonging to them.

Stockholders who have not fully paid up stocks shall bear joint and several responsibility for obligations of the society within the limits of the unpaid portion of the value of the stocks belonging to them.

Stockholders shall have the right to alienate stocks belonging to them without the consent of other stockholders and the society [added by Federal Law No. 120-ФЗ, 7 August 2001].

2. The provisions of the present Federal Law shall extend to societies with one stockholder in so far as not provided otherwise by the present Federal Law and in so far as this is not contrary to the essence of the respective relations [added by Federal Law No. 120-ФЗ, 7 August 2001].

3. The society shall be a juridical person and shall have in ownership solitary property taken into account on its autonomous balance sheet, may in its own name acquire and effectuate property and personal nonproperty rights, bear duties, and be a plaintiff and defendant in a court [renumbered by Federal Law No. 120-ФЗ, 7 August 2001].

A society shall not have the right to conclude transactions not connected with the founding of the society until 50% of the stocks of the society distributed among its founders have been paid up [added by Federal Law No. 120-ФЗ, 7 August 2001].

4. A society shall have civil rights and bear duties necessary for the effectuation of any types of activity not prohibited by federal laws.

A society may engage in individual types of activity, a List of which shall be determined by federal laws, only on the basis of a special authorisation (or license). If a requirement concerning the engaging in such activity as exclusive has been provided for by the conditions of granting a special authorisation (or license) to engage in a specified type of activity, the society during the period of operation of the special authorisation (or license) shall not have the right to effectuate other types of activity except for types of activity provided for by the special authorisation (or license) and concomitant thereto [renumbered by Federal Law No. 120-ФЗ, 7 August 2001].

5. A society shall be considered to be created as a juridical person from the moment of its State registration in the procedure established by federal laws. A society shall be created without limitation of period unless established otherwise by its charter [renumbered by Federal Law No. 120-ФЗ, 7 August 2001].

6. A society shall have the right in the established procedure to open bank accounts on the territory of the Russian Federation and beyond its limits [renumbered by Federal Law No. 120-ФЗ, 7 August 2001].

7. A society must have a circular seal containing its full firm name in the Russian language and an indication of its location. The seal also may indicate the firm name of the society in any foreign language or in the language of peoples of the Russian Federation.

A society shall have the right to have stamps and letterheads with its name, own emblem, and also trademark and other means of visual identification registered in the established procedure [renumbered by Federal Law No. 120-ФЗ, 7 August 2001].

Article 3. Responsibility of Society

1. A society shall bear responsibility for its obligations with all of the property belonging to it.

2. A society shall not be liable for the obligations of its stockholders.

3. If the insolvency (or bankruptcy) of a society is caused by the actions (or failure to act) of its stockholders or other persons who have the right to give instructions binding upon the society or otherwise have the possibility to determine its actions, then subsidiary responsibility for its obligations may be placed on the said stockholders or other persons in the event of the insufficiency of the property of the society.

The insolvency (or bankruptcy) of a society shall be considered to be caused by the actions (or failure to act) of its stockholders or other persons who have the right to give instructions binding upon the society or otherwise have the possibility to determine its actions only if they have used the said right and/or the possibility for the purposes of the commission of actions by the society knowingly knowing that as a consequence thereof the insolvency (or bankruptcy) of the society shall ensue.

4. The State and its agencies shall not bear responsibility for obligations of the society, and likewise the society shall not be liable for the obligations of the State and its agencies.

Article 4. Firm Name and Location of Society [as amended by Federal Law No. 120-ФЗ, 7 August 2001]

1. A society shall have a full and shall have the right to have an abbreviated firm name in the Russian language. A society also shall have the right to have a full and/or abbreviated name in the languages of peoples of the Russian Federation and/or foreign languages [as amended by Federal Law No. 120-ФЗ, 7 August 2001].

The full firm name of the society in the Russian language must contain the full name of the society and an indication of the type of society (closed or open). The abbreviated firm name of a society in the Russian language must contain the full or abbreviated name of the society and the words 'closed joint-stock society' or 'open joint-stock society' or the abbreviation 'ZAO' or 'OAO' [added by Federal Law No. 120-ФЗ, 7 August 2001].

The firm name of a society in the Russian language may not contain other terms and abbreviations reflecting its organisational-legal form, including borrowed from foreign languages, unless provided otherwise by federal laws and other legal acts of the Russian Federation [added by Federal Law No. 120-ФЗ, 7 August 2001].

2. The location of a society shall be determined by the place of its State registration. The constitutive documents of a society may establish that the location of a society is the place of permanent location of its management organs or principal place of its activity [as amended by Federal Law No. 120-ФЗ, 7 August 2001].

3. [as amended by Federal Law No. 120-ФЗ, 7 August 2001, and repealed by Federal Law No. 31-ФЗ, 21 March 2002].

Article 5. Branches and Representations of Society

1. A society may create branches and open representations on the territory of the Russian Federation in compliance with the requirements of the present Federal Law and other federal laws.

The creation by a society of branches and the opening of representations beyond the limits of the territory of the Russian Federation also shall be effectuated in accordance with legislation of the foreign State at the location of the branches and representations unless provided otherwise by an international treaty of the Russian Federation.

2. A branch of a society shall be the solitary subdivision thereof located outside the location of the society and effectuating all of its functions, including the functions of a representation or part thereof.

3. A representation of a society shall be a solitary subdivision thereof located outside the location of the society and representing the interests of the society and effectuating the defence thereof.

4. A branch and representation shall not be juridical persons and shall operate on the basis of a Statute confirmed by the society. A branch and representation shall be endowed with property by the society which created it, which shall be taken into account on their individual balance sheets and also on the balance sheet of the society.

The director of the branch and the director of the representation shall be appointed by the society and shall operate on the basis of a power of attorney issued by the society.

5. A branch and representation shall effectuate activity in the name of the society which created them. Responsibility for the activity of the branch and representation shall be borne by the society which created them.

6. The charter of a society must contain information concerning its branches and representations. Communications concerning changes in the charter of a society connected with the change of information concerning its branches and representations shall be submitted to the State registration agency of juridical persons in an informational procedure. The said changes in the charter of the society shall enter into force for third persons from the moment of the notification concerning such changes of the agency effectuating State registration of juridical persons [as amended by Federal Law No. 120-ФЗ, 7 August 2001].

Article 6. Subsidiary and Dependent Societies

1. A society may have subsidiary and dependent societies with the rights of a juridical person on the territory of the Russian Federation created in accordance with the present Federal Law and other federal laws, and beyond the limits of the territory of the Russian Federation—in accordance with legislation of the foreign State where the subsidiary or dependent society is located unless provided otherwise by an international treaty of the Russian Federation.

2. A society shall be deemed to be a subsidiary if another (principal) economic society (or partnership) by virtue of predominant participation in its charter capital or in accordance with a contract concluded between them, or otherwise has the possibility to determine decisions adopted by such a society.

3. A subsidiary society shall not be liable for the debts of the principal society (or partnership).

A principal society (or partnership) which has the right to give to the subsidiary society instructions binding upon the last shall be liable jointly and severally with the subsidiary society for transactions concluded by the last in execution of such instructions. The principal society (or partnership) shall be considered to have the right to give to the subsidiary society instructions which are binding upon the last only when this right is provided for in a contract with the subsidiary society or the charter of the subsidiary society.

In the event of the insolvency (or bankruptcy) of a subsidiary society through the fault of the principal society (or partnership), the last shall bear subsidiary responsibility for its debts. The insolvency (or bankruptcy) of a subsidiary society shall be considered to have occurred through the fault of the principal society (or partnership) only when the principal society (or partnership) has used the said right and/or possibility for the purposes of the commission by the subsidiary society of actions knowingly knowing that as a consequence thereof the insolvency (or bankruptcy) of the subsidiary society shall ensue.

Stockholders of a subsidiary society shall have the right to demand compensation by the principal society (or partnership) of losses caused through its fault to the subsidiary society. The losses shall be considered to be caused through the fault of the principal society (or partnership) only when the principal society (or partnership) has used a right and/or possibility which it has for the purposes of the commission by the subsidiary society of actions knowingly knowing that as a consequence thereof the subsidiary society shall incur losses.

4. A society shall be deemed to be dependent if another (predominant) society has more than 20% of the voting stocks of the first society.

A society which acquires more than 20% of the voting stocks of a society shall be obliged immediately to publish information about this in the procedure determined by the federal agency of executive power for the securities market and the federal antimonopoly agency [as amended by Federal Law No. 120-ФЗ, 7 August 2001].

Article 7. Open and Closed Societies

1. A society may be open or closed, which shall be reflected in its charter and firm name.

2. An open society shall have the right to conduct an open subscription for stocks issued by it and shall effectuate the free sale thereof taking into account the requirements of the present Federal Law and other legal acts of the Russian Federation. An open society shall have the right to conduct a closed subscription for the stocks to be issued by it except for instances when the possibility of conducting a closed subscription has been limited by the charter of the society or requirements of legal acts of the Russian Federation [as amended by Federal Law No. 120-ФЗ, 7 August 2001].

The number of stockholders of an open society shall not be limited.

The establishment of a preferential right of the society or its stockholders to acquire stocks alienated by stockholders of this society shall not be permitted in an open society [added by Federal Law No. 120-ФЗ, 7 August 2001].

3. A society whose stocks are distributed only among its founders or other previously determined group of persons shall be deemed to be a closed society. Such a society shall not have the right to conduct an open subscription for stocks to be issued by it or otherwise to offer them for acquisition to an unlimited group of persons.

The number of stockholders of a closed society must not exceed fifty.

If the number of stockholders of a closed society exceeds the limit established by the present point, the said society within one year must be transformed into an open [society]. If the number of its stockholders is not reduced up to the limit established by the present point, the society shall be subject to liquidation in a judicial proceeding.

The stockholders of a closed society shall enjoy a preferential right to acquire the stocks being sold by other stockholders of this society at the price of offer to a third person in proportion to the quantity of stocks belonging to each of them unless a different procedure for the effectuation of this right has been provided by the charter of the society. The preferential right of the society to acquire the stocks being sold by its stockholders may be provided for by the charter of a closed society unless the stockholders have used their preferential right to acquire the stocks [as amended by Federal Law No. 120-ФЗ, 7 August 2001].

A stockholder of a society intending to sell his stocks to a third person shall be obliged to notify in writing the remaining stockholders of the society thereof and the society itself, specifying the price and other conditions of the sale of the stocks. The notification of stockholders of the society shall be effectuated through the society. Unless provided otherwise by the charter of the society, notification of the stockholders of the society shall be effectuated at the expense of the stockholder intending to sell his stocks [as amended by Federal Law No. 120-ФЗ, 7 August 2001].

If the stockholders of a society and/or the society do not take advantage of the preferential right to acquire all the stocks offered for sale within two months from the day of such notification, unless a shorter period has been provided for by the charter of the society, the stocks may be sold to a third person at the price and on the conditions which have been communicated to the society and its stockholders. The period for effectuation of the preferential right provided for by the charter of the society must be not less than 10 days from the day of notification by the stockholder intending to sell his stocks to a third person of the remaining stockholders and the society. The period for effectuation of the preferential right shall terminate if before the expiry thereof written statements have been received from all stockholders of the society concerning the use or refusal to use the preferential right [added by Federal Law No. 120-ФЗ, 7 August 2001].

In the event of sale of the stocks with a violation of the preferential right of acquisition, any stockholder of the society and/or the society, if a preferential right of acquisition of stocks by the society has been provided for by the charter of the society, shall have the right within three months from the moment when the stockholder or the society knew or should have known about such violation to demand in a judicial proceeding the transfer to them of the rights and duties of the purchaser [added by Federal Law No. 120-ФЗ, 7 August 2001].

Assignment of the said preferential right shall not be permitted [added by Federal Law No. 120-ФЗ, 7 August 2001].

4. Societies whose founders are, in the instances established by federal laws, the Russian Federation, a subject of the Russian Federation, or municipal forma-

tion (except for societies formed in the process of privatisation of State and municipal enterprises) may only be open.

Chapter II. Founding, Reorganisation, and Liquidation of Society
[as amended by Federal Law No. 120-ФЗ, 7 August 2001]

Article 8. Creation of Society

A society may be created by means of being founded anew and by means of the reorganisation of an existing juridical person (merger, division, separation, transformation) [as amended by Federal Law No. 120-ФЗ, 7 August 2001].

A society shall be considered to be created from the moment of its State registration.

Article 9. Founding of Society

1. The creation of a society by means of founding shall be effectuated by decision of the founder(s). The decision concerning the founding of a society shall be adopted by the constitutive meeting. In the event of the founding of a society by one person, the decision concerning the founding thereof shall be adopted by this person alone.

2. The decision concerning the founding of a society must reflect the results of the voting of the founders and the decisions adopted by them regarding questions of the founding of the society, confirmation of the charter of the society, and election of the management organs of the society.

3. The decision concerning the founding of a society, confirmation of its charter, and confirmation of the monetary valuation of securities, other things or property rights, or other rights having monetary valuation contributed by the founders and the paying up of the stocks of the society shall be adopted by the founders unanimously.

4. The election of the management organs of the society shall be effectuated by the founders by a majority of three-quarters of the votes which represent the stocks subject to placement among the founders of the society.

5. The founders of the society shall conclude among themselves a written contract concerning its creation which determines the procedure for the effectuation by them of joint activity relating to the founding of the society, the amount of the charter capital of the society, the categories and types of stocks subject to placement among the founders, and amount and procedure for the paying up thereof, and the rights and duties of the founders relating to the creation of the society. A contract concerning the creation of a society shall not be the constitutive document of the society.

In the event a society is founded by one person, the decision concerning the founding must determine the amount of charter capital of the society, the categories (or types) of stocks, and the amount and procedure for paying them up [added by Federal Law No. 120-ФЗ, 7 August 2001].

6. The peculiarities of the founding of societies with the participation of foreign investors may be provided for by federal laws [as amended by Federal Law No. 120-ФЗ, 7 August 2001].

Article 10. Founders of Society

1. The founders of a society shall be citizens and/or juridical persons who have adopted a decision concerning the founding thereof.

State agencies and agencies of local self-government may not act as the founders of a society unless established otherwise by federal laws.

2. The number of founders of an open society shall not be limited. The number of founders of a closed society may not exceed fifty.

A society may not have as a sole founder (or stockholder) another economic society consisting of one person.

3. The founders of a society shall bear joint and several responsibility for obligations connected with its creation and arising before the State registration of the particular society.

A society shall bear responsibility for obligations of the founders connected with its creation only in the event of the subsequent approval of their actions by the general meeting of stockholders.

Article 11. Charter of Society

1. The charter of a society shall be the constitutive document of the society.

2. The requirements of the charter of a society shall be binding for execution by all organs of the society and its stockholders.

3. The charter of a society must contain the following information:
the full and abbreviated firm names of the society;
the location of the society;
the type of society (open or closed);
the number, par value, categories (common, preferred) of stocks and types of preferred stocks to be placed by the society;
the rights of the stockholders-possessors of stocks of each category (or type);
the amount of the charter capital of the society;
the structure and competence of the management organs of the society and the procedure for the adoption of decisions by them;
the procedure for the preparation and conducting of the general meeting of stockholders, including the list of questions, decisions regarding which shall be adopted by the management organs of the society by a qualified majority of votes or unanimously;

information concerning branches and representations of the society;

other provisions provided for by the present Federal Law and other federal laws [as amended by Federal Law No. 120-ФЗ, 7 August 2001].

Limitations on the quantity of stocks which belong to one stockholder, and the total par value thereof, and also the maximum number of votes to be granted to one stockholder, may be established by the charter of the society.

The charter of a society may contain other provisions which are not contrary to the present Federal Law and other federal laws.

The charter of a society must contain information concerning the use with respect to the society of the special right for participation of the Russian Federation, subject of the Russian Federation, or municipal formation in the management of the said society ('golden stock') [added by Federal Law No. 120-ФЗ, 7 August 2001].

4. At the demand of a stockholder, auditor, or any interested person, a society shall be obliged within reasonable periods to grant to it the possibility of familiarising itself with the charter of the society, including changes therein and additions thereto. The society shall be obliged to grant to a stockholder at his request a copy of the prevailing charter of the society. Payment recovered by the society for provision of a copy may not exceed the expenses for the manufacture thereof.

Article 12. Making Changes in and Additions to Charter of Society or Confirmation of Charter in New Version

1. The making of changes in and additions to the charter of a society or confirmation of a charter in a new version shall be effectuated by decision of the general meeting of stockholders, except for instances provided by points 2–5 of the present Article [as amended by Federal Law No. 120-ФЗ, 7 August 2001].

2. The making of changes in and additions to the charter of a society with regard to the results of placing stocks of the society, including changes connected with an increase of the charter capital of the society, shall be effectuated on the basis of a decision of the general meeting of stockholders concerning an increase of the charter capital of the society or a decision of the council of directors (or supervisory council) of the society, if in accordance with the charter of the society to the last belongs the right to adopt such decision, another decision which is the grounds for the placement of stocks and emission securities convertible into stocks, and registered report concerning the results of the issue of stocks. When increasing the charter capital of a society by means of the placement of additional stocks, the charter capital shall be increased by the amount of par values of the placed additional stocks, and the quantity of declared stocks of determined categories and types shall be reduced by the number of placed additional stocks of these categories and types [as amended by Federal Law No. 120-ФЗ, 7 August 2001].

3. The making of changes in and additions to the charter of a society connected with a reduction of charter capital of the society by means of the acquisition of stocks of a society for the purpose of cancellation thereof shall be effectuated on the basis of a decision of the general meeting of stockholders concerning such reduction and report confirmed by the council of directors (or supervisory council) of the society concerning the results of the acquisition of the stocks. In this event the charter capital of the society shall be reduced by the amount of par values of the cancelled stocks [added by Federal Law No. 120-ФЗ, 7 August 2001].

4. The insertion of information in the charter of a society concerning the use with respect to the society of the special right to participation of the Russian Federation, subject of the Russian Federation, or municipal formation in the management of the said society ('golden stock') shall be effectuated on the basis of the respective decision of the Government of the Russian Federation, agency of State power of the subject of the Russian Federation, or agency of local self-government of the Russian Federation concerning the use of the said special right, and the exclusion of such information—on the basis of a decision of these agencies concerning termination of the operation of such special right [added by Federal Law No. 120-ФЗ, 7 August 2001].

5. The making in the charter of a society of changes connected with the creation of branches, opening of representations of the society, and liquidation thereof shall be effectuated on the basis of a decision of the council of directors (or supervisory council) of the society [added by Federal Law No. 120-ФЗ, 7 August 2001].

Article 13. State Registration of Society

A society shall be subject to State registration in the agency effectuating the State registration of juridical persons in the procedure provided for by a federal law on the State registration of juridical persons.
[paragraph two repealed by Federal Law No. 31-ФЗ, 21 March 2002].

Article 14. State Registration of Changes in and Additions to Charter of Society or Charter of Society in New Version

1. The changes in and additions to the charter of a society or the charter of a society in a new version shall be subject to State registration in the procedure provided for by Article 13 of the present Federal Law for the registration of a society.

2. The changes in and additions to the charter of a society or the charter of a society in a new version shall acquire force for third persons from the moment of their State registration, and in the instances established by the present Federal Law, from the moment of informing the agency effectuating State registration.

Article 15. Reorganisation of Society

1. A society may be voluntarily reorganised in the procedure provided for by the present Federal Law. The peculiarities of the reorganisation of a society which is the subject of a natural monopoly, more than 25% of the stocks of which have been consolidated in federal ownership, shall be determined by a federal law establishing the grounds and procedure for the reorganisation of such society [as amended by Federal Law No. 101-ФЗ, 24 May 1999].

Other grounds and procedure of reorganisation of a society shall be determined by the Civil Code of the Russian Federation and by other federal laws.

2. The reorganisation of a society may be effectuated in the form of merger, accession, division, separation, and transformation.

3. The forming of the property of societies to be created as a result of a reorganisation shall be effectuated only at the expense of the property of the societies being reorganised [added by Federal Law No. 120-ФЗ, 7 August 2001].

4. A society shall be considered to be reorganised except for instances of reorganisation in the form of accession, from the moment of State registration of the juridical persons which arose anew.

In the event of the reorganisation of a society in the form of accession to it of another society, the first of them shall be considered to be reorganised from the moment of the making of the entry concerning the termination of the activity of the acceding society in the unified State Register of juridical persons [renumbered and amended by Federal Law No. 120-ФЗ, 7 August 2001].

5. The State registration of a society which arose anew as a result of reorganisation and the making of entries concerning the termination of activity of the reorganised societies shall be effectuated in the procedure established by federal laws [renumbered by Federal Law No. 120-ФЗ, 7 August 2001].

6. Not later than 30 days from the date of the adoption of a decision concerning reorganisation of a society, and in the event of reorganisation of a society in the form of merger or accession—from the date of adoption of the decision concerning this by the last of the societies participating in the merger or accession, a society shall be obliged in writing to inform creditors of the society thereof and to publish in a printed publication intended for the publication of data concerning the State registration of juridical persons a notice about the decision adopted. Creditors of the society within 30 days from the date of sending notifications to them or within 30 days from the date of publication of the notice concerning the decision adopted shall have the right in writing to demand the termination or the performance before time of respective obligations of the society and compensation of losses to them [renumbered and amended by Federal Law No. 120-ФЗ, 7 August 2001].

State registration of societies created as a result of reorganisation and the making of entries concerning the termination of activity of the reorganised societies shall be effectuated when there is evidence of notification of creditors in the procedure established by the present point [as amended by Federal Law No. 120-ФЗ, 7 August 2001].

If the separation balance sheet or act of transfer does not give the possibility to determine the legal successor of the reorganised society, the juridical persons created as a result of the reorganisation shall bear joint and several responsibility for obligations of the reorganised society to the creditors thereof [as amended by Federal Law No. 120-ФЗ, 7 August 2001].

Article 16. Merger of Society

1. The merger of a society shall be deemed to be the arising of a new society by means of the transfer to it of all the rights and duties of two or several societies with the termination of the last.

2. The societies participating in a merger shall conclude a contract concerning the merger in which shall be determined the procedure and conditions of the merger, and also the procedure for converting the stocks of each society into the stocks of the new society. The council of directors (or supervisory council) of the society shall submit for decision of the general meeting of stockholders of each society participating in the merger the question concerning reorganisation in the form of merger, confirmation of the contract concerning the merger, charter of the society created as a result of the merger, and confirmation of the act of transfer [as amended by Federal Law No. 120-ФЗ, 7 August 2001].

3. The formation of the organs of the society which newly arose shall be conducted at a joint general meeting of the stockholders of the societies participating in the merger. The procedure for voting at the joint general meeting of stockholders may be determined by a contract concerning the merger of the societies [as amended by Federal Law No. 120-ФЗ, 7 August 2001].

4. In the event of the merger of societies, the stocks of the society belonging to the other society participating in the merger, as well as own stocks belonging to the society participating in the merger, shall be cancelled [added by Federal Law No. 120-ФЗ, 7 August 2001].

5. In the event of the merger of societies, all the rights and duties of each of them shall pass to the society which newly arose in accordance with the act of transfer [renumbered by Federal Law No. 120-ФЗ, 7 August 2001].

Article 17. Accession of Society

1. The accession of a society shall be deemed to be the termination of one or several societies with the transfer of all their rights and duties to another society.

2. The acceding society and the society to which the accession is being effectuated shall conclude a contract concerning accession in which shall be determined the procedure and conditions of the accession, and also the procedure for converting the stocks of the acceding society to the stocks of the society to which the accession is being effectuated. The council of directors (or supervisory council) of each society shall submit for decision of the general meeting of stockholders participating in the accession the question concerning reorganisation in the form of accession and concerning confirmation of the contract concerning the accession. The council of directors (or supervisory council) of the acceding society shall also submit for decision of the general meeting of stockholders the question on confirmation of the act of transfer [as amended by Federal Law No. 120-ФЗ, 7 August 2001].

3. A joint general meeting of stockholders of the said societies shall adopt a decision concerning the making of changes in and additions to the charter and, when necessary, other questions. The procedure for voting at the joint general meeting of stockholders shall be determined by the contract on accession.

4. In the event of the accession of a society, the stocks of the acceding society belonging to the society to which the accession is being effectuated, and also own stocks belonging to the acceding society, shall be cancelled [added by Federal Law No. 120-ФЗ, 7 August 2001].

5. In the event of the accession of one society to another, to the last shall pass all the rights and duties of the acceding society in accordance with the act of transfer [renumbered by Federal Law No. 120-ФЗ, 7 August 2001].

Article 18. Division of Society

1. The division of a society shall be deemed to be the termination of a society by the transfer of all of its rights and duties to the societies created anew.

2. The council of directors (or supervisory council) of the society being reorganised in the form of division shall submit for decision of the general meeting of stockholders the question concerning the reorganisation of the society in the form of division, the procedure and conditions of the division, the creation of new societies and the procedure for converting the stocks of the society being reorganised into the stocks of the societies being created, and confirmation of the separation balance sheet [as amended by Federal Law No. 120-ФЗ, 7 August 2001].

3. The general meeting of the society being reorganised in the form of division shall adopt a decision concerning the reorganisation of the society in the form of division, the procedure and conditions of the division, the creation of the new societies, the procedure for converting the stocks of the society being reorganised into the stocks of the societies being created, and on confirmation of the division balance sheet. The general meeting of each newly-created society shall adopt a

decision concerning the confirmation of its charter and the formation of its organs [as amended by Federal Law No. 120-ФЗ, 7 August 2001].

Each stockholder of the society being reorganised who has voted against or has not taken part in the voting with regard to the question concerning reorganisation of the society must receive stocks of each society created as a result of the division granting the same rights as the stocks belonging to him in the society being reorganised in proportion to the number of stocks of that society belonging to him [added by Federal Law No. 120-ФЗ, 7 August 2001].

4. In the event of the division of a society, all of its rights and duties shall pass to the two or several societies created anew in accordance with the division balance sheet.

Article 19. Separation of Society

1. The separation of a society shall be deemed to be the creation of one or several societies with the transfer to them of part of the rights and duties of the reorganised society without the termination of the last.

2. The council of directors (or supervisory council) of the society being reorganised in the form of separation shall submit for decision of the general meeting of stockholders of the society the question concerning the reorganisation of the society in the form of separation, the procedure and the conditions of the separation, the creation of a new society (or societies), the converting of stocks of the society being reorganised into stocks of the society being created (or distribution of the stocks of the society being created among stockholders of the society being reorganised, acquisition of the stocks of the society being created by the society itself being reorganised), and the procedure for such converting (or distribution, acquisition), and confirmation of the division balance sheet [as amended by Federal Law No. 120-ФЗ, 7 August 2001].

3. The general meeting of stockholders of the society being reorganised in the form of separation shall adopt the decision concerning reorganisation of the society in the form of separation, the procedure and the conditions of the separation, the creation of a new society (or societies), the converting of stocks of the society being reorganised into stocks of the society being created (or distribution of the stocks of the society being created among the stockholders of the society being reorganised, acquisition of the stocks of the society being created by the society itself being reorganised), and the procedure for such converting (or distribution, acquisition), and confirmation of the division balance sheet [as amended by Federal Law No. 120-ФЗ, 7 August 2001].

The general meeting of stockholders of each society being created shall adopt a decision concerning confirmation of its charter and the formation of its organs. If in accordance with the decision concerning reorganisation in the form of separation the reorganised society will be the sole stockholder of the society being created, confirmation of the charter of the society being created and the formation of its organs shall be effectuated by the general meeting of stockholders of the society being reorganised [added by Federal Law No. 120-ФЗ, 7 August 2001].

If the decision concerning reorganisation of a society in the form of separation provides for converting stocks of the society being reorganised into stocks of the society being created or distribution of the stocks of the society being created among stockholders of the society being reorganised, each stockholder of the society being reorganised who voted against or who did not take part in voting with regard to the question concerning reorganisation of the society must receive stocks of each society created as a result of the separation granting the same rights that the stocks did which belonged to him in the reorganised society in proportion to the number of stocks of that society belonging to him [added by Federal Law No. 120-ФЗ, 7 August 2001].

4. In the event of the separation of one or several societies from a society, to each of them shall pass part of the rights and duties of the society being reorganised in the form of separation in accordance with the division balance sheet.

Article 20. Transformation of Society

1. A society shall have the right to transform itself into a limited responsibility society or into a production cooperative while complying with the requirements established by federal laws.

A society shall by unanimous decision of all the stockholders have the right to be transformed into a noncommercial partnership [added by Federal Law No. 120-ФЗ, 7 August 2001].

2. The council of directors (or supervisory council) of the society being transformed shall submit for decision of the general meeting of stockholders the question concerning transformation of the society, the procedure and conditions of the effectuation of the transformation, the procedure for exchange of the stocks of the society for contributions of the participants of the limited responsibility society or shares of the members of the production cooperative.

3. The general meeting of stockholders of the society being transformed shall adopt the decision concerning transformation of the society, the procedure and conditions of the effectuation of the transformation, the procedure for exchange of the stocks of the society for the contributions of the participants of the limited responsibility society or shares of the members of the production cooperative. The participants of the new juridical person being created during the transformation shall adopt at their joint session a decision concerning the confirmation of its constitutive doducments and the election (or appointment) of the management organs in accordance with the requirements of federal laws concerning these organisations.

4. In the event of the transformation of the society, to the juridical person created anew shall pass all the rights and duties of the reorganised society in accordance with the act of transfer.

Article 21. Liquidation of Society

1. A society may be liquidated voluntarily in the procedure established by the Civil Code of the Russian Federation, taking into account the requirements of the present Federal Law and the charter of the society. The society may be liquidated by decision of a court on the grounds provided for by the Civil Code of the Russian Federation.

The liquidation of a society shall entail its termination without the transfer of rights and duties by way of legal succession to other persons.

2. In the event of the voluntary liquidation of a society the council of directors (or supervisory council) of the society being liquidated shall submit for decision of the general meeting of stockholders the question concerning the liquidation of the society and the appointment of the liquidation commission.

The general meeting of stockholders of a society being liquidated voluntarily shall adopt a decision concerning liquidation of the society and the appointment of the liquidation commission.

3. From the moment of appointment of the liquidation commission, to it shall pass all the powers relating to the management of the affairs of the society. The liquidation commission shall act in the name of a society being liquidated in court.

4. When the stockholder of a society being liquidated is the State or a municipal formation, a representative of the respective committee for the administration of property or property fund or the respective agency of local self-government shall be included in the membership of the liquidation commission [as amended by Federal Law No. 31-ФЗ, 21 March 2002].

Article 22. Procedure for Liquidation of Society

1. The liquidation commission shall place in the press organs in which data concerning the registration of juridical persons is published a communication concerning the liquidation of the society and the procedure and periods for the presentation of demands by its creditors. The period for the presentation of demands by creditors may not be less than two months from the date of publication of the communication concerning the liquidation of the society.

2. If at the moment of the adoption of the decision concerning the liquidation the society has no obligations to creditors, its property shall be distributed among the stockholders in accordance with Article 23 of the present Federal Law.

3. The liquidation commission shall take measures to elicit creditors and to receive debtor indebtedness, and also shall inform in writing the creditors about the liquidation of the society.

4. At the end of the period for the presentation of demands by creditors, the liquidation commission shall draw up the interim liquidation balance sheet, which shall contain information concerning the composition of the property of the society being liquidated, the demands presented by creditors, and also the results of their consideration. The interim liquidation balance sheet shall be confirmed by the general meeting of stockholders [as amended by Federal Law No. 31-ФЗ, 21 March 2002].

5. If the monetary assets existing in the society being liquidated are insufficient to satisfy the demands of creditors, the liquidation commission shall effectuate the sale of other property of the society by public sale in the procedure established for the execution of judicial decisions.

6. Payments to creditors of a society being liquidated of monetary amounts shall be carried out by the liquidation commission in the sequence of priority established by the Civil Code of the Russian Federation in accordance with the interim liquidation balance sheet, commencing from the date of its confirmation, except for creditors of the fifth priority, payments to which shall be made upon the expiry of a month from the date of confirmation of the interim liquidation balance sheet.

7. After completion of the settlement of accounts with creditors, the liquidation commission shall draw up the liquidation balance sheet, which shall be confirmed by the general meeting of stockholders [as amended by Federal Law No. 31-ФЗ, 21 March 2002].

Article 23. Distribution of Property of Society Being Liquidated Among Stockholders

1. The property of the society being liquidated remaining after the completion of the settlement of accounts with creditors shall be distributed by the liquidation commission among the stockholders in the following priorities:

in the first priority shall be effectuated the payments relating to stocks which must be purchased in accordance with Article 75 of the present Federal Law;

in the second priority shall be effectuated payments for dividends credited but not paid with regard to preferred stocks and the liquidation value of preferred stocks determined by the charter of the society;

in the third priority shall be effectuated the distribution of property of the society being liquidated among the stockholders-possessors of common stocks and all types of preferred stocks.

2. The distribution of property of each priority shall be effectuated after the full distribution of property of the preceding priority. The payment by the society of the liquidation value of preferred stocks determined by the charter of the society being liquidated shall be effectuated after the payment in full of the liquidation value of the preferred stocks of the previous priority determined by the charter of the society being liquidated.

If the property existing in the society is insufficient for the payment of dividends credited but not paid and the liquidation value determined by the charter of the society for all stockholders-possessors of preferred stocks of one type, the property shall be distributed among the stockholders-possessors of this type of preferred stocks in proportion to the quantity of stocks of this type belonging to them.

Article 24. Completion of Liquidation of Society

The liquidation of a society shall be considered to be completed, and the society to have terminated its existence from the moment of the making by the agency of State registration of the respective entry in the unified State Register of juridical persons.

Chapter III. Charter Capital of Society. Stocks, Bonds, and Other Emission Securities of Society. Net Assets of Society
[as amended by Federal Law No. 120-ФЗ, 7 August 2001]

Article 25. Charter Capital and Stocks of Society

1. The charter capital of a society shall comprise the par value of the stocks of the society acquired by the stockholders.

The par value of all common stocks of the society must be identical.

The charter capital of a society shall determine the minimum amount of the property of a society guaranteeing the interests of its creditors.

2. A society shall place common stocks and shall have the right to place one or several types of preferred stocks. The par value of the placed preferred stocks must not exceed 25% of the charter capital of the society [as amended by Federal Law No. 120-ФЗ, 7 August 2001].

When founding a society, all of its stocks must be placed among the founders.

All stocks of a society shall be inscribed.

3. If when effectuating the preferential right for the acquisition of stocks to be sold by a stockholder of a closed society, when effectuating the preferential right for the acquisition of additional stocks, and also when consolidating stocks the acquisition by the stockholder of a round number of stocks is impossible, parts of stocks shall be formed (hereinafter: split stocks) [added by Federal Law No. 120-ФЗ, 7 August 2001].

A split stock shall grant to the stockholder-possessor thereof the rights granted by a stock of the respective category (or type) in the amount corresponding to the part of the whole stock which it comprises [added by Federal Law No. 120-Ф3, 7 August 2001].

Split stocks shall circulate equally with whole stocks. If one person acquires two or more split stocks of one category (or type), these stocks shall form a single whole and/or split stock equal to the amount of these split stocks [added by Federal Law No. 120-Ф3, 7 August 2001].

Article 26. Minimum Charter Capital of Society

The minimum charter capital of an open society must comprise not less than a thousand times the minimum amount for payment of labour established by a federal law on the date of registration of the society, and a closed society, not less than one hundred times the amount of payment of labour established by a federal law on the date of State registration of the society.

Article 27. Placed and Declared Stocks of Society

1. The quantity and par value of stocks acquired by stockholders (placed stocks), and the rights granted by these stocks, must be determined by the charter of the society. Stocks acquired and purchased by the society, and also stocks of the society the right of ownership to which has passed to the society in accordance with Article 34 of the present Federal Law, shall be placed until the cancellation thereof [as amended by Federal Law No. 120-Ф3, 7 August 2001].

The quantity, par value, categories (or types) of stocks which the society has the right to place additionally to the stocks placed (declared stocks), and the rights granted by these stocks, may be determined by the charter of the society. In the absence in the charter of the society of such provisions, the society shall not have the right to place additional stocks [as amended by Federal Law No. 120-Ф3, 7 August 2001].

The procedure and conditions for the placement by the society of declared stocks may be determined by the charter of a society.

2. A decision concerning the making of changes in and additions to the charter of a society connected with the provisions provided for by the present Article concerning declared stocks of a society, except for changes connected with a reduction of the quantity thereof according to the results of placement of additional stocks, shall be adopted by the general meeting of stockholders [as amended by Federal Law No. 120-Ф3, 7 August 2001].

In the event of the placement by a society of securities converted into stocks of a specified category (or type) the quantity of declared stocks of this category (or type) must be not less than the quantity needed for the converting during the period of circulation of these securities.

A society shall not have the right to adopt a decision concerning the change of rights granted by stocks into which securities placed by the society have been converted [as amended by Federal Law No. 120-ФЗ, 7 August 2001].

Article 28. Increase of Charter Capital of Society

1. The charter capital of a society may be increased by means of increasing the par value of stocks or the placement of additional stocks.

2. The decision concerning the increase of charter capital of a society by means of increasing the par value of stocks shall be adopted by the general meeting of stockholders.

The decision concerning the increase of charter capital of a society by means of placing additional stocks shall be adopted by the general meeting of stockholders or by the council of directors (or supervisory council) of the society if in accordance with the charter of the society it has been granted the right to adopt such decision [as amended by Federal Law No. 120-ФЗ, 7 August 2001].

The decision of the council of directors (or supervisory council) of the society concerning the increase of charter capital of a society by means of the placement of additional stocks shall be adopted by the council of directors (or supervisory council) of the society unanimously by all members of the council of directors (or supervisory council) of the society, the votes of members of the council of directors (or supervisory council) of the society who have left not being taken into account in so doing [added by Federal Law No. 120-ФЗ, 7 August 2001].

3. Additional stocks may be placed by a society only within the limits of the quantity of declared stocks established by the charter of the society.

The deciding of the question concerning an increase of charter capital by means of placing additional stocks may be adopted by the general meeting of stockholders simultaneously with the decision concerning the insertion in the charter of the society of provisions concerning declared stocks necessary in accordance with the present Federal Law in order to adopt such decision, or concerning a change of the provisions on declared stocks
[as amended by Federal Law No. 120-ФЗ, 7 August 2001].

4. The quantity of additional common stocks and preferred stocks of each type to be placed within the limits of the quantity of declared stocks of this category (or type), means of placement, price of placement of additional stocks to be placed by means of subscription, or the procedure for determining it, including the price of placement or procedure for determining the price of placing additional stocks to stockholders having a preferential right of acquisition of stocks to be placed, the form of paying up additional stocks to be placed by means of subscription, must be determined by the decision concerning an increase of charter capital of a society by means of placing additional stocks, and other conditions of

placement also may be determined [as amended by Federal Law No. 120-ФЗ, 7 August 2001].

5. An increase of charter capital of a society by means of placing additional stocks may be effectuated at the expense of property of the society. An increase of charter capital of a society by means of increasing the par value of stocks shall be effectuated only at the expense of property of the society [added by Federal Law No. 120-ФЗ, 7 August 2001].

The amount by which charter capital of a society is increased at the expense of property of the society must not exceed the difference between the value of net assets of the society and the amount of charter capital and reserve fund of the society [added by Federal Law No. 120-ФЗ, 7 August 2001].

In the event of an increase of charter capital of a society at the expense of its property by means of placing additional stocks, these stocks shall be distributed among all stockholders. In so doing stocks shall be distributed to each stockholder of the same category (or type) as the stocks which belong to it in proportion to the quantity of stocks belonging to it. An increase of charter capital of a society at the expense of its property by means of placing additional stocks, as a result of which split stocks are formed, shall not be permitted [added by Federal Law No. 120-ФЗ, 7 August 2001].

6. An increase of charter capital of a society by means of the issue of additional stocks when there is a block of stocks granting more than 25% of the votes at the general meeting of stockholders and consolidated in accordance with legal acts of the Russian Federation on privatisation in State or municipal ownership may be effectuated within the period of consolidation only if under such increase the amount of participatory share of the State or municipal formation is preserved [added by Federal Law No. 120-ФЗ, 7 August 2001].

Article 29. Reduction of Charter Capital of Society

1. A society shall have the right, and in instances provided for by the present Federal Law, shall be obliged, to reduce its charter capital [added by Federal Law No. 120-ФЗ, 7 August 2001].

The charter capital of a society may be reduced by means of reduction of the par value of stocks or a reduction of their total quantity, including by means of the acquisition of part of the stocks in the instances provided for by the present Federal Law.

A reduction of the charter capital of a society by means of the acquisition and cancellation of part of the stocks shall be permitted if such possibility has been provided for by the charter of the society.

A society shall not have the right to reduce its charter capital if as a result of such reduction the amount thereof becomes less than the minimum amount of charter capital determined in accordance with the present Federal Law on the date of submission of documents for State registration of the respective changes in the charter of the society, and in instances when in accordance with the present Federal Law a society is obliged to reduce its charter capital—on the date of State registration of the society [as amended by Federal Law No. 120-ФЗ, 7 August 2001].

2. A decision concerning a reduction of the charter capital of a society by means of reducing the par value of stocks or by means of the acquisition of part of the stocks for the purpose of reducing their total quantity shall be adopted by the general meeting of stockholders [as amended by Federal Law No. 120-ФЗ, 7 August 2001].

Article 30.   Informing of Creditors About Reduction of Charter Capital of Society [as amended by Federal Law No. 120-ФЗ, 7 August 2001]

1. Within 30 days from the date of adoption of the decision concerning a reduction of its charter capital, a society shall be obliged to inform in writing creditors of the society about the reduction of charter capital of the society and the new amount thereof, and also to publish in a printed publication intended for publication of data concerning the State registration of juridical persons a notice about the decision adopted. In so doing the creditors shall have the right within 30 days from the date of the sending to them of the notice or within 30 days from the date of publication of the notice about the decision adopted to demand in writing from the society the termination or the performance before time of respective obligations of the society and compensation of losses to them [as amended by Federal Law No. 120-ФЗ, 7 August 2001].

2. State registration of changes in the charter of a society connected with a reduction of charter capital of the society shall be effectuated when there is evidence of notification of the creditors in the procedure established by the present Article [added by Federal Law No. 120-ФЗ, 7 August 2001].

Article 31.   Rights of Stockholders-Possessors of Common Stocks of Society

1. Each common stock of a society shall grant to the stockholder-possessor thereof an identical amount of rights.

2. Stockholders-possessors of common stocks of a society may in accordance with the present Federal Law and charter of the society participate in the general meeting of stockholders with the right of vote in regard to all questions of its competence, and also have the right to receive dividends, and in instances of the liquidation of the society, the right to receive part of its property.

3. The converting of common stocks into preferred stocks, bonds, and other securities shall not be permitted [added by Federal Law No. 120-ФЗ, 7 August 2001].

Article 32. Rights of Stockholders-Possessors of Preferred Stocks of Society

1. Stockholders-possessors of preferred stocks of a society shall not have the right of vote at a general meeting of stockholders unless established otherwise by the present Federal Law [as amended by Federal Law No. 120-ФЗ, 7 August 2001].

Preferred stocks of the society of one type shall grant to the stockholders-possessors thereof an identical amount of rights and have an identical par value.

2. The amount of dividend and/or value to be paid in the event of the liquidation of a society (liquidation value) for preferred stocks of each type must be determined in the charter of a society. The amount of dividend and the liquidation value shall be determined in a fixed monetary amount or in a percentage of par value of the preferred stocks. The amount of the dividend and the liquidation value for preferred stocks shall be considered to be determined also if the procedure for determining them has been established by the charter of the society. The possessors of preferred stocks for which the amount of dividend has not been determined shall have the right to receive dividends equally with the possessors of common stocks.

If preferred stocks of two or more types have been provided for by the charter of a society, with regard to each of which the amount of dividend has been determined, then the priority of payment of the dividends with regard to each of them must also be established by the charter of the society, and if preferred stocks of two or more types have been provided for by the charter of the society with regard to each of which the liquidation value has been determined,—the priority of payment of the liquidation value with regard to each of them [as amended by Federal Law No. 120-ФЗ, 7 August 2001].

It may be established by the charter of a society that unpaid or not fully paid dividends with regard to preferred stocks of a determined type, the amount of which is determined by the charter, shall be accumulated and paid not later than the period determined by the charter (cumulative preferred stocks). If such period has not been established by the charter of the society, the preferred stocks shall not be cumulative [as amended by Federal Law No. 120-ФЗ, 7 August 2001].

[paragraph repealed by Federal Law No. 120-ФЗ, 7 August 2001].

3. The converting of preferred stocks of a determined type into common stocks or preferred stocks of other types at the demand of stockholders-possessors thereof or converting of all stocks of this type within the period determined by the charter of a society may be provided for by the charter of a society. In this event the procedure for converting them, including the quantity, category (or type) of stocks into which they are converted, and other conditions of converting must be determined by the charter of the society at the moment of adoption of the decision which is grounds for placing the preferred stocks being converted. A change

of the said provisions of the charter of a society after the adoption of the decision which is the grounds for placing the preferred stocks being converted shall not be permitted [added by Federal Law No. 120-ФЗ, 7 August 2001].

The converting of preferred stocks into bonds and other securities, except for stocks, shall not be permitted. The converting of preferred stocks into common stocks and preferred stocks of other types shall be permitted only if this is provided for by the charter of a society, and also when reorganising a society in accordance with the present Federal Law [added by Federal Law No. 120-ФЗ, 7 August 2001].

4. Stockholders-possessors of preferred stocks shall participate in the general meeting of stockholders with the right of vote when deciding questions concerning the reorganisation and liquidation of a society.

The stockholders-possessors of preferred stocks of a determined type shall acquire the right of vote when deciding questions at the general meeting of stockholders concerning the making of changes in and additions to the charter of a society which limit the right of stockholders-possessors of this type of preferred stocks, including instances of the determining or increasing the amount of dividend and/or determining or increasing the liquidation value to be paid for preferred stocks of the preceding priority, and also the granting to stockholders-possessors of preferred stocks of another type preferences in the priority of payment of a dividend and/or liquidation value of the stocks. The decision concerning the making of such changes and additions shall be considered to be adopted if not less than three-quarters of the votes of stockholders-possessors of voting stocks have voted for it taking part in the general meeting of stockholders, except for the votes of stockholders-possessors of preferred stocks, the rights with regard to which are limited, and three-quarters of the votes of all stockholders-possessors of preferred stocks of each type, the rights with regard to which are limited, unless a larger number of votes of stockholders has been established for the adoption of such a decision by the charter of the society [renumbered and amended by Federal Law No. 120-ФЗ, 7 August 2001].

5. Stockholders-possessors of preferred stocks of a specified type, the amount of dividend for which has been determined in the charter of the society, except for stockholders-possessors of cumulative preferred stocks, shall have the right to participate in the general meeting of stockholders with the right of vote in regard to all questions of its competence, commencing from the meeting following the yearly general meeting of stockholders at which, irrespective of the reasons, a decision was not adopted concerning the payment of dividends for preferred stocks of this type. The right of stockholders-possessors of preferred stocks of such type to participate in the general meeting of stockholders shall terminate from the moment of the first payment for the said stocks of dividends in full [renumbered and amended by Federal Law No. 120-ФЗ, 7 August 2001].

Stockholders-possessors of cumulative preferred stocks of a specified type shall have the right to participate in the general meeting of stockholders with the right of vote in regard to all questions of its competence, commencing from the meeting following the yearly general meeting of stockholders at which a decision should have been adopted concerning the payment of cumulated dividends in full for these stocks if such decision was not adopted or a decision was adopted concerning the payment of dividends not in full. The right of stockholders-possessors of cumulative preferred stocks of a specified type to participate in the general meeting of stockholders shall terminate from the moment of the payment of all dividends in full cumulated with regard to the said stocks.

5. [repealed by Federal Law No. 120-ФЗ, 7 August 2001].

Article 33. Bonds and Other Emission Securities of Society [as amended by Federal Law No. 120-ФЗ, 7 August 2001]

1. A society shall have the right to place bonds and other emission securities provided for by legal acts of the Russian Federation on securities [as amended by Federal Law No. 120-ФЗ, 7 August 2001].

2. The placement by a society of bonds and other emission securities shall be effectuated by decision of the council of directors (or supervisory council) of the society unless provided otherwise by the charter of the society [as amended by Federal Law No. 120-ФЗ, 7 August 2001].

The placement by the society of bonds convertible into stocks and other emission securities convertible into stocks must be effectuated by decision of the general meeting of stockholders or by decision of the council of directors (or supervisory council) of the society if in accordance with the charter of the society the right to adopt the decision concerning the placement of bonds convertible into stocks and other emission securities convertible into stocks belongs to it [added by Federal Law No. 120-ФЗ, 7 August 2001].

3. A bond shall certify the right of its possessor to demand the cancellation of the bond (or payment of par value or the par value and interest) within the established periods [as amended by Federal Law No. 120-ФЗ, 7 August 2001].

The form, periods, and other conditions for cancellation of the bonds must be determined in the decision concerning the issuance of the bonds.

A bond must have a par value. The par value of all bonds issued by a society must not exceed the amount of charter capital of the society or the amount of security granted to the society by third persons for the purpose of the issuance of the bonds. The placement of bonds by the society shall be permitted after the paying up in full of the charter capital of the society [as amended by Federal Law No. 120-ФЗ, 7 August 2001].

A society may place bonds with a single period for repayment or bonds with a repayment period by series within specified periods [as amended by Federal Law No. 120-ФЗ, 7 August 2001].

The repayment of bonds may be effectuated in monetary form or by other property in accordance with the decision concerning their issuance.

A society shall have the right to place bonds secured by the pledge of specified property of the society or bonds under a security granted to the society for the purpose of issuance of the bonds by third persons, and bonds without security [as amended by Federal Law No. 120-ФЗ, 7 August 2001].

The placement of bonds without security shall be permitted not earlier than the third year of existence of the society and on condition of the proper confirmation at this time of two annual balance sheets of the society [as amended by Federal Law No. 120-ФЗ, 7 August 2001].

Bonds may be inscribed or bearer. In the event of the issuance of inscribed bonds, a society shall be obliged to keep a register of their possessors. Lost inscribed bonds shall be reinstated by the society for a reasonable payment. The rights of a possessor of a lost bearer bond shall be reinstated by a court in the procedure established by procedure legislation of the Russian Federation.

A society shall have the right to provide for the possibility of cancellation of bonds before time at the wish of the possessors thereof. In so doing, the value of the cancellation and the period not earlier than which they may be presented for cancellation before time must be specified in the decision concerning the issuance of the bonds [as amended by Federal Law No. 120-ФЗ, 7 August 2001].

4. A society shall not have the right to place bonds and other emission securities convertible into stocks of the society if the quantity of declared stocks of the society of specified categories and types is less than the quantity of stocks of these categories and types, the right to acquire which such securities grant [as amended by Federal Law No. 120-ФЗ, 7 August 2001].

Article 34. Paying Up of Stocks and Other Emission Securities of Society When Placing Them [as amended by Federal Law No. 120-ФЗ, 7 August 2001]

1. The stocks of a society distributed when it is founded must be paid up in full within a year from the moment of State registration of the society unless a lesser period has been provided for by the contract on the creation of the society [as amended by Federal Law No. 120-ФЗ, 7 August 2001].

Not less than 50% of the stocks of a society distributed when it is founded must be paid up within three months from the moment of State registration of the society [added by Federal Law No. 120-ФЗ, 7 August 2001].

Stocks belonging to the founder of a society shall not grant the right of vote until the moment of the paying up in full thereof, unless provided otherwise by the charter of the society [added by Federal Law No. 120-ФЗ, 7 August 2001].

In the event of the failure to pay up stocks in full within the period established by paragraph one of the present point, the right of ownership to the stocks, the price for the placement of which corresponds to the unpaid amount (or value of property not transferred to pay up the stocks) shall pass to the society. The recovery of a penalty (or fine, forfeit) for the failure to perform duties with regard to pay up stocks may be provided for by the contract on the creation of the society [added by Federal Law No. 120-ФЗ, 7 August 2001].

Stocks, the right of ownership to which has passed to the society, shall not grant a right to vote, shall not be taken into account when counting votes, and dividends shall not be calculated with regard to them. Such stocks must be realised by the society at a price not lower than the par value not later than one year after their acquisition by the society; otherwise, the society shall be obliged to adopt a decision concerning the reduction of its charter capital. If the society within a reasonable period does not adopt a decision concerning a reduction of its charter capital, the agency effectuating State registration of juridical persons, or other State agencies or agencies of local self-government to whom the right to present such demand has been granted by a federal law, shall have the right to present a demand in court concerning liquidation of the society [added by Federal Law No. 120-ФЗ, 7 August 2001].

Additional stocks and other emission securities of a society placed by means of subscription shall be placed on condition of their being paid up in full [as amended by Federal Law No. 120-ФЗ, 7 August 2001].

2. The paying up of stocks to be distributed among the founders of a society when it is founded and of additional stocks to be placed by means of subscription may be effectuated by money, securities, other things or property rights, or other rights having monetary value. The form of paying up of stocks of a society when it is founded shall be determined by the contract on the creation of the society, and additional stocks—by the decision concerning the placement thereof [as amended by Federal Law No. 120-ФЗ, 7 August 2001].

The charter of a society may contain limitations on the types of property by which stocks of the society may be paid up [added by by Federal Law No. 120-ФЗ, 7 August 2001].

3. The monetary valuation of property contributed to pay up stocks when a society is founded shall be made by an agreement among the founders.

When paying up additional stocks by nonmonetary means, the monetary valuation of the property contributed to pay up the stocks shall be made by the council of directors (or supervisory council) of the society in accordance with Article 77 of the present Federal Law [as amended by Federal Law No. 120-ФЗ, 7 August 2001].

When paying up stocks by nonmonetary means an independent valuer must be enlisted to determine the market value of such property. The amount of monetary valuation of the property made by the founders of the society and the council of directors (or supervisory council) of the society may not be higher than the amount of the valuation made by the independent valuer [added by Federal Law No. 120-Ф3, 7 August 2001].

4. [repealed by Federal Law No. 120-Ф3, 7 August 2001].

Article 35. Funds and Net Assets of Society

1. A reserve fund in the amount provided for by the charter of the society, but not less than 5% of its charter capital, shall be created in the society [as amended by Federal Law No. 120-Ф3, 7 August 2001].

The reserve fund of a society shall be formed by means of obligatory annual deductions until the attainment of the amount established by the charter of the society. The amount of annual deductions shall be provided for by the charter of the society, but may not be less than 5% of net profit until the attainment of the amount established by the charter of the society.

The reserve fund of a society shall be earmarked for the covering of its losses, and also for the cancellation of bonds of the society and the purchase of stocks of the society in the event of the absence of other means.

The reserve fund may not be used for other purposes.

2. The charter of a society may provide for the formation from net profit of a special fund for the joint-stockisation of workers of the society. The assets thereof shall be spent exclusively for the acquisition of stocks of the society to be sold by stockholders of this society for subsequent placement to its workers.

In the event of the compensated realisation to workers of the society of stocks acquired at the expense of means of the fund for the joint-stockisation of workers of the society, the means received shall be directed towards the formation of the said fund [added by Federal Law No. 120-Ф3, 7 August 2001].

3. The value of net assets of the society shall be valued according to the data of bookkeeping records in the procedure established by the Ministry of Finances of the Russian Federation and the federal agency of executive power for the securities market [as amended by Federal Law No. 120-Ф3, 7 August 2001].

4. If at the end of this and each subsequent financial year in accordance with the annual bookkeeping balance sheet proposed for confirmation to the stockholders of the society or the results of an auditor verification the value of net assets of the society proves to be less than its charter capital, the society shall be obliged to declare a reduction of its charter capital up to the amount not exceeding the value of its net assets.

5. If at the end of the second and each subsequent financial year in accordance with the annual bookkeeping balance sheet proposed for confirmation to the stockholders of the society or the results of an auditor verification the value of net

assets of the society proves to be less than the amount of the minimum charter capital specified in Article 26 of the present Federal Law, the society shall be obliged to adopt a decision concerning its liquidation.

6. If in the instances provided for by points 4 and 5 of the present Article a society does not adopt the decision within a reasonable period concerning the reduction of its charter capital or liquidation, creditors shall have the right to demand from the society the termination or performance before time of obligations and compensation to them of losses. In these instances the agency effectuating State registration of juridical persons, or other State agencies or agencies of local self-government to which the right to present such a demand has been granted by a federal law, shall have the right to present a demand in court concerning liquidation of the society [as amended by Federal Law No. 120-ФЗ, 7 August 2001].

Chapter IV. Placement by Society of Stocks and Other Emission Securities
[as amended by Federal Law No. 120-ФЗ, 7 August 2001]

Article 36. Price of Placement of Stocks of Society

1. The stocks of a society shall be paid up when it is founded by the founders thereof at a price not lower than the par value of these stocks [as amended by Federal Law No. 120-ФЗ, 7 August 2001].

The paying up of additional stocks of a society to be placed by means of subscription shall be effectuated at the price determined by the council of directors (or supervisory council) of the society in accordance with Article 77 of the present Federal Law, but lower than the par value thereof [as amended by Federal Law No. 120-ФЗ, 7 August 2001].

2. The price of the placement of additional stocks to stockholders of a society in the event of the effectuation by them of a preferential right to acquire stocks may be lower than the price of placement to other persons, but not by more than 10% [as amended by Federal Law No. 120-ФЗ, 7 August 2001].

The amount of remuneration for the intermediary participation in the placement of additional stocks of the society by means of subscription must not exceed 10% of the price of the placement of the stocks [as amended by Federal Law No. 120-ФЗ, 7 August 2001].

Article 37. Procedure for Converting Emission Securities of Society into Stock [as amended by Federal Law No. 120-ФЗ, 7 August 2001]

1. The procedure for converting emission securities of the society into stock shall be established:

by the charter of the society—with respect to converting preferred stocks;

by the decision concerning the issue—with respect to converting bonds and other emission securities, except stocks.

The placement of stocks of the society within the limits of the quantity of declared stocks necessary for the converting into them of convertible stocks and other emission securities of the society shall be conducted only by means of such converting [as amended by Federal Law No. 120-ФЗ, 7 August 2001].

2. The conditions and procedure for converting stocks and other emission securities of a society when it is reorganised shall be determined by respective decisions and contracts in accordance with the present Federal Law [added by Federal Law No. 120-ФЗ, 7 August 2001].

Article 38. Price of Placement of Emission Securities [as amended by Federal Law No. 120-ФЗ, 7 August 2001]

1. The paying up of emission securities of a society to be placed by means of subscription shall be effectuated at the price determined by the council of directors (or supervisory council) of the society in accordance with Article 77 of the present Federal Law. In so doing the paying up of emission securities convertible into stocks to be placed by means of subscription shall be effectuated at a price not lower than the par value of stocks into which such securities shall be converted [as amended by Federal Law No. 120-ФЗ, 7 August 2001].

2. The price of placement of emission securities convertible into stocks to stockholders of the society in the event of their effectuation of a preferential right to acquire such securities may be lower than the price of placement to other persons, but by not more than 10%.

The amount of remuneration of an intermediary participating in the placement of emission securities by means of subscription must not exceed 10% of the price of the placement of these securities [added by Federal Law No. 120-ФЗ, 7 August 2001].

Article 39. Means of Placement by Society of Stocks and Other Emission Securities of Society [as amended by Federal Law No. 120-ФЗ, 7 August 2001]

1. A society shall have the right to effectuate the placement of additional stocks and other emission securities by means of subscription and converting. In the event of an increase of the charter capital of a society at the expense of its property a society must effectuate the placement of additional stocks by means of distribution thereof among the stockholders [as amended by Federal Law No. 120-ФЗ, 7 August 2001].

2. An open society shall have the right to conduct the placement of stocks and emission securities of a society convertible into stocks by means of both an open and a closed subscription. The possibility of conducting a closed subscription by open societies may be limited by the charter of a society and by legal acts of the Russian Federation [as amended by Federal Law No. 120-ФЗ, 7 August 2001].

A closed society shall not have the right to conduct the placement of stocks and emission securities of a society convertible into stocks by means of an open subscription or otherwise to offer them for acquisition to an unlimited group of persons [added by Federal Law No. 120-ФЗ, 7 August 2001].

3. The placement of stocks (or emission securities of the society convertible into stocks) by means of closed subscription shall be effectuated only by decision of the general meeting of stockholders concerning an increase of charter capital of the society by means of the placement of additional stocks (or concerning emission securities of the society convertible into stocks) adopted by a majority of three-quarters of the votes of the stockholders-possessors of voting stocks taking part in the general meeting of stockholders, unless the necessity of a larger number of votes for the adoption of this decision has been provided for by the charter of the society [as amended by Federal Law No. 120-ФЗ, 7 August 2001].

4. The placement by means of an open subscription of common stocks comprising more than 25% of previously placed common stocks shall be effectuated only by decision of the general meeting of stockholders-possessors of voting stocks taking part in the general meeting of stockholders, unless the necessity of a larger number of votes for the adoption of this decision has been provided for by the charter of the society [added by Federal Law No. 120-ФЗ, 7 August 2001].

The placement by means of an open subscription of emission securities convertible into common stocks which may be converted into common stocks comprising more than 25% of previously placed common stocks shall be effectuated only by decision of the general meeting of stockholders adopted by a majority of three-quarters of the votes of the stockholders-possessors of voting stocks taking part in the general meeting of stockholders, unless the necessity of a larger number of votes for the adoption of this decision has been provided for by the charter of the society [added by Federal Law No. 120-ФЗ, 7 August 2001].

5. The placement by a society of stocks and other emission securities of a society shall be effectuated in accordance with legal acts of the Russian Federation [added by Federal Law No. 120-ФЗ, 7 August 2001].

Article 40. Ensuring Rights of Stockholders in Event of Placement of Stocks and Emission Securities of Society Convertible into Stocks [as amended by Federal Law No. 120-ФЗ, 7 August 2001]

1. Stockholders of a society shall have a preferential right to acquire additional stocks and emission securities convertible into stocks to be placed by means of open subscription in a quantity proportional to the quantity of stocks of this category (or type) belonging to them [as amended by Federal Law No. 120-ФЗ, 7 August 2001].

Stockholders of a society who have voted against or who did not take part in voting with regard to the question concerning the placement by means of a closed subscription of stocks and emission securities convertible into stocks shall have a preferential right to acquire the additional stocks and emission securities convertible into stocks to be placed by means of closed subscription in the quantity proportional to the quantity of stocks of this category (or type) belonging to them. The said right shall not extend to the placement of stocks and other emission securities convertible into stocks effectuated by means of closed subscription only among stockholders, if in so doing the stockholders have the possibility to acquire a whole number of stocks to be placed and other emission securities convertible into stocks in proportion to the quantity of stocks of the respective category (or type) belonging to them [added by Federal Law No. 120-Ф3, 7 August 2001].

2. The list of persons having the preferential right to acquire additional stocks and emission securities convertible into stocks shall be drawn up on the basis of data of the register of stockholders on the date of adoption of the decision which is the grounds for the placement of additional stocks and emission securities convertible into stocks. In order to draw up a list of persons having a preferential right to acquire additional stocks and emission securities convertible into stocks the nominee holder of the stocks shall submit data concerning the persons in whose interests he possesses stocks [as amended by Federal Law No. 120-Ф3, 7 August 2001].

3. [repealed by Federal Law No. 120-Ф3, 7 August 2001]

Article 41. Procedure for Effectuation of Preferential Right to Acquire Stocks and Emission Securities Convertible into Stocks [as amended by Federal Law No. 120-Ф3, 7 August 2001]

1. Persons included in the list of persons having a preferential right to acquire additional stocks and emission securities convertible into stocks of a society must be informed about the possibility of the effectuation by them of the preferential right provided for by Article 40 of the present Federal Law in the procedure provided for by the present Federal Law for the communication of the conducting of a general meeting of stockholders [as amended by Federal Law No. 120-Ф3, 7 August 2001].

The notice must contain information concerning the quantity of stocks and emission securities convertible into stocks to be placed, the price of their placement or the procedure for determining the price of placement (including the price of their placement or procedure for determining the price of placement to stockholders of the society in the event of the effectuation by them of the preferential right of acquisition), the procedure for determining the quantity of securities which each stockholder has the right to acquire, the period of operation of the preferential right which may not be less than 45 days from the moment of sending (or handing over) or publication of the notice. A society shall not have the right before the end of the said period to place additional stocks and emission securities convertible into stocks to persons not included in the list of persons having a preferential right to acquire additional stocks and emission securities convertible into stocks [added by Federal Law No. 120-Ф3, 7 August 2001].

2. A person having a preferential right to acquire additional stocks and emission securities convertible into stocks shall have the right to fully or partially effectuate his preferential right by means of filing at the society a written application concerning the acquisition of stocks and emission securities convertible into stocks, and a document concerning the paying up of stocks and emission securities convertible into stocks to be acquired. The application must contain the name of the stockholder, indication of his place of residence (or location), and the quantity of securities to be acquired by him [as amended by Federal Law No. 120-Ф3, 7 August 2001].

If a decision which is grounds for the placement of additional stocks and emission securities convertible into stocks provides for the paying up thereof by non-monetary means, the persons effectuating the preferential right of acquisition shall have the right at his discretion to pay them up with money [added by Federal Law No. 120-Ф3, 7 August 2001].

Chapter V. Dividends of Society

Article 42. Procedure for Payment by Society of Dividends

1. A society shall have the right with regard to the results of the first quarter, half-year, and nine months of the financial year and/or with regard to the results of the financial year to adopt a decision (or declare) the payment of dividends with regard to placed stocks unless established otherwise by the present Federal Law. The decision concerning the payment (or declaration) of dividends with regard to the results of the first quarter, half-year, and nine months of the financial year may be adopted within three months after the end of the respective period [as amended by Federal Law No. 120-Ф3, 7 August 2001, and Federal Law No. 134-Ф3, 31 October 2002].

The society shall be obliged to pay the dividends declared for stocks of each category (or type). Dividends shall be paid in money, and in the instances provided for by the charter of the society,—by other property.

2. Dividends shall be paid from the net profit of the society. Dividends for preferred stocks of determined types may be paid at the expense of funds of the society specially earmarked for this [as amended by Federal Law No. 120-Ф3, 7 August 2001].

3. The decision concerning the payment (or declaration) of dividends, including the decision concerning the amount of dividends and the form of its payment with regard to the stocks of each category (or type), shall be adopted by the general meeting of stockholders. The amount of dividend may not be larger than

recommended by the council of directors (or supervisory council) of the society [as amended by Federal Law No. 120-ФЗ, 7 August 2001, and by Federal Law No. 134-ФЗ, 31 October 2002].

4. The period and procedure for payment of dividends shall be determined by the charter of the society or by decision of the general meeting of stockholders concerning the payment of dividends. If the period of payment of dividends has not been determined, the period for payment thereof must not exceed 60 days from the day of adoption of the decision concerning the payment of dividends [as amended by Federal Law No. 120-ФЗ, 7 August 2001, and by Federal Law No. 134-ФЗ, 31 October 2002].

The list of persons having the right to receive dividends shall be drawn up on the date of drawing up the list of persons having the right to participate in the general meeting of stockholders at which the decision is adopted concerning the payment of respective dividends. In order to draw up the list of persons having the right to receive dividends, the nominee holder of stocks shall submit data concerning persons in whose interests it possesses stocks [as amended by Federal Law No. 120-ФЗ, 7 August 2001, and by Federal Law No. 134-ФЗ, 31 October 2002].

Article 43. Limitations on Payment of Dividends

1. A society shall not have the right to adopt a decision (or declare) concerning the payment of dividends regarding stocks [as amended by Federal Law No. 120-ФЗ, 7 August 2001]:

until the entire charter capital of the society is paid up in full;

until the purchase of all stocks which must be purchased in accordance with Article 76 of the present Federal Law;

if on the day of adoption of such decision a society is liable by indicia of insolvency (or bankruptcy) in accordance with legislation of the Russian Federation on insolvency (or bankruptcy) or if the said indicia appear in the society as a result of the payment of dividends [as amended by Federal Law No. 120-ФЗ, 7 August 2001];

if on the day of adoption of such decision the value of net assets of the society is less than its charter capital and the reserve fund and the excess over par value of the liquidation value determined by the charter of the placed preferred stocks or becomes less than the amount thereof as a result of the adoption of such decision [as amended by Federal Law No. 120-ФЗ, 7 August 2001];

in other instances provided for by federal laws [added by Federal Law No. 120-ФЗ, 7 August 2001].

2. A society shall not have the right to adopt a decision (or declare) concerning the payment of dividends (including dividends with regard to the results of the first quarter, halfyear, or nine months of the financial year) on common stocks and

preferred stocks, the amount of the dividend for which has not been determined, unless a decision concerning the payment of the full amount of dividends (including accumulated dividends with regard to cumulative preferred stocks) with regard to all types of preferred stocks, the amount of dividends (including dividends with regard to the results of the first quarter, half-year, and nine months of the financial year) for which has been determined by the charter of the society, is adopted [as amended by Federal Law No. 120-ФЗ, 7 August 2001, and by Federal Law No. 134-ФЗ, 31 October 2002].

3. A society shall not have the right to adopt a decision (or declare) concerning the payment of dividends for preferred stocks of a determined type, for which the amount of dividend is determined by the charter of the society, unless a decision concerning the payment of dividends in full (including the full payment of all accumulated dividends with regard to cumulative preferred stocks) with regard to all types of preferred stocks granting a preference in priority to receive dividends before the preferred stocks of this type is adopted [as amended by Federal Law No. 120-ФЗ, 7 August 2001].

4. A society shall not have the right to pay declared dividends with regard to stocks:

if on the day of payment a society is liable by the indicia of insolvency (or bankruptcy) in accordance with legislation of the Russian Federation concerning insolvency (or bankruptcy) or if the said indicia appear in the society as a result of the payment of dividends;

if on the day of payment the value of net assets of the society is less than the amount of its charter capital, reserve fund, and excess over the par value of the liquidation value determined by the charter of the society of placed preferred stocks or becomes less than the said amount as a result of the payment of dividends;

in other instances provided for by federal laws.

Upon the termination of the circumstances specified in the present point the society shall be obliged to pay stockholders the declared dividends [added by Federal Law No. 120-ФЗ, 7 August 2001].

Chapter VI. Register of Stockholders of Society

Article 44. Register of Stockholders of Society

1. In the register of stockholders of a society shall be specified information concerning each registered person, the quantity and categories (or types) of stocks entered in the name of each registered person, and other information provided for by legal acts of the Russian Federation [as amended by Federal Law No. 120-ФЗ, 7 August 2001].

2. A society shall be obliged to ensure the keeping and storage of the register of stockholders of a society in accordance with legal acts of the Russian Federation from the moment of State registration of the society [as amended by Federal Law No. 120-ФЗ, 7 August 2001].

3. The holder of the register of stockholders of a society may be this society or a professional participant of the securities market effectuating activity with regard to keeping the register of possessors of inscribed securities (hereinafter: registrar).

In a society with a number of stockholders of more than fifty, a registrar must be the holder of the register of stockholders of the society [as amended by Federal Law No. 120-ФЗ, 7 August 2001].

4. A society entrusting the keeping and storage of a register of stockholders of the society to a specialised registrar shall not be relieved from responsibility for the keeping and storage thereof.

5. A person registered in the register of stockholders of a society shall be obliged to inform the holder of the register of stockholders of the society in a timely way about changes of his data. In the event of the failure to submit information concerning a change of his data, the society and the registrar shall not bear responsibility for the losses caused in connection therewith [as amended by Federal Law No. 120-ФЗ, 7 August 2001].

Article 45. Making Entries in Register of Stockholders of Society

1. The making of an entry in the register of stockholders of a society shall be effectuated at the demand of the stockholder or nominee holder of stocks not later than three days from the moment of the submission of the documents provided for by legal acts of the Russian Federation. A shorter period for making entries in the register of stockholders of a society may be established by legal acts of the Russian Federation [as amended by Federal Law No. 120-ФЗ, 7 August 2001].

2. A refusal to make an entry in the register of stockholders of a society shall not be permitted, except for instances provided for by legal acts of the Russian Federation. In the event of a refusal to make an entry in the register of stockholders of the society the holder of the said register shall not later than five days from the moment of presentation of the demand to make an entry in the register of stockholders of the society send to the person demanding the making of the entry a reasoned notice concerning the refusal to make the entry.

The refusal to make an entry in the register of stockholders of a society may be appealed to a court. By decision of the court the holder of the register of stockholders of a society shall be obliged to make the respective entry in the said register.

Article 46. Extract from Register of Stockholders of Society

The holder of the register of stockholders of a society shall at the demand of a stockholder or nominee holder of stocks be obliged to confirm his rights to stocks by means of the issuance of an extract from the register of stockholders of the society, which is not a security.

Chapter VII. General Meeting of Stockholders

Article 47. General Meeting of Stockholders

1. The highest management organ of a society shall be the general meeting of stockholders.

The society shall be obliged annually to hold a yearly general meeting of stockholders [as amended by Federal Law No. 120-ФЗ, 7 August 2001].

The yearly general meeting of stockholders shall be held within the periods established by the charter of the society, but not earlier than two months and not later than six months after the end of the financial year. At the yearly general meeting of stockholders must be decided the questions of the election of the council of directors (or supervisory council) of the society, the audit commission (or internal auditor) of the society, and confirmation of the auditor of the society, questions provided for by Article 48(1)(11) of the present Federal Law, and also may decide other questions relegated to the competence of the general meeting of stockholders. General meetings of stockholders held besides the yearly [meeting] shall be extraordinary [meetings] [as amended by Federal Law No. 120-ФЗ, 7 August 2001].

2. Requirements for the procedure of preparing, convocation, and holding of the general meeting of stockholders additional to those provided for by the present Federal Law may be established by a federal agency of executive power for the securities market [as amended by Federal Law No. 120-ФЗ, 7 August 2001].

3. In a society all voting stocks of which belong to one stockholder the decisions with regard to questions relegated to the competence of the general meeting of stockholders shall be adopted by this stockholder as one person and shall be formalised in writing. In so doing the provisions of the present Chapter determining the procedure and periods for the preparation, convocation, and holding of the general meeting of stockholders shall not apply, except for the provisions affecting the period for holding the yearly general meeting of stockholders [added by Federal Law No. 120-ФЗ, 7 August 2001].

Article 48. Competence of General Meeting of Stockholders

1. There shall be relegated to the competence of the general meeting of stockholders:

(1) the making of changes in and additions to the charter of a society or the confirmation of the charter of the society in a new version;

(2) the reorganisation of the society;

(3) the liquidation of the society, appointment of the liquidation commission, and confirmation of the interim and final liquidation balance sheets;

(4) the determination of the quantitative composition of the council of directors (or supervisory council) of the society, election of its members, and termination of their powers before time;

(5) the determination of the quantity, par value, categories (or types) of declared stocks and the rights granted by these stocks;

(6) the increase of the charter capital of the society by means of increasing the par value of the stocks or by means of the placement of additional stocks, unless the increase of charter capital of the society by means of the placement of additional stocks has been relegated to the competence of the council of directors (or supervisory council) of the society by the charter of the society in accordance with the present Federal Law;

(7) the reduction of the charter capital of the society by means of reducing the par value of the stocks by means of the acquisition by the society of part of the stocks for the purpose of reducing the total quantity thereof, and also by means of the cancellation of stocks acquired or purchased by the society;

(8) the formation of the executive organ of the society, the termination before time of its powers unless the deciding of these questions has been relegated by the charter of the society to the competence of the council of directors (or supervisory council) of the society;

(9) the election of members of the audit commission (or internal auditor) of the society and the termination before time of their powers;

(10) the confirmation of the auditor of the society;

(10^1) Payment (or declaration) of dividends with regard to the results of the first quarter, half-year, and nine months of the financial year [added by Federal Law No. 134-ФЗ, 31 October 2002];

(11) the confirmation of yearly reports, yearly bookkeeping reports, including the profits and losses reports (or profits and losses accounts) of the society, and also the distribution of profit, including the payment (or declaration) of dividends, except for profits distributed as dividends with regard to the results of the first quarter, half-year, and nine months of the financial year), and losses of the society with regard to results of the financial year [as amended by Federal Law No. 134-ФЗ, 31 October 2002];

(12) the determination of the procedure for conducting the general meeting of stockholders;

(13) the election of members of the counting commission and termination before time of their powers;

(14) the splitting and consolidation of stocks;

(15) the adoption of decisions concerning the approval of transactions in instances provided for by Article 83 of the present Federal Law;

(16) the adoption of decisions concerning the approval of large-scale transactions in instances provided for by Article 79 of the present Federal Law;

(17) the acquisition by the society of placed stocks in instances provided for by the present Federal Law;

(18) the adoption of a decision concerning participation in holding companies, financial-industrial groups, associations, and other associations of commercial organisations;

(19) the confirmation of internal documents regulating the activity of organs of the society;

(20) the deciding of other questions provided for by the present Federal Law [point 1 as amended by Federal Law No. 120-ФЗ, 7 August 2001].

2. Questions relegated to the competence of the general meeting of stockholders may not be transferred for decision to an executive organ of the society [as amended by Federal Law No. 120-ФЗ, 7 August 2001].

Questions relegated to the competence of the general meeting of stockholders may not be transferred for decision to the council of directors (or supervisory council) of the society except for questions provided for by the present Federal Law [as amended by Federal Law No. 120-ФЗ, 7 August 2001].

3. The general meeting of stockholders shall not have the right to consider and adopt decisions with regard to questions not relegated to its competence by the present Federal Law.

Article 49. Decision of General Meeting of Stockholders

1. With the exception of instances established by federal laws, there shall have the right of vote at a general meeting of stockholders with regard to questions put for voting:

stockholders-possessors of common stocks of the society;

stockholders-possessors of preferred stocks of the society in the instances provided for by the present Federal Law [as amended by Federal Law No. 120-ФЗ, 7 August 2001].

Voting stocks of the society shall be common stocks or preferred stocks granting to the stockholder-possessor thereof the right of vote when deciding a question put for voting [as amended by Federal Law No. 120-ФЗ, 7 August 2001].

2. The decision of a general meeting of stockholders with regard to a question put for voting shall be adopted by a majority of votes of the stockholders-possessors of voting stocks of the society taking part in the meeting unless established otherwise by the present Federal Law or by the charter of the society for the adoption of a decision [as amended by Federal Law No. 120-ФЗ, 7 August 2001].

The counting of votes at a general meeting of stockholders with regard to a question put for voting, the right of vote when deciding which is possessed by stockholders-possessors of common and preferred stocks of the society, shall be effectuated with regard to all voting stocks jointly unless established otherwise by the present Federal Law [as amended by Federal Law No. 120-ФЗ, 7 August 2001].

3. A decision with regard to the questions specified in Article 48(1)(2),(6) and (14)-(19) of the present Federal Law shall be adopted by a general meeting of stockholders only upon the proposal of the council of directors (or supervisory council) unless established otherwise by the charter of the society [as amended by Federal Law No. 120-ФЗ, 7 August 2001].

4. A decision with regard to the questions specified in Article 48(1)(1)-(3), (5) and (17) of the present Federal Law shall be adopted by the general meeting of stockholders by a majority of three-quarters of the votes of the stockholders-possessors of voting stocks who take part in the general meeting of stockholders [as amended by Federal Law No. 120-ФЗ, 7 August 2001].

5. The procedure for the adoption by the general meeting of stockholders of a decision regarding the procedure for conducting the general meeting of stockholders shall be established by the charter of the society or by the internal documents of the society confirmed by decision of the general meeting of stockholders.

6. The general meeting of stockholders shall not have the right to adopt decisions with regard to questions not included on the agenda of the meeting, nor to change the agenda.

7. [repealed by Federal Law No. 120-ФЗ, 7 August 2001].

7. A stockholder shall have the right to appeal to a court a decision adopted by the general meeting of stockholders in violation of the requirements of the present Federal Law, other legal acts of the Russian Federation, and the charter of the society if he did not take part in the general meeting of stockholders or he voted against the adoption of such decision and his rights and legal interests were violated by the said decision. Such application may be filed in a court within six months from the day when the stockholder knew or should have known about the decision adopted. The court shall have the right, taking into account all the circumstances of the case, to leave the decision appealed in force if the vote of the said stockholder could not influence the results of the voting, the violation permitted was not material, and the decision did not entail the causing of losses to the particular stockholder [renumbered and amended by Federal Law No. 120-ФЗ, 7 August 2001].

Article 50. General Meeting of Stockholders in Form of External Voting [as amended by Federal Law No. 120-ФЗ, 7 August 2001]

1. A decision of a general meeting of stockholders may be adopted without holding a meeting (or the joint presence of stockholders to discuss questions of the

agenda and adoption of decisions with regard to the questions put for voting) by means of conducting external voting [as amended by Federal Law No. 120-ФЗ, 7 August 2001].

2. A general meeting of stockholders whose agenda includes questions concerning the election of the council of directors (or supervisory council) of the society, audit commission (or internal auditor) of the society, confirmation of the auditor of the society, and also questions provided for by Article 48(1)(11) of the present Federal Law may not be held in the form of external voting [as amended by Federal Law No. 120-ФЗ, 7 August 2001].

3. [repealed by Federal Law No. 120-ФЗ, 7 August 2001]

Article 51. Right to Participate in General Meeting of Stockholders

1. A list of persons who have the right to participate in the general meeting of stockholders shall be drawn up on the basis of data of the register of stockholders of the society. If a special right for the participation of the Russian Federation, subject of the Russian Federation, or municipal formation in the management of the said society ('golden stock') is used with respect to the society, the representatives of the Russian Federation, subject of the Russian Federation, or municipal formation also shall be included in this list [as amended by Federal Law No. 120-ФЗ, 7 August 2001].

The date of drawing up the list of persons having the right to participate in the general meeting of stockholders may not be established earlier than the date of adoption of the decision concerning the holding of the general meeting of stockholders nor more than 50 days, and in the event provided for by Article 53(2) of the present Federal Law, —more than 65 days before the date of holding the general meeting of stockholders [as amended by Federal Law No. 120-ФЗ, 7 August 2001].

In the event a general meeting of stockholders is conducted in which ballots received by the society in accordance with Article 58(2) of the present Federal Law participate in determining the quorum and the voting, the date of drawing up the list of persons having the right to participate in the general meeting of stockholders shall be established not less than 45 days before the date of holding the general meeting of stockholders [as amended by Federal Law No. 120-ФЗ, 7 August 2001].

2. The nominee holder of stocks shall submit data concerning the persons in whose interests he possesses stocks on the date of drawing up the list in order to draw up the list of persons having the right to participate in the general meeting [as amended by Federal Law No. 120-ФЗ, 7 August 2001].

3. A list of persons having the right to participate in the general meeting of stockholders shall contain the name of each person, data necessary for the identification thereof, data concerning the quantity and category (or type) of stocks, the right of vote with regard to which he possesses, the postal address in the Russian

Federation at which a notice should be sent concerning the holding of the general meeting of stockholders and ballot for voting in the event the voting presupposes the sending of ballots for voting, and the report concerning the results of the voting [as amended by Federal Law No. 120-ФЗ, 7 August 2001].

4. A list of persons having the right to participate in the general meeting of stockholders shall be provided by the society for familiarisation at the demand of persons included in the list and possessing not less than 1% of the votes. In so doing the data of documents and the postal address of natural persons included in this list shall be provided only with the consent of those persons [as amended by Federal Law No. 120-ФЗ, 7 August 2001].

At the demand of any interested person, the society shall be obliged to provide him within three days an extract from the list of persons having the right to participate in the general meeting of stockholders containing data concerning this person or a reference that he is not included in the list of persons having the right to participate in the general meeting of stockholders [as amended by Federal Law No. 120-ФЗ, 7 August 2001].

5. Changes in the list of persons having the right to participate in the general meeting of stockholders may be made only in the event of the reinstatement of violated rights of persons not included in the said list on the date of the drawing up thereof or the correction of errors permitted when drawing it up [as amended by Federal Law No. 120-ФЗ, 7 August 2001].

Article 52. Information on Holding General Meeting of Stockholders

1. Notification about the holding of a general meeting of stockholders must be made not later than 20 days in advance, and notification concerning the holding of a general meeting of stockholders whose agenda contains the question of the reorganisation of the society,—not later than 30 days before the date of holding it [as amended by Federal Law No. 120-ФЗ, 7 August 2001].

In the event provided for by Article 53(2) of the present Federal Law, notification concerning the holding of an extraordinary general meeting of stockholders must be made not later than 50 days before the date of holding it [as amended by Federal Law No. 120-ФЗ, 7 August 2001].

Within the said periods the notification concerning the holding of a general meeting of stockholders must be sent to each person specified in the list of persons having the right to participate in a general meeting of stockholders by registered letter unless another means of sending this notification in written form has been provided for by the charter of the society, or handed over to each of the said persons under receipt, or, if this is provided for by the charter of the society, published in a printed publication determined by the charter of the society which is accessible to all stockholders of the society [as amended by Federal Law No. 120-ФЗ, 7 August 2001].

A society shall have the right additionally to inform stockholders about the holding of a general meeting of stockholders through other mass media (television, radio).

2. The communication concerning the holding of a general meeting of stockholders must specify:

the full firm name of the society and location of the society;

the form of holding the general meeting of stockholders (a meeting or external voting);

the date, time, and place of holding the general meeting of stockholders, and when in accordance with Article 60(3) of the present Federal Law ballots filled in may be sent to the society, the postal address to which ballots filled in may be sent, or in the event of holding a general meeting of stockholders in the form of external voting, the date for final receipt of the ballots for voting and the postal address to which the ballots filled in must be sent;

the date of drawing up the list of persons having the right to participate in the general meeting of stockholders;

the agenda of the general meeting of stockholders;

the procedure for familiarisation with information (or materials) subject to provision when preparing for conducting the general meeting of stockholders, and the address(es) at which it is possible to familiarise oneself with them [as amended by Federal Law No. 120-ФЗ, 7 August 2001].

3. There shall be relegated to information (or materials) subject to provision to persons having the right to participate in the general meeting of stockholders when preparing for holding the general meeting of stockholders the yearly bookkeeping report, including the opinion of the auditor, the opinion of the audit commission (or internal auditor) of the society with regard to the results of the verification of the yearly bookkeeping report, information concerning the candidate(s) for the executive organs of the society, council of directors (or supervisory council) of the society, and the audit commission (or internal auditor) of the society, the counting commission of the society, the draft changes in and additions to be made in the charter of the society, or the draft charter of the society in a new version, draft internal documents of the society, draft decisions of the general meeting of stockholders, and also information (or materials) provided for by the charter of the society [as amended by Federal Law No. 120-ФЗ, 7 August 2001].

A list of additional information (or materials) obligatory for provision to persons having the right to participate in the general meeting of stockholders when preparing for holding the general meeting of stockholders may be established by the federal executive agency for the securities market [as amended by Federal Law No. 120-ФЗ, 7 August 2001].

Information (or materials) provided for by the present Article within 20 days, and in the event of holding a general meeting of stockholders whose agenda contains the question of the reorganisation of the society, within 30 days before holding the general meeting of stockholders must be accessible to persons having the right to participate in the general meeting of stockholders for familiarisation at the premise of the executive organ of the society and other places whose addresses have been specified in the notification concerning the holding of the general meeting of stockholders. The said information (or materials) must be accessible to persons taking part in the general meeting of stockholders during the holding thereof [added by Federal Law No. 120-ФЗ, 7 August 2001].

A society shall be obliged at the demand of a person having the right to participate in the general meeting of stockholders to provide him a copy of the said documents. Payment recovered by the society for the provision of the said copies may not exceed the expenditures for the manufacture thereof [added by Federal Law No. 120-ФЗ, 7 August 2001].

4. [repealed by Federal Law No. 120-ФЗ, 7 August 2001].

4. If a person registered in the register of stockholders of a society is a nominee holder of stocks, the communication concerning the holding of the general meeting of stockholders shall be sent to the address of the nominee holder of the stocks, unless another postal address has been specified in the list of persons having the right to participate in the general meeting of stockholders to which the communication should be sent concerning the holding of the general meeting of stockholders. If the communication concerning the holding of the general meeting of stockholders has been sent to the nominee holder of stocks, it shall be obliged to bring it to the information of its clients in the procedure and within the periods which have been established by legal acts of the Russian Federation or the contract with the client [as renumbered and amended by Federal Law No. 120-ФЗ, 7 August 2001].

Article 53. Proposals for Agenda of General Meeting of Stockholders [as amended by Federal Law No. 120-ФЗ, 7 August 2001]

1. A stockholder(s) of a society who in aggregate are the possessors of not less than 2% of the voting stocks of a society shall have the right to submit questions for the agenda of the yearly general meeting of stockholders and to nominate candidates for the council of directors (or supervisory council) of the society, collegial executive organ, and the audit commission (or internal auditor) and counting commission of the society, the number of which may not exceed the quantitative composition of the respective organ, and also a candidates for the office of one-man executive organ. Such proposals must come to the society not later than 30 days after the end of the financial year unless a later period is established by the charter of the society [as amended by Federal Law No. 120-ФЗ, 7 August 2001].

2. If the proposed agenda of an extraordinary general meeting of stockholders contains a question concerning the election of members of the council of directors

(or supervisory council) of the society who should be elected by cumulative voting, the stockholder(s) of the society who in aggregate possess not less than 2% of the voting stocks of the society shall have the right to propose candidates for election to the council of directors (or supervisory council) of the society, the number of which may not exceed the quantitative composition of the council of directors (or supervisory council) of the society. Such proposals must come to the society not less than 30 days before the date of holding the extraordinary general meeting of stockholders unless a later period has been established by the charter of the society [as amended by Federal Law No. 120-ФЗ, 7 August 2001].

3. A proposal concerning the placing of questions on the agenda of a general meeting of stockholers and a proposal concerning the nomination of candidates shall be submitted in written form, specifying the name(s) of the stockholder(s) submitting them and the quantity and categories (or types) of stocks belonging to them, and must be signed by the stockholder(s) [as amended by Federal Law No. 120-ФЗ, 7 August 2001].

4. A proposal concerning the placing of questions on the agenda of a general meeting of stockholders must contain a formulation of each proposed question, and the proposal concerning the nomination of candidates—the name of each proposed candidate, name of the organ to the election of which he is proposed, and also other information about him provided for by the charter or internal documents of the society. A proposal concerning the placing of questions on the agenda of a general meeting of stockholders may contain a formulation of the decision with regard to each proposed question [added by Federal Law No. 120-ФЗ, 7 August 2001].

5. The council of directors (or supervisory council) of a society shall be obliged to consider proposals received and to adopt a decision concerning the inclusion thereof on the agenda of the general meeting of stockholders or to refuse inclusion on the said agenda not later than 5 days after the end of the periods established by points 1 and 2 of the present Article. The question proposed by a stockholder(s) shall be subject to inclusion on the agenda of a general meeting of stockholders, and likewise nominated candidates shall be included in the list of candidacies for voting for elections to the respective organ of the society, except for instances when:

the stockholder(s) have not complied with the periods established by points 1 and 2 of the present Article;

the stockholder(s) are not the possessors of the quantity of voting stocks of the society provided for by points 1 and 2 of the present Article;

the proposal does not correspond to the requirements provided for by points 3 and 4 of the present Article;

the question proposed for inclusion on the agenda of the general meeting of stockholders of the society was not relegated to its competence and/or does not correspond to the requirements of the present Federal Law and other legal acts of the Russian Federation [renumbered and amended by Federal Law No. 120-ФЗ, 7 August 2001].

6. A reasoned decision of the council of directors (or supervisory council) of a society concerning the refusal to include a proposed question on the agenda of the general meeting of stockholders or candidate on the list of candidacies for voting for elections to the respective organ of a society shall be sent to the stockholder(s) who submitted the question or nominated the candidate not later than three days from the date of the adoption thereof.

The decision of a council of directors (or supervisory council) of the society concerning the refusal to include a question on the agenda of the general meeting of stockholders or candidate on the list of candidacies for voting for elections to the respective organ of the society, and also the evasion by the council of directors (or supervisory council) of the society of adopting a decision, may be appealed to a court [as amended by Federal Law No. 120-ФЗ, 7 August 2001].

7. A council of directors (or supervisory council) of a society shall not have the right to make changes in the formulation of questions proposed for inclusion on the agenda of the general meeting of stockholders and the formulation of the decisions with regard to such questions.

Besides the questions proposed for inclusion on the agenda of a general meeting of stockholders by stockholders, and also in the absence of such proposals, the absence or insufficient quantity of candidates proposed by stockholders for the formation of the respective organ, the council of directors (or supervisory council) of a society shall have the right to include on the agenda of the general meeting of stockholders questions or candidates on the list of candidacies at its discretion [added by Federal Law No. 120-ФЗ, 7 August 2001].

Article 54. Preparation for Holding General Meeting of Stockholders

1. When preparing to hold a general meeting of stockholders the council of directors (or supervisory council) of a society shall determine:

the form of holding the general meeting of stockholders (meeting or external voting);

the date, place, and time of holding the general meeting of stockholders, and when in accordance with Article 60(3) of the present Federal Law the filled-in ballots may be sent to the society, the postal address to which filled-in ballots may be sent, or in the event of holding the general meeting of stockholders in the form of external voting, the date of the end of receiving ballots for voting and the postal address to which the filled-in ballots should be sent;

the date of drawing up the list of persons having the right to participate in the general meeting of stockholders;

the agenda of the general meeting of stockholders;

the procedure for communication to the stockholders concerning the holding of the general meeting of stockholders;

the list of information (or materials) to be provided to stockholders when preparing to hold the general meeting of stockholders, and the procedure for the provision thereof;

the form and text of the ballot for voting in the event of voting by ballots [as numbered and amended by Federal Law No. 120-ФЗ, 7 August 2001].

2. Questions concerning the election of the council of directors (or supervisory council) of a society, audit commission (or internal auditor) of a society, confirmation of the auditor of the society, and also questions provided for by Article 48(1)(11) of the present Federal Law, must obligatorily be included on the agenda of the yearly general meeting of stockholders [added by Federal Law No. 120-ФЗ, 7 August 2001].

Article 55. Extraordinary General Meeting of Stockholders

1. An extraordinary general meeting of stockholders shall be held by decision of the council of directors (or supervisory council) of the society on the basis of its own initiative, the demand of the audit commission (or internal auditor) of the society, the auditor of the society, and also a stockholder(s) who is the possessor of not less than 10% of the voting stocks of the society on the date of submitting the demand.

The convocation of an extraordinary general meeting of stockholders at the demand of the audit commission (or internal auditor) of the society, auditor of the society, or stockholder(s) who possess not less than 10% of the voting stocks of the society shall be effectuated by the council of directors (or supervisory council) of the society [as amended by Federal Law No. 120-ФЗ, 7 August 2001].

2. An extraordinary general meeting of stockholders convoked at the demand of the audit commission (or internal auditor) of the society, auditor of the society, or stockholder(s) who is the possessor of not less than 10% of the voting stocks of the society must be held within 40 days from the moment of the submission of the demand concerning the holding of the extraordinary general meeting of stockholders [as amended by Federal Law No. 120-ФЗ, 7 August 2001].

If the proposed agenda of the extraordinary general meeting of stockholders contains a question concerning the election of members of the council of directors (or supervisory council) of the society which must be elected by means of cumulative voting, then such general meeting of stockholders must be held within 70 days from the moment of submission of the demand concerning the holding of an extraordinary general meeting of stockholders unless a lesser period has been provided by the charter of the society [added by Federal Law No. 120-ФЗ, 7 August 2001].

3. In instances when in accordance with Articles 68–70 of the present Federal Law the council of directors (or supervisory council) of the society is obliged to adopt a decision concerning the holding of an extraordinary general meeting of

stockholders, such general meeting of stockholders must be held within 40 days from the moment of adoption of the decision concerning the holding thereof by the council of directors (or supervisory council) of the society unless a lesser period has been provided by the charter of the society [added by Federal Law No. 120-ФЗ, 7 August 2001].

In instances when in accordance with the present Federal Law the council of directors (or supervisory council) of a society is obliged to adopt a decision concerning the holding of an extraordinary general meeting of stockholders in order to elect members of the council of directors (or supervisory council) of the society who must be elected by cumulative voting, such general meeting of stockholders must be held within 70 days from the moment of adoption of the decision concerning the holding thereof by the council of directors (or supervisory council) of the society unless an earlier period has been provided for by the charter of the society [added by Federal Law No. 120-ФЗ, 7 August 2001].

4. In a demand concerning the holding of an extraordinary general meeting of stockholders must be formulated the questions subject to being placed on the agenda of the meeting. The demand concerning the holding of an extraordinary general meeting of stockholdes may contain a formulation of the decisions with regard to each of these questions, and also a proposal concerning the form of holding the general meeting of stockholders. If the demand concerning the convocation of an extraordinary general meeting of stockholders contains a proposal concerning the nomination of candidates, the respective provisions of Article 53 of the present Federal Law shall extend to such proposal.

The council of directors (or supervisory council) of a society shall not have the right to make changes in the formulation of questions of the agenda and formulations of decisions with regard to such questions and to change the proposed form of holding the extraordinary general meeting of stockholders to be convoked at the demand of the audit commission (or internal auditor) of the society, auditor of the society, or stockholder(s) who are the possessors of not less than 10% of the voting stocks of the society [added by Federal Law No. 120-ФЗ, 7 August 2001].

5. If the demand concerning the convocation of an extraordinary general meeting of stockholders emanates from a stockholder(s), it must contain the name of the stockholder(s) demanding the convocation of the meeting, specifying the quantity and category (or type) of stocks belonging to them [renumbered pursuant to Federal Law No. 120-ФЗ, 7 August 2001].

The demand concerning the convocation of an extraordinary general meeting of stockholders shall be signed by the person(s) demanding the convocation of an extraordinary general meeting of stockholders.

6. Within 5 days from the date of submission of the demand of the audit commission (or internal auditor) of the society, the auditor of the society, or a stockholder(s) who are the possessors of not less than 10% of the voting stocks of

the society concerning the convocation of an extraordinary general meeting of stockholders by the council of directors (or supervisory commission) of the society, a decision must be adopted concerning the convocation of an extraordinary general meeting of stockholders or concerning a refusal of the convocation.

The decision concerning a refusal of the convocation of an extraordinary general meeting of stockholders at the demand of the audit commission (or internal auditor) of a society, the auditor of the society, or a stockholder(s) who are the possessors of not less than 10% of the stocks of the society may be adopted if:

the procedure for submission of the demand concerning the convocation of an extraordinary general meeting of stockholders established by the present Article has not been complied with;

the stockholder(s) demanding the convocation of an extraordinary general meeting of stockholders are not the possessors of the quantity of voting stocks of the society provided for by point 1 of the present Article;

none of the questions proposed for submission on the agenda of the extraordinary general meeting of stockholders is relegated to its competence and/or does not correspond to the requirements of the present Federal Law and other legal acts of the Russian Federation [as renumbered pursuant to and amended by Federal Law No. 120-ФЗ, 7 August 2001].

7. A decision of the council of directors (or supervisory council) of the society concerning the convocation of an extraordinary general meeting of stockholders or a reasoned decision concerning a refusal to convoke it shall be sent to the persons demanding the convocation thereof not later than three days from the moment of adoption of such decision.

The decision of the council of directors (or supervisory council) of the society concerning the refusal of the convocation of an extraordinary general meeting of stockholders may be appealed to a court [as renumbered pursuant to and amended by Federal Law No. 120-ФЗ, 7 August 2001].

8. If within the period established by the present Federal Law a decision has not been adopted by the council of directors (or supervisory council) of the society concerning the convocation of an extraordinary general meeting of stockholders or a decision adopted concerning the refusal to convoke it, the extraordinary general meeting of stockholders may be convoked by the agencies and persons demanding the convocation thereof. In so doing the agencies and persons convoking the extraordinary general meeting of stockholders shall possess the powers provided for by the present Federal Law necessary to convoke and hold a general meeting of stockholders [as renumbered pursuant to and amended by Federal Law No. 120-ФЗ, 7 August 2001].

In this event the expenses for the preparation and holding of the general meeting of stockholders may be compensated by decision of the general meeting of stockholders at the expense of means of the society.

Article 56. Counting Commission

1. A counting commission, the quantitative and personal composition of which shall be confirmed by the general meeting of stockholders, shall be created in a society with a number of stockholders-possessors of voting stocks of the society of more than one hundred [as amended by Federal Law No. 120-ФЗ, 7 August 2001].

In a society the holder of the register of stockholders of which is a registrar, to him may be entrusted the fulfilment of the function of a counting commission. In a society with a number of stockholders-possessors of voting stocks of more than 500, the registrar shall fulfil the functions of the counting commission [added by Federal Law No. 120-ФЗ, 7 August 2001].

2. Not less than three persons may be on the counting commission. Members of the council of directors (or supervisory council) of the society, members of the audit commission (or internal auditor) of the society, members of a collegial executive organ of the society, a one-man executive organ of the society, and likewise the management organisation or manager, and also persons nominated as candidates for such offices, may not be on the counting commission.

3. In the event the period of powers of the counting commission expires or the number of members thereof has become less than three, and also in the event of the appearance for the performance of their duties of less than three members of the counting commission, the registrar may be enlisted to effectuate the functions of the counting commission [as amended by Federal Law No. 120-ФЗ, 7 August 2001].

4. The counting commission shall verify the powers and register persons participating in the general meeting of stockholders, determine the quorum of the general meeting of stockholders, explain questions arising in connection with the realisation by stockholders (or their representatives) of the right of vote at a general meeting, explain the procedure of voting with regard to questions submitted for voting, ensure the established procedure of voting and the right of stockholders to participate in the voting, count the votes and total up the results of the voting, draw up a protocol on the results of the voting, and transfer the ballots for voting to the archive [as amended by Federal Law No. 120-ФЗ, 7 August 2001].

Article 57. Procedure for Participation of Stockholders in General Meeting of Stockholders

1. The right to participate in a general meeting of stockholders shall be effectuated by the stockholder both personally or through his representative.

A stockholder shall have the right at any time to replace his representative at a general meeting of stockholders or personally to take part in the general meeting of stockholders.

The representative of a stockholder at a general meeting of stockholders shall operate in accordance with the powers based on the instructions of federal laws or acts of duly empowered State agencies or agencies of local self-government, or a power of attorney drawn up in writing. A power of attorney for voting must contain information concerning the person representing as representative (name, place of residence or location, passport data). A power of attorney for voting must be formalised in accordance with the requirements of Article 185(4) and (5) of the Civil Code of the Russian Federation or notarially certified.

2. In the event of the transfer of a stock after the date of drawing up the list of persons having the right to participate in the general meeting of stockholders and before the date of holding the general meeting of stockholders, the person included in this list shall be obliged to issue to the acquirer a power of attorney for voting or to vote at the general meeting in accordance with the instructions of the acquirer of the stocks. The said rule also shall apply to each subsequent instance of the transfer of a stock [as amended by Federal Law No. 120-ФЗ, 7 August 2001].

3. If the stock of a society is in common participatory share ownership of several persons, the powers relating to voting at the general meeting of stockholders shall be effectuated at their discretion by one of the participants of common participatory share ownership or by their common representative. The powers of each of the said persons must be duly formalised.

Article 58. Quorum of General Meeting of Stockholders

1. The general meeting of stockholders shall be empowered (have a quorum) if stockholders possessing in aggregate more than half of the votes of the placed voting stocks of the society have taken part therein [as amended by Federal Law No. 120-ФЗ, 7 August 2001].

Stockholders who have registered to participate therein, and stockholders whose ballots have been received not later than two days before the date of holding the general meeting of stockholders, shall be considered to have taken part in the general meeting of stockholders. Stockholders whose ballots have been received before the date of the end of receiving ballots shall be considered to have taken part in the general meeting of stockholders held in the form of external voting [added by Federal Law No. 120-ФЗ, 7 August 2001].

2. If the agenda of the general meeting of stockholders includes questions, the voting with regard to which is effectuated by a different composition of those voting, the determination of a quorum for the adoption of a decision with regard to these questions shall be effectuated separately. In so doing the absence of a quorum for the adoption of a decision with regard to questions, the voting with regard to which is effectuated by one composition of those voting, shall not prevent the adoption of a decision with regard to questions, voting with regard to which is effectuated by another composition of those voting, for the adoption of which there is a quorum [as amended by Federal Law No. 120-ФЗ, 7 August 2001].

3. In the absence of a quorum for conducting the yearly general meeting of stockholders, a repeated general meeting of stockholders with the same agenda must be held. In the absence of a quorum for conducting an extraordinary general meeting of stockholders a repeated general meeting of stockholders with the same agenda may be held [as amended by Federal Law No. 120-ФЗ, 7 August 2001].

A repeated general meeting of stockholders shall be empowered (or have a quorum) if stockholders possessing in aggregate not less than 30% of the votes of placed voting stocks of the society take part therein. A smaller quorum for holding a repeated general meeting of stockholders may be provided for by the charter of a society with a number of stockholders of more than 500,000 [as amended by Federal Law No. 120-ФЗ, 7 August 2001].

A communication concerning the conducting of a repeated general meeting of stockholders shall be effectuated in accordance with the requirements of Article 52 of the present Federal Law. In so doing the provisions of Article 52(1), paragraph two, of the present Federal Law shall not apply. The handing over, sending, and publication of ballots for voting when holding a repeated general meeting of stockholders shall be effectuated in accordance with the requirements of Article 60 of the present Federal Law [as amended by Federal Law No. 120-ФЗ, 7 August 2001].

4. In the event of holding a repeated general meeting of stockholdrs less than 40 days after the unconstituted general meeting of stockholders, the persons having the right to participate in the general meeting of stockholders shall be determined in accordance with the list of persons having the right to participate in the unconstituted general meeting of stockholders [as amended by Federal Law No. 120-ФЗ, 7 August 2001].

Article 59. Voting at General Meeting of Stockholders

Voting at a general meeting of stockholders shall be effectuated according to the principle of 'one voting stock of the society—one vote', except for conducting cumulative voting in the event provided for by the present Federal Law [as amended by Federal Law No. 120-ФЗ, 7 August 2001].

Article 60. Ballot for Voting

1. Voting with regard to questions of the agenda of the general meeting of stockholders may be effectuated by ballots for voting.

Voting with regard to questions of the agenda of the general meeting of stockholders of the society with a number of stockholders-possessors of voting stocks of more than one hundred, and also voting with regard to questions of the agenda of the general meeting of stockholders conducted in the form of external voting, shall be effectuated only by ballots for voting [as amended by Federal Law No. 120-ФЗ, 7 August 2001].

2. A ballot for voting must be handed over under receipt to each person specified in the list of persons having the right to participate in the general meeting of stockholders (or representative thereof) who has registered to participate in the general meeting of stockholders, except for instances provided for by paragraph two of the present point [as amended by Federal Law No. 120-ФЗ, 7 August 2001].

When holding a general meeting of stockholders in the form of external voting and holding the general meeting of stockholders of the society with a number of stockholders-possessors of voting stocks of 1000 or more, and also of another society whose charter provided for the obligatory sending (or handing over) of ballots before holding the general meeting of stockholders, the ballot for voting must be sent or handed over under receipt to each person specified in the list of persons having the right to participate in the general meeting of stockholders not later than 20 days before holding the general meeting of stockholders [added by Federal Law No. 120-ФЗ, 7 August 2001].

Sending a ballot for voting shall be effectuated by registered letter unless another means of sending ballots for voting has been provided for by the charter of the society [added by Federal Law No. 120-ФЗ, 7 August 2001].

Publication within a specified period of ballot forms for voting in a printed publication determined by the charter of the society accessible for all stockholders of a society may be provided for by the charter of a society with a number of stockholders of more than 500,000 [added by Federal Law No. 120-ФЗ, 7 August 2001].

3. When holding a general meeting of stockholders, except for a general meeting of stockholders held in the form of external voting, in socieites effectuating the sending (or handing over) of ballots or publication of forms thereof in accordance with point 2 of the present Article, the persons included in the list of persons having the right to participate in the general meeting of stockholders (or representatives thereof) shall have the right to take part in such meeting or to send filled-in ballots to the society. In so doing, when determining the quorum and adding up the results of the voting, votes submitted as ballots for voting received by the society not later than two days before the date of holding the general meeting of stockholders shall be taken into account [added by Federal Law No. 120-ФЗ, 7 August 2001].

4. Ballots for voting must specify:

the full firm name of the society and the location of the society;

the form of holding the general meeting of stockholders (meeting or external voting);

the date, place, and time for holding the general meeting of stockholders, and in the event when in accordance with point 3 of the present Article filled-in ballots may be sent to the society, the postal address to which filled-in ballots may be sent, or in the event of holding the general meeting of stockholders in the form of external voting the date of ending the receipt of ballots for voting and the postal address to which filled-in ballots must be sent;

the formulation of decisions with regard to each question (or name of each candidate), voting with regard to which is effectuated by the said ballot;

the variants of voting for each question on the agenda expressed by the formulas 'yes', 'against' or 'abstain';

a mention that the ballot for voting must be signed by the stockholder.

In the event of the effectuation of cumulative voting, the ballot for voting must contain an indication to this and an explanation of the essence of cumulative voting [as renumbered in pursuance of and as amended by Federal Law No. 120-ФЗ, 7 August 2001].

Article 61. Counting Votes in Event of Voting Effectuated by Ballots for Voting

In the event of voting effectuated by ballots for voting, the votes shall be counted with regard to those questions for which the voter has left only one of the possible variants of voting. Ballots for voting which are filled out with a violation of the aforesaid requirement shall be deemed to be invalid and the votes shall not be counted with regard to the questions contained therein.

If a ballot for voting contains several questions placed on the ballot, the failure to comply with the aforesaid requirement with respect to one or several questions shall not entail the deeming of the ballot for voting to be invalid as a whole.

Article 62. Protocol and Report on Results of Voting [as amended by Federal Law No. 120-ФЗ, 7 August 2001]

1. The counting commission shall draw up a protocol with regard to the results of voting concerning the results of the voting signed by the members of the counting commission or the person fulfilling the functions thereof. The protocol on the results of voting shall be drawn up not later than 15 days after the adjournment of the general meeting of stockholders or date of the end of the receipt of ballots when holding a general meeting of stockholders in the form of external voting [as amended by Federal Law No. 120-ФЗ, 7 August 2001].

2. After the drawing up of the protocol concerning the results of the voting and the signature of the protocol of the general meeting of stockholders, the ballots for voting shall be sealed by the counting commission and handed over to the archive of the society for storage.

3. The protocol concerning the results of the voting shall be subject to being attached to the protocol of the general meeting of stockholders.

4. Decisions adopted by the general meeting of stockholders, and also the results of the voting, shall be disclosed at the general meeting of stockholders in the course of which the voting was conducted, or brought not later than 10 days after

the drawing up of the protocol concerning the results of the voting in the form of a report concerning the results of voting to the information of persons included in the list of persons having the right to participate in the general meeting of stockholders in the procedure provided for notifying the holding of the general meeting of stockholders [as amended by Federal Law No. 120-ФЗ, 7 August 2001].

Article 63. Protocol of General Meeting of Stockholders

1. The protocol of a general meeting of stockholders shall be drawn up not later than 15 days after the closing of the general meeting of stockholders in two copies. Both copies shall be signed by the person presiding at the general meeting of stockholders and by the secretary of the general meeting of stockholders.

2. There shall be specified in the protocol of a general meeting of stockholders:
the place and time of holding the general meeting of stockholders;
the total quantity of votes which the stockholders-possessors of voting stocks of the society possess;
the quantity of votes which the stockholders taking part in the meeting possess;
the chairman (or presidium) and secretary of the meeting and the agenda of the meeting.
The basic tenets of the speeches, the questions put for voting, and the results of the voting with regard to them, and the decisions adopted by the meeting must be contained in the protocol of the general meeting of stockholders of the society.

Chapter VIII. Council of Directors (or Supervisory Council) of Society and Executive Organ of Society

Article 64. Council of Directors (or Supervisory Council) of Society

1. The council of directors (or supervisory council) of a society shall effectuate general direction over the activity of the society, except for the deciding of questions relegated by the present Federal Law to the competence of the general meeting of stockholders [as amended by Federal Law No. 120-ФЗ, 7 August 2001].

In a society with a number of stockholders-possessors of voting stocks of less than fifty the charter of the society may provide that the functions of the council of directors of the society (or supervisory council) shall be effectuated by the general meeting of stockholders. In this event the charter of the society must contain an instruction concerning the specified person or organ of the society to whose competence the deciding of the question of conducting a general meeting of stockholders and confirmation of its agenda is relegated.

2. By decision of the general meeting of stockholders the members of the council of directors (or supervisory council) of the society may in the period during which they perform their duties be paid remuneration and/or expenses be contributorily compensated which are connected with their performance of the functions of members of the council of directors (or supervisory council) of the

society. The amounts of such remuneration and contributory compensation shall be established by decision of the general meeting of stockholders.

Article 65. Competence of Council of Directors (or Supervisory Council) of Society

1. Within the competence of the council of directors (or supervisory council) of the society shall be the deciding of questions of the general direction of the activity of the society, except for questions relegated by the present Federal Law to the competence of the general meeting of stockholders [as amended by Federal Law No. 120-ФЗ, 7 August 2001].

The following questions shall be relegated to the competence of the council of directors (or supervisory council) of a society:

(1) determination of the priority orientations of activity of the society;

(2) convocation of the yearly and extraordinary general meetings of stockholders, except for the instances provided for by Article 55(8) of the present Federal Law;

(3) confirmation of the agenda of the general meeting of stockholders;

(4) determination of the date of drawing up the list of persons having the right to participate in the general meeting of stockholders and other questions relegated to the competence of the council of directors (or supervisory council) of the society in accordance with the provisions of Chapter VII of the present Federal Law and connected with the preparation and conducting of the general meeting of stockholders;

(5) increase of the charter capital of the society by means of the placement by the society of additional stocks within the limits of the quantity and categories (or types) of declared stocks if, in accordance with the present Federal Law, this has been relegated to its competence by the charter of the society;

(6) placement by the society of bonds and other emission securities in the instances provided for by the present Federal Law;

(7) determination of the price (or market value) of property and the price of placement and purchase of emission securities in instances provided for by the present Federal Law;

(8) acquisition of stocks, bonds, and other securities placed by the society in the instances provided for by the present Federal Law;

(9) formation of the executive organ of the society and termination before time of its powers, if this has been relegated to its competence by the charter of the society;

(10) recommendations relating to the amount of remuneration and contributory compensation to be paid to members of the audit commission (or internal auditor) of the society and determination of the amount of payment for the services of an auditor;

(11) recommendations relating to the amount of dividend for stocks and the procedure for the payment thereof;

(12) use of the reserve and other funds of the society;

(13) confirmation of the internal documents of the society, except for internal documents whose confirmation is relegated by the present Federal Law to the competence of the general meeting of stockholders, and also other internal documents of the society, confirmation of which is relegated by the charter of the society to the competence of executive organs of the society;

(14) creation of branches and the opening of representations of the society;

(15) approval of large-scale transactions in the instances provided for by Chapter X of the present Federal Law;

(16) approval of transactions provided for by Chapter XI of the present Federal Law;

(17) confirmation of the registrar of the society and conditions of the contract with him, and also dissolution of the contract with him;

(18) other questions provided for by the present Federal Law and the charter of the society [point 1 as amended by Federal Law No. 120-ФЗ, 7 August 2001].

2. Questions relegated to the competence of the council of directors (or supervisory council) of the society may not be transferred for decision to an executive organ of the society [as renumbered and amended by Federal Law No. 120-ФЗ, 7 August 2001].

Article 66. Election of Council of Directors (or Supervisory Council) of Society

1. Members of the council of directors (or supervisory council) of a society shall be elected by the general meeting of stockholders in the procedure provided for by the present Federal Law and the charter of the society for a term of up to the next yearly general meeting of stockholders. If the yearly general meeting of stockholders is not held within the periods established by Article 47(1) of the present Federal Law, the powers of the council of directors (or supervisory council) of the society shall terminate, except for powers with regard to the preparation, convocation, and conducting of the yearly general meeting of stockholders [as amended by Federal Law No. 120-ФЗ, 7 August 2001].

Persons elected to the council of directors (or supervisory council) of a society may be re-elected for an unlimited number of times.

By decision of the general meeting of stockholders the powers of any member (or all members) of the council of directors (or supervisory council) of the society may be terminated before time.

In the event of the election of members of the council of directors (or supervisory council) of the society by cumulative voting in accordance with point 4 of the present Article, the decision of the general meeting of stockholders concerning the termination of powers before time may be adopted only with respect to all members of the council of directors (or supervisory council) of the society.

2. Only a natural person may be a member of the council of directors (or supervisory council) of a society. A member of the council of directors (or supervisory council) of a society may not be a stockholder of the society.

Members of a collegial executive organ of a society may not comprise more than one-fourth of the composition of the council of directors (or supervisory council) of a society. A person effectuating the functions of one-man executive organ may not be simultaneously the chairman of the council of directors (or supervisory council) of a society [as amended by Federal Law No. 120-ФЗ, 7 August 2001].

3. The quantitative composition of the council of directors (or supervisory council) of a society shall be determined by the charter of the society or decision of the general meeting of stockholders in accordance with the requirements of the present Federal Law.

For an open society with a number of stockholders-possessors of voting stocks of the society of more than one thousand, the quantitative composition of the council of directors (or supervisory council) of the society may not be less than seven members, and for a society with a number of stockholders-possessors of common and other voting stocks of the society of more than ten thousand, not less than nine members [as amended by Federal Law No. 120-ФЗ, 7 August 2001].

4. Elections of members of the council of directors (or supervisory council) of a society with a number of stockholders-possessors of voting stocks of the society of more than one thousand shall be effectuated by cumulative voting. In a society with a number of stockholders-possessors of common stocks of the stock of 1000 and less, cumulative voting in the event of elections of members of the council of directors (or supervisory council) of the society may be provided for by the charter [as amended by Federal Law No. 120-ФЗ, 7 August 2001].

In the event of cumulative voting, the number of votes belonging to each stockholder shall be multiplied by the number of persons who should be elected to the council of directors (or supervisory council) of the society, and a stockholder shall have the right to cast the votes so received entirely for one candidate or to distribute them among two or more candidates [as amended by Federal Law No. 120-ФЗ, 7 August 2001].

The candidates who receive the largest number of votes shall be considered to be elected to the council of directors (or supervisory council) of the society.

Article 67. Chairman of Council of Directors (or Supervisory Council) of Society

1. The chairman of the council of directors (or supervisory council) of a society shall be elected by the members of the council of directors (or supervisory council) of the society from among their number by a majority of votes of the total

number of members of the council of directors (or supervisory council) of the society unless provided otherwise by the charter of the society.

The council of directors (or supervisory council) of a society shall have the right at any time to re-elect its chairman by a majority of votes of the total number of members of the council of directors (or supervisory council) unless provided otherwise by the charter of the society.

2. The chairman of the council of directors (or supervisory council) of the society shall organise its work, convoke sessions of the council of directors (or supervisory council) of the society and preside at them, organise the keeping of the protocol at sessions, and preside at the general meeting of stockholders unless provided otherwise by the charter of the society.

3. In the event of the absence of the chairman of the council of directors (or supervisory council) of the society, his functions shall be effectuated by one of the members of the council of directors (or supervisory council) of the society by decision of the council of directors (or supervisory council) of the society.

Article 68. Session of Council of Directors (or Supervisory Council) of Society

1. A session of the council of directors (or supervisory council) of a society shall be convoked by the chairman of the council of directors (or supervisory council) of the society at his own initiative or at the demand of a member of the council of directors (or supervisory council), or the audit commission (or internal auditor) of the society or the auditor of the society, executive organ of the society, and also other persons determined by the charter of the society. The procedure for the convocation and conducting of sessions of the council of directors (or supervisory council) of the society shall be determined by the charter of the society or internal document of the society. The possibility of taking into account when determining the existence of a quorum and the results of voting of a written opinion of a member of the council of directors (or supervisory council) of a society with regard to questions of the agenda, and also the possibility of adopting decisions by the council of directors (or supervisory council) of the society by external voting, may be provided for by the charter or internal document of the society [as amended by Federal Law No. 120-ФЗ, 7 August 2001].

2. A quorum for conducting a session of the council of directors (or supervisory council) of the society shall be determined by the charter of the society, but must not be less than half of the number of elected members of the council of directors (or supervisory council) of the society. When the number of members of the council of directors (or supervisory council) of a society becomes less than quantity comprising the said quorum, the council of directors (or supervisory council) of a society shall be obliged to adopt a decision concerning the holding of an extraordinary general meeting of stockholders in order to elect the new

membership of the council of directors (or supervisory council) of the society. The remaining members of the council of directors (or supervisory council) of the society shall have the right to adopt a decision only concerning the convocation of such an extraordinary general meeting of stockholders [as amended by Federal Law No. 120-Ф3, 7 August 2001].

3. Decisions shall be adopted at a session of the council of directors (or supervisory council) of the society by a majority of votes of members of the council of directors (or supervisory council) of the society taking part in the session, unless provided otherwise by the present Federal Law, the charter of the society, or internal document thereof determining the procedure for the convocation and conducting of sessions of the council of directors (or supervisory council). When deciding questions at a session of the council of directors (or supervisory council) of the society each member of the council of directors (or supervisory council) shall possess one vote [as amended by Federal Law No. 120-Ф3, 7 August 2001].

The transfer of the right to vote by a member of the council of directors (or supervisory council) of the society to another person, including to another member of the council of directors (or supervisory council) of the society, shall not be permitted [as amended by Federal Law No. 120-Ф3, 7 August 2001].

The right of a casting vote of the chairman of the council of directors (or supervisory council) of the society in the event of the adoption by the council of directors (or supervisory council) of the society of decisions by a tie vote of members of the council of directors (or supervisory council) of the society may be provided for by the charter of the society.

4. A protocol shall be kept at a session of the council of directors (or supervisory council) of a society.

The protocol of a session of the council of directors (or supervisory council) of a society shall be drawn up not later than three days after the conducting thereof [as amended by Federal Law No. 120-Ф3, 7 August 2001].

There shall be specified in the protocol:

the place and time of holding it;

the persons present at the session;

the agenda of the session;

the questions put for voting and the resuults of voting with regard to them;

the decisions adopted.

The protocol of a session of the council of directors (or supervisory council) of a society shall be signed by the person presiding at the session, who shall bear responsibility for the correctness of the drawing up of the protocol.

Article 69. Executive Organ of Society. One-Man Executive Organ of Society (Director, Director-General)

1. The direction of the current activity of a society shall be effectuated by a one-man executive organ of the society (director, director-general) or by a one-man executive organ of the society (director, director-general) and collegial executive organ of the society (board, directorate). The executive organs shall be accountable to the council of directors (or supervisory council) of the society and to the general meeting of stockholders [as amended by Federal Law No. 120-ФЗ, 7 August 2001].

The competence of a collegial organ must be determined by the charter of a society providing for the existence simultaneously of a one-man and a collegial executive organ. In this event the person effectuating the functions of the one-man executive organ of the society (director, director-general) shall also effectuate the functions of chairman of the collegial executive organ of the society (board, directorate) [as amended by Federal Law No. 120-ФЗ, 7 August 2001].

By decision of the general meeting of stockholders, the powers of the one-man executive organ of the society may be transferred under a contract to a commercial organisation (or management organisation) or to an individual entrepreneur (or manager). The decision concerning the transfer of powers of a one-man executive organ of a society to the management organisation or manager shall be adopted by the general meeting of stockholders only upon the proposal of the council of directors (or supervisory council) of the society [as amended by Federal Law No. 120-ФЗ, 7 August 2001].

2. To the competence of the executive organ of the society shall be relegated all questions of the direction of the current activity of the society, except for questions relegated to the competence of the general meeting of stockholders or council of directors (or supervisory council) of the society [as amended by Federal Law No. 120-ФЗ, 7 August 2001].

The executive organ of the society shall organise the fulfilment of the decisions of the general meeting of stockholders and council of directors (or supervisory council) of the society.

A one-man executive organ of a society (director, director-general) shall operate in the name of the society without a power of attorney, including represent its interests, conclude transactions in the name of the society, confirm the personnel establishment, and issue orders and give instructions binding for execution by all workers of the society.

3. The formation of the executive organs of a society and the termination of their powers before time shall be effectuated by decision of the general meeting of stockholders unless the charter of the society has relegated the deciding of these questions to the competence of the council of directors (or supervisory council) of the society [as amended by Federal Law No. 120-ФЗ, 7 August 2001].

The rights and duties of the one-man executive organ of the society (director, director-general), members of the collegial executive organ of the society (board, directorate), management organisation, or manager with regard to the effectuation of the direction of the current activity of the society shall be determined by the present Federal Law and other legal acts of the Russian Federation and by the contract concluded by each of them with the society. The contract shall be signed in the name of the society by the chairman of the council of directors (or supervisory council) of the society or by the person empowered by the council of directors (or supervisory council) of the society.

The operation of legislation of the Russian Federation on labour shall extend to relations between the society and the one-man executive organ of the society (director, director-general) and/or members of the collegial executive organ of the society (board, directorate) in that part which is not contrary to the provisions of the present Federal Law.

The combining by a person effectuating the functions of one-man executive organ of the society (director, director-general) and by members of the collegial executive organ of the society (board, directorate) of offices in the management organs of other organisations shall be permitted only with the consent of the council of directors (or supervisory council) of the society.

4. The general meeting of stockholders shall have the right, unless the formation of executive organs has been relegated by the charter of the society to the competence of the council of directors (or supervisory council) of the society, at any time to adopt a decision concerning the termination of powers of the one-man executive organ of the society (director, director-general) and members of a collegial executive organ of the society (board, directorate). The general meeting of stockholders shall have the right at any time to adopt a decision concerning termination before time of the powers of a management organisation or manager [as amended by Federal Law No. 120-ФЗ, 7 August 2001].

If the formation of executive organs has been relegated by the charter of a society to the competence of the council of directors (or supervisory council) of a society, it shall have the right at any time to adopt a decision concerning the termination before time of the powers of a one-man executive organ of a society (director, director-general) and members of a collegial executive organ of a society (board, directorate) and the formation of new executive organs [added by Federal Law No. 120-ФЗ, 7 August 2001].

If the formation of executive organs is effectuated by the general meeting of stockholders, the right of the council of directors (or supervisory council) of a society may be provided for by the charter of the society to adopt a decision concerning the suspension of powers of the one-man executive organ of the society (director, director-general). The right of a council of directors (or supervisory council) of a society to adopt a decision concerning the suspension of powers of a management organisation or manager may be provided for by the charter of a society. Simultaneously with the said decision, a council of directors (or supervisory council) of a society shall be obliged to adopt a decision concerning the formation of a temporary one-man executive organ of the society (director, director-general) and holding an extraordinary general meeting of stockholders in order to decide the question of the termination before time of the powers of the one-man executive organ of a society (director, director-general) or management organisation (or manager) and on the formation of a new one-man executive organ of the society (director, director-general) or the transfer of the powers of a one-man executive organ of the society (director, director-general) to a management organisation or manager [added by Federal Law No. 120-ФЗ, 7 August 2001].

If the formation of executive organs is effectuated by the general meeting of stockholders and the one-man executive organ of a society (director, director-general) or management organisation (or manager) cannot perform its duties, the council of directors (or supervisory council) of a society shall have the right to adopt a decision concerning the formation of a temporary one-man executive organ of the society (director, director-general) and on holding an extraordinary general meeting of stockholders in order to decide the question of the termination before time of the powers of a one-man executive organ of a society (director, director-general) or management organisation (or manager) and on the formation of a new executive organ of the society or on the transfer of powers of the one-man executive organ of a society to a management organisation or manager [added by Federal Law No. 120-ФЗ, 7 August 2001].

All decisions specified in paragraphs three and four of the present point shall be adopted by a majority of three-quarters of the votes of members of the council of directors (or supervisory council), in so doing the votes of members of the council of directors (or supervisory council) of a society who have withdrawn shall not be taken into account [added by Federal Law No. 120-ФЗ, 7 August 2001].

Temporary executive organs of a society shall effectuate direction over the current activity of the society within the limits of the competence of executive organs of a society unless the competence of temporary executive organs of a society has been limited by the charter of the society [added by Federal Law No. 120-ФЗ, 7 August 2001].

Article 70. Collegial Executive Organ of Society (Board, Directorate)

1. The collegial executive organ of a society (board, directorate) shall operate on the basis of the charter of the society, and also an internal document of the society (statute, reglament, or other document) confirmed by the general meeting of stockholders in which the periods and procedure for the convocation and conducting of its sessions, as well as the procedure for the adoption of decisions, are established [as amended by Federal Law No. 120-ФЗ, 7 August 2001].

2. A quorum for holding a session of a collegial executive organ of a society (board, directorate) shall be determined by the charter of the society or by an internal document of the society and must comprise not less than half of the number of elected members of the collegial executive organ of a society (board, directorate). If the number of members of a collegial executive organ of a society (board, directorate) becomes less than the number constituting the said quorum, the council of directors (or supervisory council) of a society shall be obliged to adopt a decision on the formation of a temporary collegial executive organ of the society (board, directorate) and on holding an extraordinary general meeting of stockholders in order to elect the collegial executive organ of a society (board, directorate) or, if in accordance with the charter of a society this has been relegated to its competence, to form the collegial executive organ of the society (board, directorate) [as amended by Federal Law No. 120-ФЗ, 7 August 2001].

A protocol shall be kept at the session of a collegial executive organ of a society (board, directorate). The protocol of a session of a collegial executive organ of a society (board, directorate) shall be provided to members of the council of directors (or supervisory council) of a society, auditing commission (or internal auditor), or auditor of the society at their demand [[as amended by Federal Law No. 120-ФЗ, 7 August 2001].

The conducting of sessions of the collegial executive organ of a society (board, directorate) shall be organised by the person effectuating the functions of one-man executive organ of the society (director, director-general), who shall sign all documents in the name of the society and protocols of sessions of the collegial executive organ of the society (board, directorate), and operate without a power of attorney in the name of the society in accordance with decisions of the collegial executive organ of the society (board, directorate) adopted within the limits of its competence.

The transfer of the right to vote by a member of a collegial executive organ of a society (board, directorate) to another person, including to another person of the collegial executive organ of a society (board, directorate), shall not be permitted [added by Federal Law No. 120-ФЗ, 7 August 2001].

Article 71. Responsibility of Members of Council of Directors (or Supervisory Council) of Society, One-Man Executive Organ of Society (Director, Director-General) and/or Members of Collegial Executive Organ of Society (Board, Directorate), Management Organisation, or Manager

1. The members of the council of directors (or supervisory council) of the society, one-man executive organ of the society (director, director-general), temporary one-man executive organ, members of the collegial executive organ of the society (board, directorate), and likewise the management organisation or manager must, when effectuating their rights and peforming duties, operate in the interests of the society and effectuate their rights and perform duties with respect

to the society in good faith and reasonably [as amended by Federal Law No. 120-ФЗ, 7 August 2001].

2. Members of the council of directors (or supervisory council) of the society, one-man executive organ of the society (director, director-general), temporary one-man executive organ, members of the collegial executive organ of the society (board, directorate), and likewise the management organisation or manager shall bear responsibility to the society for losses caused to the society by their guilty actions (or failure to act) unless other grounds and extent of responsibility have been established by federal laws [as amended by Federal Law No. 120-ФЗ, 7 August 2001].

In the council of directors (or supervisory council) of the society and the collegial executive organ of the society (board, directorate) the members who have voted against decisions which entailed the causing of losses to the society or who did not take part in the voting shall not bear responsibility.

3. When determining the grounds and extent of responsibility of members of the council of directors (or supervisory council), of the one-man executive organ of the society (director, director-general) and/or members of the collegial executive organ of the society (board, directorate), and likewise of the management organisation or manager, the ordinary conditions of business turnover and other circumstances having significance for the matter must be taken into account.

4. If in accordance with the provisions of the present Article several persons bear responsibility, their responsibility to the society shall be joint and several.

5. A society or stockholder(s) possessing in aggregate not less than 1% of the placed common stocks of the society shall have the right to apply to a court with a suit against a member of the council of directors (or supervisory council) of the society, one-man executive organ of the society (director, director-general), member of collegial executive organ of the society (board, directorate), and likewise management organisation or manager concerning compensation of losses caused to the society in the event provided for by point 2 of the present Article.

6. Representatives of the State or municipal formation in the council of directors (or supervisory council) of an open society shall bear the responsibility provided for by the prewsent Article together with other members of the council of directors (or supervisory council) of an open society [added by Federal Law No. 120-ФЗ, 7 August 2001].

Chapter IX. Acquisition and Purchase by Society of Placed Stocks

Article 72. Acquisition by Society of Placed Stocks

1. A society shall have the right to acquire stocks placed by it by a decision of the general meeting of stockholders concerning the reduction of charter capital of

the society by means of the acquisition of part of the placed stocks for the purpose of reducing the total quantity thereof, if this has been provided for by the charter of the society.

The society shall not have the right to adopt a decision concerning the reduction of charter capital of the society by means of the acquisition of part of the placed stocks for the purpose of reducing the total quantity thereof if the par value of the stocks remaining in circulation becomes lower than the minimum amount of charter capital provided for by the present Federal Law.

2. The society, if this has been provided by the charter thereof, shall have the right to acquire stocks placed by it by a decision of the council of directors (or supervisory council) of the society if in accordance with the charter of the society the right to adopt such a decision belongs to the council of directors (or supervisory council) of the society [as amended by Federal Law No. 120-ФЗ, 7 August 2001].

The society shall not have the right to adopt a decision concerning the acquisition by the society of stocks if the par value of the stocks of the society in circulation comprises less than 90% of the charter capital of the society [as amended by Federal Law No. 120-ФЗ, 7 August 2001].

3. Stocks acquired by the society on the basis of a decision adopted by the general meeting of stockholders concerning a reduction of the charter capital of the society by means of acquisition of stocks for the purpose of reducing the total quantity thereof shall be cancelled when they are acquired.

Stocks acquired by the society in accordance with point 2 of the present Article shall not grant a right of vote, they shall not be taken into account during the counting of votes, and dividends shall not be credited with respect to them. Such stocks must be realised at their market value not later than one year from the date of their acquisition. Otherwise the general meeting of stockholders must adopt a decision concerning the reduction of the charter capital of the society by means of cancelling the said stocks [as amended by Federal Law No. 120-ФЗ, 7 August 2001].

4. The categories (or types) of stocks to be acquired, the quantity of stocks to be acquired by the society of each category (or type), the price of acquisition, the form and period for paying up, and also the period during which the acquisition of stocks shall be effectuated must be determined by the decision on the acquisition of stocks.

Unless established otherwise by the charter of the society, the paying up of stocks in the event of their acquisition shall be effectuated in money. The period during which the acquisition of stocks is effectuated may not be less than 30 days. The price of acquisition by the society of stocks shall be determined in accordance with Article 77 of the present Federal Law [as amended by Federal Law No. 120-ФЗ, 7 August 2001].

Each stockholder-possessor of stocks of specified categories (or types), the decision concerning the acquisition of which is adopted, shall have the right to sell the said stocks, and the society shall be obliged to acquire them. If the total quantity of stocks with respect to which applications have been received concerning their acquisition exceeds the quantity of stocks which may be acquired by the society taking into account the limitations established by the present Article, the stocks shall be acquired from the stockholders in proportion to the stated demands.

5. Not later than 30 days before the commencement of the period during which the acquisition of stocks is effectuated the society shall be obliged to inform the stockholders-possessors of stocks of the specified categories (or types), the decision concerning the acquisition of which is adopted. The notice must contain the information specified in paragraph one of point 4 of the present Article.

6. [repealed by Federal Law No. 120-ФЗ, 7 August 2001]

Article 73. Limitations on Acquisition of Placed Stocks by Society

1. A society shall not have the right to effectuate the acquisition of common stocks placed by it:
   until payment up in full of the entire charter capital of the society;
   if at the moment of their acquisition the society is liable by the indicia of insolvency (or bankruptcy) in accordance with legal acts of the Russian Federation on the insolvency (or bankruptcy) of enterprises or the said indicia appear as a result of the acquisition of these stocks;
   if at the moment of their acquisition the value of the net assets of the society is less than its charter capital, reserve fund, and excess of the liquidation value of the placed preferred stocks over the par value determined by the charter or becomes less than the amount thereof as a result of the acquisition of the stocks.

2. A society shall not have the right to effectuate the acquisition of preferred stocks of a specified type placed by it:
   until payment up in full of the entire charter capital of the society;
   if at the moment of their acquisition the society is liable by the indicia of insolvency (or bankruptcy) in accordance with legal acts of the Russian Federation on the insolvency (or bankruptcy) of enterprises or the said indicia appear as a result of the acquisition of these stocks;
   if at the moment of their acquisition the value of the net assets of the society is less than its charter capital, reserve fund, and excess of the liquidation value of the placed preferred stocks over the par value determined by the charter, the possessors of which possess a preference in priority of payment of the liquidation value over the possessors of types of preferred stocks subject to acquisition, or becomes less than the amount thereof as a result of the acquisition of the stocks.

3. A society shall not have the right to effectuate the acquisition of placed stocks before the purchase of all stocks, demands concerning the purchase of

which have been submitted in accordance with Article 76 of the present Federal Law.

Article 74. Consolidation and Splitting of Stocks of Society

1. By decision of the general meeting of stockholders, a society shall have the right to carry out consolidation with regard to placed stocks as a result of which two or more stocks of the society shall be converted into one new stock of the same category (or type). Respective changes relative to the par value and quantity of the placed and declared stocks of the society of the respective category (or type) shall be made in the charter of the society in so doing [as amended by Federal Law No. 120-ФЗ, 7 August 2001].

[paragraph two repealed by Federal Law No. 120-ФЗ, 7 August 2001]

2. By decision of the general meeting of stockholders, a society shall have the right to carry out the splitting of placed stocks of the society, as a result of which one stock of the society is converted into two or more stocks of the society of the same category (or type). Respective changes relative to the par value and quantity of the placed and declared stocks of the society of the respective category (or type) shall be made in the charter of the society in so doing [as amended by Federal Law No. 120-ФЗ, 7 August 2001].

Article 75. Purchase of Stocks by Society at Demand of Stockholders

1. Stockholders-possessors of voting stocks shall have the right to demand the purchase by the society of all or part of the stocks belonging to them in instances of:

the reorganisation of the society or the conclusion of a large-scale transaction, the decision concerning the approval of which is adopted by the general meeting of stockholders in accordance with Article 79(2) of the present Federal Law if they voted against the adoption of the decision concerning its reorganisation or the approval of the said transaction or did not take part in the voting with regard to these questions [as amended by Federal Law No. 120-ФЗ, 7 August 2001];

making changes in and additions to the charter of the society or confirmation of the charter of the society in a new redaction which limit their rights, if they voted against the adoption of the respective decision or did not take part in the voting.

2. The list of stockholders who have the right to demand the purchase by the society of stocks belonging to them shall be drawn up on the basis of data of the register of stockholders of the society on the day of drawing up the list of persons who have the right to participate in the general meeting of stockholders, the agenda for which includes the questions, the voting with regard to which in accordance with the present Federal Law may entail the arising of the right to demand the purchase of the stocks [as amended by Federal Law No. 120-ФЗ, 7 August 2001].

3. The purchase of stocks by the society shall be effectuated at the price determined by the council of directors (or supervisory council) of the society, but not lower than the market value, which must be determined by an independent valuer without taking into account changes thereof as a result of the actions of the society which entailed the arising of the right of demand for the valuation and purchase of the stocks [as amended by Federal Law No. 120-ФЗ, 7 August 2001].

Article 76. Procedure for Effectuation by Stockholders of Right to Demand Purchase by Society of Stocks Belonging to Them

1. A society shall be obliged to inform stockholders about the existence of their right to demand the purchase by the society of stocks belonging to them, the price, and the procedure for the effectuation of the purchase.

2. The communication to the stockholders concerning the holding of a general meeting of stockholders, the agenda of which includes the questions, voting with regard to which may in accordance with the present Federal Law entail the arising of the right to demand the purchase by the society of stocks, must contain the information specified in point 1 of the present Article [as amended by Federal Law No. 120-ФЗ, 7 August 2001].

3. The written demand of a stockholder concerning the purchase of the stocks belonging to him shall be sent to the society specifying the place of residence (or location) of the stockholder and the quantity of stocks whose purchase he demands.

The demands of stockholders concerning the purchase by the society of the stocks belonging to them must be submitted to the society not later than 45 days from the date of the adoption of the respective decision by the general meeting of stockholders.

4. Upon the expiry of the period specified in paragraph two of point 3 of the present Article, the society shall be obliged to purchase the stocks from the stockholders which have submitted demands concerning the purchase within 30 days.

5. The purchase of stocks by the society shall be effectuated at the price specified in the communication concerning the conducting of the general meeting, the agenda of which shall include the questions, voting with regard to which may in accordance with the present Federal Law entail the arising of the right to demand the purchase of stocks by the society. The total amount of assets directed by the society towards the purchase of the stocks may not exceed 10% of the value of the net assets of the society on the date of the adoption of the decision which entails the arising of the right of the stockholders to demand the purchase by the society of the stocks belonging to them. If the total quantity of stocks with respect to which demands have been stated concerning purchase exceed the quantity of

stocks which may be purchased by the society taking into account the afore-established limitations, the stocks shall be purchased from the stockholders in proportion to the stated demands.

6. Stocks purchased by the society in the event of its reorganisation shall be cancelled in the event of their purchase.

Such stocks must be realised at their market value not later than one year from the date of their purchase; otherwise, the general meeting of stockholders must adopt a decision concerning the reduction of the charter capital of the society by means of cancellation of the said stocks [as amended by Federal Law No. 120-ФЗ, 7 August 2001].

Article 77. Determination of Market Value of Property

1. In instances when in accordance with the present Federal Law the price (or monetary valuation) of property, and also the price of placement or price of purchase of emission securities of a society shall be determined by a decision of the council of directors (or supervisory council) of a society, they must be determined by proceeding from the market value thereof [as amended by Federal Law No. 120-ФЗ, 7 August 2001].

If a person interested in the conclusion of one or several transactions under which the price (or monetary valuation) of property is determined by the council of directors (or supervisory council) of a society is a member of the council of directors (or supervisory council) of a society, the price (or monetary valuation) of property shall be determined by decision of the members of the council of directors (or supervisory council) of the society who are not interested in the conclusion of the transaction. In a society with a number of stockholders of 1000 or more, the price (or monetary valuation) of property shall be determined by the independent directors who are not interested in the conclusion of the transaction [added by Federal Law No. 120-ФЗ, 7 August 2001].

2. In order to determine the market value of property an independent valuer may be enlisted [as amended by Federal Law No. 120-ФЗ, 7 August 2001].

The enlistment of an independent valuer shall be obligatory in order to determine the price of purchase by a society from stockholders of stocks belonging to them in accordance with Article 76 of the present Federal Law, and also in other instances provided for by the present Federal Law [as amended by Federal Law No. 120-ФЗ, 7 August 2001].

In the event of determining the price of placement of securities, the price of purchase or price of demand and price of offer of which are regularly published in the press, the enlistment of an independent valuer shall not be obligatory, and in order to determine the market value of such securities, the price of purchase or price of demand and price of offer must be taken into account [added by Federal Law No. 120-ФЗ, 7 August 2001].

3. [paragraph one repealed by Federal Law No. 120-ФЗ, 7 August 2001]

[paragraph two repealed by Federal Law No. 120-ФЗ, 7 August 2001]

If the possessor of more than 2% of the voting stocks of the society is the State and/or a municipal formation, the involvement of a State financial control agency shall be obligatory [as amended by Federal Law No. 120-ФЗ, 7 August 2001].

[paragraph four repealed by Federal Law No. 120-ФЗ, 7 August 2001]

[paragraph five repealed by Federal Law No. 120-ФЗ, 7 August 2001]

Chapter X. Large-Scale Transactions

Article 78. Large-Scale Transaction [as amended by Federal Law No. 120-ФЗ, 7 August 2001]

1. A transaction (including loan, credit, pledge, suretyship) or several mutually-connected transactions connected with the acquisition or alienation or the possibility of alienation by the society directly or indirectly of property whose value comprises 25% or more of the balance sheet value of the assets of the society determined according to the bookkeeping report data on the last report date, except for transactions concluded in the process of ordinary economic activity of the society, transactions connected with the placement by means of subscription (or realisation) of common stocks of the society, and translations connected with the placement of emission securities convertible into common stocks of the society. Other instances also may be established by the charter of a society under which the procedure for the approval of large-scale transactions provided for by the present Federal Law extend to transactions concluded by the society [as amended by Federal Law No. 120-ФЗ, 7 August 2001].

In the event of the alienation or arising of the possibility of alienation of property with the balance-sheet value of assets of the society shall be contrasted the value of such property determiend according to bookkeeper report data, and in the event of the alienation of property—the price of acquisition thereof [added by Federal Law No. 120-ФЗ, 7 August 2001]

2. The price of alienated or acquired property (or services) shall be determined by the council of directors (or supervisory council) of the society in accordance with Article 77 of the present Federal Law for the adoption by the council of directors (or supervisory council) of the society and general meeting of stockholders of a decision concerning approval of a large-scale transaction [as amended by Federal Law No. 120-ФЗ, 7 August 2001].

Article 79. Procedure for Approval of Large-Scale Transaction [as amended by Federal Law No. 120-ФЗ, 7 August 2001]

1. A large-scale translation must be approved by the council of directors (or supervisory council) of a society or by the general meeting of stockholders in

accordance with the present Article [as amended by Federal Law No. 120-ФЗ, 7 August 2001].

2. A decision concerning the approval of a large-scale transaction, the subject of which is property whose value comprises from 25% to 50% of the balance sheet value of the assets of the society shall be adopted by all members of the council of directors (or supervisory council) of a society unanimously, but in so doing the votes of the members who have left the council of directors (or supervisory council) of the society shall not be taken into account [as amended by Federal Law No. 120-ФЗ, 7 August 2001].

If unanimity of the council of directors (or supervisory council) of a society with regard to the question of approval of a large-scale transaction is not achieved, by decision of the council of directors (or supervisory council) of the society the question concerning approval of a large-scale transaction may be submitted for decision of the general meeting of stockholders. In this event the decision concerning the approval of a large-scale transaction shall be adopted by the general meeting of stockholders by a majority of votes of stockholders-possessors of voting stocks taking part in the general meeting of stockholders [added by Federal Law No. 120-ФЗ, 7 August 2001].

3. A decision concerning approval of a large-scale transaction, the subject of which is property whose value comprises more than 50% of the balance sheet value of assets of the society shall be adopted by the general meeting of stockholders by a majority of three-quarters of the votes of stockholders-possessors of voting stocks taking part in the general meeting of stockholders [added by Federal Law No. 120-ФЗ, 7 August 2001].

4. In a decision concerning the approval of a large-scale transaction must be specified the person(s) who are the party(ies) thereof, beneficiary(ies), price, subject of the transaction, and other material conditions thereof [added by Federal Law No. 120-ФЗ, 7 August 2001].

5. If a large-scale transaction simultaneously is a transaction in the conclusion of which there is an interest, only the provisions of Chapter XI of the present Federal Law shall apply to the procedure for the conclusion thereof [added by Federal Law No. 120-ФЗ, 7 August 2001].

6. A large-scale transaction concluded in violation of the requirements of the present Article may be deemed to be invalid upon the suit of the society or a stockholder [added by Federal Law No. 120-ФЗ, 7 August 2001].

7. The provisions of the present Article shall not apply to societies consisting of one stockholder who simultaneously effectuates the functions of the one-man executive organ [added by Federal Law No. 120-ФЗ, 7 August 2001].

Article 80. Acquisition of 30% or More of Common Stocks of Society

1. A person having the intention autonomously or jointly with his affiliated person(s) to acquire 30% or more of the placed common stocks of a society with a number of stockholders-possessors of common stocks of more than 1,000, taking into account the quantity of stocks belonging to him, shall be obliged not earlier than 90 days and later than 30 days before the date of acquisition of the stocks to send to the society a written statement concerning the intention to acquire the said stocks [as amended by Federal Law No. 120-Ф3, 7 August 2001].

2. A person who autonomously or jointly with his affiliated person(s) has acquired 30% or more of the placed common stocks of the society with a number of stockholders-possessors of common stocks of more than 1000, taking into account the stocks belonging to him, shall be obliged within 30 days from the date of acquisition to offer to the stockholders to sell to him the common stocks of the society belonging to them and emission securities convertible into common stocks at the market price, but not lower than their average weighted price for the last six months preceding the date of the acquisition [as amended by Federal Law No. 120-Ф3, 7 August 2001].

An exemption from the duty specified in the present point may be provided for by the charter of the society or by a decision of the general meeting of stockholders. The decision of the general meeting of stockholders concerning the exemption from such duty may be adopted by a majority of votes of the possessors of voting stocks taking part in the general meeting of stockholders, except for votes relating to stocks belonging to the person specified in the present point and its affiliated persons [as amended by Federal Law No. 120-Ф3, 7 August 2001].

3. The offer of the person who acquired common stocks in accordance with the present Article concerning the acquisition of common stocks of the society shall be sent to all stockholders-possessors of the common stocks of the society in written form [as amended by Federal Law No. 120-Ф3, 7 August 2001].

4. A stockholder shall have the right to accept the offer concerning the acquisition of the stocks from him within a period of not more than 30 days from the moment of receipt of the offer [as amended by Federal Law No. 120-Ф3, 7 August 2001].

In the event of the acceptance by a stockholder of the offer concerning acquisition of stocks from him, such stocks must be acquired and paid up not later than 15 days from the date of acceptance of the respective offer by the stockholder [added by Federal Law No. 120-Ф3, 7 August 2001].

5. The offer to stockholders concerning the acquisition of stocks from them shall contain data concerning the person who acquired the common stocks of the society (name, address or location) in accordance with the present Article, and

also an indication of the quantity of common stocks which he acquired, the price offered to the stockholders for the acquisition of the stocks, and period for acquisition and paying up of the stocks [as amended by Federal Law No. 120-ФЗ, 7 August 2001].

6. A person who has acquired stocks in violation of the requirements of the present Article shall have the right to vote at the general meeting of stockholders with regard to stocks whose total quantity does not exceed the quantity of stocks acquired by him in compliance with the requirements of the present Article [as amended by Federal Law No. 120-ФЗ, 7 August 2001].

7. The rules of the present Article shall extend to the acquisition of each 5% of placed common stocks exceeding 30% of the placed common stocks of a society [as amended by Federal Law No. 120-ФЗ, 7 August 2001].

Chapter XI. Interest in Conclusion of Transaction by Society

Article 81. Interest in Conclusion of Transaction by Society

1. Transactions (including a loan, credit, pledge, suretyship) in the conclusion of which there is interest of a member of the council of directors (or supervisory council) of a society, person effectuating the functions of one-man executive organ of the society, including management organisation or manager, member of the collegial executive organ of the society or stockholder of the society having jointly with his affiliated persons 20% or more of voting stocks of the society, and also persons having the right to give to the society instructions binding on it, shall be concluded by the society in accordance with the provisions of the present Chapter [as renumbered and amended by Federal Law No. 120-ФЗ, 7 August 2001].

The said persons shall be deemed to be interested in the conclusion by the society of a transaction in instances when they, their spouses, parents, children, full and half brothers and sisters, adoptive and adopted persons, and/or their affiliated persons:

are a party, beneficiary, intermediary, or representative in the transaction;

possesses (each individually or in aggregate) 20% or more of the stocks (or participatory shares, shares) of a juridical person which is a party, beneficiary, intermediary, or representative in the transaction;

holds office in the management organs of the juridical person which is a party, beneficiary, intermediary, or representative in the transaction, as well as office in management organs of the management organisation of such juridical person;

in other instances determined by the charter of the society [as amended by Federal Law No. 120-ФЗ, 7 August 2001].

2. The provisions of the present Chapter shall not apply to:

societies consisting of one stockholder who simultaneously effectuates the functions of the one-man executive organ;

transactions in the conclusion of which all stockholders of a society are interested;

when effectuating a preferential right to acquire stocks placed by the society;

in the event of the acquisition and purchase of placed stocks by the society;

in the event of the reorganisation of the society in the form of merger (or accession) of societies if more than three-quarters of all voting stocks of the reorganised society belong to the other society participating in the merger (or accession) [added by Federal Law No. 120-ФЗ, 7 August 2001].

Article 82. Information on Interest in Conclusion of Transaction by Society

The persons specified in Article 81 of the present Federal Law shall be obliged to bring to the information of the council of directors (or supervisory council) of the society, audit commission (or internal auditor) of the society, and the auditor of the society information concerning:

juridical persons in which they possess autonomously or jointly with their affiliated person(s) 20% or more of the voting stocks (or participatory shares, shares);

juridical persons in whose management organs they hold office;

transactions known to them to be concluded or proposed in which they may be deemed to be interested persons.

Article 83. Procedure for Approval of Transaction in Conclusion of Which There is an Interest [as amended by Federal Law No. 120-ФЗ, 7 August 2001]

1. A transaction in the conclusion of which there is an interest must be approved before the conclusion thereof by the council of directors (or supervisory council) of the society or by the general meeting of stockholders in accordance with the present Article [as amended by Federal Law No. 120-ФЗ, 7 August 2001].

2. In a society with a number of stockholders-possessors of voting stocks of 1000 or less a decision concerning approval of the transaction in the conclusion of which there is an interest shall be adopted by the council of directors (or supervisory council) of the society by a majority of votes of the directors who are not interested in the conclusion thereof. If the number of uninterested directors comprises less than the quorum determined by the charter for holding a session of the council of directors (or supervisory council) of the society, a decision with regard to this question must be adopted by the general meeting of stockholders in the procedure provided for by point 4 of the present Article [as amended by Federal Law No. 120-ФЗ, 7 August 2001].

[paragraph two repealed by Federal Law No. 120-ФЗ, 7 August 2001]

3. In a society with a number of stockholders-possessors of voting stocks of more than 1000, the decision concerning the approval by the society of a transaction in the conclusion of which there is an interest shall be adopted by the

council of directors (or supervisory council) of a society by a majority of votes of independent directors who are not interested in the conclusion thereof. If all members of the council of directors (or supervisory council) of a society are deemed to be interested persons and/or are not independent directors, the transaction may be approved by decision of the general meeting of stockholders adopted in the procedure provided for by point 4 of the present Article [as amended by Federal Law No. 120-ФЗ, 7 August 2001].

An independent director shall be deemed to be a member of the council of directors (or supervisory council) of a society who is not and who was not within one year preceding the adoption of a decision:

a person effectuating the functions of one-man executive organ of the society, including a manager thereof, member of the collegial executive organ, or person holding office in management organs of a management organisation;

a person, spouse, parents, children, full and half brothers and sisters, adoptive and adopted persons who are persons holding office in the said management organs of a society, management organisation of a society, or managers of a society;

affiliated person of a society, except for a member of the council of directors (or supervisory council) of the society [as amended by Federal Law No. 120-ФЗ, 7 August 2001].

4. A decision concerning the approval of a transaction in the conclusion of which there is an interest shall be adopted by the general meeting of stockholders by a majority of votes of all stockholders-possessors not interested in the transaction of voting stocks in the following instances:

if the subject of a transaction or several mutually-connected transactions is property whose value according to bookkeeping account data (price of the offer for property to be acquired) of the society comprises 2% or more of the balance sheet value of assets of the society according to data of the bookkeeping report thereof on the last report date, except for transactions provided for by paragraphs three and four of the present point;

if the transaction or several mutually-connected transactions is the placement by means of subscription or realisation of stocks comprising more than 2% of the common stocks previously placed by the society and common stocks into which previously placed emission securities convertible into stocks may be converted;

if the transaction or several mutually-connected transactions is the placement by means of subscription of emission securities convertible into stocks which may be converted into common stocks comprising more than 2% of common stocks previously placed by the society and common stocks into which emission securities convertible into stocks may be converted [as amended by Federal Law No. 120-ФЗ, 7 August 2001].

5. A transaction in the commission of which there is an interest shall not require approval of the general meeting of stockholders provided for by point 4 of

the present Article in instances when the conditions of such transaction materially do not differ from the conditions of analogous transactions which have been concluded between the society and the interested person in the process of the effectuation of ordinary economic activity of the society which occurred before the moment when the interested person was deemed to be such. The said exception shall extend only to transactions in the conclusion of which there is an interest concluded in the period from the moment when the interested person was deemed to be such and until the moment of holding the next yearly general meeting of stockholders [as amended by Federal Law No. 120-Ф3, 7 August 2001].

6. In the decision concerning the approval of a transaction in the conclusion of which there is an interest must be specified the person(s) who is a party(ies) thereof, beneficiary(ies), price, subject of the transaction, and other material conditions thereof.

The general meeting of stockholders may adopt a decision concerning the approval of a transaction(s) between the society and interested person which may be concluded in the future in the process of the effectuation by the society of its ordinary economic activity. In so doing the maximum amount must be specified in the decision of the general meeting of stockholders for which such transaction(s) may be concluded. Such decision shall have force until the next yearly general meeting of stockholders [as amended by Federal Law No. 120-Ф3, 7 August 2001].

7. For the adoption by the council of directors (or supervisory council) of a society and the general meeting of stockholders of a decision concerning approval of a transaction in the conclusion of which there is an interest, the price of the property or services to be alienated or acquired shall be determined by the council of directors (or supervisory council) of the society in accordance with Article 77 of the present Federal Law [as amended by Federal Law No. 120-Ф3, 7 August 2001].

8. Additional requirements for the procedure of concluding a transaction in the conclusion of which there is an interest may be established by the federal agency of executive power for the securities market [as amended by Federal Law No. 120-Ф3, 7 August 2001].

Article 84. Consequences of Failure to Comply with Requirements for Transaction, in Conclusion of Which There is an Interest

1. A transaction in the conclusion of which there is an interest concluded with a violation of the requirements for a transaction provided for by the present Federal Law may be deemed to be invalid upon the suit of the society or stockholder [as amended by Federal Law No. 120-Ф3, 7 August 2001].

2. The interested person shall bear responsibility to the society in the amount of losses caused by him to the society. If several persons bear responsibility, their responsibility to the society shall be joint and several.

Chapter XII. Control Over Financial-Economic Activity of Society

Article 85. Audit Commission (or Internal Auditor) of Society

1. In order to effectuate control over the financial-economic activity of the society, an audit commission (or internal auditor) of the society shall be elected by the general meeting of stockholders in accordance with the charter of the society.

By decision of the general meeting of stockholders, remuneration may be paid and/or expenses be contributorily compensated connected with the performance by them of their duties to members of the audit commission (or internal auditor) of the society. The amounts of such remuneration and contributory compensation shall be established by decision of the general meeting of stockholders [added by Federal Law No. 120-ФЗ, 7 August 2001].

2. The competence of the audit commission (or internal auditor) of the society with regard to questions not provided for by the present Federal Law shall be determined by the charter of the society.

The procedure for the activity of the audit commission (or internal auditor) shall be determined by an internal document of the society confirmed by the general meeting of stockholders.

3. The verification (or audit) of the financial-economic activity of a society shall be effectuated with regard to the results of the activity of the society for the year, and also at any time at the initiative of the audit commission (or internal auditor) of the society, decision of the general meeting of stockholders, council of directors (or supervisory council), or at the demand of a stockholder(s) of the society possessing in aggregate not less than 10% of the voting stocks of the society.

4. At the demand of the audit commission (or internal auditor) of a society the persons holding office in the management organs of the society shall be obliged to submit documents concerning the financial-economic activity of the society.

5. The audit commission (or internal auditor) of a society shall have the right to demand the convocation of an extraordinary general meeting of stockholders in accordance with Article 56 of the present Federal Law.

6. The members of the audit commission (or internal auditor) of the society may not be simultaneously members of the council of directors (or supervisory council) of the society, nor hold other offices in the management organs of the society.

Stocks belonging to members of the council of directors (or supervisory council) of the society or to persons holding office in the mamangement organs of the society may not participate in the voting when electing members of the audit commission (or internal auditor) of the society.

Article 86. Auditor of Society

1. The auditor (citizen or auditing organisation) of a society shall effectuate the verification of the financial-economic activity of a society in accordance with legal acts of the Russian Federation on the basis of a contract concluded with him.

2. The general meeting of stockholders shall confirm the auditor of the society. The amount of payment for his services shall be determined by the council of directors (or supervisory council) of the society.

Article 87. Opinion of Audit Commission (or Internal Auditor) of Society or Auditor of Society

With regard to the results of the verification of the financial-economic activity of the society, the audit commission (or internal auditor) or the auditor of the society shall draw up an opinion, which must contain:

confirmation of the reliability of the data contained in the reports and other financial documents of the society;

information concerning facts of a violation of the procedure for keeping bookkeeping records and the submission of financial reports established by legal acts of the Russian Federation, and also of legal acts of the Russian Federation when effectuating financial-economic activity.

Chapter XIII. Records, Reports, and Documents of Society. Information Concerning the Society

Article 88. Bookkeeping Records and Financial Reports of Society

1. A society shall be obliged to keep the bookkeeping report and to submit the financial report in the procedure established by the present Federal Law and other legal acts of the Russian Federation.

2. Responsibility for the organisation, state, and reliability of the bookkeeping records in the society and the timely submission of the annual report and other financial reports to the respective agencies, and also information concerning the activity of the society to be submitted to the stockholders, creditors, and mass media, shall be borne by the executive organ of the society in accordance with the present Federal Law, other legal acts of the Russian Federation, and the charter of the society.

3. The reliability of the data contained in the yearly report of the society and yearly bookkeeping report must be confirmed by the audit commission (or internal auditor) of the society [as amended by Federal Law No. 120-ФЗ, 7 August 2001].

Before publication by the society of the documents specified in the present point in accordance with Article 92 of the present Federal Law, the society shall be obliged to enlist for annual verification and confirmation of the annual financial reports an auditor not connected by property interests with the society or its stockholders.

4. The yearly report of the society shall be subject to preliminary confirmation by the council of directors (or supervisory council) of the society, and in the absence in the society of a council of directors (or supervisory council) of the society—by the person effectuating the functions of one-man executive organ of the society, not later than 30 days before the date of conducting the yearly general meeting of stockholders [as amended by Federal Law No. 120-ФЗ, 7 August 2001].

Article 89. Keeping of Documents of Society

1. A society shall be obliged to keep the following documents:

the contract concerning creation of the society;

the charter of the society and changes and additions made in the charter of the society registered in the established procedure, the decision concerning the creation of the society, and the document concerning State registration of the society [as amended by Federal Law No. 31-ФЗ, 21 March 2002];

documents confirming the rights of the society to property on its balance sheet;

internal documents of the society;

the Statute on the branch or representation of the society;

the yearly reports;

documents of bookkeeping records;

documents of bookkeeping reports;

protocols of the general meetings of stockholders (or decisions of stockholder who is the possessor of all voting stocks of the society), sessions of the council of directors (or supervisory council) of the society, audit commission (or internal auditor) of the society and collegial executive organ of the society (board, directorate);

ballots for voting, and also powers of attorney (or copies of powers of attorney) for participation in the general meeting of stockholders;

reports of independent valuers;

lists of affiliated persons of the society;

lists of persons having the right to participate in the general meeting of stockholders, having the right to receive dividends, and also other lists drawn up by the society for the effectuation by stockholders of their rights in accordance with the requirements of the present Federal Law;

the opinions of the audit commission (or internal auditor) of the society, the auditor of the society, and of State and municipal financial control agencies;

emission prospectuses, quarterly reports of the emittent and other documents containing information subject to publication or divulgence by other means in accordance with the present Federal Law and other federal laws;

other documents provided for by the present Federal Law, the charter of the society, internal documents of the society, decisions of the general meeting of stockhoolders, council of directors (or supervisory council) of the society, management organs of the society, and also documents provided for by legal acts of the Russian Federation [point 1 as amended by Federal Law No. 120-Ф3, 7 August 2001].

2. The society shall keep the documents provided for by point 1 of the present Article at the location of its executive organ in the procedure and during the period which have been established by the federal agency of executive power for the securities market [as amended by Federal Law No. 120-Ф3, 7 August 2001].

Article 90. Provision of Information by Society

Information concerning the society shall be provided by it in accordance with the requirements of the present Federal Law and other legal acts of the Russian Federation.

Article 91. Provision of Information by Society to Stockholders

1. A society shall be obliged to ensure stockholders access to documents provided for by Article 89(1) of the present Federal Law. A stockholder(s) having in aggregate not less than 25% of voting stocks of the society shall have the right of access to documents of bookkeeping records and protocols of sessions of the collegial executive organ [as amended by Federal Law No. 120-Ф3, 7 August 2001].

In the event of the use with respect to an open society of a special right to participate of the Russian Federation, subject of the Russian Federation, or municipal formation in the management of the said society ('golden stock'), such society shall ensure the representatives of the Russian Federation, subject of the Russian Federation, or municipal formation of access to all of its documents [added by Federal Law No. 120-Ф3, 7 August 2001].

2. The documents provided for by point 1 of the present Article must be provided by the society within seven days from the day of submission of the respective demand for familiarisation at the premise of the executive organ of the society. The society shall be obliged at the demand of persons having the right of access to the documents provided for by point 1 of the present Article to provide copies of the said documents to them. Payment recovered by the society for provision of the said copies may not exceed expenditures for the manufacture thereof [as amended by Federal Law No. 120-Ф3, 7 August 2001].

Article 92. Obligatory Divulgence of Information by Society [as amended by Federal Law No. 120-Ф3, 7 August 2001]

1. An open society shall be obliged to divulge:
the yearly report of the society and yearly bookkeeping report;

the emission prospectus for stocks of the society in the instances provided for by legal acts of the Russian Federation;

communication concerning the holding of the general meeting of stockholders in the procedure provided for by the present Federal Law;

other information determined by the federal agency of executive power for the securities market [as amended by Federal Law No. 120-ФЗ, 7 August 2001].

2. The obligatory divulgence of information by a society, including a closed society, in the event of the public placement by it of bonds or other emission securities, shall be effectuated by the society to the extent and in the procedure which have been established by the federal agency of executive power for the securities market [as amended by Federal Law No. 120-ФЗ, 7 August 2001].

Article 93. Information Concerning Affiliated Persons of Society

1. A person shall be deemed to be affiliated in accordance with the requirements of legislation of the Russian Federation [as amended by Federal Law No. 120-ФЗ, 7 August 2001].

2. Affiliated persons of a society shall be obliged to inform the society in writing about stocks of the society belonging to them, specifying their quantity and categories (or types) not later than 10 days from the date of acquisition of the stocks.

3. If as a result of the failure to submit the said information through the fault of the affiliated person or of the untimely submission property damage is caused to the society, the affiliated person shall bear responsibility to the society in the amount of the damage caused.

4. A society shall be obliged to keep a record of its affiliated persons and to submit reports concerning them in accordance with the requirements of legislation of the Russian Federation.

Chapter XIV. Concluding Provisions

Article 94. Introduction into Operation of Present Federal Law

1. The present Federal Law shall be introduced into operation from 1 January 1996.

2. From the moment of the introduction into operation of the present Federal Law, the legal acts operating on the territory of the Russian Federation shall be applied in that part which is not contrary to the present Federal Law until the bringing thereof into conformity with the present Federal Law.

3. The constitutive documents of societies not corresponding to norms of the present Federal Law shall from the moment of introduction of the present Federal Law into operation apply in that part which is not contrary to the said norms [as

amended by Federal Law No. 65-ФЗ, 13 June 1996, and by Federal Law No. 120-ФЗ, 7 August 2001].

[paragraph two as amended by Federal Law No. 65-ФЗ, 13 June 1996; repealed by Federal Law No. 120-ФЗ, 7 August 2001].

With regard to the contributions of the State or municipal formations the rights of stockholders shall be effectuated by the respective committees for the administration of property, property funds, or other empowered State agencies or agencies of local self-government, except for instances of the transfer of the stocks within State ownership to trust management or to the charter capital of unitary enterprises.

4. The provisions of Article 7(3), paragraphs two and three, of the present Federal Law shall not apply to closed societies created before the introduction of the present Federal Law into operation [as amended by Federal Law No. 120-ФЗ, 7 August 2001].

5. Until the introduction into operation of the respective federal laws, the societies enumerated in Article 1(4) of the present Federal Law shall operate on the basis of legal acts of the Russian Federation adopted before the introduction into operation of the present Federal Law.

6. To propose to the President of the Russian Federation within the period before 1 March 1996 to bring legal acts issued by him into confirmity with the present Federal Law.

7. To charge the Government of the Russian Federation within the period before 1 March 1996 to:

bring the legal acts issued by it into conformity with the present Federal Law;

adopt legal acts ensuring the realisation of the present Federal Law.

FEDERAL LAW ON THE PECULIARITIES OF THE LEGAL STATUS OF JOINT-STOCK SOCIETIES OF WORKERS (PEOPLE'S ENTERPRISES)

[Federal Law No. 115-ФЗ, 19 July 1998, as amended by Federal Law
No. 31-ФЗ, 21 March 2002.
СЗ РФ (1998), no. 30, item 3611; (2002), no. 12, item 1093]

Article 1. Relations Regulated by Present Federal Law

1. The present Federal Law shall determine the peculiarities of the creation and legal status of joint-stock societies of workers (people's enterprises) (hereinafter: people's enterprises), the rights and duties of their stockholders, and also ensure the defence of the rights and interests of the stockholders.

2. The rules of the Federal Law on Joint-Stock Societies concerning closed joint-stock societies shall apply to people's enterprises unless provided otherwise by the present Law.

Article 2. Procedure for Creation of People's Enterprise

1. A people's enterprise may be created in the procedure provided for by the present Federal Law by means of the transformation of any commercial organisation, except for State unitary enterprises, municipal unitary enterprises, and open joint-stock societies to whose workers belong less than 49% of the charter capital.

The creation of a people's enterprise by other means shall not be permitted.

2. The participants of a commercial organisation shall in the procedure established by legislation of the Russian Federation and constitutive documents of the particular organisation adopt a decision concerning the transformation thereof into a people's enterprise.

3. The participants of a commercial organisation which have voted against the transformation of a commercial organisation into a people's enterprise shall have the right within one month after the date of adoption of the said decision to pre-

sent a demand concerning the purchase of their stocks (or participatory shares, shares) fully or partially.

4. The workers of a commercial organisation whose participants have adopted the decision specified in point 2 of the present Article by not less than three-fourths of the votes of their listed number shall give consent in the procedure established by legislation of the Russian Federation to the creation of a people's enterprise.

If the workers of a commercial organisation have not given consent to the creation of a people's enterprise, the decision of the participants of the commercial organisation concerning the transformation thereof into a people's enterprise shall be considered to be unconstituted.

5. If the workers of a commercial organisation have given consent to the creation of a people's enterprise, those of them who decided to become a stockholder of the people's enterprise and the participants of the commercial organisation subject to transformation shall conclude a contract on the creation of a people's enterprise.

If the participants of a commercial organisation and its workers, having decided to become stockholders of the people's enterprise, have not reached agreement with regard to the conditions of the contract concerning the creation of the people's enterprise specified in point 2 of the present Article, the decision shall be considered to be unconstituted.

Article 3. Contract on Creation of People's Enterprise and Charter of People's Enterprise

1. The contract concerning the creation of a people's enterprise, besides the information specified in Article 9(5) of the Federal Law on Joint-Stock Societies, must contain the following:

(1) information concerning the quantity of stocks of the people's enterprise which may be possessed at the moment of the creation of the people's enterprise:

each worker, including those who are a participant of the commercial organisation being transformed and who have decided to become a stockholder of the people's enterprise;

each participant of the commercial organisation being transformed who is not a worker thereof;

each natural person who is not a participant of the commercial organisation being transformed and/or juridical person;

(2) the monetary valuation of stocks (or participatory shares, shares) of the commercial organisation to be transformed;

(3) the conditions, periods, and procedure for the purchase by the people's enterprise of the stocks of the people's enterprise from its stockholders for the

purpose of compliance with the present Federal Law and the conditions of the contract concerning the creation of a people's enterprise;

(4) an indication of the form of payment for the stocks of the people's enterprise or procedure for the exchange of stocks (or participatory shares, shares) of the commercial organisation being transformed into stocks of the people's enterprise for each stockholder at the moment of creation of the people's enterprise.

2. The contract concerning the creation of the people's enterprise must be signed by all the persons who have decided to become stockholders of the people's enterprise.

3. A people's enterprise shall be obliged within one month after the date of its creation to conclude contracts for the purchase-sale of stocks belonging to them with the stockholders who have presented demands concerning the purchase of stocks in accordance with Article 2(3) of the present Federal Law, and also with stockholders whose quantity of stocks of the people's enterprise at the date of its creation has proved not to correspond to the requirements of Article 6(1) of the present Federal Law and the conditions of the contract concerning the creation of the people's enterprise.

4. The charter of the people's enterprise, besides the information specified in Article 11(3) of the Federal Law on Joint-Stock Societies, must contain information concerning:

the maximum participatory share of the stocks of the people's enterprise in the total quantity of stocks which natural persons who are not workers of the people's enterprise and/or juridical persons may possess in aggregate;

the maximum participatory share of stocks of the people's enterprise in the total quantity of stocks which one worker of the people's enterprise may possess.

Article 4. Charter Capital of People's Enterprise

1. A people's enterprise shall have the right to issue only common stocks. A reduction of the number of votes for a possessor of the stocks of a people's enterprise when voting according to the principle of 'one stock—one vote' shall not be permitted.

The par value of one stock of a people's enterprise shall be determined by the general meeting of stockholders of the people's enterprise (hereinafter: general meeting of stockholders) but may not be more than 20% of the minimum amount of payment for labour established by a Federal law.

2. The quantity of stocks of the people's enterprise whose par value comprises more than 75% of its charter capital must belong to workers of the people's enterprise.

The quantity of stocks of the people's enterprise whose par value comprises more than 75% of the charter capital must belong to workers of a people's enterprise, more than 45% of whose charter capital belongs to natural persons who are not its workers and/or juridical persons not later than the date of the end of the tenth financial year after the year of creation of the people's enterprise.

The quantity of stocks of the people's enterprise whose par value comprises more than 75% of the charter capital must belong to workers of the people's enterprise from 35% up to 45% of whose charter capital belongs to natural persons who are not workers thereof and/or juridical persons not later than the date of the end of the fifth financial year after the year of creation of the people's enterprise.

If within the periods established by paragraphs two and three of the present point the aforesaid quantities of stocks of a people's enterprise do not belong to workers of the people's enterprise, the people's enterprise must within one year be transformed into a commercial organisation of another form. Upon the expiry of the said period the people's enterprise shall be subject to liquidation in a judicial procedure upon the demand of the agency effectuating the State registration of juridical persons or empowered State agency or agency of local self-government.

3. The participatory share of stocks of a people's enterprise in the total quantity of stocks which a worker may possess at the moment of its creation must be equal to the participatory share of payment for his labour in the total amount of the payment for the labour of workers during the 12 months preceding the creation of the people's enterprise. Another procedure for determining the participatory share of stocks of a people's enterprise in the total quantity of stocks which a worker of a commercial organisation being transformed may possess at the moment of its creation may be provided for by the contract concerning the creation of the people's enterprise.

4. A worker of a commercial organisation being transformed who does not have a sufficient quantity of stocks (or participatory shares, shares) of the commercial organisation being transformed to exchange for the quantity of stocks of the people's enterprise which must belong to him in accordance with the contract concerning the creation of the people's enterprise shall be obliged to pay not less than 50% of the value of such quantity of stocks of the people's enterprise which must belong to him at the moment of creation of the people's enterprise.

5. The participatory share of stocks of a people's enterprise in the total quantity of stocks which participants of a commercial organisation who are not workers thereof may possess in aggregate at the moment of its creation must be less than 25% of the charter capital of the people's enterprise unless provided otherwise by the contract concerning the creation of the people's enterprise for periods not greater than established by point 2 of the present Article.

6. The participatory share of stocks of a people's enterprise in the total quantity of stocks which one worker of a people's enterprise may possess at the moment of its creation may not exceed the maximum participatory share specified in

Article 6(1) of the present Federal Law unless provided otherwise by the contract concerning the creation of the people's enterprise for periods not greater than established by point 2 of the present Article.

7. The minimum charter capital of a people's enterprise must comprise not less than 1000 times the minimum amount of payment for labour established by a Federal law on the date of State registration of the people's enterprise.

8. The purchase of stocks of a people's enterprise from stockholders specified in Article 3(3) of the present Federal Law may be effectuated only at the expense of the profit of the people's enterprise.

Article 5. Allotment of Stocks to Workers of People's Enterprise

1. A people's enterprise annually in compliance with the limitations established by Federal laws and other legal acts of the Russian Federation shall have the right to increase its charter capital by means of the issuance of additional stocks for an amount of not less than the amount of net profit actually used for the purpose of accumulation for the report financial year.

2. Additional stocks of a people's enterprise, and also stocks purchased by the people's enterprise from its stockholders, shall be distributed among all workers of the people's enterprise having the right thereto in proportion to the amounts of their payment for labour for the report financial year.

3. The operation of point 2 of the present Article shall extend to newly hired workers if they have worked not less than three months during the report financial year.

4. The procedure for determination of the amounts of payment for labour of workers of a people's enterprise for the report financial year for the purposes specified in point 2 of the present Article, and also the procedure for the allotment of stocks of the people's enterprise to workers of the people's enterprise, shall be confirmed by the general meeting of stockholders. The decision shall be adopted according to the principle of 'one stockholder—one vote'.

5. The provisions of the present Article shall enter into force after the fulfilment of the conditions of the contract concerning the creation of the people's enterprise.

Article 6. Limitations on Right to Possession and Disposition of Stocks of People's Enterprise

1. One stockholder of a people's enterprise who is a worker thereof (hereinafter: worker-stockholder) may not possess a quantity of stocks of a people's enterprise whose par value exceeds 5% of the charter capital of the people's enterprise.

The maximum participatory share of the stocks of a people's enterprise which one worker-stockholder may possess as established by paragraph one of the present point may be reduced by the charter of the people's enterprise.

If for any reasons, including as a result of the allotment of stocks in accordance with Article 5 of the present Federal Law the quantity of stocks of the people's enterprise held by one worker exceeds the maximum participatory share established by the charter of the people's enterprise, the people's enterprise shall be obliged to purchase from such worker-stockholder those stocks which form the said excess, and the worker-stockholder shall be obliged to sell them to the people's enterprise. The purchase shall be made at the par value of the stocks of the people's enterprise within three months from the date of formation of such excess.

2. A worker-stockholder may sell or otherwise alienate the stocks of a people's enterprise belonging to him to another natural person and/or juridical person only in the instances provided for by the present Federal Law.

3. A worker-stockholder shall have the right to sell at a contract price part of the stocks of the people's enterprise belonging to him on the date of the end of the report financial year within the next financial year to stockholders of the people's enterprise except for the persons specified in Article 8(3) of the present Federal Law or to the people's enterprise itself, and in the event of their refusal, to workers of the people's enterprise who are not stockholders thereof.

The quantity of stocks of a people's enterprise authorised for sale to one worker-stockholder shall be established by the general meeting of stockholders, but may not exceed 20% of the stocks of the people's enterprise belonging to the particular worker-stockholder on the said date.

4. A people's enterprise shall be obliged to purchase from a dismissed worker-stockholder, and the dismissed worker-stockholder shall be obliged to sell to the people's enterprise the stocks of the people's enterprise belonging to him at their purchase value within three months from the date of dismissal.

5. By decision of the supervisory council of the people's enterprise (hereinafter: supervisory council) or in accordance with the charter of the people's enterprise, a dismissed worker-stockholder shall have the right to sell at a contract price within three months from the date of dismissal the stocks of the people's enterprise belonging to him to workers of the people's enterprise, except for the persons specified in Article 8(3) of the present Federal Law.

If the said purchase-sale transaction for any reasons is unconstituted, the provisions of points 4 and 6 of the present Article shall enter into force. The period during which the people's enterprise is obliged to purchase the stocks of the people's enterprise which belong to a dismissed worker-stockholder shall be increased up to six months.

6. A people's enterprise shall bear responsibility for monetary obligations arising from Article 3(3) of the present Federal Law and points 1, 4, and 5 of the present Article in accordance with Article 395 of the Civil Code of the Russian Federation.

7. A dismissed worker-stockholder who does not agree with the purchase value of the stocks of the people's enterprise belonging to him shall have the right in written form to appeal it to the internal audit (or control) commission of the people's enterprise (hereinafter: control commission).

8. In the event the property of a worker-stockholder is insufficient to satisfy the demands of creditors presented to him, the people's enterprise shall be obliged by decision of a court to pay them the purchase value of the stocks or part thereof belonging to such worker-stockholder. The stocks of the people's enterprise whose purchase value is paid to creditors shall pass to the balance sheet of the people's enterprise.

9. Stockholders of a people's enterprise-natural persons who are not workers thereof and juridical persons shall have the right at any time to sell at a contract price the stocks belonging to them in priority to stockholders of the people's enterprise, and in the event of their refusal, to the people's enterprise itself or to its workers who are not stockholders thereof.

10. The operation of points 4–6 of the present Article shall extend to heirs of deceased workers-stockholders.

11. The provisions of points 1 and 2 of the present Article shall enter into force after the fulfilment of conditions of the contract concerning the creation of the people's enterprise.

12. The rules of Article 75 of the Federal Law on Joint-Stock Societies shall extend only to stockholders of the people's enterprise-natural persons who are not workers thereof and to juridical persons.

Article 7. Purchase Value of Stocks of People's Enterprise and Payment of Dividends

1. The purchase value of all stocks of a people's enterprise shall be determined quarterly according to a method confirmed by the general meeting of stockholders, the said value not comprising less than 30% of the value of the net assets of the people's enterprise and corresponding, as a rule, to the market value thereof.

A special jointstockisation fund for workers which may not be used for other purposes shall be created at a people's enterprise for the purchase of stocks of the people's enterprise from dismissed workers-stockholders.

2. Dividends relating to stocks of a people's enterprise shall be paid not less frequently than once a year.

A people's enterprise shall not have the right to adopt a decision concerning the payment of dividends if:

at the moment of payment of dividends it meets the indicia of insolvency (or bankruptcy) in accordance with legal acts of the Russian Federation concerning insolvency (or bankruptcy) or the said indicia may appear as a result of the payment of dividends;

the value of its net assets is less than the amount of its charter capital and reserve fund or will become less than such amount as a result of the payment of dividends;

it has not purchased stocks of the people's enterprise form its stockholders, the participatory share of which in the total quantity of stocks of the people's enterprise does not correspond to the requirements of Article 6 of the present Federal Law and the charter of the people's enterprise.

Article 8. Sale of Stocks of People's Enterprise on Its Balance Sheet

1. The stocks of a people's enterprise on its balance sheet may be sold fully or partially to its workers, and also to natural persons who are not workers thereof, and/or to juridical persons.

The quantity of stocks of the people's enterprise to be sold, the price at which they will be sold, and the conditions and procedure for their sale shall be confirmed by a decision of the general meeting of stockholders adopted by not less than three-fourths of the votes of the stockholders present at the general meeting.

2. The sale of stocks of a people's enterprise on its balance sheet shall be effectuated in accordance with the present Federal Law, the quantity of stocks of the people's enterprise to be sold not exceeding 50% of the total quantity of stocks of the people's enterprise earmarked for distribution among the workers in accordance with Article 5(2) of the present Federal Law.

3. The sale of the stocks of a people's enterprise on its balance sheet to the general director of the people's enterprise, his deputies, and assistants, members of the supervisory council, and members of the control commission shall not be permitted.

An additional list of persons to whom the sale of stocks of the people's enterprise is not permitted may be established by the charter of the people's enterprise.

Article 9. Number of Workers and Stockholders of People's Enterprise

1. The average listed number of workers of a people's enterprise may not comprise less than 51 persons. In the event of being lower than the said number, a people's enterprise shall be obliged within one year to bring it into accordance with the present point or to be transformed into a commercial organisation of another form.

In the event of the failure to fulfil this requirement within the said period, the people's enterprise shall be subject to liquidation in a judicial proceeding at the demand of the agency effectuating the State registration of juridical persons or empowered State agency or agency of local self-government.

2. The number of workers who are not stockholders of the people's enterprise (hereinafter: workers-nonstockholders) for the report financial year must not exceed 10% of the number of workers of the people's enterprise.

If the average listed number of workers-nonstockholders for the third full report financial year from the year of creation of the people's enterprise or for any subsequent financial year exceeds 10% of the average listed number of workers of the people's enterprise, the people's enterprise shall be obliged within one year to bring the average listed number of workers-nonstockholders into conformity with the present point or to be transformed into a commercial organisation of another form.

In the event of the failure to fulfil the said requirement within the specified period the people's enterprise shall be subject to liquidation in a judicial proceeding at the demand of the agency effectuating the State registration of juridical persons or empowered State agency or agency of local self-government.

3. When calculating the average listed number of workers of a people's enterprise for the purposes of the present Federal Law the workers with whom labour contracts have been concluded for the period of fulfilling determined work, and also seasonal workers, shall not be subject to being recorded.

4. The number of stockholders of a people's enterprise must not exceed five thousand. In the event of exceeding the said number, the people's enterprise shall be obliged within one year to bring it into conformity with the present point or to be transformed into a commercial organisation of another form.

In the event of the failure to fulfil the said requirement within the specified period the people's enterprise shall be subject to liquidation in a judicial proceeding at the demand of the agency effectuating State registration of juridical persons or empowered State agency or agency of local self-government.

Article 10. General Meeting of Stockholders

1. The following questions shall be relegated to the exclusive competence of the general meeting of stockholders:

(1) election of the general director of the people's enterprise, termination of his powers before time, and also the establishment of the amount of earnings for him;

(2) election of the chairman of the control commission, termination of his powers before time, and also the establishment of the amount of earnings for him;

(3) determination of the quantitative composition of the supervisory council, election of its members, and termination before time of their powers;

(4) determination of the maximum participatory share of stocks of a people's enterprise in the total quantity of stocks which natural persons who are not workers of the people's enterprise and/or juridical persons may possess in aggregate;

(5) determination of the maximum amount of stocks of a people's enterprise in the total quantity of stocks which one worker of a people's enterprise may possess;

(6) confirmation of the Statute on the control commission;

(7) establishment of the amount of remuneration and contributory compensation for members of the supervisory council;

(8) establishment of the amount of remuneration and contributory compensation for members of the control commission, and also confirmation of the estimate for the effectuation of its activity;

(9) confirmation of the method for determination of the purchase value of the stocks of the people's enterprise;

(10) confirmation of changes of the charter of the people's enterprise, including changes of the amount of charter capital of the people's enterprise or confirmation of the charter of the people's enterprise in a new version;

(11) confirmation of the yearly bookkeeping balance sheet and the report on profits and losses;

(12) adoption of a decision concerning the reorganisation of the people's enterprise;

(13) confirmation of the priority orientations of activity of the people's enterprise;

(14) confirmation of the report of the control commission;

(15) adoption of a decision concerning liquidation of a people's enterprise, appointment of the liquidation commission, and confirmation of the interim and final liquidation balance sheets.

Decisions relating to subpoints (1)–(6), (8), (10), (12), and (14) of the present point shall be adopted according to the principle: 'one stockholder—one vote'.

2. Questions relegated to the exclusive competence of the general meeting of stockholders may not be transferred for decision to other management organs of the people's enterprise, and the powers of the general meeting of stockholders relating to other questions may be transferred by its decision adopted by not less than three-fourths of the votes of the total number of stockholders to the supervisory council or control commission for a determined period but not more than one year. Decisions shall be adopted according to the principle: 'one stockholder—one vote'.

3. The procedure for the adoption of a decision by the general meeting of stockholders shall be confirmed by the general meeting of stockholders. The decision shall be adopted according to the principle: 'one stockholder—one vote'.

4. Decisions adopted by the general meeting of stockholders, and also the results of the voting, shall be brought to the information of all workers of the people's enterprise not later than 15 days from the date of adoption of these decisions.

5. Workers-nonstockholders may participate in the work of the general meeting of stockholders with the right of a consultative vote.

6. 2% of the stockholders or a stockholder(s) to whom not less than 2% of the stocks of the people's enterprise belong in aggregate shall have the right not later than 30 days from the date of the end of the report financial year to propose not more than two questions for inclusion on the agenda of the yearly general meeting of stockholders, and in the event of conducting elections for the supervisory council and control commission to nominate candidacies in a number not exceeding the quantitative composition of each of those organs, and also nominate candidacies for the office of general director of the people's enterprise and chairman of the control commission.

7. When submitting proposals concerning the nomination of candidacies for the office of general director of a people's enterprise and chairman of the control commission, members of the supervisory council, and members of the control commission, including self-nomination, the name of the candidate shall be specified, and if the candidate is a stockholder, the number of stocks of the people's enterprise belonging to him, and also the names of the stockholder(s) nominating the said candidacies and the quantity of stocks of the people's enterprise belonging to them.

8. The supervisory council shall be obliged to consider proposals received and adopt a decision concerning their inclusion on the agenda of the general meeting of stockholders or refuse such inclusion not later than 15 days after the end of the period established by point 6 of the present Article.

Questions submitted by a stockholder(s) shall be subject to inclusion on the agenda of the general meeting of stockholders, and likewise nominated candidacies shall be subject to inclusion in the list of candidacies for voting with regard to elections for the office of general director of the people's enterprise and chairman of the control commission, members of the supervisory council, and members of the control commission, except for instances when:

the stockholder(s) have not complied with the period established by point 6 of the present Article;

the stockholder(s) are not possessors of the quantity of votes provided for by point 6 of the present Article;

the date submitted in accordance with point 7 of the present Article is incomplete;

the proposals submitted do not conform to the present Federal Law and other normative legal acts of the Russian Federation.

9. A reasoned decision of the supervisory council concerning the refusal to include a question on the agenda of the general meeting of stockholders or candidacies on the list of candidacies for voting with regard to the elections for office of

general director of the people's enterprise or chairman of the control commission, members of the supervisory council and members of the control commission shall be sent to the stockholder(s) who submitted the question or proposal not later than three days from the date of the adoption thereof.

10. The decision of the supervisory council concerning a refusal to include a question on the agenda for the general meeting of stockholders or candidacies on the list of candidacies for voting with regard to elections for the office of general director of the people's enterprise and chairman of the control commission, members of the supervisory council, and members of the control commission may be appealed to the control commission, whose decision with regard to the question shall be binding for execution by the supervisory council.

11. On the ballot for voting at the general meeting of stockholders, besides the information established by Article 60(3) of the Federal Law on Joint-Stock Societies, there must be specified the principle for voting with regard to each question: 'one stock—one vote', or 'one stockholder—one vote'.

In the event of conducting voting with regard to elections for the office of general director of a people's enterprise and chairman of the control commission, members of the supervisory council, and members of the control commission, the ballot for voting must contain brief biographical data of the candidates.

12. The period for the powers of the counting commission of the general meeting of stockholders shall be established by decision of the particular general meeting of stockholders by not less than three-fourths of the votes of the stockholders present at the general meeting. The decision shall be adopted according to the principle: 'one stockholder—one vote'.

Article 11. Extraordinary General Meeting of Stockholders

1. An extraordinary general meeting of stockholders shall be conducted by decision of the supervisory council at its initiative, at the demand of the control commission, and also at the demand of not less than 10% of the stockholders or at the demand of a stockholder(s) to whom not less than 10% of the stocks of the people's enterprise belong on the date of presenting the demand.

The form of conducting the extraordinary general meeting of stockholders (joint presence or voting by poll) must be determined by decision of the supervisory council. The supervisory council shall not have the right to change by its decision the form of conducting an extraordinary general meeting of stockholders if the demand of the control commission, and also the said stockholder(s) concerning the conducting of an extraordinary general meeting of stockholders contains an indication of the form of conducting it.

2. Convocation of an extraordinary general meeting of stockholders at the demand of the control commission, at the demand of not less than 10% of the

stockholders, or at the demand of a stockholder(s) to whom not less than 10% of the stocks of the people's enterprise belong shall be effectuated by the supervisory council not later than45 days from the moment of presentation of the demand concerning the conducting of the extraordinary general meeting of stockholders.

The supervisory council shall not have the right to make changes in the formulations of the questions of the agenda of the extraordinary general meeting of stockholders to be convoked at the demand of the control commission, at the demand of not less than 10% of the stockholders, or the demand of stockholder(s) to whom not less than 10% of the stocks of the people's enterprise belong on the date of presenting the demand.

3. Within 10 days from the date of presentation of the demand of the control commission, demand of not less than 10% of the stockholders, or demand of the stockholder(s) to whom not less than 10% of the stocks of the people's enterprise belong concerning the convocation of an extraordinary general meeting of stockholders, the supervisory council must adopt a decision concerning the convocation of the extraordinary general meeting of stockholders or refuse to convoke it.

The decision concerning a refusal to convoke an extraordinary general meeting of stockholders upon the demand of the control commission, upon the demand of not less than 10% of the stockholders, or upon the demand of the stockholder(s) to whom not less than 10% of the stocks of the people's enterprise belong may be adopted only if:

the procedure for the presentation of a demand concerning the convocation of a general meeting of stockholders established by legislation is not complied with;

the quantity of votes provided for by point 1 of the present Article do not belong to the stockholder(s) demanding the convocation of the extraordinary general meeting of stockholders;

not one of the questions proposed for inclusion on the agenda of the extraordinary general meeting of stockholders is relegated to its competence.

Article 12. Supervisory Council of People's Enterprise

1. The supervisory council shall effectuate general guidance over the activity of the people's enterprise and may adopt decisions with regard to all questions, with the exception of questions relegated to the competence of the general meeting of stockholders, and also questions relegated by the present Federal Law and charter of the people's enterprise to the competence of the general director of the people's enterprise.

2. The following questions shall be relegated to the exclusive competence of the supervisory council:

(1) convocation of the yearly and extraordinary general meeting of stockholders, except for instances provided for by Article 55(6) of the Federal Law on Joint-Stock Societies;

(2) confirmation of the agenda of the general meeting of stockholders;

(3) determination of the date of drawing up the list of stockholders having the right to participate in the general meeting of stockholders and other questions relegated to the competence of the supervisory council in accordance with the provisions of Chapter VII of the Federal Law on Joint-Stock Societies and connected with the preparation and conducting of the general meeting of stockholders;

(4) determination of the amount of dividend for stocks of the people's enterprise and the procedure for payment thereof;

(5) use of the reserve and other funds of the people's enterprise;

(6) confirmation of internal documents of the people's enterprise provided for by the charter of the people's enterprise;

(7) creation of branches and opening of representations of people's enterprise.

3. Questions relegated to the exclusive competence of the supervisory council may not be transferred for decision to the general director of the people's enterprise.

The powers of the supervisory council with regard to other questions granted to it in accordance with the present Federal Law and the charter of the people's enterprise may be transferred by decision of the general meeting of stockholders to the general director of the people's enterprise or the control commission for a determined period, but not more than one year.

4. The general director of the people's enterprise shall be ex officio the chairman of the supervisory council unless provided otherwise by the charter of the people's enterprise.

5. The supervisory council shall be elected for a term of three years.

6. The general director of a people's enterprise and his deputies and aides may not comprise more than 30% of the quantitative composition of the supervisory council.

7. In the event the listed number of workers of the people's enterprise is more than one thousand persons and in the composition thereof more than 2% are workers-nonstockholders, one representative of the workers-nonstockholders chosen by the general meeting of workers-nonstockholders must be a member of the supervisory council.

8. Sessions of the supervisory council shall be convoked by the chairman of the supervisory council at its initiative, upon the demand of a member(s) of the supervisory council, upon the demand of the control commission, upon the demand of not less than 5% of the stockholders or upon the demand of a stockholder(s) to whom not less than 5% of the stocks of the people's enterprise belong.

9. Decisions of each session of the supervisory council shall be brought to the information of the workers of a people's enterprise.

Article 13. General Director of People's Enterprise

1. The direction of the current activity of a people's enterprise shall be effectuated by the general director of the people's enterprise, who shall be a one-man executive organ of the people's enterprise.

All questions of the direction of the current activity of a people's enterprise, except for questions relegated by the present Federal Law and by the charter of the people's enterprise to the competence of the general meeting of stockholders or supervisory council shall be relegated to the competence of the general director of the people's enterprise.

2. The general director of a people's enterprise shall be elected by decision of the general meeting of stockholders for a term determined by the charter of the people's enterprise, but not more than five years, and may be elected an unlimited number of times.

3. The amount of payment for labour of the general director of a people's enterprise for the report financial year may not by more than 10 times exceed the average amount of payment for labour of one worker of the people's enterprise for the same period.

Article 14. Audit (or Control) Commission of People's Enterprise

1. The control commission shall effectuate control over the financial-economic activity of the people's enterprise, compliance with the rights of stockholders, and also the fulfilment of rules of internal labour order of the people's enterprise.

2. Members of the control commission may not simultaneously be members of the supervisory council.

3. Members of the control commission shall have the right to participate in sessions of the supervisory council with the right of a consultative vote, and also to be present at meetings conducted by the director general of the people's enterprise.

4. Members of the supervisory council may not participate in elections of the members of the control commission.

5. The powers of the control commission, the quantitative composition thereof, the procedure for election of its members, the term of their powers, work procedure, and the adoption of decisions at sessions shall be established by the Statute on the control commission.

Decisions of the control commission shall be binding for execution by the management organs of the people's enterprise.

Decisions of the control commission may be reviewed by the general meeting of stockholders or appealed to a court.

314

6. The chairman of the control commission and members of the control commission shall be elected from among the workers-stockholders for the term determined by the charter of the people's enterprise, but not less than five years.

Article 15. Effectuation of Control Over Financial-Economic Activity of People's Enterprise

1. A verification (or internal audit) of the financial-economic activity of a people's enterprise shall be conducted with regard to the results of the work of the people's enterprise for the report financial year, and also at any other time by decision of the control commission adopted at its initiative, decision of the supervisory council, demand of not less than 10% of the stockholders, or upon the demand of the stockholder(s) to whom not less than 10% of the stocks of the people's enterprise belong.

2. The verification (or internal audit) of financial-economic activity of a people's enterprise shall be conducted, as a rule, by independent auditors on the basis of a contract. The personal composition of the auditors shall be subject to obligatory agreement with the control commission.

3. Payment for the services of independent auditors relating to the verification (or internal audit) of the financial-economic activity of the people's enterprise shall be made within the limits of the estimate for the effectuation of the activity of the control commission.

4. The control commission shall have the right to familiarise itself with the documents affecting all aspects of the activity of the people's enterprise, and also to receive necessary explanations in oral and written form.

5. The decision concerning the conclusion of a large-scale transaction, the subject of which is property whose value comprises from 15% up to 30% of the balance sheet value of the property of the people's enterprise on the date of the adoption of the decision concerning the conclusion of such transaction shall be adopted by the supervisory council unanimously (not taking into account the votes of members of the supervisory council who have withdrawn) and shall be agreed in an obligatory procedure with the control commission.

If unanimity of the supervisory council relating to the question of the conclusion of a large-scale transaction is not reached or the decision relating to it is not agreed with the control commission, the said question may be resolved only by the general meeting of stockholders.

The decision concerning the conclusion of a large-scale transaction, the subject of which is property whose value comprises more than 30% of the balance sheet value of the people's enterprise on the date of adoption of the decision concerning conclusion of such transaction shall be adopted by the general meeting of

315

stockholders by not less than three-fourths of the votes of the stockholders present at the general meeting.

6. The persons deemed to be interested in the conclusion of a transaction by a people's enterprise shall be the general director of the people's enterprise, members of the supervisory council and members of the control commission, a stockholder(s) to whom not less than 20% of the stocks of the people's enterprise belong, if the said persons, their spouses, parents, children, brothers, and sisters:

are a party to such transaction or participate in it as a representative or intermediary;

possess not less than 20% of the voting stocks (or participatory shares, shares) of the juridical person which is a party to such transaction or participates therein as a representative or intermediary;

occupy a post in the management organs of a juridical person which is a party to such transaction or participate therein as a representative or intermediary.

The said persons shall be obliged to bring to the information of the supervisory council and control commission information concerning:

juridical persons in which they possess autonomously or jointly with their affiliated persons not less than 20% of the voting stocks (or participatory shares, shares);

juridical persons in whose management organs they occupy posts;

transactions known to them to be concluded or proposed in which they might be deemed to be interested persons.

If the said persons have not submitted the said information in a timely way, the control commission shall be obliged to submit the question concerning the failure to fulfil this requirement for consideration of the general meeting of stockholders.

Article 16. Entry of Present Federal Law into Force

1. The present Federal Law shall enter into force from 1 October 1998.

2. To propose to the President of the Russian Federation and to charge the Government of the Russian Federation to bring their legal acts into conformity with the present Federal Law.

3. [repealed by Federal Law No. 31-ФЗ, 21 March 2002].

FEDERAL LAW ON
FINANCIAL-INDUSTRIAL GROUPS

[Federal Law No. 190-ФЗ, 30 November 1995.
СЗ РФ (1995), no. 49; item 4697]

Chapter I	General Provisions	317
Chapter II	State Registration of Financial-Industrial Groups	319
Chapter III	Management in Financial-Industrial Group, Conducting Affairs of Financial-Industrial Group	322
Chapter IV	Activity of Financial-Industrial Group	323
Chapter V	Control and Accountability in Financial-Industrial Group	325
Chapter VI	Liquidation of Financial-Industrial Group	326
Chapter VII	Concluding Provisions	327

Chapter I. General Provisions

Article 1. Legislation of Russian Federation on Financial-Industrial Groups

1. The present Federal Law establishes the legal foundations for the creation, activity, and liquidation of financial-industrial groups in the Russian Federation.

2. Relations arising from the participation of financial-industrial groups in the realisation of federal special-purpose programmes shall be regulated by legislation of the Russian Federation on federal special-purpose programmes. Relations arising from the participation of financial-industrial groups in the realisation of regional special-purpose programmes shall be regulated by legislative acts of subjects of the Russian Federation.

3. With regard to individual questions of the creation, activity, and liquidation of financial-industrial groups in the instances established by the present Federal Law regulation shall be effectuated by normative legal acts of the Government of the Russian Federation and by normative legal acts of other empowered agencies of executive power. State regulation of the creation, activity, and liquidation of financial-industrial groups shall be effectuated by the duly empowered federal State agency (hereinafter—empowered State agency), the said functions of which shall be exclusive.

4. Relations not regulated by the present Federal Law and other normative legal acts of the Russian Federation and subjects of the Russian Federation shall be regulated by a contract concerning the creation of the financial-industrial group and by other contracts concluded between participants of the financial-industrial group.

Article 2. Concept of Financial-Industrial Group

A financial-industrial group is the aggregate of juridical persons acting as the principal and subsidiary societies who have either entirely or partially combined their material and nonmaterial assets (system of participation) on the basis of a contract concerning the creation of the financial-industrial group for the purposes of technological or economic integration in order to realise investment and other projects and programmes directed towards increasing the competitiveness and expanding markets for the sale of goods and services, increasing the efficiency of production, and creating new jobs.

Article 3. Participants of Financial-Industrial Group

1. The participants of a financial-industrial group shall be deemed to be the juridical persons who have signed a contract concerning the creation of the financial-industrial group and the central company of the financial-industrial group founded by them (Article 11 of the present Federal Law) or the principal and subsidiary societies forming the financial-industrial group.

2. Commercial and noncommercial organisations may be within a financial-industrial group, including foreign, except for social and religious organisations (or associations). Participation in more than one financial-industrial group shall not be permitted.

3. The existence of organisations among the participants of a financial-industrial group which are operating in the sphere of the production of goods and services, and also banks or other credit organisations, shall be obligatory.

4. State and municipal unitary enterprises may be participants of a financial-industrial group in the procedure and on the conditions determined by the owner of their property.

5. Subsidiary economic societies and enterprises may be within a financial-industrial group only together with their principal society (or unitary enterprise-founder).

6. Investment institutes, non-State pension and other funds, and insurance organisations whose participation is conditioned by their role in ensuring the investment process in the financial-industrial group may be among the participants of the financial-industrial group.

Article 4. Transnational Financial-Industrial Groups

1. Financial-industrial groups among whose participants are juridical persons under the jurisdiction of States-participants of the Commonwealth of Independent States having solitary subdivisions on the territory of the said States or effectuating capital investments on their territory shall be registered as transnational financial-industrial groups in accordance with the present Federal Law.

2. In the event of the creation of a transnational financial-group on the basis of an intergovernmental agreement, the status shall be conferred on it of an inter-State (or international) financial-industrial group. The peculiarities of the creation, activity, and liquidation of an inter-State financial-industrial group shall be established by the said agreements.

3. The national regime shall be established for participants of an inter-State financial-industrial group by intergovernmental agreements on the basis of reciprocity.

4. Customs tariff privileges provided for by the Law of the Russian Federation 'On the Customs Tariff' with regard to goods moved across the boundary within the framework of activity of this financial-industrial group may be granted to participants of the inter-State financial-industrial group in the procedure and on the conditions established by the Government of the Russian Federation.

Chapter II. State Registration of Financial-Industrial Groups

Article 5. Procedure for State Registration of Financial-Industrial Groups

1. The aggregate of juridical persons forming a financial-industrial group shall acquire the status of a financial-industrial group by decision of the empowered State agency concerning its State registration.

2. The central company of a financial-industrial group shall submit for State registration the following documents to the empowered State agency:

application for the creation of a financial-industrial group (according to the form established by the Government of the Russian Federation);

contract concerning the creation of the financial-industrial group (except for financial-industrial groups formed of principal and subsidiary societies);

notarially-certified copies of the certificate concerning registration, constitutive documents, copies of stockholder registers (for joint-stock societies) of each of the participants, including the central company of the financial-industrial group);

organisational project;

notarially-certified and legalised constitutive documents of foreign participants;

opinion of the federal anti-monopoly agency.

When necessary, additional requirements with regard to the composition of documents submitted may be established by the Government of the Russian Federation.

3. The decision concerning State registration of a financial-industrial group shall be adopted on the basis of an expert examination of the documents submitted by the empowered State agency.

4. The empowered State agency shall have the right to request expert opinions of other organisations, specialists, and agencies of executive power of the respective subjects of the Russian Federation with regard to documents of the financial-industrial group.

5. With regard to the results of consideration of documents of a financial-industrial group, taking into account expert opinions, the empowered State agency shall within a two-week period from the day of submission to it of the documents adopt one of the following decisions:
concerning refusal to register the financial-industrial group;
concerning return of the documents of the financial-industrial group for reworking;
concerning registration of the financial-industrial group.

6. A refusal to register or return of the documents of the financial-industrial group for reworking shall be accompanied by a written explanation of the reasons of the empowered State agency.

7. In the event of the adoption by the empowered State agency of an unsubstantiated decision, and also in the event of a violation by it of the periods for consideration of the documents of the financial-industrial group, the operation thereof may be appealed to a court.

8. State registration shall be confirmed by the issuance of a certificate of the established form containing the full name of the financial-industrial group with the obligatory inclusion of words 'financial-industrial group', 'transnational financial-industrial group', or 'inter-State financial-industrial group' and inclusion in the State register of financial-industrial groups.
Use of the words 'financial-industrial' in the name of any juridical person except the central company of the financial-industrial group shall not be permitted.
The word combinations 'financial-industrial' and 'industrial-financial' shall be equivalents.

9. The peculiarities of State registration of financial-industrial groups not regulated by the present Federal Law shall be established by the Government of the Russian Federation.

Article 6. State Registration of Changes of Conditions of Contract on Creation of Financial-Industrial Group

1. A change of the conditions of a contract concerning the creation of a financial-industrial group or composition of participants of a financial-industrial group shall be subject to State registration by the empowered State agency.

2. State registration of changes of the composition of participants of a financial-industrial group shall be made by the empowered State agency on the basis of an opinion of the federal antimonopoly agency.

3. In the event of changes of material conditions of the contract concerning the creation of a financial-industrial group, the financial-industrial group shall be subject to a second State registration.

Article 7. Contract on Creation of Financial-Industrial Group

1. A contract concerning the creation of a financial-industrial group must determine:

the name of the financial-industrial group;

the procedure and conditions for founding the central company of the financial-industrial

group as a juridical person in the determined organisational-legal form empowered to conduct the affairs of the financial-industrial group;

the procedure for the formation, amount of powers, and other conditions of activity of the council of managers of the financial-industrial group;

the procedure for making changes in the composition of participants of the financial-industrial group;

the amount, procedure, and conditions for combining assets;

the purpose of the combining of the participants;

the period of operation of the contract.

Other conditions of a contract concerning the creation of a financial-industrial group shall be established by the participants, by proceeding from the purposes and tasks of the financial-industrial group and conformity to legislation of the Russian Federation.

Article 8. Organisational Project of Financial-Industrial Group

1. The organisational project of a financial-industrial group is the package of documents submitted by the central company to the empowered State agency and containing necessary information concerning the purposes and tasks, investment and other projects, and programmes, and proposed economic, social, and other results of activity of the financial-industrial group, and also other information necessary in order to adopt a decision concerning the registration of the financial-industrial group.

2. An exhaustive amount of requirements for the organisational project of a financial-industrial group shall be established by the Government of the Russian Federation.

Article 9. State Register of Financial-Industrial Groups

1. The State register of financial-industrial groups is a unified data bank created by the empowered State agency and containing necessary information concerning State registration of financial-industrial groups.

2. The composition of information and the structure of the State register of financial-industrial groups shall be determined by the Government of the Russian Federation.

Chapter III. Management in Financial-Industrial Group, Conducting Affairs of Financial-Industrial Group

Article 10. Council of Managers of Financial-Industrial Group

1. The council of managers of a financial-industrial group, including representatives of all participants thereof, shall be the highest management organ of the financial-industrial group.

2. The sending by a participant of the financial-industrial group of a representative to the composition of the council of managers of a financial-industrial group shall be effectuated by decision of the competent management organ of the participant of the financial-industrial group.

3. The competence of the council of managers of the financial-industrial group shall be established by the contract concerning the creation of the financial-industrial group.

Article 11. Central Company of Financial-Industrial Group

1. The central company of a financial-industrial group shall be the juridical person founded by all the participants of the contract concerning the creation of a financial-industrial group or being the principal society with respect to them and empowered by virtue of a law or contract to conduct affairs of the financial-industrial group. The registration of a newly-founded central company of a financial-industrial group shall be effectuated in the procedure established by civil legislation of the Russian Federation for the registration of juridical persons.

2. The central company of a financial-industrial group shall, as a rule, be an investment institute. The creation of a central company of a financial-industrial group in the form of an economic society, and also of an association or union, shall be permitted.

3. The words 'central company of financial-industrial group' shall be included in the name of the central company of the financial-industrial group after the

State registration of the financial-industrial group, of which the central company of the financial-industrial group shall inform the agency which effectuated the registration thereof.

4. The charter of a central company of the financial-industrial group must determine the subject and purpose of its activity and correspond to the conditions of the contract concerning the creation of the financial-industrial group. The agency which effectuated the registration of the central company of the financial-industrial group shall inform the empowered State agency about all changes made in its charter.

5. The central company of a financial-industrial group in the instances established by the present Federal Law, by other legislative acts of the Russian Federation, and by the contract concerning the creation of the financial-industrial group shall:

act in the name of the participants of the financial-industrial group in relations connected with the creation and activity of the financial-industrial group;

conduct consolidated records, reports, and the balance sheet of the financial-industrial group;

prepare the annual report on the activity of the financial-industrial group;

fulfil in the interests of participants of the financial-industrial group individual banking operations in accordance with legislation of the Russian Federation on banks and banking activity.

Other types of activity of the central company of a financial-industrial group with regard to conducting the affairs of the financial-industrial group shall be established by its charter and by the contract concerning the creation of the financial-industrial group.

Chapter IV. Activity of Financial-Industrial Group

Article 12. Concept of Activity of Financial-Industrial Group

By activity of a financial-industrial group is understood the activity of the participants, being conducted by them in accordance with the contract concerning the creation of a financial-industrial group and/or its organisational project when using solitary assets.

Article 13. Consolidated Record in Financial-Industrial Group

1. In the instances and in the procedure established by legislation of the Russian Federation on taxes and the contract concerning the creation of a financial-industrial group, the participants of the financial-industrial group engaged in the sphere of the production of goods and services may be deemed to be a consolidated group of taxpayers, and also may conduct consolidated records, reports, and balance sheet of the financial-industrial group.

2. The procedure for conducting consolidated records, reports, and balance sheet of a financial-industrial group shall be determined by the Government of the Russian Federation.

Article 14. Responsibility of Participants of Financial-Industrial Group

The participants of a financial-industrial group shall bear joint and several responsibility with regard to obligations of the central company of the financial-industrial group which arose as a result of participation in the activity of the financial-industrial group.

The peculiarities of performing a joint and several duty shall be established by the contract concerning the creation of the financial-industrial group.

Article 15. State Support of Activity of Financial-Industrial Groups

1. Measures of State support for the activity of financial-industrial groups established by decision of the Government of the Russian Federation shall be:

set-off of indebtedness of a participant of a financial-industrial group whose stocks are realised at investment competitions (or public sales) against the amount of investments provided for by the conditions of investment competitions (or public sales) for the purchaser-central company of the same financial-industrial group;

granting to participants of a financial-industrial group of the right autonomously to determine the periods of amortisation of equipment and accumulation of amortisation deductions, the means received being directed towards the activity of the financial-industrial group;

transfer to trust management by the central company of a financial-industrial group of the bloc of stocks of participants of this financial-industrial group temporarily consolidated to the State;

provision of State guarantees to attract various types of investments;

provision of investment credits and other financial support for realisation of projects of the financial-industrial group.

Agencies of State power of subjects of the Russian Federation may within the limits of their competence provide additional privileges and guarantees to financial-industrial groups.

2. Privileges providing for a reduction of norms of obligatory reserves and a change of other normative standards for the purpose of enhancing their investment activeness may be provided by the Central Bank of the Russian Federation to banks-participants of a financial-industrial group effectuating investment activity therein.

3. The Government of the Russian Federation shall work out the procedure for the provision of measures of support for financial-industrial groups in accordance with priorities in industrial and social policy declared by it annually, simul-

taneously with the submission of the draft federal budget for the respective year and shall report on the results of their application when reporting on the execution of the federal budget.

Chapter V. Control and Accountability in Financial-Industrial Group

Article 16. Yearly Report of Financial-Industrial Group

1. Not later than 90 days after the end of the financial year, the central company of a financial-industrial group shall submit to all participants of the financial-industrial group and to the empowered State agency a report concerning the activity of the financial-industrial group according to the form established by the Government of the Russian Federation, and also shall publish the said report.

2. The report shall be drawn up according to the results of the verification of the activity of the financial-industrial group by an independent auditor.

3. The auditor verification shall be conducted at the expense of means of the central company of the financial-industrial group.

Article 17. Control Over Activity of Financial-Industrial Group

1. The empowered State agency shall have the right not more often than once a year to demand a report concerning the activity of a financial-industrial group and to designate an auditor verification thereof.

2. A verification conducted at the initiative of the empowered State agency shall be conducted at its expense.

3. The participants of a financial-industrial group shall be obliged to provide to the empowered State agency at its request any information with regard to individual questions of current activity of the financial-industrial group.

4. The empowered State agency shall be obliged to take measures with regard to the results of the yearly or current report of a financial-industrial group in instances of the discovery of unreliable information in the documents submitted, evading the submission of necessary documents, discovery in the activity of the financial-industrial group of a nonconformity to the contract concerning the creation thereof and organisational project, a nonconformity of the activity of the central company of the financial-industrial group to its charter, abuse of the rights and measures of support granted, and a violation of legislation of the Russian Federation and of legislation of a subject of the Russian Federation. Depending upon the character and degree of the violation, the empowered State agency may:

propose that the participants of the financial-industrial group eliminate the shortcomings elicited and establish periods for the elimination thereof;

apply to the Government of the Russian Federation or respective agency of a subject of the Russian Federation with a proposal to deprive the financial-industrial group of all or part of the rights or measures of support provided by them;

take measures to bring to responsibility the persons guilty of the violation thereof established by legislation of the Russian Federation;

apply to the Government of the Russian Federation with a proposal to terminate the operation of a certificate concerning registration of the financial-industrial group.

The empowered State agency shall inform the Government of the Russian Federation about each of the enumerated actions.

5. A respective decision shall be adopted by the Government of the Russian Federation and agency of State power of the subject of the Russian Federation with regard to the recourse of the empowered State agency.

Chapter VI. Liquidation of Financial-Industrial Group

Article 18. Concept of Liquidation of Financial-Industrial Group

A financial-industrial group shall be considered to be liquidated from the moment of termination of the operation of a certificate concerning registration of the financial-industrial group and exclusion thereof from the State register of financial-industrial groups.

Article 19. Grounds of Liquidation

A financial-industrial group shall be liquidated in instances of:

the adoption by all participants of a financial-industrial group of a decision to terminate the activity thereof;

the entry into legal force of a decision of a court concerning the deeming of the contract concerning the creation of a financial-industrial group to be invalid;

the violation of legislation of the Russian Federation when creating the financial-industrial group established by the decision of a court which has entered into legal force;

the expiry of the period of operation of the contract concerning the creation of a financial-industrial group, unless it has been prolonged by the participants of the financial-industrial group;

the adoption by the Government of the Russian Federation of a decision concerning termination of the operation of a certificate concerning the registration of a financial-industrial group in connection with the failure of its activity to conform to the conditions of the contract concerning the creation thereof and organisational project, and also in the event of a second guilty commission of actions provided for by Article 17 of the present Federal Law if measures provided for by the said Article already have been applied to it.

Article 20. Consequences of Liquidation

1. The empowered State agency in any of the instances established by Article 19 of the present Federal Law shall terminate the operation of the certificate concerning registration of the financial-industrial group and exclude the respective entry from the State register of financial-industrial groups.

2. Obligations of participants of a financial-industrial group with regard to performance of the contract concerning the creation of a financial-industrial group in the event of its liquidation shall operate in so far as this is not contrary to the present Federal Law and the Civil Code of the Russian Federation.

Chapter VII. Concluding Provisons

Article 21. Clarification of Normative Legal Acts

Normative legal acts of federal agencies of executive power shall be brought by the Government of the Russian Federation into conformity with the present Federal Law.

Article 22. Entry of Present Federal Law into Force

1. The present Federal Law shall enter into force from the day of official publication thereof.

2. The activity and respective documents of financial-industrial groups registered at the moment of entry into force of the present Federal Law must be brought into conformity with the present Federal Law, and they must undergo re-registration within six months from the moment of entry into force thereof.

3. The empowered State agency formed by the Government of the Russian Federation shall ensure the priority procedure for re-registration of existing financial-industrial groups.

FEDERAL LAW ON BANKS AND BANKING ACTIVITY

[Adopted 2 December 1990, No. 395-I, in the version of 3
February 1996, No. 17-ФЗ, as amended 31 July 1998, No. 151-ФЗ,
5 July 1999, No. 126-ФЗ, 8 July 1999, No.
136-ФЗ; 19 June 2001, No. 82-ФЗ; 7 August 2001, No. 121-ФЗ,
21 March 2002, No. 31-ФЗ.
Ведомости СНД РСФСР и ВС РСФСР (1990), no. 27,
item 357; СЗ РФ (1996), no. 6, item 492;
(1998), no. 31, item 3829; (1999), no. 28, item 3469;
(2001), no. 26, item 2586; no. 33(I), item 3424;
(2002), no. 12, item 1093]

Chapter I	General Provisions	328
Chapter II	Procedure for Registration of Credit Organisations and Licensing of Banking Operations	338
Chapter III	Ensuring Stability of Banking System, Defence of Rights and Interests of Depositors and Creditors of Credit Organisations	355
Chapter IV	Inter-Bank Relations and Servicing of Clients	358
Chapter V	Branches, Representations, and Subsidiary Organisations of Credit Organisation on Territory of Foreign State	361
Chapter VI	Savings	361
Chapter VII	Bookkeeping Records in Credit Organisations and Supervision Over Activity Thereof	362

Chapter I. General Provisions

Article 1. Basic Concepts of Present Federal Law

A credit organisation shall be a juridical person which in order to derive profit as a principal purpose of its activity on the basis of a special authorisation (or license) of the Central Bank of the Russian Federation (Bank of Russia) has the right to effectuate banking operations provided for by the present Federal Law. A credit organisation shall be formed on the basis of any form of ownership as an economic society.

A bank shall be a credit organisation which has the exclusive right to effectuate in aggregate the following banking operations: attracting deposits of monetary means of natural and juridical persons, placement of the said means in its own name and for its own account on conditions of repayability, payability, demand, and the opening and conducting of bank accounts of natural and juridical persons.

A nonbanking credit organisation shall be a credit organisation having the right to effectuate individual banking operations provided for by the present Federal Law. The admissible combining of banking operations for nonbanking credit organisations shall be established by the Bank of Russia.

A foreign bank is a bank deemed to be such according to the legislation of the foreign State on whose territory it was registered.

Article 2. Banking System of Russian Federation and Legal Regulation of Banking Activity

The banking system of the Russian Federation includes the Bank of Russia, credit organisations, and also branches and representations of foreign banks.

The legal regulation of banking activity shall be effectuated by the Constitution of the Russian Federation, the present Federal Law, the Federal Law on the Central Bank of the Russian Federation (Bank of Russia), other federal laws, and normative acts of the Bank of Russia.

Article 3. Unions and Associations of Credit Organisations

Credit organisations may create unions and associations not pursuing the purposes of deriving profit in order to defend and represent the interests of their members, coordinate their activity, develop inter-regional and international links, satisfaction of scientific, informational, and professional interests, working out recommendations with regard to the effectuation of banking activity and deciding of other joint tasks of credit organisations. The effectuation of banking operations by unions and associations shall be prohibited.

Unions and associations of credit organisations shall be created and registered in the procedure established by legislation of the Russian Federation for noncommercial organisations.

Unions and associations of credit organisations shall inform the Bank of Russia about their creation within a month after registration.

Article 4. Banking Group and Banking Holding Companies [as amended by Federal Law No. 82-ФЗ, 19 June 2001]

An association of credit organisations which is not a juridical person in which one (head) credit organisation exerts directly or indirectly (or through a third person) material influence on decisions to be adopted by the management organs of another (or other) credit organisation(s) shall be deemed to be a banking group.

An association of juridical persons which is not a juridical person with the participation of a credit organisation(s) in which a juridical person which is not a credit organisation (head organisation of a banking holding company) has the

329

possibility directly or indirectly (or through a third person) to exert material influence on decisions to be adopted by the management organs of the credit organisation(s) shall be deemed to be a banking holding company.

By material influence for the purpose of the present Federal Law is understood the possibility to determine decisions to be adopted by management organs of a juridical person, the conditions of it conducting entrepreneurial activity by reason of participation in its charter capital and/or in accordance with the conditions of a contract to be concluded between juridical persons within the composition of the banking group and/or banking holding company, to appoint the one-man executive organ and/or more than half of the composition of a collegial executive organ of a juridical person, and also the possibility to determine the election of more than half of the composition of the council of directors (or supervisory council) of a juridical person.

The head credit organisation of a banking group and head organisation of a banking holding company shall be obliged to notify the Bank of Russia in the procedure established by it concerning the formation of the banking group and banking holding company.

A commercial organisation which in accordance with the present Federal Law may be deemed to be a head organisation of a banking holding company shall for the purpose of managing the activity of all credit organisations within the banking holding company have the right to create a management company of the banking holding company. In this event the management company of the banking holding company shall perform the duties which in accordance with the present Federal Law are placed on the head organisation of the banking holding company.

The management company of a banking holding company shall for the purposes of the present Federal Law be deemed to be an economic society, the basis of whose activity is management of the activity of credit organisations within the banking holding company. The management company of a banking holding company shall not have the right to engage insurance, banking, production, and trade activity. A commercial organisation which in accordance with the present Federal Law may be deemed to be the head organisation of a banking holding company shall be obliged to have the possibility to determine the decision of the management company of the banking holding company with regard to questions relegated to the competence of the meeting of its founders (or participants), including concerning the reorganisation and liquidation thereof [as amended by Federal Law No. 82-ФЗ, 19 June 2001].

Article 5. Banking Operations and Other Transactions of Credit Organisation

There shall be relegated to banking operations:

(1) attraction of monetary means of natural and juridical persons in deposits (on demand and for a determined period);

(2) placement of attracted means specified in point 1 of paragraph one of the present Article in their own name and on their own account;

(3) opening and conducting of bank accounts of natural and juridical persons;

(4) effectuation of settlement of accounts on behalf of natural and juridical persons, including correspondent banks, with regard to their bank accounts;

(5) encashment of monetary means, bills of exchange, payment and settlement documents and cashier servicing of natural and juridical persons;

(6) purchase-sale of foreign currency in cash and noncash forms;

(7) attraction on deposit and placement of precious metals;

(8) issuance of bank guarantees;

(9) effectuation of transfers of monetary means on behalf of natural persons without opening bank accounts (except for postal transfers) [added by Federal Law No. 151-ФЗ, 31 July 1998].

A credit organisation, besides the banking operations enumerated in paragraph one of the present Article, shall have the right to effectuate the following transactions:

(1) issuance of suretyships for third persons providing for the performance of obligations in monetary form;

(2) acquisition of the right of demand from third persons for the performance of obligations in monetary form;

(3) trust management of monetary means and other property under a contract with natural and juridical persons;

(4) effectuation of operations with precious metals and precious stones in accordance with legislation of the Russian Federation;

(5) granting on lease to natural and juridical persons of specialised premises or safes situated therein for the keeping of documents and valuables;

(6) finance lease operations;

(7) rendering consulting and information services.

A credit organisation shall have the right to effectuate other transactions in accordance with legislation of the Russian Federation.

All banking operations and other transactions shall be effectuated in rubles, and when there is a respective license of the Bank of Russia, also in foreign currency. The rules for the effectuation of banking operations, including rules for the material-technical provision thereof, shall be established by the Bank of Russia in accordance with federal laws.

It shall be prohibited for a credit organisation to engage in production, trade, and insurance activity.

Article 6. Activity of Credit Organisation on Securities Market

In accordance with the license of the Bank of Russia for the effectuation of banking operations a bank shall have the right to effectuate the issuance, purchase, sale, registration, keeping, and other securities operations fulfilling the functions of a payment document, securities confirming the attraction of monetary means for deposit and in bank accounts, and other securities, the effectuation of operations with which does not require the receipt of a special license in accordance with federal laws, and also shall have the right to effectuate trust management of the said securities under a contract with natural and juridical persons.

A credit organisation shall have the right to effectuate professional activity on the securities market in accordance with federal laws.

Article 7. Name of Credit Organisation

A credit organisation shall have firm (full official) name in the Russian language, may have a name in another language of the peoples of the Russian Federation, an abbreviated name, and a name in a foreign language.

A firm name of a credit organisation must contain an indication of the character of the activity of this juridical person by means of the use of the words 'bank' or 'nonbanking credit organisation', and also an indication of its organisational-legal form.

The Bank of Russia shall be obliged when considering an application concerning the State registration of a credit organisation to prohibit the use of the name of the credit organisation if the proposed name already is contained in the Book of State Registration of Credit Organisations. Use in the name of a credit organisation of the words 'Russia', 'Russian Federation', 'State', 'federal', and 'central' and derivative words and word combinations from them shall be permitted in the procedure established by legislative acts of the Russian Federation [as amended by Federal Law No. 31-ФЗ, 21 March 2002].

Not one juridical person in the Russian Federation, except for a license received from the Bank of Russia for the effectuation of banking operations, may use in its name the word 'bank', 'credit organisation', or otherwise indicate that the said juridical person has the right to effectuate banking operations.

Article 8. Provision of Information Concerning Activity of Credit Organisation, Banking Group, and Banking Holding Company [as amended by Federal Law No. 82-ФЗ, 19 June 2001]

A credit organisation shall be obliged to publish according to the forms and within the periods which are established by the Bank of Russia the following information concerning its activity:

quarterly—the bookkeeping balance sheet, report on profits and losses, information concerning the level of capital sufficiency and the amount of reserves for covering doubtful loans and other assets;

annually—the bookkeeping balance sheet and report on profits and losses with the opinion of an auditing firm (or auditor) concerning the reliability thereof.

A credit organisation shall be obliged upon the demand of a natural or juridical person to provide him a copy of the license for the effectuation of banking operations, copies of other authorisation (or licenses) issued to it if the need to receive the said documents has been provided for by federal laws, and also monthly book-keeping balance sheets for the current year.

A credit organisation shall bear responsibility in accordance with the present Federal Law and other federal laws for deluding natural and juridical persons by means of the failure to provide information or the provision of unreliable or incomplete information.

The head credit organisation of a banking group and head organisation of a banking holding company (or management company of a banking holding company) shall publish their consolidated bookkeeping reports and consolidated reports on profits and losses in the form, procedure, and within the periods which are established by the Bank of Russia after confirmation of their reliability by the opinion of an auditing firm (or auditor) [as amended by Federal Law No. 82-ФЗ, 19 June 2001].

Article 9. Relations Between Credit Organisation and State

A credit organisation shall not be liable for obligations of the State. The State shall not be liable for obligations of a credit organisation, except for instances when the State itself as assumed such obligations.

A credit organisation shall not be liable for obligations of the Bank of Russia. The Bank of Russia shall not be liable for obligations of a credit organisation, except for instances when the Bank of Russia has assumed such obligations.

Agencies of legislative and executive power and agencies of local self-government shall not have the right to interfere in the activity of credit organisations, except for instances provided for by federal laws.

A credit organisation under a contract specially concluded on a competitive basis may fulfil individual commissions of the Government of the Russian Federation, agencies of executive power of subjects of the Russian Federation, and agencies of local self-government, effectuate operations with means of the federal budget, budgets of subjects of the Russian Federation, and local budgets and settlements of accounts with them, ensure the special-purpose use of budgetary means allotted for the effectuation of federal and regional programmes. The respective contract must contain mutual obligations of the parties and provide for their responsibility, the conditions and form of control over the use of budgetary means.

A credit organisation may not be obliged to effectuate activity which is not provided for by its constitutive documents, except for instances when the credit organisation assumed the respective obligations or instances provided for by federal laws.

Article 10. Constitutive Documents of Credit Organisation [as amended by Federal Law No. 31-ФЗ, 21 March 2002]

A credit organisation shall have the constitutive documents provided for by federal laws for a juridical person of the respective organisational-legal form [as amended by Federal Law No. 31-ФЗ, 21 March 2002].

The charter of a credit organisation must contain:

(1) the firm (full official) name, and also all other names established by the present Federal Law;

(2) an indication of the organisational-legal form;

(3) information concerning the address (or location) of management organs and solitary subdivisions [as amended by Federal Law No. 31-ФЗ, 21 March 2002];

(4) a list of banking operations and transactions to be effectuated in accordance with Article 5 of the present Federal Law;

(5) information concerning the amount of charter capital;

(6) information concerning the system of management organs, including executive organs, and internal control organs, the procedure for forming them, and their powers;

(7) other information provided for by federal laws for the charters of juridical persons of the said organisational-legal form.

A credit organisation shall be obliged to register all changes made in its constitutive documents. The documents provided for by Article 17(1) of the Federal Law 'On the State Registration of Juridical Persons' and by normative acts of the Bank of Russia shall be submitted by the credit organisation to the Bank of Russia in the procedure established by it. The Bank of Russia within a month's period from the day of filing of all duly formalised documents shall adopt a decision concerning the State registration of changes made in the constitutive documents of the credit organisation and send to the empowered federal agency of executive power (hereinafter: empowered registering agency) in accordance with Article 2 of the Federal Law 'On the State Registration of Juridical Persons' information and documents necessary for the effectuation by this agency of the functions with regard to keeping a unified State register of juridical persons [as amended by Federal Law No. 31-ФЗ, 21 March 2002].

On the basis of the said decision adopted by the Bank of Russia and necessary information and documents submitted to it, the empowered registering agency within a period of not more than five work days from the day of receipt of the necessary information and documents shall make in the unified State register of juridical persons a respective entry and not later than the work day following the day of making the respective entry shall notify the Bank of Russia thereof. Interaction of the Bank of Russia with the empowered registering agency with regard to the question of State registration of changes made in the constitutive documents of a credit organisation shall be effectuated in the procedure agreed by the Bank of Russia with the empowered registering agency [added by Federal Law No. 31-ФЗ, 21 March 2002].

Article 11. Charter Capital of Credit Organisation

The charter capital of a credit organisation shall be comprised of the amount of deposits of its participants and determine the minimum amount of property guaranteeing the interests of its creditors.

The Bank of Russia shall establish the normative standards for the minimum amount of charter capital of credit organisation being newly registered, the maximum amounts of nonmonetary contributions to the charter capital of a credit organisation, and also the list of types of property in nonmonetary form contributed to pay up charter capital. The normative standards of the minimum charter capital of a credit organisation may be established depending upon the type of credit organisation [as amended by Federal Law No. 82-ФЗ, 19 June 2001].

A decision of the Bank of Russia concerning a change of the minimum amount of charter capital shall enter into force not earlier than 90 days after the day of official publication thereof. The normative standard of minimum amount of charter capital operating on the day of filing the documents for registration and receipt of the license shall be applied to newly registered credit organisations by the Bank of Russia.

The Bank of Russia shall not have the right to demand changes of their charter capital from previously registered credit organisations, except for instances established by federal laws [as amended by Federal Law No. 82-ФЗ, 19 June 2001].

Attracted monetary means may not be used for the forming of charter capital of a credit organisation. For the purpose of valuing the means to be contributed as paying up charter capital of a credit organisation the Bank of Russia shall have the right to establish the procedure and criteria for valuing the financial position of the founders (or participants) thereos [as amended by Federal Law No. 136-ФЗ, 8 July 1999, and by Federal Law No. 82-ФЗ, 19 June 2001].

Means of the federal budget and State extrabudgetary funds, free monetary means, and other objects of ownership in the jurisdiction of federal agencies of State power may not be used to form the charter capital of a credit organisation, except for instances provided for by federal laws.

Means of the budgets of subjects of the Russian Federation, local budgets, free monetary means, and other objects of ownership in the jurisdiction of agencies of State power of subjects of the Russian Federation and agencies of local self-government may be used to form the charter capital of a credit organisation on the basis respectively of a legislative act of the subject of the Russian Federation or decision of the agency of local self-government in the procedure provided for by the present Federal Law and other federal laws.

The acquistion and/or receipt on trust management (hereinafter: acquisition) as a result of one or several transactions by one juridical or natural person or group of juridical and/or natural persons lined by an agreement, or a group of juridical persons which are subsidiaries or dependent with respect to one another, of more than 5% of the stocks (or participatory shares) of the credit organisation shall require notification of the Bank of Russia, more than 20% the prior consent of the Bank of Russia. The Bank of Russia not later than 30 days from the moment of receipt of a petition shall notify the applicant in written form about its decision—consent or refusal. A refusal must be reasoned. If the Bank of Russia does not communicate the decision adopted within the said period, the acquisition of stocks (or participatory shares) of the credit organisation shall be considered to be authorised. The procedure for receiving the consent of the Bank of Russia for the acquisition of more than 20% of the stocks (or participatory shares) of a credit organisation and the procedure for notification of the Bank of Russia about the acquisition of more than 5% of the stocks (or participatory shares) of a credit organisation shall be established by federal laws and normative acts of the Bank of Russia adopted in accordance therewith [as amended by Federal Law No. 82-ФЗ, 19 June 2001].

The Bank of Russia shall have the right to refuse to give consent to an acquisition of more than 20% of the stocks (or participatory shares) of the credit organisation in the event of establishing the unsatisfactory financial status of the acquirers of the stocks (or participatory shares), a violation of antimonopoly rules, and also in instances when with respect to the person acquiring the stocks (or participatory shares) of a credit organisation there are judicial decisions which have entered into force that established facts of the commission by the said person of unlawful actions in the event of a bankruptcy and an international and/or fictitious bankruptcy, and in other instances provided for by federal laws [as amended by Federal Law No. 82-ФЗ, 19 June 2001].

The Bank of Russia shall refuse to give consent to the acquisition of more than 20% of the stocks (or participatory shares) of a credit organisation if the fault was previously established by a court of the person acquiring stocks (or participatory shares) of a credit organisation in causing losses to any credit organisation when performing his duties as a member of a council of directors (or supervisory council) of the credit organisation, one-man executive organ, deputy thereof, and/or member of a collegial executive organ (or board, directorate) [added by Federal Law No. 82-ФЗ, 19 June 2001].

The founders of a bank shall not have the right to withdraw from the composition of participants of the bank within the first three years from the day of registration thereof.

Article 11¹. Management Organs of Credit Organisation

The council of directors (or supervisory council), one-man executive organ, and collegial executive organ shall be the management organs of a credit organisation together with the general meeting of founders (or participants) thereof.

The current direction of the activity of a credit organisation shall be effectuated by the one-man executive organ and collegial executive organ.

The one-man executive organ, his deputies, members of the collegial executive organ (hereinafter: executive of credit organisation), chief bookkeeper of the credit organisation, and executive of the branch thereof shall not have the right to hold posts in other organisations which are credit or insurance organisations, professional participants of the securities market, and also in organisations engaging in finance leasing activity or which are affiliated persons with respect to the credit organisation in which the executive thereof, chief bookkeeper, and executive of the branch thereof works.

Candidates for the posts of members of the council of directors (or supervisory council), executive of credit organisation, chief bookkeeper, deputies of the chief bookkeeper of the credit organisation, and also for the posts of executive, deputy executive, chief bookkeeper, and deputies of the chief bookkeeper of a branch of a credit organisation, must correspond to the qualifications requirements established by federal laws and normative acts of the Bank of Russia adopted in accordance therewith.

A credit organisation shall be obliged in written form to notify the Bank of Russia about all proposed appointments to the posts of executive of the credit organisation, chief bookkeeper, and deputies of the chief bookkeeper of the credit organisation, and also the posts of executive, deputy executive, chief bookkeeper, and deputies of the chief bookkeeper of a branch of the credit organisation. The notification must contain information provided for by Article 14(8) of the present Federal Law. The Bank of Russia within a month from the day of receipt of the said notification shall give consent to the said appointments or submit a reasoned refusal in written form on the grounds provided for by Article 16 of the present Federal Law.

A credit organisation shall be obliged in written form to notify the Bank of Russia about relieving from office the executive of a credit organisation, chief bookkeeper, and deputy of the chief bookkeeper of the credit organisation, and also the executive, deputy executive, chief bookkeeper, and deputy of the chief bookkeeper of a branch of the credit organisation not later than the working day following the day of adoption of such decision.

A credit organisation shall be obliged in written form to notify the Bank of Russia about the election (or relieving) of a member of the council of directors (or supervisory council) within a three-day period from the day of adoption of such decision [as amended by Federal Law No. 82-ФЗ, 19 June 2001].

Chapter II. Procedure for Registration of Credit Organisations and Licensing of Banking Operations

Article 12. State Registration of Credit Organisations and Issuance to Them of Licenses for Effectuation of Banking Operations

Credit organisations shall be subject to State registration in accordance with the Federal Law 'On the State Registration of Juridical Persons', taking into account the special procedure for the State registration of credit organisations established by the present Federal Law [as amended by Federal Law No. 136-ФЗ, 19 June 2001 and Federal Law No. 31-ФЗ, 21 March 2002].

The decision concerning State registration of a credit organisation shall be adopted by the Bank of Russia. Inserting in the unified State register of juridical persons information concerning the creation, reorganisation, and liquidation of credit organisations, and also other information provided for by federal laws, shall be effectuated by the empowered registering agency on the basis of the decision of the Bank of Russia concerning the respective State registration. Interaction of the Bank of Russia with the empowered registering agency with regard to the State registration of credit organisations shall be effectuated in the procedure agreed by the Bank of Russia with the empowered registering agency [added by Federal Law No. 31-ФЗ, 21 March 2002].

The Bank of Russia for the purposes of the effectuation by it of control and supervisory functions shall keep the Book of State Registration of Credit Organisations in the procedure established by federal laws and normative acts of the Bank of Russia adopted in accordance therewith [added by Federal Law No. 31-ФЗ, 21 March 2002].

State duty shall be recovered for the State registration of credit organisations in the procedure and amounts which have been established by legislation of the Russian Federation [as amended by Federal Law No. 31-ФЗ, 21 March 2002].

A credit organisation shall be obliged to inform the Bank of Russia concerning a change of information specified in Article 5(1) of the Federal Law 'On the State Registration of Juridical Persons', except for information concerning licenses received, within three days from the moment of such changes. The Bank of Russia not later than one work day from the day of receipt of the respective information from a credit organisation shall inform the empowered registering agency thereof, which shall make an entry in the unified State register of juridical persons concerning the change of information about the credit organisation [added by Federal Law No. 31-ФЗ, 21 March 2002].

A license for the effectuation of banking operations of a credit organisation shall be issued after the State registration thereof in the procedure established by the present Federal Law and normative acts of the Bank of Russia adopted in accordance therewith [as amended by Federal Law No. 82-ФЗ, 19 June 2001].

A credit organisation shall have the right to effectuate banking operations from the moment of receipt of the license issued by the Bank of Russia [as amended by Federal Law No. 31-ФЗ, 21 March 2002].

A license charge shall be recovered for consideration of the question concerning issuance of a license in the amount determined by the Bank of Russia, but not more than 1% of the declared charter capital of the credit organisation. The said charge shall go to the revenue of the federal budget [added by Federal Law No. 31-ФЗ, 21 March 2002].

Article 13. Licensing of Banking Operations

Banking operations shall be effectuated only on the basis of a license issued by the Bank of Russia in the procedure established by the present Federal Law.

Licenses issued by the Bank of Russia shall be recorded in the register of issued licenses for the effectuation of banking operations.

The register of licenses issued by credit organisations shall be subject to publication of the Bank of Russia in the official publication of the Bank of Russia (Вестник Банка России) not less than once a year. Changes in and additions to the said register shall be published by the Bank of Russia within a month's period from the day of their entry in the register.

On the license for the effectuation of banking operations shall be specified the banking operations for the effectuation of which the said credit organisation has the right, and also the currency in which these banking operations may be effectuated.

A license for the effectuation of banking operations shall be issued without limitation of periods for the operation thereof.

The effectuation by a juridical person of banking operations without a license shall entail the recovery from such juridical person of all the amounts received as a result of the effectuation of such operations, and also the recovery of a fine in double the sum of this amount to the federal budget. The recovery shall be made in a judicial proceeding upon the suit of the procurator, respective federal agency of executive power empowerd by a federal law, or the Bank of Russia.

The Bank of Russia shall have the right to present a suit to an arbitrazh court concerning the liquidation of the juridical person effectuating banking operations without a license.

Citizens illegally effectuating banking operations shall bear civil-law, administrative, or criminal responsibility in the procedure established by a law.

Article 14. Documents Necessary for State Registration of Credit Organisation and Receipt of License for Effectuation of Banking Operations

The following documents shall be submitted to the Bank of Russia in the procedure established by it for the State registration of a credit organisation and receipt of a license for the effectuation of banking operations [as amended by Federal Law No. 31-ФЗ, 21 March 2002]:

(1) an application with a petition concerning State registration of a credit organisation and issuance of a license for the effectuation of banking operations; information shall be specified in the application concerning the address (or location) of the permanently operating executive organ of the credit organisation with regard to which a link with the credit organisation is effectuated [as amended by Federal Law No. 31-ФЗ, 21 March 2002];

(2) constitutive contract (original or notarially certified copy), if the signature thereof was provided for by a federal law [as amended by Federal Law No. 31-ФЗ, 21 March 2002];

(3) charter (original or notarially certified copy) [as amended by Federal Law No. 31-ФЗ, 21 March 2002];

(4) business plan confirmed by the meeting of founders (or participants) of the credit organisation, protocol of the meeting of founders (or participants) containing the decision concerning confirmation of the charter of the credit organisation, and also candidacies for appointment to the office of executive of the credit organisation and chief bookkeeper of the credit organisation. The procedure for drawing up the business plan of a credit organisation and the criteria for the evaluation thereof shall be established by normative acts of the Bank of Russia [as amended by Federal Law No. 82-ФЗ, 19 June 2001];

(5) document concerning the payment of State duty and the license charge [as amended by Federal Law No. 31-ФЗ, 21 March 2002];

(6) copies of documents concerning the State registration of the founders-juridical persons, auditor opinions concerning the reliability of their financial reporting, and also confirmations by State Tax Service agencies of the Russian Federation of the fulfilment by founders-juridical persons of obligations to the federal budget, budgets of subjects of the Russian Federation, and local budgets for the last three years [as amended by Federal Law No. 31-ФЗ, 21 March 2002];

(7) documents (according to the List established by normative acts of the Bank of Russia) confirming the sources of origin of means contributed by natural persons-founders to the charter capital of the credit organisation [as amended by Federal Law No. 82-ФЗ, 19 June 2001];

(8) questionnaires of candidates for the office of executive of credit organisation, chief bookkeeper and deputies of the chief bookkeeper of the credit organisation, and also for the offices of executive, deputy executive, chief bookkeeper, and deputies of the chief bookkeeper of a branch of the credit organisation. The said questionnaires shall be filled out by these candidates in their own hand and must contain information established by normative acts of the Bank of Russia, as well as information concerning [as amended by Federal Law No. 82-ФЗ, 19 June 2001]:

these persons having a higher legal or economic education (with submission of a copy of the diploma or document replacing it) and experience of directing a section or other subdivision of a credit organisation connected with the effectuation of banking operations not less than one year, and in the absence of specialised education, experience in directing such a subdivision for not less than two years;

the presence (or absence) of a record of conviction.

Article 15. Procedure for State Registration of Credit Organisation and Issuance of License for Effectuation of Banking Operations

In the event of the submission of the documents enumerated in Article 14 of the present Federal Law, the Bank of Russia issues to the founders of the credit organisation a written confirmation of receipt of the documents from them necessary for State registration of the credit organisation and receipt of a license for the effectuation of banking operations.

The adoption of a decision concerning State registration of the credit organisation and issuance of a license for the effectuation of banking operations or refusal to do so shall be within a period not exceeding six months from the date of submission of all documents provided for by the present Federal Law.

The Bank of Russia, after the adoption of the decision concerning State registration of the credit organisation, shall send to the empowered registering agency the information and documents necessary for the effectuation by the said agency of functions with regard to keeping the unified State register of juridical persons [as amended by Federal Law No. 31-ФЗ, 21 March 2002].

On the basis of the said decision adopted by the Bank of Russia and necessary information and documents submitted by it, the empowered registering agency within a period of not more than five work days from the day of receipt of the necessary information and documents shall make a respective entry in the unified State register of juridical persons and not later than the work day following the day of making the respective entry, inform the Bank of Russia thereof [added by Federal Law No. 31-ФЗ, 21 March 2002].

The Bank of Russia not later than three work days from the day of receipt from the empowered registering agency of information concerning the entry made in the unified State register of juridical persons about the credit organisation shall inform the foundres thereof about this with a request to make payment within a month's period of 100% of the declared charter capital of the credit organisation and issue to the founders a document confirming the fact of making the entry concerning the credit organisation in the unified State register of juridical persons [added by Federal Law No. 31-ФЗ, 21 March 2002].

The failure to pay or incomplete payment of the charter capital within the established period shall be grounds for the Bank of Russia to apply to a court with a demand concerning liquidation of the credit organisation [as amended by Federal Law No. 31-ФЗ, 21 March 2002].

For payment of the charter capital the Bank of Russia shall open a correspondent account in the Bank of Russia for the registered bank and, when necessary, nonbanking credit organisation. The requisites of the correspondent account shall be specified in the notification of the Bank of Russia concerning the State registration of the credit organisation and issuance of the license for the effectuation of banking operations.

In the event of the submission of documents confirming the payment of 100% of the declared charter capital of the credit organisation, the Bank of Russia shall within a three-day period issue a license to the credit organisation for the effectuation of banking operations.

[paragraph seven repealed by Federal Law No. 82-ФЗ, 19 June 2001].

Article 16. Grounds for Refusal of State Registration of Credit Organisation and Issuance Thereto of License for Effectuation of Banking Operations [as amended by Law of 19 June 2001]

A refusal of State registration of a credit organisation and issuance thereto of a license for the effectuation of banking operations shall be permitted only on the following grounds:

(1) failure of candidates proposed for the office of executive of a credit organisation, chief bookkeeper of a credit organisation and deputies thereof to conform to qualifications requirements established by federal laws and normative acts of the Bank of Russia adopted in accordance therewith. By failure of candidates proposed for the said offices to conform to these qualifications requirements is understood:

the absence of a higher legal or economic education and experience of direction of a section or other subdivision of a credit organisation whose activity is connected with the effectuation of banking operations, or the lack of two years' experience of directing such section or subdivision;

the presence of a record of conviction for the commission of crimes in the sphere of the economy;

the commission within one year which preceded the day of filing documents at the Bank of Russia for State registration of the credit organisation of an administrative violation in the domain of trade and finances established by the decree of an agency which has entered into legal force empowered to consider cases concerning administrative violations [as amended by Federal Law No. 31-ФЗ, 21 March 2002];

the presence in the two years which preceded the day of filing documents at the Bank of Russia for State registration of the credit organisation of facts of the dissolution with the said persons of a labour contract at the initiative of the administration on the grounds provided for by Article 254(2) of the Code of Laws on Labour of the Russian Federation [as amended by Federal Law No. 31-ФЗ, 21 March 2002];

the presentation in the three years which preceded the day of filing documents at the Bank of Russia for State registration of the credit organisation to the credit organisation in which each of the said candidates was in the office of executive of a credit organisation of a demand concerning the replacement thereof as executive of the credit organisation in the procedure provided for by the Federal Law on the Central Bank of the Russian Federation (Bank of Russia) [as amended by Federal Law No. 31-ФЗ, 21 March 2002];

the failure of the business reputation of the said candidates to conform to the requirements established by federal laws and normative acts of the Bank of Russia adopted in accordance therewith;

the presence of other grounds established by federal laws;

(2) the unsatisfactory financial status of the founders of the credit organisation or failure of them to perform their obligations to the federal budget, budgets of subjects of the Russian Federation, and local budgets for the last three years;

(3) failure of documents filed at the Bank of Russia for State registration of the credit organisation and receipt of a license for the effectuation of banking operations to conform to the requirements of federal laws and normative acts of the Bank of Russia adopted in accordance therewith;

(4) the failure of the business reputation of the candidates for office of members of the council of directors (or supervisory council) to conform to the qualifications requirements established by federal laws and normative acts of the Bank of Russia adopted in accordance therewith and the presence of a record of conviction for them for the commission of a crime in the sphere of the economy.

The decision concerning a refusal of State registration of a credit organisation and issuance thereto of a license for the effectuation of banking operations shall be notified to the founders of the credit organisation in written form and must be reasoned.

A refusal of State registration of a credit organisation and issuance thereto of a license for the effectuation of banking operations and the failure of the Bank of Russia to adopt the respective decision within the established period may be appealed to an arbitrazh court.

By business reputation in accordance with the present Article is understood the evaluation of the professional and other qualities of a person enabling him to occupy the respective office in the management organs of a credit organisation [as amended by Law of 19 June 2001].

Article 17. State Registration of Credit Organisation with Foreign Investments and Branch of Foreign Bank and Issuance of Licenses to Them for Effectuation of Banking Operations

The duly formalised documents enumerated below shall be submitted for the State registration of a credit organisation with foreign investments and branch of a foreign bank and receipt by them of a license for the effectuation of banking operations in addition to the documents specified in Article 14 of the present Federal Law.

The foriegn juridical person shall submit:

(1) the decision concerning the participation thereof in the creation of a credit organisation on the territory of the Russian Federation or opening of the branch of the bank;

(2) the document confirming the registration of the juridical person and balance sheets for the three preceding years confirmed by an auditor's opinion;

(3) the written consent of the respective control agency of the country of its whereabouts to participation in the creation of a credit organisation on the territory of the Russian Federation or opening of the branch of the bank in those instances when such authorisation is required according to the legislation of the country of its whereabouts.

A foreign natural person shall submit confirmation of a first-class (according to international practice) foreign bank of the ability of this person to pay.

Article 18. Additional Requirements for Creation and Activity of Credit Organisations with Foreign Investments and Branches of Foreign Banks

The amount (or quota) of participation of foreign capital in the banking system of the Russian Federation shall be established by a federal law upon the proposal of the Government of the Russian Federation agreed with the Bank of Russia. The said quota shall be calculated as the relationship of the total capital belonging to nonresidents in the charter capital of credit organisations with foreign investments and the capital of branches of foreign banks to the aggregate charter capital of credit organisations registered on the territory of the Russian Federation.

The Bank of Russia shall terminate the issuance of licenses for the effectuation of banking operations to banks with foreign investments and branches of foreign banks when the established quota is reached.

A credit organisation shall be obliged to receive the prior authorisation of the Bank of Russia to increase its charter capital at the expense of the means of nonresidents, the alienation (including sale) of its stocks (or participatory shares) to the benefit of nonresidents, and participants of the credit organisation—residents—to the alienation of stocks (or participatory shares) of the credit organisation belonging to them to the benefit of nonresidents. The said transactions with regard to the alienation of stocks (or participatory shares) to nonresidents concluded without the authorisation of the Bank of Russia shall be invalid, except for instances provided for by paragraph five of the present Article.

The Bank of Russia shall have the right to impose a prohibition on an increase of the charter capital of a credit organisation at the expense of the means of nonresidents and the alienation of stocks (or participatory shares) to the benefit of nonresidents if the result of the said action is exceeding the quota of participation of foreign capital in the banking system of the Russian Federation.

An application concerning the intention to increase the charter capital of a credit organisation at the expense of the means of nonresidents and the alienation of stocks (or participatory shares) to the benefit of nonresidents shall be considered by the Bank of Russia within a two-month period from the day of filing the application. The result of the consideration thereof shall be the authorisation of the Bank of Russia to conducting the operation specified in the application or a reasoned refusal in written form. If the Bank of Russia does not communicate the decision adopted within the established period, the said operation shall be considered to be authorised.

The Bank of Russia shall have the right by agreement with the Government of the Russian Federation to establish limitations for credit organisations with foreign investments and branches of the foreign banks on the effectuation of banking operations if limitations are applied in the respective foreign States with respect to banks with Russian investments and branches of Russian banks on their creation and activity.

The Bank of Russia shall have the right to establish in the procedure established by the Federal Law on the Central Bank of the Russian Federation (Bank of Russia) additional requirements for credit organisations with foreign investments and branches of foreign banks relative to obligatory normative standards, the procedure for the submission of reports, confirmation of the composition of the leadership and list of banking operations to be effectuated, and also relative to the minimum amount of charter capital of the newly registered credit organisations with foreign investments and the minimum amount of capital of branches of foreign banks being newly registered.

Article 19. Measures of Bank of Russia to be Applied by It by way of Supervision in Event of Violation by Credit Organisation of Federal Laws and Normative Acts of Bank of Russia

In the event of a violation of federal laws, normative acts, and prescriptions of the Bank of Russia, obligatory normative standards established by it, the failure to submit information, the submission of incomplete or unreliable information, and also the commission of actions creating a real threat to the interests of depositors and creditors, the Bank of Russia shall have the right by way of supervision to apply measures to the credit organisation established by the Federal Law on the Central Bank of the Russian Federation (Bank of Russia).

Article 20. Grounds for Revocation of License for Effectuation of Banking Operations by Credit Organisation [as amended by Law of 19 June 2001]

The Bank of Russia may revoke the license for the effectuation of banking operations by a credit organisation in instances of [as amended by Law of 19 June 2001]:

(1) the establishment of the unreliability of information on the basis of which the license was issued;

(2) the delay of the commencement of the effectuation of banking operations provided for by this license of more than one year from the day of issuance thereof [as amended by Law of 19 June 2001];

(3) the establishment of facts of the material unreliability of reporting data [as amended by Federal Law No. 151-ФЗ, 31 July 1998, and by Federal Law No. 82-ФЗ, 19 June 2001];

(4) the delay by more than 15 days of submitting monthly reporting (or reporting documentation) [added by Federal Law No. 82-ФЗ, 19 June 2001];

(5) the effectuation, including once, of banking operations not provided for by the said license [as amended by Federal Law No. 82-ФЗ, 19 June 2001];

(6) the failure to perform federal laws regulating banking activity, and also normative acts of the Bank of Russia, if within one year measures have been applied to the credit organisation repeatedly which are provided for by the Federal Law on the Central Bank of the Russian Federation (Bank of Russia), and also the repeated violation within one year of the requirements provided for by Articles 6 and 7 (except for Article 7[3]) of the Federal Law on Counteracting the Legalisation (or Laundering) of Revenues Received by Criminal Means [as amended by Federal Law No. 82-ФЗ, 19 June 2001, and Federal Law No. 121-ФЗ, 7 August 2001];

(7) [as amended by Federal Law No. 151-ФЗ, 31 July 1998; repealed by Federal Law No. 82-ФЗ, 19 June 2001];

(7) the repeated guilty failure to perform within one year demands contained in documents of execution of courts and arbitrazh courts concerning the recovery of monetary means from the accounts (or deposits) of clients of the credit organisation when there are monetary means in the account (or deposits) of the said persons [as amended by Federal Law No. 151-ФЗ, 31 July 1998; and renumbered and amended by Federal Law No. 82-ФЗ, 19 June 2001];

(8) the existence of a petition of a temporary administration if at the moment of the ending of the period of activity of the said administration established by the Federal Law on Insolvency (or Bankruptcy) of Credit Organisations there are grounds for the designation thereof provided for by the said Federal Law [added by Federal Law No. 82-ФЗ, 19 June 2001];

(9) the repeated failure to submit within the established period by a credit organisation to the Bank of Russia of renewed information necessary in order to make changes in the unified State register of juridical persons, except for information concerning licenses received [added by Federal Law No. 31-ФЗ, 21 March 2002].

The Bank of Russia shall be obliged to revoke a license for the effectuation of banking operations if:

(1) the sufficiency of capital of the credit organisation becomes lower than 2%;

If during the last 12 months which preceded the moment when in accordance with the present Article the said license of the credit organisation must be revoked, the Bank of Russia has changed the method of calculating capital sufficiency of credit organisations, for the purposes of the present Article that method shall apply in accordance with which the capital sufficiency of a credit organisation reaches maximum significance;

(2) if the amount of own means (or capital) of a credit organisation is lower than the minimum significance of charter capital established by the Bank of Russia on the date of State registration of the credit organisation [as amended by Federal Law No. 31-ФЗ, 21 March 2002];

(3) if a credit organisation does not perform within the period established by the Federal Law on Insolvency (or Bankruptcy) of Credit Organisations the requirements of the Bank of Russia concerning the bringing into conformity of the amount of charter capital and amount of own means (or capital);

(4) if a credit organisation is not capable of satisfying demands of creditors with regard to monetary obligations and/or to perform the duty with regard to payment of obligatory payments within one month from the ensuing of the date of their satisfaction and/or performance. In so doing the said demands in aggregate must comprise not less than 1000 times the minimum amount of payment for labour established by a federal law.

In instances provided for by paragraph two of the present Article the Bank of Russia shall revoke a license for the effectuation of banking operation by a credit organisation within 15 days from the day of receipt by agencies of the Bank of Russia resposible for the revocation of the said license of reliable information concerning the presence of grounds for revocation of that license of the credit organisation.

Revocation of the license for the effectuation of banking operations on other grounds except those grounds provided for by the present Federal Law shall not be permitted.

The decision of the Bank of Russia concerning the revocation of a license from a credit organisation for the effectuation of banking operations shall enter into force form the day of adoption of the respective act of the Bank of Russia and may be appealed within 30 days from the day of publication of the notice concerning revocation of the license for the effectuation of banking operations in Вестник Банка России. An appeal of the said decision of the Bank of Russia, and also the application of measures with regard to securing suits with respect to a credit organisation, shall not suspend the operation of the said decision of the Bank of Russia.

A notice concerning the revocation of a license from a credit organisation for the effectuation of banking operations shall be publised by the Bank of Russia in the official publication of the Bank of Russia, Вестник Банка России, within a week from the day of adoption of the respective decision.

After revocation from a credit organisation of a license for the effectuation of banking operations a credit organisation must be liquidated in accordance with the requirements of Article 23[1] of the present Federal Law, and in the event of being deemed to be bankrupt—in accordance with the requirements of the Federal Law on Insolvency (or Bankruptcy) of Credit Organisations.

After revocation from a credit organisation of a license for the effectuation of banking operations the Bank of Russia shall:

not later than the working day following the day of revocation of the said license designate temporary administration for the credit organisation in accordance with the requirements of the Federal Law on Insolvency (or Bankruptcy) of Credit Organisations;

perform the actions provided for by Article 23[1] of the present Federal Law.

From the moment of revocation of the license from a credit organisation for the effectuation of banking operations:

(1) the period of performance of obligations of the credit organisation shall be considered to have ensued. The obligations of the credit organisation in foreign currency shall be taken into account in rubles at the exchange rate of the Bank of Russia which operated on the day of revocation of the license from the credit organisation;

(2) the calculation of interest, and also of penalties (or fines, forfeits) and the imposition of other financial (or economic) sanctions with regard to obligations of the credit organisation shall terminate;

(3) the execution of documents of execution with regard to property recoveries shall be suspended (except for the execution of documents of execution issued on the basis of judicial decisions concerning the recovery of indebtedness for earnings, payment of remuneration under authors' contracts, alimony, and also compensation of harm caused to life and health, and moral harm) which entered into legal force before the moment of revocation of the license from the credit organisation for the effectuation of banking operations [as amended by Federal Law No. 82-ФЗ, 19 June 2001];

(4) before the moment of creation of the liquidation commission (or liquidator) or appointment of a bankruptcy administrator by the arbitrazh court the conclusion of transactions by the credit organisation and performance of obligations with regard to transactions of the credit organisation shall be prohibited (except for transactions connected with current municipal and operational payments of the credit organisation, and also with the payment of severance benefits and payment for the labour of persons working under a labour contract, within the limits of the estimate of expenses agreed with the Bank of Russia or with the empowered representative of the Bank of Russia in the event of his appointment) [as amended by Federal Law No. 151-ФЗ, 31 July 1998].

Article 21. Consideration of Disputes with Participation of Credit Organisation

Decisions and actions (or failure to act) of the Bank of Russia or officials thereof may be appealed by the credit organisation to a court or arbitrazh court in the procedure established by federal laws.

A credit organisation shall have the right to apply to the Bank of Russia with requests and applications in connection with decisions and actions (or failure to act) of the Bank of Russia, to which the Bank of Russia shall be obliged within a month's period to give a reply on the substance of the questions treated therein.

Disputes between a credit organisation and its clients (natural and juridical persons) shall be settled in the procedure provided for by federal laws.

Article 22. Branches and Representations of Credit Organisation

A branch of a credit organisation shall be a solitary subdivision thereof, situated outside the location of the credit organisation and effectuating in its name all or part of the banking operations provided for by the license of the Bank of Russia issued to the credit organisation.

A representation of a credit organisation shall be a solitary subdivision thereof, situated outwise the location of the credit organisation and representing the interests thereof and effectuating the defence thereof. The representation of a credit organisation shall not have the right to effectuating banking operations.

Branches and representations of a credit organisation shall not be juridical persons and shall effectuate their activity on the basis of Statutes confirmed by the credit organisation which created them.

The directors of branches and representations shall be appointed by the director of the credit organisation which created them and operate on the basis of a power of attorney issued to them in the established procedure.

A credit organisation shall open on the territory of the Russian Federation branches and representations from the moment of notifing the Bank of Russia. In the notification shall be specified the postal address of the branch (or representation), its powers and functions, information about the directors, the scale and character of planned operations, and also an impression shall be submitted of the seal and samples of the signatures of its directors.

A fee shall be recovered for opening branches of credit organisations in the amount determined by the Bank of Russia, but not more than 1000 times the minimum amount of payment for labour. The said fee shall go to the revenue of the federal budget.

Branches of a credit organisation with foreign investments on the territory of the Russian Federation shall be registered by the Bank of Russia in the procedure established by it.

Article 23. Liquidation or Reorganisation of Credit Organisation

The liquidation or reorganisation of a credit organisation shall be effectuated in conformity with federal laws, taking into account the demands of the present Federal Law. In so doing the State registration of a credit organisation in connection with the liquidation thereof and State registration of a credit organisation created by means of reorganisation shall be effectuated in the procedure provided for by the Federal Law 'On the State Registration of Juridical Persons', taking into account the peculiarities of such registration established by the present Federal

Law and normative acts of the Bank of Russia adopted in accordance with it. The information and documents necessary for the effectuation of State registration of a credit organisation shall be submitted to the Bank of Russia. The List of the said information and documents, and also the procedure for the submission thereof, shall be determined by the Bank of Russia [as amended by Federal Law No. 82-ФЗ, 19 June 2001, and by Federal Law No. 31-ФЗ, 21 March 2002].

The Bank of Russia shall, after the adoption of the decision concerning State registration of a credit organisation in connection with the liquidation thereof or a credit organisation created by means of reorganisation, send to the empowered registering agency of the information and documents necessary for effectuation by the said agency of the functions with regard to keeping the unified State register of juridical persons [added by Federal Law No. 31-ФЗ, 21 March 2002].

On the basis of the said decision adopted by the Bank of Russia and necessary information and documents submitted by it, the empowered registering agency within a period of not more than five work days from the day of receipt of the necessary information and documents shall make a respective entry in the unified State register of juridical persons and not later than the work day following the day of making the respective entry, inform the Bank of Russia thereof [added by Federal Law No. 31-ФЗ, 21 March 2002].

Interaction of the Bank of Russia with the empowered registering agency with regard to the question of State registration of a credit organisation in connection with the liqudiation thereof and credit organisation created by means of reorganisation shall be effectuated in the procedure agreed by the Bank of Russia with the empowered registering agency [added by Federal Law No. 31-ФЗ, 21 March 2002].

State registration of a credit organisation in connection with the liquidation thereof shall be effectuated within a period of not more than forty-five work days from the day of submission to the Bank of Russia of documents formalised in the established procedure [added by Federal Law No. 31-ФЗ, 21 March 2002].

State registration of a credit organisation created by means of reorganisation, if the decision was not taken to refuse the said State registration, shall be effectuated within a period of not more than six months from the day of submission to the Bank of Russia of all documents formalised in the established procedure [added by Federal Law No. 31-ФЗ, 21 March 2002].

In the event of the termination of the activity of a credit organisation on the basis of a decision of its founders (or participants) the Bank of Russia shall on the basis of a petition of the credit organisation adopt a decision concerning the annulment of the license for the effectuation of banking operations. The procedure for the submission of the said petition by the credit organisation shall be regulated by normative acts of the Bank of Russia [added by Federal Law No. 151-ФЗ, 31 July 1998].

In the event of the annulment or revocation of a license for the effectuation of banking operations a credit organisation shall within 15 days from the moment of the adoption of such decision return the said license to the Bank of Russia [added by Federal Law No. 151-ФЗ, 31 July 1998].

The founders (or participants) of a credit organisation who have adopted a decision concerning the liquidation thereof shall appoint the liquidation commission, confirm the intermediate liquidation balance sheet and liquidation balance sheet of the credit organisation by agreement with the Bank of Russia [as amended by Federal Law No. 31-ФЗ, 21 March 2002].

The liquidation of a credit organisation shall be considered to be completed, and the credit organisation to have terminated its activity, after the making of an entry thereof by the empowered registering agency in the unified State register of juridical persons [added by Federal Law No. 31-ФЗ, 21 March 2002].

Article 23[1]. Liquidation of Credit Organisation at Initiative of Bank of Russia (Compulsory Liquidation) [as amended by Federal Law No. 82-ФЗ, 19 June 2001]

The Bank of Russia shall be obliged within 30 days from the date of publication in Вестник Банка России of the notice concerning revocation from a credit organisation of the license for the effectuation of banking operations to apply to an arbitrazh court with a demand concerning the liquidation of a credit organisation, except when at the moment of revocation of the said license from the credit organisation there are indicia of insolvency (or bankruptcy) provided for by the Federal Law on Insolvency (or Bankruptcy) of Credit Organisations. Simultaneously, the Bank of Russia shall be obliged to submit to the arbitrazh court a candidacy for the liquidator corresponding to the requirements set out by the Federal Law on Insolvency (or Bankruptcy) of Credit Organisations for an arbitrazh administrator in the event of the bankruptcy of a credit organisation unless established otherwise by a federal law [added by Federal Law No. 151-ФЗ, 31 July 1998; as amended by Federal Law No. 82-ФЗ, 19 June 2001].

If at the moment of revocation from a credit organisation of a license for the effectuation of banking operations it has the indicia of insolvency (or bankruptcy) provided for by the Federal Law on Insolvency (or Bankruptcy) of Credit Organisations, or the presence of these indicia has been established by a temporary administration designated by the Bank of Russia for the credit organisation after the revocation of the said license, the Bank of Russia shall apply to an arbitrazh court with an application concerning the deeming of a credit organisation to be bankrupt in the procedure established by the Federal Law on Insolvency (or Bankruptcy) of Credit Organisations [added by Federal Law No. 82-ФЗ, 19 June 2001].

The arbitrazh court shall consider the demand concerning liquidation of the credit organisation in accordance with the rules established by the Code of Arbitrazh Procedure of the Russian Federation. The arbitrazh court shall adopt a decision concerning liquidation of the credit organisation and appointment of a liquidator from among the candidacies submitted to it by the Bank of Russia unless the presence of indicia of bankruptcy is proved at the moment of revocation from the credit organisation of the license for the effectuation of banking operations [added by Federal Law No. 82-ФЗ, 19 June 2001].

From the moment of rendering of a decision by the arbitrazh court concerning the liquidation of a credit organisation:

the management organs of the credit organisation (including the liquidation commission (or liquidator), if they have been elected (or appointed) by decision of the meeting of founders (or participants) of the credit organisation, shall be removed from the fulfilment of functions with regard to management of its affairs, including with regard to the disposition of its property, and within a three-day period shall ensure the transfer to the liquidator of bookkeeping and other documentation, material and other valuables, seals, and stamps of the credit organisation;

information concerning the financial state of the credit organisation shall cease to be relegated to the category of information having a confidential character or being a commercial secret;

the imposition of arrest previously imposed on property of the credit organisation and other limitations with regard to the disposition of its property shall be removed. The imposition of new arrests on property of the credit organisation and introduction of other limitations with regard to the disposition of its property shall not be permitted;

all demands against the credit organisation may be presentd and shall be subject to satisfaction only in the process of liquidation thereof [added by Federal Law No. 82-ФЗ, 19 June 2001].

The arbitrazh court which has adopted the decision concerning liquidation of a credit organisation shall send the said decision to the Bank of Russia and the empowered registering agency, which shall make an entry in the unified State register of juridical persons that the credit organisation is in the process of liquidation [added by Federal Law No. 31-ФЗ, 21 March 2002].

In the process of liquidation of a credit organisation the liquidator has the right to perform the duties provided for by the present Article and federal laws, and shall be obliged to act by taking into account the interests of its creditors. The founders (or participants) of the credit organisation and creditors thereof shall have the right to demand from the liquidator compensation of losses caused by its actions (or failure to act) violating legislation of the Russian Federation [added by Federal Law No. 82-ФЗ, 19 June 2001].

The liquidator shall send for publication the announcement concerning liquidation of the credit organisation to the Вестник Банка России not later than five working days from the day of his appointment. There must be specified in this announcement:

the name and other requisites of the credit organisation being liquidated on the basis of the decision of an arbitrazh court;

the name of the arbitrazh court in whose proceedings the case concerning liquidation of the credit organisation is situated;

the date of adoption by an arbitrazh court of the decision concerning liquidation of the credit organisation;

the period established for presentation of demands of creditors (may not be less than two months from the date of publication of the said announcement);

the postal address at which creditors may present their demands against the credit organisation;

information concerning the liquidator [added by Federal Law No. 82-ФЗ, 19 June 2001].

The demands of creditors of a credit organisation shall be sent to the liquidator at the postal address specified in the publication of the announcement concerning the liquidation of the credit organisation simultaneously with the documents on the basis of the consideration of which the liquidator adopts the decision concerning the deeming of the said demands to be established or to be not established. The liquidator shall consider the declared demands of creditors of a credit organisation and take them into account when drawing up the interim liquidation balance sheet. The liquidator shall be obliged to inform the creditor of the credit organisation about the results of consideration of its demands within the period not exceeding one month from the day of receipt of the said demands. Objections with regard to the results of consideration by the liquidator of demands of creditors may be declared by the creditor and shall be considered in the procedure provided for by the Federal Law on Insolvency (or Bankruptcy) in order to effectuate the procedures of a bankruptcy proceeding [added by Federal Law No. 82-ФЗ, 19 June 2001].

The demands of creditors of the credit organisation being liquidated with regard to the results of their consideration by the liquidator may be declared by the creditor in a court or arbitrazh court in the procedure established by a law [added by Federal Law No. 82-ФЗ, 19 June 2001].

The liquidator shall be obliged to conduct the first meeting of creditors of the credit organisation being liquidated not later than 60 days from the day of the end of the period established for presentation of the demands of creditors. Creditors must be informed about the day and place of conducting the said meeting not later than 15 days before the day of conducting this meeting [added by Federal Law No. 82-ФЗ, 19 June 2001].

The election of the committee of creditors shall be within the competence of the meeting of creditors [added by Federal Law No. 82-ФЗ, 19 June 2001].

The meeting of creditors and/or committee of creditors shall have the right to:

hear the report of the liquidator concerning the course of conducting liquidation procedures;

consider the interim liquidation balance sheet and liquidation balance sheet;

petition the arbitrazh court to remove the liquidator;

appeal the decision of the liquidation to the arbitrazh court;

give consent to the effectuation of transactions connected with the alienation of property of the credit organisation if the said property is not realised at a public sale;

effectuate other powers in accordance with the requirements of the present Article [added by Federal Law No. 82-ФЗ, 19 June 2001].

The procedure for conducting the meeting of creditors and sessions of the committee of creditors, including the procedure for the election of the committee of creditors and conducting voting, shall be regulated by the Federal Law on Insolvency (or Bankruptcy) [added by Federal Law No. 82-ФЗ, 19 June 2001].

After the end of the period established for the presentation of demands of creditors to the credit organisation, the liquidator shall draw up the interim liquidation balance sheet, which shall contain information concerning the composition of property of the credit organisation being liquidated, a list of demands of creditors presented, and also the results of their consideration. The interim liquidation balance sheet shall be subject to consideration at the meeting of creditors and/or at a session of the committee of creditors and after the said consideration—to agreement with the Bank of Russia. Satisfaction of demands of creditors shall be effectuated in accordance with the priority provided for by Article 64 of the Civil Code of the Russian Federation, and the interim liquidation balance sheet commencing from the day of agreement thereof with the Bank of Russia, except for creditors of the fifth priority, payments to whom shall be made upon the expiry of one month from the day of agreement of the said balance sheet with the Bank of Russia [added by Federal Law No. 82-ФЗ, 19 June 2001].

Unless established otherwise by the present Article, in instances when the credit organisation has monetary means insufficient to satisfy the demands of creditors the liquidation shall effectuate the realisation of property of the credit organisation at a public sale in the procedure established by legislation of the Russian Federation [added by Federal Law No. 82-ФЗ, 19 June 2001].

The liquidator shall draw up and submit to the Bank of Russia for agreement the interim liquidation balance sheet and the liquidation balance sheet and the bookkeeping and statistical report of the credit organisation in the procedure and within the periods which have been established by federal laws and normative acts of the Bank of Russia adopted in accordance therewith [added by Federal Law No. 82-ФЗ, 19 June 2001].

In the event of the failure to perform or the improper performance by the liquidator of duties placed on him the arbitrazh court shall have the right to:

deem invalid the transactions concluded or performed by the liquidator in the course of the conducting by him in the credit organisation of liquidation procedures on the grounds provided for by civil legislation of the Russian Federation and the Federal Law on Insolvency (or Bankruptcy);

remove the liquidator from the performance by him of his duties with regard to the petition of the Bank of Russia or meeting (or committee) of creditors and to appoint a new liquidator whose candidacy is proposed by the Bank of Russia in the procedure provided for by the Federal Law on Insolvency (or Bankruptcy) [added by Federal Law No. 82-ФЗ, 19 June 2001].

The period of liquidation of a credit organisation may not exceed 12 months from the day of adoption by the arbitrazh court of a decision concerning liquidation of the credit organisation. The said period may be extended by the arbitrazh court upon the substantiated petition of the liquidator [added by Federal Law No. 82-ФЗ, 19 June 2001].

If in the course of conducting liquidation procedures it is elicited that the value of property of the credit organisation with respect to which a decision has been adopted concerning liquidation is insufficient to satisfy the demands of creditors of the credit organisation, the liquidator shall be obliged to send to the arbitrazh court an application to deem the credit organisation to be bankrupt [added by Federal Law No. 82-ФЗ, 19 June 2001].

A report concerning the results of the liquidation of a credit organisation with the liquidation balance sheet appended shall be heard at the meeting of creditors or session of the committee of creditors and shall be confirmed in the procedure provided for by the Federal Law on Insolvency (or Bankruptcy) [added by Federal Law 82-ФЗ, 19 June 2001].

A liquidator shall be obliged within a ten-day period from the day of rendering by the arbitrazh court of a ruling concerning completion of the liquidation of the credit organisation to submit to the Bank of Russia the said ruling and other documents provided for by normative acts of the Bank of Russia for effectuating the State registration of the credit organisations in connection with its liquidation [added by Federal Law No. 82-ФЗ, 19 June 2001, as amended by Federal Law No. 31-ФЗ, 21 March 2002].

Chapter III. Ensuring Stability of Banking System, Defence of Rights and Interests of Depositors and Creditors of Credit Organisations

Article 24. Ensuring Financial Reliability of Credit Organisation

For the purposes of ensuring financial reliability, a credit organisation shall be obliged to create reserves (or funds), including the loss of value of securities, the procedure for the forming and use of which shall be established by the Bank of Russia. The minimum amounts of reserves (or funds) shall be established by the Bank of Russia. The amounts of deductions to reserves (or funds) from profit before taxation shall be established by federal laws on taxes.

A credit organisation shall be obliged to effectuate the classification of assets, separating out doubtful and hopeless debts, and to create reserves (or funds) to cover possible losses in the procedure established by the Bank of Russia.

A credit organisation shall be obliged to comply with obligatory normative standards established in accordance with the Federal Law on the Central Bank of the Russian Federation (Bank of Russia). The numerical significance of obligatory normative standards shall be established by the Bank of Russia in accordance with the said federal law.

A credit organisation shall be obliged to organise internal control ensuring the proper level of reliability corresponding to the character and scale of operations being conducted.

Article 25. Normative Standards of Obligatory Reserves of Bank

A bank shall be obliged to fulfil the normative standards of obligatory reserves deposited in the Bank of Russia, including with regard to periods, amounts, and types of attracted monetary means. The procedure for depositing the obligatory reserves shall be determined by the Bank of Russia in accordance with the Federal Law on the Central Bank of the Russian Federation (Bank of Russia).

The bank shall be obliged to have in the Bank of Russia an account for keeping obligatory reserves. The procedure for opening the said account and the effectuation of operations with regard to it shall be established by the Bank of Russia.

Article 26. Banking Secrecy

A credit organisation and the Bank of Russia shall guarantee secrecy concerning operations, accounts, and deposits of its clients and correspondents. All employees of the credit organisation shall be obliged to preserve secrecy concerning operations, accounts, and deposits of its clients and correspondents, and also other information established by the credit organisation, if this is not contrary to a federal law.

References with regard to operations and accounts of juridical persons and citizens effectuating entrepreneurial activity without the formation of a juridical person shall be issued by the credit organisation to them themselves, courts, and arbitrazh courts (or judges), the Counting Chamber of the Russian Federation, State tax service and tax police agencies, customs agencies of the Russian Federation in the instances provided for by legislative acts concerning their activity, and with the consent of the procurator, to agencies of preliminary investigation with regard to cases under proceedings therein.

References with regard to accounts and deposits of natural persons shall be issued by a credit organisation to them themselves, courts, and with the consent of a procurator, to agencies of preliminary investigation with regard to cases under proceedings therein.

References with regard to accounts and deposits in the event of the death of the possessors thereof shall be issued by a credit organisation to the persons specified by the possessor of the account or deposit in the testamentary disposition made to the credit organisation, notarial offices with regard to inheritance cases under proceedings therein concerning deposits of deceased depositors, and with respect to accounts of foreign citizens, to foreign consular institutions.

Information with regard to operations of juridical persons, citizens effectuating entrepreneurial activity without the formation of a juridical person, and natural persons shall be provided by credit organisations to the empowered agency effectuating measures with regard to counteracting the legalisation (or laundering) of revenues received by criminal means in the instances, procedure, and amount which have been provided for by the Federal Law on Counteracting the Legalisation (or Laundering) of Revenues Received by Criminal Means [added by Federal Law No. 121-ФЗ, 7 August 2001].

The Bank of Russia shall not have the right to divulge information concerning accounts, deposits, and also information concerning specific transactions and operations from the reports of credit organisations received by it as a result of the performance of licensing, supervisory, and control functions, except for instances provided for by federal laws.

Auditor organisations shall not have the right to divulge information to third persons concerning operations, accounts, and deposits of credit organisations, clients thereof, and correspondents received in the course of the verifications conducted by them, except for instances provided for by federal laws.

The empowered agency effectuating measures with regard to counteracting the legalisation (or laundering) of revenues received by criminal means shall not have the right to divulge to third persons information received from credit organisations in accordance with the Federal Law on Counteracting the Legalisation (or Laundering) of Revenues Received by Criminal Means, except for instances provided for by the said Federal Law [added by Federal Law No. 121-ФЗ, 7 August 2001].

For divulgence of bank secrecy the Bank of Russia, credit, auditor, and other organisations, empowered agency effectuating measures with regard to counteracting the legalisation (or laundering) of revenues received by criminal means, and also officials and workers thereof, shall bear responsibility, including compensation of damage inflicted, in the procedure established by a federal law [as amended by Federal Law No. 121-ФЗ, 7 August 2001].

Article 27. Imposition of Arrest and Levy of Execution Against Monetary Means and Other Valuables Situated in Credit Organisation

Arrest may be imposed on monetary means and other valuables of juridical and natural persons situated in accounts and deposits or for keeping in a credit organisation not other than by a court and arbitrazh court, judges, and also by decree of agencies of preliminary investigation when there is the sanction of a procurator.

In the event of the imposition of arrest on monetary means situated in accounts and deposits, a credit organisation immediately upon receipt of the decision concerning the imposition of arrest terminate expenditure operations with regard to the particular account (or deposit) within the limits of the means for which arrest was imposed.

Execution may be levied against monetary means and other valuables of natural and juridical persons situated in accounts and deposits or for keeping in a credit organisation only on the basis of documents of execution in accordance with legislation of the Russian Federation.

A credit organisation of the Bank of Russia shall not bear responsibility for damage caused as a result of the imposition of arrest or levy of execution against monetary means and other valuables of their clients, except for instances provided for by a law.

Monetary means and other valuables may be confiscated on the basis of the judgment of a court which has entered into legal force.

Chapter IV. Inter-Bank Relations and Servicing of Clients

Article 28. Inter-Bank Relations

Credit organisations may on contractual bases attract and place with one another means in the form of deposits, credits, effectuate settlements of accounts through settlement centres created in the established procedure and correspondent accounts opened with one another, and perform other mutual operations provided for by licenses issued by the Bank of Russia.

A credit organisation monthly shall notify the Bank of Russia about newly opened correspondent accounts on the territory of the Russian Federation and abroad.

Credit organisations shall establish correspondent relations with foreign banks registered on the territories of offshore zones of foreign States in the procedure determined by the Bank of Russia [added by Federal Law No. 126-ФЗ, 5 July 1999].

Correspondent relations between a credit organisation and the Bank of Russia shall be effectuated on contractual bases.

The withdrawal of means from the accounts of a credit organisation shall be done according to its instruction or with its consent, except for instances provided for by a federal law.

In the event of the insufficiency of means for effectuating the granting of credits to clients and the fulfilment of obligations assumed, a credit organisation may have recourse to receive credits to the Bank of Russia on the conditions determined by it.

Article 29. Interest Rates With Regard to Credits, Deposits, and Commission Agency Remuneration for Operations of Credit Organisation

Interest rates with regard to credits, deposits, and commission agency remuneration for operations shall be established by a credit organisation by agreement with clients unless provided otherwise by a federal law.

A credit organisation shall not have the right unilaterally to change interest rates with regard to credits, deposits, commission agency remuneration and the periods of operation of these contracts with clients, except for instances provided for by a federal law or the contract with the client [paragraph two was declared unconstitutional by Decree of the Constitutional Court of the Russian Federation, No. 4-п, 23 February 1999, in so far as it allowed banks unilaterally to reduce interest on demand deposits of citizens solely on the basis of a contract without the grounds for such having been determined in a federal law].

Article 30. Relations Between Bank of Russia, Credit Organisations, and Clients Thereof

Relations between the Bank of Russia, credit organisations, and the clients thereof shall be effectuated on the basis of contract, unless provided otherwise by a federal law.

In the contract must be specified the interest rates for credits and deposits, the cost of banking services and periods for fulfilling them, incuding the periods for processing payment documents, the property responsibility of the parties for a violation of the contract, including responsibility for a violation of obligations with regard to periods for the effectuation of payments, and also the procedure for the dissolution thereof and other material conditions of the contract.

Clients shall have the right to open the number of settlement, deposit, and other accounts necessary for them in any currency in banks with their consent unless established otherwise by a federal law.

The procedure for the opening, conducting, and closing of accounts of clients by the bank in rubles and foreign currency shall be established by the Bank of Russia in accordance with federal laws.

The participants of a credit organisation shall not have any preferences when considering the question of receiving a credit or rendering of other banking services to them unless provided otherwise by a federal law.

Article 31. Effectuation of Settlement of Accounts by Credit Organisation

A credit organisation shall effectuate the settlement of accounts according to the rules, forms, and standards established by the Bank of Russia; in the absence of rules for conducting individual types of settlements of accounts, by arrangement between themselves; when effectuating international settlements of accounts, in the procedure established by federal laws and rules accepted in international banking practice.

A credit organisation and the Bank of Russia shall be obliged to effectuate the transfer of means of the client and crediting of means to his account not later than the next operational day after receipt of the respective payment document, unless established otherwise by a federal law, the contract, or payment document.

In the event of the untimely or incorrect crediting to an account or withdrawal from an account of the client of monetary means, the credit organisation and the Bank of Russia shall pay interest on the amount of these means at the refinancing rate of the Bank of Russia.

Article 32. Antimonopoly Rules

It shall be prohibited for credit organisations to conclude agreements and effectuate agreed actions directed towards monopolisation of the banking services market, and also the limitation of competition in banking.

The acquisition of stocks (or participatory shares) of credit organisations, and also the conclusion of agreements providing for the effectuation of control over the activity of credit organisations (or group of credit organisations) must not be contrary to antimonopoly rules.

Compliance with antimonopoly rules in the sphere of banking services shall be controlled by the State Committee of the Russian Federation for Antimonopoly Policy and Support of New Economic Structures, jointly with the Bank of Russia.

Article 33. Securing Repayment of Credits

Credits granted by a bank may be secured by the pledge of immoveable and moveable property, including State and other securities, bank guarantees, and other means provided for by federal laws or a contract.

In the event of a violation by the borrower of obligations under a contract, the bank shall have the right to recover the credits granted before time and the interest calculated thereon, if this has been provided for by the contract, and also levy execution against pledged property in the procedure established by a federal law.

Article 34. Announcement of Debtors to be Insolvent (or Bankrupt) and Payment of Indebtedness

A credit organisation shall be obliged to undertake all measures provided for by legislation of the Russian Federation to recover indebtedness.

A credit organisation shall have the right to apply to an arbitrazh court with an application concerning the initiation of proceedings with regard to a case concerning insolvency (or bankruptcy) with respect to debtors not performing their obligations with regard to payment of indebtedness in the procedure established by a federal law.

Chapter V. Branches, Representations, and Subsidiary Organisations of Credit Organisation on Territory of Foreign State

Article 35. Branches, Representations, and Subsidiary Organisations of Credit Organisation on Territory of Foreign State

A credit organisation may with the authorisation of the Bank of Russia create on the territory of a foreign State branches and, after notifying the Bank of Russia, representations.

A credit organisation may with the authorisation of and in accordance with the requirements of the Bank of Russia have subsidiary organisations on the territory of a foreign State.

The Bank of Russia shall not later than a three-month period from the moment of receipt of the respective petition notify the applicant in written form about its decision—consent or refusal. A refusal must be reasoned. If the Bank of Russia did not communicate the decision adopted within the said period, the respective authorisation of the Bank of Russia shall be considered to be received.

Chapter VI. Savings

Article 36. Bank Deposits of Natural Persons

A deposit—monetary means in the currency of the Russian Federation or foreign currency placed by natural persons for the purposes of keeping and of receiving revenue. Revenue with regard to a deposit shall be paid in monetary form in the form of interest. A deposit shall be returned to the depositor upon his first demand in the procedure provided for the deposit of the particular type by a federal law and respective contract.

Deposits shall be accepted only by banks having such right in accordance with a license issued by the Bank of Russia. Banks shall ensure the preservation of deposits and timeliness of the performance of their obligations to depositors. The attraction of means on deposit shall be formalised by a contract in written form in two examples, one of which shall be issued to the depositor.

The right to attract deposits of monetary means of natural persons shall be granted to banks from the date of State registration of which not less than two years have elapsed. In the event of the merger of banks the said period shall be calculated according to the bank having the earliest date of State registration. In the event of the transformation of the bank, the said period shall not be interrupted.

The preservation and return of deposits of natural persons in banks created by the State and banks more than 50% of the voting stocks (or participatory shares) of whose charter capital belongs to the State shall be guaranteed in the procedure provided for by federal laws.

Article 37. Depositors of Bank

Depositors may be citizens of the Russian Federation, foreign citizens, and stateless persons.

Depositors shall be free in the choice of bank for the placement of deposits of monetary means belonging to them and may have deposits in one or several banks.

Depositors may dispose of desposts, receive revenue on deposits, and perform noncash settlements in accordance with the contract.

Article 38. Federal Fund of Obligatory Insurance of Deposits

In order to ensure the guarantees of the return of means of citizens attracted by banks and contributory compensation of loss of revenue on invested means, the federal fund of obligatory insurance of deposits shall be created.

Participants of the federal fund of obligatory insurance of deposits shall be the Bank of Russia and banks attracting the means of citizens.

The procedure for the creation, forming, and use of means of the federal fund of obligatory insurance of deposits shall be determined by a federal law.

Article 39. Funds of Voluntary Insurance of Deposits

Banks shall have the right to create funds of voluntary insurance of deposits in order to ensure the return of deposits and payment of revenues with regard to them. Funds of voluntary insurance of deposits shall be created as noncommercial organisations.

The number of banks-founders of a fund of voluntary insurance of deposits must be not less than five with aggregate charter capital of not less than twenty-times the minimum amount of charter capital established by the Bank of Russia for banks on the date of creation of the fund.

The procedure for the creation, management, and activity of funds of voluntary insurance of deposits shall be determined by the charters and federal laws.

A bank shall be obliged to bring to the knowledge of clients their participation or nonparticipation in funds of voluntary insurance of deposits. In the event of participation in a fund of voluntary insurance of deposits the bank shall inform the client about the conditions of the insurance.

Chapter VII. Bookkeeping Records in Credit Organisations and Supervision Over Activity Thereof

Article 40. Rules of Bookkeeping Records in Credit Organisation

The rules for keeping bookkeeping records, submission of financial and statistical reports, and drawing up yearly reports by credit organisations shall be established by the Bank of Russia by taking into account international banking practice.

Article 41. Supervision Over Activity of Credit Organisation

Supervision over the activity of a credit organisation shall be effectuated by the Bank of Russia in accordance with federal laws.

Article 42. Auditor Verification of Credit Organisation, Banking Groups and Banking Holding Companies [as amended by Federal Law No. 82-ФЗ, 19 June 2001]

The reporting of a credit organisation shall be subject to annual verification by an auditor organisation having in accordance with legislation of the Russian Federation a license for the effectuation of such verifications. The reporting of banking groups and reporting of banking holding companies shall be subject to annual verification by an auditor organisation having in accordance with legislation of the Russian Federation a license for the effectuation of verifications of credit organisations and effectuating auditor verification of credit organisations for not less than two years. Licenses for the effectuation of audit verifications of credit organisations shall be issued in accordance with federal laws to auditor organisations effectuating auditor activity for not less than two years [as amended by Federal Law No. 82-ФЗ, 19 June 2001].

The auditor verification of a credit organisation, banking groups, and banking holding companies shall be effectuated in accordance with legislation of the Russian Federation [as amended by Federal Law No. 82-ФЗ, 19 June 2001].

An auditor organisation shall be obliged to draw up an opinion concerning the results of the auditor verification containing information concerning the reliability of financial reporting of the credit organisation, the fulfilment by it of obligatory normative standards established by the Bank of Russia, the quality of management of the credit organisation, the state of internal control and other provisions determined by federal laws and the charter of the credit organisation.

An auditor opinion shall be sent to the Bank of Russia within a three-month period from the day of submission to the Bank of Russia of yearly reports of the credit organisation, banking groups, and banking holding companies [as amended by Federal Law No. 82-ФЗ, 19 June 2001].

Article 43. Reporting of Credit Organisation, Reporting of Banking Groups, and Reporting of Banking Holding Companies [as amended by Federal Law No. 82-ФЗ, 19 June 2001]

A credit organisation shall submit to the Bank of Russia a yearly report (including bookkeeping balance sheet and report on profits and losses) after the confirmation of the reliability thereof by an auditor organisation. If a credit organisation has the possibility to render material (direct or indirect) influence on the activity of other juridical persons (except for credit organisations), it shall draw up and submit the said report on a consolidated basis in the procedure determined by the Bank of Russia [as amended by Federal Law No. 82-ФЗ, 19 June 2001].

A credit organisation shall publish in the open press a yearly report (including bookkeeping balance sheet and report on profits and losses) in the form and within the periods which are established by the Bank of Russia after confirmation of its reliability by an auditor organisation.

The head credit organisation of a banking group and head organisation of a banking holding company (or management company of a banking holding company) shall draw up and submit to the Bank of Russia for the purposes of effectuating supervision over the activity of credit organisations on a consolidated basis in the procedure determined by the Bank of Russia a consolidated report concerning the activity of the banking group and consolidated report concerning the activity of the banking holding company, each of which shall include a consolidated bookkeeping report, consolidated report of profits and losses, and also a calculation of the risks on a consolidated basis [as amended by Federal Law No. 82-ФЗ, 19 June 2001].

For the purpose of drawing up, submitting, and publishing the consolidated report on the activity of a banking group within the composition of the said consolidated report must be included the reporting of other juridical persons with respect to which credit organisations within the banking group may exert material (direct or indirect) influence on the activity and decisions adopted by the management organs of the said juridical persons [added by Federal Law No. 82-ФЗ, 19 June 2001].

For the purpose of drawing up, submitting, and publishing the consolidated report on the activity of a banking holding company within the composition of the said consolidated report must be included the reporting of other juridical persons with respect to which the head organisation within the banking holding company (or management company of the banking holding company) and/or credit organisations within the banking holding company may exert material (direct or indirect) influence on the activity and decisions adopted by the management organs of the said juridical persons [added by Federal Law No. 82-ФЗ, 19 June 2001].

Juridical persons with respect to which the head credit organisation of a banking group, head organisation of a banking holding company (or management company of a banking holding company) exert material (direct or indirect) influence shall be obliged for the purpose of drawing up the consolidated reporting to submit to them a report on their activity [added by Federal Law No. 82-ФЗ, 19 June 2001].

The head credit organisation of a banking group and head organisation of a banking holding company (or management company of a banking holding company) shall not have the right to divulge information received from other juridical persons within the particular banking group (or particular banking holding company) concerning their activity, except for instances provided for by the present Federal Law or instances arising from the tasks of publication of consolidated reporting [added by Federal Law No. 82-ФЗ, 19 June 2001].

FEDERAL LAW ON INSOLVENCY (OR BANKRUPTCY)

[Federal Law of 26 October 2002,
No. 127-ФЗ. СЗ РФ (2002), no. 43, item 4190]

Chapter I	General Provisions	366
Chapter II	Prevention of Bankruptcy	398
Chapter III	Examination of Cases Concerning Bankruptcy in Arbitrazh Court	398
Chapter IV	Observation	417
Chapter V	Financial Recuperation	428
Chapter VI	External Administration	445
Chapter VII	Bankruptcy Proceeding	472
Chapter VIII	Amicable Agreement	494
Chapter IX	Peculiarities of Bankruptcy of Individual Categories of Debtors–Juridical Persons	507
Chapter X	Bankruptcy of Citizen	528
Chapter XI	Simplified Procedures of Bankruptcy	537
Chapter XII	Concluding and Transitional Provisions	540

Chapter I. General Provisions

Article 1. Relations Regulated by Present Federal Law

1. In accordance with the Civil Code of the Russian Federation the present Federal Law establishes the grounds for deeming a debtor to be insolvent (or bankrupt), regulates the procedure and conditions for the effectuation of measures with regard to the prevention of insolvency (or bankruptcy) and the procedure and conditions for conducting procedures of bankruptcy and other relations arising in the event of the inability of the debtor to satisfy in full the demands of creditors.

2. The operation of the present Federal Law shall extend to all juridical persons, except for treasury enterprises, institutions, political parties, and religious organizations.

3. Relations connected with the insolvency (or bankruptcy) of citizens, including individual entrepreneurs, shall be regulated by the present Federal Law.

Norms which regulate the insolvency (or bankruptcy) of citizens, including individual entrepreneurs, and are contained in other federal laws, may be applied only after the making of respective changes in and additions to the present Federal Law.

4. If other rules have been established by an international treaty of the Russian Federation than those which have been provided by the present Federal Law, the rules of the international treaty of the Russian Federation shall apply.

5. The provisions of the present Federal Law shall apply to relations regulated by the present Federal Law with the participation of foreign persons as creditors unless provided otherwise by an international treaty of the Russian Federation.

6. Decisions of courts of foreign States with regard to cases concerning insolvency (or bankruptcy) shall be recognised on the territory of the Russian Federation in accordance with international treaties of the Russian Federation. In the absence of international treaties of the Russian Federation decisions of courts of foreign States with regard to cases concerning insolvency (or bankruptcy) shall be recognised on the territory of the Russian Federation on the principle of reciprocity unless provided otherwise by a federal law.

Article 2. Basic Concepts Used in Present Federal Law

For the purposes of the present Federal Law the following basic concepts have been used:

insolvency (or bankruptcy)—the inability recognised by an arbitrazh court of a debtor to satisfy the demands of creditors in full with regard to monetary obligations and/or to perform the duty with regard to payment of obligatory payments (hereinafter—bankruptcy);

debtor—a citizen, including an individual entrepreneur, or juridical person who has proved to be unable to satisfy the demands of creditors with regard to monetary obligations and/or to perform the duty with regard to payment of obligatory payments during a period established by the present Federal Law;

monetary obligation—duty of a debtor to pay to a creditor a determined monetary amount with regard to a civil-law transaction and/or other grounds provided for by the Civil Code of the Russian Federation;

obligatory payments—the taxes, charges, and other obligatory contributions to the budget of the respective level and State extrabudgetary funds in the procedure and on the conditions which are determined by legislation of the Russian Federation;

executive of debtor—one-man executive organ of a juridical person or executive of a collegial executive organ, and also other person effectuating in accordance with a federal law activity in the name of the juridical person without a power of attorney;

creditors—persons having with respect to a debtor the right of demand with regard to monetary obligations and other obligations, concerning obligatory payments, the payment for severance benefits, and the payment of labour of persons working under a labour contract;

bankruptcy creditors—creditors with regard to monetary obligations, except for empowered agencies, citizens to whom the debtor bears responsibility for causing harm to life or health, moral harm, has obligations with regard to the payment of remuneration under authors' contracts, and also the founders (or participants) of a debtor with regard to obligations arising from such participation;

empowered agencies—federal agencies of executive power empowered by the Government of the Russian Federation to submit in a case concerning bankruptcy and in the procedures of bankruptcy demands concerning the payment of obligatory payments and demands of the Russian Federation with regard to monetary obligations, and also agencies of executive power of subjects of the Russian Federation and agencies of local self-government empowered to submit in a case concerning bankruptcy and in procedures of bankruptcy demands with regard to monetary obligations respectively of subjects of the Russian Federation and municipal formations;

pre-judicial sanation—measures with regard to the restoration of the ability to pay of a debtor taken by the owner of property of the debtor-unitary enterprise, founders (or participants) of the debtor, creditors of the debtor, and other persons for the purpose of prevention of bankruptcy;

observation—a procedure of bankruptcy applicable to a debtor for the purpose of ensuring the preservation of property of the debtor, conducting an analysis of the financial state of the debtor, drawing up a register of demands of creditors, and conducting the first meeting of creditors;

financial recuperation—a procedure of bankruptcy applicable to a debtor for the purpose of restoration of his ability to pay and repayment of indebtedness in accordance with a schedule for the repayment of indebtedness;

external administration—a procedure of bankruptcy applicable to a debtor for the purposes of restoration of his ability to pay;

bankruptcy proceeding—a procedure of bankruptcy applicable to a debtor for the purposes of the commensurate satisfaction of the demands of creditors;

amicable agreement—a procedure of bankruptcy applicable to any stage of consideration of a case concerning bankruptcy by means of reaching an agreement between the debtor and creditors;

representative of founders (or participants) of debtor—chairman of council of directors (or supervisory council) or other analogous collegial management organ of debtor, or person elected by council of directors (or supervisory council) or other analogous collegial management organ of a debtor, or person elected by founders (or participants) of a debtor to represent their legal interests when conducting procedures of bankruptcy;

representative of owner of property of debtor-unitary enterprise—person empowered by owner of property of a debtor-unitary enterprise to represent its legal interests when conducting procedures of bankruptcy;

representative of committee of creditors—person empowered by committee of creditors to participate in arbitrazh proceeding with regard to a case concerning the bankruptcy of debtor in the name of a committee of creditors;

representative of meeting of creditors—person empowered by a meeting of creditors to participate in an arbitrazh proceeding with regard to a case concerning bankruptcy of a debtor in the name of the meeting of creditors;

arbitrazh administrator (or temporary administrator, administrative administrator, external administrator, or bankruptcy administrator)—citizen of the Russian Federation confirmed by an arbitrazh court to conduct procedures of bankruptcy and to effectuate other powers established by the present Federal Law and who is a member of one of the self-regulating organizations;

temporary administrator—arbitrazh administrator confirmed by an arbitrazh court to conduct observation in accordance with the present Federal Law;

administrative administrator—arbitrazh administrator confirmed by an arbitrazh court to conduct financial recuperation in accordance with the present Federal Law;

external administrator—arbitrazh administrator confirmed by an arbitrazh court to conduct external administration and effectuate other powers established by the present Federal Law;

bankruptcy administrator—arbitrazh administrator confirmed by an arbitrazh court to conduct a bankruptcy proceeding and effectuate other powers established by the present Federal Law;

moratorium—suspension of the performance of monetary obligations by a debtor and the payment of obligatory payments;

representative of workers of debtor—person empowered by workers of a debtor to represent their legal interests when conducting procedures of bankruptcy;

self-regulating organisation of arbitrazh administrators (hereinafter also self-regulating organisation)—noncommercial organisation which is based on membership created by citizens of the Russian Federation, included in the unified State register of self-regulating organisations of arbitrazh administrators, and whose purposes of activity are the regulation and ensuring the activity of arbitrazh administrators;

regulating organization—federal agency of executive power effectuating control over activity of self-regulating organisations of arbitrazh administrators.

Article 3. Indicia of Bankruptcy

1. A citizen shall be considered not able to satisfy the demands of creditors with regard to monetary obligations and/or to perform the duty with regard to the payment of obligatory payments if the respective obligations were not performed thereby within three months from the date when they should have been performed and if the amount of obligations thereof exceeds the value of property belonging thereto.

2. A juridical person shall be considered not able to satisfy demands of creditors with regard to monetary obligations and/or to perform the duty with regard to the payment of obligatory payments if the respective obligations and/or duty has not been performed thereby within three months from the date when they should have been performed.

3. The provisions provided for by points 1 and 2 of the present Article shall apply unless established otherwise by the present Federal Law.

Article 4. Composition and Amount of Monetary Obligations and Obligatory Payments

1. The composition and amount of monetary obligations and obligatory payments shall be determined on the date of filing an application in an arbitrazh court concerning the deeming of a debtor to be bankrupt unless provided otherwise by the present Federal Law.

The composition and amount of monetary obligations and obligatory payments which arose before the acceptance by an arbitrazh court of an application concerning the deeming of a debtor to be bankrupt and declared after the acceptance by the arbitrazh court of such application and before the adoption of a decision concerning the deeming of a debtor to be bankrupt and the opening of a bankruptcy proceeding shall be determined on the date of introduction of each procedure of bankruptcy following after the ensuing of the period of performance of the respective obligation.

The composition and amount of monetary obligations and obligatory payments which arose before the acceptance by the arbitrazh court of the application concerning the deeming of a debtor to be bankrupt and declared after the adoption by the arbitrazh court of a decision concerning the deeming of a debtor to be bankrupt and the opening of a bankruptcy proceeding shall be determined on the date of opening the bankruptcy proceeding.

The composition and amount of monetary obligations and obligatory payments expressed in foreign currency shall be determined in rubles at the exchange rate established by the Central Bank of the Russian Federation on the date of the introduction of each procedure of bankruptcy following after the ensuing of the period of performance of the respective obligation.

2. In order to determine the presence of the indicia of bankruptcy of a debtor there shall be taken into account:

the amount of monetary obligations, including the amount of indebtedness for goods transferred, work fulfilled, and services rendered, and amounts of a loan, taking into account interest subject to payment by the debtor, the amount of indebtedness which arose as a consequence of unfounded enrichment, and the amount of indebtedness which arose as a consequence of the causing of harm to the property of creditors, except for obligations to citizens to whom the debtor bears responsibility for causing harm to life or health, obligations with regard to the payment of severance benefits and payment of labour of persons working under a labour contract, obligations with regard to payment of remuneration under an authors' contract, and also obligations to founders (or participants) of the debtor arising from such participation;

the amount of obligatory payments without taking into account fines (or forfeits) and other financial sanctions established by legislation of the Russian Federation.

Penalties (or fines, forfeits) subject to application for the failure to perform or improper performance of an obligation, interest for delay of payment, losses subject to compensation for the failure to perform an obligation, and also other property and/or financial sanctions, including for the failure to perform a duty with regard to the payment of obligatory payments, shall not be taken into account when determining the presence of the indicia of bankruptcy of the debtor.

3. The amount of monetary obligations or obligatory payments shall be considered to be established if it was determined by a court in the procedure provided for by the present Federal Law.

4. In instances when a debtor contests demands of creditors, the amount of monetary obligations or obligatory payments shall be determined by the arbitrazh court in the procedure provided for by the present Federal Law.

5. Demands of creditors with regard to obligations which are not monetary may be presented in a court and shall be considered by the court or arbitrazh court in the procedure provided for by procedure legislation.

Article 5. Current Payments

1. For the purposes of the present Federal Law current payments is understood as monetary obligations and obligatory payments which arose after the acceptance of an application concerning the deeming of a debtor to be a bankrupt, and also monetary obligations and obligatory payments whose period of performance has ensued after the introduction of the respective procedure of bankruptcy.

2. Demands of creditors with regard to current payments shall not be subject to inclusion in the register of demands of creditors. Creditors with regard to current payments shall when conducting respective procedures of bankruptcy not be deemed to be persons participating in the case concerning bankruptcy.

3. Satisfaction of demands of creditors with regard to current payments in the course of external administration shall be in the procedure established by the present Federal Law.

Article 6. Consideration of Cases Concerning Bankruptcy

1. Cases concerning bankruptcy shall be considered by an arbitrazh court.

2. Unless provided otherwise by the present Federal Law, a case concerning bankruptcy may be instituted by an arbitrazh court on condition that demands against a debtor-juridical person in aggregate comprise not less than one hundred thousand rubles, and against a citizen-debtor—not less than ten thousand rubles, and also there are indicia of bankruptcy established by Article 3 of the present Federal Law.

3. Demands confirmed by the decision of a court which has entered into legal force, arbitrazh court, and arbitration court shall be taken into account in order to institute a case concerning bankruptcy upon the application of a bankruptcy creditor, and also upon the application of an empowered agency with regard to monetary obligations.

Demands of empowered agencies concerning the payment of obligatory payments shall be taken into account in order to institute a case concerning bankruptcy if they have been confirmed by decision of a tax agency or customs agency concerning the recovery of indebtedness at the expense of property of the debtor.

Article 7. Right to Apply to Arbitrazh Court

1. A debtor, bankruptcy creditor, and empowered agencies shall possess the right to apply to an arbitrazh court with an application concerning the deeming of a debtor to be bankrupt.

2. The right to apply to an arbitrazh court shall arise with a bankruptcy creditor and empowered agency with regard to monetary obligations upon the expiry of thirty days from the date of sending (or presenting for execution) the document of execution to the court bailiffs service and copy thereof to the debtor.

The right to apply to an arbitrazh court shall arise with an empowered agency with regard to obligatory payments upon the expiry of thirty days from the date of adoption of the decision specified in Article 6(3), paragraph two, of the present Federal Law.

3. The partial performance of demands of a bankruptcy creditor or empowered agency shall not be grounds for the refusal by an arbitrazh court to accept an application concerning the deeming of a debtor to be a bankrupt if the amount of the unperformed demands comprises not less than the amount determined in accordance with Article 6(2) of the present Federal Law.

Article 8. Right to File Application of Debtor in Arbitrazh Court

A debtor shall have the right to file an application in an arbitrazh court in the event of foreseeing bankruptcy when circumstances are present which obviously testify to the fact that it is not in a state to perform monetary obligations and/or the duty with regard to the payment of obligatory payments within the established period.

Article 9. Duty of Debtor with Regard to Filing Application of Debtor in Arbitrazh Court

1. An executive of a debtor or individual entrepreneur shall be obliged to have recourse with an application of a debtor to an arbitrazh court if:

satisfaction of the demands of one creditor or several creditors will lead to the impossibility of performance by the debtor of monetary obligations, duties with regard to the payment of obligatory payments, and/or other payments in full to other creditors;

an organ of a debtor empowered in accordance with the constitutive documents of the debtor to adopt a decision concerning liquidation of the debtor has adopted a decision concerning recourse to an arbitrazh court with an application of the debtor;

an organ empowered by the owner of property of a debtor-unitary enterprise has adopted a decision concerning recourse to an arbitrazh court with an application of the debtor;

levy of execution against property of a debtor materially complicates or makes impossible the economic activity of the debtor;

in other instances provided for by the present Federal Law.

2. A debtor shall be obliged to apply to an arbitrazh court with an application of the debtor if when conducting the liquidation of a juridical person the impossibility is established of satisfaction of the demands of creditors in full.

3. An application of the debtor must be sent to an arbitrazh court in the instances provided for by the present Article not later than a month from the date of the arising of the respective circumstances.

Article 10. Responsibility of Citizen-Debtor and Management Organs of Debtor

1. In the event of a violation by an executive of the debtor or by a founder (or participant) of the debtor, owner of the property of a debtor-unitary enterprise, members of the management organs of the debtor, members of the liquidation commission (or liquidator), and citizen-debtor of the provisions of the present Federal Law, the said persons shall be obliged to compensate the losses caused as a result of such violation.

2. The failure to fill the application of a debtor in an arbitrazh court in the instances and within the period which have been established by Article 9 of the present Federal Law shall entail subsidiary responsibility of the persons on whom the duty has been placed by the present Federal Law with regard to the adoption of a decision concerning the filing of an application of a debtor in an arbitrazh court and the filing of such application with regard to obligations of the debtor which arose after expiry of the period provided for by Article 9(3) of the present Federal Law.

3. If the application of a debtor has been filed by a debtor in an arbitrazh court when the debtor has the possibility to satisfy demands of creditors in full or the debtor has not taken measures with regard to contesting unsubstantiated demands of the applicant, the debtor shall bear to the creditors responsibility for losses caused by instituting a case concerning bankruptcy or unsubstantiated recognition of the demands of creditors.

4. In the event of bankruptcy of a debtor through the fault of the founders (or participants) of a debtor, owner of property of a debtor-unitary enterprise, or other persons, including through the fault of an executive of the debtor who has the right to give instructions binding upon the debtor or has the possibility otherwise to determine the actions thereof, subsidiary responsibility for the obligations thereof may be placed on the founders (or participants) of the debtor or other persons in the event of the insufficiency of property of the debtor.

5. In instances established by a federal law the executive of a debtor-natural person, members of management organs of a debtor-natural person, and also a debtor citizen, may be brought to criminal or administrative responsibility.

Article 11. Rights of Creditors and Empowered Agencies

1. Empowered agencies in the procedure established by the Government of the Russian Federation and bankruptcy creditors shall possess the right to file an application concerning the deeming of a debtor to be bankrupt.

2. Agencies of executive power and organisations endowed in accordance with legislation of the Russian Federation with the right to recover indebtedness with regard to obligatory payments shall have the right to participate in judicial sessions with regard to the consideration of the substantiation of demands with regard to these payments and grounds for the inclusion of these demands in the register of demands of creditors.

Article 12. Meeting of Creditors

1. Bankruptcy creditors and empowered agencies shall be participants of a meeting of creditors with the right to vote. A representative of workers of the debtor, representative of the founders (or participants) of the debtor, and representative of the owner of property of a debtor-unitary enterprise who has the right to speak with regard to questions of the agenda of the meeting of creditors shall have the right to participate in the meeting of creditors without the right to vote. In instances when a sole bankruptcy creditor or empowered agency participates in a case concerning bankruptcy the decisions relegated to the competence of a meeting of creditors of the meeting of creditors shall be adopted by that creditor or empowered agency.

The organisation and conducting of the meeting of creditors shall be effectuated by the arbitrazh administrator.

2. There shall be relegated to the exclusive competence of the meeting of creditors:

the adoption of the decision concerning the introduction and change of the period for conducting financial recuperation, external administration, and recourse with a respective petition to an arbitrazh court;

the confirmation and change of the plan of external administration;

the confirmation of the plan of financial recuperation and schedule for repayment of indebtedness;

the confirmation of requirements for candidacies of administrative administrator, external administrator, and bankruptcy administrator;

the selection of the self-regulating organisation to submit to an arbitrazh court the candidacies for administrative administrator, external administrator, and bankruptcy administrator;

the selection of register-holder from among accredited self-regulating organisations;

the adoption of the decision concerning the conclusion of an amicable agreement;

the adoption of a decision concerning recourse to the arbitrazh court with a petition concerning the deeming of a debtor to be a bankrupt and the opening of a bankruptcy proceeding;

the adoption of decisions concerning the formation of the committee of creditors, determination of the quantitative composition, election of members of the committee of creditors, and the termination before time of the powers of the committee of creditors;

relegation to the competence of the committee of creditors the adoption of decisions which in accordance with the present Federal Law shall be adopted by the meeting of creditors or committee of creditors, except for those decisions of the meeting of creditors which in accordance with the present Article have been relegated to the exclusive competence of the meeting of creditors;

election of a representative of the meeting of creditors.

Questions relegated in accordance with the present Federal Law to the exclusive competence of the meeting of creditors may not be transferred for decision to other persons or agencies.

3. A bankruptcy creditor and empowered agency shall possess at the meeting of creditors the number of votes proportional to the amount of their demands against the total amount of demands with regard to monetary obligations and concerning payment of obligatory payments included in the register of demands of creditors on the date of conducting the meeting of creditors in accordance with the present Federal Law.

Penalties (or fine, forfeits) subject to application for the failure to perform or the improper performance of an obligation, interest for delay of payment, losses subject to compensation for failure to perform an obligation, and also other property and/or financial sanctions, including for the failure to perform a duty with regard to payment of obligatory payments, shall not be taken into account for the purpose of determining the number of votes at a meeting of creditors.

4. A meeting of creditors shall be competent if the bankruptcy creditors and empowered agencies included in the register of demands of creditors and possessing more than half of the votes of the total number of votes of bankruptcy creditors and empowered agencies included in the register of demands of creditors were present at it. A meeting of creditors convoked a second time shall be competent if bankruptcy creditors and empowered agencies included in the register of demands of creditors and possessing more than thirty per cent of the votes of the total number of votes of bankruptcy creditors and empowered agencies included in the register of demands of creditors were present at it, on condition that the bankruptcy creditors and empowered agencies were duly notified in accordance with the present Federal Law about the time and place of conducting the meeting of creditors.

5. If a meeting of creditors is not conducted by an arbitrazh administrator within the periods established by Article 14(3) of the present Federal Law, the meeting of creditors may be conducted by the persons demanding the convocation thereof.

6. By decision of the meeting of creditors or temporary administrator, the register-holder conducting the register of demands of creditors may when conducting the meeting of creditors effectuate the following functions:
    verify the powers and register persons participating in the meeting of creditors;
    ensure the established procedure for voting;
    count the votes;
    draw up the protocol concerning the results of the voting.

7. A protocol of the meeting of creditors shall be drawn up in two examples, one of which shall be sent to the arbitrazh court not later than five days from the date of conducting the meeting of creditors unless another period has been established by the present Federal Law.
    In the event of conducting a meeting of creditors in the procedure provided for by point 5 of the present Article, the protocol of the meeting of creditors shall be drawn up in three examples, the first of which shall be sent to the arbitrazh court, the second—to the arbitrazh administrator not later than five days from the date of conducting the meeting of creditors. The third example of the meeting of creditors shall be kept with the person who conducted the meeting.
    To the protocol of the meeting of creditors must be appended copies of:
    the register of demands of creditors on the date of conducting the meeting of creditors;

the ballots for voting;

the documents confirming the powers of participants of the meeting;

the materials submitted to participants of the meeting for familiarisation and/or confirmation;

the documents which are evidence testifying to proper notification of bankruptcy creditors and empowered agencies concerning the date and place of conducting the meeting of creditors;

other documents at the discretion of the arbitrazh administrator or on the basis of a decision of the meeting of creditors.

Originals of the said documents shall be subject to keeping by the arbitrazh administrator or register-holder until completion of the arbitrazh proceeding with regard to the case concerning bankruptcy unless another period has been established by the present Federal Law and shall be submitted at the request of the arbitrazh court or in other instances provided for by a federal law.

An arbitrazh administrator shall be obliged to ensure access to copies of the said documents to persons participating in the case concerning bankruptcy, and also to a representative of workers of the debtor, representative of the founders (or participants) of the debtor, and representative of the owner of the property of the debtor-unitary enterprise.

Article 13. Notifications Concerning Conducting of Meeting of Creditors

1. For the purposes of the present Federal Law proper notification shall be deemed to be the sending to a bankruptcy creditor, empowered agency, and also other person having in accordance with the present Federal Law the right to participate in the meeting of creditors, communications concerning the conducting of the meeting of creditors by post not later than fourteen days before the day of conducting the meeting of creditors or other means ensuring the receipt of such communication not later than five days before the day of conducting the meeting of creditors.

2. If the number of bankruptcy creditors and empowered agencies exceeds five hundred, the publication of a communication concerning the conducting of a meeting of creditors in the mass media in the procedure determined by Article 28 of the present Federal Law shall be deemed to be proper notification.

In the event of the impossibility of eliciting information needed for personal notification of a bankruptcy creditor at the place of permanent or preferred residing or whereabouts or other available in accordance with the present Federal Law the right to participate in the meeting of creditors of the person, or if there are other circumstances making impossible such notification of the said persons, the publication of information concerning the conducting of a meeting of creditors in the procedure determined by Article 28 of the present Federal Law shall be deemed to be proper notification of such persons.

3. The communication concerning the conducting of a meeting of creditors must contain the following information:

the name and location of the debtor and address thereof;

the date, time, and place of conducting the meeting of creditors;

the agenda of the meeting of creditors;

the procedure for familiarisation with the materials subject to consideration by the meeting of creditors;

the procedure for registration of the participants of the meeting.

Article 14. Procedure for Convocation of Meeting of Creditors

1. A meeting of creditors shall be convoked at the initiative of:

the arbitrazh administrator;

the committee of creditors;

the bankruptcy creditors and/or empowered agencies whose rights of demand comprise not less than 10 per cent of the total amount of demands of creditors with regard to monetary obligations and concerning payment of obligatory payments included in the register of demands of creditors;

one-third of the total number of bankruptcy creditors and empowered agencies.

2. The questions subject to inclusion on the agenda of the meeting of creditors must be formulated in the demand concerning the conducting of a meeting of creditors.

The arbitrazh administrator shall not have the right to include changes in the formulation of questions on the agenda of the meeting of creditors convoked at the demand of the committee of creditors, bankruptcy creditors, and/or empowered agencies.

3. A meeting of creditors at the demand of the committee of creditors, bankruptcy creditors and/or empowered agencies shall be conducted by the arbitrazh administrator not later than three weeks from the date of receipt by the arbitrazh administrator of the demand of the committee of creditors, bankruptcy creditors, and/or empowered agencies concerning the conducting of a meeting of creditors, unless another period has been established by the present Federal Law.

4. A meeting of creditors shall be conducted at the location of the debtor or management organs of the debtor unless established otherwise by the meeting of creditors.

In the event of the impossibility of conducting a meeting of creditors at the location of the debtor or management organs of the debtor, the place of conducting the meeting of creditors shall be determined by the arbitrazh administrator.

The date, time, and place of conducting the meeting of creditors must not prevent participation in such meeting of creditors or representatives thereof, and also other persons having the right in accordance with the present Federal Law to take part in a meeting of creditors.

Article 15. Procedure for Adoption of Decisions of Meeting of Creditors

1. Decisions of a meeting of creditors with regard to questions put for voting shall be adopted by a majority of votes from the number of votes of bankruptcy creditors and empowered agencies present at a meeting of creditors, unless provided otherwise by the present Federal Law.

2. Decisions shall be adopted by a majority of votes from the total number of votes of bankruptcy creditors and empowered agencies concerning:

the formation of the committee of creditors, determination of the quantitative composition and powers of the committee of creditors and election of members thereof;

the termination before time of the powers of the committee of creditors and election of a new composition of the committee of creditors;

the introduction of financial recuperation, change of the periods for teh conducting thereof, and recourse with a respective petition to an arbitrazh court;

the confirmation of the schedule for repayment of indebtedness;

the introduction and extension of external administration and recourse with a respective petition to an arbitrazh court;

the confirmation of the plan of the external administrator;

the recourse to an arbitrazh court with a petition concerning the deeming of a debtor to be a bankrupt and the opening of a bankruptcy proceeding;

the selection of a self-regulating organisation from whose members the arbitrazh court shall confirm the arbitrazh administrator;

the recourse to an arbitrazh court with a petition to remove the arbitrazh administrator;

the inclusion on the agenda of the meeting of creditors of additional questions and decisions adopted with regard to them;

the conclusion of an amicable agreement in the procedure and on the conditions which have been established by Article 150(2) of the present Federal Law.

3. If at a meeting of creditors convoked to adopt decisions provided for by pointg 2 of the present Article the number of votes of bankruptcy creditors and empowered agencies are not represented which are necessary in order to adopt decisions, a second meeting of creditors shall be convoked which is empowered to adopt such decisions if bankruptcy creditors and empowered agencies, the number of whose votes comprised more than thirty per cent of the total number of votes of bankruptcy creditors and empowered agencies voted for them, on condition that the time and place of conducting the meeting of creditors were duly notified to the bankruptcy creditors and empowered agencies.

4. If a decision of the meeting of creditors violates the rights and legal interests of persons participating in the case concerning bankruptcy, persons participating

in the arbitrazh proceeding with regard to the case concerning bankruptcy, third persons, or was adopted with a violation of the limits of competence of a meeting of creditors established by the present Federal Law, such decision may be deemed to be invalid by the arbitrazh court considering the case concerning bankruptcy upon the application of the persons participating in the case concerning bankruptcy, persons participating in the arbitrazh proceeding with regard to the case concerning bankruptcy, and third persons.

An application to deem the decision of a meeting of creditors to be invalid may be filed by a person duly notified about the conducting of the meeting of creditors which adopted such decision within twenty days from the date of adoption of such decision.

An application to deem the decision of a meeting of creditors to be invalid may be filed by a person not duly notified about the conducting of the meeting of creditors which adopted such decision within twenty days from the date when such person knew or should have known about the decisions adopted by the said meeting of creditors.

5. The ruling of an arbitrazh court concerning the deeming of the decision of a meeting of creditors to be invalid or refusal to deem invalid the decision of a meeting of creditors shall be subject to immediate execution and may be appealed in the procedure provided for by Article 61(3) of the present Federal Law.

Article 16. Register of Demands of Creditors

1. The register of demands of creditors shall be conducted by the arbitrazh administrator or register-holder.

The register of demands of creditors as register-holder shall be conducted by professional participants of the securities market effectuating activity with regard to conducting the register of possessors of securities.

A register-holder shall be obliged to effectuate its activity in accordance with the general rules of activity of the arbitrazh administrator affecting the content and procedure for conducting the register of demands of creditors and confirmed by the Government of the Russian Federation.

2. A decision concerning the enlistment of a register-holder to conduct a register of demands of creditors and the selection of a register-holder shall be adopted by the meeting of creditors. The decision before the date of conducting the first meeting of creditors concerning the enlistment of a register-holder to conduct the register of demands of creditors and the selection of a register-holder shall be adopted by the temporary administrator.

The decision of a meeting of creditors concerning the selection of a register-holder must contain the amount for payment of services of the register-holder agreed with the register-holder.

3. An arbitrazh administrator shall be obliged to conclude a respective contract with the register-holder not later than five days from the date of selection of the register-holder by the meeting of creditors.

The contract with the register-holder may be concluded only when he has a contract of insurance of responsibility in the event of causing losses to persons participating in the case concerning bankruptcy.

Information concerning the register-holder must be submitted by the arbitrazh administrator to the arbitrazh court not later than five days from the date of conclusion of the contract.

Payment of services of the register-holder shall be effectuated at the expense of means of the debtor if the meeting of creditors has not established the source for payment of services of the register-holder.

4. A register-holder shall be obliged to compensate losses caused by the failure to perform or the improper performance of duties provided for by the present Federal Law.

If the conducting of the register of demands of creditors has been transferred to a register-holder, the arbitrazh administrator shall not bear responsibility for the correctness of the conducting of the register of demands of creditors and shall not be liable for the commission by the register-holder of other actions (or failure to act) which cause or may cause damage to the debtor and creditors thereof.

5. The recording of demands of creditors shall be conducted in the currency of the Russian Federation in the register of demands of creditors. Demands of creditors expressed in a foreign currency shall be taken into account in the register of demands of creditors in the procedure established by Article 4 of the present Federal Law.

6. Demands of creditors shall be included in the register of demands of creditors and excluded therefrom by the arbitrazh administrator or register-holder exclusively on the basis of judicial acts which have entered into force establishing the composition and amount thereof unless determined otherwise by the present point.

Demands concerning the payment of severance benefits and payment for labour of persons working under a labour contract shall be included in the register of demands of creditors by the arbitrazh administrator or register-holder upon the submission of the arbitrazh administrator.

Demands concerning the payment of severance benefits and payment for labour of persons working under a labour contract shall be excluded from the register of demands of creditors by the arbitrazh administrator or register-holder exclusively on the basis of judicial acts which have entered into legal force.

If conducting the register of demands of creditors is effectuated by a register-holder, judicial acts establishing the amount of demands of creditors shall be sent by the arbitrazh court to the register-holder in order to include the respective demands in the register of demands of creditors.

7. Information concerning each creditor, the amount of demands thereof against the debtor, the priority of satisfaction of each demand of the creditor, and also the grounds for the arising of demands of creditors, shall be specified in the register of demands of creditors.

When declaring demands, a creditor shall be obliged to specify information about himself, including surname, forename, patronymic, passport data (for a natural person), name and location (for a juridical person), and also banking requisites (when there are such).

8. A person whose demands are included in the register of demands of creditors shall be obliged to inform in a timely manner the arbitrazh administrator or register-holder concerning a change of information specified in point 7 of the present Article.

In the event of the failure to submit such information or of the untimely submission thereof the arbitrazh administrator or register-holder and the debtor shall not bear responsibility for losses caused in connection therewith.

9. The arbitrazh administrator or register-holder shall be obliged at the demand of a creditor or empowered representative within five work days from the date of receipt of such demand to send to the said creditor or empowered representative thereof an extract from the register of demands of creditors concerning the amount, composition, and priority of satisfaction of his demands, and if the amount of indebtedness to the creditor comprises not less than one per cent of total creditor indebtedness, to send to the said creditor or empowered representative thereof a copy attested by the arbitrazh administrator of the register of demands of creditors.

Expenses for the preparation and sending of such extract and copy of the register shall be placed on the creditor.

10. Disagreements arising between bankruptcy creditors, empowered agencies, and the arbitrazh administrator concerning the composition, amount, and priority of satisfaction of demands of creditors with regard to monetary obligations or payment of obligatory payments shall be considered by the arbitrazh court in the procedure provided for by the present Federal Law.

Disagreements with regard to demands of creditors or empowered agencies confirmed by the decision of a court which has entered into legal force in the part of the composition and amount thereof shall not be subject to consideration by the arbitrazh court, and application concerning such disagreements shall be subject to return without consideration, except for disagreements connected with the execution of judicial acts or review thereof.

11. Disagreements arising between the representative of workers of the debtor and the arbitrazh administrator and connected with the priority, composition, and amount of demands concerning the payment of severance benefits and payment for labour of persons working under labour contracts shall be considered by an arbitrazh court in the procedure provided for by the present Federal Law.

Labour disputes between the debtor and a worker of the debtor shall be considered in the procedure determined by labour legislation and civil procedure legislation.

Article 17. Committee of Creditors

1. The committee of creditors shall represent the legal interests of bankruptcy creditors and empowered agencies and shall effectuate control over the actions of an arbitrazh administrator, and also shall realize other powers granted by the meeting of creditors in the procedure provided for by the present Federal Law.

2. If the number of bankruptcy creditors and empowered agencies comprises less than fifty, the meeting of creditors may not adopt a decision concerning the formation of the committee of creditors.

3. The committee of creditors shall in order to effectuate the functions placed on it have the right to:

demand that the arbitrazh administrator or executive of the debtor provide information concerning the financial state of the debtor and the course of the procedure of bankruptcy;

appeal to an arbitrazh court actions of the arbitrazh administrator;

adopt decisions concerning the convocation of a meeting of creditors;

adopt decisions concerning recourse to the meeting of creditors with a recommendation to remove the arbitrazh administrator from the performance of his duties;

adopt other decisions, and also perform other actions in the event of the provision of such powers to the meeting of creditors in the procedure established by the present Federal Law.

4. The quantitative composition of the committee of creditors shall be determined by the meeting of creditors, but many not be less than three persons nor more than eleven persons.

5. When deciding questions at a session of the committee of creditors each member of the committee of creditors shall possess one vote.
Transfer of the right to vote by a member of the committee of creditors to another person shall not be permitted.

6. Decisions of the committee of creditors shall be adopted by a majority of votes of the total number of members of the committee of members.

7. The committee of creditors shall in order to realize its powers have the right to elect its representative. Such decision shall be formalised by a protocol of a session of the committee of creditors.

8. The Reglament of work of the committee of creditors shall be determined by a committee of creditors.

Article 18. Election of Committee of Creditors

1. A committee of creditors shall be elected by the meeting of creditors from among natural persons upon the proposal of bankruptcy creditors and empowered agencies for the period of conducting observation, financial recuperation, external administration, and bankruptcy proceeding.

State and municipal employees may be elected as members of a committee of creditors upon the proposal of empowered agencies.

By decision of the meeting of creditors the powers of the committee of creditors may be terminated before time.

2. Elections of the committee of creditors shall be effectuated by cumulative voting.

When electing the committee of creditors each bankruptcy creditor and each empowered agency shall possess the number of votes equal to the amount of demands thereof in rubles multiplied by the number of members of the committee of creditors. A bankruptcy creditor and empowered agency shall have the right to cast votes belonging to each of them for one candidate or to distribute them among several candidates for members of the committee of creditors.

Candidates who have gathered the largest number of votes shall be considered to be elected to the composition of the committee of creditors.

3. Members of the committee of creditors shall elect from their composition the chairman of the committee of creditors.

4. The protocol of a session of the committee of creditors shall be signed by the chairman of the committee of creditors unless established otherwise by the Reglament of work of the committee of creditors.

Article 19. Interested Persons

1. For the purposes of the present Federal Law, interested persons with respect to the debtor shall be deemed to be:

juridical person which is the principal or subsidiary with respect to the debtor in accordance with civil legislation;

executive of the debtor, and also persons on the council of directors (or supervisory council) of the debtor, collegial executive organ of the debtor, chief bookkeeper (or bookkeeper) of the debtor, including the said persons released from their duties within a year before the moment of instituting the proceeding with regard to the case concerning bankruptcy;

other persons in the instances provided for by a federal law.

Interested persons with respect to the debtor shall also be deemed to be persons in relations with natural persons specified in the present point determined by point 2 of the present Article.

2. For the purposes of the present Federal Law by interested persons with respect to a citizen is understood the spouse thereof, relatives by direct ascent and descent, sisters, brothers, and relatives thereof by descent, parents, sisters, and brothers of the spouse.

3. In the instances provided for by the present Federal Law, interested persons with respect to the arbitrazh administrator and creditors shall be determined in the procedure provided for by points 1 and 2 of the present Article.

Article 20. Arbitrazh Administrators

1. A citizen of the Russian Federation who corresponds to the following requirements may be an arbitrazh administrator:

is registered as an individual entrepreneur;

has a higher education;

has experience of executive work of not less than two years in aggregate;

has taken a theoretical examination according to the syllabus for training arbitrazh administrators;

has undergone work experience for a period of not less than six months as an aide to an arbitrazh administrator;

has no record of conviction for a crime in the sphere of the economy, and also for a crime of average gravity, grave, and especially grave crime;

is a member of one of the self-regulating organisations.

2. The organisation and conducting of the theoretical examination with regard to the syllabus for training arbitrazh administrators shall be effectuated by a commission formed on conditions of equal representation by the federal agency of executive power empowered by the Government of the Russian Federation and an educational institution.

3. The organisation and conducting of the work experience of a citizen of the Russian Federation as an aide to an arbitrazh administrator shall be effectuated by the self-regulating organisations of arbitrazh administrators.

4. For the purposes of the present Federal Law executive work shall be deemed to be work as an executive of a juridical person or deputy thereof, and also activity as an arbitrazh administrator, on condition of the performance of duties of the executive of the debtor, except for instances of conducting procedures of bankruptcy with respect to an absent debtor.

5. If in accordance with the present Federal Law the powers of executive of the debtor are placed on the arbitrazh administrator, to him shall extend all

requirements and with respect to him shall apply all measures of responsibility established by federal laws and other normative legal acts of the Russian Federation for the executive of such debtor.

If execution of the powers of an arbitrazh administrator confirmed by an arbitrazh court is linked with access to information comprising a State secret, such arbitrazh administrator must have or receive access to a State secret.

6. Arbitrazh administrators may not be confirmed by an arbitrazh court as temporary administrators, administrative administrators, external administrators, or bankruptcy administrators:

who are interested persons with respect to a debtor or creditors;

with respect to whom a procedure of bankruptcy has been introduced;

which have not compensated losses due to a debtor, creditors, or third persons when performing duties of an arbitrazh administrator;

who have been disqualified or deprived in the procedure established by a federal law of the right to hold executive posts and/or to effectuate entrepreneurial activity with regard to the management of juridical persons, join a council of directors (or supervisory council), and/or manage affairs and/or the property of other persons;

who do not have contracts of insurance of responsibility concluded in accordance with the requirements of the present Federal Law in the event of causing of losses to persons participating the case concerning bankruptcy.

7. A document certifying the conformity of the candidacies for arbitrazh administrator submitted for confirmation to the requirements provided for by point 1 of the present Article shall be submitted to the arbitrazh court by the self-regulating organization of arbitrazh administrators, a member of which he is.

8. A contract of insurance of responsibility shall be deemed to be a form of financial security for the responsibility of the arbitrazh administrator and must be concluded for a period of not less than a year with the obligatory subsequent renewal thereof for the same period.

The minimum amount of financial security (insured amount under contract of insurance) may not be less than three million rubles per year.

The arbitrazh administrator must within ten days from the date of his confirmation by the arbitrazh court with regard to the case concerning bankruptcy additionally insure his responsibility for the instance of causing losses to persons participating in the case concerning bankruptcy in the amount depending upon the balance sheet value of assets of the debtor as of the last reporting date preceding the date of the introduction of the respective procedure of bankruptcy, namely:

three per cent of the balance sheet value of assets of the debtor exceeding one hundred million rubles, in the event of the balance sheet value of assets of the debtor from one hundred up to three hundred million rubles;

six million rubles and two per cent of the balance sheet value of assets of the debtor exceeding three hundred million rubles, in the event of the balance sheet value of assets of the debtor of from three hundred million rubles up to one billion rubles;

twenty million rubles and one per cent of the balance sheet value of assets of the debtor exceeding one billion rubles, in the event of the balance sheet value of assets of the debtor of more than one billion rubles.

9. Arbitrazh administrators confirmed by an arbitrazh court shall be the procedural legal successors of the preceding arbitrazh administrators.

Article 21. Self-Regulating Organisations of Arbitrazh Arbitrators

1. The status of self-regulating organisation of arbitrazh administrators shall be acquired by a noncommercial organisation from the date of inclusion of the said organization in the unified State register of self-regulating organisations of arbitrazh administrators.

2. The grounds for inclusion of a noncommercial organization in the unified State register of self-regulating organizations of arbitrazh administrators shall be the fulfilment of the following conditions by it:

the conformity of not less than one hundred members thereof to the requirements established in Article 20(1) of the present Federal Law, except for requirements concerning obligatory membership in the self-regulating organisation of arbitrazh administrators;

the participation of members of not less than one hundred (in aggregate) procedures of bankruptcy, including not completed on the date of inclusion in the unified State register of self-regulating organisations of arbitrazh administrators, except for procedures of bankruptcy with respect to absent debtors;

existence of contributory compensation fund or property with a mutual insurance society which is formed exclusively in monetary form at the expense of contributions of members in an amount of not less than fifty thousand rubles for each member.

Execution may not be levied against means of contributory compensation funds or property of a mutual insurance society with regard to obligations of the self-regulating organisation, and also with regard to the obligations of arbitrazh administrators, unless the arising of such obligations was connected with the effectuation of activity provided for by the present Federal Law.

The conditions and procedure for the placement of means of contributory compensation funds and mutual insurance societies of self-regulating organisations of arbitrazh administrators, and also the procedure for the expenditure of the said means in accordance with the special-purpose designation, recommendations concerning the liquidity of assets included in such funds, the composition thereof, and the structure shall be established by the Government of the Russian Federation.

3. A self-regulating organisation of arbitrazh administrators shall effectuate the following functions:

ensure compliance by its members with legislation of the Russian Federation and the rules of professional activity of an arbitrazh administrator;

defence of the rights and legal interests of its members;

ensuring of informational openness of the activity of its members and the procedures of bankruptcy;

promoting the raising of the level of professional training of its members.

A self-regulating organisation of arbitrazh administrators shall have the right to effectuate with respect to its members also other functions provided for by its charter and not contrary to legislation.

4. A permanently operating collegial management organ comprised of not less than seven persons shall be formed in a self-regulating organisation of arbitrazh administrators besides the executive organ. Within the competence of this organ shall be confirmation of the rules of activity and business ethics of members of the self-regulating organisation as arbitrazh administrators.

Not more than twenty five per cent of the members of the permanently operating collegial management organ of the self-regulating organisation should comprise persons who are not members of the self-regulating organisation. State and municipal employees may not be in the composition of management organs of a self-regulating organisation.

In order to ensure its activity a self-regulating organisation of arbitrazh administrators shall form a structural subdivision effectuating control over the activity of its members as arbitrazh administrators, and also organs for:

the consideration of cases concerning the imposition of measures of responsibility on members of the self-regulating organisation;

the selection of candidacies of its members for submission thereof to arbitrazh courts for confirmation in a case concerning bankruptcy.

5. A noncommercial organisation corresponding to the conditions of point 2 of the present Article shall be subject to inclusion in the unified State register of self-regulating organisations of arbitrazh administrators within seven days from the date of submission to the regulating agency determined by the Government of the Russian Federation of the following documents:

application concerning inclusion in the unified State register of self-regulating organizations of arbitrazh administrators;

duly attested copies of the constitutive documents;

duly attested copy of the certificate on State registration;

copies attested by the noncommercial organisation of certificates on the State registration of all its members as individual entrepreneurs;

copies attested by the noncommercial organisation of diplomas on the higher education of all its members;

copies attested by the noncommercial organisation of documents confirming the taking of the theoretical examination with regard to the syllabus of training arbitrazh administrators;

copies attested by the noncommercial organisation of the labour books or other documents confirming the existence of the established experience of executive work of all its members;

copies attested by a noncommercial organisation of certificates or other documents confirming the undergoing by each of its members of work experience as an aide to an arbitrazh administrator;

copies attested by a noncommercial organisation of references concerning the absence of a record of conviction on the part of all of its members.

The regulating agency shall be obliged within three days from the date of inclusion of the noncommercial organisation in the unified State register of self-regulating organisations of arbitrazh administrators to notify in written form the noncommercial organisation about such inclusion or submit a reasoned refusal to include in the register.

The regulating agency shall refuse to include a noncommercial organisation in the unified State register of self-regulating organisations of arbitrazh administrators on the following grounds:

the noncommercial organisation does not fulfil at least a single condition of the conditions provided for by point 2 of the present Article;

not all documents have been submitted as provided for by the present point.

6. On the basis of an application of the regulating agency in the event of a violation of the requirements established by point 2 of the present Article, or a repeated violation of the present Federal Law, the self-regulating organisation shall be excluded from the State register of self-regulating organisations of arbitrazh administrators.

In the event of an autonomous and voluntary declaration by a self-regulating organisation concerning a nonconformity which has arisen to any of the indicia provided for by point 2 of the present Article, the said organisation may not be excluded from the unified State register of self-regulating organisations of arbitrazh administrators for two months from the moment of the arising of such nonconformity, during which it must being its activity into accordance with the said indicia.

Article 22. Rights and Duties of Self-Regulating Organization

1. A self-regulating organisation of arbitrazh arbitrators shall have the right to:

represent the legal interests of its members in their relations with federal agencies of State power, agencies of State power of subjects of the Russian Federation, and agencies of local self-government;

notify arbitrazh courts of the Russian Federation about the acquisition of the status of self-regulating organisations of arbitrazh administrators;

appeal in a judicial procedure the acts and actions of federal agencies of State power, agencies of State power of subjects of the Russian Federation, and agencies of local self-government violating the rights and legal interests of any of its members or groups of members;

file suits concerning the defence of the rights and legal interests of persons participating in a case concerning bankruptcy;

take measures of disciplinary responsibility with respect to their members provided for by constitutive and other documents, including expulsion of members of a self-regulating organisation;

declare in an arbitrazh court petitions concerning the removal from participation in a case concerning bankruptcy of their members in whose actions (or failure to act) violations have been established of legislation on insolvency (or bankruptcy);

effectuate other powers established by the present Federal Law.

2. A self-regulating organisation of arbitrazh administrators shall be obliged to: work out and establish rules of professional activity of an arbitrazh administrator binding for fulfilment by all of its members;

control the professional activity of its members with respect to compliance with the requirements of the present Federal Law and rules of professional activity of an arbitrazh administrator established by the self-regulating organisation;

consider appeals against actions of its member performing the duties of an arbitrazh administrator in a case concerning bankruptcy;

work out and establish the requirements for citizens of the Russian Federation wishing to join the self-regulating organisation;

notify an arbitrazh court considering a case concerning bankruptcy about the expulsion of its member performing the duties of arbitrazh administrator in such case within a period of not later than three days from the date of his expulsion;

effectuate the collection, processing, and keeping of information concerning the activity of its members divulged by them to the self-regulating organisation in the form of reports in the procedure and with the periodicity which have been established by the charter and other documents of the self-regulating organisation;

effectuate the organisation and conducting of experience of a citizen of the Russian Federation as an aide to an arbitrazh administrator;

effectuate the introduction of the register of arbitrazh administrators who are members thereof and ensure free access to the information included in such register to persons interested in the receipt thereof;

ensure the formation of a contributory compensation fund or property of a mutual insurance society for financial security of the responsibility with regard to the compensation of losses caused to its members when performing the duties of arbitrazh administrator.

3. A self-regulating organisation of arbitrazh administrators shall be obliged to submit to the regulating agency for the purposes of subsequent publication the changes made in constitutive documents, rules and standards of activity and business ethics of arbitrazh administrators, and also information concerning:

the making of changes in the register of arbitrazh administrators who are members of this self-regulating organisation;

the confirmations which have occurred of arbitrazh administrators who are members of this self-regulating organisation with regard to cases concerning bankruptcy;

the application of measures of responsibility to members of this self-regulating organisation in the form of expulsion of the members of the self-regulating organisation;

the removal of arbitrazh administrators who are members of this self-regulating organisation from the performance of their duties;

the rules for the admission of arbitrazh administrators in the composition of members of the self-regulating organisation;

the rules for undergoing work experience as an aide of an arbitrazh administrator;

the amount of the contributory compensation fund or property of mutual insurance society;

the appeals received against the actions of members of the self-regulating organisation and results of consideration of such appeals;

the list of insurance organisations effectuating the insurance of civil responsibility of arbitrazh administrators and accredited self-regulating organisations;

the list of professional participants of the securities market effectuating activity with regard to conducting the register of possessors of securities and accredited self-regulating organisations.

A self-regulating organisation of arbitrazh administrators shall be obliged at the request of a regulating agency to provide reports concerning procedure of bankruptcy conducted by arbitrazh administrators who are members of the self-regulating organisation.

Article 23. Requirements for Candidacy of Arbitrazh Administrator

1. A bankruptcy creditor or empowered agency (or meeting of creditors) shall have the right to provide the following requirements for a candidacy of an arbitrazh administrator:

the presence of a higher legal or economic education with the candidate or education with regard to a speciality corresponding to the sphere of activity of the debtor;

the presence of a determined work experience with the candidate in posts of executives of organisations in the respective branch of the economy;

the establishment of the quantity of procedures of bankruptcy conducted by the candidate as an arbitrazh administrator.

A bankruptcy creditor or empowered agency (or meeting of creditors) shall not have the right to put forward requirements for a candidacy of arbitrazh administrator not provided for by the present point.

2. In the event of the putting forward by a bankruptcy creditor or empowered agency (or meeting of creditors) of requirements for a candidacy of arbitrazh administrator, the bankruptcy creditor or empowered agency (or meeting of creditors) shall have the right to indicate the amount and procedure for payment of additional remuneration for the arbitrazh administrator.

Article 24. Rights and Duties of Arbitrazh Administrator

1. An arbitrazh administrator shall be obliged in his activity to be guided by legislation of the Russian Federation.

An arbitrazh administrator shall be obliged in this activity to comply with the rules of professional activity of an arbitrazh administrator confirmed by the self-regulating organisation of which he is a member.

2. An arbitrazh administrator shall have the right to be a member of only one self-regulating organisation of arbitrazh administrators.

3. An arbitrazh administrator confirmed by an arbitrazh court shall have the right to:

convoke a meeting of creditors;

convoke a committee of creditors;

have recourse to an arbitrazh court with applications and petitions in the instances provided for by the present Federal Law;

receive remuneration in the amounts and in the procedure which have been established by the present Federal Law;

enlist in order to ensure the effectuation of his powers on a contractual basis other persons with payment of their activity at the expense of means of the debtor unless established otherwise by the present Federal Law, meeting of creditors, or by agreement of the creditors;

file in an arbitrazh court an application concerning the termination before time of the performance of his duties.

4. An arbitrazh administrator confirmed by an arbitrazh court shall be obliged to:

take measures with regard to defence of the property of the debtor;

analyse the financial state of the debtor;

analyse financial, economic, and investment activity of the debtor and his position on the goods and other markets;

conduct the register of demands of creditors, except for instances provided for by the present Federal Law;

compensate losses to a debtor, creditors, and third persons in the event of causing them losses when performing the duties placed on him from the day of entry into legal force of a judicial act concerning the compensation of such losses;

elicit the indicia of deliberate fictitious bankruptcy, and also circumstances the responsibility for which has been provided by Article 10 (3) and (4) of the present Federal Law;

effectuate other functions established by the present Federal Law.

5. Unless established otherwise by the present Federal Law, an arbitrazh administrator shall be obliged to preserve the confidentiality of information protected by a federal Law (including information comprising an employment and commercial secret) and which became known to him in connection with the performance of duties of an arbitrazh administrator.

6. When conducting the procedures of bankruptcy an arbitrazh administrator confirmed by an arbitrazh court shall be obliged to act in good faith and reasonably in the interests of the debtor, creditors, and society.

7. The powers of an arbitrazh administrator confirmed by an arbitrazh court placed personally on him in accordance with the present Federal Law may not be transferred to other persons.

Article 25. Responsibility of Arbitrazh Administrator

1. The failure to perform or improper performance of duties placed on an arbitrazh administrator in accordance with the present Federal Law and rules of professional activity of an arbitrazh administrator established by the Government of the Russian Federation shall be grounds for removal of an arbitrazh administrator by a court upon the demand of the persons participating in a case concerning bankruptcy.

In the event of the vacating of a ruling of an arbitrazh court concerning the removal of a confirmed arbitrazh administrator for the failure to perform or improper performance of the duties placed on him in accordance with the present Federal Law, and also the rules of professional activity of an arbitrazh administrator established by the Government of the Russian Federation, the arbitrazh administrator shall be subject to reinstatement by the arbitrazh court within the framework of that procedure of bankruptcy in which he was removed from professional activity.

2. The failure to perform or improper performance by an arbitrazh administrator of the rules of professional activity of an arbitrazh administrator confirmed by the self-regulating organisation, a member of which he is, may serve as grounds for expulsion of an arbitrazh administrator from the particular self-regulating organisation. In the event of the expulsion of an arbitrazh administrator from the self-regulating organisation, the arbitrazh administrator shall be removed by an

arbitrazh court from the performance of his duties on the basis of the application of the self-regulating organisation.

In the event of the vacating or deeming invalid of the decision concerning expulsion of an arbitrazh administrator from the self-regulating organisation which served as grounds for the removal by an arbitrazh court of a confirmed arbitrazh administrator, he may not be reinstated by the arbitrazh court to perform duties of an arbitrazh administrator.

3. An arbitrazh administrator who caused as a result of the failure to perform or improper performance of the requirements of the present Federal Law losses to the debtor, creditors, and other persons may not be confirmed as an arbitrazh administrator until full compensation of such losses. An arbitrazh administrator in this event also shall bear the responsibility provided for by a federal law.

Article 26. Remuneration of Arbitrazh Administrator

1. Remuneration of an arbitrazh administrator for each month of effectuation of his powers shall be established in the amount determined by the creditor (or meeting of creditors) and confirmed by the arbitrazh court unless established otherwise by the present Federal Law and must comprise not less than ten thousand rubles.

In the event of the removal of an arbitrazh administrator by an arbitrazh court in connection with the failure to perform or improper performance of the duties placed on him, the remuneration may not be paid to the arbitrazh administrator.

2. Additional remuneration may be established by a bankruptcy creditor, empowered agency, or meeting of creditors for an arbitrazh administrator at the expense of means of creditors confirmed by the arbitrazh court and paid for the results of his activity.

3. Remuneration for persons enlisted by an arbitrazh administrator to ensure his activity shall be paid at the expense of property of the debtor unless provided otherwise by the present Federal Law, meeting of creditors, or by agreement of the creditors.

Article 27. Procedures of Bankruptcy

1. When considering a case concerning bankruptcy of a debtor-juridical person, the following procedures of bankruptcy shall apply:
observation;
financial recuperation;
external administration;
bankruptcy proceeding;
amicable agreement.

2. When considering a case concerning bankruptcy of a debtor-citizen, the following procedures of bankruptcy shall apply:

bankruptcy proceeding;

amicable agreement;

other procedures of bankruptcy provided by the present Federal Law.

Article 28. Procedure for Publication of Information Provided for by Present Federal Law

1. Information subject to publication in accordance with the present Federal Law shall be published in an official publication determined by the Government of the Russian Federation. The print run of the official publication, periodicity, and period for publication of the said information, the procedure for financing services rendered, and the price for such services shall be established by the Government of the Russian Federation and must not be an obstacle to rapid and free access to the said information by any interested person. Information subject to publication in accordance with the present Federal Law also shall be published in electronic mass media in the procedure determined by the Government of the Russian Federation.

2. Compensation of expenses connected with publication of the information specified in point 1 of the present Article shall be effectuated at the expense of property of the debtor unless provided otherwise by the present Federal Law or meeting of creditors.

In the absence of property with the debtor sufficient to compensate expenses for publication, it shall be effectuated at the expense of the creditor who has had recourse with an application concerning the instituting of a case concerning bankruptcy with respect to the debtor.

3. When conducting procedures of bankruptcy information shall be subject to obligatory publication concerning the introduction of observation, deeming a debtor to be a bankrupt, and the opening of a bankruptcy proceeding, and termination of proceedings with regard to a case concerning bankruptcy. If the quantity of creditors of the debtor exceeds one hundred or the quantity thereof can not be determined, information concerning the commencement of each procedure of bankruptcy applicable with respect to a debtor also shall be subject to obligatory publication.

4. On the basis of the decision of a meeting of creditors or committee of creditors the information subject to obligatory publication may also be published in other mass media.

5. Unless provided otherwise by the present Federal Law, published information must contain:

the name of the debtor and address thereof;

the name of the arbitrazh court which adopted the judicial act, date of adoption of such judicial act and indication of the name of the procedure of bankruptcy introduced, and also the number of the case concerning the bankruptcy of a debtor;

the surname, forename, and patronymic of the confirmed arbitrazh administrator and address for sending correspondence to him, and also the name of the respective self-regulating organisation and address thereof;

the date established by the arbitrazh court of the next judicial session with regard to consideration of the case concerning bankruptcy in instances provided for by the present Federal Law;

other information in instances provided for by the present Federal Law.

Article 29. Competence of Federal Agencies of Executive Power, Agencies of State Power of Subjects of Russian Federation, and Agencies of Local Self-Government in Sphere of Financial Recuperation and Bankruptcy

1. For the purpose of conducting State policy in the sphere of financial recuperation and bankruptcy the Government of the Russian Federation shall:
determine the procedure for filing applications by empowered agencies;

determine the procedure for association and submission of demands concerning the payment of obligatory payments and demands of the Russian Federation with regard to monetary obligations in a case concerning bankruptcy and in procedures of bankruptcy;

effectuate the coordination of activity of representatives of federal agencies of executive power and representatives of State extrabudgetary funds as creditors with regard to monetary obligations and obligatory payments;
determine the procedure for conducting the recording and analysis of the ability to pay of strategic enterprises and organisations.

2. The Government of the Russian Federation shall confirm the following rules of professional activity of an arbitrazh administrator and activity of a self-regulating organization:

general rules of activity of an arbitrazh administrator affecting the content and procedure of conducting the register of demands of creditors, preparation, organisation, and conducting of meetings of creditors and committees of creditors, and preparation of reports of an arbitrazh administrator;

rules for conducting financial analysis;

rules for verification of existence of indicia of fictitious and deliberate bankruptcy;

rules for conducting and taking theoretical examination;

rules for conducting work experience as aide to arbitrazh administrator;

rules for conducting verification by self-regulating organisation of activity of its members — arbitrazh administrators.

3. Federal agencies of executive power relegated in accordance with Article 2 of the present Federal Law to empowered agencies shall within the limits of their

competence submit in a case concerning bankruptcy and in procedures of bankruptcy the demands concerning payment of obligatory payments and demands of the Russian Federation with regard to monetary obligations.

4. The regulating agency shall:

effectuate control over compliance by the self-regulating organisations of arbitrazh administrators with federal laws and other normative legal acts regulating the activity of self-regulating organisations;

conduct verifications of the activity of self-regulating organisations in the procedure established by the Government of the Russian Federation;

have recourse to an arbitrazh court with an application concerning the exclusion of a self-regulating organisation from the unified State register of self-regulating organisations of arbitrazh administrators in the instances provided for by the present Federal Law;

have recourse in the procedure established by a federal law to a court with an application concerning the disqualification of an arbitrazh administrator;

render support to self-regulating organisations and arbitrazh administrators in the course of procedures of bankruptcy connected with questions of transnational insolvency;

participate in the organisation of the training of arbitrazh administrators and taking of the theoretical examination;

confirm the unified syllabus for the training arbitrazh administrators;

conduct the unified State register of self-regulating organisations and register of arbitrazh administrators;

effectuate other powers granted to it by the present Federal Law, other federal laws, and other normative legal acts.

The functions of an empowered agency representing the legal interests of the State as a creditor with regard to monetary obligations and/or obligatory payments, and/or owner of property of a debtor-unitary enterprise, founder (or participant) of a debtor may not be placed on a regulating agency effectuating the powers specified in the present point.

5. The Government of the Russian Federation shall determine the procedure for taking into account the opinions of agencies of executive power of subjects of the Russian Federation and agencies of local self-government when determining the position of federal agencies of executive power as creditors with regard to obligatory payments in the course of procedures of bankruptcy.

6. The competence of agencies of State power of subjects of the Russian Federation and agencies of local self-government shall be determined by laws and other normative legal acts of subjects of the Russian Federation and legal acts of agencies of local self-government adopted within the limits of their competence.

Chapter II. Prevention of Bankruptcy

Article 30. Measures with Regard to Prevention of Bankruptcy of Organisations

1. In the event of the arising of the indicia of bankruptcy established by Article 3(2) of the present Federal Law, an executive of the debtor shall be obliged to send to the founders (or participants) of the debtor and owner of the property of the debtor-unitary enterprise information concerning the presence of the indicia of bankruptcy.

2. The founders (or participants) of the debtor, owner of the property of a debtor-unitary enterprise, federal agencies of executive power, agencies of executive power of subjects of the Russian Federation, and agencies of local self-government in the instances provided for by a federal law shall be obliged to take timely measures with regard to the prevention of bankruptcy of organisations.

3. For the purposes of the prevention of bankruptcy of organisations the founders (or participants) of a debtor and owner of property of a debtor-unitary enterprise before the moment of filing in an arbitrazh court an application concerning the deeming of a debtor to be a bankrupt shall take measures directed towards restoration of the ability of the debtor to pay. The measures directed towards the restoration of the ability of the debtor to pay may be adopted by the creditors or other persons on the basis of an agreement with the debtor.

Article 31. Pre-Judicial Sanation

1. Financial assistance may be provided to a debtor by the founders (or participants) of the debtor, owner of property of a debtor-unitary enterprise, creditors, and other persons within the framework of measures with regard to the prevention of bankruptcy in an amount sufficient to repay monetary obligations and obligatory payments and restore the ability of the debtor to pay (pre-judicial sanation).

2. The provision of financial assistance may be accompanied by the assumption by a debtor or other persons of obligations to the benefit of persons who provided the financial assistance.

Chapter III. Examination of Cases Concerning Bankruptcy in Arbitrazh Court

Article 32. Procedure for Consideration of Cases Concerning Bankruptcy

1. Cases concerning bankruptcy of juridical persons and citizens, including individual entrepreneurs, shall be considered by an arbitrazh court according to

the rules provided for by the Code of Arbitrazh Procedure of the Russian Federation with the peculiarities established by the present Federal Law.

2. The peculiarities of the consideration of cases concerning bankruptcy established by the present Chapter shall apply unless provided otherwise by other Chapters of the present Federal Law.

Article 33. Particular Jurisdiction and Systemic Jurisdiction of Cases Concerning Bankruptcy

1. Cases concerning bankruptcy of juridical persons and citizens, including individual entrepreneurs, shall be considered by the arbitrazh court at the location of the debtor-juridical person or place of residence of a citizen.

2. An application concerning the deeming of a debtor to be bankrupt shall be accepted by an arbitrazh court if the demands against the debtor-juridical person in aggregate comprise not less than one hundred thousand rubles, and against a debtor-citizen—not less than ten thousand rubles and the said demands were not performed within three months from the date when they should have been performed, unless provided otherwise by the present Federal Law.

3. A case concerning bankruptcy may not be transferred for consideration to an arbitration court.

Article 34. Persons Participating in Case Concerning Bankruptcy

1. Persons participating in a case concerning bankruptcy shall be:
debtor;
arbitrazh administrator;
bankruptcy creditors;
empowered agencies;
federal agencies of executive power, and also agencies of executive power of subject of the Russian Federation and agencies of local self-government at the location of the debtor in instances provided for by the present Federal Law;
person who provided security in order to conduct financial recuperation.

Article 35. Persons Participating in Arbitrazh Proceeding With Regard to Case Concerning Bankruptcy

There shall participate in an arbitrazh proceeding with regard to a case concerning bankruptcy:
representative of workers of the debtor;
representative of owner of owner of debtor-unitary enterprise;
representative of founders (or participants) of debtor;
representative of meeting of creditors or representative of committee of creditors;
other persons in the instances provided for by the Code of Arbitrazh Procedure of the Russian Federation and the present Federal Law.

Article 36. Representation in Case Concerning Bankruptcy

1. Any citizens having dispositive legal capacity and duly formalised powers to conduct cases concerning bankruptcy, including auditors, evaluators, economists, and other specialists, may act as representatives of citizens, including individual entrepreneurs and organisations which are persons participating in a case concerning bankruptcy or persons participating in an arbitrazh proceeding with regard to a case concerning bankruptcy.

2. The powers of executives of organisations operating in the name of organisations within the limits of powers provided for by a federal law, other normative legal acts, or constitutive documents shall be confirmed by documents submitted by them to the court certifying their employment position, and also by constitutive and other documents.

3. The powers of legal representatives shall be confirmed by documents submitted to the court certifying their status and powers.

4. The powers of other representatives to conduct cases concerning bankruptcy in an arbitrazh court must be expressed in a power of attorney issued and formalised in accordance with a federal law, and in instances provided for by an international treaty of the Russian Federation or federal law, in another document.

Article 37. Application of Debtor

1. An application of a debtor shall be filed in an arbitrazh court in written form. The said application shall be signed by an executive of the debtor-juridical person or person empowered in accordance with the constitutive documents of the debtor to file an application concerning the deeming of the debtor to be a bankrupt, or by a debtor-citizen.

An application of a debtor may be signed by the representative of the debtor if such power is expressly provided for in the power of attorney of the representative.

2. There must be specified in the application of a debtor:

the name of the arbitrazh court in which the said application is filed;

the amount of demands of creditors with regard to monetary obligations to the extent which they are not contested by the debtor;

the amount of indebtedness with regard to compensation of harm caused to life of health of citizens, payment for labour of workers of the debtor, and payment to them of severance benefits, amount of remuneration due for payment of remuneration under authors' contracts;

amount of indebtedness with regard to obligatory payments;

substantiation of the impossibility to satisfy demands of creditors in full or material complication of economic activity in event of levy of execution against the property of the debtor;

information concerning petitions to sue accepted for proceedings by courts of general jurisdiction, arbitrazh courts, and arbitration courts against the debtor, documents of execution, and also other documents presented for the withdrawal of monetary means from the accounts of the debtor in a nonacceptance procedure;

information concerning property which the debtor has, including monetary means and debit indebtedness;

number of accounts of the debtor in banks and other credit organisations, addresses of the banks, and other credit organisations;

name and address of the self-regulating organisation from whose members the arbitrazh court confirms the temporary administrator;

amount of remuneration of arbitrazh administrator;

list of appended documents.

Other information relevant to consideration of the case concerning bankruptcy may be specified in the application of a debtor.

Petitions which the debtor has also may be appended to the application of the debtor.

Demands against the candidacy of temporary administrator shall not be specified in the application of the debtor.

3. Information concerning obligations of the debtor not connected with entrepreneurial activity also shall be specified in the application of a citizen-debtor.

4. A debtor shall be obliged to send copies of the application of a debtor to bankruptcy creditors, empowered agencies, the owner of property of a debtor-unitary enterprise, council of directors (or supervisory council) or other analogous collegial management organ, and also to other persons in instances provided for by the present Federal Law. If before filing the application of a debtor the representative of the owner of property of a debtor-unitary enterprise has been elected (or appointed), the representative of the founders (or participants) of the debtor, and the representative of workers of the debtor, copies of the application of the debtor shall be sent to the said persons.

Article 38. Documents to be Appended to Application of Debtor

1. Besides the documents provided for by the Code of Arbitrazh Procedure of the Russian Federation to the application of a debtor shall be appended documents confirming:

the existence of indebtedness, and also the inability of the debtor to satisfy the demands of creditors in full;

other circumstances on which the application of the debtor is based.

2. To the application of a debtor also shall be appended:

constitutive documents of the debtor-juridical person, and also the certificate concerning State registration of the juridical person or document concerning State registration of an individual entrepreneur;

list of creditors and debtors of the application with an interpretation of creditor and debit indebtedness and an indication of the addresses of creditors and
debtors of the applicant;

bookkeeping balance sheet on the last reporting date or documents replacing it
or documents concerning the composition and value of property of a debtor-
citizen;

decision of the owner of property of a debtor-unitary enterprise or founders (or
participants) of the debtor, and also other empowered organ of the debtor concerning the recourse of the debtor to an arbitrazh court with an application of the
debtor when there is such a decision;

decision of the owner of property of a debtor-unitary enterprise or founders
(or participants) of the debtor, and also other empowered organ of the debtor
concerning the election (or appointment) of a representative of the founders (or
participants) of the debtor or representative of the owner of property of the
debtor-unitary enterprise;

protocol of the meeting of workers of the debtor at which the representative of
the workers of the debtor was elected in order to participate in the arbitrazh proceeding with regard to the case concerning bankruptcy if the said meeting was
conducted before the filing of the application of the debtor;

report concerning the value of property of the debtor prepared by an independent valuer, when there is such a report;

other documents in the instances provided for by the present Federal Law.

3. To the application of a debtor shall be appended originals of the documents
specified in the present Article or duly attested copies thereof.

Article 39. Application of Bankruptcy Creditor

1. An application of a bankruptcy creditor concerning the deeming of a debtor
to be bankrupt (hereinafter—application of creditor) shall be filed in an arbitrazh
court in written form. The application of a creditor-juridical person shall be
signed by the executive thereof or representative, and an application of a creditor-
citizen by this citizen or his representative.

2. There must be specified in an application of a bankruptcy creditor:
the name of the arbitrazh court in which the application of the creditor is filed;
the name (or surname, forename, patronymic) of the debtor and address
thereof;
the name (or surname, forename, patronymic) of the bankruptcy creditor and
his address;
the amount of demands of the bankruptcy creditor against the debtor, specifying the amount of interest and penalties (or fines, forfeits) subject to payment;
the obligation from which the demand of the debtor arose to the bankruptcy
creditor, and also the period of performance of such obligation;

the decision of a court, arbitrazh court, and arbitration court which has entered into legal force and which considered the demands of the bankruptcy creditor against the debtor;

evidence of sending (or presenting for execution) a document of execution to the judicial bailiff service and copy thereof to the debtor;

evidence of the grounds of the arising of the indebtedness (invoices, goods-transport waybill, and other documents);

name and address of the self-regulating organisation from among members of which must be confirmed the temporary administrator;

amount of remuneration of the arbitrazh administrator;

list of documents appended to the application of the creditor.

The bankruptcy creditor in its application shall have the right to specify the professional requirements for the candidacy of temporary administrator. In the application of the creditor may be specified other information having relevance for consideration of the case concerning bankruptcy.

To the application of a creditor also may be appended petitions which the bankruptcy creditor has.

3. A bankruptcy creditor shall be obliged to send a copy of the application of the creditor to the debtor.

4. An application of a creditor may be based on the combined indebtedness with regard to various obligations.

5. Bankruptcy creditors shall have the right to combine their demands against the debtor and to have recourse to a court with one application of a creditor. Such application shall be signed by the bankruptcy creditors who have combined their demands.

Article 40. Documents Appended to Application of Creditor

1. Besides the documents provided for by the Code of Arbitrazh Procedure of the Russian Federation to the application of a creditor shall be appended documents confirming:

obligations of the debtor to the bankruptcy creditor, and also the presence and amount of indebtedness with regard to the said obligations;

evidence of the grounds for the arising of the indebtedness (invoices, goods-transport waybills, and other documents);

other circumstances on which the application of the creditor is based.

2. To the application of a creditor signed by the representative of the bankruptcy creditor also shall be appended the power of attorney confirming the powers of the person who signed such application to file such application.

3. To the application of a creditor must be appended the decision of a court, arbitrazh court, or arbitrazh which has entered into legal force and which

considered the demand of the bankruptcy creditor against the debtor, and also evidence of sending (or presenting for execution) a document of execution to the judicial bailiff service and copy thereof to the debtor.

Article 41. Application of Empowered Agency

1. The application of an empowered agency to deem a debtor to be bankrupt must meet the requirements provided for the application of a creditor.

2. To the application of an empowered agency with regard to obligatory payments must be appended the decision of the tax agency or customs agency concerning the recovery of indebtedness at the expense of property of the debtor. To the application of the empowered agency with regard to obligatory payments to deem a debtor to be bankrupt shall be appended information concerning indebtedness with regard to obligatory payments according to data of the empowered agency.

Article 42. Acceptance of Application Concerning Deeming of Debtor to be Bankrupt

1. The judge of an arbitrazh court shall accept an application concerning the deeming of a debtor to be bankrupt filed in compliance with the demands provided for by the Code of Arbitrazh Procedure of the Russian Federation and the present Federal Law.

If recourse to an arbitrazh court with an application of the debtor is obligatory but not all documents provided for by Article 38 of the present Federal Law have been appended to the said application, the said application shall be accepted by the arbitrazh court for proceedings and the documents not supplied shall be demanded and obtained when preparing the case concerning bankruptcy for judicial examination.

2. The judge of the arbitrazh court shall render a ruling concerning the acceptance of the application to deem a debtor to be bankrupt not later than five days from the date of receipt of the said application in the arbitrazh court.

3. In the ruling concerning the acceptance of the application to deem a debtor to be bankrupt shall be specified the self-regulating organisation from among whose members the arbitrazh court shall confirm the temporary administrator (hereinafter—declared self-regulating organisation) and the date of consideration of the well-foundedness of the demands of the applicant against the debtor unless established otherwise by the present Federal Law.

The declared self-regulating organisation shall have the right to familiarise itself with the materials of the case concerning bankruptcy, to make extracts therefrom, and to make copies.

4. The arbitrazh court shall send the ruling concerning acceptance of the application to deem a debtor to be bankrupt to the applicant, debtor, regulating agency, and declared self-regulating agency.

In the ruling of the arbitrazh court sent to the declared self-regulating organisation shall be specified the requirements for the candidacy of temporary administrator. If the applicant has not specified the requirements for the candidacy of temporary administrator, the said ruling shall be sent to the declared self-regulating organisation without specifying the requirements for the candidacy of temporary administrator.

5. Unless bookkeeping reporting documents of the debtor for the last reporting date have been appended to the application concerning the deeming of the debtor to be bankrupt, the arbitrazh court shall demand and obtain such documents from the debtor. The debtor shall be obliged to submit documents of its bookkeeping reporting to the arbitrazh court not later than five days from the date of receipt of the ruling concerning the demanding and obtaining of such documents.

6. Observation shall be introduced with regard to the results of consideration the substantiation of the demands of the applicant against the debtor, except for instances provided for by Article 62(2) of the present Federal Law.

The judicial session with regard to verification of the substantiation of the demands of the applicant against the debtor shall be conducted not less than fifteen days and not more than thirty days from the date of rendering the ruling concerning acceptance of the application to deem the debtor to be bankrupt.

7. The arbitrazh court upon the petition of the person who filed the application concerning the deeming of a debtor to be bankrupt shall have the right to take the measures with regard to securing the application provided for by the Code of Arbitrazh Procedure of the Russian Federation.

A petition concerning the taking of measures with regard to securing the application concerning the deeming of the debtor to be bankrupt shall be considered by the judge not later than the day following the day of receipt of the petition without notification of the parties.

A ruling shall be rendered with regard to the results of consideration of the petition.

The ruling concerning the taking of measures with regard to securing the application shall be subject to immediate execution.

The ruling concerning the taking of measures with regard to securing the application or refusal to take measures with regard to securing the application may be appealed. Appeal of the said ruling shall not be grounds for the suspension thereof.

8. If before the session assigned by the court an application concerning the deeming of the debtor to be bankrupt is received for consideration of the arbitrazh court from other persons, all applications received shall be considered by the arbitrazh court as applications concerning entry into the case concerning bankruptcy.

The said applications must be considered within fifteen days from the date of the judicial session with regard to verification of the substantiation of the demands of the first applicant who had recourse to the arbitrazh court.

Persons, the consideration of whose applications is deferred, shall possess the rights provided for by point 7 of the present Article.

9. If the consideration of the substantiation of demands of the first applicant is postponed by the arbitrazh court, and likewise if the demands of the first applicant have been deemed to be unsubstantiated, the arbitrazh court shall combine all applications concerning the deeming of the debtor to be bankrupt and assign a date for a new judicial session with regard to verification of the substantiation of the demands of all applicants. In this instance the arbitrazh administrator shall be confirmed among among the members of the self-regulating organisation declared by the bankruptcy creditor or empowered agency whose demands will be deemed first substantiated.

Article 43. Refusal to Accept Application Concerning the Deeming of Debtor to be Bankrupt

The judge of an arbitrazh court shall refuse to accept an application concerning the deeming of a debtor to be bankrupt in the event of:

a violation of the conditions provided for by Article 33(2) of the present Federal Law;

the filing of an application concerning the deeming of a debtor to be bankrupt with respect to whom a case has been instituted by an arbitrazh court concerning bankruptcy and one of the procedures of bankruptcy introduced;

the existence of grounds for refusal to accept an application provided for by the Code of Arbitrazh Procedure of the Russian Federation.

Article 44. Return of Application Concerning the Deeming of Debtor to be Bankrupt

1. An application concerning the deeming of a debtor to be bankrupt which does not correspond to the requirements provided for by Articles 37-41 of the present Federal Law and documents appended thereto shall be returned by the arbitrazh court.

An arbitrazh court shall render a ruling concerning the return of the application concerning the deeming of a debtor to be bankrupt.

2. A ruling concerning the return of an application to deem a debtor to be bankrupt shall be sent to the debtor and the creditor-applicant.

Article 45. Procedure for Confirmation of Arbitrazh Administrator

1. After receiving a query concerning the submission of candidacies for arbitrazh administrator, the declared self-regulating organisation shall draw up a list of

its members who have expressed consent to be confirmed by the arbitrazh court as the arbitrazh administrator and to the greatest degree satisfy the requirements for the candidacy of arbitrazh administrator contained in the said query (hereinafter—list of candidacies). In the list of candidacies should be indicated three candidacies placed in declining order of their conformity to the requirements for candidacy of the arbitrazh administrator contained in the query, and in the event of equal conformity to the requirements—taking into account their professional qualities.

In the event of a query concerning the submission of candidacies of arbitrazh administrator which does not contain requirements for the candidacy of arbitrazh administrator, the declared self-regulating organisation shall conduct the selection of candidacies for arbitrazh administrator from among its members who have expressed consent to be confirmed by the arbitrazh court as arbitrazh administrator. Three candidacies must be specified on the list in descending order of their professional qualities.

2. The declared self-regulating organisation shall be obliged to ensure free access of interested persons to conducting the procedure of selection of the candidacies of arbitrazh administrator.

The decision concerning the inclusion of arbitrazh administrators in the list of candidacies shall be adopted by the declared self-regulating organisation on a collegial basis.

3. A declared self-regulating organisation shall not later than five days from the date of receipt of the query concerning the submission of candidacies for arbitrazh administrator containing the requirements for the candidacy of arbitrazh administrator send a list of candidacies containing information concerning the professional qualities of arbitrazh administrators and a reasoned opinion concerning their conformity to the requirements of candidacy of arbitrazh administrator to the arbitrazh court, applicant (or meeting of creditors or representative of the meeting of creditors), and debtor.

4. The debtor and applicant (or representative of the meeting of creditors) shall have the right to challenge each one candidacy for arbitrazh administrator specified in the list of candidacies. The remaining candidacy shall be confirmed by the arbitrazh court, except for instances of eliciting a violation of the procedure for challenge or nonconformity of the selected candidacy to the requirements of Article 20 of the present Federal Law.

If the debtor and/or applicant (or representative of the meeting of creditors) does not take advantage of the right to challenge, the arbitrazh court shall appoint the candidacy occupying the highest position in the list of candidacies submitted by the declared self-regulating organisation.

5. In the event of the failure to submit to the arbitrazh court by the declared self-regulating organisation a list of candidacies within the period

established by point 3 of the present Article, the arbitrazh court shall have recourse to the regulating agency which is obliged within seven days from the date of receipt of the recourse of the arbitrazh court to ensure the submission of a list of candidacies by other self-regulating organisations from among the self-regulating organisations of arbitrazh administrators included in the unified State register.

Article 46. Measures With Regard to Securing Declared Demands of Creditors

1. An arbitrazh court upon the application of a person participating in the case concerning bankruptcy shall have the right to take measures with regard to securing the declared demands of creditors in accordance with the Code of Arbitrazh Procedure of the Russian Federation.

2. After the introduction of observation, an arbitrazh court in addition to the measures provided for by the Code of Arbitrazh Procedure of the Russian Federation shall have the right to prohibit the conclusion of transactions without the consent of the arbitrazh administrator not provided for by Article 64(2) of the present Federal Law.

3. Measures with regard to securing declared demands of creditors shall operate until the date of rendering by the arbitrazh court of a ruling concerning the introduction of observation, refusal to accept the application, return of the application without consideration or termination of the proceedings with regard to the case concerning bankruptcy.

4. An arbitrazh court upon the petition of persons participating in a case shall have the right to vacate measures with regard to securing demands of creditors before the ensuing of the circumstances provided for by point 3 of the present Article.

5. A ruling concerning the taking of measures with regard to securing demands of creditors shall be subject to immediate execution and may be appealed. The appeal against the said ruling shall not suspend the execution thereof.

Article 47. Opinion of Debtor on Application to Deem Debtor to be Bankrupt

1. A debtor within ten days from the date of receipt of the ruling concerning the acceptance of an application of a creditor or application of an empowered agency to deem a debtor to be bankrupt shall have the right to send to the arbitrazh court, and also to the bankruptcy creditor or empowered agency (hereinafter—applicant) an opinion on such application. To the opinion of the debtor send to the arbitrazh court should be appended evidence of dispatch of a copy of the opinion to the applicant.

2. Besides the information provided for by the Code of Arbitrazh Procedure of the Russian Federation there shall be specified in the opinion of the debtor sent to the arbitrazh court and to the applicant:

objections which the debtor has relative to the demands of the applicant;

total amount of indebtedness of the debtor with regard to obligations to creditors, payment for labour of workers of the debtor, and obligatory payments;

information concerning all accounts of the debtor in credit organisations;

evidence of the unfoundedness of the demands of the applicant if there are such.

In the opinion of the debtor sent to the applicant other information relevant to consideration of the case concerning bankruptcy may be specified.

To the opinion of the debtor also may be appended petitions which the debtor has.

3. The absence of the opinion of a debtor shall not obstruct consideration of the case concerning bankruptcy.

Article 48. Consideration of Substantiation of Demands of Applicant Against Debtor

1. A judicial session of an arbitrazh court with regard to the substantiation of the demands of the applicant against the debtor shall be conducted by a judge of the arbitrazh court in the procedure established by the Code of Arbitrazh Procedure of the Russian Federation with the peculiarities established by the present Federal Law.

2. The judge of the arbitrazh court shall inform the person who has sent an application concerning the deeming of a debtor to be bankrupt, debtor, declared self-regulating organisation, and regulating agency, the failure of which to appear shall not obstruct consideration of the question concerning the introduction of observation, about the time and place of the judicial session.

3. With regard to the results of consideration of the substantiation of the demands of the applicant against the debtor the arbitrazh court shall render one of the following rulings concerning:

the deeming of the demands of the applicant to be substantiated and the introduction of observation;

the refusal to introduce observation and leave the application without consideration;

the refusal to introduce observation and termination of the proceedings with regard to the case concerning bankruptcy.

The said rulings may be appealed in the procedure established by the present Federal Law.

The ruling concerning the introduction of observation shall be rendered if the demand of the applicant corresponds to the conditions established by Article

33(2) of the present Federal Law, is substantiated, and was not satisfied by the debtor on the date of the session of the arbitrazh court.

The ruling concerning the refusal to introduce observation and leaving the application concerning the deeming of the debtor to be bankrupt without consideration shall be rendered if at the session of the arbitrazh court a demand of a person who had recourse with the application concerning the deeming of the debtor to be bankrupt was deemed unsubstantiated or established the absence of even one of the conditions provided for by Article 33(2) of the present Federal Law, on condition that there is an application of another creditor.

The ruling concerning the refusal to introduce observation and to terminate proceedings with regard to the case concerning bankruptcy shall be rendered by an arbitrazh court in the absence of applications of other creditors concerning the deeming of the debtor to be bankrupt if on the date of the session of the arbitrazh court with regard to consideration of the application concerning the deeming of the debtor to be bankrupt the demand of a person who had recourse with an application concerning the deeming of the debtor to be bankrupt is satisfied or the demand of such creditor is deemed to be unsubstantiated or the absence is established of even one of the conditions provided for by Article 33(2) of the present Federal Law.

4. In the event of the deeming by an arbitrazh court of demands of the applicant to be substantiated and the introduction of observation the demands of other applicants shall be considered in the procedure provided for by Article 71 of the present Federal Law.

In the event of the deeming of demands of the applicant to be unsubstantiated, when there are other applications of other creditors concerning the deeming of the debtor to be bankrupt the arbitrazh court shall consider the substantiation of the demands of the said creditors in the procedure provided for by the present Article.

Article 49. Ruling Concerning Introduction of Observation

1. A ruling concerning the introduction of observation shall be rendered by a judge of an arbitrazh court as one man.

2. In the ruling of an arbitrazh court concerning the introduction of observation must be contained indications of:

the deeming of the demands of the applicant to be substantiated and the introduction of observation;

the confirmation of a temporary administrator;

the amount of remuneration of the temporary administrator.

3. If when rendering a ruling concerning the introduction of observation it is impossible to determine the candidacy for temporary administrator, the arbitrazh court shall render a ruling concerning deferral of consideration of the question

concerning confirmation of the temporary administrator for a period of not more than fifteen days from the date of rendering the ruling on the introduction of observation.

4. The ruling concerning the introduction of observation, and also the ruling concerning the confirmation of a temporary administrator, shall be subject to immediate execution.

The said rulings may be appealed. An appeal of the said rulings shall not suspend the execution thereof.

Article 50. Preparation of Case Concerning Bankruptcy for Judicial Examination

1. The preparation of a case concerning bankruptcy for judicial examination shall be conducted by the judge of an arbitrazh court in the procedure provided by the Code of Arbitrazh Procedure of the Russian Federation with the peculiarities established by the present Federal Law.

2. When preparing a case for judicial examination an arbitrazh court shall consider the applications, appeals, and petitions of persons participating in the case concerning bankruptcy, establish the substantiation of the demands of creditors in the procedure determined by Article 71 of the present Federal Law, and effectuate other powers provided for by the present Federal Law.

3. Upon the petition of persons participating in a case concerning bankruptcy the arbitrazh court may designate expert examination for the purpose of eliciting the indicia of fictitious or deliberate bankruptcy.

4. A judge of an arbitrazh court may when preparing a case for judicial examination take measures to reconcile the parties. The effectuation of such measures may not be grounds for suspension of the proceedings with regard to a case concerning bankruptcy.

Article 51. Period for Consideration of Case Concerning Bankruptcy

A case concerning bankruptcy must be considered in the session of an arbitrazh court within the period not exceeding seven months from the date of receipt of the application concerning the deeming of a debtor to be bankrupt in the arbitrazh court.

Article 52. Powers of Arbitrazh Court

1. With regard to the results of consideration of a case concerning bankruptcy an arbitrazh court shall adopt one of the following judicial acts:

decision concerning the deeming of a debtor to be bankrupt and opening of a bankruptcy proceeding;

decision concerning a refusal to deem the debtor to be bankrupt;

ruling concerning the introduction of financial recuperation;

ruling concerning the introduction of external administration;

ruling concerning the termination of proceedings with regard to a case concerning bankruptcy;

ruling concerning the leaving of an application concerning the deeming of a debtor to be bankrupt without consideration;

ruling concerning confirmation of an amicable agreement.

2. Judicial acts provided for by point 1 of the present Article, and also other judicial acts of an arbitrazh court provided for by the present Federal Law, shall be subject to immediate execution unless established otherwise by the present Federal Law.

Article 53. Decision Concerning Deeming of Debtor to be Bankrupt and Opening of Bankruptcy Proceeding

1. A decision of an arbitrazh court concerning the deeming of a debtor to be bankrupt and the opening of a bankruptcy proceeding shall be adopted in instances of the establishment of the indicia of bankruptcy of the debtor provided for by Article 3 of the present Federal Law in the absence of grounds for leaving the application concerning the deeming of a debtor to be bankrupt without consideration, introduction of financial recuperation, external administration, confirmation of an amicable agreement, or termination of the proceedings with regard to a case concerning bankruptcy.

2. The decision of an arbitrazh court concerning the deeming of a debtor-juridical person to be bankrupt and the opening of a bankruptcy proceeding must contain an indication of:

deeming the debtor to be bankrupt;

opening of a bankruptcy proceeding.

3. The decision of an arbitrazh court concerning the deeming of a debtor-individual entrepreneur to be bankrupt shall indicate the deeming of the State registration of the debtor as an individual entrepreneur to have lost force.

4. The decision of an arbitrazh court concerning the deeming of a debtor to be bankrupt and the opening of a bankruptcy proceeding may be appealed.

5. In the instances provided for by the present Federal Law upon the petition of a meeting of creditors or bankruptcy administrator the court shall have the right to render a ruling concerning the termination of the bankruptcy proceeding and transition to external administration.

The ruling of an arbitrazh court concerning termination of the bankruptcy proceeding and transition to external administration may be appealed. The appeal of the said ruling shall not suspend the execution thereof.

Article 54. Publication of Information Concerning Judicial Acts Rendered by Arbitrazh Court

1. Information concerning the rendering of a ruling concerning the introduction of observation, introduction of financial recuperation, introduction of external administration, termination of a proceeding with regard to a case concerning bankruptcy, concerning the confirmation, removal, or relieving of an arbitrazh administrator, concerning the adoption of a decision concerning the deeming of a debtor to be bankrupt and the opening of a bankruptcy proceeding, and a decree concerning the repeal or change of the said acts shall be published in the procedure established by Article 28 of the present Federal Law.

An arbitrazh administrator within three days from the date of receipt of the respective judicial act shall send information subject to publication to the address of the agency determined in accordance with Article 28 of the present Federal Law. Payment for publication of such information shall be made at the expense of the debtor. In the absence of monetary means with the debtor the publication of such information shall be paid for by the arbitrazh administrator with subsequent compensation of the said means at the expense of the debtor.

2. The information sent for publication in accordance with the present Federal Law shall be published within ten days from the moment of receipt thereof.

3. Information concerning the judicial acts rendered by an arbitrazh court may be published in other mass media.

Article 55. Decision of Arbitrazh Court Concerning Refusal to Deem Debtor to be Bankrupt

A decision of an arbitrazh court to refuse to deem a debtor to be bankrupt shall be adopted in the event of:
the absence of the indicia of bankruptcy provided for by Article 3 of the present Federal Law;
the establishment of fictitious bankruptcy;
other instances provided for by the present Federal Law.

Article 56. Consequences of Adoption by Arbitrazh Court of Decision to Refuse Deeming of Debtor to be Bankrupt

The adoption by an arbitrazh court of the decision to refuse to deeming a debtor to be bankrupt shall be grounds for termination of the operation of all limitations provided for by the present Federal Law and which are consequences of the acceptance of an application concerning the deeming of a debtor to be bankrupt and/or introduction of observation.

Article 57. Grounds for Termination of Proceedings With Regard to Case Concerning Bankruptcy

1. An arbitrazh court shall terminate proceedings with regard to a case concerning bankruptcy in the event of:

restoration of the ability of the debtor to pay in the course of financial recuperation;

restoration of the ability of the debtor to pay in the course of external administration;

conclusion of an amicable agreement;

deeming in the course of observation of the demands of the applicant which served as grounds for instituting a case concerning bankruptcy to be unsubstantiated in the absence of demands of creditors declared and recognised in the procedure established by the present Federal Law and other respective provision of Article 6 of the present Federal Law;

refusal of all creditors participating in the case concerning bankruptcy of declared demands or demands concerning the deeming of the creditor to be bankrupt;

satisfaction of all demands of creditors included in the register of demands of creditors in the course of any procedure of bankruptcy;

completion of the bankruptcy proceeding;

other instances provided for by the present Federal Law.

2. In the instances provided for by point 1 of the present Article the consequences of the termination of the proceedings with regard to the case concerning bankruptcy established by Article 56 of the present Federal Law shall apply.

Article 58. Suspension of Proceedings With Regard to Case Concerning Bankruptcy

1. A proceeding with regard to a case concerning bankruptcy may be suspended upon the petition of a participating in the case concerning bankruptcy in the event of:

appeal of judicial acts provided for by Article 52 of the present Federal Law;

appeal of decisions of the meeting of creditors (or committee of creditors);

other instances provided for by the Code of Arbitrazh Procedure of the Russian Federation.

2. In the event of the suspension of proceedings with regard to a case an arbitrazh court shall not have the right to adopt judicial acts provided for by Article 52 of the present Federal Law.

3. The suspension of a proceeding with regard to a case shall not be an obstacle to the rendering of other rulings provided for by the present Federal Law, and also the effectuation by an arbitrazh administrator and other persons participat-

ing in a case concerning bankruptcy of actions provided for by the present Federal Law.

Article 59. Distribution of Judicial Expenses and Expenses for Payment of Remuneration to Arbitrazh Administrator

1. Unless provided otherwise by the present Federal Law or agreement with the creditors, all judicial expenses, including expenses for the payment of State duty, which were deferred or by installment, expenses for the publication of information in the procedure established by Article 28 of the present Federal Law, and also expenses for the payment of remuneration to the arbitrazh administrator and payment for services of persons enlisted by the arbitrazh administrator to ensure the performance of his activity, shall be relegated to the property of the debtor and compensated at the expense of this property in priority.

Another procedure for the distribution of the said expenses may be provided for by the amicable agreement.

2. If according to the results of consideration of the substantiation of the demands of creditors a ruling has been rendered by an arbitrazh court concerning the refusal to introduce observation and to terminate the proceedings with regard to the case, except for satisfaction of demands of the applicable after the filing of an application concerning the deeming of the debtor to be bankrupt specified in point 1 of the present Article, expenses shall be relegated to the applicant who had recourse to the arbitrazh court with the application of a creditor. If the application was filed in the procedure established by Article 39(5) of the present Federal Law, the expenses provided for by point 1 of the present Article shall be distributed among the applicants in proportion to the amounts of their demands.

3. In the absence of the debtor having means sufficient to repay the expenses provided for by point 1 of the present Article, the applicant shall be obliged to repay the said expenses in the part not repaid at the expense of property of the debtor.

4. The procedure for the distribution of judicial expenses and expenses for the payment of remuneration to the arbitrazh administrator shall be established in the decision of the arbitrazh court or ruling of the arbitrazh court adopted with regard to the results of the consideration of the case concerning bankruptcy.

Article 60. Consideration of Disagreements, Applications, Petitions, and Appeals in Case Concerning Bankruptcy

1. Applications and petitions of an arbitrazh administrator, including concerning disagreements which arose between him and creditors, and in instances provided for by the present Federal Law, between him and the debtor, appeals of creditors concerning a violation of the rights and legal interests thereof, shall be considered at a session of an arbitrazh court not later than a month from the date

of receipt of the said applications, petitions, and appeals unless established otherwise by the present Federal Law.

The said applications, petitions, and appeals shall be considered by a judge as one man.

A ruling shall be rendered with regard to the results of consideration of the said applications, petitions, and appeals by an arbitrazh court.

The said ruling may be appealed in the procedure and within the periods which were established by the present Federal Law.

2. Disagreements between the arbitrazh administrator and citizens to whose benefit a judicial act has been rendered concerning the recovery of damage caused to life or health, and also between arbitrazh administrators and a representative of workers of the debtor in the instances provided for by Article 16(11) of the present Federal Law, shall be considered in the procedure and within the periods which have been established by point 1 of the present Article.

3. Appeals of a representative of the founders (or participants) of a debtor, representative of the owner of property of a debtor-unitary enterprise, and other persons participating in an arbitrazh proceeding with regard to a case concerning bankruptcy against the actions of the arbitrazh administrator, decision of the meeting of creditors or committee of creditors violating the rights and legal interests of the founders (or participants) of the debtor, and owner of the property of the debtor-unitary enterprise shall be considered in the procedure and within the periods which have been established by point 1 of the present Article.

4. Applications and appeals filed by persons not having the right of appeal or with a violation of the procedure established by the present Article shall be subject to return.

5. Ruling of an arbitrazh court not provided for by the Code of Arbitrazh Procedure of the Russian Federation shall be appealed in the procedure established by the present Federal Law.

Article 61. Proceedings With Regard to Review of Rulings of Arbitrazh Court Rendered With Regard to Results of Consideration of Disagreements in Case Concerning Bankruptcy

1. Rulings of an arbitrazh court rendered with regard to the results of the consideration by an arbitrazh court of applications, petitions, and appeals in the procedure established by Articles 50, 71, and 100 of the present Federal Law may be appealed in the procedure established by the Code of Arbitrazh Procedure of the Russian Federation with the peculiarities provided for by the present Federal Law.

2. Rulings establishing the amount of demands of creditors may be appeale din accordance with the Code of Arbitrazh Procedure of the Russian Federation. When considering such cases in superior judicial instances an arbitrazh court

which rendered the ruling shall send to creditors in the procedure provided for by the Code of Arbitrazh Procedure of the Russian Federation only those materials of the case concerning bankruptcy which directly relate to the dispute of the debtor and creditor(s) concerning the establishment of the substantiation, amount, and priority of demands.

3. Other rulings of an arbitrazh court which were adopted within the framework of a case concerning bankruptcy but not provided for by the Code of Arbitrazh Procedure of the Russian Federation and with respect to which it was not established that they are subject to appeal may be appealed in an appellate procedure not later than fourteen days from the day of adoption thereof. A court of appellate instance shall adopt a decree within not later than fourteen days, which shall be final, with regard to the results of consideration of the appeal. The appeal of such rulings in an appellate instance shall not be an obstacle to the performance of procedural actions with regard to the case concerning bankruptcy and the grounds for the suspension of the operation thereof.

Chapter IV. Observation

Article 62. Introduction of Observation

1. Unless provided otherwise by the present Federal Law, observation shall be introduced with regard to the results of consideration by an arbitrazh court of the substantiation of demands of the applicant in the procedure provided for by Article 48 of the present Federal Law.

2. When instituting a case concerning bankruptcy on the basis of the application of a debtor observation shall be introduced from the date of acceptance by an arbitrazh court of the application of the debtor for proceedings, except for instances when another procedure of bankruptcy must be applied in accordance with the present Federal Law to the debtor. In the event of the instituting of a case concerning bankruptcy on the basis of the application of a debtor concerning the introduction of observation this shall be indicated in the ruling concerning the acceptance of the application of the debtor.

3. Observation must be completed by taking into account the periods for the consideration of the case concerning bankruptcy provided for by Article 51 of the present Federal Law.

Article 63. Consequences of Rendering by Arbitrazh Court of Ruling Concerning Introduction of Observation

1. From the date of rendering by an arbitrazh court of a ruling concerning the introduction of observation shall ensue the following consequences:
demands of creditors with regard to monetary obligations and the payment of obligatory payments, the period of performance with regard to which had ensued

on the date of the introduction of observation may be presented against the debtor only in compliance with the procedure established by the present Federal Law for the presentation of demands against the debtor;

proceedings with regard to cases connected with the recovery from the debtor of monetary means shall be suspended upon the petition of the creditor. The creditor in this event shall have the right to present its demands against the debtor in the procedure established by the present Federal Law;

execution of documents of execution with regard to property sanctions shall be suspended, including arrests removed against property of the debtor and other limitations with respect to the disposition of property of the debtor imposed in the course of an execution proceeding, except for documents of execution issued on the basis of judicial acts which entered into legal force before the date of the introduction of observation concerning the recovery of indebtedness with regard to earnings, payment of remuneration with regard to authors' contracts, demanding and obtaining property from another's illegal possession, compensation of harm caused to life or health, and compensation of moral harm. Grounds for the suspension of the execution of documents of execution shall be the ruling of an arbitrazh court concerning the introduction of observation;

satisfaction of demands of the founder (or participant) of the debtor concerning the apportionment of a participatory share (or share) in property of the debtor in connection with withdrawal from the composition thereof by the founders (or participants), purchase by the debtor of stocks placed or payment of the actual value of the participatory share (or share) shall be prohibited;

payment of dividends and other payments with regard to emission securities shall be prohibited;

termination of monetary obligations of the debtor by means of the set-off of a counter homogeneous demand shall not be permitted if in so doing the priority of satisfaction of demands of creditors established by Article 134(4) of the present Federal Law is violated.

Article 64. Limitations and Duties of Debtor in Course of Observation

1. The introduction of observation shall not be grounds for the removal of an executive of the debtor and other management organs of the debtor which shall continue to effectuate their powers with the limitations established by points 2 and 3 of the present Article.

2. Management organs of the debtor may conclude exclusively with the consent of the temporary administrator expressed in written form, except for instances expressly provided for by the present Federal Law, transactions and several interconnected transactions:

connected with the acquisition, alienation, or possibility of alienation directly or indirectly of property of the debtor whose balance sheet value comprises more than five per cent of the balance sheet value of assets of the debtor on the date of the introduction of observation;

connected with the receipt and issuance of loans (or credits), issuance of suretyships and guarantees, assignment of rights of demand, transfer of debt, and also with the founding of trust management of property of the debtor.

3. Management organs of the debtor shall not have the right to adopt decisions concerning:

reorganisation (merger, accession, division, separation, transformation) and liquidation of the debtor;

creation of juridical persons or participation of the debtor in other juridical persons;

creation of branches and representations;

payment of dividends or distribution of profit of the debtor among the founders (or participants);

placement by the debtor of bonds and other emission securities, except for stocks;

withdrawal from the composition of the founders (or participants) of the debtor and acquisition from stockholders of stocks previously issued;

participation in associations, unions, holding companies, financial-industrial groups, and other associations of juridical persons;
conclusion of contracts of simple partnership.

4. The executive of the debtor shall within ten days from the date of rendering of the ruling concerning the introduction of observation be obliged to have recourse to the founders (or participants) of the debtor with a proposal to conduct a general meeting of founders (or participants) of the debtor and the owner of property of a debtor-unitary enterprise for consideration of questions concerning recourse to the first meeting of creditors of the debtor with a proposal concerning the introduction with respect to the debtor of financial recuperation, conducting an additional emission of stocks, and other questions provided for by the present Federal Law.

5. A debtor shall have the right to effectuate an increase of its charter capital by means of the placement under closed subscription of additional common stocks at the expense of additional contributions of its founders (or participants) and third persons in the procedure established by federal laws and constitutive documents of the debtor. In this event State registration of the report concerning the results of the issuance of additional common stocks and changes of the constitutive documents of the debtor must be effectuated before the date of the judicial session with regard to consideration of the case concerning bankruptcy.

Article 65. Temporary Administrator

1. The temporary administrator shall be confirmed by the arbitrazh court in the procedure provided for by Article 45 of the present Federal Law.

2. In the ruling of the arbitrazh court concerning confirmation of the temporary administrator must be specified the amount of his remuneration established by the arbitrazh court.

Thereafter the initially determined amount of remuneration of the temporary administrator may be increased by the arbitrazh court on the basis of a decision of the meeting of creditors.

3. A temporary administrator may be removed by the arbitrazh court from the performance of duties of temporary administrator:

in connection with the satisfaction by the arbitrazh court of an appeal of a person participating in the case concerning bankruptcy for the failure to perform or the improper performance by the temporary administrator of duties placed on them on condition that such failure to perform or improper performance of duties violated the rights or legal interests of the applicant of the appeal, and also entailed or might entail losses of the debtor or creditors thereof;

in the event of eliciting circumstances which obstructed confirmation of the person as temporary administrator, including if such circumstances arose after confirmation of the person as temporary administrator;

in other instances provided for by a federal law.

Article 66. Rights of Temporary Administrator

1. A temporary administrator shall have the right to:

present to an arbitrazh court in his own name demands concerning the deeming invalid of transactions and decisions, and also demands concerning the application of the consequences of the invalidity of null transactions, concluded or performed by the debtor with a violation of the requirements established by Articles 63 and 64 of the present Federal Law;

declare objections relative to the demands of creditors in instances provided for by the present Federal Law;

take part in judicial sessions of the arbitrazh court with regard to the verification of the substantiation of objections submitted of the debtor relative to the demands of creditors;

apply to the arbitrazh court with a petition concerning the taking of additional measures with regard to ensuring the preservation of property of the debtor, including a prohibition to conclude translations without the consent of the temporary administrator without the consent of the temporary administrator not provided for by Article 64(2) of the present Federal Law;

apply to the arbitrazh court with a petition concerning the removal of the executive of the debtor from office;

receive any information and documents affecting the activity of the debtor;

effectuate other powers established by the present Federal Law.

2. Management organs of the debtor shall be obliged to provide to the temporary administrator at his request any information affecting the activity of the debtor.

Article 67. Duties of Temporary Administrator

1. A temporary administrator shall be obliged to:

take measures with regard to ensuring the preservation of property of the debtor;

conduct an analysis of the financial state of the debtor;

elicit creditors of the debtor;

conduct the register of demands of creditors, except for instances provided for by the present Federal Law;

inform creditors about the introduction of observation;

convoke and conduct the first meeting of creditors.

2. A temporary administrator at the end of observation but not later than five days before the established date of the session of the arbitrazh court specified in the ruling of the arbitrazh court concerning the introduction of observation shall be obliged to submit to the arbitrazh court a report concerning his activity, information concerning the financial state of the debtor, and a proposal concerning the possibility or impossibility of restoring the ability of the debtor to pay, and the protocol of the first meeting of creditors with documents appended which are determined in Article 12(7) of the present Federal Law.

Article 68. Notification Concerning Introduction of Observation

1. A temporary administrator shall be obliged within the period established by Article 54 of the present Federal Law to send a notice for publication concerning the introduction of observation in the procedure provided for by Article 28 of the present Federal Law.

2. The temporary administrator shall be obliged not later than fourteen days from the date of publication of the notice concerning the introduction of observation to inform all creditors of the debtor elicited by him, except for creditors to whom the debtor bears responsibility for causing harm to life or health, moral harm, performance of obligations with regard to the payment of severance benefits and payment for labour of persons working under a labour contract, performance of obligations concerning the payment of remuneration under authors' contracts, and rendering by an arbitrazh court of a ruling concerning the introduction of observation.

3. The executive of a debtor shall be obliged to inform workers of the debtor, founders (or participants) of the debtor, and lower of the property of a debtor-unitary enterprise about the rendering by the arbitrazh court of a ruling concerning the introduction of observation within ten days from the date of rendering such ruling.

4. The notice concerning the introduction of observation must contain:
the name of the debtor-juridical person or surname, forename, and patronymic of a debtor-citizen and his address;

name of the arbitrazh court which rendered the ruling concerning the introduction of observation, date of rendering such ruling, and number of the case concerning bankruptcy;

the surname, forename, and patronymic of the confirmed temporary administrator and address for sending correspondence to the temporary administrator;

date of the judicial session established by the arbitrazh court with regard to consideration of the case concerning bankruptcy.

Article 69. Removal of Executive of Debtor from Office

1. An arbitrazh court shall remove an executive of the debtor from office upon the petition of the temporary administrator in the event of a violation of the requirements of the present Federal Law.

2. In the event of recourse with a petition to the arbitrazh court concerning the removal of the executive of the debtor from office the temporary administrator shall be obliged to send a copy of the petition to the executive of the debtor, representative of the founders (or participants) of the debtor, or other collegial management organ of the debtor, and representative of the owner of the property of a debtor-unitary enterprise.

3. The arbitrazh court shall render a ruling concerning consideration at the judicial session of the petition of the temporary administrator concerning removal of the executive of the debtor and inform the representative of the founders (or participants) of the debtor or other collegial management organ of the debtor, and representative of the owner of property of the debtor-unitary enterprise about the date of conducting the session and the need to submit to the court a candidacy for the acting executive of the debtor during the period of conducting observation.

4. In the event of the satisfaction by the arbitrazh court of the petition of the temporary administrator concerning the removal of the executive of the debtor from office the arbitrazh court shall render a ruling concerning the removal of the executive of the debtor and placement of the performance of duties of the executive of the debtor on the person submitted as a candidacy for executive of the debtor by the representative of the founders (or participants) of the debtor or other collegial management organ of the debtor and representative of the owner of property of a debtor-unitary enterprise, and in the event of the failure of the said persons to submit a candidacy for acting executive of the debtor—on one of the deputy executives of the debtor, and in the absence of a deputy—on one of the workers of the debtor.

5. The arbitrazh court may upon the petition of the temporary administrator remove the acting executive of the debtor in the event of a violation of the requirements of the present Federal Law. In this even performance of the duties of executive of the debtor shall be placed on the person submitted as a candidacy for executive of the debtor in the procedure provided for by point 4 of the present Article, and in the even to fthe failure to submit a candidacy—on one of the deputies of the executive, and in the absence of a deputy executive of the debtor—on one of the workers of the debtor.

The arbitrazh court on the basis of the application of the temporary administrator may prohibit the acting executive of the debtor to conclude determined transactions and perform actions or to perform them without the consent of the temporary administrator.

Article 70. Analysis of Financial State of Debtor

1. An analysis of the financial state of the debtor shall be conducted for the purposes of determining the value of property belonging to the debtor in order to cover judicial expenses, expenses for the payment of remuneration to the arbitrazh administrator, and also for the purpose of determining the possibility or impossibility of restoring the ability of the debtor to pay in the procedure and within the periods which have been established by the present Federal Law.

2. The temporary administrator shall, on the basis of an analysis of the financial state of the debtor, including the results of the inventorying of property of the debtor when there is such, and an analysis of documents certifying the State registration of rights of ownership, prepare proposals concerning the possibility or impossibility of restoring the ability of the debtor to pay and a substantiation of the advisability of introducing the next procedures of bankruptcy.

3. If as a result of the analysis of the financial state of the debtor it is established that the value of property belonging to the debtor is insufficient to cover judicial expenses, the creditors shall have the right to adopt a decision concerning the introduction of external administration only when determining the sources for covering judicial expenses.

If a source for covering judicial expenses is not determined by the creditors or it proves to be impossible to cover them at the expense of the source determined by them, the creditors who voted for the decision concerning the introduction of external administration shall bear joint and several responsibility with regard to covering the said expenses.

Article 71. Establishment of Amount of Demands of Creditors

1. For the purpose of participation in the first meeting of creditors, creditors shall have the right to present their demands against the debtor within thirty days from the date of publication of the notice concerning the introduction of

observation. The said demands shall be sent to the arbitrazh court, debtor, and temporary administrator with an annex of the judicial act or other documents confirming the substantiation of these demands. The said demands shall be included in the register of demands of creditors on the basis of a ruling of the arbitrazh court concerning inclusion of the said demands in the register of demands of creditors.

2. Objections relative to demands of creditors may be presented to an arbitrazh court not later than fifteen days from the day of expiry of the period for the presentation of demands of creditors by the debtor, temporary administrator, creditors who presented demands against the debtor, representative of the founders (or participants) of the debtor, or representative of the owner of property of the debtor-unitary enterprise.

3. When there are objections relative to demands of creditors an arbitrazh court shall verify the substantiation of the demands and the existence of grounds for inclusion of the said demands in the register of demands of creditors.

4. Demands of creditors with regard to which objections have ensued shall be considered in a session of the arbitrazh court. With regard to the results of consideration shall be rendered a ruling concerning the inclusion or refusal to include the said demands in the register of demands of creditors. The amount and priority of satisfaction of such demands shall be specified in the ruling of the arbitrazh court concerning the inclusion of demands in the register of demands of creditors.

5. Demands of creditors with regard to which objections have not ensued shall be considered by the arbitrazh court in order to verify their substantiation and the presence of grounds for inclusion in the register of demands of creditors. With regard to the results of such consideration the arbitrazh court shall render a ruling concerning the inclusion or refusal to include demands in the register of demands of creditors. The said demands may be considered without involvement of the persons participating in the case.

The ruling concerning the inclusion or refusal to include demands of creditors in the register of demands of creditors shall enter into force immediately and may be appealed. The ruling concerning inclusion or refusal to include demands of creditors shall be sent by the arbitrazh court to the debtor, arbitrazh administrator, creditor which presented the demand, and register-holder.

6. In the event it is necessary to complete consideration of the demands of creditors presented within the established period, the arbitrazh court may charge the temporary administrator to defer the conducting of the first meeting of creditors.

7. Demands of creditors presented upon the expiry of the period provided for by point 1 of the present Article for the presentation of demands shall be subject

to consideration by the arbitrazh court after introduction of the procedure following the procedure of observation.

Article 72. Convocation of First Meeting of Creditors

1. The temporary administrator shall determine the date of conducting the first meeting of creditors and inform all elicited bankruptcy creditors, empowered agencies, representative of workers of the debtor, and other persons having the right to participate in the first meeting of creditors thereof. The notice concerning the conducting of the first meeting of creditors shall be effectuated by the temporary administrator in the procedure and within the periods which have been provided by Article 14 of the present Federal Law.

The first meeting of creditors must be constituted not later than ten days before the date of the end of observation.

2. The bankruptcy creditors and empowered agencies whose demands were presented in the procedure and within the periods which were provided by Article 71(1) of the present Federal Law and entered in the register of demands of creditors shall be participants of the first meeting of creditors with the right of vote.

3. The executive of the debtor, representative of the founders (or participants) of the debtor, or representative of the owner of property of a debtor-unitary enterprise and representative of workers of the debtor shall take part in the first meeting of creditors without a right of vote. The absence of the said persons shall not be grounds for deeming the first meeting of creditors to be invalid.

Article 73. Competence of First Meeting of Creditors

1. To the competence of the first meeting of creditors shall be relegated:

adoption of the decision concerning the introduction of financial recuperation and recourse to an arbitrazh court with a respective petition;

adoption of the decision concerning the introduction of external administration and recourse to an arbitrazh court with a respective petition;

adoption of the decision concerning recourse to an arbitrazh court with a petition to deeming the debtor to be bankrupt and the opening of a bankruptcy proceeding;

formation of the committee of creditors, determination of the quantitative composition and powers of the committee of creditors, and election of the members of the committee of creditors;

determination of the requirements for the candidacies of administrative administrator, external administrator, and bankruptcy administrator;

determination of the self-regulating organisation which must submit candidacies for arbitrazh administrators to the arbitrazh court;

selection of the register-holder from among register-holders accredited by the self-regulating organisation;

deciding of other questions provided for by the present Federal Law.

2. The meeting of creditors which adopted a decision concerning recourse to an arbitrazh court with a petition concerning the introduction of financial recuperation, introduction of external administration, or deeming the debtor to be bankrupt and opening of a bankruptcy proceeding shall have the right to formulate the requirements for candidacies of the administrative administrator, external administrator, and bankruptcy administrator and send to the self-regulating organisation a query concerning the submission of candidacies for such administrators.

Article 74. Decision of First Meeting of Creditors Concerning Application of Procedures of Bankruptcy

1. A decision of the first meeting of creditors concerning the introduction of financial recuperation must contain the proposed period of financial recuperation, confirmed plan of financial recuperation, and schedule of repayment of indebtedness, and also may contain requirements for candidacies if administrative administrator.

2. A decision of the first meeting of creditors concerning the introduction of external administration must contain the proposed period of external administration, and also may contain the requirements for the candidacy of external administrator.

3. The proposed period of bankruptcy administrator and requirements for the candidacy of bankruptcy administrator also may be contained in the decision of the first meeting of creditors concerning recourse to an arbitrazh court with a petition to deem the debtor to be bankrupt and open a bankruptcy proceeding.

4. The decision of the first meeting of creditors concerning the conclusion of an amicable agreement must contain the information provided for by Article 151 of the present Federal Law.

Article 75. End of Observation

1. Unless established otherwise by the present Article, an arbitrazh court shall on the basis of the decision of the first meeting of creditors render a ruling concerning the introduction of financial recuperation or external administration or adopt a decision concerning the deeming of the debtor to be bankrupt and the opening of a bankruptcy proceeding, or confirm the amicable agreement and terminate the proceedings with regard to the case concerning bankruptcy.

2. If a decision was not adopted by the first meeting of creditors concerning the application of one of the procedures of bankruptcy, the arbitrazh court shall defer consideration of the case within the limits of the period established by Article 51 of the present Federal Law and oblige the creditors to adopt a respective decision within the period established by the arbitrazh court.

In the absence of the possibility to defer consideration of the case within the limits of the period established by Article 51 of the present Federal Law, the arbitrazh court shall:

render a ruling concerning the introduction of financial recuperation if there is a petition of the founders (or participants) of the debtor, owner of the property of a debtor-unitary enterprise, empowered State agency, and also a third person(s), on condition of the provision of security for the performance of obligations of the debtor in accordance with the schedule of repayment of indebtedness, the amount of which must exceed the amount of obligations of the debtor included in the register of demands of creditors on the date of the judicial session by not less than twenty per cent. In so doing the schedule of repayment of indebtedness must provide for the commencement of repayment of indebtedness not later than a month after the rendering by the arbitrazh court of a ruling concerning the introduction of financial recuperation and repayment of demands of creditors monthly in proportion, in equal participatory shares, within a year from the date of the commencement of the satisfaction of the demands of creditors;

in the absence of grounds for the introduction of financial recuperation provided for by the present Article, render a ruling concerning the introduction of external management if the arbitrazh court has sufficient grounds to suppose that the ability of the debtor to pay may be restored;

when there are indicia of bankruptcy established by the present Federal Law and in the absence of grounds to introduce financial recuperation and external management provided for by the present Article, adopt a decision concerning the deeming of the debtor to be bankrupt and the opening of a bankruptcy proceeding.

3. If a decision is adopted by the first meeting of creditors concerning recourse to an arbitrazh court with a petition concerning the introduction of external administration or deeming the debtor to be bankrupt and opening of a bankruptcy proceeding, the arbitrazh court may render a ruling concerning the introduction of financial recuperation on condition of the granting of the petition of the founders (or participants) of the debtor, owner of the property of a debtor-unitary enterprise, empowered State agency, and also third person(s) and the provision of a bank guarantee as security for the performance of obligations of the debtor in accordance with the schedule of repayment of indebtedness. The amount for which the bank guarantee is issued must exceed the amount of obligations of the debtor included in the register of creditors on the date of conducting the first meeting of creditors by not less than twenty per cent. In so doing the schedule of repayment of indebtedness must provide for the commencement of repayment of indebtedness not later than a month after the rendering by the arbitrazh court of the ruling concerning the introduction of financial recuperation and repayment of demands of creditors monthly in proportion, in equal

participatory shares, within a year from the date of the commencement of satisfaction of demands of creditors.

From the date of introduction of financial recuperation, external administration, deeming of the debtor to be bankrupt by an arbitrazh court and opening of a bankruptcy proceeding or confirmation of an amicable agreement the observation shall terminate.

If the administrative, external, or bankruptcy administrator was not confirmed simultaneously with the introduction of the respective procedure, and also in necessary instances, the arbitrazh court shall place the performance of the duties of the respective arbitrazh administrator on the temporary administrator and oblige the temporary administrator to conduct the meeting of creditors in order to consider the question concerning the choice of self-regulating organisation from among the members of which the administrative, external, or bankruptcy administrator should be chosen and the requirements for the candidacy of such administrator.

Chapter V. Financial Recuperation

Article 76. Petition Concerning Introduction of Financial Recuperation

1. In the course of observation a debtor on the basis of the decision of its founders (or participants), agency empowered by the owner of property of a debtor-unitary enterprise, founders (or participants) of the debtor, agency empowered by the owner of the property of a debtor-unitary enterprise, and third person(s) shall have the right in the procedure established by the present Federal Law to have recourse to the first meeting of creditors, and in instances established by the present Federal Law, — to an arbitrazh court, with a petition concerning the introduction of financial recuperation.

2. When having recourse to a meeting of creditors with a petition concerning the introduction of financial recuperation the persons who adopted the decision concerning recourse with such a petition shall be obliged to submit the said petition and documents appended thereto to the temporary administrator and arbitrazh court not later than fifteen days before the date of conducting the meeting of creditors.

The temporary administrator shall be obliged to grant to the creditors the possibility to familiarise themselves with the said documents.

Article 77. Petition of Founders (or Participants) of Debtor or Owner of Property of Debtor-Unitary Enterprise Concerning Introduction of Financial Recuperation

1. A decision concerning recourse to the first meeting of creditors with a petition concerning the introduction of financial recuperation shall be adopted at the general meeting by a majority of votes of the founders (or participants) of the

debtor who took part in the said meeting or by the agency empowered by the owner of property of the debtor-unitary enterprise.

2. The general meeting of founders (or participants) of a debtor or agency empowered by the owner of property of the debtor-unitary enterprise shall, when adopting the decision concerning recourse to the first meeting of creditors with a petition concerning the introduction of financial recuperation have the right to terminate before time the powers of the executive of the debtor and to elect (or appoint) a new executive of the debtor.

3. The founders (or participants) of the debtor who voted for the adoption of the decision concerning recourse to the first meeting of creditors with a petition concerning the introduction of financial recuperation shall have the right to provide security for the performance by the debtor of obligations in accordance with the schedule for repayment of indebtedness in the procedure and amount which has been provided by the present Federal Law or to organise the provision of such security.

4. The decision concerning recourse to the first meeting of creditors concerning the introduction of financial recuperation must contain:

information concerning the security for the performance by the debtor of obligations in accordance with the schedule of repayment of indebtedness proposed by the founders (or participants) of the debtor or owner of property of a debtor-unitary enterprise;

period of financial recuperation and period of satisfaction of the demands of creditors proposed by the founders (or participants) of the debtor or owner of property of a debtor-unitary enterprise.

5. To the decision concerning recourse to the first meeting of creditors with a petition concerning the introduction of financial recuperation shall be appended:

the plan of financial recuperation;

the schedule of repayment of indebtedness;

the protocol of the general meeting of founders (or participants) of the debtor or decision of the agency empowered by the owner of property of a debtor-unitary enterprise;

the list of founders (or participants) of the debtor who voted for recourse to the meeting of creditors with a petition concerning the introduction of financial recuperation;

when there is security for the performance of obligations of the debtor in accordance with the schedule of repayment of indebtedness, the information concerning the security for performance by the debtor of obligations in accordance with the schedule of repayment of indebtedness proposed by the founders (or participants) of the debtor or owner of property of a debtor-unitary enterprise;

other documents provided for by the present Federal Law.

Article 78. Petition of Third Person(s) Concerning Introduction of Financial Recuperation

1. By agreement with the debtor the petition concerning the introduction of financial recuperation may be filed by a third person(s). The said petition must contain information about the proposed security by a third person(s) for the performance by the debtor of obligations in accordance with the schedule of repayment of indebtedness.

2. To the petition concerning the introduction of financial recuperation shall be appended:
the schedule of repayment of indebtedness signed by an empowered person;
   the documents concerning the security proposed by a third person(s) for performance by the debtor of obligations in accordance with the schedule of repayment of indebtedness.
   In the event of recourse to the meeting of creditors concerning the introduction of financial recuperation by several persons, including the founders (or participants) of the debtor, security for the performance by the debtor of obligations in accordance with the schedule of repayment of indebtedness for each of them shall be determined by an agreement among them, which shall be appended to the petition. The said agreement must provide for joint and several responsibility of the persons who concluded it.

Article 79. Security for Performance by Debtor of Obligations in Accordance with Schedule of Repayment of Indebtedness

1. Performance by a debtor of obligations in accordance with the schedule of repayment of indebtedness may be secured by a pledge (or mortgage), bank guarantee, State or municipal guarantee, suretyship, and also other means which are not contrary to the present Federal Law.
   Performance by the debtor of obligations in accordance with the schedule of repayment of indebtedness may not be secured by withholding, deposit, or penalty.
   Property and property rights which belong to a debtor by right of ownership or right of economic jurisdiction may not be a subject of security for the performance by the debtor of obligations in accordance with the schedule of repayment of indebtedness.

2. Rights and duties of a person(s) who have provided security for the performance by the debtor of obligations in accordance with the schedule of repayment of indebtedness shall flow from the said security and shall arise from the date of rendering by the arbitrazh court of a ruling concerning the introduction of financial recuperation.

3. An agreement concerning the securing of obligations of the debtor in accordance with the schedule of repayment of indebtedness shall be concluded in

written form within fifteen days from the day of the introduction of financial recuperation and shall be signed by the person(s) who provided the security, and also by the temporary administrator in the interests of creditors. In the said instance the agreement concerning the securing of obligations of the debtor in accordance with the schedule of repayment of indebtedness must be submitted to the court not later than twenty days from the date of conclusion thereof.

4. The person(s) who provided security for performance by the debtor of obligations in accordance with the schedule of repayment of indebtedness shall bear responsibility for the failure of the debtor to perform the said obligations within the limits of the value of property and property rights submitted as security for the performance by the debtor of the said obligations.

5. In the event of securing the performance by the debtor of obligations in accordance with the schedule of repayment of obligations by a bank guarantee the temporary administrator or administrative administrator who signed the agreement in the interests of creditors whose demands are subject to satisfaction iin accordance with the confirmed schedule of repayment of indebtedness shall be deemed to be the beneficiary.

In the event of securing the performance by the debtor of obligations in accordance with the schedule of repayment of indebtedness by a mortgage State registration of the mortgage shall be conducted not later than forty-five days from the date of introduction of financial recuperation on the basis of a ruling of the arbitrazh court concerning the introduction of financial recuperation and agreement concerning the securing of obligations of the debtor in accordance with the schedule of repayment of indebtedness.

6. The introduction of a new procedure of bankruptcy with respect to the debtor shall not terminate the obligation with regard to securing the performance by the debtor of obligations in accordance with the schedule of repayment of indebtedness.

Article 80. Procedure for Introduction of Financial Recuperation

1. Financial recuperation shall be introduced by an arbitrazh court on the basis of the decision of a meeting of creditors, except for instances provided for by Article 75(2) and (3) of the present Federal Law.

2. Simultaneously with the rendering of a ruling concerning the introduction of financial recuperation an arbitrazh court shall confirm the administrative administrator, except for instances provided for by Article 75(2) of the present Federal Law.

3. In the ruling concerning the introduction of financial recuperation must be specified the period of financial recuperation, and also contain the schedule of repayment of indebtedness confirmed by the court.

In the event of the provision of security for the performance of obligations in accordance with the schedule of repayment of indebtedness the ruling concerning the introduction of financial recuperation must contain information concerning the persons who provided the security and the amount and means of such security.

4. The ruling of an arbitrazh court concerning the introduction of financial recuperation shall be subject to immediate execution..

5. The ruling of an arbitrazh court concerning the introduction of financial recuperation may be appealed.

6. Financial recuperation shall be introduced for a period of not more than two years.

Article 81. Consequences of Introduction of Financial Recuperation

1. From the date of rendering by the arbitrazh court of a ruling concerning the introduction of financial recuperation the following consequences shall ensue:

demands of creditors with regard to monetary obligations and the payment of obligatory payments, the period of performance of which has ensued on the date of introduction of financial recuperation, may be presented against the debtor only in compliance with the procedure for the presentation of demands against the debtor established by the present Federal Law;

measures previously taken with regard to securing the demands of creditors shall be abolished;

arrests on the property of the debtor and other limitations of the debtor in the part of disposition of property belonging to him may be imposed exclusively within the framework of the procedure concerning bankruptcy;

execution of documents of execution with regard to property sanctions, except for execution of documents of execution issued on the basis of decisions which entered into legal force before the date of introduction of financial recuperation concerning the recovery of indebtedness for earnings, payment of remuneration with regard to authors' contracts, demanding and obtaining property from another's illegal possession, compensation of harm caused to life or health, and compensation of moral harm shall be suspended;

satisfaction of demands of the founder (or participant) of the debtor concerning the partition of a participatory share (or share) in the property of the debtor in connection with the withdrawal from the composition thereof of founders (or participants) and the buying up by the debtor of placed stocks or the payment of the actual value of a participatory share (or share) shall be prohibited;

the payment of dividends and other payments with regard to emission securities shall be prohibited;

the termination of monetary obligations of the debtor by means of the set-off of a homogeneous demand shall not be permitted if in so doing the priority of satisfaction of the demands of creditors established by Article 134(4) of the present Federal Law is violated;

penalties (or fines, forfeits) subject to the payment of interest and other financial sanctions for the failure to perform or improper performance of monetary obligations and obligatory payments arising before the date of the introduction of financial recuperation shall not be added.

2. Interest shall be added in the procedure and amount which has been provided for by Article 95(2) of the present Federal Law to the amount of demands of creditors with regard to monetary obligations and payment of obligatory payments subject to satisfaction in accordance with the schedule of repayment of indebtedness.

Interest specified in the present point shall be subject to being added to the amount of demands of a creditor from the date of rendering the ruling concerning the introduction of financial recuperation and up to the date of repayment of demands of the creditor, and if such repayment has not occurred before the date of adoption of the decision concerning the deeming of the debtor to be bankrupt and opening of a bankruptcy proceeding—before the date of adoption of such decision.

3. Penalties (or fines, forfeits), and also amounts of losses caused in the form of lost advantage, which the debtor is obliged to pay to creditors in amounts which existed on the date of the introduction of financial recuperation in accordance with the schedule of repayment of indebtedness shall be subject to repayment in the course of financial recuperation in accordance with the schedule of repayment of indebtedness after satisfaction of all other demands of creditors.

4. Settlements with regard to obligations of the debtor whose period of performance had ensued before the date of introduction of financial recuperation shall be effectuated exclusively in accordance with the present Federal Law.

5. Demands of creditors shall be considered by an arbitrazh court in the procedure provided for by Article 71 of the present Federal Law.

Demands of creditors presented in the course of financial recuperation and included in the register of demands of creditors shall be satisfied not later than a month from the date of the end of performance of obligations in accordance with the schedule of repayment of indebtedness unless provided otherwise by the present Federal Law.

Article 82. Management of Debtor in Course of Financial Recuperation

1. In the course of financial recuperation the management organs of the debtor shall effectuate their powers with the limitations established by the present Chapter.

2. On the basis of a petition of the meeting of creditors, administrative administrator, or persons who provided security containing information about the

improper performance by an executive of the debtor of the financial recuperation plan or commission by an executive of the debtor of actions violating the rights and legal interests of creditors and/or persons who provided security, the arbitrazh court may remove the executive of the debtor from office in the procedure provided for by Article 69 of the present Federal Law. The arbitrazh court shall render a ruling concerning the removal of the executive of the debtor from office, which may be appealed.

3. A debtor shall not have the right without the consent of the meeting of creditors (or committee of creditors) to conclude transactions or several interconnected transactions, in the conclusion of which there is an interest or which:

are connected with the acquisition, alienation, or possibility of alienation directly or indirectly of property of the debtor whose balance sheet value comprises more than five per cent of the balance sheet value of assets of the debtor on the last reporting date preceding the date of conclusion of the transaction;

entail the issuance of loans (or credits), issuance of suretyships and guarantees, and also the founding of trust management of property of the debtor.

A debtor shall not have the right without the consent of the meeting of creditors (or committee of creditors) and person(s) who provided security to adopt a decision concerning the reorganisation (or merger, accession, separation, division, or transformation) thereof.

If the amount of monetary obligations of the debtor which arose after the introduction of financial recuperation comprises more than twenty per cent of the amount of demands of creditors included in the register of demands of creditors, transactions entailing the arising of new obligations of the debtor may be concluded exclusively with the consent of the meeting of creditors (or committee of creditors).

4. A debtor shall not have the right without the consent of the administrative administrator to conclude a transaction or several interconnected transactions which:

entail an increase of creditor indebtedness of the debtor by more than five per cent of the amount of demands of creditors included in the register of demands of creditors on the date of the introduction of financial recuperation;

are connected with the acquisition, alienation, or possibility of alienation directly or indirectly of property of the debtor, except for the realisation of property of the debtor which is a finished product (or work, services) manufactured or realised by the debtor in the process of ordinary economic activity;

entail the assignment of rights of demand and transfer of a debt;

entail the receipt of loans (or credits).

5. Transactions concluded by the debtor with a violation of the present Article may be deemed invalid upon the application of persons participating in the case concerning bankruptcy.

6. A debtor shall have the right to alienate property which is the subject of pledge, transfer it on lease or uncompensated use to another person, or otherwise dispose of it, or encumber a subject of pledge with rights and claims of third persons only with the consent of the creditor whose demand has been secured by the pledge of such property, unless provided otherwise by a federal law or contract of pledge and does not arise from the essence of the pledge.

Property which is the subject of pledge shall be sold only at a public sale in the procedure provided for by Article 110(3)–(9) of the present Federal Law. The sale of property which is the subject of pledge shall be permitted only with the consent of a creditor whose demand has been secured by the pledge of such property. In this instance the demand of the creditor secured by a pledge shall be repaid at the expense of the value of the sold property preferentially before other creditors after the sale of the subject of pledge, except for obligations to creditors of the first and second priorities, the rights of demand with regard to which arose before the conclusion of the respective contract of pledge.

Article 83. Administrative Administrator

1. An administrative administrator shall be confirmed by an arbitrazh court in the procedure provided for by Article 45 of the present Federal Law.

2. An administrative administrator shall act from the date of his confirmation by an arbitrazh court until the termination of financial recuperation or until his removal or being relieved by an arbitrazh court.

3. An administrative administrator in the course of financial recuperation shall be obliged to:

conduct the register of demands of creditors, except for instances provided for by the present Federal Law;

convoke the meeting of creditors in instances established by the present Federal Law;

consider reports concerning the course of the fulfillment of the financial recuperation plan and schedule of repayment of indebtedness provided by the debtor and submit an opinion concerning the course of fulfillment of the financial recuperation plan and schedule of repayment of indebtedness to the meeting of creditors;

submit for consideration of the meeting of creditors (or committee of creditors) information concerning the course of fulfillment of the financial recuperation plan and schedule of repayment of indebtedness;

effectuate control over the timely performance by the debtor of current demands of creditors;

effectuate control over the course of the fulfillment of the financial recuperation plan and schedule of repayment of indebtedness;

effectuate control over the timeliness and fullness of the transfer of monetary means for repayment of the demands of creditors;

in the event of the failure of the debtor to perform obligations in accordance with the schedule of repayment of indebtedness, to demand from persons who provided security for the performance by the debtor of obligations in accordance with the schedule of repayment of indebtedness the performance of duties arising from the security provided;

perform other duties provided for by the present Federal Law.

4. An administrative administrator shall have the right to:
demand from the executive of the debtor information concerning current activity of the debtor;

take part in the inventorying in the event of its being conducted by the debtor;

agree transactions and decisions of the debtor in instances provided for by the present Federal Law and provide information to creditors concerning the said transactions and decisions;

have recourse to an arbitrazh court with a petition concerning the removal of an executive of the debtor in instances established by the present Federal Law;

have recourse to an arbitrazh court with a petition concerning the taking of additional measures with regard to ensuring the preservation of property of the debtor, and also the abolition of such measures;

present to an arbitrazh court in his own name demands concerning the deeming of transactions and decisions to be invalid, and also the application of the consequences of invalidity of null transactions concluded or performed by the debtor with a violation of the requirements of the present Federal Law;

effectuate other powers provided for by the present Federal Law.

5. An administrative administrator may be relieved by an arbitrazh court from the performance of duties as administrative administrator:
upon the application of an administrative administrator concerning the relieving thereof from the performance of duties of administrative administrator;

in other instances provided for by a federal law.

An administrative administrator may be removed by an arbitrazh court from the performance of duties of administrative administrator:

on the basis of a decision of a meeting of creditors in the event of the failure to perform or the improper performance of duties placed on an administrative administrator established by the present Federal Law;

in connection with the satisfaction by an arbitrazh court of an appeal of a person participating in the case concerning bankruptcy for the failure to perform or improper performance by an administrative administrator of the duties placed on him on condition that such failure to perform or improper performance violated the rights or legal interests of the declarant of the appeal, and also entailed or could entail losses of the debtor or creditors thereof;

in the event of eliciting circumstances which obstructed the confirmation of the person as administrative administrator, including if such circumstances arose after confirmation of the person as administrative administrator;

in other instances provided for by a federal law.

In the event of the relieving or removal of an administrative administrator an arbitrazh court shall confirm the new administrative administrator in the procedure established by the present Article.

An administrative administrator relieved or removed from the performance of duties of administrative administrator shall be obliged to ensure within three days the transfer of bookkeeping and other documentation of the juridical person, seals and stamps, material and other valuables to the newly confirmed administrative administrator.

The ruling of the arbitrazh court concerning the relieving or removal of an administrative administrator from the performance of duties of administrative administrator shall be subject to immediate execution. The ruling of an arbitrazh court concerning the relieving or removal of an administrative administrator may be appealed. The ruling of an arbitrazh court concerning the relieving or removal of an administrative administrator shall not suspend the execution of the ruling.

6. Termination of the proceedings with regard to a case concerning bankruptcy in connection with repayment of the demands of creditors in the course of financial recuperation shall entail termination of the powers of the administrative administrator.

7. If a ruling has been rendered by an arbitrazh court concerning the introduction of external administration or a decision adopted concerning the deeming of a debtor to be bankrupt and the opening of a bankruptcy proceeding and another person has been confirmed as external administrator or bankruptcy administrator, the administrative administrator shall continue to perform his duties until confirmation of the external or bankruptcy administrator.

Article 84. Financial Recuperation Plan and Schedule of Repayment of Indebtedness

1. A financial recuperation plan prepared by the founders (or participants) of the debtor or owner of property of a debtor-unitary enterprise shall be confirmed by the meeting of creditors and must provide for means of receipt by the debtor of means necessary to satisfy demands of creditors in accordance with the schedule of repayment of indebtedness in the course of financial recuperation.

2. The schedule of repayment of indebtedness shall be signed by the person empowered to do so by the founders (or participants) of the debtor or owner of property of a debtor-unitary enterprise, and a unilateral obligation of the debtor shall arise from the date of confirmation of the schedule of repayment of indebtedness by an arbitrazh court to repay the indebtedness of the debtor to creditors within the periods established by the schedule.

When there is security for performance of obligations of the debtor by the debtor in accordance with the schedule of repayment of indebtedness it shall also be signed by the person who provided such security.

3. The schedule of repayment of indebtedness must provide for repayment of all demands of creditors included in the register of demands of creditors not later than a month before the date of the end of the period of financial recuperation, and also repayment of demands of creditors of the first and second priorities, not later than six months from the date of introduction of financial recuperation.

The schedule of repayment of indebtedness with regard to obligatory payments to be recovered in accordance with legislation on taxes and charges shall be established in accordance with the requirements of legislation on taxes and charges.

In the event of the introduction of financial recuperation in the procedure established by Article 75(2) or (3) of the present Federal Law, the schedule of repayment of indebtedness must meet the requirements of Article 75 of the present Federal Law.

4. Proportional repayment of demands of creditors in the priority established by Article 134 of the present Federal Law must be provided for by the schedule of repayment of indebtedness.

5. A debtor shall have the right to perform the schedule of repayment of indebtedness before time.

Article 85. Making of Changes in Schedule of Repayment of Indebtedness

1. In the event of the failure of the debtor to perform the schedule of repayment of indebtedness (or nonrepayment of indebtedness within the established periods and/or within the established amounts) the founders (or participants) of the debtor, owner of property of a debtor-unitary enterprise, or third persons who have provided security not later than fourteen days from the date provided for by the schedule of repayment of indebtedness shall have the right to have recourse to the meeting of creditors with a petition concerning confirmation of changes made in the schedule of repayment of indebtedness or repay demands in creditors in accordance with the schedule of repayment of indebtedness. A copy of the petition shall be sent to the administrative administrator. The administrative administrator shall convoke a meeting of creditors not later than fourteen days from the date of receipt of the petition.

In the event of the adoption of a decision concerning the making of changes in the schedule of repayment of indebtedness the meeting of creditors shall have the right to have recourse to an arbitrazh court with a petition concerning confirmation of the changes made in the schedule of repayment of indebtedness.

In the event of the refusal of the meeting of creditors to confirm changes made in the schedule of repayment of indebtedness the meeting of creditors shall adopt a decision concerning recourse to an arbitrazh court with a petition concerning the termination before time of financial recuperation.

2. If the amount of demands declared by creditors in the course of financial recuperation and included in the register of demands of creditors exceeds by more than per cent the amount of demands of creditors whose repayment is provided for by the schedule of repayment of indebtedness, the administrative administrator shall be obliged not later than fourteen days from the date of inclusion of the said demands in the register of demands of creditors to convoke a meeting of creditors in order to adopt a decision concerning the making of changes in the schedule of repayment of indebtedness.

In the event of the adoption of a decision concerning the making of changes in the schedule of repayment of indebtedness the meeting of creditors shall have the right to have recourse to an arbitrazh court with a petition concerning confirmation of the changes made in the schedule of repayment of indebtedness.

In the event of the refusal of the meeting of creditors to confirm the changes made in the schedule of repayment of indebtedness the meeting of creditors shall have the right to petition concerning the termination before time of financial recuperation.

3. The meeting of creditors which adopted the decision concerning the making of changes in the schedule of repayment of indebtedness may have recourse to the person(s) who provided security for performance of obligations by the debtor in accordance with the schedule of repayment of indebtedness with a proposal concerning an increase of the amount of security for performance by the debtor of obligations in accordance with the schedule of repayment of indebtedness.

4. An arbitrazh court shall have the right to render a ruling concerning the making of changes in the schedule of repayment of indebtedness only with respect to demands included in the register of demands of creditors.

5. The making of changes in the schedule of repayment of indebtedness may not be grounds for a refusal of a person(s) who have provided security for performance of obligations by the debtor in accordance with the schedule of repayment of indebtedness to perform obligations with regard to securing the performance of obligations by the debtor in accordance with the schedule of repayment of indebtedness, concerning which an agreement has been concluded concerning the securing of obligations of the debtor.

Article 86. End of Financial Recuperation Before Time

1. In the event of repayment by the debtor of all demands of creditors provided for by the schedule of repayment of indebtedness before the expiry of the period of financial recuperation established by the arbitrazh court the debtor shall submit a report concerning the end of financial recuperation before time.

2. The procedure for the submission of a report and consideration by an arbitrazh court of the results of financial recuperation, and also the composition of the materials appended to the report, have been established by Article 88(1)–(4) of the present Federal Law.

3. With regard to results of the consideration of financial recuperation and appeals of creditors an arbitrazh court shall render one of the following rulings:

concerning termination of the proceedings with regard to the case concerning bankruptcy if there is no unpaid indebtedness and appeals of creditors have been deemed to be unsubstantiated;

concerning a refusal to terminate the proceedings with regard to a case concerning bankruptcy if the existence of unpaid indebtedness has been elicited and appeals of creditors have been deemed to be substantiated.

The said rulings shall enter into force immediately and may be appealed.

Article 87. Termination of Financial Recuperation Before Time

1. The grounds for termination of financial recuperation before time shall be:

the failure to submit to an arbitrazh court within the periods provided for by Article 79(3) of the present Federal Law an agreement concerning security for obligations of the debtor in accordance with the schedule of repayment of indebtedness;

the repeated or material (for a period of more than fifteen days) violation in the course of financial recuperation of the periods for the satisfaction of demands of creditors established by the schedule of repayment of indebtedness.

2. An administrative administrator shall be obliged within fifteen days from the date of arising of grounds for the termination before time of financial recuperation to convoke a meeting of creditors for consideration of the question concerning recourse to an arbitrazh court with a petition concerning the termination of financial recuperation before time.

3. A debtor shall be obliged to submit to the meeting of creditors convoked in accordance with point 2 of the present Article a report concerning the results of the fulfillment of the schedule of repayment of indebtedness and financial recuperation plan when there is such a plan.

To the report must be appended the balance sheet of the debtor on the last reporting date, report on profits and losses of the debtor, information concerning the amount of repaid demands of creditors, and documents confirming the repayment of demands of creditors.

Simultaneously with the report of the debtor the administrative administrator shall submit to the meeting of creditors his opinion concerning the course of the fulfillment of the financial recuperation plan and schedule of satisfaction of the demands of creditors.

4. A meeting of creditors shall have the right with regard to the results of consideration of the report of the debtor and opinion of the administrative administrator to adopt a decision concerning recourse to a court with one of the petitions concerning:

the introduction of external administration;

the deeming of the debtor to be bankrupt and the opening of a bankruptcy proceeding.

A copy of the protocol of the session of the meeting of creditors and list of creditors who voted against the decision adopted by the meeting of creditors or who did not take part in voting with regard to the particular question shall be appended to the petition of the meeting of creditors.

5. An arbitrazh court on the basis of the petition of the meeting of creditors shall adopt one of the following acts:

ruling concerning the refusal to satisfy the respective petition of the meeting of creditors if performance by the debtor of the demands of creditors in accordance with the schedule of repayment of indebtedness has been elicited and the appeals of creditors have been deemed to be unsubstantiated;

ruling concerning the introduction of external administration if there is a possibility to restore the ability of the debtor to pay;

decision concerning the deeming of a debtor to be bankrupt and the opening of a bankruptcy proceeding in the absence of grounds for the introduction of external administration and the presence of the indicia of bankruptcy.

6. If financial recuperation was introduced by an arbitrazh court in the procedure established by Article 75(3) of the present Federal Law upon the petition of a person participating in the case concerning bankruptcy an arbitrazh court may terminate financial recuperation before time on condition of a violation in the course of financial recuperation of periods to satisfy the demands of creditors established by the schedule of repayment of indebtedness. In the said event the arbitrazh court shall render a ruling concerning the introduction of procedures of bankruptcy, the petition concerning the introduction of which was adopted by the first meeting of creditors.

Article 88. End of Financial Recuperation

1. Not later than a month before the expiry of the established period of financial recuperation the debtor shall be obliged to submit to the administrative administrator a report concerning the results of conducting financial recuperation.

2. To the report shall be appended:

the balance sheet of the debtor on the last reporting date;

the report on profits and losses of the debtor;

the documents confirming the repayment of demands of creditors.

3. The administrative administrator shall consider the report of the debtor concerning the results of financial recuperation and draw up an opinion concerning the fulfillment of the financial recuperation plan, schedule of repayment of indebtedness, and satisfaction of demands of creditors which shall not later than ten days from the date of receipt of the report of the debtor concerning the results of financial recuperation be sent to creditors included in the register of demands of creditors and to the arbitrazh court. To the opinion of the administrative administrator must be appended a copy of the report of the debtor concerning the results of financial recuperation and a list of paid or unpaid demands of creditors included in the register of demands of creditors.

4. If demands of creditors included in the register of demands of creditors have not been satisfied on the date of consideration of the report of the debtor or the said report has not been submitted to the administrative administrator within the period established by point 1 of the present Article the administrative administrator shall convoke a meeting of creditors which is empowered to adopt one of the decisions concerning:

recourse with a petition to the arbitrazh court concerning the introduction of external management;

recourse with a petition to the arbitrazh court concerning the deeming of a debtor to be bankrupt and the opening of a bankruptcy proceeding.

5. After receipt of the opinion of an administrative administrator or petition of a meeting of creditors an arbitrazh court shall designate the date of the session with regard to the consideration of the results of financial recuperation and appeals of creditors against the actions of a debtor and administrative administrator. An arbitrazh court shall inform the persons participating in the case concerning bankruptcy about the date and place of the judicial session in the procedure established by the present Federal Law.

6. With regard to the results of consideration of the results of financial recuperation, and also appeals of creditors, an arbitrazh court shall adopt one of the judicial acts:

ruling concerning termination of the proceedings with regard to the case concerning bankruptcy if there is no unpaid indebtedness and appeals of creditors have been deemed to be unsubstantiated;

ruling concerning the introduction of external administration in the event of the presence of the possibility to restore the ability of the debtor to pay;

decision concerning the deeming of a debtor to be bankrupt and the opening of a bankruptcy proceeding in the absence of grounds for the introduction of external administration and the presence of indicia of bankruptcy.

Article 89. Performance of Obligations to Persons Who Provided Security for Performance of Obligations by Debtor in Accordance with Schedule of Repayment of Indebtedness

1. In the event of the failure of the debtor to perform the schedule of repayment of indebtedness within more than five days the administrative administrator shall be obliged to have recourse to the persons who provided security for performance of obligations by the debtor in accordance with the schedule of repayment of indebtedness with a demand concerning performance by the debtor of obligations in accordance with the schedule of repayment of indebtedness.

2. Monetary means received as a result of performance by persons who provided security for performance of obligations by the debtor in accordance with the schedule of repayment of indebtedness shall be transferred to the account of the debtor for settlements with creditors.

Settlements with creditors shall be effectuated by the debtor in the procedure established by Article 84(4) of the present Federal Law.

3. From the date of satisfaction of the requirements of creditors an administrative administrator or register-holder shall make a respective entry in the register of demands of creditors.

4. In the event of the satisfaction of demands of creditors by persons who have provided security for the performance of obligations by the debtor in accordance with the schedule of repayment of indebtedness the demands of persons who have provided security for performance of obligations by the debtor in accordance with the schedule of repayment of indebtedness shall be repaid by the debtor after termination of the proceedings with regard to the case concerning bankruptcy or in the course of a bankruptcy proceeding in the composition of demands of creditors of the third priority.

5. Disputes between persons who have provided security for performance of obligations by the debtor in accordance with the schedule of repayment of indebtedness and the administrative administrator, bankruptcy creditors, and empowered agencies shall be settled by the arbitrazh court considering the case concerning bankruptcy.

Article 90. Consequences of Performance of Obligations by Persons Who Provided Security for Performance of Obligations by Debtor in Accordance with Schedule of Repayment of Indebtedness

1. Persons who have provided security for performance of obligations by the debtor in accordance with the schedule of repayment of indebtedness and who have performed obligations arising from such security shall have the right to present their demands against the debtor in the general procedure provided for by a federal law.

2. If in the course of financial recuperation by persons who have provided security for performance of obligations by a debtor in accordance with the schedule of repayment of indebtedness demands of creditors have been satisfied, when introducing subsequent procedures of bankruptcy demands of the said persons shall be subject to inclusion in the register of demands of creditors as demands of bankruptcy creditors.

Article 91. Consequences of Failure to Perform Obligations by Persons Who Provided Security for Performance of Obligations by Debtor in Accordance with Schedule of Repayment of Indebtedness

The failure to perform by persons who have provided security for the performance of obligations by the debtor in accordance with the schedule of repayment of indebtedness of their obligations arising from the security provided within the period established by Article 89(1) of the present Federal Law shall entail responsibility of the said persons in accordance with civil legislation.

Article 92. Transition to External Administration

1. An arbitrazh court with regard to the results of consideration of the results of conducting financial recuperation shall have the right to render a ruling concerning the introduction of external administration in the event of:

the establishment of the real possibility to restore the ability of the debtor to pay;

the filing in an arbitrazh court of a petition of a meeting of creditors concerning the transition to external administration in instances provided for by the present Federal Law;

the conducting of the meeting of creditors at which a decision was adopted concerning recourse to an arbitrazh court with a petition concerning the deeming of a debtor to be bankrupt and the opening of a bankruptcy proceeding circumstances emerge giving grounds to suppose that the ability of the debtor to pay may be restored;

other instances provided for by the present Federal Law.

2. The aggregate period of financial recuperation and external administration may not exceed two years.

If from the date of the introduction of financial recuperation until the date of consideration by an arbitrazh court of the question concerning the introduction of external administration more than eighteen months have elapsed, the arbitrazh court may not render a ruling concerning the introduction of external administration.

Chapter VI. External Administration

Article 93. Procedure for Introduction of External Administration

1. External administration shall be introduced by an arbitrazh court on the basis of a decision of the meeting of creditors, except for instances provided for by the present Federal Law.

2. External administration shall be introduced for a period of not more than eighteen months, which may be extended in the procedure provided for by the present Federal Law, but for not more than six months, unless established otherwise by the present Federal Law.

A ruling concerning extension of the period of external administration shall be subject to immediate execution and may be appealed in the procedure established by Article 61(3) of the present Federal Law.

3. Upon the petition of a meeting of creditors or external administrator the established period of external administrated may be reduced.

Article 94. Consequences of Introduction of External Administration

1. From the date of the introduction of external administration:

the powers of the executive of the debtor shall terminate and the management of affairs shall be placed on the external administrator;

the external administrator shall have the right to publish an order concerning dismissal of the executive of the debtor or to propose to the executive of the debtor to transfer to other work in the procedure and on the conditions which have been established by labour legislation;

the powers of the management organs of the debtor and of the owner of property of a debtor-unitary enterprise shall terminate and the powers of the executive of the debtor, and other management organs of the debtor shall pass to the external administrator, except for the powers of management organs of the debtor provided for by point 2 of the present Article. Management organs of the debtor, temporary administrator, and administrative administrator shall within three days from the date of confirmation of the external administrator be obliged to ensure the transfer of bookkeeping and other documentation of the debtor, seals and stamps, material and other valuables to the external administrator;

previously taken measures with regard to securing the demands of creditors shall be abolished;

arrests on the property of the debtor and other limitations of the debtor with respect to the disposition of property belonging to them may be imposed exclusively within the framework of the procedure concerning bankruptcy;

a moratorium shall be introduced on the satisfaction of demands of creditors with regard to monetary obligations and payment of obligatory payments, except for instances provided for by the present Federal Law.

2. Management organs of the debtor within the limits of the competence established by a federal law shall have the right to adopt a decision concerning:

the making of changes in and additions to the charter of the society with respect to an increase of charter capital;

the determination of the quantity and par value of declared stocks;

the increase of charter capital of a joint-stock society by means of the placement of additional common stocks;

the recourse with a petition to the meeting of creditors concerning the inclusion in the external administration plan of the possibility of an additional emission of stocks;

the determination of the procedure for conducting the general meeting of stockholders;

the recourse with a petition concerning the sale of the enterprise of the debtor;

the substitution of assets of the debtor;

the election of a representative of the founders (or participants) of the debtor;

the conclusion of an agreement between a third person(s) and management organs of the debtor empowered in accordance with the constitutive documents to adopt a decision concerning the conclusion of large-scale transactions and the conditions of the provision of monetary means for performance of obligations of the debtor;

other decisions necessary for the placement of additional common stocks of the debtor.

The petition of management organs of the debtor concerning the sale of an enterprise must contain information concerning the minimum price of the sale of the enterprise of the debtor.

Means expended for the conducting of a meeting of stockholders and session of the council of directors (or supervisory council) and other management organ of the debtor shall be compensated at the expense of the debtor only if such possibility was provided for by the external administration plan.

Article 95. Moratorium on Satisfaction of Demands of Creditors

1. A moratorium on the satisfaction of demands of creditors shall extend to monetary obligations and obligatory payments whose periods of performance have ensued before the introduction of external administration.

2. Within the period of operation of a moratorium on the satisfaction of demands of creditors with regard to monetary obligations and the payment of obligatory payments provided for by point 1 of the present Article:

the execution of documents of execution shall be suspended with regard to property sanctions, other documents recovery under which is performed in an uncontested procedure shall not be permitted for compulsory execution except for execution of documents of execution issued on the basis of decisions which entered into force before the introduction of external administration concerning the recovery of indebtedness with regard to earnings, payment of remuneration under authors' contracts, demanding and obtaining property from another's illegal possession, compensation of harm caused to life or health, and compensation of moral harm, and also recovery of indebtedness with regard to current payments;

penalties (or fines, forfeits) and other financial sanctions shall not be added for the failure to perform or improper performance of monetary obligations and obligatory payments which arose after the acceptance of the application concerning the deeming of a debtor to be bankrupt, and also penalties (or fines, forfeits) subject to payment with regard to them.

Interest shall be added on the amount of demands of bankruptcy creditors and empowered agency in the amount established in accordance with Article 4 of the present Federal Law on the date of introduction of external administration in the procedure and amount which was provided for by the present Article.

Interest shall be added to the amount of demands of a bankruptcy creditor and empowered agency expressed in the currency of the Russian Federation in the amount of the refinancing rate established by the Central Bank of the Russian Federation on the date of the introduction of external administration.

A lower amount of interest subject to payment or shorter period for adding interest in comparison with such amount or period provided for by the present Article may be provided for by an agreement of the external administrator with a bankruptcy creditor.

Interest subject to being added and to payment in accordance with the present Article shall be added to the amount of demands of creditors of each priority from the date of the introduction of external administration and up to the date of the rendering by an arbitrazh court of a ruling concerning the commencement of settlements with creditors with regard to the demands of creditors of each priority, or up to the moment of satisfaction of the said demands by the debtor or third person in the course of external management, or up to the moment of adoption of a decision concerning the deeming of a debtor to be bankrupt and the opening of a bankruptcy proceeding.

Interest added in accordance with the present Article shall not be taken into account when determining the quantity of votes belonging to a bankruptcy creditor or empowered agency at meetings of creditors.

Interest added in accordance with the present Article in the event of deeming a debtor to be bankrupt and the opening of a bankruptcy proceeding shall be subject to satisfaction in the procedure established by Article 137(3) of the present Federal Law.

3. A moratorium on the satisfaction of demands of creditors shall extend also to demands of creditors concerning compensation of losses connected with the refusal of the external administrator to perform contracts of the debtor.

4. The rules provided for by points 2 and 3 of the present Article shall not apply to monetary obligations and obligatory payments which arose after the acceptance by the arbitrazh court of the application concerning the deeming of a debtor to be bankrupt and the period of performance of which ensued after the introduction of external administration.

5. A moratorium on the satisfaction of demands of creditors shall not extend to demands concerning the recovery of indebtedness with regard to earnings, payment of remuneration under authors' contracts, compensation of harm caused to life or health, and compensation of moral harm.

Article 96. External Administrator

1. An external administrator shall be confirmed by an arbitrazh court simultaneously with the introduction of external administration, except for instances provided for by the present Federal Law.

2. Before the date of confirmation of the external administrator the arbitrazh court shall place the performance of duties and effectuation of the rights of external administrator established by the present Federal Law, except for drawing up the external administration plan, on the person who is the acting temporary administrator or administrative administrator of the debtor.

An arbitrazh court shall render a ruling concerning the confirmation of the external administrator.

3. The ruling concerning confirmation of an external administrator shall be subject to immediate execution.

4. The ruling concerning confirmation of the external administrator may be appealed. Appeal of a ruling concerning confirmation of an external administrator shall not entail suspension of the execution thereof.

5. An external administrator shall be confirmed by an arbitrazh court in the procedure provided for by Article 45 of the present Federal Law.

Article 97. Relieving External Administrator

1. An external administrator may be relieved by an arbitrazh court from the performance of duties of external administrator:

upon the application of the external administrator concerning the relieving thereof from the performance of duties of external administrator;

in other instances provided for by a federal law.

2. A ruling of an arbitrazh court concerning the relieving of an external administrator from the performance of duties of external administrator shall be subject to immediate execution and may be appealed.

3. An external administrator relieved from the performance of duties of external administrator shall be obliged to transfer bookkeeping and other documenta-

tion of the debtor, seals and stamps, material and other valuables within three days to the newly confirmed external administrator.

4. In the event of relieving the external administrator the arbitrazh court shall confirm the new external administrator in the procedure provided for by Article 96 of the present Federal Law.

Article 98. Removal of Temporary Administrator

1. An external administrator may be removed by an arbitrazh court from the performance of duties of external administrator:

on the basis of the decision of a meeting of creditors concerning recourse to an arbitrazh court with a petition in the event of the failure to perform or improper performance by the external administrator of duties placed on him or the failure to fulfil measures provided for by the external administration plan with regard to restoration of the ability to pay;

in connection with satisfaction by the arbitrazh court of an appeal of a person participating in the case concerning bankruptcy against the failure to perform or improper performance by the external administrator of duties placed on him, on condition that such failure to perform or improper performance of duties violated the rights and legal interests of the declarant of the appeal, and also entailed or could entail losses to the debtor or his creditors;

in the event of the eliciting of circumstances obstructing the confirmation of the person as external administrator, and also in the event such circumstances arose after confirmation of the person as external administrator;

in other instances provided for by a federal law.

2. A ruling of an arbitrazh court concerning removal of an external administrator from the performance of duties of external administrator shall be subject to immediate execution and may be appealed. Appeal of a ruling of an arbitrazh court concerning the removal of an external administrator shall not suspend the execution of such ruling.

3. In the event of the removal of external administrator an arbitrazh court shall confirm the new external administrator in the procedure established by Article 96 of the present Federal Law.

4. An external administrator removed from the performance of the duties of external administrator shall be obliged to ensure the transfer of bookkeeping and other documentation of the debtor, seals and stamps, material and other valuables to the newly confirmed external administrator within three days from the moment of confirmation thereof.

Article 99. Rights and Duties of External Administrator

1. An external administrator shall have the right to:

dispose of property of the debtor in accordance with the external administration plan with the limitations provided for by the present Federal Law;

conclude an amicable agreement in the name of the debtor;

declare a refusal to perform contracts of the debtor in accordance with Article 102 of the present Federal Law;

present to an arbitrazh court in his own name demands concerning the recognition of the invalidity of transactions and decisions, and also the application of the consequences of the invalidity of null transactions concluded or performed by the debtor with a violation of the requirements of the present Federal Law;

effectuate other actions provided for by the present Federal Law.

2. An external administrator shall be obliged to:

accept for management property of the debtor and conduct the inventorying thereof;

work out the external administration plan and submit it for confirmation to the meeting of creditors;

conduct bookkeeping, financial, and statistical records and reports;

declare in the established procedure objections relative to demands of creditors presented against the debtor;

take measures with regard to the recovery of indebtedness to the debtor;

conduct the register of demands of creditors;

realize measures provided for by the external administration plan in the procedure and on the conditions which have been established by the present Federal Law;

inform the committee of creditors concerning the realisation of measures provided for by the external administration plan;

submit to the meeting of creditors a report concerning the results of the realisation of the external administration plan;

effectuate other powers provided for by the present Federal Law.

Article 100. Establishment of Amount of Demands of Creditors

1. Creditors shall have the right to present heir demands against the debtor at any moment in the course of external administration. The said demands shall be sent to the arbitrazh court and external administrator with the judicial act or other documents confirming the substantiation of these demands appended. The said demands shall be included by the external administrator or register-holder in the register of demands of creditors on the basis of a ruling of the arbitrazh court concerning the inclusion of the said demands in the register of demands of creditors.

2. An external administrator shall be obliged within five days from the date of receipt of demands of creditors to inform the representative of the founders (or participants) of the debtor or representative or the owner of property of a debtor-

unitary enterprise about receipt of the demands of creditors and to provide the said persons the possibility to familiarise themselves with the demands of creditors and documents appended thereto.

3. Objections relative to the demands of creditors may be presented to an arbitrazh court by an external administrator, representative of the founders (or participants) of the debtor, or representative of the owner of property of a debtor-unitary enterprise, and also by creditors whose demands have been included in the register of demands of creditors. Such objections shall be presented within a month from the date of receipt by the external administrator of the said demands.

4. When there are objections relative to demands of creditors the arbitrazh court shall verify the substantiation of respective demands of creditors. A ruling of an arbitrazh court shall be rendered with regard to the results of consideration concerning the inclusion or refusal to include the said demands in the register of demands of creditors. The amount and priority of satisfaction of such demands shall be specified in the ruling of the arbitrazh court concerning inclusion.

5. Demands of creditors with regard to which objections have not been received shall be considered by an arbitrazh court for verification of their substantiation and the presence of grounds for inclusion in the register of creditors. The arbitrazh court shall render a ruling with regard to the results of consideration concerning the inclusion or refusal to include the demands of creditors in the register of demands of creditors. The said demands may be considered by an arbitrazh court without the enlistment of persons participating in the case concerning bankruptcy.

6. A ruling concerning the inclusion or refusal to include demands of creditors in the register of demands of creditors shall be subject to immediate execution and may be appealed.

A ruling concerning inclusion or refusal to include demands of creditors in the register of demands of creditors shall be sent by the arbitrazh court to the external administrator or register-holder and applicant.

Article 101. Disposition of Property of Debtor

1. Large-scale transactions, and also transactions in the conclusion of which there is an interest, shall be concluded by the external administrator only with the consent of the meeting of creditors (or committee of creditors) unless provided otherwise by the present Federal Law.

2. For the purposes of the present Federal Law to large-scale transactions shall be relegated transactions or several interconnected transactions connected with the acquisition, alienation, or possibility of alienation directly or indirectly of property of the debtor whose balance sheet value is more than ten per cent of the

balance sheet value of assets of the debtor on the last reporting date preceding the date of conclusion of such transaction.

3. For the purposes of the present Federal Law transactions in the conclusion of which there is an interest shall be deemed to be transactions, a party to which are interested persons with respect to the external administrator or bankruptcy creditor.

4. Transactions entailing the receipt or issuance of loans, issue of suretyships or guarantees, assignment of rights of demands, transfer of a debt, alienation or acquisition of stocks and participatory shares of economic partnerships and societies, and the founding of trust management shall be concluded by the external administrator after agreement with the meeting of creditors (or committee of creditors). The transactions specified in the present point may be concluded by the external administrator without agreement with the meeting of creditors (or committee of creditors) if the possibility and conditions of the conclusion of such transactions was provided for by the external administration plan.

5. Property which is the subject of pledge shall be sold only at an open public sale. The sale of property which is the subject of pledge shall be permitted only with the consent of the creditor whose demands have been secured by the pledge of this property. In this instance the demands of the creditor secured by a pledge shall be repaid at the expense of the value of the sold property preferentially before other creditors after the sale of the subject of pledge, except for obligations to creditors of the first and second priorities, the rights of demand with regard to which arose before the conclusion of the respective contract of pledge.

Article 102. Refusal to Perform Transactions of Debtor

1. An external administrator within three months from the date of the introduction of external administration shall have the right to refuse to perform contracts and other transactions of the debtor.

2. The refusal to perform contracts and other transactions of the debtor may be declared only with respect to transactions not performed by the parties fully or partially if such transactions obstruct the restoration of the ability of the debtor to pay or if performance of such transactions by the debtor entails losses for the debtor in comparison with analogous transactions to be concluded under comparable circumstances.

3. In instances provided for by point 2 of the present Article a contract shall be considered to be dissolved from the date of receipt by all the parties under such contract of the statement of the external administrator concerning the refusal to perform the contract.

4. A party under a contract with respect to which is declared a refusal to perform shall have the right to demand compensation of losses from the debtor caused by the refusal to perform the contract of the debtor.

5. The provisions provided by the present Article shall not apply with respect to contracts of the debtor concluded in the course of observation with the consent of the temporary administrator or in the course of financial recuperation if such contracts were concluded in accordance with the present Federal Law.

Article 103. Invalidity of Transaction Concluded by Debtor

1. A transaction concluded by a debtor, including a transaction concluded by the debtor before the date of introduction of external management, may be deemed by a court or arbitrazh court to be invalid upon the application of the external administrator on the grounds provided for by a federal law.

2. A transaction concluded by a debtor with an interested person shall be deemed by a court or arbitrazh court to be invalid upon the application of the external administrator if as a result of the performance of the said transaction the creditors or debtor were or might be caused losses.

3. A transaction concluded or performed by a debtor with an individual creditor or other person after the acceptance by an arbitrazh court of an application concerning the deeming of a debtor to be bankrupt and/or within six months preceding the filing the application concerning the deeming of a debtor to be bankrupt may be deemed by a court to be invalid upon the application of the external administrator or creditor if the said transaction entails preferential satisfaction of demands for some creditors over other creditors.

4. A transaction concluded by a debtor-juridical person within six months preceding the filing of an application concerning the deeming of a debtor to be bankrupt and connected with the payment (or partition) of a participatory share (or share) in the property of the debtor to a founder (or participant) of the debtor in connection with the withdrawal thereof from the composition of founders (or participants) of the debtor may upon the application of the external administrator or creditor be deemed to be invalid by a court or arbitrazh court if the performance of such transaction violates the rights and legal interests of creditors.

In the event of deeming a debtor to be bankrupt and opening of a bankruptcy proceeding this founder (or participant) of the debtor shall be deemed to be a creditor of the third priority.

5. A transaction concluded by a debtor-juridical person after the acceptance of an application concerning the deeming of a debtor to be bankrupt and connected with the payment (or partition) of a participatory share (or share) in the property of the debtor to a founder (or participant) of the debtor in connection with the withdrawal thereof from the composition of the founders (or participants) of the debtor shall be null.

In the event of the deeming of a debtor to be bankrupt and the opening of a bankruptcy proceeding the demand of such founder (or participant) must be repaid from property of the debtor which remains after the full satisfaction of all demands of creditors.

6. Demands of the external administrator concerning the application of the consequences of invalidity of a null transaction provided for by point 5 of the present Article may be presented within the period of limitations established by a federal law for the application of the consequences of the invalidity of a null transaction.

7. In instances provided for by point 1 of the present Article a suit concerning the deeming of a transaction to be invalid or application of the consequences of the invalidity of a null transaction shall be presented by the external administrator in the name of the debtor.

In instances provided for by points (2)-(5) of the present Article the external administrator shall present suits concerning the deeming of transactions to be invalid or the application of the consequences of invalidity of null transactions in his own name.

Article 104. Monetary Obligations of Debtor in Course of External Administrator

1. If the amount of monetary obligations of the debtor which arose after the introduction of external administration exceeds by twenty per cent the amount of demands of bankruptcy creditors included in the register of demands of creditors, transactions which entailed new monetary obligations of the debtor, except for transactions provided for by the external administration plan may be concluded by the external administrator only with the consent of the meeting of creditors (or committee of creditors).

2. Transactions concluded with a violation of point 1 of the present Article may be deemed by a court to be invalid upon the application of a bankruptcy creditor or empowered agency and if the said transactions were concluded by a person who previously performed the rights and duties of external administration of the debtor, upon the application of the newly confirmed external administrator.

Article 105. Regulation of Consumption Funds of Debtor

Decisions entailing an increase of expenses of the debtor not provided for by the external administration plan may be accepted by the external administrator only with the consent of the meeting of creditors (or committee of creditors), except for instances provided for by the present Federal Law.

Article 106. External Administration Plan

1. Not later than a month from the date of his confirmation the external administrator shall be obliged to work out the external administration plan and submit it to the meeting of creditors for confirmation.

The external administration plan must provide measures with regard to the restoration of the ability of the debtor to pay, conditions and procedure for the realisation of the said measures, and expenses for their realisation and other expenses of the debtor.

The ability of the debtor to pay shall be deemed to be restored in the absence of indicia of bankruptcy established by Article 3 of the present Federal Law.

2. The external administration plan must:

correspond to the requirements established by federal laws;

provide for a period of restoration of the ability of the debtor to pay;

contain a substantiation of the possibility of restoration of the ability of the debtor to pay within the established period.

3. The external administration plan must provide for a delimitation of competence between the meeting of creditors and committee of creditors with respect to confirmation of transactions of the debtor if such delimitation is not established by the meeting of creditors or there are grounds for the redistribution of competence between the meeting of creditors and committee of creditors.

4. The external administrator at the request of the meeting of creditors or committee of creditors shall report to creditors concerning the course of external administration and realization of the external administration plan.

Article 107. Consideration of External Administration Plan

1. Consideration of the question concerning confirmation and change of the external administration plan shall be relegated to the exclusive competence of the meeting of creditors.

2. The external administration plan shall be considered by the meeting of creditors which shall be convoked by the external administrator not later than two months from the date of confirmation of the external administrator. The external administrator shall notify bankruptcy creditors and empowered agencies about the date, time, and place of conducting the said meeting in the procedure provided for by the present Federal Law and ensure the possibility of familiarisation with the external administration plan not less than fourteen days before the date of conducting the said meeting.

3. The meeting of creditors shall have the right to adopt one of the following decisions concerning:

confirmation of the external administration plan;

rejection of the external administration plan and recourse to an arbitrazh court with a petition concerning the deeming of the debtor to be bankrupt and the opening of a bankruptcy proceeding;

rejection of the external administration plan. The said decision must provide for a period for the convocation of the next meeting of creditors in order to consider the new external administration plan, in so doing the period of convocation of the meeting of creditors may not exceed two months from the date of adoption of the said decision;

rejection of the external administration plan and removal of the external administration with simultaneous confirmation of the self-regulating organisation from whose members the external administration must be confirmed and requirements for the candidacy of external administrator.

4. The external administration plan confirmed by the meeting of creditors shall be submitted to an arbitrazh court by the external administrator not later than five days from the date of conducting the meeting of creditors.

5. If within four months from the date of the introduction of external administration the external administration plan confirmed by the meeting of creditors is not submitted to an arbitrazh court and a petition has not been declared by the meeting of creditors provided for by the present Article, the arbitrazh court may adopt a decision concerning the deeming of the debtor to be bankrupt and the opening of a bankruptcy proceeding.

If external administration was introduced by an arbitrazh court in the procedure established by Article 87(6) of the present Federal Law and the external administration plan confirmed by the meeting of creditors was not submitted to the arbitrazh court within two months from the date of the introduction of external administration, the arbitrazh court may adopt a decision concerning the deeming of a debtor to be bankrupt and the opening of a bankruptcy proceeding.

6. The external administration plan may be deemed to be invalid fully or partially by the arbitrazh court considering the case concerning bankruptcy upon the petition of the person(s) whose rights and legal interests were violated. A ruling concerning the deeming invalid fully or partially the external administration plan may be appealed.

7. The external administration plan may be changed in the procedure established for consideration of the external administration plan.

Article 108. Extension of Period of External Administration

1. The period of external administration established by an arbitrazh court shall be extended by an arbitrazh court in the event of:

a decision adopted by the meeting of creditors concerning the confirmation or change of the external administration plan in which the period of external administration is provided which exceeds the initially established period but not more than the maximum period of external administration;

a decision adopted by the meeting of creditors with regard to the results of consideration of the report of the external administrator in connection with the results of the external administration concerning recourse to an arbitrazh court with a petition concerning the extension of external administration for a period provided for by the decision of the meeting of creditors, but not more than the maximum period of external administration.

2. External administration may not be extended for a period exceeding the aggregate period of financial recuperation and external administration established by Article 92(2) of the present Federal Law.

Article 109. Measures With Regard to Restoration of the Ability of Debtor to Pay

1. The following measures may be provided by the external administration plan with regard to restoration of the ability of the debtor to pay:

reprofiling of production;

closure of unprofitable production entities;

recovery of debtor indebtedness;

sale of part of property of debtor;

assignment of rights of demand of debtor;

performance of obligations of debtor by owner of property of debtor-unitary enterprise, founders (or participants) of debtor, or third person(s);

increase of charter capital of debtor at expense of contributions of participants and third persons;

placement of additional common stocks of debtor;

sale of enterprise of debtor;

substitution of assets of debtor;

other measures with regard to restoration of the ability of debtor to pay.

Article 110. Sale of Enterprise of Debtor

1. For the purposes of the present Federal Law by enterprise of a debtor is understood a property complex intended for the effectuation of entrepreneurial activity (hereinafter—enterprise). Branches and other structural subdivisions of a debtor-juridical person may also serve as the object of sale.

2. The sale of an enterprise may be included in the external administration plan on the basis of a decision of a management organ of the debtor empowered in accordance with the constitutive documents to adopt a decision concerning the conclusion of respective large-scale transactions of the debtor. In the decision concerning the sale of an enterprise should be contained an indication of the minimum price of the sale of the enterprise.

3. In the event of the sale of an enterprise all types of property shall be sold intended for the effectuation of entrepreneurial activity, including land plots, buildings, structures, installations, equipment, tools, raw materials, products, rights of demand, and also rights to designation which individualise the debtor, products, work, and services thereof (firm name, trademarks, service marks), and other exclusive rights belonging to a debtor, except for rights and duties which can not be sold to other persons.

In the event of the sale of an enterprise effectuated in accordance with the present Article, monetary obligations and obligatory payments of the debtor shall not be included in the composition of the enterprise, except for obligations of the debtor which arose after the acceptance of the application concerning the deeming of a debtor to be bankrupt and may be transferred to the purchase of the enterprise in the procedure and on the conditions which have been established by the present Federal Law.

In the event of the sale of an enterprise, all labour contracts operating on the date of the sale of the enterprise shall retain force, the rights and duties of employer passing to the purchase of the enterprise.

4. The sale of an enterprise shall be effectuated in the procedure established by a federal law by means of conducting an open sale in the form of an auction unless established otherwise by the present Federal Law.

If property relegated to limited circulability property is within the composition of property of the enterprise, the sale of the enterprise shall be effectuated only by means of conducting a closed public sale.

Persons shall take part in a closed public sale who in accordance with a federal law may have the said property in ownership or other right to a thing.

5. The starting price of the sale of an enterprise offered at a public sale shall be established by decision of the meeting of creditors or committee of creditors on the basis of the market value of the property determined in accordance with the report of an independent valuer enlisted by an external administrator and operating on the basis of a contract with payment for services thereof at the expense of property of the debtor.

The starting price of the sale of an enterprise may not be lower than the minimum price of the sale of an enterprise determined by the management organs of the debtor when having recourse with a petition concerning the sale of the enterprise. The procedure and conditions of conducting the public sale shall be determined by the meeting of creditors or committee of creditors.

The conditions of conducting a public sale must provide for the receipt of monetary means from the sale of the enterprise not later than a month before the expiry of the period of external administration.

The amount of deposit for participation in a public sale shall be established by the external administrator and must not exceed twenty per cent of the starting price.

The duration of the acceptance of applications (or proposals) for participation in a public sale should not be less than twenty-five days.

6. An external administrator shall act as the organiser of a public sale or on the basis of a decision of the meeting of creditors or committee of creditors enlist for these purposes a specialist organisation with payment for the services thereof at the expense of property of the debtor. The said organisation must not be an interested person with respect to the debtor and external administrator.

An external administrator (or organiser of the public sale) shall be obliged to publish a communication concerning the sale of the enterprise on a public sale in an official publication determined in accordance with Article 28 of the present Federal Law, and also in a local printed organ at the location of the debtor, not later than thirty days before the date of the conducting of the public sale.

The external administrator (or organiser of the public sale) also shall have the right to publish the said communication in other mass media. The communication concerning the sale of the enterprise must contain:

information concerning the enterprise, its characteristics and procedure for familiarisation with them;

information concerning the form of conducting the public sale and form of filing proposals concerning the price of the enterprise;

requirements for participants of the public sale if a closed public sale is conducted;

conditions of a competition in the event of the conducting thereof;

period, time, and place of filing applications and proposals concerning the price of the enterprise;

procedure for the formalisation of participation in a public sale, list of documents to be submitted by participants of the public sale, and requirements for the formalization thereof;

amount of deposit, periods, and procedure for making the deposit and requisites of accounts;

starting price of sale of enterprise;

size of increase of starting price ("auction steps") in the event of an open form of filing proposals concerning the price of the enterprise;

procedure and criteria for eliciting the winner of the public sale;

time and place of conducting the results of the public sale;

procedure and period for concluding the contract of purchase-sale;

conditions and periods for payment and requisites of accounts;

information concerning the organiser of the public sale.

When preparing for conducting the public sale, the external administrator (or organiser of the public sale) shall organise the acceptance of applications (or proposals) of participants of the public sale, and also deposits.

The external administrator (or organiser of the public sale) shall conduct the public sale, effectuating the totaling up of the results of the public sale, and determine the winner, and also sign the protocol concerning the results of the public sale. In the event of conducting a public sale by the organiser of the public sale, he shall transfer the protocol concerning the results of the public sale to the external administrator for conclusion of the contract of purchase-sale with the winner of the public sale.

7. If within the periods specified in the communication concerning the sale of an enterprise not a single application (or proposal) has been received, the external administrator (or organiser of the public sale) shall deem the first public sale to be unconstituted with regard to the enterprise and conduct a second public sale.

The second public sale shall also be conducted if the enterprise was not sold at the first public sale.

If the second public sale was deemed to be unconstituted or the enterprise was not sold, the external administrator shall within fourteen days from the date of totaling up the results of the second public sale publish a new communication concerning the sale of the enterprise in the procedure provided for by the present Article and Article 28 of the present Federal Law.

The starting price of the sale of an enterprise specified in such communication may be reduced by ten per cent of the starting price of the sale of the enterprise established by the meeting of creditors or committee of creditors, but may not be lower than the minimum price of sale of the enterprise determined by the management organs of the debtor.

If an enterprise was not sold in the procedure provided for by the present point, the procedure of sale of the enterprise at a public sale shall be established by the meeting of creditors or committee of creditors, including by means of a public proposal. In so doing the enterprise may not be sold at a price lower than the minimum price for sale of the enterprise determined by the management organs of the debtor.

8. A person who is the winner of the public sale and the external administrator not later than ten days from the date of totaling up the results of the public sale shall sign a contract of purchase-sale of the enterprise.

Unless established otherwise by the present Federal Law, in the event of the sale of an enterprise by means of a public proposal the contract of purchase-sale of an enterprise shall be concluded by the external administrator with the person who proposed the maximum price within a month from the date of publication of the communication concerning the sale of the enterprise.

9. The purchaser of the enterprise shall be obliged to pay the price of the sale of the enterprise determined at the public sale within the period specified in the communication concerning the conducting of the public sale, but not later than a month from the date of totaling up the results of the public sale.

Monetary means received from the sale of the enterprise shall be included in the composition of property of the debtor.

In the event the person who is the winner of the public sale evades signature of the protocol or contract of purchase-sale, the amount of deposit lost by this person shall be included in the composition of property of the debtor, deducting costs of the organiser of the public sale for the conducting thereof.

Article 111. Sale of Part of Property of Debtor

1. In instances provided for by the external administration plan, after the conducting the inventorying and valuation of property of the debtor the external administrator shall have the right to embark upon the sale of property of the debtor at an open public sale unless another procedure for the sale of property has been provided by the present Federal Law.

The sale of property of the debtor must not lead to the impossibility of the effectuation by the debtor of his economic activity.

2. Property of a debtor-unitary enterprise or debtor-joint-stock society subject to sale in accordance with the external administration plan, more than twenty-five per cent of whose voting stocks are in State or municipal ownership, shall be valued by an independent valuer with submission of the opinion of the State financial control agency with regard to the valuation conducted.

3. The starting price of property offered at a public sale shall be established by decision of the meeting of creditors (or committee of creditors) on the basis of the market value of the property determined in accordance with the report of the independent valuer enlisted by the external administrator and operating on the basis of a contract with payment for his services at the expense of property of the debtor.

4. If the sale of property has been provided by the external administration plan whose balance sheet value on the last reporting date before confirmation of the external administration plan comprises not less than one hundred thousand rubles, such property must be sold at an open public sale on condition that another procedure of sale is not provided for by the present Federal Law.

An open public sale shall be conducted in the procedure provided for by Article 110(4)–(9) of the present Federal Law unless established otherwise by the present Article.

5. Property of the debtor relegated to limited circulability of property may be sold only at a closed public sale.

Persons shall take part in a closed public sale who in accordance with a federal law may have the said property in ownership or other right to a thing.

A closed public sale shall be conducted in the procedure provided for by Article 110(4)–(9) of the present Federal Law unless established otherwise by the present Article.

6. Property whose balance sheet value on the last reporting date before the date of confirmation of the external administration plan comprises not less than one hundred thousand rubles shall be sold in the procedure provided for by the external administration plan.

7. The operation of provisions of the present Article shall not extend to instances of the realisation of the property of the debtor which is a product manufactured by the debtor in the process of economic activity.

Article 112. Assignment of Rights of Demand of Debtor

1. An external administrator shall have the right with the consent of the meeting of creditors (or committee of creditors) to embark upon the assignment of rights of demand of the debtor by means of the sale thereof.

2. The sale of the rights of demand of the debtor shall be effectuated by an external administrator in the procedure and on the conditions which have been determined by Article 111(3) and (5) of the present Federal Law unless established otherwise by a federal law or arises from the essence of the demand. The conditions of the contract of purchase-sale of the right of demand of the debtor must provide for:

receipt of monetary means for the sold right of demand not later than fifteen days from the date of conclusion of the contract of purchase-sale;

transfer of the right of demand shall be effectuated only after the full paying up thereof.

Article 113. Performance of Obligations of Debtor by Owner of Property of Debtor-Unitary Enterprise, Founders (or Participants) of Debtor, or Third Person(s)

1. The owner of property of a debtor-unitary enterprise, founders (or participants) of the debtor, or third person(s) shall at any time before the end of external administration for the purpose of termination of the proceedings with regard to a case concerning bankruptcy have the right to satisfy all demands of creditors in accordance with the register of demands of creditors or to provide monetary means to the debtor sufficient for satisfaction of all demands of creditors in accordance with the register of demands of creditors.

2. The owner of property of a debtor-unitary enterprise, founders (or participants) of the debtor, or third person(s) shall be obliged in written form to notify the arbitrazh administrator and creditors about the commencement of the satisfaction of demands of creditors. After receipt of the first notification by the arbitrazh administrator the performance of obligations of the debtor to creditors from other persons shall not apply. If a person who has sent the notification has not commenced the performance of obligations within a week's period after the sending of the notification or within a month's period has not satisfied the demands of

creditors in accordance with point 4 of the present Article, the notification shall be considered to be invalid.

3. In the event of satisfaction of demands of creditors or provision of monetary means to the debtor by the owner of property of a debtor-unitary enterprise, founders (or participants) of the debtor, or third person(s), the creditors of the debtor shall be obliged to accept such satisfaction and the debtor shall be obliged to satisfy the demands of creditors and empowered agencies at the expense of means provided thereto.

In the event of the impossibility of satisfying demands of creditors in accordance with point 1 of the present Article and paragraph one of the present point in connection with a violation by a creditor of the duties with regard to the provision of information necessary for the effectuation of a settlement of accounts with the said creditor, and likewise in the event of evasion by the creditor of acceptance of the performance of obligations of the debtor by other means, monetary means may be placed on deposit with a notary.

4. Monetary means shall be considered to be provided to a debtor on the conditions of a contract of an interest-free loan, the period of which is determined by the moment of demand, but not earlier than the end of the period for which the procedure of external administration was introduced.

The conclusion shall be permitted of an agreement between a third person(s) and the management organs of the debtor empowered in accordance with the constitutive documents to adopt a decision on the conclusion of large-scale transactions concerning other conditions of the provision of monetary means for the performance of obligations of the debtor.

5. In the event of the performance of obligations of the debtor by the owner of property of a debtor-unitary enterprise, founders (or participants) of the debtor, or third person(s), the completion of external administration and termination of the proceedings with regard to the case concerning bankruptcy shall occur in accordance with Article 116 of the present Federal Law.

Article 114. Placement of Additional Common Stocks of Debtor

1. For the purpose of restoring the ability of the debtor to pay an increase of charter capital of the debtor-joint-stock society may be provided by the external administration plan by means of the placement of additional common stocks.

An increase of charter capital by means of the placement of additional common stocks may be included in the external administration plan exclusively upon the petition of the management organ of the debtor which adopted the decision provided by Article 94(2) of the present Federal Law.

In the event of receiving a petition of the management organ of the debtor concerning inclusion in the external management plan for an increase of the charter capital of a debtor-joint-stock society by means of the placement of additional common stocks of the debtor the external administrator shall be obliged to conduct a meeting of creditors in order to consider the petition of the management organ of the debtor concerning the inclusion in the external administration plan a decision concerning the conducting of an emission of additional common stocks of the debtor.

2. The placement of additional common stocks of the debtor may be conducted only under closed subscription. The period for the placement of additional common stocks of the debtor may not exceed three months. State registration of the report concerning the results of the placement of additional common stocks of the debtor must be effectuated not later than a month before the date of the end of external administration.

3. Stockholders of the debtor shall have a preferential right to acquire placed additional common stocks of the debtor in the procedure provided for by a federal law.

The period provided to stockholders of the debtor for the effectuation of the preferential right to acquire additional common stocks of the debtor may not be more than forty-five days from the date of the commencement of the placement of the said stocks.

4. The emission prospectus (or decision concerning the issue) of additional common stocks of the debtor must provide for paying up of the additional common stocks only by monetary means.

5. In the event of the deeming of the issue of additional common stocks of the debtor to be unconstituted or invalid, the means received by the debtor from persons who acquired the additional common stocks of the debtor shall be returned to such persons in priority of the satisfaction of demands of creditors established by the present Federal Law.

Article 115. Substitution of Assets of Debtor

1. The substitution of assets of a debtor shall be conducted by means of the creation on the base of the property of the debtor a single open joint-stock society or several open joint-stock societies. In the event of the creation of one open joint-stock society all property shall be contributed to its charter capital, including property rights within the composition of the enterprise and intended for the effectuation of entrepreneurial activity. The composition of the enterprise shall be determined in accordance with Article 110(1) and (2) of the present Federal Law.

2. Substitution of assets of the debtor by means of the creation on the base of property of the debtor of a single open joint-stock society or several open joint-stock societies may be included in the external administration plan on the basis of the decision of the management organ of the debtor empowered in accordance

with the constitutive documents to adopt a decision concerning the conclusion of the respective transactions of the debtor.

The possibility of substitution of assets of the debtor may be included in the external administration plan on condition that all creditors whose obligations have been secured by a pledge of property of the debtor voted for the adoption of such decision.

3. The external administration plan may provide for the creation of several open joint-stock societies with paying up of their charter capital with property of the debtor intended for the effectuation of individual types of activity. The composition of property of the debtor contributed as payment for charter capital of the open joint-stock societies to be created shall be determined by the external administration plan.

The size of charter capital of the said societies shall be determined on the basis of the market value of the property contributed determined on the basis of the report of an independent valuer, taking into account proposals of the management organ of the debtor empowered in accordance with the constitutive documents to adopt a decision concerning the conclusion of respective transactions of the debtor.

4. When substituting assets of the debtor, all labour contracts prevailing on the date of adoption of the decision concerning the substitution of assets of the debtor shall retain force, in so doing the rights and duties of the employer shall pass to the newly created open joint-stock society (or open joint-stock societies).

A document confirming the presence of a license for the effectuation of individual types of activity shall be subject to reformalization into a document confirming the presence of a respective license with the open joint-stock society or open joint-stock societies in the procedure established by a federal law.

5. Stocks of an open joint-stock society or open joint-stock societies created on the base of property of the debtor shall be included in the composition of the property of the debtor and may be sold at an open public sale unless established otherwise by the present Article.

The sale of stocks of an open joint-stock society or open joint-stock societies created on the base of property of a debtor must ensure the accumulation of monetary means in order to repay demands of all creditors.

6. The sale at an open public sale of stocks of an open joint-stock society or open joint-stock societies created on the base of property of a debtor shall be effectuated in the procedure provided for by Article 110 of the present Federal Law. The sale of stocks of an open joint-stock society or open joint-stock societies on the organised securities market may be provided for by the external administration plan.

Article 116. Peculiarities of Completion of Procedures of Bankruptcy and Termination of Proceedings With Regard to Case Concerning Bankruptcy in Event of Performance of Obligations of Debtor by Owner of Property of Debtor-Unitary Enterprise, Founders (or Participants) of Debtor, or Third Person(s)

1. At the end of performance of obligations of a debtor by the owner of property of a debtor-unitary enterprise, founders (or participants) of the debtor, or third person(s), the external administrator within ten days shall be obliged to inform all creditors whose demands are included in the register of demands of creditors about the satisfaction of these demands.

2. The report of the external administrator shall not later than fourteen days be sent to the arbitrazh court without consideration of the report of the external administrator by the meeting of creditors.

3. Confirmation of the report of the external administrator shall be made by the arbitrazh court in the procedure and on the conditions which have been provided by Article 119(1) and (3)–(7) of the present Federal Law.

Article 117. Report of External Administrator

1. An external administrator shall be obliged to submit for consideration of the meeting of creditors the report of the external administrator:
with regard to the results of conducting external administration;
when there are grounds, for termination of external administration before time;
upon the request of persons having the right to convoke a meeting of creditors;
in the event of the accumulation of monetary means sufficient for satisfaction of all demands of creditors included in the register of demands of creditors.

2. If in the course of external administration all demands of creditors included in the register of demands of creditors have been satisfied in accordance with the present Federal Law, the external administrator shall within not later than a month from the date of satisfaction of all demands of creditors included in the register of demands of creditors inform persons thereof whose demands were included in the register of demands of creditors and submit the report of the external administrator to the arbitrazh court for confirmation.

3. The report of the external administrator must contain:
the balance sheet of the debtor for the last reporting date;
the report concerning the movement of monetary means;
the report on profits and losses of the debtor;
information concerning the presence of free monetary means and other means of the debtor which may be directed towards satisfaction of the demands of cred-

itors with regard to monetary obligations and payment of obligatory payments of the debtor;

deciphering of residual debtor indebtedness and information concerning residual unrealised rights of demand of the debtor;

information concerning the satisfied demands of creditors included in the register of demands of creditors;

other information concerning the possibility of repayment of residual creditor indebtedness of the debtor.

To the report of the external administrator must be appended the register of demands of creditors.

4. In the report of the external administrator must be contained one of the proposals concerning:

the termination of external administration in connection with the restoration of the ability of the debtor to pay and transition to settlements with creditors;

extension of the established period of external administration;

termination of the proceedings with regard to the case in connection with the satisfaction of all demands of creditors in accordance with the register of demands of creditors;

termination of external administration and recourse to an arbitrazh court with a petition concerning the deeming of the debtor to be bankrupt and the opening of a bankruptcy proceeding.

Article 118. Consideration by Meeting of Creditors of Report of External Administrator

1. If the report of an external administrator is subject to consideration by a meeting of creditors, the meeting of creditors shall be convoked not later than three weeks from the date of declaring the demand concerning the conducting of the meeting of creditors for consideration of the report of the external administrator or not later than three weeks from the moment of the arising of grounds for termination of external administration before time, or not later than a month before the date of the expiry of the established period of external administration.

2. An external administrator shall be obliged to provide to creditors the possibility of preliminary familiarisation with the report of the external administrator not less than forty-five days before the expiry of the established period of external administration or not less than ten days before the established date of the convocation of the meeting of creditors.

3. A meeting of creditors shall have the right to adopt, with regard to the results of consideration of the report of the external administrator, one of the decisions concerning:

recourse to an arbitrazh court with a petition concerning the termination of external administration in connection with the restoration of the ability of the debtor to pay and transition to settlements with creditors;

recourse to an arbitrazh court with a petition concerning the termination of proceedings with regard to the case in connection with the satisfaction of all demands of creditors in accordance with the register of demands of creditors;

recourse to an arbitrazh court with a petition concerning the deeming of a debtor to be bankrupt and the opening of a bankruptcy proceeding;

the conclusion of an amicable agreement.

4. When considering a report of an external administrator in connection with the expiry of the period of external administration established by an arbitrazh court the meeting of creditors shall have the right to adopt a decision concerning recourse to an arbitrazh court with a petition concerning extension of the established period of external administration on condition that the general period of external administration will not exceed the maximally permissible period of external administration in accordance with the present Federal Law.

Article 119. Confirmation by Arbitrazh Court of Report of External Administrator

1. The report of the external administrator shall be subject to obligatory consideration by an arbitrazh court, except if the report of the external administrator was considered by the meeting of creditors at the request of persons having the right to convoke a meeting of creditors and the meeting of creditors did not adopt with regard to the results of the consideration of such report one of the decisions provided for by Article 118(3) of the present Federal Law.

2. If in accordance with the present Federal Law the report of the external administrator is subject to obligatory consideration by the meeting of creditors, the report of the external administrator considered by the meeting of creditors and protocol of the meeting of creditors shall be sent to an arbitrazh court not later than five days from the date of conducting the meeting of creditors.

To the report of the external administrator must be appended the register of demands of creditors on the date of conducting the meeting of creditors and appeals of creditors who voted against the decision adopted by the meeting of creditors or who did not take part in the voting.

3. A report of the external administrator and appeals against his actions when there are such shall be considered by an arbitrazh court not later than a month from the date of receipt of the report of the external administrator.

4. A report of the external administrator shall be subject to confirmation by the arbitrazh court if:

all demands of creditors included in the register of demands of creditors have been satisfied in accordance with the present Federal Law;

a decision was adopted by the meeting of creditors concerning the termination of external administration in connection with the restoration of the ability of the debtor to pay and transition to settlements with creditors;

an amicable agreement has been concluded between creditors and the debtor;

a decision was adopted by the meeting of creditors concerning extension of the period of external administration, except for instances established by the present Federal Law.

5. An arbitrazh court shall refuse to confirm the report of an external administrator if:

demands of creditors included in the register of demands of creditors have not been satisfied;

indicia of restoration of the ability of the debtor to pay are lacking;

there are circumstances obstructing confirmation of an amicable agreement.

6. A ruling shall be rendered with regard to results of the consideration of the report of the external administrator concerning:

termination of the proceedings with regard to the case concerning bankruptcy in the event of satisfaction of all demands of creditors in accordance with the register of demands of creditors or in the event of confirmation by an arbitrazh court by an amicable agreement;

transition to settlements with creditors in the event of satisfaction of the petition of a meeting of creditors concerning the termination of external administration in connection with the restoration of the ability of the debtor to pay and transition to settlements with creditors;

extension of the period of external administration in the event of the satisfaction of a petition concerning the prolonging of the period of external administration;

refusal to confirm a report of the external administrator in the event circumstances are elicited by the court determined by point 5 of the present Article which obstruct confirmation of the report of the external administrator.

7. When there is a petition of the meeting of creditors concerning the deeming of a debtor to be bankrupt and the opening of a bankruptcy proceeding, and also in the event of the refusal of an arbitrazh court to confirm the report of an external administrator within a month from the end of the established period of external administration, the arbitrazh court may adopt a decision concerning the deeming of a debtor to be bankrupt and the opening of a bankruptcy proceeding.

Article 120. Consequences of Rendering Ruling Concerning Transition to Settlements With Creditors

1. The rendering by an arbitrazh court of a ruling concerning the transition to settlements with creditors shall be grounds for the commencement of settlements with all creditors in accordance with the register of demands of creditors.

2. In the ruling concerning the transition to settlements with creditors shall be established the period for the end of settlements with creditors which may not exceed six months from the date of rendering of the said ruling.

After the end of settlements with creditors an arbitrazh court shall render a ruling concerning the confirmation of the report of the external administrator and termination of the proceeding with regard to the case concerning bankruptcy.

3. If within the period established by an arbitrazh court settlements have not been made with creditors, the arbitrazh court shall adopt a decision concerning the deeming of the debtor to be bankrupt and the opening of a bankruptcy proceeding.

Article 121. Settlements with Creditors

1. Settlements with creditors shall be made by the external administrator in accordance with the register of demands of creditors beginning from the day of rendering of a ruling by an arbitrazh court concerning the transition to settlements with creditors or ruling concerning the commencement of settlements with creditors of a determined priority.

2. Settlements with creditors shall be made in the procedure provided for by Articles 134–138 of the present Federal Law with the peculiarities established by the present Article.

3. After satisfaction of the demand of a creditor included in the register of demands of creditors the external administrator or register-holder shall exclude such demand from the register of demands of creditors.

If the conducting of the register of demands of creditors is effectuated by a register-holder, the documents confirming satisfaction of the demand of a creditor shall be sent by the external administrator to the register-holder.

Article 122. Settlements With Creditors of Determined Priority

1. After the accumulation of monetary means sufficient for settlements with creditors of a determined priority the external administrator shall send to the arbitrazh court a petition concerning the rendering of a ruling concerning settlements with creditors of a determined priority and inform the creditors about sending the said petition whose demands have been included in the register of creditors. The petition concerning the rendering of a ruling concerning the settlement with creditors of a determined priority must contain the proposal of the external administrator on the proportion of satisfaction of demands of creditors.

2. An arbitrazh court shall consider the petition of the external administrator specified in point 1 of the present Article in a judicial session and if there are sufficient monetary means to satisfy demands of creditors of a determined priority and the absence of substantiated appeals of creditors shall render a ruling

concerning the commencement of settlements with creditors of the determined priority.

The rendering by an arbitrazh court of a ruling concerning the commencement of settlements with creditors of a determined priority shall be grounds for the commencement of settlements with creditors of this priority in accordance with the register of demands of creditors.

3. In the ruling of an arbitrazh court concerning the commencement of settlements with creditors of a determined priority shall be established:

the priority of satisfaction of demands of creditors whose demands begin to be satisfied;

the period of ending of settlements with creditors of that priority which may not exceed two months from the date of rendering the said ruling;

the proportion of satisfaction of demands of creditors of that priority.

4. In the event of the establishment by an arbitrazh court of demands of creditors subject to satisfaction within the composition of the priority with respect to creditors of which the ruling was rendered concerning the commencement of settlements with them, the arbitrazh court may render a ruling concerning a change of the procedure for satisfaction of the demands of creditors.

5. In the event settlements with creditors of a determined priority are not made within the period established by the arbitrazh court in the determined proportion, a creditor shall have the right to demand the addition of interest to the unpaid amount in the amount determined by Article 95(2) of the present Federal Law, commencing from the date of rendering of the ruling concerning the commencement of settlements with creditors of a determined priority and up to the date of satisfaction of his demand in full or in the determined proportion.

Article 123. Procedure for Termination of Powers of External Administrator

1. Termination of a proceeding with regard to a case concerning bankruptcy or the adoption by an arbitrazh court of a decision concerning the deeming of a debtor to be bankrupt and the opening of a bankruptcy proceeding shall entail termination of the powers of the external administrator.

2. If the external administration is completed by the conclusion of an amicable agreement or repayment of demands of creditors, the external administrator shall continue to perform his duties within the limits of the competence of the executive of the debtor until the date of election (or appointment) of the new executive of the debtor.

The external administrator shall be obliged to convoke the management organ of the debtor, to the powers of which in accordance with the present Federal Law and constitutive documents of the debtor have been relegated consideration of the question concerning the election (or appointment) of the executive of the debtor for consideration of the question concerning election (or appointment) of the executive of the debtor.

The powers of other management organs of the debtor and owner of the property of a debtor-unitary enterprise shall be restored.

3. If an arbitrazh court adopted a decision concerning the deeming of a debtor to be bankrupt and the opening of a bankruptcy proceeding and confirmed another person as the bankruptcy administrator or if it is impossible to confirm the bankruptcy administrator simultaneously with the adoption of such decision, the external administrator shall perform the duties of bankruptcy administrator until the date of confirmation of the bankruptcy administrator.

The external administrator shall be obliged to transfer the files of the case to the bankruptcy administrator not later than three work days from the date of confirmation of the bankruptcy administrator.

Chapter VII. Bankruptcy Proceeding

Article 124. General Provisions Concerning Bankruptcy Proceeding

1. The adoption by an arbitrazh court of a decision concerning the deeming of a debtor to be bankrupt shall entail the opening of a bankruptcy proceeding.

2. A bankruptcy proceeding shall be introduced for a period of a year. The period of the bankruptcy proceeding may be extended upon the petition of a person participating in the case by not more than six months.

3. The ruling of an arbitrazh court concerning the extension of the period of a bankruptcy proceeding shall be subject to immediate execution and may be appealed in the procedure established by Article 61(3) of the present Federal Law.

Article 125. Performance of Obligations of Debtor by Owner of Property of Debtor-Unitary Enterprise, Founders (or Participants) of Debtor, or by Third Person(s) in Bankruptcy Proceeding

1. The owner of property of a debtor-unitary enterprise or founders (or participants) of the debtor or a third person(s) at any time before the end of the bankruptcy proceeding shall have the right simultaneously to satisfy all demands of creditors in accordance with the register of demands of creditors or provide to the debtor monetary means sufficient to satisfy all demands of creditors in accordance with the register of demands of creditors in the procedure and on the conditions which have been provided by Article 113 of the present Federal Law.

2. In the event of the performance of obligations of a debtor by the owner of property of a debtor-unitary enterprise, founders (or participants) of the debtor, or third person(s) the submission of the report by the bankruptcy administrator

shall occur in the procedure provided for by Article 116(1) and (2) of the present Federal Law.

3. Confirmation of the report of the bankruptcy administrator shall be performed by the arbitrazh court in the procedure and on the conditions which were provided by Article 119(3), (4), paragraphs one and two, and (5), paragraphs one and two, of the present Federal Law.

4. An arbitrazh court shall render a ruling with regard to the results of the consideration of the report of the bankruptcy administrator with regard to a case concerning bankruptcy in the event of satisfaction of all demands of creditors in accordance with the register of demands of creditors or confirmation by the arbitrazh court of an amicable agreement.

Article 126. Consequences of Opening of Bankruptcy Proceeding

1. From the date of adoption by an arbitrazh court concerning the deeming of a debtor to be bankrupt and the opening of a bankruptcy proceeding:

the period of performance of monetary obligations which arose before the opening of the bankruptcy proceeding and payment of obligatory payments of the debtor shall be considered to have ensued;

the addition of penalties (or fines, forfeits), interest, and other financial sanctions with regard to all types of indebtedness of the debtor shall terminate;

information concerning the financial state of the debtor shall terminate relative to information deemed to be confidential or constitute a commercial secret;

the conclusion of transactions connected with the alienation of property of the debtor or entailing the transfer of the property thereof to third persons for use shall be permitted exclusively in the procedure established by the present Chapter;

the performance under documents of execution, including with regard to documents of execution executed in the course of previously introduced procedures of bankruptcy shall terminate unless provided otherwise by the present Federal Law;

all demands of creditors with regard to monetary obligations, payment of obligatory payments, and other property demands, except for demands concerning the recognition of the right of ownership, the recovery of moral harm, demanding and obtaining property from another's illegal possession, deeming null transactions to be invalid, and applying the consequences of their invalidity, and also current obligations specified in Article 134(1) of the present Federal Law, may be presented only in the course of the bankruptcy proceeding;

documents of execution, execution with regard to which has terminated in accordance with the present Federal Law shall be subject to transfer by court bailiffs-executors to the bankruptcy administrator in the procedure established by a federal law;

previously imposed arrests on property of the debtor and other limitations of the disposition of property of the debtor shall be removed. The grounds for the removal of an arrest on property of the debtor shall be the decision of a court concerning the deeming of a debtor to be bankrupt and the opening of a bankruptcy proceeding. The imposition of new arrests on property of the debtor and other limitations on the disposition of property of the debtor shall not be permitted;

the performance of obligations of the debtor shall be effectuated in the instances and in the procedure which have been established by the present Chapter.

2. From the date of adoption by an arbitrazh court of a decision concerning the deeming of a debtor to be bankrupt and the opening of a bankruptcy proceeding the powers of the executive of the debtor, other management organs of the debtor, and the owner of property of a debtor-unitary enterprise shall terminate, except for powers of management organs of the debtor empowered in accordance with the constitutive documents to adopt a decision concerning the conclusion of large-scale transactions to adopt a decision concerning the conclusion of agreements concerning conditions of providing monetary means by a third person(s) for the performance of obligations of the debtor.

An executive of the debtor, and also temporary administrator, administrative administrator, and external administrator within three days from the date of confirmation of the bankruptcy administrator shall be obliged to ensure the transfer of bookkeeping and other documentation of the debtor, seals, stamps, material and other valuables to the bankruptcy administrator.

In the event of evasion of the said duty the executive of a debtor, and also temporary administrator, administrative administrator, and external administrator shall bear responsibility in accordance with legislation of the Russian Federation.

3. Representatives of the owner of property of a debtor-unitary enterprise, and also the founders (or participants) of the debtor in the course of a bankruptcy proceeding shall possess the rights of persons participating in a case concerning bankruptcy.

Article 127. Bankruptcy Administrator

1. When adopting a decision concerning the deeming of a debtor to be bankrupt and the opening of a bankruptcy proceeding the arbitrazh court shall confirm the bankruptcy administrator in the procedure provided for by Article 45 of the present Federal Law and the amount of remuneration of the bankruptcy administrator, concerning which a ruling shall be rendered. The said ruling shall be subject to immediate execution and may be appealed.

2. The bankruptcy administrator shall operate until the date of completion of the bankruptcy proceeding.

Article 128. Publication of Information Concerning the Deeming of Debtor to be Bankrupt and Opening of Bankruptcy Proceeding

1. Publication of information concerning the deeming of a debtor to be bankrupt and the opening of a bankruptcy proceeding shall be effectuated by the bankruptcy administrator in the procedure provided for by Article 28 of the present Federal Law. The bankruptcy administrator shall not later than ten days from date of his confirmation send the said information for publication.

2. The following information shall be subject to publication concerning the deeming of a debtor to be bankrupt and the opening of a bankruptcy proceeding:

name and other requisites of the debtor deemed to be bankrupt;

name of the arbitrazh court in whose proceedings the case concerning the bankruptcy is situated and the number of the case;

date of adoption by an arbitrazh court of the decision concerning the deeming of the debtor to be bankrupt and the opening of the bankruptcy proceeding;

date of closure of the register of demands of creditors determined in accordance with Article 142(1) of the present Federal Law;

address of the debtor for the declaring by creditors of their demands against the debtor;

information concerning the bankruptcy administrator and respective self-regulating organisation.

Article 129. Powers of Bankruptcy Administrator

1. From the date of confirmation of the bankruptcy administrator to the date of termination of proceedings with regard to a case concerning bankruptcy or conclusion of an amicable agreement, or removal of the bankruptcy administrator, he shall effectuate powers of the executive of the debtor and other management organs of the debtor, and also the owner of property of a debtor-unitary enterprise, within the limits, in the procedure, and on the conditions which have been established by the present Federal Law.

2. A bankruptcy administrator shall be obliged to:

accept under jurisdiction property of the debtor and conduct the inventorying thereof;

enlist an independent valuer to value property of the debtor, except for instances provided for by the present Federal Law;

inform workers of the debtor about the forthcoming dismissal not later than a month from the date of introduction of the bankruptcy proceeding;

take measures with regard to ensuring the preservation of property of the debtor;

analyse the financial state of the debtor;

present to third persons having indebtedness to the debtor demands concerning the recovery thereof in the procedure established by the present Federal Law;

declare objections in the established procedure relative to demands of creditors presented against the debtor;

conduct the register of demands of creditors unless provided otherwise by the present Federal Law;

take measures directed towards the search for, eliciting, and return of property of the debtor situated with third persons;

perform other duties established by the present Federal Law.

3. A bankruptcy administrator shall have the right to:

dispose of property of the debtor in the procedure and on the conditions which have been established by the present Federal Law;

dismiss workers of the debtor, including the executive of the debtor, in the procedure and on the conditions which have been established by a federal law;

declare a refusal to perform contracts and other transactions in the procedure established by Article 102 of the present Federal Law. The bankruptcy administrator shall not have the right to declare a refusal to perform contracts of the debtor when there are circumstances obstructing the restoration of the ability of the debtor to pay;

transfer for keeping documents of the debtor subject to obligatory keeping in accordance with federal laws. The procedure and conditions of transfer of documents of the debtor for keeping shall be determined by federal laws and other normative legal acts;

present suits concerning the deeming of transactions concluded by the debtor to be invalid, including on grounds provided for by Article 103 of the present Federal Law, the demanding and obtaining of property of the debtor from third persons, dissolution of contracts concluded by the debtor, and perform other actions provided for by federal laws and other normative legal acts of the Russian Federation and directed towards the return of property of the debtor;

effectuate other rights connected with the performance of duties placed on him established by the present Federal Law.

4. In the instances provided for by Article 103(1) of the present Federal Law suit concerning the deeming of a transaction to be invalid or application of the consequences of invalidity of a null transaction shall be presented by the bankruptcy administrator by the bankruptcy administrator in the name of the debtor.

In the instances provided for by Article 103(2)-(5) of the present Federal Law the bankruptcy administrator shall present suits concerning the deeming of transactions to be invalid or application of the consequences of the invalidity of a null transaction in his own name.

5. When there are grounds established by a federal law the bankruptcy administrator shall present demands against third persons who in accordance with a

federal law bear subsidiary responsibility for obligations of the debtor in connection with bringing him to bankruptcy.

The amount of responsibility of persons brought to subsidiary responsibility in accordance with the present point shall be determined by proceeding from the difference between the amount of demands of creditors included in the register of demands of creditors and the monetary means received from the sale of property of the debtor or substitution of assets of organisations of the debtor.

Article 130. Valuation of Property of Debtor

1. In the course of a bankruptcy proceeding the bankruptcy administrator shall effectuate the inventorying and valuation of property of the debtor.

In order to effectuate the aid activity the bankruptcy administrator shall enlist independent valuers and other specialists with payment for their services at the expense of property of the debtor, unless another source of payment is established by the meeting of creditors (or committee of creditors).

Valuation of the property of the debtor shall be conducted by an independent valuer unless provided otherwise by the present Federal Law.

The meeting of creditors (or committee of creditors) shall have the right to determine the person on whom with his consent the duty is placed with regard to payment for the said services with subsequent contributory compensation in priority for expenses made by him at the expense of property of the debtor.

2. Property of the debtor-unitary enterprise or debtor-joint-stock society, more than twenty-five per cent of whose voting stocks are in State or municipal ownership, shall be valued by the independent valuer with the submission of the opinion of the State financial control agency with regard to the valuation conducted, except for instances provided for by point 3 of the present Article.

3. On the basis of a decision of the meeting of creditors or committee of creditors the valuation of moveable property of the debtor whose balance sheet value on the last reporting date preceding the deeming of the debtor to be bankrupt shall comprising less than one hundred thousand rubles may be conducted without enlisting an independent valuer.

The founders (or participants) of the debtor or owner of property of the debtor-unitary enterprise, bankruptcy creditors, and empowered agencies shall have the right to appeal the results of the valuation of property of the debtor in the procedure established by a federal law.

Article 131. Bankruptcy Mass

1. All property of a debtor having at the moment of opening a bankruptcy proceeding and elicited in the course of the bankruptcy proceeding shall comprise the bankruptcy mass.

2. Property removed from turnover, property rights connected with the person of the debtor, including rights based on available licenses for the effectuation of individual types of activity, and also other property provided for by the present Federal Law, shall be excluded from the property of the debtor which comprises the bankruptcy mass.

Property which is the subject of a pledge shall be taken into account in the composition of property of the debtor separately and shall be subject to obligatory valuation.

3. A bankruptcy administrator shall have the right to enlist bookkeepers, auditors, and other specialists for the purpose of the correct conducting of the recording of property of the debtor which comprises the bankruptcy mass.

Article 132. Property of Debtor Not Included in Bankruptcy Mass

1. The bankruptcy administrator shall inform the owner of property removed from turnover when there is in the composition of property of the debtor property removed from turnover.

2. The owner of property removed from turnover shall accept this property form the bankruptcy administrator or consolidate it to other persons not later than six months from the date of receipt of the notification from the bankruptcy administrator.

3. In the event of the failure of the owner of property removed from turnover to perform the duty provided for by point 2 of the present Article upon the expiry of six months from the date of receipt of notification from the bankruptcy administrator all expenses for the maintenance of the property removed from turnover shall be placed on the owner of the said property unless established otherwise by the present Article.

4. Preschool educational institutions, institutions of general education, treatment institutions, sport installations, objects of municipal infrastructure relegated to the systems of life-ensuring (hereinafter—socially significant objects) shall be sold by means of conducting a public sale in the form of a competition in the procedure established by Article 110 of the present Federal Law.

The duty of the purchaser of socially significant objects to maintain and ensure their operation and use in accordance with the special-purpose designation of the said objects must be an obligatory condition of such a competition. Other conditions for conducting a competition shall be determined by the meeting of creditors (or committee of creditors) upon the proposal of the agency of local self-government

The price of the sale of socially significant objects shall be determined by an independent valuer. Means received from the sale of socially significant objects shall be included in the bankruptcy mass.

After conducting the competition the agency of local self-government shall conclude with the purchaser of socially significant objects an agreement concerning performance of the conditions of the competition.

In the event of a material violation of or failure of the purchaser of socially significant objects to perform the agreement concerning the performance of conditions of the competition, the said agreement and contract of purchase-sale shall be subject to dissolution by a court on the basis of an application of the agency of local self-government.

In the event of dissolution by a court of the said agreement and contract of purchase-sale of socially significant objects, such objects shall be subject to transfer to the ownership of the municipal formation, and the monetary means paid under the contract of purchase-sale of socially significant objects shall be compensated to the purchaser at the expense of the local budget.

5. A housing fund of social use, and also socially significant objects, not sold in the procedure provided for by point 4 of the present Article shall be subject to transfer to the ownership of the respective municipal formation in the person of agencies of local self-government, of which the bankruptcy administrator shall inform the said agencies.

6. The transfer of objects specified in point 5 of the present Article to the ownership of a municipal formation shall be effectuated by taking into account the actual state without any additional conditions on a compensated basis at a contractual price, except for objects whose operation is loss-making. The respective budgets shall be the sources of financing the maintenance of the said objects.

Means paid by the agency of local self-government shall be included in the bankruptcy mass.

7. Officials of agencies of local self-government who do not execute the provisions of points 5 and 6 of the present Article shall bear responsibility provided for by a federal law.

8. In the event of the existence of disagreements between the bankruptcy administrator and agency of local self-government with regard to the transfer of socially significant objects to municipal ownership, the agency of local self-government shall be obliged to send to the bankruptcy administrator a protocol of disagreements to the draft contract not later than fourteen days from the date of receipt of the notification of the bankruptcy administrator.

In the absence of such protocol the bankruptcy administrator shall have the right to apply to the arbitrazh court in whose proceedings the case concerning bankruptcy is situated with an application concerning consideration of the disagreements which arose.

When considering the application the arbitrazh court shall determine the conditions of transfer of socially significant objects to municipal ownership with respect to which there are disagreements.

9. In the event of the refusal or evasion of an agency of local self-government to accept the objects specified in point 5 of the present Article the bankruptcy administrator shall have the right to have recourse to the arbitrazh court which considered the case concerning bankruptcy with an application to compel the agency of local self-government to accept the objects.

In the event of the satisfaction of such application the arbitrazh court shall establish the amount of means subject to payment by the agency of local self-government for socially significant objects to be transferred to municipal ownership.

10. In the event of the failure to perform by an agency of local self-government of the duties provided for by the present Article upon the expiry of a month from the date of receipt of notification from the bankruptcy administrator all expenses for maintenance of the housing fund of social use and socially significant objects shall be placed on the municipal formation.

11. With regard to the results of consideration of the applications specified in points 8 and 9 of the present Article the arbitrazh court shall render a ruling. The said ruling shall be subject to immediate execution and may be appealed.

Article 133. Accounts of Debtor in Course of Bankruptcy Proceeding

1. A bankruptcy administrator shall be obliged to use only one account of the debtor in a bank or other credit organisation (principal account of the debtor), and in the absence thereof or impossibility to effectuate operations with regard to available accounts, shall be obliged to open such account in the course of the bankruptcy proceeding.

When third persons have indebtedness to the debtor expressed in foreign currency, the bankruptcy administrator shall have the right to open or to use an account of the debtor in foreign currency in the procedure established by a federal law.

Other accounts of the debtor in credit organisations known at the moment of opening the bankruptcy proceeding, and also discovered in the course of the bankruptcy proceeding, except for account opened for settlements with regard to activity connected with trust management and special broker accounts of a professional participant of the securities market effectuating broker activity, shall be subject to closure by the bankruptcy administrator as they are discovered unless provided otherwise by the present Article. Residual monetary means of the debtor from the said accounts must be credited to the principal account of the debtor.

In the event of the failure of a bank or other credit organisation to perform the conditions of the contract of bank account in connection with a revocation of a license from the said organisation for the effectuation of banking activity the bankruptcy administrator shall have the right to assign the rights of demands for monetary means from the bank account in the procedure provided for by Article 140 of the present Federal Law.

2. Monetary means of the debtor received in the course of the bankruptcy proceeding shall be credited to the principal account of the debtor.

Payments to creditors shall be effectuated from the principal account of the debtor in the procedure provided for by Article 134 of the present Federal Law.

3. A report concerning the use of monetary means the bankruptcy administrator shall submit to the arbitrazh court and meeting of creditors (or committee of creditors) with regard to a demand but not more often than once a month.

Article 134. Priority of Satisfaction of Demands of Creditors

1. The following current obligations shall be paid in priority at the expense of the bankruptcy mass:

judicial expenses of the debtor, including expenses for the publication of notices provided for by Articles 28 and 54 of the present Federal Law;

expenses connected with the payment of remuneration to the arbitrazh administrator and register-holder;

current municipal and operational payments necessary for the effectuation of activity of the debtor;

demands of creditors which arose in the period after the acceptance by an arbitrazh court of an application concerning the deeming of a debtor to be bankrupt and before deeming the debtor to be bankrupt, and also demands of creditors with regard to monetary obligations which arose in the course of a bankruptcy proceeding, unless provided otherwise by the present Federal Law;

indebtedness with regard to earnings which arose after the acceptance by an arbitrazh court concerning the deeming of a debtor to be bankrupt and with regard to payment of workers of the debtor, added for the period of the bankruptcy proceeding;

other expenses connected with the conducting of the bankruptcy proceeding.

If termination of the activity of the organisation of the debtor or structural subdivisions thereof may entail technogenic and/or ecological catastrophe or perishing of people, expenses for conducting measures with regard to not permitting the said consequences to arise shall be repaid also in priority.

2. Demands of creditors with regard to current monetary obligations of the debtor expressed in foreign currency shall be satisfied in the procedure established by the present Federal Law.

3. The priority of the satisfaction of demands of creditors with regard to current monetary obligations of the debtor specified in point 1 of the present Article shall be determined in accordance with Article 855 of the Civil Code of the Russian Federation.

4. Demands of creditors shall be satisfied in the following priority:

in first priority settlements shall be made with regard to the demands of citizens to whom the debtor bears responsibility for the causing of harm to life or health by means of the capitalisation of respective time payments, and also contributory compensation of moral harm;

in second priority settlements shall be made with regard to the payment of severance benefits and payment for labour of persons working or who worked under a labour contract and with regard to the payment of remuneration under authors' contracts;

in third priority settlements shall be made with other creditors.

Demands of creditors with regard to obligations secured by the pledge of property of the debtor shall be satisfied at the expense of the value of the subject of pledge preferentially before other creditors, except for obligations to creditors of the first and second priorities, the rights of demand with regard to which arose before the conclusion of the respective contract of pledge.

5. In the event of the payment for labour of workers of the debtor who continue labour activity in the course of the bankruptcy proceeding, and also hired for work in the course of the bankruptcy proceeding, the bankruptcy administrator must make withholdings provided for by legislation (alimony, income tax, trade union and insurance contributions, and others) and payments placed on the employer in accordance with a federal law.

Article 135. Amount and Procedure of Satisfaction of Demands of Creditors of First Priority

1. Determination of the amount of demands of citizens to whom a debtor bears responsibility for the causing of harm to life or health shall be effectuated by means of the capitalisation of the respective time payments established on the date of adoption by an arbitrazh court of a decision concerning the deeming of the debtor to be bankrupt and opening of a bankruptcy proceeding and subject to payment to citizens until the attainment by them of the age of seventy years, but not less than ten years. The procedure and conditions of capitalisation of respective time payments shall be determined by the Government of the Russian Federation.

2. With the payment of capitalised time payments, the amount of which is determined in the procedure provided for by point 1 of the present Article, the respective obligation of the debtor shall terminate.

3. With the consent of a citizen his right of demand against the debtor in the amount of capitalised time payments shall pass to the Russian Federation.

The said demand in the event of the passing thereof to the Russian Federation also shall be satisfied in first priority.

In this event the obligations of the debtor to a citizen with regard to payment of capitalised time payments shall pass to the Russian Federation and shall be performed by the Russian Federation in accordance with a federal law in the procedure determined by the Government of the Russian Federation.

Demands concerning contributory compensation of moral harm shall be satisfied in the amount established by a judicial act.

Article 136. Amount and Procedure of Satisfaction of Demands of Creditors of Second Priority

1. When determining the amount of demands concerning the payment of severance benefits and payment for labour of persons working or who worked under a labour contract and payment of remuneration under authors' contracts, the unpaid indebtedness formed on the date of acceptance by an arbitrazh court of an application concerning the deeming of a debtor to be bankrupt shall be taken into account.

2. If obligations with regard to the payment for labour of persons working or who worked under a labour contract and payment of remuneration under authors' contracts were not fulfilled in full by the debtor within the period after the rendering of a ruling concerning the acceptance by the arbitrazh court of an application concerning the deeming of a debtor to be bankrupt and opening of a bankruptcy proceeding, amounts not paid before the adoption of a decision by an arbitrazh court concerning the deeming of a debtor to be bankrupt and the opening of a bankruptcy proceeding shall be subject to satisfaction in the composition of current demands.

Article 137. Demands of Creditors of Third Priority

1. When determining the amount of demands of creditors of the third priority the demands of bankruptcy creditors and empowered agencies shall be taken into account.

2. If obligatory payments have not been paid in full by the debtor in the period after the rendering by an arbitrazh court of a ruling concerning acceptance of the application concerning the deeming of the debtor to be bankrupt and before the opening of a bankruptcy proceeding, demands not paid before the adoption by an arbitrazh court of a decision to deem a debtor to be bankrupt and opening of a bankruptcy proceeding shall be paid in priority.

3. Demands of creditors of the third priority with regard to compensation of losses in the form of lost advantage, recovery of penalties (or fines, forfeits) and other financial sanctions, including for the failure to perform or improper performance of the duty with regard to the payment of obligatory payments, shall be taken into account separately in the register of demands of creditors and subject to satisfaction after repayment of the principal amount of indebtedness and interest due.

4. The peculiarities of recording and satisfaction of demands of creditors of the third priority with regard to obligations secured by a pledge of property of the debtor shall be determined by Article 138 of the present Federal Law.

Article 138. Demands of Creditors With Regard to Obligations Secured by Pledge of Property of Debtor

1. Demands of creditors with regard to obligations secured by the pledge of property of the debtor shall be taken into account in the composition of demands of creditors of the third priority.

2. Demands of creditors with regard to obligations secured by the pledge of property of the debtor shall be satisfied at the expense of means received from the sale of the subject of pledge preferentially before other creditors after the sale of the subject of pledge, except for obligations to creditors of the first and second priorities, the rights of demand with regard to which arose before conclusion of the respective contract of pledge.

Demands of creditors not satisfied at the expense of means received from the sale of the subject of pledge with regard to obligations secured by pledge of the property of the debtor shall be satisfied in the composition of demands of creditors of the third priority.

3. The sale of the subject of pledge shall be effectuated by means of conducting an open public sale.

Article 139. Sale of Property of Debtor

1. Within a month from the date of ending the conducting of inventorying and valuing the property of the debtor the bankruptcy administrator shall be obliged to submit to the meeting of creditors (or committee of creditors) for confirmation proposals concerning the procedure, periods, and conditions of sale of the property of the debtor. The conditions of sale of the property of the debtor must provide for receipt of monetary means for the sold property not later than a month from the date of conclusion of the contract of purchase-sale or seven days from the moment of the arising of the right of ownership of the purchaser.

2. If within two months from the date of submission by the bankruptcy administrator to the meeting of creditors (or committee of creditors) of proposals concerning the procedure, periods, and conditions of the sale of property of the debtor the procedure, periods, and conditions for sale of the property of the debtor have not been confirmed by the meeting of creditors (or committee of creditors), the meeting of creditors (or committee of creditors) or the bankruptcy administrator shall have the right to apply to an arbitrazh court with an application concerning the settlement of the disagreements which have arisen.

With regard to the results of consideration of the said disagreements the arbitrazh court either shall confirm the procedure, periods, and conditions of the sale or the property or shall relieve the bankruptcy administrator from the performance of his duties.

3. In the event circumstances arise in the course of a bankruptcy proceeding in connection with which the making of changes is required in the procedure, periods, and conditions of the sale of property of the debtor the bankruptcy administrator shall be obliged to submit to the meeting of creditors (or committee of creditors) respective proposals concerning changes of the procedure, periods, and conditions of the sale of property of the debtor for confirmation within a month from the moment of arising of the said circumstances.

4. After conducting the inventorying and valuation of property of the debtor the bankruptcy administrator shall embark upon the sale of property of the debtor at open public sale unless another procedure has been established by the present Federal Law for sale of the property of a debtor.

5. The starting price for the sale of property of the debtor placed on sale shall be determined by an independent valuer unless provided otherwise by the present Federal Law.

6. The sale of an enterprise, and also other property of the debtor, shall be effectuated in the procedure and on the conditions which have been established by Article 110(3)–(8) and Article 111 of the present Federal Law with the peculiarities provided for by the present Chapter.

Article 140. Assignment of Rights of Demand of Debtor

1. A bankruptcy administrator shall have the right with the consent of the meeting of creditors (or committee of creditors) to commence to assign rights of demand of a debtor by means of the sale thereof.

2. The sale of rights of demand of a debtor shall be effectuated by the bankruptcy administrator in the procedure and on the conditions which have been established by Article 111(3) and (5) of the present Federal Law unless established otherwise by a federal law or does not arise from the essence of the demand. The conditions of the contract of sale of rights of demand of a debtor must provide for:
the receipt of monetary means for the sold rights of demand of the debtor not later than fifteen days from the date of conclusion of the contract of purchase-sale of the rights of demand;
the transfer of the rights of demand only after the rights of demand have been fully paid up.

3. In the event of the presence of disagreements between the bankruptcy administrator and meeting of creditors (or committee of creditors) with regard to the question of agreeing the procedure for the sale of rights of demand of the

debtor, the said disagreements shall be settled in the procedure provided for by Article 139(2) of the present Federal Law.

Article 141. Substitution of Assets of Debtor in Course of Bankruptcy Proceeding

1. On the basis of a decision of the meeting of creditors in the course of a bankruptcy proceeding the substitution of assets of the debtor may be conducted on condition that all creditors whose obligations have been secured by a pledge of the property of the debtor have voted for the adoption of such decision.

2. The substitution of assets of the debtor shall be conducted in the procedure and on the conditions which have been determined by Article 115(2)–(6) of the present Federal Law.

Article 142. Settlement of Accounts with Creditors in Course of Bankruptcy Proceeding

1. A bankruptcy administrator or persons having in accordance with Articles 113 and 125 of the present Federal Law the right to perform obligations of the debtor shall settle accounts with creditors in accordance with the register of demands of creditors.

Establishment of the amount of demands of creditors shall be effectuated in the procedure provided for by Article 100 of the present Federal Law.

The register of demands of creditors shall be subject to closure upon the expiry of two months from the date of publication of information concerning the deeming of the debtor to be bankrupt and opening of a bankruptcy proceeding.

2. Demands of creditors of each priority shall be satisfied after the full satisfaction of demands of creditors of the preceding priority, except for instances provided for by the present Federal Law for the satisfaction of demands of creditors secured by a pledge of property of the debtor.

When the transfer of monetary means to the account (or deposit) of the creditor due to him is impossible, the monetary means shall be placed by the bankruptcy administrator on deposit at the notary at the location of the debtor, which shall be communicated to the creditor.

In the event of the failure of the creditor to demand the monetary means placed on deposit with a notary within three years from the date of placing them on deposit with the notary, the said monetary means shall be transferred by the notary to the federal budget.

3. In the event the monetary means of the debtor are insufficient to satisfy the demands of creditors of one priority, the monetary means shall be distributed among the creditors of the respective priority in proportion to the amounts of their demands included in the register of demands of creditors unless provided otherwise by the present Federal Law.

4. Demands of bankruptcy creditors and/or empowered agencies declared after closure of the register of demands of creditors, and also demands concerning the payment of obligatory payments which arose after the opening of the bankruptcy proceeding, irrespective of the period of their presentation, shall be satisfied at the expense of property of the debtor remaining after satisfaction of the demands of creditors included in the register of demands of creditors.

Settlements with creditors with regard to such demands shall be made by the bankruptcy administrator in the procedure established by the present Article.

5. Demands of creditors of the first priority declared before the end of settlements with all creditors (including after closure of the register of demands of creditors) but after completion of the settlements of accounts with creditors of the first priority who declared their demands within the established period, shall be subject to satisfaction before satisfaction of the demands of creditors of subsequent priorities. Until full satisfaction of the said demands of creditors of the first priority, satisfaction of demands of creditors of subsequent priorities shall be suspended.

If such demands were declared before completion of settlements of accounts with creditors of the first priority, they shall be subject to satisfaction after completion of the settlements with creditors of the first priority who declared their demands within the established period when there exist monetary means for the satisfaction thereof.

Demands of creditors of the second priority declared before the end of settlements with all creditors (including after closure of the register of demands of creditors) shall be subject to satisfaction in the procedure analogous to the procedure established by paragraphs one and two of the present point.

6. When there are disagreements being considered in an arbitrazh court (or court) at the moment of the commencement of settlements with creditors of the respective priority between the bankruptcy administrator and creditor with regard to a declared demand of the creditor, the bankruptcy administrator shall be obliged to reserve monetary means in an amount sufficient for the proportional satisfaction of demands of the respective creditor.

7. Demands of creditors of the third priority declared within the established period but established by the arbitrazh court after the commencement of the repayment of demands of creditors of the third priority shall be subject to satisfaction in the amount provided for repayment of demands of creditors of the third priority.

8. Satisfied demands, and also those demands in connection with which agreement has been reached concerning release-money, or the bankruptcy administrator has declared a set-off of demands, or there are other grounds for termination of obligations, shall be considered to be repaid demands.

Only property of the debtor not encumbered by a pledge may be provided as release-money.

Set-off of a demand, and also repayment of a demand by the provision of release-money, shall be permitted only on condition of compliance with the priority and proportionality of satisfaction of demands of creditors.

9. Repayment of demands of creditors by means of the conclusion of an agreement concerning release-money shall be permitted in the event of agreeing the said agreement with the meeting of creditors (or committee of creditors).

Repayment of demands of creditors by means of the conclusion of an agreement concerning the novation of an obligation shall not be permitted in a bankruptcy proceeding.

Demands of creditors not satisfied by reason of the insufficiency of property of the debtor shall be considered to be repaid.

Demands of creditors not recognised by the bankruptcy administrator shall be considered to be repaid if the creditor did not apply to an arbitrazh court or such demands were deemed by the arbitrazh court to be unsubstantiated.

10. A bankruptcy administrator shall enter in the register of demands of creditors information concerning the repayment of demands of creditors.

11. Creditors whose demands were not satisfied in full in the course of a bankruptcy proceeding shall have the right to demand levy of execution against property of the debtor illegally received by third persons in the amount of the demands which remain unpaid in a case concerning bankruptcy. In the absence of the said property or upon the application of a third person a court shall have the right to satisfy demands of the said creditors by means of levy of execution of the respective amount without levy of execution against property of the debtor. The said demand may be presented within the period established by a federal law.

Article 143. Control Over Activity of Bankruptcy Administrator

1. A bankruptcy administrator shall submit to the meeting of creditors (or committee of creditors) a report concerning his activity, information concerning the financial state of the debtor and property thereof at the moment of opening the bankruptcy proceeding and in the course of the bankruptcy proceeding, and also other information not less than once a month unless a more extended period or periods for submission of the report have been established by the meeting of creditors.

2. The report of a bankruptcy administrator must contain information concerning:

the bankruptcy mass formed, including the course and results of inventorying property of the debtor and the course and results of valuing the property of the debtor;

the amount of monetary means received in the basic account of the debtor and the sources of the said proceeds;

the course of realisation of property of the debtor, specifying the amounts received from the realisation of property;

the quantity and total amount of demands concerning recovery of indebtedness presented by the bankruptcy administrator against third persons;

the measures undertaken with regard to ensuring the preservation of property of the debtor, and also eliciting and demanding and obtaining property of the debtor in the possession of third persons;

the measures undertaken with regard to deeming invalid transactions of the debtor, and also with regard to declaring a refusal to perform contracts of the debtor;

the conducting of the register of demands of creditors, specifying the total amount of demands of creditors included in the register, and separately—relative to each priority;

the quantity of workers of the debtor continuing their activity in the course of the bankruptcy administrator, and also the quantity of workers of the debtor dismissed (or reduced) in the coure of the bankruptcy proceeding;

the work conducted by the bankruptcy administrator with regard to the closure of accounts of the debtor and results thereof;

the amount of expenses with regard to the conducting of a bankruptcy proceeding, specifying the designation thereof;

the bringing to subsidiary responsibility of third persons who in accordance with legislation of the Russian Federation bear subsidiary responsibility with regard to obligations of the debtor in connection with bringing him into bankruptcy;

other information concerning the course of the bankruptcy proceeding, the composition of which is determined by the bankruptcy administrator, and also requirements of the meeting of creditors (or committee of creditors) or arbitrazh court.

3. A bankruptcy administrator shall be obliged upon the request of an arbitrazh court to provide to the arbitrazh court all information affecting the bankruptcy proceeding, including the report on his activity.

Article 144. Relieving of Bankruptcy Administrator

1. A bankruptcy administrator may upon the application concerning the relieving thereof from the performance of duties of bankruptcy administrator and in other instances provided for by a federal law, be relieved by an arbitrazh court from the performance of duties.

2. In the event of relieving a bankruptcy administrator from the performance of duties placed on him the arbitrazh court shall confirm a new bankruptcy

administrator in the procedure established by Article 127(1) of the present Federal Law.

3. A ruling of an arbitrazh court concerning the relieving of a bankruptcy administrator from the performance of duties of bankruptcy administrator shall be subject to immediate execution and may be appealed.

Article 145. Removal of Bankruptcy Administrator

1. A bankruptcy administrator may be removed by an arbitrazh court from the performance of duties of a bankruptcy administrator:

on the basis of a petition of the meeting of creditors (or committee of creditors) in the event of the failure to perform or improper performance of duties placed on the bankruptcy administrator;

in connection with satisfaction by an arbitrazh court of an appeal of a person participating in the case concerning bankruptcy, the failure to perform or improper performance by the bankruptcy administrator of duties placed on him on condition that such failure to perform or improper performance of duties violated the rights or legal interests of the declarant of the appeal, and also entailed or could entail losses to the debtor of creditors thereof;

in the event of the eliciting of circumstances obstructing the confirmation of the person as bankruptcy administrator, and also if such circumstances arose after confirmation of the person as bankruptcy administrator.

Simultaneously with the removal of the bankruptcy administrator the court shall confirm the new bankruptcy administrator in the procedure established by Article 127(1) of the present Federal Law.

2. The ruling of an arbitrazh court concerning removal of a bankruptcy administrator from the performance of duties of a bankruptcy administrator shall be subject to immediate execution.

3. The ruling of an arbitrazh court concerning removal of a bankruptcy administrator from the performance of duties of a bankruptcy administrator may be appealed.

Article 146. Possibility of Transition to External Administration

1. If with respect to a debtor financial recuperation and/or external administration was not introduced and in the course of a bankruptcy proceeding sufficient grounds have emerged with the bankruptcy administrator, including grounds confirmed by financial analysis data, to suppose that the ability of the debtor to pay may be restored, the bankruptcy administrator shall be obliged to convoke a meeting of creditors within a month from the moment of eliciting the said circumstances for the purpose of consideration of the question concerning recourse to an arbitrazh court with a petition to terminate the bankruptcy proceeding and transition to external administration.

2. A decision of the meeting of creditors concerning recourse to an arbitrazh court with a petition concerning termination of the bankruptcy proceeding and transition to external administration shall be adopted by a majority of votes of the total number of votes of creditors whose demands are included in the register of demands of creditors and not repaid on the date of conducting the meeting of creditors considering the question concerning the adoption of such decision.

A decision of the meeting of creditors concerning recourse to an arbitrazh court with a petition concerning termination of a bankruptcy proceeding and transition to an external administrator must contain the proposed period of external administration and requirements for the candidacy of external administrator.

On the basis of a petition of the meeting of creditors concerning termination of the bankruptcy proceeding and transition to external administration an arbitrazh court may render a ruling concerning termination of the bankruptcy proceeding and transition to external administration.

The said ruling may be rendered only when the debtor has property necessary to effectuate autonomous economic activity.

3. In the event of the rendering of a ruling by an arbitrazh court concerning the termination of the bankruptcy proceeding and transition to external administration:

limitations of the management organs of the debtor provided for by the present Chapter shall terminate;

the register of demands of creditors shall be opened;

the demands of creditors with regard to monetary obligations and payment of obligatory payments which arose in the course of the bankruptcy proceeding shall be considered to be current from the date of rendering the ruling concerning the transition to external administration;

the demands of creditors with regard to obligations whose period of performance in accordance with the conditions of the obligations had not ensued at the moment of opening the bankruptcy proceeding also shall be considered to be current from the date of rendering the ruling concerning the transition to external administration;

the demands satisfied in the course of the bankruptcy proceeding shall be considered to be repaid and shall not be subject to restoration.

Interest in the amount and in the procedure which have been established by Article 95(2) of the present Federal Law shall be added in the course of the bankruptcy proceeding to demands of creditors and empowered agencies with regard to monetary obligations of the debtor and payment of obligatory payments which arose before adoption of the decision concerning the deeming of the debtor to be bankrupt and opening of the bankruptcy proceeding.

4. If on the date of rendering of a ruling by an arbitrazh court concerning the transition to external administration not more than three months have elapsed

from the date of introduction of the bankruptcy proceeding, the running of the period established by Article 102(1) of the present Federal Law shall be suspended until the confirmation of the external administrator.

Article 147. Report of Bankruptcy Administrator Concerning Results of Conducting Bankruptcy Proceeding

1. After the completion of the settlements of accounts with creditors, and also in the event of the termination of proceedings with regard to a case concerning bankruptcy in the instances provided for by Article 57 of the present Federal Law, the bankruptcy administrator shall be obliged to submit to the arbitrazh court a report concerning the results of conducting the bankruptcy proceeding.

2. To the report of the bankruptcy administrator shall be appended:
documents confirming the sale of the property of the debtor;
register of demands of creditors specifying the amount of repaid demands of creditors;
documents confirming the repayment of demands of creditors.

Article 148. Property of Debtor Remaining After Completion of Settlement of Accounts with Creditors

1. In the event of the refusal of creditors to accept property in order to repay their demands which was proposed for sale but was not sold in the course of a bankruptcy proceeding and in the absence of applications of the owner of the property of a debtor-unitary enterprise or founders (or participants) of the debtor concerning rights to the said property, the bankruptcy administrator shall notify agencies of local self-government at the location of the property of the debtor about the said property.

2. Not later than thirty days from the date of receipt of the respective notification agencies of local self-government shall accept the property specified in point 1 of the present Article on the balance sheet and bear all expenses for the maintenance thereof.

3. In the event of the refusal or evasion by the agency of local self-government to accept the property specified in point 1 of the present Article the bankruptcy administrator shall be obliged to apply to the arbitrazh court in whose proceedings the case concerning bankruptcy is situated with an application to compel the respective agency of local self-government to accept the said property.

4. In the event of disagreements between the bankruptcy administrator and agency of local self-government connected with the transfer of property specified in point 1 of the present Article the agency of local self-government shall be obliged to send to the bankruptcy administrator a protocol of disagreements not later than fourteen days from the date of receipt of the notification of the bankruptcy administrator.

When rejecting the said protocol the bankruptcy administrator shall be obliged to have recourse to an arbitrazh court in whose proceedings the case concerning bankruptcy is situated with an application concerning consideration of the disagreements which have arisen.

5. When considering an application specified in point 4 of the present Article the arbitrazh court shall determine the conditions for the transfer of property with respect to which there were disagreements to the agency of local self-government.

6. An arbitrazh court shall render a ruling with regard to the results of the consideration of the applications specified in points 3 and 4 of the present Article. From the date of rendering of the ruling of the arbitrazh court with regard to the results of consideration of the said applications of the bankruptcy administrator the expenses for the maintenance of the said property shall be at the expense of the respective budgets.

7. The ruling of an arbitrazh court rendered with regard to the results of the consideration of applications of the bankruptcy administrator shall be subject to immediate execution.

The failure to execute or untimely execution of the said ruling of the arbitrazh court by agencies of local self-government shall not be grounds for a refusal of the arbitrazh court to render a ruling concerning the completion of the bankruptcy proceeding.

8. The ruling of an arbitrazh court rendered with regard to the results of consideration of the applications of a bankruptcy administrator may be appealed.

Article 149. Completion of Bankruptcy Proceeding

1. After consideration by an arbitrazh court of the report of the bankruptcy administrator concerning the results of conducting the bankruptcy proceeding, the arbitrazh court shall render a ruling concerning completion of the bankruptcy proceeding, and in the event of repayment of demands of creditors in accordance with Article 125 of the present Federal Law—a ruling concerning termination of the proceeding with regard to the case concerning bankruptcy.

The ruling concerning completion of the bankruptcy proceeding shall be subject to immediate execution.

The ruling concerning termination of the proceeding with regard to case concerning bankruptcy shall be subject to immediate execution.

In the event of the rendering of a ruling concerning termination of the proceeding with regard to the case concerning bankruptcy the decision of the arbitrazh court concerning the deeming of the debtor to be bankrupt and the opening of a bankruptcy proceeding shall not be subject to further execution.

2. The bankruptcy administrator must within five days from the date of receipt of the ruling of the arbitrazh court concerning completion of the

bankruptcy proceeding submit the said ruling to the agency effectuating the State registration of juridical persons.

3. The ruling of an arbitrazh court concerning completion of the bankruptcy proceeding shall be grounds for making an entry in the unified State register of juridical persons concerning liquidation of the debtor.

The respective entry must be made in this register not later than five days from the date of submission of the said ruling of the arbitrazh court to the agency effectuating the State registration of juridical persons.

The ruling of the arbitrazh court concerning completion of the bankruptcy proceeding may be appealed until the date of making the entry concerning liquidation of the debtor in the unified State register of juridical persons.

4. From the date of making the entry concerning the liquidation of the debtor in the unified State register of juridical persons the bankruptcy proceeding shall be considered to be completed.

Chapter VIII. Amicable Agreement

Article 150. General Provisions on Conclusion of Amicable Agreement

1. At any stage of the consideration by an arbitrazh court of a case concerning bankruptcy the debtor, bankruptcy creditors thereof, and empowered agencies shall have the right to conclude an amicable agreement.

2. The decision concerning the conclusion of an amicable agreement on the part of bankruptcy creditors of creditors and empowered agencies shall be adopted by the meeting of creditors. The decision of a meeting of creditors concerning the conclusion of an amicable agreement shall be adopted by a majority of votes of the total number of votes of bankruptcy creditors and empowered agencies in accordance with the register of demands of creditors and shall be considered to be adopted on condition that all creditors with regard to obligations secured by a pledge of the property of the debtor voted for it.

The powers of a representative of a bankruptcy creditor and representative of an empowered agency at the voting with regard to the question of concluding an amicable agreement must be specially provided for in the power of attorney thereof.

The decision concerning the conclusion of an amicable agreement on the part of the debtor shall be adopted by a debtor-citizen or executive of a debtor-juridical person, acting executive of the debtor, external administrator, or bankruptcy administrator.

3. The participation in an amicable agreement of third persons who assume rights and duties provided for by the amicable agreement shall be permitted.

4. An amicable agreement shall be confirmed an arbitrazh court.

When confirming an amicable agreement the arbitrazh court shall render a ruling concerning confirmation of the amicable agreement in which is indicated the termination of the proceedings with regard to the case concerning bankruptcy. If the amicable agreement is concluded in the course of a bankruptcy proceeding it shall be specified in the ruling concerning confirmation of the amicable agreement that the decision to deem the debtor to be bankrupt and the opening of a bankruptcy proceeding is not subject to execution.

5. An amicable agreement shall enter into force for the debtor, bankruptcy creditors, and empowered agencies, and also for third persons participating in the amicable agreement, from the date of confirmation thereof by the arbitrazh court and shall be binding upon the debtor, bankruptcy creditors, empowered agencies, and third persons participating in the amicable agreement.

6. A unilateral refusal to perform an amicable agreement which has entered into force shall not be permitted.

Article 151. Peculiarities of Conclusion of Amicable Agreement in Course of Observation

1. A decision concerning the conclusion of an amicable agreement on the part of the debtor shall be adopted by a citizen-debtor, executive of a debtor-juridical person, or person acting as the said executive.

2. If an amicable agreement is a transaction for the debtor which in accordance with federal laws and/or constitutive documents of the debtor is concluded on the basis of a decision of the management organs of the debtor or is subject to agreement (or approval) with the management organs of the debtor, the decision concerning the conclusion of the amicable agreement in the name of the debtor may be adopted after the adoption of the respective decision by the management organs of the debtor or receipt of the respective agreement (or approval).

3. An amicable agreement shall not be subject to agreement with the temporary administrator.

4. When concluding an amicable agreement with the participation of third persons who are interested persons with respect to the debtor, temporary administrator, or bankruptcy creditor, the meeting of creditors must be informed about the existence and character of the interest in the conclusion of the transaction, and the amicable agreement must contain information about the fact that the amicable agreement is a transaction in the conclusion of which there is an interest and specifically indicate the character of such interest.

5. The provisions provided for by point 2 of the present Article shall not prohibit the meeting of creditors to adopt a decision in the name of the bankruptcy

creditors and empowered agencies concerning the conclusion of an amicable agreement.

6. In the event of the conclusion of an amicable agreement in the course of observation the amicable agreement shall extend to the demands of bankruptcy creditors and empowered agencies included in the register of demands of creditors on the date of conducting the meeting of creditors who adopted the decision concerning the conclusion of the amicable agreement.

Article 152. Peculiarities of Conclusion of Amicable Agreement in Course of Financial Recuperation

1. A decision concerning the conclusion of an amicable agreement on the part of the debtor shall be adopted by the executive of the debtor-juridical person or by the person performing the duties of the said executive.

2. If an amicable agreement is a transaction for the debtor which in accordance with federal laws and/or constitutive documents of the debtor is concluded on the basis of a decision of the management organs of the debtor or is subject to agreement with the management organs of the debtor, the decision concerning the conclusion of the amicable agreement in the name of the debtor may be adopted after the adoption of the respective decision by the management organs of the debtor or receipt of the respective agreement.

3. An amicable agreement shall not be subject to agreement with the administrative administrator.

4. When concluding an amicable agreement with the participation of third persons who are interested persons with respect to the debtor, administrative administrator, or bankruptcy creditor, the meeting of creditors must be informed about the existence and character of interest in the conclusion of the transaction, and the amicable agreement must contain information that the amicable agreement is a transaction in the conclusion of which there is an interest and specifically indicate the character of such interest.

5. The provisions provided for by point 2 of the present Article shall not prohibit the meeting of creditors to adopt a decision in the name of the bankruptcy creditors and empowered agencies concerning the conclusion of an amicable agreement.

6. In the event of the conclusion of an amicable agreement in the course of financial recuperation the amicable agreement shall extend to demands of bankruptcy creditors and empowered agencies included in the register of demands of creditors on the date of conducting the meeting of creditors who adopted the decision concerning the conclusion of the amicable agreement.

Article 153. Peculiarities of Conclusion of Amicable Agreement in Course of External Administration

1. A decision concerning the conclusion of an amicable agreement shall be taken on the part of the debtor by the external administrator.

2. If an amicable agreement is for the debtor a transaction which in accordance with federal laws and/or constitutive documents of the debtor is concluded on the basis of a decision of management organs of the debtor or subject to agreement with management organs of the debtor (or approval by these organs) the decision concerning the conclusion of an amicable agreement in the name of the debtor may be adopted after the adoption of the respective decision of the management organs of the debtor or receipt of the respective agreement (or approval).

3. When concluding an amicable agreement with the participation of third persons who are interested persons with respect to the debtor, external administrator, or bankruptcy creditor, the meeting of creditors must be informed about the presence and character of interest in the conclusion of the transaction, and the amicable agreement must contain information that the amicable agreement is a transaction in whose conclusion there is an interest and the character of such interest specifically indicated.

4. When concluding an amicable agreement in the course of external administration an amicable agreement shall extend to demands of bankruptcy creditors and empowered agencies included in the register of demands of creditors on the date of conducting the meeting of creditors which adopted the decision concerning the conclusion of the amicable agreement.

5. The provisions provided for by point 2 of the present Article shall not prohibit the meeting of creditors to adopt a decision in the name of the bankruptcy creditors and empowered agencies concerning the conclusion of an amicable agreement.

Article 154. Peculiarities of Conclusion of Amicable Agreement in Course of Bankruptcy Proceeding

1. A decision concerning the conclusion of an amicable agreement on the part of the debtor shall be adopted by the bankruptcy administrator.

2. If an amicable agreement is for the debtor a transaction which in accordance with federal laws and/or constitutive documents of the debtor is concluded on the basis of a decision of management organs of the debtor or is subject to agreement with management organs of the debtor (or approval by these organs), the decision concerning the conclusion of an amicable agreement in the name of the debtor may be adopted after the adoption of the respective decision by the management organs of the debtor or receipt of the respective agreement (or approval).

3. When concluding an amicable agreement with the participation of third persons who are interested persons with regard to the debtor, bankruptcy administrator, or bankruptcy creditor, the amicable agreement must contain information that the amicable agreement is a transaction in the conclusion of which there is an interest and specifically indicate the character of that interest.

4. When concluding an amicable agreement in the course of a bankruptcy proceeding an amicable agreement shall extend to all demands of the bankruptcy creditors and empowered agencies include in the register of demands of creditors on the date of conducting the meeting of creditors which adopted the decision concerning the conclusion of an amicable agreement.

Article 155. Form of Amicable Agreement

1. An amicable agreement shall be concluded in written form.

2. On the part of the debtor an amicable agreement shall be signed by the person who adopted in accordance with the present Federal Law a decision concerning the conclusion of an amicable agreement. In the name of bankruptcy creditors and empowered agencies an amicable agreement shall be signed by the representative of the meeting of creditors or by the person empowered by the meeting of creditors to perform such action.

3. If third persons participate in the amicable agreement, the amicable agreement shall be signed on their side by these persons or by their empowered representatives.

Article 156. Content of Amicable Agreement

1. An amicable agreement must contain provisions concerning the procedure and periods for the performance of obligations of the debtor in monetary form.

With the consent of an individual bankruptcy creditor and/or empowered agency an amicable agreement may contain provisions concerning the termination of obligations of the debtor by means of the provision of release money, exchange of demands for a participatory share in the charter capital of the debtor, stocks convertible into stocks, bonds, or other securities, novation of an obligation, forgiveness of a debt or other means provided for by a federal law if such means of the termination of obligations does not violate the rights of other creditors whose demands are included in the register of demands of creditors.

An amicable agreement may contain provisions concerning the change of periods and procedure of payment of obligatory payments included in the register of demands of creditors.

The conditions of an amicable agreement affecting the repayment of indebtedness with regard to obligatory payments to be recovered in accordance with legislation on taxes and charges must not be contrary to the requirements of legislation on taxes and charges.

The satisfaction of demands of bankruptcy creditors in nonmonetary form must not create preferences for such creditors in comparison with creditors whose demands are performed in monetary form.

2. Interest shall be added for the unpaid part of the demands of creditors subject to repayment in accordance with the amicable agreement in monetary form from the date of confirmation by the arbitrazh court of the amicable agreement and until the date of satisfaction of the respective part of the demands of creditors in the amount established by Article 95(2) of the present Federal Law.

With the consent of the creditor a lower amount of interest rate, a lesser period for adding interest rate, or relief from the payment of interest may be established by the amicable agreement.

3. The conditions of an amicable agreement for bankruptcy creditors and empowered agencies who voted against the conclusion of an amicable agreement or did not take part in the voting may not be worse than for the bankruptcy creditors and empowered agencies who voted for the conclusion thereof.

Unless provided otherwise by the amicable agreement, the pledge of property of the debtor securing the performance by the debtor of obligations assumed shall be retained.

4. The bankruptcy creditor and/or empowered agency which voted for the conclusion of an amicable agreement, founders (or participants) of the debtor, owner of property of a debtor-unitary enterprise shall have the right to perform in full and in monetary form obligations of the debtor to bankruptcy creditors or to provide to the debtor monetary means needed to satisfy the demands of empowered agencies who voted against the conclusion of an amicable agreement or who did not take part in the voting, including to pay interest added in accordance with the present Federal Law, and also amounts of penalties (or fines, forfeits). In this event the bankruptcy creditor shall be obliged to accept the performance proposed for the debtor, the debtor shall be obliged to repay the demands of empowered agencies at the expense of monetary means provided to it and to the person who performed the obligation of the debtor shall pass the rights of the bankruptcy creditor. Means provided to the debtor in order to satisfy demands of empowered agencies shall be considered to be provided on the conditions of a contract of interest-free loan, the period for return of which is determined by the moment of demand.

Article 157. Participation in Amicable Agreement of Third Persons

1. The participation in an amicable agreement of third persons shall be permitted if their participation does not violate the rights and legal interests of creditors whose demands are included in the register of demands of creditors, and also of creditors whose demands arose after the date of adoption of the application concerning the deeming of the debtor to be bankrupt and the period of

performance of the demands which ensued before the date of conclusion of the amicable agreement.

2. Third persons participating in an amicable agreement shall have the right to provide a suretyship or guarantee of performance by the debtor of obligations under an amicable agreement or otherwise ensure the proper performance thereof.

Article 158. Conditions of Confirmation of Amicable Agreement by Arbitrazh Court

1. An amicable agreement may be confirmed by an arbitrazh court only after the repayment of indebtedness with regard to demands of creditors of the first and second priorities.

2. The debtor, external administrator, or bankruptcy administrator must not earlier than five days nor later than ten days from the date of conclusion of an amicable agreement submit to the arbitrazh court an application concerning confirmation of the amicable agreement.

3. To the application concerning confirmation of the amicable agreement must be appended:

the text of the amicable agreement;

the protocol of the meeting of creditors which adopted the decision concerning conclusion of the amicable agreement;

the list of all known bankruptcy creditors and empowered agencies which have not declared their demands against the debtor, specifying their addresses and amounts of indebtedness;

the register of demands of creditors;

the documents confirming the repayment of indebtedness with regard to demands of creditors of the first and second priorities;

the decision of the management organs of the debtor-juridical person if the necessity of such a decision is provided for by the present Federal Law;

the objections in written form of the bankruptcy creditors and empowered agencies which voted against the conclusion of the amicable agreement or did not take part in the voting with regard to the question concerning the conclusion of an amicable agreement when there are such objections;

other documents, the provision of which in accordance with the present Federal Law is obligatory.

4. The date of consideration of the application concerning confirmation of an amicable agreement the arbitrazh court shall notify to the persons participating in the case concerning bankruptcy. The failure of duly notified persons to appear shall not prevent consideration of the application concerning confirmation of the amicable agreement.

5. Confirmation of an amicable agreement may be refused in connection with the fact that the representative of the creditor when voting for the conclusion of an amicable agreement exceeded the powers granted to him by the present Federal Law, power of attorney, or constitutive documents of the creditor if it is proved that the person acting on the side of the debtor knew or could not fail to know about such limitations.

An arbitrazh court shall have the right to confirm an amicable agreement even if the person acting on the side of the debtor knew or could not fail to know about the limitations of the powers of the representative of the creditor but the voting of such representative did not influence the adoption of the decision concerning the conclusion of an amicable agreement.

Article 159. Consequences of Confirmation of Amicable Agreement by Arbitrazh Court

1. Confirmation of an amicable agreement by an arbitrazh court in the course of procedures of bankruptcy shall be grounds for termination of the proceedings with regard to the case concerning bankruptcy.

2. In the event of confirmation of an amicable agreement by an arbitrazh court in the course of financial recuperation, the performance of the schedule of repayment of indebtedness shall be terminated.

In the event of confirmation of an amicable agreement in the course of external administration the operation of the moratorium on satisfaction of the demands of creditors shall be terminated.

3. If an amicable agreement is confirmed by an arbitrazh court in the course of a bankruptcy proceeding, from the date of confirmation of the amicable agreement the decision of an arbitrazh court concerning the deeming of a debtor to be bankrupt and the opening of a bankruptcy proceeding shall not be subject to further execution.

4. From the date of confirmation of an amicable agreement by an arbitrazh court the powers of the temporary administrator, administrative administrator, external administrator, and bankruptcy administrator shall terminate.

The person who performed the duties of external administrator or bankruptcy administrator of a debtor-juridical person shall perform the duties of executive of the debtor until the date of appointment (or election) of the executive of the debtor.

From the date of appointment (or election) of the executive of the debtor, the debtor shall be the procedural legal successor with regard to suits declared previously by the arbitrazh administrator.

5. From the date of confirmation of the amicable agreement the debtor or third person shall commence to repay the indebtedness to creditors.

Article 160. Refusal to Confirm Amicable Agreement by Arbitrazh Court

1. In the event of the failure to perform the duty with regard to the repayment of indebtedness with regard to the demands of creditors of the first and second priorities an arbitrazh court shall refuse to confirm the amicable agreement.

2. The grounds for refusal by an arbitrazh court to confirm an amicable agreement shall be:

violation of the procedure established by the present Federal Law to conclude an amicable agreement;

failure to conform to the form of an amicable agreement;

violation of the rights of third persons;

contradiction of the conditions of the amicable agreement to the present Federal Law, other federal laws, and other normative legal acts;

existence of other grounds for the nullity of transactions provided for by civil legislation.

3. An arbitrazh court shall render a ruling concerning the refusal to confirm an amicable agreement, which may be appealed.

Article 161. Consequences of Refusal to Confirm Amicable Agreement

1. In the event of the rendering by an arbitrazh court of a ruling to refuse to confirm an amicable agreement, the amicable agreement shall be considered to be not concluded.

2. The rendering by an arbitrazh court of a ruling to refuse to confirm an amicable agreement shall not prevent the conclusion of a new amicable agreement.

Article 162. Appeal and Review of Ruling Concerning Confirmation of Amicable Agreement

1. Upon the appeal of persons participating in a case concerning bankruptcy, third persons participating in an amicable agreement, and also other persons whose rights and legal interests have been violated or might be violated by the amicable agreement, the ruling concerning confirmation of an amicable agreement may be appealed in the procedure established by the Code of Arbitrazh Procedure of the Russian Federation.

2. The ruling concerning confirmation of an amicable agreement may be reviewed for newly discovered circumstances if:

the circumstances preventing confirmation of an amicable agreement were not and could not have been known to the applicant at the moment of confirmation of the amicable agreement;

the applicant did not participate in the conclusion of the amicable agreement but his rights and legal interests were violated by the amicable agreement.

An applicant shall have the right to file an application concerning review of the ruling on confirmation of an amicable agreement on the grounds established by the present Article within a month from the date of discovery of the circumstances which are grounds for review of the particular ruling.

Article 163. Consequences of Vacating of Ruling Concerning Confirmation of Amicable Agreement

1. The vacating of a ruling concerning confirmation of an amicable agreement shall be grounds for renewal of the proceedings with regard to a case concerning bankruptcy. An arbitrazh court shall render a ruling concerning renewal of the proceedings with regard to a case concerning bankruptcy which shall be subject to immediate execution and may be appealed.

In the event of renewal of a proceeding with regard to a case concerning bankruptcy a procedure shall be introduced with respect to a debtor in the course of which an amicable agreement was concluded. Candidacies for arbitrazh administrators shall be submitted to the arbitrazh court in the procedure provided for by Article 45 of the present Federal Law by that self-regulating organisation which submitted such candidacy in the course of the said procedure of bankruptcy.

Within a month from the date of confirmation of the arbitrazh administrator he shall be obliged to conduct a meeting of creditors which is empowered to adopt decisions provided for by Article 73(1) of the present Federal Law.

In the event of the vacating of the ruling concerning confirmation of the amicable agreement when introducing with respect to the debtor procedures of bankruptcy with regard to a new case concerning bankruptcy, the bankruptcy creditors and empowered agencies who participated in the conclusion of the amicable agreement shall have the right to declare their demands against the debtor in the new case concerning bankruptcy in the composition and amount which have been provided for by the present Article.

2. In the event of vacating the ruling concerning confirmation of an amicable agreement the demands of creditors with respect to whom a deferral and/or instalment of payments due to them or discount from the debts were made shall be reinstated in their unsatisfied part.

3. Vacating a ruling concerning confirmation of an amicable agreement shall not entail the duty of creditors of the first and second priorities to return to the debtor that received by them on account of repayment of indebtedness.

4. In the event of vacating a ruling concerning confirmation of an amicable agreement publication of the communication concerning the renewal of the proceedings with regard to a case concerning bankruptcy of the debtor shall be effectuated by the arbitrazh court which adopted the decision concerning renewal of the procedure in the procedure provided for by Article 28 of the present Federal Law.

5. Demands of creditors which whom settlements of accounts were made on the conditions of the amicable agreement which are not contrary to the present Federal Law shall be considered to be repaid. Creditors whose demands were satisfied in accordance with the conditions of an amicable agreement providing preferences for the said creditors or impinging the rights and legal interests of other creditors shall be obliged to return everything received by way of performance of the amicable agreement, in so doing the demands of the said creditors shall be restored in the register of demands of creditors.

The composition and amount of demands of creditors and empowered agencies shall be determined on the date of renewal of the proceedings with regard to the case concerning bankruptcy.

6. In the part not regulated by the present Article the consequences of invalidity of transactions provided for by civil legislation shall apply.

Article 164. Dissolution of Amicable Agreement

1. Dissolution of an amicable agreement confirmed by an arbitrazh court shall not be permitted by agreement among individual creditors and the debtor.

2. An amicable agreement may be dissolved by an arbitrazh court with respect to all bankruptcy creditors and empowered agencies upon the application of a bankruptcy creditor or bankruptcy creditors and/or empowered agencies who possessed on the date of confirmation of the amicable agreement not less than one-fourth of the demands of bankruptcy creditors and empowered agencies against the debtor.

Bankruptcy creditors or empowered agencies shall have the right to file an application concerning dissolution of an amicable agreement with respect to all bankruptcy creditors and empowered agencies in the event of the failure to perform or material violation by the debtor of the conditions of the amicable agreement with respect to demands of such bankruptcy creditors and empowered agencies who comprised in aggregate not less than one-fourth of the demands of bankruptcy creditors and empowered agencies against the debtor on the date of confirmation of the amicable agreement.

Article 165. Procedure for Consideration of Application Concerning Dissolution of Amicable Agreement

1. Disputes concerning the dissolution of an amicable agreement shall be considered by an arbitrazh court which considered the case concerning bankruptcy.

2. An application concerning dissolution of an amicable agreement shall be signed by the bankruptcy creditor or bankruptcy creditors or empowered agencies whose demands were not performed by the debtor on the conditions of the amicable agreement and/or with respect to whose demands the conditions of the amicable agreement were materially violated by the debtor.

3. In the event of the receipt in an arbitrazh court of an application concerning dissolution of an amicable agreement the arbitrazh court shall render a ruling concerning the assignment of a session with regard to consideration of the application concerning dissolution of the amicable agreement.

The debtor, bankruptcy creditor or bankruptcy creditors, or empowered agencies who had recourse with the application concerning dissolution of the amicable agreement, and also third persons participating in the amicable agreement, shall be notified about the date and time of the judicial session with regard to consideration of the application concerning dissolution of the amicable agreement with respect to an individual creditor.

Persons who participated in the case concerning bankruptcy on the date of confirmation of the amicable agreement, and also third persons who participated in the amicable agreement, shall be notified about the date and time of the judicial session with regard to consideration of the application concerning dissolution of the amicable agreement with respect to all bankruptcy creditors and empowered agencies.

4. The court shall render a ruling with regard to the results of the consideration of the application concerning dissolution of the amicable agreement confirmed by the arbitrazh court, which shall be subject to immediate execution and may be appealed in the procedure provided for by the Code of Arbitrazh Procedure of the Russian Federation.

5. In the event of a refusal to satisfy the application concerning dissolution of the amicable agreement the arbitrazh court shall render a ruling concerning the refusal to dissolve the amicable agreement.

Article 166. Consequences of Dissolution of Amicable Agreement With Respect to All Bankruptcy Creditors and Empowered Agencies

1. The dissolution of an amicable agreement with respect to all bankruptcy creditors and empowered agencies shall be grounds for the renewal of proceedings with regard to a case concerning bankruptcy, except for instances of procedures of bankruptcy with regard to a new case concerning bankruptcy being introduced with respect to the debtor.

In the event of the renewal of proceedings with regard to the case concerning bankruptcy with respect to a debtor a procedure shall be introduced in the course of which an amicable agreement is concluded. Candidacies for arbitrazh administrators shall be submitted to the arbitrazh court in the procedure provided for by Article 45 of the present Federal Law by that self-regulating organisation which submitted such candidacy in the course of the said procedure of bankruptcy.

In the event of dissolution of the amicable agreement when introducing with respect to a debtor procedures of bankruptcy with regard to a new case concerning bankruptcy the bankruptcy creditors and empowered agencies whose demands were settled by the amicable agreement shall have the right to declare their demands against the debtor in the new case concerning bankruptcy in the composition and amount which are provided for by the present Article.

2. In the event of the renewal of a case concerning bankruptcy the amount of demands of such creditors shall be determined on the basis of the register of demands of creditors as of the date of confirmation of the amicable agreement. In this event the demands of bankruptcy creditors and empowered agencies satisfied in the course of performance of the amicable agreement in accordance with the present Federal Law shall not be taken into account in the register of demands of creditors, except for instances provided for by the present Article.

3. Dissolution of the amicable agreement with respect to all bankruptcy creditors and empowered agencies shall not entail the duty of bankruptcy creditors and empowered agencies whose demands were satisfied in the course of performance of the amicable agreement to return to the debtor everything received by them in the course of performance of the amicable agreement.

Bankruptcy creditors and empowered agencies shall be obliged to return everything received by them in the course of performance of the amicable agreement if they knew or should have known that satisfaction of their demands was made with a violation of the rights and legal interests of other bankruptcy creditors and empowered agencies, the said demands being restored in the register of demands of creditors.

4. In the event of dissolution of the amicable agreement the conditions of the amicable agreement providing for instalment or deferral of satisfaction of demands of bankruptcy creditors and empowered agencies, and also a discount from debts, shall be terminated with respect to that part of the demands of creditors which were not satisfied on the date of dissolution of the amicable agreement.

5. Dissolution of the amicable agreement shall not entail the duty of creditors of the first and second priorities to return to the debtor that received by them on account of the repayment of indebtedness.

6. The composition and amount of demands of creditors and empowered agencies shall be determined on the date of renewal of the proceedings with regard to the case concerning bankruptcy.

Article 167. Consequences of Failure to Perform Amicable Agreement

1. In the event of the failure to perform an amicable agreement by the debtor, the creditors shall have the right without dissolution of the amicable agreement to present their demands in the amount provided for by the amicable agreement in the general procedure established by procedural legislation.

2. In the event of the instituting of a new case concerning bankruptcy of the debtor the amount of demands of creditors with respect to whom an amicable agreement was concluded shall be determined by the conditions provided for by the amicable agreement.

Chapter IX. Peculiarities of Bankruptcy of Individual Categories of Debtors–Juridical Persons

§1. General Provisions

Article 168. General Provisions of Bankruptcy of Individual Categories of Debtors-Juridical Persons

To relations connected with bankruptcy of urban-forming, agricultural, and financial organisations, strategic enterprises and organisations, and also subjects of natural monopolies, the provisions of the present Federal Law shall apply which regulate the bankruptcy of debtors-juridical persons unless provided otherwise by the present Chapter.

§2. Bankruptcy of Urban-Forming Organisations

Article 169. Status of Urban-Forming Organisations

1. For the purposes of the present Federal Law urban-forming organisations shall be deemed to be juridical persons whose numbers of workers comprise not less than twenty-five per cent of the number of the working population of a respective population center.

2. The provisions provided by the present paragraph shall also apply to other organisations whose numbers of workers exceed five thousand persons.

Article 170. Consideration of Case Concerning Bankruptcy of Urban-Forming Organisation

1. When considering a case concerning bankruptcy of an urban-forming organisation, the respective agency of local self-government shall be deemed to be the person participating in the case concerning bankruptcy.

2. Federal agencies of executive power and agencies of executive power of the respective subject of the Russian Federation also may be enlisted as persons participating in the case concerning bankruptcy.

3. When considering the substantiation of the demands of creditors evidence must be presented to the arbitrazh court confirming that the urban-forming organisation corresponds to the requirements of Article 169 of the present Federal Law.

Article 171. Introduction of External Administration of Urban-Forming Organisation Under Suretyship

1. In the event a decision is not adopted by the meeting of creditors concerning the introduction of external administration of an urban-forming organisation the arbitrazh court shall have the right to introduce external administration with regard to the grounds provided for by the present Federal Law, and also upon the petition of an agency of local self-government, or respective federal agency of executive power enlisted to participate in the case concerning bankruptcy, or agency of executive power of the subject of the Russian Federation on condition of the granting of a suretyship with regard to obligations of the debtor.

The suretyship with regard to obligations of the debtor may be given by the Russian Federation, subject of the Russian Federation, or municipal formation in the person of their empowered agencies.

2. An agency of local self-government or respective federal agency of executive power enlisted to participate in a case concerning the bankruptcy of an urban-forming organisation, or agency of executive power of a subject of the Russian Federation which submitted a suretyship with regard to obligations of the debtor shall determine the requirements for the candidacy of external manager and send them to the self-regulating organisations of arbitrazh administrators.

3. If the external administration of an urban-forming organisation was introduced in the procedure provided for by the present Article, the surety shall bear subsidiary responsibility with regard to obligations of the debtor to the creditors thereof.

Article 172. Extension of Financial Recuperation or External Administration with Respect to Urban-Forming Organisation Upon Petition of Agency of Local Self-Government

Financial recuperation or external administration with respect to an urban-forming organisation may be extended by an arbitrazh court for not more than a year when there is a petition of the agency of local self-government, or respective federal agency of executive power enlisted to participate in the case, or agency of executive power of a subject of the Russian Federation on condition of the granting of a suretyship with regard to the obligations of the debtor.

Article 173. Suretyship

1. For the purposes of the present Federal Law by suretyship is understood the unilateral duty of the person who gave the suretyship for a debtor to be liable for the performance by the last of all the monetary obligations thereof to creditors, and also duties with regard to the payment of obligatory payments to budgets and extrabudgetary funds.

A suretyship with regard to obligations of the debtor may be given by the Russian Federation, subject of the Russian Federation, or municipal formation in the person of their empowered agencies in the procedure and on the conditions which were provided for by a federal law.

2. A suretyship with regard to obligations of a debtor shall be granted to an arbitrazh court in written form. In the application concerning the suretyship there must be specified:

the amount of obligations of the debtor to creditors and duties with regard to the payment of obligatory payments;

the schedule for the repayment of indebtedness.

To the suretyship shall be appended the documents confirming the inclusion of obligations under the suretyship in the corresponding budget on the date of granting the suretyship;

3. The debtor and his surety shall be obliged to commence to settle accounts with creditors in accordance with the schedule of repayment of indebtedness provided for by the suretyship.

4. In the event of the failure to perform the demands of creditors and empowered agencies in the procedure and within the periods which were provided for by the schedule for repayment of demands, the creditors and empowered agencies shall have the right to present demands to the surety concerning the recovery of the unpaid amounts in the general procedure provided for by legislation.

5. A violation by the surety of his obligations with respect to creditors and empowered agencies possessing one third part of all demands against the debtor may serve as grounds for the termination before time of financial recuperation or external administration, deeming the debtor to be a bankrupt, and the opening of a bankruptcy proceeding.

Article 174. Repayment of Demands of Creditors in Course of Financial Recuperation or External Administration With Respect to Urban-Forming Organisation

1. The Russian Federation, subject of the Russian Federation, or municipal formation at any time before the end of financial recuperation of an urban-forming organisation or external administration of an urban-forming organisation shall have the right to settle accounts with all creditors or to extinguish demands of creditors with regard to monetary obligations and payment of obligatory payments by other means provided for by the present Federal Law.

2. Accounts shall be settled with creditors in the sequence of priority established by Articles 134–138 of the present Federal Law.

3. In the event of the satisfaction of demands of creditors with regard to monetary obligations and payment of obligatory payments in the procedure provided

for by points 1 and 2 of the present Article, the proceedings with regard to the case concerning bankruptcy shall be subject to termination.

Article 175. Sale of Enterprise by Urban-Forming Organisation

1. In the course of external administration or bankruptcy proceeding the sale of an enterprise of the urban-forming organisation may be effectuated.

2. When there is a petition of an agency of local self-government or enlistment for participation in a case concerning bankruptcy of the respective federal agency of executive power, or agency of executive power of a subject of the Russian Federation, a material condition of the contract of purchase-sale of the enterprise of an urban-forming organisation may be the preservation of jobs for not less than fifty per cent of the workers of such enterprise on the date of sale thereof within a determined period, but not more than three years from the moment of entry of the contract into force.

Other conditions may be established upon the proposal of the agency of local self-government or respective federal agency of executive power enlisted to partic-ipate in the case concerning bankruptcy, or agency of executive power of a subject of the Russian Federation exclusively with the consent of the meeting of creditors in the procedure provided for by Article 15 of the present Federal Law.

3. In the event of the failure of the purchaser of the enterprise of an urban-forming organisation to perform the conditions provided for by point 2 of the present Article, the contract of purchase-sale shall be subject to dissolution by an arbitrazh court on the basis of an application of the agency of local self-govern-ment or federal agency of executive power, or agency of executive power of a sub-ject of the Russian Federation upon whose petition the competition was conducted. In the event of the dissolution of the contract of purchase-sale the means expended for the purchase of the enterprise shall be compensated to the purchaser of such enterprise at the expense of means of the respective budget and investments effectuated during the period of operation of the contract, and the enterprise shall be subject to transfer to the municipal formation.

4. If the petition specified in point 2 of the present Article was not filed or the enterprise of an urban-forming organisation was not sold on the said conditions, the enterprise shall be subject to sale in the procedure and on the conditions which were established by Articles 110, 111, and 139 of the present Federal Law.

Article 176. Sale of Property of Urban-Forming Organisation Deemed to be Bankrupt

1. In the event of the sale of property of an urban-forming organisation deemed to be bankrupt, the arbitrazh administrator must place the enterprise on sale in the first public sale on the conditions provided for by Article 175 of the pre-sent Federal Law.

2. If the enterprise of the debtor was not sold in the procedure provided for by point 1 of the present Article, the sale of the property of the urban-forming organisation shall be effectuated according to the rules provided for by Article 111 of the present Federal Law.

§3. Bankruptcy of Agricultural Organisations

Article 177. General Provisions of Bankruptcy of Agricultural Organisations

1. For the purposes of the present Federal Law by agricultural organizations is understood juridical persons whose principal types of activity are the production or the production and processing of agricultural products, receipts from the realisation of which comprise not less than fifty per cent of the total amount of receipts.

2. The peculiarities of bankruptcy of agricultural organisations provided for by the present Federal Law also shall apply to fishery artels (or collective farms) whose receipts from the realisation of agricultural products produced or produced and processed and caught (or extracted) water biological resources comprises not less than seventy per cent of the total amount of receipts.

3. In the event of the sale of objects of immoveables which are used for the purposes of agricultural production and belong to an agricultural organisation deemed to be bankrupt, other conditions being equal the preferential right of acquisition of the said objects shall belong to agricultural organisations and peasant (or farmer) economies located in the particular locality.

4. When deeming an agricultural organisation to be bankrupt the land plots may be alienated or transferred to another person, to the Russian Federation, to a subject of the Russian Federation, or to a municipal formation to the extent that the turnover thereof is permitted by land legislation.

Article 178. Observation and Financial Recuperation of Agricultural Organisation and External Administration of Agricultural Organisation

1. In the course of observation when analysing the financial state of an agricultural organisation the seasonality of agricultural production must be taken into account and the dependence thereof on nature-climatic conditions, and also the possibility of satisfaction of the demands of creditors at the expense of revenues which might be received by the agricultural organisation at the end of the respective period of agricultural work.

2. Financial recuperation of an agricultural organisation shall be introduced for a period up to the end of the respective period of agricultural work, taking into account the time necessary for the realisation of the agricultural products produced or produced and processed.

If in the course of financial recuperation a decline and worsening of the financial state of the agricultural organisation occurred in connection with natural calamities, epizootics, and other circumstances of an extraordinary character, the period of financial recuperation may be extended for a year on condition of a change of the schedule for repayment of indebtedness in the procedure provided for by Article 85 of the present Federal Law.

3. External administration of an agricultural organisation shall be introduced until the end of the respective period of agricultural work, taking into account the time necessary for the realisation of agricultural products produced or produced and processed. The period of external administration may not exceed the periods established by Article 92(2) of the present Federal Law, but not more than three months.

If in the course of external administration a decline and worsening of the financial state of the agricultural organisation occurred in connection with natural calamities, epizootics, and other circumstances of an extraordinary character, the period of external administration may be extended for a year.

Article 179. Peculiarities of Sale of Property and Property Rights of Agricultural Organisations

1. In the event of the sale of property and property rights of a debtor-agricultural organisation the arbitrazh administrator must place on sale at the first public sale the enterprise of the debtor.

2. The persons engaging in the production or the production and processing of agricultural products and possessing a land plot directly adjacent to the land plot of the debtor shall have a preferential right to acquire the property of the debtor.

3. An arbitrazh administrator in the event of the sale of the property specified in point 2 of the present Article, and also the property rights, shall be obliged to conduct an independent evaluation of the value of the property and property rights and propose to persons specified in point 2 of the present Article to acquire the property and property rights at the assessed evaluation.

If the said persons within a month have not declared their wish to acquire the property and property rights, the arbitrazh administrator shall effectuate the realisation of the property and property rights in the procedure provided for by the present Federal Law.

§4. Bankruptcy of Financial Organisations

Article 180. Regulation of Bankruptcy of Financial Organisations

To relations connected with the bankruptcy of financial organisations (or credit organisations, insurance organisations, professional participants of the securities market) the present Federal Law shall apply with the peculiarities established by the federal law on insolvency (or bankruptcy) of financial organisations.

Article 181. Grounds for Deeming Credit Organisation to be Bankrupt

1. The grounds for deeming a credit organisation to be bankrupt shall be determined by the federal law on insolvency (or bankruptcy) of credit organisations.

2. An application concerning the deeming of a credit organisation to be bankrupt shall be accepted for consideration by an arbitrazh court after the revocation by the Bank of Russia of the license which the credit organisation has for the effectuation of banking operations unless provided otherwise by the federal law on insolvency (or bankruptcy) of credit organisations.

Article 182. Procedures of Bankruptcy for Credit Organisations

1. One of the following decisions may be adopted by an arbitrazh court with regard to the results of consideration of an application concerning the deeming of a credit organisation to be bankrupt:
on deeming the credit organisation to be bankrupt and opening a bankruptcy proceeding;
on refusing to deem the credit organisation to be bankrupt.

2. In the event of the adoption by an arbitrazh court concerning the deeming of a credit organisation to be bankrupt a bankruptcy proceeding shall be conducted in the procedure established by the present Federal Law, taking into account the peculiarities provided for by the federal law on insolvency (or bankruptcy) of credit organisations.

3. The bankruptcy administrator within ten days from the date of rendering a ruling of an arbitrazh court concerning the completion of the bankruptcy proceeding must submit the said ruling to the agency effectuating the State registration of juridical persons.

Article 183. Consideration of Case Concerning Bankruptcy of Insurance Organisation

1. When considering a case concerning bankruptcy of an insurance organisation the federal agency of executive power empowered by the Government of the Russian Federation to effectuate supervision over insurance activity shall be deemed the person participating in the arbitrazh proceeding with regard to a case concerning bankruptcy together with other persons specified in Article 35 of the present Federal Law.

2. The application concerning the deeming of an insurance organisation to be bankrupt may be filed in an arbitrazh court by the debtor, bankruptcy creditor, or empowered agency.

3. In the event of the introduction with respect to the debtor-insurance organisation of procedures of bankruptcy in the procedure established by the present Federal Law the debtor or bankruptcy administrator shall be obliged within ten days from the date of introduction of the procedure of observation or bankruptcy proceeding to inform the federal agency of executive power empowered by the Government of the Russian Federation to effectuate supervision over insurance activity about the introduction of the respective procedure of bankruptcy with respect to the debtor.

Article 184. Sale of Property Complex of Insurance Organisation

1. The sale of a property complex of an insurance organisation may be effectuated in the course of external administration according to the rules provided for by Article 110 of the present Federal Law and taking into account the requirements of the federal laws regulating insurance activity.

When conducting a bankruptcy proceeding the property complex of an insurance organisation may be sold only with the consent of the purchaser to assume the contracts of insurance whose period of operation has not expired and under which the insured event has not ensued on the date of deeming the insurance organisation to be bankrupt.

2. Only an insurance organisation having a license of the federal agency of executive power for supervision over insurance activity for the effectuation of the respective type of insurance and possessing assets sufficient to perform the obligations under the contracts of insurance assumed may act as the purchaser of the property complex of the insurance organisation.

3. In the event of the sale of a property complex of an insurance organisation in the course of external administration to the purchaser thereof shall pass all the rights and duties under the contracts of insurance with regard to which on the date of the sale of property of the insurance organisation the insured event has not ensued.

Article 185. Right of Demand of Insurants in Event of Bankruptcy of Insurance Organisation

1. In the event of the adoption by an arbitrazh court of a decision concerning the deeming of an insurance organisation to be bankrupt and the opening of a bankruptcy proceeding all contracts of insurance which have been concluded by such organisation as insurer and under which the insured event has not ensued on the date of adoption of the said decision shall terminate, except for instances provided for by Article 184(1) of the present Federal Law.

2. Insurants or beneficiaries under contracts of insurance which have terminated on the grounds provided for by point 1 of the present Article shall have the right to demand the return of part of the insurance premium paid to the insurer

in proportion to the difference between the period for which the contract of insurance was concluded and the period during which it operated unless provided otherwise by a federal law.

3. Insurants or beneficiaries under contracts of insurance with regard to which the insured event ensued before the moment of adoption by the arbitrazh court of a decision concerning the deeming of the insurance organisation to be bankrupt and the opening of a bankruptcy proceeding shall have the right to demand the effectuation of the insurance payment.

Article 186. Satisfaction of Demands of Creditors of Third Priority

1. In the event of the adoption by an arbitrazh court of the decision to deem an insurance organisation to be bankrupt and the opening of a bankruptcy proceeding, the demands of creditors of the third priority shall be subject to satisfaction in the following procedure:

in first priority—demands of the insured and beneficiaries under contracts of obligatory personal insurance;

in second priority—demands of beneficiaries and insurants under other contracts of obligatory insurance;

in third priority—demands of insured, beneficiaries, and insurants under contracts of personal insurance, including demands provided for by Article 185(2) of the present Federal Law;

in fourth priority—demands of other creditors.

2. Demands of creditors secured by a pledge of property of the debtor shall be satisfied in the procedure established by Article 138 of the present Federal Law.

Article 187. Peculiarities of Regulation of Bankruptcy of Professional Participants of Securities Market

1. When considering a case concerning the bankruptcy of a professional participant of the securities market an arbitrazh court shall have the right to enlist to participate in the case the federal agency of executive power for regulation of the securities market and respective self-regulating organisation on the securities market.

2. An arbitrazh administrator participating in a case concerning the bankruptcy of a professional participant of the securities market must have a respective attestation issued by the federal agency of executive power for the securities market.

3. The peculiarities of the procedures of bankruptcy of professional participants of the securities market not regulated by the present paragraph, and also measures with regard to defence of the rights and legal interests of clients of professional participants of the securities market, may be established by a federal law.

4. In the event of the introduction with respect to a debtor who is a professional participant of the securities market of the procedures of bankruptcy in the procedure established by the present Federal Law the arbitrazh administrator shall be obliged within ten days from the date of introduction of the procedures of bankruptcy to send a respective notification to the federal agency of executive power for regulation of the securities market, the self-regulating organisation, of which the professional participant is a member, and clients of the professional participant.

In the notification sent to clients of the professional participant it shall be proposed to give an instruction concerning the actions which is it necessary to perform with securities belonging to the client.

5. The provisions of the present Article and Articles 188 and 189 of the present Federal Law shall not apply in the event of the bankruptcy of a credit organisation which is a professional participant of the securities market, except for instances when the credit organisation is a professional participant of the securities market effectuating depositary activity.

Article 188. Limitations of Conclusion of Transactions by Professional Participant of Securities Market

Limitations on the conclusion of transactions or conducting of operations with regard to recording rights to securities by a professional participant of the securities market in the event of the application thereto of procedures of bankruptcy, except for a bankruptcy proceeding, shall not extend to transactions with securities of the clients thereof or conducting of operations with regard to recording rights to securities effectuated according to commissions of clients and confirmed by clients after the instituting of a proceeding with regard to the case concerning bankruptcy.

Article 189. Peculiarities of External Administration and Bankruptcy Proceeding of Professional Participant of Securities Market

1. In the course of external administration an arbitrazh administrator with the consent and in the name of clients of the debtor shall have the right to transfer securities in the management and possession of a professional participant of the securities market for keeping and/or recording with him or another organisation having a respective license of a professional participant of the securities market.

2. Securities and other property of clients, including monetary means, belonging to them and situated in a special broker account of a professional participant of the securities market effectuating broker activity shall not be included in the bankruptcy mass. Monetary means and securities within the composition of special funds intended to reduce risks of the failure to perform transactions with securities and formed by the organisers of public sales or by clearing organisations also shall not be subject to inclusion in the bankruptcy mass.

3. From the moment of the introduction of external administration or bankruptcy proceeding the securities of clients in the management or possession of a professional participant of the securities market or recorded by a professional participant of the securities market shall be subject to return to clients unless provided otherwise by an agreement of the owner of the said property with the debtor or arbitrazh administrator.

In the absence of consent of clients to the transfer of inscribed securities recorded by the debtor or other organisation having a respective license of a professional participant of the securities market, the said records shall be transferred to the professional participant of the securities market effectuating the conducting of the register of possessors of such securities.

4. If the demands of clients with respect to the return of securities belonging to them of one form (or one emittent, one category, one type, one series) exceed the number of said securities at the disposition of the professional participant of the securities market, the return of such securities shall be effectuated in proportion to the demands of clients.

The amount of monetary means belonging to each client and subject to return which are in the special broker account shall be established on the basis of bookkeeping records of the professional participant of the securities market effectuating broker activity.

Demands of clients in the unsatisfied part thereof shall be deemed to be monetary obligations and shall be satisfied (or repaid) in the procedure provided for by Chapter VII of the present Federal Law.

5. In the event of the introduction of a bankruptcy proceeding with respect to a professional participant of the securities market effectuating the keeping and/or recording of the rights to securities belonging to clients thereof the professional participant of the securities market shall be obliged to transfer these securities to another professional participant of the securities market specified by the client.

6. In the event of the introduction of a bankruptcy proceeding with respect to a professional participant of the securities market effectuating the conducting of the register of possessors of shares of a share investment fund, the register of participants of a non-State pension fund, or the register of demands of creditors, such professional participant of the securities market shall be obliged within a month from the date of introduction of the bankruptcy proceeding to transfer the information and documents within the composition of such registers to another professional participant of the securities market specified by the client or arbitrazh administrator.

§5. Bankruptcy of Strategic Enterprises and Organisations

Article 190. General Provisions of Bankruptcy of Strategic Enterprises and Organisations

1. For the purposes of the present Federal Law by strategic enterprises and organisations is understood:

federal State unitary enterprises and open joint-stock societies whose stocks are in federal ownership and which effectuate the production of products (or work, services) having strategic significance to ensure the defence capability and security of the State and defence of the morality, health, rights and legal interests of citizens of the Russian Federation;

organisations of the defence-industrial complex—production, scientific-production, scientific-research, design-construction design, experimental and other organisations effectuating work with regard to ensuring the fulfillment of a State defence order.

2. The list of strategic enterprises and organisations, including organizations of the defence-industrial complex to which the rules provided for by the present paragraph apply shall be confirmed by the Government of the Russian Federation and subject to obligatory publication.

3. Strategic enterprises and organisations shall be considered to be unable to satisfy demands of creditors with regard to monetary obligations and/or to perform the duty with regard to payment of obligatory payments if the respective obligations and/or duties have not been performed within six months from the date when they should have been performed.

4. In order to institute a case concerning the bankruptcy of strategic enterprises or organisations the demands comprising in aggregate not less than five hundred thousand rubles shall be taken into account.

Article 191. Measures With Regard to Prevention of Bankruptcy of Strategic Enterprises and Organisations

For the purposes of the prevention of bankruptcy of strategic enterprises and organisations the Government of the Russian Federation shall in the procedure established by a federal law and other normative legal acts of the Russian Federation:

organise the conducting of the recording and analysis of the financial state of strategic enterprises and organisations and their ability to pay;

conduct the reorganisation of strategic enterprises and organisations;

effectuate the repayment of indebtedness of the federal budget formed as a result of the untimely payment of a State defence order to strategic enterprises and organisations which are the executors of work under the State defence order;

ensure the conducting of the restructurisation of indebtedness (principal debt and interest, forfeits, and fines) of strategic enterprises and organisations which are executors of work under a State defence order to the federal budget and State extrabudgetary funds;

promote the achievement of agreement of strategic enterprises and organisations with creditors concerning the restructurisation of their creditor indebtedness, including by means of the provision of State guarantees;

conduct pre-judicial sanation of strategic enterprises and organisations in the procedure provided for by the present Federal Law;

effectuate other measures directed towards the prevention of bankruptcy of strategic enterprises and organisations.

Article 192. Persons Participating in Case Concerning Bankruptcy of Strategic Enterprises or Organisations

Among the persons provided for by Article 34 of the present Federal Law the federal agency of executive power ensuring the realisation of the unified State policy in the branch of the economy in which the activity of the respective strategic enterprise or organisation is effectuated shall be deemed the person participating in the case concerning bankruptcy of the strategic enterprise or organisation.

Article 193. Arbitrazh Administrator in Case Concerning Bankruptcy of Strategic Enterprise or Organisation

The Government of the Russian Federation shall besides the requirements for the candidacy of arbitrazh administrator established by Articles 20 and 23 of the present Federal Law have the right to establish the list of additional requirements which are obligatory for the arbitrazh court when confirming the candidacy of arbitrazh administrator in a case concerning the bankruptcy of a strategic enterprise or organisation.

Article 194. Financial Recuperation of Strategic Enterprises and Organisations

1. If a decision is not adopted by the first meeting of creditors concerning the introduction with respect to a strategic enterprise or organisation of one of the procedures of bankruptcy and the self-regulating organisation is not determined which submits the candidacies of arbitrazh administrators satisfying the requirements determined by the meeting of creditors, the arbitrazh court shall postpone consideration of the case concerning the bankruptcy of the strategic enterprise or organisation within the limits of the period established by Article 51 of the present Federal Law and shall oblige creditors within the period established by the arbitrazh court to adopt respective decisions.

In the absence of the possibility to postpone consideration of the case within the limits of the period established by Article 51 of the present Federal Law the arbitrazh court shall:

render a ruling concerning the introduction with respect to the strategic enterprise or organisation of financial recuperation if there is a petition of the founders (or participants) of the debtor, owner of the property of the debtor (unitary enterprise), empowered State agency, or federal agency of executive power ensuring the realization of the unified State policy in the branch of the economy in which the strategic enterprise or organisation effectuates its activity, and also other third person or third persons, on condition of the granting by the said persons of security for performance of the obligations of the debtor, including by means of the provision of State guarantees, in accordance with the schedule for the repayment of indebtedness. The amount of security provided may not be less than the amount of the obligations of the debtor reflected in the bookkeeping balance sheet on the last reporting date before conducting the first meeting of creditors. In so doing the schedule confirmed by the arbitrazh court for the repayment of indebtedness must provide for the beginning of repayment of indebtedness not later than a month after the rendering by the arbitrazh court of a ruling concerning the introduction of financial recuperation and repayment of demands of creditors monthly in equal participatory shares within a year from the date of the commencement of repayment of demands of creditors;

render a ruling concerning the introduction of external administration with respect to a strategic enterprise or organisation in the absence of grounds for the introduction of financial recuperation provided for by the present Article if the opinion of a federal agency of executive power ensuring the realisation of the unified State policy in the branch of the economy in which the strategic enterprise or organisation effectuates its activity has been submitted to the arbitrazh court concerning the possibility of restoration of the ability of the debtor to pay in the course of external administration;

in the absence of grounds for the introduction of financial recuperation and external administration provided for by the present Article a decision shall be adopted concerning the deeming of the debtor to be bankrupt and the opening of a bankruptcy proceeding.

2. If a decision is adopted by the first meeting of creditors concerning recourse to an arbitrazh court with a petition concerning the introduction of external administration or deeming the debtor-strategic enterprise or organisation to be bankrupt and the opening of a bankruptcy proceeding, the arbitrazh court may render a ruling concerning the introduction of financial recuperation on condition of the submission of a petition of the founders (or participants) of the debtor, owner of the property of the debtor (unitary enterprise), empowered State agency, and federal agency of executive power ensuring the realisation of the unified State policy in the branch of the economy in which the strategic enterprise or organisa-

tion effectuates its activity, and also of a third person or third persons and the granting by the said persons of security for the performance of obligations of the debtor, including by means of the provision of State guarantees in accordance with the schedule of repayment of indebtedness. The amount of security provided may not be less than the amount of obligations of the debtor reflected in the book-keeping balance sheet on the last reporting date before the date of conducting the first meeting of creditors. In so doing the schedule confirmed by the arbitrazh court for repayment of indebtedness must provide for the commencement of repayment of indebtedness not later than a month from the date of rendering by the arbitrazh court of a ruling concerning the introduction of financial recupera-tion and repayment of demands of creditors monthly in equal participatory shares within a year from the date of commencement of the repayment of demands of creditors.

The repayment of indebtedness with regard to obligatory payments shall be established in accordance with the requirements of tax legislation in the schedule of repayment of indebtedness provided for by the present Article.

Article 195. External Administration of Strategic Enterprises and Organisations

1. The external administrator shall be obliged to send the plan of external administration worked out by him not later than fifteen days before the date of consideration thereof by the meeting of creditors at the federal agency of execu-tive power ensuring the realisation of the unified State policy in the branch of the economy in which the strategic enterprise or organisation effectuates its activity.

2. The federal agency of executive power specified in point 1 of the present Article shall send to the meeting of creditors and to the arbitrazh court an opinion concerning the plan of external administration containing an analysis of the results provided for by the plan of external administration with regard to restora-tion of the ability of the debtor to pay in the course of external administration.

3. The federal agency of executive power ensuring the realisation of the unified State policy in the branch of the economy in which the strategic enter-prise or organisation effectuates activity shall have the right before the date of confirmation by the meeting of creditors of the plan of external administration with respect to the strategic enterprise or organisation to send to the arbitrazh court a petition concerning a transition to financial recuperation unless financial recuperation was previously applied with respect to this debtor. To the said peti-tion must be appended the schedule for repayment of indebtedness, and also information concerning the security of performance of the obligations of the debtor, including by means of the provision of State guarantees, in accordance with the schedule for the repayment of indebtedness. The amount of security provided may not be less than the amount of obligations of the debtor reflected

in the bookkeeping balance sheet on the last reporting date before conducting the first meeting of creditors. In so doing the schedule for the repayment of indebtedness confirmed by the arbitrazh court must provide for the commencement of the repayment of indebtedness not later than a month from the date of rendering by the arbitrazh court of a ruling concerning the introduction of financial recuperation and repayment of demands of creditors monthly in equal participatory shares within a year from the date of the commencement of repayment of the demands of creditors.

In this event the arbitrazh court may render a ruling concerning the transition to financial recuperation.

4. The plan of external administration with respect to a strategic enterprise or organisation may provide for transactions not related to the economic activity of the debtor which are connected with:

sale of the enterprise;

alienation or encumberment of immoveable property;

disposition of other property of the debtor whose balance sheet value comprises more than five per cent of the balance sheet value of assets of the debtor determined on the basis of the bookkeeping report for the last reporting period;

receipt and issuance of loans (or credits), issuance of suretyships and guarantees, assignment of rights of demand, transfer of debt, and also the founding of trust management over property of the debtor;

alienation and acquisition of stocks and participatory shares of economic partnerships and societies;

conclusion of contracts of a simple partnership.

5. The external administrator shall not have the right to refuse to perform contracts of the debtor connected with the fulfillment of work with regard to a State defence order ensuring federal State needs in the domain of maintaining the defence capacity and security of the Russian Federation.

6. The external administrator shall not have the right to alienate individual types of property and property and other rights which are within the composition of the property complex of the debtor-strategic enterprise or organisation intended for the effectuation of activity connected with the fulfillment of work with regard to a State defence order ensuring federal State needs in the domain of maintaining the defence capacity and security of the Russian Federation.

7. The sale of the enterprise of the debtor which was intended for the effectuation of activity connected with the fulfillment of work with regard to a State defence order ensuring federal State needs in the domain of maintaining the defence capacity and security of the Russian Federation shall be effectuated by means of conducting an open public sale in the form of a competition unless established otherwise by the present Article.

If property within the composition of the enterprise of the debtor which was intended for the effectuation of activity connected with the fulfillment of work under a State defence order ensuring federal State needs in the domain of maintaining the defence capacity and security of the Russian Federation is relegated to property limiting defence capacity, the sale of the enterprise shall be effectuated only at a closed public sale in the form of a competition.

Obligatory conditions of the competition shall be obligations of the purchaser to:

ensure the preservation of the special-purpose designation of the said property complex and property of mobilisation designation of the debtor;

fulfil contracts of the debtor connected with the fulfillment of work under a State defence order ensuring federal State needs in the domain of maintaining the defence capacity and security of the Russian Federation.

8. In the event of the sale of the enterprise of a debtor-strategic enterprise or organisation intended to effectuate activity connected with the fulfillment of work under a State defence order ensuring federal State needs in the domain of maintaining the defence capacity and security of the Russian Federation, the Russian Federation shall have the right of preferential acquisition of this enterprise.

In the event of the sale at a public sale of an enterprise of the debtor-strategic organisation which is not a federal State unitary enterprise intended for the effectuation of activity connected with the fulfillment of work under a State defence order ensuring federal State needs in the domain of maintaining the defence capacity and security of the Russian Federation, the Russian Federation shall have the right within a month from the date of signature of the protocol concerning the results of the public sale to conclude a contract of purchase-sale providing for the acquisition of the said enterprise at the price determined according to the results of the public sale and specified in the protocol concerning the results of the public sale on the conditions established for conducting the competition.

If the Russian Federation within the said period has not concluded a contract of purchase-sale, this contract shall be concluded with the winner of the public sale established in the protocol on the results of the public sale.

The winner of the public sale shall be obliged to pay the sale price of the enterprise determined at the public sale within the period which is provided for in the communication concerning the conducting of the public sale and may not exceed a month from the date of conclusion of the contract of purchase-sale.

Bankruptcy creditors and their affiliated persons shall not be permitted to participate in the public sale.

9. In the event of the sale at a public sale of the enterprise of the debtor-strategic enterprise which is a federal State unitary enterprise intended for the effectuation of activity connected with the fulfillment of work under a State defence

order ensuring federal State needs in the domain of maintaining the defence capacity and security of the Russian Federation, the Russian Federation within a month from the date of signature of the protocol concerning the results of the public sale shall have the right to provide monetary means to the debtor in an amount equal to the sale price of the said enterprise determined according to the results of the conducting of the competition and specified in the protocol on the results of the public sale. The said means the debtor shall be obliged to send to repay the demands of creditors in accordance with the register of demands of creditors.

If the Russian Federation within the said period has not provided monetary means to the debtor in accordance with the present Article, a contract of purchase-sale shall be concluded with the winner of the public sale established in the protocol on the results of the public sale.

The winner of the public sale shall be obliged to pay the sale price of the enterprise determined at the public sale within the period which is provided in the communication concerning the conducting of the public sale and which may not exceed a month from the date of conclusion of the contract of purchase-sale.

In the event of the sale of the enterprise of a debtor-strategic enterprise or organisation which is intended for the effectuation of activity connected with the fulfillment of work under a State defence order ensuring federal State needs in the domain of maintaining the defence capacity and security of the Russian Federation at a public sale in the form of a competition the federal agency of executive power ensuring the realisation of the unified State policy in the branch of the economy in which the strategic enterprise or organisation effectuated activity shall conclude with the purchaser of such enterprise of the debtor an agreement concerning the performance of conditions of the competition. In the event of a material violation or failure to perform by the purchaser of the agreement concerning the performance of conditions of the competition, this agreement and contract of purchase-sale of such enterprise of the debtor shall be subject to dissolution by the arbitrazh court upon the suit of the said federal agency. In the event of dissolution by the arbitrazh court of the said agreement and contract of purchase-sale such enterprise of the debtor shall be subject to transfer into federal ownership in the procedure established by a federal law.

Article 196. Bankruptcy Proceeding of Strategic Enterprises and Organisations

1. The sale of the enterprise of a debtor-strategic enterprise or organisation shall be effectuated in the procedure provided for by Article 195(7)-(9) of the present Federal Law.

The sale of property and property and other rights not within the property complex of the debtor intended for the effectuation of activity connected with the fulfillment of work under a State defence order ensuring federal State needs in the domain of maintaining the defence capacity and security of the Russian

Federation may be effectuated in the procedure provided for by Article 111 of the present Federal Law.

2. When there is present in the composition of property of the debtor property removed from turnover the bankruptcy administrator shall be obliged to inform the owner of the property removed from turnover thereof.

The owner of property removed from turnover shall accept this property from the bankruptcy administrator or consolidate it to other persons within a period of not later than six months from the date of receive of the notification.

§6. Bankruptcy of Subjects of Natural Monopolies

Article 197. General Provisions of Bankruptcy of Subjects of Natural Monopolies

1. For the purposes of the present Federal Law by subject of a natural monopoly is understood an organisation effectuating the production and/or the realisation of goods (or work, services) under conditions of a natural monopoly.

2. A subject of a natural monopoly shall be considered to be unable to satisfy demands of creditors with regard to monetary obligations and/or to perform the duty with regard to payment of obligatory payments if the respective obligations and/or duty has not been performed by it within six months from the date when they should have been performed.

3. The case concerning bankruptcy may be instituted by an arbitrazh court if the demands of creditors with regard to monetary obligations and payment of obligatory payments against the debtor-subject of a natural monopoly in aggregate comprise not less than five hundred thousand rubles. The said demands must be confirmed by documents of execution and not satisfied in full by means of levy of execution against the property by creditors of the first and second priorities in accordance with Article 59 of the Federal Law "On an Execution Proceeding".

Article 198. Person Participating in Case Concerning Bankruptcy of Subjects of Natural Monopolies

The federal agency of executive power empowered by the Government of the Russian Federation to conduct State policy with respect to the corresponding subject of a natural monopoly shall be deemed to be the person participating in the case concerning bankruptcy of a debtor-subject of natural monopoly together with the persons determined by the present Federal Law.

Article 199. Consideration of Case Concerning Bankruptcy of Subjects of Natural Monopolies

1. In the event a debtor-subject of a natural monopoly before the acceptance by an arbitrazh court of an application concerning the deeming of the debtor to

be bankrupt has filed a petition to sue in a court concerning the deeming invalid of acts of agencies of State power concerning the confirmation of prices (or tariffs) for goods (or work, services) produced and/or realised under conditions of a natural monopoly, the consideration of the case concerning bankruptcy of such debtor shall be suspended until the entry into legal force of the decision with regard to the case concerning the deeming invalid of the respective acts of agencies of State power.

2. The arbitrazh court may adopt a decision to refuse to deem a debtor-subject of natural monopoly to be bankrupt if the respective acts of State power in the part of confirmation of prices (or tariffs) for goods (or work, services) produced and/or realised under conditions of a natural monopoly have been deemed invalid.

Article 200. External Administration of Subject of Natural Monopoly

1. An external administrator shall not have the right to refuse to perform contracts of the debtor to consumers with respect to whom in accordance with federal laws and other normative legal acts the termination of obligations on the part of subjects of the respective natural monopolies is not permitted.

2. An external administrator shall not have the right to alienate property of a debtor which is a unified technological complex of the subject of a natural monopoly. Immoveable and other property directly used for the production and/or realisation of goods (or work, services) under conditions of a natural monopoly and reserves of raw material and materials being expended which are used for the performance of contracts connected with activity of the debtor as a subject of natural monopoly shall be relegated to the said property.

Article 201. Sale of Property of Debtor-Subject of Natural Monopoly

1. The conditions specified in point 2 of the present Article shall be established when conducting procedures of bankruptcy as an obligatory condition of the contract of purchase-sale of property of the debtor-subject of a natural monopoly for goods (or work, services) directly used for the production and/or realisation under conditions of a natural monopoly.

The property of the debtor directly used for the production and/or realisation of goods (or work, services) under conditions of a natural monopoly shall be placed in a public sale as a single lot.

2. The obligatory conditions of a contract of purchase-sale of property of the debtor-subject of natural monopoly shall be:

consent of the purchaser to assume obligations of the debtor under contracts for the delivery of goods which are the subject of regulation of legislation on natural monopolies;

assuming by the purchaser of obligations with regard to ensuring accessibility to goods (or work, services) produced or realised for consumers;

existence of a license for the effectuation of the respective type of activity if the activity of the debtor is subject to licensing.

In the event of the sale of property of the debtor directly used for production and/or realisation of goods (or work, services) under conditions of a natural monopoly by means of conducting a competition the federal agency of executive power empowered by the Government of the Russian Federation to conduct State policy with respect to relations of subjects of a natural monopoly shall conclude with the purchaser of the said property of the debtor an agreement concerning the performance of the conditions of the competition.

3. In the event of the failure of the purchaser of property of the debtor directly used for production and/or realisation of goods (or work, services) under conditions of a natural monopoly to perform the conditions provided for by point 2 of the present Article the contract shall be subject to dissolution by an arbitrazh court on the basis of the application of a respective federal agency of executive power.

In the event of the dissolution of the contract the means expended for the purchase of property and effectuation of the investments for the period which has lapsed shall be compensated to the purchaser of the property at the expense of means of the federal budget. In the event of dissolution of the contract the property shall be subject to transfer to federal ownership.

4. In the event of the sale of property directly being used for the production and/or realisation of goods (or work, services) of goods (or work, services) under conditions of a natural monopoly the Russian Federation, subjects of the Russian Federation, and municipal formations in the person of respective empowered agencies shall have the right of preferential acquisition of the property proposed for sale in the procedure provided for by Article 195(8) and (9) of the present Federal Law.

5. The Russian Federation, subjects of the Russian Federation, and municipal formations in the person of the respective empowered agencies shall have the right to suspend the sale of property directly being used for the production and/or realisation of goods (or work, services) under conditions of a natural monopoly in the course of external administration for a period of not more than three months in order to work out proposals concerning the restoration of the ability to pay of the subject of the natural monopoly.

6. The re-profiling or closure of production (or production entities) effectuating the production (or realisation) of goods (or work, services) under conditions of a natural monopoly shall be permitted in the procedure established by a federal law.

Chapter X. Bankruptcy of Citizen

§1. General Provisions

Article 202. Regulation of Bankruptcy of Citizen

1. The rules established by Chapters I–VIII of the present Federal Law shall apply to relations connected with the bankruptcy of a citizen unless provided otherwise by the present Chapter.

2. The rules provided for by the present paragraph shall apply to relations connected with the bankruptcy of an individual entrepreneur and the bankruptcy of a peasant (or farmer) economy, taking into account the peculiarities provided for by paragraphs 2 and 3 of the present Chapter.

Article 203. Application Concerning the Deeming of Citizen to be Bankrupt

1. An application concerning the deeming of a citizen to be bankrupt may be filed at an arbitrazh court a citizen-debtor, creditor, and also empowered agency.

2. Creditors shall possess the right to file an application concerning the deeming of a citizen to be bankrupt except for creditors with regard to demands concerning compensation of harm caused to life or health, the recovery of alimony, and also creditors whose demands are inextricably connected with their personality.

3. In the event of the application of procedures of bankruptcy of a citizen creditors with regard to demands concerning compensation of harm caused to life of health, recovery of alimony, and also creditors whose demands are inextricably connected their personality, shall have the right to file their own demands.

Demands of the said creditors not declared by them in the event of the application of procedures of bankruptcy of a citizen shall retain force after the completion of the procedures of bankruptcy of a citizen.

Article 204. Plan for Repayment of Debts

1. To the application of a citizen may be appended the plan for repayment of the debts thereof, copies of which shall be sent to creditors and other persons participating in the case concerning bankruptcy.

2. In the absence of objections of creditors the arbitrazh court may confirm the plan for repayment of debts, which shall be grounds for the suspension of proceedings with regard to a case concerning bankruptcy for a period of not more than three months.

3. The plan for repayment of debts must include:
the period for effectuation thereof;

the amounts left monthly to the debtor and members of his family in order to ensure their life activity;

the amounts which it is proposed to send monthly to repay the demands of creditors.

4. The arbitrazh court shall have the right with regard to a reasoned petition of the persons participating in the case concerning bankruptcy to change the plan for repayment of debts, including to increase or to reduce the period for effectuation thereof, the amounts left monthly to the debtor and members of his family to ensure their life activity.

5. If as a result of the fulfilment by the debtor of the plan for repayment of debts the demands of creditors have been repaid in full, the proceeding with regard to the case concerning bankruptcy shall be subject to termination.

Article 205. Property of Citizen Not Included in Bankruptcy Mass

1. The property of a citizen against which in accordance with civil procedure legislation execution may not be levied shall not be included in the bankruptcy mass.

2. An arbitrazh court shall have the right with regard to a reasoned petition of a citizen and other persons participating in a case concerning bankruptcy to exclude from the bankruptcy mass the property of a citizen against which in accordance with civil procedure legislation execution may be levied which is nonliquid or revenue from the realisation of which does not materially influence the satisfaction of demands of creditors. The total value of property of a citizen which is excluded from the bankruptcy mass in accordance with the provisions of the present point may not exceed one hundred minimum amounts of payment of labour established by a federal law.

A list of property of a citizen which shall be excluded from the bankruptcy mass in accordance with the provisions of the present point shall be confirmed by the arbitrazh court, concerning which a ruling shall be rendered which may be appealed.

Article 206. Invalidity of Transactions of Citizen

1. Transactions of a citizen connected with the alienation or transfer by other means of property of the citizen to interested persons a year before the institution by an arbitrazh court of proceedings with regard to a case concerning bankruptcy shall be null.

2. With regard to the demand of a creditor an arbitrazh court shall apply the consequences of invalidity of a null transaction in the form of return of the property of the citizen which is the subject of the transaction to the composition of property of the citizen or in the form of levy of execution against the respective property situated with the interested person.

Article 207. Consideration by Arbitrazh Court of Case Concerning Bankruptcy of Citizen

1. Simultaneously with the rendering of a ruling concerning the introduction of observation with respect to a citizen an arbitrazh court shall impose arrest on property of the citizen, except for property against which execution may not be levied in accordance with civil procedure legislation.

A temporary administrator shall before consideration by an arbitrazh court of a case concerning bankruptcy ensure the conducting of an independent valuation of the property of the debtor.

2. Upon the petition of a citizen an arbitrazh court may release property of the citizen (or part of the property) from arrest in the event of the submission of a suretyship or other security of performance of the obligation of the citizen by third persons.

3. On the basis of an application of a citizen an arbitrazh court may defer consideration of a case concerning bankruptcy for not more than a month for the effectuation by the citizen of the settlement of accounts with creditors or the achievement of an amicable agreement.

4. When there is information concerning the opening of an inheritance to the benefit of a citizen an arbitrazh court shall have the right to suspend the proceedings with regard to the case concerning bankruptcy until the deciding of the question concerning the fate of the inheritance in the procedure established by a federal law.

5. If within the period established by point 3 of the present Article a citizen has not submitted evidence of the satisfaction of demands of creditors and within the said period an amicable agreement has not been concluded, the arbitrazh court shall adopt a decision concerning the deeming of a citizen to be bankrupt and opening of a bankruptcy proceeding.

Article 208. Consequences of Deeming Citizen to be Bankrupt

1. From the moment of adoption by an arbitrazh court of the decision to deeming a citizen to be bankrupt and the opening of a bankruptcy proceeding the following consequences shall ensue:

the periods of performance of obligations of a citizen shall be considered to have ensued;

the calculation of penalties (or fines, forfeits), interest, and other financial sanctions with regard to all obligations of a citizen shall terminate;

the recovery from a citizen under all documents of execution shall terminate with regard to demands concerning compensation of harm caused to life or health, and also with regard to demands concerning the recovery of alimony.

2. The decision concerning the deeming of a citizen to be bankrupt and the opening of a bankruptcy proceeding an arbitrazh court shall send to all known creditors, specifying the period for the presentation by creditors of demands, which may not exceed two months.

The sending of the said decision of the arbitrazh court shall be effectuated at the expense of the citizen.

Article 209. Execution of Decision of Arbitrazh Court

1. The decision of an arbitrazh court concerning the deeming of a citizen to be bankrupt and the opening of a bankruptcy proceeding and the writ of execution concerning the levy of execution against property of the citizen shall be sent to the judicial bailiff-executor in order to effectuate the sale of property of the citizen. All property of the citizen shall be subject to sale, except property not included in the bankruptcy mass in accordance with the present Federal Law.

2. When constant management of immoveable property or valuable moveable property of the citizen is necessary, the arbitrazh court shall confirm for the said purposes a bankruptcy administrator and determine the amount of remuneration thereof. In this event the sale of property of a citizen shall be effectuated by the bankruptcy administrator.

3. Monetary means received from the sale of the property of a citizen, and also monetary means available in cash, shall be placed on deposit of the arbitrazh court which adopted the decision concerning the deeming of a citizen to be bankrupt.

Article 210. Consideration of Demands of Creditors

An arbitrazh court shall consider the demands of creditors declared by the creditors or debtor within the periods provided for by Article 208(2) of the present Federal Law. The arbitrazh court shall render a ruling with regard to the results of consideration of the said demands concerning the procedure and amount of satisfaction of the demands of creditors.

Article 211. Procedure for Satisfaction of Demands of Creditors

1. Before satisfaction of the demands of creditors at the expense of monetary means placed on deposit of an arbitrazh court the expenses connected with consideration of the case concerning bankruptcy and execution of the decision of the arbitrazh court concerning the deeming of a citizen to be bankrupt and the opening of a bankruptcy proceeding shall be covered.

2. Demands of creditors shall be satisfied in the following priority:

in first priority shall be satisfied the demands of citizens to whom the citizen bears responsibility for causing harm to life or health by means of capitalisation of the respective time payments, and also demands concerning the recovery of alimony;

in second priority accounts shall be settled with regard to the payment of severance benefits and payment for labour of persons working under a labour contract or with regard to the payment of remuneration under authors' contracts;

in third priority accounts shall be settled with other creditors.

Accounts shall be settled with creditors in the procedure provided for by Articles 135-138 of the present Federal Law.

3. Demands of creditors of each priority shall be satisfied after the full satisfaction of demands of creditors of the preceding priority, except for instances established by the present Federal Law for the satisfaction of demands of creditors secured by the pledge of property of the debtor.

4. In the event of the insufficiency of monetary means on deposit of the arbitrazh court they shall be distributed among the creditors of the respective priority in proportion to the amounts of their demands.

Article 212. Relieving Citizen from Obligations

1. After the completion of the settlement of accounts with creditors the citizen deemed to be bankrupt shall be relieved from the further performance of demands of creditors declared in the course of the procedures of bankruptcy, except for demands provided for by point 2 of the present Article

2. Demands of creditors concerning compensation of harm caused to life or health, recovery of alimony, and also demands inextricably connected with the personality of the creditor and not repaid in the procedure of execution of the decision of the arbitrazh court concerning the deeming of a citizen to be bankrupt or repaid partly, or not declared in the course of the procedures of bankruptcy shall retain force and may be presented after the end of the proceedings with regard to the case concerning bankruptcy of a citizen in full or in the unpaid part thereof.

3. In the event of eliciting facts of the concealment by a citizen of property or illegal transfer by a citizen of property to third persons the creditor whose demands were not satisfied in the course of the procedures of bankruptcy shall have the right to present the demand concerning the levy of execution against this property.

Article 213. Consequences of Second Bankruptcy of Citizen

1. Within five years after the deeming of a citizen to be bankrupt upon his application a case concerning bankruptcy may not be instituted a second time.

2. In the event of the deeming a second time of a citizen to be bankrupt upon the application of a creditor and application of an empowered agency with regard to demands concerning the payment of obligatory payments within five years after the completion of the settlement of accounts with creditors such citizen shall not be relieved from further performance of the demands of creditors.

The unsatisfied demands of creditors may be presented in the procedure established by civil legislation.

§2. Peculiarities of Bankruptcy of Individual Entrepreneurs

Article 214. Grounds for Deeming Individual Entrepreneur to be Bankrupt

The grounds for deeming an individual entrepreneur to be bankrupt shall be the inability thereof to satisfy demands of creditors with regard to monetary obligations and/or perform the duty with regard to the payment of obligatory payments.

Article 215. Application Concerning Deeming of Individual Entrepreneur to be Bankrupt

1. An application concerning the deeming of individual entrepreneur to be bankrupt may be filed by a debtor-individual entrepreneur, creditor whose demands is connected with obligations when effectuating entrepreneurial activity, and empowered agencies.

2. In the event of the application of procedures of bankruptcy of an individual entrepreneur, the creditors thereof whose demands are not linked with obligations when effectuating entrepreneurial activity, and also creditors whose demands are inextricably connected with the personality of the creditors, shall also have the right to present their demands.

Article 216. Consequences of Deeming Individual Entrepreneur to be Bankrupt

1. From the moment of adoption by an arbitrazh court of a decision concerning the deeming of an individual entrepreneur to be bankrupt and opening of a bankruptcy proceeding the State registration of a citizen as an individual entrepreneur shall lose force, and also the license for the effectuation of individual types of entrepreneurial activity issued to him shall be annulled.

2. An individual entrepreneur deemed to be bankrupt may not be registered as an individual entrepreneur within a year from the moment of the deeming thereof to be bankrupt.

3. An arbitrazh court shall send a copy of the decision concerning the deeming of an individual entrepreneur to be bankrupt and the opening of a bankruptcy proceeding to the agency which registered the citizen as an individual entrepreneur.

§3. Peculiarities of Bankruptcy of Peasant (or Farmer) Economy

Article 217. Grounds for Deeming Peasant (or Farmer) Economy to be Bankrupt

The grounds for deeming a peasant (or farmer) economy to be bankrupt shall be the inability thereof to satisfy demands of creditors with regard to monetary obligations and/or to perform the duty with regard to the payment of obligatory payments.

Article 218. Peculiarities of Procedure of Deeming Individual Entrepreneur-Head of Peasant (or Farmer) Economy to be Bankrupt

1. An application of an individual entrepreneur-head of a peasant (or farmer) economy concerning the deeming thereof to be bankrupt (hereinafter—application) may be filed in an arbitrazh court when there is consent in written form of all members of the peasant (or farmer) economy.

The application shall be signed by the individual entrepreneur-head of the peasant (or farmer) economy.

2. To an application, besides the documents provided for by Article 38 of the present Federal Law, must be appended documents concerning:

the composition and value of property of the peasant (or farmer) economy;

the composition and value of property belonging to members of the peasant (or farmer) economy by right of ownership, and also the sources at the expense of which the said property was acquired;

the amount of revenues which might be received by the peasant (or farmer) economy at the end of the respective period of agricultural work.

The said documents also shall be appended by the individual entrepreneur-head of peasant (or farmer) economy to the opinion on the application of the creditor.

Article 219. Peculiarities of Financial Recuperation of Peasant (or Farmer) Economy and External Administration of Peasant (or Farmer) Economy

1. A plan for financial recuperation and schedule of repayment of indebtedness may be submitted to an arbitrazh court by the head of a peasant (or farmer) economy within two months from the moment of rendering by an arbitrazh court of the ruling concerning the introduction of observation with respect to the peasant (or farmer) economy.

2. If the effectuation of measures provided for by the plan for financial recuperation enables the peasant (or farmer) economy, including at the expense of revenues which may be received by the peasant (or farmer) economy at the end of the respective period of agricultural work, to repay the demands of creditors with regard to monetary obligations and payment of obligatory payments in accor-

dance with the schedule of repayment of indebtedness, financial recuperation of the peasant (or farmer) economy shall be introduced.

A ruling shall be rendered concerning the introduction of financial recuperation of a peasant (or farmer) economy by an arbitrazh court which may be repealed.

3. Financial recuperation of a peasant (or farmer) economy shall be introduced at the end of the respective period of agricultural work, taking into account the time necessary for the realization of agricultural products produced or produced and processes.

If during financial recuperation a decline and worsening of the financial state of the peasant (or farmer) economy occurred in connection with natural calamities, epizootics, or other circumstances of an extraordinary character the period of financial recuperation may be extended for a year on condition of a change of the schedule of repayment of indebtedness in the procedure provided for by Article 85 of the present Federal Law.

4. On the basis of a decision of a meeting of creditors when there is the possibility of the restoration of the ability of the peasant (or farmer) economy to pay, external administration shall be introduced by an arbitrazh court. External administration of a peasant (or farmer) economy shall be introduced before the end of the respective period of agricultural work, taking into account the time necessary for the realisation of the agricultural products produced or produced and processed. The period of external administration may not exceed the periods established by Article 92(2) of the present Federal Law by more than three months.

If in the course of external administration a decline or worsening of the financial state of the peasant (or farmer) economy occurred in connection with natural calamities, epizootics, and other circumstances having an extraordinary character, the period of external administration, the period of external administration may be extended by a year.

5. External administration of a peasant (or farmer) economy may be terminated before time by an arbitrazh court on the basis of an application of the external administrator or any of the creditors in the event of:

the failure to fulfil measures provided for by the plan of external administration;

the presence of other circumstances testifying to the impossibility of restoration of the ability of the peasant (or farmer) economy to pay.

The termination before time of external administration of a peasant (or farmer) economy shall entail the deeming thereof bankrupt and the opening of a bankruptcy proceeding.

Article 220. External Administrator

1. An external administrator shall be confirmed by an arbitrazh court in order to conduct the external administration of a peasant (or farmer) economy/

2. A person not corresponding to the requirements of external administrator presented by the present Federal Law may be appointed external administrator.

3. The powers of external administrator may be effectuated by the head of the peasant (or farmer) economy with the consent of the external administrator.

Article 221. Bankruptcy Mass of Peasant (or Farmer) Economy

1. In the event of the deeming by an arbitrazh court of a peasant (or farmer) economy to be bankrupt and the opening of a bankruptcy proceeding, in the bankruptcy mass of the peasant (or farmer) economy shall be included immoveable property included in common ownership of members of the peasant (or farmer) economy, including plantings, economic and other structures, soil conservation and other installations, pedigree, dairy, and working livestock, poultry, agricultural and other technology and equipment, means of transport, tools, and other property acquired for the peasant (or farmer) economy for the common means of its members, and also the right of lease belonging to the peasant (or farmer) economy to a land plot and other property rights belonging to the peasant (or farmer) economy and having monetary value.

2. In the event of bankruptcy of a peasant (or farmer) economy the land plot belonging to the peasant (or farmer) economy may be alienated or pass to another person, the Russian Federation, subject of the Russian Federation, and municipal formation in that measure to which the turnover thereof is permitted by land legislation.

3. Property belonging to the head of a peasant (or farmer) economy and members of the peasant (or farmer) economy by right of ownership, and also other property with respect to which it is proved that it was acquired for revenues which were not common means of the peasant (or farmer) economy, shall not be included in the bankruptcy mass.

Article 222. Procedure for Sale of Property and Property Rights of Peasant (or Farmer) Economy

1. In the event of the sale of property of a peasant (or farmer) economy the arbitrazh administrator must put on sale the enterprise of the debtor-peasant (or farmer) economy by means of conducting a public sale.

2. Persons engaging in the production of agricultural products and possessing land plots directly adjacent to the land plot belonging to the peasant (or farmer) economy shall have a preferential right of acquisition of the property.

3. An arbitrazh administrator when realizing the property specified in point 2 of the present Article, and also property rights of the peasant (or farmer) economy, shall be obliged to conduct an independent valuation of the value of the property and property rights and to propose to the persons specified in point 2

of the present Article to acquire the property and property rights at the valuation value.

If the said persons within a month from the date of receipt of the proposal concerning the acquisition of the property and property rights have not declared their wish to acquire the property and rights of demands, the arbitrazh administrator or head of the peasant (or farmer) economy shall effectuate the realisation of the property and property rights in the procedure provided for by the present Federal Law.

Article 223. Consequences of Deeming Peasant (or Farmer) Economy to be Bankrupt

1. From the moment of the adoption of a decision concerning the deeming of a peasant (or farmer) economy to be bankrupt and the opening of a bankruptcy proceeding State registration of the head of the peasant (or farmer) economy as an individual entrepreneur shall lose force.

2. An arbitrazh court shall send a copy of the decision concerning the deeming of a peasant (or farmer) economy to be bankrupt and the opening of a bankruptcy proceeding to the agency which registered the head of the peasant (or farmer) economy as an individual entrepreneur.

Chapter XI. Simplified Procedures of Bankruptcy

§1. Peculiarities of Bankruptcy of Debtor Being Liquidated

Article 224. Bankruptcy of Debtor Being Liquidated

1. If the value of property of a debtor-juridical person with respect to which a decision is adopted concerning liquidation is insufficient to satisfy the demands of creditors, such juridical person shall be liquidated in the procedure provided for by the present Federal Law.

2. In the event of the discovery of circumstances provided for by point 1 of the present Article, the liquidation commission (or liquidator) shall be obliged to have recourse to an arbitrazh court with an application concerning the deeming of a debtor to be bankrupt.

3. In the even to the discovery of circumstances provided for by point 1 of the present Article after the adoption of the decision concerning liquidation of the juridical person and before the creation of the liquidation commission (or appointment of the liquidator), the application concerning the deeming of a debtor to be bankrupt must be filed in an arbitrazh court by the owner of the property of the debtor-unitary enterprise, founder (or participant) of the debtor, or executives of the debtor.

Article 225. Peculiarities of Consideration of Case Concerning Bankruptcy of Debtor Being Liquidated

1. An arbitrazh court shall adopt a decision concerning the deeming of a debtor being liquidated to be bankrupt and the opening of a bankruptcy proceeding and confirm the bankruptcy administrator.

Observation, financial recuperation, and external administration shall not apply in the event of the bankruptcy of a debtor being liquidated.

2. Creditors shall have the right to present their demands against the debtor being liquidated within a month from the date of publication of the announcement concerning the deeming of the debtor being liquidated to be bankrupt.

3. If a case concerning is instituted on the basis of an application of the owner of property of the debtor-unitary enterprise, founder (or participant) of the debtor, or executive of the debtor filed before the creation of the liquidation commission (or appointment of the liquidator), consideration of the case concerning bankruptcy shall be effectuated without taking into account the peculiarities provided for by the present paragraph.

Article 226. Consequences of Refusal to Liquidate Debtor by way of Bankruptcy

1. Violation of the requirements provided for by Article 224(2) of the present Federal Law shall be grounds for a refusal to enter in the unified State register of juridical; persons an entry concerning liquidation of the juridical person.

2. The owner of property of a debtor-unitary enterprise, founders (or participants) of the debtor, executive of the debtor, and chairman of the liquidation commission (or liquidator) who have committed the violation of the requirements provided for by Article 224(2) and (3) of the present Federal Law shall bear subsidiary responsibility for the unsatisfied demands of creditors with regard to monetary obligations and payment of obligatory payments of the debtor.

§2. Bankruptcy of Absent Debtor

Article 227. Peculiarities of Filing Application Concerning Deeming of Absent Debtor to be Bankrupt

1. If a citizen-debtor or executive of a debtor-juridical person actually has terminated its activity is absent or it is not possible to establish the whereabouts thereof, an application concerning the deeming of the absent debtor to be bankrupt may be filed by the bankruptcy administrator or empowered agency irrespective of the amount of creditor indebtedness.

2. An application concerning the deeming of an absent debtor to be bankrupt is filed by an empowered agency only when there are means necessary to financial

procedures of bankruptcy. The procedure and conditions of financing the procedures of bankruptcy with respect to an absent debtor, including the amount of remuneration of the bankruptcy administrator, shall be determined by the Government of the Russian Federation.

Article 228. Consideration of Case Concerning Bankruptcy of Absent Debtor

1. An arbitrazh court within a month from the date of acceptance for proceedings the application concerning the deeming of an absent debtor to be bankrupt shall adopt a decision concerning the deeming of an absent debtor to be bankrupt and the opening of a bankruptcy proceeding.

Observation, financial recuperation, and external administration shall not apply in the event of the bankruptcy of an absent debtor.

2. A bankruptcy administrator shall notify in written form the bankruptcy of an absent debtor to all creditors of the absent debtor known thereto, who within a month from the day of receipt of the notification may present their demands to the bankruptcy administrator.

3. Upon the petition of a bankruptcy administrator, in the event of the discovery by him of property of an absent debtor the arbitrazh court may render a ruling concerning the termination of the simplified procedure of bankruptcy and transition to procedures of bankruptcy provided for by the present Federal Law.

4. A case concerning bankruptcy of an absent debtor shall be considered by a judge alone.

Article 229. Distribution of Receipts

Satisfaction of demands of creditors shall be effectuated in the priorities provided for by Article 134 of the present Federal Law. In so doing the covering of court expenses and expenses for the payment of remuneration to the bankruptcy administrator shall be effectuated outside the priorities.

Article 230. Application of Provisions on Bankruptcy of Absent Debtor

The provisions provided for by the present paragraph also shall apply if the property of a debtor-juridical person the court expenses are known not to be enabled to be covered in connection with a case concerning bankruptcy or if within the last twelve months before the date of filing the application concerning the deeming of a debtor to be bankrupt operations were not conducted with regard to the bank accounts of the debtor, and also when there are other indicia testifying to the absence of entrepreneurial or other activity of the debtor.

Chapter XII. Concluding and Transitional Provisions

Article 231. Entry of Present Federal Law into Force

1. The present Federal Law shall enter into force upon the expiry of thirty days from the day of official publication, except for point 3 of the present Article, the provisions of which shall enter into force from the day of official publication of the present Federal Law, and Chapter XI, paragraph 6, of the present Federal Law, whose provisions shall enter into force from 1 January 2005.

The provision of Article 29(4), paragraph eleven, of the present Federal Law shall enter into force upon the expiry of three months after the day of entry of the present Federal Law into force.

2. The provisions provided for by the present Federal Law concerning the bankruptcy of citizens who are not individual entrepreneurs shall enter into force from the day of entry into force of the Federal Law on making respective changes in and additions to federal laws.

3. Within a year from the day of entry of the present Federal Law into force the regulating agency with respect to arbitrazh administrators who are not members of a self-regulating organisation of arbitrazh administrators shall:

control compliance by them in the activity of arbitrazh administrators of the requirements of legislation of the Russian Federation and rules of professional activity of arbitrazh administrators confirmed by the Government of the Russian Federation;

conduct verifications of the activity of arbitrazh administrators;

have recourse to an arbitrazh court with an application concerning the removal of an arbitrazh administrator from the performance by them of the duties of arbitrazh administrator in the event of eliciting a violation of the requirements of legislation of the Russian Federation and rules of professional activity of arbitrazh administrators confirmed by the Government of the Russian Federation.

4. Persons corresponding to the requirements established by Article 20 of the present Federal Law may be confirmed by an arbitrazh court as arbitrazh administrators.

Within a year from the day of entry of the present Federal Law into force persons corresponding to the requirements of Article 20(1) and (8) of the present Federal Law may be members of self-regulating organisations of arbitrazh administrators and may be confirmed by an arbitrazh court as arbitrazh administrators in cases concerning bankruptcy, except for requirements established by Article 20(1), paragraphs five, six, and eight, and who have had a license of arbitrazh administrator, except for instances when such license was revoked or annulled.

During the period provided for by point 3 of the present Article as experience of executive work sufficient for appointment as arbitrazh administrator also shall be taken into account experience with regard to the performance of duties of an arbitrazh administrator for a period of not less than a year, except for experience with regard to the performance of such duties with respect to an absent debtor.

During a year from the day of entry of the present Federal Law into force the documents provided for by Article 21(5), paragraphs seven and nine, of the present Federal Law may not be presented.

5. During a year from the day of entry of the present Federal Law into force a creditor and debtor shall have the right not to specify in an application concerning the deeming of a debtor to be bankrupt the self-regulating organisation from a member of which the temporary administrator must be confirmed.

During a year from the day of entry of the present Federal Law into force, unless a self-regulating organisation is specified in the application, the arbitrazh court shall send to the regulating agency a query concerning the submission of candidacies for temporary administrator. The regulating agency within five days from the day of receipt of the said query shall submit to the arbitrazh court three candidacies for temporary administrator. The creditor upon whose application the case concerning bankruptcy was instituted, and also the debtor in the course of a judicial session, shall have the right to each reject one of the candidacies submitted. The arbitrazh court shall confirm the candidacy of the temporary administrator from among the candidacies with respect to whom a challenged was not declared in the established procedure.

Within the period specified in paragraph one of the present point confirmation of the candidacy of arbitrazh administrator shall be effectuated in the procedure established by Articles 15 and 45 of the present Federal Law or the meeting of creditors may determined and submit to the arbitrazh court three candidacies for arbitrazh administrator (or administrative administrator, external administrator, or bankruptcy administrator). In so doing the debtor shall have the right to declare a challenge of one of the candidacies submitted for arbitrazh administrator. The regulating agency shall have the right to declare a reasoned challenged of one of the candidacies or several candidacies of arbitrazh administrator in the event of the failure to conform to the requirements of point 4 of the present Article.

The arbitrazh court shall confirm the candidacy of arbitrazh administrator, external administrator, or bankruptcy administrator from among the candidacies with respect to which a challenge was not declared in the established procedure.

6. Until the determination by the Government of the Russian Federation of the official publication in which in accordance with Article 28 of the present Federal Law information is subject to publication with regard to questions connected with bankruptcy, the said information shall be subject to publication in Российская газета.

7. Within a year from the day of entry into force of the present Federal Law an external administrator or bankruptcy administrator in order to organise a public

sale with regard to the sale of property of a debtor whose balance sheet value on the last reporting date comprises not less than two hundred million rubles shall enlist on an uncompensated basis the State specialised organisation empowered by the Government of the Russian Federation.

8. Until the making of respective changes in legislation concerning tases and charges and/or budget legislation the rule of proportional satisfaction of demands provided for by Article 84(4) of the present Federal Law shall extend only to demands of bankruptcy creditors and demands of empowered agencies with regard to monetary obligations.

Article 232. Regulation of Relations Connected With Bankruptcy

1. From the day of entry into force of the present Federal Law, to deem to have lost force:
Federal Law of 8 January 1998, No. 6-ФЗ "On Insolvency (or Bankruptcy)" (СЗ РФ (1998), no. 2, item 222);
Article 2(30) of the Federal Law of 21 March 2002, No. 31-ФЗ "On Bringing Legislative Acts into Conformity with the Federal Law 'On State Registration of Juridical Persons'" (СЗ РФ (2002), no. 12, item 1093);
Article 1(3) of the Federal Law of 25 April 2002, No. 41-ФЗ "On Making Changes in and Additions to Legislative Acts of the Russian Federation in Connection with the Adoption of the Federal Law 'On Obligatory Insurance of Civil Responsibility and Possessors of Means of Transport'" (СЗ РФ (2002), no. 18, item 1721);

2. To deem to have lost force from 1 January 2005 the Federal Law of 24 June 1999, No. 122-ФЗ "On the Peculiarities of Insolvency (or Bankruptcy) of Subjects of Natural Monopolies of the Fuel and Electric Power Complex" (СЗ РФ (1999), no. 26, item 3179).

3. Until the bringing of laws and other normative legal acts operating on the territory of the Russian Federation and regulating relations connected with bankruptcy into conformity with the present Federal Law the said laws and other normative legal acts shall apply insofar as they are not contrary to the present Federal Law.

Article 233. Application of Present Federal Law by Arbitrazh Courts

1. The present Federal Law shall be applied by arbitrazh courts when considering cases concerning bankruptcy, the proceedings with regard to which were instituted after the entry thereof into force.

2. With regard to cases, proceedings with regard to which were instituted before the entry of the present Federal Law into force, the norms of the Federal Law of 8 January 1998, No. 6-ФЗ (СЗ РФ (1998), no. 2, item 222; (2002),

no. 12, item 1093; no. 18, item 1721) shall apply until the moment of completion of the procedures of bankruptcy (external administration, bankruptcy proceeding, or amicable agreement) introduced before the entry of the present Federal Law into force.

3. From the moment of completion of a procedure of bankruptcy introduced before the entry of the present Federal Law into force, the provisions of the present Federal Law shall apply to legal relations which arose from the moment of the completion of this procedure of bankruptcy. The procedures of bankruptcy provided for by the present Federal Law (financial recuperation, external administration, or amicable agreement) shall be introduced in the event of the consideration by arbitrazh courts of cases concerning bankruptcy after the entry of the present Federal Law into force irrespective of the date of adoption of the said cases for proceedings. The further consideration of a case concerning bankruptcy shall be effectuated in accordance with the present Federal Law, except for an instance of the opening of a bankruptcy proceeding after the completion of the procedure of bankruptcy introduced before the entry of the present Federal Law into force. In this event the norms of the Federal Law of 8 January 1998, No. 6-ФЗ "On Insolvency (or Bankruptcy)" (СЗ РФ (1998), no. 2, item 222; (2002), no. 12, item 1093; no. 18, item 1721) shall apply to the procedure of bankruptcy proceeding.

4. In the event of the consideration by arbitrazh courts of cases concerning bankruptcy in accordance with the Federal Law of 8 January 1998, No. 6-ФЗ "On Insolvency (or Bankruptcy)" СЗ РФ (1998), no. 2, item 222; (2002), no. 12, item 1093; no. 18, item 1721) and the Law of the Russian Federation of 19 November 1992, No. 3929-1 "On Insolvency (or Bankruptcy) of Enterprises" (*Ведомости Съезеда народных депутатов Российской Федерации и Верховного Совета Российской Федерации* (1993), no. 1, item 6), the requirements for a candidacy of arbitrazh administrator must correspond to the provisions of Article 231 of the present Federal Law.

5. In the event of the consideration by an arbitrazh court of cases concerning bankruptcy in accordance with the Federal Law of 8 January 1998, No. 6-ФЗ, "On Insolvency (or Bankruptcy)" СЗ РФ (1998), no. 2, item 222; (2002), no. 12, item 1093); no. 18, item 1721) the regulating agency shall have the powers provided for by Article 231 of the present Federal Law.

FEDERAL LAW ON THE INSOLVENCY (OR BANKRUPTCY) OF CREDIT ORGANISATIONS

[Federal Law of 25 February 1999, No. 40-ФЗ, as amended
2 January 2000, No. 6-ФЗ, 19 June 2001, No. 86-ФЗ
7 August 2001, No. 116-ФЗ,
and 21 March 2002, No 31-ФЗ, with changes introduced
by the Constitutional Court of the Russian Federation,
3 July 2001, No. 10-П. СЗ РФ (1999), no.
9, item 1097; (2000), no. 2, item 127;
(2001), no. 26, item 2590; no. 33(I), item 3419;
(2002), no. 12, item 1093; (2001), no. 29, item 3058]

Chapter I	General Provisions	544
Chapter II	Financial Recuperation of Credit Organisation	547
Chapter III	Temporary Administration	553
Chapter IV	Reorganisation of Credit Organisation	562
Chapter V	Peculiarities of Consideration of Case Concerning Bankruptcy by Arbitrazh Court	563
Chapter VI	Peculiarities of Bankruptcy Proceeding of Credit Organisation Deemed to be Bankrupt	568
Chapter VII	Peculiarities of Deeming Credit Organisation Being Liquidated and Absent Credit Organisation to be Bankrupt	573
Chapter VIII	Concluding Provisions	574

Chapter I. General Provisions

Article 1. Subject of Regulation of Present Federal Law

1. The present Federal Law shall establish the procedure and conditions for the effectuation of measures relating to the prevention of insolvency (or bankruptcy) of credit organisations, and also the peculiarities of the grounds and procedures for deeming credit organisations to be insolvent (or bankrupt) and the liquidation thereof by way of a bankruptcy proceeding.

2. The relations connected with the effectuation of measures relating to the prevention of insolvency (or bankruptcy) of credit organisations not regulated by

the present Federal Law shall be regulated by other federal laws and normative acts of the Central Bank of the Russian Federation (hereinafter—Bank of Russia) adopted in accordance with them.

3. Relations connected with insolvency (or bankruptcy) of credit organisations which are not regulated by the present Federal Law shall be regulated by the Federal Law on Insolvency (or Bankruptcy) also in the instances provided for by the present Federal Law and normative acts of the Bank of Russia.

Article 2. Insolvency (or Bankruptcy) of Credit Organisation

1. By insolvency (or bankruptcy) of a credit organisation is understood the inability thereof deemed by an arbitrazh court to satisfy demands of creditors with regard to monetary obligations and/or perform the duty with regard to the payment of obligatory payments (hereinafter—bankruptcy).

2. A credit organisation shall be considered to be unable to satisfy demands of creditors with regard to monetary obligations and/or perform the duty with regard to payment of obligatory payments if the respective duties have not been performed by it within one month from the moment of ensuing of the date of performance thereof, and/or if after the revocation of the license of a credit organisation for the effectuation of banking operations the value of its property (or assets) is insufficient for the performance of obligations of the credit organisation to its creditors [as amended by Law of 19 June 2001].

Article 3. Measures Relating to Prevention of Bankruptcy of Credit Organisations

1. In accordance with the present Federal Law the following measures shall be effectuated with regard to the prevention of the bankruptcy of credit organisations:
(1) financial recuperation of the credit organisation;
(2) appointment of temporary administration for management of credit organisation (hereinafter: temporary administration);
(3) reorganisation of credit organisation.

2. Measures relating to the prevention of the bankruptcy of credit organisations shall be effectuated when the grounds arise established by Article 4 of the present Federal Law.
A credit organisation and the founders (or participants) thereof shall in the event the said grounds arise take necessary and timely measures with regard to the financial recuperation and/or reorganisation of the credit organisation.
The Bank of Russia in the event the said grounds arise shall have the right to demand from the credit organisation the effectuation of measures for its financial recuperation, reorganisation, and also shall have the right to appoint a temporary administration.

Article 4. Grounds for Effectuation of Measures Relating to Prevention of Bankruptcy of Credit Organisation

Unless provided otherwise by the present Federal Law, measures relating to the prevention of the bankruptcy of a credit organisation provided for by Article 3 of the present Federal Law shall be effectuated in instances when the credit organisation:

does not satisfy repeatedly for a duration of the last six months the demands of individual creditors with regard to monetary obligations and/or does not perform the duty with regard to the payment of obligatory payments within a period of up to three days from the moment of the ensuing of the date of their performance in connection with the absence or insufficiency of monetary means in the correspondent accounts of the credit organisation;

does not satisfy the demands of individual creditors with regard to monetary obligations and/or does not perform the duty with regard to the payment of obligatory payments within periods exceeding three days from the moment of ensuing of the date of their satisfaction and/or the date of their performance in connection with the absence or insufficiency of monetary means in the correspondent accounts of a credit organisation;

permits an absolute reduction of own means (capital) in comparison with the maximum size thereof achieved for the last 12 months by more than 20% with the simultaneous violation of one of the obligatory normative standards established by the Bank of Russia;

violates the normative standards of sufficiency of own means (capital) established by the Bank of Russia;

violates the normative standards of current liquidity of the credit organisation established by the Bank of Russia during the last month by more than 10%;

permits a reduction of the amount of own means (or capital) according to the results of the reporting month lower than the amount of charter capital determined by the constitutive documents of the credit organisation registered in the procedure established by federal laws and normative acts of the Bank of Russia adopted in accordance with them [added by Federal Law No. 86-ФЗ, 19 June 2001].

Article 5. Procedures in Case Concerning Bankruptcy of Credit Organisation

1. The following procedures shall apply in the event of the consideration by an arbitrazh court of a case concerning bankruptcy of a credit organisation (hereinafter: case concerning bankruptcy):

(1) observation;

(2) bankruptcy proceeding.

2. External administration and amicable agreement provided for by the Federal Law on Insolvency (or Bankruptcy) shall not apply in the event of the

bankruptcy of a credit organisation [as amended by Federal Law No. 86-ФЗ, 19 June 2001].

Article 6. Attestation of Arbitrazh Administrators in Event of Bankruptcy of Credit Organisation [as amended by Federal Law No. 86-ФЗ, 19 June 2001]

1. [repealed by Federal Law No. 86-ФЗ, 19 June 2001]

1. An arbitrazh administrator must in the event of the bankruptcy of a credit organisation have the license of an arbitrazh administrator issued to State agencies of the Russian Federation for cases concerning bankruptcy and financial recuperation, and also meet the qualifications requirements of the Bank of Russia and have a certificate issued by the Bank of Russia.

The functions of an arbitrazh administrator in the event of the bankruptcy of an absent credit organisation an employee of the Bank of Russia shall have the right to effectuate irrespective of whether he has a license of an arbitrazh administrator and a certificate of an arbitrazh administrator in the event of the bankruptcy of a credit organisation [added by Federal Law No. 86-ФЗ, 19 June 2001].

2. The amount of qualifications requirements of the Bank of Russia, the procedure and conditions for conducting attestation, including the grounds, procedure for issuance, and annulment of attestation certificates shall be determined by normative acts of the Bank of Russia [as amended by Law of 19 June 2001].

Chapter II. Financial Recuperation of Credit Organisation

Article 7. Measures Relating to Financial Recuperation of Credit Organisation

For the purposes of the financial recuperation of a credit organisation the following measures may be effectuated:

the rendering of financial assistance to the credit organisation by its founders (or participants) and other persons;

a change of the structure of assets and structure of liabilities of the credit organisation;

a change of the organisational structure of the credit organisation;

bringing into conformity the amount of charter capital of the credit organisation and the amount of its own means (or capital) [added by Law of 19 June 2001];

other measures effectuated in accordance with federal laws.

Article 8. Rendering Financial Assistance to Credit Organisation by Founders (or Participants) Thereof and Other Persons

1. Financial assistance to a credit organisation by the founders (or participants) thereof and by other persons may be rendered in the following forms:

(1) placement of monetary means on deposit in the credit organisation for a period of return of not less than six months and with the calculation of interest at a rate not exceeding the refinancing interest rate (or bank rate) of the Bank of Russia;

(2) granting of suretyships (or bank guarantees) with regard to credits for the credit organisation;

(3) granting of deferral and/or instalment payment;

(4) transfer of debt of credit organisation with consent of creditors thereof;

(5) refusal to distribute profit of credit organisation as dividends and directing it to the effectuation of measures with regard to the financial recuperation of the particular credit organisation;

(6) additional contribution to the charter capital of the particular credit organisation;

(7) forgiveness of debt of credit organisation;

(8) novation, and tate in other forms facilitating the elimination of the reasons causing the necessity to take measures with regard to financial recuperation of the credit organisation.

2. Monetary means in the bank accounts and in deposits in the credit organisation may be used by the creditors thereof in order to increase the charter capital of the credit organisation in the procedure established by the Bank of Russia.

3. The decision concerning the forms and conditions of rendering financial assistance to the credit organisation shall be adopted by the credit organisation itself and by the person rendering financial assistance to it.

Article 9. Change of Structure of Assets and Structure of Liabilities of Credit Organisation

1. A change of the structure of assets of the credit organisation may provide for:

(1) improvement of the quality of its credit portfolio, including replacement of nonliquid assets with liquid assets;

(2) bringing the structure of assets on demand into conformity with the periods of obligations which ensure the performance thereof;

(3) reduction of expenses of the credit organisation, including for servicing the debt of the credit organisation, and expenses for the management thereof;

(4) sale of assets not bringing revenue, and also of assets whose sale will not obstruct the fulfilment of banking operations by the credit organisation;

(5) other measures with regard to a change of the structure of the assets thereof.

2. A change of the structure of liabilities of the credit organisation may provide for:

(1) an increase of own means (or capital);

(2) a reduction of the amount and/or weight of current and short-term obligations in the general structure of liabilities;

(3) an increase of the weight of medium-term and long-term obligations in the
general structure of liabilities;

(4) other measures relating to the structure of liabilities thereof.

3. [repealed by Federal Law No. 86-ФЗ, 19 June 2001].

Article 9¹. Bringing into Conformity the Amount of Charter Capital of Credit Organisation and Amount of Own Means (or Capital) of Credit Organisation

1. If the amount of own means (or capital) of a credit organisation according
to the results of the reporting month proves to be less than the amount of its charter capital, the credit organisation shall be obliged to bring into conformity the
amount of charter capital and the amount of own means (or capital).

2. A credit organisation shall be obliged to adopt a decision concerning liquidation if the amount of own means (or capital) of a credit organisation at the end
of the second and each consecutive financial year becomes less than the minimum
amount of charter capital established by the Federal Law on Joint-Stock Societies
or the Federal Law on Limited Responsibility Societies [added by Federal Law No.
86-ФЗ, 19 June 2001].

Article 10. Change of Organisational Structure of Credit Organisation

A change of the organisational structure of a credit organisation may be effectuated by:

a change of the composition and number of personnel of the credit organisation;

a change of the structure, reduction, and liquidation of solitary and other structural subdivisions of the credit organisation, and also by other means facilitating
the elimination of the reasons which caused the necessity of effectuating measures
with regard to the financial recuperation of a credit organisation.

Article 11. Petition of One-Man Executive Organ of Credit Organisation Concerning Effectuation of Measures With Regard to Prevention of Bankruptcy of Credit Organisation

1. The one-man executive organ of a credit organisation (hereinafter: executive of credit organisation) shall in the event of the arising of the circumstances
provided for by Article 4 of the present Federal Law within 10 days from the
moment of their arising be obliged to apply to the council of directors (or supervisory council) of the credit organisation, and if the formation thereof has not
been provided for by its constitutive documents, to the general meeting of
founders (or participants) of the credit organisation with a petition concerning

the effectuation of measures relating to financial recuperation of the credit organisation or a petition concerning reorganisation of the credit organisation on condition that the reasons for the arising of the said circumstances cannot be eliminated by the executive organs of the credit organisation.

2. The petition of the executive of a credit organisation concerning the effectuation of measures with relating to financial recuperation of the credit organisation or petition concerning the reorganisation of the credit organisation must contain a recommendation concerning the forms, character, and periods of their effectuation.

3. The management organs of a credit organisation to which the petition has been sent in accordance with point 1 of the present Article concerning the effectuation of measures relating to financial recuperation of the credit organisation or petition concerning reorganisation of the credit organisation must adopt a decision with regard to the petition sent within 10 days from the moment of sending thereof and inform the Bank of Russia about the decision adopted.

4. The executive of a credit organisation shall be obliged to apply to the Bank of Russia with a petition concerning the effectuation of measures with regard to the prevention of bankruptcy of the credit organisation if the founders (or participants) thereof refused to take part in the effectuation of measures relating to its financial recuperation or reorganisation or did not take the respective decision within the period provided for by point 3 of the present Article.

Article 12. Effectuation of Measures With Regard to Financial Recuperation of Credit Organisation Upon Demand of Bank of Russia

1. The Bank of Russia shall have the right to send a demand to the credit organisation concerning the effectuation of measures relating to its financial recuperation when there are grounds provided for by Article 4 (except for grounds provided for by paragraph seven of that Article) of the present Federal Law and Article 75 of the Federal Law on the Central Bank of the Russian Federation (Bank of Russia). The said demand of the Bank of Russia must contain a list of the reasons serving as the grounds for sending it, and als a recommendation concerning the forms and periods of the effectuation of measures relating to financial recuperation of the credit organisation [as amended by Federal Law No. 86-ФЗ, 19 June 2001].

2. In the event of the receipt of a demand of the Bank of Russia concerning the effectuation of measures relating to financial recuperation of the credit organisation, the executive of the credit organisation shall be obliged within five days from the moment of receipt thereof to apply to the management organs of the credit organisation specified in Article 11(1) of the present Federal Law with a petition concerning the effectuation of measures relating to financial recuper-

ation of the credit organisation or with a petition concerning the credit organisation.

3. The Bank of Russia shall be obliged to send a demand to a credit organisation concerning the bringing into conformity the amount of charter of the credit organisation and the amount of its own means (or capital) if on the basis of data of the reporting of the credit organisation and/or according to the results of a verification conducted in accordance with the requirements of the Federal Law on the Central Bank of the Russian Federation (Bank of Russia) it is elicited that the amount of own means (or capital) of a credit organisation has proved to be less than the amount of its charter capital.

If within the last 12 months which preceded the moment when in accordance with the present Article the Bank of Russia was obliged to send to the credit organisation a demand concerning the bringing into conformity of the amount of charter capital of a credit organisation and the amount of its own means (or capital) the Bank of Russia has changed the method of calculating the amount of own means (or capital) of a credit organisation, for the purposes of the present Article that method shall apply in accordance with which the amount of own means (or capital) of the credit organisation reaches maximum significance.

A credit organisation shall within 45 days from the moment of receipt of the said demand of the Bank of Russia in the event of the impossibility of increasing the amount of own means (or capital) up to the amount of charter capital be obliged to reduce the amount of charter capital to an amount not exceeding the amount of own means (or capital) and to make respective changes in the constitutive documents.

Creditors of a credit organisation shall not have the right to demand the termination or performance before time of its obligations on the basis of a reduction of the amount of charter capital of a credit organisation made in accordance with the requirements of the present Article. In so doing the provisions of legislation of the Russian Federation concerning obligatory notification of creditors concerning their right to demand from a credit organisation termination or performance before time of its obligations and compensation connected with these losses [added by Federal Law No. 86-ФЗ, 19 June 2001].

4. From the moment of receipt of the demand of the Bank of Russia concerning the effectuation of measures relating to financial recuperation of the credit organisation up to the moment of receipt of the authorisation of the Bank of Russia, the credit organisation shall not have the right to adopt a decision concerning the distribution of profit among the founders (or participants) thereof, payment (or announcement) of dividends, distribute profit among the founders (or participants) thereof and pay dividends to them, and also satisfy demands of founders (or participants) concerning the apportionment to them of a

participatory share (or part of a participatory share) or payment of the actual value thereof or purchase stocks.

The Bank of Russia shall send to the credit organisation an authorisation concerning the distribution of profit among the founders (or participants) thereof and the payment (or announcement) of dividends, and also satisfy demands of founders (or participants) concerning the apportionment to them of a participatory share (or part of a participatory share) or payment of the actual value thereof or purchase stocks if the grounds which served as the reason for sending the demand of the Bank of Russia concerning the effectuation of measures relating to financial recuperation of the credit organisation have been eliminated [as amended by Federal Law No. 86-ФЗ, 19 June 2001].

Article 13. Plan of Measures for Financial Recuperation of Credit Organisation

1. The Bank of Russia shall have the right to demand of a credit organisation the working out and effectuation of a plan of measures for its financial recuperation.

2. The plan of measures for the financial recuperation of a credit organisation must obligatorily contain:

an assessment of the financial state of the credit organisation;

an indication of the form and extent of participation of the founders (or participants) of the credit organisation and other persons in the financial recuperation thereof;

the measures relating to the reduction of expenses for maintenance of the credit organisation;

the measures relating to the receipt of additional revenues;

the measures relating to the return of delayed debtor indebtedness;

the measures relating to the change of organisational structure of the credit organisation;

the period for restoration of the level of sufficiency of own means (capital) and current liquidity of the credit organisation.

The form of the plan of measures relating to financial recuperation of the credit organisation shall be established by normative acts of the Bank of Russia.

3. The plan of measures relating to the financial recuperation of the credit organisation shall be submitted to the Bank of Russia within the period established by it.

The Bank of Russia shall control fulfilment of the plan of measures relating to financial recuperation of the credit organisation.

Article 14. Responsibility of Executive of Credit Organisation

In the event of the failure to take measures with regard to financial recuperation of a credit organisation, and also in the event of a violation of the requirements of

Articles 11 and 12 of the present Federal Law, the executive of a credit organisation may be brought to responsibility in accordance with federal laws.

Article 15. Consequences of Failure to Perform Requirements of Present Federal Law

The failure to perform the requirements provided for by Article 9(3), Article 11(3) and (4), Article 12(2), and Article 13(3) of the present Federal Law shall be grounds for the application by the Bank of Russia of measures by way of supervision established by federal laws.

Chapter III. Temporary Administration

Article 16. Temporary Administration

1. The temporary administration shall be a special management organ of a credit organisation designated by the Bank of Russia in the procedure established by the present Federal Law and normative acts of the Bank of Russia.

2. The temporary administration shall operate in accordance with the present Federal Law and other federal laws and normative acts of the Bank of Russia.

3. In the period of activity of the temporary administration the powers of the executive organs of the credit organisation may be either limited, or suspended, in the procedure and on the conditions which have been established by the present Federal Law by an act of the Bank of Russia concerning the designation of the temporary administration.

Article 17. Grounds for Designation of Temporary Administration

1. The Bank of Russia shall have the right to designate temporary administration if:
(1) the credit organisation does not satisfy the demands of individual creditors with regard to monetary obligations and/or does not perform the duty with regard to the payment of obligatory payments within the periods exceeding seven days and more from the moment of the ensuing of the date of their satisfaction and/or performance in connection with the absence or insufficiency of monetary means in correspondent accounts of the credit organisation;
(2) the credit organisation permits a reduction of own means (or capital) in comparison with the maximum size thereof achieved for the last 12 months by more than 30% with simultaneous violation of one of the obligatory normative standards established by the Bank of Russia;
(3) the credit organisation violates the normative standards of current liquidity established by the Bank of Russia wihtin the last month by more than 20%;
(4) the credit organisation does not perform the demand of the Bank of Russia concerning the replacement of the executive of the credit organisation or

effectuation of measures relating to financial recuperation or reorganisation of the credit organisation within the established period;

(5) in accordance with the Federal Law on Banks and Banking Activity there are grounds for revocation of the license of the credit organisation for the effectuation of banking operations.

2. The Bank of Russia shall be obliged to designate temporary administration in a credit organisation not later than the day following the day of revocation of the license for the effectuation of banking operations by the credit organisation [added by Federal Law No. 86-ФЗ, 19 June 2001].

3. The act of the Bank of Russia concerning the designation of the temporary administration shall be published by the Bank of Russia in the Вестник Банка России within 10 days from the moment of adoption thereof [as amended by Federal Law No. 86-ФЗ, 19 June 2001].

Article 18. Period of Operation of Temporary Administration

1. The temporary administration shall be designated by the Bank of Russia for a term of not more than nine months [as amended by Fedeal Law No. 86-ФЗ, 19 June 2001].

2. The Bank of Russia shall have the right to extend the period of operation of the temporary administration for not more than three months. The operation of the present point shall not extend to instances of the designation of temporary administration in accordance with point 4 of the present Article [as amended by Federal Law No. 86-ФЗ, 19 June 2001].

3. If at the moment of the end of the period of operation of temporary administration established by the present Federal Law as before there are grounds for the designation thereof provided for by the present Federal Law, the temporary administration shall send to the Bank of Russia a petition concerning the revocation of the license for the effectuation of banking operations by the credit organisation [added by Federal Law No. 86-ФЗ, 19 June 2001].

4. A temporary administration designated by the Bank of Russia after revocation of a license for the effectuation of banking operations by a credit organisation shall effectuate its activity in the credit organisation from the moment of its designation until the moment of appointment of a liquidator or until the moment of appointment of a bankruptcy administrator [added by Federal Law No. 86-ФЗ, 19 June 2001].

Article 19. Director of Temporary Administration

1. An employee of the Bank of Russia shall be appointed the head of temporary administration, and in instances provided for by the Federal Law on the Restructuring of Credit Organisations, an employee of the State Corporation

'Agency for the Restructuring of Credit Organisations' may be appointed the head of a temporary administration [as amended by Federal Law No. 86-ФЗ, 19 June 2001].

2. The director of the temporary administration shall form the composition of the temporary administration and bear responsibility for its activity.

3. The director of the temporary administration in the event of the suspension of the powers of the executive organs of the credit organisation shall effectuate activity in the name of the credit organisation without a power of attorney.

Article 20. Responsibility of Head of Temporary Administration for Failure to Perform or Improper Performance of His Duties [as amended by Law of 19 June 2001]

In the event of the failure to perform or improper performance by the director of the temporary administration of his duties he shall bear responsibility in accordance with federal laws [as amended by Federal Law No. 86-ФЗ, 19 June 2001].

Article 21. Functions of Temporary Administration in Event of Limitation of Powers of Executive Organs of Credit Organisation

1. In the event of the limitation of the powers of executive organs of the credit organisation the temporary administration shall effectuate the following functions:

conduct an investigation of the credit organisation [added by Federal Law No. 86-ФЗ, 19 June 2001];

establish the existence of grounds for revocation of a license for the effectuation of banking operations provided for by Article 20 of the Federal Law on Banks and Banking Activity [added by Federal Law No. 86-ФЗ, 19 June 2001];

participate in working out measures relating to the financial recuperation of the credit organisation and control the realisation thereof;

control the disposition of property of the credit organisation within the limits established by the present Article;

other functions in accordance with federal laws.

2. When effectuating the functions specified in point 1 of the present Article the temporary administrator shall:

receive from the management organs of the credit organisation necessary information and documents affecting the activity of the credit organisation;

give consent to the conclusion by management organs of the credit organisation of transactions specified in point 3 of the present Article;

turn to the Bank of Russia with a petition concerning the suspension of the powers of the management organs of the credit organisation if they counteract the effectuation of the functions of the temporary administration or if this is necessary in order to effectuate measures with regard to the prevention of the bankruptcy of the credit organisation.

3. The management organs of a credit organisation shall have the right only with the consent of the temporary administration to conclude transactions:

connected with the transfer of immoveable property of the credit organisation on lease, pledge, making a contribution thereof to the charter capital of third persons, and also the disposition of such property otherwise;

connected with the disposition of other property of the credit organisation whose balance sheet value comprises more than 1% of the balance sheet value of the assets of the credit organisation, including the receipt and issuance of credits and loans, issuance of guarantees and suretyships, assignment of the rights of demand, transfer and forgiveness of debt, novation, release-money, and also the establishment of trust management;

with interested persons with respect to the credit organisation determined in accordance with the Federal Law on Insolvency (or Bankruptcy).

Article 22. Functions of Temporary Administration in Event of Suspension of Powers of Executive Organs of Credit Organisation

1. In the event of the suspension of the powers of executive organs of the credit organisation the temporary administration shall effectuate the following functions:

realise the powers of the executive organs of the credit organisation;

conduct an investigation of the credit organisation [added by Federal Law No. 86-ФЗ, 19 June 2001];

establish the existence of grounds for revocation of a license for the effectuation of banking operations provided for by Article 20 of the Federal Law on Banks and Banking Activity [added by Federal Law No. 86-ФЗ, 19 June 2001];

work out measures relating to the financial recuperation of the credit organisation and organise and control their execution;

take measures relating to ensuring the preservation of the property and documentation of the credit organisation;

establish the creditors of the credit organisation and amounts of their demands with regard to monetary obligations;

take measures with regard to the recovery of indebtedness to the credit organisation;

apply to the Bank of Russia with a petition concerning the introduction of a moratorium on the satisfaction of demands of creditors of the credit organisation;

other functions in accordance with federal laws.

2. When effectuating the functions specified in point 1 of the present Article, the temporary administration shall:

receive from management organs of the credit organisation necessary information and documents affecting the activity of the credit organisation;

file suits in the name of the credit organisation in courts of general jurisdiction, arbitrazh courts, and arbitration courts;

appoint representatives of the temporary administration in branches of the credit organisation,and also in the management organs of its subsidiary organisations;

agree decisions of the council of directors (or supervisory council) of the credit organisation or general meeting of its founders (or participants), except for decisions concerning the conclusion of transactions provided for by point 3 of the present Article;

have the right to remove members of the executive organs of the credit organisation from work (or relieved from post occupied) and suspend the payment of earnings to them;

have the right to assemble a meeting of founders (or participants) of the credit organisation in the procedure established by federal laws [added by Federal Law No. 86-ФЗ, 19 June 2001];

have the right to apply in the name of the credit organisation to a court with a demand concerning the bringing to responsibility members of the council of directors (or supervisory council) of a credit organisation, one-man executive organ of the credit organisation (director, general director), and/or members of the collegial executive organ of the credit organisation (board, directorate) if by their guilty actions (or failure to act) losses were caused to the credit organisation in the amount of losses caused unless other grounds and measure of responsibility have been established by federal laws [added by Federal Law No. 86-ФЗ, 19 June 2001];

apply in the name of the credit organisation to a court or arbitrazh court with a demand concerning the deeming of transactions concluded by the credit organisation within three years from the day of designation of temporary administration invalid if the said transactions meet the indicia of invalidity of transactions specified in Article 28 [as amended by Federal Law No. 86-ФЗ, 19 June 2001].

3. The temporary administration shall have the right only with the consent of the council of directors (or supervisory council) of the credit organisation or general meeting of its founders (or participants) within the limits of their competence established by federal laws and the constitutive documents of the credit organisation to conclude transactions connected with:

the transfer of immoveable property of the credit organisation on lease, pledge, making of contribution to charter capital of third persons, and also the disposition of such property otherwise;

the disposition of other property of the credit organisation whose balance sheet value comprises more than 5% of the balance sheet value of the assets of the credit organisation, including the receipt and issuance of credits and loans, issuance of guaratees and suretyships, assignment of rights of demand, transfer and forgiveness of debt, novation, release-money, and also with the establishment of trust management.

4. The council of directors (or supervisory council) of a credit organisation or general meeting of its founders (or participants) within the limits of their competence established by federal laws and constitutive documents of the credit organisation shall have the right to expand the powers of the temporary administration with regard to the disposition of property of the credit organisation.

Article 22¹. Functions of Temporary Administration in Event of Designation Thereof After Revocation of License for Effectuation of Banking Operations by Credit Organisation [added by Federal Law No. 86-Ф3, 19 June 2001]

1. A temporary administration designated by the Bank of Russia after the revocation of the license for the effectuation of banking operations by the credit organisation shall effectuate the same functions and possess the powers which have been granted to a temporary administration in accordance with Article 22 of the present Federal Law, except for functions of working out measures with regard to the financial recuperation of the credit organisation, the organisation thereof, and control over the performance thereof.

2. A temporary administration designated by the Bank of Russia after revocation of the license for the effectuation of banking operations by the credit organisation shall be obliged to conduct an investigation of the credit organisation and to determine the existence of the indicia of insolvency (or bankruptcy) provided for by Article 2(2) of the present Federal Law. In the event of the discovery of the said indicia a temporary administration designaged by the Bank of Russia after revocation of the license for the effectuation of banking operations by the credit organisation shall send to the Bank of Russia a petition concerning the sending by the Bank of Russia of an application to an arbitrazh court concerning the credit organisation to be bankrupt [added by Federal Law No. 86-Ф3, 19 June 2001].

Article 23. Consequences of Suspension of Powers of Executive Organs of Credit Organisation for Period of Activity of Temporary Administration

1. In the event of the suspension of the powers of the executive organs of a credit organisation for the period of activity of the temporary administration:

the executive organs of the credit organisation shall not have the right to adopt decisions with regard to questions relegated to their competence by federal laws and constitutive documents of the credit organisation;

decisions of other management organs of the credit organisation shall enter into force after their being agreed with the temporary administration.

2. The executive organs of the credit organisation shall in the event of the suspension of their powers for the period of activity of the temporary administration

not later than the day following the day of the designation of temporary administration be obliged to transfer to it the seals and stamps of the credit organisation, and within the periods agreed with the temporary administration, the bookkeeping and other documentation and the material and other valuables of the credit organisation.

3. Counteraction on the part of members of the management organs and other workers of the credit organisation to the effectuation of the functions of the temporary administration shall entail the ensuing of responsibility established in the procedure provided for by federal laws.

Article 24. Petition of Director of Temporary Administration Concerning Revocation of License for Effectuation of Banking Operations

In the event of the establishment of grounds for revocation of the license of the credit organisation for the effectuation of banking operations provided for by Article 20 of the Federal Law on Banks and Banking Activity, the director of the temporary administration shall be obliged to send to the Bank of Russia a petition concerning revocation of the said license.

Article 25. Disputes Concerning Activity of Temporary Administration

1. A credit organisation shall have the right to appeal the decision of the Bank of Russia concerning the designation of temporary administration to the arbitrazh court in the procedure established by federal laws.

The appeal of a decision of the Bank of Russia concerning the designation of temporary administration, and also the application of measures with regard to securing suits with respect to the credit organisation, shall not suspend the activity of the temporary administration [as amended by Federal Law No. 86-ФЗ, 19 June 2001].

2. [repealed by Federal Law No. 86-ФЗ, 19 June 2001].

2. The founders (or participants) of a credit organisation possessing in aggregate not less than 1% of the charter capital of the credit organisation shall have the right to apply to an arbitrazh court with a suit against the Bank of Russia concerning compensation of the credit organisation for real damage if it was inflicted as a result of the unfounded designation of temporary administration [as amended by Federal Law No. 86-ФЗ, 19 June 2001].

Article 26. Moratorium on Satisfaction of Demands of Creditors of Credit Organisation

1. In the event of the suspension of the powers of the executive organs of a credit organisation and the presence of grounds provided for by Article 17(1), subpoint (1), of the present Federal Law, the Bank of Russia shall have the right to introduce a moratorium on the satisfaction of demands of creditors of the credit

organisation (hereinafter—moratorium) for a period of not more than three months. The operation of the said moratorium shall extend to monetary obligations and duties with regard to the payment of obligatory payments which arose before the moment of the designation of the temporary administration [Article 26(1) and (2) were declared unconstitutional by Decree of the Constitutional Court of the Russian Federation, 3 July 2001, No. 10-П, to the extent that they do not make provision for the subject empowered to introduce a moratorium on the satisfaction of demands of citizen depositors against a credit organisation in the process of restructuring and the grounds for extending such moratorium; these provisions also limit the rights of citizens excessively and impinge upon their right to judicial defence].

2. During the period of operation of the moratorium:
penalties (or fines, forfeits) and other financial (or economic) sanctions shall not be calculated for the failure to perform or the improper performance of monetary obligations and duties with regard to the payment of obligatory payments, and also interest subject to payment;
recovery under execution and other documents, the recovery under which is made in an uncontested (or nonacceptance) proceeding shall not be permitted;
the execution of documents of execution with regard to property recoveries shall be suspended, except for the execution of documents of execution issued on the basis of decisions concerning the recovery of indebtedness for earnings, payment of remuneration under authors' contracts, and also compensation of harm caused to life and health, and moral harm which entered into legal force before the moment of the designation of the temporary administration;
the satisfaction of demands of the founder (or participant) of the credit organisation concerning the partition to him of a participatory share (or contribution) to the charter capital of the credit organisation shall be prohibited in connection with his withdraal from the composition of the founders (or participants) thereof.
Interest shall be calculated in the amount of two-thirds of the refinancing rate of the Bank of Russia on the amount of demands of a creditor with regard to monetary obligations and/or obligatory payments in the amount established at the moment of the introduction of the moratorium (without taking into account calculated interest), and also on the amount of applied penalties (or fines, forfeits) and other financial (or economic) sanctions [as amended by Federal Law No. 86-ФЗ, 19 June 2001].

3. The operation of a moratorium shall not extend to:
demands of citizens to whom the credit organisation bears responsibility for causing harm to life or health;
demands of citizens with regard to the payment of severance benefits and payment for labour of citizens working under a labour contract, and with regard to the payment of remuneration under authors' contracts;

demands with regard to the payment of organisational-economic expenses necessary for the activity of the credit organisation.

Article 27. Refusal to Perform Contract of Credit Organisation

The director of the temporary administration shall have the right in the event of the suspension of the powers of the executive organs of the credit organisation from the moment of the designation of the temporary administration to refuse to perform the contract of the credit organisation in the procedure provided for by the Federal Law on Insolvency (or Bankruptcy).

Article 28. Invalidity of Transactions of Credit Organisation

1. A transaction of a credit organisation concluded by it before the moment of designation of a temporary administration may be deemed by an arbitrazh court to be invalid upon the application of the director of the temporary administration on the grounds provided for by civil legislation of the Russian Federation and the Federal Law on Insolvency (or Bankruptcy) [as amended by Federal Law No. 86-ФЗ, 19 June 2001].

2. A transaction concluded or performed by a credit organisation within the three years which preceded the designation of a temporary administration may be deemed by a court to be invalid upon the application of a temporary administration or creditor of a credit organisation in instances when the price of the said transaction and other conditions materially worse for the credit organisation differ from the price and other conditions under which in comparable circumstances analogous transactions are concluded, and if the parties who participated in the transaction at the moment of concluding it knew or should have known that as a result of the particular transaction the indicia of insolvency (or bankruptcy) of the credit organisation appear at the credit organisation specified in Article 2 of the present Federal Law, or the transaction was concluded with persons who directly or indirectly control the credit organisation, directly or indirectly are controlling it, or directly or indirectly are under common control with it [added by Federal Law No. 86-ФЗ, 19 June 2001].

Article 29. Expenses of Temporary Administration

Expenses of the temporary administration, including expenses for the payment of members of the temporary administration connected with the activity thereof, shall be effectuated at the expense of the credit organisation.

The estimate of expenses of the temporary administration shall be confirmed by the Bank of Russia.

Article 30. Report of Temporary Administration

The temporary administration shall report to the Bank of Russia in the procedure established by normative acts of the Bank of Russia.

Article 31. Termination of Activity of Temporary Administration

1. The Bank of Russia shall adopt a decision concerning the termination of the activity of temporary administration:

in the event of elimination of the reasons serving as grounds for its designation;

in the event of the transfer of the files to an arbitrazh administrator;

on other grounds provided for by the present Federal Law and normative acts of the Bank of Russia.

2. The procedure for termination of the activity of temporary administration shall be established by normative acts of the Bank of Russia.

3. Termination of the activity of temporary administration when eliminating the reasons serving as the grounds for the designation thereof shall entail the restoration of the powers of the executive organs of the credit organisation.

The powers of the executives of the credit organisation removed for the period of activity of the temporary administration from the performance of their duties shall be restored after termination of the activity of the temporary administration if the executives of the credit organisation have not been relieved from them in accordance with legislation of the Russian Federation on labour.

4. Notification concerning the termination of the activity of the temporary administration shall be published by the Bank of Russia in the Вестник Банка России.

Chapter IV. Reorganisation of Credit Organisation

Article 32. Demand of Bank of Russia Concerning Reorganisation of Credit Organisation

1. The Bank of Russia shall have the right to demand the reorganisation of a credit organisation in the instances established by Article 17(1), subpoints (1)-(3), of the present Federal Law. The procedure for sending the demand of the Bank of Russia concerning the reorganisation of a credit organisation shall be established by Article 12(1) of the present Federal Law.

2. The reorganisation of a credit organisation shall be effectuated in the form of merger or accession in the procedure established by federal laws and normative acts of the Bank of Russia adopted in accordance with them.

Article 33. Actions of Credit Organisation in Event of Receipt of Demand of Bank of Russia Concerning Reorganisation Thereof

1. In the event of receiving the demand of the Bank of Russia concerning reorganisation of the credit organisation the director thereof shall be obliged within five days from the moment of receipt to apply to the management organs of the credit organisation specified in Article 11(1) of the present

Federal Law with a petition concerning the necessity to reorganise the credit organisation.

The management organs of the credit organisation specified in Article 11(1) of the present Federal Law shall be obliged within a period of not later than 10 days from the moment of receipt of the demand of the Bank of Russia concerning reorganisation to notify the Bank of Russia about the decision adopted.

2. Requirements for the stability of credit organisations arising when merging credit organisations shall be determined by normative acts of the Bank of Russia.

Chapter V. Peculiarities of Consideration of Case Concerning Bankruptcy by Arbitrazh Court

Article 34. Procedure for Consideration of Cases Concerning Bankruptcy

Cases concerning bankruptcy shall be considered by an arbitrazh court according to the rules provided for by the Code of Arbitrazh Procedure of the Russian Federation and the Federal Law on Insolvency (or Bankruptcy), with the peculiarities established by the present Federal Law.

Article 35. Recourse to Arbitrazh Court

1. There shall possess the right of recourse to an arbitrazh court with an application concerning the deeming of a credit organisation to be bankrupt:

(1) a creditor organisation-debtor (hereinafter—credit organisation);

(2) a creditor of the credit organisation, including citizens having the right of demand against the credit organisation under a contract of bank deposit and/or contract of bank account;

(3) the Bank of Russia, including in instances when the Bank of Russia is not a creditor of the credit organisation [as amended by Federal Law No. 86-ФЗ, 19 June 2001];

(4) the procurator—in instances provided for by the Federal Law on Insolvency (or Bankruptcy);

(5) a tax or other agency empowered in accordance with a federal law—with regard to payment of obligatory payments to the budget and extrabudgetary funds.

2. If at the moment of revocation of a license for the effectuation of banking operations by a credit organisation the credit organisation has the indicia of insolvency (or bankruptcy) provided for by the present Federal Law, the Bank of Russia within five days from the day of publication of the decision concerning the revocation of the license for the effectuation of banking operations by the credit organisation in Вестник Банка России shall be obliged to apply to an arbitrazh court with an application concerning the deeming of the credit organisation to be bankrupt. In the event of the Bank of Russia sending to the arbitrazh court

an application concerning the deeming of a credit organisation to be bankrupt, the Bank of Russia shall within 15 days from the day of acceptance of the said application by the arbitrazh court be obliged to submit to the arbitrazh court a candidacy for appointment as arbitrazh administrator.

In the event of the eliciting by a temporary administration designated by the Bank of Russia after revocation of the license for the effectuation of banking operations by the credit organisation the indicia of insolvency (or bankruptcy) of the credit organisation, the Bank of Russia within five days from the day of receipt of the petition of the said temporary administration shall send to the arbitrazh court an application concerning the deeming of the credit organisation to be bankrupt. In the event of the Bank of Russia sending to an arbitrazh court an application concerning the deeming of a credit organisation to be bankrupt, the Bank of Russia shall within 15 days from the day of acceptance of the said application by the arbitrazh court be obliged to submit to the arbitrazh court a candidacy for appointment as arbitrazh administrator [added by Federal Law No. 86-ФЗ, 19 June 2001].

3. The persons specified in point 1, subpoints (1), (2), (4), and (5), of the present Article shall have the right to send to the Bank of Russia an application concerning revocation of the license of the credit organisation for the effectuation of banking operations when the indicia of the bankruptcy thereof ensue specified in Article 2 of the present Federal Law with documents appended showing the presence of monetary obligations of the credit organisation and the amount thereof which have been established in accordance with the requirements of Article 4 of the Federal Law on Insolvency (or Bankruptcy) [as amended by Federal Law No. 86-ФЗ, 19 June 2001].

4. The persons specified in point 1, subpoints (1), (2), (4), and (5), of the present Article who have sent an application to the Bank of Russia concerning the revocation of the license of the credit organisation for the effectuation of banking operations shall in the event of the failure to receive a reply of the Bank of Russia upon the expiry of two months after the sending of the said application have the right to apply to the arbitrazh court with an application concerning the deeming of the credit organisation to be bankrupt.

When receiving the application concerning the deeming of a credit organisation to be bankrupt at the arbitrazh court, the judge shall before initiating a proceeding with regard to a case concerning bankruptcy propose to the Bank of Russia to submit an opinion of the Bank of Russia concerning the advisability of revocation of the license of the credit organisation for the effectuation of banking operations or a copy of the order of the Bank of Russia concerning revocation of the said license. The Bank of Russia shall be obliged to send the said documents to the arbitrazh court within a month's period after receipt of the proposal of the arbitrazh court.

The submission to the arbitrazh court of a copy of the order of the Bank of Russia concerning revocation of the license for the effectuation of banking operations within the aforesaid period shall be grounds for initiation of the proceedings with regard to the case concerning bankruptcy.

In the event of receiving within a month's period the opinion of the Bank of Russia concerning the inadvisability of revocation of the license of the credit organisation for the effectuation of banking operations, the application concerning the deeming thereof to be bankrupt shall be returned to the creditor.

In the event of the failure to receive the aforesaid opinion of the Bank of Russia within a month's period the arbitrazh court shall return the application to the creditor concerning the deeming of the credit organisation to be bankrupt. In this event the person who sent an application to the Bank of Russia concerning revocation of the license of the credit organisation for the effectuation of banking operations shall have the right to demand in an arbitrazh court compensation by the Bank of Russia of losses caused by the failure of the Bank of Russia to adopt a decision concerning revocation of the said license of the credit organisation or the failure of the Bank of Russia to adopt decisions provided for by the present Federal Law and relegated to the competence of the Bank of Russia concerning the effectuation of measures with regard to the prevention of the bankruptcy of the credit organisation [as amended by Federal Law No. 86-ФЗ, 19 June 2001].

Article 36. Initiation of Case Concerning Bankruptcy

A case concerning bankruptcy may be initiated by the arbitrazh court only after revocation of the license of the credit organisation for the effectuation of banking operations on the basis of the application of the persons specified in Article 35 of the present Federal Law if the demands against the credit organisation in aggregate comprise not less than one thousand minimum amounts of payment for labour established by a federal law and if these demands are not performed within one month from the moment of ensuing of the date of the performance thereof, or if after revocation of a license for the effectuation of banking operations by the credit organisation the value of its property (or assets) is insufficient for performance of obligations of a credit organisation to its creditors. The value of property (or assets) and obligations of a credit organisation shall be subject to determination on the basis of the methods established by normative acts of the Bank of Russia [as amended by Federal Law No. 86-ФЗ, 19 June 2001].

Article 37. Persons Participating in Case Concerning Bankruptcy

1. Persons participating in a case concerning bankruptcy shall be the persons specified in the Federal Law on Insolvency (or Bankruptcy), and also the Bank of Russia when initiating the proceedings with regard to a case concerning bankruptcy upon the application of the Bank of Russia concerning the deeming of the

credit organisation to be bankrupt [as amended by Federal Law No. 86-ФЗ, 19 June 2001].

2. [repealed by Federal Law No. 86-ФЗ, 19 June 2001].

Article 38. Persons Participating in Arbitrazh Proceeding

The persons specified in the Federal Law on Insolvency (or Bankruptcy), and also the Bank of Russia in instances when the application concerning the deeming of a credit organisation to be bankrupt was sent to the arbitrazh court by another person, shall participate in the arbitrazh proceeding with regard to a case concerning bankruptcy.

Article 39. Application Concerning Deeming of Credit Organisation to be Bankrupt

1. An application of a credit organisation concerning the deeming thereof to be bankrupt must meet the requirements provided for by the Federal Law on Insolvency (or Bankruptcy) for the application of a debtor.

The application concerning the deeming of a credit organisation to be bankrupt of other persons having in accordance with the present Federal Law the right to file the said application must meet the requirements provided for by the Federal Law on Insolvency (or Bankruptcy) for the application of a creditor, unless arises otherwise from the essence of legal relations.

2. A copy of the application of the credit organisation concerning the deeming thereof to be bankrupt shall be sent to the Bank of Russia.

Copies of the application of the persons specified in Article 35 of the present Federal Law concerning the deeming of a credit organisation to be bankrupt shall be sent by this credit organisation to the Bank of Russia.

3. The Bank of Russia may when filing applications concerning the deeming of a credit organisation to be bankrupt submit the candidacy of the arbitrazh administrator to the arbitrazh court.

Article 40. Documents to be Appended to Application Concerning Deeming of Credit Organisation to be Bankrupt

Besides the documents provided for by the Code of Arbitrazh Procedure of the Russian Federation and the Federal Law on Insolvency (or Bankruptcy), to an application concerning the deeming of a credit organisation to be bankrupt shall be appended a copy of the order of the Bank of Russia concerning revocation of the license of the credit organisation for the effectuation of banking operations published in the Вестник Банка России or a copy of the said order attested by the Bank of Russia.

Article 41. Acceptance of Application Concerning Deeming of Credit Organisation to be Bankrupt

The ruling of an arbitrazh court concerning the acceptance of an application concerning the deeming of a credit organisation to be bankrupt shall specify the introduction of observation and appointment of the temporary administrator.

Article 42. Refusal to Accept Application Concerning Deeming of Credit Organisation to be Bankrupt

The judge of an arbitrazh court shall refuse to accept an application concerning the deeming of a credit organisation to be bankrupt if even one of the conditions provided for by Article 36 of the present Federal Law was violated.

Article 43. Return of Application Concerning Deeming of Credit Organisation to be Bankrupt

The application concerning the deeming of a credit organisation to be bankrupt as not corresponding to the requirements provided for by Articles 39 and 40 of the present Federal Law shall be returned by the arbitrazh court to the person who sent the said application with the documents appended to this application.

Article 44. Sending of Judicial Acts by Arbitrazh Court With Regard to Case Concerning Bankruptcy

An arbitrazh court shall send judicial acts with regard to a case concerning bankruptcy within a five-day period from the moment of adoption thereof to the persons participating in the case concerning bankruptcy and in the arbitrazh proceeding.

Article 45. Consequences of Failure to Perform or Improper Performance of Duties by Arbitrazh Administrator

1. In the event of the failure to perform or improper performance by the arbitrazh administrator of his duties the Bank of Russia shall have the right to annul the qualifications certificate of the Bank of Russia issued to him in the procedure determined by normative acts of the Bank of Russia.

The decision of the Bank of Russia concerning annulment of the said certificate may be appealed by the arbitrazh administrator to the arbitrazh court.

2. The failure to perform or improper performance by the arbitrazh administrator of his duties which entailed losses for the credit organisation may be grounds for revocation of the license of the arbitrazh administrator.

In the event of the failure to perform or improper performance by the arbitrazh administrator of his duties the Bank of Russia shall have the right to apply to the State agency of the Russian Federation for cases concerning bankruptcy and financial recuperation with a petition concerning revocation of his license of an arbitrazh administrator.

Chapter VI. Peculiarities of Bankruptcy Proceeding of Credit Organisation Deemed to be Bankrupt

Article 46. Account of Credit Organisation in Course of Bankruptcy Proceeding

1. A bankruptcy administrator shall be obliged to use in the course of the bankruptcy proceeding only the correspondent account of the credit organisation deemed to be bankrupt which is open in an institution of the Bank of Russia. The procedure for opening the said account and effectuation of the settlement of accounts with regard to the particular account shall be determined by normative acts of the Bank of Russia.

2. Within 10 days from the moment of submission of documents by the bankruptcy administrator to the Bank of Russia confirming the right of the bankruptcy administrator to perform operations with regard to the correspondent account of the credit organisation deemed to be bankrupt, the balances of monetary means shall be transferred from the correspondent accounts of the credit organisation open in other credit organisations to the said account in the procedure determined by normative acts of the Bank of Russia, and also other monetary means of the credit organisation, including obligatory reserves deposited by the credit organisation in the Bank of Russia.

Article 47. Publication of Information Concerning Bankruptcy of Credit Organisation

1. The bankruptcy administrator within 15 days from the moment of the submission by him to the Bank of Russia of documents confirming the right of the bankruptcy administrator to perform operations with regard to the correspondent account of the credit organisation deemed to be bankrupt shall send for publication in the Вестник Высшего Арбитражного Суда Российской Федерации and the Вестник Банка России, and also shall publish in the local press at the location of the credit organisation, at the expense of the means thereof an announcement concerning the decision of the arbitrazh court about deeming the credit organisation to be bankrupt and the opening of a bankruptcy proceeding [as amended by Federal Law No. 116-ФЗ, 7 August 2001].

2. The bankruptcy administrator within 70 days from the day of publication of information concerning the deeming of a credit organisation to be bankrupt and the opening of a bankruptcy proceeding provided for by Article 100 of the Federal Law on Insolvency (or Bankruptcy) and the present Article shall send for publication in the Вестник Высшего Арбитражного Суда Российской

Федерации and the Вестник Банка России, and also in the periodical printed publication at the location of the credit organisation deemed to be bankrupt, at the expense of the means thereof an announcement concerning the effectuation by the credit organisation of preliminary payments to creditors of the first priority, specifying the procedure and conditions of these payments [added by Federal Law No. 116-ФЗ, 7 August 2001].

3. If the information concerning the deeming of a debtor to be bankrupt and the opening of a bankruptcy proceeding was published in the official publications specified in point 2 of the present Article at different times, the period for presentation of demands of creditors shall be calculated from the day of first publication of this information [added by Federal Law No. 116-ФЗ, 7 August 2001].

Article 47[1]. Duties of Bankruptcy Administrator in Process of Bankruptcy Proceeding of Credit Organisation

1. A bankruptcy administrator shall in the event of the bankruptcy of a credit organisation be obliged to fulfil the functions placed on him in good faith, taking into account the rights and legal interests of all creditors.

2. In the event of the discovery in the process of a bankruptcy proceeding of a credit organisation of transactions effectuated by the credit organisation during the period after the revocation of a license for the effectuation of banking operations by the credit organisation (except for transactions connected with current municipal and operational payments of the credit organisation, and also with the payment of severance benefits and payment for labour of persons working under a labour contract, which have been provided for by Article 20 of the Federal Law on Banks and Banking Activity), the bankruptcy administrator shall be obliged to apply to a court with a demand concerning the application to the said transactions of the consequences of the invalidity of null transactions.

3. The bankruptcy administrator shall be obliged to turn to a court with a demand concerning the deeming of transactions concluded by the credit organisation within the three years which preceded the day of deeming by an arbitrazh court of the credit organisation to be bankrupt invalid, if the said transactions meet the indicia of invalidity of transactions specified in Article 28 of the present Federal Law (except for transactions, the decision concerning the inadvisability of applying to a court with regard to which the committee of creditors has adopted).

4. The bankruptcy administrator shall be obliged to turn to a court or arbitrazh court with a demand concerning the bringing of founders (or participants), members of the council of directors (or supervisory council), and executives of the credit organisation to subsidiary responsibility for obligations of the credit organisation in accordance with the requirements of Article 50 of the present Federal Law [added by Federal Law No. 86-ФЗ, 19 June 2001].

Article 47². Peculiarities of Effectuation of Preliminary Payments to Creditors of First Priority

1. The bankruptcy administrator shall keep a register of demands of creditors of the first priority for the purpose of effectuation by the credit organisation of preliminary payments to creditors of the first priority in which shall be specified information concerning each creditor of the first priority and the amount of its demands with regard to monetary obligations. The period for drawing up the said register shall comprise two months from the day of publication of information concerning the deeming of a credit organisation to be bankrupt and the opening of a bankruptcy proceeding.

2. Preliminary payments to creditors of the first priority shall commence no later than the third working day from the day of publication of the first announcement concerning the procedure and the conditions of payments to creditors of the first priority and shall be effectuated within three months from the said date.

3. For the effectuation by a credit organisation of preliminary payments to creditors of the first priority shall be sent 70% of the monetary means in the correspondent account of the credit organisation deemed to be bankrupt to be used in the course of the bankruptcy proceeding on the day of the closure of the register of demands of creditors of the first priority for the prupose of effectuation by the credit organisation of preliminary payments. If the means are insufficient to satisfy the demands of creditors of the first priority in full, the means shall be distributed in proportion to the amounts of demands subject to satisfaction.

4. The amount of demands of creditors of the first priority shall be subject to reduction by the amount paid to them in the course of the effectuation by the credit organisation of preliminary payments and shall be reflected in the register of demands of creditors of the credit organistion deemed to be bankrupt. The report of the bankruptcy administrator concerning the conducting of preliminary payments to creditors of the first priority, appending the register of demands of creditors of the first priority for the purpose of effectuating preliminary payments, shall be submitted by the credit organisation deemed to be bankrupt to the Bank of Russia, arbitrazh court, and committee of creditors.

5. Demands of creditors of the first priority in the amount exceeding the amount of preliminary payments to be effectuated, as well as demands declared after the closure of the register of demands of creditors of the first priority, for the purpose of effectuation of preliminary payments shall be satisfied in the procedure determined by Article 49 of the present Federal Law. In so doing the proportional satisfaction of demands of all creditors of the first priority shall be ensured [added by Federal Law No. 116-ФЗ, 7 August 2001].

Article 48. Procedure for Liquidation of Credit Organisation

1. The arbitrazh court which has adopted a decision concerning the bankruptcy of a credit organisation shall send the said decision to the Bank of Russia, and also the federal agency of executive power empowered in accordance with Article 2 of the Federal Law 'On the State Registration of Juridical Persons' (hereinafter: empowered registering agency), which shall make an entry concerning the fact that the credit organisation is in the process of liquidation in the unified State register of juridical persons [as amended by Federal Law No. 31-ФЗ, 21 March 2002].

2. The bankruptcy administrator monthly shall submit to the Bank of Russia the bookkeeping and statistical report of the credit organisation being liquidated in accordance with the List and in the procedure which is established by the Bank of Russia.

3. After drawing up the register of demands of creditors, the bankruptcy administrator shall within a period of not later than six months from the day of opening the bankruptcy proceeding draw up an interim liquidation balance sheet, which shall contain information concerning the composition of the property of the credit organisation being liquidated, a List of demands presented by creditors, the results of the consideration of these demands, and also information concerning the preliminary payments effectuated to creditors of the first priority. The period for drawing up the register of demands of creditors and the period for drawing up the interim liquidation balance sheet may be extended by the arbitrazh court upon the application of bankruptcy administrator.

The interim liquidation balance sheet and liquidation balance sheet shall be drawn up and submitted to the Bank of Russia in accordance with normative acts of the Bank of Russia [as amended by Federal Law No. 116-ФЗ, 7 August 2001].

4. On the basis of the ruling of an arbitrazh court rendered in accordance with Article 119 of the Federal Law 'On Insolvency (or Bankruptcy)' concerning the completion of the bankruptcy proceeding, the Bank of Russia shall send to the empowered registering agency information and documents concerning the credit organisation necessary for the effectuation by the said agency of the functions with regard to keeping the unified State register of juridical persons and making in the said register an entry concerning liquidation of the credit organisation.

The liquidation of a credit organisation shall be considered to be completed, and the credit organisation to have terminated its activity, after the making the entry thereof by the empowered registering agency in the unified State register of juridical persons [as amended by Federal Law No. 31-ФЗ, 21 March 2002].

5. After completion of the procedure for a bankruptcy proceeding and liquidation of the credit organisation, documents shall be transferred to the Archive

Fund of the Russian Federation in the procedure and in accordance with the List which shall be confirmed by the State agency effectuating State policy in the domain of archives and by the Bank of Russia.

Article 49. Peculiarities of Distribution of Bankruptcy Mass

1. Demands of natural persons who are creditors of the credit organisation under contract of bank deposit concluded with them and contracts of bank account, and the demands of citizens to whom the credit bears responsibility for causing harm to life or health shall be satisfied in first priority at the expense of the property of the credit organisation which comprises the bankruptcy mass [as amended by Federal Law No. 86-ФЗ, 19 June 2001].

2. Demands of creditors with regard to subordinated credits (or loans) shall be satisfied after the full satisfaction of demands of all other creditors. For the purposes of the present Federal Law by subordinated credit (or loan) is understood a credit (or loan) if it simultaneously satisfies the following conditions:

the period of provision of the credit (or loan) constitutes not less than five years;

the contract of credit (or loan) contains a provision concerning the impossibility of dissolution before time;

the conditions of provision of the credit (or loan) materially do not differ from market conditions for the provision of analogous credits (or loans) at the moment of the provision thereof;

the contract of credit (or loan) contains a provision that in the event of the bankruptcy of a credit organisation demands with regard to that credit (or loan) shall be satisfied after the satisfaction of the demands of all other creditors [added by Federal Law No. 86-ФЗ, 19 June 2001].

Article 50. Responsibility of Founders (or Participants), Members of Council of Directors (or Supervisory Council), and Executives of Credit Organisation for Bringing it into Bankruptcy [as amended by Federal Law No. 86-ФЗ, 19 June 2001]

1. In the event of the bankruptcy of a credit organisation through the fault of its founders (or participants), members of the council of directors (or supervisory council), or executives of the credit organisation who have the right to give instructions binding upon the particular credit organisation or have the possibility otherwise to determine its actions, subsidiary responsibility for obligations of the credit organisation may be placed on the said persons by a court.

The bankruptcy of a credit organisation shall be considered to have ensued through the fault of its executives who have the right to give instructions binding upon the particular credit organisation or have the possibility otherwise to determine its actions if it is established by a court that the said persons gave instructions directly or indirectly directed towards bringing the credit organisation to bankruptcy, or if it was established by a court that the said persons did not perform those actions which they were obliged in accordance with the present Federal Law to perform in order to prevent the bankruptcy of the credit organisation.

The bankruptcy of a credit organisation shall be considered to have ensued through the fault of its founders (or participants) and members of the council of directors (or supervisory council) who have the right to give instructions binding upon the particular credit organisation or have the possibility otherwise to determine its actions if it is established by a court that the said persons gave instructions directly or indirectly directed towards bringing the credit organisation to bankruptcy.

2. The founders (or participants) of a credit organisation deemed by a court to be at fault in bringing the credit organisation to bankruptcy shall not have the right for 10 years from the day of rendering of a decision by an arbitrazh court concerning the deeming of the credit organisation to be bankrupt to acquire stocks (or participatory shares) of another credit organisation comprising more than 5% of the charter capital thereof.

3. Members of the council of directors (or supervisory council) and executives of a credit organisation deemed by a court to be at fault in the bankruptcy thereof in accordance with the requirements of point 1 of the present Article shall not have the right for five years from the day of rendering of a decision by an arbitrazh court concerning the deeming of the credit organisation to be bankrupt to hold the office of executives of credit organisations.

4. The persons specified as executives of a credit organisation in the Federal Law on Banks and Banking Activity shall be deemed to be the executives of a credit organisation [as amended by Federal Law No. 86-ФЗ, 19 June 2001].

Chapter VII. Peculiarities of Deeming Credit Organisation Being Liquidated and Absent Credit Organisation to be Bankrupt

Article 51. Deeming Credit Organisation Being Liquidated to be Bankrupt

1. If the value of the property of a credit organisation with respect to which a decision has been adopted concerning liquidation is insufficient in order to satisfy the demands of creditors of the credit organisation, such credit organisation shall be liquidated in the procedure provided for by the Federal Law on Insolvency (or Bankruptcy), with the peculiarities established by the present Federal Law.

2. In the event of the discovery of the circumstance provided for by point 1 of the present Article, the right to file an application concerning the deeming of the credit organisation being liquidated to be bankrupt shall belong to creditors of the credit organisation and the Bank of Russia.

3. In the event of the discovery of the circumstance provided for by point 1 of the present Article, the liquidation commission (or liquidator) of the credit

organisation being liquidated shall be obliged to apply to the arbitrazh court with an application concerning the deeming of the credit organisation being liquidated to be bankrupt.

4. The arbitrazh court shall designate consideration of the case concerning the deeming of the credit organisation being liquidated to be bankrupt upon the application of persons specified in points 2 and 3 of the present Article not later than one month after the rendering by the arbitrazh court of a ruling concerning the acceptance of the said application.

Article 52. Bankruptcy of Absent Credit Organisation

The decision of an arbitrazh court concerning the deeming of an absent credit organisation to be bankrupt shall be sent to the Bank of Russia, and also to the empowered registering agency, which shall make an entry in the unified State register of juridical persons that the credit organisation is in the process of liquidation. The Bank of Russia within a two-week period from the day of receipt of the decision of the arbitrazh court concerning the deeming of the absent credit organisation to be bankrupt shall submit to the arbitrazh court a candidacy for bankruptcy administrator [as amended by Federal Law No. 31-ФЗ, 21 March 2002].

Chapter VIII. Concluding Provisions

Article 53. Introduction of Present Federal Law into Operation

1. To introduce the present Federal Law into operation from the day of official publication thereof, except for the provisions for which other periods of introduction into operation have been established by the present Federal Law.

2. Article 6 of the present Federal Law in the part affecting the attestation of arbitrazh administrators shall enter into force from 1 March 1999. Articles 6 and 19 of the present Federal Law in the part affecting the attestation of directors of temporary administrations, and also Article 25(2) of the present Federal Law, shall enter into force from 1 January 2000 [as amended by Federal Law No. 6-ФЗ, 2 January 2000].

3. Until 1 January 2000 the certificate of the director of a temporary administration may be issued by the Bank of Russia to a person corresponding to the requirements for the director of a credit organisation [as amended by Federal Law No. 6-ФЗ, 2 January 2000].

The provisions of Article 25(2) of the present Federal Law shall not extend to the directors of temporary administrations having the certificate of a director of temporary administration issued in accordance with the present point by the Bank of Russia before 1 January 2000 [as amended by Federal Law No. 6-ФЗ, 2 January 2000].

4. The certificate of a director of a temporary administration issued by the Bank of Russia before 1 January 2000 shall be valid for three years from the moment of the adoption of the decision concerning its issuance [as amended by Federal Law No. 6-ФЗ, 2 January 2000].

5. Article 52 of the present Federal Law shall enter into force from 1 September 1999.

Article 54. Bringing of Normative Acts into Conformity with Present Federal Law

To charge the Government of the Russian Federation and the Bank of Russia to bring their normative acts into conformity with the present Federal Law.

FEDERAL LAW ON STATE AND MUNICIPAL UNITARY ENTERPRISES

[Federal Law of 14 November 2002, No. 161-ФЗ.
СЗ РФ (2002), no. 48, item 4746]

Chapter I	General Provisions	577
Chapter II	Founding of Unitary Enterprise	581
Chapter III	Property and Charter Fund of Unitary Enterprise	584
Chapter IV	Management of Unitary Enterprise	589
Chapter V	Reorganisation and Liquidation of Unitary Enterprises	595
Chapter VI	Concluding and Transitional Provisions	599

Chapter I. General Provisions

Article 1. Relations Regulated by Present Federal Law

The present Federal Law shall determine in accordance with the Civil Code of the Russian Federation the legal status of a State unitary enterprise and municipal unitary enterprise (hereinafter—unitary enterprise), the rights and duties of owners of their property, and the procedure for the creation, reorganisation, and liquidation of a unitary enterprise.

Article 2. Unitary Enterprise

1. A commercial organisation not endowed with the right of ownership to property consolidated to it by the owner shall be deemed to be a unitary enterprise. Only State and municipal enterprises may be created in the form of unitary enterprises. Property of a unitary enterprise shall belong by right of ownership to the Russian Federation, subject of the Russian Federation, or municipal formation.

Agencies of State power of the Russian Federation or agencies of State power of a subject of the Russian Federation shall be effectuated in the name of the Russian Federation or subject of the Russian Federation within the framework of their competence established by acts determining the status of those agencies. Agencies of local self-government shall be effectuated in the name of the municipal formation the rights of owner of property of the unitary enterprise within the framework of their competence established by acts determining the status of those agencies.

Property of a unitary enterprise shall belong to it by right of economic jurisdiction or by right of operative management, shall be indivisible, and may not be distributed according to contributions (or participatory shares, shares), including among workers of the unitary enterprise.

A unitary enterprise shall not have the right to create another unitary enterprise as a juridical person by means of the transfer to it of part of its property (subsidiary enterprise).

A unitary enterprise may in its own name acquire and effectuate property and personal nonproperty rights, bear duties, and be a plaintiff and defendant in court.

A unitary enterprise must have an autonomous balance sheet.

2. The following types of unitary enterprises shall be created and operate in the Russian Federation:

unitary enterprises based on the right of economic jurisdiction—federal State enterprise and State enterprise of a subject of the Russian Federation (hereinafter also—State enterprise) and municipal enterprise;

unitary enterprises based on the right of operative management—federal treasury enterprise, treasury enterprise of a subject of the Russian Federation, and municipal enterprise (hereinafter also—treasury enterprise).

3. A unitary enterprise must have a circular seal containing its full firm name in the Russian language and indication of the location of the unitary enterprise. The seal of the unitary enterprise may also contain its firm name in the languages of the peoples of the Russian Federation and/or a foreign language.

A unitary enterprise shall have the right to have stamps and stationery with its firm name, own emblem, and also trademark registered in the established procedure and other means of individualisation.

4. The creation of unitary enterprises on the basis of the combining of property in the ownership of the Russian Federation, subjects of the Russian Federation, or municipal formations shall not be permitted.

Article 3. Legal Capacity of Unitary Enterprise

1. A unitary enterprise may have civil rights corresponding to the subject and purposes of its activity provided for in the charter of this unitary enterprise and bear duties connected with this activity.

2. A unitary enterprise shall be considered to be created as a juridical person from the day of making of the respective entry in the unified State register of juridical persons with the peculiarities established by Article 10 of the present Federal Law.

A unitary enterprise shall be created without limitation of period unless established otherwise by its charter.

A unitary enterprise shall have the right in the established procedure to open bank accounts on the territory of the Russian Federation and beyond its limits.

A State or municipal enterprise before the moment of completion of the formalisation by the owner of its property of the charter fund shall not have the right to conclude transactions not connected with the founding of the State or municipal enterprise.

3. Individual types of activity, a list of which shall be determined by a federal law, a unitary enterprise may effectuate only on the basis of a license.

Article 4. Firm Name of Unitary Enterprise and Location Thereof

1. A unitary enterprise must have a full firm name and shall have the right to have an abbreviated firm name in the Russian language. A unitary enterprise shall have the right to have also a full and/or abbreviated firm name in the languages of peoples of the Russian Federation and/or a foreign language.

The full firm name of a State or municipal enterprise in the Russian language must contain the words "federal State enterprise", "State enterprise" or "municipal enterprise" and an indication of the owner of its property—Russian Federation, subject of the Russian Federation, or municipal formation.

The full firm name of a treasury enterprise in the Russian language must contain the words "federal treasury enterprise", "treasury enterprise" or "municipal treasury enterprise" and an indication of the owner of its property—Russian Federation, subject of the Russian Federation, or municipal formation.

The firm name of a unitary enterprise in the Russian language may not contain other terms reflecting its organisational-legal form, including borrowed from foreign languages, unless provided otherwise by federal laws and other normative legal acts of the Russian Federation.

2. The location of a unitary enterprise shall be determined by the place of its State registration.

3. A unitary enterprise must have a postal address at which communication is effectuated with it and shall be obliged to inform the agency effectuating the State registration of juridical persons about a change of its postal address.

Article 5. Branches and Representations of Unitary Enterprise

1. A unitary enterprise by agreement with the owner of its property may create branches and open representations.

The creation by a unitary enterprise of branches and the opening of representations on the territory of the Russian Federation shall be effectuated in compliance with the requirements of the present Federal Law and other federal laws, and beyond the limits of the territory of the Russian Federation, also in accordance with legislation of the foreign State on whose territory the branches are created or the representations are opened of the unitary enterprise, unless provided otherwise by international treaties of the Russian Federation.

2. A branch of a unitary enterprise shall be a solitary subdivision thereof located outside the location of the unitary enterprise and effectuating all of its functions or part thereof, including the function of representation.

3. A representation of a unitary enterprise shall be a solitary subdivision thereof located outside the location of the unitary enterprise, representing the interests of the unitary enterprise, and effectuating the defence thereof.

4. A branch and representation of a unitary enterprise shall not be juridical persons and shall operate on the basis of statutes confirmed by the unitary enterprise. A branch and representation shall be endowed with property by the unitary enterprise which created it.

The executive of a branch or representation of a unitary enterprise shall be appointed by the unitary enterprise and operate on the basis of a power of attorney thereof. In the event of the termination of a labour contract with the executive of a branch or representation the power of attorney must be revoked by the unitary enterprise which issued it.

A branch and representation of a unitary enterprise shall effectuate its activity in the name of the unitary enterprise which created it. Responsibility for the activity of the branch and representation of the unitary enterprise shall be borne by the unitary enterprise which created them.

5. The charter of a unitary enterprise must contain information concerning the branches and representations thereof. A communication of information concerning changes in the charter of a unitary enterprise which concern its branches and representations shall be submitted to the agency effectuating the State registration of juridical persons. The said changes in the charter of a unitary enterprise shall enter into force for third persons from the moment of notification concerning such changes of the agency effectuating the State registration of juridical persons.

Article 6. Participation of Unitary Enterprises in Commercial and Noncommercial Organisations

1. Unitary enterprises may be participants (or members) of commercial organisations, and also noncommercial organisations in which the participation of juridical persons is permitted in accordance with a federal law.

Unitary enterprises shall not have the right to act as founders (or participants) of credit organisations.

2. A decision concerning the participation of a unitary enterprise in a commercial or noncommercial organisation may be adopted only with the consent of the owner of property of the unitary enterprise.

The disposition of a contribution (or participatory share) in the charter (or contributed) capital of an economic society or partnership, and also stocks belonging to a unitary enterprise, shall be effectuated by the unitary enterprise only with the consent of the owner of its property.

Article 7. Responsibility of Unitary Enterprise

1. A unitary enterprise shall bear responsibility for its obligations with all of the property belonging to it.

A unitary enterprise shall not bear responsibility for obligations of the owner of its property (Russian Federation, subject of the Russian Federation, and municipal formation).

2. The Russian Federation, subject of the Russian Federation, and municipal formation shall not bear responsibility for obligations of a State or municipal enterprise, except for instances when the insolvency (or bankruptcy) of such enterprise has been caused by the owner of its property. In the said instances in the event of the insufficiency of property on the owner of the State or municipal enterprise may be placed subsidiary responsibility for its obligations.

3. The Russian Federation, subjects of the Russian Federation, or municipal formations shall bear subsidiary responsibility for obligations of its treasury enterprises in the event of the insufficiency of their property.

Chapter II. Founding of Unitary Enterprise

Article 8. Founding of Unitary Enterprise

1. The Russian Federation, subject of the Russian Federation, or municipal formation may act as the founder of a unitary enterprise.

2. A decision concerning the founding of a federal State enterprise shall be adopted by the Government of the Russian Federation or federal agencies of executive power in accordance with acts determining the competence of such agencies.

A decision concerning the founding of a State enterprise of a subject of the Russian Federation or municipal enterprise shall be adopted by an empowered agency of State power of the subject of the Russian Federation or agency of local self-government in accordance with acts determining the competence of such agencies.

3. A federal treasury enterprise shall be founded by decision of the Government of the Russian Federation.

A treasury enterprise of a subject of the Russian Federation shall be founded by decision of an agency of State power of a subject of the Russian Federation to which in accordance with acts determining the status of such agency the right to adopt such decision was granted.

A municipal treasury enterprise shall be founded by decision of the agency of local self-government to which in accordance with acts determining the status of this agency the right to adopt such decision was granted.

4. A state or municipal enterprise may be created in the event of:

the necessity to use property, the privatisation of which is prohibited, including property which is necessary in order to ensure the security of the Russian Federation;

the necessity of the effectuation of activity for the purposes of resolving social tasks (including the realisation of determined goods or services at minimum prices), and also the organisation and conducting of purchasing and goods interventions in order to ensure the foodstuffs security of the State;

the necessity of effectuating activity provided for by federal laws exclusively for State unitary enterprises;

the necessity of effectuating scientific and scientific-technical activity in branches connected with ensuring the security of the Russian Federation;

the necessity of working out and manufacturing individual types of products in the sphere of interests of the Russian Federation and ensuring the security of the Russian Federation;

the necessity of the production of individual types of products removed from turnover or of limited circulability.

A treasury enterprise may be created in the event of:

the predominant or significant part of products to be produced, work to be fulfilled, or services to be rendered are intended for federal State needs, needs of a subject of the Russian Federation, or municipal formation;

the necessity of using property whose privatisation is prohibited, including property necessary in order to ensure the security of the Russian Federation, functioning of air, railway, and water transport, and realisation of other strategic interests of the Russian Federation;

the necessity of effectuating activity with regard to the production of goods, fulfillment of work, and rendering of services to be realised at prices established by the State for the purposes of resolving social tasks;

the necessity of working out and production of individual types of products ensuring the security of the Russian Federation;

the necessity of the production of individual types of products removed from turnover or of limited circulability;

the necessity of effectuating individual subsidised types of activity and conducting of loss-making production entities;

the necessity of effectuating activity provided for by federal laws exclusively for treasury enterprises.

5. A decision concerning the founding of a unitary enterprise must determine the purposes and subject of activity of the unitary enterprise.

The procedure for determining the composition of property consolidated to a unitary enterprise by right of economic jurisdiction or right of operative management, and also the procedure for confirmation of the charter of a unitary enterprise and conclusion of a contract with its executive, shall be established by the Government of the Russian Federation, empowered agencies of State power of subjects of the Russian Federation, or agencies of local self-government.

The value of property consolidated to a unitary enterprise by right of economic jurisdiction or by right of operative management during the founding thereof shall be determined in accordance with legislation on valuation activity.

Article 9. Charter of Unitary Enterprise

1. The charter thereof shall be the constitutive document of a unitary enterprise.

2. The charter of a unitary enterprise shall be confirmed by empowered State agencies of the Russian Federation, State agencies of a subject of the Russian Federation, or agencies of local self-government.

3. The charter of a unitary enterprise must contain:
the full or abbreviated firm name of the unitary enterprise;
an indication of the location of the unitary enterprise;
the purposes, subject, and types of activity of the unitary enterprise;
the information concerning the agency or agencies effectuating the powers of owner of the property of the unitary enterprise;
the name of the organ of the unitary enterprise (executive, director, general director);
the procedure for appointment to office of executive of the unitary enterprise, and also the procedure for the conclusion, change, and termination of a labour contract with him in accordance with labour legislation and other normative legal acts containing norms of labour law;
the list of funds to be created by the unitary enterprise, amounts, procedure for formation, and use of these funds;
other information provided for by the present Federal Law.

4. The charter of a State or municipal enterprise must, besides the information specified in point 3 of the present Article, contain information concerning the amount of its charter fund, procedure and sources for the formation thereof, and also the orientations of the use of profit.

5. The charter of a treasury enterprise must, besides the information specified in point 3 of the present Article, contain information concerning the distribution and use of revenues of the treasury enterprise.

6. The charter of a unitary enterprise also may contain other provisions which are not contrary to the present Federal Law and other federal laws.

7. Changes in the charter of a unitary enterprise shall be made by decision of the State agency of the Russian Federation, State agency of a subject of the Russian Federation, or agency of local self-government empowered to confirm the charter of a unitary enterprise.

Changes made in the charter of a unitary enterprise or charter of a unitary enterprise in a new version shall be subject to State registration in the procedure provided for by Article 10 of the present Federal Law for the State registration of a unitary enterprise.

Changes made in the charter of a unitary enterprise or charter of a unitary enterprise in a new version shall acquire force for third persons from the moment of their State registration, and in instances established by the present Federal Law, from the moment of notification of the agency effectuating the State registration of juridical persons.

Article 10. State Registration of Unitary Enterprise

1. A unitary enterprise shall be subject to State registration in the agency effectuating the State registration of juridical persons in the procedure established by the Federal Law on the State Registration of Juridical Persons.

2. The decision of the empowered State agency of the Russian Federation, empowered State agency of a subject of the Russian Federation, or agency of local self-government concerning the creation of the unitary enterprise, charter of the unitary enterprise, information concerning the composition and value of property consolidated to it by right of economic jurisdiction or by right of operative management shall be provided for State registration of a unitary enterprise.

Chapter III. Property and Charter Fund of Unitary Enterprise

Article 11. Property of Unitary Enterprise

1. The property of a unitary enterprise shall be formed at the expense of:
property consolidated to a unitary enterprise by right of economic jurisdiction or by right of operative management by the owner of this property;
revenues of the unitary enterprise from its activity;
other sources which are not contrary to legislation.

2. The right to property consolidated to a unitary enterprise by right of economic jurisdiction or right of operative management by the owner of this property shall arise from the moment of transfer of such property to the unitary enterprise unless provided otherwise by a federal law or established by decision of the owner concerning the transfer of property to the unitary enterprise.

The peculiarities of the effectuating of the right of economic jurisdiction or right of operative management with respect to immoveable property situated beyond the limits of the Russian Federation and being federal ownership, and also securities, participatory shares, shares in juridical persons beyond the limits of the Russian Federation, shall be established by the Government of the Russian Federation.

3. In the event of the transfer of the right of ownership to a State or municipal enterprise as a property complex to another owner of State or municipal property such enterprise shall retain the right of economic jurisdiction or right of operative management to the property belonging to it.

Article 12. Charter Fund of Unitary Enterprise

1. The minimum amount of its property guaranteeing the interests of creditors of such enterprise shall be determined by the charter fund of the State or municipal enterprise.

2. The charter fund of a State or municipal enterprise may be formed at the expense of money, and also securities, other things, property rights, and other rights having monetary value.

The amount of the charter fund of a State or municipal enterprise shall be determined in rubles.

3. The amount of the charter fund of a State enterprise must comprise not less than five thousand minimum amounts of payment for labour established by a federal law on the date of State registration of the State enterprise.

The amount of the charter fund of a municipal enterprise must comprise not less than one thousand minimum amounts of payment for labour established by a federal law on the date of State registration of the municipal enterprise.

4. Types of property may be determined by federal laws or other normative legal acts at the expense of which the charter fund of a State or municipal enterprise may not be formed.

5. A fund shall not be formed in a treasury enterprise.

Article 13. Procedure of Formation of Charter Fund

1. The charter fund of a State or municipal enterprise must be fully formed by the owner of its property within three months from the moment of State registration of such enterprise.

2. The charter fund shall be considered to be formed from the moment of crediting the respective monetary amounts in a bank account opened for these purposes and/or transfer in the established procedure to the State or municipal enterprise of other property consolidated to it by right of economic jurisdiction in full.

Article 14. Increase of Charter Fund

1. An increase of the charter fund of a State or municipal enterprise shall be permitted only after the forming thereof in full, including after the transfer to the

State or municipal enterprise of immoveable and other property intended for consolidation thereto by right of economic jurisdiction.

2. An increase of the charter fund of a State or municipal enterprise may be effectuated at the expense of property additionally transferred by the owner, and also revenues received as a result of the activity of this enterprise.

3. A decision concerning an increase of the charter fund of a State or municipal enterprise may be adopted by the owner of its property only on the basis of data confirmed by the yearly bookkeeping reporting of such enterprise for the last financial year.

The amount of the charter fund of a State or municipal enterprise, taking into account the amount of its reserve fund, may not exceed the value of the net assets of such enterprise.

4. Simultaneously with the adoption of the decision concerning an increase of the charter fund of a State or municipal enterprise the owner of its property shall adopt a decision concerning the making of the respective changes in the charter of such enterprise.

Documents for State registration of changes made in the charter of a State or municipal enterprise in connection with the increase of its charter fund, and also documents confirming an increase of the charter fund of the State or municipal enterprise, must be submitted to the agency effectuating the State registration of juridical persons.

The failure to submit the documents specified in the present point shall be grounds for a refusal of State registration of the changes made in the charter of the State or municipal enterprise.

Article 15. Decrease of Charter Fund

1. The owner of the property of a State or municipal enterprise shall have the right, and in the instances provided for by the present Article, shall be obliged to decrease the charter fund of such enterprise.

The charter fund of a State or municipal enterprise may not be decreased if as a result of such decrease the amount thereof becomes less than the minimum amount of charter fund determined in accordance with the present Federal Law.

2. If at the end of the financial year the value of net assets of a State or municipal enterprise proves to be less than the amount of its charter fund, the owner of the property of such enterprise shall be obliged to adopt a decision concerning a decrease of the amount of the charter fund of the State or municipal enterprise to the amount not exceeding the value of its net assets and to register these changes in the procedure established by the present Federal Law.

If at the end of the financial year the value of net assets of a State or municipal enterprise proves to be less than the minimum amount of the charter fund established by the present Federal Law on the date of State registration of such enterprise and within three months the value of net assets is not restored to the minimum amount of the charter fund, the owner of the property of a State or municipal enterprise must adopt a decision concerning the liquidation or reorganisation of such enterprise.

The value of net assets of a State or municipal enterprise shall be determined on the basis of bookkeeping reporting data in the procedure established by normative legal acts of the Russian Federation.

3. If in the instances provided for by the present Article the owner of the property of a State or municipal enterprise within six calendar months after the end of the financial year does not adopt a decision concerning a decrease of the charter fund, restoration of the amount of net assets to the minimum amount of a charter fund, or liquidation or reorganisation of the State or municipal enterprise, the creditors shall have the right to demand from the State or municipal enterprise the termination or performance before time of obligations and compensation of losses caused to them.

4. Within thirty days from the date of adoption of a decision concerning a decrease of its charter fund the State or municipal enterprise shall be obliged in written form to notify all creditors known to it about the decrease of its charter fund and the new amount thereof, and also to publish in a press organ in which data is published concerning the State registration of juridical persons a communication concerning the decision adopted. In so doing the creditors of the State or municipal enterprise shall have the right within thirty days from the date of sending notification concerning the decision adopted or within thirty days from the date of publication of the said communication to demand the termination or performance before time of obligations of the State or municipal enterprise and compensation of losses caused to them.

State registration of the decrease of the charter fund of a State or municipal enterprise shall be effectuated only in the event of the submission by the said enterprise of evidence of notification concerning the creditors thereof in the procedure established by the present point.

Article 16. Reserve Fund and Other Funds of Unitary Enterprise

1. A unitary enterprise shall at the expense of net profit remaining at its disposition create a reserve fund in the procedure and in the amounts which have been provided by the charter of the unitary enterprise.

Means of the reserve fund shall be used exclusively to cover losses of the unitary enterprise.

2. A unitary enterprise shall at the expense of net profit also create other funds in accordance with the list thereof and in the procedure which has been provided by the charter of the unitary enterprise.

Means credited to such funds may be used by the unitary enterprise only for the purposed determined by federal laws, other normative legal acts, and the charter of the unitary enterprise.

Article 17. Procedure for Realisation by Owner of Property of Unitary Enterprise of Right to Receive Profit from Use of Property Belonging to Unitary Enterprise

1. The owner of property of a State or municipal enterprise shall have the right to receive part of the profit from the use of property in economic jurisdiction of such enterprise.

2. A State or municipal enterprise annually shall transfer to the respective budget part of the profit remaining at its disposition after the payment of taxes and other obligatory payments in the procedure, in the amounts, and within the periods which are determined by the Government of the Russian Federation, empowered agencies of State power of subjects of the Russian Federation, or agencies of local self-government.

3. The procedure for the distribution of revenues of a treasury enterprise shall be determined by the Government of the Russian Federation, empowered agencies of State power of subjects of the Russian Federation, or agencies of local self-government.

Article 18. Disposition of Property of State or Municipal Enterprise

1. A State or municipal enterprise shall dispose of moveable property belonging to it by right of economic jurisdiction autonomously, except for instances established by the present Federal Law, other federal laws, and other normative legal acts.

2. A State or municipal enterprise shall not have the right to sell immoveable property belonging to it, lease it out, pledge, or submit it as a contribution to the charter (or contributed) capital of an economic society or partnership or by other means dispose of such property without the consent of the owner of the property of the State or municipal enterprise.

3. Moveable and immoveable property a State or municipal enterprise shall dispose of only within limits not depriving it of the possibility to effectuate activity, the purposes, subject, and types of which have been determined by the charter of such enterprise. Transactions concluded by a State or municipal enterprise with a violation of this requirement shall be null.

4. A State or municipal enterprise shall not have the right without the consent of the owner to conclude transactions connected with the granting of loans, suretyships, receipt of bank guarantees, and other encumberments, assignment of demands, transfer of debt, and also conclude contracts of simple partnership.

Types and/or the amount of other transactions, the conclusion of which may not be effectuated without the consent of the owner of the property of such enterprise, may be provided for by the charter of the State or municipal enterprise.

Article 19. Disposition of Property of Treasury Enterprise

1. A federal treasury enterprise shall have the right to alienate or by other means dispose of property belonging to it only with the consent of the Government of the Russian Federation or federal agency of executive power empowered by it.

A treasury enterprise of a subject of the Russian Federation shall have the right to alienate or by other means dispose of property belonging to it only with the consent of the empowered agency of State power of a subject of the Russian Federation.

A municipal treasury enterprise shall have the right to alienate or by other means dispose of property belonging to it only with the consent of the empowered agency of local self-government.

Types and/or an amount of other transactions, the conclusion of which may not be effectuated without the consent of the owner of property of such enterprise, may be provided for by the charter of a treasury enterprise.

A treasury enterprise autonomously shall realise the products (or work, services) produced by it unless established otherwise by federal laws or by other normative legal acts of the Russian Federation.

2. A treasury enterprise shall have the right to dispose of property belonging to it, including with the consent of the owner of such property, only within limits not depriving it of the possibility to effectuate activity, the subject and purpose of which has been determined by the charter of such enterprise. The activity of a treasury enterprise shall be effectuated in accordance with the estimate of revenues and expenses confirmed by the owner of the property of the treasury enterprise.

Chapter IV. Management of Unitary Enterprise

Article 20. Rights of Owner of Property of Unitary Enterprise

1. The owner of property of a unitary enterprise with respect to the said enterprise shall:

(1) adopt a decision concerning the creation of the unitary enterprise;

(2) determine the purpose, subject, and types of activity of the unitary enterprise, and also give consent to the participation of the unitary enterprise in associations and other amalgamations of commercial organisations;

(3) determine the procedure for the drawing up, confirmation, and establishment of the indicia of plans (or programs) of financial-economic activity of the unitary enterprise;

(4) confirm the charter of the unitary enterprise and make changes therein, including confirm the charter of the unitary enterprise in a new version;

(5) adopt a decision concerning the reorganisation or liquidation of the unitary enterprise in the procedure established by legislation, appoint the liquidation commission, and confirm the liquidation balance sheet of the unitary enterprise;

(6) form the charter fund of the State or municipal enterprise;

(7) appoint to office the executive of the unitary enterprise, conclude with him, change, and terminate a labour contract in accordance with labour legislation and other normative legal acts containing norms of labour law;

(8) agree the hiring of the chief bookkeeper of a unitary enterprise and conclude with him, change, and terminate a labour contract;

(9) confirm the bookkeeping reporting and reports of the unitary enterprise;

(10) give consent to the disposition of immoveable property, and in instances established by federal laws, other normative legal acts, or the charter of the unitary enterprise, to conclude other transactions;

(11) effectuate control over the use for designation and preservation of property belonging to the unitary enterprise;

(12) confirm the indicia of economic effectiveness of the activity of the unitary enterprise and control the fulfillment thereof;

(13) give consent to the creation of branches and opening of representations of a unitary enterprise;

(14) give consent to the participation of the unitary enterprise in other juridical persons;

(15) give consent in instances provided for by the present Federal Law to the conclusion of large-scale transactions in the conclusion of which there is an interest, and other transactions;

(16) adopt decisions concerning the conducting of auditor verifications, confirm the auditor, and determining the amount of payment of services thereof;

(17) have other rights and bear other duties determined by legislation of the Russian Federation.

2. The owner of property of a treasury enterprise shall besides the powers specified in point 1 of the present Article, have the right to:

remove from a treasury enterprise property surplus to, unused, or used not for designation;

bring to a treasury enterprise orders binding for performance for delivery of goods, fulfillment of work, and rendering of services for State or municipal needs;

confirm the estimate of revenues and expenses of the treasury enterprise.

3. The owner of property of a unitary enterprise shall have the right to have recourse to a court with suits concerning the deeming of a contested transaction with property of the unitary enterprise to be invalid, and also with a demand concerning the application of the consequences of invalidity of a null transaction in instances established by the Civil Code of the Russian Federation and the present Federal Law.

4. The owner of property of a unitary enterprise shall have the right to demand and obtain property of the unitary enterprise from another's illegal possession.

5. The powers of an owner of property of a federal treasury enterprise with regard to the creation, reorganisation, and liquidation of a federal treasury enterprise, confirmation of the charter and making of changes in the charter of such enterprise shall be effectuated by the Government of the Russian Federation.

Other powers of the owner of property of a federal treasury enterprise shall be effectuated by the Government of the Russian Federation or empowered federal agencies of executive power.

The powers of the owner of property of a unitary enterprise whose property is in the ownership may not be transferred by the Russian Federation to a subject of the Russian Federation or municipal formation.

The powers of the owner of property of a unitary enterprise of property which is in the ownership of a subject of the Russian Federation may not be transferred by a subject of the Russian Federation to the Russian Federation, other subject of the Russian Federation, or municipal formation.

The powers of the owner of property of a unitary enterprise whose property is in the ownership of a municipal formation may not be transferred by a municipal formation to the Russian Federation, subject of the Russian Federation, or other municipal formation.

Article 21. Executive of Unitary Enterprise

1. The executive of a unitary enterprise (director, general director) shall be a one-man executive organ of the unitary enterprise. The executive of a unitary enterprise shall be appointed by the owner of the property of the unitary enterprise. The executive of a unitary enterprise shall be accountable to the owner of the property of the unitary enterprise.

The executive of a unitary enterprise shall operate in the name of the unitary enterprise without a power of attorney, including represent its interests, conclude transactions in the established procedure in the name of the unitary enterprise, confirm the structure and personnel establishment of the unitary enterprise, effectuate the hiring of workers of such enterprise, conclude with them, change, and terminate labour contracts, issue orders, and issue powers of attorney in the procedure established by legislation.

The executive of a unitary enterprise shall organise the fulfillment of decisions of the owner of property of the unitary enterprise.

2. The executive of a unitary enterprise shall not have the right to be the founder (or participant) of a juridical person, hold office or engage in other paid activity in State agencies, agencies of local self-government, commercial and non-commercial organisations except teaching, scientific, and other creative activity, engage in entrepreneurial activity, be a one-man executive organ or member of a

collegial executive organ of a commercial organisation, except for instances when participation in organs of a commercial organisation is within the post duties of the particular executive, nor to take part in strikes.

The executive of a unitary enterprise shall be subject to attestation in the procedure established by the owner of the property of the unitary enterprise.

3. The executive of a unitary enterprise shall be accountable concerning the activity of the enterprise in the procedure and within the periods which are determined by the owner of the property of the unitary enterprise.

4. In instances provided for by federal laws and legal acts issued in accordance therewith advisory organs (learned, pedagogical, scientific, scientific-technical councils and others) may be formed in a unitary enterprise. The structure of such organs and their composition and competence must be determined by the charter of the unitary enterprise.

Article 22. Interest in Conclusion of Transactions by Unitary Enterprise

1. A transaction in the conclusion of which there is an interest of the executive of a unitary enterprise may not be concluded by the unitary enterprise without the consent of the owner of the property of the unitary enterprise.

The executive of a unitary enterprise shall be deemed to be interested in the conclusion of a transaction by the unitary enterprise if he, his spouse, parents, children, brothers, sisters, and/or affiliated persons thereof deemed to be such in accordance with legislation of the Russian Federation:

are a party to the transaction or act in the interests of third persons in their relations with the unitary enterprise;

possess (each individually or in aggregate) twenty or more per cent of the stocks (or participatory shares, shares) of a juridical person who is a party to the transaction or act in the interests of third persons in their relations with the unitary enterprise;

hold an office in management organs of a juridical person which is a party to the transaction or acting in the interests of third persons in their relations with a unitary enterprise;

in other instances determined by the charter of the unitary enterprise.

2. The executive of a unitary enterprise must bring to the information of the owner of property of the unitary enterprise information concerning:

juridical persons in which he, his spouse, parents, children, brothers, sisters, and/or affiliated persons thereof deemed to be such in accordance with legislation of the Russian Federation possess twenty or more per cent of the stocks (or participatory shares, shares) in aggregate;

juridical persons in which he, his spouse, parents, children, brothers, sisters, and/or affiliated persons thereof deemed to be such in accordance with legislation of the Russian Federation hold posts in the management organs;

transactions known to him to be concluded or proposed, in the conclusion of which he may be deemed to be interested.

3. A transaction in the conclusion of which there is an interest of the executive of a unitary enterprise and which is concluded with a violation of the requirements provided for by the present Article may be deemed to be invalid upon the suit of a unitary enterprise or owner of the property of a unitary enterprise.

Article 23. Large-Scale Transaction

1. A large-scale transaction shall be a transaction or several interconnected transactions connected with the acquisition, alienation, or possibility of alienation by the unitary enterprise directly or indirectly of property whose value comprises more than ten per cent of the charter fund of the unitary enterprise or more than 50 thousand times exceeds the minimum amount of payment for labour established by a federal law.

2. For the purposes of the present Article the value of property alienated by a unitary enterprise as a result of a large-scale transaction shall be determined on the basis of the bookkeeping records data thereof, and the value of property to be acquired by a unitary enterprise—on the basis of the price of the proposal of such property.

3. The decision concerning the conclusion of a large-scale transaction shall be adopted with the consent of the owner of property of the unitary enterprise.

Article 24. Borrowing by Unitary Enterprise

1. Borrowing by a unitary enterprise may be effectuated in the form of:
credits under contracts with credit organisations;
budget credits provided on the conditions and within the limits of ceilings which have been provided by budget legislation of the Russian Federation.
A State or municipal enterprise also shall have the right to effectuate borrowing by means of the placement of bonds or issuance of bills of exchange.

2. A unitary enterprise shall have the right to effectuate borrowing only by agreement with the owner of property of the unitary enterprise of the amount and orientations of the use of means attracted. The procedure for the effectuation of borrowings by a unitary enterprise shall be determined by the Government of the Russian Federation, agencies of State power of subjects of the Russian Federation, or agencies of local self-government.

Article 25. Responsibility of Executive of Unitary Enterprise

1. The executive of a unitary enterprise must when effectuating his rights and performing duties act in the interests of the unitary enterprise in good faith and reasonably.

2. The executive of a unitary enterprise shall bear in the procedure established by a law responsibility for losses caused to the unitary enterprise by his guilty actions (or failure to act), including in the event of the loss of property of the unitary enterprise.

3. The owner of property of a unitary enterprise shall have the right to present a suit concerning compensation of losses caused to the unitary enterprise against the executive of the unitary enterprise.

Article 26. Control Over Activity of Unitary Enterprise

1. Bookkeeping reporting of a unitary enterprise in instances determined by the owner of property of a unitary enterprise shall be subject to obligatory annual audit verification by an independent auditor.

2. Control over the activity of a unitary enterprise shall be effectuated by the agency effectuating the power of the owner and by other empowered agencies.

3. A unitary enterprise at the end of the reporting period shall submit to the empowered agencies of State power of the Russian Federation, agencies of State power of a subject of the Russian Federation, or agencies of local self-government bookkeeping reports and other documents, a list of which shall be determined by the Government of the Russian Federation, agencies of executive power of the Russian Federation, or agencies of local self-government.

Article 27. Public Report of Unitary Enterprise

A unitary enterprise shall be obliged to publish a report concerning its activity in the instances provided for by federal laws or other normative legal acts of the Russian Federation.

Article 28. Keeping of Documents of Unitary Enterprise

1. A unitary enterprise shall be obliged to keep the following documents:
constitutive documents of the unitary enterprise, and also changes and additions made in the constitutive documents of a unitary enterprise and registered in the established procedure;
decisions of the owner of property of the unitary enterprise concerning the creation of the unitary enterprise and confirmation of the list of property to be transferred to the unitary enterprise in economic jurisdiction or operative management, the monetary valuation of the charter fund of the State or municipal enterprise, and also other decisions connected with the creation of the unitary enterprise;
document confirming the State registration of the unitary enterprise;
documents confirming the rights of the unitary enterprise to property on its balance sheet;
internal documents of the unitary enterprise;

statutes on branches and representations of the unitary enterprise;

decisions of the owner of property of the unitary enterprise affecting the activity of the unitary enterprise;

lists of affiliated persons of the unitary enterprise;

auditor opinions and the opinions of agencies of State or municipal financial control;

other documents provided for by federal laws and other normative legal acts, charter of the unitary enterprise, internal documents of the unitary enterprise, decisions of the owner of property of the unitary enterprise, and executive of the unitary enterprise.

2. A unitary enterprise shall keep documents provided for by point 1 of the present Article at the location of its executive or in another place determined by the charter of the unitary enterprise.

3. In the event of the liquidation of the unitary enterprise the documents provided for by point 1 of the present Article shall be transferred for keeping to a State archive in the procedure established by legislation of the Russian Federation.

Chapter V. Reorganisation and Liquidation of Unitary Enterprises

Article 29. Reorganisation of Unitary Enterprise

1. A unitary enterprise may be reorganised by decision of the owner of its property in the procedure provided for by the Civil Code of the Russian Federation, present Federal Law, and other federal laws.

In instances established by a federal law the reorganisation of a unitary enterprise in the form of the division or separation thereof of one or several unitary enterprises from the composition thereof shall be effectuated on the basis of a decision of the empowered State agency or decision of a court.

2. The reorganisation of a unitary enterprise may be effectuated in the form of:

merger of two or several unitary enterprises;

accession to a unitary enterprise of one or several unitary enterprises;

division of a unitary enterprise into two or several unitary enterprises;

separation from a unitary enterprise of one or several unitary enterprises;

transformation of a unitary enterprise into a juridical person of another organisational-legal form in the instances provided for by the present Federal Law or other federal laws.

3. Unitary enterprises may be reorganised in the form of merger or accession if the property thereof belongs to one and the same owner.

4. A change of type of unitary enterprise, and also a change of the legal status of a unitary enterprise as a consequence of the transfer of the right of ownership to its property to another owner of a State or municipal property (Russian

Federation, subject of the Russian Federation, or municipal formation) shall not be a reorganisation.

In the event of a change of type of unitary enterprise, and also the transfer of property of a unitary enterprise to another owner of State or municipal property (Russian Federation, subject of the Russian Federation, or municipal formation), respective changes shall be made in the charter of the unitary enterprise.

The transfer of property shall be considered to be constituted from the moment of State registration of the changes made in the charter of the unitary enterprise.

5. Unless provided otherwise by a federal law, the property of unitary enterprises which arose as a result of a reorganisation in the form of division or separation shall belong to the same owner as the property of the reorganised unitary enterprise.

In the event of the transformation of a treasury enterprise into a State or municipal enterprise the owner of property of a treasury enterprise shall within six months bear subsidiary responsibility for obligations which passed to the State or municipal enterprise.

6. A unitary enterprise shall be considered to be reorganised, except for instances of reorganisation in the form of accession, from the moment of State registration of the juridical persons which newly arose.

In the event of the reorganisation of a unitary enterprise in the form of accession thereto of another unitary enterprise the first of them shall be considered to be reorganised from the moment of the making of an entry in the unified State register of juridical persons concerning the termination of the unitary enterprise which acceded.

7. A unitary enterprise shall not later than thirty days from the date of adoption of the decision concerning reorganisation be obliged to notify in written form all creditors of the unitary enterprise known to it, and also place in press organs in which data are published concerning the State registration of juridical persons a communication concerning such decision. In so doing the creditors of a unitary enterprise shall within thirty days from the date of sending the notice to them or within thirty days from the date of publication of the communication concerning such decision have the right in written form to demand the termination or performance before time of respective obligations of the unitary enterprise and compensation of losses to them.

8. State registration of unitary enterprises newly arisen as a result of a reorganisation and the making of an entry concerning the termination of unitary enterprises, and also the State registration of changes in and additions to the charter, shall be effectuated in the procedure established by the Federal Law on State Registration of Juridical Persons only in the event of the submission of evidence of notice of creditors in the procedure established by point 7 of the present Article.

If the separation balance sheet does not give the possibility to determine the legal successor of the reorganised unitary enterprise, the unitary enterprises newly arisen shall bear joint and several responsibility for obligations of the reorganised unitary enterprise to its creditors in proportion to the participatory share of the property (or rights) of the reorganised unitary enterprise which passed thereto determined in an expression of value.

Article 30. Merger of Unitary Enterprises

1. The creation of a new unitary enterprise with the transfer thereto of rights and duties or two or several unitary enterprises and the termination of the last shall be deemed to be the merger of unitary enterprises.

2. The owner of property of a unitary enterprise shall adopt a decision concerning confirmation of the act of transfer, charter of the unitary enterprise newly arisen, and appointment of its executive.

3. In the event of the merger of unitary enterprises the rights and duties of each of them shall pass to a newly arisen unitary enterprise in accordance with the act of transfer.

Article 31. Accession to Unitary Enterprise

1. Accession to a unitary enterprise shall be deemed to be the termination of one or several unitary enterprises with the transfer of their rights and duties to the unitary enterprise to which accession is effectuated.

2. The owner of property of a unitary enterprise shall adopt decisions concerning the confirmation of the act of transfer, making of changes in and additions to the charter of a unitary enterprise to which accession is effectuated, and, when necessary, the appointment of the executive of this unitary enterprise.

3. In the event of the accession of one or several unitary enterprises to another unitary enterprise, to the last shall pass the rights and duties of the acceding unitary enterprises in accordance with the act of transfer.

Article 32. Division of Unitary Enterprise

1. The termination of a unitary enterprise with the transfer of its rights and duties to the newly created unitary enterprises shall be deemed to be a division of the unitary enterprise.

2. The owner of property of a unitary enterprise shall adopt decisions concerning confirmation of the division balance sheet, charters of the newly unitary enterprises, and appointment of their executives.

3. In the event of the division of a unitary enterprise its rights and duties shall pass to the newly created unitary enterprises in accordance with the division balance sheet.

Article 33. Separation from Unitary Enterprise

1. The creation of one or several unitary enterprises with the transfer to each of them of part of the rights and duties of the reorganised unitary enterprise without termination of the last shall be deemed to be separation from a unitary enterprise.

2. The owner of property of a unitary enterprise shall adopt decisions concerning the confirmation of the separation balance sheet, charters of the newly created unitary enterprises, and appointment of their executives, and also the making of changes in and additions to the charter of the reorganised unitary enterprise and, when necessary, appointment of the executive thereof.

3. In the event of separation from a unitary enterprise of one or several unitary enterprises to each of them shall pass part of the rights and duties of the reorganised unitary enterprise in accordance with the division balance sheet.

Article 34. Transformation of Unitary Enterprise

A unitary enterprise may be transformed by decision of the owner of its property into a State or municipal institution. The transformation of a unitary enterprise into an organisation of another organisational-legal form shall be effectuated in accordance with legislation on privatisation.

Article 35. Liquidation of Unitary Enterprise

1. A unitary enterprise may be liquidated by decision of the owner of its property.

2. A unitary enterprise may also be liquidated by decision of the court on the grounds and in the procedure which have been established by the Civil Code of the Russian Federation and other federal laws.

3. The liquidation of a unitary enterprise shall entail the termination thereof without transfer of the rights and duties by way of legal succession to other persons.

4. In the event of the adoption of a decision concerning liquidation of a unitary enterprise the owner of its property shall appoint the liquidation commission.

From the moment of appointment of the liquidation commission to it shall pass the powers with regard to management of the affairs of the unitary enterprise. The liquidation commission shall act in court in the name of the unitary enterprise being liquidated.

5. If when conducting the liquidation of a State or municipal enterprise its inability to satisfy the demands of creditors in full is established, the executive of

such enterprise or liquidation commission must have recourse to an arbitrazh court with an application concerning the deeming of a State or municipal enterprise to be bankrupt.

6. The procedure for liquidation of a unitary enterprise shall be determined by the Civil Code of the Russian Federation, the present Federal Law, and other normative legal acts.

Chapter VI. Concluding and Transitional Provisions

Article 36. Entry into Force of Present Federal Law

The present Federal Law shall enter into force from the day of official publication thereof.

Article 37. Transitional Provisions

1. Until the bringing of laws and other normative legal acts operating on the territory of the Russian Federation into conformity with the present Federal Law, the laws and other legal acts shall be applied insofar as they are not contrary to the present Federal Law.

The charters of unitary enterprises from the day of entry into force of the present Federal Law shall apply in the part which is not contrary to the present Federal Law.

2. The charters of unitary enterprises shall be subject to being brought into conformity with the norms of the present Federal Law within the period before 1 July 2003.

3. Subsidiary enterprises created by unitary enterprises before the entry into force of the present Federal Law shall be subject to reorganisation in the form of accession to the unitary enterprises which created them within six months from the day of entry into force of the present Federal Law.

Article 38. On Bringing Normative Legal Acts into Conformity With Present Federal Law

1. To make the following changes and additions to Part One of the Civil Code of the Russian Federation (СЗ РФ (1994), no. 32, item 3301; (2002), no. 12, item 1093):

in paragraph three of Article 48(2) the words "including subsidiary enterprises" shall be deleted;

the second sentence of Article 54(1) shall be set out in the following version: "The names of noncommercial organisations, and in the instances provided for by a law the names of commercial organisations, must contain an indication of the character of activity of the juridical person";

in paragraph two of Article 113(1) the words "except for treasury enterprises" shall be added;

in Article 114:

point 4 shall be set out in the following version:

"4. The procedure for forming the charter fund of an enterprise based on the right of economic jurisdiction shall be determined by the Law on State and Municipal Unitary Enterprises";

point 7 shall be deleted;

point 8 shall be considered to be point 7;

Article 115 shall be set out in the following version:

"Article 115. Unitary Enterprise Based on Right of Operative Management

1. In the instances and in the procedure which have been provided by the Law on State and Municipal Unitary Enterprises a unitary enterprise may be created on the base of State or municipal property by right of operative management (treasury enterprise).

2. The constitutive document of a treasury enterprise shall be its charter, confirmed by the empowered State agency or agency of local self-government.

3. The firm name of a unitary enterprise based on the right of operative management must contain an indication that such enterprise is a treasury [enterprise].

4. The rights of a treasury enterprise to the property consolidated to it shall be determined in accordance with Articles 296 and 297 of the present Code and by the Law on State and Municipal Unitary Enterprises.

5. The owner of property of a treasury enterprise shall bear subsidiary responsibility for the obligations of such enterprise in the event of the insufficiency of its property.

6. A treasury enterprise may be reorganised or liquidated in accordance with the Law on State and Municipal Unitary Enterprises";

Article 300(1), after the words "right of economic jurisdiction" shall be supplemented with the words "or right of operative management".

2. The President of the Russian Federation and Government of the Russian Federation shall bring their normative legal acts into conformity with the present Federal Law.

FEDERAL LAW ON NONCOMMERCIAL ORGANISATIONS

[Federal Law No. 7-ФЗ, 12 January 1996,
as amended by Federal Law No. 174-ФЗ, 26 November 1998
Federal Law No. 149-ФЗ, 8 July 1999, Federal Law No. 31-ФЗ,
21 March 2002; and Federal Law No. 185-ФЗ, 28 December 2002.
СЗ РФ (1996), no. 3, item 145; (1998), no. 48, item 5849;
(1999), no. 28, item 3473; (2002), no. 12, item 1093; no. 52(II), item 5141]

Chapter I	General Provisions	601
Chapter II	Forms of Noncommercial Organisations	604
Chapter III	Creation, Reorganisation, and Liquidation of Noncommercial Organisation	609
Chapter IV	Activity of Noncommercial Organisation	614
Chapter V	Management of Noncommercial Organisation	617
Chapter VI	Noncommercial Organisations and Agencies of State Power	619
Chapter VII	Concluding Provisions	620

Chapter I. General Provisions

Article 1. Subject of Regulation in Domain of Operation of Present Federal Law

1. The present Federal Law shall determine the legal status, procedure for the creation, activity, reorganisation, and liquidation of noncommercial organisations as juridical persons, formation and use of property of noncommercial organisations, rights and duties of their founders (or participants), fundamental principles of management of noncommercial organisations and possible forms of support thereof by agencies of State power and agencies of local self-government.

2. The present Federal Law shall apply with respect to all noncommercial organisations created or to be created on the territory of the Russian Federation insofar as not established otherwise by the present Federal Law and other federal laws.

3. The present Federal Law shall not extend to consumer cooperatives. The activity of consumer cooperatives shall be regulated by norms of the Civil Code of the Russian Federation, laws on consumer cooperatives, other laws, and legal acts.

4. The operation of Articles 13–19, 21–23, and 28–30 of the present Federal Law shall not extend to religious organisations [added by Federal Law No. 173-ФЗ, 26 November 1998].

Article 2. Noncommercial Organisation

1. A noncommercial organisation is an organisation not having the deriving of profit as a principal purpose of its activity and not distributing the profit received among the participants.

2. Noncommercial organisations may be created in order to achieve social, philanthropic, cultural, educational, scientific, and management purposes, for the purposes of protection of the health of citizens, development of physical culture and sport, satisfaction of spiritual and other nonmaterial requirements of citizens, defence of the rights and legal interests of citizens and organisations, the settlement of disputes and conflicts, rendering legal assistance, and also for other purposes directed towards the achievement of social benefits.

3. Noncommercial organisations may be created in the form of social or religious organisations (or associations), noncommercial partnerships, institutions, autonomous noncommercial organisations, social, philanthropic, and other foundations, associations, and unions, and also in other forms provided for by federal laws.

Article 3. Legal Status of Noncommercial Organisation

1. A noncommercial organisation shall be considered to be created as a juridical person from the moment of its State registration in the procedure established by a law, having in ownership or operative management solitary property, be liable (except for institutions) for their obligations with this property, may in their own name acquire and effectuate property and nonproperty rights, bear duties, and be a plaintiff and defendant in a court.

A noncommercial organisation must have an autonomous balance sheet or estimate.

2. A noncommercial organisation shall be created without limitation of period of activity unless established otherwise by the constitutive documents of the noncommercial organisation.

3. A noncommercial organisation shall have the right in the established procedure to open accounts in banks on the territory of the Russian Federation and beyond the limits of the territory thereof.

4. A noncommercial organisation shall have seals and letterheads with its own name, and also an emblem registered in the established procedure.

Article 4. Name and Location of Noncommercial Organisation

1. A noncommercial organisation shall have a name containing a reference to its organisational-legal form and the character of activity.

A noncommercial organisation whose name has been registered in the established procedure shall have the exclusive right to the use thereof.

2. The location of a noncommercial organisation shall be determined by the place of State registration thereof [as amended by Federal Law No. 31-ФЗ, 21 March 2002].

3. The name and location of a noncommercial organisation shall be specified in its constitutive documents.

Article 5. Branches and Representations of Noncommercial Organisation

1. A noncommercial organisation may create branches and open representations on the territory of the Russian Federation in accordance with legislation of the Russian Federation.

2. A branch of a noncommercial organisation shall be the solitary subdivision thereof located outside the location of the noncommercial organisation and effectuating all of its functions or parts thereof, including the functions of a representation.

3. A representation of a noncommercial organisation shall be a solitary subdivision which is situated outside the location of the noncommercial organisation, represent the interests of the noncommercial organisation, and effectuate the defence thereof.

4. A branch and representation of a noncommercial organisation shall not be juridical persons, shall be endowed with property of the noncommercial organisation which created them, and shall operate on the basis of a Statute confirmed by it. The property of a branch or representation shall be taken into account on a separate balance sheet and on the balance sheet of the noncommercial organisation which created them.

The directors of the branch and representation shall be appointed by the noncommercial organisation and operate on the basis of a power of attorney issued by the noncommercial organisation.

5. A branch and representation shall effectuate activity in the name of the noncommercial organisation which created them. Responsibility for the activity of branch and representation thereof shall be borne by the noncommercial organisation which created them.

Chapter II. Forms of Noncommercial Organisations

Article 6. Social and Religious Organisations (or Associations)

1. Voluntary associations of citizens who have combined in the procedure established by a law on the basis of the community of their interests in order to satisfy spiritual or other nonmaterial requirements shall be deemed to be social and religious organisations (or associations).

Social and religious organisations (or associations) shall have the right to effectuate entrepreneurial activity corresponding to the purposes for the attainment of which they have been created.

2. The participants (or members) of social and religious organisations (or associations) shall not retain the rights to property transferred by them to these organisations in ownership, including membership dues. The participants (or members) of social and religious organisations (or associations) shall not be liable for obligations of the said organisations (or associations), and the said organisations (or associations) shall not be liable for obligations of their members.

3. The peculiarities of the legal status of social organisations (or associations) shall be determined by other federal laws [as amended by Federal Law No. 174-ФЗ, 26 November 1998].

4. The peculiarities of the legal status, creation, reorganisation, and liquidation of religious organisations and the management of religious organisations shall be determined by a Federal Law on religious organisations [as amended by Federal Law No. 174-ФЗ, 26 November 1998].

Article 7. Foundations

1. For the purposes of the present Federal Law, a foundation shall be deemed to be a noncommercial organisation not having membership, founded by citizens and/or juridical persons on the basis of voluntary property dues and pursuing social, philanthropic, cultural, educational, or other socially-useful purposes.

Property transferred to a foundation by its founder(s) shall be the ownership of the foundation. The founders shall not be liable for obligations of the foundation created by them, and the foundation shall not be liable for obligations of its founders.

2. A foundation shall use property for the purposes determined by the charter of the foundation. A foundation shall have the right to engage in entrepreneurial activity corresponding to these purposes and necessary in order to achieve socially-useful purposes for which the foundation was created. In order to effectuate entrepreneurial activity foundations shall have the right to create economic societies or participate in them.

A foundation shall be obliged annually to publish reports concerning the use of its property.

3. A trustee council of the foundation shall be the organ of the foundation and shall effectuate supervision over the activity of the foundation, the adoption by other organs of the foundation of decisions, and ensure the execution thereof, and use of the means of the foundation and compliance with legislation by the foundation.

The trustee council of the foundation shall effectuate its activity on social principles.

The procedure for the formation and activity of the trustee council of a foundation shall be determined by the charter of the foundation confirmed by its founders.

Article 7¹. State Corporation

1. A noncommercial organisation founded by the Russian Federation on the basis of a property contribution and created for the effectuation of social, administrative, or other socially-useful functions and not having membership shall be deemed to be a State corporation. A State corporation shall be created on the basis of a Federal Law.

Property transferred to a State corporation of the Russian Federation shall be the ownership of the State corporation.

A State corporation shall not be liable for obligations of the Russian Federation, and the Russian Federation shall not be liable for obligations of the State corporation unless provided otherwise by the Law providing for the creation of the State corporation.

2. A State corporation shall use property for the purposes determined by the Law providing for the creation of the State corporation. The State corporation may effectuate entrepreneurial activity only insofar as this serves the achievement of the purposes for which it was created and corresponding to these purposes.

A State corporation shall be obliged annually to publish reports concerning the use of its property in accordance with the Law providing for the creation of the State corporation.

3. The peculiarities of the legal status of a State corporation shall be established by the Law providing for the creation of the State corporation. Constitutive documents provided for by Article 52 of the Civil Code of the Russian Federation shall not be required in order to create a State corporation.

In the Law providing for the creation of a State corporation must be determined the name of the State corporation, the purposes of its activity, the location thereof, the procedure for the management of its activity (including the management organs of the State corporation and procedure for their formation, and the procedure for the appointment of officials of the State corporation and relieving thereof), procedure for reorganisation and liquidation of the State corporation, and the procedure for the use of the property of the State corporation in the event of the liquidation thereof.

4. The provisions of the present Federal Law shall apply to State corporations unless provided otherwise by the present Article or by the Law provided for the creation of the State corporation [Article 7–1 added by Federal Law No. 140-ФЗ, 8 July 1999]

Article 8. Noncommercial Partnerships

1. A noncommercial organisation based on membership, founded by citizens and/or juridical persons in order to assist its members in the effectuation of activity directed towards the achievement of purposes provided for by Article 2(2) of the present Federal Law shall be deemed to be a noncommercial partnership.

2. A noncommercial partnership shall have the right to effectuate entrepreneurial activity corresponding to the purposes for the achievement of which it was created.

3. Members of a noncommercial partnership shall have the right to:
participate in the management of affairs of the noncommercial partnership;
receive information concerning the activity of the noncommercial partnership in the procedure established by the constitutive documents;
at their discretion withdraw from the noncommercial partnership;
unless established otherwise by a federal law or constitutive documents of the noncommercial partnership, receive in the event of the withdrawal from the noncommercial partnership part of its property or the value of this property within the limits of the value of the property transferred by members of the noncommecial partnership to its ownership, except for membership contributions, in the procedure provided for by the constitutive documents of the noncommercial partnership;
receive in the event of the liquidation of the noncommercial partnership part of its property remaining after the settlement of accounts with creditors, or the value of this property within the limits of the value of the property transferred by members of the noncommercial partnership to its ownership, unless provided otherwise by a federal law or constitutive documents of the noncommercial partnership.

4. A member of a noncommercial partnership may be expelled therefrom by decision of the remaining members in the instances and in the procedure which have been provided for by the constitutive documents of the noncommercial partnership.
A member of a noncommercial partnership expelled therefrom shall have the right to receive the part of the property or the noncommercial partnership or

value of this property in accordance with point 3, paragraph five, of the present Article.

5. Members of a noncommercial partnership may also have other rights provided for by its constitutive documents and which are not contrary to legislation.

Article 9. Institutions

1. A noncommercial organisation created by the owner for the effectuation of management, socio-cultural, or other functions of a noncommercial character and financed fully or partially by this owner shall be deemed to be an institution.

The property of an institution shall be consolidated to it by right of operative management in accordance with the Civil Code of the Russian Federation.

The rights of the institution to the property consolidated to it shall be determined in accordance with the Civil Code of the Russian Federation.

2. An institution shall be liable for its obligations with the monetary means at its disposition. In the event of the insufficiency thereof, its owner shall bear subsidiary responsibility for obligations of the institution.

3. The peculiarities of the legal status of individual types of State and other institutions shall be determined by a law and other legal acts.

Article 10. Autonomous Noncommercial Organisation

1. An autonomous noncommercial organisation shall be deemed to be a noncommercial organisation not having membership founded by citizens and/or juridical persons on the basis of voluntary property contributions for the purposes of provision of services in the domain of education, public health, culture, science, law, physical culture, and sport and other services.

Property transferred to an autonomous noncommecial organisation by its founder(s) shall be the ownership of the autonomous noncommercial organisation. The founders of an autonomous noncommercial organisation shall not retain rights to the property transferred by them to the ownership of this organisation. The founders shall not be liable for obligations of an autonomous noncommercial organisation created by them, and it shall not be liable for the obligations of its founders.

2. An autonomous noncommercial organisation shall have the right to effectuate entrepreneurial activity corresponding to the purposes for whose achievement the said organisation was created.

3. Supervision over the activity of an autonomous noncommercial organisation shall be effectuated by its founders in the procedure provided for by its constitutive documents.

4. The founders of an autonomous noncommercial organisation may use its services only on equal conditions with other persons.

Article 11. Associations of Juridical Persons (Associations and Unions)

1. Commercial organisations may for the purposes of coordinating their entrepreneurial activity, and also of representation and defence of common property interests, by contract between them create associations in the form of associations or unions which are noncommercial organisations.

If by decision of the participants the conducting of entrepreneurial activity is placed on an association (or union), such association (or union) shall be transformed into an economic society or partnership in the procedure provided for by the Civil Code of the Russian Federation, or may create an economic society in order to effectuate entrepreneurial activity or participate in such society.

2. Noncommercial organisations may voluntarily combine into associations (or unions) of noncommercial organisations.

An association (or union) of noncommercial organisations shall be a noncommercial organisation.

3. Members of an association (or union) shall retain their autonomy and rights of a juridical person.

4. An association (or union) shall not be liable for obligations of its members. Members of an association (or union) shall bear subsidiary responsibility for obligations of this association (or union) in the amount and in the procedure provided for by its constitutive documents.

5. The name of an association (or union) must contain an indication of the principal subject of activity of members of the association (or union) with inclusion of the words 'association' or 'union'.

Article 12. Rights and Duties of Members of Associations and Unions

1. Members of an association (or union) shall have the right to use its services without compensation.

2. A member of an association (or union) shall have the right at his discretion to withdraw from the association (or union) at the end of the financial year. In this event the member of the association (or union) shall bear subsidiary responsibility for its obligations in proportion to his contribution for two years from the moment of withdrawal.

A member of an association (or union) may be expelled from it by decision of the remaining members in the instances and in the procedure which has been established by the constitutive documents of the association (or union). The rules relating to withdrawal from an association (or union) shall apply with respect to the responsibility of an expelled member of the association (or union).

3. With the consent of members of an association (or union) a new member may join. The entry of a new member in an association (or union) may be condi-

tiond by his subsidiary responsibility for obligations of the association (or union) which arose before his entry.

Chapter III. Creation, Reorganisation, and Liquidation of Noncommercial Organisation

Article 13. Creation of Noncommercial Organisation

1. A noncommercial organisation may be created as a result of the founding thereof, and also as a result of the reorganisation of an existing noncommercial organisation.

2. The creation of a noncommercial organisation as a result of the founding thereof shall be effectuated by decision of the founder(s).

Article 14. Constitutive Documents of Noncommercial Organisation

1. The constitutive documents of noncommercial organisations shall be:
the charter, confirmed by the founders (or participants) for the social organisa-tion (or association), foundation, noncommercial partnership, and autonomous noncommercial organisation [as amended by Federal Law No. 174-ФЗ, 26 November 1998];
the constitutive contract concludes by the members thereof and the charter confirmed by them for the association or union;
the decision of the owner concerning the creation of the institution and the charter confirmed by the owner for the institution.
The founders (or participants) of noncommercial partnerships, and also of autonomous noncommercial organisations, shall have the right to conclude a constitutive contract.
In the instances provided for by a law, a noncommercial organisation may oper-ate on the basis of a general statute on organisations of the given type.

2. The requirements for the constitutive documents of a noncommercial organisation shall be obligatory for execution by the noncommercial organisation itself and by its founders (or participants).

3. In the constitutive documents of a noncommercial organisation must be determined the name of the noncommercial organisation containing a reference to the character of its activity and organisational-legal form, location of the non-commercial organisation, procedure for management of activity, subject and pur-pose of activity, information concerning branches and representations, rights and duties of members, conditions and procedure for admitting members to and withdrawal from the noncommercial organisation (if the noncommercial organi-sation has membership), sources of forming the property of the noncommercial organisation, procedure for making changes in the constitutive documents of the noncommercial organisation, procedure for use of the property in the event of

liquidation of the noncommercial organisation, and other provisions provided for by the present Federal Law and other federal laws.

In the constitutive contract the founders shall be obliged to create a noncommercial organisation, determine the procedure for joint activity with regard to the creation of a noncommercial organisation, conditions for the transfer of their property to it and participation in its activity, and the conditions and procedure for the withdrawal of founders (or participants) from its membership.

The charter of a foundation also must contain the name of the foundation which includes the word 'foundation', information concerning the purposes of the foundation; indications concerning the organs of the foundation, including the trustee council, and the procedure of the forming thereof, the procedure for the appointment of officials of the foundation and the relieving thereof, the location of the foundation, and the fate of the property of the foundation in the event of its liquidation.

The constitutive documents of an association (or union) and noncommercial partnership also must contain conditions concerning the composition and competence of their management organs, procedure for adoption of decisions by them, including with regard to questions the decisions concerning which are adopted unanimously or by a qualified majority of votes, and the procedure for the distribution of property remaining after liquidation of the association (or union) or noncommercial partnership.

The constitutive documents of a noncommercial organisation may contain other provisions which are not contrary to legislation.

4. Changes in the charter of a noncommercial organisation shall be made by decision of its highest management organ, except for the charter of the foundation, which may be changed by organs of the foundation if the possibility of a change of his charter in such a procedure has been provided for by the charter of the foundation.

If retention of the charter of the foundation in unchanged form entails consequences which are impossible to foresee when founding the foundation and the possibility of changing its charter have not been provided for or the charter is not changed by competent persons, the right to make changes in accordance with the Civil Code of the Russian Federation shall belong to a court upon the application of organs of the foundation or agency empowered to effectuate supervision over the activity of the foundation.

Article 15. Founders of Noncommercial Organisation

1. Citizens and/or juridical persons may act as the founders of a noncommercial organisation, depending upon its organisational-legal forms.

2. The number of founders of a noncommercial organisation shall not be limited unless established otherwise by a federal law.

A noncommercial organisation may be founded by one person, except for instances of the founding of noncommercial partnerships, associations (or unions), and other instances provided for by a federal law.

Article 16. Reorganisation of Noncommercial Organisation

1. A noncommercial organisation may be reorganised in the procedure provided for by the Civil Code of the Russian Federation, the present Federal Law, and other federal laws.

2. The reorganisation of a noncommercial organisation may be effectuated in the form of merger, accession, separation, division, and transformation.

3. A noncommercial organisation shall be considered to be reorganised, except for instances of reorganisation in the form of accession, from the moment of State registration of the organisation(s) which newly arose.

In the event of the reorganisation of a noncommercial organisation in the form of accession to it of another organisation, the first of them shall be considered to be reorganised from the moment of the making of an entry in the unified State register of juridical persons concerning the termination of activity of the acceding organisation.

4. State registration of an organisation(s) which newly arose as a result of reorganisation and the making of an entry in the unified State register of juridical persons concerning the termination of activity of the reorganised organisation(s) shall be effectuated in the procedure established by federal laws [as amended by Federal Law No. 31-Ф3, 21 March 2002].

Article 17. Transformation of Noncommercial Organisation

1. A noncommercial partnership shall have the right to be transformed into a social organisation (or association), foundation, or autonomous noncommercial organisation, and also into an economic society in the instances and procedure established by a Federal Law (as amended by Federal Law No. 174-Ф3, 26 November 1998; and by Federal Law No. 185-Ф3, 28 December 2002.

2. An institution may be transformed into a foundation, autonomous noncommercial organisation, and economic society. The transformation of State or municipal institutions into noncommercial organisations of other forms or an economic society shall be permitted in the instances and in the procedure which has been established by a law.

3. An autonomous noncommercial organisation shall have the right to be transformed into a social organisation (or association) or into a foundation [as amended by Federal Law No. 174-Ф3, 26 November 1998].

4. An association or union shall have the right to be transformed into a foundation, autonomous noncommercial organisation, economic society, or partnership.

5. The decision concerning transformation of a noncommercial partnership shall be adopted by the founders unanimously, and of an association (or union) by all the members who concluded on the contract on the creation thereof.

The decision concerning the transformation of an institution shall be adopted by its owner.

The decision concerning the transformation of an autonomous noncommercial organisation shall be adopted by its highest management organ in accordance with the present Federal Law in the procedure provided for by the charter of the autonomous noncommercial organisation.

6. When transforming a noncommercial organisation, the rights and duties of the reorganised noncommercial organisation shall pass to the organisation which newly arose in accordance with the act of transfer.

Article 18. Liquidation of Noncommercial Organisation

1. A noncommercial organisation may be liquidated on the basis and in the procedure which has been provided by the Civil Code of the Russian Federation, the present Federal Law, and other federal laws.

2. The decision concerning the liquidation of a foundation may be adopted only by a court upon the application of the interested persons.

A foundation may be liquidated:

if the property of the foundation is insufficient for the effectuation of its purposes and the probability of receiving the necessary property is unrealistic;

if the purposes of the foundation cannot be achieved, and necessary changes of the purposes of the foundation cannot be made;

in the event of the foundation evading in its activity the purposes provided for by its charter;

in other instances provided for by a federal law.

3. The founders (or participants) of a noncommercial organisation or organ which adopted the decision concerning the liquidation of a noncommercial organisation shall appoint by a liquidation commission (or liquidator) and establish in accordance with the Civil Code of the Russian Federation and the present Federal Law the procedure and periods for liquidation of the noncommercial organisation [as amended by Federal Law No. 31-ФЗ, 21 March 2002].

4. From the moment of appointment of the liquidation commission to it shall pass the powers relating to the management of affairs of the noncommercial organisation. The liquidation commission shall act in court in the name of the noncommercial organisation being liquidated.

Article 19. Procedure for Liquidation of Noncommercial Organisation

1. A liquidation commission shall place in press organs in which data is published concerning the State registration of juridical persons a publication

concerning the liquidation of a noncommercial organisation and the procedure and period for declaring demands by creditors thereof. The period for declaring demands by creditors may not be less than two months from the day of publication concerning the liquidation of the noncommercial organisation.

2. The liquidation commission shall take measures with regard to eliciting creditors and receiving debtor indebtedness, and also inform creditors in written form about the liquidation of the noncommercial organisation.

3. Upon the end of the period for presenting demands by creditors the liquidation commission shall draw up the interim balance sheet, which shall contain information concerning the composition of the property of the noncommercial organisation being liquidated, a List of the demands presented by creditors, and also the results of the consideration thereof.

The interim liquidation balance sheet shall be confirmed by the founders (or participants) of the noncommercial organisation or agency which adopted the decision concerning its liquidation [as amended by Federal Law No. 31-v, 21 March 2002].

4. If monetary means available with the noncommercial organisation being liquidated (except for institutions) are insufficient in order to satisfy the demands of creditors, the liquidation commission shall effectuate the sale of property of the noncommercial organisation at a public sale in the procedure established for the execution of judicial decisions.

In the event of the insufficiency of monetary means with an institution being liquidated in order to satisfy the demands of creditors, the last shall have the right to apply to a court with a suit concerning satisfaction of the remaining part of the demands at the expense of the owner of this institution.

5. Payment of monetary amounts to creditors of a noncommercial organisation being liquidated shall be made by the liquidation commission in the priority established by the Civil Code of the Russian Federation in accordance with the interim liquidation balance sheet beginning from the day of confirmation thereof, except for creditors of the fifth priority, payments to whom shall be made upon the expiry of a month from the day of confirmation of the interim liquidation balance sheet.

6. After completion of the settlement of accounts with creditors a liquidation commission shall draw up the liquidation balance sheet, which shall be confirmed by the founders (or participants) of the noncommercial organisation or agency which adopted the decision concerning the liquidation of the noncommercial organisation [as amended by Federal Law No. 31-ФЗ, 21 March 2002].

Article 20. Property of Noncommercial Organisation Being Liquidated

1. In the event of the liquidation of a noncommercial organisation the property remaining after satisfaction of the demands of creditors, unless established

otherwise by the present Federal Law and other federal laws, shall be directed in accordance with the constitutive documents of the noncommercial organisation to the purposes in whose interests it was created and/or to philanthropic purposes. If use of the property of the noncommercial organisation being liquidated is not possible in accordance with its constitutive documents, it shall be applied to the revenue of the State.

2. In the event of the liquidation of a noncommercial partnership, the property remaining after satisfaction of demands of creditors shall be subject to distribution among the members of the noncommercial partnership in accordance with their property contribution, the amount of which shall not exceed the amount of their property contributions unless established otherwise by federal laws or constitutive documents of the noncommercial partnership.

The procedure for the use of property of a noncommercial partnership whose value exceeds the amount of property contributions of its members shall be determined in accordance with point 1 of the present Article.

3. The property of an institution remaining after satisfaction of the demands of creditors shall be transferred to its owner unless provided otherwise by laws and other legal acts of the Russian Federation or constitutive documents of the institution.

Article 21. Completion of Liquidation of Noncommercial Organisation

The liquidation of a noncommercial organisation shall be considered to be completed, and a noncommercial organisation to have terminated existence, after the making of the entry thereof in the unified State register of juridical persons.

Article 22. Entry Concerning Termination of Activity of Noncommercial Organisation [repealed by Federal Law No. 31-ФЗ, 21 March 2002]

Article 23. State Registration of Changes of Constitutive Documents of Noncommercial Organisation

1. State registration of changes of constitutive documents of a noncommercial organisation shall be effectuated in the procedure established by federal laws [as amended by Federal Law No. 31-ФЗ, 21 March 2002].

2. Changes of constitutive documents of a noncommercial organisation shall enter into force from the moment of their State registration.

Chapter IV. Activity of Noncommercial Organisation

Article 24. Types of Activity of Noncommercial Organisation

1. A noncommercial organisation may effectuate one type of activity or several types of activity not prohibited by legislation of the Russian Federation and

respective purposes of activity of the noncommercial organisation which have been provided for by its constitutive documents.

Limitations on types of activity which noncommercial organisations of individual types have the right to engage in may be established by legislation of the Russian Federation.

Individual types of activity may be effectuated by noncommercial organisations only on the basis of special authorisations (or licenses). A List of these types of activity shall be determined by a law.

2. A noncommercial organisation may effectuate entrepreneurial activity only insofar as this serves the achievement of the purposes for which it was created. Such activity shall be deemed to be the production of goods and services bringing profit which meets the purposes of the creation of the noncommercial organisation, and also the acquisition and realisation of securities, property and nonproperty rights, and participation in economic societies and participation in limited partnerships as a contributor.

Limitations on entrepreneurial activity of noncommercial organisations of individual types may be established by legislation of the Russian Federation.

3. A noncommercial organisation shall keep a record of revenues and expenses with regard to entrepreneurial activity.

4. In the interests of achieving the purposes provided for by the charter, a noncommercial organisation may create other noncommercial organisations and join associations and unions.

Article 25. Property of Noncommercial Organisation

1. A noncommercial organisation may have in ownership or in operative management buildings, installations, housing fund, equipment, inventory, monetary means in rubles and foreign currency, securities, and other property. A noncommercial organisation may have land plots in ownership or in use for perpetuity.

2. A noncommercial organisation shall be liable for its obligations with that of its property against which execution may be levied according to legislation of the Russian Federation.

Article 26. Sources of Forming Property of Noncommercial Organisation

1. The sources of forming the property of a noncommercial organisation in monetary and other forms shall be:
regular and one-off proceeds from the founders (or participants, members);
voluntary property contributions and donations;
receipts from the realisation of goods, work, and services;
dividends (or revenues, interest) received with regard to stocks, bonds, other securities, and deposits;

revenues received from the ownership of the noncommercial organisation; other proceeds not prohibited by a law.

Limitations on the sources of revenues of noncommercial organisations of individual types may be established by laws.

2. The procedure for regular proceeds from the founders (or participants, members) shall be determined by the constitutive documents of a noncommercial organisation.

3. Profit received by a noncommercial organisation shall not be subject to distribution among the participants (or members) of the noncommercial organisation.

Article 27. Conflict of Interests

1. For the purposes of the present Federal Law, persons interested in the performance of particular actions by a noncommercial organisation, including transactions with other organisations or citizens (hereinafter: interested persons), shall be deemed to be the director (or deputy director) of the noncommercial organisation, and also person who is a member of the management organs of the noncommercial organisation or agencies of supervision over its activity, if the said persons are in labour relations with these organisations or citizens, are participants or creditors of these organisations, or are close relatives of these citizens or are creditors of these citizens. The said organisations or citizens are suppliers of goods (or services) for a noncommercial organisation, large-scale consumers of goods (or services) produced by the noncommercial organisation, possess property which is fully or partially formed by the noncommercial organisation, or may derive advantage from the use or disposition of property of the noncommercial organisation.

Interest in the performance by a noncommercial organisation of particular actions, including the conclusion of transactions, shall entail a conflict of interests of the interested persons and the noncommercial organisation.

2. Interested persons shall be obliged to comply with the interests of the noncommercial organisation, above all with respect to the purposes of its activity, and must not use the possibilities of the noncommercial organisation or permit the use thereof for other purposes besides those provided for by the constitutive documents of the noncommercial organisation.

By the term 'possibilities of a noncommercial organisation' is understood for the purposes of the present Article property belonging to a noncommercial organisation, property and nonproperty rights, possibilities in the domain of entrepreneurial activity, and information concerning the activity and plans of the noncommercial organisation having value for it.

3. If an interested person has an interest in a transaction, a party to which is or is intended to be a noncommercial organisation, and also in the event of other

contradiction of interests of the said person and the noncommercial organisation with respect to an existing or proposed transaction:

he shall be obliged to notify his interest to the management organ of the noncommercial organisation or agency of supervision over its activity before the moment of adoption of the decision concerning conclusion of the transaction;

the transaction must be approved by the management organ of the noncommercial organisation or agency of supervision over its activity.

4. A transaction in whose conclusion there is an interest and which is concluded in violation of the requirements of the present Article may be deemed by a court to be invalid.

The interested person shall bear responsibility to the noncommercial organisation in the amount of losses caused to him to this noncommercial organisation. If the losses were caused to the noncommercial organisation by several interested persons, their responsibility to the noncommercial organisation shall be joint and several.

Chapter V. Management of Noncommercial Organisation

Article 28. Fundamental Principles of Management of Noncommercial Organisation

The structure, competence, procedure for formation, and period of powers of the management organs of a noncommercial organisation, the procedure for the adoption of decisions by them, and acting in the name of a noncommercial organisation shall be established by the constitutive documents of the noncommercial organisation in accordance with the present Law and other federal laws.

Article 29. Highest Management Organ of Noncommercial Organisation

1. The highest management organs of noncommercial organisations shall in accordance with their constitutive documents be:

the collegial highest management organ for an autonomous noncommercial organisation;

the general meeting of members for a noncommercial partnership, association (or union).

The procedure for the management of a foundation shall be determined by its charter.

The composition and competence of management organs of social organisations (or associations) shall be established in accordance with laws on their organisations (or associations) [as amended by Federal Law No. 174-ФЗ, 26 November 1998].

2. The principal function of the highest management of a noncommercial organisation shall be ensuring compliance by the noncommercial organisation with the purposes in whose interests it was created.

3. Deciding the following questions shall be relegated to the competence of the highest management organ of a noncommercial organisation:

change of the charter of the noncommercial organisation;

determination of the priority orientations of the activity of a noncommercial organisation and the principles of forming and using its property;

formation of executive organs of the noncommercial organisation and termination of their powers before time;

confirmation of the yearly report and yearly bookkeeping balance sheet;

confirmation of the financial plan of the noncommercial organisation and making of changes therein;

creation of branches and opening of representations of a noncommercial organisation;

participation in other organisations;

reorganisation and liquidation of the noncommercial organisation (except for the liquidation of a foundation).

The constitutive documents of a noncommercial organisation may provide for the creation of a permanently operating collegial management organ to whose jurisdiction may be relegated the deciding of questions provided for by paragraphs five to eight of the present point.

Questions provided for by paragraphs two to four and nine of the present point shall be relegated to the exclusive competence of the highest management organ of the noncommercial organisation.

4. The general meeting of members of a noncommercial organisation or session of the collegial highest management organ of a noncommercial organisation shall be competent if more than half of its members are present at the said meeting or session.

A decision of the said general meeting or session shall be adopted by a majority of votes of members present at the meeting or session. The decision of the general meeting or session with regard to questions of the exclusive competence of the highest management organ of a noncommercial organisation shall be adopted unanimously or by a qualified majority of votes in accordance with the present Federal Law, other federal laws, and constitutive documents.

5. For an autonomous noncommercial organisation, persons who are workers of this noncommercial organisation may not comprise more than one-third of the total number of members of the collegial highest management organ of the autonomous noncommercial organisation.

A noncommercial organisation shall not have the right to effectuate the payment of remuneration to members of its highest management organ for the fulfilment by them of functions placed on them, except for contributory compensation for expenses directly connected with participation in the work of the highest management organ.

Article 30. Executive Organ of Noncommercial Organisation

1. The executive organ of a noncommercial organisation may be collegial and/or one-man. It shall effectuate the current direction of the activity of the noncommercial organisation and shall be accountable to the highest management organ of the noncommercial organisation.

2. To the competence of the executive organ of a noncommercial organisation shall be relegated the deciding of all questions which do not comprise the exclusive competence of other management organs of the noncommercial organisation determined by the present Federal Law, other federal laws, and constitutive documents of the noncommercial organisation.

Chapter VI. Noncommercial Organisations and Agencies of State Power

Article 31. Economic Support of Noncommercial Organisations by Agencies of State Power and Agencies of Local Self-Government

1. Agencies of State power and agencies of local self-government shall create State and municipal institutions, consolidate property to them by right of operative management in accordance with the Civil Code of the Russian Federation, and effectuate the full or partial financing thereof.

Agencies of State power and agencies of local self-government may within the limits of their competence render economic support in various forms to noncommercial organisations, including:

granting of privileges in accordance with legislation with regard to the payment of taxes, customs, and other fees and payments to noncommercial organisations created for philanthropic, educational, cultural, and scientific purposes, for the purposes of protection of the health of citizens, development of physical culture and sport, other purposes established by legislation, taking into account the organisational-legal forms of noncommercial organisations;

granting other privileges to noncommercial organisations, including full or partial exemption from payment for the use of State and municipal property;

placing State and municipal social orders on a competitive basis among noncommercial organisations;

granting privileges in accordance with a law with regard to the payment of taxes to citizens and juridical persons rendering material support to noncommercial organisations.

2. The granting of privileges shall not be permitted with regard to taxes individually to individual noncommercial organisations, and also to individual citizens and juridical persons rendering material support to these noncommercial organisations.

Article 32. Control Over Activity of Noncommercial Organisation

1. A noncommercial organisation shall keep bookkeeping records and statistical reports in the procedure established by legislation of the Russian Federation.

A noncommercial organisation shall provide information concerning its activity to agencies of State statistics and tax agencies, founders, and other persons in accordance with legislation of the Russian Federation and constitutive documents of the noncommercial organisation.

2. The amounts and structure of revenues of a noncommercial organisation, and also information concerning the amounts and composition of property of the noncommercial organisation, the expenses thereof, numbers and composition of workers, payment of their labour, use of labour without compensation of citizens in the activity of the noncommercial organisation may not be the subject of commercial secrecy.

Chapter VII. Concluding Provisions

Article 33. Responsibility of Noncommercial Organisation

1. A noncommercial organisation shall in the event of a violation of the present Federal Law bear responsibility in accordance with legislation of the Russian Federation.

2. If a noncommercial organisation has performed actions which are contrary to its purposes and to the present Federal Law, warning may be rendered to the noncommercial organisation in written form by the agency effectuating State registration of juridical persons or a recommendation made by a procurator concerning the elimination of the violations.

3. In the event of the rendering by a noncommercial organisation of more than two warnings in written form or recommendations concerning elimination of the violations, the noncommercial organisation may be liquidated by decision of a court in the procedure provided for by Article 19 of the present Federal Law and by the Civil Code of the Russian Federation.

Article 34. Entry into Force of Present Federal Law

1. The present Federal Law shall enter into force from the day of its official publication.

2. To propose to the President of the Russian Federation and to charge the Government of the Russian Federation to bring their legal acts into conformity with the present Federal Law.

FEDERAL LAW ON PHILANTHROPIC ACTIVITY AND PHILANTHROPIC ORGANISATIONS

[Federal Law No. 135-ФЗ, 11 August 1995,
as amended by Federal Law No. 31-ФЗ, 21 March 2002;
and Federal Law No. 135-ФЗ, 25 July 2002.
СЗ РФ (1995), no. 33, item 3340; (2002), no. 12,
item 1093; no. 30, item 3029]

Section I	General Provisions	621
Section II	Procedure for Creation and Termination of Activity of Philanthropic Organisation	624
Section III	Conditions and Procedure for Effectuation of Activity of Philanthropic Organisation	625
Section IV	State Guarantees of Philanthropic Activity	628
Section V	Concluding Provisions	632

The present Federal Law establishes the fundamental principles for the legal regulation of philanthropic activity, determines the possible forms of support thereof by agencies of State power and agencies of local self-government, the peculiarities of the creation and activity of philanthropic organisations for the purposes of the extensive dissemination and development of philanthropic activity in the Russian Federation.

Section I. General Provisions

Article 1. Philanthropic Activity

By philanthropic activity is understood the voluntary activity of citizens and juridical persons with regard to disinterested (without compensation or on privileged conditions) transfer to citizens or juridical persons of property, including monetary means, the disinterested fulfilment of work, provision of services, and rendering of other support.

Article 2. Purposes of Philanthropic Activity

1. Philanthropic activity shall be effectuated for the purposes of:

social support and defence of citizens, including improvement of the material status of indigent, social rehabilitation of the unemployed, disabled persons, and other persons who by virtue of their physical or intellectual characteristics and other circumstances are not capable autonomously of realising their rights and legal interests;

training of the population to overcome the consequences of natural disasters, ecological, industrial, or other catastrophes, and to prevention of accidents;

rendering assistance to persons who have suffered as a result of natural calamities, ecological, industrial, or other catastrophes, social, nationality, and religious conflicts, victims of repressions, refugees, and forced resettlers;

facilitating the strengthening of peace, friendship, and amity among peoples, prevention of social, nationality, and religious conflicts;

promoting the strengthening of the prestige and role of the family in society;

promoting the defence of motherhood, childhood, and fatherhood;

promoting activity in the sphere of education, science, culture, art, enlightenment, and spiritual development of the individual;

promoting activity in the sphere of the prevention and protection of health of citizens, and also propaganda of a healthy way of life, and improvement of the moral-psychological state of citizens;

promoting activity in the sphere of physical culture and mass sport;

protection of the natural environment and defence of fauna;

protection and proper maintenance of buildings, objects, and territories having historical, cult, cultural, or nature protection significance, and burial sites.

2. The sending of monetary and other material means, rendering assistance in various forms to commercial organisations, and also support of political parties, movements, groups, and campaigns shall not be philanthropic activity.

Article 3. Legislation on Philanthropic Activity

1. Legislation on philanthropic activity shall consist of the respective provisions of the Constitution of the Russian Federation, Civil Code of the Russian Federation, present Federal Law, and federal laws and laws of subjects of the Russian Federation adopted in accordance with them.

2. Norms contained in other laws regulating philanthropic activity must not be contrary to the present Federal Law.

3. If other rules have been established by an international treaty of the Russian Federation than those which are provided for by the present Federal Law, the rules of the international treaty of the Russian Federation shall apply.

Article 4. Right to Effectuate Philanthropic Activity

1. Citizens and juridical persons shall have the right without obstruction to effectuate philanthropic activity on the basis of voluntariness and freedom of choice of the purposes thereof.

2. Citizens and juridical persons shall have the right freely to effectuate philanthropic activity individually or having combined with or without the formation of a philanthropic organisation.

3. No one shall have the right to limit the freedom of choice established by the present Federal Law of the purposes of philanthropic activity and the forms of effectuation thereof.

Article 5. Participants of Philanthropic Activity

By participants of philanthropic activity for the purposes of the present Federal Law are understood citizens and juridical persons effectuating philanthropic activity, including by means of support of existing or creation of a new philanthropic organisation, and also citizens and juridical persons in whose interests philanthropic activity is effectuated: philanthropists, volunteers, recipients.

Philanthropists—persons effectuating philanthropic donations in the forms of:

disinterested (without compensation or on privileged conditions) transfer in ownership of property, including monetary means and/or objects of intellectual property;

disinterested (without compensation or on privileged conditions) endowing of rights of possession, use, and disposition of any objects of the right of ownership;

disinterested (without compensation or on privileged conditions) of the fulfilment of work and provision of services by philanthropists-juridical persons.

Philanthropists shall have the right to determine the purposes and procedure for the use of their donations.

Volunteers—citizens effectuating philanthropic activity in the form of labour without compensation in the interests of the recipient, inclujding in the interests of a philanthropic organisation. A philanthropic organisation may pay expenses of volunteers connected with their activity in this organisation (business trip expenses, expenditures for transport, and others).

Recipients—persons receiving philanthropic donations from philanthropists and the assistance of volunteers.

Article 6. Philanthropic Organisation

1. A nongovernmental (non-State and nonmunicipal) noncommercial organisation created for the realisation of the purposes provided for by the present Federal Law by means of the effectuation of philanthropic activity in the interests of society as a whole or of individual categories of persons shall be a philanthropic organisation.

2. In the event of the revenues of a philanthropic organisation exceeding expenses, the amount of excess shall not be subject to distribution among the founders (or members) thereof, but shall be sent for realisation of the purposes for which this philanthropic organisation was created.

Article 7. Forms of Philanthropic Organisations

Philanthropic organisations shall be created in the forms of social organisations (or associations), foundations, institutions, and other forms provided for by federal laws for philanthropic organisations.

A philanthropic organisation may be created in the form of an institution if the founder thereof is a philanthropic organisation.

Section II. Procedure for Creation and Termination of Activity of Philanthropic Organisation

Article 8. Founders of Philanthropic Organisation

Natural and/or juridical persons may act as the founders of a philanthropic organisation depending upon the form thereof. Agencies of State power and agencies of local self-government, and also State and municipal unitary enterprises, and State and municipal institutions, may not act as the founders of a philanthropic organisation.

Article 9. State Registration of Philanthropic Organisation

1. The State registration of a philanthropic organisation shall be effectuated in the procedure established by federal laws.

2. A refusal of State registration of a philanthropic organisation in connection with the provision of the legal address thereof by a citizen at his place of residence shall not be permitted.

3. The decision concerning a refusal of State registration of a philanthropic organisation, and also the evasion of such registration, may be appealed in a judicial proceeding [as amended by Federal Law No. 31-ФЗ, 21 March 2002].

Article 10. Highest Management Organ of Philanthropic Organisation

1. The highest management organ of a philanthropic organisation shall be its collegial organ formed in the procedure provided for by the charter of a philanthropic organisation.

2. There shall be relegated to the competence of the highest management organ of a philanthropic organisation:
a change of the charter of the philanthropic organisation;
the formation of the executive organs of the philanthropic organisation, its control-internal audit organs, and the termination of the powers thereof before time;
the confirmation of philanthropic programmes;
the confirmation of the yearly plan, the budget of the philanthropic organisation, and the yearly report thereof;

the adoption of decisions concerning the creation of commercial and noncommercial organisations, participation in such organisations, and the opening of branches and representations;

the adoption of decisions concerning reorganisation and liquidation of a philanthropic organisation (except for a philanthropic foundation).

3. Members of the highest management organ of a philanthropic organisation shall fulfil their duties in this organ as volunteers. There may be not more than one worker of the executive organ thereof in the highest management organ of a philanthropic organisation (with or without the right of casting vote).

4. The members of the highest management organ of a philanthropic organisation and officials of a philanthropic organisation shall not have the right to hold establishment posts in the administration of commercial and noncommercial organisations, founder (or participant) of which the philanthropic organisation is.

Article 11. Reorganisation and Liquidation of Philanthropic Organisation

1. The reorganisation and liquidation of a philanthropic organisation shall be effectuated in the procedure established by a law.

2. A philanthropic organisation may not be reorganised into an economic partnership or society.

3. In the event of the liquidation of a philanthropic organisation the property thereof remaining after the satisfaction of the demands of creditors shall be used for philanthropic purposes in the procedure provided for by the charter or by decision of the liquidation commission unless the procedure for the use of the property of the philanthropic organisation has been provided for in its charter, or unless established otherwise by a federal law [as amended by Federal Law No. 112-ФЗ, 25 July 2002].

Section III. Conditions and Procedure for Effectuation of Activity of Philanthropic Organisation

Article 12. Activity of Philanthropic Organisation

1. A philanthropic organisation shall have the right to effectuate philanthropic activity directed towards achievement of the purposes for which it was created, and also philanthropic activity directed towards the achievement of the purposes provided for by the present Federal Law.

2. A philanthropic organisation shall have the right to engage in activity relating to attracting resources and conducting extra-realisation operations.

3. A philanthropic organisation shall have the right to effectuate entrepreneurial activity only in order to achieve the purposes thanks to which it was created and corresponding to these purposes.

4. In order to create the material conditions for the realisation of philanthropic purposes, a philanthropic organisation shall have the right to found economic societies. The participation of a philanthropic organisation in economic societies jointly with other persons shall not be permitted.

5. A philanthropic organisation shall not have the right to expend its means and use its property in order to support political parties, movements, groups, and campaigns.

Article 13. Branches and Representations of Philanthropic Organisation

1. A philanthropic organisation shall have the right to create branches and open representations on the territory of the Russian Federation in compliance with the requirements of legislation of the Russian Federation.

2. The creation by a Russian philanthropic organisation of branches and the opening of representations on the territories of foreign States shall be effectuated in accordance with the legislation of these States, unless provided otherwise by international treaties of the Russian Federation.

3. Branches and representations shall not be juridical persons, shall be endowed with the property of the philanthropic organisation which created them, and shall operate on the basis of Statutes confirmed by it. The property of branches and representations shall be taken into account on their individual balance sheet and on the balance sheet of the philanthropic organisation which created them.

4. The directors of branches and representations shall be appointed by the highest management organ of the philanthropic organisation and shall operate on the basis of a power of attorney issued by the philanthropic organisation.

5. Branches and representations shall effectuate activity in the name of the philanthropic organisation which created them. Responsibility for the activity of branches and representations shall be borne by the philanthropic organisation which created them.

Article 14. Associations (or Associations [assotsiatsiia] and Unions) of Philanthropic Organisations

1. Philanthropic organisations may combine into associations and unions created on a contractual basis in order to expand their possibilities in the realisation of the charter purposes.

2. An association (or association, union) of philanthropic organisations shall be a noncommercial organisation.

3. Members of the association (or association, union) of philanthropic organisations shall retain their autonomy and rights of a juridical person.

4. An association (or association, union) of philanthropic organisations shall not be liable for the obligations of its members. Members of an association (or association, union) of philanthropic organisations shall bear subsidiary responsibility for its obligations in the amount and in the procedure provided for by the constitutive documents of the association (or association, union) of philanthropic organisations.

Article 15. Sources of Forming Property of Philanthropic Organisation

The sources of forming property of a philanthropic organisation may be:
contributions of founders of the philanthropic organisation;
membership dues (for philanthropic organisations based on membership);
philanthropic donations, including those having a special-purpose character (philanthropic grants) to be granted by citizens and juridical persons in monetary for or in kind;
revenues from extra-realisation operations, including revenues from securities;
proceeds from activity relating to the attraction of resources (conducting of campaigns with regard to the attraction of philanthropists and volunteers, including the organisation of entertainment, cultural, sport, and other mass measures, conducting of campaigns relating to the collection of philanthropic donations, conducting lotteries and auctions in accordance with legislation of the Russian Federation, realisation of property and donations received from philanthropists in accordance with their wishes);
revenues from entrepreneurial activity authorised by a law;
proceeds from the federal budget, the budgets of subjects of the Russian Federation, local budgets, and extrabudgetary funds;
revenues from activity of economic societies founded by a philanthropic organisation;
labour of volunteers;
other sources not prohibited by a law.

Article 16. Property of Philanthropic Organisation

1. There may be in the ownership or other right to a thing of a philanthropic organisation: buildings, installations, equipment, monetary means, securities, informational resources, other property unless provided otherwise by federal laws, and the results of intellectual activity.

2. A philanthropic organisation may conclude with respect to property in its ownership or other right to a thing any transactions which are not contrary to legislation of the Russian Federation, the charter of this organisation, and the wishes of a philanthropist.

3. A philanthropic organisation shall not have the right to use with payment for labour of administrative-management personnel more than 20% of the

financial means expended by this organisation for the financial year. The said limitation shall not extend to payment of labour for persons participation in the realisation of the philanthropic programmes.

4. Unless established otherwise by the philanthropist or philanthropic programme, not less than 80% of a philanthropic donation in monetary form must be used for philanthropic purposes within a year from the moment of receipt by the philanthropic organisation of this donation. Philanthropic donations in kind shall be sent for philanthropic purposes within one year from the moment of receipt thereof unless established otherwise by the philanthropist or philanthropic programme.

5. The property of a philanthropic organisation may not be transferred (in the forms of sale, payment for goods, work, services, and other forms) to the founders (or members) of this organisation on conditions more advantageous to them than for other persons.

Article 17. Philanthropic Programme

1. A complex of measures confirmed by the highest management organ of a philanthropic organisation and directed towards resolving specific tasks corresponding to the charter purposes of this organisation shall be a philanthropic programme.

2. A philanthropic programme shall include an estimate of proposed proceeds and planned expenses (including payment for labour of persons participating in the realisation of the philanthropic programme) and establish stages and periods for the realisation thereof.

3. Not less than 80% of revenues received for the financial year from extra-realisation operations, proceeds from economic societies founded by the philanthropic organisation, and revenues from entrepreneurial activity authorised by a law must be used for the financing of philanthropic programmes (including expenses for their material-technical, organisational, and other provision, for the payment of labour of persons participating in the realisation of philanthropic programmes, and other expenses connected with the realisation of philanthropic programmes). In the event of the realisation of long-term philanthropic programmes the means received shall be used within the periods established by these programmes.

Section IV. State Guarantees of Philanthropic Activity

Article 18. Support of Philanthropic Activity by Agencies of State Power and Agencies of Local Self-Government

1. The defence of the rights and legal interests of citizens and juridical persons-participants of philanthropic activity shall be guaranteed and ensured.

2. Officials obstructing the realisation of the rights of citizens and juridical persons in the effectuation of philanthropic activity shall bear responsibility in accordance with legislation of the Russian Federation.

3. Agencies of State power and agencies of local self-government, in acknowledging the social significance of philanthropic activity, may render support to participants of philanthropic activity in the following forms:

granting in accordance with federal laws privileges with regard to the payment of taxes, customs and other charges and payments, and other privileges;

granting by agencies of State power of subjects of the Russian Federation and agencies of local self-government tax and other privileges within the limits of their competence;

material-technical provision and subsidising of philanthropic organisations (including full or partial exemption from payment for services rendered by State and municipal organisations, from payment for the use of State and municipal property) by decision of the respective agencies of State power and agencies of local self-government;

financing on a competitive basis of philanthropic programmes worked out by philanthropic organisations;

placement on a competitive basis of State and municipal social orders;

transfer to ownership of philanthropic organisations on a free of charge or privileged basis of State or municipal property in the process of its destatisation and privatisation effectuated in the procedure provided for by legislation.

4. For the purposes of support of philanthropic activity, effectuation of the interaction of agencies of State power, agencies of local self-government, and philanthropic organisations councils (or committees) may be created for the support of philanthropy, in the composition of which are representatives of agencies of legislative and executive power, philanthropic organisations, social organisations, and public figures. These councils (or committees) shall not possess rights of power with regard to participants of philanthropic activity, and their decisions shall have a recommendatory character.

5. The granting of tax privileges individually to separate philanthropic organisations, their founders (or members), and other participants of philanthropic activity shall be prohibited.

6. The right to tax and other privileges established by legislation a philanthropic organisation shall receive from the moment of the State registration thereof.

Article 19. Control Over Effectuation of Philanthropic Activity

1. A philanthropic organisation shall keep bookkeeping records and reports in the procedure established by legislation of the Russian Federation.

2. The agency which adopted the decision concerning State registration of a philanthropic organisation shall effectuate control over the conformity of its activity to the purposes for which it was created. A philanthropic organisation annually shall submit to the agency which adopted the decision concerning its State registration a report concerning its activity containing information concerning [as amended by Federal Law No. 31-ФЗ, 21 March 2002]:

financial-economic activity confirming compliance with the requirements of the present Federal Law for the use of property and expenditure of means of the philanthropic organisation;

personal composition of the highest management organ of the philanthropic organisation;

composition and content of philanthropic programmes of the philanthropic organisation (list and description of said programmes);

content and results of activity of philanthropic organisation;

violations of requirements of present Federal Law elicited as a result of verifications conducted by tax agencies and measures taken to eliminate them.

3. The annual report shall be submitted by the philanthropic organisation to the agency which adopted the decision concerning its State registration within the same period as the yearly report concerning financial-economic activity submitted to tax agencies [as amended by Federal Law No. 31-ФЗ, 21 March 2002].

4. The agency which adopted the decision concerning State registration of the philanthropic organisation shall ensure open access, including access to the mass media, to annual reports of the philanthropic organisation received by it [as amended by Federal Law No. 31-ФЗ, 21 March 2002].

5. A philanthropic organisation shall ensure open access, including access of the mass media, to its annual reports.

6. Means expended for the publication of the annual report and information concerning the activity of a philanthropic organisation shall be calculated as expenses for philanthropic purposes.

7. Information concerning the amounts and structure of revenues of a philanthropic organisation, and also information concerning the amounts of its property, its expenses, numbers of workers, payment for their labour, and enlisting volunteers may not constitute a commercial secret.

8. Tax agencies shall effectuate control over the sources of revenues of philanthropic organisations, the amounts of means received by them, and the payment of taxes in accordance with legislation of the Russian Federation on taxes.

Article 20. Responsibility of Philanthropic Organisation

1. In instances of a violation of the present Federal Law a philanthropic organisation shall bear responsibility in accordance with legislation of the Russian Federation.

2. In the event of the performance of actions by a philanthropic organisation which are contrary to its purposes, and also to the present Federal Law, the agency which adopted the decision to register that philanthropic organisation may send a warning to it in written form which may be appealed by the philanthropic organisation in a judicial proceeding [as amended by Federal Law No. 31-ФЗ, 21 March 2002].

3. In the event of the repeated warning of a philanthropic organisation in written form, it may be liquidated in the procedure provided for by the Civil Code of the Russian Federation.

4. All means received by a philanthropic organisation from the effectuation of entrepreneurial activity in violation of Article 12 of the present Federal Law shall be recovered to the revenue of the local budget at the location of the philanthropic organisation in the procedure determined by legislation of the Russian Federation and subject to use for philanthropic purposes in the procedure determined by municipal social defence agencies.

5. Disputes between a philanthropic organisation and citizens and juridical persons who have transferred means to it for philanthropic purposes concerning the use of these means shall be considered in a judicial proceeding.

Article 21. Effectuation of International Philanthropic Activity

1. The participants of philanthropic activity shall have the right to effectuate international philanthropic activity in the procedure established by legislation of the Russian Federation and international treaties of the Russian Federation.

2. International philanthropic activity shall be effectuated by means of participation in international philanthropic projects, participation in the work of international philanthropic organisations, interaction with foreign partners in respective spheres of philanthropic activity, and also in any other form accepted in international practice and not contrary to legislation of the Russian Federation and the norms and principles of international law.

3. A philanthropic organisation shall have the right to open accounts in institutions of banks of other States in accordance with legislation of the Russian Federation.

4. A philanthropic organisation shall have the right to receive philanthropic donations from foreign citizens, stateless persons, and also from foreign and

international organisations. Use of the said donations shall be effectuated in the procedure established by the present Federal Law.

Article 22. Philanthropic Activity of Foreign Citizens, Stateless Persons, Foreign and International Organisations on Territory of Russian Federation

Foreign citizens, stateless persons, and foreign and international organisations shall have the right to act as participants of philanthropic activity on the territory of the Russian Federation in accordance with the present Federal Law.

Section V. Concluding Provisions

Article 23. On Entry into Force of Present Federal Law

1. The present Federal Law shall enter into force from the day of official publication thereof.

2. The provisions of the present Federal Law shall extent to philanthropic organisations created before the entry into force of the present Federal Law.

3. The charters of philanthropic organisations created before the entry of the present Federal Law into force shall operate only in the part which is not contrary to the present Federal Law.

Article 24. On Re-Registration of Philanthropic Organisations Created Before Entry into Force of Present Federal Law

The charters of philanthropic organisations created before the entry of the present Federal Law into force must be brought into conformity with the present Federal Law.

The re-registration of philanthropic organisations created before the entry into force of the present Federal Law must be carried out before 1 July 1999 with exemption of such organisations from the registration fee. Philanthropic organisations who have not undergone re-registration within the said period shall be subject to liquidation in a judicial proceeding upon the demand of the registering agency.

Article 25. On Bringing Legal Acts into Conformity with Present Federal Law

To propose to the President of the Russian Federation and to charge the Government of the Russian Federation to bring their legal acts into conformity with the present Federal Law.

OBJECTS OF CIVIL RIGHTS

FEDERAL LAW ON
THE SECURITIES MARKET

[Federal Law No. 39-ФЗ, 20 March 1996,
as amended by Federal Law No. 182-ФЗ, 26 November 1998,
Federal Law No. 139-ФЗ, 8 July 1999, Federal Law
No. 121-ФЗ, 7 August 2001, and Federal Law No. 185-ФЗ,
28 December 2002. СЗ РФ (1996), no. 17,
item 1918; (1998), no. 48, item 5857 (1999), no. 28,
item 3472; (2001), no. 33(I), item 3424;
(2002), no. 52(II), item 5141]

Section I	General Provisions	634
Chapter 1	Relations Determined by Present Federal Law	634
Section II	Professional Participants of Securities Market	636
Chapter 2	Types of Professional Activity on Securities Market	636
Chapter 3	Stock Market	649
Section III	On Emission Securities	652
Chapter 4	Basic Provisions on Emission Securities	652
Chapter 5	Emission of Securities	658
Chapter 6	Circulation of Emission Securities	677
Section IV	Informational Provision of Securities Market	679
Chapter 7	On Disclosure of Information on Securities	679
Chapter 8	On Use of Employment Information on Securities Market	682
Chapter 9	On Advertising on the Securities Market	682
Section V	Regulation of Securities Market	684
Chapter 10	Foundations of Regulation of Securities Market	684
Chapter 11	Regulation of Activity of Professional Participants of Securities Market	685
Chapter 12	Federal Agency of Executive Power for Securities Market	685
Chapter 13	Self-Regulating Organisations of Professional Participants of the Securities Market	695
Section VI	Concluding Provisions	699

Section I. General Provisions

Chapter 1. Relations Determined by Present Federal Law

Article 1. Subject of Regulation of Present Federal Law

Relations which arise during the emission and circulation of emission securities, irrespective of the type of emitent, when circulating other securities in instances provided for by federal laws, and also the peculiarities of the creation and activity of professional participants of the securities market, shall be regulated by the present Federal Law [as amended by Federal Law No. 185-ФЗ, 28 December 2002].

Article 2. Basic Terms Used in Present Federal Law

Emission security: any security, including paperless, which is characterized simultaneously by the following indicia:

—consolidates the aggregate of property and nonproperty rights subject to certification, assignment, and unconditional effectuation in compliance with the forms and procedure established by the present Federal Law;

—is placed by issues;

—has an equal amount and periods for the effectuation of rights within a single issue irrespective of the time of acquisition of the security.

Stock: emission security consolidating the rights of its possessor (stockholder) to receive part of the profit of a joint-stock society in the form of dividends, to participation in the management of the joint-stock society, and to part of the property remaining after the liquidation thereof. A stock shall be an inscribed security [as amended by Federal Law No. 185-ФЗ, 28 December 2002].

Bond: an emission security consolidating the right of the possessor thereof to receive from the emitent of the bond within the period provided for by it the par value or other property equivalent. A bond may also provide for the right of the possessor thereof to receive interest fixed therein on the par value of the bond or other property rights. Interest and/or a discount shall be revenue with regard to the bond [as amended by Federal Law No. 185-ФЗ, 28 December 2002].

Option of emitent: an emission security consolidating the right of the possessor to purchase within the period provided therein and/or in the event of the ensuing of circumstances specified therein of a determined quantity of stocks of the emitent of such option at the price determined in the option of the emitent. An option of an emitent shall be an inscribed security. The adoption of the decision concerning the placement of options of an emitent and the placement thereof shall be effectuated in accordance with the rules established by federal laws for the placement of securities convertible into stocks. In so doing the price of the placement of stocks in performance of the requirements with regard to options of an emitent shall be determined in accordance with the price determined in such option [added by Federal Law No. 185-ФЗ, 28 December 2002].

Issue of emission securities: aggregate of all securities of one emitent granting an identical volume of rights to possessors thereof and having identical par value in instances when the presence of par value has been provided by legislation of the Russian Federation. A single State registration number which shall extend to all securities of the particular issue shall be conferred on an issue of emission securities [as amended by Federal Law No. 185-ФЗ, 28 December 2002].

Additional issue of emission securities: aggregate of securities placed additionally to the securities previously placed of the same issue of emission securities. Securities of an additional issue shall be placed on identical conditions [added by Federal Law No. 185-ФЗ, 28 December 2002].

Emitent: juridical person or agencies of executive power or agencies of local self-government bearing in its name obligations to possessors of securities with regard to the effectuation of the rights consolidated by them.

Inscribed emission securities: securities, information concerning the possessors of which must be accessible to the emitent in the form of a register of possessors of securities, the transfer of the rights to which and the effectuation of the rights consolidated by them requires obligatory identification of the possessor.

Emission bearer securities: securities, the transfer of the rights to which and the effectuation of the rights consolidated by them shall not require identification of the possessor.

Documentary form of emission securities: form of emission securities under which the possessor is established on the basis of the presentation of a duly formalized certificate of the security or, in the event of the deposit of such, on the basis of an entry relating to the deposit account.

Paperless form of emission securities: form of emission securities under which the possessor is established on the basis of an entry in the system of keeping the register of possessors of securities or, in the event of the deposit of securities, on the basis of an entry relating to the deposit account.

Decision concerning issue of securities: document containing data sufficient to establish the volume of rights consolidated by the security [as amended by Federal Law No. 185-ФЗ, 28 December 2002].

Certificate of emission security: document to be issued by emitent and certifying the aggregate of rights to the quantity of securities specified in the certificate. The possessor of securities shall have the right to demand from the emitent the performance of its obligations on the basis of such certificate.

Possessor: person to whom securities belong by right of ownership or other right to a thing.

Circulation of securities: conclusion of civil-law transactions entailing the transfer of the rights of ownership to securities.

Placement of emission securities: alienation of emission securities by emitent to primary possessors by means of conclusion of civil-law transactions.

Emission of securities: sequence of actions of emitent established by present Federal Law with regard to placement of emission securities.

Professional participants of securities market: juridical persons which effectuate the types of activity specified in Chapter 2 of the present Federal Law [as amended by Federal Law No. 185-ФЗ, 28 December 2002].

Financial consultant on securities market: juridical person having a license for the effectuation of broker and/or dealer activity on the securities market rendering services to an emitent with regard to the preparation of a securities prospectus [added by Federal Law No. 185-ФЗ, 28 December 2002].

Good-faith acquirer: person who has acquired securities, paid them up, and at the moment of acquisition did not know and could not know abut the rights of third persons to such securities, unless it is proved otherwise.

State registration number: figure (or letter, symbolic) code which identifies a specific issue of emission securities.

Public placement of securities: placement of securities by means of an open subscription, including the placement of securities for public sale of stock exchanges and/or other organizers of trade on the securities market [added by Federal Law No. 185-ФЗ, 28 December 2002].

Public circulation of securities: circulation of securities for public sale of stock exchanges and/or other organisers of trade on the securities market and circulation of securities by means of proposing securities to an indeterminate group of persons, including with the use of advertisment [added by Federal Law No. 185-ФЗ, 28 December 2002].

Listing: inclusion of securities on a quoted list [added by Federal Law No. 185-ФЗ, 28 December 2002].

Delisting: exclusion of securities from a quoted list [added by Federal Law No. 185-ФЗ, 28 December 2002].

Section II. Professional Participants of Securities Market

Chapter 2. Types of Professional Activity on Securities Market

Article 3. Broker Activity

1. Activity with regard to the conclusion of civil-law securities transactions in the name of and at the expense of a client (including the emitent of emission securities in the event of the placement thereof) or in one's own name and at the expense of a client on the basic of compensated contracts with a client, shall be deemed to be broker activity [as amended by Federal Law No. 185-ФЗ, 28 December 2002].

A professional participant of the securites market effectuating broker activity shall be named a broker [as amended by Federal Law No. 185-ФЗ, 28 December 2002].

In the event of the rendering of services by a broker with regard to the placement of emission securities, the broker shall have the right to acquire at his own expense securities not placed within the period provided for by the contract [added by Federal Law No. 185-ФЗ, 28 December 2002].

2. A broker must fulfil the commissions of clients in good faith and in the order of receiving them. Transactions to be effectuated on behalf of clients shall in all instances be subject to priority execution in comparison with dealer operations of the broker himself when he combines the activity of broker and dealer [as amended by Federal Law No. 185-ФЗ, 28 December 2002].

If a conflict of interests of a broker and his client, of which the client was not informed before receipt by the broker of the respective commission led to causing losses to the client, the broker shall be obliged to compensate them in the procedure established by civil legislation of the Russian Federation [as amended by Federal Law No. 185-ФЗ, 28 December 2002].

3. Monetary means of clients transferred by them to a broker for investing in securities, and also monetary means received under transactions concluded by the broker on the basis of contracts with clients, must be in a separate bank account(s) opened by the broker in a credit organisation (special broker account). A broker shall be obliged to keep a record of the monetary means of each client in a special broker account(s) and shall be accountable to the client. Execution may not be levied for obligations of the broker against monetary means of clients in a special broker account(s). A broker shall not have the right to deposit own monetary means in a special broker account(s), except for instances of the return thereof to a client and/or provision of a loan to a client in the procedure established by the present Article [added by Federal Law No. 185-ФЗ, 28 December 2002].

A broker shall have the right to use monetary means in his interests which are in a special broker account(s) if this has been provided for by a contract concerning broker servicing, guaranteeing to the client the execution of his commissions at the expense of the said monetary means or the return thereof at the demand of the client. Monetary means of clients who have granted the right to the use thereof to a broker in his interests must be in a special broker account(s) separate from the special broker account(s) in which the monetary means of clients are situated who have not granted such right to the broker. Monetary means of clients who have granted to a broker the right to the use thereof may be credited by the broker to his own bank account [added by Federal Law No. 185-ФЗ, 28 December 2002].

The requirements of the present point shall not extend to credit organisations [added by Federal Law No. 185-ФЗ, 28 December 2002].

4. A brok er shall have the right to provide a loan of monetary means to a client and/or securities for the conclusion of purchase-sale securities transactions on condition of the provision by the client of security by the means provided for by the present point. Transactions concluded with the use of monetary means and/or

securities transferred by a broker on loan shall be called margin transactions [added by Federal Law No. 185-Ф3, 28 December 2002].

The conditions of a contract of loan, including the amount of the loan or procedure for determination thereof, may be determined by a contract on broker servicing. In so doing the document certifying the transfer of a determined monetary amount on loan or determined quantity of securities shall be deemed to be the report of the broker concerning margin transactions concluded or another document determined by the conditions of the contract [added by Federal Law No. 185-Ф3, 28 December 2002].

A broker shall have the right to recover interest from a client for the loans provided. A broker shall have the right to accept as security for obligations of a client with regard to loans provided only securities belonging to the client and/or acquired by the broker for the client under margin transactions [added by Federal Law No. 185-Ф3, 28 December 2002].

The amount of security provided by a client shall be determined by the broker at the market cost of securities acting as security which has formed in public sales of a stock exchange and/or other organisers of trade on the securities market, deducting the discount established by the contract. Securities acting as security for the obligations of a client with regard to loans provided by a broker shall be subject to re-valuation [added by Federal Law No. 185-Ф3, 28 December 2002].

In instances of the failure to return the amount of the loan and/or securities engaged within the period, the failure to pay interest within the period under the loan provided, and also if the amount of security becomes less than the amount of loan provided to the client (market value of securities engaged which has formed in public sales of a stock exchange, and/or other organisers of trade on the securities market), the broker shall levy execution against monetary means and/or securities acting as security of obligations of the client for loans provided by the broker in an extra-judicial procedure by means of the realisation of such securities in public sales of a stock exchange and/or other organisers of trade on the securities market [added by Federal Law No. 185-Ф3, 28 December 2002].

Only liquid securities included in a quoted list of organisers of trade on the securities market may be accepted as security for obligations of a client with regard to loans provided by a broker. The criteria of liquidity of the said securities accepted by a broker as security and the procedure and conditions of re-valuation thereof, and also requirements for periods and the procedure and conditions of the realisation of securities acting as security for the obligations of a client with regard to loans provided by a broker, shall be established by normative legal acts of the federal agency of executive power for securities [added by Federal Law No. 185-Ф3, 28 December 2002].

Article 4. Dealer Activity

The conclusion of purchase-sale securities transactions in his own name and for his own account by means of the public announcement of the prices of purchase and/or sale of determined securities with the obligation of purchase and/or sale of these securities at the prices declared by the person effectuating such activity shall be deemed to be dealer activity.

A professional participant of the securities market effectuating dealer activity shall be named a dealer. Only a juridical person which is a commercial organisation may be a dealer.

Besides prices, a dealer shall have the right to announce other material conditions of the contract of purchase-sale of securities: the minimum and maximum quantity of securities to be purchased and/or sold, and also the period during which the announced prices operate. In the absence in the announcement of an indication of other material conditions the dealer shall be obliged to conclude a contract on the material conditions offered by his client. In the event the dealer evades the conclusion of the contract, a suit may be brought against him concerning the compulsory conclusion of such contract and/or compensation of the losses caused to the client.

Article 5. Activity Relating to Management of Securities

For the purpose of the present Federal Law activity relating to the management of securities shall be deemed to be the effectuation by a juridical person in its own name for remuneration during a determined period which are transferred to it in possession and which belong to another person in the interests of this person or of third persons specified by this person the trust management of [as amended by Federal Law No. 185-ФЗ, 28 December 2002]:

—securities;

—monetary means intended for investing in securities;

—monetary means and securities received in the process of management of the securities.

A professional participant of the securities market effectuating activity relating to the management of securities shall be named a manager.

The presence of a license for the effectuation of activity relating to the management of securities shall not be required if trust management is connected only with the management of rights with regard to securities [added by Federal Law No. 185-ФЗ, 28 December 2002];

The procedure for the effectuation of activity relating to the management of securities and the rights and duties of the manager shall be determined by legislation of the Russian Federation and by contracts.

The manager when effectuating his activity shall be obliged to specify that he is acting as a manager.

If a conflict of interests of the manager and his client or of various clients of one manager, of which all the parties were not informed beforehand, had led to actions of the manager which inflicted damage on the interests of the client, the manager shall be obliged on his own account to compensate the losses in the procedure established by civil legislation.

Article 6. Activity Relating to Determination of Mutual Obligations (Clearing)

Clearing activity is activity relating to the determination of mutual obligations (collection, verification, and adjustment of information relating to securities transactions and the preparation of bookkeeping doucments regarding them) and the set-off thereof with regard to deliveries of securities and settlements of accounts regarding them.

Organisations effectuating clearing with regard to securities in connection with the settlement of accounts regarding securities operations shall accept for execution bookkeeping documents prepared when determining mutual obligations on the basis of their contracts with participants of the securities market for which the settlement of accounts is made.

A clearing organisation effectuating the settlement of accounts with regard to securities transactions shall be obliged to form special funds in order to reduce the risks of the failure to perform securities transactions. The minimum amount of special funds of clearing organisations shall be established by the federal agency of executive power for the securities market by agreement with the Central Bank of the Russian Federation [as amended by Federal Law No. 185-ФЗ, 28 December 2002].

A clearing organisation shall be obliged to confirm rules for the effectuation of clearing activity [added by Federal Law No. 185-ФЗ, 28 December 2002].

A clearing organisation shall be obliged to register the rules for the effectuation of clearing activity, and also changes in and additions thereto, at the federal agency of executive power for the securities market [added by Federal Law No. 185-ФЗ, 28 December 2002].

Article 7. Depositary Activity

The rendering of services relating to the keeping of securities certificates and/or the recording and transfer of the rights to securities shall be deemed to be depositary activity.

A professional participant of the securities market effectuating depositary activity shall be named a depositary. Only a juridical person may be a depositary.

A person enjoying the services of a depositary with regard to keeping securities and/or recording rights to securities shall be named the depositor.

A contract between the depositary and the depositor regulating their relations in the process of depositary activity shall be named a depositary contract (or contract on deposit account). The depositary contract must be concluded in written form. The depositary shall be obliged to confirm the conditions of the effectuation of depositary activity by him, which shall be an integral constituent part of the depositary contract concluded.

The conclusion of a depositary contract shall not entail the transfer to the depositary of the right of ownership to securities of the depositor. Depositaries shall not have the right to dispose of securities of the depositor, to manage them, or to effectuate in the name of the depositor any actions with securities except those to be effectuated on behalf of the depositor in instances provided for by the depositary contract. Depositaries shall not have the right to condition the conclusion of a depositary contract upon the waiver by the depositor of any one of the rights consolidated by the securities. Depositaries shall bear civil-law responsibility for the preservation of securities certificates deposited with them.

Execution may not be levied with regard to obligations of a depositary on securities of the depositors.

Depositaries shall have the right on the basis of agreements with other depositaries to involve them in the performance of their duties relating to keeping securities certificates and/or recording rights of depositors to securities (that is, to become the depositor of another depositary or to accept another depositary as depositor), unless this is expressly prohibited by the depositary contract.

If the depositor of one depositary is another depositary, then the deposit contract between them must provide for a procedure to receive information in the instances provided for by legislation of the Russian Federation concerning the possessors of securities, the recording of which is conducted in the depositary-depositor, and also in its depositaries-depositors.

The depositary contract must contain the following material conditions:

—an unequivocal determination of the subject of the contract: the granting of services relating to keeping securities certificates and/or recording the rights to securities;

—the procedure for the transfer by the depositor to the depositary of information concerning the disposition of securities of the depositor deposited in the depositary;

—the period of operation of the contract;

—the amount and procedure for paying for the services of the depositary provided by the contract;

—the form and periodicity of a report of the depositary to the depositor;

—the duties of the depositary.

There shall be within the duties of the depositary:

—the registration of facts of encumberment of securities of the depositor with obligations;

—the conducting of a deposit of the depositor separately from other account, specifying the date and grounds for each operation relating to the account;

—the transfer to the depositor of all information concerning the securities received by the depositary from the emitent or holder of the register of possessors of securities.

Depositaries shall have the right to be registered in the system of conducting the register of possessors of securities or with another depositary as a nominee holder in accordance with the depositary contract.

Depositaries shall bear responsibility for the failure to perform or the improper performance of its duties with regard to recording the rights to securities, including for the completeness and correctness of the entries relating to deposit accounts.

Depositaries shall in accordance with a depositary contract have the right to receive revenues in their account relating to securities which are being kept for the purpose of crediting to the accounts of depositors.

Article 8. Activity Relating to Conducting Register of Possessors of Securities

1. The collection, fixation, processing, keeping, and provision of data constituting the system of conducting the register of possessors of securities shall be deemed to be activity relating to the conducting of the register of possessors of securities.

Only juridical persons shall have the right to engage in activity relating to the conducting of the register of possessors of securities.

Persons effectuating activity relating to conducting the register of possessors of securities shall be called holders of the register (registrars).

A juridical person effectuating activity relating to conducting the register of possessors of securities shall not have the right to effectuate transactions with securities registered in the system of conducting the register of possessors of securities of an emitent.

The system of conducting the register of possessors of securities is understood to be the aggregate of data fixed on a paper bearer and/or with the use of electronic databases ensuring the identification of nominee holders and possessors of securities registered in the system of conducting the register of possessors of securities and recording their rights with respect to securities registered in their name enabling them to receive and send information to the said persons and to compile the register of possessors of securities.

The system of conducting the register of possessors of securities must ensure the collection and keeping during the periods established by legislation of the Russian Federation of information concerning all facts and documents entailing the necessity to make changes in the system of conducting the register of possessors of securities and all actions of the holder of the register relating to making these changes.

A system for conducting the register of possessors of securities shall not be conducted for bearer securities.

The register of possessors of securities (hereinafter: register) is part of the system of conducting the register, representing a list of registered possessors with an indication of the quantity, par value, and categories of inscribed securities belonging to them drawn up as of any established date and enabling these possessors and the quantity and category of securities belonging to them to be identified.

The possessors and nominee holders of securities shall be obliged to comply with the rules for the submission of information to the system of conducting the register.

The holder of the register may be the emitent or professional participant of the securities market effectuating activity relating to conducting the register on the basis of a commission of the emitent. If the number of possessors exceeds 500, the holder of the register must be an independent specialized organisation which is a professional participant of the securities market and effectuating activity relating to conducting the register. The registrar shall have the right to delegate part of his functions with regard to the collection of information to be entered in the system for conducting the register to other registrars. The transfer of functions shall not relieve the registrar form responsibility to the emitent.

A contract for conducting the register shall be concluded only with one juridical person. The registrar may conduct the registers of possessors of securities of an unlimited number of emitents.

2. The nominee holder of securities is a person registered in the system of conducting the register, including the depositor of a depositary and who is not the possessor with respect to these securities.

Professional participants of the securities market may act as nominee holders of securities. Depositaries may be registered as a nominee holder of securities in accordance with the depositary contract. A broker may be registered as a nominee holder of securities in accordance with the contract on the basis of which he services a client.

A nominee holder of securities may effectuate the rights consolidated by the security only in the event of receiving the respective power from the possessor.

Data concerning a nominee holder of securities shall be subject to entry in the system of conducting the register by the holder of the register on behalf of the possessor or nominee holder of securities if the last persons have been registered in this system for conducting the register.

The entry of the name of a nominee holder of securities in the system of conducting the register, and also the re-registration of securities in the name of a nominee holder, shall not entail the transfer of the right of ownership and/or other right to a thing to securities to the last. Securities of clients of a nominee holder of securities shall not be subject to levy to the benefit of creditors of the last.

Securities operations between the possessors of securities of one nominee holder of securities shall not be reflected with the holder of the register or depositary of which he is a client.

The nominee holder with respect to inscribed securities of which he is the holder shall be obliged in the interests of the other person to:

—perform all necessary actions directed towards ensuring the receipt by this person of all payments which are due to him with regard to these securities;

—effectuate transactions and securities operations exclusively on behalf of the person in whose interests he is a nominee holder of securities and in accordance with the contract concluded with this person;

—effectuate the recording of securities which he holds in the interests of other persons on separate balanced accounts and permanently has in separate balanced accounts a sufficient quantity of securities for the purpose of satisfying the demands of persons in whose interests he holds these securities.

A nominee holder of securities shall at the demand of the possessor be obliged to ensure the making of an entry in the system of conducting the register concerning the transfer of securities in the name of the possessor.

In order for possessors to effectuate the rights consolidated by securities the holder of a register shall have the right to demand from the nominee holder of the securities the granting of a list of possessors for whom he is a nominee holder as of a determined date. The nominee holder of securities shall be obliged to draw up the list demanded and to send it to the holder of the register within seven days after receipt of the demand. If the list demanded is necessary in order to draw up the register, then the nominee holder of securities shall not receive remuneration for drawing up this list.

The nominee holder of securities shall bear responsibility for the refusal to grant the said lists to the holder of the register to his clients, the holder of the register and the emitent in accordance with legislation of the Russian Federation.

3. The emitent who has charged the conducting the system for conducting the register to the registrar may once a year demand from the last the granting of the register for remuneration not exceeding the expenditures for the drawing up thereof, and the registrar shall be obliged to grant the register for such remuneration. In remaining instances the amount of remuneration shall be determined by the contract of the emitent and the registrar.

The holder of the register shall have the right to recover payment from the parties to a transaction corresponding to the quantity of dispositions concerning the transfer of securities and identical for all juridical and natural persons. The holder of the register shall not have the right to recover payment from the parties to a transaction in the form of interest on the volume of the transaction.

The procedure for determining the maximum amount of payment for services of the holder of the register with regard to inserting data in the register and issuing extracts from the register shall be determined by the federal agency of executive power for the securities market [as amended by Federal Law No. 185-ФЗ, 28 December 2002].

A suit concerning compensation for damage (including lost advantage) which arose from the impossibility to effectuate the rights consolidated by securities may be brought against the person who permitted the improper performance of the procedure for maintenance of the system of conducting and drawing up the register and a violation of the forms of report (against the emitent, registrar, depositary, possessor).

The holder of the register shall be obliged upon the demand of the possessor or of the person acting in his name, and also the nominee holder of securities, to grant an extract from the system of conducting the register with regard to his personal account within five working days. The possessor of securities shall not have the right to demand inclusion in the extract from the system of conducting the register information not relevant to him, including information concerning other possessors of securities and the quantity of securities belonging to them.

A document issued by the holder of the register specifying the possessor of the personal account, quantity of securities of each issue included in this account at the moment of the issuance of the extract, facts of the encumberment thereof by obligations, and also other information relevant to these securities, shall be an extract from the system of conducting the register.

An extract from the system of conducting the register must contain a notation concerning all limitations or facts of encumberment with obligations of securities for which the extract is issued fixed on the date of drawing up in the system of conducting the register.

Extracts from the system of conducting the register formalized when placing securities shall be issued to possessors free of charge.

The person who issued the said extract shall bear responsibility for the completeness and reliability of the information contained therein.

The rights and duties of the holder of the register, the procedure for the effectuation of activity with regard to conducting the register shall be determined by prevailing legislation and by the contract concluded between the registrar and the emitent.

There shall be within the duties of the holder of the register:

—to open for each possessor expressing the wish to be registered with the holder of the register, and also for the nominee holder of securities, a personal account in the system of conducting the register on the basis of notification concerning the assignment of a demand or instruction concerning the transfer of securities, and when placing emission securities, on the basis of a notification of the seller of the securities;

—insert in the system of conducting the register all necessary changes and additions;

—perform operations in personal accounts of possessors and nominee holders of securities only on their behalf;

—bring to registered persons information granted by the emitent;

—grant to possessors and nominee holders of securities registered in the system of conducting the register who possess more than 1% of the voting stocks of the emitent data from the register concerning the names of the possesors registered in the register and the quantity, categories, and par value of the securities belonging to them;

—inform the possessors and nominee holders of securities registered in the system of conducting the register about the rights consolidated by the securities and on the means and procedure for effectuating these rights;

—strictly comply with the procedure for the transfer of the system of conducting the register when dissolving the contract with the emitent.

The form of instruction concerning the transfer of securities and information specified therein shall be established by the federal agency of executive power for the securities market [as amended by Federal Law No. 185-ФЗ, 28 December 2002].

The holder of the register shall not have the right to present additional requirements when making changes in the data of the system of conducting the register except those which are established in the procedure provided for by the present Federal Law.

In the event of the termination of the operation of the contract for the maintenance of the system of conducting the register between the emitent and the registrar, the last shall transfer to another holder of the register for the said emitent the information received from the emitent, all data and documents comprising the system of conducting the register, and also the register drawn up on the date of termination of the operation of the contract. The transfer shall be made on the day of dissolution of the contract.

In the event of the replacement of the holder of the register, the emitent shall make an announcement thereof in the mass media or inform all possessors of the securities in writing at its expense.

All extracts issued by the holder of the register after the date of termination of the contract with the emitent shall be invalid.

The holder of the register shall make changes in the system of conducting the register on the basis of:

—an instruction of the possessor concerning the transfer of securities or the person acting in his name, or the nominee holder of securities who is registered in the system of conducting the register in accordance with the rules for conducting the register established by legislation of the Russian Federation, and when placing emission securities, in accordance with the procedure established by the present Article;

—other documents confirming the transfer of the right of ownership to securities in accordance with civil legislation of the Russian Federation.

In the event of the documentary form of emission securities providing for the securities to be situated with the possessors thereof, in addition to the said documents the certificate of the security also shall be submitted. In so doing the name of the person specified in the certificate as the possessor of the inscribed security must correspond to the name of the registered person specified in the instruction concerning the transfer of securities.

A refusal to make an entry in the system of conducting the register or the evasion of such entry, including with respect to a good faith acquirer, shall not be permitted except for the instances provided for by Federal laws.

Article 9. Activity Relating to Organisation of Trade on Securities Market

The provision of services directly facilitating the conclusion of civil-law securities transactions between participants of the securities market shall be deemed to be activity relating to organisation of trade on the securities market.

A professional participant of the securities market effectuating activity relating to the organisation of trade on the securities market shall be called the organiser of trade on the securities market.

The organiser of trade on the securities market shall be obliged to disclose the following information to any interested person:

the rules for admitting a participant of the securities market to public sales;

the rules for admittance to public sales of securities;

the rules for the conclusion and verification of transactions;

the rules for the registration of transactions;

the procedure for the performance of transactions;

the rules limiting the manipulation of prices;

the schedule for granting of services by the organiser of trade on the securities market;

the reglament for making changes in and additions to the aforesaid provisions;

the list of securities permitted for public sale.

The following information shall be granted to any interested person concerning each transaction concluded in accordance with the rules established by the organiser of trade:

the date and time of conclusion of a transaction;

the name of the securities which are the subject of the transaction;

the State registration number of the securities;

the price of a single security;

the quantity of securities.

An organiser of trade on the securities market shall be obliged to register at the federal agency of executive power for the securities market documents containing information specified in paragraph three of the present Article, and also changes in and additions thereto [added by Federal Law No. 185-ФЗ, 28 December 2002].

Article 10. Combining of Professional Types of Activity on Securities Market

The effectuation of activity with regard to keeping the register shall not permit the combining thereof with other types of professional activity on the securities market.

Limitations on the combining of types of activity and securities operations shall be established by the federal agency of executive power for the securities market [as amended by Federal Law No. 185-ФЗ, 28 December 2002].

Article 10¹. Requirements for Officials of Professional Participants of Securities Market

1. The functions of a one-man executive organ of a professional participant of the securities market may not be effectuated by:

persons who have effectuated the function of one-man executive organ or entered the composition of a collegial executive organ of a management company of joint-stock investment funds, share investment funds, and non-State pension funds, specialized depositary of joint-stock investment funds, share investment funds, and non-State pension funds, joint-stock investment fund, professional participant of the securities market, credit organisation, insurance organisation, and non-State pension fund at the moment of the annulment (or revocation) of licenses of those organisations for the effectuation of the respective types of activity for a violation of licensing requirements or at the moment of rendering of a decision concerning the application of procedures of bankruptcy, if at the moment of such annulment or moment of completion of the procedures of bankruptcy less than three years have elapsed;

persons having a record of conviction for a crime in the sphere of economic activity or crime against State power.

The said persons also may not be within the composition of the council of directors (or supervisory council) and collegial executive organ of a professional participant of the securities market, and also effectuate the functions of an executive of a control subdivision (or controller) of a professional participant of the securities market.

2. The federal agency of executive power for the securities market must be informed about the person elected to the office of one-man executive organ and about the person appointed as executive of the control subdivision (or controller) of a stock exchange and professional participant of the securities market effectuating clearing activity and depositary effectuating settlements of accounts with regard to the results of transactions concluded in public sales of stock exchanges and/or other organisers of trade on the securities market by agreement with such stock exchanges and/or organisers of trade (or settlement depositary) [Article added by Federal Law No. 185-ФЗ, 28 December 2002].

Chapter 3. Stock Market

Article 11. Stock Exchange [as amended by Federal Law No. 185-ФЗ, 28 December 2002]

1. An organiser of trade on the securities market which meets the requirements established by the present Chapter shall be deemed to be a stock exchange [as amended by Federal Law No. 185-ФЗ, 28 December 2002].

2. A juridical person may effectuate the activity of a stock exchange if it is a noncommercial partnership or joint-stock society [as amended by Federal Law No. 185-ФЗ, 28 December 2002].

3. To one stockholder of a stock exchange and affiliated persons thereof may not belong 20% or more of the stocks of each category (or type), and to one member of a stock exchange of a noncommercial partnership may not belong 20% or more of the votes at a general meeting of the members of such exchange.

The limitations specified in paragraph one of the present point shall not apply to stockholders (or members) of a stock exchange which are stock exchanges.

Only professional participants of the securities market may be members of a stock exchange which is a noncommercial partnership. In so doing the procedure for joining such a stock exchange, and the withdrawal and expulsion of members of a stock exchange, shall be determined by such stock exchange autonomously on the basis of its internal documents [as amended by Federal Law No. 185-ФЗ, 28 December 2002].

4. A juridical person effectuating the activity of a stock exchange shall not have the right to combine the said activity with other types of activity, except for activity of a currency exchange, goods exchange (or activity with regard to the organisation of exchange trade), clearing activity connected with the effectuation of clearing with regard to securities operations and investment shares of share investment funds, activity with regard to the dissemination of information, publishing activity, and also the effectuation of activity with regard to leasing out property.

In the event of the combining by a juridical person of activity of a currency exchange and/or goods exchange (or activity with regard to the organisation of exchange trade), and/or with the activity of a stock exchange, for the effectuation of each of the said types of activity an individual structural subdivision must be created [as amended by Federal Law No. 185-ФЗ, 28 December 2002].

5. A person effectuating the functions of one-man executive organ, executive of a control subdivision (or controller) of a stock exchange, and other workers of a stock exchange may not be workers and/or participants of professional participants of the stock market who are participants of public sales for the particular and/or other stock exchanges [as amended by Federal Law No. 185-ФЗ, 28 December 2002].

6. Stock exchanges which are noncommercial partnerships may be transformed into joint-stock societies. A decision concerning such transformation shall be adopted by members of such stock exchange by a majority of three-quarters of the votes of all members of this stock exchange [as amended by Federal Law No. 185-ФЗ, 28 December 2002].

Article 12. Participants of Public Sales on Stock Exchange [as amended by Federal Law No. 185-ФЗ, 28 December 2002]

Only brokers, dealers, and managers may be participants in public sales on a stock exchange.

Participants in public sales on a stock exchange created in the form of a non-commercial partnership may be only members of such an exchange.

The procedure for admission to participate in public sales and expel from among the participants of public sales shall be determined by the rules established by the stock exchange.

An unequal status of participants in public sales on a stock exchange, and also the transfer of the right to participate in public sales on a stock exchange to third persons, shall not be permitted [as amended by Federal Law No. 185-ФЗ, 28 December 2002].

Article 13. Requirements for Activity of Stock Exchange

1. A stock exchange shall be obliged to confirm:

the rules for admission to participate in public sales on the stock exchange;

the rules for conducting public sales on a stock exchange which must contain rules for the conclusion and registration of transactions, measures directed towards prevention of the manipulation of prices and use of employment information.

A stock exchange rendering services directly facilitating the conclusion of securities transactions, including with investment shares of share investment funds, also shall be obliged to confirm the rules of listing/delisting securities and/or rules for the admission of securities to public sales without undergoing the procedure of listing, and a stock exchange rendering services directly facilitating the conclusion of transactions, the performance of obligations under which depends upon changes of prices for securities or changes of the significance of indices calculated on the basis of aggregate prices for securities (stock exchange indices), including transactions providing for exclusively the duty of the parties to pay monetary amounts depending upon the change of prices for securities or changes of the significance of stock exchange indices, shall be obliged also to confirm the specifications of such transactions which conform to the requirements of normative legal acts of the federal agency of executive power for the securities market.

A stock exchange shall be obliged to register at the federal agency of executive power for the securities market documents specified in the present point, and also changes in and additions thereto [as amended by Federal Law No. 185-ФЗ, 28 December 2002].

2. A stock exchange must effectuate permanent control over transactions concluded on the stock exchange for the purpose of eliciting instances of the use of employment information, manipulation of prices, and compliance by participants of public sales and emitents whose securities are included on the quoted lists with requirements of legislation of the Russian Federation concerning securities and normative legal acts of the federal agency of executive power for the securities market.

The participants of public sales shall be obliged to provide to the stock exchange at its request information necessary for the effectuation of control by it in accordance with the rules for conducting public sales on the stock exchange [as amended by Federal Law No. 185-ФЗ, 28 December 2002].

3. A stock exchange shall be obliged to ensure glasnost and publicity of public sales being conducted by means of notification of participants in public sales about the place and time of conducting public sales, the list and quoting of securities admitted to public sales on the stock exchange, the results of trading sessions, and also provide other information specified in Article 9 of the present Federal Law [as amended by Federal Law No. 185-ФЗ, 28 December 2002].

4. A stock exchange shall have the right to establish the amount and procedure for levying contributions, charges, and other payments from participants in public sales for services rendered by it, and also the amount and procedure for the recovery of fines for a violation of the rules established by it.

A stock exchange shall not have the right to establish the amount of remuneration recovered by participants of public sales for the conclusion of stock-exchange transactions [as amended by Federal Law No. 185-ФЗ, 28 December 2002].

Article 14. Admittance of Securities to Public Sales on Stock Exchange [as amended by Federal Law No. 185-ФЗ, 28 December 2002]

Emission securities corresponding to the requirements of legislation of the Russian Federation may be admitted to public sales on a stock exchange in the process of their placement and circulation, and also other securities, including investment shares of share investment funds in the process of their issuance and circulation. Investment shares of share investment funds shall be admitted for issuance and circulation on a stock exchange in the instances and procedure which have been established by normative legal acts of the federal agency of executive power for the securities market.

The rules for listing/delisting of securities, including investment shares of share investment funds, must correspond to the requirements of normative legal acts of the federal agency of executive power for the securities market. The listing of emission securities shall be effectuated by a stock exchange on the basis of a contract with the emitent of securities, and the listing of investment shares of a share investment fund—on the basis of a contract with the management company of this share investment fund. Only securities which correspond to the requirements of legislation of the Russian Federation and normative legal acts of the federal agency of executive power for the securities market may be included in quotation lists. In so doing a stock exchange shall have the right to establish additional requirements for securities included in quotation lists.

Securities may be admitted to public sales on a stock exchange without undergoing the procedure of listing in accordance with the rules of the admittance of securities to public sales without undergoing the procedure of listing [as amended by Federal Law No. 185-ФЗ, 28 December 2002].

Article 15. Settlement of Disputes Arising in Connection with Effectuation of Trade in Securities on Stock Exchange

Disputes between participants in public sales on a stock exchange and participants in public sales on a stock exchange and their clients shall be considered by a court, arbitrazh court, or arbitration court [as amended by Federal Law No. 185-ФЗ, 28 December 2002].

Section III. On Emission Securities

Chapter 4. Basic Provisions on Emission Securities

Article 16. General Provisions

Emission securities may be inscribed or bearer. Inscribed emission securities may be issued only in paperless form, except for instances provided for by federal laws. Bearer emission securities may be issued only in documentary form [as amended by Federal Law No. 185-ФЗ, 28 December 2002].

A certificate shall be issued for each bearer emission security to the possessor thereof. Upon the demand of a possessor one certificate may be issued for two or more bearer emission securities of one issue acquired by him. The present provision shall not apply to bearer emission securities with obligatory centralised keeping [as amended by Federal Law No. 185-ФЗ, 28 December 2002].

A certificate of bearer emission securities must contain the requisites provided for by the present Federal Law. The requirements for blanks of certificates of bearer emission securities, except for blanks of certificates of bearer emission securities with obligatory centralised keeping, shall be established by normative legal acts of the Russian Federation [as amended by Federal Law No. 185-ФЗ, 28 December 2002].

The total quantity of bearer emission securities specified on all certificates issued by the emitent must not exceed the quantity of bearer emission securities in the particular issue [as amended by Federal Law No. 185-ФЗ, 28 December 2002].

By decision concerning the issue of bearer emission securities, and in the instances provided for by federal laws, by decision concerning the issue of inscribed emission securities, it may be determined that such securities are subject to obligatory keeping in a depositary determined by the emitent (emission securities with obligatory centralised keeping). A certificate of bearer emission securities with obligatory centralised keeping may not be issued by hand to the possessor(s) of such securities [as amended by Federal Law No. 185-ФЗ, 28 December 2002].

[paragraph six repealed by Federal Law No. 185-ФЗ, 28 December 2002]

[paragraph seven repealed by Federal Law No. 185-ФЗ, 28 December 2002]

[paragraph eight repealed by Federal Law No. 185-ФЗ, 28 December 2002]

[paragraph nine repealed by Federal Law No. 185-ФЗ, 28 December 2002]

[paragraph ten repealed by Federal Law No. 185-ФЗ, 28 December 2002]

[paragraph eleven repealed by Federal Law No. 185-ФЗ, 28 December 2002]

[paragraph twelve repealed by Federal Law No. 185-ФЗ, 28 December 2002]

Any property and nonproperty rights consolidated in documentary or paperless form, irrespective of the name thereof, shall be emission securities if the conditions of their arising and circulation correspond to the aggregate of indicia of an emission security specified in Article 2 of the present Federal Law.

[paragraph fourteen repealed by Federal Law No. 185-ФЗ, 28 December 2002]

Russian emitents shall have the right to place securities beyond the limits of the Russian Federation, including by means of placement in accordance with foreign law of securities of foreign emitents certifying rights with respect to emission securities of Russian emitents, only upon the authorisation of the federal agency of executive power for the securities market [paragraph seven instead of fifteen by Federal Law No. 185-ФЗ, 28 December 2002].

Organisation of the circulation of emission securities of a Russian emitent beyond the limits of the Russian Federation on the basis of a contract with the Russian emitent, including by means of placement in accordance with foreign law of securities of foreign emitents certifying rights with respect to emission securities of Russian emitents, shall be permitted only upon the authorisation of the federal agency of executive power for the securities market [paragraph eight added by Federal Law No. 185-ФЗ, 28 December 2002].

The said authorisations shall be issued by the federal agency of executive power for the securities market in compliance with the following conditions:

if the State registration of the issue (or additional issue) of securities of the Russian emitent has been effectuated;

if the securities of the Russian emitent have been included in the quotation list by at least one organiser of trade on the securities market;

if the quantity of securities of the Russian emitent whose placement or circulation is proposed beyond the limits of the Russian Federation, including by means of placement in accordance with foreign law of securities of foreign emitents certifying rights with respect to such securities, do not exceed normative standards established by normative legal acts of the federal agency of executive for the securities market;

if the contract on the basis of which the placement is effectuated in accordance with foreign law of securities of foreign emitents certifying rights with respect to stocks of Russian emitents provides that the right of vote with regard to the said stocks is effectuated not other than in accordance with the instructions of the possessors of the said securities of foreign emitents;

if other requirements established by federal laws have been complied with [paragraph nine added by Federal Law No. 185-ФЗ, 28 December 2002].

An authorisation for the placement and/or circulation of securities of Russian emitents beyond the limits of the Russian Federation shall be issued by the federal agency of executive power for the securities market on the basis of an application, to which shall be attached documents confirming compliance by the emitent with the requirements of the present Article. An exhaustive list of such documents shall be determined by normative legal acts of the federal agency of executive power for the securities market [paragraph ten added by Federal Law No. 185-ФЗ, 28 December 2002].

An authorisation for the placement of securities of Russian emitents beyond the limits of the Russian Federation may be issued simultaneously with the State registration of the issue (or additional issue) of such securities [paragraph eleven added by Federal Law No. 185-ФЗ, 28 December 2002].

The federal agency of executive power for the securities market shall be obliged to issue the said authorisation or adopt a reasoned decision concerning refusal of the issuance thereof within 30 days from the date of receipt of all necessary documents [paragraph twelve added by Federal Law No. 185-ФЗ, 28 December 2002].

The federal agency of executive power for the securities market shall have the right to conduct a verification of the reliability of the information contained in documents submitted for receipt of an authorisation. In this event the running of the period provided for by paragraph twelve of the present Article may be suspended for the time of conducting the verification, but not more than 30 days [paragraph thirteen added by Federal Law No. 185-ФЗ, 28 December 2002].

Article 17. Decision on Issue (or Additional Issue) of Emission Securities [as amended by Federal Law No. 185-ФЗ, 28 December 2002]

1. A decision concerning the issue (or additional issue) of emission securities must contain the following:

the full name of the emitent, location thereof, and postal address;

the date of adoption of the decision concerning the placement of the emission securities;

the name of the empowered organ of the emitent which adopted the decision concerning placement of the emission securities;

the date of confirmation of the decision concerning the issue (or additional issue) of emission securities;

the name of the empowered organ of the emitent which confirmed the decision concerning the issue (or additional issue) of emission securities;

the type and category (or type) of emission securities;

the rights of the possessor consolidated by an emission security;

the conditions for the placement of emission securities;

an indication of the quantity of the emission securities in the particular issue (or additional issuance) of emission securities;

an indication of the total quantity of emission securities in the particular issue previously placed (in the event of the placement of an additional issue of emission securities);

an indication of whether the emission securities are inscribed or bearer;

the par value of the emission securities if the presence of a par value has been provided for by legislation of the Russian Federation;

the signature of the person effectuating the functions of executive organ of the emitent and the seal of the emitent;

other information provided for by the present Federal Law or other federal laws on securities.

A description or sample of the certificate shall be appended to the decision concerning the issue (or additional issue) of emission securities in documentary form [point 1 as amended by Federal Law No. 185-ФЗ, 28 December 2002].

2. The decision concerning the issue (or additional issue) of emission securities of an economic society shall be confirmed by the council of directors (or supervisory council) or organ effectuating in accordance with federal laws the functions of the council of directors (or supervisory council) of this economic society. The decision concerning the issue (or additional issue) of emission securities of juridical persons of other organisational-legal forms shall be confirmed by the highest management organ unless established otherwise by federal laws.

The decision concerning the issue of bonds and the performance of the obligations with regard to which is secured by a pledge, bank guarantee, or other means provided for by the present Federal Law, also must contain information concerning the person who provided the security and the conditions of the security. The composition of information concerning the person providing the security shall be determined by the federal agency of executive power for the securities market. In this event the decision concerning the issue of bonds must also be signed by the person providing such security. A bond, performance of the obligations with regard to which is secured by one of the said means, also shall provide to the possessor thereof the right of demand against the person who provided such security.

The decision concerning the issue of inscribed bonds or documentary bonds with obligatory centralised keeping also must contain an indication of the date on which the list of possessors of bonds is drawn up for performance by the emitent of obligations with regard to the bonds. Such date may not be earlier than 14 days before the ensuing of the period of performance of the obligations with regard to the bonds. In so doing performance of an obligation with respect to a possessor included in the list of possessors of bonds shall be deemed to be proper, including in the event of the alienation of bonds after the date of drawing up the list of possessors of bonds [point 2 as amended by Federal Law No. 185-ФЗ, 28 December 2002].

3. An emitent shall not have the right to change a decision concerning the issue (or additional issue) of emission securities with respect to the amount of rights under the emission security established by this decision after the State registration of the issue (or additional issue) of emission securities [point 3 as amended by Federal Law No. 185-ФЗ, 28 December 2002].

4. The decision concerning the issue (or additional issue) of emission securities shall be drawn up in three examples. After State registration of an issue (or additional issue) of emission securities, one example of the decision concerning the issue of emission securities shall remain for keeping in the registering agency, and the two other examples shall be issued to the emitent. If the conducting of the register of possessors of inscribed emission securities of an emitent is effectuated by the registrar, and also if bearer emission securities placed by the emitent are emission securities with obligatory centralised keeping, one example of the decision concerning the issue of emission securities shall be transferred by the emitent for keeping to the registrar or depositary effectuating the obligatory centralised keeping. When there are divergencies in the texts of examples of a decision concerning the issue (or additional issue) of emission securities, the text of the document kept in the registering agency shall have preferential force [point 4 as amended by Federal Law No. 185-ФЗ, 28 December 2002].

5. In the event of the State registration of an issue (or additional issue) of emission securities a notation shall be made on each example of the decision concerning the issue (or additional issue) of emission securities concerning the State registration of the issue (or additional issue) of emission securities and the State registration number conferred on the issue (or additional issue) of emission securities shall be specified [point 5 as amended by Federal Law No. 185-ФЗ, 28 December 2002].

6. An emitent and/or registrar shall at the request of an interested person be obliged to provide him a copy of the decision concerning the issue (or additional issue) of emission securities for payment not exceeding the expenditures for the manufacture thereof [point 6 as amended by Federal Law No. 185-ФЗ, 28 December 2002].

Article 18. Form of Certification of Rights Comprising Emission Security

In the event of the documentary form of emission securities the certificate and decision concerning the issuance of securities shall be documents certifying the rights consolidated by the security.

In the event of the paperless form of emission securities the decision concerning the issuance of the securities shall be the document certifying the rights consolidated by the security.

An emission security shall consolidate property rights in that volume in which they have been established in the decision concerning the issuance of the particular securities and in accordance with legislation of the Russian Federation.

The certificate of an emission security must contain the following obligatory requisites:

full name of the emitent, location thereof, and postal address;

type and category (or type) of emission securities;

State registration number of issue of emission securities and date of State registration;

rights of possessor consolidated by emission security;

conditions of performance of obligations by person who provided security and information concerning this person in the event of the issue of bonds with security;

an indication of the quantity of emission securities certified by particular certificate;

an indication of the total quantity of emission securities in the particular issue of emission securities;

an indication of whether the emission securities are subject to obligatory centralised keeping, and if so subject—the name of the depositary effectuating the centralised keeping thereof;

an indication whether the emission securities are bearer emission securities;

signature of the person effectuating the functions of executive organ of the emitent and the seal of the emitent;

other requisites provided for by legislation of the Russian Federation for the particular type of emission securities [paragraph four as amended by Federal Law No. 185-ФЗ, 28 December 2002].

[paragraph five repealed by Federal Law No. 185-ФЗ, 28 December 2002]

In the event of a divergence between the text of the decision concerning the issuance of securities and data quoted in the certificate of an emission security, the possessor shall have the right to demand the effectuation of the rights consolidated by this security in the amount established by the certificate. The emitent shall bear responsibility for the failure of the data contained in the certificate of the emission security to coincide with the data contained in the decision concerning the issuance of securities, in accordance with legislation of the Russian Federation.

[paragraph seven repealed by Federal Law No. 185-ФЗ, 28 December 2002]

Chapter 5. Emission of Securities

Article 19. Procedure for Emission and Stages Thereof

1. The procedure for the emission of emission securities, unless provided otherwise by federal laws, shall include the following stages:

adoption of a decision concerning the placement of emission securities;

confirmation of the decision concerning the issue (or additional issue) of emission securities;

State registration of the issue (or additional issue) of emission securities;

the placement of emission securities;

State registration of the report concerning the results of the issue (or additional issue) of emission securities.

Emission securities whose issue (or additional issue) did not undergo State registration in accordance with the requirements of the present Federal Law shall not be subject to placement.

In the event of the founding of a joint-stock society or reorganisation of juridical persons effectuated in the form of a merger, division, separation, and transformation, the placement of emission securities shall be effectuated before State registration of the issue thereof, and State registration of the report concerning the results of the issue of emission securities shall be effectuated simultaneously with State registration of the issue of emission securities [point one as amended by Federal Law No. 185-ФЗ, 28 December 2002].

2. State registration of an issue (or additional issue) of emission securities shall be accompanied by registration of the prospectus thereof in the event of the placement of emission securities by means of open subscription or by means of closed subscription among a group of persons, the number of which exceeds 500.

If State registration of an issue (or additional issue) of emission securities is accompanied by registration of the prospectus of securities, each stage of the procedure for the emission of securities shall be accompanied by the divulgence of information [point two as amended by Federal Law No. 185-ФЗ, 28 December 2002].

3. If State registration of an issue (or additional issue) of emission securities has not been accompanied by registration of the prospectus thereof, it may be registered subsequently. In so doing registration of the securities prospectus shall be effectuated by the registering agency within 30 days from the date of receipt of the securities prospectus and other documents necessary for the registration thereof [point three as amended by Federal Law No. 185-ФЗ, 28 December 2002].

4. The peculiarities of the procedure for the issue of bonds of the Bank of Russia shall be determined by the Government of the Russian Federation in

accordance with legislation of the Russian Federation [point four as amended by Federal Law No. 185-ФЗ, 28 December 2002].

5. The procedure for emission of State and municipal securities, and also the conditions of their placement, shall be regulated by federal laws or in the procedure established by federal laws [point five as amended by Federal Law No. 185-ФЗ, 28 December 2002].

Article 20. State Registration of Issues (or Additional Issues) of Emission Securities [as amended by Federal Law No. 185-ФЗ, 28 December 2002]

1. State registration of issues (or additional issues) of emission securities shall be effectuated by the federal agency of executive power for the securities market or other registering agency determined by a federal law (hereinafter—registering agency) [as amended by Federal Law No. 185-ФЗ, 28 December 2002].

2. State registration of an issue (or additional issue) of emission securities shall be effectuated on the basis of an application of the emitent.

To an application concerning State registration of an issue (or additional issue) of emission securities shall be appended the decision concerning the issue (or additional issue) of securities, documents confirming compliance by the emitent with the requirements of legislation of the Russian Federation determining the procedure and conditions of adoption of the decision concerning placement of securities, confirmation of the decision concerning the issue of securities, and other requirements, compliance with which is necessary when effectuating an emission of securities, and if registration of an issue (or additional issue) of securities in accordance with the present Federal Law must be accompanied by registration of a securities prospectus, the securities prospectus. An exhaustive list of such documents shall be determined by normative legal acts of the federal agency of executive power for the securities market [as amended by Federal Law No. 185-ФЗ, 28 December 2002].

3. The registering agency shall be obliged to effectuate State registration of an issue (or additional issue) of emission securities or to adopt a reasoned decision concerning a refusal of State registration of an issue (or additional issue) of emission securities within 30 days from the date of receipt of the documents submitted for State registration.

A registering agency shall have the right to conduct a verification of the reliability of information contained in documents submitted for State registration of an issue (or additional issue) of emission securities. In this event the running of the period provided for by paragraph one of the present point may be suspended for the time of conducting the verification, but not more than 30 days [as amended by Federal Law No. 185-ФЗ, 28 December 2002].

4. In the event of the State registration of an issue of emission securities an individual State registration number shall be conferred on it.

In the event of the State registration of each additional issue of emission securities an individual State registration number shall be conferred on it consisting of the individual State registration number conferred on the issue of emission securities and the individual number (or code) of this additional issue of emission securities.

Upon the expiry of three months from the moment of State registration of the report concerning the results of an additional issue of emission securities, the individual number (or code) of the additional issue shall be annulled.

The procedure for conferment of the State registration numbers of issues of emission securities and annulment of individual numbers (or codes) of additional issues of emission securities shall be established by the federal agency of executive power for the securities market [as amended by Federal Law No. 185-ФЗ, 28 December 2002].

5. A registering agency shall be liable only for the fullness of information contained in documents submitted for State registration of the issue (or additional issue) of emission securities [as amended by Federal Law No. 185-ФЗ, 28 December 2002].

Article 21. Grounds for Refusal of Registration of Issue (or Additional Issue) of Emission Securities [as amended by Federal Law No. 185-ФЗ, 28 December 2002]

The grounds for the refusal of State registration of an issue (or additional issue) of emission securities and registration of a securities prospectus shall be [as amended by Federal Law No. 185-ФЗ, 28 December 2002]:

violation by the emitent of the requirements of legislation of the Russian Federation on securities, including the existence in the documents submitted of information enabling the conclusion to be drawn that the conditions of emission and circulation of emission securities are contrary to legislation of the Russian Federation and the nonconformity of the conditions of the issuance of emission securities to legislation of the Russian Federation on securities;

the failure of the documents submitted for State registration of an issue (or additional issue) of emission securities, or the registration of a securities prospectus, and the composition of information contained therein to conform to the requirements of the present Federal Law and normative legal acts of the federal agency of executive power for the securities market [as amended by Federal Law No. 185-ФЗ, 28 December 2002];

the failure to submit within 30 days at the request of the registering agency all documents necessary for State registration of an issue (or additional issue) of emission securities or registration of a securities prospectus [added by Federal Law No. 185-ФЗ, 28 December 2002];

the failure of a financial consultant on the securities market who signed the securities prospectus to conform to the established requirements [added by Federal Law No. 185-ФЗ, 28 December 2002];

the insertion in the securities prospectus or decision concerning the issue of securities (or other documents which are the grounds for registration of the issue of securities) of false information or information not corresponding to reality (unreliable information) [as amended by Federal Law No. 185-ФЗ, 28 December 2002].

The decision concerning a refusal of registration of the issue of securities and securities prospectus may be appealed to a court or arbitrazh court [as amended by Federal Law No. 185-ФЗ, 28 December 2002].

Article 22. General Requirements for Content of Securities Prospectus [as amended by Federal Law No. 185-ФЗ, 28 December 2002]

1. A securities prospectus must contain:

brief information concerning the persons within the composition of management organs of an emitent, information concerning bank accounts, auditor, valuer, and financial consultant of the emitent, and also other persons who have signed the prospectus;

brief information concerning the amount, periods, procedure, and conditions of the placement of emission securities;

basic information concerning the financial-economic state of the emitent and factors of risk;

detailed information concerning the emitent;

information concerning the financial-economic activity of the emitent;

detailed information concerning persons within the composition of the management organs of the emitent, organs of the emitent for control over its financial-economic activity and brief information concerning personnel (or workers) of the emitent;

information concerning participants (or stockholders) of the emitent and transactions concluded by the emitent in the conclusion of which there was an interest;

bookkeeping reports of the emitent and other financial information;

detailed information concerning the procedure and conditions for the placement of emission securities;

additional information concerning the emitent and placement by it of emission securities.

The requirements for information which must be specified on the title page of a securities prospectus shall be established by the standards for emission and securities prospectuses. A securities prospectus also must contain an introduction in which the basic information to be set out further in the securities prospectus is concisely set forth [as amended by Federal Law No. 185-ФЗ, 28 December 2002].

2. To the brief information concerning persons within the composition of management organs of the emitent, information concerning bank accounts, auditor, valuer, and financial consultant of the emitent, and also other persons who have signed the prospectus, shall be relegated:

indication of the persons within the composition of management organs of the emitent;

information concerning bank accounts of the emitent, information concerning the auditor(s) of the emitent who have drawn up an opinion with respect to the yearly bookkeeping reports of the emitent for the last three completed financial years or for each completed financial year if the emitent effectuates its activity for less than three years;

information concerning the valuer and consultants of the emitent [as amended by Federal Law No. 185-ФЗ, 28 December 2002].

3. To brief information concerning the amount, periods, procedure, and conditions of the placement for each type or category (or type) of emission securities to be placed shall be relegated:

type or category (or type) and form of emission securities to be placed;

par value of each type or category (or type), and series of emission securities to be placed if the presence of par value has been provided for by legislation of the Russian Federation;

proposed size of the issue expressed in money and the quantity of emission securities which it is proposed to place;

price (or procedure for determining price) of placement of emission securities;

procedure and periods for placement of emission securities;

procedure and conditions of paying up emission securities to be placed;

procedure and conditions for conclusion of contracts in course of placement of emission securities;

group of potential acquirers of emission securities to be placed;

procedure for divulgence of information concerning placement and results of placement of emission securities [as amended by Federal Law No. 185-ФЗ, 28 December 2002].

4. To basic information concerning financial-economic state of emitent shall be relegated information for the five last completed financial years or for each completed financial year if the emitent effectuates its activity for less than five years, and also for the last completed reporting period, including information concerning:

indicators of financial-economic activity of the emitent;

market capitalisation of the emitent and obligations thereof;

purposes of emission and orientations of the use of means received as a result of the placement of emission securities;

risks which arose in connection with the acquisition of emission securities to be placed [as amended by Federal Law No. 185-ФЗ, 28 December 2002].

5. To detailed information concerning the emitent shall be relegated information concerning:

the history of the creation and development of the emitent;

the basic economic activity of the emitent;

the plans for future activity of the emitent;

the participation of the emitent in industrial, banking, and financial groups, holding companies, concerns, and associations, and also subsidiary and dependent economic societies of the emitent;

the composition, structure, and value of basic means of the emitent, including plans with regard to the acquisition, replacement, and withdrawal of basic means, and also information concerning all facts of encumberment of basic means of the emitent [as amended by Federal Law No. 185-ФЗ, 28 December 2002].

6. To information concerning financial-economic activity of the emitent shall be relegated information concerning the financial state of the emitent and dynamics of the changes thereof for the five last completed financial years or for each completed financial year if the emitent effectuates his activity for less than five years, and also an indication of the reasons and factors which, in the opinion of the management organs of the emitent, led to such changes, including concerning:

the results of financial-economic activity of the emitent, factors which have exerted an influence on a change of the amount of receipts from the sale by the emitent of goods, products, work, services, and profit (or losses) of the emitent from the basic activity, including the influence of inflation, change of exchange rates of foreign currencies, decisions of State agencies, other economic, financial, political, and other factors;

the liquidity of the emitent, amount, structure, and sufficiency of capital and circulating means of the emitent;

the policy and expenses of the emitent in the domain of scientific-technical development with respect to licenses and patents, new works, and research;

an analysis of the trends of development in the sphere of the basic activity of the emitent [as amended by Federal Law No. 185-ФЗ, 28 December 2002].

7. To detailed information concerning persons within the composition of management organs of the emitent, organs of the emitent for control over its financial-economic activity, and concise information concerning personnel (or workers) of the emitent shall be relegated:

information concerning persons within the composition of management organs of the emitent, including who are members of the council of directors (or supervisory council) of the emitent and members of the collegial executive management organ of the emitent, information concerning the person effectuating the functions of one-man executive management organ of the emitent (including information concerning a management organisation), information concerning persons effectuating the functions of internal auditor and/or members of the internal audit commission of the emitent, and also information concerning the character of any kinship links between any of the said persons;

information concerning the amount of remuneration, privileges, and/or contributory compensation of expenses for each management organ of the emitent (except for a natural person effectuating the functions of one-man executive organ) and organ of control over its financial-economic activity which has been paid by the emitent for the last completed financial year, and also information concerning existing agreements relative to such payments in the current financial year;

information concerning the structure and competence of management organs of the emitent and organs of control over its financial-economic activity;

data concerning the number and summarised data concerning the formation and composition of personnel (or workers) of the emitent, and also changes of the number of personnel (or workers) of the emitent if such change is material for the emitent;

information concerning any obligations of the emitent to personnel (or workers) affecting the possibility of their participation in the charter (or contributed) capital (or share fund) of the emitent (or acquisition of stocks of the emitent), including any agreements which provide for the issue or provision of options of the emitent to personnel (or workers);

amount of participatory share of participation of persons specified in paragraph one of the present point in the charter (or contributed) capital (or share fund) of the emitent and its subsidiary and dependent societies, participatory shares belonging to the said persons of common stocks of the emitent and its subsidiary and dependent societies, and also information concerning options of the emitent and its subsidiary and dependent societies providing stocks of the emitent to such persons [as amended by Federal Law No. 185-ФЗ, 28 December 2002].

8. To information concerning participants (or stockholders) of the emitent and transactions concluded by the emitent in the conclusion of which there was an interest, shall be relegated:

information concerning the total quantity of participants (or stockholders) of the emitent;

information concerning the participants (or stockholders) of the emitent possessing not less than 5% of its charter (or contributed) capital (or share fund) or not less than 5% of its common stocks, including the amount of the participatory share of participant (or stockholder) of the emitent in its charter (or contributed) capital (or share fund), and also the participatory share of common stocks of the emitent belonging to it;

for participants (or stockholders) of the emitent possessing not less than 5% of its charter (or contributed) capital (or share fund) or not less than 5% of its common stocks, information concerning the participants (or stockholders) thereof possessing not less than 20% of the charter (or contributed) capital (or share fund) or not less than 20% of their common stocks, including an indication of their participatory share in the charter (or contributed) capital (or share fund) of the emitent, and also the participatory share belonging to them of the common stocks of the emitent;

information concerning the participatory share of participation of the State or municipal formation in the charter (or contributed) capital (or share fund) of the emitent and the presence of a special right ("golden stock");

information concerning limitations on participation in the charter (or contributed) capital (or share fund) of the emitent;

information concerning changes in the composition and amount of participation of participants (or stockholders) of the emitent possessing not less than 5% of its charter (or contributed) capital (or share fund) or not less than 5% of its common stocks for the five last completed financial years or for each completed financial year if the emitent effectuates its activity for less than five years;

information concerning the transactions concluded by the emitent, in the conclusion of which there was an interest, for the five last completed financial years or for each completed financial year if the emitent effectuates its activity for less than five years, and also for the period up to the date of confirmation of the securities prospectus;

information concerning the amount of debtor indebtedness for the five last completed financial years or for each completed financial year if the emitent effectuates its activity for less than five years, including a breakdown by debtors, the amount of indebtedness which comprises not less than 10% of the total amount of debtor indebtedness, and also information concerning debtor indebtedness to affiliated persons [as amended by Federal Law No. 185-ФЗ, 28 December 2002].

9. Bookkeeping reports of the emitent and other financial information shall be:

yearly bookkeeping reporting of the emitent for the three last completed financial years or for each completed financial year if the emitent effectuates its activity for less than three years, to which the opinion of an auditor(s) shall be appended with respect to the said bookkeeping reporting;

quarterly bookkeeping reporting of the emitent for the last completed reporting quarter;

composite bookkeeping reporting of the emitent for the three last completed financial years or for each completed financial year;

information concerning the total amount of export, and also the participatory share which export comprises in the total volume of sales;

information concerning material changes which have occurred in the composition of property of the emitent after the date of the end of the last completed financial year;

information concerning participation of the emitent in judicial proceedings if such participation may materially reflect on the financial-economic activity of the emitent [as amended by Federal Law No. 185-ФЗ, 28 December 2002].

10. To detailed information concerning the procedure and conditions for placement of emission securities shall be relegated information concerning:

emission securities to be placed, price of the placement (or procedure for determining it), presence of preferential or other rights for the acquisition of emission securities to be placed, any limitations on the acquisition and circulation of emission securities to be placed;

dynamics of the change of prices for emission securities of the emitent if such securites were admitted to circulation by an organiser of trade on the securities market, including a stock exchange;

persons rendering services with regard to organisation of the placement and/or placement of the emission securities;

group of potential acquirers of emission securities;

organisers of trade on the securities market, including stock exchanges, on which the placement and/or circulation of the emission securities to be placed is proposed;

possible changes of the participatory share of participation of stockholders in the charter capital of the emitent as a result of the placement of emission securities;

expenses connected with the emission of securities;

means and procedure for the return of means received in payment of emission securities to be placed in the event of the issue (or additional issue) of emission securities being deemed to be unconstituted or invalid, and also in other instances provided for by legislation of the Russian Federation [as amended by Federal Law No. 185-ФЗ, 28 December 2002].

11. To additional information concerning an emitent and emission securities to be placed by it shall be relegated:

information concerning the amount, structure of the charter (or contributed) capital (or share fund) of the emitent and changes thereof for the five last completed financial years or for each completed financial year if the emitent effectuates its activity for less than five years, indicating the decision of empowered management organs of the emitent which are the basis for such changes;

information concerning each category (or type) of stocks of the emitent, indicating the rights granted by stocks to the possessors thereof, par value of each stock, quantity of stocks in circulation, quantity of additional stocks in the process of placement, quantity of declared stocks, quantity of stocks on the balance sheet of the emitent, quantity of additional stocks which may be placed as a result of converting placed emission securities convertible into stocks, or as a result of performance of obligations with regard to options of the emitent;

information concerning preceding issues of emission securities of the emitent, except for stocks of the emitent;

information concerning the structure of management organs of the emitent and their competence, and also the structure of organs of the emitent for control over its financial-economic activity and the competence thereof;

information concerning the procedure for the convocation and conducting of a meeting (or session) of the highest management organ of the emitent;

information concerning material transactions concluded by the emitent for the five last completed financial years or for each completed financial year if the emitent effectuates its activity for less than five years, the amount of obligations under which comprise not less than 10% of the balance sheet value of assets of the emitent according to data of its bookkeeping reporting for the last completed reporting period;

information concerning legislative acts regulating questions of the import and export of capital which may influence the payment of dividends, interest, and other payments to nonresidents;

description of the procedure for the taxation of revenues with regard to emission securities of the emitent placed and to be placed;

information concerning declared (or accumulated) and paid dividends with regard to stocks of the emitent, and also revenues with regard to bonds of the emitent for the five last completed financial years or for each completed financial year if the emitent effectuates its activity for less than five years, including the procedure for the payment of dividends and other revenues;

information concerning persons who provided security in the event of the issue of bonds with security by the emitent, and also the conditions for securing the performance of obligations with regard to bonds of the emitent;

information concerning credit ratings of the emitent, and also the change thereof for the five last completed financial years or for each completed financial year if the emitent effectuates its activity for less than five years;

information concerning commercial organisations in which the emitent possesses not less than 5% of the charter (or contributed) capital (or share fund) or not less than 5% of the common stocks;

information concerning the forming and use of the reserve fund, and also other funds of the emitent, for the last five completed financial years or for each completed financial year if the emitent effectuates its activity for less than five years;

information concerning organisations effectuating the recording of rights to emission securities of the emitent;

other information provided for by the present Federal Law or other federal laws [as amended by Federal Law No. 185-ФЗ, 28 December 2002].

12. The composition of information specified in points 2–11 of the present Article shall be determined by the federal agency of executive power for the

securities market [as amended by Federal Law No. 185-ФЗ, 28 December 2002].

13. Unless established otherwise by the present Federal Law or other federal laws, information contained in a securities prospectus shall indicate the date of its confirmation by the empowered management organ of the emitent [as amended by Federal Law No. 185-ФЗ, 28 December 2002].

14. If the registration of a securities prospectus is effectuated after the State registration of the issue of emission securities, the requirements of point 3 and point 10 (except for paragraph seven) of the present Article shall not apply [as amended by Federal Law No. 185-ФЗ, 28 December 2002].

Article 22¹. Confirmation and Signature of Securities Prospectus. Responsibility of Persons Who Have Signed Securities Prospectus [added by Federal Law No. 185-ФЗ, 28 December 2002]

1. A securities prospectus of an economic society shall be confirmed by the council of directors (or supervisory council) or organ effectuating in accordance with federal laws the functions of the council of directors (or supervisory council) of this economic society. The securities prospectus of juridical persons of other organisational-legal forms shall be confirmed by the person effectuating the functions of executive organ of the emitent unless established otherwise by federal laws.

2. A securities prospectus must be signed by the person effectuating the functions of one-man executive organ of the emitent, chief bookkeeper thereof (or other person fulfilling the functions thereof), thereby confirming the reliability and fullness of all information contained in the securities prospectus. A securities prospectus also must be signed by the auditor, and in instances provided for by normative legal acts of the federal agency of executive power for the securities market, an independent valuer, confirming the reliability of information in the part of the securities prospectus specified by them. In instances of a public placement and/or public circulation of emission securities the securities prospectus must be signed by a financial consultant for the securities market, thereby confirming the reliability and fullness of all information contained in the securities prospectus, except for the part confirmed by the auditor and/or valuer. A financial consultant for the securities market may not be an affiliated person of the emitent.

The involvement of a financial consultant for the securities market when privatising stocks shall be effectuated in the instances and procedure which have been provided by legislation of the Russian Federation on privatisation.

In the event of the issue of bonds with security the person who has provided the security shall be obliged to sign the securities prospectus, thereby confirming the reliability of information concerning the security.

3. Persons who have signed the securities prospectus shall, in the event of their fault, bear jointly and severally between themselves subsidiary responsibility with the emitent for damage caused to the possessor of securities as a consequence of unreliable or incomplete information and/or information deluding an investor which was confirmed by them. In so doing the period of limitations for compensation of damage on the grounds specified in the present Article shall comprise three years from the day of commencement of the placement of the securities, and if State registration of the issue (or additional issue) of emission securities was not accompanied by the registration of the securities prospectus, from the day of commencement of public circulation of the emission securities.

Article 23. Information on Issue (or Additional Issue) of Emission Securities Disclosed by Emitent [as amended by Federal Law No. 185-ФЗ, 28 December 2002]

In the event of the registration of a securities prospectus, the emitent shall be obliged to ensure access to information contained in the securities prospectus to any persons interested in such irrespective of the purpose of receiving such information [as amended by Federal Law No. 185-ФЗ, 28 December 2002].

In the event of an open subscription the emitent shall be obliged to publish a communication concerning State registration of the issue (or additional issue) of emission securities, in so doing having indicated the procedure for access of any interested persons to information contained in the securities prospectus, in a printed organ of the mass media distributed in a print-run of not less than 10,000 examples. In the event of a closed subscription accompanied by the registration of a securities prospectus an emitent shall be obliged to publish a communication concerning the State registration of the issue (or additional issue) of emission securities, in so doing having indicated the procedure for access of potential possessors of emission securities to information contained in the securities prospectus in a printed organ of the mass media distributed in a print-run of not less than 1,000 examples [as amended by Federal Law No. 185-ФЗ, 28 December 2002].

[paragraphs three to seven repealed by Federal Law No. 185-ФЗ, 28 December 2002]

Article 24. Conditions of Placement of Emission Securities Issued

An emitent shall have the right to commence the placement of emission securities only after State registration of the issue thereof, unless established otherwise by the present Federal Law [as amended by Federal Law No. 185-ФЗ, 28 December 2002].

The quantity of placed emission securities must not exceed the quantity specified in the decision concerning the issue (or additional issue) of emission securities [as amended by Federal Law No. 185-ФЗ, 28 December 2002].

The emitent may place a lesser quantity of emission securities than was specified in the decision concerning the issue (or additional issue) of emission securities. The actual quantity of placed securities shall be specified in the report concerning the results of the issuance submitted for registration. The participatory share of the unplaced securities from among those specified in the decision concerning the issue (or additional issue) of emission securities under which the emission is considered to be unconstituted shall be established by the federal agency of executive power for the securities market [as amended by Federal Law No. 185-ФЗ, 28 December 2002].

The means of investors in the event of an unconstituted emission shall be returned in the procedure established by the federal agency of executive power for the securities market [as amended by Federal Law No. 185-ФЗ, 28 December 2002].

The emitent shall be obliged to complete the placement of emission securities issued not later than one year from the date of State registration of the issue (or additional issue) of such securities [as amended by Federal Law No. 185-ФЗ, 28 December 2002].

The placement by means of subscription to emission securities of an issue whose State rgistration is accompanied by the registration of a securities prospectus earlier than two weeks after publication of the communication concerning State registration of the issue of emission securities in accordance with Article 23 of the present Federal Law shall be prohibited. Information concerning the price of placement of emission securities may be disclosed on the day of the commencement of emission securities [as amended by Federal Law No. 185-ФЗ, 28 December 2002].

It shall be prohibited in the event of the public placement or circulation of the issue of emission securities to prefer one potential possessor over others when acquiring securities. The present provision shall not apply in the following instances:

(1) in the event of the emission of State securities;

(2) in the event of the granting to stockholders of joint-stock societies a preferential right of purchase of a new emission of securities in a quantity proportional to the number of stocks belonging to them at the moment of the adoption of the decision concerning emission;

(3) in the event of the introduction by the emitent of limitations on the acquisition of securities by nonresidents.

Article 25. Report on Results of Issue (or Additional Issue) of Emission Securities [as amended by Federal Law No. 185-ФЗ, 28 December 2002]

Not later than 30 days after the completion of the placement of emission securities the emitent shall be obliged to submit a report concerning the results of the issue (or additional issue) of emission securities to the registering agency.

The report concerning the results of the issue (or additional issue) of emission securities must contain the following information:

(1) the date of commencement and ending of the placement of the securities;

(2) the actual price of placement of the securities (by types of securities within the framework of the particular issuance);

(3) the quantity of securities placed;

(4) the total amount of proceeds for the placed securities, including:

(a) the amount of monetary means in rubles as payment for placed securities;

(b) the amount of foreign currency as payment for placed securities expressed in currency of the Russian Federation at the exchange rate of the Central Bank of the Russian Federation at the moment of payment;

(c) the amount of material and nonmaterial assets as payment for placed securities expressed in the currency of the Russian Federation.

The list of possessors possessing a block of emission securities, the amount of which is determined by the federal agency of executive power for the securities market, shall be specified additionally for stocks in the report concerning the results of the issue (or additional issue) of emission securities.

Simultaneously with the report concerning the results of the issue (or additional issue) of emission securities an application shall be submitted to the registering agency concerning the registration thereof and documents confirming compliance by the emitent with the requirements of legislation of the Russian Federation determining the procedure and conditions for placement of the securities, confirmation of the report concerning the results of the issue of securities, disclosure of information, and other requirements, compliance with which is necessary when placing securities. An exhaustive list of such documents shall be determined by normative legal acts of the federal agency of executive power for the securities market [paragraph four added by Federal Law No. 185-ФЗ, 28 December 2002].

The registering agency shall consider the report concerning the results of the issue (or additional issue) of emission securities within a two-week period and in the absence of violations connected with the issue of securities, shall register it. The registering agency shall be liable for the completeness of the report registered by it.

Article 26. Emission Not in Good Faith

Actions expressed in a violation of the procedure for an emission established in the present Section which are grounds for a refusal by registering agencies of the State registration of an issue (or additional issue) of emission securities, deeming the issue of emission securities to be unconstituted, or suspension of the emission of emission securities shall be deemed to be an emission not in good faith [as amended by Federal Law No. 185-ФЗ, 28 December 2002].

In the event of the discovery by a registering agency of the indicia of an emission not in good faith, it shall be obliged within seven days to communicate this to the federal agency of executive power for the securities market (regional division of federal agency of executive power for the securities market) [as amended by Federal Law No. 185-ФЗ, 28 December 2002].

The State registration of an issue (or additional issue) of emission securities may be refused when there are grounds provided for in Article 21 of the present Federal Law [as amended by Federal Law No. 185-ФЗ, 28 December 2002].

The issue of emission securities may be suspended or deemed to be unconstituted in the event of the discovery by the registering agency of the following violations:

violation by the emitent in the course of the emission of the requirements of legislation of the Russian Federation;

discovery in documents on the basis of which the issuance of securities was registered of unreliable information.

In the event of eliciting violations of the established procedure of an emission the registering agency may also suspend the emission until the elimination of violations within the limits of a period for placement of the securities. The renewal of the emission shall be effectuated according to a special decision of the registering agency.

In the event of the deeming of the issue of emission securities to be invalid, all securities of the particular issue shall be subject to return to the emitent, and the means received by the emitent from the placement of the issue of securities deemed to be invalid must be returned to the possessors. The federal agency of executive power for the securities market shall have the right to apply to a court for the return of the means to possessors [as amended by Federal Law No. 185-ФЗ, 28 December 2002].

All costs connected with deeming the issuance of emission securities to be invalid (or unconstituted) and return of means to possessors shall be relegated to the expense of the emitent.

In the event of a violation expressed in the issue of securities into circulation in excess of that declared in the securities prospectus, the emitent shall be obliged to ensure the purchase and cancellation of securities issued into circulation in excess of the quantity announced for issue [as amended by Federal Law No. 185-ФЗ, 28 December 2002].

If the emitent within two months does not ensure the purchase and cancellation of securities issued into circulation in excess of the quantity announced for issue, the federal agency of executive power for the securities market shall have the right to apply to a court concerning the recovery of the means unfoundedly received by the emitent [as amended by Federal Law No. 185-ФЗ, 28 December 2002].

The period of limitations for deeming invalid an issue (or additional issue) of emission securities, transactions concluded in the process of the placement of emission securities, and the report concerning the results of their issue shall comprise three months from the moment of registration of the report concerning the results of the issue (or additional issue) of these securities [paragraph added by Federal Law No. 185-ФЗ, 28 December 2002]

Article 27. Peculiarities of Emission of Stocks by Credit Organisations

The accumulation of means in the process of the emission of stocks by credit organisations shall be effectuated by the opening by the emitent bank of a cumulation account.

The regime of the cumulation account shall be established by the Central Bank of the Russian Federation.

Article 27¹. Peculiarities of Emission of Options of Emitent [added by Federal Law No. 185-ФЗ, 28 December 2002]

An emitent shall not have the right to place options of the emitent if the quantity of declared stocks of the emitent is less than the quantity of stocks, the right to the acquisition of which grant such options.

The quantity of stocks of a determined category (or type), the right to the acquisition of which grants options of the emitent, may not exceed 5% of the stocks of this category (or type) placed on the date of submission of the documents for State registration of the issue of options of the emitent.

The decision concerning the issue of options of an emitent may provide for limitations on the circulation thereof.

The placement of options of the emitent shall be possible only after the paying up in full of the charter capital of a joint-stock society.

Article 27². Peculiarities of Emission and Circulation of Bonds With Security [added by Federal Law No. 185-ФЗ, 28 December 2002]

1. Bonds, the performance of obligations under which is secured by a pledge (hereinafter—bonds with pledge security), suretyship, bank guarantee, State or municipal guarantee) shall be deemed to be bonds with security.

To relations connected with securing the performance of obligations under bonds with the pledge of property of the emitent or a third person shall apply the provisions of the Civil Code of the Russian Federation and other federal laws, taking into account the peculiarities established by the present Federal Law.

A bond with security shall grant to the possessor thereof all rights arising from such security. With the transfer of rights to a bond with security shall pass all rights to the new possessor (or acquirer) arising from such security. The transfer of rights which arose from the security provided without the transfer of rights to the bond shall be invalid.

2. In the event of the emission of bonds with security the conditions of the secured obligation must be contained in the decision concerning the issue of

bonds and, if in accordance with the present Federal Law, State registration of the issue of bonds is accompanied by the registration of a bond prospectus, in the bond prospectus, and in the event of the documentary form of the issue, also in the bond certificates.

3. If security with regard to bonds has been provided by a third person, the decision concerning the issue of bonds and/or bond prospectus, and in the event of the documentary form of issue, also a certificate, must be signed also by the person who provided such security.

4. If security with regard to bonds has been provided by a foreign person, to the relations connected with the securing of bonds shall apply norms of law of the Russian Federation. All disputes which arose as a consequence of the failure to perform or improper performance by the person who provided the security of his duties shall be within the systemic jurisdiction of the courts of the Russian Federation.

Article 27³. Bonds with Pledge Security [added by Federal Law No. 185-ФЗ, 28 December 2002]

1. Only securities and immoveable property may be the subject of a pledge with regard to bonds with pledge security.

Property which is the subject of a pledge with regard to bonds with pledge security shall be subject to valuation by a valuer.

2. Each possessor of a bond with pledge security of one issue shall have rights equal with all other possessors of bonds of this same issue with respect to property which is the subject of pledge, and also insurance compensation and the amounts of compensation due to the pledgor in the event of the withdrawal (or purchase) of pledged property for State or municipal needs and the requisition or nationalisation thereof.

3. A contract of pledge by which the performance is secured of obligations with regard to bonds shall be considered to be concluded from the moment of the arising with the first possessor (or acquirer) thereof of the rights to such bonds. In so doing the written form of the contract on pledge shall be considered to be complied with. If the performance of obligations under bonds is secured by the pledge of immoveable property (mortgage), demands concerning the notarial form of the contract of mortgage and the State registration thereof shall be considered to be complied with on condition of notarial certification and State registration by a justice institution of the decision concerning the issue of bonds with pledge security.

4. Notarial certification and State registration by a justice institution of a decision concerning the issue of bonds secured by a mortgage shall be effectuated after the State registration of the issue of such bonds. State registration of a mortgage

shall be effectuated by a justice institution simultaneously with the State registration of the decision concerning the issue of bonds secured by the mortgage.

The placement of bonds secured by a mortgage before State registration of the mortgage shall be prohibited.

5. If the performance of obligations with regard to bonds is secured by a pledge of immoveable property (mortgage), for State registration of the mortgage, instead of a notarially certified contract concerning the mortgage and a copy thereof, and also a document confirming the arising of the obligation secured by the mortgage, there shall be submitted a notarially certified decision concerning the issue of bonds secured by a mortgage and a copy of such decision. In the event of the State registration of a mortgage as information concerning the initial pledgeholder the registration entry concerning the mortgage in the unified State register of rights to immoveable property must contain the registration number of the issue of bonds and the date of State registration thereof, and also an indication that the possessors of bonds of the issue with the said State registration number are the pledgeholders.

In the event of the deeming of the issue of bonds secured by a pledge to be unconstituted, the registration entry concerning the mortgage shall be cancelled on the basis of an application of the pledgor, to which shall be appended a document confirming the adoption by the registering agency of a decision to deem the respective issue of bonds to be unconstituted.

6. If securities are not inscribed, they may be provided as security with regard to bonds only on condition of recording the rights thereto in a depositary.

7. If bonds have been secured by a pledge of securities, the rights to which have been recorded in the system of keeping a register (or in the register) or in a depositary, after the State registration of the issue of such bonds and before the commencement of their placement the pledgor shall be obliged to fix the encumberment of the securities by a pledge with the person effectuating the recording of rights to these securities and to submit evidence of such fixation in the agency effectuating State registration of the respective issue of bonds, with State registration of the report concerning the results of the issue.

8. In the event of the failure to perform or improper performance of obligations with regard to bonds with pledge security, property which is the subject of a pledge shall be subject to realisation upon the written demand of any of the possessors of such securities sent to the pledgeholder, person specified in the decision concerning the issue as the person who will effectuate the realisation of the pledged property, and also to the emitent of such securities if the pledgor is a third person.

Possessors of bonds with pledge security shall have the right to declare the said demands within two months from the day of ensuing of the period of performance of the obligation (or expiry of the last day of the period if performance of obligations was provided for within a determined period of time).

Public sales with regard to the realisation of pledged property by which obligations have been secured with regard to bonds may not be conducted earlier than the expiry of the period established for the presentation of demands of possessors of the said bonds.

Monetary means received from the realisation of pledged property shall be sent to persons who are possessors of bonds with pledge security having the right to effectuate the rights certified by the said securities and who have declared their own demands during the period established by the present Article for sending demands concerning the realisation of pledged property or upon the expiry of that period, but not later than the last day of the period established by the decision concerning the issue of these securities for realisation of the pledged property. If the amount received in the event of realisation of pledged property exceeds the amount of demands secured by the pledge with regard to bonds, the difference after withholding the amounts therefrom necessary to cover expenses connected with the levy of execution against this property and the realisation thereof shall be returned to the pledgor. The amount received from realisation of pledged property and remaining after the satisfaction of the demands of possessors of bonds with pledge security within the said procedure not exceeding the amount of demands secured by the pledge with regard to bonds shall be subject to being credited to a deposit with a notary. Possessors who have not sent the said written demands concerning the realisation of pledged property and not received means from the realisation thereof shall have the right to receive them through the deposit with the notary in the procedure established by a law.

If on the grounds provided for by legislation of the Russian Federation pledged property must pass to the ownership of the possessors of bonds with pledge security, the property which is the subject of pledge with regard to bonds shall pass to the common participatory share ownership of all possessors of bonds secured by such pledge.

Article 27⁴. Bonds Secured by Suretyship [added by Federal Law No. 185-ФЗ, 28 December 2002]

A contract of suretyship by which the performance of obligations is secured with regard to bonds shall be considered to be concluded from the moment of the arising with the first possessor thereof of rights to such bonds. In so doing the written form of the contract of suretyship shall be considered to be complied with.

A contract of suretyship by which the performance of obligations is secured with regard to bonds may provide only for joint and several responsibility of the surety and the emitent for the failure to perform or improper performance by the emitent of obligations with regard to the bonds.

Article 27⁵. Bonds Secured by Bank Guarantee and State or Municipal Guarantee [added by Federal Law No. 185-ФЗ, 28 December 2002]

A bank guarantee provided to secure the performance of obligations with regard to bonds may not be revoked.

The period for which a bank guarantee is issued must not by more than six months exceed the date (or period of ending) of cancellation of the bonds secured by such guarantee.

It must be provided by the conditions of a bank guarantee that the rights of demand against the guarantor shall pass to the person to whom the rights to the bond pass.

A bank guarantee which is secured by the performance of obligations with regard to bonds must provide only for the joint and several responsibility of the guarantor and emitent for the failure to perform or improper performance by the emitent of obligations with regard to the bonds.

State and municipal guarantees with regard to bonds shall be provided in accordance with budget legislation of the Russian Federation and legislation of the Russian Federation on State (or municipal) securities.

Chapter 6. Circulation of Emission Securities

Article 27⁶. Limitations on Circulation of Emission Securities [added by Federal Law No. 185-ФЗ, 28 December 2002]

The circulation of emission securities before the paying up thereof in full and State registration of the report concerning the results of their issue shall be prohibited. In so doing the public circulation of emission securities, including securities of foreign emitents, before registration of the securities prospectus shall be prohibited.

Article 28. Form of Certification of Right of Ownership to Emission Securites

The rights of possessors to emission securities of the documentary form of issuance shall be certified by certificates (if certificates are situated with possessors) or by certificates and entries in deposit accounts at depositaries (if the certificates are transferred for keeping to the depositary).

The rights of possessors to emission securities of paperless form of issue shall be certified in the system of keeping the register by entries in personal accounts with the holder of the register or in the event of the recording of rights to securities at the depositary, by entries in the deposit accounts at the depositaries.

Article 29. Transfer of Rights to Securities and Realisation of Rights Consolidated by Securities

The right to a bearer documentary security shall pass to the acquirer:

in the event of the certificate thereof being with the possessor: at the moment of transfer of this certificate to the acquirer;

in the event of the keeping of certificates of bearer documentary securities and/or recording of rights to such securities in a depositary: at the moment of effectuation of the arrival entry in the deposit account of the acquirer.

The right to an inscribed paperless security shall pass to the acquirer:

in the event of the recording of the rights to securities with the person effectuating depositary activity: from the moment of making the arrival entry in the deposit account of the acquirer;

in the event of the recording of the rights to securities in the system of keeping the register: from the moment of making the arrival entry in the personal account of the acquirer.

[paragraph three repealed by Federal Law No. 185-ФЗ, 28 December 2002]

The rights consolidated by an emission security shall pass to the acquirer thereof from the moment of transfer of the rights to this security. The transfer of the rights consolidated by an inscribed emission security must be accompanied by informing the holder of the register or the depositary or the nominee holder of the securities.

The rights relating to bearer emission securities shall be effectuated upon presentation by the possessor thereof or his entrusted person.

[paragraph six repealed by Federal Law No. 185-ФЗ, 28 December 2002]

In the event certificates of documentary emission securities are kept in depositaries, the rights consolidated by securities shall be effectuated on the basis of certificates presented by these depositaries under a commission of the possessors granted by depositary contracts with the list of such possessors appended. The emitent in this instance shall ensure the realisation of the rights relating to bearer securities of the person specified in this list.

The effectuation of rights relating to inscribed paperless emission securities shall be by the emitent with respect to the persons specified in the system of conducting the register.

If the data concerning the new possessor of such security was not communicated to the holder of the register of the particular issuance or to the nominee holder of the security at the moment of closing the register in order to execute the performance of obligations of the emitent comprising the security (voting, receipt of revenue, and others), the performance of obligations with respect to the possessor registered in the register at the moment of closure thereof shall be deemed to be proper. Responsibility for the timely notification lies on the acquirer of the security.

If by legislation of the Russian Federation or other normative legal acts of the Russian Federation limitations have been established on the participatory share of participation of foreign persons in the capital of Russian emitents, the conclusion of transactions with regard to the acquisition by foreign possessors of stocks issued by such Russian emitents, the parties under the transaction shall inform the federal agency of executive power for the securities market and other agencies in the instances provided for by federal laws [as amended by Federal Law No. 185-ФЗ, 28 December 2002].

[paragraph eleven repealed by Federal Law No. 185-ФЗ, 28 December 2002]

The authenticity of the signature of natural persons on documents concerning the transfer of rights to securities and rights consolidated by securities (except for instances provided for by legislation of the Russian Federation) may be attested notarially or professional participant of the securities market.

Section IV. Informational Provision of Securities Market

Chapter 7. On Disclosure of Information on Securities

Article 30. Disclosure of Information

Disclosure of information shall be understood to be ensuring the accessibility thereof to all persons interested therein irrespective of the purpose of receiving the said information with regard to the procedure guaranteeing the location and receipt thereof.

Information with respect to which actions have been conducted with regard to disclosing it shall be deemed to be disclosed information on the securities market.

Generally-accessible information on the securities market shall be deemed to be information not requiring privileges for access thereto or subject to disclosure in accordance with the present Federal Law.

In the event of the registration of a securities prospectus the emitent shall be obliged to effectuate the disclosure of information in the form of:

the quarterly report of the emitent of emission securities (quarterly report);

a communication concerning material facts (or events, actions) affecting the financial-economic activity of the emitent of emission securities (communication concerning material facts) [as amended by Federal Law No. 185-ФЗ, 28 December 2002].

The quarterly report must contain information, the composition and amount of which corresponds to the requirements of the present Federal Law for a securities prospectus, except for information concerning the procedure and conditions of placement of emission securities [as amended by Federal Law No. 185-ФЗ, 28 December 2002].

The yearly bookkeeping report for the last completed financial year shall be included in the composition of the quarterly report for the first quarter [as amended by Federal Law No. 185-ФЗ, 28 December 2002].

In the event of drawing up a composite bookkeeping report of the emitent such bookkeeping report for the last completed financial year shall be included in the composition of the quarterly report for the second quarter [added by Federal Law No. 185-ФЗ, 28 December 2002].

The yearly bookkeeping report of the emitent, and also composite bookkeeping report of the emitent for two completed financial years preceding the last completed financial year, shall not be submitted in the composition of the quarterly report [added by Federal Law No. 185-ФЗ, 28 December 2002].

The bookkeeping report for the fourth quarter shall not be included in the quarterly report [added by Federal Law No. 185-ФЗ, 28 December 2002].

The quarterly report shall be submitted to the registering agency not later than 45 days from the date of the end of the reporting quarter [added by Federal Law No. 185-ФЗ, 28 December 2002].

The quarterly report must be signed by the person effectuating the functions of one-man executive organ of the emitent, the chief bookkeeper thereof (or other person fulfilling his functions), thereby confirming the reliability of all information contained therein. A quarterly report must be provided to possessions of emission securities of the emitent upon their request for payment not exceeding expenditures for the manufacture of brochures. Persons who have signed the quarterly report shall bear responsibility for the fullness and reliability of the information communicated therein [added by Federal Law No. 185-ФЗ, 28 December 2002].

Communications concerning material facts shall be deemed to be [as amended by Federal Law No. 185-ФЗ, 28 December 2002]:

information concerning the reorganisation of the emitent and its subsidiary and dependent societies;

information concerning facts which entailed the one-off increase or reduction of the value of assets of the emitent by more than 10%, concerning facts which entailed the one-off increase of net profit or net losses of the emitent of more than 10%, concerning facts of one-off transactions of the emitent, the amount of which or the value of the property with regard to which comprises 10% and more of the assets of the emitent as of the date of the transaction;

information concerning the issue by the emitent of securities and concerning credited and/or paid revenues with regard to securities of the emitent;

information concerning the emergence in the register of the emitent of a person possessing more than 25% of its emission securities of any individual type;

information concerning the dates of the closure of the register, the periods for the performance of obligations of the emitent to possessors, and decisions of general meetings;

information concerning the adoption by the empowered organ of the emitent of a decision concerning the issuance of emission securities.

Communications concerning material facts must be sent by the emitent to the federal agency of executive power for the securities market or agency empowered by it, and also shall be published by the emitent not later than five days from the moment of the ensuing of these facts in printed mass media disseminated by a print run accessible to the majority of possessors of securities of the emitent [as amended by Federal Law No. 185-ФЗ, 28 December 2002].

The possessor shall be obliged to effectuate the disclosure of information concerning its possession of emission securities of any emitent whatsoever, except for bonds not convertible into stocks, in the following instances [as amended by Federal Law No. 185-ФЗ, 28 December 2002]:

the possessor entered into possession of 20% or more of any type of emission securities of the emitent;

the possessor increased its participatory share of possession of any type of emission securities of the emitent up to a level by a multiple of 5% above the 20% of this type of securities;

the possessor reduced its participatory share of possession of any type of emission securities of the emitent up to a level by a multiple of 5% above 20% of this type of securities.

The possessor shall disclose the said information (containing the name of the possessor, type and State registration number of the securities, name of the emitent, quantity of securities belonging to it) not later than five days after the respective actions by means in notifying the federal agency of executive power for the securities market or agency empowered by it [as amended by Federal Law No. 185-ФЗ, 28 December 2002].

Professional participants of the securities market shall be obliged to effectuate the disclosure of information concerning its securities operations in the following instances:

the professional participant of the securities market performed operations within one quarter with a single type of securities of a single emitent, if the quantity of securities relating to these operations comprised not less than 100% of the total number of the said securities;

the professional participant of the securities market performed a one-off operation with a single type of securities of a single emitent, if the quantity of securities relating to this operation comprised not less than 15% of the total quantity of the said securities.

Professional participants of the securities market shall disclose the said information (containing the name of the professional participant of the securities market, type and State registration code of the securities, name of the emitent, price of one security, quantity of securities with regard to respective transactions) not later than five days after the end of the respective quarter or after the respective one-off operation by means of informing the federal agency of executive power for the securities market or agency empowered by it [as amended by Federal Law No. 185-ФЗ, 28 December 2002].

A professional participant of the securities market shall when offering and/or announcing prices for the purchase and/or sale of emission securities, be obliged to disclose generally accessible information which he has disclosed by the emitent of these emission securities or communicate the fact that he lacks such information.

The composition, procedure, and periods for the disclosure of information, and also the submission of reports by professional participants of the securities market, shall be determined by normative legal acts of the federal agency of executive power for the securities market [as amended by Federal Law No. 185-ФЗ, 28 December 2002].

Chapter 8. On Use of Employment Information on Securities Market

Article 31. Employment Information

Employment information for the purposes of the present Federal Law shall be deemed to be any information which is not generally accessible concerning the emitent and emission securities issued by it which places persons possessing such information by virtue of their employment position, labour duties, or a contract concluded with the emitent in a preferential position in comparison with other subjects of the securities market.

Article 32. On Persons Disposing of Employment Information

There shall be relegated to persons disposing of employment information:
members of the management organs of the emitent or professional participant of the securities market connected with this emitent by a contract;
[paragraph three repealed by Federal Law No. 185-ФЗ, 28 December 2002]
auditors of the emitent or professional participant of the securities market connected with this emitent by a contract;
employees of State agencies having by virtue of control, supervisory, and other powers access to the said information.

In so doing members of management organs of the emitent and a professional participant of the securities market shall be understood to be persons occupying posts permanently or temporarily which are connected with the fulfilment of organisational-administrative or administrative-economic duties, and also fulfilling such duties under a special power [as amended by Federal Law No. 185-ФЗ, 28 December 2002].

Article 33. Transactions Performed With Use of Employment Information

Persons disposing of employment information shall not have the right to use this information in order to conclude transactions, and also to transfer employment information to conclude transactions with third persons.

Persons who have violated the said requirement shall bear responsibility in accordance with legislation of the Russian Federation.

Chapter 9. On Advertising on the Securities Market

Article 34. Requirements for Advertising

An advertisement must contain the name of the advertiser. The advertiser who is a professional participant of the securities market shall also be obliged to include

in the advertisement information concerning the types of activity effectuated by
him on the securities market in accordance with the advertised announcement.

Advertisers shall be prohibited to:

specify in the advertisement reliable information concerning its activity and the
types and characteristics of securities offered for purchase or sale or other transactions therewith and the conditions of such transactions and other information
directed towards fraud or deceiving the possessors and other participants of the
securities market;

specify in the advertisement the proposed amount of revenues with regard to
the securities and the forecast of the growth of their rated value;

use the advertisement for the purposes of unfair competition by means of indicating real or fictitious shortcomings of professional participants of the securities
market engaging in analogous activity or emitents issuing analogous securities.

When one of the circumstances specified in paragraph two of the present
Article is present in an advertisement, the advertisement of the securities shall be
deemed to be not in good faith.

The public guarantee or otherwise bringing to the information of potential
possessors of data concerning the profitability of securities, ensuring thereof in
comparison with other securities or other financial instruments, and also communicating information known to be false or unreliable capable of entailing or
which entailed the deception of potential possessors relative to the securities being
acquired shall be deemed to be an advertisement not in good faith.

The advertiser shall bear responsibility for damage caused by an advertisement
not in good faith in accordance with legislation of the Russian Federation.

In the event of deeming an advertisement to be not in good faith, the contracts
of the advertiser with the disseminator of the advertisement shall be invalid.

Article 35. On Information Which Is Not Advertising on Securities Market

Generally accessible information on securities and emitents specified in Article
30 of the present Federal Law, and also information granted to empowered agencies in connection with the fulfilment by them of functions relating to regulation
of the securities market in accordance with legislation of the Russian Federation,
shall not be advertising on the securities market.

Information concerning the issue by the emitent of securities and dividends
calculated and/or paid shall be advertising.

Article 36. On Prohibition to Advertise Unregistered Issues of Emission Securities

The advertising of emission securities before the date of State registration of
their issues (or additional issues) in accordance with legislation of the Russian
Federation shall be prohibited. Contracts for advertising unregistered issues of

emission securities shall be invalid. Agencies which effectuated the State registration of an issue (or additional issue) of emission securities shall have the right to bring a suit with regard to the consequences which have arisen because of the invalidity of the contracts [as amended by Federal Law No. 185-ФЗ, 28 December 2002].

Article 37. On Grounds for Termination of Contract for Advertising Emission Securities

The deeming of the issue of emission securities to be unconstituted shall be grounds for the termination of a contract for advertising these securities. The contract for advertising emission securities, the issue of which is deemed to be unconstituted, shall terminate from the moment of notification of the advertisement disseminator by the registering agency which has deemed the issue of emission securities to be unconstituted. The advertisement disseminator shall have the right to demand from the advertiser compensation of losses caused as a result of the termination of the contract for advertising.

Section V. Regulation of Securities Market

Chapter 10. Foundations of Regulation of Securities Market

Article 38. Foundations of Regulation of Securities Market

State regulation of the securities market shall be effectuated by means of:

the establishment of obligatory requirements for the activity of emitents, professional participants of the securities market, and standards thereof;

the State registration of issues of emission securities and securities prospectuses and control over compliance by emitents with the conditions and obligations provided for therein [as amended by Federal Law No. 185-ФЗ, 28 December 2002];

the licensing of the activity of professional participants of the securities market;

the creation of a system for the defence of the rights of possessors and control over compliance with their rights by emitents and professional participants of the securities market;

the prohibitions and suppression of the activity of persons effectuating entrepreneurial activity on the securities market without a respective license.

Representative agencies of State power and agencies of local self-government shall establish maximum amounts of the emission of securities emitted by agencies of power of the respective level.

Chapter 11. Regulation of Activity of Professional Participants of Securities Market

Article 39. Licensing of Activity of Professional Participants of Securities Market

All types of professional activity on the securities market specified in Chapter 2 of the present Federal Law shall be effectuated on the basis of a special authorisation—a license issued by the federal agency of executive power for the securities market or agencies empowered by it on the basis of a general license [as amended by Federal Law No. 185-ФЗ, 28 December 2002].

Credit organisations shall effectuate professional activity on the securities market in the procedure established by the present Federal Law for professional participants of the securities market. An additional ground for refusal to issue a license to a credit organisation for the effectuation of professional activity on the securities market, suspension or annulment thereof shall be the annulment or revocation of a license for the effectuation of banking operations issued by the Bank of Russia [as amended by Federal Law No. 185-ФЗ, 28 December 2002].

The agencies which issued the license shall control the activity of professional participants of the securities market and shall adopt a decision concerning the revocation of the license issued in the event of a violation of legislation of the Russian Federation on securities.

The activity of professional participants of the securities market shall be licensed by three types of licenses: the license of a professional participant of the securities market; the license to effectuate activity with regard to keeping the register; and the license of the stock exchange.

A condition of the rendering of services by the broker and/or dealer with regard to the preparation of a securities prospectus shall be the conformity thereof to the requirements established by normative legal acts of the federal agency of executive power for the securities market to the extent of own capital and and skills requirements for personnel (or workers) [added by Federal Law No. 185-ФЗ, 28 December 2002].

Chapter 12. Federal Agency of Executive Power for Securities Market
[as amended by Federal Law No. 185-ФЗ, 28 December 2002]

Article 40. Organisation of Federal Agency of Executive Power for Securities Market [as amended by Federal Law No. 185-ФЗ, 28 December 2002]

The federal agency of executive power for the securities market shall be the federal agency of executive power for conducting State policy in the domain of the securities market, control over the activity of professional participants of the securities market through the determination of the procedure for their activity and determination of the standards of the emission of securities [as amended by Federal Law No. 185-Ф3, 28 December 2002].

The director of the federal agency of executive power for the securities market shall be *ex officio* a federal minister [as amended by Federal Law No. 185-Ф3, 28 December 2002].

The posts of five members of the federal agency of executive power for the securities market (first deputy chairman, deputy chairmen of the federal agency of executive power for the securities market, secretary of the federal agency of executive power for the securities market) shall be State posts of the State service and shall be filled in the established procedure [as amended by Federal Law No. 185-Ф3, 28 December 2002].

The basic functions and powers of the federal agency of executive power for the securities market shall be determined by the present Federal Law [as amended by Federal Law No. 185-Ф3, 28 December 2002].

The federal agency of executive power for the securities market shall in order to effectuate its powers create its own territorial agencies [as amended by Federal Law No. 185-Ф3, 28 December 2002].

The powers of the federal agency of executive power for the securities market shall not extend to the procedure for the emission of debt obligations of the Government of the Russian Federation and securities of subjects of the Russian Federation [as amended by Federal Law No. 185-Ф3, 28 December 2002].

Article 41. Collegium of Federal Agency of Executive Power for Securities Market [as amended by Federal Law No. 185-Ф3, 28 December 2002]

The collegium of the federal agency of executive power for the securities market shall consist of 15 members, including the chairman of the federal agency of executive power for the securities market, the first deputy and deputy chairmen of the federal agency of executive power for the securities market, and the secretary of the federal agency of executive power for the securities market [as amended by Federal Law No. 185-Ф3, 28 December 2002].

Five members of the collegium of the federal agency of executive power for the securities market shall be representatives of federal agencies of executive power within whose competence are questions connected with the securities market. The representative of the Ministry of Finances of the Russian Federation shall be obligatorily included in the membership thereof [as amended by Federal Law No. 185-Ф3, 28 December 2002].

One member of the collegium of the federal agency of executive power for the securities market shall be a representative of the Central Bank of the Russian Federation [as amended by Federal Law No. 185-Ф3, 28 December 2002].

The chairman of the Expert Council attached to the federal agency of executive power for the securities market shall be a member of the collegium of the federal agency of executive power for the securities market *ex officio* [as amended by Federal Law No. 185-ФЗ, 28 December 2002].

Two members of the collegium of the federal agency of executive power for the securities market shall be representatives of the chambers of the Federal Assembly of the Russian Federation [as amended by Federal Law No. 185-ФЗ, 28 December 2002].

A consultative-advisory organ—Expert Council attached to the federal agency of executive power for the securities market—shall be created by the federal agency of executive power for the securities market and shall have 25 members: representatives of State agencies and organisations whose activity is connected with the regulation of the financial market and the securities market, professional participants of the securities market, self-regulating organisations of professional participants of the securities market, unions and associations thereof, and other social associations and independent experts [as amended by Federal Law No. 185-ФЗ, 28 December 2002].

A member of the Expert Council attached to the federal agency of executive power for the securities market shall be appointed for a term of two years with the possibility of appointment any number of times [as amended by Federal Law No. 185-ФЗ, 28 December 2002].

Work in the collegium of the federal agency of executive power for the securities market and the Expert Council attached to the federal agency of executive power for the securities market of representatives of State agencies and other organisations specified in the present Article shall be effectuated on an uncompensated basis [as amended by Federal Law No. 185-ФЗ, 28 December 2002].

The collegium of the federal agency of executive power for the securities market autonomously shall confirm the Reglament of work and activity of the Expert Council attached to the federal agency of executive power for the securities market.

Article 42. Functions of Federal Agency of Executive Power for Securities Market [as amended by Federal Law No. 185-ФЗ, 28 December 2002]

The federal agency of executive power for the securities market shall [as amended by Federal Law No. 185-ФЗ, 28 December 2002]:

(1) effectuate the working out of the basic orientations of the development of the securities market and coordination of the activity of federal agencies of executive power for the securities market with regard to questions of the regulation of the securities market [as amended by Federal Law No. 185-ФЗ, 28 December 2002];

(2) confirm the standards for the emission of securities, securities prospectuses of emitents, including foreign emitents effectuating the emission of securities on the territory of the Russian Federation and the procedure for the State registration of the issue (or additional issue) of emission securities, State registration of reports concerning the results of the issue (or additional issue) of emission securities, and

the registration of securities prospectuses [as amended by Federal Law No. 185-ФЗ, 28 December 2002];

(3) work out and confirm unified requirements for rules for the effectuation of professional securities activity;

(4) establish obligatory requirements for securities operations, norms for the access of securities for public placement, circulation, quotation and listing, and settlement and depositary activity. The rules for keeping records and drawing up reports by emitents and professional participants of the securities market shall be established by the federal agency of executive power for the securities market jointly with the Ministry of Finances of the Russian Federation [as amended by Federal Law No. 185-ФЗ, 28 December 2002];

(5) establish obligatory requirements for the procedure of conducting the register;

(6) establish the procedure and effectuate the licensing of various types of professional activity on the securities market, and also suspend and annul the said licenses in the event of a violation of the requirements of legislation of the Russian Federation on securities;

(7) issue general licenses for the effectuation of activity with regard to the licensing of activity of professional participants of the securities market, and also suspend or annul the said licenses. The annulment of a general license issued to the empowered agency shall not entail the annulment of licenses issued by it to the professional participants of the securities market;

(8) establish the procedure, effectuate licensing, and conduct the register of self-regulating organisations of professional participants of the securities market and annul the said licenses in the event of a violation of the requirements of legislation of the Russian Federation on securities, and also standards and requirements confirmed by the federal agency of executive power for the securities market [as amended by Federal Law No. 185-ФЗ, 28 December 2002];

(9) determine the standards of activity of investment, non-State pension and insurance funds and their management companies, and also of insurance companies, on the securities market;

(10) effectuate control over compliance by emitents, professional participants of the securities market, and self-regulating organisations of professional participants of the securities market with the requirements of legislation of the Russian Federation on securities, standards, and requirements confirmed by the federal agency of executive power for the securities market [as amended by Federal Law No. 185-ФЗ, 28 December 2002];

(11) for the purposes of counteracting the legalisation (or laundering) of revenues received by criminal means, control the procedure for conducting operations with monetary means or other property performed by professional participants of the securities market [added by Federal Law No. 121-ФЗ, 7 August 2002];

(12) ensure the disclosure of information concerning registered issues of securities, professional participants of the securities market, and the regulation of the securities market;

(13) ensure the creation of a generally-accessible system for the disclosure of information on the securities market;

(14) confirm the qualifications requirements for executives and personnel (or workers) of professional participants of the securities market, effectuate the attestation thereof (or verification of conformity to qualifications of executives and workers to the qualification requirements) in the form of taking a qualifications examination and issuing a qualifications attestation, determine the procedure for conducting attestation, list of documents to be filed together with the application concerning admittance to attestation, quantity and types of attestants, syllabus of qualifications examination, and the procedure for taking it [as amended by Federal Law No. 185-ФЗ, 28 December 2002];

(15) work out draft legislative and other normative acts connected with questions of regulation of the securities market, licensing the activity of the professional participants thereof, and self-regulating organisations of professional participants of the securities market, control over compliance with legislative and normative acts on securities, and conduct the expert examination thereof;

(16) work out recommendations with regard to the application of legislation of the Russian Federation regulating relations connected with the functioning of the securities market [as amended by Federal Law No. 185-ФЗ, 28 December 2002];

(17) effectuate the direction of regional divisions of the federal agency of executive power for the securities market [as amended by Federal Law No. 185-ФЗ, 28 December 2002];

(18) conduct the register of issued, suspended, and annulled licenses;

(19) establish and determine the procedure for admittance to primary placement and circulation outside the territory of the Russian Federation of securities issued by emitents registered in the Russian Federation;

(20) apply to the arbitrazh court with a suit concerning the liquidation of a juridical person which has violated the requirements of legislation of the Russian Federation concerning securites and concerning the application to offenders of the sanctions established by legislation of the Russian Federation;

(21) effectuate supervision over the conformity of the amount of the issue of emission securities to the quantity thereof in circulation;

(22) [repealed by Federal Law No. 185-ФЗ, 28 December 2002].

Article 43. Decisions of Federal Agency of Executive Power for Securities Market [as amended by Federal Law No. 185-ФЗ, 28 December 2002]

The federal agency of executive power for the securities market shall adopt decisions with regard to questions of the regulation of the securities market, the activity of professional participants of the securities market, self-regulating organisations of professional participants of the securities market, and control over compliance with legislation of the Russian Federation and normative acts on securities [as amended by Federal Law No. 185-ФЗ, 28 December 2002].

Decisions of the federal agency of executive power for the securities market shall be adopted in the form of decrees [as amended by Federal Law No. 185-ФЗ, 28 December 2002].

Decrees adopted by the federal agency of executive power for the securities market shall be signed by the chairman of the federal agency of executive power for the securities market, and in his absence, by his first deputy [as amended by Federal Law No. 185-ФЗ, 28 December 2002].

Protocols of the federal agency of executive power for the securities market shall be signed by the chairman of the federal agency of executive power for the securities market and by the secretary of the federal agency of executive power for the securities market [as amended by Federal Law No. 185-ФЗ, 28 December 2002].

Members of the federal agency of executive power for the securities market shall have the right to submit their opinion with regard to individual questions in the protocol, and also append to the protocol in written form a special opinion and individual materials [as amended by Federal Law No. 185-ФЗ, 28 December 2002].

The preparation and adoption of documents in which a credit organisation is specially singled out by the federal agency of executive power for the securities market shall be by agreement with the Central Bank of the Russian Federation [as amended by Federal Law No. 185-ФЗ, 28 December 2002].

The operations with currency exchange valuables shall be regulated by the federal agency by agreement with the Central Bank of the Russian Federation [as amended by Federal Law No. 185-ФЗ, 28 December 2002].

Decrees of the federal agency of executive power for the securities market with regard to questions relegated to its competence are binding for execution by federal ministries and other federal agencies of executive power, agencies of executive power of subjects of the Russian Federation, and agencies of local self-government, and also professional participants of the securities market and self-regulating organisations [as amended by Federal Law No. 185-ФЗ, 28 December 2002].

The adoption of decrees of the federal agency of executive power for the securities market without preliminary consideration thereof at the Expert Council attached to the federal agency of executive power for the securities market shall not be permitted [as amended by Federal Law No. 185-ФЗ, 28 December 2002].

Decrees of the federal agency of executive power for the securities market shall be subject to obligatory publication [as amended by Federal Law No. 185-ФЗ, 28 December 2002].

Decrees of the federal agency of executive power for the securities market having a normative character shall be subject to State registration in the instances and in the procedure which has been provided for normative legal acts of federal agencies of executive power [added by Federal Law No. 182-ФЗ, 26 November 1998, as amended by Federal Law No. 185-ФЗ, 28 December 2002].

Decrees of the federal agency of executive power for the securities market having a normative character shall enter into force upon the expiry of ten days from the day of their official publication unless another period for their entry into force has been provided for in those decrees [added by Federal Law No. 182-ФЗ, 26 November 1998, as amended by Federal Law No. 185-ФЗ, 28 December 2002].

Decrees of the federal agency of executive power for the securities market may be appealed by natural and juridical persons to a court or arbitrazh court [as amended by Federal Law No. 185-ФЗ, 28 December 2002].

Normative acts with regard to questions of the regulation of the securities market, the activity of professional participants of the securities market, and self-regulating organisations of professional participants of the securities market shall be adopted by federal ministries and other federal agencies of executive power within the limits of their competence only by agreement with the federal agency of executive power for the securities market [as amended by Federal Law No. 185-ФЗ, 28 December 2002].

Article 44. Rights of Federal Agency of Executive Power for Securities Market [as amended by Federal Law No. 185-ФЗ, 28 December 2002]

The federal agency of executive power for the securities market shall have the right to [as amended by Federal Law No. 185-ФЗ, 28 December 2002]:

(1) issue general licenses for the effectuation of licensing of professional participants of the securities market, and also for the effectuation of control over the securities market, to federal agencies of executive power (with the right to delegate functions relating to licensing to their territorial agencies);

(2) classify securities and determine their types in accordance with legislation of the Russian Federation;

(3) establish normative standards which are binding upon professional participants of the securities market, except for credit organisations, for sufficiency of own means and other requirements directed towards reducing risks of professional activity on the securities market, and also excluding conflicts of interests, including in the event of the rendering by a broker who is a financial consultant of services with regard to the placement of emission securities [as amended by Federal Law No. 185-ФЗ, 28 December 2002];

(4) in the event of a repeated violation within one year by professional participants of the securities market of legislation of the Russian Federation concerning securities, adopt a decision concerning the suspension of the operation or annulment of the license for the effectuation of professional activity on the securities market. Immediately after the entry into force of a decision of the federal agency of executive power for the securities market concerning the suspension of the

operation of the license, the State agency which issued the respective license must adopt measures with regard to the elimination of violations or annul the license [as amended by Federal Law No. 185-ФЗ, 28 December 2002];

in the event of a repeated violation within one year by professional participants of the securities market of demands provided for by Articles 6 and 7 (except for Article 7(3)) of the Federal Law "On Counteracting the Legalisation (of Laundering) of Revenues Received by Criminal Means", adopt a decision concerning annulment of the license for the effectuation of professional activity on the securities market [as amended by Federal Law No. 121-ФЗ, 7 August 2001];

(5) on the grounds provided for by legislation of the Russian Federation, refuse to issue a license to a self-regulating organisation of professional participants of the securities market and annul the license issued to it with obligatory publication of a communication thereof in the mass media;

(6) establish the procedure for conducting verifications of emitents, professional participants of the securities market, and self-regulating organisations of professional participants of the securities market, and also other organisations licensed by it, effectuate autonomously or jointly with respective federal agencies of executive power the verification of the activity of emitents, professional participants of the securities market, and self-regulating organisations of professional participants of the securities market, and also other organisations licensed by it, and appoint and recall inspectors for control over the activity of the said organisations [as amended by Federal Law No. 185-ФЗ, 28 December 2002];

(7) send to emitents and professional participants of the securities market, and also to their self-regulating organisations, prescriptions binding for execution and also demand from them the submission of documents necessary in order to decide questions within the competence of the federal agency of executive power for the securities market [as amended by Federal Law No. 185-ФЗ, 28 December 2002];

(8) send materials to law enforcement agencies and apply with suits to a court (or arbitrazh court) with regard to questions relegated to the competence of the federal agency of executive power for the securities market (including the invalidity of securities transactions) [as amended by Federal Law No. 185-ФЗ, 28 December 2002];

(9) adopt decisions concerning the creation and liquidation of regional divisions of the federal agency of executive power for the securities market [as amended by Federal Law No. 185-ФЗ, 28 December 2002];

(10) annul qualifications attestations of natural persons in the event of the repeated or flagrant violation by them of legislation of the Russian Federation on securities [as amended by Federal Law No. 185-ФЗ, 28 December 2002];

(11) establish normative standards obligatory for compliance by emitents of securities and the rules for the application thereof.

Article 44¹. Duties of Federal Agency of Executive Power for Securities Market [added by Federal Law No. 185-ФЗ, 28 December 2002]

When effectuating the powers granted by the present Federal Law, the federal agency of executive power for the securities market shall be obliged to:

(1) ensure the confidentiality of information provided to it, except for information disclosed in accordance with legislation of the Russian Federation on securities;

(2) when sending to emitents, professional participants of the securities market, and self-regulating organisations of professional participants of the securities market queries concerning the provision of information to substantiate with reasons the necessity to receive the information requested;

(3) effectuate the registration of documents of professional participants of the securities market and self-regulating organisations of professional participants of the securities market subject to registration in accordance with the present Federal Law not later than 30 days from the date of receipt of the respective documents or to provide within the said period a reasoned refusal of registration unless other periods for registration have been established by the present Federal Law;

(4) provide within 30 days reasoned replies to queries of juridical persons and citizens with regard to questions relegated to the competence of the federal agency of executive power for the securities market.

Article 45. Expert Council Attached to Federal Agency of Executive Power for Securities Market [as amended by Federal Law No. 185-ФЗ, 28 December 2002]

Professional participants of the securities market shall elect their candidates to the Expert Council attached to the federal agency of executive power for the securities market at the All-Russian Conference of Professional Participants of the Securities Market, organised by the federal agency of executive power for the securities market [as amended by Federal Law No. 185-ФЗ, 28 December 2002].

Candidates elected by professional participants of the securities market shall be confirmed as members of the Expert Council attached to the federal agency of executive power for the securities market by decision of the federal agency of executive power for the securities market [as amended by Federal Law No. 185-ФЗ, 28 December 2002].

The chairman of the Expert Council attached to the federal agency of executive power for the securities market shall be elected by the members of the Expert Council and shall be confirmed by the chairman of the federal agency of executive power for the securities market [as amended by Federal Law No. 185-ФЗ, 28 December 2002].

The procedure for the submission of candidacies for election as member of the Expert Council attached to the federal agency of executive power for the securities market from professional participants of the securities market and the conducting and totalling of the results of voting shall be established by decision of the All-Russian Conference of Professional Participants of the Securities Market [as amended by Federal Law No. 185-ФЗ, 28 December 2002].

Candidates for the Expert Council attached to the federal agency of executive power for the securities market from State agencies shall be submitted by these State agencies and shall be confirmed by decision of the federal agency of executive power for the securities market [as amended by Federal Law No. 185-ФЗ, 28 December 2002].

The Expert Council attached to the federal agency of executive power for the securities market shall effectuate [as amended by Federal Law No. 185-ФЗ, 28 December 2002]:

the preparation and preliminary consideration of questions connected with the execution of powers of the federal agency of executive power for the securities market [as amended by Federal Law No. 185-ФЗ, 28 December 2002];

the working out of proposals with regard to the basic orientations of regulation of the securities market;

the preliminary consideration of draft decrees to be adopted by the federal agency of executive power for the securities market, and their publication at the demand of any member of the Expert Council attached to the federal agency of executive power for the securities market [as amended by Federal Law No. 185-ФЗ, 28 December 2002].

The Expert Council attached to the federal agency of executive power for the securities market shall have the right by a majority vote of its members to suspend for a term of up to six months the introduction into operation of decrees of the federal agency of executive power for the securities market [as amended by Federal Law No. 185-ФЗ, 28 December 2002].

Article 46. Ensuring Activity of Federal Agency of Executive Power for Securities Market [as amended by Federal Law No. 185-ФЗ, 28 December 2002]

The activity of the federal agency of executive power for the securities market shall be ensured by the working apparatus [as amended by Federal Law No. 185-ФЗ, 28 December 2002].

The expenses connected with the activity of the federal agency of executive power for the securities market shall be effectuated at the expense of means of the federal budget directed towards the maintenance of federal agencies of executive power [as amended by Federal Law No. 185-ФЗ, 28 December 2002].

The federal agency of executive power for the securities market shall be a juridical person and have a seal depicting the State Arms of the Russian Federation and its own name [as amended by Federal Law No. 185-ФЗ, 28 December 2002].

The federal agency of executive power for the securities market shall have a settlement account and other accounts, including hard currency [as amended by Federal Law No. 185-ФЗ, 28 December 2002].

The location of the federal agency of executive power for the securities market shall be the City of Moscow [as amended by Federal Law No. 185-ФЗ, 28 December 2002].

Article 47. Regional Divisions of Federal Agency of Executive Power for Securities Market [as amended by Federal Law No. 185-ФЗ, 28 December 2002]

Regional divisions of the federal agency of executive power for the securities market shall be formed by decision of the federal agency of executive power for the securities market by agreement with agencies of executive power of subjects of the Russian Federation in order to ensure the fulfilment of the norms, rules, and conditions established by legislation of the Russian Federation for the functioning of the stock market, the practical realisation of decisions to be adopted by the federal agency of executive power for the securities market, and control over activity of professional participants of the securities market [as amended by Federal Law No. 185-ФЗ, 28 December 2002].

A regional division of the federal agency of executive power for the securities market shall operate on the basis of a Statute confirmed by the federal agency of executive power for the securities market [as amended by Federal Law No. 185-ФЗ, 28 December 2002].

The chairman of a regional division shall be confirmed by the federal agency of executive power for the securities market on the basis of the joint recommendation of the head of executive power of the subject of the Russian Federation and the chairman of the federal agency of executive power for the securities market [as amended by Federal Law No. 185-ФЗ, 28 December 2002].

Chapter 13. Self-Regulating Organisations of Professional Participants of the Securities Market

Article 48. Concept of Self-Regulating Organisation of Professional Participants of Securities Market

A voluntary association of professional participants of the securities market acting in accordance with the present Federal Law and functioning on the principles of a nomcommercial organisation shall be called a self-regulating organisation of professional participants of the securities market (hereinafter: self-regulating organisation).

A self-regulating organisation shall be founded by professional participants of the securities market in order to ensure the conditions of professional activity of participants of the securities market, compliance with the standards of professional ethics on the securities market, defence of the interests of the possessors of securities and other clients of professional participants of the securities market who are members of the self-regulating organisation, the establishment of rules and standards for conducting securities operations, and ensuring the effective activity of the securities market.

All revenues of the self-regulating organisation shall be used by it exclusively in order to fulfil the charter tasks and shall not be distributed among its members.

A self-regulating organisation shall, in accordance with the requirements for the effectuation of professional activity and the conducting of securities operations which are confirmed by the federal agency of executive power for the securities market, establish rules binding upon its members for the effectuation of professional activity on the securities market and standards for conducting securities operations and effectuate control over compliance therewith [as amended by Federal Law No. 185-Ф3, 28 December 2002].

Article 49. Rights of Self-Regulating Organisations in Regulating Securities Market

A self-regulating organisation shall have the right to:

receive information relating to the results of verifications of the activity of their members effectuated in the procedure established by the federal agency of executive power for the securities market (or regional division of the federal agency of executive power for the securities market) [as amended by Federal Law No. 185-Ф3, 28 December 2002];

work out in accordance with the present Federal Law the rules and standards for the effectuation of professional activity and securities operations by their members and effectuate control over compliance therewith;

control compliance by their members with the rules and standards adopted by the self-regulating organisation for the effectuation of professional activity and securities operations;

in accordance with the qualifications requirements of the federal agency of executive power for the securities market, work out instructional syllabi and plans, effectuate the training of officials and personnel of organisations effectuating professional activity on the securities market, determine the qualifications of the said persons, and issue them qualifications attestations [as amended by Federal Law No. 185-Ф3, 28 December 2002].

Article 50. Requirements for Self-Regulating Organisations

An organisation founded by not less than ten professional participants of the securities market shall have the right to file a statement at the federal agency of executive power for the securities market concerning the acquisition thereof of the status of a self-regulating organisation [as amended by Federal Law No. 185-Ф3, 28 December 2002].

An organisation created by professional participants of the securities market shall acquire the status of a self-regulating organisation on the basis of an authorisation issued by the federal agency of executive power for the securities market. The authorisation issued by the federal agency of executive power for the securities market to a self-regulating organisation shall include all the rights provided for by the present Article [as amended by Federal Law No. 185-ФЗ, 28 December 2002].

In order to receive an authorisation there shall be submitted to the federal agency of executive power for the securities market [as amended by Federal Law No. 185-ФЗ, 28 December 2002]:

certified copies of documents concerning the creation of the self-regulating organisation;

the rules and statutes of the organisation adopted by its members and obligatory for execution by all members of the self-regulating organisation.

The rules and statutes of a self-regulating organisation must contain the requirements for a self-regulating organisation and its members with respect to:

(1) the professional qualification of personnel (except technical);

(2) the rules and standards for the effectuation of professional activity;

(3) the rules limiting the manipulation of prices;

(4) documentation, the keeping of records and reports;

(5) the minimum amount of their own means;

(6) the rules for a professional participant of the securities market joining the organisation and with withdrawal or expulsion therefrom;

(7) equal rights to representation in elections to management organs of the organisation and participation in the management of the organisation;

(8) the procedure for the distribution of costs, payments, and fees among members of the organisation;

(9) defence of the rights of clients, including the procedure for the consideration of claims and appeals of clients of members of the organisation;

(10) obligations of its members with respect to clients and other persons in regard to compensation of damage by reason of mistakes or omissions when a member of the organisation is effectuating its professional activity, and also unlawful actions of a member of the organisation or its officials and/or personnel;

(11) compliance with the procedure for the consideration of claims and appeals of members of the organisation;

(12) procedure for conducting verifications of compliance by members of the organisation with the established rules and standards, including the creation of a control organ and the procedure for familiarisation with the results of the verifications of other members of the organisation;

(13) sanctions and other measures with respect to members of the organisation and their officials and/or other personnel and the procedure for applying them;

(14) requirements relating to ensuring openness of information for verifications to be conducted at the initiative of the organisation;

(15) control over the execution of sanctions and measures to be applied to members of the organisation and the procedure for recording them.

A self-regulating organisation which is an organiser of trade shall be obliged, in addition to the requirements provided for by point 3 of the present Article and by Article 10 of the present Federal Law, to establish and comply with rules for:

the conclusion, registration, and confirmation of securities transactions;

the conducting of operations ensuring securities trades (clearing and/or account settlement operations);

the formalisation and recording of documents to be used by members of the organisation when concluding transactions and conducting securities operations;

the settlement of disputes arising between members of the organisation when performing securities operations and the settlement of accounts with regard to them, including monetary;

procedures for the provision of information concerning the prices of demands and offers, concerning prices, and concerning the volume of securities transactions performed by members of the organisation;

rendering services to persons who are not members of the organisation.

The issuance of an authorisation may be refused if the documents submitted by the organisation of professional participants of the securities market do not contain even one the respective requirements enumerated in the present Article, as well as any of the following provisions which provide for:

the possibility of discrimination against the rights of clients who use the services of members of the organisation;

unsubstantiated discrimination against members of the organisation;

unsubstantiated limitation on joining the organisation or withdrawing from it;

limitations obstructing the development of competition of professional participants of the securities market, including the regulation of rates of remuneration and revenues from the professional activity of members of the organisation;

the regulation of questions not relegated to the competence nor corresponding to the purposes of the activity of a self-regulating organisation;

the granting of unreliable or incomplete information.

A refusal to issue an authorisation on other grounds shall not be permitted.

The authorisation of a self-regulating organisation shall be revoked in the event of the establishment by the federal agency of executive power for the securities market of violations of legislation of the Russian Federation on securities, the requirements and standards established by the federal agency of executive power for the securities market, the rules and statutes of the self-regulating organisation, and the granting of unreliable or incomplete information [as amended by Federal Law No. 185-ФЗ, 28 December 2002].

The self-regulating organisation shall be obliged to submit to the federal agency of executive power for the securities market data concerning all changes to be made in the documents concerning the creation and the statutes and rules of the self-reg-

698

ulating organisation with a brief substantiation of the reasons and purposes for such changes [as amended by Federal Law No. 185-ФЗ, 28 December 2002].

Changes and additions shall be considered to be adopted if within 30 calendar days from the moment of their receipt by the federal agency of executive power for the securities market a written notification has not been sent concerning a refusal, specifying the reasons therefor [as amended by Federal Law No. 185-ФЗ, 28 December 2002].

Section VI. Concluding Provisions

Article 51. Responsibility for Violation of Legislation of Russian Federation on Securities

1. Persons shall bear responsibility for a violation of the present Federal Law and other legislative acts of the Russian Federation on securities in the instances and procedure provided for by civil, administrative, or criminal legislation of the Russian Federation.

The harm caused as a result of a violation of legislation of the Russian Federation on securities shall be subject to compensation in the procedure established by civil legislation of the Russian Federation.

2. Professional participants of the securities market shall not have the right to manipulate prices on the securities market nor to compel the purchase or sale of securities by means of granting deliberately distorted information on securities, the emitents of emission securities, and prices for securities, including information presented in an advertisement.

By manipulation of prices is understood actions committed for the creation of the appearance of raising and/or reducing prices and/or trading activeness on the securities market relative to the existing level of prices and/or existing trading activeness on the securities market for the purpose of persuading investors to sell or to acquire publicly placed and/or publicly circulated securities, including:

the dissemination of false or unreliable information;

the conclusion of securities transactions in public sales of stock exchanges and other organisers of trade on the securities market, as a result of which the possessor of these securities does not change;

the simultaneous placing of commissions for purchase and sale of securities at prices having a material deviation from current market prices under analogous transactions;

an agreement of two or several participants of a public sale or representatives thereof concerning the purchase (or sale) of securities at prices having material deviation from current market prices under analogous transactions [paragraphs two to six added by Federal Law No. 185-ФЗ, 28 December 2002].

The commission of the said actions by professional participants of the securities market shall be grounds for the suspension or annulment of the authorisation issued thereto, and also other sanctions provided for members of self-regulating organisations.

In the event of the discovery of facts giving grounds to suppose the presence in the actions of persons of the indicia of the manipulation of prices determined by the present point the federal agency of executive power for the securities market shall conduct a verification of the said facts in the procedure established by legislation of the Russian Federation and normative legal acts of the federal agency of executive power for the securities market. With regard to the results of the verification conducted and taking into account the explanations of the said persons the federal agency of executive power for the securities market shall render a decision concerning the deeming of a fact of manipulation of prices on the securities market and bring the guilty person(s) to responsibility provided for by legislation of the Russian Federation and/or suspension (or annulment) of the license issued to a professional participant of the securities market who is guilty of manipulation of prices or sending the materials of the verification to law enforcement agencies [as amended by Federal Law No. 185-ФЗ, 28 December 2002].

The said decision of the federal agency of executive power for the securities market concerning the suspension (or annulment) of a license issued to a professional participant of the securities market shall enter into force upon the expiry of 15 days from the moment of receipt thereof by the professional participant of the securities market, and in the event of an appeal against the said decision to a court —from the moment of entry into legal force of the decision of the court. The decision of the federal agency of executive power for the securities market shall be considered to be received by the professional participant of the securities market from the moment of handing over a copy of the decision to a representative of the professional participant of the securities market under receipt or upon the expiry of six days from the moment of sending a copy of the decision to the professional participant of the securities market by registered letter [added by Federal Law No. 185-ФЗ, 28 December 2002].

3. With respect to emitents effectuating the emission of securities not in good faith the federal agency of executive power for the securities market shall [as amended by Federal Law No. 185-ФЗ, 28 December 2002]:

take measures to suspend the further placement of securities issued as a result of the emission not in good faith;

publish in the mass media information concerning the fact of the emission not in good faith and the grounds for the suspension of the placement of securities issued as a result of an emission not in good faith;

notify in writing the necessity to eliminate violations, make changes in the securities prospectus and other conditions of the issue, and also establish periods for the elimination of the violations [as amended by Federal Law No. 185-ФЗ, 28 December 2002];

send materials of a verification with regard to the facts of the emission not in good faith to a court for the application of measures of administrative responsibility against officials of the emitent in accordance with legislation of the Russian Federation;

send materials of a verification with regard to the facts of an emission not in good faith to procuracy agencies when there are in the actions of the officials of the emitent the indicia of the constituent elements of a crime;

issue a written directive concerning the authorisation of the further placement of securities in the event of the elimination by the emitent of violations connected with the emission of securities not in good faith;

apply to a court with a suit to deem the issue of securities to be invalid if the emission not in good faith entailed the deluding of possessors having material significance, or if the purposes of the emission are contrary to the foundations of legal order and morality.

4. Officials of the emitent who adopted the decision concerning the issue of securities into circulation which did not undergo State registration shall bear administrative or criminal responsibility in accordance with legislation of the Russian Federation.

5. The issue of securities may be deemed invalid upon the suit of the federal agency of executive power for the securities market, regional divisions of the federal agency of executive power for the securities market, the State registering agency, State tax service agency, procurator, and also the suits of other State agencies effectuating powers in the sphere of the securities market in accordance with legislation of the Russian Federation [as amended by Federal Law No. 185-ФЗ, 28 December 2002].

The deeming of the issue of securities to be invalid shall entail the withdrawal of the securities from circulation which were issued in violation of the established procedure for registration or emission of securities and the return to the possessors of the monetary means (or other property) received by the emitent as payment for the securities.

6. Professional activity on the securities market effectuated without a license shall be illegal.

With respect to the persons effectuating unlicensed activity the federal agency of executive power for the securities market shall [as amended by Federal Law No. 185-ФЗ, 28 December 2002]:

take measures to suspend the unlicensed activity;

publish in the mass media information concerning the fact of unlicensed activity of a participant of the securities market;

notify in writing about the necessity to receive a license, and also establish the periods for this;

send materials of a verification with regard to the facts of unlicensed activity to a court for the application of measures of administrative responsibility against the officials of the participant of the securities market in accordance with legislation of the Russian Federation;

apply to an arbitrazh court with a suit concerning the recovery to the revenue of the State of the revenues received as a result of unlicensed activity on the securities market;

apply to an arbitrazh court with a suit concerning the compulsory liquidation of the participant of the securities market in the event of the failure thereof to receive a license within the established periods.

7. In the event of the discovery of facts of an advertisement not in good faith the federal agency of executive power for the securities market shall [as amended by Federal Law No. 185-ФЗ, 28 December 2002]:

take measures to suspend the advertisement not in good faith;

notify in writing the advertiser about the necessity of terminating the advertisement not in good faith and also establish the periods for this;

publish in the mass media information concerning the facts of the advertisement not in good faith and the advertisers not in good faith;

send materials of a verification with regard to the facts of an advertisement not in good faith to a court for the application of measures of administrative responsibility against officials of a participant of the securities market-advertiser in accordance with legislation of the Russian Federation;

suspend the operation of a license for the effectuation of activity of professional participants of the securities market effectuating the advertisement of securities not in good faith;

apply to a court with a suit concerning the deeming of the issue of securities to be invalid if the advertisement not in good faith entailed the deluding of possessors having material significance.

8. Professional participants of the securities market and emitents of securities, and also their officials, shall have the right to appeal against the actions of the federal agency of executive power for the securities market with regard to suppressing violation of legislation of the Russian Federation on securities and the application of measures of responsibility in the procedure provided for by legislation of the Russian Federation [as amended by Federal Law No. 185-ФЗ, 28 December 2002].

9. In the instances provided for by the present Federal Law and other legislative acts of the Russian Federation on securities, the participants of the securities market shall be obliged to secure the property interests of the possessors with a pledge, guarantee, and by other means provided for by civil legislation of the Russian Federation, and also to insure the property and risks connected with activity on the securities market.

Article 51¹. Peculiarities of Placement and Circulation of Securities of Foreign Emitents [added by Federal Law No. 185-ФЗ, 28 December 2002]

1. Securities of foreign emitents, except for securities of international financial organisations, admitted for placement and public circulation in the Russian Federation, when there is an international treaty of the Russian Federation or agreement concluded between the federal agency of executive power for the securities market on the basis of a decision of the Government of the Russian Federation and respective agency (or organisation) of the country of the foreign emitent and providing for the procedure of their interaction.

A list of international financial organisations whose securities are admitted for placement and public circulation in the Russian Federation shall be confirmed by the Government of the Russian Federation.

2. In the event of the public placement and/or public circulation of securities of foreign emitents, including international financial organisations, the recording of the rights to such securities shall be effectuated by depositaries which are juridical persons in accordance with legislation of the Russian Federation and respective requirements of normative legal acts of the federal agency of executive power for the securities market for such depositaries.

3. Requirements for documents to be submitted for State registration of an issue (or additional issue) of emission securities of foreign emitents, including international financial organisations, for the registration of securities prospectuses and State registration of reports concerning the results of issues (or additional issues) of emission securities of such emitents, the composition of information to be included in these documents, the formalisation thereof, and also the composition of information and procedure for the disclosure of information by foreign emitents, including international financial organisations, shall apply by taking into account exceptions determined by normative legal acts of the federal agency of executive power for the securities market.

Article 52. Transitional Provisions in Connection With Entry into Force of Present Federal Law

Credit organisations shall have the right to effectuate professional activity on the securities market on the basis of a license for the effectuation of banking operations within one year from the entry into force of the present Federal Law. The federal agency of executive power for the securities market shall have the right to extend the said period up to two years [as amended by Federal Law No. 185-ФЗ, 28 December 2002].

Investment institutes effectuating professional activity on the securities market on the basis of a license issued before the entry into force of the present Federal Law, and also stock exchanges must bring their constitutive and internal documents (reglaments) into conformity with it within one year from the date of its official publication. The federal agency of executive power for the securities market shall have the right to extend the said period up to two years [as amended by Federal Law No. 185-ФЗ, 28 December 2002].

Article 53. Procedure for Entry into Force of Present Federal Law

1. The present Federal Law shall enter into force from the date of its official publication.

2. To propose to the President of the Russian Federation and charge the Government of the Russian Federation to bring their normative legal acts into conformity with the present Federal Law.

FEDERAL LAW ON DEFENCE OF THE RIGHTS AND LEGAL INTERESTS OF INVESTORS ON THE SECURITIES MARKET

[Federal Law No. 46-ФЗ, 5 March 1999, as amended by
Federal Law No. 150-ФЗ, 27 December 2000,
Federal Law No. 194-ФЗ, 30 December 2001,
Federal Law No. 196-ФЗ, 30 December 2001, Federal Law No. 162-ФЗ,
9 December 2002, and Federal Law No. 176-ФЗ, 24 December 2002.
СЗ РФ (1999), no. 10, item 1163; (2001), no. 1(I), item 2; no. 53(I),
item 5030; (2002), no. 1(I), item 2; no. 50, item 4923; no. 52(I) item 5132]

Article 1. Purposes of Present Federal Law

The purposes of the present Federal Law shall be ensuring State and social defence of the rights and legal interests of natural and juridical persons, the object of whose investing are emission securities (hereinafter: investors), and also determination of the procedure for the payment of contributory compensation and granting of other forms of compensation for damage to investors-natural persons caused by the unlawful actions of emittents and other participants of the securities market (hereinafter: professional participants) on the securities market.

Article 2. Sphere of Application of Present Federal Law

1. There shall be established by the present Federal Law:

the conditions of the provision by professional participants of services to investors who are not professional participants;

the additional requirements for professional participants providing services to investors on the securities market;

the additional conditions for the placement of emission securities among an unlimited group of investors on the securities market;

the additional measures with regard to defence of the rights and legal interests of investors on the securities market and responsibility of the emittents and other persons for a violation of these rights and interests.

2. The present Federal Law shall not apply to relations connected with attracting monetary means for deposits by banks and other credit organisations, insurance companies, and non-State pension funds, circulation of deposit and savings certificates of credit organisations. cheques, bills of exchange, and other securities which are not in accordance with legislation of the Russian Federation emission securities, nor to the circulation of State securities of the Russian Federation, State securities of subjects of the Russian Federation, and securities of municipal formations.

Article 3. Legislation of Russian Federation on Defence of Rights and Legal Interests of Investors on Securities Market

Relations connected with defence of the rights and legal interests of investors on the securities market shall be regulated by the present Federal Law, other federal laws, and other normative legal acts of the Russian Federation.

Article 4. Limitations on Securities Market for Purpose of Defence of Rights and Legal Interests of Investors

1. It shall be prohibited to advertise and/or to propose to an unlimited group of persons securities of emittents without disclosing information to the extent and in the procedure which has been provided for by legislation of the Russian Federation concerning securities for emittents publicly placing the securities.

2. The conditions of contracts concluded with investors which limit the rights of the investors in comparison with the rights provided for by legislation of the Russian Federation concerning defence of the rights and legal interests of the investors on the securities market shall be null.

3. A violation of points 1 and 2 of the present Article by a professional participant shall be grounds for the annulment or suspension of the operation of the license thereof for the effectuation of professional activity on the securities market and/or imposition of a fine.

Article 5. Limitations Connected with Emission and Circulation of Securities

1. The public placement, advertising, and proposal in any other form of securities to an unlimited group of persons, the issue of which did not undergo State registration, of securities the public placement of which has been prohibited or is not provided for by federal laws and other normative legal acts of the Russian Federation, and also of documents certifying monetary and other obligations but in so doing are not securities in accordance with legislation of the Russian Federation, shall be prohibited on the securities market.

2. The conclusion by the possessor of securities of any transactions with securities belonging to him before the paying up thereof in full and registration of the report concerning the results of the issue thereof shall be prohibited.

3. The emission of bonds and other emission securities by noncommercial organisations shall be permitted only in the instances provided for by federal laws and other normative legal acts of the Russian Federation when there is the security determined by the said normative acts.

4. [repealed by Federal Law No. 162-ФЗ, 9 December 2002].

5. Persons who have signed the emission prospectus for securities shall bear joint and several subsidiary responsibility for damage caused by the emittent to the investor as a consequence of the unreliable and/or deceptive information contained in the said prospectus.

An independent valuer and auditor who have signed an emission prospectus for securities shall bear jointly and severally with the other persons who have signed the emission prospectus for securities subsidiary responsibility with the emittent for damage caused to an investor by the emittent as a consequence of the unreliable and/or deceptive information contained in the said prospectus and confirmed by them.

A suit concerning compensation of damage on the grounds specified in paragraphs one and two of the present point may be filed in a court within one year from the day of discovery of the violation, but not later than three years from the day of the commencement of the placement of the securities.

Article 6. Provision of Information to Investor in Connection with Circulation of Securities

1. The emittent shall be obliged to provide information to the investor determined by legislation of the Russian Federation.

2. A professional participant proposing services to the investor on the securities market shall be obliged upon the demand of the investor to provide him the following documents and information:

a copy of the license for effectuation of professional activity on the securities market;

a copy of the document concerning State registration of the professional participant as a juridical person or individual entrepreneur;

information concerning the agency which issued the license for effectuation of professional activity on the securities market (its name, address, and telephone);

information concerning the charter capital, and the amount of own means of the professional participant and the reserve fund thereof.

3. A professional participant, in the event of the acquisition of securities from him by an investor or in the event of the acquisition by him of securities on behalf of an investor shall be obliged upon the demand of the investor, in addition to the information whose composition has been determined by federal laws and other normative legal acts of the Russian Federation, provide the following information:

information concerning State registration of the issue of these securities and the State registration number of this issue;

information contained in the decision concerning the issue of these securities and the emission prospectus thereof;

information concerning the prices and quotations of these securities of the organised securities markets during the six weeks which preceded the date of presentation of the demand by the investor concerning the provision of information if these securities were included in the listing of the organisers of trade, or information concerning the absence of these securities in the listing of the organisers of trade;

information concerning the prices under which these securities were purchased or sold by this professional participant within the six weeks which preceded the date of the presentation by the investor of the demand concerning the provision of information, or information concerning the fact that such operations were not conducted;

information concerning the valuation of these securities by a rating agency recognised in the procedure established by legislation of the Russian Federation.

4. A professional participant shall in the event of the alienation of securities by an investor be obliged upon the demand of the investor, besides the information whose composition has been determined by federal laws and other normative legal acts of the Russian Federation, to provide information concerning:

prices and quotations of these securities or organised securities markets within the six weeks which preceded the date of the presentation by the investor of the demand concerning the provision of information if these securities were included in the listing of organisers of trade, or information concerning the absence of these securities in the listing of organisers of trade;

prices at which these securities were purchased and sold by this professional participant within the six weeks which preceded the date of presentation by the investor of the demand concerning the provision of the information, or information concerning the fact that such operations were not conducted.

5. A professional participant shall in any event be obliged to inform the investor about his right to receive the information specified in the present Article. In so doing the professional participant shall in providing services to investors-natural persons be obliged to inform the last about the rights and guarantees provided to them in accordance with the present Federal Law.

6. A professional participant shall have the right to demand from the investor payment for information provided to him in written form specified in points 3 and 4 of the present Article in an amount not exceeding the expenditures for the copying thereof.

Control over the well-foundedness of the amounts of payment for the provision of information to be recovered by professional participants or emittents shall be placed on the federal agency of executive power for the securities market.

7. A violation of the requirements established by the present Article, including the provision of unreliable, incomplete, and/or deceptive information to the investor shall be grounds for a change of or dissolution of the contract between the investor and professional participant (or emittent) upon the demand of the investor in the procedure established by civil legislation of the Russian Federation.

8. An investor shall have the right in connection with the acquisition or alienation of securities to demand from a professional participant or emittent the provision of information in accordance with the present Federal Law and other federal laws and bear the risk of the consequences of the failure to present such demand.

Article 7. Period for Consideration of Appeals and Applications of Investors by Federal Agency of Executive Power for Securities Market and Other Federal Agencies of Executive Power Regulating Securities Market

Appeals and applications of investors shall be subject to consideration by the federal agency of executive power for the securities market and other federal agencies of executive power regulating the securities market within a period not exceeding two weeks from the day of filing the appeal or application.

Article 8. Informing of Investors by Federal Agency of Executive Power for Securities Market

1. For the purposes of informing investors and warning them about committed and possible violations on the securities market the federal agency of executive power for the securities market shall publish information in its official publication concerning:

annulment or suspension of the operation of licenses for the effectuation of professional activity on the securities market;

self-regulating organisations of professional participants (hereinafter: self-regulating organisations);

administrative sanctions imposed by the federal agency of executive power for the securities market;

judicial decisions rendered with regard to suits of the federal agency of executive power for the securities market.

2. The federal agency of executive power for the securities market shall be obliged to keep information data bases containing information open and accessible to each interested person concerning sanctions applied by it with respect to persons who have committed violations on the securites market, the persons who

have committed the said violations, registered issues of securities, and licenses issued by it.

Article 9. Informing of Investors by Federal Agencies of Executive Power Effectuating Registration of Issues of Securities and Licensing of Activity of Professional Participants of Securities Market

1. Federal agencies of executive power effectuating the registration of issues of securities shall be obliged to keep information data bases of data containing information open and accessible to each interested person concerning registered issues of securities, annulled issues of securities, and issues of securites, the placement of which was suspended.

2. Federal agencies of executive power effectuating the licensing of the activity of professional participants of the securities market shall be obliged to keep information data bases containing information open and accessible to each interested person concerning all licenses issued, suspended, and annulled by them.

3. The requirements for the maintenance and procedure for keeping the information data bases specified in points 1 and 2 of the present Article shall be established by federal laws and other normative legal acts of the Russian Federation.

Article 10. Conducting by Federal Agencies of Executive Power of Public Hearings With Regard to Questions of Execution and Improvement of Legislation of Russian Federation on Securities

1. The federal agency of executive power for the securities market, other federal agencies of executive power regulating the securities market, and tax and law enforcement agencies shall have the right to conduct public hearings with regard to questions of the execution and improvement of legislation of the Russian Federation on securities.

The said hearings shall be conducted at the initiative of the federal agency of executive power for the securities market, other federal agencies of executive power regulating the securities market, tax and law enforcement agencies, and self-regulating organisations of professional participants.

2. The decision concerning the conducting of public hearings with regard to questions of the execution and improvement of legislation of the Russian Federation on securities and on topics thereof, the date of conducting, and the composition of participants shall be adopted by the heads of the federal agency of executive power for the securities market, other federal agencies of executive power regulating the securities market, tax and law enforcement agencies, and the deputies thereof.

Recommendations shall be adopted at the said public hearings which may be taken into account in the activity of the federal agency of executive power for the securities market, other federal agencies of executive power regulating the securities market, tax and law enforcement agencies, and also the preparation of proposals relating to the improvement of legislation of the Russian Federation.

The recommendations shall be adopted by a majority of the participants of the public hearings. The recommendations and materials of the hearings conducted shall be subject to publication.

In the event of eliciting in the course of the said public hearings of facts of violations on the securities market respective proposals shall be sent to the federal agency of executive power for the securities market, law enforcement, and other federal agencies of executive power in accordance with the competence thereof in order to decide questions concerning the bringing to responsibility provided for by legislation of the Russian Federation.

3. The Reglament for conducting public hearings with regard to questions of the execution and improvement of legislation of the Russian Federation on securities shall be confirmed by the federal agency which adopted the decision to conduct the said public hearings.

Article 11. Prescriptions of Federal Agency of Executive Power for Securities

1. The prescriptions of the federal agency of executive power for the securities market shall be obligatory for execution by commercial and noncommercial organisations and officials thereof, individual entrepreneurs, and natural persons on the territory of the Russian Federation.

2. The prescriptions of the federal agency of executive power for the securities market shall be rendered with regard to questions provided for by the present Federal Law, other federal laws, and other normative legal acts of the Russian Federation for the purposes of the termination and prevention of violations on the securities market, and also with regard to other questions relegated to the competence of the federal agency of executive power for the securities market.

In the event of eliciting a violation of the rights and legal interests of investors by a professional participant or if actions committed by a professional participant create a threat to the rights and legal interests of investors, the federal agency of executive power for the securities market shall have the right to prohibit or limit by their prescriptions the conducting by a professional participant of individual operations on the securities market for a term of up to six months.

3. The prescriptions of the federal agency of executive power for the securities market shall be changed or vacated by the federal agency of executive power for the securities market in connection with the decision of a court which has entered into legal force or at the initiative of the said federal agency of executive power.

Article 12. Distribution of Amounts of Fines Paid for Violation of Legislation on Defence of Rights and Legal Interests of Investors on Securities Market [as amended by Federal Law No. 196-ФЗ, 30 December 2001]

The amounts of fines paid for a violation of legislation on the defence of rights and legal interests of investors on the securities market shall be distributed as follows:

20%—to the federal budget;

40%—to the budget of the subject of the Russian Federation at the location of the regional division of the federal agency of executive power for the securities market which adopted the decision concerning the imposition of a fine or drew up the protocol concerning the administrative violation if the decision concerning imposition of a fine was adopted by a court;

40%—to the budget of the subject of the Russian Federation at the place of commission of the violation [as amended by Federal Law No. 196-ФЗ, 30 December 2001].

Article 13. Period of Limitations With Regard to Cases Concerning the Deeming of Issue of Securities to be Invalid

The period of limitations with regard to cases concerning the deeming of the issue of securities to be invalid shall be one year from the date of the commencement of the placement of the securities.

Article 14. Defence of Rights and Legal Interests by Federal Agency of Executive Power for Securities Market in Judicial Proceeding

1. In the event of the consideration in a court of disputes with regard to suits or applications concerning defence of the rights and legal interests of investors, the federal agency of executive power for the securities market shall have the right to act in the proceeding at its own initiative in order to give an opinion with regard to the case for the purposes of effectuation of the duties placed on it and in order to defend the rights of investors-natural persons and the interests of the State.

2. For the purposes of defence of the rights and legal interests of investors the federal agency of executive power for the securities market shall have the right to apply to a court with suits and applications:

in defence of State and social interests and the interests of investors protected by a law;

the liquidation of juridical persons or termination of the activity of individual entrepreneurs effectuating professional activity on the securities market without a license, annulment of the issue of securities, deeming securities transactions to be invalid, and also in other instances established by legislation of the Russian Federation concerning defence of the rights and legal interests of investors on the securities market.

Article 15. Defence of Rights and Legal Interests of Investors by Self-Regulating Organisations

1. Self-regulating organisations shall in accordance with the present Federal Law, the Federal Law on the Securities Market, other normative legal acts of the Russian Federation, and also in accordance with rules and standards of their activity, effectuate control over the performance by their participants (or members) of legislation of the Russian Federation concerning the defence of the rights and legal interests of investors on the securities market.

2. Self-regulating organisations shall effectuate the control specified in point 1 of the present Article at own initiative on the basis of a recourse of the federal agency of executive power for the securities market and other federal agencies of executive power, and also appeals and applications of investors.

The forms, periods, and procedure for conducting the said control shall be determined by the constitutive documents, rules, and standards of activity of the self-regulating organisation.

Article 16. Procedure for Consideration by Self-Regulating Organisation of Appeals and Applications of Investors

1. A self-regulating organisation shall consider appeals and applications of investors against the actions of a participant (or member) thereof, officials thereof, and specialists in the procedure provided for by the constitutive documents, rules, and standards of its activity.

2. According to the results of consideration of an appeal and application the self-regulating organisation shall have the right to adopt the following decision:

apply to the violator the sanctions established by the rules and standards for the activity of this organisation;

recommend to its participant (or member) to compensate the investor for damage caused in an extra-judicial procedure;

expel the professional participant from among its participants (or members) and apply to the federal agency of executive power for the securities market with an application concerning the taking of measures for annulment or suspension of the operation of the license of the said professional participant for effectuation of professional activity on the securities market;

send the materials with regard to the appeal or application to law enforcement and other federal agencies of executive power for consideration in accordance with the competence thereof.

3. A self-regulating organisation shall be obliged to notify the federal agency of executive power for the securities market about the results of the consideration of appeals and applications of investors and the decisions adopted concerning them.

4. In the event of the failure to take measures with regard to legal and substantiated appeals and applications of investors and the failure to execute legislation of the Russian Federation concerning the rights and legal interests of investors on the securities market, the federal agency of executive power for the securities market shall have the right to apply to the self-regulating organisation the sanctions established by the Federal Law on the Securities Market and normative legal acts of the Russian Federation.

Article 17. Contributory Compensation and Other Funds of Self-Regulating Organisations

For the purpose of compensation for damage incurred by investors-natural persons as a result of the activity of professional participants who are participants (or members) of a self-regulating organisation, a self-regulating organisation shall have the right to create contributory compensation and other funds.

Article 18. Defence of Rights and Legal Interests of Investors-Natural Persons by Social Associations Thereof

1. Social associations of investors-natural persons of the federal, inter-regional, and regional levels shall have the right to effectuate defence of the rights and legal interests of investors-natural persons in the forms and procedure which has been provided for by legislation of the Russian Federation.

2. Social associations of investors-natural persons shall have the right to:
apply to a court with applications concerning defence of the rights and legal interests of investors-natural persons who have sustained damage on the securities market in the procedure established by procedure legislation of the Russian Federation;
effectuate control over compliance with the conditions for keeping and realisation of property of debtors intended for the satisfaction of property requirements of investors-natural persons in connection with unlawful actions on the securities market in the procedure established by legislation of the Russian Federation;
create own contributory compensation and other funds for the purposes of ensuring defence of the rights and legal interests of investors-juridical persons;
combine into associations and unions.

Article 19. Programme for Payment of Contributory Compensation to Investors-Natural Persons

1. For the purposes of the realisation of the State Programme for Defence of the Rights of Investors with respect to payment of contributory compensation to investors-natural persons the Federal Contributory Compensation Fund shall be created as a noncommercial organisation (hereinafter: Fund), the principal purposes of whose activity shall be:
payment of contributory compensation to investors-natural persons;

formation of information data banks and conducting of the register of investors-natural persons having the right to receive the said contributory compensation;

representation and defence of property interests of investors-natural persons who have resorted to the Fund in a court and in the course of an execution proceeding, filing suits concerning defence of the rights and legal interests of an undetermined group of investors-natural persons;

keeping of property intended for satisfaction of the property rights of investors-natural persons and participation in the realisation thereof or ensuring control for the purposes of the proper keeping and realisation of the said property in the course of an execution proceeding.

Management of the monetary means and other property intended for payment of compensation to investors-natural persons, and also the keeping of the said property, shall be effectuated in the procedure provided for by federal laws and other normative legal acts of the Russian Federation.

The charter of the Fund shall be confirmed by the Government of the Russian Federation.

A trusteeship council of the fund shall be created in order to effectuate supervision over the activity of the Fund consisting of representatives of the Federal Assembly of the Russian Federation, federal agency of executive power for the securities market, other federal agencies of executive power, self-regulating organisations, and social associations of investors-natural persons.

The Fund annually shall report on its activity in the procedure established by the Government of the Russian Federation. The Report concerning the activity of the Fund shall be published in the printed organ of the Federal agency of executive power for the securities market.

2. The Fund shall effectuate payments of compensation to investors-natural persons who would not receive compensation under judicial decisions and orders in view of the debtor lacking monetary means and other property.

Investors-natural persons shall have the right to receive contributory compensation in connection with the causing to them of damage by a professional participant having a license for effectuation of the respective type of professional activity on the securities market, and also in the instances provided for by normative legal acts of the Russian Federation.

The sources of the formation of the means of the Fund shall be means of the federal budget in the instances and procedure which has been provided for by the federal law on the federal budget, and also other sources provided for by the charter fund in accordance with legislation of the Russian Federation [the operation of this paragraph of Article 19 is suspended from 1 January to 31 December 2002 inclusive by Federal Law No. 194-ФЗ, 20 December 2001 and from 1 January to 31 December 2003 by Federal Law No. 176-ФЗ, 24 December 2002].

Article 20. Procedure for Entry of Present Federal Law into Force

1. The present Federal Law shall enter into force from the day of its official publication.

2. Article 8 of the present Federal Law shall enter into force upon the expiry of six months from the day of entry into force of the present Federal Law.

3. [repealed by Federal Law No. 162-ФЗ, 9 December 2002].

3. Article 17 of the present Federal Law shall operate until the entry into force of respective changes in the Federal Law on the Securities Market [renumbered by Federal Law No. 162-ФЗ, 9 December 2002].

4. To propose to the President of the Russian Federation within three months from the day of entry into force of the present Federal Law to bring his normative legal acts into conformity with the present Federal Law [renumbered by Federal Law No. 162-ФЗ, 9 December 2002].

5. To charge the Government of the Russian Federation within three months from the day of entry into force of the present Federal Law to bring its normative legal acts into conformity with the present Federal Law and to adopt necessary normative legal acts in accordance with the present Federal Law [renumbered by Federal Law No. 162-ФЗ, 9 December 2002].

FEDERAL LAW ON COUNTERACTING THE LEGALISATION (OR LAUNDERING) OF REVENUES RECEIVED BY CRIMINAL MEANS AND FINANCING OF TERRORISM

[as amended by Federal Law of 30 October 2002]

[Federal Law No. 115-ФЗ, 7 August 2001,
as amended by Federal Law No. 112-ФЗ, 25 July 2002, and
Federal Law No. 131-ФЗ, 30 October 2002.
СЗ РФ (2001), no. 33(I), item 3418; (2002),
no. 30, item 3029; no. 44, item 1234]

Chapter I	General Provisions	717
Chapter II	Prevention of Legalisation (or Laundering) of Revenues Received by Criminal Means and the Financing of Terrorism	719
Chapter III	Organisation of Activity With Regard to Counteracting Legalisation (or Laundering) of Revenues Received by Criminal Means and the Financing of Terrorism	726
Chapter IV	International Cooperation in Sphere of Struggle Against Legalisation (or Laundering) of Revenues Received by Criminal Means and Financing of Terrorism	728
Chapter V	Concluding Provisions	730

Chapter I. General Provisions

Article 1. Purposes of Present Federal Law

The present Federal Law is directed towards defence of the rights and legal interests of citizens, society, and the State by means of the creation of a legal mechanism to counteract the legalisation (or laundering) of revenues received by criminal means and the financing of terrorism [as amended by Federal Law of 30 October 2002].

717

Article 2. Sphere of Application of Present Federal Law

The present Federal Law shall regulate relations of citizens of the Russian Federation, foreign citizens, and stateless persons permanently residing in the Russian Federation, organisations effectuating operations with monetary means or other property, and also State agencies effectuating control on the territory of the Russian Federation over the conducting of operations with monetary means or other property for the purposes of prevention of the eliciting and suppression of acts connected with the legalisation (or laundering) of revenues received by criminal means and the financing of terrorism [as amended by Federal Law of 30 October 2002].

In accordance with international treaties of the Russian Federation the operation of the present Federal Law shall extend to natural and juridical persons which effectuate operations with monetary means or other property beyond the limits of the Russian Federation.

Article 3. Basic Concepts Used in Present Federal Law

For the purposes of the present Federal Law the following basic concepts shall be used:

revenues received by criminal means—monetary means or other property received as a result of the commission of a crime;

legalisation (or laundering) of revenues received by criminal means—imparting a lawful appearance to the possession, use, or disposition of monetary means or other property received as a result of the commission of a crime, except for crimes provided for by Articles 193, 194, 198, and 199 of the Criminal Code of the Russian Federation, responsibility for which has been established by the said Articles;

operations with monetary means or other property—actions of natural and juridical persons with monetary means or other property irrespective of the form and means of the effectuation thereof directed towards the establishment, change, or termination of civil rights and duties connected with them;

empowered agency—federal agency of executive power taking measures with regard to counteracting the legalisation (or laundering) of revenues received by criminal means and the financing of terrorism in accordance with the present Federal Law [as amended by Federal Law of 30 October 2002];

obligatory control—the aggregate of measures taken by the empowered agency with regard to control over operations with monetary means and other property effectuated on the basis of information submitted to it by organisations effectuating such operations, and also verification of this information in accordance with legislation of the Russian Federation;

internal control—the activity of organisations effectuating operations with monetary means or other property with regard to eliciting operations subject to obligatory control and other operations with monetary means or other property connected with the legalisation (or laundering) of revenues received by criminal means and the financing of terrorism [as amended by Federal Law of 30 October 2002].

Chapter II. Prevention of Legalisation (or Laundering) of Revenues Received by Criminal Means and the Financing of Terrorism
[as amended by Federal Law of 30 October 2002]

Article 4. Measures Directed Towards Counteracting Legalisation (or Laundering) of Revenues Received by Criminal Means and the Financing of Terrorism [as amended by Federal Law of 30 Ocober 2002]

There shall be relegated to measures directed towards counteracting the legalisation (or laundering) of revenues received by criminal means and financing of terrorism [as amended by Federal Law of 30 October 2002]:

obligatory procedures of internal control;

obligatory control;

prohibition against informing clients and other persons about measures being taken of counteracting legalisation (or laundering) revenues received by criminal means and financing of terrorism [as amended by Federal Law of 30 October 2002];

other measures taken in accordance with federal laws.

Article 5. Organisations Effectuating Operations with Monetary Means or Other Property

For the purposes of the present Federal Law there shall be relegated to organisations effectuating operations with monetary means or other property:

credit organisations;

professional participants of the securities market;

insurance and finance lease companies;

organisations of federal postal communications [as amended by Federal Law of 30 October 2002];

pawnshops;

organisations effectuating the buying up and purchase-sale of precious metals and precious stones, jewellery manufactures from them, and scrap of such manufactures [added by Federal Law of 30 October 2002];

organisations maintaining totalisers and bookmaker offices, and also conducting lotteries and other games in which the organiser draws a prize fund among the participants, including in electronic form [added by Federal Law of 30 October 2002];

organisations effectuating the management of investment funds or non-State pension funds [added by Federal Law of 30 October 2002].

Article 6. Operations with Monetary Means or Other Property Subject to Obligatory Control

1. Operations with monetary means or other property shall be subject to obligatory control if the amount for which it was concluded is equal to or exceeds 600,000 rubles, or equal to an amount in foreign currency equivalent to 600,000 rubles or exceeds it, and by its character the said operation is relegated to one of the following types of operations:

(1) operations with monetary means in cash form:

withdrawal from an account or credit to an account of a juridical person of monetary means in cash form in the instances if this is not stipulated by the character of economic activity thereof;

purchase or sale of cash foreign currency;

acquisition by a natural person of securities for cash settlement;

receipt by a natural person of monetary means by bearer cheque issued by a nonresident;

exchange of banknotes of one denomination for banknotes of another denomination;

contribution of monetary means by natural person in charter (or constributed) capital of organisation in cash form;

(2) transfer or remittance of monetary means to an account, provision or receipt of a credit (or loan), securities operations if any of the parties is a natural or juridical person having respectively a registration, place of residence, or location in the State (or territory) which does not participate in international cooperation in the sphere of counteracting the legalisation (or laundering) of revenues received by criminal means and the financing of terrorism or one of the parties is a person possessing an account in a bank registered in the said State (or said territory). The List of such States (or territories) shall be determined in the procedure established by the Government of the Russian Federation on the basis of a list confirmed by international organisations engaging in the counteracting of the legalisation (or laundering) of revenues received by criminal means and the financing of terrorism and shall be subject to publication;

(3) operations with regard to bank accounts (or deposits):

placement of monetary means on deposit with the formalisation of documents certifying a bearer deposit;

opening of a deposit in favour of third persons with the placement therein of monetary means in cash form;

remittance of monetary means abroad to an account (or deposit) opened for an anonymous possessor and the receipt of monetary means from abroad from an account (or deposit) opened for an anonymous possessor;

crediting of monetary means to an account (or deposit) of a juridical person from an account (or deposit) of a juridical person whose period of activity does not exceed three months from the date of registration thereof, or crediting of monetary means to an account (or deposit) or withdrawal of monetary means from an account (or deposit) of a juridical person if the operations with regard to the said account (or deposit) were not made from the moment of opening thereof;

(4) other transactions with moveable property:

placing securities, precious metals, precious stones, jewellery manufactures from them and scrap of such manufactures and other valuables in a pawnshop;

payment to a natural person of insurance compensation or receipt of an insurance from him for the insurance of life or other types of cumulative insurance and pension security;

receipt or provision of property under a contract of financial lease (finance leasing);

remittances of monetary means effectuated by noncredit organisations on behalf of a client;

buying up and purchase-sale of precious metals and precious stones, jewellery manufactures from them, and scrap of such manufactures;

receipt of monetary means in the form of payment for participation in a game in a lottery, totaliser (or mutual betting) or other games based on risk in the form of winnings received from participation in the said games [point 1 as amended by Federal Law of 30 October 2002].

2. Operations with monetary means or other property shall be subject to obligatory control if any of the parties is an organization or natural person with respect to which there is information received in the procedure established in accordance with the present Federal Law concerning their participation in extremist activity, or a juridical person directly or indirectly in ownership or under the control of such organisations or person, or a natural or juridical person acting in the name or under the instruction of such organisation or person.

The procedure for determining and bringing to the information of organisations effectuating operations with monetary means or other property and the lists of such organisations and persons shall be established by the Government of the Russian Federation.

The grounds for the inclusion of an organisation or natural person in the said List shall be:

the decision of a court of the Russian Federation which has entered into legal force concerning the liquidation or prohibition of activity of the organisation in connection with the effectuation by it of extremist activity;

the judgment of a court of the Russian Federation which has entered into legal force concerning the deeming of a natural person to be guilty in the commission of a crime of a terrorist character;

the decision of the Procurator General of the Russian Federation or procurator subordinate to him concerning the suspension of the activity of an organisation in connection with its recourse to a court with an application to bring the organisation to responsibility for terrorist activity;

the decree of an investigator or procurator concerning the instituting of a criminal case with respect to a person who committed a crime of a terrorist character;

the lists of organisations and natural persons connected with terrorist organisations or terrorists drawn up by international organisations effectuating the struggle against terrorism or aencies empowered by them and recognised by the Russian Federation;

the judgments (or decisions) of courts and decisions of other competent agencies of foreign States with respect to organisations or natural persons effectuating terrorist activity recognized in the Russian Federation in accordance with international treaties of the Russian Federation and federal laws [point 2 as amended by Federal Law of 25 July 2002 in the version of Federal Law of 30 October 2002].

3. If an operation with monetary means or other property is effectuated in foreign currency, the amount thereof in Russian rubles shall be determined according to the official exchange rate of the Central Bank of the Russian Federation operating on the date of the performance of such operation [added by Federal Law of 30 October 2002].

4. Information concerning operations with monetary means or other property subject to obligatory control shall be submitted directly to the empowered agency by organisations effectuating operations with monetary means or other property [renumbered and amended by Federal Law of 30 October 2002].

Article 7. Rights and Duties of Organisations Effectuating Operations with Monetary Means or Other Property [as amended by Federal Law of 30 October 2002]

1. Organisations effectuating operations with monetary means or other property shall be obliged to:

(1) identify the person present for servicing in the organisation effectuating operations with monetary means or other property [as amended by Federal Law of 30 October 2002];

(2) documentarily fix and submit to the empowered agency not later than the work day following the day of performance of the operation the following information with regard to operations with monetary means or other property subject to obligatory control:

the type of operation and grounds for performing it;

the date of performance of the operation with monetary means or other property, and also the amount for which it was performed;

information necessary for identification of the natural person who performed the operation with monetary means or other property (passport data or other document certifying identity), taxpayer identification number (when there is such), address of the place of residence or whereabouts thereof [as amended by Federal Law of 30 October 2002];

the name, taxpayer identification number, registration number, place of registration, and address of the location of a juridical person performing an operation with monetary means or other property;

information necessary for identification of the natural or juridical person on whose behalf or in whose name the operation with monetary means or other property is performed, taxpayer identification number (when there is such), address of the place of residence or location of the natural or juridical person;

information necessary for identification of the representative of the natural or juridical person performing an operation with monetary means or other property in the name of another person by virtue of powers based on a power of attorney, law, or act of duly empowered State agency or agency of local self-government, address of the place of residence of the representative of the natural or juridical person;

information necessary for identification of the recipient with regard to operation with monetary means or other property and his representative, including taxpayer identification number (if there is such), address of the place of residence or location of the recipient and his representaive, if this is provided for by the rules for performance of the respective operation;

(3) submit to the empowered agency at its written request information specified in subpoint (2) of the present point both with respect to operations subject to obligatory control and with respect to operations specified in point 3 of the present Article.

The procedure for sending by the empowered agency the said requests shall be determined by the Government of the Russian Federation by agreement with the Central Bank of the Russian Federation.

The empowered agency shall not have the right to request documents an dinformation with regard to operations performed before the entry into force of the present Federal Law, except for documents and information which are submitted on the basis of a respective international treaty of the Russian Federation.

2. Organisations effectuating operations with monetary means or other property shall be obliged for the purposes of preventing the legalisation (or laundering) of revenues received by criminal means and the financing of terrorism to work out rules for internal control and programmes for the effectuation thereof, appoint special officials responsible for compliance with the said rules and realisation of the said programmes, and also undertake other internal organisational measures for the said purposes [as amended by Federal Law of 30 October 2002].

The rules of internal control of an organisation effectuating operations with monetary means or other property must include the procedure for the documentary fixing of the necessary information, the procedure for ensuring confidentiality of the information, skills requirements for the preparation and training of cadres, and also criteria for eliciting and the indicia of unusual transactions, taking into account the peculiarities of activity of this organisation.

Organisations effectuating operations with monetary means or other property in accordance with rules of internal order shall be obliged documentarily to fix the information received as a result of applying the said rules and realisation of the programmes for effectuation of internal control and to preserve the confidential character thereof.

The grounds for documentary fixing of information shall be:

the confusing or unusual character of a transaction not having obvious economic sense or obvious legal purpose;

the failure of a transaction to conform to the purposes of the activity of the organisation established by constitutive documents of this organisation;

eliciting the repeated performance of operations or transactions whose character gives grounds to suppose that the purpose of the effectuation thereof is evasion of the procedures of obligatory control provided for by the present Federal Law;

other circumstances giving grounds to suppose that transactions are effectuated for the purposes of legalisation (or laundering) of revenues received by crminal means or the financing of terrorism [as amended by Federal Law of 30 October 2002].

The rules of internal control shall be worked out by taking into account recommendations confirmed by the Government of the Russian Federation, and for credit organisations—by the Central Bank of the Russian Federation, and shall be confirmed in accordance with the procedure established by the Government of the Russian Federation [as amended by Federal Law of 30 October 2002].

3. If suspicion arises among workers of an organisation effectuating opeations with monetary means or other property on the basis of the realisation of the programmes specified in point 2 of the present Article for the effectuation of internal control that any operations are being effectuated for the purposes of legalisation (or laundering) of revenues received by criminal means or financing of terrorism, this organisation shall be obliged to send information to the empowered agency concerning such operations irrespective of whether they are or are not relegated to operations provided for by Article 6 of the present Federal Law [as amended by Federal Law of 30 October 2002].

4. Documents confirming information specified in the present Article, and also copies of documents necessary for identification of identity, shall be subject to keeping for not less than five years.

5. Credit organisations shall have the right to refuse to conclude a contract of bank account (or deposit) with a natural or juridical person in the event of the failure of the respective person to submit documents confirming the information

specified in the present Article or the submission by him of unreliable documents, and also if with respect to the particular person there is information concerning participation in terrorist activity received in accordance with the present Federal Law [as amended by Federal Law of 30 October 2002].

6. Workers of organisation submitting respective information to the empowered agency shall not have the right to inform clients of these organisations thereof or other persons.

7. The procedure for the submission of information to the empowered agency shall be established by the Government of the Russian Federation, and with respect to credit organisations, by the Central Bank of the Russian Federation.

8. The submission to the empowered agency of information and documents by workers of organisations effectuating operations with monetary means or other property with respect to operations and for the purposes and in the procedure which have been provided by the present Federal Law shall not be a violation of employment, banking, tax, and commercial secrecy and secrecy of communications (with respect to information concerning postal remittances of monetary means) [as amended by Federal Law of 30 October 2002].

9. Control over the execution by natural and juridical persons of the present Federal Law with regard to fixing, keeping, and submitting information concerning operations subject to obligatory control, and also over the organisation of internal control, shall be effectuated by respective supervisory agencies in accordance with their competence and in the procedure established by legislation of the Russian Federation, and also by the empowered agency in the absence of supervisory agencies in the sphere of activity of individual organisations effectuating operations with monetary means or other property.

In the absence of supervisory agencies in the sphere of activity of individual organisations effectuating operations with monetary means or other property, such organisations shall be subject to recording in an empowered agency in the procedure established by the Government of the Russian Federation [paragraph added by Federal Law of 30 October 2002].

10. Organisations effectuating operations with monetary means or other property shall suspend such operations, except for operations with regard to crediting monetary means received in an account of a natural or juridical person for two working days from the date when the instruction of the clients concerning the effectuation thereof must be fulfilled and not later than the working day following that day of suspension of the operation shall submit information concerning them to the empowered agency if any of the parties is an organisation or natural person with respect to which there is information received in the procedure established in accordance with Article 6(2) of the present Federal Law concerning their participation in terrorist activity, or a juridical person directly or indirectly in the

ownerhsip or under the control of such organisations or person, or a natural or juridical person operating in the name or under the instruction of such organisation or person.

In the event of the failure to receive within the said period a decree of the empowered agency concerning suspension of the respective operation for an additional period on the basis of Article 8, paragraph three, of the present Federal Law the organisation shall effectuate the operation with monetary means or other property at the instruction of the client unless in accordance with legislation of the Russian Federation another decision has been adopted limiting the effectuation thereof [point 10 added by Federal Law of 30 October 2002].

11. Organisations effectuating operations with monetary means or other property shall have the right to refuse to fulfil an instruction of a client concerning the performance of an operation, except for operations with regard to the crediting of monetary means received in the account of a natural or juridical person with regard to which documents have not been submitted necessary for the fixation of information in accordance with the provisions of the present Federal Law [point 11 added by Federal Law of 30 October 2002].

12. The suspension of operations in accordance with point 10 of the present Article and the refusal to fulfil operations in accordance with point 11 of the present Article shall not be grounds for the arising of civil-law responsibility of the organisations effectuating operations with monetary means or other property for a violation of conditions of the respective contracts [point 12 added by Federal Law of 30 October 2002].

Chapter III. Organisation of Activity With Regard to Counteracting Legalisation (or Laundering) of Revenues Received by Criminal Means and the Financing of Terrorism
[as amended by Federal Law of 30 October 2002]

Article 8. Empowered Agency

The empowered agency determined by the President of the Russian Federation shall be the federal agency of executive power whose tasks, functions, and powers in the sphere of counteracting the legalisation (or laundering) of revenues received by criminal means and the financing of terrorism is established in accordance with the present Federal Law [as amended by Federal Law of 30 October 2002].

When there are sufficient grounds attesting to the fact that an operation or transaction is connected with the legalisation (or laundering) of revenues received by criminal means or with the financing of terrorism, the empowered agency shall send the respective information and materials to law enforcement agencies in accordance with their competence [as amended by Federal Law of 30 October 2002].

An empowered agency shall issue a decree concerning the suspension of operations with monetary means or other property specified in Article 6(2) of the present Federal Law for a period of up to five working days if information received by it in accordance with Article 7(10) of the present Federal Law with regard to the results of the preliminary verification are deemed by it to be substantiated [added by Federal Law of 30 October 2002].

Workers of the empowered agency shall when executing the present Federal Law ensure the preservation of information which became known to them connected with the activity of the empowered agency constituting an employment, banking, tax, and commercial secret or secrecy of communications and shall bear the responsibility established by legislation of the Russian Federation for the divulgence of this information [as amended by Federal Law of 30 October 2002].

The harm caused to natural and juridical persons by illegal actions of the empowered agency or its workers in connection with the fulfilment of functions by the empowered agency shall be subject to compensation at the expense of means of the federal budget in accordance with legislation of the Russian Federation.

Article 9. Submission of Information and Documents

Agencies of State power of the Russian Federation, agencies of State power of subjects of the Russian Federation, and agencies of local self-government shall provide to the empowered agency information and documents necessary for the effectuation of its functions (except for information concerning the private life of citizens) in the procedure established by the Government of the Russian Federation.

The Central Bank of the Russian Federation shall provide information and documents to the empowered agency necessary for the effectuation of its functions in the procedure agreed by the Central Bank of the Russian Federation with the empowered agency.

The provision with regard to a request of the empowered agency of information and documents by agencies of State power of the Russian Federation, agencies of State power of subjects of the Russian Federation, by agencies of local self-government, and by the Central Bank of the Russian Federation for the purposes and in the procedure which has been provided for by the present Federal Law shall not be a violation of employment, banking, tax, commercial secrecy, and secrecy of communications (with respect to information concerning postal remittances of monetary means) [as amended by Federal Law of 30 October 2002].

The provisions of the present Article shall not extend to information and documents which in accordance with Articles 6 and 7 of the present Federal Law the empowered agency does not have the right to request from organisations effectuating operations with monetary means or other property, or must be submitted by these organisations directly to the empowered agency [as amended by Federal Law of 30 October 2002].

Chapter IV. International Cooperation in Sphere of Struggle Against Legalisation (or Laundering) of Revenues Received by Criminal Means and Financing of Terrorism
[as amended by Federal Law of 30 October 2002]

Article 10. Exchange of Information and Legal Assistance

Agencies of State power of the Russian Federation effectuating activity connected with counteracting the legalisation (or laundering) of revenues received by criminal means and the financing of terrorism shall, in accordance with international treaties of the Russian Federation, cooperate with competent agencies of foreign States at the stages of collecting information, preliminary investigation, judicial examination, and execution of judicial decisions [as amended by Federal Law of 30 October 2002].

The empowered agency and other agencies of State power of the Russian Federation effectuating activity connected with counteracting the legalisation (or laundering) of revenues received by criminal means and the financing of terrorism shall provide respective information to competent agencies of foreign States at their requests or at its own initiative in the procedure and on the grounds which have been provided for by international treaties of the Russian Federation [as amended by Federal Law of 30 October 2002].

The transfer to competent agencies of a foreign State of information connected with eliciting, seizure, and confiscation of revenues received by criminal means shall be effectuated if it does not cause damage to the interests of national security of the Russian Federation and may enable competent agencies of this State to commence an investigation or formulate a request.

Information connected with the eliciting, seizure, and confiscation of revenues received by criminal means shall be provided at the request of the competent agency of the foreign State on condition that it will not be used without the prior consent of the respective agencies of State power of the Russian Federation which provided it for purposes not specified in the request.

Agencies of State power of the Russian Federation shall send to competent agencies of foreign States requests concerning the provision of necessary information and give replies to requests made by the said competent agencies in the procedure provided for by international treaties of the Russian Federation.

Agencies of State power of the Russian Federation effectuating activity connected with counteracting the legalisation (or laundering) of revenues received by criminal means and the financing of terrorism, having sent a request, shall ensure the confidentiality of the information provided and use it only for the purposes specified in the request [as amended by Federal Law of 30 October 2002].

Agencies of State power of the Russian Federation effectuating activity connected with counteracting the legalisation (or laundering) of revenues received by criminal means and the financing of terrorism shall, in accordance with international treaties of the Russian Federation and federal laws, execute within the limits of their competence requests of competent agencies of foreign States concerning the confiscation of revenues received by criminal means, and also the performance of individual procedural actions with regard to cases concerning the eliciting of revenues received by criminal means, imposition of arrest on property, and seizure of property, including conduct expert examinations, interrogations of suspects, accused, witnesses, victims, and other persons, searches, searches and seizures, transfer material evidence, impose arrest on property, and effectuate the handing over and sending of documents [as amended by Federal Law of 30 October 2002].

Expenses connected with execution of the said requests shall be compensated in accordance with international treaties of the Russian Federation.

Article 11. Recognition of Judgment (or Decision) Rendered by Court of Foreign State

Judgments (or decisions) with respect to persons having revenues received by criminal means rendered by courts of foreign States and which have entered into legal force shall be recognised in the Russian Federation in accordance with international treaties of the Russian Federation and federal laws.

Judgments (or decisions) rendered by courts of foreign States and which have entered into legal force concerning the confiscation of revenues on the territory of the Russian Federation received by criminal means or property equivalent thereto shall be recognised and executed in the Russian Federation in accordance with international treaties of the Russian Federation.

Confiscated revenues received by criminal means or property equivalent thereto may be transferred wholly or partly to a foreign State by the court which rendered the decision concerning confiscation on the basis of a respective international treaty of the Russian Federation.

Article 12. Extradition and Transit Carriage

A decision concerning extradition to a foreign State of persons who have committed crimes connected with the legalisation (or laundering) of revenues received by criminal means shall be adopted on the basis of obligations of the Russian Federation arising from an international treaty of the Russian Federation. A decision concerning the transit carriage of the said persons about the territory of the Russian Federation shall be adopted in the same procedure.

If the Russian Federation has no respective treaty with the foreign State which requests extradition, the said persons may be extradited for crimes connected with the legalisation (or laundering) of revenues received by criminal means on condition of compliance with the principle of reciprocity.

Chapter V. Concluding Provisions

Article 13. Responsibility for Violation of Present Federal Law

A violation by organisations effectuating operations with monetary means or other property and operating on the basis of a license of the requirements provided for by Articles 6 and 7 of the present Federal Law, except for Article 7(3) of the present Federal Law, may entail revocation (or annulment) of the license in the procedure provided for by legislation of the Russian Federation.

Persons guilty of a violation of the present Federal Law shall bear administrative, civil, and criminal responsibility in accordance with legislation of the Russian Federation.

Article 14. Procuracy Supervision

Supervision over the execution of the present Federal Law shall be effectuated by the Procurator General of the Russian Federation and procurators subordinate to him.

Article 15. Appeal of Actions of Empowered Agency and Officials Thereof

An interested person shall have the right to apply to a court for the defence of his violated or contested rights and legal interests in the procedure established by a law.

Article 16. Entry into Force of Present Federal Law

The present Federal Law shall enter into force from 1 February 2002.

Article 17. Bringing Normative Legal Acts into Conformity with Present Federal Law

Normative legal acts of the President of the Russian Federation and the Government of the Russian Federation, laws, and other federal normative acts of subjects of the Russian Federation shall be brought into conformity with the present Federal Law before the entry thereof into force.

LAW OF THE RUSSIAN FEDERATION ON PLEDGE

[Law No. 2872–1, 29 May 1992.
Ведомости СНД и ВС РФ (1992), no. 23, item 1239;
as affected by Federal Law No. 102-ФЗ. СЗ РФ (1998),
no. 29, item 3400]

Section I	General Provisions	731
Section II	Pledge While Leaving Property With Pledgor	739
Chapter 1	General Questions	739
Chapter 2	Pledge of Enterprise, Structure, Building, Installation, and Other Object Directly Connected with Land (Mortgage)	741
Chapter 3	Pledge of Goods in Turnover and Processing	742
Section III	Pledge with Transfer of Pledged Property (or Thing) to Pledgeholder (Pawn)	743
Section IV	Pledge of Rights	744
Section V	Guarantees of Rights of Parties in Event of Pledge	746

Section I. General Provisions

Article 1. Concept of Pledge

Pledge is a means of securing obligations under which the creditor-pledgeholder acquires the right in the event of the failure of the debtor to perform the obligation to receive satisfaction at the expense of the pledged property preferentially before other creditors, with the exceptions provided for by law.

Article 2. Legislation of Russian Federation on Pledge

The basic provisions on pledge shall be determined by the present Law.

Relations of pledge not regulated by the present Law shall be regulated by other acts of legislation of the Russian Federation.

If other rules on pledge have been established by an international treaty of the Russian Federation than those which are contained in acts of legislation of the Russian Federation, the rules of the international treaty shall apply.

Article 3. Grounds for Pledge to Arise

1. Pledge shall arise by virtue of contract or law.

2. A law providing for a pledge to arise must contain a specification of by virtue of which obligation and precisely which property must be deemed to be under pledge.

Article 4. Sphere of Application of Law

1. A valid demand may be secured by a pledge, in particular arising from a contract of loan, including a bank loan, contracts of purchase-sale, property hire, carriage of goods, and other contracts.

2. Things, securities, and other property and property rights may be the subject of a pledge. Demands of a personal character, and also other demands whose pledge has been expressly prohibited by law, may not be the subject of a pledge.

3. A pledge may be established with respect to demands which arise in the future on condition that the parties agree about the extent such demands are secured by pledge.

4. A pledge shall be derivative from the demands secured by it. The existence of the rights of the pledgeholder are dependent upon the fate of the obligation secured by the pledge.

Article 5. Types of Pledge

It may be provided by law or contract that pledged property shall remain in the possession of the pledgor or shall be transferred to the possession of the pledge-holder (pawn).

The pledge of goods may be effectuated by means of the transfer to the pledge-holder of a goods-disposition document which is a security. Pledged securities may be transferred for deposit with a notarial office or bank.

Article 6. Property as Subject of Pledge

1. Any property which in accordance with legislation of the Russian Federation may be alienated by a pledgeholder may be the subject of a pledge.

2. Unless provided otherwise by law or contract, the right of pledge to a thing shall encompass the appurtenances and inseparable fruits. The right of pledge to a thing may include separable fruits only in the instances, within the limits, and in the procedure provided for by law or contract.

3. The extension of pledge to things which might be acquired by the pledgor in future may be provided for by contract or law.

Article 7. Pledge of Property in Common Ownership

1. Property in common joint ownership may be transferred on pledge only with the consent of all the owners.

2. The pledge by an owner of his participatory share in common participatory share ownership shall not require the consent of the remaining owners.

3. The owner of an apartment shall autonomously decide the question of pledging it.

Article 8. Replacement of Subject of Pledge

The replacement of the subject of a pledge shall be permitted only with the consent of the pledgeholder. The procedure for replacement of the subject of a pledge when goods in turnover are pledged shall be regulated by Articles 46 and 47 of the present Law.

Article 9. Pledge and Insurance

1. Law or contract may impose on the pledgeholder the duty to insure the pledged property transferred to his possession.
A pawnshop shall be obliged to insure property accepted on pledge at the expense of the pledgor at its full value according to the valuation made by agreement of the parties when accepting the property on pledge.

2. Law or contract may impose on the pledgor the duty to insure against the performance of actions and adoption of acts by State agencies terminating its economic activity, or obstructing it, or unfavourably influencing it (confiscation or requisition of property), and also against liquidation or the debtor being deemed to be insolvent.

3. When insured events ensue, the pledgeholder shall have the right to preferential satisfaction of his demands from the amount of insurance compensation.

Article 10. Content and Form of Contract on Pledge

1. A contract on pledge must contain conditions providing for the type of pledge, the essence of the demand secured by pledge, the amount thereof, the periods for performance of the obligation, the composition and value of the pledged property, and also any other conditions relative to which consent must be reached according to the statement of one of the parties.

2. A contract on pledge must be concluded in written form.

3. A contract on pledge securing an obligation arising from a basic contract which is subject to notarial certification or is notarially certified by agreement of the parties, also must be notarially certified at the agency which certified the basic contract.

4. A condition on pledge may be incorporated in a contract with regard to which the obligation secured by pledge arises. Such contract must be concluded in the form established for a contract on pledge.

5. The form of a contract on pledge shall be determined according to the legislation of the place where it is concluded. A contract on pledge concluded beyond the limits of the Russian Federation may not be deemed to be void as a consequence of the failure to comply with the form if the requirements of legislation of the Russian Federation have been complied with.

The form of contract on the pledge of buildings, installations, enterprises, land plots, and other objects situated on the territory of the Russian Federation, and also movable railway stock, civil aircraft, sea-going and river ships, and space objects registered in the Russian Federation, irrespective of the place where such a contract is concluded, shall be determined by legislation of the Russian Federation.

6. The rights and duties of the parties of a contract on pledge shall be determined according to the legislation of the country where the party which is the pledgor has been founded, has a place of residence, or basic place of activity, unless established otherwise by agreement of the parties.

Article 11. State Registration of Pledge

The pledge of an enterprise as a whole or other property subject to State registration must be registered in the agency which effectuated such registration, unless another procedure of registration has been established by the present Law.

If a pledge of property is subject to State registration, then the contract on pledge shall be considered to be concluded from the moment of its registration.

Article 12. Consequences of Failure to Comply with the Form of Contract on Pledge

The failure to comply with the form of a contract on pledge shall entail the voidness of the contract with the consequences provided for by legislation of the Russian Federation.

Article 13. Appeal Against Actions Connected with Registration of Pledge

An interested person shall have the right to appeal against a refusal of registration or the illegal performance of the registration of a pledge to a court at the place where the agency is located which effectuated the registration.

Article 14. Information on Registration of Pledge

An agency effectuating the State registration of a pledge shall be obliged to issue to the pledgeholder and the pledgor a certificate of registration, and also extracts from the register at the request of the pledgeholder, pledgor, and other interested persons.

Article 15. State Duty for Registration of Pledge

State duty in an amount determined by legislative acts of the Russian Federation shall be recovered from the registration of a pledge, the issuance of a certificate concerning registration, and also providing extracts from the register. The applicant shall provide to the agency effectuating registration evidence of payment of the State duty. In the absence of such evidence, the application shall remain without movement.

Article 16. Responsibility of Agency Effectuating Registration

The agency to which the registration of pledge is entrusted shall bear responsibility for harm caused as a result of the violation of the registration rules by its workers.

Article 17. Registration of Performance of Obligation Secured by Pledge

1. The pledgeholder shall, at the demand of the pledgor, be obliged to issue documents to him confirming the full or partial performance of an obligation for subsequent entry of the respective information in the register.

2. When receiving documents confirming the full or partial performance of an obligation secured by pledge, the agency effectuating registration of a pledge shall be obliged immediately to make a respective entry in the register.

Article 18. Keeping of Pledge Registration Books by Pledgor

1. Pledgor-juridical persons and natural persons registered as entrepreneurs shall be obliged to:
—keep a pledge registration book;
—not later than 10 days after a pledge arises to make an entry in the book containing data on the type and subject of pledge, and also the amount of the obligation secured by the pledge;
—give the book to any interest person for familiarisation.

2. The pledgor shall bear responsibility for the timeliness and correctness of information entered on pledge in the pledge registration book. The pledgor shall be obliged to compensate to the victim in full losses caused by the untimeliness of making entries in the book, for the incompleteness or inaccuracy thereof, and also for evading the duty to provide the pledge registration book for familiarisation.

Article 19. Pledgor

1. The person to whom the subject of the pledge belongs by right of ownership or full economic jurisdiction may be a pledgor.

2. An enterprise to whom property has been allocated by right of full economic jurisdiction shall effectuate the pledge of an enterprise as a whole, its structural entities and subdivisions as property complexes, and also individual buildings and installations, with the consent of the owner of this property or agency empowered by it.

3. An institution may transfer on pledge property with respect to which it has acquired in accordance with law the right of autonomous disposition.

4. A person to whom a right transferred on pledge belongs may be a pledgor.

A lessee may transfer his lease rights on pledge without the consent of the lessor unless provided otherwise for by contract of lease.

Article 20. Right of Disposition of Pledged Property

Unless provided otherwise by law or contract on pledge, a pledgor shall retain the right of disposition of pledged property.

In this connection the transfer of a right to pledged property is possible only with the transfer of the basic debt secured by the pledge to the new pledgor.

Article 21. Subsequent Pledge of Pledged Property

Subsequent pledges of property already pledged shall be permitted unless provided otherwise by the present Law and preceding contracts on pledge.

Article 22. Rights of Preceding Pledgeholder

1. If pledged property which already serves as pledged security for another obligation becomes the subject of a pledge, the right of pledge of the preceding pledgeholder shall retain force.

The demands of the subsequent pledgeholder shall be satisfied from the value of the subject of the pledge after the demands of the preceding pledgeholder have been satisfied.

2. A pledgor shall be obliged to inform each subsequent pledgeholder about all existing pledges of the particular property, and also about the character and amount of obligations secured by these pledges. The pledgor shall be obliged to compensate losses which arose from any of his pledgeholders as a consequence of his failure to perform this duty.

Article 23. Demands of Pledgeholder Satisfied at Expense of Pledged Property

A pledgeholder shall, at the expense of the pledge property, have the right to satisfy his demands in full, determined at the moment of actual satisfaction, including interest, losses caused by delay of performance, and in the instances provided for by law or contract, a penalty; necessary costs for the maintenance of the pledged property and expenses for the effectuation of the demand secured by the pledge also shall be subject to compensation.

Article 24. Arising of Right to Levy Execution Against Subject of Pledge

The pledgeholder shall acquire the right to levy execution against the subject of the pledge if at the moment the period for performance of the obligation secured by pledge ensues it will not have been performed, with the exception of instances when by law or contract such right arises later or by virtue of law execution may be levied earlier.

Article 25. Subject of Pledge in Event of Partial Performance of Obligation

In the event of the partial performance by a debtor of the obligation secured by pledge, the pledge shall be retained in the initial amount until full performance of the obligation secured by it unless provided otherwise by the law or contract.

Article 26. Satisfaction of Demand of Pledgeholder from Subject of Pledge Consisting of Several Things (or Rights)

If the subject of a pledge is several things or rights, the pledgeholder may at his choice receive satisfaction at the expense of all this property or at the expense of any of the things (or rights), retaining the possibility of subsequently receiving satisfaction at the expense of other things (or rights) comprising the subject of the pledge.

Article 27. Consequences of Satisfying Demand of Pledgeholder by Third Person

In the event of the satisfaction of the demand of a pledgeholder by a third person to him shall pass, together with the right of demand, the right of pledge securing it in the procedure providing for by legislation of the Russian Federation for the assignment of a demand.

Article 28. Procedure for Levying Execution Against Pledge Property

1. Unless provided otherwise by law, execution shall be levied against pledged property by decision of a court, arbitrazh court, or arbitration court. In instances provided for by legislation of the Russian Federation, levying execution against pledged property shall be effectuated in an uncontested proceeding on the basis of the executory endorsement of a notary.

2. The realisation of pledged property against which execution is levied shall, unless provided otherwise by the present Law or contract, be effectuated in accordance with civil procedure legislation of the Russian Federation.

A list of the property of citizens against which execution may not be levied shall be established by the Code of Civil Procedure of the Russian Federation.

Article 29. Satisfaction of Demands of Pledgeholder in Event of Insufficiency of Amounts Received from Realisation Subject of Pledge

In the event that amounts received from the sale of the subject of a pledge are insufficient to fully satisfy the demands of the pledgeholder, he shall have the right, unless provided otherwise by law or contract, to receive the amount lacking from other property of the debtor against which execution may be levied in accordance with legislation of the Russian Federation without using in so doing a preference based on the right of pledge.

Article 30. Reimbursement to Pledgor of Amount Received When Realising Subject of Pledge

If when realising the subject of a pledge the amount received exceeds the amount of demands of the pledgeholder secured by this pledge, the difference shall be returned to the pledgor.

Article 31. Termination of Levying Execution Against Pledged Property by Performance of Obligation

1. The pledgor shall have the right at any time before the moment of realisation of the subject of the pledge to terminate the levy of execution against pledged property by means of performing the obligation secured by the pledge.

2. If an obligation secured by pledge provides for performance by parts, the pledgor shall have the right to terminate the levy of execution against the pledged property by means of performance of the deferred part of the obligation.

3. An agreement limiting the right of the pledgor provided for by points 1 and 2 of the present Article shall be void.

Article 32. Preservation of Pledge When Transferring Subject of Pledge to Third Person

A pledge shall retain force if the right of ownership or full economic jurisdiction to a pledged thing or a right comprising the subject of a pledge passes to a third person.

Article 33. Preservation of Pledge In Event of Assignment of Demand and Transfer of Debt

In instances when in the procedure established by law an assignment occurs by the pledgeholder of the demand secured by pledge to a third person or the transfer by the pledgor of the debt arising from the obligation secured by pledge to another person, the pledge shall retain force.

Article 34. Grounds and Consequences of Termination of Pledge

The right of pledge shall terminate:

(1) in the event of the termination of the obligation secured by pledge;

(2) in the event of the perishing of pledged property;

(3) in the event of the expiry of the period of operation of the right comprising the subject of pledge;

(4) in the event of the transfer of the rights to the subject of the pledge to the pledgeholder;

(5) in other instances provided for by law.

Section II. Pledge While Leaving Pledged Property With Pledgor

Chapter 1. General Questions

Article 35. Subject of Pledge While Leaving Pledged Property With Pledgor

1. The subject of a pledge while leaving the pledged property with the pledgor may be enterprises, buildings, installations, apartments, means of transport, space objects, and other property specified in Article 6 of the present Law.

2. Separable fruits may be the subject of pledge specified in point 1 of the present Article on condition that they do not become from the moment of separation the object of the rights of a third person.

3. The pledge of property transferred by the pledgor for a period to the possession or use of a third person shall be considered to be a pledge while leaving it with the pledgor.

Article 36. Rights of Pledgeholder in Event of Pledge of Property Left With Pledgor

In the event of a pledge while leaving property with the pledgor, the pledgeholder shall have the right, unless provided otherwise by the contract, to:

(1) verify through documents and actual presence the amount, state, and conditions of keeping the subject of the pledge;

(2) demand of the pledgor the taking of measures needed to preserve the subject of the pledge;

(3) demand of any person the termination of any infringement against the subject of the pledge threatening it with loss or damage.

If the subject of pledge is lost not through the fault of the pledgeholder and pledgor and the pledgor does not restore it or with the consent of the pledgeholder has not replaced it with other property equal in value, the pledgeholder shall have the right to demand performance before time of the obligation secured by the pledge.

Article 37. Rights of Pledgor in Event of Pledge While Leaving Property with Pledgor

Unless provided otherwise by contract and law, the pledgor shall have the right, in the event of the pledge while leaving property with the pledgor, to:

(a) possess and use the subject of pledge in accordance with its purpose;

(b) dispose of the subject of pledge by means of alienating it with the transfer to the acquirer of the debt relating to the obligation secured by pledge or by leasing it out.

Article 38. Duties of Pledgor in Event of Pledge While Leaving Property with Pledgor

1. The pledgor shall, in the event of the pledge while leaving property with the pledgor, be obliged unless otherwise provided by the contract on pledge to:

(1) insure at his own expense the subject of the pledge for its full value;

(2) take measures needed to preserve the subject of pledge, including capital and current repairs;

(3) inform the pledgeholder about leasing out the subject of pledge.

Article 39. Consequences of Violation of Duties by Pledgor in Event of Pledge While Leaving Property With Pledgor

In the event of a violation by a pledgor of the duties provided for by Article 38(1) and (2) of the present Law, the pledgeholder shall have the right to levy execution against the subject of pledge before the period for performance of the obligation secured by pledge ensues.

Article 40. Form and Registration of Contract on Pledge of Means of Transport and Space Objects

1. A contract on the pledge of civil aircraft, sea-going and river vessels, moveable railway stock, and space objects must be notarially certified.

2. The pledge of means of transport shall be subject to registration in registers which are kept by State organisations effectuating the registration of civil aircraft and sea-going and river vessels and other means of transport.

3. The pledge of an object intended for research or use for civilian purposes of outer space, the moon, and other celestial bodies shall be subject to registration in a special State Register.

The pledge of an object in outer space, on the moon, and other celestial bodies shall be subject to registration in a Register, the keeping of which shall be effectuated in accordance with norms of international space law.

Article 41. Pledge of Land Plots

The pledge of land plots to whom they belong by right of ownership, if such pledge does not fall under the rules of Chapter 2 of the present Section, shall be effectuated in the procedure established by land and other legislation of the Russian Federation.

Chapter 2. Pledge of Enterprise, Structure, Building, Installation, and Other Object Directly Connected with Land (Mortgage)

Article 42. Concept of Mortgage

The pledge of an enterprise, structure, building, installation, and other object directly connected with land, together with the respective land plot or right to use it, shall be deemed to be a mortgage.

Article 43. Form of Contract on Mortgage. Registration of Mortgage

1. A contract on mortgage must be notarially certified.

2. A mortgage shall be registered in the land book at the place where the enterprise, structure, building, installation, or other object is located.

The transfer of the right of ownership or full economic jurisdiction to the subject of the mortgage from the pledgor to another person shall be subject to registration in the same land book in which the mortgage has been registered.

3. The agency effectuating State registration of the pledge of an enterprise as a whole shall be obliged to transmit information concerning the registration of a pledge to the agencies keeping the land book, including also at the place where territorially solitary subdivisions of the enterprise are situated.

Article 44. Mortgage of Enterprise

1. The mortgage of an enterprise shall extend to all of its property, including the basic funds and circulating assets, and also other valuables reflected on the autonomous balance sheet of the enterprise, unless established otherwise by law or contract.

2. An enterprise-pledgor shall be obliged upon the demand of the pledgeholder to provide it with the annual balance sheet.

3. In the event of the failure to perform an obligation secured by the mortgage of an enterprise, the pledgeholder shall have the right to take measures to restore the financial position of the enterprise provided for by the contract on mortgage, including the appointment of representatives to executive organs of the enterprise and the limitation of the right to dispose of products produced and other property of the enterprise. If the said measures do not give the proper results, the pledgeholder shall have the right to levy execution against the mortgaged enterprise.

4. When execution is levied against a mortgaged enterprise, it shall be sold at auction as a single complex in the procedure provided for by legislation of the Russian Federation.

Article 45. Performance Before Time of Obligation Secured by Mortgage

The pledgor shall have the right at any time to perform the obligation secured by the mortgage in full before time, if the contract on mortgage excludes the possibility of subsequent pledge of the same subject of pledge.

Chapter 3. Pledge of Goods in Turnover and Processing

Article 46. Peculiarities of Pledge of Goods in Turnover and Processing

1. In the event of the pledge of goods in turnover and processing, a change of the composition and natural form of the subject of pledge (goods stocks, raw material, materials, semi-fabricates, finished product, and those similar thereto) shall be permitted on condition that the total value does not become less than that specified in the contract on pledge.

Unless provided otherwise by contract, a reduction of the value of the pledged goods in turnover and processing shall be permitted commensurate to the portion of the obligation secured by the pledge performed.

2. In the event of the pledge of goods in turnover and processing, the goods realised by the pledgor shall cease to be the object of pledge from the moment of their transfer to the ownership, full economic jurisdiction, or operative management of the acquirer, and the goods acquired by the pledgor provided for in a contract on pledge shall become the subject of pledge from the moment the right of ownership or full economic jurisdiction arises in them for the pledgor.

Article 47. Content of Contract on Pledge of Goods in Turnover and Processing

A contract on the pledge of goods in turnover and processing must specify the type of good pledged, its other generic characteristics, the total value of the subject of the pledge, the place in which they are situated, and also the types of goods by which the subject of the pledge may be replaced.

Article 48. Rights of Pledgor in Event of Pledge of Goods in Turnover and Processing

In the event of the pledge of goods in turnover and processing, the pledgor shall retain the right to possess, use, and dispose of the subject of the pledge while complying with the rules of the present Chapter.

Article 49. Concept of Pawn

1. A contract on pledge according to the conditions of which the pledged property is transferred to the pledgeholder in possession shall be deemed to be a pawn.

2. By agreement of the pledgeholder with the pledgor, the subject of pawn may be left with the pledgor under lock and seal of the pledgeholder (fixed pawn). An individually specified thing may be left with the pledgor with the affixing of marks testifying to the pawn.

The rules of the present Section shall apply to a fixed pledge insofar as their application is not contrary to the essence of the relations of the pledgeholder with the pledgor under such a pledge.

Article 50. Duties of Pledgeholder in Event of Pawn

In the event of a pawn, the pledgeholder shall, unless provided otherwise by contract, be obliged to:

(1) insure the subject of the pawn for its full value at the expense of and in the interests of the pledgor;

(2) take measures necessary for the preservation of the subject of the pawn;

(3) immediately notify the pledgor about a threat of loss or damage to the subject of the pawn which has arisen;

(4) regularly send a report to the pledgor about the use of the subject of the pawn, if the use is permitted in accordance with Article 51(1) of the present Law;

(5) immediately return the subject of the pawn after the performance of the obligation by the pledgor or a third person which is secured by the pawn.

The pledgeholder must derive revenues from the subject of the pawn in the interests of the pledgor when this has been provided for by contract.

Article 51. Rights of Pledgeholder in Event of Pawn

1. In the instances expressly provided for by the contract on pledge, the pledgeholder shall have the right to use the subject of the pawn. The revenues and other property advantages acquired by the pledgeholder as a result of the use of the subject of pawn shall be directed towards covering the expenses for maintenance of the subject of the pawn, and also shall be credited towards the payment of interest on the debt or the debt itself with regard to the obligation secured by the pawn.

2. If the threat of loss, shortage, or damage of the subject of the pawn arises not through the fault of the pledgeholder, he shall have the right to demand the

replacement of the subject of the pawn, and in the event the pledgor refuses to fulfil this demand, to levy execution against the subject of the pawn before the period of performance of the obligations secured by the pawn ensues.

Article 52. Possibility of Performance Before Time of Obligation Secured by Pawn

If the pledgeholder keeps or uses the subject of the pawn improperly, the pledgor shall have the right at any time to demand the termination of the pledge or to perform the demand secured by the pawn before time.

Article 53. Responsibility of Pledgeholder for Loss, Shortage, or Damage to Subject of Pawn

1. A pledgeholder shall be liable for the loss, shortage, or damaging of the subject of the pawn if it is proved that the loss, shortage, or damaging occurred not through his fault.

If the pledgeholder is a pawnshop or other entrepreneur for which the granting of credits under pawn of property is the subject of its activity, relief from responsibility may occur only when the pledgeholder proves that the loss, shortage, or damage of the subject of pawn occurred as a consequence of insuperable force or the intent or gross negligence of the pledgor.

2. The pledgeholder shall, in the event of pawn, bear responsibility for the loss and shortage of the subject of pawn in the amount of the value of the loss (or shortage), and for damage to the subject of pawn, in the amount by which the value of the pledged thing was reduced. If when accepting a thing on pawn a valuation was done of the subject of pawn, the responsibility of the pledgeholder must not exceed the said valuation.

The pledgeholder shall be obliged to compensate the pledgor in full for losses caused by the loss, shortage, or damage to the subject of pawn if this has been provided for by law or contract.

Section IV. Pledge of Rights

Article 54. Rights as Subject of Pledge

1. The rights of possession and use, including the rights of a lessee, and other rights (or demands) arising from obligations, and other property rights belonging to a pledgor may be the subject of a pledge.

2. A right with a specified period of operation may be the subject of pledge only until the expiry of the period of its operation.

3. In a contract on the pledge of rights which do not have a monetary valuation, the value of the subject of pledge shall be determined by agreement of the parties.

Article 55. Content of Contract on Pledge of Rights

In a contract on the pledge of rights, together with the conditions provided for by Article 10 of the present Law, the person who is the debtor with respect to the pledgor must be specified. The pledgor shall be obliged to inform his debtor about the pledge or rights which occurred.

Article 56. Duties of Pledgor in Event of Pledge of Rights

Unless provided otherwise by contract, in the event of the pledge of rights the pledgor shall be obliged to:

(1) perform actions which are necessary in order to ensure the validity of the pledged right;

(2) not perform an assignment of the pledged right;

(3) not perform actions entailing the termination of the pledged right or a reduction of its value;

(4) take measures which are necessary in order to defend the pledged right against infringements on the part of third persons;

(5) communicate to the pledgeholder information concerning changes which have occurred in the pledged right, about violations thereof on the part of third persons, and on the claims of third persons to this right.

Article 57. Rights of Pledgeholder in Event of Pledge of Rights

Unless provided otherwise by contract, in the event of a pledge of rights the pledgeholder shall have the right to:

(1) demand in court or an arbitrazh court irrespective of the ensuing of the period of performance of an obligation secured by pledge the transfer of the pledged right to himself, if the pledgor has not performed the duties provided for by Article 56 of the present Law;

(2) act as a third person in a case in which the suit concerning the pledged right is considered;

(3) in the event of the failure of the pledgor to perform the duties provided for by Article 56(4) of the present Law, autonomously undertake measures necessary to protect the pledged right against violations on the part of third persons.

Article 58. Consequences of Performance by Debtor of Obligation to Pledgor

1. If the debtor of a pledgor before the performance of an obligation by the pledgor which is secured by a pledge performs his own obligation, everything received by the pledgor in so doing shall become the subject of a pledge, the pledgor being obliged immediately to notify the pledgeholder thereof.

2. When receiving monetary amounts from a debtor as performance of an obligation, the pledgor shall be obliged upon the demand of the pledgeholder to

credit the respective amounts to the account of performing the obligation secured by the pledge, unless established otherwise by the contract on pledge.

Section V. Guarantees of Rights of Parties in Event of Pledge

Article 59. Protection of Interests of Pledgeholder in Event of Termination of His Rights and Rights of Pledgor to Pledged Property on Grounds Provided for by Law

1. In the event of the adoption by the Russian Federation or republic within the Russian Federation of legislative acts terminating the right of pledge or the right of the pledgor to pledged property, the losses caused to the pledgeholder as a result of the adoption of these acts shall be compensated to it in full by the Russian Federation or the respective republic within the Russian Federation. Disputes concerning the compensation of losses shall be settled by a court.

2. In instances of the termination of the right of ownership to pledged property or termination of pledged rights in connection with a decision of a State agency of power and administration not aimed directly at seizing pledged property or pledged rights, including a decision to seize a land plot on which a pledged house, other structures, installations, or plantings are situated, the losses caused to the pledgeholder as a result of this decision shall be compensated by the pledgeholder in full by this State agency at the expense of assets at its disposition. Disputes concerning compensation of losses shall be settled by a court or arbitrazh court.

Article 60. Invalidity of Acts Violating Pledged Right

1. If as a result of the publication of an act by an agency of State administration or local agency of self-government not conforming to legislation the rights of the pledgeholder are violated, such act shall be deemed to be void by a court or arbitrazh court upon the application of the pledgeholder.

2. Losses caused to the pledgeholder as a result of the publication of an act specified in point 1 of the present Article shall be subject to compensation in full by the respective agency of State administration or agency of local self-government.

FEDERAL LAW ON MORTGAGE (OR PLEDGE OF IMMOVEABLE)

[Federal Law No. 102-ФЗ, 16 July 1998,
as amended by Federal Law No. 143-ФЗ, 9 November
2001, Federal Law No. 18-ФЗ, 11 February 2002 and Federal
Law No. 179-ФЗ, 24 December 2002, СЗ РФ (1998), no. 29, item 3400;
(2001), no. 46, item 4308; (2002), no. 7, item 629; no. 52(I), item 5135]

Chapter I	General Provisions	747
Chapter II	Conclusion of Contract on Mortgage	751
Chapter III	Zakladnaia	754
Chapter IV	State Registration of Mortgage	761
Chapter V	Ensuring Preservation of Property Pledged Under Contract on Mortgage	766
Chapter VI	Transfer of Rights to Property Pledged Under Contract on Mortgage to Other Persons and Encumberment of this Property by Rights of Other Persons	769
Chapter VII	Subsequent Mortgage	772
Chapter VIII	Assignment of Rights Under Contract of Mortgage. Transfer and Pledge of Zakladnaia	774
Chapter IX	Levy of Execution Against Property Pledged Under Contract on Mortgage	777
Chapter X	Realisation of Pledged Property Against Which Execution is Levied	781
Chapter XI	Peculiarities of Mortgage of Land Plots	785
Chapter XII	Peculiarities of Mortgage of Enterprises, Buildings, and Installations	788
Chapter XIII	Peculiarities of Mortgage of Dwelling Houses and Apartments	790
Chapter XIV	Concluding Provisions	793

Chapter I. General Provisions

Article 1. Grounds for Arising of Mortgage and Regulation Thereof

1. Under a contract on the pledge of immoveable property (or contract on mortgage), one party—the pledgeholder who is the creditor with regard to the obligation secured by a mortgage, shall have the right to receive satisfaction of his monetary demands against the debtor with regard to this obligation from the value of the pledged immoveable property of the other party—the pledgor preferentially before other creditors of the pledgor, with the exceptions established by the present Law.

The pledgor may be the debtor himself under the obligation secured by a mortgage or a person not participating in this obligation (third person).

Property on which a mortage is established shall remain with the pledgor in his possession and use.

2. To a pledge of immoveable property arising on the basis of a federal law in the event of the ensuing of the circumstances specified therein (hereinafter—mortgage by virtue of law) respectively shall apply the rules on pledge arising by virtue of a contract on mortgage unless established otherwise by a federal law [as amended by Federal Law No. 18-ФЗ, 11 February 2002].

3. The general rules on pledge contained in the Civil Code of the Russian Federation shall apply to relations with regard to a contract on mortgage in instances when other rules have not been established by the said Code or present Federal Law.

4. The pledge of land plots, enterprises, buildings, installations, apartments, and other immoveable property may arise only insofar as their turnover is permitted by federal laws.

Article 2. Obligation Secured by Mortgage

A mortgage may be established to secure an obligation under a credit contract, under a contract of loan or other obligation, including an obligation based on purchase-sale, lease, independent-work, or other contract, or causing of harm, unless provided otherwise by a federal law.

Obligations secured by a mortgage shall be subject to bookkeeping recording by the creditor and debtor if they are juridical persons in the procedure established by legislation of the Russian Federation on bookkeeping.

Article 3. Demands Secured by Mortgage

1. A mortage shall ensure payment to the pledgeholder of the principal amount of the debt under a credit contract or other obligation secured by the mortgage fully or in the part provided for by the contract on mortgage.

A mortgage established to secure the performance of a credit contract or contract of loan with a condition of payment of interest shall also ensure payment to the creditor (or lender) of the interest due to him for use of the credit (or loan means).

Unless provided otherwise by a contract, the mortgage also shall secure payment to the pledgeholder of the amounts due to him:

(1) in compensation of losses and/or as a penalty (or fine, forfeit) as a consequence of the failure to perform, delay of performance, or other improper performance of an obligacion secured by a mortgage;

(2) in the form of interest for the unlawful use of another's monetary means provided for by an obligation secured by a mortgage or by a federal law;

(3) in compensation of judicial costs and other expenses caused by the levy of execution against pledged property;

(4) in compensation of expenses for the realisation of pledged property.

2. Unless provided otherwise by a contract, a mortgage shall secure demands of a pledgeholder in that amount which they have at the moment of satisfaction thereof at the expense of pledged property.

3. If in a contract on mortgage a total firm amount of demands of the pledge-holder has been specified which are secured by a mortgage, the obligations of the debtor to the pledgeholder in the part exceeding this amount shall not be considered to be secured by the mortgage, except for demands based on point 1, subpoints (3) and (4), of the present Article or on Article 4 of the present Federal Law.

Article 4. Securing Additional Expenses of Pledgeholder by Mortgage

In instances when a pledgeholder in accordance with the conditions of a contract on mortgage or by virtue of the need to ensure the preservation of property pledged under this contract is forced to bear expenses for the maintenance thereof and/or protection or to replay indebtedness of the pledgor with regard to taxes, charges, or municipal payments connected with this property, compensation to the pledgeholder of such necessary expenses shall be secured at the expense of the pledged property.

Article 5. Property Which May Be Subject of Mortgage

1. Under a contract on mortgage immoveable property specified in Article 130(1) of the Civil Code of the Russian Federation may be pledged, the right to which has been registered in the procedure established for the State registration of rights to immoveable property, including:

(1) land plots, except for land plots specified in Article 63 of the present Federal Law;

(2) enterprises, as well as buildings, installations, and other immoveable property to be used in entrepreneurial activity;

(3) dwelling houses, apartments, and parts of dwelling houses and apartments consisting of one or several isolated rooms;

(4) dachas, garden homes, garages, and other structures of consumption designation;

(5) aircraft and sea-going vessels, vessels of internal navigation, and space objects.

Buildings, including dwelling houses and other structures, and installations directly connected with land, may be the subject of a mortgage on condition of compliance with the rules of Article 69 of the present Federal Law.

2. The rules of the present Federal Law shall apply to the pledge of uncompleted construction of immoveable property erected on a land plot in accordance

with the requirements of legislation of the Russian Federation, including buildings and installations on condition of compliance with the rules of Article 69 of
the present Federal Law [as amended by Federal Law No. 18-ФЗ, 11 February
2002].

3. Unless provided otherwise by a contract, a thing which is the subject of a
mortgage shall be considered to be pledged together with appurtenances (Article
135, Civil Code of the Russian Federation) as a single whole.

4. Part of property whose division in kind is impossible without changing the
designation thereof (indivisible thing) may not be an autonomous subject of a
mortgage.

5. The rules concerning mortgage of immoveable property respectively shall
apply to the pledge of rights of a lessee under a contract concerning lease of such
property (or right of lease) insofar as not established otherwise by a federal law and
is not contrary to the essence of the lease relations.

Article 6. Right to Pledge Out Property Under Contract on Mortgage

1. A mortgage may be established on property specified in Article 5 of the present Federal Law which belongs to the pledgor by right of ownership or by right
of economic jurisdiction.

2. A mortgage of property removed from turnover, property against which in
accordance with a federal law executed may not be levied, and also property
with respect to which obligatory privatisation is provided for in a procedure
established by a federal law or whose privatisation is prohibited shall not be
permitted.

3. If property whose alienation requires the consent or authorisation of
another person or agency is the subject of a mortgage, such consent or authorisation shall be necessary for a mortgage of this property.

Decisions concerning the pledge of immoveable property in State ownership
and not consolidated by right of economic jurisdiction shall be adopted by the
Government of the Russian Federation or by the government (or administration)
of a subject of the Russian Federation.

4. The right of lease may be the subject of a mortgage with the consent of the
lessor unless provided otherwise by a federal law or by the contract of lease. In
instances provided for by Article 335(3) of the Civil Code of the Russian
Federation, the consent of the owner of the leased property or person having the
right of economic jurisdiction over it also shall be necessary.

5. The pledge of immoveable property shall not be grounds for releasing the
person who is the pledgor under a contract on mortgage from the fulfilment by
him of conditions on which he participated in an investment (or commercial)

competition, auction, or otherwise in the process of privatisation of property which is the subject of the said pledge.

Article 7. Mortgage of Property in Common Ownership

1. A mortgage may be established on property in common joint ownership (without determination of the participatory share of each of the owners in the right of ownership) when there is consent to this of all owners. The consent must be given in written form unless established otherwise by a federal law.

2. A participant of common participatory share ownership may pledge his participatory share in the right to common property without the consent of the other owners.

In the event of levy of execution upon the demand of the pledgeholder against this participatory share, the rules of Articles 250 and 255 of the Civil Code of the Russian Federation shall apply in the event of the sale thereof concerning the preferential right of purchase belonging to the other owners, and concerning levy of execution against a participatory share in the right of common ownership, except for instances of levy of execution against a participatory share in the right of ownership to common property in a dwelling house (Article 290 of the Civil Code of the Russian Federation) in connection with levy of execution against an apartment in this house.

Chapter II. Conclusion of Contract on Mortgage

Article 8. General Rules of Conclusion of Contract on Mortgage

A contract on mortgage shall be concluded in compliance with the general rules of the Civil Code of the Russian Federation on the conclusion of contracts, and also the provisions of the present Federal Law.

Article 9. Content of Contract on Mortgage

1. The subject of mortgage must be specified in a contract on mortgage, the valuation thereof, the essence, amount, and period for performance of the obligation secured by the mortgage.

2. The subject of a mortgage shall be determined in the contract by specifying the name thereof, location, and a description sufficient for the identification of this subject.

The right by virtue of which property is the subject of a mortgage, belongs to the pledgor, and the name of the agency of State registration of rights to immoveable property which registered this right of the pledgor must be specified in the contract on mortgage.

If the right of lease belonging to a pledgor is the subject of a mortgage, the leased property must be determined in the contract on mortgage as though it itself were the subject of the mortgage and the period of lease must be specified.

751

3. The valuation of the subject of a mortgage shall be determined in accordance with legislation of the Russian Federation by agreement of the pledgor with the pledgeholder in compliance with the requirements of Article 67 of the present Federal Law in the event of the mortgage of a land plot and specified in the contract on mortgage in monetary expression.

In the event of the mortgage of State and municipal property, the valuation thereof shall be effectuated in accordance with the requirements established by a federal law or in the procedure determined by it.

[paragraph repealed by Federal Law No. 143-ФЗ, 9 November 2001].

In the event of the pledge of uncompleted construction of immoveable property in State or municipal ownership, the valuation shall be effectuated at the market value of this property [added by Federal Law No. 143-ФЗ, 9 November 2001].

4. An obligation secured by a mortgage must be named in the contract on mortgage, specifying the amount thereof, grounds for arising, and period of performance. In those instances when this obligation is based on some contract, the parties to this contract and the date and place of conclusion thereof must be specified. If the amount of the obligation secured by a mortgage is subject to determination in the future, the procedure and other necessary conditions for determining it must be specified in the contract on mortgage.

5. If an obligation secured by a mortgage is subject to performance by parts, the periods (or periodicity) of the respective payments and the amounts thereof or conditions enabling these amounts to be determined must be specified.

6. If the rights of pledgeholder in accordance with Article 13 of the present Federal Law are certified by a zakladnaia, this shall be specified in the contract on mortgage, except for instances of the issuance of a zakladnaia in the event of a mortgage by virtue of a law [as amended by Federal Law No. 18-ФЗ, 11 February 2002].

Article 10. Notarial Certification and State Registration of Contract on Mortgage

1. A contract on mortgage must be notarially certified and shall be subject to State registration.

A contract in which any data specified in Article 9 of the present Federal Law are absent or the rules of Article 13(4) of the present Federal Law have been violated shall not be subject to notarial certification and State registration as a contract on mortgage.

The failure to comply with the rules on notarial certification and State registration of the contract on mortgage shall entail the invalidity thereof. Such contract shall be considered to be null.

2. A contract on mortgage shall be considered to be concluded and shall enter into force from the moment of its State registration.

3. When including an agreement on mortgage in a credit or other contract containing an obligation secured by the mortgage, compliance with the requirements established for a contract on mortgage must be complied with in respect of the form and State registration of this contract.

4. If it has been specified in a contract on mortgage that the rights of the pledgeholder in accordance with Article 13 of the present Federal Law are certified by a zakladnaia, together with such contract the zakladnaia shall be submitted to the notary. The notary shall gave a notation on the zakladnaia concerning the time and place of notarial certification of the contract on mortgage, and shall number and seal the sheets of the zakladnaia in accordance with Article 14(3), paragraph two, of the present Federal Law.

Article 11. Arising of Mortgage as Encumberment

1. State registration of a contract on mortgage shall be grounds for making an entry concerning the mortgage in the Unified State Register of Rights to Immoveable Property and Transactions Therewith.

State registration of a contract entailing the arising of a mortgage by virtue of a law shall be grounds for making an entry concerning the arising of a mortgage by virtue of a law in the Unified State Register of Rights to Immoveable Property and Transactions Therewith.

Payment for making an entry concerning the encumberment of immoveable property by a mortgage in the Unified State Register of Rights to Immoveable Property and Transactions Therewith shall not be recovered.

2. A mortgage as an encumberment of property pledged under a contract on mortgage shall arise from the moment of conclusion of this contract.

In the event of a mortgage by virtue of a law, a mortgage as an encumberment of property shall arise from the moment of State registration of the right of ownership to this property unless established otherwise by a contract.

3. The rights of the pledgeholder (right of pledge) to property provided for by the present Federal Law and contract on mortgage shall be considered to have arisen from the moment of making the entry concerning the mortgage in the Unified State Register of Rights to Immoveable Property and Transactions Therewith, unless established otherwise by a federal law. If an obligation secured by a mortgage arose after making an entry in the Unified State Register of Rights to Immoveable Property and Transactions Therewith concerning a mortgage, the rights of the pledgeholder shall arise from the moment of arising of this obligation.

The rights of a pledgeholder (right of pledge) to pledged property shall not be subject to State registration.

753

Article 12. Warning of Pledgeholder About Rights of Third Persons to Subject of Mortgage

In the event of the conclusion of a contract on mortgage the pledgor shall be obliged in written form to warn the pledgeholder about all rights of third persons to the subject of mortgage (rights of pledge, use for life, lease, servitudes, and other rights) known to him at the moment of State registration. The failure to perform this duty shall give to the pledgeholder the right to demand performance before time of the obligation secured by the mortgage or a change of conditions of the contract on pledge.

Chapter III. Zakladnaia

Article 13. Basic Provisions on Zakladnaia

1. The rights of a pledgeholder with regard to an obligation secured by a mortgage and under a contract on mortgage may be certified by a zakladnaia insofar as not established otherwise by the present Federal Law.

The rights of a pledgeholder under a mortgage by virtue of a law and with regard to an obligation secured by the said mortgage may be certified by a zakladnaia unless established otherwise by the present Federal Law [paragraph added by Federal Law No. 18-ФЗ, 11 February 2002].

2. A zakladnaia shall be an inscribed security certifying the following rights of the legal possessor thereof:

the right to receive performance under a monetary obligation secured by a mortgage without the submission of other evidence of the existence of this obligation;

the right of pledge on property encumbered by the mortgage [as amended by Federal Law No. 18-ФЗ, 11 February 2002].

3. The debtor with regard to the obligation secured by a mortgage and the pledgor shall be the persons obliged under the zakladnaia.

4. The drawing up and issuance of a zakladnaia shall not be permitted if:
(1) the subject of mortgage is:
an enterprise as a property complex;
land plots from lands of agricultural designation to which the operation of the present Federal Law extends;
forests;
the right of lease of property enumerated in the present subpoint;
(2) a monetary obligation, the amount of debt under which at the moment of conclusion of the contract is not determined and which does not contain conditions enabling this amount to be determined at the proper moment, is secured by a mortgage.

In the instances provided for by the present point the conditions on zakladnaia in a contract on mortgage shall be invalid.

5. A zakladnaia shall be drawn up by the pledgor, and if he is a third person, also by the debtor with regard to the obligation secured by the mortgage.

A zakladnaia shall be issued to the initial pledgeholder by the agency effectuating the State registration of the mortgage after the State registration of the mortgage.

The transfer of rights under a zakladnaia and pledge of a zakladnaia shall be effectuated in the procedure established by Articles 48 and 49 of the present Federal Law.

6. In the event of the part performance of an obligation secured by a mortgage, the debtor with regard to it, the pledgor, and the legal possessor of the zakladnaia shall have the right to conclude an agreement providing that:

such change of the subject of mortgage under which the part of the property previously pledged under the said contract on mortgage is deemed to be pledged if the said part of the property may be an autonomous object of pledge;

such change of the amount of security under which the amount of demands which arose from the credit or other contract and secured under the said contract on mortgage is increased or decreased in comparison with that which was previously secured by the mortgage.

The said agreement must be notarially certified.

7. When concluding agreements specified in point 6 of the present Article and Article 36(3) of the present Federal Law and in the event of the transfer of the debt with regard to the obligation secured by a mortgage there shall be provided in such agreements:

either the making of changes in the content of the zakladnaia by means of attaching thereto a notarially certified copy of the said agreement and an indication on the agreement as a document which is an integral part of the zakladnaia and in the text of the zakladnaia itself in accordance with the rules of Article 15, paragraph two, of the present Federal Law;

or the annulment of the zakladnaia and simultaneously therewith the issuance of a new zakladnaia drawn up by taking into account the respective changes.

In the last instance simultaneously with the statement concerning the making of changes in the said unified State register of rights to immoveable property the pledgor shall transfer to the agency which effectuated the State registration of the mortgage the new zakladnaia, which shall be handed over to the pledgeholder in exchange for the zakladnaia in his legal possession.

The annulled zakladnaia shall be kept in the archive of the agency which effectuated the State registration of the mortgage until the moment of cancellation of the registration entry concerning the mortgage.

Article 14. Content of Zakladnaia

1. A zakladnaia at the moment of issuance thereof to the initial pledgeholder by the agency effectuating State registration of the mortgage must contain [as amended by Federal Law No. 18-ФЗ, 11 February 2002]:

(1) the word 'zakladnaia' incorporated into the name of the document;

(2) the name of the pledgor and indication of place of his residence or the name and indication of location, if the pledgor is a juridical person;

(3) name of the initial pledgeholder and indication of place of his residence or the name and indication of location if the pledgeholder is a juridical person;

(4) name of the credit contract or other monetary obligation whose performance is secured by the mortgage, specifying the date and place of conclusion of such contract or grounds of arising of the obligation secured by the mortgage;

(5) name of the debtor with regard to the obligation secured by the mortgage, if the debtor is not the pledgor, and indication of the place of residence of the debtor or its name and indication of location if the debtor is a juridical person;

(6) indication of the amount of the obligation secured by the mortgage and the amount of interest, if it is subject to payment with regard to the obligation, or conditions enabling this amount and interest to be determined at the proper moment;

(7) indication of the period of payment of the amount of the obligation secured by the mortgage, and if this amount is subject to payment by parts, the periods (or periodicity) of the respective payments and amount of each of them or the conditions enabling these periods and the amounts of payments (or plan for repayment of the debt) to be determined;

(8) name and description of the property sufficient for identification on which the mortgage is established and indication of the location of such property;

(9) monetary valuation of the property on which the mortgage is established, and in instances if the establishment of a mortgage is obligatory by virtue of a law, the monetary valuation of the property confirmed by an opinion of a valuer (as amended by Federal Law No. 143-ФЗ, 9 November 2001];

(10) name of the right by virtue of which the property which is the subject of mortgage belongs to the pledgor and the agency which registered this right, specifying the number, date, and place of State registration, and if the subject of mortgage is a right of lease belonging to the pledgor—the precise name of the property which is the subject of lease, in accordance with subpoint 8 and the period of operation of this right;

(11) indication whether the property which is the subject of mortgage has been encumbered by a right of use for life, lease, servitude, or other right or is not encumbered by any rights of third persons subject to State registration at the moment of State registration of the mortgage;

(12) signature of the pledgor, and if he is a third person, also of the debtor with regard to the obligation secured by the mortgage;

(13) information concerning the time and place of notarial certification of the contract on the mortgage, except for instances of the issuance of a zakladnaia in the event of a mortgage by virtue of a law, and also information provided for by Article 22(2) of the present Federal Law concerning State registration of a mortgage [as amended by Federal Law No. 18-ФЗ, 22 February 2002];

(14) indication of the date of issuance of a zakladnaia to the initial pledgeholder. In the event of the issuance of a zakladnaia by reason of a mortgage by virtue of a law, the incorporation in the zakladnaia of data specified in subpoint 10 of the present point shall be ensured by the agency effectuating the State registration of the mortgage. The procedure for the incorporation of this data in the zakladnaia shall be determined by Article 22 of the present Federal Law [as amended by Federal Law No. 18-ФЗ, 11 February 2002].

A document named a 'zakladnaia' in which nonetheless any data specified in subpoints (1) to (14) of the present point are absent shall not be a zakladnaia and shall not be subject to issuance to the initial pledgeholder.

2. By agreement between the pledgor and the pledgeholder, data and conditions not provided for by point 1 of the present Article also may be included in a zakladnaia.

3. In the event the place on the zakladnaia itself is insufficient for notations concerning new possessors and part performance of the obligation secured by the mortgage or the entry of other necessary information, an additional sheet shall be attached to the zakladnaia, the inscriptions and notations on which shall be so made that they commenced on the zakladnaia and end on this sheet [as amended by Federal Law No. 18-ФЗ, 11 February 2002].

All sheets of a zakladnaia shall comprise a single whole. They must be numbered and sealed by the notary. Individual sheets of a zakladnaia may not be the subject of a transaction.

4. In the event of the failure of a zakladnaia to conform to the contract on mortgage or contract, an obligation from which is secured by a mortgage, the content of the zakladnaia shall be considered to be true if the acquirer thereof at the moment of conclusion of the transaction did not know and should not have known about such nonconformity. This rule shall not extend to instances when the initial pledgeholder is the possessor of the zakladnaia.

The legal possessor of a zakladnaia shall have the right to demand the elimination of the said nonconformity by means of annulment of the zakladnaia in his possession and issuance simultaneously with this of a new zakladnaia, if the demand was declared immediately after such nonconformity became know to the legal possessor.

The compiler of the zakladnaia shall bear responsibility for losses which arose in connection with the said nonconformity and the elimination thereof.

Article 15. Annexes to Zakladnaia

Documents determining the conditions of a mortgage or necessary for the effectuation by the pledgeholder of his rights under the zakladnaia may be appended to a zakladnaia.

If the documents appended to a zakladnaia have not been named in it with that degree of specificity which is sufficient for their identification, and it is not said in the zakladnaia that such documents are an integral part thereof, such documents shall not be binding for persons to whom the rights under the zakladnaia have passed as a result of the sale thereof, pledge, or otherwise.

Article 16. Registration of Possessors of Zakladnaia

1. Any legal possessor of a zakladnaia shall have the right to demand from the agency which effectuated the State registration of the mortgage to register him in the unified State register of rights to immoveable property as pledgeholder, specifying his name and place of residence, and if the possessor of the zakladnaia is a juridical person—its name and location.

2. A debtor with regard to an obligation secured by a mortgage who has received from the legal possessor of a zakladnaia written notification concerning registration of the last in the unified State register of rights to immoveable property with a properly attested extract from this register shall be obliged to effectuate interim payments with regard to the said obligation without requiring presentation of the zakladnaia to him at any time. Such duty of the debtor shall be terminated upon receipt of the written notification from this or another legal possessor of the zakladnaia concerning assignment of the rights with regard to the zakladnaia.

3. The registration entry concerning the legal possessor of a zakladnaia must be effectuated within one day from the moment of recourse of the applicant to the agency which effectuated State registration of the mortgage when presenting the zakladnaia on the basis of:

the transfer of a right under a zakladnaia conlcuded in accordance with the present Federal Law and notation made on the zakladnaia if the person who performed such inscription was the legal possessor of the zakladnaia or pledgeholder of the zakladnaia in whose name the special pledge inscription of endorsement was made and who sold the zakladnaia upon the expiry of the period determined therein (Article 49(4)) [as amended by Federal Law No. 18-ФЗ, 11 February 2002];

the documents confirming the transfer of rights under a zakladnaia to other persons as a result of the reorganisation of a juridical person or by way of inheriting;

the decision of a court recognising the rights under a zakladnaia for the applicant.

Article 17. Effectuation of Rights With Regard to Zakladnaia and Performance of Obligation Secured by Pledge

1. When effectuating their rights provided for by a federal law or by a contract, the possessor of the zakladnaia shall be obliged to present the zakladnaia to the obliged person (debtor or pledgor) with respect to which the respective right is effectuated upon the demand thereof only if in the event of the pledge of the zakladnaia it was not transferred on deposit to a notary or was not pledged with the transfer of the zakladnaia to the pledgeholder thereof [as amended by Federal Law No. 18-ФЗ, 11 February 2002].

2. The pledgeholder with regard to performance of the obligation secured by a mortgage in full shall be obliged to transfer the zakladnaia to the pledgor, and in instances when an obligation is performed by parts, to certify the partial performance thereof by a means sufficient for the pledgor and evident to possible subsequent possessors of the zakladnaia, including by appending respective financial documents or performing an entry on the zakladnaia concerning partial performance of the obligation [as amended by Federal Law No. 18-ФЗ, 11 February 2002].

3. The location of the zakladnaia with the pledgeholder or absence of a notation thereon or certification otherwise of partial performance of the obligation secured by the mortgage shall testify, unless proved otherwise, that this obligation or respective part thereof has not been performed, except for the instance specified in Article 48(2) of the present Federal Law [as amended by Federal Law No. 18-ФЗ, 11 February 2002].

4. The debtor with regard to an obligation secured by a mortgage shall pay his debt in full or in part by the proper performance of his duties under the zakladnaia in accordance with the plan for the repayment of the debt to the legal possessor thereof or to the person empowered in writing by the legal possessor of the zakladnaia to effectuate the rights with regard to it.

5. In the event of the transfer of a zakladnaia on deposit to a notary in the event of the pledge of the zakladnaia, the debtor with regard to the obligation secured by the mortgage shall perform his obligation by placing the debt on deposit with a notary.

6. A person obliged with regard to a zakladnaia shall have the right to refuse to the presenter of the zakladnaia the effectuation of rights by him under the zakladnaia if:

a suit has been accepted for consideration by a court to deem invalid the assignment of rights under the said zakladnaia or to apply the consequences of the invalidity of that transaction;

the zakladnaia presented is invalid in connection with the loss thereof by the legal possessor and issuance of a duplicate zakladnaia (Article 18) or in connection with a violation of the procedure for the issuance of a zakladnaia or duplicate thereof for which the person obliged with regard to it is not liable;

the debtor with regard to the grounds specified in Article 48(2) of the present Federal Law is deemed partially to have performed the obligation [added by Federal Law No. 18-ФЗ, 11 February 2002].

A person obliged with regard to a zakladnaia shall not have the right to cite against the demands of the legal possessor of the zakladnaia any objections concerning the effectuation of rights under it which are not based on the zakladnaia.

7. The location of a zakladnaia with any of the person obliged with regard to it or at the agency which effectuated the State registration of the mortgage shall testify, unless proved otherwise or established by the present Federal Law, that the obligation secured by the mortgage has been performed. The person in whose possessoin the zakladnaia proves to be shall be obliged immediately to notify other persons thereof from among the aforesaid.

In instances when in accordance with the present Federal Law the zakladnaia is annulled, the agency which effectuated the State registration of the mortgage immediately upon receipt of the zakladnaia by it shall annul it by means of placing on the face side the stamp 'paid' or otherwise not permitting the possibility of its circulation, except for physical destruction of the zakladnaia.

Article 18. Restoration of Rights Under Lost Zakladnaia

1. Restoration of rights with regard to a lost zakladnaia shall be performed by the pledgor, and if he is a third person, also by the debtor with regard to the obligation secured by the mortgage on the basis of:

the application to their address of the person signified in the unified State register of rights to immoveable property as the pledgeholder if according to the date in the said register in accordance with Article 16 of the present Federal Law it is possible to establish the legality of the rights to be restored under the lost zakladnaia [as amended by Federal Law No. 18-ФЗ, 11 February 2002];

the decision of a court rendered with regard to the results of the consideration by way of a special proceeding concerning the establishment of facts having legal significance in accordance with procedural legislation of the Russian Federation.

2. The pledgor, and if he is a third person, also the debtor with regard to the obligation secured by a mortgage shall be obliged within the minimally possible periods to draw up a duplicate zakladnaia with a notation thereon 'duplicate' and transfer it to the agency which effectuated State registration of the mortgage.

3. The duplicate of a zakladnaia shall be issued by the agency which effectuated State registration of the mortgage by means of handing it over to the person who lost the zakladnaia.

4. The duplicate of a zakladnaia shall fully correspond to the lost zakladnaia.

The compiler of the duplicate of the zakladnaia shall bear responsibility for losses which arose in connection with the failure of the duplicate of the zakladnaia to conform to the lost zakladnaia. Persons obliged under the zakladnaia shall not have the right to refuse to the legal possessor of the duplicate of the zakladnaia the effectuation of rights with regard to it in connection with the said nonconformity if they are liable for it.

Chapter IV. State Registration of Mortgage

Article 19. Basic Provisions on State Registration of Mortgage

1. A mortgage shall be subject to State registration by justice institutions in the unified State register of rights to immoveable property in the procedure established by the federal law on the State registration of rights to immoveable property and transactions therewith.

2. State registration of a mortgage shall be effectuated at the location of the property which is the subject of the mortgage.

Article 20. Procedure for State Registration of Mortgage

1. State registration of a mortgage arising by virtue of a contract on mortgage shall be effectuated on the basis of an application of the pledgor or pledgeholder.

For the State registration of a mortgage arising by virtue of a contract on mortgage there must be submitted:

the notarially certified contract on mortgage and a copy thereof;

the documents specified in the contract on mortgage as annexes;

the document concerning payment of State registration;

other documents necessary for State registration of a mortgage in accordance with legislation of the Russian Federation on the State registration of rights to immoveable property and transactions therewith [as amended by Federal Law No. 18-ФЗ, 11 February 2002].

2. A mortgage by virtue of a law shall be subject to State registration. State registration of a mortgage by virtue of a law shall be effectuated by a justice institution without the submission of an individual application and without payment of State registration.

State registration of a mortgage by virtue of a law shall be effectuated simultaneously with the State registration of the right of ownership of the person whose rights are enumbered by the mortgage. The rights of the pledgeholder with regard to a mortgage by virtue of a law may be certified by a zakladnaia [as amended by Federal Law No. 18-ФЗ, 11 February 2002].

3. If the rights of a pledgeholder are certified by a zakladnaia, there also shall be submitted to the agency effectuating the State registration of a mortgage

simultaneously with the documents specified in point 1 of the present Article [as amended by Federal Law No. 18-ФЗ, 11 February 2002]:

a zakladnaia whose content must satisfy the requirements of Article 14(1) of the present Federal Law, except for requirements with respect to the date of issuance of the zakladnaia and information concerning the State registration of the mortgage, and a copy thereof.

4. State registration of a change of pledgeholder shall as a consequence of the assignment of rights under a basic obligation or under a contract on mortgage be effectuated by joint application of the former and new pledgeholders. For State registration of a change of pledgeholder there must be submitted:

the contract of assignment of rights;

the document concerning payment of State registration;

the contract on mortgage previously registered [added by Federal Law No. 18-ФЗ, 11 February 2002].

5. A mortgage must be registered within one month from the day of receipt of the documents necessary for the registration thereof to the agency effectuating the State registration of a mortgage.

6. State registration of a mortgage shall be effectuated by means of performing a registration entry concerning the mortgage in the unified State register of rights to immoveable property.

The date of State registration of a mortgage shall be the day of performing the registration entry concerning the mortgage in the unified State register of rights to immoveable property. The registration entries in the unified State register of rights to immoveable property shall be performed in the priority determined on the basis of dates of receipt of all necessary documents at the agency effectuating the conducting of the said register.

7. For third persons a mortgage shall be considered to have arisen from the moment of State registration thereof.

Article 21. Refusal of State Registration of Mortgage and Deferral of State Registration of Mortgage

1. State registration of a mortgage may be refused in the instances provided for by the federal law on the State registration of rights to immoveable property and transactions therewith.

2. State registration of a mortgage may be deferred for not more than one month in the event of:

the failure to submit to the agency effectuating State registration of a mortgage any of the documents specified in Article 20(2) and (3) of the present Federal Law;

the failure of a contract on mortgage, zakladnaia, and documents appended thereto to conform to the requirements provided for by legislation of the Russian Federation;

the need to verify the genuineness of the documents submitted.

3. In adopting a decision concerning deferral of State registration of a mortgage, the agency effectuating the State registration thereof shall request necessary documents or demand the elimination of nonconformities elicited.

In the event of the failure to fulfil requirements of the said agency within the period established by it, State registration of the mortgage must be refused.

4. When there is a judicial dispute with regard to rights to property which is the subject of a mortgage, or with regard to levy of execution against it, State registration of a mortgage may be deferred until settlement of the dispute by a court.

5. A reasoned refusal of State registration of a mortgage must be sent to the pledgor within the period established for the State registration thereof.

Article 22. Registration Entry Concerning Mortgage and Certification of State Registration of Mortgage

1. A registration entry concerning a mortgage in the unified State register of rights to immoveable property must contain information concerning the initial pledgeholder, subject of the mortgage, and amount of the obligation secured by it. If the contract on mortgage provides tht the rights of the pledgeholder shall be certified by a zakladnaia, this also shall be specified in the registration entry concerning the mortgage.

This data shall be inserted in the registration entry concerning the mortgage on the basis of the contract on mortgage.

2. State registration of a mortgage shall be certified by means of an inscription on the contract on mortgage, and in the event of State registration of a mortgage by virtue of a law—on the document which is the basis of the arising of the right of ownership of the pledgor to the property encumbered by the mortgage. The inscription must contain the full name of the agency which registered the mortgage, date, place of State registration of the mortgage, and number under which it was registered. This data shall be attested by the signature of the official and seal of the agency which effectuated the State registration of the mortgage [as amended by Federal Law No. 18-ФЗ, 11 February 2002].

3. If the rights of the pledgeholder are certified by a zakladnaia, the agency which effectuated State registration of the mortgage shall be obliged to ensure at the moment of issuance of the zakladnaia the presence of the information therein provided for by point 2 of the present Article, and also by Article 14(1), subpoints (10) and (13), of the present Federal Law [as amended by Federal Law No. 18-ФЗ, 11 February 2002].

4. The agency which effectuated State registration of the mortgage shall retain in its archive a copy of the contract on mortgage, and in the event of State registration of a mortgage by virtue of a law—a copy of the document which is the basis for arising of the right of ownership of the pledgor in the property encumbered by the mortgage. If the rights of the pledgeholder are certified by a zakladnaia, the agency which effectuated State registration of the mortgage shall retain in its archive also a copy of the zakladnaia with annexes [as amended by Federal Law No. 18-ФЗ, 11 February 2002].

Article 23. Correction, Change, and Addition to Registration Entry Concerning Mortgage

1. The correction of technical mistakes in a registration entry concerning a mortgage shall be permitted on the basis of an application of the pledgor or pledgeholder with notification of the other party about the correction made and on condition that the said correction cannot cause damage to third persons or violate their legal interests.

2. Changes in and additions to a registration entry concerning a mortgage shall be made on the basis of an agreement between the pledgor and pledgeholder about the change in or addition to the conditions of the contract concerning the mortgage. Such agreement must be notarially certified.

Changes in and additions to a registration entry concerning a mortgage shall not be permitted if the rights of the pledgeholder have been certified by a zakladnaia, except for the instance provided for by Article 13(6), paragraph three, of the present Federal Law.

In instances when after State registration of a mortgage by virtue of a law the pledgor and pledgeholder have concluded a contract on mortgage, respective changes shall be made in the registration entry concerning the mortgage previously performed [as amended by Federal Law No. 18-ФЗ, 11 February 2002].

Article 24. Expenses for State Registration of Mortgage

Expenses with regard to payment of charges for State registration of a mortgage and making of changes in and additions to a registration entry concerning a mortgage shall be placed on the pledgor unless established otherwise by an agreement between him and the pledgeholder.

Article 25. Cancellation of Registration Entry Concerning Mortgage

A registration entry concerning a mortgage shall be cancelled on the basis of an application of the legal possessor of a zakladnaia, joint application of the pledgor and pledgeholder, or on the basis of the decision of a court, arbitrazh court, or arbitration court concerning termination of the mortgage.

In the event of cancellation of a registration entry concerning a mortgage in connection with termination of the mortgage, the zakladnaia shall be annulled in the procedure established by the present Federal Law. An annulled zakladnaia shall be transferred to the person previously obliged with regard to it at his request.

Article 26. Public Character of State Registration of Mortgage

State registration of a mortgage shall be public. Any person shall have the right to receive information at the agency effectuating State registration of rights to immoveable property concerning whether there is a registration entry concerning a mortgage of respective property and an attested extract from the registration entry concerning the mortgage.

A copy of the zakladnaia in the archive of the agency effectuating State registration of a mortgage shall not be relegated to documents of a public character.

Article 27. Appeal of Actions Connected with State Registration of Mortgage

A refusal of State registration of a mortgage or evasion by the respective agency from registration thereof or issuing a zakladnaia to the initial pledgeholder, refusal to make corrections in the registration entry concerning a mortgage, to cancel a registration entry concerning a mortgage in violation of the established rules, the registration of a nonexistent mortgage, refusal to effectuate rights provided for by Article 26 of the present Federal Law, and also other actions of the agency effectuating State registration of rights to immoveable property not corresponding to a federal law, may be appealed by the interested person to a court or arbitrazh court, in accordance with procedural legislation of the Russian Federation.

Article 28. Responsibility of Agency Registering Mortgage

An agency which has registered or should have registered a mortgage shall be obliged in accordance with the Civil Code of the Russian Federation to compensate the interested person for losses caused by its illegal actions (or failure to act), including:

unsubstantiated refusal of State registration of a mortgage;

unsubstantiated refusal to make corrections in a registration entry;

delay in the State registration of a mortgage above the established period;

State registration of a mortgage in violation of the requirements of legislation of the Russian Federation to maintain a registration entry, or other mistakes;

failure to comply with the requirements of Article 22(3) of the present Federal Law;

evasion of issuance of a zakladnaia (or duplicate of a zakladnaia);

unlawful cancellation of a registration entry;

unsubstantiated refusal to perform actions provided for by Article 26 of the present Federal Law.

Chapter V. Ensuring Preservation of Property Pledged Under Contract on Mortgage

Article 29. Use of Pledged Property by Pledgor

1. The pledgor shall retain the right of use of property pledged under a contract on mortgage. The pledgor shall have the right to use this property in accordance with its designation.

The conditions of a contract on mortgage limiting this right of the pledgor shall be null.

Unless provided otherwise by a contract, when using pledged property the pledgor should not permit deterioration of the property and a reduction of its value above that caused by normal wear and tear.

2. The pledgor shall have the right to derive fruits and revenues from property pledged under a contract on mortgage. The pledgeholder shall not have the right to these fruits and revenues unless provided otherwise by the contract on mortgage.

Article 30. Maintenance and Repair of Pledged Property

1. Unless provided otherwise by the contract on mortgage, the pledgor shall be obliged to maintain property pledged under a contract on mortgage in proper condition and bear expenses for the maintenance of this property until termination of the mortgage.

2. Unless provided otherwise by a contract on mortgage, the pledgor shall be obliged to perform current and capital repair of property pledged under a contract on mortgage within the periods established by a federal law, other legal acts of the Russian Federation (Article 3(3) and (4) of the Civil Code of the Russian Federation) or in the procedure provided for by them, and if such periods have not been established—within reasonable periods.

Article 31. Insurance of Pledged Property

1. The insurance of property pledged under a contract on mortgage shall be effectuated in accordance with the conditions of this contract.

2. In the absence in the contract on mortgage of other conditions concerning insurance of the pledged property, the pledgor shall be obliged to insure this property at his own expense for the full value against risks of loss and damage, and if the full value of the property exceeds the amount of the obligation secured by the mortgage—for an amount not lower than the amount of this obligation.

3. The pledgeholder shall have the right to satisfaction of his demand with regard to an obligation secured by the mortgage directly from the insurance compensation for loss or damage of the pledged property irrespective of to whose

benefit it was insured. This demand shall be subject to satisfaction preferentially before the demands of other creditors of the pledgor and persons to whose benefit the insurance was effectuated, with the exceptions established by a federal law.

The pledgeholder shall be deprived of the right to satisfaction of his demand from insurance compensation if the loss or damage of the property occurred for reasons for which he is liable.

Article 32. Measures With Regard to Preserving Pledged Property Against Loss and Damage

1. In order to ensure the preservation of pledged property, including to defend it against infringements of third persons, fire, and natural calamities, the pledgor shall be obliged to take measures established by a federal law, other legal acts of the Russian Federation (Article 3(3) and (4) of the Civil Code of the Russian Federation), and the contract on mortgage, and if they have not been established—necessary measures corresponding to requirements usually presented.

In the event of a real threat of loss or damage of pledged property, the pledgor shall be obliged to inform the pledgeholder thereof, if he is known to him.

Article 33. Defence of Pledged Property Against Claims of Third Persons

1. In instances of the presentation of demands against the pledgor by third persons concerning the recognition for them of the right of ownership or other rights to the pledged property, concerning the seizure (or demanding and obtaining) or encumberment of the said property, or other demands whose satisfaction may entail a reduction of the value or deterioration of this property, the pledgor shall be obliged immediately to inform the pledgeholder thereof if he is known to him. In the event of bringing a respective suit in court, arbitrazh court, or arbitration court against the pledgor (hereinafter—court), he should enlist such pledgeholder to participate in the case.

2. In the instances specified in point 1 of the present Article, the pledgor must use the means of defence of his rights to the pledged property corresponding to the circumstances provided for by Article 12 of the Civil Code of the Russian Federation. If the pledgor renounced defence of his rights to the pledged property or does not effectuate it, the pledgeholder shall have the right to use these means of defence in the name of the pledgor without a special power of attorney and to demand from the pledgor compensation of necessary expenses incurred in connection with this.

3. If property pledged under a contract on mortgage proved to be in the illegal possession of third persons, the pledgeholder shall have the right, acting in his own name, to demand and obtain this property from another's illegal possession in accordance with Articles 301–303 of the Civil Code of the Russian Federation in order to transfer it to the possession of the pledgor.

Article 34. Right of Pledgeholder to Verify Pledged Property

A pledgeholder shall have the right to verify according to documents and the actual existence, state, and conditions of maintenance of the property pledged under the contract on mortgage. This right also shall belong to the pledgeholder if the pledged property has been transferred by the pledgor for a time to the possession of third persons.

A verification effectuated by the pledgeholder must not create unjustified hindrances for use of the pledged property by the pledgor or other persons in whose possession it is situated.

Article 35. Rights of Pledgeholder in Event of Improper Ensuring Preservation of Pledged Property

In the event of a flagrant violation by the pledgor of rules for the use of pledged property (Article 29(1)), rules for maintenance or repair of pledged property (Article 30), duty to take measures for preservation of the said property (Article 32), if such violation creates a threat of loss or damage of the pledged property, and also in the event of a violation of duties with regard to insurance of the pledged property (Article 31(1) and (2)) or in the event of an unsubstantiated refusal to the pledgeholder to verify the pledged property (Article 34), the pledgeholder shall have the right to demand performance before time of the obligation secured by the mortgage.

If satisfaction of such demand is refused or it is not satisfied within the period provided for by the contract, and if such period has not been provided for, within one month, the pledgeholder shall have the right to levy execution against the property pledged under the contract on mortgage.

Article 36. Consequences of Loss or Damage to Pledged Property

1. A pledgor shall bear the risk of accidental perishing and accidental damage to property pledged under a contract on mortgage unless provided otherwise by such contract.

2. If under circumstances for which the pledgeholder is not liable pledged property has been lost or damaged such that as a consequence thereof security of the obligation by the mortgage has materially worsened, the pledgeholder shall have the right to demand performance before time of the obligation secured by the mortgage, including at the expense of insurance compensation in accordance with Article 31(3) of the present Federal Law.

3. A pledgeholder may not effectuate rights provided for by point 2 of the present Article if an agreement has been concluded between him and the pledgor in written form concerning restoration or replacement of the perished or damaged property and the pledgor duly fulfils the conditions of this agreement.

Chapter VI. Transfer of Rights to Property Pledged Under Contract on Mortgage to Other Persons and Encumberment of this Property by Rights of Other Persons

Article 37. Alienation of Pledged Property

1. Property pledged under a contract on mortgage may be alienated by the pledgor to another person by means of sale, gift, exchange, contributing it as a contribution to the property of an economic partnership or society or share contribution to the proeprty of a production cooperative or by other means only with the consent of the pledgeholder, unless provided otherwise by the contract on mortgage.

2. In the event of the issuance of a zakladnaia the alienation of the pledged property shall be permitted if the right of the pledgor to do so has been provided for in the zakladnaia in compliance with the conditions which have been established therein.

3. The pledgor shall have the right to bequeath pledged property. The conditions of the contract on mortgage or other agreement limiting this right of the pledgor shall be null.

Article 38. Preservation of Mortgage in Event of Transfer of Rights to Pledged Property to Other Person

1. A person who has acquired property pledged under a contract on mortgage as a result of its alienation or by way of universal legal succession, including as a result of the reorganisation of a juridical person or by way of inheritance, shall take the place of the pledgor and shall bear all duties of the last under the contract on mortgage, including those which were not properly fulfilled by the initial pledgor.
The new pledgor may be relieved from any of these duties only by agreement with the pledgeholder. Such agreement shall not be binding upon subsequent acquirers of the zakladnaia if it was not certified notarially and does not comply with the rules of Article 15 of the present Federal Law.

2. If property pledged under the contract on mortgage has passed on the grounds specified in point 1 of the present Article to several persons, each of the legal successors of the initial pledgor shall bear the consequences arising from relations of mortgage of the failure to perform the obligation secured by the mortgage commensurate to the part of the pledged property which has passed to it. If the subject of mortgage is indivisible or on other grounds is in the common ownership of the legal successors of the pledgor, the legal successors shall become joint and several pledgors.

3. The pledge of property under a contract on mortgage shall retain force irrespective of whether in the event of the transfer of this property to other persons any of the rules established for such transfer were violated.

Article 39. Consequences of Violation of Rules on Alienation of Pledged Property

In the event of the alienation of property pledged under a contract on mortgage with a violation of the rules of Article 37(1) and (2) of the present Federal Law, the pledgeholder shall have the right at its choice to demand:

the deeming of the transaction concerning alienation of the pledged property to be invalid and the application of the consequences provided for by Article 167 of the Civil Code of the Russian Federation;

the performance before time of the obligation secured by the mortgage and levy execution against the pledged property irrespective of to whom it belongs.

In the last instance, if it is proved that the acquirer of the property pledged under a contract on mortgage at the moment of its acquisition knew or should have known that the property is being alienated with a violation of the rules of Article 37 of the present Federal Law, such acquirer shall bear within the limits of the value of the said property responsibility for the failure to perform the obligation secured by the mortgage jointly and severally with the debtor under this obligation. If the pledged property is alienated with a violation of the said rules by the pledgor who is not a debtor under the obligation secured by the mortgage, both the acquirer of the property and the former pledgor shall bear responsibility jointly and severally with this debtor.

Article 40. Encumberment of Pledged Property by Rights of Other Persons

1. Unless provided otherwise by a Federal Law or the contract on mortgage, the pledgor shall have the right without the consent of the pledgeholder to lease out the pledged property, transfer it for temporary uncompensated use, and by agreement with another person grant to the last the right of limited use of this property (servitude) on condition that:

the period for which the property is granted for use does not exceed the period of the obligation secured by the mortgage;

the property is granted for use for purposes corresponding to the designation of this property.

2. In the event of levy of execution by the pledgeholder against pledged property on the grounds provided for by a Federal Law or the contract on mortgage, all the rights of lease and other rights of use to such property granted by the pledgor to third persons without the consent of the pledgeholder after the conclusion of the contract on mortgage shall terminate from the moment of entry into legal force of the decision of a court concerning the levy of execution against the property, and if the demand of the pledgeholder is satisfied without recourse to a court, from the moment of notarial certification of the agreement between the pledgor and the pledgeholder concerning levy of execution in accordance with Article 55 of the present Federal Law.

3. Pledged property may be granted by the pledgor for use to third persons for a period exceeding the period of the obligatino secured by a mortgage, or for purposes not corresponding to the designation of the property, only with the consent of the pledgeholder. In the event of the issuance of a zakladnaia, the granting of the right of use of pledged property on these conditions to third persons shall be permitted if the right of the pledgor to do so has been provided in the zakladnaia.

4. The granting by the pledgor of pledged property for use to another person shall not relieve the pledgor from the performance of duties under the contract on mortgage unless provided otherwise by this contract.

5. The encumberment of property pledged under a contract on mortgage by other pledges shall be regulated by the rules of Chapter VII of the present Federal Law.

Article 41. Consequences of Compulsory Seizure by State of Pledged Property

1. If the right of ownership of the pledgor to property which is the subject of mortgage terminates on the grounds and in the procedure which has been established by a Federal Law, the subsequent seizure (or purchase) of the property for State or municipal needs or the requisition or nationalisation thereof and to the pledgor is granted other property or respective compensation, the mortgage shall extend to the property granted in its stead or the pledgeholder shall acquire the right of preferential satisfaction of its demands from the amount of compensation due to the pledgor.

The pledgeholder whose interests may not in full measure be defended by the rights provided for by paragraph one of the present point shall have the right to demand performance before time of the obligation secured by the mortgage and levy execution against the property granted to the pledgor in the stead of that seized.

2. In instances when the property which is the subject of a mortgage is seized from the pledgor by the State in the form of a sanction for the commission of a crime or other violation of law (confiscation), the mortgage shall retain force and the rules of Article 38 of the present Federal Law shall apply. However, the pledgeholder whose interests cannot in full measure be defended by the application of these rules shall have the right to require the performance before time of the obligation secured by the mortgage and levy of execution against the confiscated property.

Article 42. Consequences of Vindication of Pledged Property

In instances when property which is the subject of mortgage is seized from the pledgor in the procedure established by a Federal Law on the grounds that in reality the owner of this property is another person (vindicatio), the mortgage with respect to this property shall terminate. The pledgeholder after the entry into legal force of the respective decision of a court shall have the right to demand performance before time of the obligation which was secured by the mortgage.

Chapter VII. Subsequent Mortgage

Article 43. Concept of Subsequent Mortgage and Conditions Under Which It Is Permitted

1. Property pledged under a contract on mortgage to secure the performance of one obligation (preceding mortgage) may be granted on pledge to secure the performance of another obligation of the same or another debtor to the same or to another pledgeholder (subsequent mortgage).

The priority of pledgeholders shall be established on the basis of the data of the unified State register of rights to immoveable property concerning the moment of arising of the mortgage determined in accordance with the rules of Article 20(5) and (6) of the present Federal Law.

2. A subsequent mortgage shall be permitted unless prohibited by the preceding contracts on mortgage of the same property, the operation of which has not terminated at the moment of conclusion of the subsequent contract on mortgage.

If the preceding contract on mortgage provides conditions on which a subsequent contract on mortgage may be concluded, the last must be concluded in compliance with these conditions.

3. A subsequent contract on mortgage concluded notwithstanding the prohibition established by the preceding contract on mortgage may be deemed by a court to be invalid upon the suit of the pledgeholder under the preceding contract irrespective of whether the pledgeholder under the subsequent contract knew about such prohibition.

If the subsequent mortgage is not prohibited but the subsequent contract was concluded with a violation of the conditions provided for it by the preceding contract, the demands of the pledgeholder under the subsequent contract shall be satisfied to the degree to which their satisfaction is possible in accordance with the conditions of the preceding contract on mortgage.

4. The rules of points 2 and 3 of the present Article shall not apply if the parties to the preceding and subsequent contracts on mortgage are one and the same persons.

5. The conclusion of a subsequent contract on mortgage providing for the compilation and issuance of a zakladnaia shall not be permitted.

Article 44. Warning of Pledgeholders About Preceding and Subsequent Mortgages. Change of Preceding Contract on Mortgage

1. The pledgor shall be obliged to communicate to each subsequent pledgeholder before the conclusion of a contract with him concerning a subsequent

mortgage information concerning all already existing mortgages of the particular property provided for by Article 9(1) of the present Federal Law.

The failure of the pledgor to fulfil this duty shall give to the pledgeholder under the subsequent contract the right to demand dissolution of the contract and compensation of losses caused unless it is proved that he could receive the necessary information about the preceding mortgages on the basis of Article 26 of the present Federal Law from data concerning their State registration.

2. The pledgor who has concluded a subsequent contract on mortgage must immediately inform the pledgeholders thereof under the preceding mortgages and upon their demand communicate to them information about the subsequent mortgage provided for by Article 9(1) of the present Federal Law.

3. After the conclusion of a subsequent contract on mortgage a change of the preceding contract entailing the security of new demands of the preceding pledgeholder or increase of the amount of demands already secured under this contract (Article 3) shall be permitted only with the consent of the pledgeholder under the subsequent contract, unless provided otherwise by the preceding contract on mortgage [as amended by Federal Law No. 18-ФЗ, 11 February 2002].

4. The rules of the present Article shall not apply if the parties to the preceding and subsequent contracts on mortgage are one and the same persons.

Article 45. State Registration of Subsequent Mortgage

State registration of a subsequent mortgage shall be effectuated in compliance with the rules of Chapter IV of the present Federal Law.

Notations shall be made on the subsequent contract on mortgage concerning all registration entries on preceding mortgages of the same property.

A notation concerning a subsequent mortgage shall be entered in the registration entries concerning all preceding mortgages of the same property.

Article 46. Satisfaction of Demands of Pledgeholders Under Preceding and Subsequent Mortgages

1. The demands of a pledgeholder under a subsequent contract on mortgage shall be satisfied from the value of the pledged property in compliance with the demands concerning the existence with the pledgeholder under the preceding contract on mortgage of the right of preferential satisfaction of his demands.

2. In the event of levy of execution against pledged property with regard to demands secured by a subsequent mortgage, performance before time of the obligation secured by the mortgage may be demanded and execution levied against this property also with regard to demands secured by a preceding mortgage, the period for the presentation of which has not yet ensued for levy. If the pledgeholder under the preceding contract on mortgage does not take advantage of this right, the

property against which execution is levied with regard to demands secured by a subsequent mortgage shall pass to its acquirer encumbered by the preceding mortgage [as amended by Federal Law No. 18-ФЗ, 11 February 2002].

3. In the event of levy of execution against pledged property with regard to demands secured by a preceding mortgage, the simultaneous levy of execution against this property shall be permitted also with regard to demands secured by a subsequent mortgage, the period for the presentation of which has not yet ensued for levy. Demands secured by a subsequent mortgage shall not be subject to satisfaction before time if the levy of execution against part of the pledged property is sufficient to satisfy the demands secured by the preceding mortgage.

4. Before levy of execution against property, by the pledge of which demands have been secured under a preceding and subsequent mortgages, the pledgeholder who intended to present his demands for levy shall be obliged in written form to inform the pledgeholder under the other contract on mortgage of the same property thereof.

5. The rules contained in the present Article shall not apply if the pledgeholder under the preceding and subsequent mortgages is one and the same person. In this event the demands secured by each of the mortgages shall be satisfied by way of priority of the respective periods for performance of the respective obligations unless provided otherwise by a Federal Law or by agreement of the parties.

Chapter VIII. Assignment of Rights Under Contract on Mortgage. Transfer and Pledge of Zakladnaia

Article 47. Assignment of Rights Under Contract on Mortgage or Obligation Secured by Mortgage [as amended by Federal Law No 18-ФЗ, 11 February 2002]

1. A pledgeholder shall have the right to transfer his rights to another person unless provided otherwise by a contract:
under the contract on mortgage;
under the obligation secured by the mortgage (principal obligation) [as amended by Federal Law No 18-ФЗ, 11 February 2002].

2. The person to whom the rights under a contract on mortgage have been transferred shall take the place of the previous pledgeholder under this contract.
Unless proved otherwise, the assignment of rights under a contract on mortgage shall also mean the assignment of rights under the obligation secured by the mortgage [as amended by Federal Law No 18-ФЗ, 11 February 2002].

3. Unless provided otherwise by a contract, the rights securing performance of an obligation shall also pass to the person to whom the rights under the obligation (or principal obligation) were transferred.

Such person shall take the place of the previous pledgeholder under the contract on mortgage.

The assignment of rights with regard to an obligation secured by a mortgage (or principal obligation) in accordance with Article 389(1) of the Civil Code of the Russian Federation must be concluded in that form in which the obligation secured by the mortgage was concluded (or principal obligation) [as amended by Federal Law No 18-ФЗ, 11 February 2002].

4. To relations between the person to whom rights are assigned and the pledgeholder shall apply the norms of Articles 382, 384–386, 388, and 390 of the Civil Code of the Russian Federation on the transfer of rights of a creditor by means of the assignment of a demand [as amended by Federal Law No 18-ФЗ, 11 February 2002].

5. The assignment of rights under a contract on mortgage or obligation secured by the mortgage, the rights from which have been certified by a zakladnaia, shall not be permitted. In the event of the conclusion of such a transaction, it shall be deemed to be null.

Article 48. Transfer of Rights Under Zakladnaia

1. The transfer of rights under a zakladnaia shall be performed by means of the conclusion of a transaction in simple written form.

In the event of the transfer of rights under a zaklandaia, the person transferring the right shall make a notation on the zakladnaia concerning the new possessor.

The name of the person to whom the rights under the zakladnaia have been transferred and the grounds of such transfer must be precisely and fully indicated in the notation.

The notation must be signed by the pledgeholder specified in the zakladnaia, and if this inscription is not the first—by the possessor of the zakladnaia specified in the preceding notation [as amended by Federal Law No. 18-ФЗ, 11 February 2002].

2. The transfer of the rights under the zakladnaia to another person shall mean the transfer thereby to this person of all the rights certified by it in aggregate [as amended by Federal Law No. 18-ФЗ, 11 February 2002].

All the rights certified by it, including the rights of the pledgeholder and the rights of a creditor with regard to the obligation secured by the mortgage, irrespective of the rights of the initial pledgeholder and preceding possessors of the zakladnaia, shall belong to the legal possessor of the zakladnaia.

3. The possessor of a zakladnaia shall be considered to be legal if his rights to the zakladnaia are based on a transaction with regard to the transfer of rights under the zakladnaia and the last notation on the zakladnaia made by the preceding possessor. He shall not be considered to be a legal possessor of a zakladnaia if it is

proved that the zakladnaia left the possession of any of the persons who have made endorsements of transfer as a result of stealing or otherwise other than by the will of this person, of which the possessor of the zakladnaia, in acquiring it, knew or should have known [as amended by Federal Law No. 18-ФЗ, 11 February 2002].

4. Endorsements on a zakladnaia prohibiting its subsequent transfer to other persons shall be null.

5. If a third person in accordance with Article 313(2) of the Civil Code of the Russian Federation has fully executed the obligation secured by the mortgage for the debtor, it shall have the right to demand the transfer to it of the rights under the zakladnaia. In the event of the refusal of the pledgeholder to transfer these rights, the third person may demand the transfer of these rights to itself in a judicial proceeding.

Article 49. Pledge of Zakladnaia

1. A zakladnaia may be pledged under a contract of pledge by zakladnaia with or without the transfer thereof to another person (or pledgeholder of the zakladnaia) to secure an obligation under a credit contract or other obligation arising between this person and the pledgeholder initially named in the zakladnaia, or other legal possessor thereof [as amended by Federal Law No. 18-ФЗ, 11 February 2002].

2. In the event of the pledge of a zakladnaia without the transfer thereof to the pledgeholder of the zakladnaia, the procedure for levy of execution against the pledged zakladnaia shall be regulated by Article 349 of the Civil Code of the Russian Federation [as amended by Federal Law No. 18-ФЗ, 11 February 2002].

3. When concluding a contract on pledge by a zakladnaia with the transfer thereof to the pledgeholder of the zakladnaia, the parties shall have the right to provide for:

(1) levy of execution against pledged property in the procedure established by Article 349 of the Civil Code of the Russian Federation;

(2) transfer of rights under the zakladnaia in the procedure, on the conditions, and with the consequences which have been provided for by Article 48 of the present Federal Law;

(3) effectuation by the mortgage pledgeholder on the zakladnaia of a special pledge inscription giving to the pledgeholder of the zakladnaia the right upon the expiry of a determined period to sell the zakladnaia and to withhold from the monies received the amount of the obligation secured by the pledge [as amended by Federal Law No. 18-ФЗ, 11 February 2002].

4. A special pledge endorsement of transfer giving to the pledgeholder of the zakladnaia the right upon the expiry of a determined period to sell the zakladnaia while withholding from the monies received the amount of the obligation secured

by the pledge thereof may be made by the mortgage pledgeholder on the zakladnaia.

Chapter IX. Levy of Execution Against Property Pledged Under Contract on Mortgage

Article 50. Grounds for Levy of Execution Against Pledged Property

1. The pledgeholder shall have the right to levy execution against property pledged under a contract on mortgage in order to satisfy demands at the expense of this property named in Article 3 of the present Federal Law caused by the failure to perform or by the improper performance of the obligation secured by the mortgage, in particular, the failure to pay or the untimely payment of the amount of the debt in full or in part unless provided otherwise by the contract.

In the event of a divergence between the conditions of the contract on mortgage and the conditions of the obligation secured by the mortgage with respect to demands which may be satisfied by means of levy of execution against pledged property, preference shall be given to the conditions of the contract on mortgage.

2. Unless provided otherwise by the contract on mortgage, levy of execution against property pledged to secure an obligation to be performed by periodic payments shall be permitted in the event of the systematic violation of the periods for making them, that is, in the event of the violation of the periods for making payments more than three times during 12 months even if each delay is insignificant.

3. With regard to demands caused by the failure to perform or by the improper performance of an obligation secured by a mortgage, levy of execution may not be made if in accordance with the conditions of this obligation and with Federal laws and other legal acts of the Russian Federation applicable thereto (Article 3(3) and (4) of the Civil Code of the Russian Federation) the debtor is relieved from responsibility for such failure to perform or improper performance.

4. In the instances provided for by Articles 35, 39, and 41 of the present Federal Law, the pledgeholder shall have the right to demand the performance before time of the obligation secured by a mortgage, and in the event of the failure to fulfil this demand, levy of execution against the pledged property even if the obligation secured by the mortgage is duly performed.

Article 51. Judicial Procedure for Levy of Execution Against Pledged Property

Execution shall be levied with regard to the demands of a pledgeholder against property pledged under a contract on mortgage by decision of a court, except for instances when in accordance with Article 55 of the present Federal Law the satisfaction of such demands without recourse to a court is permitted.

Article 52. Jurisdiction of Cases Concerning Levy of Execution Against Pledged Property

A suit concerning levy of execution against property pledged under a contract on mortgage shall be presented in accordance with the rules of jurisdiction of cases established by procedural legislation of the Russian Federation.

Article 53. Measures Relating to Defence of Interests of Other Pledgeholders, Absent Pledgor, and Other Persons

1. In the event of levy of execution against property pledged under two or more contracts on mortgage, the pledgeholder must submit to the court in which the respective suit is presented evidence of the performance of the duty provided for by Article 46(4) of the present Federal Law.

2. If from the materials of the case concerning levy of execution against pledged property it is evident that the mortgage was or should have been effectuated with the consent of another person or agency, the court in which the suit is presented concerning levy of execution shall inform the respective person or agency thereof and grant to it the possibility to participate in the particular case.

3. Persons having a right of use of pledged property (lessees, tenants, members of the family of the owner of a dwelling premise, and other persons) or the right to a thing to such property (servitude, right of use for life, and other rights) based on a law or contract shall have the right to participate in the consideration of the case on levy of execution against the pledged property.

Article 54. Questions To Be Settled by Court When Considering Case Concerning Levy of Execution Against Pledged Property

1. Levy of execution against property pledged undeer a contract on mortgage may be refused if a violation of the obligation secured by the mortgage permitted by the debtor is extremely insignificant and the amount of the demands of the pledgeholder as a consequence thereof are clearly incommensurate with the value of the pledged property, except for the instance provided for by Article 50(2) of the present Federal Law.

2. In adopting the decision concerning levy of execution against property pledged under the contract on mortgage the court must determine and specify therein:

(1) the amounts subject to payment to the pledgeholder from the value of the pledged property, except for amounts of expenses relating to the protection and realisation of the property, which shall be determined upon the completion of the realisation thereof. The amount against which interest is calculated, the amount of interest, and the period for which it is subject to calculation must be specified for the amounts calculated in a percentage;

(2) the property which is the subject of the mortgage from whose value the demands of the pledgeholder are satisfied;

(3) the means of realisation of the property against which execution is levied;

(4) the starting sale price of the pledged property in the event of its realisation. The starting sale price of the property at a public sale shall be determined on the basis of an agreement between the pledgor and pledgeholder, and in the event of a dispute, by the court itself;

(5) measures relating to ensuring the preservation of the property until the realisation thereof if such are necessary.

3. Upon the application of the pledgor, the court shall have the right when there are justifiable reasons in the decision to levy execution against pledged property to defer the realisation thereof for a period of up to one year in instances when [as amended by Federal Law No. 18-ФЗ, 11 February 2002]:

the pledgor is a citizen, irrespective of what property has been pledged by him under the contract on mortgage, on condition that the pledge is not connected with the effectuation of entrepreneurial activity by this citizen;

the subject of mortgage is a land plot from lands of agricultural designation to which the operation of the present Federal Law extends.

In determining the period for which deferral of the realisation of the pledged property is to be granted, the court shall take into account, inter alia, the fact that the amount of demands of the pledgeholder subject to satisfaction from the value of the pledged property at the moment of the expiry of the deferral must not exceed the value of the pledged property according to the valuation specified in the contract on mortgage.

The deferral of the realisation of the pledged property shall not affect the rights and duties of the parties with regard to the obligation secured by the mortgage of this property and shall not relieve the debtor from compensation of the losses of the creditor which grew during the time of deferral nor the interest and penalties due to the creditor.

If the debtor within the limits of the time of deferral granted to him satisfies the demands of the creditor secured by the mortgage in the amount which they have at the moment of satisfaction of the demand, the court upon the application of the pledgor shall vacate the decision concerning levy of execution [as amended by Federal Law No. 18-ФЗ, 11 February 2002].

4. Deferral of the realisation of pledged property shall not be permitted if:

it may entail a material worsening of the financial position of the pledgeholder;

with respect to the pledgor or pledgeholder a case is initiated to deem him insolvent (or bankrupt).

Article 55. Levy of Execution Against Pledged Property in Extrajudicial Proceeding

1. Satisfaction of the demands of the pledgeholder at the expense of the property pledged under the contract on mortgage without recourse to a court shall be permitted on the basis of a notarially certified agreement between the pledgeholder and pledgor concluded after the grounds arise for levy of execution against the subject of the mortgage.

The agreement concerning satisfaction of the demands of the pledgeholder under a subsequent contract on mortgage shall be valid if it was concluded with the participation of the pledgeholders under the preceding contracts on mortgage.

2. The satisfaction of demands of the pledgeholder in the procedure provided for by point 1 of the present Article shall not be permitted if:

(1) the consent or authorisation of another person or agency is required in order to mortgage the property;

(2) an enterprise as a property complex is the subject of mortgage;

(3) property having significant historical, artistic, or other cultural value for society is the subject of mortgage;

(4) property in common ownership is the subject of mortgage and any of its owners do not give consent in written or other form established by the Federal Law to satisfy the demands of the pledgeholder in an extrajudicial procedure.

In the said instances execution shall be levied against the pledged property by decision of a court.

3. In an agreement concerning the satisfaction of demands of the pledgeholder concluded in accordance with point 1 of the present Article the parties may provide for:

(1) the realisation of the pledged property in the procedure established in Article 56 of the present Federal Law [as amended by Federal Law No 18-ФЗ, 11 February 2002];

(2) the acquisition of pledged property by the pledgeholder for himself or third persons, less the purchase price of the demands of the pledgeholder against the debtor which are secured by the mortgage. The acquisition of the pledged property may not be provided for in the said agreement if the subject of mortgage is a land plot.

The rules of civil legislation of the Russian Federation on the contract of purchase-sale, and in the event of the acquisition of property by the pledgeholder for third persons, also on the contract of commission agency, shall apply to the agreement concerning the acquisition of pledged property by the pledgeholder.

4. In the event of the conclusion of an agreement concerning the satisfaction of the demands of the pledgeholder in accordance with point 1 of the present Article the parties must specify therein:

(1) the name of the pledged property under the contract on mortgage of the property at the expense of which the demands of the pledgeholder shall be satisfied and the value of this property;

(2) the amounts subject to payment to the pledgeholder by the debtor on the basis of the obligation secured by the mortgage and the contract on mortgage, and if the pledgor is a third person, also by the pledgor;

(3) the means of realisation of the pledged property or the condition concerning the acquisition thereof by the pledgeholder;

(4) preceding and subsequent mortgages of the particular property and the right to a thing and the rights of use which third persons have with respect to this property known to the parties at the moment of conclusion of the agreement.

5. An agreement concerning the satisfaction of demands of the pledgeholder in an extrajudicial procedure concluded on the basis of point 1 of the present Article may be deemed by a court to be invalid upon the suit of the person whose rights have been violated by this agreement.

Chapter X. Realisation of Pledged Property Against Which Execution is Levied

Article 56. Means of Realisation of Pledged Property

1. Property pledged under a contract on mortgage against which by decision of a court execution is levied in accordance with the present Federal Law shall be realised by means of sale at a public sale, except for instances provided for by the present Federal Law.

The procedure for conducting a public sale with regard to the sale of property pledged under a contract on mortgage shall be determined by procedural legislation of the Russian Federation insofar as other rules have not been established by the present Federal Law.

2. In adopting a decision concerning levy of execution against pledged property a court may, with the consent of the pledgor and pledgeholder, establish in the decision that the property is subject to realisation in the procedure provided for by Article 59 of the present Federal Law. Such means of the realisation of the pledged property may be provided for by the pledgor and pledgeholder in an agreement concerning the satisfaction of demands of the pledgeholder in an extrajudicial procedure concluded in accordance with Article 55(1) of the present Federal Law [as amended by Federal Law No. 18-ФЗ, 11 February 2002].

The realisation of the pledged property in the procedure provided for by Article 59 of the present Federal Law shall not be permitted in instances when execution may not be levied against this property in accordance with Article 55(2) of the present Federal Law in an extrajudicial procedure [as amended by Federal Law No. 18-ФЗ, 11 February 2002].

The procedure for the sale of property pledged under a contract on mortgage at an auction shall be determined by the rules of Articles 447–449 of the Civil Code of the Russian Federation and the present Federal Law, and with regard to that not provided for by them, shall be determined by an agreement concerning the satisfaction of demands of the pledgeholder in an extrajudicial procedure.

3. In instances of levy of execution against a pledged right of lease of immoveable property, it shall be realised in accordance with the rules of the present Federal Law with subsequent formalisation of the assignment of the said right.

Article 57. Procedure for Conducting Public Sale by Decision of Court [as amended by Federal Law No. 18-ФЗ, 11 February 2002]

1. A public sale for the sale of pledged property shall be organised and conducted by the agencies on which in accordance with procedural legislation of the Russian Federation the execution of judicial decisions has been placed, unless established otherwise by a Federal law.

2. A public sale for the sale of pledged property shall be conducted at the location of this property.

3. The organiser of a public sale shall give notice of the forthcoming public sale not later than 30 days, but not earlier than 60 days, before the conducting thereof in a periodical publication which is the official information organ of the agency of executive power of the respective subject of the Russian Federation, specifying the date, time, and place of conducting the public sale, the character of the property being sold, and the starting sale price thereof [as amended by Federal Law No. 18-ФЗ, 11 February 2002].

4. The persons wishing to take part in the public sale shall make a deposit in the amount, within the periods, and in the procedure which must be specified in the notice on the public sale. The amount of the deposit may not exceed 5% of the starting sale price of the pledged property.

The deposit shall be refunded immediately upon the end of the public sale to the persons who participated in the public sale but did not win. The deposit also shall be subject to return if the public sale is unconstituted.

5. The presence at a public sale with regard to the sale of pledged property of persons not participating therein may be limited only by the agencies of local self-government in the interests of the maintenance of public order. The persons having the right of use of the property being sold or the rights to a thing to this property shall have the right to be present at the public sale in any event, as well as the pledgeholders with regard to subsequent mortgages [as amended by Federal Law No. 18-ФЗ, 11 February 2002].

6. The person who has offered at a public sale the highest price for the property being sold shall be deemed to have won the public sale. This person and the organiser of the public sale shall sign a protocol on the date of the conducting thereof concerning the results of the public sale. Evasion by any of them of signature of the protocol shall entail the consequences provided for by Article 448(5) of the Civil Code of the Russian Federation.

7. The person who has won the public sale must within five days after the end thereof pay the amount for which the pledged property has been purchased by him (purchase price) less the deposit previously made to the account specified by the organiser of the public sale. In the event of the failure to pay this amount, the deposit shall not be returned.

8. Within five days from the moment of payment of the purchase price by the person who won the public sale, the organiser of the public sale shall conclude a contract of purchase-sale with him. This contract and the protocol concerning the results of the public sale shall be the grounds for making the necessary entries in the unified State register of rights to immoveable property.

Article 58. Declaration of Public Sale to be Unconstituted

1. The organiser of a public sale shall announce it to be unconstituted in instances when:
(1) less than two purchasers were at the public sale;
(2) an increment above the starting sale price of the pledged property is not made at the public sale;
(3) the person who has won the public sale has not paid the purchase price within the established period.
A public sale must be announced to be unconstituted not later than the day following that on which the said circumstances occurred.

2. Within 10 days after the announcement of the public sale as unconstituted, the pledgeholder shall have the right by agreement with the pledgor to acquire the pledged property at its starting sale price at the public sale less his demands secured by the morgage of this property from the purchase price.
To such agreement shall apply the rules of civil legislation of the Russian Federation on the contract of purchase-sale. The mortgage in this event shall terminate.

3. If the agreement on the acquisition of property by the pledgeholder provided for by point 2 of the present Article is unconstituted, a second public sale shall be conducted not later than a month after the first public sale. The starting sale price of the pledged property at the second sale, if it was caused by the reasons specified in point 1(1) and (2) of the present Article, shall be reduced by 15%. The public sale shall be conducted in the procedure provided for by Article 57 of the present Federal Law.

4. In the event of the announcement of the second public sale to be unconstituted for the reasons specified in point 1 of the present Article, the pledgeholder shall have the right to acquire (or retain) the pledged property at the price of not more than 25% lower than its starting sale price at the first public sale and deducting from the purchase price his demands secured by the mortgage of the property.

If the pledgeholder has retained the pledged property which by its character and designation cannot belong to him, including property having significant historical, artistic, or other cultural value for society or a land plot, he shall be obliged within a year to alienate the particular property in accordance with Article 238 of the Civil Code of the Russian Federation.

5. If the pledgeholder does not take advantage of the right to retain the subject of mortgage within a month after the announcement of the second public sale to be unconstituted, the mortgage shall terminate.

Article 59. Realisation of Pledged Property by Agreement of Parties at Auction [as amended by Federal Law No 18-ФЗ, 11 February 2002]

1. A specialised organisation chosen by the pledgeholder with the consent of the pledgor which operates on the basis of a contract with the pledgeholder and acts in his or in its own name shall act as the organisor of the auction for the sale of pledged property.

2. The sale of pledged property at an auction shall be permitted if the auction is open.

The sale of pledged property at a closed auction shall be permitted in the instances provided for by a Federal Law.

3. Within five days from the moment of the fulfilment of the demand concerning the payment of the property by the person who won the auction, the organiser of the auction shall conclude with him a contract of purchase-sale. This contract and the protocol concerning the results of the auction shall be the grounds for making the necessary entries in the unified State register of rights to immoveable propeerty.

Article 60. Termination of Levy of Execution Against Pledged Property and Realisation Thereof

1. The debtor under the obligation secured by a mortgage and the pledgor who is a third person shall have the right to terminate levy of execution against the pledged property, having satisfied all demands of the pledgeholder secured by the mortgage, the failure to fulfil which served as the grounds for the levy of execution against the property to the extent that these demands have at the moment of the payment of the respective amounts. This right may be effectuated at any time up to the moment of sale of the pledged property at a public sale, auction, or compe-

tition or acquisition of the right to this property by the pledgeholder in the established procedure.

2. The person demanding termination of levy of execution against the pledged property or the realisation thereof shall be obliged to compensate the pledgeholder for expenses incurred in connection with the levy of execution against this proeprty and the realisation thereof.

Article 61. Distribution of Amount Received from Realisation of Pledged Property

The amount derived from the realisation of the property pledged under a contract on mortgage after the withholding therefrom of amounts necessary to cover expenses in connection with the levy of execution against this property and the realisation thereof shall be distributed between those pledgeholders who have declared their demands against for levy, other creditors of the pledgor, and the pledgor himself. The distribution shall be conducted by the agency effectuating the execution of the judicial decisions, and if execution was levied against pledged property in an extrajudicial procedure, by the notary certifying the agreement concerning such procedure of recovery in compliance with the rules of Article 319, Article 334(1), and Article 350(5) and (6) of the Civil Code of the Russian Federation, and also Article 46 of the present Federal Law.

If the subject of the mortgage against which execution is levied is State or municipal property, the amounts subject to being credited to the pledgor in the procedure and priority which has been determined by the present Article shall be credited to the respective budget.

Chapter XI. Peculiarities of Mortgage of Land Plots

Article 62. Land Plots Which May Be Subject of Mortgage

1. Under a contract on mortgage land plots in the ownership of citizens, associations thereof, juridical persons, and granted for gardening, livestock farming, individual housing, dacha, and garage construction, farm land plots of personal subsidiary husbandry, and land plots occupied by buildings, structures, or installations in a size necessary for the economic servicing (or functional provision) thereof may be pledged.

2. In the event of common participatory share or joint ownership to land plots specified in point 1 of the present Article the mortgage may be established only on the land plots belonging to a citizen or juridical person allotted in kind from land in general participatory share or joint ownership.

Article 63. Land Plots Not Subject to Mortgage

1. The mortgage of land in State or municipal ownership, and also agricultural lands from lands of agricultural organisations, peasant (or farmer) economies, and

field land plots of personal subsidiary husbandries in accordance with the present Federal Law shall not be permitted.

2. The mortgage of part of a land plot, the area of which is less than the minimum amount established by normative acts of subjects of the Russian Federation and normative acts of agencies of local self-government for lands of various special-purpose designations and authorised use shall not be permitted.

Article 64. Mortgage of Land Plot on Which There Are Buildings or Installations Belonging to Pledgor

1. Unless provided otherwise by the contract on mortgage, in the event of the mortgage of a land plot the right of pledge shall not extend to the buildings and installations of the pledgor situated or erected on this plot, including to dwelling structures.

In the absence in the contract of a condition providing that the building or installations situated or erected on the land plot has been pledged to the same pledgeholder, the pledgor shall in the event of levy of execution against the land plot retain the right to this building or installation and acquire the right of limited use (servitude) of that part of the plot which is necessary for the use of the building or installation in accordance with its purpose. The conditions of use of this part of the plot shall be determined by agreement between the pledgor and the pledgeholder, and in the event of a dispute, by a court.

2. The pledgor of a land plot shall have the right without the consent of the pledgeholder to dispose of the buildings and installations belonging to him on this plot to which in accordance with point 1 of the present Article the right of pledge does not extend.

In the event of the alienation of such building or installation to another person and the absence of an agreement with the pledgeholder otherwise, the rights which this person may acquire to the pledged land plot shall be limited by the conditions provided for by point 1, paragraph two, of the present Article.

3. If a building or installation belonging to the pledgor of a land plot situated or erected on this land plot has been pledged to the same pledgeholder, the right of the pledgor to dispose of this building or installations and the conditions and consequences of the transfer of the rights to this building or installation to other persons shall be determined by the rules of Chapter VI of the present Federal Law.

Article 65. Erection of Buildings or Installations by Pledgor on Pledged Land Plot

1. On a land plot pledged under a contract on mortgage the pledgor shall have the right without the consent of the pledgeholder to erect a building or installation in the established procedure unless provided otherwise by the contract on mortgage. The mortgage shall extend to these buildings and installations unless

provided otherwise by the contract on mortgage [as amended by Federal Law No. 18-ФЗ, 11 February 2002].

If the erection by the pledgor of a building or installation on a pledged land plot entails or may entail a worsening of the security granted to the pledgeholder by the mortgage of this plot, the pledgeholder shall have the right in accordance with Article 450(2) of the Civil Code of the Russian Federation to demand a change of the contract on mortgage, including, if this is necessary, by means of extending the mortgage to the erected building or installation.

2. The erection of buildings or installations on a pledged land plot, if the rights of the pledgeholder have been certified by a zakladnaia, shall be permitted only if the right of the pledgor thereto has been provided for in the zakladnaia in compliance with the conditions which have been reflected therein.

Article 66. Mortgage of Land Plot on Which There Are Buildings or Installations Belonging to Third Persons

If a mortgage has been established on a land plot on which a building of installation is situated belonging not to the pledgor, but to another person, in the event of the levy of execution by the pledgeholder against this plot and the realisation thereof, the rights and duties which with respect to this person the pledgor had as possessor of the plot shall pass to the acquirer of the plot.

Article 67. Valuation of Land Plot in Event of Mortgage Thereof

The valuation of a land plot may not be established in the contract on mortgage lower than its normative price.

To the contract on mortgage of a land plot must be appended as an obligatory annexe a copy of the plan (or drawing of the boundaries) of this plot issued by the respective committee for land resources and land tenure.

Article 68. Peculiarities of Levy of Execution Against Pledged Land Plots and the Realisation Thereof

1. The requirements concerning authorised use shall extend to a land plot acquired in the event of a sale at a public sale, auction, or competition.

The person who acquired the land plot in the event of a sale at a public sale, auction, or competiton shall have the right to change the designation of the plot only in the instances provided for by land legislation of the Russian Federation or in the procedure established by this legislation.

2. The sale and acquisition at a public sale, auction, or competition of pledged land plots shall be effectuated in compliance with the limitations established by a Federal law with respect to the group of persons who may acquire such plots.

Chapter XII. Peculiarities of Mortgage of Enterprises, Buildings, and Installations

Article 69. Mortgage of Enterprises, Buildings, or Installations With Land Plot On Which They Are Situated

In the event of the mortgage of an enterprise as a property complex (hereinafter: enterprise) the right of pledge shall extend to all property within the composition thereof (Article 340(2) of the Civil Code of the Russian Federation).

The mortgage of a building or installation shall be permitted only with the simultanous mortgage under the same contract of the land plot on which this building or installation is situated, or part of this plot, functionally securing the pledged object or the rights of lease of this plot or respective part thereof belonging to the pledgor.

The right of pledge shall not extend to the right of permanent use of a land plot on which the enterprise, building, or installation is situated belonging to the pledgor. In the event of levy of execution against such enterprise, building, or installation the person who acquires this property in ownership shall acquire the right of use of the land plot on the same conditions and in the same amount as the former owner (or pledgor) of the immoveable property.

Article 70. Mortgage of Enterprise as Property Complex

1. The transfer of an enterprise on mortgage shall be permitted when there is the consent of the owner of the property relating to the enterprise or agency empowered by it. The contract on the mortgage of an enterprise concluded in violation of this requirement shall be null.

2. If the subject of the mortgage is an enterprise and unless provided otherwise by the contract, the material and nonmaterial assets, including the buildings, installations, equipment, tools, raw material, finished products, rights of demand, and exclusive rights relating to the enterprise shall be in the composition of the pledged property.

3. The composition of property relating to the enterprise and transferred on mortgage and the valuation of its value shall be determined on the basis of the full inventorisation of the particular property. The act of inventorisation, bookkeeping balance sheet, and opinion of an independent auditor concerning the composition and value of the property relating to the enterprise shall be obligatory annexes to the contract on mortgage.

If the conducting of a valuation is obligatory by virtue of a law, the report concerning the valuation of property relating to the enterprise also shall be an obligatory annexe to the contract [added by Federal Law No. 143-ФЗ, 9 November 2001].

Article 71. Obligations Which May be Secured by Mortgage of Enterprise

1. An obligation, the amount of which constitutes not less than half of the value of the property relating to the enterprise may be secured by the mortgage of the enterprise.

2. A monetary obligation subject to performance not earlier than a year after the conclusion of the contract on mortgage shall be secured by a mortgage of the enterprise. When it is provided by a contract that an obligation with a lesser period of performance is secured by a mortgage of the enterprise, the right to levy execution against the subject of the mortgage for the failure to perform or an improperly performed obligation arises with the pledgeholder upon the expiry of a year from the moment of conclusion of the contract on mortgage.

Article 72. Rights of Pledgor With Respect to Pledged Property

1. The pledgor shall have the right to sell, exchange, lease out, or grant on loan relating to an enterprise transferred on mortgage and otherwise dispose of the said property, and also make changes in the composition of the said property unless this entails a reduction of the total value of the property specified in the contract on mortgage relating to the enterprise, and also does not violate other conditions of the contract on mortgage.

Without the authorisation of the pledgeholder, the pledgor shall not have the right to transfer property relating to the enterprise on pledge, conclude transactions directed towards an alienation of immoveable property relating to the enterprise unless established otherwise by the contract on mortgage.

2. In the event of the failure of the pledgor to undertake measures relating to ensuring the preservation of the pledged property or of the inefficient use of this property which may lead to a reduction of the value of the enterprise, the pledgeholder shall have the right to apply to a court with a demand concerning the fulfilment before time of the obligation secured by the mortgage or the introduction of mortgage control over the activity of the pledgor.

By decision of a court the pledgeholder may by way of mortgage control be empowered to:

demand the pledgor regularly submit bookkeeping and other report documents, agree questions in advance connected with the conclusion of transactions with property relating to the enterprise;

apply to the owner of the property relating to the enterprise or agency empowered by it with a demand concerning dissolution of the contract with the director of the enterprise;

present suits in court concerning the deeming of transactions concluded by the pledgor to be invalid;

effectuate other rights provided for by mortgage control over the activity of the pledgor.

Article 73. Levy of Execution Against Pledged Enterprise

1. In the event of the failure of the pledgor to perform the obligation secured by the mortgage of an enterprise, execution may be levied against the pledged property only by decision of a court.

2. To the purchaser who has acquired an enterprise at a public sale shall pass the rights and duties of the owner of the enterprise relating to the latter from the moment of State registration of the right of ownership to the acquired property.

Chapter XIII. Peculiarities of Mortgage of Dwelling Houses and Apartments

Article 74. Application of Rules on Mortgage to Dwelling Houses and Apartments

1. The rules of the present Chapter shall apply to the mortgage of individual and apartment dwelling houses and apartments intended for permanent residence which belong by right of ownership to citizens or juridical persons.

2. The mortgage of individual and apartment dwelling houses and apartments in State or municipal ownership shall not be permitted.

3. Hotels, houses of leisure, dachas, garden houses, and other structures and premises not intended for permanent residence may be the subject of a mortgage on the general grounds. The rules established for the mortgage of dwelling house or apartments shall not extend to them.

4. When part of a dwelling house or part of an apartment consisting of one or several isolated rooms is the subject of a mortgage, to such mortgage respectively shall apply the rules of the present Federal Law on the mortgage of a dwelling house and apartment.

5. The mortgage of a dwelling house or apartment in the ownership of minor citizens, persons of limited dispositive legal capacity or lacking dispositive legal capacity over whom a trusteeship or guardianship has been established shall be effectuated in the procedure established by legislation of the Russian Federation for the conclusion of transactions with the property of wards.

6. [repealed by Federal Law No. 18-ФЗ, 11 February 2002].

Article 75. Mortgage of Apartments in Apartment Dwelling House

In the event of the mortgage of an apartment in an apartment dwelling house, parts of which in accordance with Article 290(1) of the Civil Code of the Russian Federation are in the common participatory share ownership of the pledgor and other persons, the respective participatory share in the right of common ownership to the dwelling house shall be considered to be pledged together with the dwelling premise.

Article 76. Mortgage of Dwelling Houses Being Built

When granting a credit or special-purpose loan for the erection of a dwelling house, securing of the obligation with the uncompleted construction and the materials and equipment belonging to the pledgor which have been procured for the construction may be provided for by the contract on mortgage [as amended by Federal Law No. 179-ФЗ, 24 December 2002].

Article 77. Mortgage of Dwelling Houses and Apartments Acquired at Expense of Credit of Bank or Other Credit Organisation [as amended by Federal Law No. 18-ФЗ, 11 February 2002]

1. Unless provided otherwise by a federal law or contract, a dwelling house or an apartment acquired or built with the use of credit means of a bank or other credit organisation or means of a special-purpose loan granted by a juridical person for the aquisition or construction of a dwelling house or apartment shall be considered to be under pledge from the moment of State registration of the right of ownership of the borrower to the dwelling house or apartment [as amended by Federal Law No. 18-ФЗ, 11 February 2002, and by Federal Law No. 179-ФЗ, 24 December 2002].

The bank or other credit organisation or juridical person which granted the credit or special-purpose loan for the acquisition or construction of the dwelling house or apartment shall be the pledgeholder under the particular pledge [as amended by Federal Law No. 18-ФЗ, 11 February 2002, and by Federal Law No. 179-ФЗ, 24 December 2002].

2. The rules concerning pledge of immoveable property which arise by virtue of a contract shall apply respectively to the pledge of a dwelling house or apartment arising on the basis of point 1 of the present Article.

3. Trusteeship and guardianship agencies shall have the right to give consent (or authorisation) to legal representatives of minors and members of the family lacking dispositive legal capacity or limited in dispositive legal capacity of the owner of a dwelling premise in which the said persons live to the alienation and/or transfer on mortgage of this dwelling premise if the trusteeship and guardianship agencies lack grounds for deeming the rights and interested protected by a law of minors or persons lacking dispositive legal capacity or limited in dispositive legal capacity are violated.

The decision of trusteeship and guardianship agencies to give consent (or authorisation) to the alienation and/or transfer on mortgage of a dwelling premise in which minors and members of the family lacking dispositive legal capacity or limited in dispositive legal capacity of the owner reside must be submitted by the applicant in written form not later than 30 calendar days from the date of filing the application concerning the giving of such consent (or authorisation).

A refusal to give consent (or authorisation) to alienation and/or transfer on mortgage of a dwelling premise in which minors and members of the family lacking dispositive legal capacity or limited in dispositive legal capacity of the owner reside must be reasoned.

The applicant shall have the right to contest the decision of trusteeship and guardianship agencies in a court [point 3 added by Federal Law No. 18-ФЗ, 11 February 2002].

Article 78. Levy of Execution Against Pledged Dwelling House or Apartment [as amended by Federal Law No. 179-ФЗ, 24 December 2002].

1. Levy of execution by the pledgeholder against a pledged dwelling house or apartment and the realisation of this property shall be grounds for the termination of the right of use of the pledgor and members of his family (or former member of the family) jointly living in this dwelling house or apartment on condition that such dwelling house or apartment was pledged under a contract on mortgage or under a mortgage by operation of law to secure return of the credit or special-purpose loan provided by a bank or other credit organisation juridical person for the acquisition or construction of such dwelling house or apartment [as amended by Federal Law No. 18-ФЗ, 11 February 2002 and by Federal Law No. 179-ФЗ, 24 December 2002].

The vacating of such dwelling house or apartment shall be effectuated in the procedure established by a federal law [added by Federal Law No. 179-ФЗ, 24 December 2002].

2. Levy of execution against a pledged dwelling house or apartment shall be possible either in a judicial or extrajudicial procedure in compliance with the rules established by Chapter IX of the present Federal Law.

A dwelling house or apartment which was pledged under a contract on mortgage and against which execution was levied shall be realised by means of public sale conducted in the form of an open auction or competition [point 2 as amended by Federal Law No. 18-ФЗ, 11 February 2002 and by Federal Law No. 179-ФЗ, 24 December 2002].

3. Persons residing in pledged dwelling houses or apartments on conditions of a contract of hire or contract of lease of a dwelling premise shall not be subject to eviction in the event of the realisation of the pledged dwelling house or apartment. A contract of hire or contract of lease of a dwelling premise concluded with them before the conclusion of the contract on mortgage shall retain force. The conditions of the dissolution thereof shall be determined by the Civil Code of the

Russian Federation and housing legislation of the Russian Federation [as amended by Federal Law No. 179-Ф3, 24 December 2002].

Chapter XIV. Concluding Provisions

Article 79. Introduction of Present Federal Law into Operation

1. To introduce the present Federal Law into operation from the date of its official publication.

2. The norms of the Law of the Russian Federation 'On Pledge' from the date of introduction of the present Federal Law into operation shall be subject to application to the pledge of immoveable property (mortgage) only insofar as they are not contrary to the present Federal Law.

Until Federal laws and other legal acts of the Russian Federation (Article 3(3) and (4) of the Civil Code of the Russian Federation) are brought into accordance with the present Federal Law, these Federal laws and other legal acts of the Russian Federation shall apply in the part which is not contrary to the present Federal Law.

3. The rules of the present Federal Law shall apply to relations arising in connection with the pledge of immoveable property (mortgage) after its introduction into operation.

With regard to relations which arose before the introduction into operation of the present Federal Law the present Federal Law shall apply to those rights and duties which arise after its introduction into operation.

4. To propose that the President of the Russian Federation shall bring legal acts issued by him into conformity with the present Federal Law.

5. To charge the Government of the Russian Federation:
to bring legal acts issued by it into conformity with the present Federal Law;
to adopt legal acts ensuring the realisation of the present Federal Law.

FEDERAL LAW ON FINANCE LEASE (FINANCE LEASING)

[Federal Law No. 164-ФЗ,
29 October 1998, as amended by Federal Law
No. 10-ФЗ, 29 January 2002, and Federal Law No. 176-ФЗ,
24 December 2002. СЗ РФ (1998), no. 44, item 5394;
(2002), no. 5, item 376, no. 52(I), item 5132]

Chapter I   General Provisions   794
Chapter II   Legal Foundations of Finance Leasing Relations   797
Chapter III   Economic Foundations of Finance Leasing   805
Chapter IV   State Support of Finance Leasing Activity   808
Chapter V   Right of Inspection and Control   809
Chapter VI   Concluding Provisions   809

The purposes of the present Federal Law are the development of the forms of investments in the means of production on the basis of finance lease (finance leasing), defence of the rights of ownership and the rights of participants of the investment process, and ensuring the effectiveness of investing [as amended by Federal Law No. 10-ФЗ, 29 January 2002].

The legal and organisational-economic peculiarities of finance leasing have been determined in the present Federal Law.

Chapter I. General Provisions

Article 1. Sphere of Application of Present Federal Law

The sphere of application of the present Federal Law shall be the finance leasing of property relegated to nonconsumer things (except land plots and other natural objects) to be transferred in temporary possession and use to natural and juridical persons.

Article 2. Basic Concepts Used in Present Federal Law

The following basic concepts shall be used in the present Federal Law:

finance leasing: the aggregate of economic and legal relations arising in connection with the realisation of a contract of finance leasing, including acquisition of the subject of finance leasing [as amended by Federal Law No. 10-ФЗ, 29 January 2002];

finance leasing contract: contract in accordance with which the lessor (hereinafter: finance lessor) is obliged to acquire in ownership property specified by the lessee (hereinafter: finance leasing recipient) from the seller determined by it and to grant this property to the finance leasing recipient for payment in temporary possession and use. It may be provided by the contract of finance leasing that the choice of the seller and property to be acquired shall be effectuated by the finance leasing recipient [as amended by Federal Law No. 10-ФЗ, 29 January 2002];

finance leasing activity: type of investment activity with regard to the acquisition of property and transfer thereof on finance leasing [added by Federal Law No. 10-ФЗ, 29 January 2002].

Article 3. Subject of Finance Leasing

1. Any nonconsumption things, including enterprises and other property complexes, buildings, installations, equipment, means of transport, and other moveable and immoveable property which may be used for entrepreneurial activity may be the subject of finance leasing.

2. Land plots and other natural objects, and also property which is prohibited by federal laws for free circulation or for which a special procedure for circulation has been established has been prohibited by federal laws, may not be a subject of finance leasing.

Article 4. Subjects of Finance Leasing

1. The subjects of finance leasing shall be:

the finance lessor shall be a natural or juridical person who at the expense of attracted and/or own means acquires in the course of realisation of a contract of finance leasing property in ownership and provides it as a subject of finance leasing to a finance lessee for a determined payment, for a determined period, and on determined conditions for temporary possession and use with or without transfer of the right of ownership to the subject of finance leasing to the finance lessee [as amended by Federal Law No. 10-ФЗ, 29 January 2002];

the finance lessee shall be a natural or juridical person who in accordance with a contract of finance leasing is obliged to accept a subject of finance leasing for determined payment, for a determined period, and on determined conditions in temporary possession and use in accordance with a contract of finance leasing;

the seller shall be a natural or juridical person who in accordance with a contract of purchase-sale with the finance lessor sells to the finance lessor within the stipulated period property which is the subject of finance leasing. The seller shall be obliged to transfer the subject of finance leasing to the finance lessor or to the finance lessee in accordance with the conditions of the contract of purchase-sale.

The seller may simultaneously act as the finance leasing recipient within the limits of one finance leasing legal relation [as amended by Federal Law No. 10-ФЗ, 29 January 2002].

2. Any of the subjects of finance leasing may be a resident of the Russian Federation or nonresident of the Russian Federation [as amended by Federal Law No. 10-ФЗ, 29 January 2002].

Article 5. Finance Leasing Companies (or Firms)

1. Finance leasing companies (or firms) shall be commercial organisations (residents of the Russian Federation or nonresidents of the Russian Federation) fulfilling in accordance with legislation of the Russian Federation and their constitutive documents the functions of a finance lessor [as amended by Federal Law No. 10-ФЗ, 29 January 2002].

2. Juridical and natural persons (residents of the Russian Federation or nonresidents of the Russian Federation) may be founders of finance leasing companies (or firms) [as amended by Federal Law No. 10-ФЗ, 29 January 2002].

3. A finance leasing company-nonresident of the Russian Federation shall be a foreign juridical person effectuating finance leasing activity on the territory of the Russian Federation [as amended by Federal Law No. 10-ФЗ, 29 January 2002].

4. Finance leasing companies shall have the right to attract means of juridical and/or natural persons (residents of the Russian Federation and nonresidents of the Russian Federation) in order to effectuate finance leasing activity in the procedure established by legislation of the Russian Federation [as amended by Federal Law No. 10-ФЗ, 29 January 2002].

Article 6. Finance Leasing Activity [repealed by Federal Law No. 10-ФЗ, 29 January 2002]

Article 7. Forms of Finance Leasing [as amended by Federal Law No. 10-ФЗ, 29 January 2002]

1. Internal finance leasing and international finance leasing shall be the basic forms of finance leasing [as amended by Federal Law No. 10-ФЗ, 29 January 2002].

When effectuating internal finance leasing the finance lessor and finance leasing lessee shall be residents of the Russian Federation [as amended by Federal Law No. 10-ФЗ, 29 January 2002].

When effectuating international finance leasing the finance lessor or finance lessee shall be a nonresident of the Russian Federation.

[paragraphs four and five repealed by Federal Law No. 10-ФЗ, 29 January 2002].

2. [repealed by Federal Law No. 10-ФЗ, 29 January 2002].

3. [repealed by Federal Law No. 10-ФЗ, 29 January 2002].

2. A contract of finance leasing may include conditions of rendering additional services and conducting additional work.

Additional services (or work): services (or work) of any nature rendered by the finance lessor either before the commencement of use and also in the process of use of the subject of finance leasing by the finance lessee and directly connected with the realisation of the contract of finance leasing.

The List, amount, and cost of the additional services (or work) shall be determined by agreement of the parties [as renumbered and amended by Federal Law No. 10-ФЗ, 29 January 2002].

Article 8. Sub-Finance Leasing

1. Sub-finance leasing is a type of sub-hire of the subject of finance leasing under which the finance lessee under a contract of finance leasing transfers to third persons (or finance lessee under the contract of sub-finance leasing) in possession and use for payment and for a period in accordance with the conditions of the contract of sub-finance leasing property received earlier from the finance lessee under the contract of finance leasing and comprising the subject of finance leasing [as amended by Federal Law No. 10-ФЗ, 29 January 2002].

In the event of the transfer of property on sub-finance leasing the right of demand against the seller shall pass to the finance lessee under the contract of sub-finance leasing [added by Federal Law No. 10-ФЗ, 29 January 2002].

2. [repealed by Federal Law No. 10-ФЗ, 29 January 2002]

3. [repealed by Federal Law No. 10-ФЗ, 29 January 2002]

2. In the event of the transfer of the subject of finance leasing on sub-finance leasing the consent of the finance lessor in written form shall be obligatory [renumbered by Federal Law No. 10-ФЗ, 29 January 2002].

5. [repealed by Federal Law No. 10-ФЗ, 29 January 2002]

Article 9. Prohibitions Against Combining of Obligations by Participant of Finance Leasing [repealed by Federal Law No. 10-ФЗ, 29 January 2002]

Chapter II. Legal Foundations of Finance Leasing Relations

Article 10. Rights and Duties of Participants of Contract of Finance Leasing

1. The rights and duties of parties of a contract of finance leasing shall be regulated by civil legislation of the Russian Federation, the present Federal Law, and the contract of finance leasing [as amended by Federal Law No. 10-ФЗ, 29 January 2002].

2. [repealed by Federal Law No. 10-ФЗ, 29 January 2002]

3. [repealed by Federal Law No. 10-ФЗ, 29 January 2002]

2. When effectuating finance leasing, the finance lessee shall have the right to bring demands directly against the seller of the subject of finance leasing with regard to the quality and completeness, periods for performance of the duty to transfer the good, and other demands established by legislation of the Russian Federation and the contract of purchase-sale between the seller and the finance lessor [as renumbered and amended by Federal Law No. 10-ФЗ, 29 January 2002].

5. [repealed by Federal Law No. 10-ФЗ, 29 January 2002]

6. [repealed by Federal Law No. 10-ФЗ, 29 January 2002]

7. [repealed by Federal Law No. 10-ФЗ, 29 January 2002]

Article 11. Right of Ownership in Subject of Finance Leasing [as amended by Federal Law No. 10-ФЗ, 29 January 2002]

1. The subject of finance leasing transferred in temporary possession and use to the finance lessee shall be the ownership of the finance lessor [as amended by Federal Law No. 10-ФЗ, 29 January 2002].

2. The right of possession and use of the subject of finance leasing shall pass to the finance lessee in full unless established otherwise by the contract of finance leasing.

3. The right of the finance lessor to dispose of the subject of finance leasing shall include the right to remove the subject of finance leasing from the possession and use of the finance lessee in the instances and in the procedure which have been provided for by legislation of the Russian Federation and by the contract of finance leasing [as amended by Federal Law No. 10-ФЗ, 29 January 2002].

Article 12. Recording of Subject of Finance Leasing [repealed by Federal Law No. 10-ФЗ, 29 January 2002]

Article 13. Securing Rights of Finance Lessor [as amended by Federal Law No. 10-ФЗ, 29 January 2002]

1. In the event of the failure of the finance lessor to transfer finance lease payments more than two times in succession upon the expiry of the period for payment established by the contract of finance leasing, the withdrawal thereof from the account of the finance lessee shall be effectuated in an uncontested proceeding by means of the sending by the finance lessor to the bank or other credit organisation in which the account of the finance lessee is opened an instruction for the withdrawal from his account of monetary means within the limits of the amounts of delayed finance lease payments. The uncontested withdrawal of monetary

means shall not deprive the finance lessee of the right to apply to a court [as amended by Federal Law No. 10-ФЗ, 29 January 2002].

2. The finance lessor shall have the right to demand dissolution before time of the contract of finance leasing and the return within a reasonable period by the finance lessee of property in instances provided for by legislation of the Russian Federation, the present Federal Law, and the contract of finance leasing.

In this event all expenses connected with the return of the property, including expenses for the disassembly thereof, insurance, and transport, shall be borne by the finance lessee [as amended by Federal Law No. 10-ФЗ, 29 January 2002].

3. [repealed by Federal Law No. 10-ФЗ, 29 January 2002]

4. [repealed by Federal Law No. 10-ФЗ, 29 January 2002]

5. [repealed by Federal Law No. 10-ФЗ, 29 January 2002]

Article 14. Procedure for Use of Subject of Finance Leasing as Pledge
[repealed by Federal Law No. 10-ФЗ, 29 January 2002]

Article 15. Content of Contract of Finance Leasing

1. A contract of finance leasing shall irrespective of the period be concluded in written form.

2. [repealed by Federal Law No. 10-ФЗ, 29 January 2002]

2. In order to fulfil their obligations under a contract of finance leasing the subjects of finance leasing shall conclude obligatory and concomitant contracts [as amended by Federal Law No. 10-ФЗ, 29 January 2002].

The contract of purchase-sale shall be relegated to obligatory contracts.

The contract on the attraction of means, contract of pledge, contract of guarantee, contract of suretyship, and others shall be relegated to concomitant contracts [as renumbered and amended by Federal Law No. 10-ФЗ, 29 January 2002].

3. In a contract of finance leasing must be specified data enabling the property subject to transfer to the finance lessee as the subject of finance leasing to be precisely established. In the absence of such data the condition in the contract of finance leasing concerning the subject which is subject to transfer on finance leasing shall be considered not to be agreed by the parties, and the contract of finance leasing shall be considered to be nonconcluded [as renumbered and amended by Federal Law No. 10-ФЗ, 29 January 2002].

4. On the basis of a contract of finance leasing the finance lessor shall be obliged to:

acquire from a determined seller determined property in ownership for the transfer thereof for determined payment for a determined period and on determined conditions as the subject of finance leasing to the finance lessee [as renumbered and amended by Federal Law No. 10-ФЗ, 29 January 2002];

fulfil other obligations arising out of the content of the contract of finance leasing.

5. Under a contract of finance leasing the finance lessee shall be obliged to:

accept the subject of finance leasing in the procedure provided for by the contract of finance leasing;

pay the finance lease payments to the finance lessor in the procedure and within the periods which have been provided for by the contract of finance leasing [as renumbered and amended by Federal Law No. 10-ФЗ, 29 January 2002];

upon the ending of the period of operation of the contract of finance leasing, return the subject of finance leasing unless provided otherwise by the said contract of finance leasing or acquire the subject of finance leasing in ownership on the basis of the contract of purchase-sale;

fulfil other obligations arising from the content of the contract of finance leasing.

6. Obligations may be stipulated in a contract of finance leasing which the parties consider to be an uncontested and obvious violation of obligations and which will lead to termination of the operation of the contract of finance leasing and the removal of the subject of finance leasing [as renumbered and amended by Federal Law No. 10-ФЗ, 29 January 2002].

7. A contract of finance leasing may provide for the right of the finance lessee to extend for term of finance leasing with retention or a change of the conditions of the contract of finance leasing [as renumbered by Federal Law No. 10-ФЗ, 29 January 2002].

Article 16. Obligatory Indicia and Conditions of Contract of Finance Leasing [repealed by Federal Law No. 10-ФЗ, 29 January 2002]

Article 17. Granting for Temporary Possession and Use of Subject of Contract of Finance Leasing, Servicing and Return Thereof [as amended by Federal Law No. 10-ФЗ, 29 January 2002]

1. The finance lessor shall be obliged to grant to the finance lessee the property which is the subject of finance leasing in a state corresponding to the conditions of the contract of finance leasing and the designation of the particular property.

2. The subject of finance leasing shall be transferred on finance leasing together with all of the documents (technical passport and others) unless provided otherwise by the contract of finance leasing.

3. [repealed by Federal Law No. 10-ФЗ, 29 January 2002]

4. [repealed by Federal Law No. 10-ФЗ, 29 January 2002]

3. The finance lessee shall at his own expense effectuate technical servicing of the subject of finance leasing and ensure the preservation thereof, and also effectuate capital and current repair of the subject of finance leasing, unless provided otherwise by the contract of finance leasing [as renumbered and amended by Federal Law No. 10-ФЗ, 29 January 2002].

4. In the event of the termination of the contract of finance leasing the finance lessee shall be obliged to return to the finance lessor the subject of finance leasing in the state in which it was received, taking into account normal wear and tear or the wear and tear stipulated by the contract of finance leasing [as renumbered by Federal Law No. 10-ФЗ, 29 January 2002].

5. If the finance lessee has not returned the subject of finance leasing or has returned it in an untimely manner, the finance lessor shall have the right to demand the making of payments for the time of delay. If the said payment does not cover the losses caused to the finance lessor, he may demand compensation thereof [as renumbered by Federal Law No. 10-ФЗ, 29 January 2002].

6. If a penalty has been provided for the untimely return of the subject of finance leasing to the finance lessor, the losses may be recovered from the finance lessee in the full amount above the penalty unless provided otherwise by the contract of finance leasing [as renumbered by Federal Law No. 10-ФЗ, 29 January 2002].

7. Separable improvements to the subject of finance leasing made by the finance lessee shall be his ownership unless provided otherwise by the contract of finance leasing [as renumbered by Federal Law No. 10-ФЗ, 29 January 2002].

8. If the finance lessee with the consent in written form from the finance lessor made at the expense of own means improvements in the subject of finance leasing which are inseparable without harm to the subject of finance leasing, the finance lessee shall have the right after termination of the contract of finance leasing to compensation for the cost of such improvements unless provided otherwise by the contract of finance leasing [as renumbered by Federal Law No. 10-ФЗ, 29 January 2002].

9. If the finance lessee without the consent of the finance lessor in written form has made improvements at the expense of own means in the subject of finance leasing which are inseparable without harm to the subject of finance leasing, and unless provided otherwise by a federal law, the finance lessee shall not have the right after termination of the contract of finance leasing to compensation for the cost of these improvements [as renumbered and amended by Federal Law No. 10-ФЗ, 29 January 2002].

Article 18. Assignment of Rights Under Contract of Finance Leasing to Third Persons and Pledge of Subject of Finance Leasing [as amended by Federal Law No. 10-ФЗ, 29 January 2002]

1. The finance lessor may assign his rights to a third person wholly or partially under a contract of finance leasing [as amended by Federal Law No. 10-ФЗ, 29 January 2002].

2. [repealed by Federal Law No. 10-ФЗ, 29 January 2002]

2. The finance lessor shall have the right for the purpose of attracting monetary means to use the subject of finance leasing as a pledge which will be acquired in the future under the conditions of a contract of finance leasing [as renumbered and amended by Federal Law No. –10-ФЗ, 29 January 2002].

3. A finance lessor shall be obliged to warn the finance lessee about all rights of third persons in the subject of finance leasing [added by Federal Law No. 10-ФЗ, 29 January 2002].

4. [repealed by Federal Law No. 10-ФЗ, 29 January 2002]

5. [repealed by Federal Law No. 10-ФЗ, 29 January 2002]

Article 19. Transfer of Right of Ownership to Subject of Finance Leasing

1. It may be provided by a contract of finance leasing that the subject of finance leasing shall pass to the ownership of the finance lessee upon the expiry of the period of the contract of finance leasing or before the expiry thereof on the conditions provided for by agreement of the parties [as amended by Federal Law No. 10-ФЗ, 29 January 2002].

2. Instances may be established by a Federal Law of prohibiting the transfer of the right of ownership to the subject of finance leasing to the finance lessee [as amended by Federal Law No. 10-ФЗ, 29 January 2002].

Article 20. Procedure for Registration of Property (or Subject of Contract of Finance Leasing) and Rights Thereto [as amended by Federal Law No. 10-ФЗ, 29 January 2002]

1. In instances provided for by legislation of the Russian Federation the rights to property which are transferred in finance leasing and/or a contract of finance leasing, the subject of which is particular property, shall be subject to State registration.

Special requirements presented by legislation of the Russian Federation to the owner of registered property (aviation technology, sea-going and other vessels, other property) shall extent to the finance lessor or finance lessee by mutual agreement [as amended by Federal Law No. 10-ФЗ, 29 January 2002].

2. The subjects of finance leasing subject to registration in State agencies (means of transport, equipment of increased danger, and other subjects of finance leasing) shall be registered by agreement of the parties in the name of the finance lessor or the finance lessee.

3. By agreement of the parties the finance lessor shall have the right to charge the finance lessee with the registration of the subject of finance leasing in the name of the finance lessor. In so doing information concerning the owner and the possessor (or user) of the property shall obligatorily be specified in the registration documents. In the event of the dissolution of the contract and removal by the finance lessor of the subject of finance leasing upon the application of the last the State agencies which effectuated the registration shall be obliged to annul the entry concerning the possessor (or user).

Article 21. Insurance of Subject of Finance Leasing and Entrepreneurial (or Financial) Risks [as amended by Federal Law No. 10-ФЗ, 29 January 2002]

1. The subject of finance leasing may be insured against risks of loss (or perishing), shortage, or damage from the moment of delivery of the property by the seller and until the moment of ending of the period of operation of the contract of finance leasing, unless provided otherwise by the contract. The parties acting as insurer and beneficiary, and also the period of insurance of the subject of finance leasing, shall be determined by the contract of finance leasing [as amended by Federal Law No. 10-ФЗ, 29 January 2002].

2. The insuring of entrepreneurial (or financial) risks shall be effectuated by agreement of the parties to the contract of finance leasing and is not obligatory.

3. [repealed by Federal Law No. 10-ФЗ, 29 January 2002]

3. The finance lessee in the instances determined by legislation of the Russian Federation must insure its responsibility for the fulfilment of obligations arising as a consequence of the causing of harm to life, health, or property of other persons in the process of the use of the finance lease property [as renumbered by Federal Law No. 10-ФЗ, 29 January 2002].

4. A finance lessee shall have the right to insure the risk of his responsibility for a violation of the contract of finance leasing to the benefit of the finance lessor [added by Federal Law No. 10-ФЗ, 29 January 2002].

Article 22. Distribution of Risks Between Parties to Contract of Finance Leasing [as amended by Federal Law No. 10-ФЗ, 29 January 2002]

1. Responsibility for preservation of the subject of finance leasing against all the types of property damage, and also the risks connected with its perishing, loss, spoilage, stealing, premature breakage, error committed during the assemmbly or operation thereof, and other property risks from the moment of actual acceptance

of the subject of finance leasing shall be borne by the finance lessee unless provided otherwise by the contract of finance leasing.

2. The risk of the failure of the seller to fulfil duties under the contract of purchase-sale of the subject of finance leasing and losses connected therewith shall be borne by the party to the contract of finance leasing which chose the seller unless provided otherwise by the contract of finance leasing [as amended by Federal Law No. 10-ФЗ, 29 January 2002].

3. The risk of the failure of the subject of finance leasing to conform to the purposes for the use of this subject under the contract of finance leasing and losses connected therewith shall be borne by the party which chose the subject of finance leasing unless provided otherwise by the contract of finance leasing [as amended by Federal Law No. 10-ФЗ, 29 January 2002].

Article 23. Levy of Execution by Third Persons Against Subject of Finance Leasing [as amended by Federal Law No. 10-ФЗ, 29 January 2002]

1. [repealed by Federal Law No. 10-ФЗ, 29 January 2002]

1. Execution may not be levied against a subject of finance leasing by a third person with regard to obligations of the finance lessee, including in instances when the subject of finance leasing was registered in the name of the finance lessee [as renumbered by Federal Law No. 10-ФЗ, 29 January 2002].

2. The levy of third persons executed against the property of the finance lessor may be relegated only to the particular object of the right of ownership of the finance lessor with respect to the subject of finance leasing. To the acquirer of the rights of finance lessor with respect to the subject of finance leasing as a result of the satisfaction of the levy shall pass in an obligatory procedure not only the rights but also the duties of the finance lessor determined in the contract of finance leasing [as renumbered by Federal Law No. 10-ФЗ, 29 January 2002].

Article 24. Procedure for Settlement of Disputes of Participants of International Finance Leasing Transactions [repealed by Federal Law No. 10-ФЗ, 29 January 2002]

Article 25. Removal of Subject of Finance Leasing from Finance Lessee [repealed by Federal Law No. 10-ФЗ, 29 January 2002]

Article 26. Duties of Finance Lessee in Event of Loss of Subject of Finance Leasing

The loss of the subject of finance leasing or loss by the subject of finance leasing of its functions through the fault of the finance lessee shall not relieve the finance lessee from obligations under the contract of finance leasing unless established otherwise by the contract of finance leasing [as amended by Federal Law No. 10-ФЗ, 29 January 2002].

Chapter III. Economic Foundations of Finance Leasing

Article 27. Economic Content of Contract of Finance Leasing [repealed by Federal Law No. 10-ФЗ, 29 January 2002]

Article 28. Finance Leasing Payments [as amended by Federal Law No. 10-ФЗ, 29 January 2002]

1. By finance leasing payments are understood the total amount of payments under a contract of finance leasing for the entire period of operation of a contract of finance leasing in which there is compensation of expenditures of the finance lessor connected with the acquisition and transfer of the subject of finance leasing to the finance lessee, compensation of expenditures connected with the rendering of other services provided for by the contract of finance leasing, and also revenue of the finance lessor. In the total amount of the contract of finance leasing may be included the purchase price of the subject of finance leasing if the transfer of the right of ownership to the subject of finance leasing to the finance lessee has been provided for in the contract of finance leasing [as amended by Federal Law No. 10-ФЗ, 29 January 2002].

2. The amount and the means for the effectuation and the periodicity of finance leasing payments shall be determined by the contract of finance leasing, taking into account the present Federal Law.

If the finance lessee and the finance lessor effectuate the settlement of accounts with regard to finance leasing payments in products (in kind) produced with the assistance of the subject of finance leasing, the price for such product shall be determined by agreement of the parties to the contract of finance leasing.

Unless provided otherwise by the contract of finance leasing, the amount of finance leasing payments may be changed by agreement of the parties within the periods provided for by the particular contract, but not more often than once every three months [added by Federal Law No. 10-ФЗ, 29 January 2002].

3. [repealed by Federal Law No. 10-ФЗ, 29 January 2002]

3. Obligations of the finance lessee with regard to the payment of finance leasing payments shall ensue from the moment of the commencement of the use by the finance lessee of the subject of finance leasing unless provided otherwise by the contract of finance leasing [as renumbered by Federal Law No. 10-ФЗ, 29 January 2002].

5. [repealed by Federal Law No. 10-ФЗ, 29 January 2002]

4. For the purposes of taxation of profit, finance leasing payments shall be relegated in accordance with legislation on taxes and charges to expenses connected with production and/or realisation [as renumbered and amended by Federal Law No. 10-ФЗ, 29 January 2002].

Article 29. Finance Leasing Payments [repealed by Federal Law No. 10-ФЗ, 29 January 2002]

Article 30. Composition of Remuneration of Finance Lessor [repealed by Federal Law No. 10-ФЗ, 29 January 2002]

Article 31. Right of Parties of Contract of Finance Leasing to Apply Mechanism of Accelerated Amortisation of Subject of Finance Leasing [as amended by Federal Law No. 10-ФЗ, 29 January 2002]

1. The subject of finance leasing transferred to the finance lessee under a contract of finance leasing shall be taken into account on the balance sheet of the finance lessor or finance lessee by mutual agreement.

The parties of a contract of finance leasing shall have the right by mutual agreement to apply accelerated amortisation of the subject of finance leasing [as amended by Federal Law No. 10-ФЗ, 29 January 2002].

2. Amortisation deductions shall be made by the party of the contract of finance leasing on whose balance sheet the subject of finance leasing is situated [as amended by Federal Law No. 10-ФЗ, 29 January 2002].

3. [repealed by Federal Law No. 10-ФЗ, 29 January 2002]

Article 32. Revenue and Profit of Finance Lessor Under Contract of Finance Leasing [repealed by Federal Law No. 10-ФЗ, 29 January 2002]

Article 33. Revaluation of Subject of Finance Leasing and Obligations of Parties When Effectuating Finance Leasing Transaction [repealed by Federal Law No. 10-ФЗ, 29 January 2002]

Article 34. Peculiarities of International Operations Effectuated by Subjects of Finance Leasing

1. The finance lessor shall have the right without a license of the Central Bank of the Russian Federation to effectuate international operations connected with the movement of capital and to attract monetary means from nonresidents of the Russian Federation for the purpose of acquiring the subject of finance leasing for a period of not more than six months (180 days), but not exceeding the period of operation of the contract of finance leasing.

2. Finance leasing companies shall have the right without a license of the Central Bank of the Russian Federation for the effectuation of operations connected with the movement of capital, to pay interest for the use of an instalment payment granted by the seller of the subject of finance leasing irrespective of the period of actual receipt of the subject of finance leasing (current currency operations and operations connected with the movement of capital) [as amended by Federal Law No. 10-ФЗ, 29 January 2002].

3. In order to effectuate international finance leasing the present Federal Law shall establish that:

the bringing into the territory of the Russian Federation and taking out of the territory of the Russian Federation (movement across the customs boundary of the Russian Federation) of a subject of finance leasing for the purpose of the use thereof under a contract of finance leasing for a term of more than six months, and also the payment of the full amount of the contract of finance leasing for a period exceeding six months shall not be operations connected with the movement of capital in accordance with legislation of the Russian Federation on currency control and currency regulation;

[paragraph three repealed by Federal Law No. 10-ФЗ, 29 January 2002]

In the event of the bringing on the territory of the Russian Federation or taking from the territory of the Russian Federation (movement across the customs boundary of the Russian Federation) of a subject of finance leasing all types of customs payments shall be calculated for the full customs value of the property. The customs payments shall be paid [as amended by Federal Law No. 10-ФЗ, 29 January 2002]:

at the moment of the bringing (or taking) of the subject of finance leasing for the amount of the paid portion of the customs value of the property of the property, which shall be confirmed by banking documents;

thereafter the payment of customs payments shall be made simultaneously with the finance leasing payments or within 20 days from the moment of receipt of the finance leasing payments [as amended by Federal Law No. 10-ФЗ, 29 January 2002; the operation of this point is suspended from 1 January to 31 December by Federal Law No. 176-ФЗ, 24 December 2002].

4. The procedure (or system) established by the present Article for the payment of customs payments shall not be considered to be deferral of customs payments or an investment tax credit [as amended by Federal Law No. 10-ФЗ, 29 January 2002; the operation of this point is suspended from 1 January to 31 December by Federal Law No. 176-ФЗ, 24 December 2002].

Article 35. Warning, Limitation, and Suppression of Monopolistic Activity and Unfair Competition

A warning, limitation, and suppression of monopolistic activity and unfair competition on the market of services relating to finance leasing shall be provided by the federal anti-monopoly agency in accordance with anti-monopoly legislation of the Russian Federation.

Chapter IV. State Support of Finance Leasing Activity

Article 36. Measures of State Support of Finance Leasing Activity [as amended by Federal Law No. 10-ФЗ, 29 January 2002]

Measures of State support of activity of finance leasing organisations (or companies, firms) established by laws of the Russian Federation and decisions of the Government of the Russian Federation, and also by decisions by agencies of State power of subjects of the Russian Federation within the limits of their competence, may be:

the working out and realisation of a federal programme for the development of finance leasing activity in the Russian Federation or an individual region as part of the programme for medium-term and long-term socio-economic development of the Russian Federation or a region;

the creation of pledge funds in order to secure banking investments in finance leasing with the use of State property;

the participatory share participation of State capital in the creation of the infrastructure for finance leasing activity in individual special-purpose investment-finance leasing projects;

[paragraph five repealed by Federal Law No. 10-ФЗ, 29 January 2002];

the measures of State protectionism in the sphere of working out, production, and use of scientific-intensive high-technology equipment;

the financing from the federal budget and granting of State guarantees for the purpose of the realisation of finance leasing projects (budget for the development of the Russian Federation), including with the participation of nonresident firms;

the granting of investment credits for the realisation of finance leasing projects;

the granting to banks and other credit institutions in the procedure established by legislation of the Russian Federation of an exemption from the payment of tax on profit received by them from the granting of credits to subjects of finance leasing for a term of not less than three years for the realisation of a contract of finance leasing;

the granting by way of legislation of tax and credit privileges to finance leasing companies (or firms) for the purpose of creating favourable economic conditions for their activity;

the creation, development, formation, and improvement of a normative-legal base ensuring the defence of legal and property interests of participants of finance leasing activity [as amended by Federal Law No. 10-ФЗ, 29 January 2002];

[repealed by Federal Law No. 10-ФЗ, 29 January 2002];

the granting to finance lessees conducting the processing or procurement of agricultural products the right to effectuate finance leasing payments for deliveries of products on the conditions provided for by the contracts of finance leasing;

the relegation of pedigree animals to the subject of finance leasing when effectuating finance leasing operations in the agroindustrial complex;

the creation of the State guarantees fund for export when effectuating international finance leasing of fatherland machines and equipment.

Chapter V. Right of Inspection and Control

Article 37. Right to Inspection Under Finance Leasing Transaction

1. A finance lessor shall have the right to effectuate control over compliance by the finance lessee with the conditions of the contract of finance leasing and other concomitant contracts.

2. The purposes and procedure of inspecting shall be stipulated in the contract of finance leasing and other concomitant contracts between the participants thereof.

3. The finance lessee shall be obliged to ensure the finance lessor unobstructed access to the financial documents and subject of finance leasing.

Article 38. Right of Finance Lessor to Financial Control

1. The finance lessor shall have the right to financial control over the activity of the finance lessee in that part thereof which relates to the subject of finance leasing, the forming of the financial results of the activity of the finance lessee and the fulfilment by the finance lessee of the obligations under the contract of finance leasing.

2. The purpose and procedure of financial control shall be provided for by the contract of finance leasing.

3. The finance lessor shall have the right to send to the finance lessee in written form queries concerning the provision of information necessary in order to effectuate financial control, and the finance lessee shall be obliged to satisfy such queries.

4. [repealed by Federal Law No. 10-ФЗ, 29 January 2002].

Chapter VI. Concluding Provisions

Article 39. Entry into Force of Present Federal Law

The present Federal Law shall enter into force from the day of its official publication.

To propose to the President of the Russian Federation to bring his normative acts into conformity with the present Federal Law.

The Government of the Russian Federation shall within six months bring its normative acts into conformity with the present Federal Law.

FOREIGN INVESTMENT AND INTERNATIONAL
ARBITRATION

FEDERAL LAW ON FOREIGN INVESTMENTS IN THE RUSSIAN FEDERATION

[Federal Law No. 160-Ф3, 9 July 1999,
as amended by Federal Law No. 31-Ф3, 21 March 2002;
and Federal Law No. 117-Ф3, 25 July 2002.
СЗ РФ (1999), no. 28, item 3493; (2002),
no. 12, item 1093; no. 30, item 3034]

The present Federal Law determines the basic guarantees of the rights of foreign investors to investments and revenues and profit received therefrom and the conditions of entrepreneurial activity of foreign investors on the territory of the Russian Federation.

The present Federal Law is directed towards the attraction and effective use in the economy of the Russian Federation of foreign material and financial resources, progressive techniques and technologies, and management experience and ensuring the stability of the conditions of the activity of foreign investors and compliance with the conformity of the legal regime of foreign investments to the norms of international law and international practice of investment cooperation.

Article 1. Relations Regulated by Present Federal Law and Sphere of Application Thereof

1. The present Federal Law shall regulate relations connected with State guarantees of the rights of foreign investors in the event of the effectuation by them of investments on the territory of the Russian Federation.

2. The present Federal Law shall not extend to relations connected with investments of foreign capital in banks and other credit organisations, nor to insurance organisations, which are regulated respectively by legislation of the Russian Federation on banks and banking activity and by legislation of the Russian Federation on insurance.

The present Federal Law also shall not extend to relations connected with the investment of foreign capital in noncommercial organisations for the achievement of a determined socially useful purpose, including educational, philanthropic, scientific, or religious, which shall be regulated by legislation of the Russian Federation on noncommercial organisations.

Article 2. Basic Concepts Used in Present Federal Law

For the purposes of the present Federal Law the following basic concepts shall be used:

foreign investor—foreign juridical person, the civil law capacity of which is determined in accordance with legislation of the State in which it was founded and which has the right in accordance with legislation of the said State to effectuate investments on the territory of the Russian Federation; foreign organisation which is not a juridical person, the civil law capacity of which is determined in accordance with legislation of the State in which it was founded and which has the right in accordance with legislation of the said State to effectuate investments on the territory of the Russian Federation; a foreign citizen, the civil law capacity and dispositive legal capacity of whom is determined in accordance with legislation of the State of his citizenship and who has the right in accordance with the legislation of the said State to effectuate investments on the territory of the Russian Federation; a stateless person who permanently resides beyond the limits of the Russian Federation, the civil law capacity and dispositive legal capacity of whom is determined in accordance with legislation of the State of his permanent place of residence and who has the right in accordance with legislation of the said State to effectuate investments on the territory of the Russian Federation; an international organisation which has the right in conformity with an international treaty of the Russian Federation to effectuate investments on the territory of the Russian Federation; foreign States in accordance with the procedure deteermined by federal laws;

foreign investment—the investing of foreign capital in an object of entrepreneurial activity on the territory of the Russian Federation in the form of objects of civil rights which belong to the foreign investor if such objects of civil rights have not been withdrawn from turnover or have not been limited in turnover in the Russian Federation in accordance with federal legislation, including money, securities (in foreign currency and in currency of the Russian Federation), other property, property rights having the monetary value of exclusive rights to the results of intellectual activity (intellectual property), and also services and information;

direct foreign investment—the acquisition by a foreign investor of not less than 10% of a participatory share(s) (or contribution) in the charter capital of a commercial organisation created or newly created on the territory of the Russian Federation in the form of an economic partnership or society in accordance with civil legislation of the Russian Federation; the investing of capital in the basic funds of a branch of a foreign juridical person created on the territory of the Russian Federation; the effectuation on the territory of the Russian Federation by a foreign investor as lessor of a finance lease (finance leasing) of the equipment specified in Sections XVI and XVII of the Goods Nomenclature of Foreign Activity of the Commonwealth of Independent States (ТН ВЭД СНГ) with a customs value of not less than 1 million rubles;

investment project—substantiation of the economic advisability and the amount and periods for the effectuation of a direct foreign investment including design-estimate documentation which has been worked out in accordance with standards provided for by legislation of the Russian Federation;

priority investment project—an investment project, the total volume of foreign investments in which constitutes not less than 1 billion rubles (or not less than the equivalent amount in foreign currency at the exchange rate of the Central Bank of the Russian Federation on the day of entry into force of the present Federal Law), or an investment project in which the minimum participatory share (or contribution) of foreign investors in the charter (or contributed) capital comprises not less than 100 million rubles (or not less than the equivalent amount in foreign currency at the exchange rate of the Central Bank of the Russian Federation on the day of entry into force of the present Federal Law) included in a List to be confirmed by the Government of the Russian Federation;

period of recoupment of investment project—the period from the day of commencement of the financing of an investment project with the use of a direct foreign investment until the day when the difference between the accumulated amount of net profit with amortisation deductions and the amount of investment expenditures of a commercial organisation with foreign investments or the branch of a foreign juridical person or lessor under a contract of finance lease (finance leasing) acquires a positive significance;

reinvestment—the effectuation of capital investments in objects of entrepreneurial activity on the territory of the Russian Federation at the expense of revenues or profit of a foreign investor or commercial organisation with foreign investments which have been received by them from the foreign investments;

aggregate tax load—settlement summary amount of monetary means subject to payment in the form of import customs duties (except for customs duties caused by the application of measures relating to the defence of economic interests of the Russian Federation in the event of the effectuation of foreign trade in goods in accordance with legislation of the Russian Federation), federal taxes (except excises and value-added tax on goods produced on the territory of the Russian Federation), and contributions to State extrabudgetary funds (except for contributions to the Pension Fund of the Russian Federation) by a foreign investor and commercial organisation with foreign investments effectuating an investment project at the expense of foreign investments at the moment of the commencement of the financing of the investment project.

Article 3. Legal Regulation of Foreign Investments on Territory of Russian Federation

1. The legal regulation of foreign investments on the territory of the Russian Federation shall be effectuated by the present Federal Law, other federal laws, and other normative legal acts of the Russian Federation, and also by international treaties of the Russian Federation.

2. Subjects of the Russian Federation shall have the right to adopt laws and other normative legal acts regulating foreign investments with regard to questions relegated to their jurisdiction, and also to the joint jurisdiction of the Russian Federation and subjects of the Russian Federation, in accordance with the present Federal Law and other federal laws.

Article 4. Legal Regime of Activity of Foreign Investors and Commercial Organisations with Foreign Investments

1. The legal regime of the activity of foreign investors and the use of profit received from investments may not be less favourable than the legal regime of activity and the use of profit received from investments granted to Russian investors, with the exceptions established by federal laws.

2. Exceptions of a limited character for foreign investors may be established by federal laws only to the extent that this is necessary for the purposes of defence of the foundations of the constitutional system, morality, public health, and the rights and legal interests of other persons and ensuring the defence of the country and the security of the State.

Exceptions of an incentive character in the form of privileges for foreign investors may be established in the interests of the socio-economic development of the Russian Federation. The types of privileges and procedure for granting them shall be established by legislation of the Russian Federation.

3. A branch of a foreign juridical person created on the territory of the Russian Federation shall fulfil part of the functions or all of the functions, including the function of representation, in the name of the foreign juridical person which created it (hereinafter: head organisation) on condition that the purposes of the creation and activity of the head organisation shall have a commercial character and the head organisation bears direct property responsibility for obligations accepted by it in connection with the conducting of the said activity on the territory of the Russian Federation.

4. Subsidiary and dependent societies of a commercial organisation with foreign investments shall not enjoy the legal defence, guarantees, and privileges established by the present Federal Law in the event of the effectuation by them of entrepreneurial activity on the territory of the Russian Federation.

5. A foreign investor, commercial organisation with foreign investments created on the territory of the Russian Federation in which the foreign investor(s) possess not less than 10% of the participatory share(s) (or contribution) in the charter (or contributed) capital of the said organisation shall in the event of the effectuation of reinvesting by them enjoy in full the legal defence, guarantees, and privileges established by the present Federal Law.

6. A Russian commercial organisation shall receive the status of a commercial organisation with foreign investments from the day of the entry of participants of the foreign investor into the composition thereof. From this day the commercial organisation with foreign investments and the foreign investor shall enjoy the legal defence, guarantees, and privileges established by the present Federal Law.

A commercial organisation shall lose the status of a commercial organisation with foreign investments from the day of withdrawal of the foreign investor from the composition of the participants thereof (when there are several foreign investors in the composition of its participants, in the event of the withdrawal of all foreign investors). From this day the said commercial organisation shall lose the legal defence, guarantees, and privileges established by the present Federal Law.

Article 5. Guarantee of Legal Defence of Activity of Foreign Investors on Territory of Russian Federation

1. Full and unconditional defence of the rights and interests which are ensured by the present Federal Law, other federal laws, and other normative legal acts of the Russian Federation, and also international treaties of the Russian Federation, shall be granted to a foreign investor on the territory of the Russian Federation.

2. A foreign investor shall have the right to compensation of losses caused to it as a result of the illegal actions (or failure to act) of State agencies, agencies of local self-government, or officials of these agencies in accordance with civil legislation of the Russian Federation.

Article 6. Guarantee of Use by Foreign Investor of Various Forms of Effectuation of Investments on Territory of Russian Federation

A foreign investor shall have the right to effectuate investments on the territory of the Russian Federation in any forms not prohibited by legislation of the Russian Federation.

The investing of capital in the charter (or contributed) capital of a commercial organisation with foreign investments shall be valued in accordance with legislation of the Russian Federation.

The valuation of the investing of capital shall be effectuated in the currency of the Russian Federation.

Article 7. Guarantee of Transfer of Rights and Duties of Foreign Investor to Another Person

1. A foreign investor by virtue of a contract shall have the right to transfer his rights (or assign demands) and duties (or transfer a debt), and on the basis of a law or decision of a court shall be obliged to transfer his rights (or assign demands) and duties (or transfer a debt) to another person in accordance with civil legislation of the Russian Federation.

2. If a foreign State or State agency empowered by it makes payment to the benefit of a foreign investor under a guarantee (or contract of insurance) granted to a foreign investor with respect to investments effectuated by it on the territory of the Russian Federation, and to this foreign State or State agency empowered by it the rights (or demands) of the foreign investor to the said investments pass (or are assigned), then in the Russian Federation such a transfer of rights (or assignment of demand) shall be deemed to be lawful.

Article 8. Guarantee of Contributory Compensation in Event of Nationalisation and Requisition of Property of Foreign Investor or Commercial Organisation with Foreign Investments

1. The property of a foreign investor or commercial organisation with foreign investments shall not be subject to compulsory seizure, including nationalisation or requisition, except for instances and on the grounds which have been established by a federal law or international treaty of the Russian Federation.

2. In the event of requisition to a foreign investor or commercial organisation with foreign investments shall be paid the value of the requisitioned property. In the event of the termination of the operation of the circumstances in connection with which the requisition was performed, the foreign investor or commercial organisation with foreign investments shall have the right to demand in a judicial proceeding the return of the preserved property, but in so doing shall be obliged to return the amount of contributory compensation received by them, taking into account the loss from the reduction of the value of the property.

In the event of nationalisation to a foreign investor or commercial organisation with foreign investments shall be compensated the value of the property nationalised and other losses. Disputes concerning compensation of losses shall be settled in the procedure provided for by Article 10 of the present Federal Law.

Article 9. Guarantee Against Unfavourable Change for Foreign Investor or Commercial Organisation with Foreign Investments of Legislation of Russian Federation

1. In the event new federal laws and other normative legal acts of the Russian Federation enter into force which change the amounts of import customs duties

(except for customs duties caused by the application of measures relating to the defence of the economic interests of the Russian Federation when effectuating foreign trade in goods in accordance with legislation of the Russian Federation), federal taxes (except for excises and value-added tax on goods produced on the territory of the Russian Federation) and contributions to State extrabudgetary funds (except for contributions to the Pension Fund of the Russian Federation), or changes and additions are made in prevailing federal laws and other normative legal acts of the Russian Federation which lead to an increase of the aggregate tax load on the activity of a foreign investor or commercial organisation with foreign investments with regard to the realisation of priority investments projects, or they establish a regime of prohibitions and limitations with respect to foreign investments in the Russian Federation in comparison with the aggregate tax load and regime which operated in accordance with federal laws and other normative legal acts of the Russian Federation on the day of the commencement of the financing of a priority investment project at the expense of foreign investments, then such new federal laws and other normative legal acts of the Russian Federation, and also the changes in and additions made in prevailing federal laws and other normative legal acts of the Russian Federation, shall not be applied during the periods specified in point 2 of the present Article with respect to the foreign investor and commercial organisation with foreign investments on condition that the goods imported to the customs territory of the Russian Federation by the foreign investor and commercial organisation with foreign investments are used for the special-purpose designation in order to realise the priority investment projects.

The provisions of paragraph one of the present point shall extend to a commercial organisation with foreign investments if the participatory share(s) (or contribution) of foreign investors in the charter (or contributed) capital of such organisation comprise more than 25%, and also to a commercial organisation with foreign investments realising a priority investment project irrespective of the participatory share(s) (or contribution) of foreign investors to the charter (or contributed) capital of such organisation.

2. Stability for a foreign investor effectuating an investment project and the conditions and regime specified in point 1 of the present Article shall be guaranteed for the period of recoupment of the investment project, but not more than seven years from the day of commencement of the financing of the said project at the expense of foreign investments. Differentiation of the period of recoupment of investment projects shall, depending upon their types, be determined in the procedure established by the Government of the Russian Federation.

3. In exceptional instances in the event of the realisation by a foreign investor and commercial organisation with foreign investments of priority investment projects in the sphere of production or creation of a transport or other infrastructure with a total amunt of foreign investments of not less than 1 billion rubles (or

not less than the equivalent amount in foreign currency at the exchange rate of the Central Bank of the Russian Federation on the day of entry into force of the present Federal Law), the period of recoupment of which exceeds seven years, the Government of the Russian Federation shall adopt a decision concerning extension for the said foreign investor and commercial organisation with foreign investments of the period of operation of the conditions and regime specified in point 1 of the present Article.

4. The provisions of point 1 of the present Article shall not extend to changes and additions which are made in legislative acts of the Russian Federation or adopted new federal laws and other normative legal acts of the Russian Federation for the purpose of defence of the foundations of the constitutional system, morality, public health, rights and legal interests of other persons, and ensuring the defence of the country and security of the State.

5. The Government of the Russian Federation shall:

establish the criteria for evaluating changes of conditions for the recovery of import customs duties, federal taxes, and contributions to State extrabudgetary funds, and the regime of prohibitions and limitations for the effectuation of foreign investments on the territory of the Russian Federation which are unfavourable for a foreign investor or commercial organisation with foreign investments;

confirm the procedure for the registration of priority investment projects by a federal agency of executive power specified in Article 24 of the present Federal Law;

effectuate control over the performance by the foreign investor and commercial organisation with foreign investments of obligations assumed by them with regard to the realisation of priority investment projects within the periods specified in points 2 and 3 of the present Article.

In the event of the failure of the foreign investor or commercial organisation with foreign investments to perform obligations specified in paragraph one of the present point, they shall be deprived of the privileges granted to them in accordance with the present Article. The amount of monetary means not paid as a result of the granting of the said privileges shall be subject to return in the procedure established by legislation of the Russian Federation.

Article 10. Guarantee of Ensuring Proper Settlement of Dispute Which Arose in Connection with Effectuation of Investments and Entrepreneurial Activity on Territory of Russian Federation by Foreign Investor

A dispute of a foreign investor which has arisen in connection with the effectuation of investments and entrepreneurial activity on the territory of the Russian Federation shall be settled in accordance with international treaties of the Russian Federation and federal laws in a court or arbitrazh court or in international arbitration (or arbitration court).

Article 11. Guarantee of Use on Territory of Russian Federation and Transfer Beyond Limits of Russian Federation of Revenues, Profit, and Other Lawfully Receivd Monetary Amounts

A foreign investor shall after payment of the taxes and charges provided for by legislation of the Russian Federation have the right to free use of revenues and profits on the territory of the Russian Federation for reinvesting in compliance with the provisions of Article 4(2) of the present Federal Law or for other purposes which are not contrary to legislation of the Russian Federation and to unhindered transfer beyond the limits of the Russian Federation of revenues and other lawfully received monetary amounts in foreign currency in connection with investments previously effectuated by him, including:

revenues from investments received in the form of profit, dividends, interest, and other revenues;

monetary amounts in performance of obligations of a commercial organisation with foreign investments or a foreign juridical person which opened its branch on the territory of the Russian Federation with regard to contracts and other transactions;

monetary amounts received by a foreign investor in connection with the liquidation of a commercial organisation with foreign investments or branch of a foreign juridical person or alienation of invested property, property rights, and exclusive rights to the results of intellectual activity;

contributory compensation provided for by Article 8 of the present Federal Law.

Article 12. Guarantee of Right of Foreign Investor to Unhindered Export Beyond Limits of Russian Federation of Property and Information in Documentary Form or in Form of Entry of Electronic Carriers Which Were Initially Imported to Territory of Russian Federation as Foreign Investment

A foreign investor which initially imported to the territory of the Russian Federation property and information in documentary form or in the form of entries on electronic carriers as a foreign investment shall have the right to unhindered (without quotas, licensing, and application to it of other measures of non-tariff regulation of foreign trade activity) export of the said property and information beyond the limits of the Russian Federation.

Article 13. Guarantee of Right of Foreign Investor to Acquisition of Securities

A foreign investor shall have the right to acquire stocks and other securities of Russian commercial organisations and State securities in accordance with legislation of the Russian Federation on securities.

Article 14. Guarantee of Participation of Foreign Investor in Privatisation

A foreign investor may participate in the privatisation of objects of State and municipal ownership by means of the acquisition of the rights of ownership to State and municipal property or participatory share(s) (or contribution) to charter (or contributed) capital of organisation being privatised on the conditions and in the procedure which have been established by legislation of the Russian Federation on privatisation of State and municipal property.

Article 15. Guarantee of Granting to Foreign Investor of Right to Land Plots, Other Natural Resources, Buildings, Installations, and Other Immoveable Property

The acquisition by a foreign investor of the right to land plots, other natural resources, buildings, installations, and other immoveable property shall be effectuated in accordance with legislation of the Russian Federation and legislation of subjects of the Russian Federation.

The right of lease of a land plot may be acquired by a commercial organisation with foreign investments at a public sale (or auction, competition) unless provided otherwise by legislation of the Russian Federation.

Article 16. Privileges to be Granted to Foreign Investor or Commercial Organisation with Foreign Investments With Regard to Payment of Customs Payments

Privileges with regard to the payment of customs duties shall be granted to foreign investors and commercial organisations with foreign investments in the event of the effectuation by them of a priority investment project in accordance with customs legislation of the Russian Federation and legislation of the Russian Federation on taxes and charges.

Article 17. Privileges and Guarantees to be Granted to Foreign Investor by Subjects of Russian Federation and Agencies of Local Self-Government

Subjects of the Russian Federation and agencies of local self-government may within the limits of their competence grant to a foreign investor privileges and guarantees to effectuate the financing and render other forms of support for the investment project effectuated by a foreign investor at the expense of means of the budgets of subjects of the Russian Federation and local budgets, and also extra-budgetary means.

Article 18. Anti-Monopoly Legislation of Russian Federation and Compliance with Good-Faith Competition by Foreign Investor

A foreign investor shall be obliged to comply with anti-monopoly legislation of the Russian Federation and not permit unfair competition and restrictive business practices, including by means of the creation on the territory of the Russian Federation of a commercial organisation with foreign investments or branch of a foreign juridical person for the production of any good enjoying increased demand and then self-liquidation for the purposes of putting forward on the market an analogous good of foreign origin, and also by means of an ill-intentioned agreement concerning prices or distribution of markets for the sale of the good or concerning participation in a public sale (or auction, competition).

Article 19. Property Insurance Effectuated by Commercial Organisation with Foreign Investments and Head Organisation of Branch of Foreign Juridical Person

Property insurance of the risk of loss (or perishing), shortage, or damage to property, risk of civil responsibility and entrepreneurial risk shall be effectuated by a commercial organisation with foreign investments at its discretion, and by the branch of a foreign juridical person, at the discretion of the head organisation, unless provided otherwise by legislation of the Russian Federation.

Article 20. Creation and Liquidation of Commercial Organisation with Foreign Investments

1. The creation and liquidation of a commercial organisation with foreign investments shall be effectuated on the conditions and in the procedure which has been provided for by the Civil Code of the Russian Federation and other federal laws, with the exceptions which may be established by federal laws in accordance with Article 4(2) of the present Law.

2. Juridical persons which are commercial organisations with foreign investments shall be subject to State registration the procedure determined by the Federal Law 'On the State Registration of Juridical Persons' [as amended by Federal Law No. 31-ФЗ, 21 March 2002, and by Federal Law No. 117-ФЗ, 25 July 2002].

Article 21. Creation and Liquidation of Branch of Foreign Juridical Person

The branch of a foreign juridical person shall be created for the purposes of the effectuation on the territory of the Russian Federation of activity which the head organisation effectuates beyond the limits of the Russian Federation and shall be liquidated on the basis of a decision of the foreign juridical person-head organisation.

State control over the creation, activity, and liquidation of a branch of a foriegn juridical person shall be effectuated by means of the accreditation thereof in the procedure determined by the Government of the Russian Federation.

The federal agency of executive power specified in Article 24 of the present Federal Law shall effectuate the accreditation of the branch of a foreign juridical person.

The branch of a foreign juridical person may be refused accreditation for the purposes of defence of the constitutional system, morality, public health, the rights and interests of other persons, ensuring defence of the country and the security of the State.

Article 22. Requirements for Statute on Branch of Foreign Juridical Person

1. A head organisation shall submit to the federal agency of executive power specified in Article 24 of the present Federal Law the Statute on the branch of the foreign juridical person and other documents, a List of and the requirements for the content of which, taking into account points 2 and 3 of the present Article, shall be confirmed by the Government of the Russian Federation.

2. The Statute on the branch of a foreign juridical person must specify the name of the branch and its head organisation, the organisational-legal form of the head organisation, the location of the branch on the territory of the Russian Federation and legal address of its head organisation, the purposes for the creation and the types of activity of the branch, the composition, amount, and periods for investing capital in the basic funds of the branch, and the procedure for management of the branch. Other information reflecting the peculiarities of the activity of the branch of a foreign juridical person on the territory of the Russian Federation and not contrary to legislation of the Russian Federation may be included in the Statute on the branch of a foreign juridical person.

3. Investing of capital in the basic funds of the branch of a foreign juridical person shall be valued by the head organisation on the basis of internal prices or world prices. Valuation of the investing of capital shall be effectuated in the currency of the Russian Federation. The increase of the value valuation of the investing of capital in the basic funds of the branch of a foreign juridical person must be specified in the Statute on the branch of a foreign juridical person.

4. The branch of a foreign juridical person shall have the right to effectuate entrepreneurial activity on the territory of the Russian Federation from the day of its accreditation.

The branch of a foreign juridical person shall terminate entrepreneurial activity on the territory of the Russian Federation from the day of deprivation of the accreditation thereof.

Article 23. Working Out and Realisation of State Policy in Domain of Foreign Investments

In accordance with the Federal Constitutional Law on the Government of the Russian Federation, the Government of the Russian Federation shall work out and realise State policy in the sphere of international investment cooperation.

The Government of the Russian Federation shall:

determine the advisability of introducing prohibitions and limitations on the effectuation of foreign investments on the territory of the Russian Federation and work out draft laws concerning lists of the said prohibitions and limitations;

determine the measures relating to control over the activity of foreign investors in the Russian Federation;

confirm the List of priority investment projects specified in Article 2 of the present Federal Law;

work out and ensure the realisation of federal programmes for attracting foreign investments;

attract investment credits of international financial organisations and foreign States for financing of the Development Budget of the Russian Federation and investment projects of federal significance;

effectuate interaction with subjects of the Russian Federation with regard to questions of international investment cooperation;

effectuate control over the preparation and conclusion of investment agreements concerning the realisation by them of large-scale investment projects;

effectuate control over the preparation and conclusion of international treaties of the Russian Federation on encouraging and mutual defence of investments.

Article 24. Federal Agency of Executive Power With Regard to Coordination of Attraction of Direct Foreign Investments

The Government of the Russian Federation shall determine the federal agency of executive power responsible for the coordination of attracting direct foreign investments to the economy of the Russian Federation.

Article 25. Deeming to Have Lost Force Previously Adopted Legislative Acts of Russian Federation and Individual Provisions Thereof in Connection With Adoption of Present Federal Law

In connection with the adoption of the present Federal Law, to deem to have lost force:

the Law of the RSFSR on Foreign Investments in the RSFSR (Ведомости Съезда народных депутатов РСФСР и Совета РСФСР (1991), no. 29, item 1008);

the Decree of the Supreme Soviet of the RSFSR 'On the Introduction into Operation of the Law of the RSFSR on Foreign Investments in the RSFSR' (Ведомости Съезда народных депутатов РСФСР и Верховного Совета РСФСР (1991), no. 29, item 1009);

Article 6 of the Federal Law on Making Changes in and Additions to Legislative Acts of the Russian Federation in Connection with the Adoption of the Laws of the Russian Federation on Standardisation, On Ensuring the Unity of Measurements, and On Certification of Products and Services (Собрание законодательства Российской Федерации Article 1(4) of the Federal

Law on Making Changes in and Additions to Laws and Other Legal Acts of the Russian Federation in Connection with the Adoption of the Federal Constitutional Law on Arbitrazh Courts in the Russian Federation and the Code of Arbitrazh Procedure of the Russian Federation (Собрание законодательства Российской Федерации (1997), no. 47, item 5341).

Article 26. Bringing Legislation of Russian Federation into Conformity with Present Federal Law

1. To propose to the President of the Russian Federation and to the Government of the Russian Federation to bring their normative legal acts into conformity with the present Federal Law.

2. The Government of the Russian Federation shall submit proposals in the established procedure to the State Duma of the Federal Assembly of the Russian Federation concerning the making of changes in and additions to legislative acts of the Russian Federation which arise from the present Federal Law.

Article 27. Bringing Statutes of Branches of Foreign Juridical Persons Created on Territory of Russian Federation into Conformity with Present Federal Law

Head organisations whose branches have been created on the territory of the Russian Federation before the entry into force of the present Federal Law shall be obliged to:

bring the Statutes on the branches of foreign juridical persons into conformity with the present Federal Law within six months from the day of the entry thereof into force;

conduct the accreditation of branches of foreign juridical persons within one year from the day of entry into force of the present Federal Law.

Article 28. Entry of Present Federal Law into Force

The present Federal Law shall enter into force from the day of official publication thereof.

FEDERAL LAW ON INVESTMENT ACTIVITY IN THE RUSSIAN FEDERATION EFFECTUATED IN THE FORM OF CAPITAL INVESTMENTS

[Federal Law No. 39-ФЗ, 25 February 1999,
as amended by Federal Law No. 22-ФЗ,
2 January 2000. СЗ РФ (1999), no. 9, item 1096;
(2000), no. 2, item 143]

Chapter I	General Provisions	825
Chapter II	Legal and Economic Foundations of Investment Activity Effectuated in Form of Capital Investments	828
Chapter III	State Regulation of Investment Activity Effectuated in Form of Capital Investments	829
Chapter IV	Foundations of Regulation of Investment Activity Effectuated in Form of Capital Investments by Agencies of Local Self-Government	836
Chapter V	Concluding Provisions	838

The present Federal Law determines the legal and economic foundations of investment activity effectuated in the form of capital investments on the territory of the Russian Federation, and also establishes guarantees of the equal defence of the rights, interests, and property of the subjects of investment activity effectuated in the form of capital investments irrespective of the forms of ownership.

Chapter I. General Provisions

Article 1. Basic Concepts

For the purposes of the present Federal Law the following basic concepts are used:

investments: monetary means, securities, other property, including property rights, other rights having monetary value contributed to objects of entrepreneurial and/or other activity for the purposes of receiving profit and/or achieving another useful effect;

investment activity: the investing of investments and the effectuation of practical actions for the purposes of receiving profit and/or achieving another useful effect;

capital investments: investments in the basic capital (or basic means), including expenditures for new construction, expansion, conversion, and technical re-equipping of operating enterprises, the acquisition of machines, equipment, tools, inventory, and design-prospecting work and other expenditures;

investment project: substantiation of the economic advisability, amount, and periods for the effectuation of capital investments, including necessary design-estimate documentation worked out in accordance with legislation of the Russian Federation and standards (or norms, rules) confirmed in the established procedure, and also a description of the practical actions relating to the effectuation of the investments (business plan);

priority investment project: an investment project, the total amount of capital investments in which corresponds to the requirements of legislation of the Russian Federation included in the List confirmed by the Government of the Russian Federation [added by Federal Law No. 22-ФЗ, 2 January 2000];

period of recoupment of investment project: the period from the day of commencement of the financing of an investment project up to the day when the difference between the accumulation of the amount of net profit with amortisation deductions and the amount of investment expenditures acquires positive significance [added by Federal Law No. 22-ФЗ, 2 January 2000];

aggregate tax load: account settlement total amount of monetary means subject to payment in the form of import customs duties (except for special types of duties caused by the application of measures with regard to the defence of the economic interests of the Russian Federation when effectuating foreign trade in goods in accordance with legislation of the Russian Federation), federal taxes (except for excises and value-added tax on goods produced on the territory of the Russian Federation), and contributions to State extrabudgetary funds (except for contributions to the Pension Fund of the Russian Federation) by the investor effectuating the investment project on the day of commencement of the financing of the investment project [added by Federal Law No. 22-ФЗ, 2 January 2000].

Article 2. Relations Regulated by Present Federal Law

The operation of the present Federal Law shall extend to relations connected with investment activity effectuated in the form of capital investments.

The present Federal Law shall not extend to relations connected with the making of investments in banks and other credit organisations, nor also to insurance organisations, which shall be regulated respectively by legislation of the Russian Federation on banks and banking activity and by legislation of the Russian Federation on insurance [added by Federal Law No. 22-ФЗ, 2 January 2000].

Article 3. Objects of Capital Investments

1. Various types of newly created and/or modernised property, with the exceptions established by federal laws, which are in private, State, municipal and other

forms of ownership shall be objects of capital investments in the Russian Federation.

2. Capital investments shall be prohibited in objects whose creation and use does not correspond to legislation of the Russian Federation and to standards (or norms and rules) confirmed in the established procedure.

Article 4. Subjects of Investment Activity Effectuated in Form of Capital Investments

1. Investors, customers, independent-work contractors, and users of the objects of capital investments, and other persons shall be the subjects of investment activity effectuated in the form of capital investments (hereinafter: subjects of investment activity).

2. Investors shall effectuate capital investments on the territory of the Russian Federation with the use of own and/or attracted means in accordance with legislation of the Russian Federation. Natural and juridical persons created on the basis of a contract on joint activity and not having the status of a juridical person, associations of juridical persons, State agencies, agencies of local self-government, and also foreign subjects of entrepreneurial activity (hereinafter: foreign investors) may be investors.

3. Customers shall be natural and juridical persons empowered by investors which effectuate the realisation of investment projects. In so doing they shall not interfere in entrepreneurial and/or other activity of other subjects of investment activity unless provided otherwise by the contract between them. Investors may be customers.

A customer who is not an investor shall be endowed with the rights of possession, use, and disposition of capital investments in the period and within the limits of the powers which have been established by the contract and/or State contract in accordance with legislation of the Russian Federation.

4. Independent-work contractors shall be natural and juridical persons who fulfil work under an independent-work contract and/or State contract concluded with the customers in accordance with the Civil Code of the Russian Federation. Independent-work contractors shall be obliged to have a license for the effectuation by them of those types of activity which are subject to licensing in accordance with a federal law.

5. The users of objects of capital investments shall be natural and juridical persons, including foreign, and also State agencies, agencies of local self-government, foreign States, international associations, and organisations for which the said objects are created. Investors may be the users of objects of capital investments.

6. A subject of investment activity shall have the right to combine the functions of two and more subjects unless established by the contract and/or State contract concluded between them.

Article 5. Activity of Foreign Investors on Territory of Russian Federation

Relations connected with investment activity effectuated in the form of capital investments by foreign investors on the territory of the Russian Federation shall be regulated by international treaties of the Russian Federation, the Civil Code of the Russian Federation, the present Federal Law, other federal laws and other normative legal acts of the Russian Federation. If other rules than those provided for by the present Federal Law have been established by an international treaty of the Russian Federation, the rules of the international treaty shall apply.

Chapter II. Legal and Economic Foundations of Investment Activity Effectuated in Form of Capital Investments

Article 6. Rights of Investors

Investors shall have equal rights to:
the effectuation of investment activity in the form of capital investments, with the exceptions established by federal laws;
autonomous determination of the amounts and orientations of capital investments, and also the conclusion of contracts with other subjects of investment activity, in accordance with the Civil Code of the Russian Federation;
the possession, use, and disposition of objects of capital investments and the results of the effectuated capital investments;
the transfer under a contract and/or State contract of their rights to the effectuation of capital investments and to the results thereof to natural and juridical persons, State agencies, and agencies of local self-government in accordance with legislation of the Russian Federation;
the effectuation of control over the special-purpose use of means directed towards capital investments;
the combining own and attracted means with the means of other investors for the purposes of joint effectuation of capital investments on the basis of a contract and in accordance with legislation of the Russian Federation;
the effectuation of other rights provided for by the contract and/or State contract in accordance with legislation of the Russian Federation.

Article 7. Duties of Subjects of Investment Activity

Subjects of investment activity shall be obliged to:
effectuate investment activity in accordance with international treaties of the Russian Federation, federal laws, and other normative legal acts of the Russian Federation, laws of subjects of the Russian Federation, and other normative legal

acts of subjects of the Russian Federation, and also with standards (or norms and rules) confirmed in the established procedure;

execute demands presented by State agencies and officials thereof which are not contrary to norms of legislation of the Russian Federation;

use means directed towards capital investments for their special-purpose designation.

Article 8. Relations between Subjects of Investment Activity

1. Relations between subjects of investment activity shall be effectuated on the basis of a contract and/or State contract concluded between them in accordance with the Civil Code of the Russian Federation.

2. The conditions of contracts and/or State contracts concluded between subjects of investment activity shall retain their force for the entire period of their operation, except for instances provided for by the present Federal Law and other federal laws.

Article 9. Sources of Financing of Capital Investments

The financing of capital investments shall be effectuated by investors at the expense of own and/or attracted means.

Article 10. Interaction of Agencies of State Power of Russian Federation, Agencies of State Power of Subjects of Russian Federation and Agencies of Local Self-Government in Investment Activity Effectuated in Form of Capital Investments

Agencies of State power of the Russian Federation, agencies of State power of subjects of the Russian Federation, and agencies of local self-government by agreement between them may effectuate interaction in investment activity effectuated in the form of capital investments in accordance with the Constitution of the Russian Federation, the present Federal Law, and other federal laws.

Chapter III. State Regulation of Investment Activity Effectuated in Form of Capital Investments

Article 11. Forms and Methods of State Regulation of Investment Activity Effectuated in Form of Capital Investments

1. State regulation of investment activity effectuated in the form of capital investments shall be effectuated by agencies of State power of the Russian Federation and by agencies of State power of subjects of the Russian Federation.

2. State regulation of investment activity effectuated in the form of capital investments shall provide for:

(1) the creation of favourable conditions for the development of investment activity effectuated in the form of capital investments by means of:

improvement of the system of taxes, mechanism of calculating amortisation and the use of amortisation deductions;

establishment for subjects of investment activity of special tax regimes not of an individual character;

defence of the interests of investors;

granting to subjects of investment activity privileged conditions for the use of land and other natural resources which are not contrary to legislation of the Russian Federation;

expansion of the use of means of the populace and other extrabudgetary sources for the financing of housing construction and the construction of objects of socio-cultural designation;

creation and development of the network of informational-analytical centres effectuating the regular conducting of ratings and the publication of rating evaluations of subjects of investment activity;

adoption of anti-monopoly measures;

expansion of the possibilities of the use of pledges when effectuating the granting of credits;

development of finance leasing in the Russian Federation;

conducting of the revaluation of basic funds in accordance with the rates of inflation;

creation of possibilities for the formation of own investment funds by subjects of investment activity;

(2) direct participation of the State in investment activity effectuated in the form of capital investments by means of:

working out, confirmation, and financing of investment projects effectuated by the Russian Federation jointly with foreign States, and also investment projects to be financed at the expense of means of the federal budget and means of the budgets of subjects of the Russian Federation;

formation of the List of construction sites and objects of technical re-equipping for federal State needs and financing thereof at the expense of means of the federal budget. The procedure for the formation of the said List shall be determined by the Government of the Russian Federation;

granting on a competitive basis of State guarantees with regard to investment projects at the expense of means of the federal budget (Development Budget of the Russian Federation), and also at the expense of means of budgets of subjects of the Russian Federation. The procedure for the granting of State guarantees at the expense of means of the federal budget (Development Budget of the Russian Federation) shall be determined by the Government of the Russian Federation at the expense of means of the budgets of subjects of the Russian Federation, by agencies of executive power of the respective subjects of the Russian Federation;

placing on a competitive basis means of the federal budget (Development Budget of the Russian Federation) and means of the budgets of the subjects of the Russian

Federation for the financing of investment projects. The placement of the said means shall be effectuated on repayment and fixed-term bases with the payment of interests for the use thereof in the amounts determined by the federal law on the federal budget for the respective year and/or the law on the budget of the subject of the Russian Federation, or on conditions of consolidation in State ownership of a respective part of the stocks of a joint-stock society being created which shall be realised within a determined period on the securities market with the receipts from the realisation being directed to the revenues of the respective budgets. The procedure for the placement on a competitive basis of the means of the federal budget (Development Budget of the Russian Federation) shall be determined by the Government of the Russian Federation, and means of the budgets of subjects of the Russian Federation, by agencies of executive power of the respective subjects of the Russian Federation;

conducting an expert examination of investment projects in accordance with legislation of the Russian Federation;

defence of Russian organisations against the deliveries of morally obsolete and material-intensive, energy-intensive, or nonscientific-intensive technologies, equipment, construction designs, and materials (including when realising the Development Budget of the Russian Federation);

working out and confirmation of standards (or norms and rules) and effectuation of control over compliance therewith;

issuance of bond loans and guaranteed special-purpose loans;

involvement in the investment process of temporarily suspended and shut-down construction sites and objects in State ownership;

granting of concessions to Russian and foreign investors with regard to the results of public sales (or auctions and competitions) in accordance with legislation of the Russian Federation.

3. State regulation of investment activity effectuated in the form of capital investments may be effectuated with the use of other forms and methods in accordance with legislation of the Russian Federation.

Article 12. State Regulation of Investment Activity Effectuated in Form of Capital Investments under Conditions of Arising of Extraordinary Situations

Under conditions of the arising of extraordinary situations on the territory of the Russian Federation the activity of subjects of investment activity which prove to be in the zone of the extraordinary situation shall be effectuated in accordance with legislation of the Russian Federation.

Article 13. Procedure for Adoption of Decisions on Effectuation of State Capital Investments

1. Decisions concerning the effectuation of State capital investments shall be adopted by agencies of State power in accordance with legislation of the Russian Federation.

2. Expenses for the financing of State capital investments shall be provided:

in the federal budget—on condition that these expenses are part of the expenses for the realisation of the respective federal special-purpose programmes, and also on the basis of proposals of the President of the Russian Federation or Government of the Russian Federation;

in budgets of subjects of the Russian Federation—on condition that these expenses are part of the expenses for the realisation of the respective regional special-purpose programmes, and also on the basis of proposals of agencies of executive power of the subjects of the Russian Federation.

3. The working out, consideration, and confirmation of investment projects financed at the expense of means of the federal budget shall be in accordance with legislation of the Russian Federation in the procedure provided for federal special-purpose programmes. The Lists of investment projects financed at the expense of means of the federal budget shall form federal investment programmes.

4. The procedure for financing investment projects at the expense of means of the federal budget shall be determined by the Government of the Russian Federation, and the procedure for financing investment projects at the expense of means of the budgets of subjects of the Russian Federation, by agencies of executive power of the respective subjects of the Russian Federation. The Lists of investment projects financed at the expense of means of the budgets of subjects of the Russian Federation shall form regional investment programmes.

5. Decisions concerning the use of means of the federal budget for financing of investment projects and/or investment programmes effectuated by the Russian Federation jointly with foreign States shall be adopted after the conclusion by the Russian Federation of the respective inter-State agreements.

6. The placement of orders for independent-work contract construction work for State needs at the expense of means of the federal budget and means of the budgets of subjects of the Russian Federation when realising the respective investment projects shall be by State customers by means of conducting competitions in accordance with legislation of the Russian Federation.

7. Control over the special-purpose and effective use of means of the federal budget directed towards capital investments in accordance with legislation of the Russian Federation shall be effectuated by the Counting Chamber of the Russian Federation, and also empowered federal agencies of executive power. Control over the special-purpose and effective use of means of budgets of subjects of the Russian Federation shall be effectuated by empowers agencies of the respective subjects of the Russian Federation.

Article 14. Expert Examination of Investment Projects

1. All investment projects irrespective of the sources of financing and forms of ownership of objects of capital investments shall before the confirmation thereof

be subject to expert examination in accordance with legislation of the Russian Federation.

Expert examination of investment projects shall be conducted for the purposes of preventing the creation of objects whose use violates the rights of natural and juridical persons and the interests of the State or does not meet the requirements of standards (or norms and rules) confirmed in the established procedure, and also to assess the effectiveness of the capital investments to be effectuated.

2. Investment projects financed at the expense of means of the federal budget, means of the budgets of subjects of the Russian Federation, and also investment projects having important national economic significance, irrespective of the sources of financing and forms of ownership of the objects of capital investments, shall be subject to State expert examination effectuated by empowered State agencies.

The procedure for conducting State expert examination of investment projects shall be determined by the Government of the Russian Federation.

3. All investment projects shall be subject to ecological expert examination in accordance with legislation of the Russian Federation.

Article 15. State Guarantees of Rights of Subjects of Investment Activity

1. The State in accordance with the present Federal Law, other federal laws, and other normative legal acts of the Russian Federation, laws of subjects of the Russian Federation, and other normative legal acts of subjects of the Russian Federation shall guarantee to all subjects of investment activity irrespective of the forms of ownership:

ensuring of equal rights when effectuating investment activity;

glasnost in the discussion of investment projects;

the right to appeal to a court the decisions and actions (or failure to act) of agencies of State power, agencies of local self-government, and officials thereof;

defence of capital investments [as amended by Federal Law No. 22-ФЗ, 2 January 2000].

2. If new federal laws and other normative legal acts of the Russian Federation enter into force which change the amounts of import customs duties (except for special types of duties caused by the application of measures with regard to defence of the economic interests of the Russian Federation when effectuating foreign trade in goods in accordance with legislation of the Russian Federation), federal taxes (except for excises, value-added tax on goods produced on the territory of the Russian Federation), and contributions to State extrabudgetary funds (except for contribution to the Pension Fund of the Russian Federation), or make changes in and additions to prevailing federal laws and other normative legal acts of the Russian Federation which lead to an increase of the aggregate tax load on the activity of the investor with regard to the realisation of a priority investment

project on the territory of the Russian Federation or establish a regime of prohibitions and limitations with respect to the effectuation of capital investments on the territory of the Russian Federation in comparison with the aggregate tax load and regime which operated in accordance with federal laws and other normative legal acts of the Russian Federation on the day of the commencement of the financing of a priority investment project, then such new federal laws and other normative legal acts of the Russian Federation, and also changes and additions made in prevailing federal laws and other normative legal acts of the Russian Federation, shall not apply during the periods specified in point 3 of the present Article with respect to an investor effectuating a priority investment project, on condition that the goods imported to the customs territory of the Russian Federation by the investor are used for their special-purpose designation in order to realise a priority investment project [added by Federal Law No. 22-ФЗ, 2 January 2000].

3. The stability for an investor effectuating an investment project and the conditions and regime specified in the present Article shall be guaranteed for the period of recoupment of the investment project, but not more than seven years from the day of the commencement of financing of the said project. Differentiation of the periods of recoupment of investment projects depending upon the types thereof shall be determined in the procedure established by the Government of the Russian Federation [added by Federal Law No. 22-ФЗ, 2 January 2000].

4. In exceptional instances in the event of the realisation of a priority investment project by an investor in the sphere of production or the creation of transport or other infrastructure, the period of recoupment of which exceeds seven years, the Government of the Russian Federation shall adopt a decision concerning the extension of the periods of operation of the conditions and regime specified in point 2 of the present Article for the said investor [added by Federal Law No. 22-ФЗ, 2 January 2000].

5. The provisions of point 2 of the present Article shall not extend to changes and additions which are made in legislative acts of the Russian Federation or new federal laws and other normative legal acts of the Russian Federation adopted for the purposes of the defence of the constitutional system, morality, health, rights and legal interests of other persons, and ensuring the defence of the country and security of the State [added by Federal Law No. 22-ФЗ, 2 January 2000].

6. The Government of the Russian Federation shall:
establish the criteria for assessing the changes in conditions for the recovery of import customs duties, federal taxes and contributions to the State extrabudgetary funds, regime of prohibitions and limitations with respect to the effectuation of capital investments on the territory of the Russian Federation which are unfavourable for the investor effectuating a priority investment project on the ter-

ritory of the Russian Federation [added by Federal Law No. 22-ФЗ, 2 January 2000];

confirm the procedure determining the day of the commencement of financing of an investment project, including with the participation of foreign investors;

confirm the procedure for the registration of priority investment projects;

effectuate control over the performance by the investor of obligations assumed by him with regard to the realisation of the priority investment project within the periods specified in points 3 and 4 of the present Article.

In the event of the failure of the investor to perform obligations specified in paragraph one of the present point, he shall be deprived of the privileges granted to him in accordance with the present Article. The amount of monetary means not paid as a result of the granting of the said privileges shall be subject to refund in the procedure established by legislation of the Russian Federation [added by Federal Law No. 22-ФЗ, 2 January 2000].

Article 16. Defence of Capital Investments

1. Capital investments may be:

nationalised only on condition of the prior and fair compensation by the State of losses caused to subjects of investment activity in accordance with the Constitution of the Russian Federation and the Civil Code of the Russian Federation;

requisitioned by decision of State agencies in the instances, procedure, and conditions which have been determined by the Civil Code of the Russian Federation.

2. Insurance of capital investments shall be effectuated in accordance with legislation of the Russian Federation.

Article 17. Responsibility of Subjects of Investment Activity

1. In the event of a violation of the requirements of legislation of the Russian Federation, conditions of the contract, and/or State contract subjects of investment activity shall bear responsibility in accordance with legislation of the Russian Federation.

2. Disputes connected with investment activity effectuated in the form of capital investments shall be settled in the procedure established by legislation of the Russian Federation and international treaties of the Russian Federation.

Article 18. Termination or Suspension of Investment Activity Effectuated in Form of Capital Investments

1. The termination or suspension of investment activity effectuated in the form of capital investments shall be in the procedure established by legislation of the Russian Federation.

2. The procedure for compensation of losses to subjects of investment activity in the event of the termination or suspension of investment activity effectuated in the form of capital investments shall be determined by legislation of the Russian Federation and contracts and/or State contracts concluded.

Chapter IV. Foundations of Regulation of Investment Activity Effectuated in Form of Capital Investments by Agencies of Local Self-Government

Article 19. Forms and Methods of Regulation of Investment Activity Effectuated in Form of Capital Investments by Agencies of Local Self-Government

1. The regulation by agencies of local self-government of investment activity effectuated in the form of capital investments shall provide for:

(1) the creation in municipal formations of favourable conditions for the development of investment activity effectuated in the form of capital investments by means of:

establishment of privileges with regard to the payment of local taxes for subjects of investment activity;

defence of the interests of investors;

granting to subjects of investment activity privileged conditions for the use of land and other natural resources in municipal ownership which are not contrary to legislation of the Russian Federation;

expansion of the use of means of the populace and other extrabudgetary sources of financing of housing construction and the construction of objects of socio-cultural designation;

(2) direct participation of agencies of local self-government in investment activity effectuated in the form of capital investments by means of:

the working out, confirmation, and financing of investment projects effectuated by municipal formations;

placement on a competitive basis of means of local budgets to finance investment projects. Placement of the said means shall be effectuated on a repayable and fixed-term basis with the payment of interest for the use thereof in the amounts determined by normative legal acts concerning local budgets, or on conditions of consolidation in municipal ownership of the respective part of the stocks of a joint-stock society to be created which shall be realised within a determined period on the securities market with the receipts from the realisation to be directed to the revenues of the local budgets. The procedure for the placement of a competitive basis of means of the local budgets for the financing of investment projects shall be confirmed by the representative agency of local self-government in accordance with legislation of the Russian Federation;

conducting of expert examination of investment projects in accordance with legislation of the Russian Federation;

issuance of municipal loans in accordance with legislation of the Russian Federation;

involvement in the investment process of temporarily suspended or shut-down construction sites and objects in municipal ownership.

2. Agencies of local self-government shall grant municipal guarantees on a competitive basis with regard to investment projects at the expense of means of the local budgets. The procedure for granting municipal guarantees at the expense means of the local budgets shall be confirmed by the representative agency of local self-government in accordance with legislation of the Russian Federation.

3. Expenses for financing investment activity effectuated in the form of capital investments by agencies of local self-government shall be provided for by the local budgets. Control over special-purpose and effective use of the means of local budgets directed towards capital investments shall be effectuated by the agencies empowered by representative agencies of local self-government.

4. In the event of the participation of agencies of local self-government in the financing of investment projects effectuated by the Russian Federation and subjects of the Russian Federation, the working out and confirmation of these investment projects shall be effectuated by agreement with the agencies of local self-government.

5. When effectuating investment activity agencies of local self-government shall have the right to interact with agencies of local self-government of other municipal formations, including by means of combining own and attracted means on the basis of a contract between them and in accordance with legislation of the Russian Federation.

6. The regulation by agencies of local self-government of investment activity effectuated in the form of capital investments may be effectuated with the use of other forms and methods in accordance with legislation of the Russian Federation.

Article 20. Municipal Guarantees of Rights of Subjects of Investment Activity

Agencies of local self-government within the limits of their powers in accordance with the present Federal Law, other federal laws, and other normative legal acts of the Russian Federation, laws of subjects of the Russian Federation, and other normative legal acts of subjects of the Russian Federation shall guarantee to all subjects of investment activity:

ensuring of equal rights when effectuating investment activity;

glasnost in the discussion of investment projects;

stability of the rights of subjects of investment activity.

Chapter V. Concluding Provisions

Article 21. On Deeming Certain Legislative Acts to Have Lost Force in Connection With Adoption of Present Federal Law

In connection with the adoption of the present Federal Law to deem to have lost force in the part of norms which are contrary to the present Federal Law:

Law of the RSFSR on Investment Activity in the RSFSR (Ведомости Съезда народных депутатов РСФСР и Верховного Совета РСФСР (1991), no. 29, item 1005);

Decree of the supreme Soviet of the RSFSR on the Introduction into Operation of the Law of the RSFSR on Investment Activity in the RSFSR (Ведомости Съезда народных депутатов РСФСР и Верховного Совета РСФСР (1991), no. 29, item 1006);

Article 5 of the Federal Law on Making Changes in and Additions to Legislative Acts of the Russian Federation in Connection with the Adoption of Laws of the Russian Federation on Standardisation, on Ensuring the Unity of Measurements, and on the Certification of Products and Services (Собрание законодательства Российской Федерации (1995), no. 26, item 2397).

Article 22. Entry into Force of Present Federal Law

The present Federal Law shall enter into force from the day of the official publication thereof.

Article 23. Bringing Legal Acts into Conformity with Present Federal Law

The President of the Russian Federation and the Government of the Russian Federation shall bring their legal acts into conformity with the present Federal Law.

LAW OF THE RUSSIAN FEDERATION ON INTERNATIONAL COMMERCIAL ARBITRATION

[Adopted by the Supreme Soviet of the Russian Federation,
No. 5338–1, 7 July 1993. Ведомости СНД и ВС РФ (1993), no. 32, item
1240]

Section I	General Provisions	840
Section II	Arbitration Agreement	842
Section III	Composition of Arbitration Court	843
Section IV	Competence of Arbitration Court	845
Section V	Conducting of Arbitration Examination	846
Section VI	Rendering of Arbitration Award and Termination of Examination	849
Section VII	Contesting Arbitration Award	851
Section VIII	Recognition and Enforcement of Arbitration Awards	852
Annexe 1	Statute on International Commercial Arbitration Court Attached to the Chamber of Commerce and Industry of the Russian Federation	854
Annexe 2	Statute on the Maritime Arbitration Commission Attached to the Chamber of Commerce and Industry of the Russian Federation	855
	Decree on the Introduction into Operation of the Law of the Russian Federation 'On International Commercial Arbitration'	857

The present Law:

proceeds from recognition of the usefulness of arbitration (or arbitration court) as a widely used method of settling disputes arising in the sphere of international trade and the need for the integrated regulation of international commercial arbitration in a legislative procedure;

takes into account the provisions concerning such arbitration contained in international treaties of the Russian Federation, and also in the Model Law adopted in 1985 by the United Nations Commission for International Trade Law and approved by the United Nations General Assembly for possible use by States in their legislation.

Section I. General Provisions

Article 1. Sphere of Application

1. The present Law shall apply to international commercial arbitration if the place of arbitration is situated on the territory of the Russian Federation. However, the provisions provided for by Articles 8, 9, 35, and 36 also shall apply in those instances when the place of arbitration is situated abroad.

2. By agreement of the parties there may be transferred to international commercial arbitration:

disputes from contractual and other civil-law relations arising when effectuating foreign trade and other types of international economic links if a commercial enterprise which is one of the parties is situated abroad, and also

disputes of enterprises with foreign investments and international associations and organisations created on the territory of the Russian Federation between themselves, disputes between their participants, and likewise their disputes with other subjects of law of the Russian Federation.

3. For the purposes of point 2 of the present Article:

if a party has more than one commercial enterprise, the commercial enterprise shall be considered that which has the closest relationship to the arbitration agreement;

if a party does not have a commercial enterprise, its permanent place of residence shall be taken into account.

4. The present Law shall not affect the operation of any other Law of the Russian Federation by virtue of which certain disputes may not be transferred to arbitration or may be transferred to arbitration only in accordance with provisions other than those which are contained in the present Law.

5. If other rules have been established by an international treaty of the Russian Federation than those which are contained in Russian legislation on arbitration (or arbitration court), the rules of the international treaty shall apply.

Article 2. Definitions of Terms and Rules of Interpretation

For the purposes of the present Law:

'arbitration' shall mean any arbitration (or arbitration court), irrespective of whether it is formed specially for consideration of an individual case or is effectuated by a permanently operating arbitration institution, in particular the International Commercial Arbitration Court or the Maritime Arbitration Commission attached to the Chamber of Commerce and Industry of the Russian Federation (Annexes I and II to the present Law);

'arbitration court' shall mean a sole arbitrator or a panel of arbitrators (or arbitration judges);

'court' shall mean the respective agency of the judicial system of the State;

when any provision of the present Law, except for Article 28, grants to the parties the possibility to adopt decisions regarding the respective question the parties may entrust the adoption of such decision to any third person, including an institution;

if in any provision of the present Law there is a reference to the fact that the parties have agreed or that they may agree, or in any other form there is a reference to an agreement of the parties, such agreement shall include any arbitration rules specified in this agreement;

when in any provision of the present Law, excluding Article 25, paragraph one, and Article 32(2), there is a reference to a suit, it also shall apply to a counterclaim, and when there is a reference therein to an objection, it also shall apply to an objection to such counterclaim.

Article 3. Receipt of Written Communications

1. Unless the parties have agreed otherwise:

any written communication shall be considered to be received if it is delivered to the addressee personally or to his commercial enterprise, permanent place of residence, or postal address; when such cannot be established by reasonable inquiry, a written communication shall be considered to be received if it is sent to the last known location of the commercial enterprise, permanent place of residence or postal address of the addressee by registered letter or by other means providing for the registration of attempts to deliver such communication;

the communication shall be considered to be received on the day of such delivery.

2. The provisions of the present Article shall not apply to communications in the course of a proceeding in the courts.

Article 4. Waiver of Right to Object

If a party who knows that any provision of the present Law from which a party may derogate or any requirement provided for by the arbitration agreement has not been complied with and nonetheless continues to participate in an arbitration examination and has not objected to such failure to comply without unjustified delay, and if for this purpose a period has been provided, then within this period he shall be considered to have waived his right to object.

Article 5. Limits of Intervention of Court

With regard to questions regulated by the present Law no judicial intervention shall take place except in the instances when this has been provided for in the present Law.

Article 6. Agencies for Fulfilment of Specified Functions of Assistance and Control With Respect to Arbitration

1. The functions specified in Article 11(3) and (4), Article 13(3), and Article 14 shall be fulfilled by the President of the Chamber of Commerce and Industry of the Russian Federation.

2. The functions specified in Article 16(3) and Article 34(2) shall be fulfilled by the Supreme Court of a republic within the Russian Federation, territory, region, or city court, autonomous region court, and autonomous national area court at the place of the arbitration.

Section II. Arbitration Agreement

Article 7. Definition and Form of Arbitration Agreement

1. An arbitration agreement—is an agreement of the parties to transfer to arbitration all or specified disputes which have arisen or may arise between them in connection with a specific legal relation, irrespective of whether it is of a contractual nature or not. An arbitration agreement may be concluded in the form of an arbitration clause in a contract or in the form of a separate agreement.

2. An arbitration agreement shall be concluded in writing. The agreement shall be considered to be concluded in writing if it is contained in a document signed by the parties, or has been concluded by an exchange of letters, communications by teletype, telegraph, or with the use of other means of electronic communications ensuring the fixation of such agreement, or by means of an exchange of petitions to sue and reply to a suit in which one of the parties asserts the existence of the agreement and the other does not object to it. A reference in the contract to a document containing an arbitration clause shall be an arbitration agreement on condition that the contract was concluded in writing and the particular reference is such as to make the said clause part of the contract.

Article 8. Arbitration Agreement and Filing of Suit Regarding Essence of Dispute in Court

1. A court in which a suit has been filed with regard to a question which is the subject of an arbitration agreement must, if any of the parties so requests not later than the submission of its first application regarding the essence of the dispute, terminate the proceeding and refer the parties to arbitration unless it finds that the agreement is invalid, has lost force, or cannot be performed.

2. In the event a suit specified in point 1 of the present Article is filed, the arbitration examination may nonetheless be commenced or continued and the arbitration award rendered while the arguments concerning jurisdiction await settlement in the court.

Article 9. Arbitration Agreement and Security Measures of Court

The application of a party to a court either before or during an arbitration examination with a request to take measures to secure a suit and the ruling rendered by a court to take such measures shall not be incompatible with the arbitration agreement.

Section III. Composition of Arbitration Court

Article 10. Number of Arbitrators

1. The parties may at their discretion determine the number of arbitrators.

2. If the parties do not determine this number, three arbitrators shall be appointed.

Article 11. Appointment of Arbitrators

1. No person may be deprived of the right to act as an arbitrator by reason of his citizenship unless the parties have agreed otherwise.

2. The parties may at their discretion agree the procedure for the appointment of an arbitrator or arbitrators on condition of complying with the provisions of points 4 and 5 of the present Article.

3. In the absence of such agreement:
in the event of an arbitration with three arbitrators, each party shall appoint one arbitrator, and the two arbitrators thus appointed shall appoint the third arbitrator; if a party does not appoint the arbitrator within 30 days upon receipt of the request therefor from the other party or if two arbitrators within 30 days from the moment of their appointment do not agree on the third arbitrator, at the request of any party the appointment shall be made by the agency specified in Article 6(1);
in the event of an arbitration with a sole arbitrator, if the parties do not agree on the arbitrator, at the request of any party the appointment shall be made by the agency specified in Article 6(1).

4. If under the appointment procedure agreed by the parties:
one of the parties does not comply with such procedure; or
the parties or two arbitrators cannot reach agreement in accordance with such procedure; or
a third person, including an institution, does not fulfil any function entrusted to it in accordance with this procedure, —
any party may request the agency specified in Article 6(1) to take necessary measures unless the agreement on appointment procedure does not make provision for other means of securing the appointment.

5. A decision of the agency specified in Article 6(1) with regard to any of the questions which have been relegated to its jurisdiction in accordance with point 3

843

or 4 of the present Article shall not be subject to appeal. When appointing an arbitrator this agency shall take into account any requirements submitted with regard to the qualifications of the arbitrator by agreement of the parties, and also considerations which may secure the appointment of an independent and impartial arbitrator, and in the event of the appointment of a sole or third arbitrator also shall take into account the desirability of the appointment as an arbitrator of a person who is not a citizen of those States to which the parties belong.

Article 12. Grounds for Challenge of Arbitrator

1. In the event of approaching any person in connection with his possible appointment as an arbitrator, this person must communicate any circumstances which might give rise to justifiable doubts relative to his impartiality or independence. An arbitrator from the moment of his appointment and throughout the entire arbitration examination must communicate without delay to the parties any such circumstances unless he has informed them of such circumstances previously.

2. A challenge to an arbitrator may be filed only if circumstances exist that give rise to justifiable doubts relative to his impartiality and independence, or if he does not possess the qualifications stipulated by the agreement of the parties. A party may challenge an arbitrator who he has appointed or in whose appointment it has participated only for reasons which became known to it after the appointment thereof.

Article 13. Procedure for Challenge of Arbitrator

1. The parties may at their discretion agree on a procedure for challenging an arbitrator on condition of complying with the provisions of point 3 of the present Article.

2. In the absence of such arrangement, a party who intends to challenge an arbitrator must within 15 days after the formation of the arbitration court or after becoming aware of any circumstances specified in Article 12(2), communicate in writing the reasons for the challenge to the arbitration court. Unless the arbitrator who has been challenged disqualifies himself or the other party agrees to the challenge, the question of the challenge shall be decided by the arbitration court.

3. If the challenge when applying any procedure agreed by the parties or the procedure provided for in point 2 of the present Article has not been satisfied, the party making the challenge may within 30 days upon receipt of notice of the decision to reject the challenge request the agency specified in Article 6(1) to adopt a decision regarding the challenge; the last decision shall not be subject to appeal. While the request of the party awaits resolution, the arbitration court, including the arbitrator who has been challenged, may continue the arbitration examination and render an arbitration award.

Article 14. Termination of Powers (or Mandate) of Arbitrator

1. If an arbitrator turns out to be legally or factually incapable of fulfilling his functions or for other reasons does not effectuate them without unjustified delay, his powers (or mandate) shall terminate if the arbitrator disqualifies himself or the parties agree to terminate the mandate. In other instances when disagreements relative to any of these grounds remain, any party may have recourse to the agency specified in Article 6(1) with a request to settle the question of termination of the mandate; such decision shall not be subject to appeal.

2. The disqualification of an arbitrator or consent of a party to terminate his mandate in accordance with the present Article or with Article 13(2) shall not mean recognition of any of the grounds mentioned in the present Article or in Article 12(2).

Article 15. Replacement of Arbitrator

If the mandate of an arbitrator terminates on the basis of Article 13 or 14, or in view of the fact that he has disqualified himself for any other reason, or in view of the revocation of his mandate by agreement of the parties, and likewise in any other event of the termination of his mandate, another arbitrator shall be appointed in accordance with the rules which were applicable to the appointment of the arbitrator being replaced.

Section IV. Competence of Arbitration Court

Article 16. Right of Arbitration Court to Render Decree Concerning Its Competence

1. An arbitration court may itself render a decree concerning its own competence, including any objections with respect to the existence or validity of an arbitration agreement. For that purpose an arbitration clause which is part of a contract must be treated as an agreement independent of the other conditions of the contract. A decision of the arbitration court that the contract is null shall not entail *ipso jure* the invalidity of the arbitration clause.

2. An application concerning the lack of competence of an arbitration court may be made not later than the submission of objections relating to the suit. The appointment by a party of an arbitrator or its participation in the appointment of an arbitrator shall not deprive a party of the right to make such an application. An application that the arbitration court is exceeding the limits of its competence must be made as soon as the question which, in the opinion of the party, exceeds these limits is put in the course of the arbitration examination. The arbitration court may in either of these instances accept an application made later if it considers the delay justified.

3. An arbitration court may render a decree regarding the application specified in point 2 of the present Article either as a preliminary question or in the
award relating to the essence of the dispute. If the arbitration court decrees with
regard to the preliminary question that it possesses competence, any party may
within 30 days after receipt of notification of the decree thereon request the
court specified in Article 6(2) to adopt a decision regarding the particular question; such decision shall not be subject to appeal. While the request of the party
awaits resolution, the arbitration court may continue the examination and render an arbitration award.

Article 17. Power of Arbitration Court to Order the Taking of Security Measures

Unless the parties have agreed otherwise, an arbitration court may at the
request of any party order the taking by any party of those security measures with
respect to the subject of the dispute which it considers to be necessary. The arbitration court may require of any party the provision of proper security in connection with such measures.

Section V. Conducting of Arbitration Examination

Article 18. Equal Relationship of Parties

The parties must be in a relationship of equality, and each party must be
granted a full opportunity to set out its position.

Article 19. Determination of Rules of Procedure

1. On condition of compliance with the provisions of the present Law the parties may at their discretion agree on the procedure for conducting the examination
by the arbitration court.

2. In the absence of such agreement the arbitration court may, in compliance
with the provisions of the present Law, conduct the arbitration examination as it
considers appropriate. The powers granted to the arbitration court shall include
the powers to determine the admissibility, relevance, materiality, and significance
of any evidence.

Article 20. Place of Arbitration

1. The parties may at their discretion agree on the place of arbitration. In the
absence of such agreement the place of arbitration shall be determined by the arbitration court taking into account the circumstances of the case, including the factor of convenience for the parties.

2. Notwithstanding the provisions of point 1 of the present Article, an
arbitration court may, unless the parties agree otherwise, assemble at another
place which it considers to be appropriate for consultations among the arbitrators,

hearing witnesses, experts, or the parties, or for the inspection of goods, other property, or documents.

Article 21. Commencement of Arbitration Examination

Unless the parties have agreed otherwise, an arbitration examination in respect of a specific dispute shall commence on the date when the request concerning the transfer of this dispute to arbitration is received by the defendant.

Article 22. Language

1. The parties may at their discretion agree on the language or languages which will be used in the course of the arbitration examination. In the absence of such arrangement the arbitration court shall determine the language or languages which must be used during the examination. Such type of arrangement or determination, unless stipulated otherwise, shall apply to any written application of a party, any hearing of the case, and any arbitration award, decree, or other communication of the arbitration court.

2. An arbitration court may order that any documentary evidence be accompanied by a translation into the language or languages which the parties have agreed or which were determined by the arbitration court.

Article 23. Petition to Sue and Objections Relating to Suit

1. Within the period agreed by the parties or determined by the arbitration court, the plaintiff must state all the circumstances confirming his suit demands, questions in dispute, and satisfaction demanded, and the defendant must state his objections with regard to these points unless the parties have agreed otherwise with respect to the necessary requisites of such statements. The parties may submit together with their statements all documents which they consider to be relevant to the case or may make a reference to documents and other evidence which they will submit in future.

2. Unless the parties have agreed otherwise, any party may in the course of an arbitration examination change or add to his suit demands or objections relating to the suit unless the arbitration court deems it inappropriate to authorise such a change, taking into account the delay in making it.

Article 24. Hearing and Examination Relating to Documents

1. On condition of compliance with any other agreement of the parties, the arbitration court shall adopt a decision whether to hold an oral hearing of the case for the submission of evidence or for oral arguments or to effectuate the examination only on the basis of documents and other materials. However, except when the parties have agreed not to hold an oral hearing, the arbitration must hold such a hearing at an appropriate stage of the arbitration examination if any of the parties so requests.

2. Notification must be sent to the parties sufficiently in advance concerning any hearing and concerning any session of the arbitration court being held for the purposes of inspection of goods, other property, or documents.

3. All applications, documents, or other information submitted by one party to the arbitration court must be transferred to the other party. Any opinions of experts or other documents having evidentiary significance on which the arbitration court may rely when rendering its award must be transferred to the parties.

Article 25. Failure to Submit Documents or Failure of Party to Appear

Unless the parties have agreed otherwise, in those instances when without specifying a justifiable reason:

the plaintiff fails to submit his petition to sue, as is required in accordance with Article 23(1): the arbitration court shall terminate the examination;

the defendant fails to submit his objections to the suit, as is required in accordance with Article 23(1): the arbitration court shall continue the examination without considering such failure to submit in and of itself to be recognition of the assertions of the plaintiff;

any party fails to appear at a hearing or to submit documentary evidence: the arbitration court may continue the examination and render a decision on the basis of the evidence available to it.

Article 26. Expert Appointed by Arbitration Court

1. Unless the parties have agreed otherwise, an arbitration court may:

appoint one or several experts to submit a report to it on specific questions which are to be determined by the arbitration court;

require a party to provide to the expert any information relevant to the case or to grant the opportunity to inspect documents, goods, or other property relevant to the case.

2. In the absence of an arrangement of the parties otherwise, the expert, if a party so requests or if the arbitration court considers this necessary, must after the submission of his written or oral opinion take part in a hearing at which the parties shall be granted the opportunity to put questions to him and to present specialists to give testimony regarding questions at issue.

Article 27. Assistance of Court in Obtaining Evidence

The arbitration court or a party with the consent of the arbitration court may apply to a competent court of the Russian Federation with a request for assistance in obtaining evidence. The court may fulfil this request, being guided by the rules affecting the securing of evidence, including judicial commissions.

Section VI. Rendering of Arbitration Award and Termination of Examination

Article 28. Norms Applicable to Substance of Dispute

1. The arbitration court shall settle the dispute in accordance with such norms of law as the parties have chosen as applicable to the substance of the dispute. Any specification of the law or system of law of any State must be interpreted as directly referring to the material law of that State and not to its conflicts of law norms.

2. In the absence of any specification of the parties, the arbitration court shall apply the law determined in accordance with the conflicts of law norms which it considers applicable.

3. In all instances the arbitration court shall adopt an award in accordance with the conditions of the contract and taking into account trade customs applicable to the particular transaction.

Article 29. Rendering of Award by Panel of Arbitrators

In an arbitration examination effectuated by a panel of arbitrators, any award of the arbitration court, unless the parties have agreed otherwise, must be rendered by a majority of the arbitrators. However, questions of procedure may be settled by the arbitrator who is the chairman of the arbitration court if he is empowered to do so by the parties or by all the other arbitrators.

Article 30. Amicable Settlement

1. If in the course of an arbitration examination the parties settle the dispute, the arbitration court shall terminate the examination and at the request of the parties and in the absence objections on its part shall fix the settlement in the form of an arbitration award on agreed conditions.

2. An arbitration award on agreed conditions must be rendered in accordance with the provisions of Article 31 and must contain a reference to the fact that it is an arbitration award. Such an arbitration award shall have the same force as and shall be subject to execution as any other arbitration award on the substance of the dispute.

Article 31. Form and Content of Arbitration Award

1. The arbitration award must be rendered in writing and be signed by the sole arbitrator or arbitrators. In an arbitration examination effectuated by a panel of arbitrators, the presence of the signatures of a majority of members of the arbitration court shall be sufficient on condition of specifying the reason for the absence of the other signatures.

2. The arbitration award must specify the reasons upon which it is based, the conclusion concerning the satisfaction or rejection of the suit demands, the

amount of the arbitration fee and expenses regarding the case, and the distribution thereof among the parties.

3. The arbitration award must specify its date and the place of arbitration as determined in accordance with Article 20(1). The arbitration award shall be considered to have been rendered at that place.

4. After the arbitration award is rendered, a copy thereof signed by the arbitrators in accordance with point 1 of the present Article must be transferred to each party.

Article 32. Termination of Arbitration Examination

1. An arbitration examination shall be terminated by the final arbitration award or decree of the arbitration court rendered in accordance with point 2 of the present Article.

2. The arbitration court shall render a decree on termination of the arbitration examination when:

the plaintiff withdraws his demand, unless the defendant advances objections to the termination of the examination and the arbitration court recognises a legal interest of the defendant in a final settlement of the dispute;

the parties agree on the termination of the examination;

the arbitration court finds that a continuation of the examination has become for any reason unnecessary or impossible.

3. The mandate of the arbitration court terminates simultaneously with the termination of the arbitration examination without prejudice, however, to the provisions of Article 33 and Article 34(4).

Article 33. Correction and Interpretation of Award. Additional Award

1. Within 30 days of receipt of the arbitration award, unless another period has been agreed by the parties:

any of the parties, having notified the other party thereof, may request the arbitration court to correct any errors in the award in computations or clerical or typographic errors or other errors of an analogous nature;

if there is a respective arrangement between the parties, any of the parties, having notified the other party, may request the arbitration court to give an interpretation of any specific point or part of the award.

The arbitration court, if it considers the request to be justified, must within 30 days of receipt thereof make the corresponding corrections or give the interpretation. Such interpretation shall become an integral part of the arbitration award.

2. The arbitration court may within 30 days of the date of the arbitration award correct at its own initiative any errors specified in point 1, paragraph two, of the present Article.

3. Unless the parties have agreed otherwise, any of the parties, having notified the other party, may within 30 days of receipt of the arbitration award request the arbitration court to render an additional award with respect to demands which were states in the court of the arbitration examination but were not reflected in the award. The arbitration court, if it considers the request to be justified, must within 60 days of receipt thereof render the additional arbitration award.

4. The arbitration court may, if necessary, extend the period during which it must correct errors, give an interpretation, or render an additional arbitration award in accordance with point 1 or 3 of the present Article.

5. The provisions of Article 31 must apply to a correction or interpretation of the arbitration award or to an additional award.

Section VII. Contesting Arbitration Award

Article 34. Petition Concerning Vacating as Exclusive Means of Contesting Arbitration Award

1. An arbitration award may be contested in a court only by means of filing a petition to vacate in accordance with points 2 and 3 of the present Article.

2. An arbitration award may be vacated by a court specified in Article 6(2) only if:

(1) the party filing the petition to vacate submits evidence that:

one of the parties to the arbitration agreement specified in Article 7 did in any measure whatever lack dispositive legal capacity, or this agreement is invalid according to the law to which the parties thereof have subordinated it, and in the absence of such indication, according to the law of the Russian Federation; or

it was not duly informed about the appointment of the arbitrator or about the arbitration examination, or for other reasons could not submit its explanations; or

the award was rendered with regard to a dispute not provided for by the arbitration agreement or not falling within its conditions, or it contains decrees with regard to questions beyond the limits of the arbitration agreement, on condition however that if the decrees regarding questions encompassed by the arbitration agreement can be separated from those which are not encompassed by such agreement, only that part of the arbitration award may be vacated which contains decrees relating to questions not encompassed by the arbitration agreement; or

the composition of the arbitration court or the arbitration procedure did not correspond to the agreement of the parties, unless such agreement is contrary to any provision of the present Law from which a party may not derogate, or in the absence of such agreement did not correspond to the present Law; or

(2) the court determines that:

the object of the dispute cannot be the subject of an arbitration examination according to the law of the Russian Federation; or the arbitration award is contrary to the public order of the Russian Federation.

3. A petition to vacate may not be filed upon the expiry of three months from the date of receipt by the party which filed this petition of the arbitration award, and if the request was filed in accordance with Article 33—from the date of the arbitration court rendering an award with regard to this request.

4. The court in which the petition is filed to vacate an arbitration award may, if it considers this appropriate and if one of the parties requests this, suspend the proceedings with regard to this question for an established period in order to grant to the arbitration court the opportunity to resume the arbitration examination or undertake other actions which, in the opinion of the arbitration court, enable the grounds for vacating the arbitration award to be eliminated.

Section VIII. Recognition and Enforcement of Arbitration Awards

Article 35. Recognition and Enforcement of Arbitration Award

1. An arbitration award, irrespective of the country in which it was rendered, shall be deemed to be binding and when a written petition is filed in a competent court, shall be enforced by taking into account the provisions of the present Article and Article 36.

2. The party relying on an arbitration award or petitioning for enforcement must submit a duly authenticated original arbitration award or duly authenticated copy thereof, and also the original arbitration agreement specified in Article 7, or duly authenticated copy of such. If the arbitration award or agreement has been set out in a foreign language, the party must submit a duly authenticated translation of these documents into the Russian language.

Article 36. Grounds for Refusing Recognition or Enforcement of Arbitration Award

1. Recognition or enforcement of an arbitration award may be refused, irrespective of in which country it was rendered, only:

(1) at the request of the party against which it was directed if this party submits to a competent court in which recognition or enforcement is requested evidence that:

one of the parties to the arbitration agreement specified in Article 7 did in any measure lack dispositive legal capacity; or this agreement is invalid according to the law to which the parties thereto have subordinated it, and in the absence of such indication, according to the law of the country where the decision was rendered; or

the party against whom the award was rendered was not duly informed about the appointment of the arbitrator or the arbitration examination or for other reasons could not submit his explanations; or the award was rendered with regard to a dispute not provided for by the arbitration agreement or did not fall within its conditions, or it contains decrees with regard to questions beyond the limits of the arbitration agreement, on condition however that if the decrees regarding questions encompassed by the arbitration agreement can be separated from those which are not encompassed by such agreement, then that part of the arbitration award which contains provisions regarding questions encompassed by the arbitration agreement may be recognised and enforced; or

the composition of the arbitration court or the arbitration procedure did not correspond to the agreement of the parties or in the absence of such did not correspond to the law of that country where the arbitration occurred; or

the award has not yet become binding on the parties, or was vacated, or the enforcement thereof was suspended by the court of the country in which or in accordance with the law of which it was rendered; or

(2) if the court finds that:

the subject-matter of the dispute may not be the subject of an arbitration examination according to the law of the Russian Federation; or

recognition and enforcement of this arbitration award is contrary to the public order of the Russian Federation.

2. If in the court specified in point 1, subpoint 1, paragraph five, of the present Article a petition has been filed to vacate or suspend the execution of an arbitration award, the court in which recognition or enforcement is requested may, if it considers this to be appropriate, defer rendering its award and also may upon the petition of that party who requests recognition or enforcement of the arbitration award oblige the other party to submit appropriate security.

Annexe 1 to the Law of the Russian Federation 'On International Commercial Arbitration' of 7 July 1993, No. 5338–1

STATUTE ON INTERNATIONAL COMMERCIAL ARBITRATION COURT ATTACHED TO THE CHAMBER OF COMMERCE AND INDUSTRY OF THE RUSSIAN FEDERATION

1. The International Commercial Arbitration Court shall be an autonomous permanently operating arbitration institution (or arbitration court) effectuating its activity in accordance with the Law of the Russian Federation 'On International Commercial Arbitration'.

The Chamber of Commerce and Industry of the Russian Federation shall confirm the Reglament of the International Commercial Arbitration Court, the procedure for calculating the arbitration fee, the rates of honorariums for arbitrators, and other expenses of the court, and shall render other assistance in its activity.

2. By agreement of the parties there may be transferred to the International Commercial Arbitration Court:

disputes from contractual and other civil-law relations arising during the effectuation of foreign trade and other types of international economic links if a commercial enterprise which is one of the parties to the dispute is situated abroad, and also

disputes of enterprises with foreign investments and international associations and organisations created on the territory of the Russian Federation between themselves, disputes between their participants, and likewise their disputes with other subjects of law of the Russian Federation.

Civil-law relations, disputes from which may be transferred for settlement to the International Commercial Arbitration Court, shall include, in particular, relations relating to the purchase-sale (or delivery) of goods, fulfilment of work, rendering of services, exchange of goods and/or services, carriage of freight and passengers, trade representation and intermediary activity, lease (or leasing), scientific-technical exchange, exchange other results of creative activity, installation of industrial and other objects, licensing operations, investments, credit-settlement of account operations, insurance, joint entrepreneurship, and other forms of industrial and entrepreneurial cooperation.

3. The International Commercial Arbitration Court shall accept for consideration also disputes subject to its jurisdiction by virtue of international treaties of the Russian Federation.

4. The International Commercial Arbitration Court attached to the Chamber of Commerce and Industry of the Russian Federation shall be the legal successor of the Arbitration Court attached to the Chamber of Commerce and Industry of the USSR formed in 1932 and, in particular, shall have the right to settle disputes on the basis of agreement of the parties concerning the transfer of their disputes to the Arbitration Court attached to the Chamber of Commerce and Industry of the USSR.

5. An award of the International Commercial Arbitration Court shall be executed by the parties within the period specified by it. If the period of execution has not been specified in the award, it shall be subject to immediate execution. Awards not executed within the period shall be executed in accordance with law and international treaties.

6. The chairman of the Court may, at the request of a party, establish the amount and form of securing a demand with regard to cases subject to consideration in the International Commercial Arbitration Court.

Annexe 2 to the Law of the Russian Federation 'On International Commercial Arbitration' of 7 July 1993, No. 5338–1

STATUTE ON THE MARITIME ARBITRATION COMMISSION ATTACHED TO THE CHAMBER OF COMMERCE AND INDUSTRY OF THE RUSSIAN FEDERATION

1. The Maritime Arbitration Commission shall be an autonomous permanently operating arbitration institution (or arbitration court) effectuating its activity relating to the settlement of disputes relegated to its competence by Article 2 of the present Statute in accordance with the Law of the Russian Federation 'On International Commercial Arbitration'.

The Chamber of Commerce and Industry of the Russian Federation shall confirm the Reglament of the Maritime Arbitration Commission, the procedure for calculating the arbitration fee, the rates of honorariums of arbitrators and other expenses of the Commission, and shall render assistance in its activity.

2. The Maritime Arbitration Commission shall settle disputes which emanate from contractual and other civil-law relations arising from merchant shipping, irrespective of whether subjects of Russian and foreign or only Russian or only foreign law are the parties of such relations. In particular, the Maritime Arbitration Commission shall settle disputes arising from relations:

(1) relating to the chartering of vessels, the carriage of goods by sea, and also the carriage of goods in mixed navigation (river-sea);

(2) relating to maritime towing of vessels and other floating objects;

(3) relating to marine insurance and reinsurance;

(4) connected with the purchase-sale, pledge, and repair of sea-going vessels and other floating objects;

(5) relating to pilot and icebreaker escort, agents' and other servicing of sea-going vessels, and also vessels of internal navigation, insofar as the respective operations are connected with the navigation of such vessels along sea routes;

(6) connected with the use of vessels for the effectuation of scientific research, extraction of minerals, hydro-engineering, and other work;

(7) relating to the rescue of sea-going vessels or of a vessel of internal navigation by a sea-going vessel, and also the rescue in sea waters by a vessel of internal navigation of another vessel of internal navigation;

(8) connected with the salvage of vessels and other property sunken at sea;

(9) connected with the collision of sea-going vessels, of a sea-going vessel and vessel of internal navigation, vessels of internal navigation in sea waters, and also with the causing by a vessel of damage to port installations, navigation means, and other objects;

(10) connected with causing damage to fishing nets and other fishing implements, and also other causing of harm when effectuating commercial sea fishing.

The Maritime Arbitration Commission also shall settle disputes arising in connection with the navigation of sea-going vessels and vessels of internal navigation along international rivers in the instances specified in the present Article, and likewise disputes connected with the effectuation of foreign carriages by vessels of internal navigation.

3. The Maritime Arbitration Commission shall accept disputes for consideration when there is an agreement between the parties concerning the transfer thereof for settlement by it.

The Commission shall also accept disputes for consideration which the parties are obliged to transfer for its consideration by virtue of international treaties of the Russian Federation.

4. The Chairman of the Commission may at the request of a party establish the amount and form of security for a demand and, in particular, render a decree

concerning the imposition of arrest on a vessel or cargo of another party situated in a Russian port with regard to cases subject to consideration of the Maritime Arbitration Commission.

5. Awards of the Maritime Arbitation Commission shall be executed by the parties voluntarily. An award of the Commission not executed by a party voluntarily shall be enforced in accordance with the law and international treaties.

6. The procedure for the realisation of security provided on the basis of Article 4 of the present Statute shall be established by the Chairman of the Maritime Arbitration Commission upon the entry of its award into legal force.

7. The Maritime Arbitration Commission attached to the Chamber of Commerce and Industry of the Russian Federation shall be the successor of the Maritime Arbitration Commission attached to the Chamber of Commerce and Industry of the USSR, formed in 1930, and, in particular, shall have the right to settle disputes on the basis of agreements of the parties concerning the transfer thereof to the Maritime Arbitration Commission attached to the Chamber of Commerce and Industry of the USSR.

DECREE ON THE INTRODUCTION INTO OPERATION OF THE LAW OF THE RUSSIAN FEDERATION 'ON INTERNATIONAL COMMERCIAL ARBITRATION'

[Decree of the Supreme Soviet of the Russian Federation, No. 5339–1, 7 July 1993. Ведомости СНД и ВС РФ (1993), no. 32, item 1241]

The Supreme Soviet of the Russian Federation shall decree:

1. To introduce the Law of the Russian Federation 'On International Commercial Arbitration' into operation from the moment of publication.

2. To rename the Arbitration Court attached to the Chamber of Commerce and Industry of the Russian Federation as the International Commercial Arbitration Court attached to the Chamber of Commerce and Industry of the Russian Federation.

3. The Council of Ministers-Government of the Russian Federation shall within a three-month period ensure the transfer to the International Commercial Arbitration Court, the Maritime Arbitration Commission, and other arbitration agencies attached to the Chamber of Commerce and Industry of the Russian Federation of a proper premise necessary for the fulfilment of the functions entrusted to them by the said Law and corresponding to their status.

4. To deem to have lost force:

the Edict of the Presidium of the Supreme Soviet of the USSR of 9 October 1980 'On Confirmation of the Statute on the Maritime Arbitration Commission attached to the Chamber of Commerce and Industry of the USSR' (Ведомости Верховного Совета СССР (1980), no. 42, item 868);

the Edict of the Presidium of the Supreme Soviet of the USSR of 14 December 1987 'On the Arbitration Court attached to the Chamber of Commerce and Industry of the USSR' (Ведомости Верховного Совета СССР (1987), no. 50, item 806).

FEDERAL LAW ON ARBITRATION COURTS IN THE RUSSIAN FEDERATION

[Federal Law No. 102-ФЗ, 24 July 2002.
СЗ РФ (2002), no. 30, item 3019]

Chapter I	General Provisions	859
Chapter II	Arbitration Agreement	862
Chapter III	Composition of Arbitration Court	863
Chapter IV	Expenses Connected with Settlement of Dispute in Arbitration Court	866
Chapter V	Arbitral Examination	867
Chapter VI	Award of Arbitration Court	873
Chapter VII	Contesting Award of Arbitration Court	876
Chapter VIII	Execution of Award of Arbitration Court	877
Chapter IX	Concluding Provisions	880

Chapter I. General Provisions

Article 1. Sphere of Application of Present Federal Law

1. The present Federal Law shall regulate the procedure for the formation and activity of arbitration courts situated on the territory of the Russian Federation.

2. Any dispute arising from civil-law relations may be transferred to an arbitration court by agreement of the parties for arbitral examination (hereinafter: parties) unless established otherwise by a federal law.

3. The operation of the present Federal Law shall not extend to international commercial arbitration.

4. If another procedure for the formation and activity of arbitration courts than is provided by the present Federal Law has been established by an international treaty of the Russian Federation, the rules of the international treaty shall apply.

Article 2. Basic Concepts Used in Present Federal Law

The following basic concepts shall be used in the present Federal Law:
arbitration court—permanently operating arbitration court or arbitration

court formed by the parties to decide a specific dispute (hereinafter: arbitration court for settlement of specific dispute);

arbitration judge—natural person selected by the parties or appointed in a procedure agreed by the parties to settle the dispute in an arbitration court;

arbitral examination—process of settlement of the dispute in an arbitration court and adoption of award by the arbitration court;

arbitration agreement—agreement of the parties concerning the transfer of the dispute for settlement of an arbitration court;

rules of permanently operating arbitration court—charters, statutes, reglaments containing rules of an arbitral examination and confirmed by the organisation-juridical person which formed the permanently operating arbitration court;

parties to arbitral examination—organisations-juridical persons and citizens effectuating entrepreneurial activity without the formation of a juridical person and having the status of an individual entrepreneur acquired in the procedure established by a law (hereinafter: citizen-entrepreneurs), natural persons (hereinafter: citizens) who have filed suit in an arbitration court in defence of their rights and interests or against whom suit has been filed;

competent court—arbitrazh court of a subject of the Russian Federation with regard to disputes within the jurisdiction of arbitrazh courts, district court with regard to disputes within the jurisdiction of courts of general jurisdiction, in accordance with the subject-matter jurisdiction established by arbitrazh procedure or civil procedure legislation of the Russian Federation.

Article 3. Procedure for Formation and Activity of Arbitration Courts

1. Permanently-operating arbitration courts and arbitration courts for the settlement of a specific dispute may be formed in the Russian Federation.

2. Permanently-operating arbitration courts shall be formed by chambers of commerces, stock exchanges, social associations of entrepreneurs and consumers, and other organisations-juridical persons created in accordance with legislation of the Russian Federation and associations (or associations, unions) thereof and operate attached to these organisations-juridical persons.

Permanently-operating arbitration courts may not be formed attached to federal agencies of State power, agencies of State power of subjects of the Russian Federation, and agencies of local self-government.

3. A permanently-operating arbitration court shall be considered to be formed when the organisation-juridical person has:

(1) adopted a decision concerning the formation of the permanently-operating arbitration court;

(2) confirmed the statute on the permanently-operating arbitration court;

(3) confirmed the list of arbitration judges, which may have an obligatory or recommendatory character for the parties.

4. The organisation-juridical person which has formed a permanently-operating arbitration court shall send to the competent court effectuating judicial power on that territory where the permanently-operating arbitration court is located copies of the documents attesting to the formation of the permanently-operating arbitration court in accordance with point 3 of the present Article.

5. The procedure for the formation of an arbitration court for the consideration of a specific dispute shall be determined by agreement of the parties, which may not be contrary to the provisions of Article 8(1), (2), (4) and (5), Article 9(1), Article 11, Article 13(1) and (2), and Article 14 of the present Federal Law. If the procedure for the formation of an arbitration court in order to settle a specific dispute has not been determined in an agreement of the parties, the provisions of Articles 8–14 of the present Federal Law shall apply.

6. The rules of an arbitral consideration shall be determined in accordance with Article 19 of the present Federal Law.

Article 4. Receipt of Documents and Other Materials

1. Documents and other materials shall be sent to the parties in the procedure agreed by them and to the addresses specified by them.

2. Unless the parties have a different procedure, the documents and other materials shall be sent to the last known location of an organisation which is a party to an arbitral examination, or place of residence of a citizen-entrepreneur, or citizen who is a party to an arbitral examination by registered letter with notice of handing over or by other means providing for the fixation of delivery of the said documents and materials. Documents and other materials shall be considered to be received on the day of delivery thereof, even though the addressee is not situated or does not live at this address.

Article 5. Transfer of Dispute for Settlement of Arbitration Court

1. A dispute may be transferred for consideration of an arbitration court when there is an arbitration agreement concluded between the parties.

2. An arbitration agreement may be concluded by the parties with respect to all or determined disputes which arose or may arise between the parties in connection with any specific legal relation.

3. An arbitration agreement concerning the settlement of a dispute under a contract whose conditions have been determined by one of the parties in a formulation or other standard forms and could be accepted by the other party not other by means of accession to the proposed contract as a whole (contract of adhesion) shall be valid if such agreement was concluded after the arising of the grounds for filing the suit.

4. An arbitration agreement with respect to a dispute which is situated for settlement in a court of general jurisdiction or arbitrazh court may be concluded before the adoption of a decision with regard to the dispute by the competent court.

Article 6. Norms Applicable by Arbitration Court When Settling Disputes

1. Arbitration court shall settle disputes on the basis of the Constitution of the Russian Federation, federal constitutional laws, federal laws, normative edicts of the President of the Russian Federation and decrees of the Government of the Russian Federation, normative legal acts of federal agencies of executive power, normative legal acts of subjects of the Russian Federation, and agencies of local self-government, international treaties of the Russian Federation, and other normative legal acts acting on the territory of the Russian Federation.

2. If other rules than provided for by a law have been established by an international treaty of the Russian Federation, the rules of the international treaty shall apply.

3. An arbitration court shall adopt an award in accordance with the conditions of the contract and taking into account customs of business turnover.

4. If relations of the parties are not directly regulated by norms of law or agreement of the parties and a custom of business turnover applicable to these relations is lacking, the arbitration court shall apply norms of law regulating similar relations, and in the absence of such norms, shall settle the dispute by proceeding from the general principles and sense of laws and other normative legal acts.

Chapter II. Arbitration Agreement

Article 7. Form and Content of Arbitration Agreement

1. An arbitration agreement shall be concluded in written form. An arbitration agreement shall be considered to be concluded in written form if it is contained in a document signed by the parties, or concluded by means of the exchange of letters, communications by teletype, telegraph, or with the use of other means of electronic or other communications ensuring the fixation of such agreement. A reference in the contract to a document containing a condition concerning the transfer of a dispute for settlement to an arbitration court shall be an arbitration agreement on condition that the contract was concluded in written form and the said reference is such that it makes the arbitration agreement part of the contract.

2. In the event of the failure to comply with the rules provided for by point 1 of the present Article, an arbitration agreement shall be nonconcluded.

3. Unless the parties have agreed otherwise, then in the event of the transfer of a dispute to a permanently-operating arbitration court the rules of the perma-

nently-operating arbitration court shall be considered as an integral part of the arbitration agreement.

Chapter III. Composition of Arbitration Court

Article 8. Requirements for Arbitration Court

1. A natural person capable of ensuring an impartial settlement of a dispute, directly or indirectly not interested in the outcome of the case, being independent of the parties and having given consent to performing the duties of arbitration judge shall be selected (or appointed) as arbitration judge.

2. An arbitration judge settling a dispute as one person must have a higher legal education. In the event of the collegial settlement of a dispute the chairman of the composition of the arbitration court must have a higher legal education.

3. The requirements for qualifications of an arbitration judge may be agreed by the parties directly or determined by the rules of the arbitral examination.

4. A natural person who doe snot possess full legal capacity or who is under trusteeship or guardianship may not be an arbitration judge.

5. A natural person who has a record of conviction or brought to criminal responsibility may not be an arbitration judge.

6. A natural person whose powers as a judge of a court of general jurisdiction or arbitrazh court, advocate, notary, investigator, procurator, or other worker of law enforcement agencies were terminated in the procedure established by a law for the commission of offences incompatible with the professional activity thereof may not be an arbitration judge.

7. A natural person who in accordance with his official status determined by a federal law may not be selected (or appointed) as an arbitration judge may not be an arbitration judge.

Article 9. Number of Arbitration Judges

1. The parties may determine the number of arbitration judges, which must be uneven.

2. Unless the parties have agreed otherwise, then three arbitration judges shall be selected (or appointed) to settle a specific dispute.

3. Unless the rules of a permanently-operating arbitration court have determined the number of arbitration judges, three arbitration judges shall be selected (or appointed).

Article 10. Forming of Composition of Arbitration Court

1. The composition of an arbitration court shall be formed by means of selection (or appointment) of arbitration judges (or arbitration judge).

2. In a permanently-operating arbitration court the composition of an arbitration court shall be formed in the procedure established by the rules of the permanently-operating arbitration court.

3. In an arbitration court for the settlement of a specific dispute the composition of the arbitration court shall be formed in the procedure agreed by the parties.

4. Unless the parties have agreed otherwise, the composition of an arbitration court for the settlement of a specific dispute shall be formed in the following procedure:

(1) when forming the composition of an arbitration court consisting of three arbitration judges, each party shall select one arbitration judge, and the two arbitration judges so selected shall select the third arbitration judge.

If one of the parties does not select an arbitration judge within 15 days after receipt of the request thereof from another party or the two selected arbitration judges within 15 days after their selection do not select the third arbitration judge, consideration of the dispute in an arbitration court shall terminate and the said dispute may be transferred for settlement by the competent court;

(2) if a dispute is subject to settlement by an arbitration judge as one person and after the recourse of one party to the other with a proposal to select an arbitration judge the parties within 15 days do not select an arbitration judge, consideration of the dispute in an arbitration court shall terminate and the said dispute may be transferred for consideration by a competent court.

Article 11. Grounds for Challenge of Arbitration Judge

A challenge of an arbitration judge may be declared in instances of the failure to comply with the requirements provided for by Article 8 of the present Federal Law.

Article 12. Procedure for Challenge of Arbitration Judge

1. In the event of recourse to any natural person in connection with his possible selection (or appointment) as an arbitration judge the said person must communicate the existence of circumstances which are grounds for his challenge in accordance with Article 11 of the present Federal Law.

If the said circumstances arose during the arbitral examination, the arbitration judge must without delay notify the parties thereof and declare a self-challenge.

2. A party may declare a challenge of the arbitration judge selected by it in accordance with Article 11 of the present Federal Law only if the circumstances which are grounds for challenge became known to the party after the selection by it of the arbitration judge being challenged.

3. In a permanently-operating arbitration court the procedure for challenge of an arbitration judge may be determined by the rules of the permanently-operating arbitration court.

4. In an arbitration court for the settlement of a specific dispute the procedure of challenge of an arbitration judge may be agreed by the parties.

5. If the procedure for challenge of an arbitration judge is not agreed by the parties or is not determined by the rules of the permanently-operating arbitration court, then a written reasoned declaration concerning the challenge of an arbitration judge must be filed by the party within five days after it became known to the party that the composition of the arbitration court was formed and there are grounds for challenge of an arbitration judge in accordance with Article 11 of the present Federal Law.

If an arbitration judge with regard to whom a challenge was declared does not challenge himself or the other party does not agree with the challenge of the arbitration judge, the question concerning challenge of an arbitration judge shall be settled by the other arbitration judges in the composition of the arbitration court within a ten-day period from the moment of receipt of the written reasoned declaration of the party. The question concerning challenge of an arbitration judge settling a dispute as one person shall be settled by this arbitration judge.

Article 13. Termination of Powers of Arbitration Judge

1. The powers of an arbitration judge may be terminated by agreement of the parties in connection with the self-challenge of an arbitration judge or challenge of an arbitration judge on the grounds provided for by Articles 11 and 12 of the present Federal Law, and also in the event of the death of an arbitration judge.

2. The powers of an arbitration judge shall terminate after the adoption of an award with regard to the specific case. In instances provided for by Articles 34–36 of the present Federal Law, the powers of an arbitration judge shall be renewed, and then shall terminate after the performance of the procedural actions provided for by the said Articles.

3. The legal or actual inability of an arbitration judge to participate in the consideration of a dispute and other reasons for which an arbitration judge does not participate in the consideration of a dispute for an unjustifiably long period shall be grounds for termination of the powers of an arbitration judge by agreement of the parties, as well as for self-challenge of an arbitration judge.

Article 14. Replacement of Arbitration Judge

In the event of the termination of powers of an arbitration judge, another arbitration judge shall be selected (or appointed) in accordance with the rules which were applied when selecting (or appointing) a replacement arbitration judge.

Chapter IV. Expenses Connected with Settlement of Dispute in Arbitration Court

Article 15. Composition of Expenses Connected with Settlement of Dispute in Arbitration Court

1. Expenses connected with the settlement of a dispute in an arbitration court shall include:

honorarium of the arbitration judges;

expenses incurred by the arbitration judges in connection with participation in an arbitral examination, including expenses for payment of travel to the place of consideration of the dispute;

amounts subject to payment to experts and interpreters;

expenses incurred by arbitration judges in connection with the inspection and study of written and material evidence at the location thereof;

expenses incurred by witnesses;

expenses for payment of services of representative of party to whose benefit the award of the arbitration court was made;

expenses of organisational, material, and other provision of the arbitral examination;

other expenses determined by the arbitration court.

2. If the rules of a permanently-operating arbitration court have not determined that the parties bear expenses specified in point 1 of the present Article, such expenses shall be included in the composition of expenses of the permanently-operating arbitration court (arbitration fee).

3. The amount of honorarium of arbitration judges shall be determined by taking into account the price of the suit, complexity of the dispute, time expended by the arbitration judges at the arbitral examination, and any other relevant circumstances.

4. In a permanently-operating arbitration court the amount of honorarium of arbitration judges shall be determined by the composition of the arbitration court in accordance with the scale of honorariums of arbitration judges provided for by the rules of the permanently-operating arbitration court, and in the absence of such—by taking into account the requirements of point 3 of the present Article.

5. In an arbitration court for the settlement of a specific dispute the amount of honorarium of arbitration judges shall be determined by agreement of the parties, and in the absence of such—by the arbitration court for the settlement of a specific dispute, by taking into account the requirements of point 3 of the present article.

Article 16. Distribution of Expenses Connected with Settlement of Dispute in Arbitration Court

1. Expenses connected with the settlement of a dispute in an arbitration court shall be distributed between the parties by the arbitration court in accordance with the agreement of the parties, and in the absence of such—in proportion to the demands satisfied and rejected.

2. Expenses for the payment of services of the representative of the party to whose benefit the award of the arbitration court is, and also other expenses connected with the arbitral examination, may by decision of the arbitration court be relegated to the other party if the demand concerning compensation of expenses incurred was declared in the court of the arbitral examination and satisfied by the arbitration court.

3. Distribution of expenses connected with settlement of the dispute in an arbitration court shall be specified in the award or ruling of the arbitration court.

Chapter V. Arbitral Examination

Article 17. Competence of Arbitration Court

1. An arbitration court autonomously shall decide the question of the existence or absence of competence to consider a dispute transferred for its consideration, including in instances when one of the parties objects to the arbitral examination by reason of the absence of invalidity of the arbitration agreement. For this purpose an arbitration agreement concluded in the form of a clause in a contract must be regarded as not dependent upon the other conditions of the contract. The conclusion of the arbitration court concerning the fact that the contract containing the clause is invalid shall not entail the invalidity of the clause by virtue of a law.

2. A party shall have the right to declare the lack of competence of an arbitration court to consider a dispute transferred for settlement thereof before the submission of the first statement by it with regard to the essence of the dispute.

3. A party shall have the right to declare that an arbitration court is exceeding its competence if in the course of the arbitral examination the subject of the arbitral examination becomes a question whose consideration is not provided for by the arbitration agreement or which cannot be the subject of arbitral examination in accordance with a federal law or the rules of an arbitral examination.

4. An arbitration court shall be obliged to consider a declaration made in accordance with points 2 and 3 of the present Article. A ruling shall be rendered with regard to the results of consideration of the declaration.

5. If an arbitration court when considering the question of its competence renders a ruling concerning the lack of competence of the arbitration court to

consider the dispute, the arbitration court may not consider the dispute with regard to substance.

Article 18. Principles of Arbitral Examination

An arbitral examination shall be effectuated on the basis of the principles of legality, confidentiality, independence, and impartiality for the arbitration judges, dispositiveness, contentiousness, and equality of the parties.

Article 19. Determination of Rules of Arbitral Examination

1. A permanently-operating arbitration court shall effectuate an arbitral examination in accordance with the rules of the permanently-operating arbitration court unless the parties have agreed concerning the application of other rules of arbitral consideration.

2. An arbitration court for the consideration of a specific dispute shall effectuate an arbitral examination in accordance with the rules agreed by the parties.

3. The rules of an arbitral examination agreed by the parties in accordance with points 1 and 2 of the present Article may not be contrary to obligatory provisions of the present Federal Law which do not provide to the parties the right to agree with regard to individual questions.

In the part not agreed by the parties nor determined by the rules of the permanently-operating arbitration court and the present Federal Law, the rules of the arbitral examination shall be determined by the arbitration court.

Article 20. Place of Arbitral Examination

1. In an arbitration court for the settlement of a specific dispute the parties may at their discretion agree about the place of the arbitral examination.

If the parties have not agreed otherwise, the place of the arbitral examination shall be determined by the arbitration court for the settlement of a specific dispute, taking into account all circumstances of the case, including the factor of convenience for the parties.

2. In a permanently-operating arbitration court the place of the arbitral examination shall be determined in accordance with the rules of the permanently-operating arbitration court.

If in the rules of the permanently-operating arbitration court there is no indication of the place of arbitral examination or procedure for determining it, the place of the arbitral examination shall be determined by the composition of the arbitration court, taking into account all circumstances of the case, including the factor of convenience for the parties.

Article 21. Language(s) of Arbitral Examination

1. Unless the parties have agreed otherwise, the arbitral examination shall be conducted in the Russian language.

2. The party submitting documents and other materials not in the language(s) of the arbitral examination shall ensure the translation thereof.

3. An arbitration court may demand from the parties the translation of documents and other materials into the language(s) of the arbitral examination.

Article 22. Confidentiality of Arbitral Examination

1. An arbitration judge shall not have the right to divulge information which became known to him in the court of an arbitral examination without the consent of the parties or the legal successors thereof.

2. An arbitration judge may not be questioned as a witness concerning information which became known to him in the court of an arbitral examination.

Article 23. Petition to Sue and Reply to Petition to Sue

1. The plaintiff may set out his demands in a petition to sue, which shall be transferred in written form to the arbitration court. A copy of the petition to sue shall be transferred to the defendant.

2. There must be specified in a petition to sue:
(1) the date of the petition to sue;
(2) the name and location of the organisations which are parties to the arbitral examination; surnames, forenames, and patronymics, date and place of birth, place of residence, and place of work of citizen-entrepreneurs and citizens who are parties to the arbitral examination;
(3) substantiation of the competence of the arbitration court;
(4) demands of the plaintiff;
(5) circumstance son which the plaintiff bases his demands;
(6) evidence confirming the grounds of the suit demands;
(7) value of the suit;
(8) list of documents and other materials appended to the petition to sue.
The petition to sue must be signed by the plaintiff or representative thereof. If the petition to sue was signed by the representative of the plaintiff, a power of attorney or other document certifying the powers of the representative must be appended to the petition to sue.

3. Additional requirements for the content of the petition to sue may be provided for by the rules of the arbitral examination.

4. The defendant shall have the right to submit to the plaintiff and arbitration court a reply to the petition to sue, setting out therein his objections to the suit. The reply to the petition to sue shall be submitted to the plaintiff and to the arbitration court in the procedure and within the periods which have been provided for by the rules of arbitral examination.

If the period for the submission of a reply to the petition to sue has not been provided for by the rules of the arbitral examination, the said reply shall be submitted before the first session of the arbitration court.

5. In the course of an arbitral examination a party shall have the right to change or add to its suit demands or objections to the suit.

Article 24. Counter Suit and Set-off of Suit Demands

1. A defendant shall have the right to file against the plaintiff a counter suit on condition that a mutual link exists between the counter demand and the demands of the plaintiff, and also on condition that the counter suit may be considered by an arbitration court in accordance with the arbitration agreement.

2. A counter suit may be filed in the course of the arbitral examination until the adoption of an award by the arbitration court unless the parties have agreed another period for the filing of a counter suit.

3. A counter suit must satisfy the requirements of Article 23(2) of the present Federal Law.

4. A plaintiff shall have the right to submit objections to the counter suit in the procedure and within the periods which have been provided by the rules of the arbitral examination.

5. If the parties have not agreed otherwise, the defendant shall have the right in accordance with civil legislation of the Russian Federation to demand a set-off of the counter demand, in compliance with the requirements of points 1 and 4 of the present Article.

Article 25. Powers of Arbitration Court to Order Taking of Security Measures

1. Unless the parties have agreed otherwise, an arbitration court may at the request of any party order the taking of such security measures by any party with respect to the subject of the dispute which it considers to be necessary.

2. An arbitration court may demand that any party submit proper security in connection with such measures.

3. Recourse of a party to a competence court with an application concerning securing of the suit and the taking by the competent court of security measures may not be regarded as incompatible with the agreement concerning the transfer of the dispute to an arbitration court or as a renunciation of such agreement.

4. An application concerning the securing of a suit considered in an arbitration court shall be filed by a party at the competent court at the place of effectuation of the arbitral examination or at the location of property with respect to which security measures may be taken.

To an application concerning the securing of a suit shall be appended evidence of the filing of suit in the arbitration court, ruling of the arbitration court concerning the taking of security measures, and also evidence of payment of State duty in the procedure and amount which have been established by a federal law.

5. Consideration by a competent court of an application concerning the securing of a suit being considered in an arbitration court and the rendering of a ruling by it concerning the security of the suit or refusal to secure it shall be effectuated in the procedure established by arbitrazh procedure or civil procedure legislation of the Russian Federation.

6. A ruling concerning the securing of a suit being considered in an arbitration court may be vacated by the competent court which rendered this ruling upon application of one of the parties. The award of an arbitration court concerning the refusal to satisfy suit demands shall be grounds for vacating of the security measures by the competent court.

Article 26. Submission of Evidence

Each party party must prove those circumstances to which it refers as substantiation of its demands and objections. An arbitration court shall have the right, if it considers the evidence submitted to be insufficient, to propose the parties submit additional evidence.

Article 27. Participation of Parties in Session of Arbitration Court

1. Equal possibilities must be provided to each party to set out its position and defence of its rights and interests.

2. Unless the parties have agreed otherwise, arbitral examination shall be effectuated in the session of the arbitration court with the participation of the parties or their representatives.

3. Notice must be sent in good time to the parties concerning the time and place of session of the arbitration court. The said notice shall be sent and handed over in the procedure provided for by Article 4 of the present Federal Law.

Unless the parties have agreed otherwise, copies of all documents and other materials, and also other information which one of the parties submits to the arbitration court, must be transferred by the arbitration court to the other party. Expert opinions on which the arbitration court bases its award must be transferred by the arbitration court to the parties.

4. Unless the parties have agreed otherwise, the composition of the arbitration court shall consider the case in closed session.

Article 28. Consequences of Failure of Parties to Submit Documents and Other Materials or Failure of Parties to Appear

1. The failure of the parties to submit documents and other materials, including the failure to appear for the session of the arbitration court, or their representatives duly notified about the time and place of the session of the arbitration court shall not be an obstacle to the arbitral examination and adoption of an award by the arbitration court if the reason for the failure to submit documents and other materials or the failure of the parties to appear at the session of the arbitration court is deemed by it to be not important.

2. The failure of the defendant to object to a suit may not be considered as recognition of the demands of the plaintiff.

Article 29. Designation and Conducting of Expert Examination

1. Unless the parties have agreed otherwise, the arbitration court may designate an expert examination in order to elucidate questions arising during the settlement of the dispute requiring special knowledge and demand from any of the parties the submission of documents, other materials, or articles necessary for conducting the expert examination.
Unless the parties have agreed otherwise, the arbitration court may designate one or several experts.

2. Unless the parties have agreed otherwise, the candidacy of the expert, and also questions which should be elucidated when conducting the expert examination, shall be determined by the arbitration court, taking into account the opinion of the parties.

3. Unless the parties have agreed otherwise, the arbitration court shall distribute the expenses incurred when conducting an expert examination in accordance with Article 16 of the present Federal Law.

4. An expert opinion shall be submitted in written form.

5. Unless the parties have agreed otherwise, an expert, on condition that any of the parties requests this or the arbitration considers this necessary, must after the submission of the expert opinion take part in the session of the arbitration court, at which the possibility shall be granted to the parties and to the arbitration judges to put questions to the expert connected with conducting the expert examination and the expert opinion submitted.

Article 30. Protocol of Session of Arbitration Court

Unless the parties have agreed otherwise, a protocol shall be kept in the session of the arbitration court.

Chapter VI. Award of Arbitration Court

Article 31. Obligatoriness of Award of Arbitration Court

The parties who have concluded an arbitration agreement shall assume the duty voluntarily to execute the award of the arbitration court. The parties and the arbitration court shall make all efforts so that the award of the arbitration court is legally executable.

Article 32. Adoption of Award by Arbitration Court

1. After investigation of the circumstances of the case, an arbitration by a majority vote of the arbitration judges within the composition of the arbitration court shall adopt an award.

The award shall be announced in the session of the arbitration court. An arbitration court shall have the right to announce only the resolutive part of the award. If the parties have not agreed a period for sending the award, the reasoned award must be sent to the parties within a period not exceeding 15 days from the day of announcement of the resolutive part of the award.

2. An arbitration court shall have the right, if it deems this to be necessary, to postpone adoption of an award and summon the parties for an additional session on condition of compliance with the provisions of Article 27(3) of the present Federal Law.

3. Upon the petition of the parties, the arbitration court shall adopt an award concerning the confirmation of an amicable agreement unless the amicable agreement is contrary to laws and other normative legal acts and violates the rights and legal interests of other persons. The content of the amicable agreement shall be set out in the award of the arbitration court.

4. An award of an arbitration court shall be considered to be adopted at the place of the arbitral examination and on the day when it was signed by the arbitration judges within the composition of the arbitration court.

Article 33. Form and Content of Award of Arbitration Court

1. An award of an arbitration court shall be set out in written form and shall be signed by the arbitration judges within the composition of the arbitration court, including the arbitration judge having a dissenting opinion. The dissenting opinion of an arbitration judge shall be appended to the award of the arbitration court. If the arbitral examination was effectuated collegially, the award may be signed by the majority of arbitration judges within the composition of the arbitration court on conditions of indicating the important reason for the absence of the signatures of the other arbitration judges.

2. There must be specified in the award of the arbitration court:

(1) date of adoption of the award, determined in accordance with Article 32(4) of the present Federal Law;

(2) place of the arbitral examination determined in accordance with Article 20 of the present Federal Law;

(3) composition of the arbitration court and procedure of forming thereof;

(4) name and location of the organisations which are parties to the arbitral examination, surnames, forenames, and patronymics, dates and places of birth, place of residence, and place of work of citizen-entrepreneurs and citizens who are parties to the arbitral examination;

(5) substantiation of the competence of the arbitration court;

(6) demands of the plaintiff and objections of the defendant, and petitions of the parties;

(7) circumstances of the case established by the arbitration court, evidence on which the conclusions of the arbitration court are based concerning these circumstances, laws and other normative legal acts by which the arbitration was guided when adopting the award.

The resolutive part of the award must contain conclusions of the arbitration court concerning satisfaction or refusal to satisfy each declared suit demand. In the resolutive part shall be indicated the amount of expenses connected with settlement of the dispute in the arbitration court, distribution of the said expenses between the parties, and, when necessary—the period and procedure for execution of the adopted award.

3. After adoption of the award, an example of the award formalized in accordance with point 1 of the present Article must be handed over or sent to each party.

Article 34. Supplementary Award

1. Unless the parties have agreed otherwise, any of the parties, having informed the other party thereof, may within 10 days after receipt of the award of the arbitration court apply to this same arbitration court with an application concerning the adoption of a supplementary award with respect to demands which were declared in the court of the arbitral examination but, however, did not find reflection in the award. The said application must be considered within 10 days after receipt thereof by the composition of the arbitration court which settled the dispute.

2. With regard to the results of consideration of the respective application either a supplementary award which is an integral part of the award of the arbitration court or a ruling concerning a refusal to satisfy the application concerning the adoption of a supplementary award shall be adopted.

Article 35. Explanation of Award

1. Unless the parties have agreed otherwise, any of the parties, having informed the other party thereof, may within 10 days after receipt of the award of the arbitration court apply to this same arbitration court with an application concerning an explanation of the award. The application concerning explanation of the award must be considered within 10 days after receipt thereof by the composition of the arbitration court which settled the dispute.

3. Either a ruling concerning explanation of the award, which shall be an integral part of the award of the arbitration court, or a ruling concerning a refusal to explain the award, shall be rendered with regard to the results of the consideration of the respective application.

Article 36. Rectification of Slips of Pen, Misprints, and Arithmetical Errors

1. An arbitration court shall have the right upon the application of any of the parties or at its own initiative to rectify slips of the pen, misprints, and arithmetical errors permitted.

2. The arbitration court shall render a ruling, which shall be an integral part of the award, concerning the rectification of slips of the pen, misprints, and arithmetical errors.

Article 37. Ruling of Arbitration Court

An arbitration court shall render a ruling with regard to questions not affecting the essence of the dispute.

Article 38. Termination of Arbitral Examination

An arbitration court shall render a ruling concerning the termination of the arbitral examination in instances if:

the plaintiff renounces his demand, provided that the defendant does not declare an objection to termination of the arbitral examination in connection with the existence of his legal interest in a settlement of the dispute in substance;

the parties have reached an agreement concerning termination of the arbitral examination;

the arbitration court has rendered a ruling concerning the lack of competence of the arbitration court to consider the dispute transferred for its consideration;

the arbitration court has adopted an award concerning confirmation of a written amicable agreement;

the organisation which is a party to the arbitral examination has been liquidated;

the citizen-entrepreneur or citizen which is a party to the arbitral examination dies or is declared to be deceased or missing;

there is the decision of a court of general jurisdiction or arbitrazh court or award of an arbitration court which has entered into legal force adopted with regard to a dispute between the same parties, the same subject, and the same grounds.

Article 39. Keeping of Awards and Files of Case

1. The award of an arbitration court for the settlement of a specific case shall be sent within a month's period after the adoption thereof together with the materials with regard to the case for keeping to the competent court.

2. Unless another period has been determined by the rules of a permanently-operating arbitration court, the file of a case considered in the permanently-operating arbitration court shall be kept in that arbitration court for five years from the date of adoption of an award with regard to it.

Chapter VII. Contesting Award of Arbitration Court

Article 40. Contesting Award of Arbitration Court in Competent Court

Unless provided in an arbitration agreement that the award of the arbitration court is final, the award of an arbitration court may be contested by a party participating in the case by means of filing an application concerning the vacating of the award in a competent court within three months from the day of receipt by the party which filed the application of the award of the arbitration court.

Article 41. Procedure for Contesting Award of Arbitration Court

The procedure for contesting an award of an arbitration court in a competent court, consideration by the competent court of an application concerning the vacating of the award of the arbitration court, and adoption of a decision (or ruling) concerning the satisfaction or refusal to satisfy the application shall be determined by arbitrazh procedure or civil procedure legislation of the Russian Federation.

Article 42. Grounds for Vacating Award of Arbitration Court

An award of an arbitration court may be vacated by a competent court only in instances if:

(1) the party which filed the application concerning vacating of the award of the arbitration court submits evidence that:

the arbitration agreement is invalid on the grounds provided for by the present Federal Law or other federal law;

the award of the arbitration court was rendered with regard to a dispute not provided for by the arbitration agreement or not falling under the conditions thereof, or contains decrees with regard to questions exceeding the limits of the arbitration agreement. If the decrees of the arbitration court with regard to questions which are encompassed by the arbitration agreement may be separated from the decrees with regard to questions which are not encompassed by such agreement, only that part of the award of the arbitration court may be vacated which contain decrees with regard to questions not encompassed by the arbitration agreement;

the composition of the arbitration court or arbitral examination did not correspond to the provisions of Articles 8, 10, 11, or 19 of the present Federal Law;

the party against which the award of the arbitration court was adopted was not duly notified about the selection (or appointment) or arbitration judges or about the time and place of the session of the arbitration court or for other reasons could not submit its explanations to the arbitration court;

(2) the competent court establishes that:

the dispute considered by the arbitration court could not in accordance with a federal law be the subject of an arbitral examination;

the award of the arbitration court violates fundamental principles of Russian law.

Article 43. Consequences of Vacating of Award of Arbitration Court

In the event of the vacating of the award of an arbitration court by a competent court, any of the parties shall have the right in accordance with the arbitration agreement to apply to an arbitration court. However, if the award of the arbitration court was vacated fully or partially as a consequence of the invalidity of the arbitration agreement or because the award was adopted with regard to a dispute not provided for by the arbitration agreement, or not falling under the conditions thereof, or contains decrees with regard to questions not encompassed by the arbitration agreement, the respective dispute shall not be subject to further consideration in an arbitration court.

Chapter VIII. Execution of Award of Arbitration Court

Article 44. Execution of Award of Arbitration Court

1. An award of an arbitration court shall be executed voluntarily in the procedure and within the periods which have been established in the particular award.

2. If a period has not been established in the award of an arbitration court, it shall be subject to immediate execution.

Article 45. Compulsory Execution of Award of Arbitration Court

1. If an award of an arbitration court has not been executed voluntarily within the established period, it shall be subject to compulsory execution. Compulsory execution of the award of an arbitration court shall be effectuated according to the rules of the execution proceeding operating at the moment of execution of the award of the arbitration court on the basis of a writ of execution issued by a

competent court for compulsory execution of the award of the arbitration court (hereinafter: writ of execution).

2. An application concerning the issuance of a writ of execution shall be filed at the competent court by the party to whose benefit the award was rendered.

3. There shall be appended to the application concerning issuance of a writ of execution:

(1) the original or copy of the award of the arbitration court. A copy of the award of a permanently-operating arbitration court shall be attested by the chairman of this arbitration court, and a copy of the award of an arbitration court for the settlement of a specific dispute must be notarially certified;

(2) the original or copy of the arbitration agreement concluded in accordance with the provisions of Article 7 of the present Federal Law;

(3) the documents confirming payment of the State duty in the procedure and in the amount which have been established by a federal law.

4. An application concerning the issuance of a writ of execution may be filed not later than three years from the day of ending of the period for voluntary execution of the award of an arbitration court.

5. An application concerning the issuance of a writ of execution which was filed with lapse of the established period or to which the necessary documents were not appended shall be returned by the competent court without consideration, concerning which a ruling shall be rendered which may be appealed in the procedure established by arbitrazh procedure or civil procedure legislation of the Russian Federation.

6. The competent court shall have the right to restore the period for filing an application concerning the issuance of a writ of execution if it finds the reasons for the lapse of the said period to be important.

7. An application concerning the issuance of a writ of execution shall be considered by a judge of the competent court as one person within one month from the day of receipt of the application at the competent court. The parties shall be notified about the time and place of consideration of the said application; however, the failure of the parties or one party to appear shall not be an obstruction to consideration of the application.

8. The competent court shall render a ruling concerning the issuance of a writ of execution or refuse to issue a writ of execution with regard to the results of consideration of the application concerning issuance of a writ of execution.

The ruling of the competent court concerning the issuance of a writ of execution shall be subject to immediate execution.

9. The ruling of the competent court concerning the issuance of a writ of execution or refusal to issue a writ of execution may be appealed in the procedure

established by arbitrazh procedure or civil procedure legislation of the Russian Federation.

Article 46. Grounds for Refusal to Issue Writ of Execution

1. When considering an application concerning the issuance of a writ of execution the competent court shall not have the right to investigate the circumstances established by the arbitration court or to review the award of the arbitration court with regard to the substance.

2. The competent court shall issue a ruling concerning a refusal to issue a writ of execution in instances if:

(1) the party against whom the award of the arbitration court was adopted submits evidence to the competent court that:

the arbitration agreement is invalid, including on the grounds provided for by Article 7 of the present Federal Law;

the award of the arbitration court was adopted with regard to a dispute not provided for by the arbitration agreement or does not fall under its conditions, or contains decrees with regard to questions exceeding the limits of the arbitration agreement. If the decrees of the arbitration court with regard to questions encompassed by the arbitration agreement can be separated from those which are not encompassed by such agreement, then issuance of a writ of execution for compulsory execution of that part of the award of the arbitration court which contains provisions with regard to questions encompassed by the arbitration agreement may not be refused;

the composition of the arbitration court or arbitral examination did not correspond to the requirements of Articles 8, 10, 11, or 19 of the present Federal Law;

the party against whom the award of the arbitration court was adopted was not duly notified about the selection (or appointment) of the arbitration judges or the time and place of the session of the arbitration court, or for other reasons could not submit its explanations to the arbitration court;

(2) the competent court establishes that:

the dispute may not be the subject of arbitral examination in accordance with a federal law;

the award of the arbitration court violates fundamental principles of Russian law.

3. In the event of the rendering by a competent court of a ruling to refuse to issue a writ of execution the parties shall have the right in accordance with the arbitration agreement to apply to an arbitration court or competent court in compliance with the rules for jurisdiction and subject-matter jurisdiction, except for instances provided for by Article 43 of the present Federal Law.

Chapter IX. Concluding Provisions

Article 47. Entry into Force of Present Federal Law

1. The present Federal Law shall enter into force from the day of official publication thereof.

2. From the day of entry into force of the present Federal Law, to deem to have lost force:

Annex No. 3 to the Code of Civil Procedure of the RSFSR (Ведомости Верховного Совета РСФСР (1964), no. 24, item 407);

Decree of the Supreme Soviet of the Russian Federation, 24 June 1992, No. 3115–I 'On Confirmation of the Provisional Statute on an Arbitration Court for the Settlement of Economic Disputes' (Ведомости Съезда народных депутатов Российской Федерации и Верховного Совета Российской Федерации (1992), no. 30, item 1790);

Article 1(7) of the Federal Law of 16 November 1997, No. 144-ФЗ 'On Making Changes in and Additions to Laws and Other Legal Acts of the Russian Federation in Connection with the Adoption of the Federal Constitutional Law "On Arbitrazh Courts in the Russian Federation" and the Code of Arbitrazh Procedure of the Russian Federation' (Собрание законодательства Российской Федерации (1997), no. 47, item 5341).

3. To propose to the President of the Russian Federation and to charge the Government of the Russian Federation to bring their normative legal acts into conformity with the present Federal Law.